A Note from the Author

When I took leave from Columbia University in September 2006 to take a position as a member (governor) of the Board of Governors of the Federal Reserve System, I never imagined how exciting—and stressful—the job was likely to be. The Fed was going through major changes as the new Chairman, Ben Bernanke, settled in. At the same time, the economy was hit by a perfect storm of formidable shocks: the more than doubling of prices for oil and other commodities, which led to high inflation, and the onset of the subprime financial crisis in August 2007. The resulting contraction in the U.S. economy reverberated throughout the rest of the world.

When I returned to Columbia in September of 2008, the subprime financial crisis had reached a particularly virulent stage, with credit markets completely frozen and some of our largest financial institutions in very deep trouble. The subprime crisis, the worst financial crisis the world has experienced since the Great Depression, has completely changed the nature of money, banking, and financial markets. The field of money and banking will never be the same, making all previously published money and banking textbooks obsolete, including my own. The bad news is that this required me to completely rewrite large portions of this textbook, which has indeed been a challenge. The good news is that the money and banking field has never been as much fun to teach or as intriguing to study.

The Ninth Edition of *The Economics of Money, Banking, and Financial Markets* is the most extensive and exciting revision that I have ever done. I hope that students reading this book will have as much satisfaction learning from it as I had in writing it.

Frederic S. Mishkin

April 2009

Applying Theory to the Real World: Applications and Boxes

Applications

Simple Present Value, p. 71

How Much Is That Jackpot Worth?, p. 71

Yield to Maturity on a Simple Loan, p. 73

Yield to Maturity and the Yearly Payment on a Fixed-Payment Loan, p. 74

Yield to Maturity and the Bond Price for a Coupon Bond, p. 76

Perpetuity, p. 78

Calculating Real Interest Rates, p. 85

Changes in the Interest Rate Due to Expected Inflation: The Fisher Effect, p. 103

Changes in the Interest Rate Due to a Business Cycle Expansion, p. 104

Explaining Low Japanese Interest Rates, p. 106

Reading the *Wall Street Journal* "Credit Markets" Column, p. 107

Changes in the Equilibrium Interest Rate Due to Changes in Income, the Price Level, or the Money Supply, p. 112

Money and Interest Rates, p. 114

The Subprime Collapse and the Baa-Treasury Spread, p. 127

Effects of the Bush Tax Cut and Its Possible Repeal on Bond Interest Rates, p. 130

Interpreting Yield Curves, 1980–2009, p. 141

Monetary Policy and Stock Prices, p. 151

The Subprime Financial Crisis and the Stock Market, p. 152

Practical Guide to Investing in the Stock Market, p. 158

What Do the Black Monday Crash of 1987 and the Tech Crash of 2000 Tell Us About Rational Expectations and Efficient Markets?, p. 161

Financial Development and Economic Growth, p. 186

Is China a Counter-Example to the Importance of Financial Development?, p. 188

The Mother of All Financial Crises: The Great Depression, p. 206

Financial Crises in Mexico, 1994–1995; East Asia, 1997–1998; and Argentina, 2001–2002, p. 217

Strategies for Managing Bank Capital, p. 239

How a Capital Crunch Caused a Credit Crunch in 2008, p. 240

Strategies for Managing Interest-Rate Risk, p. 247

The Great Depression Bank Panics, 1930–1933, p. 366

How the Federal Reserve's Operating Procedures Limit Fluctuations in the Federal Funds Rate, p. 380

Changes in the Equilibrium Exchange Rate: Two Examples, p. 448

Why Do Some Nations Peg Their Currencies?, p. 452

The Euro Foreign Exchange Rate and Oil Prices, p. 452

The Global Financial Crisis and the Euro, p. 454

Reading the *Financial Times:* The "LEX" Column, p. 454

How Did China Accumulate Over $2 Trillion of International Reserves?, p. 474

The Foreign Exchange Crisis of September 1992, p. 477

Recent Foreign Exchange Crises in Emerging Market Countries: Mexico 1994, East Asia 1997, Brazil 1999, and Argentina 2002, p. 478

The Collapse of Investment Spending and the Great Depression, p. 527

The Economic Stimulus Act of 2008, p. 550

Targeting Money Supply Versus Interest Rates, p. 554

Explaining Past Business Cycle Episodes, p. 580

The Debate on the Importance of Monetary Policy to Economic Fluctuations, p. 591

The Subprime Recession, p. 609

Applying the Monetary Policy Lessons to Japan, p. 612

Explaining the Rise in U.S. Inflation, 1960–1980, p. 630

Importance of Credibility to Volcker's Victory over Inflation, p. 639

Credibility and the Reagan Budget Deficits, p. 660

Following the Financial News

Money Market Rates, p. 31

Capital Market Interest Rates, p. 34

Foreign Stock Market Indexes, p. 38

How the U.K. Monetary Aggregates Differ from Those of the ECB, p. 61

The "Credit Markets" Column, p. 108

Yield Curves, p. 131

Foreign Exchange Rates, p. 435

The "LEX" Column, p. 455

Aggregate Output, Unemployment, and the Price Level, p. 566

Global Boxes

Are U.S. Capital Markets Losing Their Edge?, p. 36

The Importance of Financial Intermediaries Relative to Securities Markets: An International Comparison, p. 40

Negative T-Bill Rates? It Can Happen, p. 79

The Treasury Asset Relief Plan and Government Bailouts, p. 212

The Perversion of the Financial Liberalization/Globalization Process, p. 219

Barings, Daiwa, Sumitomo, and Société Générale: Rogue Traders and the Principal-Agent Problem, p. 249

The Spread of Government Deposit Insurance Throughout the World: Is This a Good Thing?, p. 257

Basel 2: How Well Will It Work?, p. 262

International Financial Regulation, p. 269

Comparison of Banking Structure in the United States and Abroad, p. 301

Ironic Birth of the Eurodollar Market, p. 307

Will the Monetary Union of the Six-Nation Arab Gulf Cooperation Council be Acheived?, p. 334

The European Central Bank's Monetary Policy Strategy, p. 398

Why the Large U.S. Current Account Deficit Worries Economists, p. 469

The Euro's Challenge to the Dollar, p. 471

The Subprime Financial Crisis and the IMF, p. 484

Argentina's Currency Board, p. 491

Ending the Bolivian Hyperinflation: A Successful Anti-inflation Program, p. 660

Inside the Fed Boxes

How Bernanke's Style Differs from Greenspan's, p. 331

Why Does the Fed Need to Pay Interest on Reserves?, p. 375

Using Discount Policy to Prevent a Financial Panic, p. 386

Federal Reserve Lender-of-Last-Resort Facilities During the Subprime Financial Crisis, p. 387

Chairman Bernanke and Inflation Targeting, p. 407

Fed Watchers, p. 414

Bank Panics of 1930–1933: Why Did the Fed Let Them Happen?, p. 420

A Day at the Federal Reserve Bank of New York's Foreign Exchange Desk, p. 464

FYI

Are We Headed for a Cashless Society?, p. 59

Where Are All the U.S. Dollars and the Euros?, p. 63

Helping Investors to Select Desired Interest-Rate Risk, p. 83

With TIPS, Real Interest Rates Have Become Observable in the United States, p. 87

The Yield Curve as a Forecasting Tool for Inflation and the Business Cycle, p. 141

Should You Hire an Ape as Your Investment Adviser?, p. 160

The Enron Implosion, p. 177

Should We Kill *All* the Lawyers?, p. 188

The Demise of Arthur Andersen, p. 192

Credit-Rating Agencies and the Subprime Financial Crisis, p. 193

Has Sarbanes-Oxley Led to a Decline in U.S. Capital Markets?, p. 195

Mark-to-Market Accounting and the Subprime Financial Crisis, p. 266

The Subprime Mortgage Crisis and Consumer Protection Regulation, p. 268

Will "Clicks" Dominate "Bricks" in the Banking Industry?, p. 288

Bruce Bent and the Money Market Mutual Fund Panic of 2008, p. 291

The Subprime Financial Crisis and the Demise of Large, Free-Standing Investment Banks, p. 304

Meaning of the Word Investment, p. 523

Perils of Reverse Causation: A Russian Folk Tale, p. 590

Perils of Ignoring an Outside Driving Factor: How to Lose a Presidential Election, p. 591

Real Business Cycle Theory and the Debate on Money and Economic Activity, p. 600

Consumers' Balance Sheets and the Great Depression, p. 608

Proof of the Policy Ineffectiveness Proposition, p. 648

THE ECONOMICS OF
MONEY,
BANKING
AND FINANCIAL
MARKETS

GLOBAL EDITION

The Addison-Wesley Series in Economics

Abel/Bernanke/Croushore
*Macroeconomics**

Bade/Parkin
*Foundations of Economics**

Bierman/Fernandez
Game Theory with Economic Applications

Binger/Hoffman
Microeconomics with Calculus

Boyer
Principles of Transportation Economics

Branson
Macroeconomic Theory and Policy

Bruce
Public Finance and the American Economy

Byrns/Stone
Economics

Carlton/Perloff
Modern Industrial Organization

Caves/Frankel/Jones
World Trade and Payments: An Introduction

Chapman
Environmental Economics: Theory, Application, and Policy

Cooter/Ulen
Law & Economics

Downs
An Economic Theory of Democracy

Ehrenberg/Smith
Modern Labor Economics

Ekelund/Ressler/Tollison
*Economics**

Fusfeld
The Age of the Economist

Gerber
International Economics

Ghiara
Learning Economics

Gordon
Macroeconomics

Gregory
Essentials of Economics

Gregory/Stuart
Russian and Soviet Economic Performance and Structure

Hartwick/Olewiler
The Economics of Natural Resource Use

Hoffman/Averett
Women and the Economy: Family, Work, and Pay

Holt
Markets, Games and Strategic Behavior

Hubbard
Money, the Financial System, and the Economy

Hughes/Cain
American Economic History

Husted/Melvin
International Economics

Jehle/Reny
Advanced Microeconomic Theory

Johnson-Lans
A Health Economics Primer

Klein
Mathematical Methods for Economics

Krugman/Obstfeld
*International Economics: Theory & Policy**

Laidler
The Demand for Money

Leeds/von Allmen
The Economics of Sports

Leeds/von Allmen/Schiming
*Economics**

Lipsey/Ragan/Storer
*Economics**

Melvin
International Money and Finance

Miller
*Economics Today**

Miller
Understanding Modern Economics

Miller/Benjamin
The Economics of Macro Issues

Miller/Benjamin/North
The Economics of Public Issues

Mills/Hamilton
Urban Economics

Mishkin
*The Economics of Money, Banking, and Financial Markets**

Mishkin
*The Economics of Money, Banking, and Financial Markets, Business School Edition**

Murray
Econometrics: A Modern Introduction

Parkin
*Economics**

Perloff
*Microeconomics**

Perloff
Microeconomics: Theory and Applications with Calculus

Perman/Common/McGilvray/Ma
Natural Resources and Environmental Economics

Phelps
Health Economics

Riddell/Shackelford/Stamos/ Schneider
Economics: A Tool for Critically Understanding Society

Ritter/Silber/Udell
*Principles of Money, Banking & Financial Markets**

Rohlf
Introduction to Economic Reasoning

Ruffin/Gregory
Principles of Economics

Sargent
Rational Expectations and Inflation

Scherer
Industry Structure, Strategy, and Public Policy

Sherman
Market Regulation

Stock/Watson
Introduction to Econometrics

Stock/Watson
Introduction to Econometrics, Brief Edition

Studenmund
Using Econometrics: A Practical Guide

Tietenberg
Environmental Economics and Policy

Tietenberg/Lewis
Environmental and Natural Resource Economics

Todaro/Smith
Economic Development

Waldman
Microeconomics

Waldman/Jensen
Industrial Organization: Theory and Practice

Weil
Economic Growth

Williamson
Macroeconomics

*denotes **myeconlab** titles   Log onto www.myeconlab.com to learn more

THE ECONOMICS OF
Money, Banking and Financial Markets

NINTH EDITION

GLOBAL EDITION

Frederic S. Mishkin
Columbia University

Boston   Columbus   Indianapolis   New York   San Francisco   Upper Saddle River
Amsterdam   Cape Town   Dubai   London   Madrid   Milan   Munich   Paris   Montreal   Toronto
Delhi   Mexico City   Sao Paulo   Hong Kong   Seoul   Singapore   Taipei   Tokyo

Editor in Chief: Donna Battista
Acquisitions Editor: Noel Kamm Seibert
Project Manager: Kerri McQueen
International Acquisitions Editor: Laura Dent
Managing Editor: Nancy H. Fenton
Senior Production Supervisor: Kathryn Dinovo
Supplements Production Coordinator: Alison Eusden
Director of Media: Susan Schoenberg
Senior Media Producer: Melissa Honig
Content Leads, MyEconLab: Douglas A. Ruby and Noel Lotz
Senior Author Support/Technology Specialist: Joe Vetere
Marketing Manager: Elizabeth A. Averbeck
Permissions Project Manager: Shannon Barbe
Permissions Project Supervisor: Michael Joyce
Senior Manufacturing Buyer: Carol Melville
Senior Media Buyer: Ginny Michaud
Cover Designer: Jodi Notowitz
Production Coordination, Text Design, and Illustrations: Thompson Steele
Composition: Nesbitt Graphics, Inc.
Cover image: © Image Source Pink/Alamy

For permission to use copyrighted material, grateful acknowledgment is made to the copyright holders on p. C-1, which are hereby part of this copyright page.

If you purchased this book within the United States or Canada you should be aware that it has been imported without the approval of the Publisher or the Author.

1 2 3 4 5 6 7 8 9 10—CRK—13 12 11 10 09

ISBN-10: 0-321-64936-2
ISBN-13: 978-0-321-64936-2

To Sally

BRIEF CONTENTS

PART 1   Introduction   1
  1 Why Study Money, Banking, and Financial Markets? 3
  2 An Overview of the Financial System 25
  3 What Is Money?: A Comparative Approach to Measuring Money 53

PART 2   Financial Markets   67
  4 Understanding Interest Rates 69
  5 The Behavior of Interest Rates 91
  6 The Risk and Term Structure of Interest Rates 123
  7 The Stock Market, the Theory of Rational Expectations,
     and the Efficient Market Hypothesis 147

PART 3   Financial Institutions   167
  8 An Economic Analysis of Financial Structure 169
  9 Financial Crises and the Subprime Meltdown 199
  10 Banking and the Management of Financial Institutions 225
  11 Economic Analysis of Financial Regulation 255
  12 Banking Industry: Structure and Competition 281

PART 4   Central Banking and the Conduct
                of Monetary Policy   313
  13 Central Banks: A Global Perspective 315
  14 The Money Supply Process 345
  15 The Tools of Monetary Policy 373
  16 The Conduct of Monetary Policy: Strategy and Tactics 395

PART 5   International Finance and Monetary Policy   431
  17 The Foreign Exchange Market: Exchange Rates and Applications 433
  18 The International Financial System 463

PART 6   Monetary Theory   497
  19 The Demand for Money 499
  20 The *ISLM* Model 519
  21 Monetary and Fiscal Policy in the *ISLM* Model 543
  22 Aggregate Demand and Supply Analysis 565
  23 Transmission Mechanisms of Monetary Policy: The Evidence 587
  24 Money and Inflation 617
  25 Rational Expectations: Implications for Policy 643

PART 1　Introduction　1

CHAPTER 1
Why Study Money, Banking, and Financial Markets?　3

Why Study Financial Markets? 3
    The Bond Market and Interest Rates 3
    The Stock Market 5
Why Study Financial Institutions and Banking? 5
    Structure of the Financial System 6
    Financial Crises 7
    Banks and Other Financial Institutions 7
    Financial Innovation 7
Why Study Money and Monetary Policy? 8
    Money and Business Cycles 8
    Money and Inflation 8
    Money and Interest Rates 10
    Conduct of Monetary Policy 10
    Fiscal Policy and Monetary Policy 12
Why Study International Finance? 13
    The Foreign Exchange Market 13
    The International Financial System 14
How We Will Study Money, Banking, and Financial Markets 14
    Exploring the Web 15
    Collecting and Graphing Data 15
Web Exercises 16
Concluding Remarks 17
Summary 18　•　Key Terms 19　•　Questions and Problems 19　•
    Web Exercises 20　•　Web References 20

APPENDIX TO CHAPTER 1
**Defining Aggregate Output, Income, the Price Level,
and the Inflation Rate　21**

Aggregate Output and Income 21
Real Versus Nominal Magnitudes 21
Aggregate Price Level 22
Growth Rates and the Inflation Rate 23

CHAPTER 2
An Overview of the Financial System　25

Function of Financial Markets 25
Structure of Financial Markets 27

Debt and Equity Markets 27
Primary and Secondary Markets 28
Exchanges and Over-the-Counter Markets 29
Money and Capital Markets 29
Financial Market Instruments 30
Money Market Instruments 30

Following the Financial News Money Market Rates   31

Capital Market Instruments 33

Following the Financial News Capital Market Interest Rates   34

Internationalization of Financial Markets 36

Global Are U.S. Capital Markets Losing Their Edge?   36

International Bond Market, Eurobonds, and Eurocurrencies 37
World Stock Markets 37

Following the Financial News Foreign Stock Market Indexes   38

Function of Financial Intermediaries: Indirect Finance 39
Transaction Costs 39

Global The Importance of Financial Intermediaries Relative to Securities Markets:
An International Comparison   40

Risk Sharing 40
Asymmetric Information: Adverse Selection and Moral Hazard 41
Types of Financial Intermediaries 42
Depository Institutions 43
Contractual Savings Institutions 44
Investment Intermediaries 45
Regulation of the Financial System 46
Increasing Information Available to Investors 46
Ensuring the Soundness of Financial Intermediaries 47
Financial Regulation Abroad 49
Summary 49   •   Key Terms 50   •   Questions and Problems 51   •
Web Exercises 51   •   Web References 52

CHAPTER 3
**What Is Money?: A Comparative Approach
to Measuring Money   53**
Meaning of Money 53
Functions of Money 54
Medium of Exchange 54
Unit of Account 55
Store of Value 56
Evolution of the Payments System 57
Commodity Money 57
Fiat Money 57
Checks 57

Electronic Payment 58
E-Money 58

FYI Are We Headed for a Cashless Society? 59

Measuring Money 60
Definitions of Monetary Aggregates 60

Following the Financial News How the U.K. Monetary Aggregates Differ
from Those of the ECB 61

FYI Where Are All the U.S. Dollars and the Euros? 63

Which is the Most Accurate Monetary Aggregate? 63

Summary 64 • Key Terms 65 • Questions and Problems 65 •
Web Exercises 66 • Web References 66

PART 2 Financial Markets 67

CHAPTER 4
Understanding Interest Rates 69

Measuring Interest Rates 69
Present Value 69

Application Simple Present Value 71

Application How Much is That Jackpot Worth? 71
Four Types of Credit Market Instruments 72
Yield to Maturity 72

Application Yield to Maturity on a Simple Loan 73

Application Yield to Maturity and the Yearly Payment
on a Fixed-Payment Loan 74

Application Yield to Maturity and the Bond Price for a Coupon Bond 76

Application Perpetuity 78

Global Negative T-Bill Rates? It Can Happen 79

The Distinction Between Interest Rates and Returns 80
Maturity and the Volatility of Bond Returns: Interest-Rate Risk 82

FYI Helping Investors to Select Desired Interest-Rate Risk 83

Summary 84

The Distinction Between Real and Nominal Interest Rates 84

Application Calculating Real Interest Rates 85

FYI With TIPS, Real Interest Rates Have Become Observable
in the United States 87

Summary 87 • Key Terms 87 • Questions and Problems 88 •
Web Exercises 88 • Web References 89

CHAPTER 5
The Behavior of Interest Rates   91

Determinants of Asset Demand 91
    Wealth 92
    Expected Returns 92
    Risk 92
    Liquidity 93
    Theory of Asset Demand 93
Supply and Demand in the Bond Market 94
    Demand Curve 94
    Supply Curve 95
    Market Equilibrium 96
    Supply and Demand Analysis 97
Changes in Equilibrium Interest Rates 97
    Shifts in the Demand for Bonds 97
    Shifts in the Supply of Bonds 101

Application Changes in the Interest Rate Due to Expected Inflation:
    The Fisher Effect 103

Application Changes in the Interest Rate Due to a Business Cycle Expansion . . . 104

Application Explaining Low Japanese Interest Rates 106

Application Reading the *Wall Street Journal* "Credit Markets" Column 107

Following the Financial News The "Credit Markets" Column   108

Supply and Demand in the Market for Money: The Liquidity Preference Framework .109
Changes in Equilibrium Interest Rates in the Liquidity Preference Framework 111
    Shifts in the Demand for Money 111
    Shifts in the Supply of Money 111

Application Changes in the Equilibrium Interest Rate Due to Changes
    in Income, the Price Level, or the Money Supply 112
    Changes in Income 113
    Changes in the Price Level 113
    Changes in the Money Supply 113

Application Money and Interest Rates 114
    Does a Higher Rate of Growth of the Money Supply Lower Interest Rates? 115
Summary 119 • Key Terms 119 • Questions and Problems 119 •
    Web Exercises 120 • Web References 121

CHAPTER 6
The Risk and Term Structure of Interest Rates   123

Risk Structure of Interest Rates 123
    Default Risk 123

Application The Subprime Collapse and the Baa-Treasury Spread 127
    Liquidity 127
    Income Tax Considerations 128
    Summary 129

Application Effects of the Bush Tax Cut and Its Possible Repeal
    on Bond Interest Rates 130

Term Structure of Interest Rates 130

Following the Financial News Yield Curves 131

    Expectations Theory 132
    Segmented Markets Theory 135
    Liquidity Premium and Preferred Habitat Theories 136
    Evidence on the Term Structure 140
    Summary 140

FYI The Yield Curve as a Forecasting Tool for Inflation and the Business Cycle 141

Application Interpreting Yield Curves, 1980–2009 141

Summary 142 • Key Terms 143 • Questions and Problems 143 •
    Web Exercises 144 • Web References 144

CHAPTER 7
The Stock Market, the Theory of Rational Expectations, and the Efficient Market Hypothesis 147

Computing the Price of Common Stock 147
    The One-Period Valuation Model 148
    The Generalized Dividend Valuation Model 149
    The Gordon Growth Model 149

How the Market Sets Stock Prices 150

Application Monetary Policy and Stock Prices 151

Application The Subprime Financial Crisis and the Stock Market 152

The Theory of Rational Expectations 152
    Formal Statement of the Theory 154
    Rationale Behind the Theory 154
    Implications of the Theory 155

The Efficient Market Hypothesis: Rational Expectations in Financial Markets 155
    Rationale Behind the Hypothesis 157
    Stronger Version of the Efficient Market Hypothesis 158

Application Practical Guide to Investing in the Stock Market 158
    How Valuable Are Published Reports by Investment Advisers? 158
    Should You Be Skeptical of Hot Tips? 159

FYI Should You Hire an Ape as Your Investment Adviser? 160

    Do Stock Prices Always Rise When There Is Good News? 160
    Efficient Market Prescription for the Investor 160

Application What Do the Black Monday Crash of 1987 and the Tech Crash
    of 2000 Tell Us About Rational Expectations and Efficient Markets? 161

Behavioral Finance 162

Summary 163 • Key Terms 164 • Questions and Problems 164 •
    Web Exercises 165 • Web References 165

PART 3   Financial Institutions   167

CHAPTER 8
An Economic Analysis of Financial Structure   169

Basic Facts about Financial Structure Throughout the World 169
Transaction Costs 172
    How Transaction Costs Influence Financial Structure 172
    How Financial Intermediaries Reduce Transaction Costs 173
Asymmetric Information: Adverse Selection and Moral Hazard 174
The Lemons Problem: How Adverse Selection Influences Financial Structure 174
    Lemons in the Stock and Bond Markets 175
    Tools to Help Solve Adverse Selection Problems 176

FYI The Enron Implosion   177

How Moral Hazard Affects the Choice Between Debt and Equity Contracts 180
    Moral Hazard in Equity Contracts: The Principal–Agent Problem 180
    Tools to Help Solve the Principal–Agent Problem 181
How Moral Hazard Influences Financial Structure in Debt Markets 183
    Tools to Help Solve Moral Hazard in Debt Contracts 183
    Summary 185

Application Financial Development and Economic Growth 186

FYI Should We Kill *All* the Lawyers?   188

Application Is China a Counter-Example to the Importance
    of Financial Development? 188
Conflicts of Interest 189
    What Are Conflicts of Interest and Why Do We Care? 190
    Why Do Conflicts of Interest Arise? 190
    What Has Been Done to Remedy Conflicts of Interest? 192

FYI The Demise of Arthur Andersen   192

FYI Credit-Rating Agencies and the Subprime Financial Crisis   193

FYI Has Sarbanes-Oxley Led to a Decline in U.S. Capital Markets?   195

Summary 195 • Key Terms 196 • Questions and Problems 196 •
    Web Exercises 197 • Web References 197

CHAPTER 9
Financial Crises and the Subprime Meltdown   199

Factors Causing Financial Crises 199
    Asset Market Effects on Balance Sheets 200
    Deterioration in Financial Institutions' Balance Sheets 201
    Banking Crisis 201
    Increases in Uncertainty 201
    Increases in Interest Rates 201
    Government Fiscal Imbalances 202

Dynamics of Past U.S. Financial Crises 202
   Stage One: Initiation of Financial Crisis 202
   Stage Two: Banking Crisis 205
   Stage Three: Debt Deflation 206

Application The Mother of all Financial Crises: The Great Depression 206

The Subprime Financial Crisis of 2007–2008 207
   Financial Innovations Emerge in the Mortgage Markets 207
   Housing Price Bubble Forms 208
   Agency Problems Arise 208
   Information Problems Surface 209
   Housing Price Bubble Bursts 209
   Crisis Spreads Globally 209
   Banks' Balance Sheets Deteriorate 210
   High-Profile Firms Fail 210
   Bailout Package Debated 211
   Recovery in Sight? 211

Global The Treasury Asset Relief Plan and Government Bailouts   212

Dynamics of Financial Crises in Emerging Market Economies 212
   Stage One: Initiation of Financial Crisis 212
   Stage Two: Currency Crisis 215
   Stage Three: Full-Fledged Financial Crisis 216

Application Financial Crises in Mexico, 1994–1995; East Asia, 1997–1998;
   and Argentina, 2001–2002 217

Global The Perversion of the Financial Liberalization/Globalization Process   219

Summary 222 • Key Terms 222 • Questions and Problems 223 •
   Web Exercise 223 • Web References 224

CHAPTER 10
Banking and the Management of Financial Institutions   225

The Bank Balance Sheet 225
   Liabilities 225
   Assets 228

Basic Banking 229

General Principles of Bank Management 232
   Liquidity Management and the Role of Reserves 232
   Asset Management 235
   Liability Management 236
   Capital Adequacy Management 237

Application Strategies for Managing Bank Capital 239

Application How a Capital Crunch Caused a Credit Crunch
   in 2008 240

Managing Credit Risk 241
   Screening and Monitoring 241
   Long-Term Customer Relationships 242

Loan Commitments 243
Collateral and Compensating Balances 243
Credit Rationing 244

Managing Interest-Rate Risk 245
Gap and Duration Analysis 245

Application Strategies for Managing Interest-Rate Risk 247

Off-Balance-Sheet Activities 247
Loan Sales 247
Generation of Fee Income 248
Trading Activities and Risk Management Techniques 248

Global Barings, Daiwa, Sumitomo, and Société Générale: Rogue Traders
and the Principal-Agent Problem 249

Summary 250 • Key Terms 251 • Questions and Problems 251 •
Web Exercises 252 • Web References 253

CHAPTER 11
Economic Analysis of Financial Regulation 255

Asymmetric Information and Financial Regulation 255
Government Safety Net 255

Global The Spread of Government Deposit Insurance Throughout the World:
Is This a Good Thing? 257

Restrictions on Asset Holdings 260
Capital Requirements 260
Prompt Corrective Action 261

Global Basel 2: How Well Will It Work? 262

Financial Supervision: Chartering and Examination 263
Assessment of Risk Management 264
Disclosure Requirements 265
Consumer Protection 266

FYI Mark-to-Market Accounting and the Subprime Financial Crisis 266

Restrictions on Competition 267
Summary 267

FYI The Subprime Mortgage Crisis and Consumer Protection Regulation 268

Global International Financial Regulation 269

The 1980s Savings and Loan and Banking Crisis 271

Banking Crises Throughout the World 273
"Déjà vu All Over Again" 273

Whither Financial Regulation After the Subprime Financial Crisis? 275
Increased Regulation of Mortgage Brokers 276
Fewer Subprime Mortgage Products 276
Regulation Compensation 276
Higher Capital Requirements 276

Additional Regulation of Privately Owned Government-Sponsored Enterprises 277
Heightened Regulation to Limit Financial Institutions' Risk Taking 277
Increased Regulation of Credit-Rating Agencies 277
Additional Regulation of Derivatives 277
The Danger of Overregulation 278

Summary 278 • Key Terms 278 • Questions and Problems 278 •
   Web Exercises 279 • Web References 279

CHAPTER 12
Banking Industry: Structure and Competition 281

Historical Development of the Banking System 281
   Multiple Regulatory Agencies 283
Financial Innovation and the Growth of The "Shadow Banking System" 284
   Responses to Changes in Demand Conditions: Interest-Rate Volatility 285
   Responses to Changes in Supply Conditions: Information Technology 286

FYI Will "Clicks" Dominate "Bricks" in the Banking Industry? 288

   Avoidance of Existing Regulations 289

FYI Bruce Bent and the Money Market Mutual Fund Panic of 2008 291

   Financial Innovation and the Decline of Traditional Banking 292
Structure of the U.S. Commercial Banking Industry 295
   Restrictions on Branching 296
   Response to Branching Restrictions 297
Bank Consolidation and Nationwide Banking 298
   The Riegle-Neal Interstate Banking and Branching Efficiency Act of 1994 300
   What Will the Structure of the U.S. Banking Industry Look Like
      in the Future? 300

Global Comparison of Banking Structure in the United States
      and Abroad 301

   Are Bank Consolidation and Nationwide Banking Good Things? 301
Separation of the Banking and Other Financial Service Industries 302
   Erosion of Glass-Steagall 302
   The Gramm-Leach-Bliley Financial Services Modernization Act of 1999:
      Repeal of Glass-Steagall 303
   Implications for Financial Consolidation 303
   Separation of Banking and Other Financial Services Industries Throughout
      the World 303

FYI The Subprime Financial Crisis and the Demise of Large, Free-Standing
      Investment Banks 304

Thrift Industry: Regulation and Structure 304
   Savings and Loan Associations 304
   Mutual Savings Banks 305
   Credit Unions 305
International Banking 306
   Eurodollar Market 306

Global Ironic Birth of the Eurodollar Market 307

Structure of U.S. Banking Overseas 307
Foreign Banks in the United States 308

Summary 309 • Key Terms 310 • Questions and Problems 310 •
Web Exercises 311 • Web References 311

PART 4 Central Banking and the Conduct of Monetary Policy 313

CHAPTER 13
Central Banks: A Global Perspective 315

The Price Stability Goal and the Nominal Anchor 315
The Role of a Nominal Anchor 316
The Time-Inconsistency Problem 316
Other Goals of Monetary Policy 317
High Employment 317
Economic Growth 318
Stability of Financial Markets 318
Interest-Rate Stability 318
Stability in Foreign Exchange Markets 319
Should Price Stability Be the Primary Goal of Monetary Policy? 319
Hierarchical Versus Dual Mandates 319
Price Stability as the Primary, Long-Run Goal of Monetary Policy 320
Origins of the Federal Reserve System 320
Structure of the Federal Reserve System 321
Federal Reserve Banks 321
Member Banks 323
Board of Governors of the Federal Reserve System 323
Federal Open Market Committee (FOMC) 324
How Independent is the Fed? 324

Inside the Fed How Bernanke's Style Differs from Greenspan's 325

Structure and Independence of the European Central Bank 326
Governing Council Executive Board and General Council 328
Central Banks Round the World 331
Bank of Canada 331
Bank of England 331
Bank of Japan 332
Central Banks in Transition Economies 332
Central Banks in Developing Countries and Emerging Economies 333

Global Will the Monetary Union of the Six-Nation Arab Gulf Cooperation Council
be Achieved? 334

People's Bank of China 335
Multinational Central Banks in Developing Countries 335
Central Bank Reforms in South America 336
Currency Unions in Developing Nations 336
The Trend Toward Greater Independence 336

Explaining Central Bank Behavior 337

Should the Central Banks Be Independent? 337
The Case for Independence 338
The Case Against Independence 339
Central Bank Independence and Macroeconomic Performance Throughout the World . . 339

Summary 340 • Key Terms 341 • Questions and Problems 341 •
     Web Exercises 342 • Web References 342

CHAPTER 14
The Money Supply Process   345

Three Players in the Money Supply Process 345

The Fed's Balance Sheet 345
Liabilities 346
Assets 347

Control of the Monetary Base 347
Federal Reserve Open Market Operations 348
Shifts from Deposits into Currency 351
Discount Loans 352
Other Factors That Affect the Monetary Base 353
Overview of the Fed's Ability to Control the Monetary Base 353

Multiple Deposit Creation: A Simple Model 354
Deposit Creation: The Single Bank 354
Deposit Creation: The Banking System 355
Deriving the Formula for Multiple Deposit Creation 358
Critique of the Simple Model 359

Factors that Determine the Money Supply 360
Changes in the Nonborrowed Monetary Base, MB_n 360
Changes in Borrowed Reserves, BR, from the Fed 360
Changes in the Required Reserve Ratio, r 360
Changes in Currency Holdings 361
Changes in Excess Reserves 361

Overview of the Money Supply Process 361

The Money Multiplier 362
Deriving the Money Multiplier 362
Intuition Behind the Money Multiplier 364
Money Supply Response to Changes in the Factors 365

Application The Great Depression Bank Panics, 1930–1933 366

Summary 369 • Key Terms 370 • Questions and Problems 370 •
Web Exercises 371 • Web References 372

CHAPTER 15
Tools of Monetary Policy   373
The Market for Reserves and the Federal Funds Rate 373
    Demand and Supply in the Market for Reserves 373

Inside the Fed Why Does the Fed Need to Pay Interest on Reserves?   375
    How Changes in the Tools of Monetary Policy Affect the Federal Funds Rate 376

Application How the Federal Reserve's Operating Procedures
        Limit Fluctuations in the Federal Funds Rate 380
Open Market Operations 381
    A Day at the Trading Desk 381
    Advantages of Open Market Operations 383
Discount Policy 384
    Operation of the Discount Window 384
    Lender of Last Resort 384

Inside the Fed Using Discount Policy to Prevent a Financial Panic   386

Inside the Fed Federal Reserve Lender-of-Last-Resort Facilities During
        the Subprime Financial Crisis   387
    Advantages and Disadvantages of Discount Policy 388
Reserve Requirements 389
    Disadvantages of Reserve Requirements as a Policy Tool 389
Monetary Policy Tools of the European Central Bank 390
    Open Market Operations 390
    Lending to Banks 390
    Reserve Requirements 391
Summary 391 • Key Terms 391 • Questions and Problems 392 •
Web Exercises 392 • Web References 393

CHAPTER 16
The Conduct of Monetary Policy: Strategy and Tactics   395
Monetary Targeting 395
    Monetary Targeting in the United States, Japan, and Germany 395

Global The European Central Bank's Monetary Policy Strategy   398
    Advantages of Monetary Targeting 399
    Disadvantages of Monetary Targeting 399
Inflation Targeting 399
    Inflation Targeting in New Zealand, Canada, and the United Kingdom 400
    Advantages of Inflation Targeting 402
    Disadvantages of Inflation Targeting 403
Monetary Policy With an Implicit Nominal Anchor 405

Advantages of the "Just Do It" Approach 406
Disadvantages of the "Just Do It" Approach 406

Inside the Fed Chairman Bernanke and Inflation Targeting   407

Tactics: Choosing the Policy Instrument 408
Criteria for Choosing the Policy Instrument 410

Tactics: The Taylor Rule 412

Inside the Fed Fed Watchers   414

Central Banks' Response to Asset-Price Bubbles: Lessons from the Subprime Crisis   415
Two Types of Asset-Price Bubbles 415
Should Central Banks Respond to Bubbles? 416
Should Monetary Policy Try to Prick Asset-Price Bubbles? 417
Are Other Types of Policy Responses Appropriate? 417

Fed Policy Procedures: Historical Perspective 418
The Early Years: Discount Policy as the Primary Tool 418
Discovery of Open Market Operations 419
The Great Depression 419

Inside the Fed Bank Panics of 1930–1933: Why Did the Fed Let Them Happen?   420

Reserve Requirements as a Policy Tool 420
War Finance and the Pegging of Interest Rates: 1942–1951 421
Targeting Money Market Conditions: the 1950s and 1960s 421
Targeting Monetary Aggregates: the 1970s 422
New Fed Operating Procedures: October 1979–October 1982 423
De-Emphasis of Monetary Aggregates: October 1982–Early 1990s 424
Federal Funds Targeting Again: Early 1990s and Beyond 425
Preemptive Strikes Against Inflation 425
Preemptive Strikes Against Economic Downturns and Financial Disruptions:
LTCM, Enron, and the Subprime Meltdown 425
International Considerations 426

Summary 427 • Key Terms 428 • Questions and Problems 428 •
Web Exercises 429 • Web References 429

PART 5   International Finance and Monetary Policy   431

CHAPTER 17
**The Foreign Exchange Market: Exchange Rates
and Applications 433**

Foreign Exchange Market 433
What Are Foreign Exchange Rates? 434

Following the Financial News Foreign Exchange Rates   435

Why Are Exchange Rates Important? 436
How Is Foreign Exchange Traded? 436

Exchange Rates in the Long Run 437
Law of One Price 437
Theory of Purchasing Power Parity 437

Why the Theory of Purchasing Power Parity Cannot Fully Explain Exchange Rates 439
Factors That Affect Exchange Rates in the Long Run 439

Exchange Rates in the Short Run: A Supply and Demand Analysis 440
Supply Curve for Domestic Assets 442
Demand Curve for Domestic Assets 442
Equilibrium in the Foreign Exchange Market 443

Explaining Changes in Exchange Rates 443
Shifts in the Demand for Domestic Assets 443
Recap: Factors That Change the Exchange Rate 446

Application   Changes in the Equilibrium Exchange Rate: Two Examples 448
Changes in Interest Rates 448
Changes in the Money Supply 449
Exchange Rate Overshooting 450

Application   Why Do Some Nations Peg Their Currencies? 452

Application   The Euro Foreign Exchange Rate and Oil Prices 452

Application   The Global Financial Crisis and the Euro 454

Application   Reading the Financial Times: The "LEX" Column 454

Following the Financial News   The "LEX" Column   455

Summary 456   •   Key Terms 456   •   Questions and Problems 457   •
Web Exercises 457   •   Web References 458

APPENDIX TO CHAPTER 17
The Interest Parity Condition   459
Comparing Expected Returns on Domestic and Foreign Assets 459
Interest Parity Condition 461

CHAPTER 18
The International Financial System   463
Intervention in the Foreign Exchange Market 463
Foreign Exchange Intervention and the Money Supply 463

Inside the Fed   A Day at the Federal Reserve Bank of New York's
                  Foreign Exchange Desk   464

Unsterilized Intervention 466
Sterilized Intervention 467

Balance of Payments 468

Global   Why the Large U.S. Current Account Deficit Worries Economists   469

Exchange Rate Regimes in the International Financial System 470
Gold Standard 470
The Bretton Woods System 470

Global   The Euro's Challenge to the Dollar   471

How a Fixed Exchange Rate Regime Works 472

Application How Did China Accumulate Over $2 Trillion
    of International Reserves? 474
    Managed Float 475
    European Monetary System (EMS) 476

Application The Foreign Exchange Crisis of September 1992 477

Application Recent Foreign Exchange Crises in Emerging Market Countries:
    Mexico 1994, East Asia 1997, Brazil 1999, and Argentina 2002 478
Capital Controls 480
    Controls on Capital Outflows 480
    Controls on Capital Inflows 480
The Role of the IMF 481
    Should the IMF Be an International Lender of Last Resort? 481
    How Should the IMF Operate? 482

Global The Subprime Financial Crisis and the IMF 484

International Considerations and Monetary Policy 484
    Direct Effects of the Foreign Exchange Market on the Money Supply 484
    Balance-of-Payments Considerations 485
    Exchange Rate Considerations 485
To Peg or Not to Peg: Exchange-Rate Targeting as an Alternative
    Monetary Policy Strategy 486
    Advantages of Exchange-Rate Targeting 486
    Disadvantages of Exchange-Rate Targeting 487
    When Is Exchange-Rate Targeting Desirable for Industrialized Countries? 489
    When Is Exchange-Rate Targeting Desirable for Emerging Market Countries? . . . 489
    Currency Boards 490
    Dollarization 490

Global Argentina's Currency Board 491

Summary 492 • Key Terms 493 • Questions and Problems 493 •
    Web Exercises 494 • Web References 495

PART 6   Monetary Theory   497

CHAPTER 19
The Demand for Money   499

Quantity Theory of Money 499
    Velocity of Money and Equation of Exchange 500
    Quantity Theory 501
    Quantity Theory of Money Demand 501
Is Velocity a Constant? 502
Keynes's Liquidity Preference Theory 503
    Transactions Motive 504
    Precautionary Motive 504

Speculative Motive 504
Putting the Three Motives Together 505

Further Developments in the Keynesian Approach 507
Transactions Demand 507
Precautionary Demand 509
Speculative Demand 509

Friedman's Modern Quantity Theory of Money 511

Distinguishing Between the Friedman and Keynesian Theories 512

Empirical Evidence on the Demand for Money 515
Interest Rates and Money Demand 515
Stability of Money Demand 516

Summary 516 • Key Terms 517 • Questions and Problems 517 •
Web Exercises 518 • Web References 518

CHAPTER 20
The *ISLM* Model 519

Determination of Aggregate Output 519
Consumer Expenditure and the Consumption Function 520
Investment Spending 522

FYI Meaning of the Word *Investment* 523

Equilibrium and the Keynesian Cross Diagram 523
Expenditure Multiplier 525

Application The Collapse of Investment Spending and the Great Depression 527
Government's Role 528
Role of International Trade 530
Summary of the Determinants of Aggregate Output 531

The *ISLM* Model 534
Equilibrium in the Goods Market: The *IS* Curve 534
Equilibrium in the Market for Money: The *LM* Curve 537

ISLM Approach to Aggregate Output and Interest Rates 539

Summary 541 • Key Terms 541 • Questions and Problems 541 •
Web Exercises 542 • Web References 542

CHAPTER 21
Monetary and Fiscal Policy in the *ISLM* Model 543

Factors That Cause The *IS* Curve to Shift 543

Factors That Cause The *LM* Curve to Shift 546

Changes in Equilibrium Level of the Interest Rate and Aggregate Output 548
Response to a Change in Monetary Policy 548
Response to a Change in Fiscal Policy 549

Application The Economic Stimulus Act of 2008 550

Effectiveness of Monetary Versus Fiscal Policy 552
Monetary Policy Versus Fiscal Policy: The Case of Complete Crowding Out 552

Application Targeting Money Supply Versus Interest Rates 554

ISLM Model in the Long Run 557

ISLM Model and the Aggregate Demand Curve 559

Deriving the Aggregate Demand Curve 560

Factors That Cause the Aggregate Demand Curve to Shift 561

Summary 563 • Key Terms 563 • Questions and Problems 563 •
    Web Exercises 564 • Web References 564

CHAPTER 22
Aggregate Demand and Supply Analysis   565

Aggregate Demand 565

Following the Financial News Aggregate Output, Unemployment,
                        and the Price Level   566

Deriving the Aggregate Demand Curve 566

Factors That Shift the Aggregate Demand Curve 567

Aggregate Supply 568

Long-Run Aggregate Supply Curve 568

Short-Run Aggregate Supply Curve 570

Shifts in the Short-Run Aggregate Supply Curve 571

Factors That Shift the Short-Run Aggregate Supply Curve 571

Equilibrium in Aggregate Supply and Demand Analysis 574

Equilibrium in the Short Run 574

Equilibrium in the Long Run 575

Changes in Equilibrium Caused by Aggregate Demand Shocks 577

Changes in Equilibrium Caused by Aggregate Supply Shocks 578

Shifts in the Long-Run Aggregate Supply Curve: Real Business Cycle Theory
    and Hysteresis 579

Conclusions 580

Application **Explaining Past Business Cycle Episodes** 580

Vietnam War Buildup, 1964–1970 580

Negative Supply Shocks, 1973–1975 and 1978–1980 581

Favorable Supply Shocks, 1995–1999 582

Negative Demand Shocks, 2001–2004 582

The Perfect Storm of 2007–2008: Negative Supply Shocks and the Subprime
    Financial Crisis 583

Summary 584 • Key Terms 584 • Questions and Problems 585 •
    Web Exercises 585 • Web References 586

CHAPTER 23
Transmission Mechanisms of Monetary Policy: The Evidence   587

Framework for Evaluating Empirical Evidence 587

Structural Model Evidence 588

Reduced-Form Evidence 588

Advantages and Disadvantages of Structural Model Evidence 589

Advantages and Disadvantages of Reduced-Form Evidence 589

FYI Perils of Reverse Causation: A Russian Folk Tale   590

Conclusions 590

FYI Perils of Ignoring an Outside Driving Factor:
How to Lose a Presidential Election   591

Application The Debate on the Importance of Monetary Policy
to Economic Fluctuations 591
    Early Keynesian Evidence on the Importance of Money 591
    Objections to Early Keynesian Evidence 592
    Early Monetarist Evidence on the Importance of Money 594
    Overview of the Monetarist Evidence 599

FYI Real Business Cycle Theory and the Debate on Money and Economic Activity   600

Transmission Mechanisms of Monetary Policy 600
    Traditional Interest-Rate Channels 601
    Other Asset Price Channels 602
    Credit View 605

FYI Consumers' Balance Sheets and the Great Depression   608

    Why Are Credit Channels Likely to Be Important? 609

Application The Subprime Recession 609

Lessons for Monetary Policy 610

Application Applying the Monetary Policy Lessons to Japan 612

Summary 613 • Key Terms 613 • Questions and Problems 614 •
    Web Exercises 614 • Web References 615

CHAPTER 24
Money and Inflation   617

Money and Inflation: Evidence 617
    German Hyperinflation, 1921–1923 618
    Recent Episodes of Rapid Inflation 618

Meaning of Inflation 619

Views of Inflation 620
    How Money Growth Produces Inflation 620
    Can Other Factors Besides Money Growth Produce a Sustained Inflation? 621
    Summary 624

Origins of Inflationary Monetary Policy 624
    High Employment Targets and Inflation 624
    Budget Deficits and Inflation 627

Application Explaining the Rise in U.S. Inflation, 1960–1980 630

The Discretionary/Nondiscretionary Policy Debate 634
    Responses to High Unemployment 635
    Discretionary and Nondiscretionary Positions 636
    Expectations and the Discretionary/Nondiscretionary Debate 637
    Discretionary Versus Nondiscretionary: Conclusions 638

Application Importance of Credibility to Volcker's Victory
Over Inflation 639

Summary 640 • Key Terms 640 • Questions and Problems 640 •
    Web Exercises 641 • Web References 641

CHAPTER 25
Rational Expectations: Implications for Policy 643

The Lucas Critique of Policy Evaluation 644
   Econometric Policy Evaluation 644
   Example: The Term Structure of Interest Rates 644
New Classical Macroeconomic Model 645
   Effects of Unanticipated and Anticipated Policy 646

FYI Proof of the Policy Ineffectiveness Proposition 648

   Can an Expansionary Policy Lead to a Decline in Aggregate Output? 648
   Implications for Policymakers 649
New Keynesian Model 650
   Effects of Unanticipated and Anticipated Policy 651
   Implications for Policymakers 653
Comparison of the Two New Models With the Traditional Model 653
   Short-Run Output and Price Responses 653
   Stabilization Policy 656
   Anti-inflation Policies 656
   Credibility in Fighting Inflation 659

Global Ending the Bolivian Hyperinflation: A Successful Anti-inflation Program 660

Application **Credibility and the Reagan Budget Deficits** 660
Impact of the Rational Expectations Revolution 661
Summary 662 • Key Terms 663 • Questions and Problems 663 •
   Web Exercises 664 • Web References 664

Glossary G-1
Credits C-1
Index I-1

HALLMARKS

Although this text has undergone a major revision, it retains the basic hallmarks that have made it the best-selling textbook on money and banking over the past eight editions:

- A unifying, analytic framework that uses a few basic economic principles to organize students' thinking about the structure of financial markets, the foreign exchange markets, financial institution management, and the role of monetary policy in the economy
- A careful, step-by-step development of models (an approach found in the best principles of economics textbooks), which makes it easier for students to learn
- The complete integration of an international perspective throughout the text
- A thoroughly up-to-date treatment of the latest developments in monetary theory
- Special features called "Following the Financial News" and "Reading the *Wall Street Journal*" to encourage reading of a financial newspaper
- An applications-oriented perspective with numerous applications and special-topic boxes that increase students' interest by showing them how to apply theory to real-world examples

WHAT'S NEW IN THE NINTH EDITION

In addition to the expected updating of all data through the end of 2008 whenever possible, there is major new material in every part of the text.

The Business School Edition

I am pleased to continue providing two versions of *The Economics of Money, Banking, and Financial Markets*. While both versions contain the core chapters that all professors want to cover, *The Economics of Money, Banking, and Financial Markets*, Business School Edition (formerly the Alternate Edition), is designed for those professors who prefer to focus more on finance, or who simply do not cover *ISLM*. The Business School Edition includes not only chapters on nonbank finance and financial derivatives, but also an entire chapter on the conflicts of interest in the financial industry. The Business School Edition omits the two *ISLM* chapters and the chapter on the implications of rational expectations for policy. For those professors whose courses have less of an emphasis on monetary theory, *The Economics of Money, Banking, and Financial Markets*, Business School Edition, will more closely fit your needs.

For those professors who want a comprehensive discussion of monetary theory and monetary policy, *The Economics of Money, Banking, and Financial Markets*, Ninth Edition, contains all of the chapters on monetary theory. Professors who do want this coverage are often hard-pressed to cover all the finance and institutions chapters. To that end, the

Ninth Edition omits the chapters on nonbank finance, financial derivatives, and conflicts of interest. The MyEconLab course for each edition provides the omitted chapters making them readily available for those who do wish to utilize them in their courses.

The Subprime Financial Crisis

The subprime financial crisis has led to a series of events that have completely changed the structure of the financial system and the way central banks operate. This has required a rewriting of almost the entire textbook, including a new chapter, a rewrite of one whole chapter, and the addition of many timely new sections, applications, and boxes throughout the rest of the book.

New Chapter 9: Financial Crises and the Subprime Meltdown

With the coming of the subprime financial crisis, a money and banking course would not be complete without an extensive analysis of why financial crises like the subprime crisis occur and why they have such devastating effects on the economy. Using an economic analysis of the effects of asymmetric information on financial markets and the economy, this new chapter examines why financial crises occur and why they have such devastating effects on the economy. This analysis is used to explain the course of events in a number of past financial crises throughout the world, with a particular focus on explaining the recent subprime crisis. Because the recent events in the subprime crisis have been so dramatic, the material in this chapter is very exciting for students. Indeed, when teaching this chapter after I returned to Columbia, the students were more engaged with this material than with anything else I have taught in my entire teaching career of over 30 years.

Reordering of Part 3, Financial Institutions, and Rewrite of Chapter 11, The Economic Analysis of Financial Regulation

In past editions, the chapter on the structure of the banking industry was followed by the chapter on banking regulation. This ordering no longer makes sense in the aftermath of the subprime financial crisis, because nonbank financial institutions like investment banks have for the most part disappeared as free-standing institutions and are now part of banking organizations. To reflect the new financial world that we have entered, we first discuss the financial industry as a whole and then look at the specifics of how the now more broadly based banking industry is structured. To do this, I have placed the chapter on regulation before the chapter on the structure of the banking industry and have rewritten it to focus less on bank regulation and more on regulation of the overall financial system.

Revised Chapter 13, Central Banks: A Global Perspective

Monal Abdel-Baki at the American University in Cairo has contributed a revised chapter with expanded coverage of the role and structure of the ECB, and coverage of central banks in transition and emerging economies.

Compelling New Material Throughout the Text

The subprime financial crisis has had such far-reaching effects on the field of money and banking that almost every chapter has required changes to reflect what has happened.

Throughout the book, I have also added a large amount of substantive new material on the impact of the subprime financial crisis including:

- A new application on the subprime collapse and the Baa-Treasury spread (Chapter 5)
- A new application on the subprime financial crisis and the stock market (Chapter 7)
- A new box on credit-rating agencies and the subprime financial crisis (Chapter 8)
- A new application on how a capital crunch caused a credit crunch in 2008 (Chapter 10)
- A new box on mark-to-market accounting and the subprime financial crisis (Chapter 11)
- A new box on the subprime mortgage crisis and consumer protection regulation (Chapter 11)
- A new section on where financial regulation is heading after the subprime financial crisis (Chapter 11)
- A new box on the money market mutual fund panic of 2008 (Chapter 12)
- A new box on the subprime financial crisis and the demise of large, free-standing investment banks (Chapter 12)
- A new Inside the Fed box on Federal Reserve lender-of-last-resort facilities during the subprime financial crisis (Chapter 15)
- A new section on preemptive strikes against economic downturns and financial disruption during the subprime meltdown (Chapter 16)
- A new section on lessons from the subprime crisis as to how central banks should respond to asset price bubbles (Chapter 16)
- A new application on the global financial crisis and the euro (Chapter 17)
- A new box on the subprime financial crisis and the IMF (Chapter 18)
- A new application on the Economic Stimulus Act of 2008 (Chapter 21)
- A new application on the perfect storm of shocks: negative supply shocks and the subprime financial crisis (Chapter 22)
- A new application on the subprime recession (Chapter 23)
- A new box on the AIG blowup (Web Chapter 1)
- A new box on the subprime financial crisis and the monoline insurers (Web Chapter 1)
- A new box on the subprime financial crisis and the bailout of Fannie Mae and Freddie Mac (Web Chapter 1)
- A new application on lessons from the subprime financial crisis: when are financial derivatives likely to be a worldwide time bomb? (Web Chapter 2)

Additional New Material on Financial Markets and Institutions

There have also been changes in financial markets and institutions in recent years that have not been directly related to the subprime financial crisis, and I have added the following new material to keep the text current:

- A new section on the positive role that lawyers play in our financial system, entitled "Should We Kill All the Lawyers?" (Chapter 8)
- A new box on whether Sarbanes-Oxley led to a decline in U.S. capital markets (Chapter 8)
- A new box on how well Basel 2 will work (Chapter 11)

- A rewritten section on financial innovation and the growth of the "shadow banking system" (Chapter 12)
- A new section on credit insurance (Web Chapter 1)
- A new section on private equity and venture capital funds (Web Chapter 1)
- A new box on sovereign wealth funds and whether they pose a danger (Web Chapter 1)

New Material on Monetary Theory and Policy

Drawing on my two years as a governor of the Federal Reserve, I have added new material on monetary theory and policy over and above that which was related to the subprime financial crisis:

- A new Inside the Fed box on how Bernanke's style differs from Greenspan's (Chapter 13)
- A new Inside the Fed box on why the Fed needs to pay interest on reserves (Chapter 15)
- A rewrite of the section on the market for reserves and the federal funds rate to reflect the new policy of paying interest on reserves (Chapter 15)
- A new application on how the Federal Reserve's operating procedures limit fluctuations in the federal funds rate (Chapter 15)
- An update on the Inside the Fed box on Chairman Bernanke and inflation targeting (Chapter 16)
- A expanded discussion of the Taylor Rule (Chapter 16)
- A new section on preemptive strikes against inflation (Chapter 16)
- A new section on preemptive strikes against economic downturns and financial disruptions (Chapter 16)

Further Simplification of the Supply and Demand Analysis of the Foreign Exchange Market

The chapter on the determination of exchange rates has always been challenging for some students. In the Eighth Edition, I moved the analysis closer to a more traditional supply and demand analysis to make it more intuitive for students. Although this change has been very well received by instructors, I decided that the model of exchange rate determination could be made even easier for the students if I relegated the calculation comparing expected returns and the interest parity conditions to an appendix. Doing so in the Ninth Edition simplifies discussion appreciably and should make the analysis of exchange rate determination much more accessible to students.

Improved Exposition and Organization

Helpful comments from reviewers prompted me to improve the exposition throughout the book. The reviewers convinced me that material on what central banks should do would be better placed at the beginning of the discussion of Part 4 on central banking. As a result, I moved the material on the goals of monetary policy from Chapter 16, which now has a slightly new title, "The Conduct of Monetary Policy: Strategy and Tactics" to the revised Chapter 13, "Central Banks: A Global Perspective".

Reviewers also suggested that I could simplify and condense the discussion of how the money supply is determined by combining Chapters 13 and 14 from the Eighth Edition into a new chapter. The resulting new chapter entitled "The Money Supply Process" does not lose any content and works even better in the classroom than the two chapters in the Eighth Edition. Also, at the suggestion of several reviewers, I simplified the exposition at the beginning of Chapter 22 of how the aggregate demand curve is derived.

Chapters and Appendices on the Web

The Web site for the book, www.pearsonglobaleditions.com/mishkin, is an essential resource for additional content.

The Web chapters for the Ninth Edition of *The Economics of Money, Banking, and Financial Markets* include the unique chapters from the Business School Edition. These chapters are:

Web Chapter 1:   Nonbank Finance
Web Chapter 2:   Financial Derivatives
Web Chapter 3:   Conflicts of Interest in the Financial Industry

The Web appendices include:

Chapter 4:   Measuring Interest-Rate Risk: Duration
Chapter 5:   Models of Asset Pricing
Chapter 5:   Applying the Asset Market Approach to a Commodity Market: The Case of Gold
Chapter 5:   Loanable Funds Framework
Chapter 7:   Evidence on the Efficient Market Hypothesis
Chapter 10:   Duration Gap Analysis
Chapter 10:   Measuring Bank Performance
Chapter 11:   The Savings and Loan Crisis and Its Aftermath
Chapter 11:   Banking Crises Throughout the World
Chapter 14:   The Fed's Balance Sheet and the Monetary Base
Chapter 14:   The M2 Money Multiplier
Chapter 14:   Explaining the Behavior of the Currency Ratio
Chapter 19:   A Mathematical Treatment of the Baumol-Tobin and Tobin Mean Variance Model
Chapter 19:   Empirical Evidence on the Demand for Money
Chapter 21:   Algebra of the *ISLM* Model
Chapter 22:   Aggregate Supply and the Phillips Curve

Instructors can either use these Web Chapters or appendices in class to supplement the material in the textbook or recommend them to students who want to expand their knowledge of the money and banking field.

FLEXIBILITY

In using previous editions, adopters, reviewers, and survey respondents have continually praised this text's flexibility. There are as many ways to teach money, banking, and financial markets as there are instructors. To satisfy the diverse needs of instructors, the text achieves flexibility as follows:

- Core chapters provide the basic analysis used throughout the book, and other chapters or sections of chapters can be used or omitted according to instructor preferences. For example, Chapter 2 introduces the financial system and basic concepts such as transaction costs, adverse selection, and moral hazard. After covering Chapter 2, the instructor may decide to give more detailed coverage of financial structure by assigning Chapter 8, or may choose to skip Chapter 8 and take any of a number of different paths through the book.
- The text also allows instructors to cover the most important issues in monetary theory and policy without having to use the *ISLM* model in Chapters 20 and 21, while more complete treatments of monetary theory make use of the *ISLM* chapters.
- The internationalization of the text through marked international sections within chapters, as well as through complete separate chapters on the foreign exchange market and the international monetary system, is comprehensive yet flexible. Although many instructors will teach all the international material, others will not. Instructors who want less emphasis on international topics can easily skip Chapter 17 on the foreign exchange market and Chapter 18 on the international financial system and monetary policy. The international sections within chapters are self-contained and can be omitted with little loss of continuity.

To illustrate how this book can be used for courses with varying emphases, several course outlines are suggested for a semester teaching schedule. More detailed information about how the text can be used flexibly in your course is available in the Instructor's Manual.

- *General Money and Banking Course:* Chapters 1–5, 10–13, 15, 16, 22, 24, with a choice of 6 of the remaining 12 chapters.
- *General Money and Banking Course with an International Emphasis:* Chapters 1–5, 10–13, 15–18, 22, 24 with a choice of 4 of the remaining 10 chapters.
- *Financial Markets and Institutions Course:* Chapters 1–12, with a choice of 7 of the remaining 13 chapters.
- *Monetary Theory and Policy Course:* Chapters 1–5, 13–16, 19, 22–25, with a choice of 5 of the remaining 11 chapters.

PEDAGOGICAL AIDS

In teaching theory or its applications, a textbook must be a solid motivational tool. To this end, I have incorporated a wide variety of pedagogical features to make the material easy to learn:

1. **Previews** at the beginning of each chapter tell students where the chapter is heading, why specific topics are important, and how they relate to other topics in the book.
2. **Applications**, numbering around 50, demonstrate how the analysis in the book can be used to explain many important real-world situations. A special set of applications, called "Reading the *Wall Street Journal*," shows students how to read daily columns in this leading financial newspaper.
3. **Following the Financial News boxes** introduce students to relevant news articles and data that are reported daily in the press and explain how to read them.

4. **Inside the Fed boxes** give students a feel for what is important in the operation and structure of the Federal Reserve System.

5. **Global boxes** include interesting material with an international focus.

6. **FYI boxes** highlight dramatic historical episodes, interesting ideas, and intriguing facts related to the subject matter.

7. **Summary tables** provide a useful study aid in reviewing material.

8. **Key statements** are important points set in boldface italic type so that students can easily find them for later reference.

9. **Graphs** with captions, numbering more than 150, help students clearly understand the interrelationship of the variables plotted and the principles of analysis.

10. **Summary** at the end of each chapter lists the main points covered.

11. **Key terms** are important words or phrases, boldface when they are defined for the first time and listed by page number at the end of the chapter.

12. **End-of-chapter questions and problems**, numbering more than 400, help students learn the subject matter by applying economic concepts, including a special class of problems that students find particularly relevant, under the heading "Using Economic Analysis to Predict the Future."

13. **Web Exercises** encourage students to collect information from online sources or use online resources to enhance their learning experience.

14. **Web Sources** report the Web URL source of the data used to create the many tables and charts.

15. **Web References** point the student to Web sites that provide information or data that supplement the text material.

16. **Glossary** at the back of the book provides definitions of all the key terms.

AN EASIER WAY TO TEACH: SUPPLEMENTS TO ACCOMPANY THE NINTH EDITION

The Economics of Money, Banking, and Financial Markets, Global Edition, Ninth Edition, includes the most comprehensive program of supplements of any money, banking, and financial markets textbook. These items are available to qualified domestic adopters but in some cases may not be available to international adopters.

MyEconLab is the premier online assessment and tutorial system, pairing rich online content with innovative learning tools. The MyEconLab course for the Ninth Edition of *The Economics of Money, Banking, and Financial Markets, Global Edition,* includes all end-of-chapter problems from the text, which can be easily assigned and automatically graded.

Students and MyEconLab   This online homework and tutorial system puts students in control of their own learning through a suite of study and practice tools correlated with the online, interactive version of the textbook and other media tools. Within MyEconLab's structured environment, students practice what they learn, test their understanding, and then pursue a study plan that MyEconLab generates for them based on their performance on practice tests.

Instructors and MyEconLab   MyEconLab provides flexible tools that allow instructors to easily and effectively customize online course materials to suit their needs. Instructors can create and assign tests, quizzes, or homework assignments. MyEconLab saves time by automatically grading all questions and tracking results in an online grade book. MyEconLab can even grade assignments that require students to draw a graph.

After registering for MyEconLab, instructors have access to downloadable supplements such as an instructor's manual, PowerPoint lecture notes, and the test bank. The test bank can also be used within MyEconLab, giving instructors ample material from which they can create assignments.

Additional MyEconLab features include:

- *Animated Figures.* Key figures from the textbook are presented in step-by-step animations with audio explanations of the action.
- *Applications.* The applications from the text are available with assignable questions.
- *Mishkin Interviewed on the Financial Crisis.* Watch video footage from a recent interview with the author, complete with assignable questions.
- *Weekly News Updates.* Each week, a relevant and current article from a newspaper or journal is posted with Discussion Questions.
- *Research Navigator* (CourseCompass version only). Extensive help on the research process and four exclusive databases of accredited and reliable source material including the *Financial Times* and peer-reviewed journals.

For more information and to register, please visit www.myeconlab.com.

Additional Instructor Resources

1. **Instructor's Manual**, an online supplement prepared by me and offering conventional elements such as sample course outlines, chapter outlines, and answers to questions and problems in the text.
2. **PowerPoint® Slides**. New to this edition is a far more comprehensive set of PowerPoint slides—greatly expanded from the previous edition and now numbering over 550—that provides not only all the tables and graphs in the text, but very detailed lecture notes for all the material in the course. The basis of the lecture notes is, in fact, the notes I use in class—and they should help other instructors prepare their lectures as they have helped me. In this edition, Martin Pereyra of the University of Missouri has enhanced the presentation by adding additional lecture notes. Some instructors might use these PowerPoint slides as their own class notes and prefer to teach with a blackboard. But for those who prefer to teach with visual aids, the PowerPoint slides, which are fully customizable, afford the flexibility to take this approach.
3. **Computerized Test Bank**, allowing the instructor to produce exams efficiently. Updated and revised by Richard G. Stahl of Louisiana State University and Kathy Kelly of the University of Texas at Arlington, comprising more than 2,500 multiple-choice and essay test items, this product consists of the multiple-choice and essay questions in the printed Test Bank and offers editing capabilities. It is available in Windows and Macintosh versions.

4. **Mishkin Web site**, located at www.pearsonglobaleditions.com/mishkin, which features appendices on a wide variety of topics (see "Appendices on the Web"), omitted chapters, and links to the URLs that appear at the end of the chapters.

Additional Student Resources

1. **Study Guide**, fully revised and updated by David Hakes of the University of Northern Iowa and Ed Gamber of Lafayette College, includes chapter synopses and completions, exercises, self-tests, and answers to the exercises and self-tests.
2. **Readings on Money, Banking, and Financial Markets**, edited by James W. Eaton of Bridgewater College and me, updated annually, with over half the articles new each year to enable instructors to keep the content of their course current throughout the life of an edition of the text. The readings are available within MyEconLab.

ACKNOWLEDGMENTS

As always in so large a project, there are many people to thank. My gratitude goes especially to Donna Battista, economics and finance editor-in-chief at Pearson and Rebecca Ferris-Caruso, my development editor. I would also like to thank Noel Seibert, Kathryn Dinovo, and Kerri McQueen for their contributions as well. I also have been assisted by comments from my colleagues at Columbia and from my students.

In addition, I have been guided by the thoughtful commentary of outside reviewers and correspondents, especially Jim Eaton. Their feedback has made this a better book. In particular, I thank the following:

Burt Abrams, University of Delaware
Stefania Albanesi, Columbia University
Mike Carew, Barauch University
Tina Carter, University of Florida
Imran Farooqi, University of Iowa
Shirley Gedeon, University of Vermont
Lance Girton, University of Utah
Ralph Gunderson, University of Wisconsin
Scott Hein, Texas Tech
Chad Hogan, University of Michigan
James Hueng, Western Michigan
Ahmed Kalifa, Colorado State University
Elham Mafi-Kreft, Indiana University
James Maloy, University of Pittsburgh
Carrie Meyer, George Mason University
Steve Russell, IUPUI
Joe Santos, South Dakota State University
John Shea, University of Maryland
Rajesh Singh, Iowa State University
Aditi Thapar, New York University
Chao Wei, George Washing University
Elliot Willman, New Mexico State University

JaeJoon Woo, DePaul University
Ed Zajicek, Winston Salem State University

My special thanks go to the following individuals who analyzed the manuscript in previous editions:

Francis W. Ahking, University of Connecticut
Mohammed Akacem, Metropolitan State College of Denver
Muhammad Anwar, University of Massachusetts
Harjit K. Arora, Le Moyne College
Stacie Beck, University of Delaware
Gerry Bialka, University of North Florida
Daniel K. Biederman, University of North Dakota
John Bishop, East Carolina University
Daniel Blake, California State University, Northridge
Robert Boatler, Texas Christian University
Henning Bohn, University of California, Santa Barbara
Michael W. Brandl, University of Texas at Austin
Oscar T. Brookins, Northeastern University
William Walter Brown, California State University, Northridge
James L. Butkiewicz, University of Delaware
Colleen M. Callahan, Lehigh University
Ray Canterbery, Florida State University
Sergio Castello, University of Mobile
Jen-Chi Cheng, Wichita State University
Patrick Crowley, Middlebury College
Sarah E. Culver, University of Alabama, Birmingham
Maria Davis, San Antonio College
Ranjit S. Dighe, State University of New York, Oswego
Richard Douglas, Bowling Green University
Donald H. Dutkowsky, Syracuse University
Richard Eichhorn, Colorado State University
Paul Emberton, Southwest Texas State University
Erick Eschker, Humboldt State University
Robert Eyler, Sonoma State University
L. S. Fan, Colorado State University
Sasan Fayazmanesh, California State University, Fresno
Dennis Fixler, George Washington University
Gary Fleming, Roanoke College
Grant D. Forsyth, Eastern Washington University
Timothy Fuerst, Bowling Green State University
James Gale, Michigan Technological University
Stuart M. Glosser, University of Wisconsin, Whitewater
Fred C. Graham, American University
Jo Anna Gray, University of Oregon
David Gulley, Bentley College
Daniel Haak, Stanford University
Larbi Hammami, McGill University
Bassan Harik, Western Michigan University
J. C. Hartline, Rutgers University
Robert Stanley Herren, North Dakota State University

Jane Himarios, University of Texas, Arlington
Linda Hooks, Washington and Lee University
Dar-Yeh Hwang, National Taiwan University
Jayvanth Ishwaran, Stephen F. Austin State University
Jonatan Jelen, Queens College and City College of CUNY
U Jin Jhun, State University of New York, Oswego
Frederick L. Joutz, George Washington University
Bryce Kanago, University of Northern Iowa
Magda Kandil, International Monetary Fund
Theodore Kariotis, Towson University
George G. Kaufman, Loyola University Chicago
Richard H. Keehn, University of Wisconsin, Parkside
Elizabeth Sawyer Kelly, University of Wisconsin, Madison
Fritz Laux, Northeastern State University
Jim Lee, Fort Hays State University
Robert Leeson, University of Western Ontario
Tony Lima, California State University, Hayward
Fiona Maclachlan, Manhattan College
Bernard Malamud, University of Nevada, Las Vegas
James Marchand, Mercer University
Marvin Margolis, Millersville University
Elaine McBeth, College of William and Mary
Stephen McCafferty, Ohio State University
James McCown, Ohio State University
Cheryl McGaughey, Angelo State University
W. Douglas McMillin, Louisiana State University
William Merrill, Iowa State University
Stephen M. Miller, University of Connecticut
Masoud Moghaddam, Saint Cloud State University
Thomas S. Mondschean, DePaul University
Clair Morris, U.S. Naval Academy
Jon Nadenichek, California State University, Northridge
John Nader, Grand Valley State University
Leonce Ndikumana, University of Massachusetts, Amherst
Ray Nelson, Brigham Young University
Inder P. Nijhawan, Fayetteville State University
Nick Noble, Miami University of Ohio
Dennis O'Toole, Virginia Commonwealth University
Mark J. Perry, University of Michigan, Flint
Chung Pham, University of New Mexico
Marvin M. Phaup, George Washington University
Ganga P. Ramdas, Lincoln University
Ronald A. Ratti, University of Missouri, Columbia
Hans Rau, Ball State University
Prosper Raynold, Miami University
Javier Reyes, Texas A&M University
Jack Russ, San Diego State University
Robert S. Rycroft, Mary Washington College
Lynn Schneider, Auburn University, Montgomery
Walter Schwarm, Colorado State University

Harinder Singh, Grand Valley State University
Larry Taylor, Lehigh University
Leigh Tesfatsion, Iowa State University
Frederick D. Thum, University of Texas, Austin
Robert Tokle, Idaho State University
C. Van Marrewijk, Erasmus University
Christopher J. Waller, Indiana University
Maurice Weinrobe, Clark University
James R. Wible, University of New Hampshire
Philip R. Wiest, George Mason University
William Wilkes, Athens State University
Thomas Williams, William Paterson University
Donald Wills, University of Washington, Tacoma
Laura Wolff, Southern Illinois University, Edwardsville
Robert Wright, University of Virginia
Ben T. Yu, California State University, Northridge
Ky H. Yuhn, Florida Atlantic University
Jeffrey Zimmerman, Methodist College

Finally, I want to thank my wife, Sally; my son, Matthew; and my daughter, Laura, who provide me with a warm and happy environment that enables me to do my work, and my father, Sidney, now deceased, who a long time ago put me on the path that led to this book.

FREDERIC S. MISHKIN

International Contributions
Monal Abdel-Baki, American University in Cairo, contributed international content to chapters 3, 13, and 17.

International Reviewers
Amina Tyabiji, National University of Singapore
Andy Cheuk-Chiu Kwan, Chinese University of Hong Kong
Cigdem Celik, Istanbul Bilgi University
Edward N. Gamber, Lafayette College, USA
Ng Beoy Kui, Nanyang Technological University
Rosylin Mohd, University of Bahrain
Salina Kassim, International Islamic University Malaysia
Tiong Yang Thong, Singapore Management University
Yue-cheong Chan, The Hong Kong Polytechnic University

Frederic S. Mishkin is the Alfred Lerner Professor of Banking and Financial Institutions at the Graduate School of Business, Columbia University. He is also a Research Associate at the National Bureau of Economic Research and past president of the Eastern Economics Association. Since receiving his Ph.D. from the Massachusetts Institute of Technology in 1976, he has taught at the University of Chicago, Northwestern University, Princeton University, and Columbia. He has also received an honorary professorship from the People's (Renmin) University of China. From 1994 to 1997, he was Executive Vice President and Director of Research at the Federal Reserve Bank of New York and an associate economist of the Federal Open Market Committee of the Federal Reserve System. From September 2006 to August 2008, he was a member (governor) of the Board of Governors of the Federal Reserve System.

Professor Mishkin's research focuses on monetary policy and its impact on financial markets and the aggregate economy. He is the author of more than fifteen books, including *Financial Markets and Institutions*, Sixth Edition (Addison-Wesley, 2009); *Monetary Policy Strategy*, (MIT Press, 2007) *The Next Great Globalization: How Disadvantaged Nations Can Harness Their Financial Systems to Get Rich* (Princeton University Press, 2006); *Inflation Targeting: Lessons from the International Experience* (Princeton University Press, 1999); *Money, Interest Rates, and Inflation* (Edward Elgar, 1993); and *A Rational Expectations Approach to Macroeconometrics: Testing Policy Ineffectiveness and Efficient Markets Models* (University of Chicago Press, 1983). In addition, he has published more than 150 articles in such journals as *American Economic Review*, *Journal of Political Economy*, *Econometrica*, *Quarterly Journal of Economics*, *Journal of Finance*, and *Journal of Monetary Economics*.

Professor Mishkin has served on the editorial board of *American Economic Review* and has been an associate editor at *Journal of Business and Economic Statistics*, the *Journal of Applied Econometrics*, and *Journal of Money, Credit and Banking*; he also served as the editor of the Federal Reserve Bank of New York's *Economic Policy Review*. He is currently an associate editor (member of the editorial board) at six academic journals, including *Macroeconomics and Monetary Economics Abstracts*; *Journal of International Money and Finance*; *International Finance*; *Finance India*; *Economic Policy Review;* and *Emerging Markets, Finance and Trade*. He has been a consultant to the Board of Governors of the Federal Reserve System, the World Bank, and the International Monetary Fund, as well as to many central banks throughout the world. He was also a member of the International Advisory Board to the Financial Supervisory Service of South Korea and an advisor to the Institute for Monetary and Economic Research at the Bank of Korea. Professor Mishkin was a Senior Fellow at the Federal Deposit Insurance Corporation's Center for Banking Research and was an academic consultant to and served on the Economic Advisory Panel of the Federal Reserve Bank of New York.

PART 1

Introduction

CHAPTER 1
Why Study Money, Banking, and
Financial Markets?

•

CHAPTER 2
An Overview of the Financial
System

•

CHAPTER 3
What Is Money?: A Comparative
Approach to Measuring Money

1 Why Study Money, Banking, and Financial Markets?

Preview

On the evening news you have just heard that the Federal Reserve is raising the federal funds rate by $\frac{1}{2}$ of a percentage point. What effect might this have on the interest rate of an automobile loan when you finance your purchase of a sleek new sports car? Does it mean that a house will be more or less affordable in the future? Will it make it easier or harder for you to get a job next year?

This book provides answers to these and other questions by examining how financial markets (such as those for bonds, stocks, and foreign exchange) and financial institutions (banks, insurance companies, mutual funds, and other institutions) work and by exploring the role of money in the economy. Financial markets and institutions not only affect your everyday life but also involve flows of trillions of dollars of funds throughout our economy, which in turn affect business profits, the production of goods and services, and even the economic well-being of countries other than the United States. What happens to financial markets, financial institutions, and money is of great concern to politicians and can even have a major impact on elections. The study of money, banking, and financial markets will reward you with an understanding of many exciting issues. In this chapter, we provide a road map of the book by outlining these issues and exploring why they are worth studying.

WHY STUDY FINANCIAL MARKETS?

Part 2 of this book focuses on **financial markets**, markets in which funds are transferred from people who have an excess of available funds to people who have a shortage. Financial markets such as bond and stock markets are crucial to promoting greater economic efficiency by channeling funds from people who do not have a productive use for them to those who do. Indeed, well-functioning financial markets are a key factor in producing high economic growth, and poorly performing financial markets are one reason that many countries in the world remain desperately poor. Activities in financial markets also have direct effects on personal wealth, the behavior of businesses and consumers, and the cyclical performance of the economy.

The Bond Market and Interest Rates

A **security** (also called a *financial instrument*) is a claim on the issuer's future income or **assets** (any financial claim or piece of property that is subject to ownership). A **bond** is a debt security that promises to make payments periodically for a specified period of

3

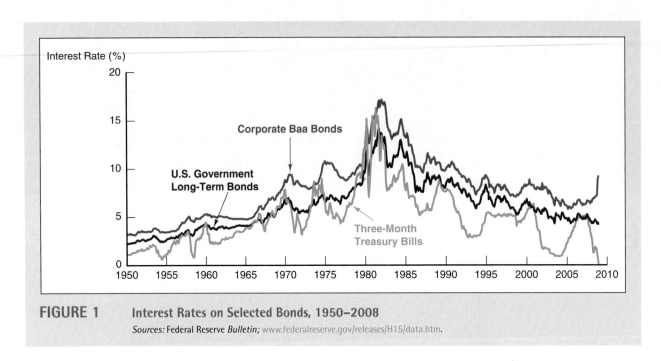

FIGURE 1   **Interest Rates on Selected Bonds, 1950–2008**

Sources: Federal Reserve *Bulletin;* www.federalreserve.gov/releases/H15/data.htm.

time.[1] The bond market is especially important to economic activity because it enables corporations and governments to borrow to finance their activities and because it is where interest rates are determined. An **interest rate** is the cost of borrowing or the price paid for the rental of funds (usually expressed as a percentage of the rental of $100 per year). There are many interest rates in the economy—mortgage interest rates, car loan rates, and interest rates on many different types of bonds.

Interest rates are important on a number of levels. On a personal level, high interest rates could deter you from buying a house or a car because the cost of financing it would be high. Conversely, high interest rates could encourage you to save because you can earn more interest income by putting aside some of your earnings as savings. On a more general level, interest rates have an impact on the overall health of the economy because they affect not only consumers' willingness to spend or save but also businesses' investment decisions. High interest rates, for example, might cause a corporation to postpone building a new plant that would provide more jobs.

Because changes in interest rates have important effects on individuals, financial institutions, businesses, and the overall economy, it is important to explain fluctuations in interest rates that have been substantial over the past thirty years. For example, the interest rate on three-month Treasury bills peaked at over 16% in 1981. This interest rate fell to 3% in late 1992 and 1993, rose to above 5% in the mid- to late 1990s, fell to below 1% in 2004, rose to 5% by 2007, only to fall to zero in 2008.

Because different interest rates have a tendency to move in unison, economists frequently lump interest rates together and refer to "the" interest rate. As Figure 1 shows, however, interest rates on several types of bonds can differ substantially. The interest

---

[1]The definition of *bond* used throughout this book is the broad one in common use by academics, which covers both short- and long-term debt instruments. However, some practitioners in financial markets use the word *bond* to describe only specific long-term debt instruments such as corporate bonds or U.S. Treasury bonds.

rate on three-month Treasury bills, for example, fluctuates more than the other interest rates and is lower, on average. The interest rate on Baa (medium-quality) corporate bonds is higher, on average, than the other interest rates, and the spread between it and the other rates became larger in the 1970s, narrowed in the 1990s, and rose briefly in the early 2000s, narrowed again, only to rise sharply starting in the summer of 2007.

In Chapter 2 we study the role of bond markets in the economy, and in Chapters 4 through 6 we examine what an interest rate is, how the common movements in interest rates come about, and why the interest rates on different bonds vary.

The Stock Market

A **common stock** (typically just called a **stock**) represents a share of ownership in a corporation. It is a security that is a claim on the earnings and assets of the corporation. Issuing stock and selling it to the public is a way for corporations to raise funds to finance their activities. The stock market, in which claims on the earnings of corporations (shares of stock) are traded, is the most widely followed financial market in almost every country that has one; that's why it is often called simply "the market." A big swing in the prices of shares in the stock market is always a major story on the evening news. People often speculate on where the market is heading and get very excited when they can brag about their latest "big killing," but they become depressed when they suffer a big loss. The attention the market receives can probably be best explained by one simple fact: It is a place where people can get rich—or poor—quickly.

As Figure 2 indicates, stock prices are extremely volatile. After the market rose in the 1980s, on "Black Monday," October 19, 1987, it experienced the worst one-day drop in its entire history, with the Dow Jones Industrial Average (DJIA) falling by 22%. From then until 2000, the stock market experienced one of the greatest bull markets in its history, with the Dow climbing to a peak of over 11,000. With the collapse of the high-tech bubble in 2000, the stock market fell sharply, dropping by over 30% by late 2002. It then recovered again and reached the 14,000 level in 2007, only to fall below the 8,000 level early in 2009. These considerable fluctuations in stock prices affect the size of people's wealth and as a result may affect their willingness to spend.

The stock market is also an important factor in business investment decisions, because the price of shares affects the amount of funds that can be raised by selling newly issued stock to finance investment spending. A higher price for a firm's shares means that it can raise a larger amount of funds, which it can use to buy production facilities and equipment.

In Chapter 2 we examine the role that the stock market plays in the financial system, and we return to the issue of how stock prices behave and respond to information in the marketplace in Chapter 7.

WHY STUDY FINANCIAL INSTITUTIONS AND BANKING?

Part 3 of this book focuses on financial institutions and the business of banking. Banks and other financial institutions are what make financial markets work. Without them, financial markets would not be able to move funds from people who save to people who have productive investment opportunities. Thus they play a crucial role in the economy.

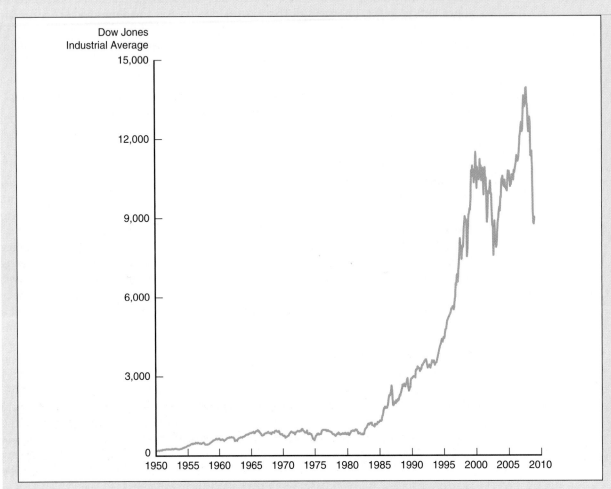

FIGURE 2   **Stock Prices as Measured by the Dow Jones Industrial Average, 1950–2008**

Source: Dow Jones Indexes: http://finance.yahoo.com/?u.

Structure of the Financial System

The financial system is complex, comprising many different types of private sector financial institutions, including banks, insurance companies, mutual funds, finance companies, and investment banks, all of which are heavily regulated by the government. If an individual wanted to make a loan to IBM or General Motors, for example, he or she would not go directly to the president of the company and offer a loan. Instead, he or she would lend to such companies indirectly through **financial intermediaries**, institutions that borrow funds from people who have saved and in turn make loans to others.

Why are financial intermediaries so crucial to well-functioning financial markets? Why do they extend credit to one party but not to another? Why do they usually write complicated legal documents when they extend loans? Why are they the most heavily regulated businesses in the economy?

We answer these questions in Chapter 8 by developing a coherent framework for analyzing financial structure in the United States and in the rest of the world.

Financial Crises

At times, the financial system seizes up and produces **financial crises**, major disruptions in financial markets that are characterized by sharp declines in asset prices and the failures of many financial and nonfinancial firms. Financial crises have been a feature of capitalist economies for hundreds of years and are typically followed by the worst business cycle downturns. Starting in August of 2007, the United States economy was hit by the worst financial crisis since the Great Depression. Defaults in subprime residential mortgages led to major losses in financial institutions, producing not only numerous bank failures, but also to the demise of Bear Stearns and Lehman Brothers, two of the largest investment banks in the United States.

Why these crises occur and do so much damage to the economy is discussed in Chapter 9.

Banks and Other Financial Institutions

Banks are financial institutions that accept deposits and make loans. Included under the term *banks* are firms such as commercial banks, savings and loan associations, mutual savings banks, and credit unions. Banks are the financial intermediaries that the average person interacts with most frequently. A person who needs a loan to buy a house or a car usually obtains it from a local bank. Most Americans keep a large proportion of their financial wealth in banks in the form of checking accounts, savings accounts, or other types of bank deposits. Because banks are the largest financial intermediaries in our economy, they deserve the most careful study. However, banks are not the only important financial institutions. Indeed, in recent years, other financial institutions such as insurance companies, finance companies, pension funds, mutual funds, and investment banks have been growing at the expense of banks, so we need to study them as well.

In Chapter 10, we examine how banks and other financial institutions manage their assets and liabilities to make profits. In Chapter 11, we extend the economic analysis in Chapter 8 to understand why financial regulation takes the form it does and what can go wrong in the regulatory process. In Chapter 12, we look at the banking industry; we examine how the competitive environment has changed in this industry and learn why some financial institutions have been growing at the expense of others.

Financial Innovation

In the good old days, when you took cash out of the bank or wanted to check your account balance, you got to say hello to a friendly human teller. Nowadays you are more likely to interact with an automatic teller machine (ATM) when withdrawing cash, and you can get your account balance from your home computer. To see why these options have developed, in Chapter 12 we study why and how financial innovation takes place, with particular emphasis on how the dramatic improvements in information technology have led to new means of delivering financial services electronically, in what has become known as **e-finance**. We also study financial innovation, because it shows us how creative thinking on the part of financial institutions can lead to higher profits. By seeing how and why financial institutions have been creative in the past, we obtain a better grasp of how they may be creative in the future. This knowledge provides us with useful clues about how the financial system may change over time and will help keep our knowledge about banks and other financial institutions from becoming obsolete.

WHY STUDY MONEY AND MONETARY POLICY?

Money, also referred to as the **money supply**, is defined as anything that is generally accepted in payment for goods or services or in the repayment of debts. Money is linked to changes in economic variables that affect all of us and are important to the health of the economy. The final two parts of the book examine the role of money in the economy.

Money and Business Cycles

In 1981–1982, total production of goods and services (called **aggregate output**) in the U.S. economy fell and the **unemployment rate** (the percentage of the available labor force unemployed) rose to over 10%. After 1982, the economy began to expand rapidly, and by 1989 the unemployment rate had declined to 5%. In 1990, the eight-year expansion came to an end, with the unemployment rate rising above 7%. The economy bottomed out in 1991, and the subsequent recovery was the longest in U.S. history, with the unemployment rate falling to around 4%. A mild economic downturn began in March 2001, with unemployment rising to 6%; the economy began to recover in November 2001 with unemployment eventually declining to a low of 4.4%. Starting in December 2007, the economy went into recession and the unemployment rate rose to well all over 7%.

Why did the economy expand from 1982 to 1990, contract in 1990 to 1991, boom again from 1991 to 2001, contract again in 2001, recover thereafter, and contract again in 2007? Evidence suggests that money plays an important role in generating **business cycles**, the upward and downward movement of aggregate output produced in the economy. Business cycles affect all of us in immediate and important ways. When output is rising, for example, it is easier to find a good job; when output is falling, finding a good job might be difficult. Figure 3 shows the movements of the rate of money growth over the 1950–2008 period, with the shaded areas representing **recessions**, periods of declining aggregate output. What we see is that the rate of money growth has declined before every recession, indicating that changes in money might be a driving force behind business cycle fluctuations. However, not every decline in the rate of money growth is followed by a recession.

We explore how money might affect aggregate output in Chapters 19 through 25 in Part 6 of this book, where we study **monetary theory**, the theory that relates changes in the quantity of money to changes in aggregate economic activity and the price level.

Money and Inflation

Thirty years ago, the movie you might have paid $10 to see last week would have set you back only a dollar or two. In fact, for $10 you could probably have had dinner, seen the movie, and bought yourself a big bucket of hot buttered popcorn. As shown in Figure 4, which illustrates the movement of average prices in the U.S. economy from 1950 to 2008, the prices of most items are quite a bit higher now than they were then. The average price of goods and services in an economy is called the **aggregate price level**, or, more simply, the *price level* (a more precise definition is found in the appendix to this chapter). From 1950 to 2008, the price level has increased more than sixfold. **Inflation**, a continual increase in the price level, affects individuals, businesses, and the government. It is generally regarded as an important problem to be solved and is often at the top of the political and policymaking agendas. To solve the inflation problem, we need to know something about its causes.

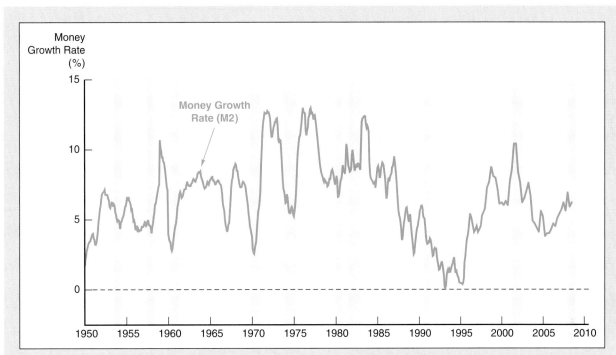

FIGURE 3   **Money Growth (M2 Annual Rate) and the Business Cycle in the United States, 1950–2008**

Note: Shaded areas represent recessions.

Source: Federal Reserve *Bulletin*, p. A4, Table 1.10; www.federalreserve.gov/releases/h6/hist/h6hist1.txt.

What explains inflation? One clue to answering this question is found in Figure 4, which plots the money supply and the price level. As we can see, the price level and the money supply generally rise together. These data seem to indicate that a continuing increase in the money supply might be an important factor in causing the continuing increase in the price level that we call inflation.

Further evidence that inflation may be tied to continuing increases in the money supply is found in Figure 5. For a number of countries, it plots the average **inflation rate** (the rate of change of the price level, usually measured as a percentage change per year) over the ten-year period 1995–2007 against the average rate of money growth over the same period. As you can see, there is a positive association between inflation and the growth rate of the money supply: The countries with the highest inflation rates are also the ones with the highest money growth rates. Belarus, Brazil, Romania, and Russia, for example, experienced high inflation during this period, and their rates of money growth were high. By contrast, the United Kingdom and the United States had low inflation rates over the same period, and their rates of money growth have been low. Such evidence led Milton Friedman, a Nobel laureate in economics, to make the famous statement, "Inflation is always and everywhere a monetary phenomenon."[2] We look at money's role in creating inflation in Chapter 24.

---

[2]Milton Friedman, *Dollars and Deficits* (Upper Saddle River, NJ: Prentice Hall, 1968), p. 39.

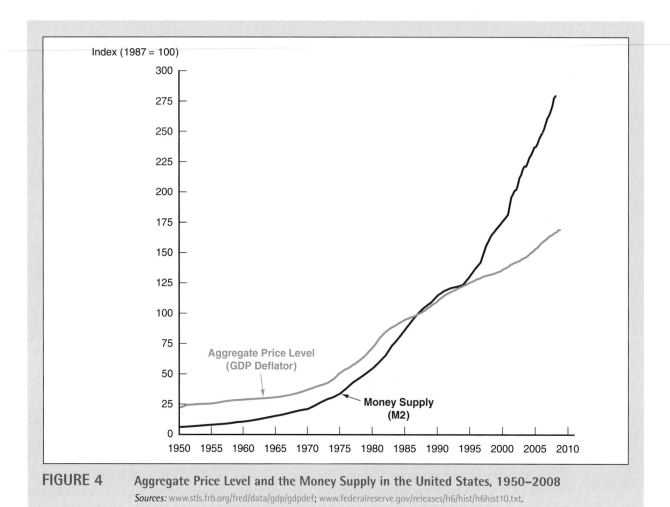

FIGURE 4   **Aggregate Price Level and the Money Supply in the United States, 1950–2008**

Sources: www.stls.frb.org/fred/data/gdp/gdpdef; www.federalreserve.gov/releases/h6/hist/h6hist10.txt.

Money and Interest Rates

In addition to other factors, money plays an important role in interest-rate fluctuations, which are of great concern to businesses and consumers. Figure 6 shows the changes in the interest rate on long-term Treasury bonds and the rate of money growth. As the money growth rate rose in the 1960s and 1970s, the long-term bond rate rose with it. However, the relationship between money growth and interest rates has been less clear-cut since 1980. We analyze the relationship between money and interest rates when we examine the behavior of interest rates in Chapter 5.

Conduct of Monetary Policy

Because money can affect many economic variables that are important to the well-being of our economy, politicians and policymakers throughout the world care about the conduct of **monetary policy**, the management of money and interest rates. The organization responsible for the conduct of a nation's monetary policy is the **central bank**. The

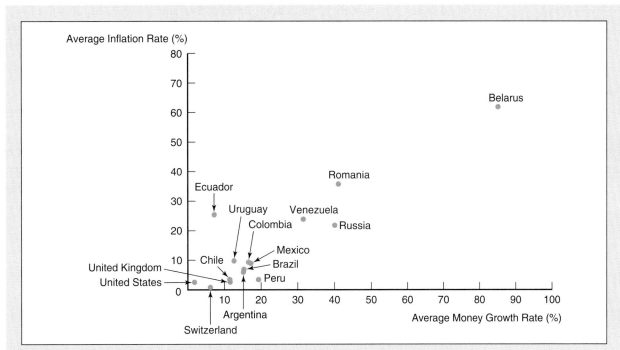

FIGURE 5   Average Inflation Rate Versus Average Rate of Money Growth for Selected Countries, 1997–2007

Source: International Financial Statistics.

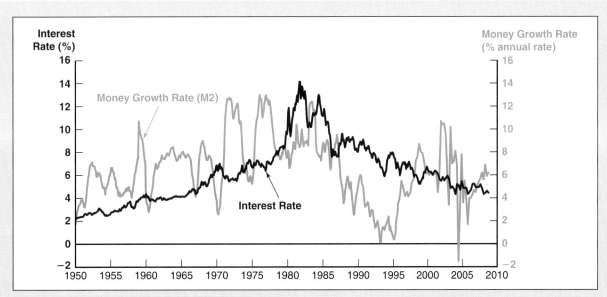

FIGURE 6   Money Growth (M2 Annual Rate) and Interest Rates (Long-Term U.S. Treasury Bonds), 1950–2008

Sources: Federal Reserve *Bulletin,* p. A4, Table 1.10; www.federalreserve.gov/releases/h6/hist/h6hist1.txt.

United States' central bank is the **Federal Reserve System** (also called simply **the Fed**). In Chapters 13–16 (Part 4), we study how central banks around the world can affect the quantity of money and interest rates in the economy and then we look at how monetary policy is actually conducted in the United States and elsewhere.

Fiscal Policy and Monetary Policy

Fiscal policy involves decisions about government spending and taxation. A **budget deficit** is the excess of government expenditures over tax revenues for a particular time period, typically a year, while a **budget surplus** arises when tax revenues exceed government expenditures. The government must finance any deficit by borrowing, while a budget surplus leads to a lower government debt burden. As Figure 7 shows, the budget deficit, relative to the size of the U.S. economy, peaked in 1983 at 6% of national output (as calculated by the **gross domestic product**, or *GDP*, a measure of aggregate output described in the appendix to this chapter). Since then, the budget deficit at first declined to less than 3% of GDP, rose again to 5% by the early 1990s, and fell subsequently, leading to budget surpluses from 1999 to 2001. In the aftermath of the terrorist attacks of September 11, 2001, the war in Iraq that began in March 2003, and the fiscal stimulus package in 2009 the budget has swung back again into deficit. What to do about budget deficits and surpluses has been the subject of legislation and bitter battles between the president and Congress in recent years.

You may have heard statements in newspapers or on TV that budget surpluses are a good thing while deficits are undesirable. We explore the accuracy of such claims in Chapters 9 and 18 by seeing how budget deficits might lead to a financial crisis as they did in Argentina in 2001. In Chapter 24, we examine why deficits might result in a higher rate of money growth, a higher rate of inflation, and higher interest rates.

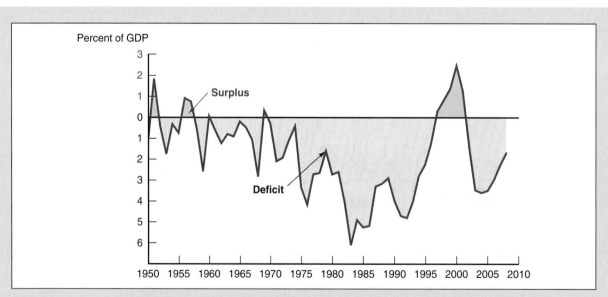

FIGURE 7   **Government Budget Surplus or Deficit as a Percentage of Gross Domestic Product, 1950–2008**

Source: www.gpoaccess.gov/usbudget/fy06/sheets/hist01z2.xls.

WHY STUDY INTERNATIONAL FINANCE?

The globalization of financial markets has accelerated at a rapid pace in recent years. Financial markets have become increasingly integrated throughout the world. American companies often borrow in foreign financial markets and foreign companies borrow in U.S. financial markets. Banks and other financial institutions, such as JP Morgan Chase, Citgroup, UBS, and Deutschebank, have become increasingly international, with operations in many countries throughout the world. Part 5 of this book explores the foreign exchange market and the international financial system.

The Foreign Exchange Market

For funds to be transferred from one country to another, they have to be converted from the currency in the country of origin (say, dollars) into the currency of the country they are going to (say, euros). The **foreign exchange market** is where this conversion takes place, so it is instrumental in moving funds between countries. It is also important because it is where the **foreign exchange rate**, the price of one country's currency in terms of another's, is determined.

Figure 8 shows the exchange rate for the U.S. dollar from 1970 to 2008 (measured as the value of the U.S. dollar in terms of a basket of major foreign currencies). The fluctuations in prices in this market have also been substantial: The dollar's value weakened considerably from 1971 to 1973, rose slightly until 1976, and then reached a low point in the 1978–1980 period. From 1980 to early 1985, the dollar's value appreciated dramatically, and then declined again reaching another low in 1995. The dollar appreciated from 1995 to 2000, only to depreciate thereafter.

What have these fluctuations in the exchange rate meant to the American public and businesses? A change in the exchange rate has a direct effect on American consumers because it affects the cost of imports. In 2001 when the euro was worth around 85 cents, 100 euros of European goods (say, French wine) cost $85. When the dollar subsequently weakened, raising the cost of a euro near $1.50, the same 100 euros of

FIGURE 8   **Exchange Rate of the U.S. Dollar, 1970–2008**

Source: Federal Reserve: www.federalreserve.gov/releases/H10/summary/indexbc_m.txt/.

wine now cost $150. Thus a weaker dollar leads to more expensive foreign goods, makes vacationing abroad more expensive, and raises the cost of indulging your desire for imported delicacies. When the value of the dollar drops, Americans decrease their purchases of foreign goods and increase their consumption of domestic goods (such as travel in the United States or American-made wine).

Conversely, a strong dollar means that U.S. goods exported abroad will cost more in foreign countries, and hence foreigners will buy fewer of them. Exports of steel, for example, declined sharply when the dollar strengthened in the 1980–1985 and 1995–2001 periods. A strong dollar benefited American consumers by making foreign goods cheaper but hurt American businesses and eliminated some jobs by cutting both domestic and foreign sales of their products. The decline in the value of the dollar from 1985 to 1995 and 2001 to 2008 had the opposite effect: It made foreign goods more expensive, but made American businesses more competitive. Fluctuations in the foreign exchange markets have major consequences for the American economy.

In Chapter 17 we study how exchange rates are determined in the foreign exchange market in which dollars are bought and sold for foreign currencies.

The International Financial System

The tremendous increase in capital flows among countries heightens the international financial system's impact on domestic economies. Issues we will explore in Chapter 18 include:

- How does a country's decision to fix its exchange rate to that of another nation shape the conduct of monetary policy?
- What is the impact of capital controls that restrict mobility of capital across national borders on domestic financial systems and the performance of the economy?
- What role should international financial institutions such as the International Monetary Fund play in the international financial system?

HOW WE WILL STUDY MONEY, BANKING, AND FINANCIAL MARKETS

This textbook stresses the economic way of thinking by developing a unifying framework to study money, banking, and financial markets. This analytic framework uses a few basic economic concepts to organize your thinking about the determination of asset prices, the structure of financial markets, bank management, and the role of money in the economy. It encompasses the following basic concepts:

- A simplified approach to the demand for assets
- The concept of equilibrium
- Basic supply and demand to explain behavior in financial markets
- The search for profits
- An approach to financial structure based on transaction costs and asymmetric information
- Aggregate supply and demand analysis

The unifying framework used in this book will keep your knowledge from becoming obsolete and make the material more interesting. It will enable you to learn what *really* matters without having to memorize a mass of dull facts that you will forget soon after the final exam. This framework will also provide you with the tools you need to understand trends in the financial marketplace and in variables such as interest rates, exchange rates, inflation, and aggregate output.

To help you understand and apply the unifying analytic framework, simple models are constructed in which the variables held constant are carefully delineated, each step in the derivation of the model is clearly and carefully laid out, and the models are then used to explain various phenomena by focusing on changes in one variable at a time, holding all other variables constant.

To reinforce the models' usefulness, this text uses case studies, applications, and special-interest boxes to present evidence that supports or casts doubts on the theories being discussed. This exposure to real-life events and empirical data should dissuade you from thinking that all economists make abstract assumptions and develop theories that have little to do with actual behavior.

To function better in the real world outside the classroom, you must have the tools to follow the financial news that appears in leading financial publications such as the *Wall Street Journal*. To help and encourage you to read the financial section of the newspaper, this book contains two unique features. The first is a set of special boxed inserts titled Following the Financial News that contain actual columns and data from the *Wall Street Journal*, which typically appear daily or periodically. These boxes give you the detailed information and definitions you need to evaluate the data being presented. The second feature is a set of special applications titled "Reading the *Wall Street Journal*" that expand on the Following the Financial News boxes. These applications show you how you can use the analytic framework in the book directly to make sense of the daily columns in the United States' leading financial newspaper. In addition to these applications, this book also contains nearly 400 end-of-chapter problems that ask you to apply the analytic concepts you have learned to other real-world issues. Particularly relevant is a special class of problems headed "Using Economic Analysis to Predict the Future." So that you can work on many of these problems on your own, answers to half of them are found at the end of the book. These give you an opportunity to review and apply many of the important financial concepts and tools presented throughout the book.

Exploring the Web

The World Wide Web has become an extremely valuable and convenient resource for financial research. We emphasize the importance of this tool in several ways. First, wherever we utilize the Web to find information to build the charts and tables that appear throughout the text, we include the source site's URL. These sites often contain additional information and are updated frequently. Second, we have Web exercises to the end of each chapter. These exercises prompt you to visit sites related to the chapter and to work with real-time data and information. We also have Web references to the end of each chapter that list the URLs of sites related to the material being discussed. Visit these sites to further explore a topic you find of particular interest. Website URLs are subject to frequent change. We have tried to select stable sites, but we realize that even government URLs change. The publisher's website (www.myeconlab.com/mishkin) will maintain an updated list of current URLs for your reference.

Collecting and Graphing Data

The following Web exercise is especially important because it demonstrates how to export data from a web site into Microsoft® Excel for further analysis. We suggest you work through this problem on your own so that you will be able to perform this activity when prompted in subsequent Web exercises.

WEB EXERCISES

You have been hired by Risky Ventures, Inc., as a consultant to help the company analyze interest-rate trends. Your employers are initially interested in determining the historical relationship between long- and short-term interest rates. The biggest task you must immediately undertake is collecting market interest-rate data. You know the best source of this information is the Web.

1. You decide that your best indicator of long-term interest rates is the ten-year U.S. Treasury note. Your first task is to gather historical data. Go to www.federalreserve.gov/releases/H15. The site should look like Figure 9. At the top click on Historical data. Now scroll down to "Treasury constant maturities" and click on the Annual tag to the right of the 10-year category.

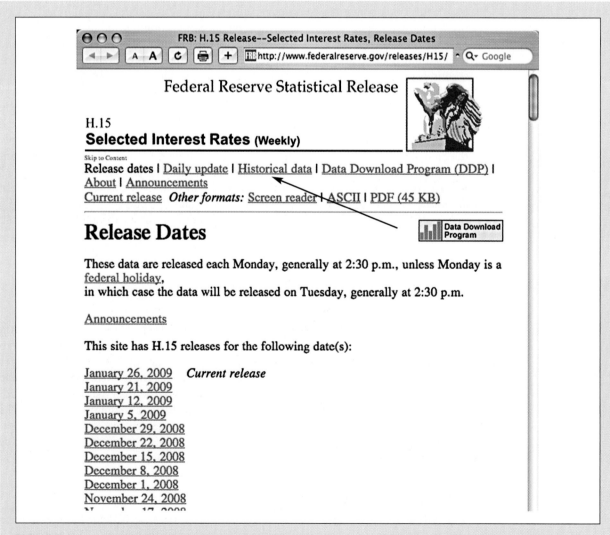

FIGURE 9   Federal Reserve Board Website

FIGURE 10 **Excel Spreadsheet with Interest-Rate Data**

2. Now that you have located an accurate source of historical interest rate data, the next step is getting it onto a spreadsheet. You recall that Excel will let you convert text data into columns. Begin by highlighting the two columns of data (the year and rate). Right-click on the mouse and choose COPY. Now open Excel and put the cursor in a cell. Click PASTE. Now choose DATA from the tool bar and click on TEXT TO COLUMNS. Follow the wizard (Figure 10), checking the fixed-width option. The list of interest rates should now have the year in one column and the interest rate in the next column. Label your columns.

    Repeat the preceding steps to collect the one-year interest rate series. Put it in the column next to the ten-year series. Be sure to line up the years correctly and delete any years that are not included in both series.

3. You now want to analyze the interest rates by graphing them. Again highlight the two columns of data you just created in Excel. Click on the charts icon on the toolbar (or INSERT/CHART). Select scatter diagram and choose any type of scatter diagram that connects the dots. Let the Excel wizard take you through the steps of completing the graph (see Figure 11).

CONCLUDING REMARKS

The topic of money, banking, and financial markets is an exciting field that directly affects your life—interest rates influence earnings on your savings and the payments on loans you may seek on a car or a house, and monetary policy may affect your job

FIGURE 11   Excel Graph of Interest-Rate Data

prospects and the prices of goods in the future. Your study of money, banking, and financial markets will introduce you to many of the controversies about the conduct of economic policy that are hotly debated in the political arena and will help you gain a clearer understanding of economic phenomena you hear about in the news media. The knowledge you gain will stay with you and benefit you long after the course is done.

SUMMARY

1. Activities in financial markets have direct effects on individuals' wealth, the behavior of businesses, and the efficiency of our economy. Three financial markets deserve particular attention: the bond market (where interest rates are determined), the stock market (which has a major effect on people's wealth and on firms' investment decisions), and the foreign exchange market (because fluctuations in the foreign exchange rate have major consequences for the U.S. economy).

2. Banks and other financial institutions channel funds from people who might not put them to productive use to people who can do so and thus play a crucial role in improving the efficiency of the economy.

3. Money appears to be a major influence on inflation, business cycles, and interest rates. Because these economic variables are so important to the health of the economy, we need to understand how monetary policy is and should be conducted. We also need to study government fiscal policy because it can be an influential factor in the conduct of monetary policy.

4. This textbook stresses the economic way of thinking by developing a unifying analytic framework for the study of money, banking, and financial markets using a few basic economic principles. This textbook also emphasizes the interaction of theoretical analysis and empirical data.

KEY TERMS

aggregate income, p. 21

aggregate output, p. 8

aggregate price level, p. 8

asset, p. 3

banks, p. 7

bond, p. 3

budget deficit, p. 12

budget surplus, p. 12

business cycles, p. 8

central bank, p. 10

common stock, p. 5

e-finance, p. 7

Federal Reserve System (the Fed), p. 12

financial crises, p. 7

financial intermediaries, p. 6

financial markets, p. 3

fiscal policy, p. 12

foreign exchange market, p. 13

foreign exchange rate, p. 13

gross domestic product, 12, 21

inflation, p. 8

inflation rate, p. 9

interest rate, p. 4

monetary policy, p. 10

monetary theory, p. 8

money (money supply), p. 8

recession, p. 8

security, p. 3

stock, p. 5

unemployment rate, p. 8

QUESTIONS AND PROBLEMS

All questions and problems are available in ⓦ myeconlab *at* www.myeconlab.com/mishkin.

1. Has the inflation rate in the United States increased or decreased in the past few years? What about interest rates?

2. If history repeats itself and we see a decline in the rate of money growth, what might you expect to happen to
   a. real output?
   b. the inflation rate?
   c. interest rates?

3. When was the most recent recession?

4. When interest rates fall, how might you change your economic behavior?

5. Can you think of any financial innovation in the past ten years that has affected you personally? Has it made you better off or worse off? Why?

6. Is everybody worse off when interest rates rise?

7. What is the basic activity of banks?

8. Why are financial markets important to the health of the economy?

9. What is the typical relationship between interest rates on three-month Treasury bills, long-term Treasury bonds, and Baa corporate bonds?

10. What effect might a fall in stock prices have on business investment?

11. What effect might a rise in stock prices have on consumers' decisions to spend?

12. How does a fall in the value of the pound sterling affect British consumers?

13. How does an increase in the value of the pound sterling affect American businesses?

14. Looking at Figure 8, in which years would an American have chosen to visit the Grand Canyon in Arizona rather than the Tower of London?

15. When the dollar is worth more in relation to currencies of other countries, would an American be more likely to buy American-made or foreign-made jeans? Are U.S. companies that manufacture jeans happier when the dollar is strong or when it is weak? What about an American company that is in the business of importing jeans into the United States?

WEB EXERCISES

1. In this exercise we will practice collecting data from the Web and graphing it using Excel. Use the example on page 18 as a guide. Go to www.forecasts.org/data/index.htm, click on "Stock Index Data" at the top of the page, then choose the U.S. Stock Indices—Monthly option. Finally, choose the Dow Jones Industrial Average option.
   a. Using the method presented in this chapter, move the data into an Excel spreadsheet.
   b. Using the data from part a, prepare a graph. Use the graphing wizard to properly label your axes.

2. In Web Exercise 1 you collected and graphed the Dow Jones Industrial Average. This same site reports forecast values of the DJIA. Go to www.forecasts.org/data/index.htm and click on "FFC Home" at the top of the page. Click on the Dow Jones Industrial link under Forecasts in the far left column.
   a. What is the Dow forecast to be in six months?
   b. What percentage increase is forecast for the next six months?

WEB REFERENCES

www.federalreserve.gov/releases/

Daily, weekly, monthly, quarterly, and annual releases and historical data for selected interest rates, foreign exchange rates, and so on.

http://stockcharts.com/charts/historical/

Historical charts of various stock indexes over differing time periods.

www.federalreserve.gov

General information, monetary policy, banking system, research, and economic data of the Federal Reserve.

www.bls.gov/data/inflation_calculator.htm

Calculator lets you compute how the dollar's buying power has changed since 1913.

www.kowaldesign.com/budget/

This site reports the current federal budget deficit or surplus and how it has changed since the 1950s. It also reports how the federal budget is spent.

www.brillig.com/debt_clock/

National debt clock. This site reports the exact national debt at each point in time.

 MyEconLab CAN HELP YOU GET A BETTER GRADE

If your exam were tomorrow, would you be ready? For each chapter, MyEconLab Practice Tests and Study Plans pinpoint which sections you have mastered and which ones you need to study. That way, you are more efficient with your study time, and you are better prepared for your exams.

Here's how it works:

1. Register and log in at: www.myeconlab.com/mishkin
2. Click on "Take a Test" and select Sample Test A for this chapter.
3. Take the diagnostic test. MyEconLab will grade it automatically and create a personalized Study Plan so you see which sections of the chapter you should study further.
4. The Study Plan will serve up additional practice problems and tutorials to help you master the specific areas on which you need to focus. By practicing online, you can track your progress in the Study Plan.
5. After you have mastered the sections, go to "Take a Test" and select Sample Test B for this chapter. Take the test and see how you do!

1 Defining Aggregate Output, Income, the Price Level, and the Inflation Rate

Because these terms are used so frequently throughout the text, we need to have a clear understanding of the definitions of *aggregate output*, *income*, the *price level*, and the *inflation rate*.

AGGREGATE OUTPUT AND INCOME

The most commonly reported measure of aggregate output, the **gross domestic product (GDP)**, is the market value of all final goods and services produced in a country during the course of the year. This measure excludes two sets of items that at first glance you might think it would include. Purchases of goods that have been produced in the past, whether a Rembrandt painting or a house built twenty years ago, are not counted as part of GDP, nor are purchases of stocks or bonds. None of these enter into GDP because they are not goods and services produced during the course of the year. Intermediate goods, which are used up in producing final goods and services, such as the sugar in a candy bar or the energy used to produce steel, are also not counted separately as part of GDP. Because the value of the final goods already includes the value of the intermediate goods, to count them separately would be to count them twice.

Aggregate income, the total income of *factors of production* (land, labor, and capital) from producing goods and services in the economy during the course of the year, is best thought of as being equal to aggregate output. Because the payments for final goods and services must eventually flow back to the owners of the factors of production as income, income payments must equal payments for final goods and services. For example, if the economy has an aggregate output of $10 trillion, total income payments in the economy (aggregate income) are also $10 trillion.

REAL VERSUS NOMINAL MAGNITUDES

When the total value of final goods and services is calculated using current prices, the resulting GDP measure is referred to as *nominal GDP*. The word *nominal* indicates that values are measured using current prices. If all prices doubled but actual production of goods and services remained the same, nominal GDP would double even though people would not enjoy the benefits of twice as many goods and services. As a result, nominal variables can be misleading measures of economic well-being.

A more reliable measure of economic production expresses values in terms of prices for an arbitrary base year, currently 2000. GDP measured with constant prices is referred to as *real GDP*, the word *real* indicating that values are measured in terms of fixed prices. Real variables thus measure the quantities of goods and services and do not change because prices have changed, but rather only if actual quantities have changed.

A brief example will make the distinction clearer. Suppose that you have a nominal income of $30,000 in 2010 and that your nominal income was $15,000 in 2000. If all prices doubled between 2000 and 2010, are you better off? The answer is no: Although your income has doubled, your $30,000 buys you only the same amount of goods because prices have also doubled. A real income measure indicates that your income in terms of the goods it can buy is the same. Measured in 2000 prices, the $30,000 of nominal income in 2010 turns out to be only $15,000 of real income. Because your real income is actually the same in the two years, you are no better or worse off in 2010 than you were in 2000.

Because real variables measure quantities in terms of real goods and services, they are typically of more interest than nominal variables. In this text, discussion of aggregate output or aggregate income always refers to real measures (such as real GDP).

AGGREGATE PRICE LEVEL

In this chapter, we defined the aggregate price level as a measure of average prices in the economy. Three measures of the aggregate price level are commonly encountered in economic data. The first is the *GDP deflator*, which is defined as nominal GDP divided by real GDP. Thus, if 2010 nominal GDP is $10 trillion but 2010 real GDP in 2000 prices is $9 trillion,

$$\text{GDP deflator} = \frac{\$10 \text{ trillion}}{\$9 \text{ trillion}} = 1.11$$

The GDP deflator equation indicates that, on average, prices have risen 11% since 2000. Typically, measures of the price level are presented in the form of a price index, which expresses the price level for the base year (in our example, 2000) as 100. Thus the GDP deflator for 2010 would be 111.

Another popular measure of the aggregate price level (which officials in the Fed frequently focus on) is the *PCE deflator*, which is similar to the GDP deflator and is defined as nominal personal consumption expenditures (PCE) divided by real PCE.

The measure of the aggregate price level that is most frequently reported in the press is the *consumer price index (CPI)*. The CPI is measured by pricing a "basket" of goods and services bought by a typical urban household. If, over the course of the year, the cost of this basket of goods and services rises from $500 to $600, the CPI has risen by 20%. The CPI is also expressed as a price index with the base year equal to 100.

The CPI, the PCE deflator, and the GDP deflator measures of the price level can be used to convert or deflate a nominal magnitude into a real magnitude. This is accomplished by dividing the nominal magnitude by the price index. In our example, in which the GDP deflator for 2010 is 1.11 (expressed as an index value of 111), real GDP for 2010 equals

$$\frac{\$10 \text{ trillion}}{1.11} = \$9 \text{ trillion in 2000 prices}$$

which corresponds to the real GDP figure for 2010 assumed earlier.

GROWTH RATES AND THE INFLATION RATE

The media often talk about the economy's growth rate, and particularly the growth rate of real GDP. A growth rate is defined as the percentage change in a variable, i.e.,

$$\text{growth rate} = \frac{x_t - x_{t-1}}{x_{t-1}} \times 100$$

where t indicates today and $t - 1$ a year earlier.

For example, if real GDP grew from \$9 trillion in 2010 to \$9.5 trillion in 2011, then the GDP growth rate for 2011 would be 5.6%:

$$\text{GDP growth rate} = \frac{\$9.5 \text{ trillion} - \$9 \text{ trillion}}{\$9 \text{ trillion}} \times 100 = 5.6\%$$

The inflation rate is defined as the growth rate of the aggregate price level. Thus, if the GDP deflator rose from 111 in 2010 to 113 in 2011, the inflation rate using the GDP deflator would be 1.8%:

$$\text{inflation rate} = \frac{113 - 111}{111} \times 100 = 1.8\%$$

If the growth rate is for a period less than one year, it is usually reported on an annualized basis; that is, it is converted to the growth rate over a year's time, assuming that the growth rate remains constant. For GDP, which is reported quarterly, the annualized growth rate would be approximately four times the percentage change in GDP from the previous quarter. For example, if GDP rose $\frac{1}{2}$% from the first quarter of 2010 to the second quarter of 2010, then the annualized GDP growth rate for the second quarter of 2010 would be reported as 2% (= 4 × $\frac{1}{2}$%). (A more accurate calculation would be 2.02%, because a precise quarterly growth rate should be compounded on a quarterly basis.)

2

An Overview of the Financial System

Preview

Inez the Inventor has designed a low-cost robot that cleans house (even does windows), washes the car, and mows the lawn, but she has no funds to put her wonderful invention into production. Walter the Widower has plenty of savings, which he and his wife accumulated over the years. If Inez and Walter could get together so that Walter could provide funds to Inez, Inez's robot would see the light of day, and the economy would be better off: We would have cleaner houses, shinier cars, and more beautiful lawns.

Financial markets (bond and stock markets) and financial intermediaries (such as banks, insurance companies, pension funds) have the basic function of getting people like Inez and Walter together by moving funds from those who have a surplus of funds (Walter) to those who have a shortage of funds (Inez). More realistically, when Apple invents a better iPod, it may need funds to bring its new product to market. Similarly, when a local government needs to build a road or a school, it may need more funds than local property taxes provide. Well-functioning financial markets and financial intermediaries are crucial to economic health.

To study the effects of financial markets and financial intermediaries on the economy, we need to acquire an understanding of their general structure and operation. In this chapter, we learn about the major financial intermediaries and the instruments that are traded in financial markets as well as how these markets are regulated.

This chapter presents an overview of the fascinating study of financial markets and institutions. We return to a more detailed treatment of the regulation, structure, and evolution of the financial system in Chapters 8 through 12.

FUNCTION OF FINANCIAL MARKETS

Financial markets perform the essential economic function of channeling funds from households, firms, and governments that have saved surplus funds by spending less than their income to those that have a shortage of funds because they wish to spend more than their income. This function is shown schematically in Figure 1. Those who have saved and are lending funds, the lender-savers, are at the left, and those who must borrow funds to finance their spending, the borrower-spenders, are at the right. The principal lender-savers are households, but business enterprises and the government (particularly state and local government), as well as foreigners and their governments, sometimes also find themselves with excess funds and so lend them out. The most important borrower-spenders are businesses and the government (particularly the federal

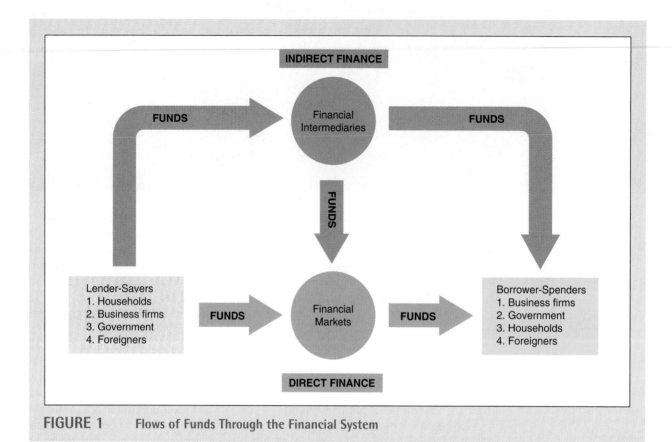

FIGURE 1   **Flows of Funds Through the Financial System**

government), but households and foreigners also borrow to finance their purchases of cars, furniture, and houses. The arrows show that funds flow from lender-savers to borrower-spenders via two routes.

In *direct finance* (the route at the bottom of Figure 1), borrowers borrow funds directly from lenders in financial markets by selling them *securities* (also called *financial instruments*), which are claims on the borrower's future income or assets. Securities are assets for the person who buys them but **liabilities** (IOUs or debts) for the individual or firm that sells (issues) them. For example, if Ford needs to borrow funds to pay for a new factory to manufacture electric cars, it might borrow the funds from savers by selling them a *bond*, a debt security, that promises to make payments periodically for a specified period of time, or a *stock*, a security that entitles the owner to a share of the company's profits and assets.

Why is this channeling of funds from savers to spenders so important to the economy? The answer is that the people who save are frequently not the same people who have profitable investment opportunities available to them, the entrepreneurs. Let's first think about this on a personal level. Suppose that you have saved $1,000 this year, but no borrowing or lending is possible because there are no financial markets. If you do not have an investment opportunity that will permit you to earn income with your savings, you will just hold on to the $1,000 and will earn no interest. However, Carl the Carpenter has a productive use for your $1,000: He can use it to purchase a new tool that will shorten the time it takes him to build a house, thereby earning an extra $200 per year. If you could get in touch with Carl, you could lend him the $1,000 at a rental fee (interest) of $100 per year, and both of you would be better off. You would earn $100 per year on your $1,000, instead of the zero amount that you would earn otherwise, while Carl would earn $100 more income per year (the $200 extra earnings per year minus the $100 rental fee for the use of the funds).

In the absence of financial markets, you and Carl the Carpenter might never get together. You would both be stuck with the status quo, and both of you would be worse off. Without financial markets, it is hard to transfer funds from a person who has no investment opportunities to one who has them. Financial markets are thus essential to promoting economic efficiency.

The existence of financial markets is beneficial even if someone borrows for a purpose other than increasing production in a business. Say that you are recently married, have a good job, and want to buy a house. You earn a good salary, but because you have just started to work, you have not saved much. Over time, you would have no problem saving enough to buy the house of your dreams, but by then you would be too old to get full enjoyment from it. Without financial markets, you are stuck; you cannot buy the house and must continue to live in your tiny apartment.

If a financial market were set up so that people who had built up savings could lend you the funds to buy the house, you would be more than happy to pay them some interest so that you could own a home while you are still young enough to enjoy it. Then, over time, you would pay back your loan. If this loan could occur, you would be better off, as would the persons who made you the loan. They would now earn some interest, whereas they would not if the financial market did not exist.

Now we can see why financial markets have such an important function in the economy. They allow funds to move from people who lack productive investment opportunities to people who have such opportunities. Financial markets are critical for producing an efficient allocation of **capital**, (wealth, either financial or physical, that is employed to produce more wealth), which contributes to higher production and efficiency for the overall economy. Indeed, as we will explore in Chapter 9, when financial markets break down during financial crises, as they have in Mexico, East Asia, and Argentina in recent years, severe economic hardship results, which can even lead to dangerous political instability.

Well-functioning financial markets also directly improve the well-being of consumers by allowing them to time their purchases better. They provide funds to young people to buy what they need and can eventually afford without forcing them to wait until they have saved up the entire purchase price. Financial markets that are operating efficiently improve the economic welfare of everyone in the society.

STRUCTURE OF FINANCIAL MARKETS

Now that we understand the basic function of financial markets, let's look at their structure. The following descriptions of several categorizations of financial markets illustrate essential features of these markets.

Debt and Equity Markets

A firm or an individual can obtain funds in a financial market in two ways. The most common method is to issue a debt instrument, such as a bond or a mortgage, which is a contractual agreement by the borrower to pay the holder of the instrument fixed dollar amounts at regular intervals (interest and principal payments) until a specified date (the maturity date), when a final payment is made. The **maturity** of a debt instrument is the number of years (term) until that instrument's expiration date. A debt instrument is **short-term** if its maturity is less than a year and **long-term** if its maturity is ten years or longer. Debt instruments with a maturity between one and ten years are said to be **intermediate-term**.

The second method of raising funds is by issuing **equities**, such as common stock, which are claims to share in the net income (income after expenses and taxes) and the assets of a business. If you own one share of common stock in a company that has issued one million shares, you are entitled to 1 one-millionth of the firm's net income and 1 one-millionth of the firm's assets. Equities often make periodic payments (**dividends**) to their holders and are considered long-term securities because they have no maturity date. In addition, owning stock means that you own a portion of the firm and thus have the right to vote on issues important to the firm and to elect its directors.

The main disadvantage of owning a corporation's equities rather than its debt is that an equity holder is a *residual claimant*; that is, the corporation must pay all its debt holders before it pays its equity holders. The advantage of holding equities is that equity holders benefit directly from any increases in the corporation's profitability or asset value because equities confer ownership rights on the equity holders. Debt holders do not share in this benefit, because their dollar payments are fixed. We examine the pros and cons of debt versus equity instruments in more detail in Chapter 8, which provides an economic analysis of financial structure.

The total value of equities in the United States has typically fluctuated between $4 and $20 trillion since the early 1990s, depending on the prices of shares. Although the average person is more aware of the stock market than any other financial market, the size of the debt market is often substantially larger than the size of the equities market: The value of debt instruments was $35 trillion at the end of 2008, while the value of equities was $19.5 trillion at the end of 2008.

Primary and Secondary Markets

A **primary market** is a financial market in which new issues of a security, such as a bond or a stock, are sold to initial buyers by the corporation or government agency borrowing the funds. A **secondary market** is a financial market in which securities that have been previously issued can be resold.

The primary markets for securities are not well known to the public because the selling of securities to initial buyers often takes place behind closed doors. An important financial institution that assists in the initial sale of securities in the primary market is the **investment bank**. It does this by **underwriting** securities: It guarantees a price for a corporation's securities and then sells them to the public.

The New York Stock Exchange and NASDAQ (National Association of Securities Dealers Automated Quotation System), in which previously issued stocks are traded, are the best-known examples of secondary markets, although the bond markets, in which previously issued bonds of major corporations and the U.S. government are bought and sold, actually have a larger trading volume. Other examples of secondary markets are foreign exchange markets, futures markets, and options markets. Securities brokers and dealers are crucial to a well-functioning secondary market. **Brokers** are agents of investors who match buyers with sellers of securities; **dealers** link buyers and sellers by buying and selling securities at stated prices.

When an individual buys a security in the secondary market, the person who has sold the security receives money in exchange for the security, but the corporation that issued the security acquires no new funds. A corporation acquires new funds only when its securities are first sold in the primary market. Nonetheless, secondary markets serve two important functions. First, they make it easier and quicker to sell these financial instruments to raise cash; that is, they make the financial instruments more **liquid**. The increased liquidity of these instruments then makes them more desirable and thus easier for the issuing firm to sell in the primary market. Second, they determine the price of the security that the issuing firm sells in the primary market. The investors who buy securities in the primary market will pay the issuing corporation no more than the price they think the secondary market will set for this security. The higher the security's price in the secondary market, the higher the price that the issuing firm will receive for a new security in the primary market, and hence the greater the amount of financial capital it can raise. Conditions in the secondary market are therefore the most relevant to corporations issuing securities. It is for this reason that books like this one, which deal with financial markets, focus on the behavior of secondary markets rather than primary markets.

Exchanges and Over-the-Counter Markets

Secondary markets can be organized in two ways. One method is to organize **exchanges**, where buyers and sellers of securities (or their agents or brokers) meet in one central location to conduct trades. The New York Stock Exchange for stocks and the Chicago Board of Trade for commodities (wheat, corn, silver, and other raw materials) are examples of organized exchanges.

The other method of organizing a secondary market is to have an **over-the-counter (OTC) market**, in which dealers at different locations who have an inventory of securities stand ready to buy and sell securities "over the counter" to anyone who comes to them and is willing to accept their prices. Because over-the-counter dealers are in computer contact and know the prices set by one another, the OTC market is very competitive and not very different from a market with an organized exchange.

Many common stocks are traded over-the-counter, although a majority of the largest corporations have their shares traded at organized stock exchanges. The U.S. government bond market, with a larger trading volume than the New York Stock Exchange, by contrast, is set up as an over-the-counter market. Forty or so dealers establish a "market" in these securities by standing ready to buy and sell U.S. government bonds. Other over-the-counter markets include those that trade other types of financial instruments such as negotiable certificates of deposit, federal funds, and foreign exchange.

Money and Capital Markets

Another way of distinguishing between markets is on the basis of the maturity of the securities traded in each market. The **money market** is a financial market in which only short-term debt instruments (generally those with original maturity of less than one year) are traded; the **capital market** is the market in which longer-term debt (generally those with original maturity of one year or greater) and equity instruments are traded. Money market securities are usually more widely traded than longer-term securities and so tend to be more liquid. In addition, as we will see in Chapter 4, short-term securities have smaller fluctuations in prices than long-term securities, making them safer investments. As a result, corporations and banks actively use the money market to earn interest on surplus funds that they expect to have only temporarily. Capital market securities, such as stocks and long-term bonds, are often held by financial intermediaries such as insurance companies and pension funds, which have little uncertainty about the amount of funds they will have available in the future.

FINANCIAL MARKET INSTRUMENTS

To complete our understanding of how financial markets perform the important role of channeling funds from lender-savers to borrower-spenders, we need to examine the securities (instruments) traded in financial markets. We first focus on the instruments traded in the money market and then turn to those traded in the capital market.

Money Market Instruments

Because of their short terms to maturity, the debt instruments traded in the money market undergo the least price fluctuations and so are the least risky investments. The money market has undergone great changes in the past three decades, with the amount of some financial instruments growing at a far more rapid rate than others.

The principal money market instruments are listed in Table 1 along with the amount outstanding at the end of 1980, 1990, 2000, and 2008. The Following the Financial News box illustrates how the interest rates on many of the instruments are reported.

United States Treasury Bills   These short-term debt instruments of the U.S. government are issued in one-, three-, and six-month maturities to finance the federal government. They pay a set amount at maturity and have no interest payments, but they effectively pay interest by initially selling at a discount, that is, at a price lower than the set amount paid at maturity. For instance, in May 2010 you might buy a six-month Treasury bill for $9,000 that can be redeemed in November 2010 for $10,000.

U.S. Treasury bills are the most liquid of all the money market instruments because they are the most actively traded. They are also the safest of all money market instruments because there is almost no possibility of **default**, a situation in which the party issuing the debt instrument (the federal government in this case) is unable to make interest payments or pay off the amount owed when the instrument matures. The federal government is always able to meet its debt obligations because it can raise taxes or issue **currency** (paper money or coins) to pay off its debts. Treasury bills are held mainly by banks, although small amounts are held by households, corporations, and other financial intermediaries.

TABLE 1

Principal Money Market Instruments

Type of Instrument	Amount Outstanding ($ billions, end of year)			
	1980	1990	2000	2008
U.S. Treasury bills	216	527	647	1060
Negotiable bank certificates of deposit (large denominations)	317	543	1053	2385
Commercial paper	122	557	1619	1732
Federal funds and Security repurchase agreements	64	387.9	768.2	2118.1

Sources: Federal Reserve Flow of Funds Accounts; Federal Reserve *Bulletin; Economic Report of the President.*

Negotiable Bank Certificates of Deposit   A *certificate of deposit (CD)* is a debt instrument sold by a bank to depositors that pays annual interest of a given amount and at maturity pays back the original purchase price. Negotiable CDs are CDs that are sold in secondary markets, with the amount outstanding currently around $2.4 trillion. Negotiable CDs are an extremely important source of funds for commercial banks, from corporations, money market mutual funds, charitable institutions, and government agencies.

Commercial Paper   *Commercial paper* is a short-term debt instrument issued by large banks and well-known corporations, such as Microsoft and General Motors. Growth of the commercial paper market has been substantial: The amount of commercial paper outstanding has increased by over 1,200% (from $122 billion to $1,732 billion) in the period 1980–2008. We will discuss why the commercial paper market has had such tremendous growth in Chapter 12.

Repurchase Agreements   *Repurchase agreements (repos)* are effectively short-term loans (usually with a maturity of less than two weeks) for which Treasury bills serve as *collateral,* an asset that the lender receives if the borrower does not pay back the loan. Repos are made as follows: A large corporation, such as Microsoft, may have some idle funds in its bank account, say $1 million, which it would like to lend for a week. Microsoft uses this excess $1 million to buy Treasury bills from a bank, which agrees to repurchase them the next week at a price slightly above Microsoft's purchase price. The effect of this agreement is that Microsoft makes a loan of $1 million to the bank and holds $1 million of the bank's Treasury bills until the bank repurchases the bills to pay off the loan. Repurchase agreements are now an important source of bank funds (over $500 billion). The most important lenders in this market are large corporations.

Federal (Fed) Funds   These instruments are typically overnight loans between banks of their deposits at the Federal Reserve. The *federal funds* designation is somewhat confusing because these loans are not made by the federal government or by the Federal Reserve but rather by banks to other banks. One reason why a bank might borrow in the federal funds market is that it might find it does not have enough deposits at the

Following the Financial News   **Money Market Rates**

The *Wall Street Journal* publishes daily a listing of interest rates on many different financial instruments in its "Money Rates" column in the Money and Investing section.

The four interest rates in the "Money Rates" column that are discussed most frequently in the media are these:

Prime rate: The base interest rate on corporate bank loans, an indicator of the cost of business borrowing from banks

Federal funds rate: The interest rate charged on overnight loans in the federal funds market, a sensitive indicator of the cost to banks of borrowing funds from other banks and the stance of monetary policy

Treasury bill rate: The interest rate on U.S. Treasury bills, an indicator of general interest-rate movements

Libor rate: The British Banker's Association average of interbank rates for dollar deposits in the London market.

(*continued*)

Money Rates

January 9, 2009

Key annual interest rates paid to borrow or lend money in U.S. and international markets. Rates below are a guide to general levels but don't always represent actual transactions.

Inflation

	Nov. index level	CHG FROM (%) Oct. '08	CHG FROM (%) Nov. '07
U.S. consumer price index			
All items	**212.425**	−1.9	1.1
Core	**216.690**	−0.2	2.0

International rates

	Latest	Week ago	—52-WEEK— High	—52-WEEK— Low
Prime rates				
U.S.	**3.25**	3.25	7.25	3.25
Canada	**3.50**	3.50	6.00	3.50
Euro zone	**2.50**	2.50	4.25	2.50
Japan	**1.675**	1.675	1.875	1.675
Switzerland	**0.52**	2.02	4.56	0.52
Britain	**1.50**	2.00	5.50	1.50
Australia	**4.25**	4.25	7.25	4.25
Hong Kong	**5.00**	5.00	7.00	5.00
Overnight repurchase				
U.S.	**0.10**	0.10	4.17	0.08
U.K. (BBA)	**1.353**	1.883	5.742	1.270
Euro zone	**2.07**	2.16	4.50	2.07

U.S. government rates

Discount				
	0.50	0.50	4.75	0.50

Federal funds				
Effective rate	**0.13**	0.13	4.25	0.12
High	**0.4000**	0.5000	10.0000	0.4000
Low	**0.0313**	0.0100	4.0000	0.0000
Bid	**0.0625**	0.0313	4.1875	0.0000
Offer	**0.1875**	0.1250	7.0000	0.0500

Treasury bill auction				
4 weeks	**0.060**	0.030	3.240	0.000
13 weeks	**0.150**	0.050	3.180	0.005
26 weeks	**0.320**	0.250	3.170	0.250

Secondary market

Freddie Mac 30-year mortgage yields				
30 days	**4.00**	4.67	6.49	4.00
60 days	**4.14**	4.80	6.56	4.14
One-year RNY	**3.375**	3.375	3.375	3.375

Fannie Mae 30-year mortgage yields				
30 days	**4.188**	4.488	6.566	4.099
60 days	**4.318**	4.635	6.618	4.186

Bankers acceptances				
30 days	**0.50**	0.50	5.13	0.50
60 days	**0.75**	0.95	5.13	0.75
90 days	**1.00**	1.25	5.00	1.00
120 days	**1.25**	1.50	5.00	1.15

	Latest	Week ago	—52-WEEK— High	—52-WEEK— Low
150 days	**1.25**	1.50	5.00	1.25
180 days	**1.50**	1.75	5.00	1.50

Other short-term rates

	Latest	Week ago	—52-WEEK— High	—52-WEEK— Low
Call money	**2.00**	2.00	6.00	2.00
Commercial paper				
30 to 59 days	**n.q.**	...	...	...
60 to 89 days	**0.15**	...	...	...
90 to 119 days	**0.20**	...	...	...
120 to 149 days	**0.25**	...	...	...
150 to 165 days	**0.35**	...	...	...
166 to 180 days	**0.40**	...	...	...
181 to 270 days	**n.q.**	...	...	...
Dealer commercial paper				
30 days	**0.59**	0.52	5.95	0.52
60 days	**0.69**	0.97	5.95	0.69
90 days	**0.84**	1.12	5.95	0.84
Euro commercial paper				
30 day	**1.94**	2.34	4.75	1.94
Two month	**2.12**	2.50	4.80	2.12
Three month	**2.20**	2.61	5.00	2.20
Four month	**2.35**	2.70	5.00	2.35
Five month	**2.37**	2.71	5.02	2.37
Six month	**2.40**	2.73	5.07	2.40

London interbank offered rate, or Libor

	Latest	Week ago	52-WEEK High	52-WEEK Low
One month	**0.36625**	0.43000	4.58750	0.36625
Three month	**1.26000**	1.41250	4.81875	1.26000
Six month	**1.60000**	1.75250	4.39375	1.60000
One year	**1.85500**	2.02375	4.23375	1.85500

New York Funding Rate

	Latest	Week ago	52-WEEK High	52-WEEK Low
One month	**0.3800**	0.4533	4.8273	0.3800
Three month	**1.1800**	1.4167	4.9000	1.1800

	Latest	Week ago	—52-WEEK— High	—52-WEEK— Low
Libor Swaps (USD)				
Two year	**1.308**	1.643	3.978	1.308
Three year	**1.634**	1.922	4.325	1.634
Five year	**2.039**	2.327	4.661	1.996
Ten year	**2.540**	2.793	4.968	2.304
20 year	**2.859**	3.001	5.200	2.438
30 year	**2.865**	2.941	5.248	2.365
Euro Libor				
One month	**2.402**	2.555	5.186	2.402
Three month	**2.689**	2.849	5.391	2.689
Six month	**2.768**	2.946	5.438	2.768
One year	**2.841**	3.027	5.514	2.841
Euro interbank offered rate (Euribor)				
One month	**2.412**	2.570	5.197	2.412
Three month	**2.692**	2.859	5.393	2.692
Six month	**2.765**	2.945	5.448	2.765
One year	**2.834**	3.025	5.526	2.834
Hibor				
One month	**0.151**	0.204	4.993	0.151
Three month	**0.841**	0.949	4.442	0.841
Six month	**1.184**	1.450	4.100	1.184
One year	**1.683**	1.850	3.950	1.671
Asian dollars				
One month	**0.372**	0.430	4.588	0.372
Three month	**1.296**	1.415	4.780	1.296
Six month	**1.642**	1.773	4.438	1.642
One year	**1.866**	2.035	5.408	1.866

	LATEST Offer	LATEST Bid	Week ago	52-WEEK High	52-WEEK Low
Eurodollars (mid rates)					
One month	**0.30**	0.75	0.75	6.25	0.50
Two month	**0.50**	1.00	1.25	5.50	0.75
Three month	**0.75**	1.25	1.50	5.75	1.00
Four month	**0.85**	1.35	1.75	5.25	1.10
Five month	**1.00**	1.40	1.75	5.25	1.20
Six month	**1.25**	1.75	1.93	5.25	1.50

Notes on data:
U.S. prime rate and discount rate are effective December 16, 2008. **U.S. prime rate** is the base rate on corporate loans posted by at least 70% of the 10 largest U.S. banks.; **Other prime rates** aren't directly comparable; lending practices vary widely by location; **Discount rate** is the charge on loans to depository institutions by the New York Federal Reserve Banks; **Federal-funds rate** is on reserves traded among commercial banks for overnight use in amounts of $1 million or more; **Call money rate** is the charge on loans to brokers on stock-exchange collateral; **Dealer commercial paper rates** are for high-grade unsecured notes sold through dealers by major corporations; **Freddie Mac RNY** is the required net yield for the one-year 2% rate-capped ARM. **Libor** is the British Bankers' Association average of interbank offered rates for dollar deposits in the London market; **Libor Swaps** quoted are mid-market, semi-annual swap rates and pay the floating 3-month Libor rate. **New York Funding Rate** is the survey-based average of unsecured bank funding costs.

Sources: Merrill Lynch; Bureau of Labor Statistics; ICAP plc.; Thomson Reuters; General Electric Capital Corp.; Tullett Prebon Information, Ltd.

Reuters Group PLC is the primary data provider for several statistical tables in The Wall Street Journal, including foreign stock quotations, futures and foreign exchange tables. Reuters real-time data feeds are used to calculate various Dow Jones Indexes.

Source: Wall Street Journal, Monday, January 12, 2009, p. C6.

Fed to meet the amount required by regulators. It can then borrow these deposits from another bank, which transfers them to the borrowing bank using the Fed's wire transfer system. This market is very sensitive to the credit needs of the banks, so the interest rate on these loans, called the **federal funds rate**, is a closely watched barometer of the tightness of credit market conditions in the banking system and the stance of monetary policy. When it is high, it indicates that the banks are strapped for funds; when it is low, banks' credit needs are low.

Capital Market Instruments

Capital market instruments are debt and equity instruments with maturities of greater than one year. They have far wider price fluctuations than money market instruments and are considered to be fairly risky investments. The principal capital market instruments are listed in Table 2, which shows the amount outstanding at the end of 1980, 1990, 2000, and 2008. The Following the Financial News box illustrates how the interest rates on many of these instruments are reported.

Stocks   *Stocks* are equity claims on the net income and assets of a corporation. Their value of $20 trillion at the end of 2008 exceeds that of any other type of security in the capital market. However, the amount of new stock issues in any given year is typically quite small, less than 1% of the total value of shares outstanding. Individuals hold around half of the value of stocks; the rest are held by pension funds, mutual funds, and insurance companies.

Mortgages   *Mortgages* are loans to households or firms to purchase housing, land, or other real structures, where the structure or land itself serves as collateral for the loans. The mortgage market is the largest debt market in the United States, with the amount of residential mortgages (used to purchase residential housing) outstanding more than

TABLE 2

Principal Capital Market Instruments

Type of Instrument	Amount Outstanding ($ billions, end of year)			
	1980	1990	2000	2008
Corporate stocks (market value)	1,601	4,146	17,627	19,648
Residential mortgages	1,106	2,886	5,463	12,033
Corporate bonds	366	1,008	2,230	3,703
U.S. government securities (marketable long-term)	407	1,653	2,184	3,621
U.S. government agency securities	193	435	1,616	8,073
State and local government bonds	310	870	1,192	2,225
Bank commercial loans	459	818	1,091	1,605
Consumer loans	355	813	536	871
Commercial and farm mortgages	352	829	1,214	2,526

Sources: Federal Reserve Flow of Funds Accounts; Federal Reserve *Bulletin.* 2008, 3rd Quarter.

quadruple the amount of commercial and farm mortgages. Savings and loan associations and mutual savings banks have been the primary lenders in the residential mortgage market, although commercial banks have started to enter this market more

Following the Financial News   Capital Market Interest Rates

The *Wall Street Journal* publishes daily a list of interest rates on many different capital market instruments in its "Bonds, Rates & Yields" column in the Money and Investing section.

The five interest rates on capital market instruments in the "Bonds, Rates & Yields" column that are discussed most frequently in the media are:

30-year mortgage: the interest rate on a 30-year fixed-rate residential mortgage that is less than $417,000 in amount and is guaranteed by the FHA.

Jumbo mortgages: the interest rate on a 30-year fixed-rate residential mortgage for prime customers that is in excess of $417,000 in amount.

Five-year adjustable mortgages (ARMs): the interest rate for the first five years on a residential mortgage that adjusts after five years for prime customers.

New-car loans: the interest rate on a four-year fixed-rate new-car loan.

10-year Treasury: the interest rate on U.S. Treasury bonds maturing in ten years.

⟦BONDS, RATES & YIELDS⟧

Consumer Rates and Returns to Investor

U.S. consumer rates
A consumer rate against its benchmark over the past year

5.40%

5-year adjustable-rate mortgage (ARM) 4.30

3.20

5-year Treasury note yield 2.10

1.00

F M A M J J A S O N D J
2008

Selected rates
Five-year ARM, APR

Bankrate.com avg:	**5.66%**
Bethpage FCU	**3.51%**
Bethpage, NY	800-628-7070
Third Federal Savings & Loan	**3.80%**
Cleveland, OH	888-844-7333
Third Federal S&LA	**3.80%**
Cleveland, OH	888-THIRDFED
Total Mortgage Services	**3.80%**
Milford, CT	800-592-1501
Park View Federal Savings Bank	**3.82%**
Cleveland, OH	440-248-7171

Interest rate	YIELD/RATE (%) Last (●)	Week ago	52-WEEK RANGE (%) Low 0 2 4 6 8 High	3-yr chg (pct pts)
Federal-funds rate target	**0-0.25**	0.00	0.00 — 4.25	**unch.**
Prime rate*	**3.25**	3.25	3.25 — 7.25	**-4.00**
Libor, 3-month	**1.14**	1.26	1.08 — 4.82	**-3.46**
Money market, annual yield	**1.96**	2.03	1.96 — 3.32	**-0.82**
Five-year CD, annual yield	**2.96**	3.03	2.96 — 4.28	**-1.54**
30-year mortgage, fixed†	**5.32**	5.33	5.30 — 6.61	**-0.39**
15-year mortgage, fixed†	**4.95**	4.90	4.90 — 6.22	**-0.35**
Jumbo mortgages, $417,000-plus†	**6.75**	6.75	6.49 — 7.89	**0.74**
Five-year adj mortgage (ARM)†	**5.66**	5.84	5.01 — 6.14	**0.34**
New-car loan, 48-month	**7.10**	7.11	6.45 — 7.14	**0.63**
Home-equity loan, $30,000	**5.18**	5.18	4.64 — 6.85	**-0.81**

Bankrate.com rates based on survey of over 4,800 online banks. *Base rate posted by 75% of the nation's largest banks.† Excludes closing costs.
Sources: Thomson Reuters; WSJ Market Data Group; Bankrate.com

Benchmark Yields and Rates

Treasury yield curve
Yield to maturity of current bills, notes and bonds

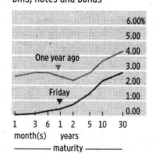

6.00%
5.00
One year ago 4.00
3.00
2.00
Friday 1.00
0.00

1   3   6   1   2   5 10   30
month(s)   years
—— maturity ——

Libor-swap curve
Fixed mid rates* to be paid against three-month Libor

Libor ◄ ► Swap 6.00%
One year ago 5.00
4.00
3.00
Friday 2.00
1.00
0.00

1   3   6   1 2 3 5 10 20 30
month(s)   year(s)
—— maturity ——

*Semiannual swaps maturing in 2 yrs–30 yrs   Sources: Ryan ALM; ICAP plc.

Corporate Borrowing Rates and Yields

Bond total return index	YIELD (%) Last	Wk ago	SPREAD +/– TREASURYS, in basis pts, 52-WK RANGE Last	Low	High	TOTAL RETURN 52-wk	3-yr
10-yr Treasury, Ryan ALM	**2.322**	2.409				16.70	10.21
DJ Corporate	**6.417**	6.514				2.59	4.19
Aggregate, Barclays Capital	**3.750**	3.590	194.0	97.0	258.0	4.09	5.90
High Yield 100, Merrill Lynch	**12.156**	12.236	1083.0	553.0	1482.0	-15.27	n.a.
Fixed-Rate MBS, Barclays	**3.080**	2.650	95.0	59.0	181.0	7.75	7.48
Muni Master, Merrill	**3.228**	3.506	45.0	-8.0	47.0	3.75	4.66
EMBI Global, J.P. Morgan	**9.267**	9.136	708.0	6.6	890.9	-10.71	n.a.

Sources: J.P. Morgan; Ryan ALM; Ryan Labs; Barclays Capital; Merrill Lynch

Source: Wall Street Journal Tuesday, January 20, 2009, p. C4.

aggressively. The majority of commercial and farm mortgages are made by commercial banks and life insurance companies. The federal government plays an active role in the mortgage market via the three government agencies—the Federal National Mortgage Association (FNMA, "Fannie Mae"), the Government National Mortgage Association (GNMA, "Ginnie Mae"), and the Federal Home Loan Mortgage Corporation (FHLMC, "Freddie Mac")—that provide funds to the mortgage market by selling bonds and using the proceeds to buy mortgages.

Corporate Bonds   These long-term bonds are issued by corporations with very strong credit ratings. The typical *corporate bond* sends the holder an interest payment twice a year and pays off the face value when the bond matures. Some corporate bonds, called *convertible bonds,* have the additional feature of allowing the holder to convert them into a specified number of shares of stock at any time up to the maturity date. This feature makes these convertible bonds more desirable to prospective purchasers than bonds without it and allows the corporation to reduce its interest payments because these bonds can increase in value if the price of the stock appreciates sufficiently. Because the outstanding amount of both convertible and nonconvertible bonds for any given corporation is small, they are not nearly as liquid as other securities such as U.S. government bonds.

Although the size of the corporate bond market is substantially smaller than that of the stock market, with the amount of corporate bonds outstanding less than one-fifth that of stocks, the volume of new corporate bonds issued each year is substantially greater than the volume of new stock issues. Thus the behavior of the corporate bond market is probably far more important to a firm's financing decisions than the behavior of the stock market. The principal buyers of corporate bonds are life insurance companies; pension funds and households are other large holders.

U.S. Government Securities   These long-term debt instruments are issued by the U.S. Treasury to finance the deficits of the federal government. Because they are the most widely traded bonds in the United States (the volume of transactions on average exceeds $100 billion daily), they are the most liquid security traded in the capital market. They are held by the Federal Reserve, banks, households, and foreigners.

U.S. Government Agency Securities   These long-term bonds are issued by various government agencies such as Ginnie Mae, the Federal Farm Credit Bank, and the Tennessee Valley Authority to finance such items as mortgages, farm loans, or power-generating equipment. Many of these securities are guaranteed by the federal government. They function much like U.S. government bonds and are held by similar parties.

State and Local Government Bonds   State and local bonds, also called *municipal bonds,* are long-term debt instruments issued by state and local governments to finance expenditures on schools, roads, and other large programs. An important feature of these bonds is that their interest payments are exempt from federal income tax and generally from state taxes in the issuing state. Commercial banks, with their high income tax rate, are the biggest buyers of these securities, owning over half the total amount outstanding. The next biggest group of holders consists of wealthy individuals in high income tax brackets, followed by insurance companies.

Consumer and Bank Commercial Loans   These loans to consumers and businesses are made principally by banks but, in the case of consumer loans, also by finance companies.

INTERNATIONALIZATION OF FINANCIAL MARKETS

The growing internationalization of financial markets has become an important trend. Before the 1980s, U.S. financial markets were much larger than financial markets outside the United States, but in recent years the dominance of U.S. markets has been disappearing. (See the Global box "Are U.S. Capital Markets Losing Their Edge?") The extraordinary growth of foreign financial markets has been the result of both large increases in the pool of savings in foreign countries such as Japan and the deregulation of foreign financial markets, which has enabled foreign markets to expand their activities. American corporations and banks are now more likely to tap international capital markets to raise needed funds, and American investors often seek investment opportunities abroad. Similarly, foreign corporations and banks raise funds from Americans, and foreigners have become important investors in the United States. A look at international

---

Global   Are U.S. Capital Markets Losing Their Edge?

Over the past few decades the United States lost its international dominance in a number of manufacturing industries, including automobiles and consumer electronics, as other countries became more competitive in global markets. Recent evidence suggests that financial markets now are undergoing a similar trend: Just as Ford and General Motors have lost global market share to Toyota and Honda, U.S. stock and bond markets recently have seen their share of sales of newly issued corporate securities slip. In 2008 the London and Hong Kong stock exchanges each handled a larger share of initial public offerings (IPO) of stock than did the New York Stock Exchange, which had been by far the dominant exchange in terms of IPO value just five years before. Likewise, the portion of new corporate bonds issued worldwide that are initially sold in U.S. capital markets has fallen below the share sold in European debt markets in each of the past two years.*

Why do corporations that issue new securities to raise capital now conduct more of this business in financial markets in Europe and Asia? Among the factors contributing to this trend are quicker adoption of technological innovation by foreign financial markets, tighter immigration controls in the United States following the terrorist attacks in 2001, and perceptions that listing on American exchanges will expose

foreign securities issuers to greater risks of lawsuits. Many people see burdensome financial regulation as the main cause, however, and point specifically to the Sarbanes-Oxley Act of 2002. Congress passed this act after a number of accounting scandals involving U.S. corporations and the accounting firms that audited them came to light. Sarbanes-Oxley aims to strengthen the integrity of the auditing process and the quality of information provided in corporate financial statements. The costs to corporations of complying with the new rules and procedures are high, especially for smaller firms, but largely avoidable if firms choose to issue their securities in financial markets outside the United States. For this reason, there is much support for revising Sarbanes-Oxley to lessen its alleged harmful effects and induce more securities issuers back to United States financial markets. However, there is not conclusive evidence to support the view that Sarbanes-Oxley is the main cause of the relative decline of U.S. financial markets and therefore in need of reform.

Discussion of the relative decline of U.S. financial markets and debate about the factors that are contributing to it likely will continue. Chapter 8 provides more detail on the Sarbanes-Oxley Act and its effects on the U.S. financial system.

*"Down on the Street," *The Economist*, November 25, 2006, pp. 69–71.

bond markets and world stock markets will give us a picture of how this globalization of financial markets is taking place.

International Bond Market, Eurobonds, and Eurocurrencies

The traditional instruments in the international bond market are known as **foreign bonds**. Foreign bonds are sold in a foreign country and are denominated in that country's currency. For example, if the German automaker Porsche sells a bond in the United States denominated in U.S. dollars, it is classified as a foreign bond. Foreign bonds have been an important instrument in the international capital market for centuries. In fact, a large percentage of U.S. railroads built in the nineteenth century were financed by sales of foreign bonds in Britain.

A more recent innovation in the international bond market is the **Eurobond**, a bond denominated in a currency other than that of the country in which it is sold—for example, a bond denominated in U.S. dollars sold in London. Currently, over 80% of the new issues in the international bond market are Eurobonds, and the market for these securities has grown very rapidly. As a result, the Eurobond market is now larger than the U.S. corporate bond market.

A variant of the Eurobond is **Eurocurrencies**, which are foreign currencies deposited in banks outside the home country. The most important of the Eurocurrencies are **Eurodollars**, which are U.S. dollars deposited in foreign banks outside the United States or in foreign branches of U.S. banks. Because these short-term deposits earn interest, they are similar to short-term Eurobonds. American banks borrow Eurodollar deposits from other banks or from their own foreign branches, and Eurodollars are now an important source of funds for American banks.

Note that the new currency, the euro, can create some confusion about the terms Eurobond, Eurocurrencies, and Eurodollars. A bond denominated in euros is called a Eurobond only *if it is sold outside the countries that have adopted the euro.* In fact, most Eurobonds are not denominated in euros but are instead denominated in U.S. dollars. Similarly, Eurodollars have nothing to do with euros, but are instead U.S. dollars deposited in banks outside the United States.

World Stock Markets

Until recently, the U.S. stock market was by far the largest in the world, but foreign stock markets have been growing in importance, with the United States not always being number one. The increased interest in foreign stocks has prompted the development in the United States of mutual funds that specialize in trading in foreign stock markets. American investors now pay attention not only to the Dow Jones Industrial Average but also to stock price indexes for foreign stock markets such as the Nikkei 300 Average (Tokyo) and the Financial Times Stock Exchange (FTSE) 100-Share Index (London).

The internationalization of financial markets is having profound effects on the United States. Foreigners, particularly Japanese investors, are not only providing funds to corporations in the United States, but are also helping finance the federal government. Without these foreign funds, the U.S. economy would have grown far less rapidly in the last twenty years. The internationalization of financial markets is also leading the way to a more integrated world economy in which flows of goods and technology between countries are more commonplace. In later chapters, we will encounter many examples of the important roles that international factors play in the U.S. economy (see the Following the Financial News box).

Following the Financial News   Foreign Stock Market Indexes

Foreign Stock market indexes are published daily in the *Wall Street Journal* which reports developments in foreign stock markets.

The first column identifies the country of the foreign stock exchange followed by the market index; for example, the circled entry for the Nikkei 300 Average in Japan. The second column,

"CLOSE," gives the closing value of the index, which was 8836.80 for the Nikkei 300 Average on January 9, 2009. The "% CHG" column indicates the percentage change in the index, −0.26%. The "YTD % CHG" column indicates the percentage change in the index from the beginning of the year, −0.3%.

International Stock Indexes

Region/Country	Index	Close	% chg	Low	Close (●)	High	YTD % chg
World	**The Global Dow**	1537.63	−2.38	1264.68		2774.34	0.7
	DJ World Index	172.52	−2.23	143.63		297.12	0.3
	DJ World ex U.S.	149.08	−0.65	123.87		270.51	1.6
	MSCI EAFE*	1255.32	−0.81	1044.24		2206.72	1.4
DJ Wilshire	**Global**	1740.22	−2.31	1452.88		3041.34	0.3
	Global ex U.S.	1465.19	−0.89	1225.96		2723.67	1.4
	Global Dev. ex U.S.	1436.66	−0.72	1198.66		2584.38	1.5
	Global Small-Cap	1881.14	−1.94	1546.11		3457.48	0.1
	Global Large-Cap	1705.44	−2.36	1426.47		2962.78	0.3
Americas	**DJ Americas**	225.17	−3.58	186.51		375.06	−0.4
Brazil	**Sao Paulo Bovespa**	41582.94	3.33	29435.11		73516.80	10.7
Canada	**S&P/TSX Comp**	9085.18	−1.61	7724.76		15073.13	1.1
Mexico	**IPC All-Share**	21741.29	−6.49	16868.66		32095.04	−2.9
Venezuela	**Caracas General**	35187.85	0.28	33894.41		41450.77	0.7
Europe	**DJ Stoxx 600**	207.82	1.64	182.13		344.78	5.5
	DJ Stoxx 50	2158.95	0.72	1894.31		3539.20	4.5
Eurozone	**DJ Euro Stoxx**	228.20	−1.03	198.93		395.38	2.4
	DJ Euro Stoxx 50	2486.59	−1.97	2165.91		4236.68	1.4
Belgium	**Bel-20**	1973.95	−0.34	1783.70		4022.93	3.4
France	**CAC 40**	3299.50	−1.50	2881.26		5403.51	2.5
Germany	**DAX**	4783.89	−3.80	4127.41		7732	−0.5
Israel	**Tel Aviv**	677.14	1.46	592.07		1170.54	3.4
Italy	**S&P/MIB**	20093	0.70	17968		37547	3.3
Netherlands	**AEX**	266.18	3.08	222.93		496.12	8.2
Spain	**IBEX 35**	9378.5	−1.14	7905.4		14458.0	2.0
Sweden	**SX All Share**	212.28	−0.81	176.54		334.77	3.9
Switzerland	**Swiss Market**	5697.24	2.94	5144.02		8193.36	2.9
U.K.	**FTSE 100**	4448.54	−2.48	3780.96		6376.50	0.3
Asia-Pacific	**DJ Asia-Pacific**	93.73	−0.02	79.11		157.77	0.1
Australia	**S&P/ASX 200**	3735.7	0.59	3352.9		5981.6	0.4
China	**Shanghai Composite**	1904.86	4.62	1706.70		5497.90	4.6
Hong Kong	**Hang Seng**	14377.44	−4.42	11015.84		26867.01	−0.1
India	**Bombay Sensex**	9406.47	−5.54	8451.01		20827.45	−2.5
Japan	**Nikkei Stock Avg**	8836.80	−0.26	7162.90		14489.44	−0.3
Singapore	**Straits Times**	1806.02	−1.29	1600.28		3287.34	2.5
South Korea	**Kospi**	1180.96	2.04	938.75		1888.88	5.0
Taiwan	**Weighted**	4502.74	−1.93	4089.93		9295.20	−1.9

*Europe, Australia, Far East, U.S.-dollar terms   Source: Thomson Reuters; WSJ Market Data Group

Source: *Wall Street Journal*, Monday, January 12, 2009, p. C4.

FUNCTION OF FINANCIAL INTERMEDIARIES: INDIRECT FINANCE

As shown in Figure 1 (p. 26), funds can move from lenders to borrowers by a second route, called *indirect finance* because it involves a financial intermediary that stands between the lender-savers and the borrower-spenders and helps transfer funds from one to the other. A financial intermediary does this by borrowing funds from the lender-savers and then using these funds to make loans to borrower-spenders. For example, a bank might acquire funds by issuing a liability to the public (an asset for the public) in the form of savings deposits. It might then use the funds to acquire an asset by making a loan to General Motors or by buying a U.S. Treasury bond in the financial market. The ultimate result is that funds have been transferred from the public (the lender-savers) to GM or the U.S. Treasury (the borrower-spender) with the help of the financial intermediary (the bank).

The process of indirect finance using financial intermediaries, called **financial intermediation**, is the primary route for moving funds from lenders to borrowers. Indeed, although the media focus much of their attention on securities markets, particularly the stock market, financial intermediaries are a far more important source of financing for corporations than securities markets are. This is true not only for the United States but for other industrialized countries as well (see the Global box). Why are financial intermediaries and indirect finance so important in financial markets? To answer this question, we need to understand the role of transaction costs, risk sharing, and information costs in financial markets.

Transaction Costs

Transaction costs, the time and money spent in carrying out financial transactions, are a major problem for people who have excess funds to lend. As we have seen, Carl the Carpenter needs $1,000 for his new tool, and you know that it is an excellent investment opportunity. You have the cash and would like to lend him the money, but to protect your investment, you have to hire a lawyer to write up the loan contract that specifies how much interest Carl will pay you, when he will make these interest payments, and when he will repay you the $1,000. Obtaining the contract will cost you $500. When you figure in this transaction cost for making the loan, you realize that you can't earn enough from the deal (you spend $500 to make perhaps $100) and reluctantly tell Carl that he will have to look elsewhere.

This example illustrates that small savers like you or potential borrowers like Carl might be frozen out of financial markets and thus be unable to benefit from them. Can anyone come to the rescue? Financial intermediaries can.

Financial intermediaries can substantially reduce transaction costs because they have developed expertise in lowering them; and because their large size allows them to take advantage of **economies of scale**, the reduction in transaction costs per dollar of transactions as the size (scale) of transactions increases. For example, a bank knows how to find a good lawyer to produce an airtight loan contract, and this contract can be used over and over again in its loan transactions, thus lowering the legal cost per transaction. Instead of a loan contract (which may not be all that well written) costing $500, a bank can hire a topflight lawyer for $5,000 to draw up an airtight loan contract that can be used for 2,000 loans at a cost of $2.50 per loan. At a cost of $2.50 per loan, it now becomes profitable for the financial intermediary to lend Carl the $1,000.

Because financial intermediaries are able to reduce transaction costs substantially, they make it possible for you to provide funds indirectly to people like Carl with

Global   The Importance of Financial Intermediaries Relative to Securities Markets: An International Comparison

Patterns of financing corporations differ across countries, but one key fact emerges: Studies of the major developed countries, including the United States, Canada, the United Kingdom, Japan, Italy, Germany, and France, show that when businesses go looking for funds to finance their activities, they usually obtain them indirectly through financial intermediaries and not directly from securities markets.* Even in the United States and Canada, which have the most developed securities markets in the world, loans from financial intermediaries are far more important for corporate finance than securities markets are. The countries that have made the least use of securities markets are Germany and Japan; in these two countries, financing from financial intermediaries has been almost ten times greater than that from securities markets. However, after the deregulation of Japanese securities markets in recent years, the share of corporate financing by financial intermediaries has been declining relative to the use of securities markets.

Although the dominance of financial intermediaries over securities markets is clear in all countries, the relative importance of bond versus stock markets differs widely across countries. In the United States, the bond market is far more important as a source of corporate finance: On average, the amount of new financing raised using bonds is ten times the amount raised using stocks. By contrast, countries such as France and Italy make more use of equities markets than of the bond market to raise capital.

*See, for example, Colin Mayer, "Financial Systems, Corporate Finance, and Economic Development," in *Asymmetric Information, Corporate Finance, and Investment*, ed. R. Glenn Hubbard (Chicago: University of Chicago Press, 1990), pp. 307–332.

productive investment opportunities. In addition, a financial intermediary's low transaction costs mean that it can provide its customers with **liquidity services**, services that make it easier for customers to conduct transactions. For example, banks provide depositors with checking accounts that enable them to pay their bills easily. In addition, depositors can earn interest on checking and savings accounts and yet still convert them into goods and services whenever necessary.

Risk Sharing

Another benefit made possible by the low transaction costs of financial institutions is that they can help reduce the exposure of investors to **risk**—that is, uncertainty about the returns investors will earn on assets. Financial intermediaries do this through the process known as **risk sharing**: They create and sell assets with risk characteristics that people are comfortable with, and the intermediaries then use the funds they acquire by selling these assets to purchase other assets that may have far more risk. Low transaction costs allow financial intermediaries to share risk at low cost, enabling them to earn a profit on the spread between the returns they earn on risky assets and the payments they make on the assets they have sold. This process of risk sharing is also sometimes referred to as **asset transformation**, because in a sense, risky assets are turned into safer assets for investors.

Financial intermediaries also promote risk sharing by helping individuals to diversify and thereby lower the amount of risk to which they are exposed. **Diversification** entails investing in a collection (**portfolio**) of assets whose returns do not always move together, with the result that overall risk is lower than for individual assets. (Diversification is just another name for the old adage, "You shouldn't put all your eggs in one basket.") Low transaction costs allow financial intermediaries to do this by pooling a collection of assets into a new asset and then selling it to individuals.

Asymmetric Information: Adverse Selection and Moral Hazard

The presence of transaction costs in financial markets explains, in part, why financial intermediaries and indirect finance play such an important role in financial markets. An additional reason is that in financial markets, one party often does not know enough about the other party to make accurate decisions. This inequality is called **asymmetric information**. For example, a borrower who takes out a loan usually has better information about the potential returns and risk associated with the investment projects for which the funds are earmarked than the lender does. Lack of information creates problems in the financial system on two fronts: before the transaction is entered into and after.[1]

Adverse selection is the problem created by asymmetric information *before* the transaction occurs. Adverse selection in financial markets occurs when the potential borrowers who are the most likely to produce an undesirable (*adverse*) outcome—the bad credit risks—are the ones who most actively seek out a loan and are thus most likely to be selected. Because adverse selection makes it more likely that loans might be made to bad credit risks, lenders may decide not to make any loans even though there are good credit risks in the marketplace.

To understand why adverse selection occurs, suppose that you have two aunts to whom you might make a loan—Aunt Louise and Aunt Sheila. Aunt Louise is a conservative type who borrows only when she has an investment she is quite sure will pay off. Aunt Sheila, by contrast, is an inveterate gambler who has just come across a get-rich-quick scheme that will make her a millionaire if she can just borrow $1,000 to invest in it. Unfortunately, as with most get-rich-quick schemes, there is a high probability that the investment won't pay off and that Aunt Sheila will lose the $1,000.

Which of your aunts is more likely to call you to ask for a loan? Aunt Sheila, of course, because she has so much to gain if the investment pays off. You, however, would not want to make a loan to her because there is a high probability that her investment will turn sour and she will be unable to pay you back.

If you knew both your aunts very well—that is, if your information were not asymmetric—you wouldn't have a problem, because you would know that Aunt Sheila is a bad risk and so you would not lend to her. Suppose, though, that you don't know your aunts well. You are more likely to lend to Aunt Sheila than to Aunt Louise because Aunt Sheila would be hounding you for the loan. Because of the possibility of adverse selection, you might decide not to lend to either of your aunts, even though there are times when Aunt Louise, who is an excellent credit risk, might need a loan for a worthwhile investment.

Moral hazard is the problem created by asymmetric information *after* the transaction occurs. Moral hazard in financial markets is the risk (*hazard*) that the borrower might engage in activities that are undesirable (*immoral*) from the lender's point of view, because they make it less likely that the loan will be paid back. Because moral hazard lowers the probability that the loan will be repaid, lenders may decide that they would rather not make a loan.

---

[1]Asymmetric information and the adverse selection and moral hazard concepts are also crucial problems for the insurance industry.

As an example of moral hazard, suppose that you made a $1,000 loan to another relative, Uncle Melvin, who needs the money to purchase a computer so he can set up a business typing students' term papers. Once you have made the loan, however, Uncle Melvin is more likely to slip off to the track and play the horses. If he bets on a 20-to-1 long shot and wins with your money, he is able to pay you back your $1,000 and live high off the hog with the remaining $19,000. But if he loses, as is likely, you don't get paid back, and all he has lost is his reputation as a reliable, upstanding uncle. Uncle Melvin therefore has an incentive to go to the track because his gains ($19,000) if he bets correctly are much greater than the cost to him (his reputation) if he bets incorrectly. If you knew what Uncle Melvin was up to, you would prevent him from going to the track, and he would not be able to increase the moral hazard. However, because it is hard for you to keep informed about his whereabouts—that is, because information is asymmetric—there is a good chance that Uncle Melvin will go to the track and you will not get paid back. The risk of moral hazard might therefore discourage you from making the $1,000 loan to Uncle Melvin, even if you were sure that you would be paid back if he used it to set up his business.

The problems created by adverse selection and moral hazard are an important impediment to well-functioning financial markets. Again, financial intermediaries can alleviate these problems.

With financial intermediaries in the economy, small savers can provide their funds to the financial markets by lending these funds to a trustworthy intermediary—say, the Honest John Bank—which in turn lends the funds out either by making loans or by buying securities such as stocks or bonds. Successful financial intermediaries have higher earnings on their investments than small savers, because they are better equipped than individuals to screen out bad credit risks from good ones, thereby reducing losses due to adverse selection. In addition, financial intermediaries have high earnings because they develop expertise in monitoring the parties they lend to, thus reducing losses due to moral hazard. The result is that financial intermediaries can afford to pay lender-savers interest or provide substantial services and still earn a profit.

As we have seen, financial intermediaries play an important role in the economy because they provide liquidity services, promote risk sharing, and solve information problems, thereby allowing small savers and borrowers to benefit from the existence of financial markets. The success of financial intermediaries in performing this role is evidenced by the fact that most Americans invest their savings with them and obtain loans from them. Financial intermediaries play a key role in improving economic efficiency because they help financial markets channel funds from lender-savers to people with productive investment opportunities. Without a well-functioning set of financial intermediaries, it is very hard for an economy to reach its full potential. We will explore further the role of financial intermediaries in the economy in Part 3.

TYPES OF FINANCIAL INTERMEDIARIES

We have seen why financial intermediaries play such an important role in the economy. Now we look at the principal financial intermediaries themselves and how they perform the intermediation function. They fall into three categories: depository institutions (banks), contractual savings institutions, and investment intermediaries. Table 3 provides a guide to the discussion of the financial intermediaries that fit into these three categories by describing their primary liabilities (sources of funds) and assets (uses of funds). The

TABLE 3

Primary Assets and Liabilities of Financial Intermediaries

Type of Intermediary	Primary Liabilities (Sources of Funds)	Primary Assets (Uses of Funds)
Depository institutions (banks)		
Commercial banks	Deposits	Business and consumer loans, mortgages, U.S. government securities and municipal bonds
Savings and loan associations	Deposits	Mortgages
Mutual savings banks	Deposits	Mortgages
Credit unions	Deposits	Consumer loans
Contractual savings institutions		
Life insurance companies	Premiums from policies	Corporate bonds and mortgages
Fire and casualty insurance companies	Premiums from policies	Municipal bonds, corporate bonds and stock, U.S. government securities
Pension funds, government retirement funds	Employer and employee contributions	Corporate bonds and stock
Investment intermediaries		
Finance companies	Commercial paper, stocks, bonds	Consumer and business loans
Mutual funds	Shares	Stocks, bonds
Money market mutual funds	Shares	Money market instruments

relative size of these intermediaries in the United States is indicated in Table 4, which lists the amount of their assets at the end of 1980, 1990, 2000, and 2008.

Depository Institutions

Depository institutions (for simplicity, we refer to these as *banks* throughout this text) are financial intermediaries that accept deposits from individuals and institutions and make loans. The study of money and banking focuses special attention on this group of financial institutions, because they are involved in the creation of deposits, an important component of the money supply. These institutions include commercial banks and the so-called **thrift institutions (thrifts)**: savings and loan associations, mutual savings banks, and credit unions.

Commercial Banks   These financial intermediaries raise funds primarily by issuing checkable deposits (deposits on which checks can be written), savings deposits (deposits that are payable on demand but do not allow their owner to write checks), and time deposits (deposits with fixed terms to maturity). They then use these funds to make commercial, consumer, and mortgage loans and to buy U.S. government securities

TABLE 4

Principal Financial Intermediaries and Value of Their Assets

Type of Intermediary	Value of Assets ($ billions, end of year)			
	1980	1990	2000	2008
Depository institutions (banks)				
Commercial banks	1,481	3,334	6,469	12,272
Savings and loan associations and mutual savings banks	792	1,365	1,218	1,518
Credit unions	67	215	441	801
Contractual savings institutions				
Life insurance companies	464	1,367	3,136	4,798
Fire and casualty insurance companies	182	533	862	1,337
Pension funds (private)	504	1,629	4,355	5,193
State and local government retirement funds	197	737	2,293	2,730
Investment intermediaries				
Finance companies	205	610	1,140	1,910
Mutual funds	70	654	4,435	6,588
Money market mutual funds	76	498	1,812	3,376

Source: Federal Reserve Flow of Funds Accounts: www.federalreserve.gov/releases/Z1/.

and municipal bonds. There are slightly fewer than 7,150 commercial banks in the United States, and as a group, they are the largest financial intermediary and have the most diversified portfolios (collections) of assets.

Savings and Loan Associations (S&Ls) and Mutual Savings Banks
These depository institutions, of which there are approximately 1,225, obtain funds primarily through savings deposits (often called *shares*) and time and checkable deposits. In the past, these institutions were constrained in their activities and mostly made mortgage loans for residential housing. Over time, these restrictions have been loosened so that the distinction between these depository institutions and commercial banks has blurred. These intermediaries have become more alike and are now more competitive with each other.

Credit Unions   These financial institutions, numbering about 8,100, are typically very small cooperative lending institutions organized around a particular group: union members, employees of a particular firm, and so forth. They acquire funds from deposits called *shares* and primarily make consumer loans.

Contractual Savings Institutions

Contractual savings institutions, such as insurance companies and pension funds, are financial intermediaries that acquire funds at periodic intervals on a contractual basis.

Because they can predict with reasonable accuracy how much they will have to pay out in benefits in the coming years, they do not have to worry as much as depository institutions about losing funds quickly. As a result, the liquidity of assets is not as important a consideration for them as it is for depository institutions, and they tend to invest their funds primarily in long-term securities such as corporate bonds, stocks, and mortgages.

Life Insurance Companies   Life insurance companies insure people against financial hazards following a death and sell annuities (annual income payments upon retirement). They acquire funds from the premiums that people pay to keep their policies in force and use them mainly to buy corporate bonds and mortgages. They also purchase stocks, but are restricted in the amount that they can hold. Currently, with $4.8 trillion in assets, they are among the largest of the contractual savings institutions.

Fire and Casualty Insurance Companies   These companies insure their policyholders against loss from theft, fire, and accidents. They are very much like life insurance companies, receiving funds through premiums for their policies, but they have a greater possibility of loss of funds if major disasters occur. For this reason, they use their funds to buy more liquid assets than life insurance companies do. Their largest holding of assets is municipal bonds; they also hold corporate bonds and stocks and U.S. government securities.

Pension Funds and Government Retirement Funds   Private pension funds and state and local retirement funds provide retirement income in the form of annuities to employees who are covered by a pension plan. Funds are acquired by contributions from employers and from employees, who either have a contribution automatically deducted from their paychecks or contribute voluntarily. The largest asset holdings of pension funds are corporate bonds and stocks. The establishment of pension funds has been actively encouraged by the federal government, both through legislation requiring pension plans and through tax incentives to encourage contributions.

Investment Intermediaries

This category of financial intermediaries includes finance companies, mutual funds, and money market mutual funds.

Finance Companies   Finance companies raise funds by selling commercial paper (a short-term debt instrument) and by issuing stocks and bonds. They lend these funds to consumers, who make purchases of such items as furniture, automobiles, and home improvements, and to small businesses. Some finance companies are organized by a parent corporation to help sell its product. For example, Ford Motor Credit Company makes loans to consumers who purchase Ford automobiles.

Mutual Funds   These financial intermediaries acquire funds by selling shares to many individuals and use the proceeds to purchase diversified portfolios of stocks and bonds. Mutual funds allow shareholders to pool their resources so that they can take advantage of lower transaction costs when buying large blocks of stocks or bonds. In addition, mutual funds allow shareholders to hold more diversified portfolios than they otherwise would. Shareholders can sell (redeem) shares at any time, but the value of these shares will be determined by the value of the mutual fund's holdings of securities. Because these fluctuate greatly, the value of mutual fund shares will, too; therefore, investments in mutual funds can be risky.

Money Market Mutual Funds   These financial institutions have the characteristics of a mutual fund but also function to some extent as a depository institution because they offer deposit-type accounts. Like most mutual funds, they sell shares to acquire funds that are then used to buy money market instruments that are both safe and very liquid. The interest on these assets is paid out to the shareholders.

A key feature of these funds is that shareholders can write checks against the value of their shareholdings. In effect, shares in a money market mutual fund function like checking account deposits that pay interest. Money market mutual funds have experienced extraordinary growth since 1971, when they first appeared. By 2008, their assets had climbed to nearly $3.4 trillion.

Investment Banks   Despite its name, an investment bank is not a bank or a financial intermediary in the ordinary sense; that is, it does not take in deposits and then lend them out. Instead, an investment bank is a different type of intermediary that helps a corporation issue securities. First it advises the corporation on which type of securities to issue (stocks or bonds); then it helps sell (**underwrite**) the securities by purchasing them from the corporation at a predetermined price and reselling them in the market. Investment banks also act as deal makers and earn enormous fees by helping corporations acquire other companies through mergers or acquisitions.

REGULATION OF THE FINANCIAL SYSTEM

The financial system is among the most heavily regulated sectors of the American economy. The government regulates financial markets for two main reasons: to increase the information available to investors and to ensure the soundness of the financial system. We will examine how these two reasons have led to the present regulatory environment. As a study aid, the principal regulatory agencies of the U.S. financial system are listed in Table 5.

Increasing Information Available to Investors

Asymmetric information in financial markets means that investors may be subject to adverse selection and moral hazard problems that may hinder the efficient operation of financial markets. Risky firms or outright crooks may be the most eager to sell securities to unwary investors, and the resulting adverse selection problem may keep investors out of financial markets. Furthermore, once an investor has bought a security, thereby lending money to a firm, the borrower may have incentives to engage in risky activities or to commit outright fraud. The presence of this moral hazard problem may also keep investors away from financial markets. Government regulation can reduce adverse selection and moral hazard problems in financial markets and increase their efficiency by increasing the amount of information available to investors.

As a result of the stock market crash in 1929 and revelations of widespread fraud in the aftermath, political demands for regulation culminated in the Securities Act of 1933 and the establishment of the Securities and Exchange Commission (SEC) in 1934. The SEC requires corporations issuing securities to disclose certain information about their sales, assets, and earnings to the public and restricts trading by the largest stockholders (known as *insiders*) in the corporation. By requiring disclosure of this information and by discouraging insider trading, which could be used to manipulate security prices, the SEC hopes that investors will be better informed and protected from some

TABLE 5

Principal Regulatory Agencies of the U.S. Financial System

Regulatory Agency	Subject of Regulation	Nature of Regulations
Securities and Exchange Commission (SEC)	Organized exchanges and financial markets	Requires disclosure of information, restricts insider trading
Commodities Futures Trading Commission (CFTC)	Futures market exchanges	Regulates procedures for trading in futures markets
Office of the Comptroller of the Currency	Federally chartered commercial banks	Charters and examines the books of federally chartered commercial banks and imposes restrictions on assets they can hold
National Credit Union Administration (NCUA)	Federally chartered credit unions	Charters and examines the books of federally chartered credit unions and imposes restrictions on assets they can hold
State banking and insurance commissions	State-chartered depository institutions	Charter and examine the books of state-chartered banks and insurance companies, impose restrictions on assets they can hold, and impose restrictions on branching
Federal Deposit Insurance Corporation (FDIC)	Commercial banks, mutual savings banks, savings and loan associations	Provides insurance of up to $100,000 (temporarily $250,000) for each depositor at a bank, examines the books of insured banks, and imposes restrictions on assets they can hold
Federal Reserve System	All depository institutions	Examines the books of commercial banks that are members of the system, sets reserve requirements for all banks
Office of Thrift Supervision	Savings and loan associations	Examines the books of savings and loan associations, imposes restrictions on assets they can hold

of the abuses in financial markets that occurred before 1933. Indeed, in recent years, the SEC has been particularly active in prosecuting people involved in insider trading.

Ensuring the Soundness of Financial Intermediaries

Asymmetric information can lead to the widespread collapse of financial intermediaries, referred to as a **financial panic**. Because providers of funds to financial intermediaries may not be able to assess whether the institutions holding their funds are sound, if they have doubts about the overall health of financial intermediaries, they may want to pull their funds out of both sound and unsound institutions. The possible outcome is a financial panic that produces large losses for the public and causes serious damage to the economy. To protect the public and the economy from financial panics, the government has implemented six types of regulations.

Restrictions on Entry   State banking and insurance commissions, as well as the Office of the Comptroller of the Currency (an agency of the federal government), have created tight regulations governing who is allowed to set up a financial intermediary. Individuals or groups that want to establish a financial intermediary, such as a bank or an insurance company, must obtain a charter from the state or the federal government. Only if they are upstanding citizens with impeccable credentials and a large amount of initial funds will they be given a charter.

Disclosure   There are stringent reporting requirements for financial intermediaries. Their bookkeeping must follow certain strict principles, their books are subject to periodic inspection, and they must make certain information available to the public.

Restrictions on Assets and Activities   There are restrictions on what financial intermediaries are allowed to do and what assets they can hold. Before you put your funds into a bank or some other such institution, you would want to know that your funds are safe and that the bank or other financial intermediary will be able to meet its obligations to you. One way of doing this is to restrict the financial intermediary from engaging in certain risky activities. Legislation passed in 1933 (repealed in 1999) separated commercial banking from the securities industry so that banks could not engage in risky ventures associated with this industry. Another way to limit a financial intermediary's risky behavior is to restrict it from holding certain risky assets, or at least from holding a greater quantity of these risky assets than is prudent. For example, commercial banks and other depository institutions are not allowed to hold common stock because stock prices experience substantial fluctuations. Insurance companies are allowed to hold common stock, but their holdings cannot exceed a certain fraction of their total assets.

Deposit Insurance   The government can insure people's deposits so that they do not suffer great financial loss if the financial intermediary that holds these deposits should fail. The most important government agency that provides this type of insurance is the Federal Deposit Insurance Corporation (FDIC), which insures each depositor at a commercial bank or mutual savings bank up to a loss of $100,000 per account (temporarily $250,000). Premiums paid by these financial institutions go into the FDIC's Deposit Insurance Fund, which is used to pay off depositors if an institution fails. The FDIC was created in 1934 after the massive bank failures of 1930–1933, in which the savings of many depositors at commercial banks were wiped out. The National Credit Union Share Insurance Fund (NCUSIF) does the same for credit unions.

Limits on Competition   Politicians have often declared that unbridled competition among financial intermediaries promotes failures that will harm the public. Although the evidence that competition has this effect is extremely weak, state and federal governments at times have imposed restrictions on the opening of additional locations (branches). In the past, banks were not allowed to open up branches in other states, and in some states, banks were restricted from opening branches in additional locations.

Restrictions on Interest Rates   Competition has also been inhibited by regulations that impose restrictions on interest rates that can be paid on deposits. For decades after 1933, banks were prohibited from paying interest on checking accounts. In addition, until 1986, the Federal Reserve System had the power under *Regulation Q* to set maximum interest rates that banks could pay on savings deposits. These regulations were instituted because of the widespread belief that unrestricted interest-rate competition helped encourage bank failures during the Great Depression. Later evidence does not seem to support this view, and Regulation Q has been abolished (although there are still restrictions on paying interest on checking accounts held by businesses).

In later chapters, we will look more closely at government regulation of financial markets and will see whether it has improved their functioning.

Financial Regulation Abroad

Not surprisingly, given the similarity of the economic system here and in Japan, Canada, and the nations of Western Europe, financial regulation in these countries is similar to financial regulation in the United States. The provision of information is improved by requiring corporations issuing securities to report details about assets and liabilities, earnings, and sales of stock, and by prohibiting insider trading. The soundness of intermediaries is ensured by licensing, periodic inspection of financial intermediaries' books, and the provision of deposit insurance (although its coverage is smaller than in the United States and its existence is often intentionally not advertised).

The major differences between financial regulation in the United States and abroad relate to bank regulation. In the past, the United States was the only industrialized country to subject banks to restrictions on branching, which limited banks' size and restricted them to certain geographic regions. (These restrictions were abolished by legislation in 1994.) U.S. banks are also the most restricted in the range of assets they may hold. Banks abroad frequently hold shares in commercial firms; in Japan and Germany, those stakes can be sizable.

SUMMARY

1. The basic function of financial markets is to channel funds from savers who have an excess of funds to spenders who have a shortage of funds. Financial markets can do this either through direct finance, in which borrowers borrow funds directly from lenders by selling them securities, or through indirect finance, which involves a financial intermediary that stands between the lender-savers and the borrower-spenders and helps transfer funds from one to the other. This channeling of funds improves the economic welfare of everyone in the society. Because they allow funds to move from people who have no productive investment opportunities to those who have such opportunities, financial markets contribute to economic efficiency. In addition, channeling of funds directly benefits consumers by allowing them to make purchases when they need them most.

2. Financial markets can be classified as debt and equity markets, primary and secondary markets, exchanges and over-the-counter markets, and money and capital markets.

3. The principal money market instruments (debt instruments with maturities of less than one year) are U.S. Treasury bills, negotiable bank certificates of deposit, commercial paper, repurchase agreements, federal

funds, and Eurodollars. The principal capital market instruments (debt and equity instruments with maturities greater than one year) are stocks, mortgages, corporate bonds, U.S. government securities, U.S. government agency securities, state and local government bonds, and consumer and bank commercial loans.

4. An important trend in recent years is the growing internationalization of financial markets. Eurobonds, which are denominated in a currency other than that of the country in which they are sold, are now the dominant security in the international bond market and have surpassed U.S. corporate bonds as a source of new funds. Eurodollars, which are U.S. dollars deposited in foreign banks, are an important source of funds for American banks.

5. Financial intermediaries are financial institutions that acquire funds by issuing liabilities and, in turn, use those funds to acquire assets by purchasing securities or making loans. Financial intermediaries play an important role in the financial system because they reduce transaction costs, allow risk sharing, and solve problems created by adverse selection and moral hazard. As a result, financial intermediaries allow small savers and borrowers to benefit from the existence of financial markets, thereby increasing the efficiency of the economy.

6. The principal financial intermediaries fall into three categories: (a) banks—commercial banks, savings and loan associations, mutual savings banks, and credit unions; (b) contractual savings institutions—life insurance companies, fire and casualty insurance companies, and pension funds; and (c) investment intermediaries—finance companies, mutual funds, and money market mutual funds.

7. The government regulates financial markets and financial intermediaries for two main reasons: to increase the information available to investors and to ensure the soundness of the financial system. Regulations include requiring disclosure of information to the public, restrictions on who can set up a financial intermediary, restrictions on what assets financial intermediaries can hold, the provision of deposit insurance, limits on competition, and restrictions on interest rates.

KEY TERMS

adverse selection, p. 41
asset transformation, p. 40
asymmetric information, p. 41
brokers, p. 28
capital, p. 27
capital market, p. 29
currency, p. 30
dealers, p. 28
default, p. 30
diversification, p. 40
dividends, p. 28
economies of scale, p. 39
equities, p. 28
Eurobond, p. 37

Eurocurrencies, p. 37
Eurodollars, p. 37
exchanges, p. 29
federal funds rate, p. 33
financial intermediation, p. 39
financial panic, p. 47
foreign bonds, p. 37
intermediate-term, p. 28
investment bank, p. 28
liabilities, p. 26
liquid, p. 29
liquidity services, p. 40
long-term, p. 28
maturity, p. 28

money market, p. 29
moral hazard, p. 41
over-the-counter (OTC) market, p. 29
portfolio, p. 40
primary market, p. 28
risk, p. 40
risk sharing, p. 40
secondary market, p. 28
short-term, p. 28
thrift institutions (thrifts), p. 43
transaction costs, p. 39
underwrite, p. 46
underwriting, p. 28

QUESTIONS AND PROBLEMS

All questions and problems are available in myeconlab *at* www.myeconlab.com/mishkin.

1. Why is a share of Microsoft common stock an asset for its owner and a liability for Microsoft?

2. If I can buy a car today for $5,000 and it is worth $10,000 in extra income next year to me because it enables me to get a job as a traveling anvil seller, should I take out a loan from Larry the Loan Shark at a 90% interest rate if no one else will give me a loan? Will I be better or worse off as a result of taking out this loan? Can you make a case for legalizing loan-sharking?

3. Some economists suspect that one of the reasons that economies in developing countries grow so slowly is that they do not have well-developed financial markets. Does this argument make sense?

4. The U.S. economy borrowed heavily from the British in the nineteenth century to build a railroad system. What was the principal debt instrument used? Why did this make both countries better off?

5. "Because corporations do not actually raise any funds in secondary markets, they are less important to the economy than primary markets." Comment.

6. If you suspect that a company will go bankrupt next year, which would you rather hold, bonds issued by the company or equities issued by the company? Why?

7. How can the adverse selection problem explain why you are more likely to make a loan to a family member than to a stranger?

8. Think of one example in which you have had to deal with the adverse selection problem.

9. Why do loan sharks worry less about moral hazard in connection with their borrowers than some other lenders do?

10. If you are an employer, what kinds of moral hazard problems might you worry about with your employees?

11. If there were no asymmetry in the information that a borrower and a lender had, could there still be a moral hazard problem?

12. "In a world without information and transaction costs, financial intermediaries would not exist." Is this statement true, false, or uncertain? Explain your answer.

13. Why might you be willing to make a loan to your neighbor by putting funds in a savings account earning a 5% interest rate at the bank and having the bank lend her the funds at a 10% interest rate rather than lend her the funds yourself?

14. How does risk sharing benefit both financial intermediaries and private investors?

15. Discuss some of the manifestations of the globalization of world capital markets.

WEB EXERCISES

1. One of the single best sources of information about U.S. financial institutions is the U.S. Flow of Funds report produced by the Federal Reserve. This document contains data on most financial intermediaries. Go to www.federalreserve.gov/releases/Z1/. Go to the most current release. You may have to load Acrobat Reader if your computer does not already have it; the site has a link for a free patch. Go to the Level Tables and answer the following.
   a. What percentage of assets do commercial banks hold in loans? What percentage of assets are held in mortgage loans?
   b. What percentage of assets do savings and loans hold in mortgage loans?
   c. What percentage of assets do credit unions hold in mortgage loans and in consumer loans?

2. The most famous financial market in the world is the New York Stock Exchange. Go to www.nyse.com.
   a. What is the mission of the NYSE?
   b. Firms must pay a fee to list their shares for sale on the NYSE. What would be the fee for a firm with five million common shares outstanding?

WEB REFERENCES

http://stockcharts.com/charts/historical

This page contains historical stock index charts for the Dow Jones Industrial Average, S&P 500, NASDAQ, 30-year Treasury Bond, and Gold prices.

www.nyse.com

New York Stock Exchange. Find listed companies, quotes, company historical data, real-time market indexes, and more.

www.nasdaq.com

Detailed market and security information for the Nasdaq OTC stock exchange.

http://finance.yahoo.com/intlindices?e=americas

Major world stock indexes, with charts, news, and components.

www.sec.gov

The United States Securities and Exchange Commission home page. It contains vast SEC resources, laws and regulations, investor information, and litigation.

 MyEconLab CAN HELP YOU GET A BETTER GRADE

If your exam were tomorrow, would you be ready? For each chapter, MyEconLab Practice Test and Study Plans pinpoint which sections you have mastered and which ones you need to study. That way, you are more efficient with your study time, and you are better prepared for your exams.

To see how it works, turn to page 20 and then go to: www.myeconlab.com/mishkin

3

What Is Money?: A Comparative Approach to Measuring Money

Preview

If you had lived in America before the Revolutionary War, your money might have consisted primarily of Spanish doubloons (silver coins that were also called *pieces of eight*). Before the Civil War, the principal forms of money in the United States were gold and silver coins and paper notes, called *banknotes*, issued by private banks. Today, you use not only coins and dollar bills issued by the government as money, but also checks written on accounts held at banks. Money has been different things at different times, but it has *always* been important to people and to the economy.

To understand the effects of money on the economy, we must understand exactly what money is. In this chapter, we develop precise definitions by exploring the functions of money, looking at why and how it promotes economic efficiency, tracing how its forms have evolved over time, and examining how money is currently measured.

MEANING OF MONEY

As the word *money* is used in everyday conversation, it can mean many things, but to economists, it has a very specific meaning. To avoid confusion, we must clarify how economists' use of the word *money* differs from conventional usage.

Economists define *money* (also referred to as the *money supply*) as anything that is generally accepted in payment for goods or services or in the repayment of debts. Currency, consisting of dollar bills and coins, clearly fits this definition and is one type of money. When most people talk about money, they're talking about **currency** (paper money and coins). If, for example, someone comes up to you and says, "Your money or your life," you should quickly hand over all your currency rather than ask, "What exactly do you mean by 'money'?"

To define money merely as currency is much too narrow for economists. Because checks are also accepted as payment for purchases, checking account deposits are considered money as well. An even broader definition of money is often needed, because other items such as savings deposits can in effect function as money if they can be quickly and easily converted into currency or checking account deposits. As you can see, there is no single, precise definition of money or the money supply, even for economists.

To complicate matters further, the word *money* is frequently used synonymously with *wealth*. When people say, "Joe is rich—he has an awful lot of money," they probably mean that Joe not only has a lot of currency and a high balance in his checking account but also has stocks, bonds, four cars, three houses, and a yacht. Thus, while "currency" is too narrow a definition of money, this other popular usage is much too broad. Economists make a distinction between money in the form of currency, demand deposits, and other items that are used to make purchases and **wealth**, the total collection of pieces of property that serve to store value. Wealth includes not only money but also other assets such as bonds, common stock, art, land, furniture, cars, and houses.

People also use the word *money* to describe what economists call *income*, as in the sentence "Sheila would be a wonderful catch; she has a good job and earns a lot of money." **Income** is a *flow* of earnings per unit of time. Money, by contrast, is a *stock*: It is a certain amount at a given point in time. If someone tells you that he has an income of $1,000, you cannot tell whether he earned a lot or a little without knowing whether this $1,000 is earned per year, per month, or even per day. But if someone tells you that she has $1,000 in her pocket, you know exactly how much this is.

Keep in mind that the money discussed in this book refers to anything that is generally accepted in payment for goods and services or in the repayment of debts and is distinct from income and wealth.

FUNCTIONS OF MONEY

Whether money is shells or rocks or gold or paper, it has three primary functions in any economy: as a medium of exchange, as a unit of account, and as a store of value. Of the three functions, its function as a medium of exchange is what distinguishes money from other assets such as stocks, bonds, and houses.

Medium of Exchange

In almost all market transactions in our economy, money in the form of currency or checks is a **medium of exchange**; it is used to pay for goods and services. The use of money as a medium of exchange promotes economic efficiency by minimizing the time spent in exchanging goods and services. To see why, let's look at a *barter economy*, one without money, in which goods and services are exchanged directly for other goods and services.

Take the case of Ellen the Economics Professor, who can do just one thing well: give brilliant economics lectures. In a barter economy, if Ellen wants to eat, she must find a farmer who not only produces the food she likes but also wants to learn economics. As you might expect, this search will be difficult and time-consuming, and Ellen might spend more time looking for such an economics-hungry farmer than she will teaching. It is even possible that she will have to quit lecturing and go into farming herself. Even so, she may still starve to death.

The time spent trying to exchange goods or services is called a *transaction cost*. In a barter economy, transaction costs are high because people have to satisfy a "double coincidence of wants"—they have to find someone who has a good or service they want and who also wants the good or service they have to offer.

Let's see what happens if we introduce money into Ellen the Economics Professor's world. Ellen can teach anyone who is willing to pay money to hear her lecture. She can then go to any farmer (or his representative at the supermarket) and buy the food she needs with the money she has been paid. The problem of the double coincidence of wants is avoided, and Ellen saves a lot of time, which she may spend doing what she does best: teaching.

As this example shows, money promotes economic efficiency by eliminating much of the time spent exchanging goods and services. It also promotes efficiency by allowing people to specialize in what they do best. Money is therefore essential in an economy: It is a lubricant that allows the economy to run more smoothly by lowering transaction costs, thereby encouraging specialization and the division of labor.

The need for money is so strong that almost every society beyond the most primitive invents it. For a commodity to function effectively as money, it has to meet several criteria: (1) It must be easily standardized, making it simple to ascertain its value; (2) it must be widely accepted; (3) it must be divisible, so that it is easy to "make change"; (4) it must be easy to carry; and (5) it must not deteriorate quickly. Forms of money that have satisfied these criteria have taken many unusual forms throughout human history, ranging from wampum (strings of beads) used by Native Americans, to tobacco and whiskey, used by the early American colonists, to cigarettes, used in prisoner-of-war camps during World War II.[1] The diversity of forms of money that have been developed over the years is as much a testament to the inventiveness of the human race as the development of tools and language.

Unit of Account

The second role of money is to provide a **unit of account**; that is, it is used to measure value in the economy. We measure the value of goods and services in terms of money, just as we measure weight in terms of pounds or distance in terms of miles. To see why this function is important, let's look again at a barter economy where money does not perform this function. If the economy has only three goods—say, peaches, economics lectures, and movies—then we need to know only three prices to tell us how to exchange one for another: the price of peaches in terms of economics lectures (that is, how many economics lectures you have to pay for a peach), the price of peaches in terms of movies, and the price of economics lectures in terms of movies. If there were ten goods, we would need to know 45 prices to exchange one good for another; with 100 goods, we would need 4,950 prices; and with 1,000 goods, 499,500 prices.[2]

Imagine how hard it would be in a barter economy to shop at a supermarket with 1,000 different items on its shelves, having to decide whether chicken or fish is a better buy if the price of a pound of chicken were quoted as 4 pounds of butter and the price of a pound of fish as 8 pounds of tomatoes. To make it possible to compare prices, the tag on each item would have to list up to 999 different prices, and the time spent reading them would result in very high transaction costs.

The solution to the problem is to introduce money into the economy and have all prices quoted in terms of units of that money, enabling us to quote the price of economics

---

[1]An extremely entertaining article on the development of money in a prisoner-of-war camp during World War II is R. A. Radford, "The Economic Organization of a P.O.W. Camp," *Economica* 12 (November 1945): 189–201.

[2]The formula for telling us the number of prices we need when we have N goods is the same formula that tells us the number of pairs when there are N items. It is

$$\frac{N(N-1)}{2}$$

In the case of ten goods, for example, we would need

$$\frac{10(10-1)}{2} = \frac{90}{2} = 45$$

lectures, peaches, and movies in terms of, say, dollars. If there were only three goods in the economy, this would not be a great advantage over the barter system, because we would still need three prices to conduct transactions. But for ten goods we now need only ten prices; for 100 goods, 100 prices; and so on. At the 1,000-goods supermarket, there are now only 1,000 prices to look at, not 499,500!

We can see that using money as a unit of account reduces transaction costs in an economy by reducing the number of prices that need to be considered. The benefits of this function of money grow as the economy becomes more complex.

Store of Value

Money also functions as a **store of value**; it is a repository of purchasing power over time. A store of value is used to save purchasing power from the time income is received until the time it is spent. This function of money is useful, because most of us do not want to spend our income immediately upon receiving it, but rather prefer to wait until we have the time or the desire to shop.

Money is not unique as a store of value; any asset—whether money, stocks, bonds, land, houses, art, or jewelry—can be used to store wealth. Many such assets have advantages over money as a store of value: They often pay the owner a higher interest rate than money, experience price appreciation, and deliver services such as providing a roof over one's head. If these assets are a more desirable store of value than money, why do people hold money at all?

The answer to this question relates to the important economic concept of **liquidity**, the relative ease and speed with which an asset can be converted into a medium of exchange. Liquidity is highly desirable. Money is the most liquid asset of all because it *is* the medium of exchange; it does not have to be converted into anything else to make purchases. Other assets involve transaction costs when they are converted into money. When you sell your house, for example, you have to pay a brokerage commission (usually 5% to 7% of the sales price), and if you need cash immediately to pay some pressing bills, you might have to settle for a lower price if you want to sell the house quickly. Because money is the most liquid asset, people are willing to hold it even if it is not the most attractive store of value.

How good a store of value money is depends on the price level. A doubling of all prices, for example, means that the value of money has dropped by half; conversely, a halving of all prices means that the value of money has doubled. During inflation, when the price level is increasing rapidly, money loses value rapidly, and people will be more reluctant to hold their wealth in this form. This is especially true during periods of extreme inflation, known as **hyperinflation**, in which the inflation rate exceeds 50% per month.

Hyperinflation occurred in Germany after World War I, with inflation rates sometimes exceeding 1,000% per month. By the end of the hyperinflation in 1923, the price level had risen to more than 30 billion times what it had been just two years before. The quantity of money needed to purchase even the most basic items became excessive. There are stories, for example, that near the end of the hyperinflation, a wheelbarrow of cash would be required to pay for a loaf of bread. Money was losing its value so rapidly that workers were paid and given time off several times during the day to spend their wages before the money became worthless. No one wanted to hold on to money, so the use of money to carry out transactions declined and barter became more and more dominant. Transaction costs skyrocketed, and as we would expect, output in the economy fell sharply.

EVOLUTION OF THE PAYMENTS SYSTEM

We can obtain a better picture of the functions of money and the forms it has taken over time by looking at the evolution of the **payments system**, the method of conducting transactions in the economy. The payments system has been evolving over centuries, and with it the form of money. At one point, precious metals such as gold were used as the principal means of payment and were the main form of money. Later, paper assets such as checks and currency began to be used in the payments system and viewed as money. Where the payments system is heading has an important bearing on how money will be defined in the future.

Commodity Money

To obtain perspective on where the payments system is heading, it is worth exploring how it has evolved. For any object to function as money, it must be universally acceptable; everyone must be willing to take it in payment for goods and services. An object that clearly has value to everyone is a likely candidate to serve as money, and a natural choice is a precious metal such as gold or silver. Money made up of precious metals or another valuable commodity is called **commodity money**, and from ancient times until several hundred years ago, commodity money functioned as the medium of exchange in all but the most primitive societies. The problem with a payments system based exclusively on precious metals is that such a form of money is very heavy and is hard to transport from one place to another. Imagine the holes you'd wear in your pockets if you had to buy things only with coins! Indeed, for large purchases such as a house, you'd have to rent a truck to transport the money payment.

Fiat Money

The next development in the payments system was *paper currency* (pieces of paper that function as a medium of exchange). Initially, paper currency carried a guarantee that it was convertible into coins or into a fixed quantity of precious metal. However, currency has evolved into **fiat money**, paper currency decreed by governments as legal tender (meaning that legally it must be accepted as payment for debts) but not convertible into coins or precious metal. Paper currency has the advantage of being much lighter than coins or precious metal, but it can be accepted as a medium of exchange only if there is some trust in the authorities who issue it and if printing has reached a sufficiently advanced stage that counterfeiting is extremely difficult. Because paper currency has evolved into a legal arrangement, countries can change the currency that they use at will. Indeed, this is what many European countries did when they abandoned their currencies for the euro in 2002.

Major drawbacks of paper currency and coins are that they are easily stolen and can be expensive to transport in large amounts because of their bulk. To combat this problem, another step in the evolution of the payments system occurred with the development of modern banking: the invention of *checks*.

Checks

A check is an instruction from you to your bank to transfer money from your account to someone else's account when she deposits the check. Checks allow transactions to take place without the need to carry around large amounts of currency.

The introduction of checks was a major innovation that improved the efficiency of the payments system. Frequently, payments made back and forth cancel each other; without checks, this would involve the movement of a lot of currency. With checks, payments that cancel each other can be settled by canceling the checks, and no currency need be moved. The use of checks thus reduces the transportation costs associated with the payments system and improves economic efficiency. Another advantage of checks is that they can be written for any amount up to the balance in the account, making transactions for large amounts much easier. Checks are also advantageous in that loss from theft is greatly reduced, and because they provide convenient receipts for purchases.

There are, however, two problems with a payments system based on checks. First, it takes time to get checks from one place to another, a particularly serious problem if you are paying someone in a different location who needs to be paid quickly. In addition, if you have a checking account, you know that it usually takes several business days before a bank will allow you to make use of the funds from a check you have deposited. If your need for cash is urgent, this feature of paying by check can be frustrating. Second, all the paper shuffling required to process checks is costly; it is estimated that it currently costs over $10 billion per year to process all the checks written in the United States.

Electronic Payment

The development of inexpensive computers and the spread of the Internet now make it cheap to pay bills electronically. In the past, you had to pay your bills by mailing a check, but now banks provide websites at which you just log on, make a few clicks, and thereby transmit your payment electronically. Not only do you save the cost of the stamp, but paying bills becomes (almost) a pleasure, requiring little effort. Electronic payment systems provided by banks now even spare you the step of logging on to pay the bill. Instead, recurring bills can be automatically deducted from your bank account. Estimated cost savings when a bill is paid electronically rather than by a check exceed one dollar per transaction. Electronic payment is thus becoming far more common in the United States.

E-Money

Electronic payments technology can substitute not only for checks, but also for cash, in the form of **electronic money** (or **e-money**)—money that exists only in electronic form. The first form of e-money was the *debit card*. Debit cards, which look like credit cards, enable consumers to purchase goods and services by electronically transferring funds directly from their bank accounts to a merchant's account. Debit cards are used in many of the same places that accept credit cards and are now often becoming faster to use than cash. At most supermarkets, for example, you can swipe your debit card through the card reader at the checkout station, press a button, and the amount of your purchases is deducted from your bank account. Most banks and companies such as Visa and MasterCard issue debit cards, and your ATM card typically can function as a debit card.

A more advanced form of e-money is the *stored-value card*. The simplest form of stored-value card is purchased for a preset dollar amount that the consumer pays up front, like a prepaid phone card. The more sophisticated stored-value card is known as a **smart card**. It contains a computer chip that allows it to be loaded with digital cash from the owner's bank account whenever needed. In Asian countries, such as Japan and Korea, cell phones now have a smart card feature that raises the expression, "pay by phone," to a new level. Smart cards can be loaded from ATM machines, personal computers with a smart card reader, or specially equipped telephones.

A third form of electronic money is often referred to as **e-cash**, which is used on the Internet to purchase goods or services. A consumer gets e-cash by setting up an account with a bank that has links to the Internet and then has the e-cash transferred to her PC. When she wants to buy something with e-cash, she surfs to a store on the Web and clicks the "buy" option for a particular item, whereupon the e-cash is automatically transferred from her computer to the merchant's computer. The merchant can then have the funds transferred from the consumer's bank account to his before the goods are shipped.

Given the convenience of e-money, you might think that we would move quickly to a cashless society in which all payments are made electronically. However, this hasn't happened, as discussed in the FYI box, "Are We Headed for a Cashless Society?"

FYI   Are We Headed for a Cashless Society?

Predictions of a cashless society have been around for decades, but they have not come to fruition. For example, *Business Week* predicted in 1975 that electronic means of payment "would soon revolutionize the very concept of money itself," only to reverse itself several years later. Pilot projects in recent years with smart cards to convert consumers to the use of e-money have not been a success. Mondex, one of the widely touted, early stored-value cards that was launched in Great Britain in 1995, is only used on a few British university campuses. In Germany and Belgium, millions of people carry bank cards with computer chips embedded in them that enable them to make use of e-money, but very few use them. Why has the movement to a cashless society been so slow in coming?

Although e-money might be more convenient and may be more efficient than a payments system based on paper, several factors work against the disappearance of the paper system. First, it is very expensive to set up the computer, card reader, and telecommunications networks necessary to make electronic money the dominant form of payment. Second, electronic means of payment raise security and privacy concerns. We often hear media reports that an unauthorized hacker has been able to access a computer database and to alter information stored there. Because this is not an uncommon occurrence, unscrupulous persons might be able to access bank accounts in electronic payments systems and steal funds by moving them from someone else's accounts into their own. The prevention of this type of fraud is no easy task, and a whole new field of computer science has developed to cope with security issues. A further concern is that the use of electronic means of payment leaves an electronic trail that contains a large amount of personal data on buying habits. There are worries that government, employers, and marketers might be able to access these data, thereby encroaching on our privacy.

The conclusion from this discussion is that although the use of e-money will surely increase in the future, to paraphrase Mark Twain, "the reports of cash's death are greatly exaggerated."

MEASURING MONEY

The definition of money as anything that is generally accepted in payment for goods and services tells us that money is defined by people's behavior. People consider an asset as money if they believe it will be accepted by others when making payment. As we have seen, many different assets have performed this role over the centuries, ranging from gold to paper currency to checking accounts. For that reason, this behavioral definition does not tell us which assets in an economy should be considered as money. To measure money, we need a precise definition that tells us exactly which assets should be included.

Definitions of Monetary Aggregates

The method by which central banks define money differs from one economy to another. Variations among definitions of money supply, also referred to as **monetary aggregates** arise from differences in the norms of money holders, the innovation of financial instruments and the variety of issuers of money. Let us see how each of these factors affects the definition of monetary aggregates.

First, the dissimilarity in definitions of money partly stems from the differences in what members of each society accept as a means of exchange. For example, the Bank of Mexico includes all deposits in both pesos and U.S. dollars in its monetary aggregates. This is because Mexicans are known for holding substantial amounts of their savings in U.S. dollars. Conversely, the People's Bank of China does not include foreign currency deposits in its monetary aggregates, since the Chinese keep most savings in their domestic currency.

Moreover, in view of the immense financial innovations mentioned earlier, some assets are accepted as money in some societies but not others. In those countries where banks and depository institutions are not widespread to attract household savings, most of the money supply would be in the form of cash. Besides, as people's norms change, the definition of monetary aggregates also changes. Hence, every few years, central banks tend to change their definition of money supply whenever they sense a change in the behavioral patterns and conceptions of members of the society.

One last factor that affects the money in the economy is the institutions responsible for issuing monetary aggregates, normally the central bank and depository institutions. Let us compare the United States, the European Union and China to show how money issuers differ immensely in these three nations. In the U.S., issuers of money are: the Federal Reserve Banks, which issue currency; the U.S. Treasury, which mints coins; and depository institutions, which hold all other components of monetary aggregates. In the Euro area, monetary financial institutions (**MFIs**) are responsible for issuing money. MFIs include: the European Central Bank (**ECB**); the National Central Banks (**NCBs**) of the Euro area countries that have adopted the euro; credit institutions and money market funds located in the Euro area (refer to chapter 13 for a detailed explanation of how the NCBs work under the umbrella of the ECB). Finally, money issuers in China are: the People's Bank of China (PCB or the central bank of China) for currency and coins; and banks and Postal Savings Bureau for other money components.

For this reason, you would never find a central bank copying the definition of money adopted by another central bank, but generally most central banks range monetary aggregates from narrow to broad. Table 1 compares how the Federal Reserve System (the Fed), the ECB and the PCB each defines its monetary aggregates. However, the eleven European Union member states that have not adopted the euro as their currency hold a different definition of monetary aggregates. The box "How the U.K. Monetary Aggregates Differ from those of the ECB" shows the disparities between the definitions of the ECB and the U.K., which is an EU member, albeit using the Sterling pound as its domestic currency.

TABLE 1

Comparison of Compositions of Monetary Aggregates in the U.S., the Euro Zone and China

	USA	Euro Zone	China
M1	Currency + Traveler's checks + Demand deposits + Other checkable deposits	Currency + Overnight and similar deposits	Money** Currency in circulation + Demand deposits
M2	M1 + Small Denomination Time Deposits + Savings deposits and MMDA + Retail MMMF shares	M1 + Deposits (2 year maturity) + Deposits redeemable in 3 months	Quasi money*** Time deposits and CDs + Savings deposits + Other deposits
M3	N.A.*	M2 + Repurchase agreements + MMF shares/units + Debt securities up to 2 years	N.A.

*The Fed discontinued calculating M3 in mid-March 2006.

**China's narrowest monetary aggregate is known as "money" and not M1. Neither currency in depository institutions nor foreign currency is included in the cash in circulation.

***China's broad monetary aggregate is known as "quasi-money" and not M2. It does not include values of the narrow definition "money" but only the sum of time, savings and other deposits. Bank of China also calculates a variable "Money and Quasi Money" which is a mere addition of both monetary aggregates.

Following the Financial News

How the U.K. Monetary Aggregates Differ from Those of the ECB

The U.K. has a special situation since it is an EU state yet it has chosen to maintain the Sterling pound as its domestic currency. Hence, it defines its monetary aggregates in two different ways. First, it adopts the ECB's definition for M1, M2, and M3. It simultaneously publishes its own definitions of the broadest and narrowest values of money supply. Currently, the Bank of England publishes the narrow definition as "Notes and Coin in Circulation", which was previously known as M0 prior to its Money Market Reform in May 2006. The broadest money supply is known as M4 and comprises:

- Sterling pound notes and coin
- Sterling deposits, including certificates of deposit
- Commercial paper, bonds, FRNs* and other instruments of up to and including five years' original maturity issued by UK monetary financial institutions (MFIs)
- Claims on U.K. MFIs arising from repos
- Estimated holdings of Sterling bank bills.

*FRNs or Floating Rate Notes are bonds that have a variable coupon

Source: Explanatory Notes—M4. *Bank of England* http://www.bankofengland.co.uk/mfsd/iadb/notesiadb/m4.htm

The narrowest measure of money that central banks report is **M1** and it is more or less the same for most countries. M1 consists of currency in circulation as well as demand deposits and other checkable deposits held in depository institutions. Canada is a noteworthy exception, since it adds checkable deposits at credit unions and other non-bank depository institutions in M1. Currency in the vaults of banks and ATMs are not included in M1. Surprisingly, there is more than $2000 cash in circulation for each person in the United States and €2200 for each citizen of the Euro area (see the FYI box). Demand deposits include all deposits in depository institutions that can be withdrawn without prior notice; most of these are non-interest bearing. Checkable deposits may be either interest-bearing, or non-interest bearing.

On the other hand, monetary aggregates broader than M1 considerably differ from one country to another. Even so, we generally find that savings deposits and most time deposits are usually included in M2. Savings deposits are interest-bearing non-transaction accounts that can be drawn upon demand at no costs. Time deposits are also interest-bearing deposits or certificates of deposits (CDs) held for a given period of time and can be withdrawn with prior written notice, usually at very low costs. Small-denomination time deposits have a value of less than $100,000. Only the US includes *money market mutual fund shares* (MMMF) in M2. MMMF shares are retail accounts issued by banks, on which households can issue checks.

M3 is the broadest definition of money and is calculated by many central banks such as the ECB. Table 2 shows how the ECB measures its monetary aggregates. Some other countries that calculate M3 are Japan, Canada, Switzerland, Australia, New Zealand, Iceland, Thailand, the Philippines, Mexico, and Turkey. The definitions of M3

TABLE 2

Components of Monetary Aggregates in the Euro Area

	Value as of February 2009 (EUR billions)
M1 = Currency	721.0
+ Overnight and similar deposits	3,417.0
Total M1	4,138.0
M2 = M1	
+ Deposits with agreed maturity within 2 years	2,331.3
+ Deposits redeemable in 3 months	1,621.2
Total M2	8,090.5
M3 = M2	
+ Repurchase agreements	330.9
+ MMF shares/units	782.2
+ Debt securities up to 2 years	223.5
Total M3	9,427.1

Source: Based on European Central Bank. "Money, Banking and Investment Funds," *Monetary Statistics.* March 2009, p. S13 https://stats.ecb.europa.eu/stats/download/bsi_easch02_update/bsi_easch02_update/easch02_update.pdf.

FYI   **Where Are All the U.S. Dollars and the Euros?**

The fact that each person in the United States holds more than $2,000 in cash and each person in the Euro area holds more than €2200 in cash is surprising. These currencies are bulky, can be easily stolen, and pay no interest, so it doesn't make sense to keep a lot of it. Do you know anyone who carries these sums in his or her pockets? We have a puzzle: Where are all these dollars and euros and who is holding them and why?

Criminals are one group who hold a lot of cash. If you were engaged in illegal activity, you would not conduct your transactions with checks because they are traceable and, therefore, a potentially powerful piece of evidence against you. That explains why Tony Soprano has so much cash in his backyard. Some businesses also like to retain a lot of cash because if they operate as a cash business that makes their transactions less traceable; thus, they can avoid declaring income on which they would have to pay taxes

People outside the United States also routinely hold U.S. dollars and euros. In many countries, people do not trust their own currency because they often experience high inflation, which erodes the value of that cur-rency. The currencies of the two largest economic entities in the globe, the European Union and the United States, have become the two major and widely sought after currencies. Foreigners hold U.S. dollars and euros as a hedge against this inflation risk. Lack of trust in the ruble, for example, has led Russians to hoard enormous amounts of U.S. dollars. More than half the quantity of U.S. dollars is held abroad.

vastly differ from one country to another. A number of central banks no longer calculate M3; for example, the Fed discontinued measuring M3 in March 2006.

WHICH IS THE MOST ACCURATE MONETARY AGGREGATE?

By influencing money supply, the central bank can control inflation. If there is too much money in the economy, the result will be more money chasing fewer products, hence leading to inflation. Central banks resort to an expansion of money supply in order to boost GDP growth, albeit with the understanding that this is apt to result in inflation.

But the question that we should ask ourselves is which measurement should central banks consider when they try to affect variables in the economy, such as GDP growth and inflation? Because we cannot be sure which of the monetary aggregates is the true measure of money, it is logical to question if their movements closely parallel one another. If they do, then using one monetary aggregate to predict future economic performance and to conduct policy will produce the same results as using another, and it does not matter much that we are not sure of the appropriate definition of money for a given policy decision. However, if the monetary aggregates do not move together, then what one monetary aggregate tells us is happening to the money supply might be quite different from what another monetary aggregate would tell us.

Figure 1 plots the growth rates of M1 and M3 in the Euro area from 1999 to 2008. These two measures have more-or-less moved together till 2006, after which they appear to have taken opposite directions. This is especially apparent during the global financial crisis. Since the second half of 2008, when the crisis hit the financial sector hard, the ECB has consistently expanded the currency in circulation at an approximate rate of 13% per month, in order to try to make up for the decrease in customer deposits.

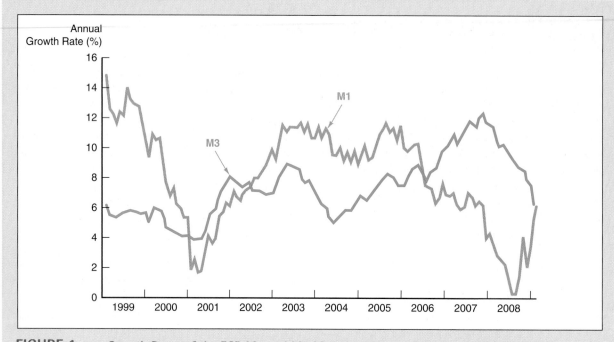

FIGURE 1   **Growth Rates of the ECB M1 and M3 Monetary Aggregates 1999–2008**

Sources: ECB. "Money, Banking and Investment Funds," *Monetary Statistics.* March 2009, p. S12. Copyright © European Central Bank, Frankfurt am Main, Germany. Figures are available free of charge via the ECB website.

The volume of deposits maturing within two years have declined substantially where the lowest level of decrease was in January 2009, amounting to 24%. To compensate for this drop in money supply, the ECB decided to increase currency notes and accordingly M1. This led to inflation levels reaching 4% during this period, a major deviation from the primary goal of the ECB, which is to maintain inflation below 2%. Yet, this was a temporary and necessary policy needed to solve the more serious problem of a deep recession.

Hence, from all the above you can see that obtaining a single precise, correct measure of money does seem to matter and that it does make a difference which monetary aggregate policymakers and economists choose as the true measure of money. However, many central banks prefer to keep a close watch on various monetary aggregates, to intervene and make up for any change in any of the components of money supply.

SUMMARY

1. To economists, the word *money* has a different meaning from *income* or *wealth*. Money is anything that is generally accepted as payment for goods or services or in the repayment of debts.

2. Money serves three primary functions: as a medium of exchange, as a unit of account, and as a store of value. Money as a medium of exchange avoids the problem of double coincidence of wants that arises in a barter

economy, and thus lowers transaction costs and encourages specialization and the division of labor. Money as a unit of account reduces the number of prices needed in the economy, which also reduces transaction costs. Money also functions as a store of value, but performs this role poorly if it is rapidly losing value due to inflation.

3. The payments system has evolved over time. Until several hundred years ago, the payments system in all but the most primitive societies was based primarily on precious metals. The introduction of paper currency lowered the cost of transporting money. The next major advance was the introduction of checks, which lowered transaction costs still further. We are currently moving toward an electronic payments system in which paper is eliminated and all transactions are handled by computers. Despite the potential efficiency of such a system, obstacles are slowing the movement to the checkless society and the development of new forms of electronic money.

4. There is no uniform definition of monetary aggregates, but in general monetary aggregates range from narrow to broad definitions. Since monetary aggregates do not usually move together, they cannot be used interchangeably by policy makers. It is imperative to measure different monetary aggregates so that the central bank can intervene if any of the components change.

5. Another problem in the measurement of money is that the data are not always as accurate as we would like. Substantial revisions in the data do occur; they indicate that initially released money data are not a reliable guide to short-run (say, month-to-month) movements in the money supply, although they are more reliable over longer periods of time, such as a year.

KEY TERMS

commodity money, p. 57

currency, p. 53

e-cash, p. 59

electronic money (e-money), p. 58

fiat money, p. 57

hyperinflation, p. 56

income, p. 54

liquidity, p. 56

M1, p. 62

M2, p. 62

medium of exchange, p. 54

monetary aggregates, p. 60

payments system, p. 57

smart card, p. 59

store of value, p. 56

unit of account, p. 55

wealth, p. 54

QUESTIONS AND PROBLEMS

All questions and problems are available in myeconlab *at* www.myeconlab.com/mishkin.

1. Which of the following three expressions uses the economists' definition of money?
   a. "How much money did you earn last week?"
   b. "When I go to the store, I always make sure that I have enough money."
   c. "The love of money is the root of all evil."

2. There are three goods produced in an economy by three individuals:

Good	Producer
Apples	Orchard owner
Bananas	Banana grower
Chocolate	Chocolatier

   If the orchard owner likes only bananas, the banana grower likes only chocolate, and the chocolatier likes only apples, will any trade between these three persons take place in a barter economy? How will introducing money into the economy benefit these three producers?

3. Why did cavemen not need money?

4. Why were people in the United States in the nineteenth century sometimes willing to be paid by check rather than with gold, even though they knew that there was a possibility that the check might bounce?

5. In ancient Greece, why was gold a more likely candidate for use as money than wine was?

6. Was money a better store of value in the United States in the 1950s than it was in the 1970s? Why or why

not? In which period would you have been more willing to hold money?

7. Would you be willing to give up your checkbook and instead use an electronic means of payment if it were made available? Why or why not?

8. Rank the following assets from most liquid to least liquid:
   a. Checking account deposits
   b. Houses
   c. Currency
   d. Washing machines
   e. Savings deposits
   f. Common stock

9. Why have some economists described money during a hyperinflation as a "hot potato" that is quickly passed from one person to another?

10. In Brazil, a country that underwent a rapid inflation before 1994, many transactions were conducted in dollars rather than in reals, the domestic currency. Why?

11. Suppose that a researcher discovers that a measure of the total amount of debt in the U.S. economy over the past twenty years was a better predictor of inflation and the business cycle than M1 or M2. Does this discovery

mean that we should define money as equal to the total amount of debt in the economy?

12. Look up the numbers of the M1, M2 and M3 monetary aggregates in the European Central Bank *Euro Area Statistics* for the most recent last-year period since the outburst of the global financial crisis. Have their growth rates been similar? What implications does this have for the conduct of monetary policy?

13. Which of the Federal Reserve's measures of the monetary aggregates—M1 or M2—is composed of the most liquid assets? Which is the largest measure?

14. For each of the following assets, indicate which of the monetary aggregates (M1 and M2) includes them:
   a. Currency
   b. Money market mutual funds
   c. Small-denomination time deposits
   d. Checkable deposits

15. Why are revisions of monetary aggregates less of a problem for measuring long-run movements of the money supply than they are for measuring short-run movements?

WEB EXERCISES

1. Go to www.federalreserve.gov/releases/h6/Current/.
   a. What has been the growth rate in M1 and M2 over the last twelve months?
   b. From what you know about the state of the economy, does this seem expansionary or restrictive?

2. Go to www.federalreserve.gov/paymentsys.htm and select one topic on which the Federal Reserve has a written policy. Write a one-paragraph summary of this policy.

WEB REFERENCES

www.federalreserve.gov/paymentsystems/default.htm

This site reports on the Federal Reserve's policies regarding payments systems.

www.federalreserve.gov/releases/h6/Current/

The Federal Reserve reports the current levels of M1 and M2 on its website.

https://stats.ecb.europa.eu/stats/ download/ bsi_easch02_update/bsi_easch02_update/easch02_update.pdf

The European Central Bank reports the details of its monetary aggregates on its website.

 MyEconLab CAN HELP YOU GET A BETTER GRADE

If your exam were tomorrow, would you be ready? For each chapter, MyEconLab Practice Tests and Study Plans pinpoint which sections you have mastered and which ones you need to study. That way, you are more efficient with your study time, and you are better prepared for your exams.

To see how it works, turn to page 20 and then go to: www.myeconlab.com/mishkin

PART 2

Financial Markets

CHAPTER 4
Understanding Interest Rates

•

CHAPTER 5
The Behavior of Interest Rates

•

CHAPTER 6
The Risk and Term Structure of
Interest Rates

•

CHAPTER 7
The Stock Market, the Theory of
Rational Expectations, and the
Efficient Market Hypothesis

Crisis and Response: Credit Market Turmoil and the Stock Market Crash in October 2008

The subprime financial crisis began snowballing as the value of mortgage-backed securities on financial institutions' balance sheets plummeted. When the House of Representatives, fearing the wrath of constituents who were angry about bailing out Wall Street, voted down a $700 billion dollar bailout package proposed by the Bush administration on Monday, September 29, 2008, the subprime financial crisis took an even more virulent turn, despite the bailout package that was passed four days later.

A "flight to quality" drove three-month Treasury bill rates down to almost zero, which had last happened during the Great Depression of the 1930s. Credit spreads—an indicator of risk—shot through the roof, with the Treasury bill to Eurodollar rate (TED) spread going from around 40 basis points (0.40 percentage points) before the subprime crisis started to over 450 basis points in mid-October, the highest value in its history. After earlier sharp declines, the stock market crashed further, with the week beginning on October 6, 2008, showing the worst weekly decline in U.S. history.

The subprime crisis illustrates how volatile financial markets can be. This volatility hit financial consumers directly with difficulty getting loans, falling home values, declining retirement account values, and jobs in jeopardy. How can policy respond to disruptions in financial markets? We begin addressing this question by examining the inner workings of financial markets, particularly interest rate dynamics. Chapter 4 explains what an interest rate is, and the relationship between interest rates, bond prices, and returns. Chapter 5 examines how the overall level of interest rates is determined. In Chapter 6, we extend the analysis of the bond market to explain changes in credit spreads and the relationship of long-term to short-term interest rates. Chapter 7 looks at the role of expectations in the stock market and what drives stock prices.

4

Understanding Interest Rates

Preview

Interest rates are among the most closely watched variables in the economy. Their movements are reported almost daily by the news media, because they directly affect our everyday lives and have important consequences for the health of the economy. They affect personal decisions such as whether to consume or save, whether to buy a house, and whether to purchase bonds or put funds into a savings account. Interest rates also affect the economic decisions of businesses and households, such as whether to use their funds to invest in new equipment for factories or to save their money in a bank.

Before we can go on with the study of money, banking, and financial markets, we must understand exactly what the phrase *interest rates* means. In this chapter, we see that a concept known as the *yield to maturity* is the most accurate measure of interest rates; the yield to maturity is what economists mean when they use the term *interest rate*. We discuss how the yield to maturity is measured. We'll also see that a bond's interest rate does not necessarily indicate how good an investment the bond is because what it earns (its rate of return) does not necessarily equal its interest rate. Finally, we explore the distinction between real interest rates, which are adjusted for inflation, and nominal interest rates, which are not.

Although learning definitions is not always the most exciting of pursuits, it is important to read carefully and understand the concepts presented in this chapter. Not only are they continually used throughout the remainder of this text, but a firm grasp of these terms will give you a clearer understanding of the role that interest rates play in your life as well as in the general economy.

MEASURING INTEREST RATES

Different debt instruments have very different streams of cash payments to the holder (known as **cash flows**) with very different timing. Thus we first need to understand how we can compare the value of one kind of debt instrument with another before we see how interest rates are measured. To do this, we make use of the concept of *present value*.

Present Value

The concept of **present value** (or **present discounted value**) is based on the common-sense notion that a dollar paid to you one year from now is less valuable to you than a dollar paid to you today: This notion is true because you can deposit a dollar today in a savings account that earns interest and have more than a dollar in one year. Economists use a more formal definition, as explained in this section.

Let's look at the simplest kind of debt instrument, which we will call a **simple loan**. In this loan, the lender provides the borrower with an amount of funds (called the principal) that must be repaid to the lender at the *maturity date*, along with an additional payment for the interest. For example, if you made your friend, Jane, a simple loan of $100 for one year, you would require her to repay the principal of $100 in one year's time along with an additional payment for interest—say, $10. In the case of a simple loan like this one, the interest payment divided by the amount of the loan is a natural and sensible way to measure the interest rate. This measure of the so-called *simple interest rate*, i, is

$$i = \frac{\$10}{\$100} = 0.10 = 10\%$$

If you make this $100 loan, at the end of the year you would have $110, which can be rewritten as

$$\$100 \times (1 + 0.10) = \$110$$

If you then lent out the $110, at the end of the second year you would have

$$\$110 \times (1 + 0.10) = \$121$$

or, equivalently,

$$\$100 \times (1 + 0.10) \times (1 + 0.10) = \$100 \times (1 + 0.10)^2 = \$121$$

Continuing with the loan again, you would have at the end of the third year

$$\$121 \times (1 + 0.10) = \$100 \times (1 + 0.10)^3 = \$133$$

Generalizing, we can see that at the end of n years, your $100 would turn into

$$\$100 \times (1 + i)^n$$

The amounts you would have at the end of each year by making the $100 loan today can be seen in the following timeline:

This timeline immediately tells you that you are just as happy having $100 today as having $110 a year from now (of course, as long as you are sure that Jane will pay you back). You are also just as happy having $100 today as having $121 two years from now, or $133 three years from now or $100 \times (1 + 0.10)^n$ n years from now. The timeline tells us that we can also work backward from future amounts to the present. For example, $133 = \$100 \times (1 + 0.10)^3$ three years from now is worth $100 today, so that

$$\$100 = \frac{\$133}{(1 + 0.10)^3}$$

The process of calculating today's value of dollars received in the future, as we have done above, is called *discounting the future*. We can generalize this process by writing today's (present) value of $100 as PV, the future cash flow (payment) of $133 as CF, and replacing 0.10 (the 10% interest rate) by i. This leads to the following formula:

$$PV = \frac{CF}{(1 + i)^n} \tag{1}$$

Intuitively, Equation 1 tells us that if you are promised $1 of cash flow for certain ten years from now, this dollar would not be as valuable to you as $1 is today because if you had the $1 today, you could invest it and end up with more than $1 in ten years.

The concept of present value is extremely useful, because it allows us to figure out today's value (price) of a credit (debt) market instrument at a given simple interest rate i by just adding up the individual present values of all the future payments received. This information allows us to compare the values of two or more instruments with very different timing of their payments.

APPLICATION ✦ Simple Present Value

What is the present value of $250 to be paid in two years if the interest rate is 15%?

Solution

The present value would be $189.04. Using Equation 1

$$PV = \frac{CF}{(1 + i)^n}$$

where

$$CF = \text{cash flow in two years} = \$250$$
$$i = \text{annual interest rate} = 0.15$$
$$n = \text{number of years} = 2$$

Thus

$$PV = \frac{\$250}{(1 + 0.15)^2} = \frac{\$250}{1.3225} = \$189.04$$

Today 0	Year 1	Year 2

$250

$189.04

APPLICATION ✦ How Much Is That Jackpot Worth?

Assume that you just hit the $20 million jackpot in the New York State Lottery, which promises you a payment of $1 million for the next twenty years. You are clearly excited, but have you really won $20 million?

Solution

No, not in the present value sense. In today's dollars, that $20 million is worth a lot less. If we assume an interest rate of 10% as in the earlier examples, the first payment of $1 million is clearly worth $1 million today, but the next payment next year is only worth $1 million/(1 + 0.10) = $909,090, a lot less than $1 million. The following year the payment is worth $1 million/(1 + 0.10)^2 = $826,446 in today's dollars, and so on. When you add all these up, they come to $9.4 million. You are still pretty excited (who wouldn't be?), but because you understand the concept of present value, you recognize that you are the victim of false advertising. In present value terms, you didn't really win $20 million, but instead won less than half as much.

Four Types of Credit Market Instruments

In terms of the timing of their cash flow payments, there are four basic types of credit market instruments.

1. A simple loan, which we have already discussed, in which the lender provides the borrower with an amount of funds, which must be repaid to the lender at the maturity date along with an additional payment for the interest. Many money market instruments are of this type—for example, commercial loans to businesses.

2. A **fixed-payment loan** (which is also called a **fully amortized loan**) in which the lender provides the borrower with an amount of funds, which must be repaid by making the same payment every period (such as a month), consisting of part of the principal and interest for a set number of years. For example, if you borrowed $1,000, a fixed-payment loan might require you to pay $126 every year for 25 years. Installment loans (such as auto loans) and mortgages are frequently of the fixed-payment type.

3. A **coupon bond** pays the owner of the bond a fixed interest payment (coupon payment) every year until the maturity date, when a specified final amount (**face value** or **par value**) is repaid. (The coupon payment is so named because the bondholder used to obtain payment by clipping a coupon off the bond and sending it to the bond issuer, who then sent the payment to the holder. Nowadays, it is no longer necessary to send in coupons to receive these payments.) A coupon bond with $1,000 face value, for example, might pay you a coupon payment of $100 per year for ten years, and at the maturity date repay you the face value amount of $1,000. (The face value of a bond is usually in $1,000 increments.)

   A coupon bond is identified by three pieces of information. First is the corporation or government agency that issues the bond. Second is the maturity date of the bond. Third is the bond's **coupon rate**, the dollar amount of the yearly coupon payment expressed as a percentage of the face value of the bond. In our example, the coupon bond has a yearly coupon payment of $100 and a face value of $1,000. The coupon rate is then $100/$1,000 = 0.10, or 10%. Capital market instruments such as U.S. Treasury bonds and notes and corporate bonds are examples of coupon bonds.

4. A **discount bond** (also called a **zero-coupon bond**) is bought at a price below its face value (at a discount), and the face value is repaid at the maturity date. Unlike a coupon bond, a discount bond does not make any interest payments; it just pays off the face value. For example, a one-year discount bond with a face value of $1,000 might be bought for $900; in a year's time the owner would be repaid the face value of $1,000. U.S. Treasury bills, U.S. savings bonds, and long-term zero-coupon bonds are examples of discount bonds.

These four types of instruments require payments at different times: Simple loans and discount bonds make payment only at their maturity dates, whereas fixed-payment loans and coupon bonds have payments periodically until maturity. How would you decide which of these instruments provides you with more income? They all seem so different because they make payments at different times. To solve this problem, we use the concept of present value, explained earlier, to provide us with a procedure for measuring interest rates on these different types of instruments.

Yield to Maturity

Of the several common ways of calculating interest rates, the most important is the **yield to maturity**, the interest rate that equates the present value of cash flow payments received from a debt instrument with its value today.[1] Because the concept behind the calculation of the yield to maturity makes good economic sense, economists consider it the most accurate measure of interest rates.

To understand the yield to maturity better, we now look at how it is calculated for the four types of credit market instruments. In all these examples, the key to understanding the calculation of the yield to maturity is equating today's value of the debt instrument with the present value of all of its future cash flow payments.

Simple Loan   Using the concept of present value, the yield to maturity on a simple loan is easy to calculate. For the one-year loan we discussed, today's value is $100, and the payments in one year's time would be $110 (the repayment of $100 plus the interest payment of $10). We can use this information to solve for the yield to maturity i by recognizing that the present value of the future payments must equal today's value of a loan.

APPLICATION ✦ Yield to Maturity on a Simple Loan

If Pete borrows $100 from his sister and next year she wants $110 back from him, what is the yield to maturity on this loan?

Solution

The yield to maturity on the loan is 10%.

$$PV = \frac{CF}{(1 + i)^n}$$

where

PV = amount borrowed   = $100
CF = cash flow in one year   = $110
n = number of years   = 1

Thus

$$\$100 = \frac{\$110}{(1 + i)}$$

$$(1 + i)\$100 = \$110$$

$$(1 + i) = \frac{\$110}{\$100}$$

$$i = 1.10 - 1 = 0.10 = 10\%$$

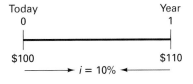

---

[1]In other contexts, it is also called the *internal rate of return*.

This calculation of the yield to maturity should look familiar, because it equals the interest payment of $10 divided by the loan amount of $100; that is, it equals the simple interest rate on the loan. An important point to recognize is that *for simple loans, the simple interest rate equals the yield to maturity*. Hence the same term i is used to denote both the yield to maturity and the simple interest rate.

Fixed-Payment Loan   Recall that this type of loan has the same cash flow payment every period throughout the life of the loan. On a fixed-rate mortgage, for example, the borrower makes the same payment to the bank every month until the maturity date, when the loan will be completely paid off. To calculate the yield to maturity for a fixed-payment loan, we follow the same strategy we used for the simple loan—we equate today's value of the loan with its present value. Because the fixed-payment loan involves more than one cash flow payment, the present value of the fixed-payment loan is calculated as the sum of the present values of all cash flow payments (using Equation 1).

In the case of our earlier example, the loan is $1,000 and the yearly payment is $126 for the next 25 years. The present value is calculated as follows: At the end of one year, there is a $126 payment with a PV of $126/(1 + i)$; at the end of two years, there is another $126 payment with a PV of $126/(1 + i)^2$; and so on until at the end of the twenty-fifth year, the last payment of $126 with a PV of $126/(1 + i)^{25}$; is made. Making today's value of the loan ($1,000) equal to the sum of the present values of all the yearly payments gives us

$$\$1,000 = \frac{\$126}{1 + i} + \frac{\$126}{(1 + i)^2} + \frac{\$126}{(1 + i)^3} + \cdots + \frac{\$126}{(1 + i)^{25}}$$

More generally, for any fixed-payment loan,

$$LV = \frac{FP}{1 + i} + \frac{FP}{(1 + i)^2} + \frac{FP}{(1 + i)^3} + \cdots + \frac{FP}{(1 + i)^n} \tag{2}$$

where

LV = loan value
FP = fixed yearly payment
n = number of years until maturity

For a fixed-payment loan amount, the fixed yearly payment and the number of years until maturity are known quantities, and only the yield to maturity is not. So we can solve this equation for the yield to maturity i. Because this calculation is not easy, many pocket calculators have programs that allow you to find i given the loan's numbers for LV, FP, and n. For example, in the case of a 25-year loan with yearly payments of $85.81, the yield to maturity that solves Equation 2 is 7%. Real estate brokers always have a pocket calculator that can solve such equations so that they can immediately tell the prospective house buyer exactly what the yearly (or monthly) payments will be if the house purchase is financed by taking out a mortgage.

APPLICATION ✦ Yield to Maturity and the Yearly Payment on a Fixed–Payment Loan

You decide to purchase a new home and need a $100,000 mortgage. You take out a loan from the bank that has an interest rate of 7%. What is the yearly payment to the bank to pay off the loan in twenty years?

Solution

The yearly payment to the bank is $9,439.29.

$$LV = \frac{FP}{1 + i} + \frac{FP}{(1 + i)^2} + \frac{FP}{(1 + i)^3} + \cdots + \frac{FP}{(1 + i)^n}$$

where

LV = loan value amount = $100,000
i = annual interest rate = 0.07
n = number of years   = 20

Thus

$$\$100,000 = \frac{FP}{1 + 0.07} + \frac{FP}{(1 + 0.07)^2} + \frac{FP}{(1 + 0.07)^3} + \cdots + \frac{FP}{(1 + 0.07)^{20}}$$

To find the monthly payment for the loan using a financial calculator:

n = number of years   = 20
PV = amount of the loan (LV)   = −100,000
FV = amount of the loan after 20 years = 0
i = annual interest rate   = .07

Then push the PMT button = fixed yearly payment (FP) = $9,439.29.

Coupon Bond   To calculate the yield to maturity for a coupon bond, follow the same strategy used for the fixed-payment loan: Equate today's value of the bond with its present value. Because coupon bonds also have more than one cash flow payment, the present value of the bond is calculated as the sum of the present values of all the coupon payments plus the present value of the final payment of the face value of the bond.

The present value of a $1,000-face-value bond with ten years to maturity and yearly coupon payments of $100 (a 10% coupon rate) can be calculated as follows: At the end of one year, there is a $100 coupon payment with a PV of $100/(1 + i)$; at the end of the second year, there is another $100 coupon payment with a PV of $100/(1 + i)^2$; and so on until at maturity, there is a $100 coupon payment with a PV of $100/(1 + i)^{10}$ plus the repayment of the $1,000 face value with a PV of $1,000/(1 + i)^{10}$. Setting today's value of the bond (its current price, denoted by P) equal to the sum of the present values of all the cash flow payments for this bond gives

$$P = \frac{\$100}{1 + i} + \frac{\$100}{(1 + i)^2} + \frac{\$100}{(1 + i)^3} + \cdots + \frac{\$100}{(1 + i)^{10}} + \frac{\$1,000}{(1 + i)^{10}}$$

More generally, for any coupon bond,[2]

$$P = \frac{C}{1 + i} + \frac{C}{(1 + i)^2} + \frac{C}{(1 + i)^3} + \cdots + \frac{C}{(1 + i)^n} + \frac{F}{(1 + i)^n} \qquad (3)$$

---

[2]Most coupon bonds actually make coupon payments on a semiannual basis rather than once a year as assumed here. The effect on the calculations is only very slight and will be ignored here.

where P = price of coupon bond
        C = yearly coupon payment
        F = face value of the bond
        n = years to maturity date

In Equation 3, the coupon payment, the face value, the years to maturity, and the price of the bond are known quantities, and only the yield to maturity is not. Hence we can solve this equation for the yield to maturity i. Just as in the case of the fixed-payment loan, this calculation is not easy, so business-oriented software and pocket calculators have built-in programs that solve this equation for you.

APPLICATION ✦ Yield to Maturity and the Bond Price for a Coupon Bond

Find the price of a 10% coupon bond with a face value of $1000, a 12.25% yield to maturity, and eight years to maturity.

Solution

The price of the bond is $889.20. To solve using a financial calculator:

       n = years to maturity   = 8
    FV = face value of the bond (F) = 1,000
       i = annual interest rate   = 12.25%
  PMT = yearly coupon payments (C) = 100

Then push the PV button = price of the bond = $889.20.

Alternatively, you could solve for the yield to maturity given the bond price by putting in $889.20 for PV and pushing the i button to get a yield to maturity of 12.25%.

Table 1 shows the yields to maturity calculated for several bond prices. Three interesting facts emerge:

1. When the coupon bond is priced at its face value, the yield to maturity equals the coupon rate.
2. The price of a coupon bond and the yield to maturity are negatively related; that is, as the yield to maturity rises, the price of the bond falls. As the yield to maturity falls, the price of the bond rises.
3. The yield to maturity is greater than the coupon rate when the bond price is below its face value.

TABLE 1	
Yields to Maturity on a 10%-Coupon-Rate Bond Maturing in Ten Years (Face Value = $1,000)	
Price of Bond ($)	**Yield to Maturity (%)**
1,200	7.13
1,100	8.48
1,000	10.00
900	11.75
800	13.81

These three facts are true for any coupon bond and are really not surprising if you think about the reasoning behind the calculation of the yield to maturity. When you put $1,000 in a bank account with an interest rate of 10%, you can take out $100 every year and you will be left with the $1,000 at the end of ten years. This is similar to buying the $1,000 bond with a 10% coupon rate analyzed in Table 1, which pays a $100 coupon payment every year and then repays $1,000 at the end of ten years. If the bond is purchased at the par value of $1,000, its yield to maturity must equal 10%, which is also equal to the coupon rate of 10%. The same reasoning applied to any coupon bond demonstrates that if the coupon bond is purchased at its par value, the yield to maturity and the coupon rate must be equal.

It is straightforward to show that the bond price and the yield to maturity are negatively related. As i, the yield to maturity, increases, all denominators in the bond price formula (Equation 3) must necessarily increase. Hence a rise in the interest rate as measured by the yield to maturity means that the price of the bond must fall. Another way to explain why the bond price falls when the interest rate rises is that a higher interest rate implies that the future coupon payments and final payment are worth less when discounted back to the present; hence the price of the bond must be lower.

The third fact, that the yield to maturity is greater than the coupon rate when the bond price is below its par value, follows directly from facts 1 and 2. When the yield to maturity equals the coupon rate, then the bond price is at the face value; when the yield to maturity rises above the coupon rate, the bond price necessarily falls and so must be below the face value of the bond.

There is one special case of a coupon bond that is worth discussing because its yield to maturity is particularly easy to calculate. This bond is called a **consol** or a **perpetuity**; it is a perpetual bond with no maturity date and no repayment of principal that makes fixed coupon payments of C forever. Consols were first sold by the British Treasury during the Napoleonic Wars and are still traded today; they are quite rare, however, in American capital markets. The formula in Equation 3 for the price of the consol P_c simplifies to the following:[3]

$$P_c = \frac{C}{i_c} \qquad\qquad (4)$$

---

[3]The bond price formula for a consol is

$$P = \frac{C}{1+i} + \frac{C}{(1+i)^2} + \frac{C}{(1+i)^3} + \cdots$$

which can be written as

$$P = C(x + x^2 + x^3 + \cdots)$$

in which $x = 1/(1+i)$. The formula for an infinite sum is

$$1 + x + x^2 + x^3 + \cdots = \frac{1}{1-x} \quad \text{for } x < 1$$

and so

$$P = C\left(\frac{1}{1-x} - 1\right) = C\left[\frac{1}{1 - 1/(1+i)} - 1\right]$$

which by suitable algebraic manipulation becomes

$$P = C\left(\frac{1+i}{i} - \frac{i}{i}\right) = \frac{C}{i}$$

where
$$P_c = \text{price of the perpetuity (consol)}$$
$$C = \text{yearly payment}$$
$$i_c = \text{yield to maturity of the perpetuity (consol)}$$

One nice feature of perpetuities is that you can immediately see that as i_c increases, the price of the bond falls. For example, if a perpetuity pays $100 per year forever and the interest rate is 10%, its price will be $1,000 = $100/0.10. If the interest rate rises to 20%, its price will fall to $500 = $100/0.20. We can also rewrite this formula as

$$i_c = \frac{C}{P_c} \qquad (5)$$

APPLICATION ✦ Perpetuity

What is the yield to maturity on a bond that has a price of $2,000 and pays $100 of interest annually forever?

Solution

The yield to maturity would be 5%.

$$i_c = \frac{C}{P_c}$$

where
$$C = \text{yearly payment} \qquad\quad = \$100$$
$$P_c = \text{price of perpetuity (consol)} = \$2,000$$

Thus

$$i_c = \frac{\$100}{\$2,000}$$

$$i_c = 0.05 = 5\%$$

The formula in Equation 5, which describes the calculation of the yield to maturity for a perpetuity, also provides a useful approximation for the yield to maturity on coupon bonds. When a coupon bond has a long term to maturity (say, twenty years or more), it is very much like a perpetuity, which pays coupon payments forever. This is because the cash flows more than twenty years in the future have such small present discounted values that the value of a long-term coupon bond is very close to the value of a perpetuity with the same coupon rate. Thus i_c in Equation 5 will be very close to the yield to maturity for any long-term bond. For this reason, i_c, the yearly coupon payment divided by the price of the security, has been given the name **current yield** and is frequently used as an approximation to describe interest rates on long-term bonds.

Discount Bond   The yield-to-maturity calculation for a discount bond is similar to that for the simple loan. Let us consider a discount bond such as a one-year U.S. Treasury bill, which pays a face value of $1,000 in one year's time. If the current purchase price of this bill is $900, then equating this price to the present value of the $1,000 received in one year, using Equation 1, gives

$$\$900 = \frac{\$1,000}{1 + i}$$

Solving for i,

$$(1 + i) \times \$900 = \$1,000$$

$$\$900 + \$900i = \$1,000$$

$$\$900i = \$1,000 - \$900$$

$$i = \frac{\$1,000 - \$900}{\$900} = 0.111 = 11.1\%$$

More generally, for any one-year discount bond, the yield to maturity can be written as

$$i = \frac{F - P}{P} \tag{6}$$

where $\qquad\qquad F$ = face value of the discount bond
$\qquad\qquad\qquad\quad P$ = current price of the discount bond

In other words, the yield to maturity equals the increase in price over the year $(F - P)$ divided by the initial price (P). In normal circumstances, investors earn positive returns from holding these securities and so they sell at a discount, meaning that the current price of the bond is below the face value. Therefore, $F - P$ should be positive, and the yield to maturity should be positive as well. However, this is not always the case, as recent extraordinary events in Japan indicate (see the Global box).

An important feature of this equation is that it indicates that for a discount bond, the yield to maturity is negatively related to the current bond price. This is the same conclusion that we reached for a coupon bond. For example, Equation 6 shows that a rise in the bond price, say from $900 to $950, means that the bond will have a smaller increase in its price at maturity, and the yield to maturity falls, from 11.1% to 5.3%. Similarly, a fall in the yield to maturity means that the price of the discount bond has risen.

Global   Negative T-Bill Rates? It Can Happen

We normally assume that interest rates must always be positive. Negative interest rates would imply that you are willing to pay more for a bond today than you will receive for it in the future (as our formula for yield to maturity on a discount bond demonstrates). Negative interest rates therefore seem like an impossibility because you would do better by holding cash that has the same value in the future as it does today.

Events in Japan in the late 1990s and in the United States during the subprime financial crisis of 2008 have demonstrated that this reasoning is not quite correct. In November 1998, interest rates on Japanese six-month Treasury bills became negative, yielding an interest rate of −0.004%. In September 2008, interest rates on three-month T-bills fell very slightly below zero for a very brief period. Negative interest rates are an extremely unusual event. How could this happen?

As we will see in Chapter 5, the weakness of the economy and a flight to quality during a financial crisis can drive interest rates to low levels, but these two factors can't explain the negative rates. The answer is that large investors found it more convenient to hold these Treasury bills as a store of value rather than holding cash because the bills are denominated in larger amounts and can be stored electronically. For that reason, some investors were willing to hold them, despite their negative rates, even though in monetary terms the investors would be better off holding cash. Clearly, the convenience of T-bills goes only so far, and thus their interest rates can go only a little bit below zero.

Summary   The concept of present value tells you that a dollar in the future is not as valuable to you as a dollar today because you can earn interest on this dollar. Specifically, a dollar received n years from now is worth only $\$1/(1 + i)^n$ today. The present value of a set of future cash flow payments on a debt instrument equals the sum of the present values of each of the future payments. The yield to maturity for an instrument is the interest rate that equates the present value of the future payments on that instrument to its value today. Because the procedure for calculating the yield to maturity is based on sound economic principles, this is the measure that economists think most accurately describes the interest rate.

Our calculations of the yield to maturity for a variety of bonds reveal the important fact that *current bond prices and interest rates are negatively related: When the interest rate rises, the price of the bond falls, and vice versa.*

THE DISTINCTION BETWEEN INTEREST RATES AND RETURNS

Many people think that the interest rate on a bond tells them all they need to know about how well off they are as a result of owning it. If Irving the Investor thinks he is better off when he owns a long-term bond yielding a 10% interest rate and the interest rate rises to 20%, he will have a rude awakening: As we will shortly see, if he has to sell the bond, Irving has lost his shirt! How well a person does by holding a bond or any other security over a particular time period is accurately measured by the **return**, or, in more precise terminology, the **rate of return**. We will use the concept of *return* continually throughout this book: Understanding it will make the material presented later in the book easier to follow.

For any security, the rate of return is defined as the payments to the owner plus the change in its value, expressed as a fraction of its purchase price. To make this definition clearer, let us see what the return would look like for a $1,000-face-value coupon bond with a coupon rate of 10% that is bought for $1,000, held for one year, and then sold for $1,200. The payments to the owner are the yearly coupon payments of $100, and the change in its value is $1,200 - $1,000 = $200. Adding these together and expressing them as a fraction of the purchase price of $1,000 gives us the one-year holding-period return for this bond:

$$\frac{\$100 + \$200}{\$1,000} = \frac{\$300}{\$1,000} = 0.30 = 30\%$$

You may have noticed something quite surprising about the return that we have just calculated: It equals 30%, yet as Table 1 indicates, initially the yield to maturity was only 10%. This demonstrates that **the return on a bond will not necessarily equal the yield to maturity on that bond**. We now see that the distinction between interest rate and return can be important, although for many securities the two may be closely related.

More generally, the return on a bond held from time t to time $t + 1$ can be written as

$$R = \frac{C + P_{t+1} - P_t}{P_t} \tag{7}$$

where

$R =$ return from holding the bond from time t to time $t + 1$
$P_t =$ price of the bond at time t
$P_{t+1} =$ price of the bond at time $t + 1$
$C =$ coupon payment

A convenient way to rewrite the return formula in Equation 7 is to recognize that it can be split into two separate terms:

$$R = \frac{C}{P_t} + \frac{P_{t+1} - P_t}{P_t}$$

The first term is the current yield i_c (the coupon payment over the purchase price):

$$\frac{C}{P_t} = i_c$$

The second term is the **rate of capital gain**, or the change in the bond's price relative to the initial purchase price:

$$\frac{P_{t+1} - P_t}{P_t} = g$$

where g is the rate of capital gain. Equation 7 can then be rewritten as

$$R = i_c + g \qquad (8)$$

which shows that the return on a bond is the current yield i_c plus the rate of capital gain g. This rewritten formula illustrates the point we just discovered: Even for a bond for which the current yield i_c is an accurate measure of the yield to maturity, the return can differ substantially from the interest rate. Returns will differ from the interest rate, especially if there are sizable fluctuations in the price of the bond that produce substantial capital gains or losses.

To explore this point even further, let's look at what happens to the returns on bonds of different maturities when interest rates rise. Table 2 calculates the one-year return using Equation 8 above on several 10%-coupon-rate bonds all purchased at par when interest rates on all these bonds rise from 10% to 20%. Several key findings in this table are generally true of all bonds:

- The only bond whose return equals the initial yield to maturity is one whose time to maturity is the same as the holding period (see the last bond in Table 2).

TABLE 2

One-Year Returns on Different-Maturity 10%–Coupon-Rate Bonds When Interest Rates Rise from 10% to 20%

(1) Years to Maturity When Bond Is Purchased	(2) Initial Current Yield (%)	(3) Initial Price ($)	(4) Price Next Year* ($)	(5) Rate of Capital Gain (%)	(6) Rate of Return (2 + 5) (%)
30	10	1,000	503	−49.7	−39.7
20	10	1,000	516	−48.4	−38.4
10	10	1,000	597	−40.3	−30.3
5	10	1,000	741	−25.9	−15.9
2	10	1,000	917	−8.3	+1.7
1	10	1,000	1,000	0.0	+10.0

*Calculated with a financial calculator using Equation 3.

- A rise in interest rates is associated with a fall in bond prices, resulting in capital losses on bonds whose terms to maturity are longer than the holding period.
- The more distant a bond's maturity, the greater the size of the percentage price change associated with an interest-rate change.
- The more distant a bond's maturity, the lower the rate of return that occurs as a result of the increase in the interest rate.
- Even though a bond has a substantial initial interest rate, its return can turn out to be negative if interest rates rise.

At first it frequently puzzles students (as it puzzles poor Irving the Investor) that a rise in interest rates can mean that a bond has been a poor investment. The trick to understanding this is to recognize that a rise in the interest rate means that the price of a bond has fallen. A rise in interest rates therefore means that a capital loss has occurred. If this loss is large enough, the bond can be a poor investment indeed. For example, we see in Table 2 that the bond that has 30 years to maturity when purchased has a capital loss of 49.7% when the interest rate rises from 10% to 20%. This loss is so large that it exceeds the current yield of 10%, resulting in a negative return (loss) of −39.7%. If Irving does not sell the bond, his capital loss is often referred to as a "paper loss." This is a loss nonetheless because if he had not bought this bond and had instead put his money in the bank, he would now be able to buy more bonds at their lower price than he presently owns.

Maturity and the Volatility of Bond Returns: Interest-Rate Risk

The finding that the prices of longer-maturity bonds respond more dramatically to changes in interest rates helps explain an important fact about the behavior of bond markets: *Prices and returns for long-term bonds are more volatile than those for shorter-term bonds.* Price changes of +20% and −20% within a year, with corresponding variations in returns, are common for bonds more than twenty years away from maturity.

We now see that changes in interest rates make investments in long-term bonds quite risky. Indeed, the riskiness of an asset's return that results from interest-rate changes is so important that it has been given a special name, **interest-rate risk**.[4] Dealing with interest-rate risk is a major concern of managers of financial institutions and investors, as we will see in later chapters (see also the FYI box).

Although long-term debt instruments have substantial interest-rate risk, short-term debt instruments do not. Indeed, bonds with a maturity that is as short as the holding period have no interest-rate risk.[5] We see this for the coupon bond at the

---

[4]Interest-rate risk can be quantitatively measured using the concept of *duration*. This concept and its calculation are discussed in an appendix to this chapter, which can be found on this book's web site at www.myeconlab.com/mishkin.

[5]The statement that there is no interest-rate risk for any bond whose time to maturity matches the holding period is literally true only for discount bonds and zero-coupon bonds that make no intermediate cash payments before the holding period is over. A coupon bond that makes an intermediate cash payment before the holding period is over requires that this payment be reinvested. Because the interest rate at which this payment can be reinvested is uncertain, there is some uncertainty about the return on this coupon bond even when the time to maturity equals the holding period. However, the riskiness of the return on a coupon bond from reinvesting the coupon payments is typically quite small, so the basic point that a coupon bond with a time to maturity equaling the holding period has very little risk still holds true.

FYI   **Helping Investors to Select Desired Interest–Rate Risk**

Because many investors want to know how much interest-rate risk they are exposed to, some mutual fund companies try to educate investors about the perils of interest-rate risk, as well as to offer investment alternatives that match their investors' preferences.

Vanguard Group, for example, offers eight separate high-grade bond mutual funds. In its prospectus, Vanguard separates the funds by the average maturity of the bonds they hold and demonstrates the effect of interest-rate changes by computing the percentage change in bond value resulting from a 1% increase and decrease in interest rates. Three of the bond funds

invest in bonds with average maturities of one to three years, which Vanguard rates as having the lowest interest-rate risk. Three other funds hold bonds with average maturities of five to ten years, which Vanguard rates as having medium interest-rate risk. Two funds hold long-term bonds with maturities of 15 to 30 years, which Vanguard rates as having high interest-rate risk.

By providing this information, Vanguard hopes to increase its market share in the sales of bond funds. Not surprisingly, Vanguard is one of the most successful mutual fund companies in the business.

bottom of Table 2, which has no uncertainty about the rate of return because it equals the yield to maturity, which is known at the time the bond is purchased. The key to understanding why there is no interest-rate risk for *any* bond whose time to maturity matches the holding period is to recognize that (in this case) the price at the end of the holding period is already fixed at the face value. The change in interest rates can then have no effect on the price at the end of the holding period for these bonds, and the return will therefore be equal to the yield to maturity known at the time the bond is purchased.[6]

---

[6]In the text, we are assuming that all holding periods are short and equal to the maturity on short-term bonds and are thus not subject to interest-rate risk. However, if an investor's holding period is longer than the term to maturity of the bond, the investor is exposed to a type of interest-rate risk called *reinvestment risk*. Reinvestment risk occurs because the proceeds from the short-term bond need to be reinvested at a future interest rate that is uncertain.

To understand reinvestment risk, suppose that Irving the Investor has a holding period of two years and decides to purchase a $1,000 one-year bond at face value and will then purchase another one at the end of the first year. If the initial interest rate is 10%, Irving will have $1,100 at the end of the year. If the interest rate rises to 20%, as in Table 2, Irving will find that buying $1,100 worth of another one-year bond will leave him at the end of the second year with $1,100 \times (1 + 0.20) = $1,320$. Thus Irving's two-year return will be ($1,320 − $1,000)/1,000 = 0.32 = 32\%$, which equals 14.9% at an annual rate. In this case, Irving has earned more by buying the one-year bonds than if he had initially purchased the two-year bond with an interest rate of 10%. Thus, when Irving has a holding period that is longer than the term to maturity of the bonds he purchases, he benefits from a rise in interest rates. Conversely, if interest rates fall to 5%, Irving will have only $1,155 at the end of two years: $1,100 \times (1 + 0.05)$. His two-year return will be ($1,155 − $1,000)/1,000 = 0.115 = 15.5\%$, which is 7.2% at an annual rate. With a holding period greater than the term to maturity of the bond, Irving now loses from a decline in interest rates.

We have thus seen that when the holding period is longer than the term to maturity of a bond, the return is uncertain because the future interest rate when reinvestment occurs is also uncertain—in short, there is reinvestment risk. We also see that if the holding period is longer than the term to maturity of the bond, the investor benefits from a rise in interest rates and is hurt by a fall in interest rates.

Summary

The return on a bond, which tells you how good an investment it has been over the holding period, is equal to the yield to maturity in only one special case: when the holding period and the maturity of the bond are identical. Bonds whose term to maturity is longer than the holding period are subject to interest-rate risk: Changes in interest rates lead to capital gains and losses that produce substantial differences between the return and the yield to maturity known at the time the bond is purchased. Interest-rate risk is especially important for long-term bonds, where the capital gains and losses can be substantial. This is why long-term bonds are not considered to be safe assets with a sure return over short holding periods.

THE DISTINCTION BETWEEN REAL AND NOMINAL INTEREST RATES

So far in our discussion of interest rates, we have ignored the effects of inflation on the cost of borrowing. What we have up to now been calling the interest rate makes no allowance for inflation, and it is more precisely referred to as the **nominal interest rate**. We distinguish it from the **real interest rate**, the interest rate that is adjusted by subtracting expected changes in the price level (inflation) so that it more accurately reflects the true cost of borrowing. This interest rate is more precisely referred to as the *ex ante real interest rate* because it is adjusted for *expected* changes in the price level. The ex ante real interest rate that is most important to economic decisions, and typically it is what economists mean when they make reference to the "real" interest rate. The interest rate that is adjusted for *actual* changes in the price level is called the *ex post real interest rate*. It describes how well a lender has done in real terms *after the fact*.

The real interest rate is more accurately defined from the *Fisher equation*, named for Irving Fisher, one of the great monetary economists of the twentieth century. The Fisher equation states that the nominal interest rate i equals the real interest rate i_r plus the expected rate of inflation π^e:[7]

$$i = i_r + \pi^e \tag{9}$$

Rearranging terms, we find that the real interest rate equals the nominal interest rate minus the expected inflation rate:

$$i_r = i - \pi^e \tag{10}$$

To see why this definition makes sense, let us first consider a situation in which you have made a one-year simple loan with a 5% interest rate ($i = 5\%$) and you expect the

---

[7]A more precise formulation of the Fisher equation is

$$i = i_r + \pi^e + (i_r \times \pi^e)$$

because

$$1 + i = (1 + i_r)(1 + \pi^e) = 1 + i_r + \pi^e + (i_r \times \pi^e)$$

and subtracting 1 from both sides gives us the first equation. For small values of i_r and π^e, the term $i_r \times \pi^e$ is so small that we ignore it, as in the text.

price level to rise by 3% over the course of the year ($\pi^e = 3\%$). As a result of making the loan, at the end of the year you expect to have 2% more in **real terms**—that is, in terms of real goods and services you can buy. In this case, the interest rate you expect to earn in terms of real goods and services is 2%:

$$i_r = 5\% - 3\% = 2\%$$

as indicated by the definition in Equation 10.

APPLICATION ✦ Calculating Real Interest Rates

What is the real interest rate if the nominal interest rate is 8% and the expected inflation rate is 10% over the course of a year?

Solution

The real interest rate is −2%. Although you will be receiving 8% more dollars at the end of the year, you will be paying 10% more for goods. The result is that you will be able to buy 2% fewer goods at the end of the year, and you will be 2% worse off in real terms.

$$i_r = i - \pi^e$$

where
$$i = \text{nominal interest rate} = 0.08$$
$$\pi^e = \text{expected inflation rate} = 0.10$$

Thus

$$i_r = 0.08 - 0.10 = -0.02 = -2\%$$

As a lender, you are clearly less eager to make a loan in this case, because in terms of real goods and services you have actually earned a negative interest rate of 2%. By contrast, as the borrower, you fare quite well because at the end of the year, the amounts you will have to pay back will be worth 2% less in terms of goods and services—you as the borrower will be ahead by 2% in real terms. *When the real interest rate is low, there are greater incentives to borrow and fewer incentives to lend.*

A similar distinction can be made between nominal returns and real returns. Nominal returns, which do not allow for inflation, are what we have been referring to as simply "returns." When inflation is subtracted from a nominal return, we have the real return, which indicates the amount of extra goods and services that we can purchase as a result of holding the security.

The distinction between real and nominal interest rates is important because the real interest rate, which reflects the real cost of borrowing, is likely to be a better indicator of the incentives to borrow and lend. It appears to be a better guide to how people will be affected by what is happening in credit markets. Figure 1, which presents estimates from 1953 to 2008 of the real and nominal interest rates on three-month U.S. Treasury bills, shows us that nominal and real rates often do not move together. (This is also true for nominal and real interest rates in the rest of the world.) In particular, when nominal rates in the United States were high in the 1970s, real rates were actually extremely low—often negative. By the standard of nominal interest rates, you would have thought that credit market conditions were tight in this period, because it was expensive to borrow. However, the estimates of the real rates indicate

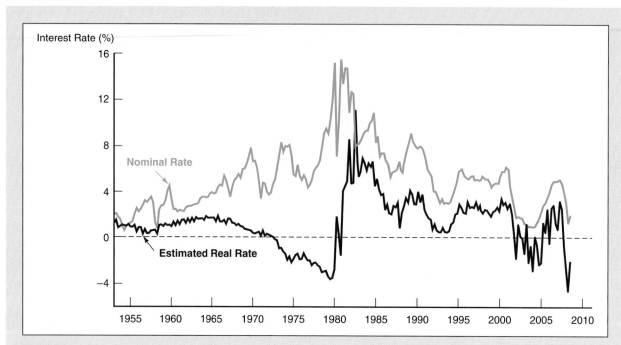

FIGURE 1 Real and Nominal Interest Rates (Three-Month Treasury Bill), 1953–2008

Sources: Nominal rates from www.federalreserve.gov/releases/H15. The real rate is constructed using the procedure outlined in Frederic S. Mishkin, "The Real Interest Rate: An Empirical Investigation," *Carnegie-Rochester Conference Series on Public Policy* 15 (1981): 151–200. This procedure involves estimating expected inflation as a function of past interest rates, inflation, and time trends and then subtracting the expected inflation measure from the nominal interest rate.

that you would have been mistaken. In real terms, the cost of borrowing was actually quite low.[8]

Until recently, real interest rates in the United States were not observable; only nominal rates were reported. This all changed when, in January 1997, the U.S. Treasury began to issue **indexed bonds**, whose interest and principal payments are adjusted for changes in the price level (see the FYI box on TIPS).

---

[8]Because most interest income in the United States is subject to federal income taxes, the true earnings in real terms from holding a debt instrument are not reflected by the real interest rate defined by the Fisher equation but rather by the *after-tax real interest rate,* which equals the nominal interest rate *after income tax payments have been subtracted,* minus the expected inflation rate. For a person facing a 30% tax rate, the after-tax interest rate earned on a bond yielding 10% is only 7% because 30% of the interest income must be paid to the Internal Revenue Service. Thus the after-tax real interest rate on this bond when expected inflation is 5% equals 2% (=7% − 5%). More generally, the after-tax real interest rate can be expressed as

$$i(1 - \tau) - \pi^e$$

where τ = the income tax rate.

This formula for the after-tax real interest rate also provides a better measure of the effective cost of borrowing for many corporations and homeowners in the United States because in calculating income taxes, they can deduct interest payments on loans from their income. Thus, if you face a 30% tax rate and take out a mortgage loan with a 10% interest rate, you are able to deduct the 10% interest payment and lower your taxes by 30% of this amount. Your after-tax nominal cost of borrowing is then 7% (10% minus 30% of the 10% interest payment), and when the expected inflation rate is 5%, the effective cost of borrowing in real terms is again 2% (=7% − 5%).

As the example (and the formula) indicates, after-tax real interest rates are always below the real interest rate defined by the Fisher equation. For a further discussion of measures of after-tax real interest rates, see Frederic S. Mishkin, "The Real Interest Rate: An Empirical Investigation," *Carnegie-Rochester Conference Series on Public Policy* 15 (1981): 151–200.

FYI   **With TIPS, Real Interest Rates Have Become Observable in the United States**

When the U.S. Treasury decided to issue TIPS (Treasury Inflation Protection Securities), a version of indexed Treasury coupon bonds, in January 1997, it was somewhat late in the game. Other countries such as the United Kingdom, Canada, Australia, and Sweden had already beaten the United States to the punch. (In September 1998, the U.S. Treasury also began issuing the Series I savings bond, which provides inflation protection for small investors.)

These indexed securities have successfully carved out a niche in the bond market, enabling governments to raise more funds. In addition, because their interest and principal payments are adjusted for changes in the price level, the interest rate on these bonds provides a direct measure of a real interest rate. These indexed bonds are very useful to policymakers, especially monetary policymakers, because by subtracting their interest rate from a nominal interest rate on a nonindexed bond, they generate more insight into expected inflation, a valuable piece of information. For example, on February 27, 2009, the interest rate on the ten-year Treasury bond was 3.02%, while that on the ten-year TIPS was 2.06%. Thus, the implied expected inflation rate for the next ten years, derived from the difference between these two rates, was 0.96%. The private sector finds the information provided by TIPS very useful: Many commercial and investment banks routinely publish the expected U.S. inflation rates derived from these bonds.

SUMMARY

1. The yield to maturity, which is the measure that most accurately reflects the interest rate, is the interest rate that equates the present value of future payments of a debt instrument with its value today. Application of this principle reveals that bond prices and interest rates are negatively related: When the interest rate rises, the price of the bond must fall, and vice versa.

2. The return on a security, which tells you how well you have done by holding this security over a stated period of time, can differ substantially from the interest rate as measured by the yield to maturity. Long-term bond prices have substantial fluctuations when interest rates change and thus bear interest-rate risk. The resulting capital gains and losses can be large, which is why long-term bonds are not considered to be safe assets with a sure return.

3. The real interest rate is defined as the nominal interest rate minus the expected rate of inflation. It is a better measure of the incentives to borrow and lend than the nominal interest rate, and it is a more accurate indicator of the tightness of credit market conditions than the nominal interest rate.

KEY TERMS

cash flows, p. 69

consol or perpetuity, p. 77

coupon bond, p. 72

coupon rate, p. 72

current yield, p. 78

discount bond (zero-coupon bond), p. 72

face value (par value), p. 72

fixed-payment loan (fully amortized loan), p. 72

indexed bond, p. 86

interest-rate risk, p. 82

nominal interest rate, p. 84

present discounted value, p. 69

present value, p. 69

rate of capital gain, p. 81

real interest rate, p. 84

real terms, p. 85

return (rate of return), p. 80

simple loan, p. 70

yield to maturity, p. 72

QUESTIONS AND PROBLEMS

All questions and problems are available in myeconlab *at* www.myeconlab.com/mishkin.

1. Would a dollar tomorrow be worth more to you today when the interest rate is 20% or when it is 10%?

2. You have just won $10 million in the local lottery, which promises to pay you $1 million (tax free) every year for the next ten years. Have you really won $10 million?

3. If the interest rate is 10%, what is the present value of a security that pays you $1,100 next year, $1,210 the year after, and $1,331 the year after that?

4. If the security in Problem 3 sold for $3,500, is the yield to maturity greater or less than 10%? Why?

5. Write down the formula that is used to calculate the yield to maturity on a twenty-year 10% coupon bond with $1,000 face value that sells for $2,000.

6. What is the yield to maturity on a $1,000-face-value discount bond maturing in one year that sells for $800?

7. What is the yield to maturity on a simple loan for $1 million that requires a repayment of $2 million in five years' time?

8. To pay for college, you have just taken out a $1,000 government loan that makes you pay $126 per year for 25 years. However, you don't have to start making these payments until you graduate from college two years from now. Why is the yield to maturity necessarily less than 12%, the yield to maturity on a normal $1,000 fixed-payment loan in which you pay $126 per year for 25 years?

9. Which $1,000 bond has the higher yield to maturity, a twenty-year bond selling for $800 with a current yield of 15% or a one-year bond selling for $800 with a current yield of 5%?

10. Pick five U.S. Treasury bonds from the bond page of the newspaper, and calculate the current yield. Note when the current yield is a good approximation of the yield to maturity.

11. You are offered two bonds, a one-year U.S. Treasury bond with a yield to maturity of 9% and a one-year U.S. Treasury bill with a yield on a discount basis of 8.9%. Which would you rather own?

12. If there is a decline in interest rates, which would you rather be holding, long-term bonds or short-term bonds? Why? Which type of bond has the greater interest-rate risk?

13. Francine the Financial Advisor has just given you the following advice: "Long-term bonds are a great investment because their interest rate is over 20%." Is Francine necessarily right?

14. If mortgage rates rise from 5% to 10% but the expected rate of increase in housing prices rises from 2% to 9%, are people more or less likely to buy houses?

15. Interest rates were lower in the mid-1980s than they were in the late 1970s, yet many economists have commented that real interest rates were actually much higher in the mid-1980s than in the late 1970s. Does this make sense? Do you think that these economists are right?

WEB EXERCISES

1. Investigate the data available from the Federal Reserve at www.federalreserve.gov/releases/. Answer the following questions:
   a. What is the difference in the interest rates on commercial paper for financial firms when compared to nonfinancial firms?
   b. What was the interest rate on the one-month Eurodollar at the end of 2002?
   c. What is the most recent interest rate report for the 30-year Treasury note?

2. Figure 1 in the text shows the estimated real and nominal rates for three-month Treasury bills. Go to www.martincapital.com/main/charts.htm and click on "Nominal vs. Real Rates," then on "Nominal vs. Real Market Rates."
   a. Compare the three-month real rate to the long-term real rate. Which is greater?
   b. Compare the short-term nominal rate to the long-term nominal rate. Which appears most volatile?

3. In this chapter we discussed long-term bonds as if there were only one type, coupon bonds. In fact, there are also long-term discount bonds. A discount bond is sold at a low price and the whole return comes in the form of a price appreciation. You can easily compute the current price of a discount bond using the financial calculator at www.treasurydirect.gov/indiv/tools/tools_savingsbondcalc.htm.

To compute the values for savings bonds, read the instructions on the page and click "Get Started." Fill in the information (you do not need to fill in the "Bond Serial Number" field) and click on "calculate."

WEB REFERENCES

www.bloomberg.com/markets/

Under "Rates & Bonds," you can access information on key interest rates, U.S. Treasuries, government bonds, and municipal bonds.

www.teachmefinance.com

A review of the key financial concepts: time value of money, annuities, perpetuities, and so on.

www.martincapital.com/main/charts.htm

Go to charts of real versus nominal rates to view 30 years of nominal interest rates compared to real rates for the 30-year T-bond and 90-day T-bill.

 MyEconLab CAN HELP YOU GET A BETTER GRADE

If your exam were tomorrow, would you be ready? For each chapter, MyEconLab Practice Tests and Study Plans pinpoint which sections you have mastered and which ones you need to study. That way, you are more efficient with your study time, and you are better prepared for your exams.

To see how it works, turn to page 20 and then go to: www.myeconlab.com/mishkin

5

The Behavior of Interest Rates

Preview

In the early 1950s, nominal interest rates on three-month Treasury bills were about 1% at an annual rate; by 1981, they had reached over 15%; in 2003 they fell below 1%, rose to 5% in 2 007 and then fell to zero in 2008. What explains these substantial fluctuations in interest rates? One reason why we study money, banking, and financial markets is to provide some answers to this question.

In this chapter, we examine how the overall level of *nominal* interest rates (which we refer to as simply "interest rates") is determined and which factors influence their behavior. We learned in Chapter 4 that interest rates are negatively related to the price of bonds, so if we can explain why bond prices change, we can also explain why interest rates fluctuate. We make use of supply and demand analysis for bond markets and money markets to examine how interest rates change.

To derive a demand curve for assets such as money or bonds, the first step in our analysis, we must first understand what determines the demand for these assets. We do this by examining the *theory of asset demand*, an economic theory that outlines criteria that are important when deciding how much of an asset to buy. Armed with this theory, we can then go on to derive the demand curve for bonds or money. After deriving supply curves for these assets, we develop the concept of *market equilibrium*, the point at which the quantity supplied equals the quantity demanded. Then we use this model to explain changes in equilibrium interest rates.

Because interest rates on different securities tend to move together, in this chapter we will proceed as if there were only one type of security and one interest rate in the entire economy. In the following chapter, we expand our analysis to look at why interest rates on different types of securities differ.

DETERMINANTS OF ASSET DEMAND

Before going on to our supply and demand analysis of the bond market and the market for money, we must first understand what determines the quantity demanded of an asset. Recall that an asset is a piece of property that is a store of value. Items such as money, bonds, stocks, art, land, houses, farm equipment, and manufacturing machinery are all assets. Facing the question of whether to buy and hold an asset or whether to buy one asset rather than another, an individual must consider the following factors:

1. **Wealth**, the total resources owned by the individual, including all assets
2. **Expected return** (the return expected over the next period) on one asset relative to alternative assets

3. **Risk** (the degree of uncertainty associated with the return) on one asset relative to alternative assets
4. **Liquidity** (the ease and speed with which an asset can be turned into cash) relative to alternative assets

Wealth

When we find that our wealth has increased, we have more resources available with which to purchase assets, and so, not surprisingly, the quantity of assets we demand increases. Therefore, the effect of changes in wealth on the quantity demanded of an asset can be summarized as follows: *Holding everything else constant, an increase in wealth raises the quantity demanded of an asset*.

Expected Returns

In Chapter 4, we saw that the return on an asset (such as a bond) measures how much we gain from holding that asset. When we make a decision to buy an asset, we are influenced by what we expect the return on that asset to be. If an Exxon Mobil Corporation bond, for example, has a return of 15% half the time and 5% the other half of the time, its expected return (which you can think of as the average return) is 10% (= $0.5 \times 15\% + 0.5 \times 5\%$)[1] If the expected return on the Exxon Mobil bond rises relative to expected returns on alternative assets, holding everything else constant, then it becomes more desirable to purchase it, and the quantity demanded increases. This can occur in either of two ways: (1) when the expected return on the Exxon Mobil bond rises while the return on an alternative asset—say, stock in Google—remains unchanged or (2) when the return on the alternative asset, the Google stock, falls while the return on the Exxon Mobil bond remains unchanged. To summarize, *an increase in an asset's expected return relative to that of an alternative asset, holding everything else unchanged, raises the quantity demanded of the asset*.

Risk

The degree of risk or uncertainty of an asset's returns also affects the demand for the asset. Consider two assets, stock in Fly-by-Night Airlines and stock in Feet-on-the-Ground Bus Company. Suppose that Fly-by-Night stock has a return of 15% half the time and 5% the other half of the time, making its expected return 10%, while stock in Feet-on-the-Ground has a fixed return of 10%. Fly-by-Night stock has uncertainty associated with its returns and so has greater risk than stock in Feet-on-the-Ground, whose return is a sure thing.

A *risk-averse* person prefers stock in Feet-on-the-Ground (the sure thing) to Fly-by-Night stock (the riskier asset), even though the stocks have the same expected return, 10%. By contrast, a person who prefers risk is a *risk preferrer* or *risk lover*. Most people are risk-averse, especially in their financial decisions: Everything else being equal, they

---

[1]If you are interested in finding out more information on how to calculate expected returns, as well as standard deviations of returns that measure risk, you can look at an appendix to this chapter describing models of asset pricing that is on this book's website at www.myeconlab.com/mishkin. This appendix also describes how diversification lowers the overall risk of a portfolio and has a discussion of systematic risk and basic asset pricing models such as the capital asset pricing model and arbitrage pricing theory.

prefer to hold the less risky asset. Hence, *holding everything else constant, if an asset's risk rises relative to that of alternative assets, its quantity demanded will fall*.

Liquidity

Another factor that affects the demand for an asset is how quickly it can be converted into cash at low costs—its liquidity. An asset is liquid if the market in which it is traded has depth and breadth; that is, if the market has many buyers and sellers. A house is not a very liquid asset, because it may be hard to find a buyer quickly; if a house must be sold to pay off bills, it might have to be sold for a much lower price. And the transaction costs in selling a house (broker's commissions, lawyer's fees, and so on) are substantial. A U.S. Treasury bill, by contrast, is a highly liquid asset. It can be sold in a well-organized market where there are many buyers, so it can be sold quickly at low cost. *The more liquid an asset is relative to alternative assets, holding everything else unchanged, the more desirable it is, and the greater will be the quantity demanded*.

Theory of Asset Demand

All the determining factors we have just discussed can be assembled into the **theory of asset demand**, which states that, holding all of the other factors constant:

1. The quantity demanded of an asset is positively related to wealth.
2. The quantity demanded of an asset is positively related to its expected return relative to alternative assets.
3. The quantity demanded of an asset is negatively related to the risk of its returns relative to alternative assets.
4. The quantity demanded of an asset is positively related to its liquidity relative to alternative assets.

These results are summarized in Table 1.

SUMMARY TABLE 1		
Response of the Quantity of an Asset Demanded to Changes in Wealth, Expected Returns, Risk, and Liquidity		
Variable	**Change in Variable**	**Change in Quantity Demanded**
Wealth	↑	↑
Expected return relative to other assets	↑	↑
Risk relative to other assets	↑	↓
Liquidity relative to other assets	↑	↑

Note: Only increases in the variables are shown. The effect of decreases in the variables on the change in quantity demanded would be the opposite of those indicated in the rightmost column.

SUPPLY AND DEMAND IN THE BOND MARKET

Our first approach to the analysis of interest-rate determination looks at supply and demand in the bond market to see how the price of bonds is determined. Thanks to our understanding of how interest rates are measured from Chapter 4, we know that each bond price is associated with a particular level of the interest rate. Specifically, the negative relationship between bond prices and interest rates means that when a bond price rises, its interest rate falls, and vice versa.

The first step in the analysis is to obtain a bond **demand curve**, which shows the relationship between the quantity demanded and the price when all other economic variables are held constant (that is, values of other variables are taken as given). You may recall from previous economics courses that the assumption that all other economic variables are held constant is called *ceteris paribus*, which means "other things being equal" in Latin.

Demand Curve

To clarify our analysis, let us consider the demand for one-year discount bonds, which make no coupon payments but pay the owner the $1,000 face value in a year. If the holding period is one year, then as we have seen in Chapter 4, the return on the bonds is known absolutely and is equal to the interest rate as measured by the yield to maturity. This means that the expected return on this bond is equal to the interest rate i, which, using Equation 6 in Chapter 4, is

$$i = R^e = \frac{F - P}{P}$$

where
$$i = \text{interest rate} = \text{yield to maturity}$$
$$R^e = \text{expected return}$$
$$F = \text{face value of the discount bond}$$
$$P = \text{initial purchase price of the discount bond}$$

This formula shows that a particular value of the interest rate corresponds to each bond price. If the bond sells for $950, the interest rate and expected return are

$$\frac{\$1,000 - \$950}{\$950} = 0.053 = 5.3\%$$

At this 5.3% interest rate and expected return corresponding to a bond price of $950, let us assume that the quantity of bonds demanded is $100 billion, which is plotted as point A in Figure 1.

At a price of $900, the interest rate and expected return are

$$\frac{\$1,000 - \$900}{\$900} = 0.111 = 11.1\%$$

Because the expected return on these bonds is higher, with all other economic variables (such as income, expected returns on other assets, risk, and liquidity) held constant, the quantity demanded of bonds will be higher as predicted by the theory of asset demand. Point B in Figure 1 shows that the quantity of bonds demanded at the price of $900 has risen to $200 billion. Continuing with this reasoning, if the bond price is $850 (interest rate and expected return = 17.6%), the quantity of bonds demanded (point C) will be greater than at point B. Similarly, at the lower prices of $800 (interest

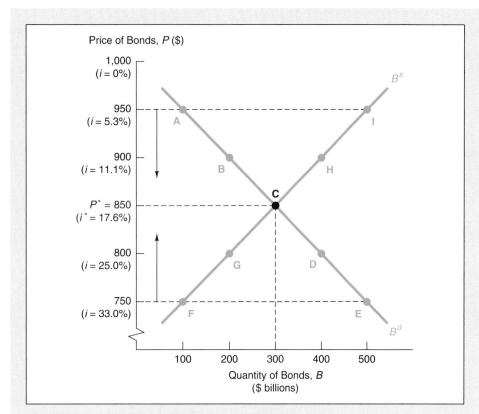

Price of Bonds, *P* ($)

FIGURE 1   **Supply and Demand for Bonds**
Equilibrium in the bond market occurs at point C, the intersection of the
demand curve *B^d* and the bond supply curve *B^s*. The equilibrium price is
P* = $850, and the equilibrium interest rate is *i** = 17.6%.

rate = 25%) and $750 (interest rate = 33.3%), the quantity of bonds demanded will be
even higher (points D and E). The curve *B^d*, which connects these points, is the demand
curve for bonds. It has the usual downward slope, indicating that at lower prices of the
bond (everything else being equal), the quantity demanded is higher.[2]

Supply Curve

An important assumption behind the demand curve for bonds in Figure 1 is that all other
economic variables besides the bond's price and interest rate are held constant. We use the
same assumption in deriving a **supply curve**, which shows the relationship between the
quantity supplied and the price when all other economic variables are held constant.

When the price of the bonds is $750 (interest rate = 33.3%), point F shows that
the quantity of bonds supplied is $100 billion for the example we are considering. If
the price is $800, the interest rate is the lower rate of 25%. Because at this interest rate
it is now less costly to borrow by issuing bonds, firms will be willing to borrow more
through bond issues, and the quantity of bonds supplied is at the higher level of $200
billion (point G). An even higher price of $850, corresponding to a lower interest rate

---

[2]Although our analysis indicates that the demand curve is downward-sloping, it does not imply that the curve is a
straight line. For ease of exposition, however, we will draw demand curves and supply curves as straight lines.

of 17.6%, results in a larger quantity of bonds supplied of $300 billion (point C). Higher prices of $900 and $950 result in even greater quantities of bonds supplied (points H and I). The B^s curve, which connects these points, is the supply curve for bonds. It has the usual upward slope found in supply curves, indicating that as the price increases (everything else being equal), the quantity supplied increases.

Market Equilibrium

In economics, **market equilibrium** occurs when the amount that people are willing to buy (*demand*) equals the amount that people are willing to sell (*supply*) at a given price. In the bond market, this is achieved when the quantity of bonds demanded equals the quantity of bonds supplied:

$$B^d = B^s \tag{1}$$

In Figure 1, equilibrium occurs at point C, where the demand and supply curves intersect at a bond price of $850 (interest rate of 17.6%) and a quantity of bonds of $300 billion. The price of $P^* = \$850$, where the quantity demanded equals the quantity supplied, is called the *equilibrium* or *market-clearing* price. Similarly, the interest rate of $i^* = 17.6\%$ that corresponds to this price is called the equilibrium or market-clearing interest rate.

The concepts of market equilibrium and equilibrium price or interest rate are useful, because there is a tendency for the market to head toward them. We can see that it does in Figure 1 by first looking at what happens when we have a bond price that is above the equilibrium price. When the price of bonds is set too high, at, say, $950, the quantity of bonds supplied at point I is greater than the quantity of bonds demanded at point A. A situation like this, in which the quantity of bonds supplied exceeds the quantity of bonds demanded, is called a condition of **excess supply**. Because people want to sell more bonds than others want to buy, the price of the bonds will fall, which is why the downward arrow is drawn in the figure at the bond price of $950. As long as the bond price remains above the equilibrium price, there will continue to be an excess supply of bonds, and the price will continue to fall. This decline will stop only when the price has reached the equilibrium price of $850, where the excess supply of bonds has been eliminated.

Now let's look at what happens when the price of bonds is below the equilibrium price. If the price of the bonds is set too low, at, say, $750, the quantity demanded at point E is greater than the quantity supplied at point F. This is called a condition of **excess demand**. People now want to buy more bonds than others are willing to sell, so the price of bonds will be driven up. This is illustrated by the upward arrow drawn in the figure at the bond price of $750. Only when the excess demand for bonds is eliminated by the price rising to the equilibrium level of $850 is there no further tendency for the price to rise.

We can see that the concept of equilibrium price is a useful one because it indicates where the market will settle. Because each price on the vertical axis of Figure 1 corresponds to a particular value of the interest rate, the same diagram also shows that the interest rate will head toward the equilibrium interest rate of 17.6%. When the interest rate is below the equilibrium interest rate, as it is when it is at 5.3%, the price of the bond is above the equilibrium price, and there will be an excess supply of bonds. The price of the bond then falls, leading to a rise in the interest rate toward the equilibrium level. Similarly, when the interest rate is above the equilibrium level, as it is when it is at 33.3%, there is excess demand for bonds, and the bond price will rise, driving the interest rate back down to the equilibrium level of 17.6%.

Supply and Demand Analysis

Our Figure 1 is a conventional supply and demand diagram with price on the vertical axis and quantity on the horizontal axis. Because the interest rate that corresponds to each bond price is also marked on the vertical axis, this diagram allows us to read the equilibrium interest rate, giving us a model that describes the determination of interest rates. It is important to recognize that a supply and demand diagram like Figure 1 can be drawn for *any* type of bond because the interest rate and price of a bond are *always* negatively related for any type of bond, whether a discount bond or a coupon bond.

An important feature of the analysis here is that supply and demand are always in terms of *stocks* (amounts at a given point in time) of assets, not in terms of *flows*. The **asset market approach** for understanding behavior in financial markets—which emphasizes stocks of assets rather than flows in determining asset prices—is the dominant methodology used by economists, because correctly conducting analyses in terms of flows is very tricky, especially when we encounter inflation.[3]

CHANGES IN EQUILIBRIUM INTEREST RATES

We will now use the supply and demand framework for bonds to analyze why interest rates change. To avoid confusion, it is important to make the distinction between *movements along* a demand (or supply) curve and *shifts in* a demand (or supply) curve. When quantity demanded (or supplied) changes as a result of a change in the price of the bond (or, equivalently, a change in the interest rate), we have a *movement along* the demand (or supply) curve. The change in the quantity demanded when we move from point A to B to C in Figure 1, for example, is a movement along a demand curve. A *shift in* the demand (or supply) curve, by contrast, occurs when the quantity demanded (or supplied) changes *at each given price (or interest rate)* of the bond in response to a change in some other factor besides the bond's price or interest rate. When one of these factors changes, causing a shift in the demand or supply curve, there will be a new equilibrium value for the interest rate.

In the following pages, we will look at how the supply and demand curves shift in response to changes in variables, such as expected inflation and wealth, and what effects these changes have on the equilibrium value of interest rates.

Shifts in the Demand for Bonds

The theory of asset demand demonstrated at the beginning of the chapter provides a framework for deciding which factors cause the demand curve for bonds to shift. These factors include changes in four parameters:

1. Wealth
2. Expected returns on bonds relative to alternative assets

---

[3]The asset market approach developed in the text is useful in understanding not only how interest rates behave but also how any asset price is determined. A second appendix to this chapter, which is on this book's website at www.myeconlab.com/mishkin, shows how the asset market approach can be applied to understanding the behavior of commodity markets; in particular, the gold market. The analysis of the bond market that we have developed here has another interpretation using a different terminology and framework involving the supply and demand for loanable funds. This loanable funds framework is discussed in a third appendix to this chapter, which is also on the book's website.

3. Risk of bonds relative to alternative assets
4. Liquidity of bonds relative to alternative assets

To see how a change in each of these factors (holding all other factors constant) can shift the demand curve, let us look at some examples. (As a study aid, Table 2 summarizes the effects of changes in these factors on the bond demand curve.)

Wealth   When the economy is growing rapidly in a business cycle expansion and wealth is increasing, the quantity of bonds demanded at each bond price (or interest rate) increases as shown in Figure 2. To see how this works, consider point B on the initial demand curve for bonds B_1^d. With higher wealth, the quantity of bonds demanded at the same price must rise, to point B'. Similarly, for point D the higher wealth causes the quantity demanded at the same bond price to rise to point D'. Continuing with this reasoning for every point on the initial demand curve B_1^d, we can see that the demand curve shifts to the right from B_1^d to B_2^d as is indicated by the arrows.

The conclusion we have reached is that **in a business cycle expansion with growing wealth, the demand for bonds rises and the demand curve for bonds shifts to the right.** Using the same reasoning, **in a recession, when income and wealth are falling, the demand for bonds falls, and the demand curve shifts to the left.**

Another factor that affects wealth is the public's propensity to save. If households save more, wealth increases and, as we have seen, the demand for bonds rises and the demand curve for bonds shifts to the right. Conversely, if people save less, wealth and the demand for bonds will fall and the demand curve shifts to the left.

Expected Returns   For a one-year discount bond and a one-year holding period, the expected return and the interest rate are identical, so nothing besides today's interest rate affects the expected return.

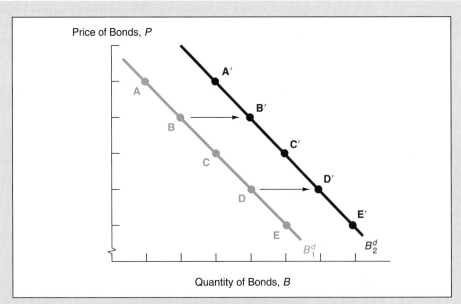

FIGURE 2   **Shift in the Demand Curve for Bonds**
When the demand for bonds increases, the demand curve shifts to the right as shown.

SUMMARY TABLE 2

Factors That Shift the Demand Curve for Bonds

Variable	Change in Variable	Change in Quantity Demanded at Each Bond Price	Shift in Demand Curve
Wealth	↑	↑	
Expected interest rate	↑	↓	
Expected inflation	↑	↓	
Riskiness of bonds relative to other assets	↑	↓	
Liquidity of bonds relative to other assets	↑	↑	

Note: Only increases in the variables are shown. The effect of decreases in the variables on the change in demand would be the opposite of those indicated in the remaining columns.

For bonds with maturities of greater than one year, the expected return may differ from the interest rate. For example, we saw in Chapter 4, Table 2, that a rise in the interest rate on a long-term bond from 10% to 20% would lead to a sharp decline in price and a very large negative return. Hence, if people began to think that interest rates would be higher next year than they had originally anticipated, the expected return today on long-term bonds would fall, and the quantity demanded would fall at each interest rate. *Higher expected interest rates in the future lower the expected return for long-term bonds, decrease the demand, and shift the demand curve to the left.*

By contrast, a revision downward of expectations of future interest rates would mean that long-term bond prices would be expected to rise more than originally anticipated, and the resulting higher expected return today would raise the quantity demanded at each bond price and interest rate. *Lower expected interest rates in the future increase the demand for long-term bonds and shift the demand curve to the right* (as in Figure 2).

Changes in expected returns on other assets can also shift the demand curve for bonds. If people suddenly became more optimistic about the stock market and began to expect higher stock prices in the future, both expected capital gains and expected returns on stocks would rise. With the expected return on bonds held constant, the expected return on bonds today relative to stocks would fall, lowering the demand for bonds and shifting the demand curve to the left.

A change in expected inflation is likely to alter expected returns on physical assets (also called *real assets*) such as automobiles and houses, which affect the demand for bonds. An increase in expected inflation, say, from 5% to 10%, will lead to higher prices on cars and houses in the future and hence higher nominal capital gains. The resulting rise in the expected returns today on these real assets will lead to a fall in the expected return on bonds relative to the expected return on real assets today and thus cause the demand for bonds to fall. Alternatively, we can think of the rise in expected inflation as lowering the real interest rate on bonds, and the resulting decline in the relative expected return on bonds will cause the demand for bonds to fall. *An increase in the expected rate of inflation lowers the expected return for bonds, causing their demand to decline and the demand curve to shift to the left.*

Risk   If prices in the bond market become more volatile, the risk associated with bonds increases, and bonds become a less attractive asset. *An increase in the riskiness of bonds causes the demand for bonds to fall and the demand curve to shift to the left.*

Conversely, an increase in the volatility of prices in another asset market, such as the stock market, would make bonds more attractive. *An increase in the riskiness of alternative assets causes the demand for bonds to rise and the demand curve to shift to the right* (as in Figure 2).

Liquidity   If more people started trading in the bond market, and as a result it became easier to sell bonds quickly, the increase in their liquidity would cause the quantity of bonds demanded at each interest rate to rise. *Increased liquidity of bonds results in an increased demand for bonds, and the demand curve shifts to the right* (see Figure 2). *Similarly, increased liquidity of alternative assets lowers the demand for bonds and shifts the demand curve to the left.* The reduction of brokerage commissions for trading common stocks that occurred when the fixed-rate commission structure was abolished in 1975, for example, increased the liquidity of stocks relative to bonds, and the resulting lower demand for bonds shifted the demand curve to the left.

Shifts in the Supply of Bonds

Certain factors can cause the supply curve for bonds to shift, among them these:

1. Expected profitability of investment opportunities
2. Expected inflation
3. Government budget

We will look at how the supply curve shifts when each of these factors changes (all others remaining constant). (As a study aid, Table 3 summarizes the effects of changes in these factors on the bond supply curve.)

SUMMARY TABLE 3

Factors That Shift the Supply of Bonds

Variable	Change in Variable	Change in Quantity Supplied at Each Bond Price	Shift in Supply Curve
Profitability of investments	↑	↑	
Expected inflation	↑	↑	
Government deficit	↑	↑	

Note: Only increases in the variables are shown. The effect of decreases in the variables on the change in supply would be the opposite of those indicated in the remaining columns.

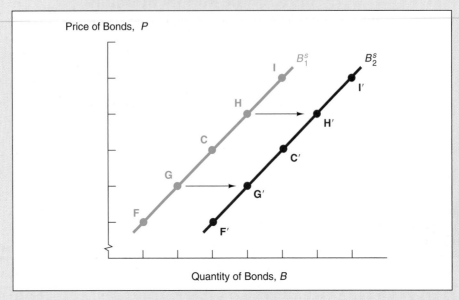

FIGURE 3   Shift in the Supply Curve for Bonds
When the supply of bonds increases, the supply curve shifts to the right.

Expected Profitability of Investment Opportunities   The more profitable plant and equipment investments that a firm expects it can make, the more willing it will be to borrow to finance these investments. When the economy is growing rapidly, as in a business cycle expansion, investment opportunities that are expected to be profitable abound, and the quantity of bonds supplied at any given bond price will increase (see Figure 3). *Therefore, in a business cycle expansion, the supply of bonds increases, and the supply curve shifts to the right. Likewise, in a recession, when there are far fewer expected profitable investment opportunities, the supply of bonds falls, and the supply curve shifts to the left.*

Expected Inflation   As we saw in Chapter 4, the real cost of borrowing is more accurately measured by the real interest rate, which equals the (nominal) interest rate minus the expected inflation rate. For a given interest rate (and bond price), when expected inflation increases, the real cost of borrowing falls; hence the quantity of bonds supplied increases at any given bond price. *An increase in expected inflation causes the supply of bonds to increase and the supply curve to shift to the right* (see Figure 3).

Government Budget   The activities of the government can influence the supply of bonds in several ways. The U.S. Treasury issues bonds to finance government deficits, the gap between the government's expenditures and its revenues. When these deficits are large, the Treasury sells more bonds, and the quantity of bonds supplied at each bond price increases. *Higher government deficits increase the supply of bonds and shift the supply curve to the right* (see Figure 3). *On the other hand, government surpluses, as occurred in the late 1990s, decrease the supply of bonds and shift the supply curve to the left.*

U.S. state and local governments and other government agencies also issue bonds to finance their expenditures, and this can also affect the supply of bonds. We will see in later chapters that the conduct of monetary policy involves the purchase and sale of bonds, which in turn influences the supply of bonds.

We now can use our knowledge of how supply and demand curves shift to analyze how the equilibrium interest rate can change. The best way to do this is to pursue several applications that are particularly relevant to our understanding of how monetary policy affects interest rates. In going through these applications, keep two things in mind:

1. When you examine the effect of a variable change, remember that we are assuming that all other variables are unchanged; that is, we are making use of the *ceteris paribus* assumption.
2. Remember that the interest rate is negatively related to the bond price, so when the equilibrium bond price rises, the equilibrium interest rate falls. Conversely, if the equilibrium bond price moves downward, the equilibrium interest rate rises.

APPLICATION ✦ Changes in the Interest Rate Due to Expected Inflation: The Fisher Effect

We have already done most of the work to evaluate how a change in expected inflation affects the nominal interest rate, in that we have already analyzed how a change in expected inflation shifts the supply and demand curves. Figure 4 shows the effect on the equilibrium interest rate of an increase in expected inflation.

Suppose that expected inflation is initially 5% and the initial supply and demand curves B_1^s and B_1^d intersect at point 1, where the equilibrium bond price is P_1. If expected inflation rises to 10%, the expected return on bonds relative to real assets falls for any

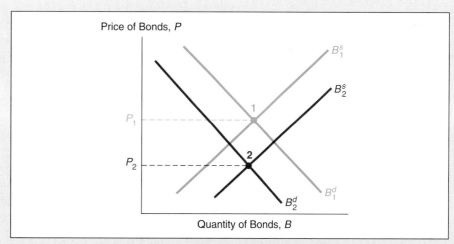

FIGURE 4   **Response to a Change in Expected Inflation**
When expected inflation rises, the supply curve shifts from B_1^s to B_2^s, and the demand curve shifts from B_1^d to B_2^d. The equilibrium moves from point 1 to point 2, with the result that the equilibrium bond price falls from P_1 to P_2 and the equilibrium interest rate rises.

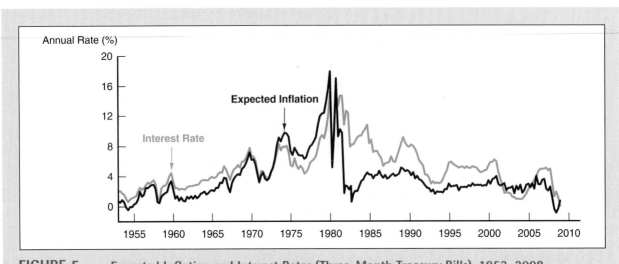

FIGURE 5   **Expected Inflation and Interest Rates (Three-Month Treasury Bills), 1953–2008**

Source: Expected inflation calculated using procedures outlined in Frederic S. Mishkin, "The Real Interest Rate: An Empirical Investigation," *Carnegie-Rochester Conference Series on Public Policy* 15 (1981): 151–200. These procedures involve estimating expected inflation as a function of past interest rates, inflation, and time trends.

given bond price and interest rate. As a result, the demand for bonds falls, and the demand curve shifts to the left from B_1^d to B_2^d. The rise in expected inflation also shifts the supply curve. At any given bond price and interest rate, the real cost of borrowing has declined, causing the quantity of bonds supplied to increase, and the supply curve shifts to the right, from B_1^s to B_2^s.

When the demand and supply curves shift in response to the change in expected inflation, the equilibrium moves from point 1 to point 2, the intersection of B_2^d and B_2^s. The equilibrium bond price has fallen from P_1 to P_2, and because the bond price is negatively related to the interest rate, this means that the interest rate has risen. Note that Figure 4 has been drawn so that the equilibrium quantity of bonds remains the same for both point 1 and point 2. However, depending on the size of the shifts in the supply and demand curves, the equilibrium quantity of bonds could either rise or fall when expected inflation rises.

Our supply and demand analysis has led us to an important observation: **When expected inflation rises, interest rates will rise**. This result has been named the **Fisher effect**, after Irving Fisher, the economist who first pointed out the relationship of expected inflation to interest rates. The accuracy of this prediction is shown in Figure 5. The interest rate on three-month Treasury bills has usually moved along with the expected inflation rate. Consequently, it is understandable that many economists recommend that inflation must be kept low if we want to keep nominal interest rates low.

APPLICATION ✦ Changes in the Interest Rate Due to a Business Cycle Expansion

Figure 6 analyzes the effects of a business cycle expansion on interest rates. In a business cycle expansion, the amounts of goods and services being produced in the economy increase, so national income increases. When this occurs, businesses will be more

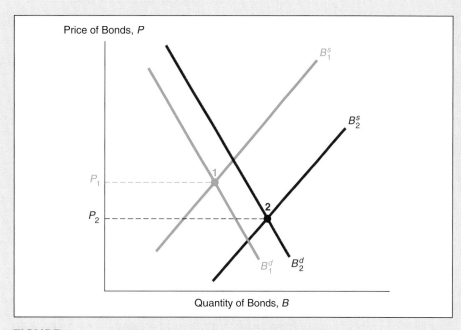

FIGURE 6   **Response to a Business Cycle Expansion**
In a business cycle expansion, when income and wealth are rising, the demand curve shifts rightward from B_1^d to B_2^d, and the supply curve shifts rightward from B_1^s to B_2^s. If the supply curve shifts to the right more than the demand curve, as in this figure, the equilibrium bond price moves down from P_1 to P_2, and the equilibrium interest rate rises.

willing to borrow, because they are likely to have many profitable investment opportunities for which they need financing. Hence at a given bond price, the quantity of bonds that firms want to sell (that is, the supply of bonds) will increase. This means that in a business cycle expansion, the supply curve for bonds shifts to the right (see Figure 6) from B_1^s to B_2^s.

Expansion in the economy will also affect the demand for bonds. As the business cycle expands, wealth is likely to increase, and the theory of asset demand tells us that the demand for bonds will rise as well. We see this in Figure 6, where the demand curve has shifted to the right, from B_1^d to B_2^d.

Given that both the supply and demand curves have shifted to the right, we know that the new equilibrium reached at the intersection of B_2^d and B_2^s must also move to the right. However, depending on whether the supply curve shifts more than the demand curve, or vice versa, the new equilibrium interest rate can either rise or fall.

The supply and demand analysis used here gives us an ambiguous answer to the question of what will happen to interest rates in a business cycle expansion. Figure 6 has been drawn so that the shift in the supply curve is greater than the shift in the demand curve, causing the equilibrium bond price to fall to P_2, leading to a rise in the equilibrium interest rate. The reason the figure has been drawn so that a business cycle expansion and a rise in income lead to a higher interest rate is that this is the

FIGURE 7   **Business Cycle and Interest Rates (Three–Month Treasury Bills), 1951–2008**
Shaded areas indicate periods of recession. The figure shows that interest rates rise during business cycle expansions and fall during contractions, which is what Figure 6 suggests would happen.
Source: Federal Reserve: www.federalreserve.gov/releases/H15/data.htm.

outcome we actually see in the data. Figure 7 plots the movement of the interest rate on three-month U.S. Treasury bills from 1951 to 2008 and indicates when the business cycle is undergoing recessions (shaded areas). As you can see, the interest rate tends to rise during business cycle expansions and fall during recessions, which is what the supply and demand diagram indicates.

APPLICATION   ✦   Explaining Low Japanese Interest Rates

In the 1990s and early 2000s, Japanese interest rates became the lowest in the world. Indeed, in November 1998, an extraordinary event occurred: Interest rates on Japanese six-month Treasury bills turned slightly negative (see Chapter 4). Why did Japanese interest rates drop to such low levels?

In the late 1990s and early 2000s, Japan experienced a prolonged recession, which was accompanied by deflation, a negative inflation rate. Using these facts, analysis similar to that used in the preceding application explains the low Japanese interest rates.

Negative inflation caused the demand for bonds to rise because the expected return on real assets fell, thereby raising the relative expected return on bonds and in turn causing the demand curve to shift to the right. The negative inflation also raised the real interest rate and therefore the real cost of borrowing for any given nominal rate, thereby causing the supply of bonds to contract and the supply curve to shift to the left. The outcome was then exactly the opposite of that graphed in Figure 4: The rightward shift of the demand curve and leftward shift of the supply curve led to a rise in the bond price and a fall in interest rates.

The business cycle contraction and the resulting lack of profitable investment opportunities in Japan also led to lower interest rates, by decreasing the supply of bonds and shifting the supply curve to the left. Although the demand curve also would shift to the left because wealth decreased during the business cycle contraction, we have seen in the preceding application that the demand curve would shift less than the supply curve. Thus, the bond price rose and interest rates fell (the opposite outcome to that in Figure 6).

Usually, we think that low interest rates are a good thing, because they make it cheap to borrow. But the Japanese example shows that just as there is a fallacy in the adage, "You can never be too rich or too thin" (maybe you can't be too rich, but you can certainly be too thin and do damage to your health), there is a fallacy in always thinking that lower interest rates are better. In Japan, the low and even negative interest rates were a sign that the Japanese economy was in real trouble, with falling prices and a contracting economy. Only when the Japanese economy returns to health will interest rates rise back to more normal levels.

APPLICATION ✦ Reading the *Wall Street Journal* "Credit Markets" Column

Now that we have an understanding of how supply and demand determine prices and interest rates in the bond market, we can use our analysis to understand discussions about bond prices and interest rates appearing in the financial press. Every day, the *Wall Street Journal* reports on developments in the bond market on the previous business day in its "Credit Markets" column, an example of which is found in the Following the Financial News box on the next page. Let's see how statements in the "Credit Markets" column can be explained using our supply and demand framework.

The column outlines how U.S. households may help prop up the Treasury bond market. Let's see how our supply and demand framework explains how this would occur.

The column expresses the concern that foreigners may find Treasiury bonds unattractive because their expected returns might be low. Specifically, it mentions that this could happen because the dollar could fall in value and so in local (foreign) currency, their returns would be low. Our supply and demand analysis then indicates that the lower expected return on Treasury bonds would lead to a decline in demand for them by foreigners, a shift of the demand curve to the left and therefore result in a decline in the price of Treasury bonds.

U.S. households could come to the rescue for two reasons. First, as the column points out, Treasury bonds could become more attractive because the swings in the stock market have raised the riskiness of stocks and have led to lower expected returns. The relative expected return on bonds would then be higher and the relative risk lower, both of which would increase the demand for Treasury bonds by U.S. households. The result is that the demand curve would shift back out to the right, and, according to our supply and demand analysis, would help prop up Treasury bond prices.

The second reason given by the column is that the rise in savings rates should be supportive of the Treasury market. Increased savings by households would need to go into some financial instruments, but because stocks are less attractive, a lot of these savings

Following the Financial News   The "Credit Markets" Column

The "Credit Markets" column appears daily in the   tion; an example is presented here.
Wall Street Journal in the Money and Investing sec-

U.S. Households May Lend Treasurys a Hand

By Min Zeng

The Treasury market faces an onslaught of supply this year. It could get help in dealing with it from an unexpected corner: U.S. households.

The recession has turned once-spendthrift U.S. consumers into savers who could well become a buying force in the Treasury market as they opt for safety. In-

CREDIT MARKETS

creased domestic demand will come as a relief for the government amid rising concerns that foreign investors, major players in gobbling up U.S. Treasurys over the past few years, may slow their purchases.

For foreign investors, who already hold more than half the roughly $5 trillion in Treasurys outstanding, current low returns make U.S. government debt unattractive. They also face the risk that the Fed's efforts to reflate the economy could undermine the dollar, reducing the value of their Treasury holdings in local currency terms.

U.S. households, however, battered by the swings in stock markets, are likely to rediscover the attractions of holding government bonds. That will help keep yields low, meaning the

Treasury Yields
— 10-year note: **2.301%**
— 2-year note: **0.747%**

2008   '09

Source: Ryan ALM via WSJ Market Data Group

government can continue to borrow cheaply to fund its more than $700 billion economic stimulus programs.

"The rise in savings rates is a good development and should be supportive to the Treasury market," said Jim O'Neill, head of global economic research at Goldman Sachs.

Mr. O'Neill expects Treasury yields to remain relatively low, with the 10-year Treasury yield to be capped at 2.75% in the first half of the year. Tuesday, the 10-year yield stood at 2.301%, with the price up 2/32

point, or $0.625 for every $1,000 invested. Yields move inversely to prices.

For sure, U.S. investors have a variety of places to park their savings. But over the past five to 10 years, households have underinvested in liquid assets such as Treasurys, said James Caron, head of U.S. interest-rate strategy at Morgan Stanley. Now with stock prices worldwide tumbling, they are likely to increase the share of Treasurys in their portfolios as a way to preserve capital.

The personal savings rate, which dipped below zero as recently as 2005 and has hovered around that level for the past few years, rose to 2.4% in October and 2.8% in November.

Economists expect the rate to rise to about 3% to 5%, or even higher, in 2009, among the sharpest reversals seen since World War II as consumers, shaken by the extent of the current financial and economic crisis, radically retrench. Goldman Sachs predicts the 2009 saving rate could be as high as 6% to 10%.

The annual personal savings rate averaged around 10% during the recession of the early 1980s and was at 7% during the recession of the early 1990s.

Source: Wall Street Journal, Wednesday, January 14, 2009, p. C2.

might be used to purchase Treasury bonds. Increased savings would then increase the demand for Treasury bonds, shift the demand curve to the right and, as our supply and demand framework suggests, raise the price of Treasury bonds.

SUPPLY AND DEMAND IN THE MARKET FOR MONEY: THE LIQUIDITY PREFERENCE FRAMEWORK

Instead of determining the equilibrium interest rate using the supply of and demand for bonds, an alternative model developed by John Maynard Keynes, known as the **liquidity preference framework**, determines the equilibrium interest rate in terms of the supply of and demand for money. Although the two frameworks look different, the liquidity preference analysis of the market for money is closely related to the supply and demand framework of the bond market.[4]

The starting point of Keynes's analysis is his assumption that there are two main categories of assets that people use to store their wealth: money and bonds. Therefore, total wealth in the economy must equal the total quantity of bonds plus money in the economy, which equals the quantity of bonds supplied (B^s) plus the quantity of money supplied (M^s). The quantity of bonds (B^d) and money (M^d) that people want to hold and thus demand must also equal the total amount of wealth, because people cannot purchase more assets than their available resources allow. The conclusion is that the quantity of bonds and money supplied must equal the quantity of bonds and money demanded:

$$B^s + M^s = B^d + M^d \tag{2}$$

Collecting the bond terms on one side of the equation and the money terms on the other, this equation can be rewritten as

$$B^s - B^d = M^d - M^s \tag{3}$$

The rewritten equation tells us that if the market for money is in equilibrium ($M^s = M^d$), the right-hand side of Equation 3 equals zero, implying that $B^s = B^d$, meaning that the bond market is also in equilibrium.

Thus it is the same to think about determining the equilibrium interest rate by equating the supply and demand for bonds or by equating the supply and demand for money. In this sense, the liquidity preference framework, which analyzes the market for money, is equivalent to a framework analyzing supply and demand in the bond market. In practice, the approaches differ, because by assuming that there are only two kinds of assets, money and bonds, the liquidity preference approach implicitly ignores any effects on interest rates that arise from changes in the expected returns on real assets such as automobiles and houses. In most instances, however, both frameworks yield the same predictions.

The reason that we approach the determination of interest rates with both frameworks is that the bond supply and demand framework is easier to use when analyzing the effects from changes in expected inflation, whereas the liquidity preference framework provides a simpler analysis of the effects from changes in income, the price level, and the supply of money.

Because the definition of money that Keynes used includes currency (which earns no interest) and checking account deposits (which in his time typically earned little or no interest), he assumed that money has a zero rate of return. Bonds, the only alternative asset to money in Keynes's framework, have an expected return equal to the interest rate i.[5] As this interest rate rises (holding everything else unchanged), the expected return on

---

[4]Note that the term *market for money* refers to the market for the medium of exchange, money. This market differs from the *money market* referred to by finance practitioners, which, as discussed in Chapter 2, is the financial market in which short-term debt instruments are traded.

[5]Keynes did not actually assume that the expected returns on bonds equaled the interest rate but rather argued that they were closely related. This distinction makes no appreciable difference in our analysis.

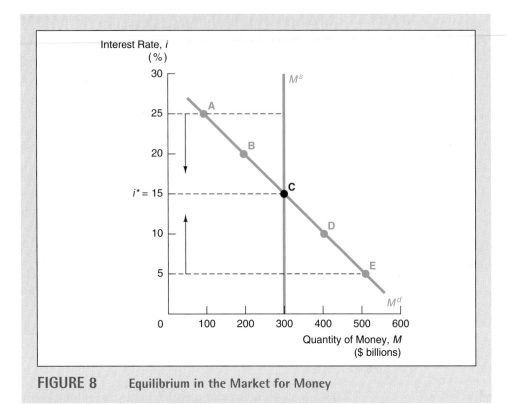

FIGURE 8   **Equilibrium in the Market for Money**

money falls relative to the expected return on bonds, and as the theory of asset demand tells us, this causes the quantity of money demanded to fall.

We can also see that the quantity of money demanded and the interest rate should be negatively related by using the concept of **opportunity cost**, the amount of interest (expected return) sacrificed by not holding the alternative asset—in this case, a bond. As the interest rate on bonds, i, rises, the opportunity cost of holding money rises; thus money is less desirable and the quantity of money demanded must fall.

Figure 8 shows the quantity of money demanded at a number of interest rates, with all other economic variables, such as income and the price level, held constant. At an interest rate of 25%, point A shows that the quantity of money demanded is $100 billion. If the interest rate is at the lower rate of 20%, the opportunity cost of holding money is lower, and the quantity of money demanded rises to $200 billion, as indicated by the move from point A to point B. If the interest rate is even lower, the quantity of money demanded is even higher, as is indicated by points C, D, and E. The curve M^d connecting these points is the demand curve for money, and it slopes downward.

At this point in our analysis, we will assume that a central bank controls the amount of money supplied at a fixed quantity of $300 billion, so the supply curve for money M^s in the figure is a vertical line at $300 billion. The equilibrium where the quantity of money demanded equals the quantity of money supplied occurs at the intersection of the supply and demand curves at point C, where

$$M^d = M^s \tag{4}$$

The resulting equilibrium interest rate is at $i^* = 15\%$.

We can again see that there is a tendency to approach this equilibrium by first looking at the relationship of money demand and supply when the interest rate is above the equilibrium interest rate. When the interest rate is 25%, the quantity of money demanded at point A is $100 billion, yet the quantity of money supplied is $300 billion. The excess supply of money means that people are holding more money than they desire, so they will try to get rid of their excess money balances by trying to buy bonds. Accordingly, they will bid up the price of bonds. As the bond price rises, the interest rate will fall toward the equilibrium interest rate of 15%. This tendency is shown by the downward arrow drawn at the interest rate of 25%.

Likewise, if the interest rate is 5%, the quantity of money demanded at point E is $500 billion, but the quantity of money supplied is only $300 billion. There is now an excess demand for money because people want to hold more money than they currently have. To try to obtain more money, they will sell their only other asset—bonds—and the price will fall. As the price of bonds falls, the interest rate will rise toward the equilibrium rate of 15%. Only when the interest rate is at its equilibrium value will there be no tendency for it to move further, and the interest rate will settle to its equilibrium value.

CHANGES IN EQUILIBRIUM INTEREST RATES IN THE LIQUIDITY PREFERENCE FRAMEWORK

Analyzing how the equilibrium interest rate changes using the liquidity preference framework requires that we understand what causes the demand and supply curves for money to shift.

Shifts in the Demand for Money

In Keynes's liquidity preference analysis, two factors cause the demand curve for money to shift: income and the price level.

Income Effect   In Keynes's view, there were two reasons why income would affect the demand for money. First, as an economy expands and income rises, wealth increases and people will want to hold more money as a store of value. Second, as the economy expands and income rises, people will want to carry out more transactions using money as a medium of exchange, with the result that they will also want to hold more money. The conclusion is that *a higher level of income causes the demand for money at each interest rate to increase and the demand curve to shift to the right*.

Price-Level Effect   Keynes took the view that people care about the amount of money they hold in real terms—that is, in terms of the goods and services that it can buy. When the price level rises, the same nominal quantity of money is no longer as valuable; it cannot be used to purchase as many real goods or services. To restore their holdings of money in real terms to its former level, people will want to hold a greater nominal quantity of money, so *a rise in the price level causes the demand for money at each interest rate to increase and the demand curve to shift to the right*.

Shifts in the Supply of Money

We will assume that the supply of money is completely controlled by the central bank, which in the United States is the Federal Reserve. (Actually, the process that determines the money supply is substantially more complicated, involving banks, depositors, and borrowers from banks. We will study it in more detail later in the book.) For now, all we need to know is that *an increase in the money supply engineered by the Federal Reserve will shift the supply curve for money to the right*.

APPLICATION ✦ Changes in the Equilibrium Interest Rate Due to Changes in Income, the Price Level, or the Money Supply

To see how we can use the liquidity preference framework to analyze the movement of interest rates, we will again look at several applications that will be useful in evaluating the effect of monetary policy on interest rates. In going through these applications, remember to use the *ceteris paribus* assumption: When examining the effect of a change in one variable, hold all other variables constant. (As a study aid, Table 4 summarizes the shifts in the demand and supply curves for money.)

SUMMARY TABLE 4

Factors That Shift the Demand for and Supply of Money

Variable	Change in Variable	Change in Money Demand (M^d) or Supply (M^s) at Each Interest Rate	Change in Interest Rate	
Income	↑	M^d ↑	↑	
Price level	↑	M^d ↑	↑	
Money supply	↑	M^s ↑	↓	

Note: Only increases in the variables are shown. The effect of decreases in the variables on the change in demand would be the opposite of those indicated in the remaining columns.

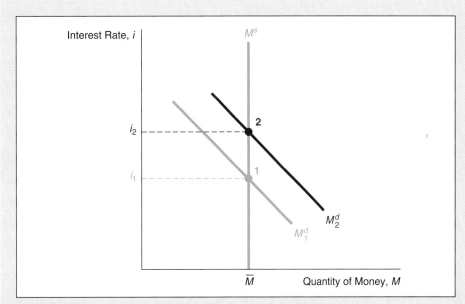

FIGURE 9   **Response to a Change in Income or the Price Level**
In a business cycle expansion, when income is rising, or when the price level rises, the demand curve shifts from M_1^d to M_2^d. The supply curve is fixed at $M^s = \overline{M}$. The equilibrium interest rate rises from i_1 to i_2.

Changes in Income

When income is rising during a business cycle expansion, we have seen that the demand for money will rise, shown in Figure 9 by the shift rightward in the demand curve from M_1^d to M_2^d. The new equilibrium is reached at point 2 at the intersection of the M_2^d curve with the money supply curve M^s. As you can see, the equilibrium interest rate rises from i_1 to i_2. The liquidity preference framework thus generates the conclusion that **when income is rising during a business cycle expansion (holding other economic variables constant), interest rates will rise**. This conclusion is unambiguous when contrasted to the conclusion reached about the effects of a business cycle expansion on interest rates using the bond supply and demand framework.

Changes in the Price Level

When the price level rises, the value of money in terms of what it can purchase is lower. To restore their purchasing power in real terms to its former level, people will want to hold a greater nominal quantity of money. A higher price level shifts the demand curve for money to the right from M_1^d to M_2^d (see Figure 9). The equilibrium moves from point 1 to point 2, where the equilibrium interest rate has risen from i_1 to i_2, illustrating that **when the price level increases, with the supply of money and other economic variables held constant, interest rates will rise**.

Changes in the Money Supply

An increase in the money supply due to expansionary monetary policy by the Federal Reserve implies that the supply curve for money shifts to the right. As is shown in Figure 10 by the movement of the supply curve from M_1^s to M_2^s, the equilibrium moves

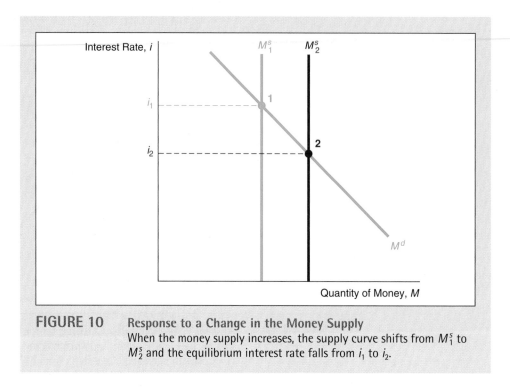

FIGURE 10   **Response to a Change in the Money Supply**
When the money supply increases, the supply curve shifts from M_1^s to M_2^s and the equilibrium interest rate falls from i_1 to i_2.

from point 1 down to point 2, where the M_2^s supply curve intersects with the demand curve M^d and the equilibrium interest rate has fallen from i_1 to i_2. **When the money supply increases (everything else remaining equal), interest rates will decline.**[6]

APPLICATION ✦ Money and Interest Rates

The liquidity preference analysis in Figure 10 seems to lead to the conclusion that an increase in the money supply will lower interest rates. This conclusion has important policy implications because it has frequently caused politicians to call for a more rapid growth of the money supply in an effort to drive down interest rates.

But is this conclusion that money and interest rates should be negatively related correct? Might there be other important factors left out of the liquidity preference analysis in Figure 10 that would reverse this conclusion? We will provide answers to these questions by applying the supply and demand analysis we have used in this chapter to obtain a deeper understanding of the relationship between money and interest rates.

An important criticism of the conclusion that an increase in the money supply lowers interest rates was raised by Milton Friedman, a Nobel laureate in economics. He acknowledged that the liquidity preference analysis was correct and called the result—that an increase in the money supply (*everything else remaining equal*) lowers interest rates—the *liquidity effect*. However, he viewed the liquidity effect as merely part of the story: An increase in the money supply might not leave "everything else equal" and will have other

---

[6]This same result can be generated using the bond supply and demand framework. As we will see in Chapter 14, the primary way that a central bank produces an increase in the money supply is by buying bonds and thereby decreasing the supply of bonds to the public. The resulting shift to the left of the supply curve for bonds will lead to an increase in the equilibrium price of bonds and a decline in the equilibrium interest rate.

effects on the economy that may make interest rates rise. If these effects are substantial, it is entirely possible that when the money supply increases, interest rates may also increase.

We have already laid the groundwork to discuss these other effects because we have shown how changes in income, the price level, and expected inflation affect the equilibrium interest rate.

1. *Income Effect.* Because an increasing money supply is an expansionary influence on the economy, it should raise national income and wealth. Both the liquidity preference and bond supply and demand frameworks indicate that interest rates will then rise (see Figures 6 and 9). Thus **the income effect of an increase in the money supply is a rise in interest rates in response to the higher level of income**.

2. *Price-Level Effect.* An increase in the money supply can also cause the overall price level in the economy to rise. The liquidity preference framework predicts that this will lead to a rise in interest rates. Thus **the price-level effect from an increase in the money supply is a rise in interest rates in response to the rise in the price level**.

3. *Expected-Inflation Effect.* The higher inflation rate that results from an increase in the money supply also affects interest rates by affecting the expected inflation rate. Specifically, an increase in the money supply may lead people to expect a higher price level in the future—and hence the expected inflation rate will be higher. The bond supply and demand framework has shown us that this increase in expected inflation will lead to a higher level of interest rates. Therefore, **the expected-inflation effect of an increase in the money supply is a rise in interest rates in response to the rise in the expected inflation rate**.

At first glance it might appear that the price-level effect and the expected-inflation effect are the same thing. They both indicate that increases in the price level induced by an increase in the money supply will raise interest rates. However, there is a subtle difference between the two, and this is why they are discussed as two separate effects.

Suppose that there is a onetime increase in the money supply today that leads to a rise in prices to a permanently higher level by next year. As the price level rises over the course of this year, the interest rate will rise via the price-level effect. Only at the end of the year, when the price level has risen to its peak, will the price-level effect be at a maximum.

The rising price level will also raise interest rates via the expected-inflation effect, because people will expect that inflation will be higher over the course of the year. However, when the price level stops rising next year, inflation and the expected inflation rate will return to zero. Any rise in interest rates as a result of the earlier rise in expected inflation will then be reversed. We thus see that in contrast to the price-level effect, which reaches its greatest impact next year, the expected-inflation effect will have its smallest impact (zero impact) next year. The basic difference between the two effects, then, is that the price-level effect remains even after prices have stopped rising, whereas the expected-inflation effect disappears.

An important point is that the expected-inflation effect will persist only as long as the price level continues to rise. As we will see in our discussion of monetary theory in subsequent chapters, a one-time increase in the money supply will not produce a continually rising price level; only a higher rate of money supply growth will. Thus a higher rate of money supply growth is needed if the expected-inflation effect is to persist.

Does a Higher Rate of Growth of the Money Supply Lower Interest Rates?

We can now put together all the effects we have discussed to help us decide whether our analysis supports the politicians who advocate a greater rate of growth of the money supply when they feel that interest rates are too high. Of all the effects, only the liquidity effect indicates that a higher rate of money growth will cause a decline in interest rates. In contrast, the income, price-level, and expected-inflation effects indicate that interest rates will rise when money growth is higher. Which of these effects are largest, and how quickly do they take effect? The answers are critical in determining whether interest rates will rise or fall when money supply growth is increased.

Generally, the liquidity effect from the greater money growth takes effect immediately, because the rising money supply leads to an immediate decline in the equilibrium interest rate. The income and price-level effects take time to work, because it takes time for the increasing money supply to raise the price level and income, which in turn raise interest rates. The expected-inflation effect, which also raises interest rates, can be slow or fast, depending on whether people adjust their expectations of inflation slowly or quickly when the money growth rate is increased.

Three possibilities are outlined in Figure 11; each shows how interest rates respond over time to an increased rate of money supply growth starting at time T. Panel (a) shows a case in which the liquidity effect dominates the other effects so that the interest rate falls from i_1 at time T to a final level of i_2. The liquidity effect operates quickly to lower the interest rate, but as time goes by, the other effects start to reverse some of the decline. Because the liquidity effect is larger than the others, however, the interest rate never rises back to its initial level.

Panel (b) has a smaller liquidity effect than the other effects, with the expected-inflation effect operating slowly because expectations of inflation are slow to adjust upward. Initially, the liquidity effect drives down the interest rate. Then the income, price-level, and expected-inflation effects begin to raise it. Because these effects are dominant, the interest rate eventually rises above its initial level to i_2. In the short run, lower interest rates result from increased money growth, but eventually they end up climbing above the initial level.

Panel (c) has the expected-inflation effect dominating as well as operating rapidly because people quickly raise their expectations of inflation when the rate of money growth increases. The expected-inflation effect begins immediately to overpower the liquidity effect, and the interest rate immediately starts to climb. Over time, as the income and price-level effects start to take hold, the interest rate rises even higher, and the eventual outcome is an interest rate that is substantially higher than the initial interest rate. The result shows clearly that increasing money supply growth is not the answer to reducing interest rates; rather, money growth should be reduced to lower interest rates!

An important issue for economic policymakers is which of these three scenarios is closest to reality. If a decline in interest rates is desired, then an increase in money supply growth is called for when the liquidity effect dominates the other effects, as in panel (a). A decrease in money growth is appropriate when the other effects dominate the liquidity effect and expectations of inflation adjust rapidly, as in panel (c). If the other effects dominate the liquidity effect but expectations of inflation adjust only slowly, as in panel (b), then whether you want to increase or decrease money growth depends on whether you care more about what happens in the short run or the long run.

Which scenario is supported by the evidence? The relationship of interest rates and money growth from 1950 to 2008 is plotted in Figure 12. When the rate of money supply growth began to climb in the mid-1960s, interest rates rose, indicating that the liquidity effect was dominated by the price-level, income, and expected-inflation effects. By the 1970s, interest rates reached levels unprecedented in the post–World War II period, as did the rate of money supply growth.

The scenario depicted in panel (a) of Figure 11 seems doubtful, and the case for lowering interest rates by raising the rate of money growth is much weakened. Looking

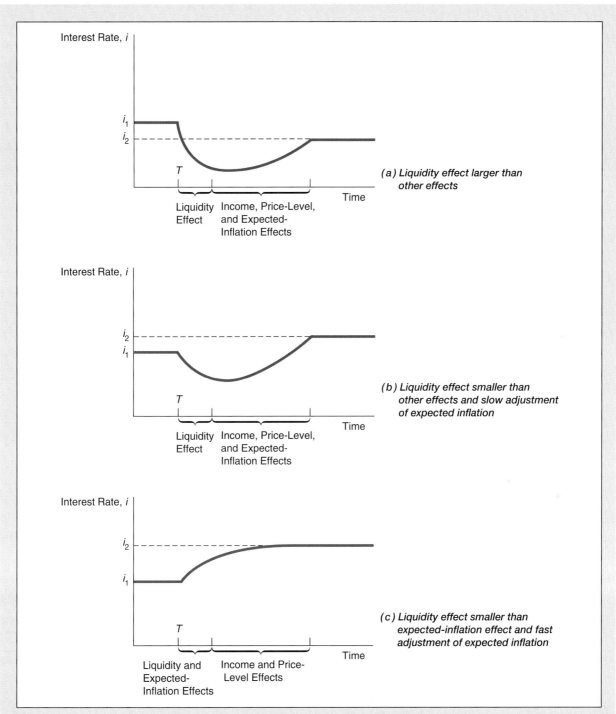

FIGURE 11   Response over Time to an Increase in Money Supply Growth

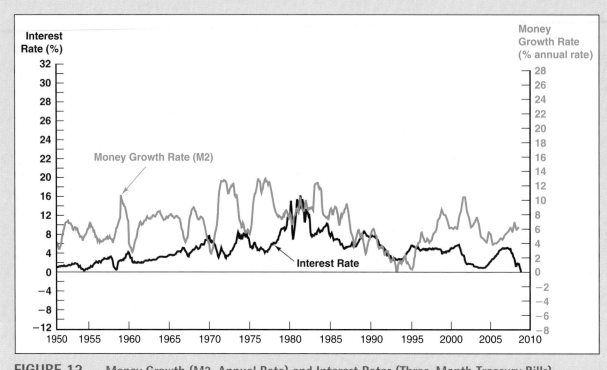

FIGURE 12   Money Growth (M2, Annual Rate) and Interest Rates (Three-Month Treasury Bills), 1950–2008

Sources: Federal Reserve: www.federalreserve.gov/releases/h6/hist/h6hist1.txt.

back at Figure 5, which shows the relationship between interest rates and expected inflation, you should not find this too surprising. The rise in the rate of money supply growth in the 1960s and 1970s is matched by a large rise in expected inflation, which would lead us to predict that the expected-inflation effect would be dominant. It is the most plausible explanation for why interest rates rose in the face of higher money growth. However, Figure 12 does not really tell us which one of the two scenarios, panel (b) or panel (c) of Figure 11, is more accurate. It depends critically on how fast people's expectations about inflation adjust. However, recent research using more sophisticated methods than just looking at a graph like Figure 12 do indicate that increased money growth temporarily lowers short-term interest rates.[7]

---

[7]See Lawrence J. Christiano and Martin Eichenbaum, "Identification and the Liquidity Effect of a Monetary Policy Shock," in *Business Cycles, Growth, and Political Economy*, ed. Alex Cukierman, Zvi Hercowitz, and Leonardo Leiderman (Cambridge, MA: MIT Press, 1992), pp. 335–370; Eric M. Leeper and David B. Gordon, "In Search of the Liquidity Effect," *Journal of Monetary Economics* 29 (1992): 341–370; Steven Strongin, "The Identification of Monetary Policy Disturbances: Explaining the Liquidity Puzzle," *Journal of Monetary Economics* 35 (1995): 463–497; Adrian Pagan and John C. Robertson, "Resolving the Liquidity Effect," *Federal Reserve Bank of St. Louis Review* 77 (May–June 1995): 33–54; and Ben S. Bernanke and Ilian Mihov, "Measuring Monetary Policy," *Quarterly Journal of Economics* 113, 3 (August 1998), pp. 869–902.

SUMMARY

1. The theory of asset demand tells us that the quantity demanded of an asset is (a) positively related to wealth, (b) positively related to the expected return on the asset relative to alternative assets, (c) negatively related to the riskiness of the asset relative to alternative assets, and (d) positively related to the liquidity of the asset relative to alternative assets.

2. The supply and demand analysis for bonds provides one theory of how interest rates are determined. It predicts that interest rates will change when there is a change in demand because of changes in income (or wealth), expected returns, risk, or liquidity or when there is a change in supply because of changes in the attractiveness of investment opportunities, the real cost of borrowing, or the government budget.

3. An alternative theory of how interest rates are determined is provided by the liquidity preference frame-

work, which analyzes the supply of and demand for money. It shows that interest rates will change when there is a change in the demand for money because of changes in income or the price level or when there is a change in the supply of money.

4. There are four possible effects of an increase in the money supply on interest rates: the liquidity effect, the income effect, the price-level effect, and the expected-inflation effect. The liquidity effect indicates that a rise in money supply growth will lead to a decline in interest rates; the other effects work in the opposite direction. The evidence seems to indicate that the income, price-level, and expected-inflation effects dominate the liquidity effect such that an increase in money supply growth leads to higher—rather than lower—interest rates.

KEY TERMS

asset market approach, p. 97

demand curve, p. 94

excess demand, p. 96

excess supply, p. 96

expected return, p. 91

Fisher effect, p. 104

liquidity, p. 92

liquidity preference framework, p. 109

market equilibrium, p. 96

opportunity cost, p. 110

risk, p. 92

supply curve, p. 95

theory of asset demand, p. 93

wealth, p. 91

QUESTIONS AND PROBLEMS

All questions and problems are available in (myeconlab) *at* www.myeconlab.com/mishkin.

1. Explain why you would be more or less willing to buy a share of Microsoft stock in the following situations:
   a. Your wealth falls.
   b. You expect the stock to appreciate in value.
   c. The bond market becomes more liquid.
   d. You expect gold to appreciate in value.
   e. Prices in the bond market become more volatile.

2. Explain why you would be more or less willing to buy a house under the following circumstances:
   a. You just inherited $100,000.
   b. Real estate commissions fall from 6% of the sales price to 5% of the sales price.
   c. You expect Microsoft stock to double in value next year.
   d. Prices in the stock market become more volatile.
   e. You expect housing prices to fall.

3. Explain why you would be more or less willing to buy gold under the following circumstances:
   a. Gold again becomes acceptable as a medium of exchange.
   b. Prices in the gold market become more volatile.
   c. You expect inflation to rise, and gold prices tend to move with the aggregate price level.
   d. You expect interest rates to rise.

4. Explain why you would be more or less willing to buy long-term AT&T bonds under the following circumstances:
   a. Trading in these bonds increases, making them easier to sell.
   b. You expect a bear market in stocks (stock prices are expected to decline).
   c. Brokerage commissions on stocks fall.
   d. You expect interest rates to rise.
   e. Brokerage commissions on bonds fall.

5. What would happen to the demand for Rembrandt paintings if the stock market undergoes a boom? Why?

Answer each question by drawing the appropriate supply and demand diagrams.

6. An important way in which the Federal Reserve decreases the money supply is by selling bonds to the public. Using a supply and demand analysis for bonds, show what effect this action has on interest rates. Is your answer consistent with what you would expect to find with the liquidity preference framework?

7. Using both the liquidity preference framework and the supply and demand for bonds framework, show why interest rates are procyclical (rising when the economy is expanding and falling during recessions).

8. Why should a rise in the price level (but not in expected inflation) cause interest rates to rise when the nominal money supply is fixed?

9. Find the "Credit Markets" column in the *Wall Street Journal*. Underline the statements in the column that explain bond price movements, and draw the appropri-ate supply and demand diagrams that support these statements.

10. What effect will a sudden increase in the volatility of gold prices have on interest rates?

11. How might a sudden increase in people's expectations of future real estate prices affect interest rates?

12. Explain what effect a large federal deficit might have on interest rates.

13. Using both the supply and demand for bonds and liquidity preference frameworks, show what the effect is on interest rates when the riskiness of bonds rises. Are the results the same in the two frameworks?

14. If the price level falls next year, remaining fixed thereafter, and the money supply is fixed, what is likely to happen to interest rates over the next two years? (*Hint:* Take account of both the price-level effect and the expected-inflation effect.)

15. Will there be an effect on interest rates if brokerage commissions on stocks fall? Explain your answer.

Using Economic Analysis to Predict the Future

16. The president of the United States announces in a press conference that he will fight the higher inflation rate with a new anti-inflation program. Predict what will happen to interest rates if the public believes him.

17. The chairman of the Fed announces that interest rates will rise sharply next year, and the market believes him. What will happen to today's interest rate on AT&T bonds, such as the $8\frac{1}{8}$s of 2022?

18. Predict what will happen to interest rates if the public suddenly expects a large increase in stock prices.

19. Predict what will happen to interest rates if prices in the bond market become more volatile.

20. If the next chair of the Federal Reserve Board has a reputation for advocating an even slower rate of money growth than the current chair, what will happen to interest rates? Discuss the possible resulting situations.

WEB EXERCISES

1. One of the largest single influences on the level of interest rates is inflation. There are a number of sites that report inflation over time. Go to ftp://ftp.bls.gov/pub/special.requests/cpi/cpiai.txt and review the data available. Note that the last columns report various averages. Move these data into a spreadsheet using the method discussed in the Web exploration at the end of Chapter 1. What has the average rate of inflation been since 1950, 1960, 1970, 1980, and 1990? Which year had the lowest level of inflation? Which year had the highest level of inflation?

2. Increasing prices erode the purchasing power of the dollar. It is interesting to compute what goods would have cost at some point in the past after adjusting for inflation. Go to http://minneapolisfed.org/index.cfm. What would a car that cost $22,000 today have cost the year that you were born?

3. One of the points made in this chapter is that inflation erodes investment returns. Go to www.moneychimp .com/articles/econ/inflation_calculator.htm and review how changes in inflation alter your real return. What happens to the difference between the adjusted value of an investment compared to its inflation-adjusted value as

   a. Inflation increases?

   b. The investment horizon lengthens?

   c. Expected returns increase?

WEB REFERENCES

ftp://ftp.bls.gov/pub/special.requests/cpi/cpiai.txt

Contains historical information about inflation.

www.federalreserve.gov/releases/H6/Current

The Federal Reserve reports money supply data at 4:30 p.m. every Thursday.

 ## MyEconLab CAN HELP YOU GET A BETTER GRADE

If your exam were tomorrow, would you be ready? For each chapter, MyEconLab Practice Test and Study Plans pinpoint which sections you have mastered and which ones you need to study. That way, you are more efficient with your study time, and you are better prepared for your exams.

To see how it works, turn to page 20 and then go to: www.myeconlab.com/mishkin

The Risk and Term Structure of Interest Rates

Preview

In our supply and demand analysis of interest-rate behavior in Chapter 5, we examined the determination of just one interest rate. Yet we saw earlier that there are enormous numbers of bonds on which the interest rates can and do differ. In this chapter, we complete the interest-rate picture by examining the relationship of the various interest rates to one another. Understanding why they differ from bond to bond can help businesses, banks, insurance companies, and private investors decide which bonds to purchase as investments and which ones to sell.

We first look at why bonds with the same term to maturity have different interest rates. The relationship among these interest rates is called the **risk structure of interest rates**, although risk, liquidity, and income tax rules all play a role in determining the risk structure. A bond's term to maturity also affects its interest rate, and the relationship among interest rates on bonds with different terms to maturity is called the **term structure of interest rates**. In this chapter, we examine the sources and causes of fluctuations in interest rates relative to one another and look at a number of theories that explain these fluctuations.

RISK STRUCTURE OF INTEREST RATES

Figure 1 shows the yields to maturity for several categories of long-term bonds from 1919 to 2008. It shows us two important features of interest-rate behavior for bonds of the same maturity: Interest rates on different categories of bonds differ from one another in any given year, and the spread (or difference) between the interest rates varies over time. The interest rates on municipal bonds, for example, are higher than those on U.S. government (Treasury) bonds in the late 1930s but lower thereafter. In addition, the spread between the interest rates on Baa corporate bonds (riskier than Aaa corporate bonds) and U.S. government bonds is very large during the Great Depression years 1930–1933, is smaller during the 1940s–1960s, and then widens again afterward. Which factors are responsible for these phenomena?

Default Risk

One attribute of a bond that influences its interest rate is its risk of **default**, which occurs when the issuer of the bond is unable or unwilling to make interest payments when promised or pay off the face value when the bond matures. A corporation suffering big losses, such as the major airline companies like United, Delta, US Airways, and

FIGURE 1   **Long-Term Bond Yields, 1919–2008**

Sources: Board of Governors of the Federal Reserve System, *Banking and Monetary Statistics, 1941–1970*; Federal Reserve: www.federalreserve.gov/releases/h15/data.htm.

Northwest in the mid-2000s, might be more likely to suspend interest payments on its bonds. The default risk on its bonds would therefore be quite high. By contrast, U.S. Treasury bonds have usually been considered to have no default risk because the federal government can always increase taxes to pay off its obligations. Bonds like these with no default risk are called **default-free bonds**. (However, during the budget negotiations in Congress in 1995 and 1996, the Republicans threatened to let Treasury bonds default, and this had an impact on the bond market. The spread between the interest rates on bonds with default risk and default-free bonds, both of the same maturity, called the **risk premium**, indicates how much additional interest people must earn to be willing to hold that risky bond. Our supply and demand analysis of the bond market in Chapter 5 can be used to explain why a bond with default risk always has a positive risk premium and why the higher the default risk is, the larger the risk premium will be.

To examine the effect of default risk on interest rates, let us look at the supply and demand diagrams for the default-free (U.S. Treasury) and corporate long-term bond markets in Figure 2. To make the diagrams somewhat easier to read, let's assume that initially corporate bonds have the same default risk as U.S. Treasury bonds. In this case, these two bonds have the same attributes (identical risk and maturity); their equilibrium prices and interest rates will initially be equal ($P_1^c = P_1^T$ and $i_1^c = i_1^T$), and the risk premium on corporate bonds ($i_1^c - i_1^T$) will be zero.

If the possibility of a default increases because a corporation begins to suffer large losses, the default risk on corporate bonds will increase, and the expected return on these bonds will decrease. In addition, the corporate bond's return will be more uncertain.

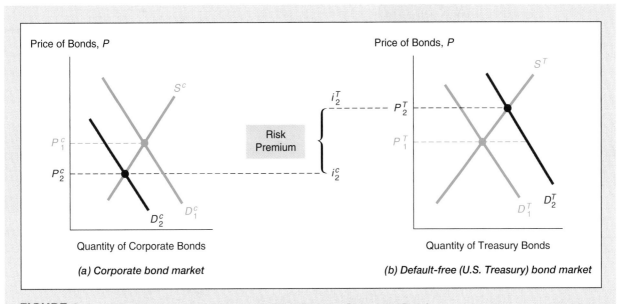

Price of Bonds, *P*   **Price of Bonds, *P***

Quantity of Corporate Bonds   Quantity of Treasury Bonds

(a) Corporate bond market   *(b) Default-free (U.S. Treasury) bond market*

FIGURE 2   **Response to an Increase in Default Risk on Corporate Bonds**
Initially $P_1^c = P_1^T$ and the risk premium is zero. An increase in default risk on corporate bonds shifts the demand curve from D_1^c to D_2^c. Simultaneously, it shifts the demand curve for Treasury bonds from D_1^T to D_2^T. The equilibrium price for corporate bonds falls from P_1^c to P_2^c, and the equilibrium interest rate on corporate bonds rises to i_2^c. In the Treasury market, the equilibrium bond price rises from P_1^T to P_2^T, and the equilibrium interest rate falls to i_2^T. The brace indicates the difference between i_2^c and i_2^T, the risk premium on corporate bonds. (Note that because P_2^c is lower than P_2^T, i_2^c is greater than i_2^T.)

The theory of asset demand predicts that because the expected return on the corporate bond falls relative to the expected return on the default-free Treasury bond while its relative riskiness rises, the corporate bond is less desirable (holding everything else equal), and demand for it will fall. Another way of thinking about this is that if you were an investor, you would want to hold (demand) a smaller amount of corporate bonds. The demand curve for corporate bonds in panel (a) of Figure 2 then shifts to the left, from to D_1^c to D_2^c.

At the same time, the expected return on default-free Treasury bonds increases relative to the expected return on corporate bonds, while their relative riskiness declines. The Treasury bonds thus become more desirable, and demand rises, as shown in panel (b) by the rightward shift in the demand curve for these bonds from D_1^T to D_2^T.

As we can see in Figure 2, the equilibrium price for corporate bonds falls from P_1^c to P_2^c, and since the bond price is negatively related to the interest rate, the equilibrium interest rate on corporate bonds rises to i_2^c. At the same time, however, the equilibrium price for the Treasury bonds rises from P_1^T to P_2^T and the equilibrium interest rate falls to i_2^T. The spread between the interest rates on corporate and default-free bonds—that is, the risk premium on corporate bonds—has risen from zero to $i_2^c - i_2^T$. We can now conclude that **a bond with default risk will always have a positive risk premium, and an increase in its default risk will raise the risk premium**.

Because default risk is so important to the size of the risk premium, purchasers of bonds need to know whether a corporation is likely to default on its bonds. This

TABLE 1

Bond Ratings by Moody's, Standard and Poor's, and Fitch

Rating			
Moody's	S&P	Fitch	Definitions
Aaa	AAA	AAA	Prime Maximum Safety
Aa1	AA-	AA-	High Grade High Quality
Aa2	AA	AA	
Aa3	AA-	AA-	
A1	A+	A+	Upper Medium Grade
A2	A	A	
A3	A-	A-	
Baa1	BBB+	BBB+	Lower Medium Grade
Baa2	BBB	BBB	
Baa3	BBB-	BBB-	
Ba1	BB+	BB+	Non Investment Grade
Ba2	BB	BB	Speculative
Ba3	BB-	BB-	
B1	B-	B-	Highly Speculative
B2	B	B	
B3	B-	B-	
Caa1	CCC+	CCC	Substantial Risk
Caa2	CCC	—	In Poor Standing
Caa3	CCC-	—	
Ca	—	—	Extremely Speculative
C	—	—	May be in Default
—	—	DDD	Default
—	—	DD	—
—	D	D	

information is provided by **credit-rating agencies**, investment advisory firms that rate the quality of corporate and municipal bonds in terms of the probability of default. Table 1 provides the ratings and their description for the three largest credit-rating agencies, Moody's Investor Service, Standard and Poor's Corporation and Fitch Ratings. Bonds with relatively low risk of default are called *investment-grade* securities and have a rating of Baa (or BBB) and above. Bonds with ratings below Baa (or BBB) have higher default risk and have been aptly dubbed speculative-grade or **junk bonds**. Because these bonds always have higher interest rates than investment-grade securities, they are also referred to as high-yield bonds.

Next let's look at Figure 1 at the beginning of the chapter and see if we can explain the relationship between interest rates on corporate and U.S. Treasury bonds. Corporate bonds always have higher interest rates than U.S. Treasury bonds because they always have some risk of default, whereas U.S. Treasury bonds do not. Because Baa-rated corporate bonds have a greater default risk than the higher-rated Aaa bonds, their risk premium is greater, and the Baa rate therefore always exceeds the Aaa rate. We can use the same analysis to explain the huge jump in the risk premium on Baa corporate bond rates during the Great Depression years 1930–1933 and the rise in the risk premium after 1970 (see Figure 1). The depression period saw a very high rate of business failures and defaults. As we would expect, these factors led to a substantial increase in the default risk for bonds issued by vulnerable corporations, and the risk premium for Baa bonds reached unprecedentedly high levels. Since 1970, we have again seen higher levels of business failures and defaults, although they were still well below Great Depression levels. Again, as expected, both default risks and risk premiums for corporate bonds rose, widening the spread between interest rates on corporate bonds and Treasury bonds.

APPLICATION   ✦   The Subprime Collapse and the Baa-Treasury Spread

Starting in August 2007, the collapse of the subprime mortgage market led to large losses in financial institutions (which we will discuss more extensively in Chapter 9). As a consequence of the subprime collapse, many investors began to doubt the financial health of corporations with low credit ratings such as Baa and even the reliability of the ratings themselves. The perceived increase in default risk for Baa bonds made them less desirable at any given interest rate, decreased the quantity demanded, and shifted the demand curve for Baa bonds to the left. As shown in panel (a) of Figure 2, the interest rate on Baa bonds should have risen, which is indeed what happened. Interest rates on Baa bonds rose by 280 basis points (2.80 percentage points) from 6.63% at the end of July 2007 to 9.43% at the most virulent stage of the crisis in mid-October, 2008. But the increase in perceived default risk for Baa bonds after the subprime collapse made default-free U.S. Treasury bonds relatively more attractive and shifted the demand curve for these securities to the right—an outcome described by some analysts as a "flight to quality." Just as our analysis predicts in Figure 2, interest rates on Treasury bonds fell by 80 basis points, from 4.78% at the end of July 2007 to 3.98% in mid-October, 2008. The spread between interest rates on Baa and Treasury bonds rose by 360 basis points from 1.85% before the crisis to 5.45% afterward.

Liquidity

Another attribute of a bond that influences its interest rate is its liquidity. As we learned in Chapter 5, a liquid asset is one that can be quickly and cheaply converted into cash if the need arises. The more liquid an asset is, the more desirable it is (holding everything else constant). United States Treasury bonds are the most liquid of all long-term bonds, because they are so widely traded that they are the easiest to sell quickly and the cost of selling them is low. Corporate bonds are not as liquid, because fewer bonds for any one corporation are traded; thus it can be costly to sell these bonds in an emergency, because it might be hard to find buyers quickly.

How does the reduced liquidity of the corporate bonds affect their interest rates relative to the interest rate on Treasury bonds? We can use supply and demand analysis with the same figure that was used to analyze the effect of default risk, Figure 2, to show that the lower liquidity of corporate bonds relative to Treasury bonds increases the spread between the interest rates on these two bonds. Let us start the analysis by assuming that initially corporate and Treasury bonds are equally liquid and all their other attributes are the same. As shown in Figure 2, their equilibrium prices and interest rates will initially be equal: $P_1^c = P_1^T$ and $i_1^c = i_1^T$. If the corporate bond becomes less liquid than the Treasury bond because it is less widely traded, then (as the theory of asset demand indicates) demand for it will fall, shifting its demand curve from D_1^c to D_2^c as in panel (a). The Treasury bond now becomes relatively more liquid in comparison with the corporate bond, so its demand curve shifts rightward from D_1^T to D_2^T as in panel (b). The shifts in the curves in Figure 2 show that the price of the less liquid corporate bond falls and its interest rate rises, while the price of the more liquid Treasury bond rises and its interest rate falls.

The result is that the spread between the interest rates on the two bond types has risen. Therefore, the differences between interest rates on corporate bonds and Treasury bonds (that is, the risk premiums) reflect not only the corporate bond's default risk but also its liquidity. This is why a risk premium is more accurately a "risk and liquidity premium," but convention dictates that it is called a *risk premium*.

Income Tax Considerations

Returning to Figure 1, we are still left with one puzzle—the behavior of municipal bond rates. Municipal bonds are certainly not default-free: U.S. state and local governments have defaulted on the municipal bonds they have issued in the past, particularly during the Great Depression and even more recently in the case of Orange County, California, in 1994. Also, municipal bonds are not as liquid as U.S. Treasury bonds.

Why is it, then, that these bonds have had lower interest rates than U.S. Treasury bonds for at least 40 years, as indicated in Figure 1? The explanation lies in the fact that interest payments on municipal bonds are exempt from federal income taxes, a factor that has the same effect on the demand for municipal bonds as an increase in their expected return.

Let us imagine that you have a high enough income to put you in the 35% income tax bracket, where for every extra dollar of income you have to pay 35 cents to the federal government. If you own a $1,000-face-value U.S. Treasury bond that sells for $1,000 and has a coupon payment of $100, you get to keep only $65 of the payment after taxes. Although the bond has a 10% interest rate, you actually earn only 6.5% after taxes.

Suppose, however, that you put your savings into a $1,000-face-value municipal bond that sells for $1,000 and pays only $80 in coupon payments. Its interest rate is only 8%, but because it is a tax-exempt security, you pay no federal income taxes on the $80 coupon payment, so you earn 8% after taxes. Clearly, you earn more on the municipal bond after taxes, so you are willing to hold the riskier and less liquid municipal bond even though it has a lower interest rate than the U.S. Treasury bond. (This was not true before World War II, when the tax-exempt status of municipal bonds did not convey much of an advantage because federal income tax rates were extremely low.)

Another way of understanding why municipal bonds have lower interest rates than Treasury bonds is to use the supply and demand analysis depicted in Figure 3. We initially assume that municipal and Treasury bonds have identical attributes and so have the same bond prices as drawn in the figure: $P_1^m = P_1^T$, and the same interest rates. Once the municipal bonds are given a tax advantage that raises their after-tax expected return relative to Treasury bonds and makes them more desirable, demand for them rises, and their demand curve shifts to the right, from D_1^m to D_2^m. The result is that their equilibrium bond price rises from P_1^m to P_2^m, and their equilibrium interest rate falls. By contrast,

FIGURE 3   **Interest Rates on Municipal and Treasury Bonds**
When the municipal bond is given tax-free status, demand for the municipal bond shifts rightward from D_1^m to D_2^m and demand for the Treasury bond shifts leftward from D_1^T to D_2^T. The equilibrium price of the municipal bond rises from P_1^m to P_2^m, so its interest rate falls, while the equilibrium price of the Treasury bond falls from P_1^T to P_2^T and its interest rate rises. The result is that municipal bonds end up with lower interest rates than those on Treasury bonds.

Treasury bonds have now become less desirable relative to municipal bonds; demand for Treasury bonds decreases, and D_1^T shifts to D_2^T. The Treasury bond price falls from P_1^T to P_2^T, and the interest rate rises. The resulting lower interest rates for municipal bonds and higher interest rates for Treasury bonds explain why municipal bonds can have interest rates below those of Treasury bonds.[1]

Summary

The risk structure of interest rates (the relationship among interest rates on bonds with the same maturity) is explained by three factors: default risk, liquidity, and the income tax treatment of a bond's interest payments. As a bond's default risk increases, the risk premium on that bond (the spread between its interest rate and the interest rate on a default-free Treasury bond) rises. The greater liquidity of Treasury bonds also explains why their interest rates are lower than interest rates on less liquid bonds. If a bond has a favorable tax treatment, as do municipal bonds, whose interest payments are exempt from federal income taxes, its interest rate will be lower.

---

[1]In contrast to corporate bonds, Treasury bonds are exempt from U.S. state and local income taxes. Using the analysis in the text, you should be able to show that this feature of Treasury bonds provides an additional reason why interest rates on corporate bonds are higher than those on Treasury bonds.

APPLICATION ✦ Effects of the Bush Tax Cut and Its Possible Repeal on Bond Interest Rates

The Bush tax cut passed in 2001 scheduled a reduction of the top income tax bracket from 39% to 35% over a ten-year period. What is the effect of this income tax decrease on interest rates in the municipal bond market relative to those in the Treasury bond market?

Our supply and demand analysis provides the answer. A decreased income tax rate for wealthy people means that the after-tax expected return on tax-free municipal bonds relative to that on Treasury bonds is lower, because the interest on Treasury bonds is now taxed at a lower rate. Because municipal bonds now become less desirable, their demand decreases, shifting the demand curve to the left, which lowers their price and raises their interest rate. Conversely, the lower income tax rate makes Treasury bonds more desirable; this change shifts their demand curve to the right, raises their price, and lowers their interest rates.

Our analysis thus shows that the Bush tax cut raised the interest rates on municipal bonds relative to the interest rate on Treasury bonds.

With the possible repeal of the Bush tax cuts for wealthy people that may occur under President Obama, the analysis would be reversed. Higher tax rates would raise the after-tax expected return on tax-free municipal bonds relative to Treasurys. Demand for municipal bonds would increase, shifting the demand curve to the right, which raises their price and lowers their interest rate. Conversely, the higher tax rate would make Treasury bonds less desirable, shifting their demand curve to the left, lowering their price, and raising their interest rate. Higher tax rates would thus result in lower interest rates on municipal bonds relative to the interest rate on Treasury bonds.

TERM STRUCTURE OF INTEREST RATES

We have seen how risk, liquidity, and tax considerations (collectively embedded in the risk structure) can influence interest rates. Another factor that influences the interest rate on a bond is its term to maturity: Bonds with identical risk, liquidity, and tax characteristics may have different interest rates because their time remaining to maturity is different. A plot of the yields on bonds with differing terms to maturity but the same risk, liquidity, and tax considerations is called a **yield curve**, and it describes the term structure of interest rates for particular types of bonds, such as government bonds. The Following the Financial News box shows several yield curves for Treasury securities that were published in the *Wall Street Journal*. Yield curves can be classified as upward-sloping, flat, and downward-sloping (the last sort is often referred to as an **inverted yield curve**). When yield curves slope upward, the most usual case, the long-term interest rates are above the short-term interest rates; when yield curves are flat, as in the Following the Financial News box, short- and long-term interest rates are the same; and when yield curves are inverted, long-term interest rates are below short-term interest rates. Yield curves can also have more complicated shapes in which they first slope up and then down, or vice versa. Why do we usually see upward slopes of the yield curve but sometimes other shapes?

Following the Financial News   Yield Curves

The *Wall Street Journal* publishes a daily plot of the yield curves for Treasury securities, an example of which is presented here. It is found in the Money and Investing section.

The numbers on the vertical axis indicate the interest rate for the Treasury security, with the maturity given by the numbers on the horizontal axis.

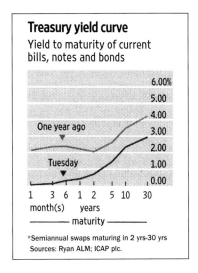

Source: Wall Street Journal, Wednesday, January 21, 2009. p. C4

Besides explaining why yield curves take on different shapes at different times, a good theory of the term structure of interest rates must explain the following three important empirical facts:

1. As we see in Figure 4, interest rates on bonds of different maturities move together over time.
2. When short-term interest rates are low, yield curves are more likely to have an upward slope; when short-term interest rates are high, yield curves are more likely to slope downward and be inverted.
3. Yield curves almost always slope upward, as in the Following the Financial News box.

Three theories have been put forward to explain the term structure of interest rates—that is, the relationship among interest rates on bonds of different maturities reflected in yield curve patterns: (1) the expectations theory, (2) the segmented markets theory, and (3) the liquidity premium theory, each of which is described in the following sections. The expectations theory does a good job of explaining the first two facts on our list, but not the third. The segmented markets theory can explain fact 3 but not the other two facts, which are well explained by the expectations theory. Because each theory explains facts that the other cannot, a natural way to seek a better understanding of the term structure is to combine features of both theories, which leads us to the liquidity premium theory, which can explain all three facts.

If the liquidity premium theory does a better job of explaining the facts and is hence the most widely accepted theory, why do we spend time discussing the other two theories? There are two reasons. First, the ideas in these two theories lay the groundwork

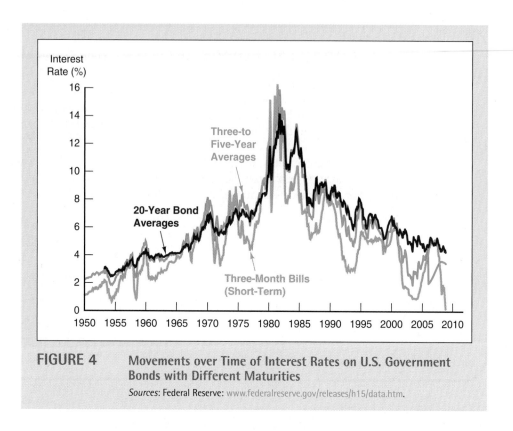

FIGURE 4   Movements over Time of Interest Rates on U.S. Government Bonds with Different Maturities

Sources: Federal Reserve: www.federalreserve.gov/releases/h15/data.htm.

for the liquidity premium theory. Second, it is important to see how economists modify theories to improve them when they find that the predicted results are inconsistent with the empirical evidence.

Expectations Theory

The **expectations theory** of the term structure states the following commonsense proposition: The interest rate on a long-term bond will equal an average of the short-term interest rates that people expect to occur over the life of the long-term bond. For example, if people expect that short-term interest rates will be 10% on average over the coming five years, the expectations theory predicts that the interest rate on bonds with five years to maturity will be 10%, too. If short-term interest rates were expected to rise even higher after this five-year period, so that the average short-term interest rate over the coming 20 years is 11%, then the interest rate on 20-year bonds would equal 11% and would be higher than the interest rate on five-year bonds. We can see that the explanation provided by the expectations theory for why interest rates on bonds of different maturities differ is that short-term interest rates are expected to have different values at future dates.

The key assumption behind this theory is that buyers of bonds do not prefer bonds of one maturity over another, so they will not hold any quantity of a bond if its expected return is less than that of another bond with a different maturity. Bonds that have this characteristic are said to be *perfect substitutes*. What this means in practice is that if bonds with different maturities are perfect substitutes, the expected return on these bonds must be equal.

To see how the assumption that bonds with different maturities are perfect substitutes leads to the expectations theory, let us consider the following two investment strategies:

1. Purchase a one-year bond, and when it matures in one year, purchase another one-year bond.
2. Purchase a two-year bond and hold it until maturity.

Because both strategies must have the same expected return if people are holding both one- and two-year bonds, the interest rate on the two-year bond must equal the average of the two one-year interest rates. For example, let's say that the current interest rate on the one-year bond is 9% and you expect the interest rate on the one-year bond next year to be 11%. If you pursue the first strategy of buying the two one-year bonds, the expected return over the two years will average out to be (9% + 11%)/2 = 10% per year. You will be willing to hold both the one- and two-year bonds only if the expected return per year of the two-year bond equals this return. Therefore, the interest rate on the two-year bond must equal 10%, the average interest rate on the two one-year bonds.

We can make this argument more general. For an investment of $1, consider the choice of holding, for two periods, a two-period bond or two one-period bonds. Using the definitions

i_t = today's (time t) interest rate on a one-period bond

i_{t+1}^e = interest rate on a one-period bond expected for next period (time $t + 1$)

i_{2t} = today's (time t) interest rate on the two-period bond

the expected return over the two periods from investing $1 in the two-period bond and holding it for the two periods can be calculated as

$$(1 + i_{2t})(1 + i_{2t}) - 1 = 1 + 2i_{2t} + (i_{2t})^2 - 1 = 2i_{2t} + (i_{2t})^2$$

After the second period, the $1 investment is worth $(1 + i_{2t})(1 + i_{2t})$. Subtracting the $1 initial investment from this amount and dividing by the initial $1 investment gives the rate of return calculated in the previous equation. Because $(i_{2t})^2$ is extremely small—if $i_{2t} = 10\% = 0.10$, then $(i_{2t})^2 = 0.01$—we can simplify the expected return for holding the two-period bond for the two periods to

$$2i_{2t}$$

With the other strategy, in which one-period bonds are bought, the expected return on the $1 investment over the two periods is

$$(1 + i_t)(1 + i_{t+1}^e) - 1 = 1 + i_t + i_{t+1}^e + i_t(i_{t+1}^e) - 1 = i_t + i_{t+1}^e + i_t(i_{t+1}^e)$$

This calculation is derived by recognizing that after the first period, the $1 investment becomes $1 + i_t$, and this is reinvested in the one-period bond for the next period, yielding an amount $(1 + i_t)(1 + i_{t+1}^e)$. Then subtracting the $1 initial investment from this amount and dividing by the initial investment of $1 gives the expected return for the strategy of holding one-period bonds for the two periods. Because $i_t(i_{t+1}^e)$ is also extremely small—if $i_t = i_{t+1}^e = 0.10$, then $i_t(i_{t+1}^e) = 0.01$—we can simplify this to

$$i_t + i_{t+1}^e$$

Both bonds will be held only if these expected returns are equal—that is, when

$$2i_{2t} = i_t + i_{t+1}^e$$

Solving for i_{2t} in terms of the one-period rates, we have

$$i_{2t} = \frac{i_t + i_{t+1}^e}{2} \tag{1}$$

which tells us that the two-period rate must equal the average of the two one-period rates. Graphically, this can be shown as

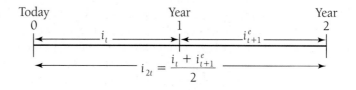

We can conduct the same steps for bonds with a longer maturity so that we can examine the whole term structure of interest rates. Doing so, we will find that the interest rate of i_{nt} on an n-period bond must be

$$i_{nt} = \frac{i_t + i_{t+1}^e + i_{t+2}^e + \ldots + i_{t+(n-1)}^e}{n} \tag{2}$$

Equation 2 states that the n-period interest rate equals the average of the one-period interest rates expected to occur over the n-period life of the bond. This is a restatement of the expectations theory in more precise terms.[2]

A simple numerical example might clarify what the expectations theory in Equation 2 is saying. If the one-year interest rate over the next five years is expected to be 5%, 6%, 7%, 8%, and 9%, Equation 2 indicates that the interest rate on the two-year bond would be

$$\frac{5\% + 6\%}{2} = 5.5\%$$

For the five-year bond it would be

$$\frac{5\% + 6\% + 7\% + 8\% + 9\%}{5} = 7\%$$

Doing a similar calculation for the one-, three-, and four-year interest rates, you should be able to verify that the one- to five-year interest rates are 5.0%, 5.5%, 6.0%, 6.5%, and 7.0%, respectively. Thus we see that the rising trend in expected short-term interest rates produces an upward-sloping yield curve along which interest rates rise as maturity lengthens.

The expectations theory is an elegant theory that explains why the term structure of interest rates (as represented by yield curves) changes at different times. When the yield curve is upward-sloping, the expectations theory suggests that short-term interest

---

[2]The analysis here has been conducted for discount bonds. Formulas for interest rates on coupon bonds would differ slightly from those used here, but would convey the same principle.

rates are expected to rise in the future, as we have seen in our numerical example. In this situation, in which the long-term rate is currently higher than the short-term rate, the average of future short-term rates is expected to be higher than the current short-term rate, which can occur only if short-term interest rates are expected to rise. This is what we see in our numerical example. When the yield curve is inverted (slopes downward), the average of future short-term interest rates is expected to be lower than the current short-term rate, implying that short-term interest rates are expected to fall, on average, in the future. Only when the yield curve is flat does the expectations theory suggest that short-term interest rates are not expected to change, on average, in the future.

The expectations theory also explains fact 1, which states that interest rates on bonds with different maturities move together over time. Historically, short-term interest rates have had the characteristic that if they increase today, they will tend to be higher in the future. Hence a rise in short-term rates will raise people's expectations of future short-term rates. Because long-term rates are the average of expected future short-term rates, a rise in short-term rates will also raise long-term rates, causing short- and long-term rates to move together.

The expectations theory also explains fact 2, which states that yield curves tend to have an upward slope when short-term interest rates are low and are inverted when short-term rates are high. When short-term rates are low, people generally expect them to rise to some normal level in the future, and the average of future expected short-term rates is high relative to the current short-term rate. Therefore, long-term interest rates will be substantially higher than current short-term rates, and the yield curve would then have an upward slope. Conversely, if short-term rates are high, people usually expect them to come back down. Long-term rates would then drop below short-term rates because the average of expected future short-term rates would be lower than current short-term rates and the yield curve would slope downward and become inverted.[3]

The expectations theory is an attractive theory because it provides a simple explanation of the behavior of the term structure, but unfortunately it has a major shortcoming: It cannot explain fact 3, which says that yield curves usually slope upward. The typical upward slope of yield curves implies that short-term interest rates are usually expected to rise in the future. In practice, short-term interest rates are just as likely to fall as they are to rise, and so the expectations theory suggests that the typical yield curve should be flat rather than upward-sloping.

Segmented Markets Theory

As the name suggests, the **segmented markets theory** of the term structure sees markets for different-maturity bonds as completely separate and segmented. The interest rate for each bond with a different maturity is then determined by the supply of and demand for that bond, with no effects from expected returns on other bonds with other maturities.

---

[3]The expectations theory explains another important fact about the relationship between short-term and long-term interest rates. As you can see in Figure 4, short-term interest rates are more volatile than long-term rates. If interest rates are *mean-reverting*—that is, if they tend to head back down after they are at unusually high levels or go back up when they are at unusually low levels—then an average of these short-term rates must necessarily have less volatility than the short-term rates themselves. Because the expectations theory suggests that the long-term rate will be an average of future short-term rates, it implies that the long-term rate will have less volatility than short-term rates.

The key assumption in the segmented markets theory is that bonds of different maturities are not substitutes at all, so the expected return from holding a bond of one maturity has no effect on the demand for a bond of another maturity. This theory of the term structure is at the opposite extreme to the expectations theory, which assumes that bonds of different maturities are perfect substitutes.

The argument for why bonds of different maturities are not substitutes is that investors have very strong preferences for bonds of one maturity but not for another, so they will be concerned with the expected returns only for bonds of the maturity they prefer. This might occur because they have a particular holding period in mind, and if they match the maturity of the bond to the desired holding period, they can obtain a certain return with no risk at all.[4] (We have seen in Chapter 4 that if the term to maturity equals the holding period, the return is known for certain because it equals the yield exactly, and there is no interest-rate risk.) For example, people who have a short holding period would prefer to hold short-term bonds. Conversely, if you were putting funds away for your young child to go to college, your desired holding period might be much longer, and you would want to hold longer-term bonds.

In the segmented markets theory, differing yield curve patterns are accounted for by supply and demand differences associated with bonds of different maturities. If, as seems sensible, investors have short desired holding periods and generally prefer bonds with shorter maturities that have less interest-rate risk, the segmented markets theory can explain fact 3, which states that yield curves typically slope upward. Because in the typical situation the demand for long-term bonds is relatively lower than that for short-term bonds, long-term bonds will have lower prices and higher interest rates, and hence the yield curve will typically slope upward.

Although the segmented markets theory can explain why yield curves usually tend to slope upward, it has a major flaw in that it cannot explain facts 1 and 2. First, because it views the market for bonds of different maturities as completely segmented, there is no reason for a rise in interest rates on a bond of one maturity to affect the interest rate on a bond of another maturity. Therefore, it cannot explain why interest rates on bonds of different maturities tend to move together (fact 1). Second, because it is not clear how demand and supply for short- versus long-term bonds change with the level of short-term interest rates, the theory cannot explain why yield curves tend to slope upward when short-term interest rates are low and to be inverted when short-term interest rates are high (fact 2).

Because each of our two theories explains empirical facts that the other cannot, a logical step is to combine the theories, which leads us to the liquidity premium theory.

Liquidity Premium and Preferred Habitat Theories

The **liquidity premium theory** of the term structure states that the interest rate on a long-term bond will equal an average of short-term interest rates expected to occur over the life of the long-term bond plus a liquidity premium (also referred to as a term premium) that responds to supply and demand conditions for that bond.

---

[4]The statement that there is no uncertainty about the return if the term to maturity equals the holding period is literally true only for a discount bond. For a coupon bond with a long holding period, there is some risk because coupon payments must be reinvested before the bond matures. Our analysis here is thus being conducted for discount bonds. However, the gist of the analysis remains the same for coupon bonds because the amount of this risk from reinvestment is small when coupon bonds have the same term to maturity as the holding period.

The liquidity premium theory's key assumption is that bonds of different maturities are substitutes, which means that the expected return on one bond *does* influence the expected return on a bond of a different maturity, but it allows investors to prefer one bond maturity over another. In other words, bonds of different maturities are assumed to be substitutes but not perfect substitutes. Investors tend to prefer shorter-term bonds because these bonds bear less interest-rate risk. For these reasons, investors must be offered a positive liquidity premium to induce them to hold longer-term bonds. Such an outcome would modify the expectations theory by adding a positive liquidity premium to the equation that describes the relationship between long- and short-term interest rates. The liquidity premium theory is thus written as

$$i_{nt} = \frac{i_t + i_{t+1}^e + i_{t+2}^e + \cdots + i_{t+(n-1)}^e}{n} + l_{nt} \tag{3}$$

where l_{nt} is the liquidity (term) premium for the n-period bond at time t, which is always positive and rises with the term to maturity of the bond, n.

Closely related to the liquidity premium theory is the **preferred habitat theory**, which takes a somewhat less direct approach to modifying the expectations hypothesis but comes to a similar conclusion. It assumes that investors have a preference for bonds of one maturity over another, a particular bond maturity (preferred habitat) in which they prefer to invest. Because they prefer bonds of one maturity over another, they will be willing to buy bonds that do not have the preferred maturity (habitat) only if they earn a somewhat higher expected return. Because investors are likely to prefer the habitat of short-term bonds over that of longer-term bonds, they are willing to hold long-term bonds only if they have higher expected returns. This reasoning leads to the same Equation 3 implied by the liquidity premium theory with a term premium that typically rises with maturity.

The relationship between the expectations theory and the liquidity premium and preferred habitat theories is shown in Figure 5. There we see that because the liquidity premium is always positive and typically grows as the term to maturity increases, the yield curve implied by the liquidity premium theory is always above the yield curve implied by the expectations theory and generally has a steeper slope. (Note that for simplicity we are assuming that the expectations theory yield curve is flat.)

A simple numerical example similar to the one we used for the expectations hypothesis further clarifies what the liquidity premium and preferred habitat theories in Equation 3 are saying. Again suppose that the one-year interest rate over the next five years is expected to be 5%, 6%, 7%, 8%, and 9%, while investors' preferences for holding short-term bonds means that the liquidity premiums for one- to five-year bonds are 0%, 0.25%, 0.5%, 0.75%, and 1.0%, respectively. Equation 3 then indicates that the interest rate on the two-year bond would be

$$\frac{5\% + 6\%}{2} + 0.25\% = 5.75\%$$

For the five-year bond it would be

$$\frac{5\% + 6\% + 7\% + 8\% + 9\%}{5} + 1\% = 8\%$$

Doing a similar calculation for the one-, three-, and four-year interest rates, you should be able to verify that the one- to five-year interest rates are 5.0%, 5.75%, 6.5%, 7.25%, and

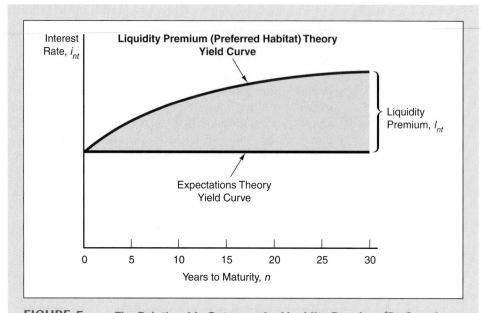

FIGURE 5   The Relationship Between the Liquidity Premium (Preferred Habitat) and Expectations Theory
Because the liquidity premium is always positive and grows as the term to maturity increases, the yield curve implied by the liquidity premium and preferred habitat theories is always above the yield curve implied by the expectations theory and has a steeper slope. For simplicity the yield curve implied by the expectations theory is drawn under the scenario of unchanging future one-year interest rates.

8.0%, respectively. Comparing these findings with those for the expectations theory, we see that the liquidity premium and preferred habitat theories produce yield curves that slope more steeply upward because of investors' preferences for short-term bonds.

Let's see if the liquidity premium and preferred habitat theories are consistent with all three empirical facts we have discussed. They explain fact 1, which states that interest rates on different-maturity bonds move together over time: A rise in short-term interest rates indicates that short-term interest rates will, on average, be higher in the future, and the first term in Equation 3 then implies that long-term interest rates will rise along with them.

They also explain why yield curves tend to have an especially steep upward slope when short-term interest rates are low and to be inverted when short-term rates are high (fact 2). Because investors generally expect short-term interest rates to rise to some normal level when they are low, the average of future expected short-term rates will be high relative to the current short-term rate. With the additional boost of a positive liquidity premium, long-term interest rates will be substantially higher than current short-term rates, and the yield curve will then have a steep upward slope. Conversely, if short-term rates are high, people usually expect them to come back down. Long-term rates will then drop below short-term rates because the average of expected future short-term rates will be so far below current short-term rates that despite positive liquidity premiums, the yield curve will slope downward.

The liquidity premium and preferred habitat theories explain fact 3, which states that yield curves typically slope upward, by recognizing that the liquidity premium rises with a bond's maturity because of investors' preferences for short-term bonds. Even if short-term interest rates are expected to stay the same on average in the future, long-term interest rates will be above short-term interest rates, and yield curves will typically slope upward.

How can the liquidity premium and preferred habitat theories explain the occasional appearance of inverted yield curves if the liquidity premium is positive? It must be that at times short-term interest rates are expected to fall so much in the future that the average of the expected short-term rates is well below the current short-term rate. Even when the positive liquidity premium is added to this average, the resulting long-term rate will still be lower than the current short-term interest rate.

As our discussion indicates, a particularly attractive feature of the liquidity premium and preferred habitat theories is that they tell you what the market is predicting about future short-term interest rates just from the slope of the yield curve. A steeply rising yield curve, as in panel (a) of Figure 6, indicates that short-term interest rates are

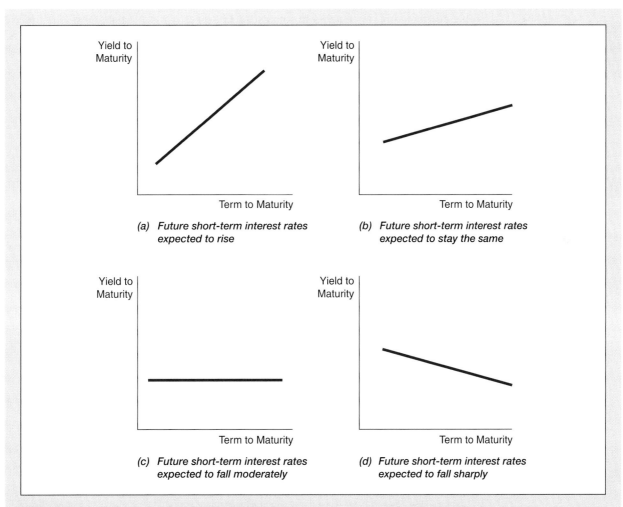

(a) *Future short-term interest rates expected to rise*

(b) *Future short-term interest rates expected to stay the same*

(c) *Future short-term interest rates expected to fall moderately*

(d) *Future short-term interest rates expected to fall sharply*

FIGURE 6   Yield Curves and the Market's Expectations of Future Short–Term Interest Rates According to the Liquidity Premium (Preferred Habitat) Theory

expected to rise in the future. A moderately steep yield curve, as in panel (b), indicates that short-term interest rates are not expected to rise or fall much in the future. A flat yield curve, as in panel (c), indicates that short-term rates are expected to fall moderately in the future. Finally, an inverted yield curve, as in panel (d), indicates that short-term interest rates are expected to fall sharply in the future.

Evidence on the Term Structure

In the 1980s, researchers examining the term structure of interest rates questioned whether the slope of the yield curve provides information about movements of future short-term interest rates.[5] They found that the spread between long- and short-term interest rates does not always help predict future short-term interest rates, a finding that may stem from substantial fluctuations in the liquidity (term) premium for long-term bonds. More recent research using more discriminating tests now favors a different view. It shows that the term structure contains quite a bit of information for the very short run (over the next several months) and the long run (over several years) but is unreliable at predicting movements in interest rates over the intermediate term (the time in between).[6] Research also finds that the yield curve helps forecast future inflation and business cycles (see the FYI box).

Summary

The liquidity premium and preferred habitat theories are the most widely accepted theories of the term structure of interest rates because they explain the major empirical facts about the term structure so well. They combine the features of both the expectations theory and the segmented markets theory by asserting that a long-term interest rate will be the sum of a liquidity (term) premium and the average of the short-term interest rates that are expected to occur over the life of the bond.

The liquidity premium and preferred habitat theories explain the following facts: (1) Interest rates on bonds of different maturities tend to move together over time, (2) yield curves usually slope upward, and (3) when short-term interest rates are low, yield curves are more likely to have a steep upward slope, whereas when short-term interest rates are high, yield curves are more likely to be inverted.

The theories also help us predict the movement of short-term interest rates in the future. A steep upward slope of the yield curve means that short-term rates are expected to rise, a mild upward slope means that short-term rates are expected to remain the same, a flat slope means that short-term rates are expected to fall moderately, and an inverted yield curve means that short-term rates are expected to fall sharply.

---

[5]Robert J. Shiller, John Y. Campbell, and Kermit L. Schoenholtz, "Forward Rates and Future Policy: Interpreting the Term Structure of Interest Rates," *Brookings Papers on Economic Activity* 1 (1983): 173–217; N. Gregory Mankiw and Lawrence H. Summers, "Do Long-Term Interest Rates Overreact to Short-Term Interest Rates?" *Brookings Papers on Economic Activity* 1 (1984): 223–242.

[6]Eugene Fama, "The Information in the Term Structure," *Journal of Financial Economics* 13 (1984): 509–528; Eugene Fama and Robert Bliss, "The Information in Long-Maturity Forward Rates," *American Economic Review* 77 (1987): 680–692; John Y. Campbell and Robert J. Shiller, "Cointegration and Tests of the Present Value Models," *Journal of Political Economy* 95 (1987): 1062–1088; John Y. Campbell and Robert J. Shiller, "Yield Spreads and Interest Rate Movements: A Bird's Eye View," *Review of Economic Studies* 58 (1991): 495–514.

FYI   **The Yield Curve as a Forecasting Tool for Inflation and the Business Cycle**

Because the yield curve contains information about future expected interest rates, it should also have the capacity to help forecast inflation and real output fluctuations. To see why, recall from Chapter 5 that rising interest rates are associated with economic booms and falling interest rates with recessions. When the yield curve is either flat or downward-sloping, it suggests that future short-term interest rates are expected to fall and, therefore, that the economy is more likely to enter a recession. Indeed, the yield curve is found to be an accurate predictor of the business cycle.[a]

In Chapter 4, we also learned that a nominal interest rate is composed of a real interest rate and expected inflation, implying that the yield curve contains information about both the future path of nominal interest rates and future inflation. A steep yield curve predicts a future increase in inflation, while a flat or downward-sloping yield curve forecasts a future decline in inflation.[b]

The ability of the yield curve to forecast business cycles and inflation is one reason why the slope of the yield curve is part of the tool kit of many economic forecasters and is often viewed as a useful indicator of the stance of monetary policy, with a steep yield curve indicating loose policy and a flat or downward-sloping yield curve indicating tight policy.

[a]For example, see Arturo Estrella and Frederic S. Mishkin, "Predicting U.S. Recessions: Financial Variables as Leading Indicators," *Review of Economics and Statistics*, 80 (February 1998): 45–61.

[b]Frederic S. Mishkin, "What Does the Term Structure Tell Us About Future Inflation?" *Journal of Monetary Economics* 25 (January 1990): 77–95; and Frederic S. Mishkin, "The Information in the Longer-Maturity Term Structure About Future Inflation," *Quarterly Journal of Economics* 55 (August 1990): 815–828.

APPLICATION ✦ Interpreting Yield Curves, 1980–2009

Figure 7 illustrates several yield curves that have appeared for U.S. government bonds in recent years. What do these yield curves tell us about the public's expectations of future movements of short-term interest rates?

The steep inverted yield curve that occurred on January 15, 1981, indicated that short-term interest rates were expected to decline sharply in the future. For longer-term interest rates with their positive liquidity premium to be well below the short-term interest rate, short-term interest rates must be expected to decline so sharply that their average is far below the current short-term rate. Indeed, the public's expectations of sharply lower short-term interest rates evident in the yield curve were realized soon after January 15; by March, three-month Treasury bill rates had declined from the 16% level to 13%.

The steep upward-sloping yield curves on March 28, 1985 and January 15, 2009 indicated that short-term interest rates would climb in the future. The long-term interest rate is higher than the short-term interest rate when short-term interest rates are expected to rise because their average plus the liquidity premium will be higher than the current short-term rate. The moderately upward-sloping yield curves on May 16, 1980, and March 3, 1997, indicated that short-term interest rates were expected neither to rise nor to fall in the near future. In this case, their average remains the same as the current short-term rate, and the positive liquidity premium for longer-term bonds explains the moderate upward slope of the yield curve. The flat yield curve of February 6, 2006 indicated that short-term interest rates were expected to fall slightly.

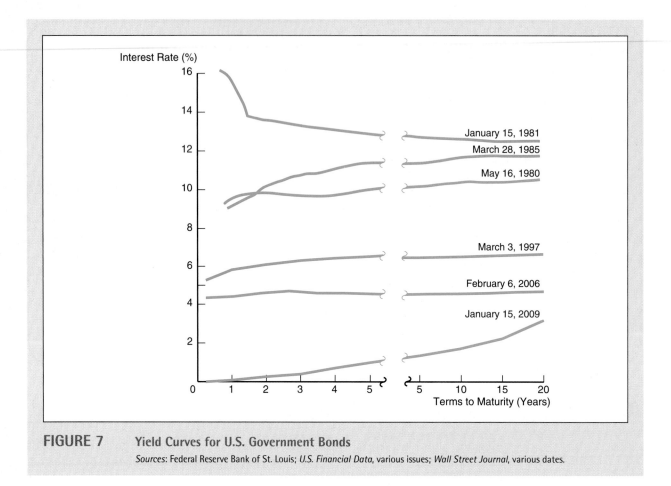

FIGURE 7 Yield Curves for U.S. Government Bonds

Sources: Federal Reserve Bank of St. Louis; *U.S. Financial Data,* various issues; *Wall Street Journal,* various dates.

SUMMARY

1. Bonds with the same maturity will have different interest rates because of three factors: default risk, liquidity, and tax considerations. The greater a bond's default risk, the higher its interest rate relative to other bonds; the greater a bond's liquidity, the lower its interest rate; and bonds with tax-exempt status will have lower interest rates than they otherwise would. The relationship among interest rates on bonds with the same maturity that arises because of these three factors is known as the *risk structure of interest rates*.

2. Four theories of the term structure provide explanations of how interest rates on bonds with different terms to maturity are related. The expectations theory views long-term interest rates as equaling the average of future short-term interest rates expected to occur over the life of the bond. By contrast, the segmented markets theory treats the determination of interest rates for each bond's maturity as the outcome of supply and demand in that market only. Neither of these theories by itself can explain the fact that interest rates on bonds of different maturities move together over time and that yield curves usually slope upward.

3. The liquidity premium (preferred habitat) theory combines the features of the other two theories, and by so doing are able to explain the facts just mentioned. It views long-term interest rates as equaling the average of future short-term interest rates expected to occur over the life of the bond plus a liquidity premium. This theory allows us to infer the market's expectations about the movement of future short-term interest

rates from the yield curve. A steeply upward-sloping curve indicates that future short-term rates are expected to rise, a mildly upward-sloping curve indicates that short-term rates are expected to stay the same, a flat curve indicates that short-term rates are expected to decline slightly, and an inverted yield curve indicates that a substantial decline in short-term rates is expected in the future.

KEY TERMS

credit-rating agencies, p. 126

default, p. 123

default-free bonds, p. 124

expectations theory, p. 132

inverted yield curve, p. 130

junk bonds, p. 126

liquidity premium theory, p. 136

preferred habitat theory, p. 137

risk premium, p. 124

risk structure of interest rates, p. 123

segmented markets theory, p. 135

term structure of interest rates, p. 123

yield curve, p. 130

QUESTIONS AND PROBLEMS

All questions and problems are available in myeconlab *at* www.myeconlab.com/mishkin.

1. Which should have the higher risk premium on its interest rates, a corporate bond with a Moody's Baa rating or a corporate bond with a C rating? Why?

2. Why do U.S. Treasury bills have lower interest rates than large-denomination negotiable bank CDs?

3. Risk premiums on corporate bonds are usually *anticyclical*; that is, they decrease during business cycle expansions and increase during recessions. Why is this so?

4. "If bonds of different maturities are close substitutes, their interest rates are more likely to move together." Is this statement true, false, or uncertain? Explain your answer.

5. If yield curves, on average, were flat, what would this say about the liquidity (term) premiums in the term structure? Would you be more or less willing to accept the expectations theory?

6. Assuming that the expectations theory is the correct theory of the term structure, calculate the interest rates in the term structure for maturities of one to five years, and plot the resulting yield curves for the following series of one-year interest rates over the next five years:
   a. 5%, 7%, 7%, 7%, 7%
   b. 5%, 4%, 4%, 4%, 4%
   How would your yield curves change if people preferred shorter-term bonds over longer-term bonds?

7. Assuming that the expectations theory is the correct theory of the term structure, calculate the interest rates in the term structure for maturities of one to five years, and plot the resulting yield curves for the following paths of one-year interest rates over the next five years:
   a. 5%, 6%, 7%, 6%, 5%
   b. 5%, 4%, 3%, 4%, 5%
   How would your yield curves change if people preferred shorter-term bonds over longer-term bonds?

8. If a yield curve looks like the one shown in Figure (a) below, what is the market predicting about the movement of future short-term interest rates? What might the yield curve indicate about the market's predictions for the inflation rate in the future?

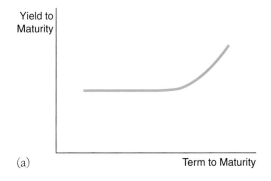

(a)

9. If a yield curve looks like the one shown in Figure (b) below, what is the market predicting about the movement of future short-term interest rates? What might

the yield curve indicate about the market's predictions for the inflation rate in the future?

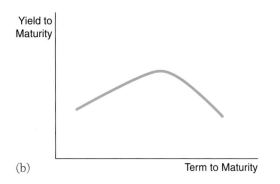

(b)

10. What effect would reducing income tax rates have on the interest rates of municipal bonds? Would interest rates of Treasury securities be affected, and if so, how?

Using Economic Analysis to Predict the Future

11. Predict what will happen to interest rates on a corporation's bonds if the U.S. government guarantees today that it will pay creditors if the corporation goes bankrupt in the future. What will happen to the interest rates on U.S. Treasury securities?

12. Predict what would happen to the risk premiums on corporate bonds if brokerage commissions were lowered in the corporate bond market.

13. If the U.S. federal income tax exemption on municipal bonds were abolished, what would happen to the interest rates on these bonds? What effect would the change have on interest rates on U.S. Treasury securities?

14. If the yield curve suddenly becomes steeper, how would you revise your predictions of interest rates in the future?

15. If expectations of future short-term interest rates suddenly fall, what would happen to the slope of the yield curve?

WEB EXERCISES

1. The amount of additional interest investors receive due to the various risk premiums changes over time. Sometimes the risk premiums are much larger than at other times. For example, the default risk premium was very small in the late 1990s when the economy was so healthy that business failures were rare. This risk premium increases during recessions.

   Go to www.federalreserve.gov/releases/h15 (historical data) and find the interest rate listings for AAA- and Baa-rated bonds at three points in time: the most recent; June 1, 1995; and June 1, 1992. Prepare a graph that shows these three time periods (see Figure 1 for an example). Are the risk premiums stable or do they change over time?

2. Figure 7 shows a number of yield curves at various points in time. Go to www.bloomberg.com/markets/rates/index.html and find the Treasury yield curve.

Does the current yield curve fall above or below the most recent one listed in Figure 7? Is the current yield curve flatter or steeper than the most recent one reported in Figure 7?

3. Investment companies attempt to explain to investors the nature of the risk the investor incurs when buying shares in their mutual funds. For example, Vanguard carefully explains interest-rate risk and offers alternative funds with different interest rate risks. Go to https://personal.vanguard.com/us/funds.
   a. Select the bond fund you would recommend to an investor who has a very low tolerance for risk and a short investment horizon. Justify your answer.
   b. Select the bond fund you would recommend to an investor who has a very high tolerance for risk and a long investment horizon. Justify your answer.

WEB REFERENCES

www.federalreserve.gov/Releases/h15/update/

The Federal Reserve reports the yields on different quality bonds. Look at the bottom of the listing of interest rates for AAA- and BBB- rated bonds.

http://stockcharts.com/charts/YieldCurve.html

This site lets you look at the dynamic yield curve at any point in time since 1995.

MyEconLab CAN HELP YOU GET A BETTER GRADE

If your exam were tomorrow, would you be ready? For each chapter, MyEconLab Practice Test and Study Plans pinpoint which sections you have mastered and which ones you need to study. That way, you are more efficient with your study time, and you are better prepared for your exams.

To see how it works, turn to page 20 and then go to: www.myeconlab.com/mishkin

The Stock Market, the Theory of Rational Expectations, and the Efficient Market Hypothesis

Preview

Rarely does a day go by that the stock market isn't a major news item. We have witnessed huge swings in the stock market in recent years. The 1990s were an extraordinary decade for stocks: The Dow Jones and S&P 500 indexes increased more than 400%, while the tech-laden NASDAQ index rose more than 1,000%. By early 2000, all three indexes had reached record highs. Unfortunately, the good times did not last, and many investors lost their shirts. Starting in early 2000, the stock market began to decline: The NASDAQ crashed, falling by more than 50%, while the Dow Jones and S&P 500 indexes fell by 30% through January 2003. After subsequently rising over 30%, the stock market crashed again during the subprime financial crisis, falling by over 50% from its peak in the fall of 2007.

Because so many people invest in the stock market and the price of stocks affects the ability of people to retire comfortably, the market for stocks is undoubtedly the financial market that receives the most attention and scrutiny. In this chapter, we look first at how this important market works.

We begin by discussing the fundamental theories that underlie the valuation of stocks. These theories are critical to understanding the forces that cause the value of stocks to rise and fall minute by minute and day by day. Once we have learned the methods for stock valuation, we need to explore how expectations about the market affect its behavior. We do so by examining the *theory of rational expectations*. When this theory is applied to financial markets, the outcome is the *efficient market hypothesis*, which has some general implications for how markets in other securities besides stocks operate. The theory of rational expectations is also central to debates about the conduct of monetary policy, to be discussed in Chapter 25.

COMPUTING THE PRICE OF COMMON STOCK

Common stock is the principal way that corporations raise equity capital. Holders of common stock own an interest in the corporation consistent with the percentage of outstanding shares owned. This ownership interest gives **stockholders**—those who hold stock in a corporation—a bundle of rights. The most important are the right to vote and to be the **residual claimant** of all funds flowing into the firm (known as **cash flows**), meaning that the stockholder receives whatever remains after all other claims against the firm's assets have been satisfied. Stockholders are paid dividends from the net earnings of the corporation. **Dividends** are payments made periodically, usually every quarter, to stockholders. The board of directors of the firm sets the level of the dividend, usually based on the recommendation of management. In addition, the stockholder has the right to sell the stock.

One basic principle of finance is that the value of any investment is found by computing the present value of all cash flows the investment will generate over its life. For example, a commercial building will sell for a price that reflects the net cash flows (rents − expenses) it is projected to have over its useful life. Similarly, we value common stock as the value in today's dollars of all future cash flows. The cash flows a stockholder might earn from stock are dividends, the sales price, or both.

To develop the theory of stock valuation, we begin with the simplest possible scenario: You buy the stock, hold it for one period to get a dividend, then sell the stock. We call this the *one-period valuation model*.

The One-Period Valuation Model

Suppose that you have some extra money to invest for one year. After a year, you will need to sell your investment to pay tuition. After watching CNBC or *Nightly Business Report* on TV, you decide that you want to buy Intel Corp. stock. You call your broker and find that Intel is currently selling for $50 per share and pays $0.16 per year in dividends. The analyst on CNBC predicts that the stock will be selling for $60 in one year. Should you buy this stock?

To answer this question, you need to determine whether the current price accurately reflects the analyst's forecast. To value the stock today, you need to find the present discounted value of the expected cash flows (future payments) using the formula in Equation 1 of Chapter 4. In this equation, the discount factor used to discount the cash flows is the required return on investments in equity rather than the interest rate. The cash flows consist of one dividend payment plus a final sales price. When these cash flows are discounted back to the present, the following equation computes the current price of the stock:

$$P_0 = \frac{Div_1}{(1 + k_e)} + \frac{P_1}{(1 + k_e)} \tag{1}$$

where P_0 = the current price of the stock. The zero subscript refers to time period zero, or the present.

Div_1 = the dividend paid at the end of year 1.

k_e = the required return on investments in equity.

P_1 = the price at the end of the first period; the assumed sales price of the stock.

To see how Equation 1 works, let's compute the price of the Intel stock if, after careful consideration, you decide that you would be satisfied to earn a 12% return on the investment. If you have decided that $k_e = 0.12$, are told that Intel pays $0.16 per year in dividends ($Div_1 = 0.16$), and forecast the share price of $60 for next year ($P_1 = \$60$), you get the following from Equation 1:

$$P_0 = \frac{0.16}{1 + 0.12} + \frac{\$60}{1 + 0.12} = \$0.14 + \$53.57 = \$53.71$$

Based on your analysis, you find that the present value of all cash flows from the stock is $53.71. Because the stock is currently priced at $50 per share, you would choose to buy it. However, you should be aware that the stock may be selling for less than $53.71, because other investors place a different risk on the cash flows or estimate the cash flows to be less than you do.

The Generalized Dividend Valuation Model

Using the present value concept, the one-period dividend valuation model can be extended to any number of periods: The value of a stock today is the present value of all future cash flows. The only cash flows that an investor will receive are dividends and a final sales price when the stock is ultimately sold in period *n*. The generalized multi-period formula for stock valuation can be written as

$$P_0 = \frac{D_1}{(1 + k_e)^1} + \frac{D_2}{(1 + k_e)^2} + \cdots + \frac{D_n}{(1 + k_e)^n} + \frac{P_n}{(1 + k_e)^n} \tag{2}$$

If you tried to use Equation 2 to find the value of a share of stock, you would soon realize that you must first estimate the value the stock will have at some point in the future before you can estimate its value today. In other words, you must find P_n before you can find P_0. However, if P_n is far in the future, it will not affect P_0. For example, the present value of a share of stock that sells for $50 seventy-five years from now using a 12% discount rate is just one cent [$50/(1.12^{75}) = $0.01]. This reasoning implies that the current value of a share of stock can be calculated as simply the present value of the future dividend stream. The **generalized dividend model** is rewritten in Equation 3 without the final sales price:

$$P_0 = \sum_{t=1}^{\infty} \frac{D_t}{(1 + k_e)^t} \tag{3}$$

Consider the implications of Equation 3 for a moment. The generalized dividend model says that the price of stock is determined only by the present value of the dividends and that nothing else matters. Many stocks do not pay dividends, so how is it that these stocks have value? *Buyers of the stock expect that the firm will pay dividends someday.* Most of the time a firm institutes dividends as soon as it has completed the rapid growth phase of its life cycle.

The generalized dividend valuation model requires that we compute the present value of an infinite stream of dividends, a process that could be difficult, to say the least. Therefore, simplified models have been developed to make the calculations easier. One such model is the **Gordon growth model**, which assumes constant dividend growth.

The Gordon Growth Model

Many firms strive to increase their dividends at a constant rate each year. Equation 4 rewrites Equation 3 to reflect this constant growth in dividends:

$$P_0 = \frac{D_0 \times (1 + g)^1}{(1 + k_e)^1} + \frac{D_0 \times (1 + g)^2}{(1 + k_e)^2} + \cdots + \frac{D_0 \times (1 + g)^\infty}{(1 + k_e)^\infty} \tag{4}$$

where
D_0 = the most recent dividend paid
g = the expected constant growth rate in dividends
k_e = the required return on an investment in equity

Equation 4 has been simplified to obtain Equation 5:[1]

$$P_0 = \frac{D_0 \times (1 + g)}{(k_e - g)} = \frac{D_1}{(k_e - g)} \tag{5}$$

This model is useful for finding the value of stock, given a few assumptions:

1. *Dividends are assumed to continue growing at a constant rate forever.* Actually, as long as they are expected to grow at a constant rate for an extended period of time, the model should yield reasonable results. This is because errors about distant cash flows become small when discounted to the present.
2. *The growth rate is assumed to be less than the required return on equity, k_e.* Myron Gordon, in his development of the model, demonstrated that this is a reasonable assumption. In theory, if the growth rate were faster than the rate demanded by holders of the firm's equity, in the long run the firm would grow impossibly large.

HOW THE MARKET SETS STOCK PRICES

Suppose you go to an auto auction. The cars are available for inspection before the auction begins, and you find a little Mazda Miata that you like. You test-drive it in the parking lot and notice that it makes a few strange noises, but you decide that you would still like the car. You decide $5,000 would be a fair price that would allow you to pay some repair bills should the noises turn out to be serious. You see that the auction is ready to begin, so you go in and wait for the Miata to enter.

Suppose another buyer also spots the Miata. He test-drives the car and recognizes that the noises are simply the result of worn brake pads that he can fix himself at a nominal cost. He decides that the car is worth $7,000. He also goes in and waits for the Miata to come up for auction.

Who will buy the car and for how much? Suppose only the two of you are interested in the Miata. You begin the bidding at $4,000. Your competitor ups your bid to $4,500. You bid your top price of $5,000. He counters with $5,100. The price is now higher than you are willing to pay, so you stop bidding. The car is sold to the more informed buyer for $5,100.

---

[1]To generate Equation 5 from Equation 4, first multiply both sides of Equation 4 by $(1 + k_e)/(1 + g)$ and subtract Equation 4 from the result. This yields

$$\frac{P_0 \times (1 + k_e)}{(1 + g)} - P_0 = D_0 - \frac{D_0 \times (1 + g)^\infty}{(1 + k_e)^\infty}$$

Assuming that k_e is greater than g, the term on the far right will approach zero and can be dropped. Thus, after factoring P_0 out of the left-hand side,

$$P_0 \times \left[\frac{1 + k_e}{1 + g} - 1 \right] = D_0$$

Next, simplify by combining terms:

$$P_0 \times \frac{(1 + k_e) - (1 + g)}{1 + g} = D_0$$

$$P_0 = \frac{D_0 \times (1 + g)}{k_e - g} = \frac{D_1}{k_e - g}$$

This simple example raises a number of points. First, the price is set by the buyer willing to pay the highest price. The price is not necessarily the highest price the asset could fetch, but it is incrementally greater than what any other buyer is willing to pay.

Second, the market price will be set by the buyer who can take best advantage of the asset. The buyer who purchased the car knew that he could fix the noise easily and cheaply. As a consequence, he was willing to pay more for the car than you were. The same concept holds for other assets. For example, a piece of property or a building will sell to the buyer who can put the asset to the most productive use.

Finally, the example shows the role played by information in asset pricing. Superior information about an asset can increase its value by reducing its risk. When you consider buying a stock, there are many unknowns about the future cash flows. The buyer who has the best information about these cash flows will discount them at a lower interest rate than will a buyer who is very uncertain.

Now let us apply these ideas to stock valuation. Suppose that you are considering the purchase of stock expected to pay a $2 dividend next year. Market analysts expect the firm to grow at 3% indefinitely. You are *uncertain* about both the constancy of the dividend stream and the accuracy of the estimated growth rate. To compensate yourself for this uncertainty (risk), you require a return of 15%.

Now suppose Jennifer, another investor, has spoken with industry insiders and feels more confident about the projected cash flows. Jennifer requires only a 12% return because her perceived risk is lower than yours. Bud, on the other hand, is dating the CEO of the company. He knows with more certainty what the future of the firm actually is, and thus requires only a 10% return.

What are the values each investor will give to the stock? Applying the Gordon growth model yields the following stock prices:

Investor	Discount Rate	Stock Price
You	15%	$16.67
Jennifer	12%	$22.22
Bud	10%	$28.57

You are willing to pay $16.67 for the stock. Jennifer would pay up to $22.22, and Bud would pay $28.57. The investor with the lowest perceived risk is willing to pay the most for the stock. If there were no other traders but these three, the market price would be between $22.22 and $28.57. If you already held the stock, you would sell it to Bud.

We thus see that the players in the market, bidding against one another, establish the market price. When new information is released about a firm, expectations change and with them, prices change. New information can cause changes in expectations about the level of future dividends or the risk of those dividends. Because market participants are constantly receiving new information and revising their expectations, it is reasonable that stock prices are constantly changing as well.

APPLICATION ✦ Monetary Policy and Stock Prices

Stock market analysts tend to hang on every word that the chairman of the Federal Reserve utters because they know that an important determinant of stock prices is monetary policy. But how does monetary policy affect stock prices?

The Gordon growth model in Equation 5 explains this relationship. Monetary policy can affect stock prices in two ways. First, when the Fed lowers interest rates, the return on bonds (an alternative asset to stocks) declines, and investors are likely to accept a lower required rate of return on an investment in equity (k_e). The resulting decline in k_e would lower the denominator in the Gordon growth model (Equation 5), lead to a higher value of P_0, and raise stock prices. Furthermore, a lowering of interest rates is likely to stimulate the economy, so that the growth rate in dividends, g, is likely to be somewhat higher. This rise in g also causes the denominator in Equation 5 to decrease, which also leads to a higher P_0 and a rise in stock prices.

As we will see in Chapter 24, the impact of monetary policy on stock prices is one of the key ways in which monetary policy affects the economy.

APPLICATION: ✦ The Subprime Financial Crisis and the Stock Market

The subprime financial crisis that started in August 2007 led to one of the worst bear markets in the last 50 years. Our analysis of stock price valuation, again using the Gordon growth model, can help us understand how this event affected stock prices.

The subprime financial crisis had a major negative impact on the economy leading to a downward revision of the growth prospects for U.S. companies, thus lowering the dividend growth rate (g) in the Gordon model. The resulting increase in the denominator in Equation 5 would lead to a decline in P_0 and hence a decline in stock prices.

Increased uncertainty for the U.S. economy and the widening credit spreads resulting from the subprime crisis would also raise the required return on investment in equity. A higher k_e also leads to an increase in the denominator in Equation 5, a decline in P_0, and a general fall in stock prices.

In the early stages of the financial crisis, the decline in growth prospects and credit spreads were moderate and so, as the Gordon model predicts, the stock market decline was also moderate. However, when the crisis entered a particularly virulent stage in October of 2008, credit spreads shot through the roof, the economy tanked, and as the Gordon model predicts, the stock market crashed, falling by over 40% from its peak value a year earlier.

THE THEORY OF RATIONAL EXPECTATIONS

The analysis of stock price evaluation we outlined in the previous section depends on people's expectations—especially of cash flows. Indeed, it is difficult to think of any sector in the economy in which expectations are not crucial; this is why it is important to examine how expectations are formed. We do so by outlining the *theory of rational expectations*, currently the most widely used theory to describe the formation of business and consumer expectations.

In the 1950s and 1960s, economists regularly viewed expectations as formed from past experience only. Expectations of inflation, for example, were typically viewed as being an average of past inflation rates. This view of expectation formation, called **adaptive expectations**, suggests that changes in expectations will occur slowly over time as past data change.[2] So if inflation had formerly been steady at a 5% rate, expectations of future inflation would be 5%, too. If inflation rose to a steady rate of 10%, expectations of future inflation would rise toward 10%, but slowly: In the first year, expected inflation might rise only to 6%; in the second year, to 7%; and so on.

Adaptive expectations have been faulted on the grounds that people use more information than just past data on a single variable to form their expectations of that variable. Their expectations of inflation will almost surely be affected by their predictions of future monetary policy as well as by current and past monetary policy. In addition, people often change their expectations quickly in the light of new information. To meet these objections to adaptive expectations, John Muth developed an alternative theory of expectations, called **rational expectations**, which can be stated as follows: ***Expectations will be identical to optimal forecasts (the best guess of the future) using all available information.***[3]

What exactly does this mean? To explain it more clearly, let's use the theory of rational expectations to examine how expectations are formed in a situation that most of us encounter at some point in our lifetime: our drive to work. Suppose that if Joe Commuter travels when it is not rush hour, it takes an average of 30 minutes for his trip. Sometimes it takes him 35 minutes, other times 25 minutes, but the average non-rush-hour driving time is 30 minutes. If, however, Joe leaves for work during the rush hour, it takes him, on average, an additional 10 minutes to get to work. Given that he leaves for work during the rush hour, the best guess of the driving time—the **optimal forecast**— is 40 minutes.

If the only information available to Joe before he leaves for work that would have a potential effect on his driving time is that he is leaving during the rush hour, what does rational expectations theory allow you to predict about Joe's expectations of his driving time? Since the best guess of his driving time using all available information is 40 minutes, Joe's expectation should also be the same. Clearly, an expectation of 35 minutes would not be rational, because it is not equal to the optimal forecast, the best guess of the driving time.

Suppose that the next day, given the same conditions and the same expectations, it takes Joe 45 minutes to drive because he hits an abnormally large number of red lights, and the day after that he hits all the lights right and it takes him only 35 minutes. Do these variations mean that Joe's 40-minute expectation is irrational? No, an expectation of 40 minutes' driving time is still a rational expectation. In both cases, the forecast is off by five minutes, so the expectation has not been perfectly accurate. However, the forecast does not have to be perfectly accurate to be rational—it need only be the *best possible* given the available information; that is, it has to be correct *on average,* and the 40-minute expectation meets this requirement. As there is bound to be some randomness in Joe's driving time regardless of driving conditions, an optimal forecast will never be completely accurate.

---

[2]More specifically, adaptive expectations—say, of inflation—are written as a weighted average of past inflation rates:

$$\pi_t^e = (1 - \lambda) \sum_{j=0}^{\infty} \lambda^j \pi_{t-j}$$

where π_t^e = adaptive expectation of inflation at time t

π_{t-j} = inflation at time $t - j$

λ = a constant between the values of 0 and 1

[3]John Muth, "Rational Expectations and the Theory of Price Movements," *Econometrica* 29 (1961): 315–335.

The example makes the following important point about rational expectations: *Even though a rational expectation equals the optimal forecast using all available information, a prediction based on it may not always be perfectly accurate.*

What if an item of information relevant to predicting driving time is unavailable or ignored? Suppose that on Joe's usual route to work there is an accident that causes a two-hour traffic jam. If Joe has no way of ascertaining this information, his rush-hour expectation of 40 minutes' driving time is still rational, because the accident information is not available to him for incorporation into his optimal forecast. However, if there was a radio or TV traffic report about the accident that Joe did not bother to listen to or heard but ignored, his 40-minute expectation is no longer rational. In light of the availability of this information, Joe's optimal forecast should have been two hours and 40 minutes.

Accordingly, there are two reasons why an expectation may fail to be rational:

1. People might be aware of all available information but find it takes too much effort to make their expectation the best guess possible.
2. People might be unaware of some available relevant information, so their best guess of the future will not be accurate.

Nonetheless, it is important to recognize that if an additional factor is important but information about it is not available, an expectation that does not take account of it can still be rational.

Formal Statement of the Theory

We can state the theory of rational expectations somewhat more formally. If X stands for the variable that is being forecast (in our example, Joe Commuter's driving time), X^e for the expectation of this variable (Joe's expectation of his driving time), and X^{of} for the optimal forecast of X using all available information (the best guess possible of his driving time), the theory of rational expectations then simply says

$$X^e = X^{of} \tag{6}$$

That is, the expectation of X equals the optimal forecast using all available information.

Rationale Behind the Theory

Why do people try to make their expectations match their best possible guess of the future using all available information? The simplest explanation is that it is costly for people not to do so. Joe Commuter has a strong incentive to make his expectation of the time it takes him to drive to work as accurate as possible. If he underpredicts his driving time, he will often be late to work and risk being fired. If he overpredicts, he will, on average, get to work too early and will have given up sleep or leisure time unnecessarily. Accurate expectations are desirable, and there are strong incentives for people to try to make them equal to optimal forecasts by using all available information.

The same principle applies to businesses. Suppose that an appliance manufacturer—say, General Electric—knows that interest-rate movements are important to the sales of appliances. If GE makes poor forecasts of interest rates, it will earn less profit, because it might produce either too many appliances or too few. There are strong incentives for GE to acquire all available information to help it forecast interest rates and use the information to make the best possible guess of future interest-rate movements.

The incentives for equating expectations with optimal forecasts are especially strong in financial markets. In these markets, people with better forecasts of the future get rich. The application of the theory of rational expectations to financial markets (where it is called the **efficient market hypothesis** or the **theory of efficient capital markets**) is thus particularly useful.

Implications of the Theory

Rational expectations theory leads to two commonsense implications for the forming of expectations that are important in the analysis of both the stock market and the aggregate economy:

1. *If there is a change in the way a variable moves, the way in which expectations of this variable are formed will change as well*. This tenet of rational expectations theory can be most easily understood through a concrete example. Suppose that interest rates move in such a way that they tend to return to a "normal" level in the future. If today's interest rate is high relative to the normal level, an optimal forecast of the interest rate in the future is that it will decline to the normal level. Rational expectations theory would imply that when today's interest rate is high, the expectation is that it will fall in the future.

Suppose now that the way in which the interest rate moves changes so that when the interest rate is high, it stays high. In this case, when today's interest rate is high, the optimal forecast of the future interest rate, and hence the rational expectation, is that it will stay high. Expectations of the future interest rate will no longer indicate that the interest rate will fall. The change in the way the interest-rate variable moves has therefore led to a change in the way that expectations of future interest rates are formed. The rational expectations analysis here is generalizable to expectations of any variable. Hence, when there is a change in the way any variable moves, the way in which expectations of this variable are formed will change, too.

2. *The forecast errors of expectations will, on average, be zero and cannot be predicted ahead of time*. The forecast error of an expectation is $X - X^e$, the difference between the realization of a variable X and the expectation of the variable. That is, if Joe Commuter's driving time on a particular day is 45 minutes and his expectation of the driving time is 40 minutes, the forecast error is five minutes.

Suppose that in violation of the rational expectations tenet, Joe's forecast error is not, on average, equal to zero; instead, it equals five minutes. The forecast error is now predictable ahead of time because Joe will soon notice that he is, on average, five minutes late for work and can improve his forecast by increasing it by five minutes. Rational expectations theory implies that this is exactly what Joe will do because he will want his forecast to be the best guess possible. When Joe has revised his forecast upward by five minutes, on average, the forecast error will equal zero so that it cannot be predicted ahead of time. Rational expectations theory implies that forecast errors of expectations cannot be predicted.

THE EFFICIENT MARKET HYPOTHESIS: RATIONAL EXPECTATIONS IN FINANCIAL MARKETS

While monetary economists were developing the theory of rational expectations, financial economists were developing a parallel theory of expectations formation in financial markets. It led them to the same conclusion as that of the rational expectations theorists:

Expectations in financial markets are equal to optimal forecasts using all available information.[4] Although financial economists gave their theory another name, calling it *the efficient market hypothesis,* in fact their theory is just an application of rational expectations to the pricing of stocks and also other securities.

The efficient market hypothesis is based on the assumption that prices of securities in financial markets fully reflect all available information. You may recall from Chapter 4 that the rate of return from holding a security equals the sum of the capital gain on the security (the change in the price), plus any cash payments, divided by the initial purchase price of the security:

$$R = \frac{P_{t+1} - P_t + C}{P_t} \tag{7}$$

where
R = rate of return on the security held from time t to $t + 1$
  (say, the end of 2010 to the end of 2011)
P_{t+1} = price of the security at time $t + 1$, the end of the holding period
P_t = price of the security at time t, the beginning of the holding period
C = cash payment (coupon or dividend payments) made in the
  period t to $t + 1$

Let's look at the expectation of this return at time t, the beginning of the holding period. Because the current price P_t and the cash payment C are known at the beginning, the only variable in the definition of the return that is uncertain is the price next period, P_{t+1}.[5] Denoting the expectation of the security's price at the end of the holding period as P^e_{t+1}, the expected return R^e is

$$R^e = \frac{P^e_{t+1} - P_t + C}{P_t}$$

The efficient market hypothesis views expectations of future prices as equal to optimal forecasts using all currently available information. In other words, the market's expectations of future securities prices are rational, so that

$$P^e_{t+1} = P^{of}_{t+1}$$

which in turn implies that the expected return on the security will equal the optimal forecast of the return:

$$R^e = R^{of} \tag{8}$$

Unfortunately, we cannot observe either R^e or P^e_{t+1}, so the rational expectations equations by themselves do not tell us much about how the financial market behaves. However, if we can devise some way to measure the value of R^e, these equations will have important implications for how prices of securities change in financial markets.

The supply and demand analysis of the bond market developed in Chapter 5 shows us that the expected return on a security (the interest rate, in the case of the bond examined) will have a tendency to head toward the equilibrium return that equates the quantity demanded to the quantity supplied. Supply and demand analysis enables us to determine the expected return on a security with the following equilibrium condition:

---

[4]The development of the efficient market hypothesis was not wholly independent of the development of rational expectations theory, in that financial economists were aware of Muth's work.

[5]There are cases where C might not be known at the beginning of the period, but that does not make a substantial difference to the analysis. We would in that case assume that not only price expectations but also the expectations of C are optimal forecasts using all available information.

The expected return on a security R^e equals the equilibrium return R^*, which equates the quantity of the security demanded to the quantity supplied; that is,

$$R^e = R^* \tag{9}$$

The academic field of finance explores the factors (risk and liquidity, for example) that influence the equilibrium returns on securities. For our purposes, it is sufficient to know that we can determine the equilibrium return and thus determine the expected return with the equilibrium condition.

We can derive an equation to describe pricing behavior in an efficient market by using the equilibrium condition to replace R^e with R^* in the rational expectations equation (Equation 8). In this way, we obtain

$$R^{of} = R^* \tag{10}$$

This equation tells us that **current prices in a financial market will be set so that the optimal forecast of a security's return using all available information equals the security's equilibrium return**. Financial economists state it more simply: In an efficient market, a security's price fully reflects all available information.

Rationale Behind the Hypothesis

To see why the efficient market efficient hypothesis makes sense, we make use of the concept of **arbitrage**, in which market participants (*arbitrageurs*) eliminate **unexploited profit opportunities**, i.e., returns on a security that are larger than what is justified by the characteristics of that security. There are two types of arbitrage, *pure arbitrage*, in which the elimination of unexploited profit opportunities involves no risk, and the type of arbitrage we discuss here in which the arbitrageur takes on some risk when eliminating the unexploited profit opportunities. To see how arbitrage leads to the efficient market hypothesis, suppose that, given its risk characteristics, the normal return on a security, say, ExxonMobil common stock, is 10% at an annual rate, and its current price P_t is lower than the optimal forecast of tomorrow's price P^{of}_{t+1} so that the optimal forecast of the return at an annual rate is 50%, which is greater than the equilibrium return of 10%. We are now able to predict that, on average, ExxonMobil's return would be abnormally high so that there is an unexploited profit opportunity. Knowing that, on average, you can earn such an abnormally high rate of return on ExxonMobil because $R^{of} > R^*$, you would buy more, which would in turn drive up its current price P_t relative to the expected future price P^{of}_{t+1}, thereby lowering R^{of}. When the current price had risen sufficiently so that R^{of} equaled R^* and the efficient market condition (Equation 10) was satisfied, the buying of ExxonMobil would stop, and the unexploited profit opportunity would disappear.

Similarly, a security for which the optimal forecast of the return is −5% and the equilibrium return is 10% ($R^{of} < R^*$) would be a poor investment, because, on average, it earns less than the equilibrium return. In such a case, you would sell the security and drive down its current price relative to the expected future price until R^{of} rose to the level of R^* and the efficient market condition was again satisfied. What we have shown can be summarized as follows:

$$R^{of} > R^* \rightarrow P_t \uparrow \rightarrow R^{of} \downarrow$$
$$R^{of} < R^* \rightarrow P_t \downarrow \rightarrow R^{of} \uparrow$$
$$\text{until}$$
$$R^{of} = R^*$$

Another way to state the efficient market condition is this: **In an efficient market, all unexploited profit opportunities will be eliminated**.

An extremely important factor in this reasoning is that ***not everyone in a financial market must be well informed about a security or have rational expectations for its price to be driven to the point at which the efficient market condition holds***. Financial markets are structured so that many participants can play. As long as a few keep their eyes open for unexploited profit opportunities (often referred to as "smart money"), they will eliminate the profit opportunities that appear, because in so doing, they make a profit. The efficient market hypothesis makes sense, because it does not require everyone in a market to be cognizant of what is happening to every security.

Stronger Version of the Efficient Market Hypothesis

Many financial economists take the efficient market hypothesis one step further in their analysis of financial markets. Not only do they define efficient markets as those in which expectations are rational—that is, equal to optimal forecasts using all available information—but they also add the condition that an efficient market is one in which prices reflect the true fundamental (intrinsic) value of the securities. Thus, in an efficient market, all prices are always correct and reflect **market fundamentals** (items that have a direct impact on future income streams of the securities). This stronger view of market efficiency has several important implications in the academic field of finance. First, it implies that in an efficient capital market, one investment is as good as any other because the securities' prices are correct. Second, it implies that a security's price reflects all available information about the intrinsic value of the security. Third, it implies that security prices can be used by managers of both financial and nonfinancial firms to assess their cost of capital (cost of financing their investments) accurately and hence that security prices can be used to help them make the correct decisions about whether a specific investment is worth making. The stronger version of market efficiency is a basic tenet of much analysis in the finance field.

APPLICATION ✦ Practical Guide to Investing in the Stock Market

The efficient market hypothesis has numerous applications to the real world.[6] It is especially valuable because it can be applied directly to an issue that concerns many of us: how to get rich (or at least not get poor) in the stock market. (The Following the Financial News box shows how stock prices are reported daily.) A practical guide to investing in the stock market, which we develop here, provides a better understanding of the use and implications of the efficient market hypothesis.

How Valuable Are Published Reports by Investment Advisers?

Suppose you have just read in the "Heard on the Street" column of the *Wall Street Journal* that investment advisers are predicting a boom in oil stocks because an oil shortage is developing. Should you proceed to withdraw all your hard-earned savings from the bank and invest it in oil stocks?

The efficient market hypothesis tells us that when purchasing a security, we cannot expect to earn an abnormally high return, a return greater than the equilibrium return.

---

[6]The empirical evidence on the efficient markets hypothesis is discussed in an appendix to this chapter, which can be found on this book's website at www.myeconlab.com/mishkin.

Information in newspapers and in the published reports of investment advisers is readily available to many market participants and is already reflected in market prices. So acting on this information will not yield abnormally high returns, on average. The empirical evidence for the most part confirms that recommendations from investment advisers cannot help us outperform the general market. Indeed, as the FYI box suggests, human investment advisers in San Francisco do not, on average, even outperform an orangutan!

Probably no other conclusion is met with more skepticism by students than this one when they first hear it. We all know or have heard of someone who has been successful in the stock market for a period of many years. We wonder, "How could someone be so consistently successful if he or she did not really know how to predict when returns would be abnormally high?" The following story, reported in the press, illustrates why such anecdotal evidence is not reliable.

A get-rich-quick artist invented a clever scam. Every week, he wrote two letters. In letter A, he would pick team A to win a particular football game; in letter B, he would pick the opponent, team B. He would then separate a mailing list into two groups, and he would send letter A to the people in one group and letter B to the people in the other. The following week he would do the same thing but would send these letters only to the group who had received the first letter with the correct prediction. After doing this for ten games, he had a small cluster of people who had received letters predicting the correct winning team for every game. He then mailed a final letter to them, declaring that since he was obviously an expert predictor of the outcome of football games (he had picked winners ten weeks in a row) and since his predictions were profitable for the recipients who bet on the games, he would continue to send his predictions only if he were paid a substantial amount of money. When one of his clients figured out what he was up to, the con man was prosecuted and thrown in jail!

What is the lesson of the story? Even if no forecaster is an accurate predictor of the market, there will always be a group of consistent winners. A person who has done well regularly in the past cannot guarantee that he or she will do well in the future. Note that there will also be a group of persistent losers, but you rarely hear about them because no one brags about a poor forecasting record.

Should You Be Skeptical of Hot Tips?

Suppose your broker phones you with a hot tip to buy stock in the Happy Feet Corporation (HFC) because it has just developed a product that is completely effective in curing athlete's foot. The stock price is sure to go up. Should you follow this advice and buy HFC stock?

The efficient market hypothesis indicates that you should be skeptical of such news. If the stock market is efficient, it has already priced HFC stock so that its expected return will equal the equilibrium return. The hot tip is not particularly valuable and will not enable you to earn an abnormally high return.

You might wonder, though, if the hot tip is based on new information and would give you an edge on the rest of the market. If other market participants have gotten this information before you, the answer is no. As soon as the information hits the street, the unexploited profit opportunity it creates will be quickly eliminated. The stock's price will already reflect the information, and you should expect to realize only the equilibrium return. But if you are one of the first to gain the new information, it can do you some good. Only then can you be one of the lucky ones who, on average, will earn an abnormally high return by helping eliminate the profit opportunity by buying HFC stock.

FYI   Should You Hire an Ape as Your Investment Adviser?

The *San Francisco Chronicle* came up with an amusing way of evaluating how successful investment advisers are at picking stocks. They asked eight analysts to pick five stocks at the beginning of the year and then compared the performance of their stock picks to those chosen by Jolyn, an orangutan living at Marine World/Africa USA in Vallejo, California. Consistent with the results found in the "Investment Dartboard" feature of the *Wall Street Journal*, Jolyn beat the investment advisers as often as they beat her. Given this result, you might be just as well off hiring an orangutan as your investment adviser as you would hiring a human being!

Do Stock Prices Always Rise When There Is Good News?

If you follow the stock market, you might have noticed a puzzling phenomenon: When good news about a stock, such as a particularly favorable earnings report, is announced, the price of the stock frequently does not rise. The efficient market hypothesis explains this phenomenon.

Because changes in stock prices are unpredictable, when information is announced that has already been expected by the market, the stock price will remain unchanged. The announcement does not contain any new information that should lead to a change in stock prices. If this were not the case and the announcement led to a change in stock prices, it would mean that the change was predictable. Because that is ruled out in an efficient market, **stock prices will respond to announcements only when the information being announced is new and unexpected**. If the news is expected, there will be no stock price response. This is exactly what the evidence shows: stock prices do reflect publicly available information.

Sometimes an individual stock price declines when good news is announced. Although this seems somewhat peculiar, it is completely consistent with the workings of an efficient market. Suppose that although the announced news is good, it is not as good as expected. HFC's earnings may have risen 15%, but if the market expected earnings to rise by 20%, the new information is actually unfavorable, and the stock price declines.

Efficient Market Prescription for the Investor

What does the efficient market hypothesis recommend for investing in the stock market? It tells us that hot tips and investment advisers' published recommendations—all of which make use of publicly available information—cannot help an investor outperform the market. Indeed, it indicates that anyone without better information than other market participants cannot expect to beat the market. So what is an investor to do?

The efficient market hypothesis leads to the conclusion that such an investor (and almost all of us fit into this category) should not try to outguess the market by constantly buying and selling securities. This process does nothing but boost the income of brokers, who earn commissions on each trade.[7] Instead, the investor should pursue a "buy and hold" strategy—purchase stocks and hold them for long periods of time. This will lead to the same returns, on average, but the investor's net profits will be higher, because fewer brokerage commissions will have to be paid.

It is frequently a sensible strategy for a small investor, whose costs of managing a portfolio may be high relative to its size, to buy into a mutual fund rather than to buy individual stocks. Because the efficient market hypothesis indicates that no mutual fund can consistently outperform the market, an investor should not buy into one that has high management fees or that pays sales commissions to brokers, but rather should purchase a no-load (commission-free) mutual fund that has low management fees.

The evidence indicates that it will not be easy to beat the prescription suggested here, although some anomalies to the efficient market hypothesis suggest that an extremely clever investor (which rules out most of us) may be able to outperform a buy-and-hold strategy.

APPLICATION ✦ What Do the Black Monday Crash of 1987 and the Tech Crash of 2000 Tell Us About Rational Expectations and Efficient Markets?

On October 19, 1987, dubbed "Black Monday," the Dow Jones Industrial Average declined more than 20%, the largest one-day decline in U.S. history. The collapse of the high-tech companies' share prices from their peaks in March 2000 caused the heavily tech-laden NASDAQ index to fall from around 5,000 in March 2000 to around 1,500 in 2001 and 2002, a decline of well over 60%. These two crashes have caused many economists to question the validity of the efficient market hypothesis and rational expectations. They do not believe that a rational marketplace could have produced such a massive swing in share prices. To what degree should these stock market crashes make us doubt the validity of rational expectations and the efficient market hypothesis?

Nothing in rational expectations theory rules out large changes in stock prices. A large change in stock prices can result from new information that produces a dramatic decline in optimal forecasts of the future valuation of firms. However, economists are hard pressed to come up with fundamental changes in the economy that can explain the Black Monday and tech crashes. One lesson from these crashes is that factors other than market fundamentals probably have an effect on stock prices. Hence these crashes have convinced many economists that the stronger version of the efficient market hypothesis, which states that asset prices reflect the true fundamental (intrinsic) value of securities, is incorrect. They attribute a large role in determination of stock prices to market psychology and to the institutional structure of the marketplace. However, nothing in this view contradicts the basic reasoning behind rational expectations or the efficient market hypothesis—that market participants eliminate unexploited profit opportunities. Even though stock market prices may not always solely reflect market fundamentals, this does not mean that rational expectations do not hold. As long as stock market crashes are unpredictable, the basic lessons of the theory of rational expectations hold.

Some economists have come up with theories of what they call *rational bubbles* to explain stock market crashes. A **bubble** is a situation in which the price of an asset differs from its fundamental market value. In a rational bubble, investors can have

---

[7]The investor may also have to pay Uncle Sam capital gains taxes on any profits that are realized when a security is sold—an additional reason why continual buying and selling does not make sense.

rational expectations that a bubble is occurring because the asset price is higher than its fundamental value but continue to hold the asset anyway. They might do so because they believe that someone else will buy the asset for a higher price in the future. In a rational bubble, asset prices can therefore deviate from their fundamental value for a long time because the bursting of the bubble cannot be predicted and so there are no unexploited profit opportunities.

However, other economists believe that the Black Monday crash of 1987 and the tech crash of 2000 suggest that there may be unexploited profit opportunities and that the theory of rational expectations and the efficient market hypothesis might be fundamentally flawed. The controversy over whether capital markets are efficient or expectations are rational continues.

BEHAVIORAL FINANCE

Doubts about the efficient market hypothesis, particularly after the stock market crash of 1987, have led to the emergence of a new field of study, **behavioral finance**. It applies concepts from other social sciences such as anthropology, sociology, and, particularly, psychology to understand the behavior of securities prices.[8]

As we have seen, the efficient market hypothesis assumes that unexploited profit opportunities are eliminated by "smart money" market participants. But can smart money dominate ordinary investors so that financial markets are efficient? Specifically, the efficient market hypothesis suggests that smart money participants will sell when a stock price goes up irrationally, with the result that the stock price falls back down to a level that is justified by fundamentals. For this to occur, smart money investors must be able to engage in **short sales**; that is, they must borrow stock from brokers and then sell it in the market, with the aim that they earn a profit by buying the stock back again ("covering the short") after it has fallen in price. Work by psychologists, however, suggests that people are subject to loss aversion: They are more unhappy when they suffer losses than they are happy when they achieve gains. Short sales can result in losses far in excess of an investor's initial investment if the stock price climbs sharply higher than the price at which the short sale is made (and losses have the possibility of being unlimited if the stock price climbs to astronomical heights).

Loss aversion can thus explain an important phenomenon: Very little short selling actually takes place. Short selling may also be constrained by rules restricting it because it seems unsavory for someone to make money from another person's misfortune. The existence of so little short selling can explain why stock prices are sometimes overvalued. That is, the lack of enough short selling means that smart money does not drive stock prices back down to their fundamental value.

Psychologists have also found that people tend to be overconfident in their own judgments. As a result, investors tend to believe that they are smarter than other investors. Because investors are willing to assume that the market typically doesn't get

---

[8]Surveys of this field can be found in Hersh Shefrin, *Beyond Greed and Fear: Understanding of Behavioral Finance and the Psychology of Investing* (Boston: Harvard Business School Press, 2000); Andrei Shleifer, *Inefficient Markets* (Oxford, UK: Oxford University Press, 2000); and Robert J. Shiller, "From Efficient Market Theory to Behavioral Finance," Cowles Foundation Discussion Paper No. 1385 (October 2002).

it right, they trade on their beliefs, rather than on pure facts. This theory may explain why securities markets have such a large trading volume—something that the efficient market hypothesis does not predict.

Overconfidence and social contagion (fads) provide an explanation for stock market bubbles. When stock prices go up, investors attribute their profits to their intelligence and talk up the stock market. This word-of-mouth enthusiasm and glowing media reports then can produce an environment in which even more investors think stock prices will rise in the future. The result is a positive feedback loop in which prices continue to rise, producing a speculative bubble, which finally crashes when prices get too far out of line with fundamentals.[9]

The field of behavioral finance is a young one, but it holds out hope that we might be able to explain some features of securities markets' behavior that are not well explained by the efficient market hypothesis.

---

[9]See Robert J. Shiller, *Irrational Exuberance* (New York: Broadway Books, 2001).

SUMMARY

1. Stocks are valued as the present value of future dividends. Unfortunately, we do not know very precisely what these dividends will be. This uncertainty introduces a great deal of error into the valuation process. The Gordon growth model is a simplified method of computing stock value that depends on the assumption that the dividends are growing at a constant rate forever. Given our uncertainty regarding future dividends, this assumption is often the best we can do.

2. The interaction among traders in the market is what actually sets prices on a day-to-day basis. The trader who values the security the most (either because of less uncertainty about the cash flows or because of greater estimated cash flows) will be willing to pay the most. As new information is released, investors will revise their estimates of the true value of the security and will either buy or sell it depending on how the market price compares to their estimated valuation. Because small changes in estimated growth rates or required return result in large changes in price, it is not surprising that the markets are often volatile.

3. The efficient market hypothesis states that current security prices will fully reflect all available information, because in an efficient market, all unexploited profit opportunities are eliminated. The elimination of unexploited profit opportunities necessary for a financial market to be efficient does not require that all market participants be well informed.

4. The efficient market hypothesis indicates that hot tips, investment advisers' published recommendations cannot help an investor outperform the market. The prescription for investors is to pursue a buy-and-hold strategy—purchase stocks and hold them for long periods of time. Empirical evidence generally supports these implications of the efficient market hypothesis in the stock market.

5. The stock market crash of 1987 and the tech crash of 2000 have convinced many financial economists that the stronger version of the efficient market hypothesis, which states that asset prices reflect the true fundamental (intrinsic) value of securities, is not correct. It is less clear that these crashes show that the weaker version of the efficient market hypothesis is wrong. Even if the stock market was driven by factors other than fundamentals, these crashes do not clearly demonstrate that many of the basic lessons of the efficient market hypothesis are no longer valid, as long as these crashes could not have been predicted.

6. The new field of behavioral finance applies concepts from other social sciences such as anthropology, sociology, and psychology to understand the behavior of securities prices. Loss aversion, overconfidence, and social contagion can explain why trading volume is so high, stock prices become overvalued, and speculative bubbles occur.

KEY TERMS

adaptive expectations, p. 152

arbitrage, p. 157

behavioral finance, p. 162

bubble, p. 161

cash flows, p. 147

dividends, p. 147

efficient market hypothesis, p. 155

generalized dividend model, p. 149

Gordon growth model, p. 149

market fundamentals, p. 158

optimal forecast, p. 153

rational expectations, p. 153

residual claimant, p. 147

short sales, p. 162

stockholders, p. 147

theory of efficient capital
   markets, p. 155

unexploited profit opportunity, p. 157

QUESTIONS AND PROBLEMS

All questions and problems are available in myeconlab *at*
www.myeconlab.com/mishkin.

1. What basic principle of finance can be applied to the valuation of any investment asset?

2. Identify the cash flows available to an investor in stock. How reliably can these cash flows be estimated? Compare the problem of estimating stock cash flows to estimating bond cash flows. Which security would you predict to be more volatile?

3. Compute the price of a share of stock that pays a $1 per year dividend and that you expect to be able to sell in one year for $20, assuming you require a 15% return.

4. After careful analysis, you have determined that a firm's dividends should grow at 7% on average in the foreseeable future. The firm's last dividend was $3. Compute the current price of this stock, assuming the required return is 18%.

5. Some economists think that the central banks should try to prick bubbles in the stock market before they get out of hand and cause later damage when they burst. How can monetary policy be used to prick a bubble? Explain how it can do this using the Gordon growth model.

6. "Forecasters' predictions of inflation are notoriously inaccurate, so their expectations of inflation cannot be rational." Is this statement true, false, or uncertain? Explain your answer.

7. "Whenever it is snowing when Joe Commuter gets up in the morning, he misjudges how long it will take him to drive to work. Otherwise, his expectations of the driving time are perfectly accurate. Considering that it snows only once every ten years where Joe lives, Joe's expectations are almost always perfectly accurate." Are Joe's expectations rational? Why or why not?

8. If a forecaster spends hours every day studying data to forecast interest rates but his expectations are not as accurate as predicting that tomorrow's interest rates will be identical to today's interest rate, are his expectations rational?

9. "If stock prices did not follow a random walk, there would be unexploited profit opportunities in the market." Is this statement true, false, or uncertain? Explain your answer.

10. Suppose that increases in the money supply lead to a rise in stock prices. Does this mean that when you see that the money supply has had a sharp increase in the past week, you should go out and buy stocks? Why or why not?

11. If the public expects a corporation to lose $5 per share this quarter and it actually loses $4, which is still the largest loss in the history of the company, what does the efficient market hypothesis say will happen to the price of the stock when the $4 loss is announced?

12. If you read in the *Wall Street Journal* that the "smart money" on Wall Street expects stock prices to fall, should you follow that lead and sell all your stocks?

13. If your broker has been right in her five previous buy and sell recommendations, should you continue listening to her advice?

14. Can a person with rational expectations expect the price of a share of Google to rise by 10% in the next month?

15. "If most participants in the stock market do not follow what is happening to the monetary aggregates, prices of common stocks will not fully reflect information about them." Is this statement true, false, or uncertain? Explain your answer.

16. "An efficient market is one in which no one ever profits from having better information than the rest." Is this statement true, false, or uncertain? Explain your answer.

17. If higher money growth is associated with higher future inflation, and if announced money growth turns out to be extremely high but is still less than the market expected, what do you think would happen to long-term bond prices?

18. "Foreign exchange rates, like stock prices, should follow a random walk." Is this statement true, false, or uncertain? Explain your answer.

19. Can we expect the value of the dollar to rise by 2% next week if our expectations are rational?

20. "Human fear is the source of stock market crashes, so these crashes indicate that expectations in the stock market cannot be rational." Is this statement true, false, or uncertain? Explain your answer.

WEB EXERCISES

1. Visit www.forecasts.org/data/index.htm. Click on "Stock Index" at the very top of the page. Now choose "U.S. Stock Indices—monthly." Review the indexes for the DJIA, the S&P 500, and the NASDAQ composite. Which index appears most volatile? In which index would you have rather invested in 1985 if the investment had been allowed to compound until now?

2. The Internet is a great source of information on stock prices and stock price movements. Yahoo Finance is a great source for stock market data. Go to http://finance.yahoo.com and click on the DOW ticker in the Market Summary section to view current data on the Dow Jones Industrial Average. Click on the chart to manipulate the different variables. Change the time range and observe the stock trend over various intervals. Have stock prices been going up or down over the last day, week, three months, and year?

WEB REFERENCES

http://stocks.tradingcharts.com

Access detailed stock quotes, charts, and historical stock data.

www.investorhome.com/emh.htm

Learn more about the efficient market hypothesis.

 MyEconLab CAN HELP YOU GET A BETTER GRADE

If your exam were tomorrow, would you be ready? For each chapter, MyEconLab Practice Test and Study Plans pinpoint which sections you have mastered and which ones you need to study. That way, you are more efficient with your study time, and you are better prepared for your exams.

To see how it works, turn to page 20 and then go to: www.myeconlab.com/mishkin

PART 3

Financial Institutions

CHAPTER 8
An Economic Analysis of
Financial Structure

•

CHAPTER 9
Financial Crises and the
Subprime Meltdown

•

CHAPTER 10
Banking and the
Management of
Financial Institutions

•

CHAPTER 11
Economic Analysis
of Financial Regulation

•

CHAPTER 12
Banking Industry:
Structure and Competition

Crisis and Response:
The U.S. $700 Billion Bailout Package

After a heated national debate, the U.S. House of Representatives passed the Emergency Economic Stabilization Act on October 3, 2008. This stunning $700 billion bailout package sought to promote recovery from the subprime financial crisis by authorizing the U.S. Treasury to purchase troubled mortgage assets from struggling financial institutions or to inject capital into banking institutions. To calm fears further, the Act raised the federal deposit insurance limit temporarily from $100,000 to $250,000.

The initial bill was voted down on September 29 when constituents flooded their representatives with complaints about bailing out the greedy Wall Street executives behind the crisis. The national debate pitted Wall Street against Main Street: Bailing out financial institutions was seen as being in opposition to helping struggling homeowners. How could injecting capital into the financial system help those fearful of losing their job or, worse yet, suddenly without work?

The central role of financial institutions in the working of the economy—the focus of Part 3—was overlooked. Banks and other financial institutions make financial markets work by moving funds from people who save to people who have productive investment opportunities. That bank branch on Main Street was not going to be able to lend freely to a small business owner or recent college graduate looking to fund a new car purchase until capital once again flowed.

The subprime crisis highlights how the financial system changes over time, be it from financial innovations or hard lessons from crises such as the one at hand. Chapter 8 analyzes financial structure in the United States and in the rest of the world. In Chapter 9, we develop a framework to understand the dynamics of financial crises—and focus in particular on the red-hot subprime crisis of 2007–2008. In Chapter 10, we look at the business and process of banking. In Chapter 11, we extend the economic analysis developed in Chapter 8 to understand the motivations for bank regulation and we examine the pitfalls in the regulatory process. Chapter 12 examines the development of the American banking system over time and the growing internationalization of banking.

8

An Economic Analysis of Financial Structure

Preview

A healthy and vibrant economy requires a financial system that moves funds from people who save to people who have productive investment opportunities. But how does the financial system make sure that your hard-earned savings get channeled to Paula the Productive Investor rather than to Benny the Bum?

This chapter answers that question by providing an economic analysis of how our financial structure is designed to promote economic efficiency. The analysis focuses on a few simple but powerful economic concepts that enable us to explain features of our financial system, such as why financial contracts are written as they are and why financial intermediaries are more important than securities markets for getting funds to borrowers. The analysis also demonstrates the important link between the financial system and the performance of the aggregate economy, which is the subject of Part 5 of the book.

BASIC FACTS ABOUT FINANCIAL STRUCTURE THROUGHOUT THE WORLD

The financial system is complex in structure and function throughout the world. It includes many different types of institutions: banks, insurance companies, mutual funds, stock and bond markets, and so on—all of which are regulated by government. The financial system channels trillions of dollars per year from savers to people with productive investment opportunities. If we take a close look at financial structure all over the world, we find eight basic facts, some of which are quite surprising, that we need to explain to understand how the financial system works.

The bar chart in Figure 1 shows how American businesses financed their activities using external funds (those obtained from outside the business itself) in the period 1970–2000 and compares U.S. data to those of Germany, Japan, and Canada. The *Bank Loans* category is made up primarily of loans from depository institutions; *Nonbank Loans* is composed primarily of loans by other financial intermediaries; the *Bonds* category includes marketable debt securities such as corporate bonds and commercial paper; and *Stock* consists of new issues of new equity (stock market shares).

Now let us explore the eight facts.

1. Stocks are not the most important source of external financing for businesses. Because so much attention in the media is focused on the stock market, many people have the impression that stocks are the most important sources of financing for

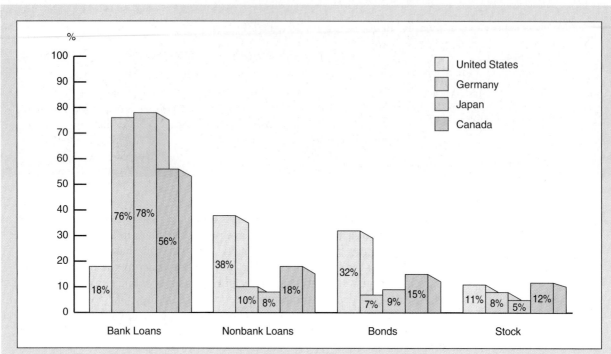

FIGURE 1   Sources of External Funds for Nonfinancial Businesses: A Comparison of the United States with Germany, Japan, and Canada

Source: Andreas Hackethal and Reinhard H. Schmidt, "Financing Patterns: Measurement Concepts and Empirical Results," Johann Wolfgang Goethe-Universitat Working Paper No. 125, January 2004. The data are from 1970–2000 and are gross flows as percentage of the total, not including trade and other credit data, which are not available.

American corporations. However, as we can see from the bar chart in Figure 1, the stock market accounted for only a small fraction of the external financing of American businesses in the 1970–2000 period: 11%.[1] Similarly small figures apply in the other countries presented in Figure 1 as well. Why is the stock market less important than other sources of financing in the United States and other countries?

2. *Issuing marketable debt and equity securities is not the primary way in which businesses finance their operations*. Figure 1 shows that bonds are a far more important source of financing than stocks in the United States (32% versus 11%). However, stocks and bonds combined (43%), which make up the total share of marketable securities, still

---

[1]The 11% figure for the percentage of external financing provided by stocks is based on the flows of external funds to corporations. However, this flow figure is somewhat misleading, because when a share of stock is issued, it raises funds permanently; whereas when a bond is issued, it raises funds only temporarily until they are paid back at maturity. To see this, suppose that a firm raises $1,000 by selling a share of stock and another $1,000 by selling a $1,000 one-year bond. In the case of the stock issue, the firm can hold on to the $1,000 it raised this way, but to hold on to the $1,000 it raised through debt, it has to issue a new $1,000 bond every year. If we look at the flow of funds to corporations over a 30-year period, as in Figure 1, the firm will have raised $1,000 with a stock issue only once in the 30-year period, while it will have raised $1,000 with debt 30 times, once in each of the 30 years. Thus it will look as though debt is 30 times more important than stocks in raising funds, even though our example indicates that they are actually equally important for the firm.

supply less than one-half of the external funds corporations need to finance their activities. The fact that issuing marketable securities is not the most important source of financing is true elsewhere in the world as well. Indeed, as we see in Figure 1, other countries have a much smaller share of external financing supplied by marketable securities than the United States. Why don't businesses use marketable securities more extensively to finance their activities?

3. *Indirect finance, which involves the activities of financial intermediaries, is many times more important than direct finance, in which businesses raise funds directly from lenders in financial markets*. Direct finance involves the sale to households of marketable securities such as stocks and bonds. The 43% share of stocks and bonds as a source of external financing for American businesses actually greatly overstates the importance of direct finance in our financial system. Since 1970, less than 5% of newly issued corporate bonds and commercial paper and less than one-third of stocks have been sold directly to American households. The rest of these securities have been bought primarily by financial intermediaries such as insurance companies, pension funds, and mutual funds. These figures indicate that direct finance is used in less than 10% of the external funding of American business. Because in most countries marketable securities are an even less important source of finance than in the United States, direct finance is also far less important than indirect finance in the rest of the world. Why are financial intermediaries and indirect finance so important in financial markets? In recent years, indirect finance has been declining in importance. Why is this happening?

4. *Financial intermediaries, particularly banks, are the most important source of external funds used to finance businesses*. As we can see in Figure 1, the primary source of external funds for businesses throughout the world comprises loans made by banks and other nonbank financial intermediaries such as insurance companies, pension funds, and finance companies (56% in the United States, but more than 70% in Germany, Japan, and Canada). In other industrialized countries, bank loans are the largest category of sources of external finance (more than 70% in Germany and Japan and more than 50% in Canada). Thus the data suggest that banks in these countries have the most important role in financing business activities. In developing countries, banks play an even more important role in the financial system than they do in the industrialized countries. What makes banks so important to the workings of the financial system? Although banks remain important, their share of external funds for businesses has been declining in recent years. What is driving this decline?

5. *The financial system is among the most heavily regulated sectors of the economy*. The financial system is heavily regulated in the United States and all other developed countries. Governments regulate financial markets primarily to promote the provision of information, and to ensure the soundness (stability) of the financial system. Why are financial markets so extensively regulated throughout the world?

6. *Only large, well-established corporations have easy access to securities markets to finance their activities*. Individuals and smaller businesses that are not well established are less likely to raise funds by issuing marketable securities. Instead, they most often obtain their financing from banks. Why do only large, well-known corporations find it easier to raise funds in securities markets?

7. *Collateral is a prevalent feature of debt contracts for both households and businesses*. **Collateral** is property that is pledged to a lender to guarantee payment in the event that the borrower is unable to make debt payments. Collateralized debt (also known as **secured debt** to contrast it with **unsecured debt**, such as credit card debt, which is not collateralized) is the predominant form of household debt and is widely

used in business borrowing as well. The majority of household debt in the United States consists of collateralized loans: Your automobile is collateral for your auto loan, and your house is collateral for your mortgage. Commercial and farm mortgages, for which property is pledged as collateral, make up one-quarter of borrowing by nonfinancial businesses; corporate bonds and other bank loans also often involve pledges of collateral. Why is collateral such an important feature of debt contracts?

8. *Debt contracts typically are extremely complicated legal documents that place substantial restrictions on the behavior of the borrower*. Many students think of a debt contract as a simple IOU that can be written on a single piece of paper. The reality of debt contracts is far different, however. In all countries, bond or loan contracts typically are long legal documents with provisions (called **restrictive covenants**) that restrict and specify certain activities that the borrower can engage in. Restrictive covenants are not just a feature of debt contracts for businesses; for example, personal automobile loan and home mortgage contracts have covenants that require the borrower to maintain sufficient insurance on the automobile or house purchased with the loan. Why are debt contracts so complex and restrictive?

As you may recall from Chapter 2, an important feature of financial markets is that they have substantial transaction and information costs. An economic analysis of how these costs affect financial markets provides us with explanations of the eight facts, which in turn provide us with a much deeper understanding of how our financial system works. In the next section, we examine the impact of transaction costs on the structure of our financial system. Then we turn to the effect of information costs on financial structure.

TRANSACTION COSTS

Transaction costs are a major problem in financial markets. An example will make this clear.

How Transaction Costs Influence Financial Structure

Say you have $5,000 you would like to invest, and you think about investing in the stock market. Because you have only $5,000, you can buy only a small number of shares. Even if you use online trading, your purchase is so small that the brokerage commission for buying the stock you picked will be a large percentage of the purchase price of the shares. If instead you decide to buy a bond, the problem is even worse, because the smallest denomination for some bonds you might want to buy is as much as $10,000, and you do not have that much to invest. You are disappointed and realize that you will not be able to use financial markets to earn a return on your hard-earned savings. You can take some consolation, however, in the fact that you are not alone in being stymied by high transaction costs. This is a fact of life for many of us: Only around one-half of American households own any securities.

You also face another problem because of transaction costs. Because you have only a small amount of funds available, you can make only a restricted number of investments because a large number of small transactions would result in very high transaction costs.

That is, you have to put all your eggs in one basket, and your inability to diversify will subject you to a lot of risk.

How Financial Intermediaries Reduce Transaction Costs

This example of the problems posed by transaction costs and the example outlined in Chapter 2 when legal costs kept you from making a loan to Carl the Carpenter illustrate that small savers like you are frozen out of financial markets and are unable to benefit from them. Fortunately, financial intermediaries, an important part of the financial structure, have evolved to reduce transaction costs and allow small savers and borrowers to benefit from the existence of financial markets.

Economies of Scale   One solution to the problem of high transaction costs is to bundle the funds of many investors together so that they can take advantage of *economies of scale*, the reduction in transaction costs per dollar of investment as the size (scale) of transactions increases. Bundling investors' funds together reduces transaction costs for each individual investor. Economies of scale exist because the total cost of carrying out a transaction in financial markets increases only a little as the size of the transaction grows. For example, the cost of arranging a purchase of 10,000 shares of stock is not much greater than the cost of arranging a purchase of 50 shares of stock.

The presence of economies of scale in financial markets helps explain why financial intermediaries developed and have become such an important part of our financial structure. The clearest example of a financial intermediary that arose because of economies of scale is a mutual fund. A *mutual fund* is a financial intermediary that sells shares to individuals and then invests the proceeds in bonds or stocks. Because it buys large blocks of stocks or bonds, a mutual fund can take advantage of lower transaction costs. These cost savings are then passed on to individual investors after the mutual fund has taken its cut in the form of management fees for administering their accounts. An additional benefit for individual investors is that a mutual fund is large enough to purchase a widely diversified portfolio of securities. The increased diversification for individual investors reduces their risk, making them better off.

Economies of scale are also important in lowering the costs of things such as computer technology that financial institutions need to accomplish their tasks. Once a large mutual fund has invested a lot of money in setting up a telecommunications system, for example, the system can be used for a huge number of transactions at a low cost per transaction.

Expertise   Financial intermediaries are also better able to develop expertise to lower transaction costs. Their expertise in computer technology enables them to offer customers convenient services like being able to call a toll-free number for information on how well their investments are doing and to write checks on their accounts.

An important outcome of a financial intermediary's low transaction costs is the ability to provide its customers with *liquidity services*, services that make it easier for customers to conduct transactions. Money market mutual funds, for example, not only pay shareholders high interest rates, but also allow them to write checks for convenient bill-paying.

ASYMMETRIC INFORMATION: ADVERSE SELECTION AND MORAL HAZARD

The presence of transaction costs in financial markets explains in part why financial intermediaries and indirect finance play such an important role in financial markets (fact 3). To understand financial structure more fully, however, we turn to the role of information in financial markets.[2]

Asymmetric information—a situation that arises when one party's insufficient knowledge about the other party involved in a transaction makes it impossible to make accurate decisions when conducting the transaction—is an important aspect of financial markets. For example, managers of a corporation know whether they are honest or have better information about how well their business is doing than the stockholders do. The presence of asymmetric information leads to adverse selection and moral hazard problems, which were introduced in Chapter 2.

Adverse selection is an asymmetric information problem that occurs *before* the transaction: Potential bad credit risks are the ones who most actively seek out loans. Thus the parties who are the most likely to produce an undesirable outcome are the ones most likely to want to engage in the transaction. For example, big risk takers or outright crooks might be the most eager to take out a loan because they know that they are unlikely to pay it back. Because adverse selection increases the chances that a loan might be made to a bad credit risk, lenders might decide not to make any loans, even though there are good credit risks in the marketplace.

Moral hazard arises *after* the transaction occurs: The lender runs the risk that the borrower will engage in activities that are undesirable from the lender's point of view because they make it less likely that the loan will be paid back. For example, once borrowers have obtained a loan, they may take on big risks (which have possible high returns but also run a greater risk of default) because they are playing with someone else's money. Because moral hazard lowers the probability that the loan will be repaid, lenders may decide that they would rather not make a loan.

The analysis of how asymmetric information problems affect economic behavior is called **agency theory**. We will apply this theory here to explain why financial structure takes the form it does, thereby explaining the facts outlined at the beginning of the chapter.

THE LEMONS PROBLEM: HOW ADVERSE SELECTION INFLUENCES FINANCIAL STRUCTURE

A particular aspect of the way the adverse selection problem interferes with the efficient functioning of a market was outlined in a famous article by Nobel Prize winner George Akerlof. It is called the "lemons problem," because it resembles the problem created by

---

[2]An excellent survey of the literature on information and financial structure that expands on the topics discussed in the rest of this chapter is contained in Mark Gertler, "Financial Structure and Aggregate Economic Activity: An Overview," *Journal of Money, Credit and Banking* 20 (1988): 559–588.

lemons in the used-car market.[3] Potential buyers of used cars are frequently unable to assess the quality of the car; that is, they can't tell whether a particular used car is a car that will run well or a lemon that will continually give them grief. The price that a buyer pays must therefore reflect the *average* quality of the cars in the market, somewhere between the low value of a lemon and the high value of a good car.

The owner of a used car, by contrast, is more likely to know whether the car is a peach or a lemon. If the car is a lemon, the owner is more than happy to sell it at the price the buyer is willing to pay, which, being somewhere between the value of a lemon and a good car, is greater than the lemon's value. However, if the car is a peach, the owner knows that the car is undervalued at the price the buyer is willing to pay, and so the owner may not want to sell it. As a result of this adverse selection, few good used cars will come to the market. Because the average quality of a used car available in the market will be low and because few people want to buy a lemon, there will be few sales. The used-car market will function poorly, if at all.

Lemons in the Stock and Bond Markets

A similar lemons problem arises in securities markets—that is, the debt (bond) and equity (stock) markets. Suppose that our friend Irving the Investor, a potential buyer of securities such as common stock, can't distinguish between good firms with high expected profits and low risk and bad firms with low expected profits and high risk. In this situation, Irving will be willing to pay only a price that reflects the *average* quality of firms issuing securities—a price that lies between the value of securities from bad firms and the value of those from good firms. If the owners or managers of a good firm have better information than Irving and *know* that they are a good firm, they know that their securities are undervalued and will not want to sell them to Irving at the price he is willing to pay. The only firms willing to sell Irving securities will be bad firms (because his price is higher than the securities are worth). Our friend Irving is not stupid; he does not want to hold securities in bad firms, and hence he will decide not to purchase securities in the market. In an outcome similar to that in the used-car market, this securities market will not work very well because few firms will sell securities in it to raise capital.

The analysis is similar if Irving considers purchasing a corporate debt instrument in the bond market rather than an equity share. Irving will buy a bond only if its interest rate is high enough to compensate him for the average default risk of the good and bad firms trying to sell the debt. The knowledgeable owners of a good firm realize that they will be paying a higher interest rate than they should, so they are unlikely to want to borrow in this market. Only the bad firms will be willing to borrow, and because investors like Irving are not eager to buy bonds issued by bad firms, they will probably not buy any bonds at all. Few bonds are likely to sell in this market, so it will not be a good source of financing.

The analysis we have just conducted explains fact 2—why marketable securities are not the primary source of financing for businesses in any country in the world. It also partly explains fact 1—why stocks are not the most important source of financing for

---

[3]George Akerlof, "The Market for 'Lemons': Quality, Uncertainty and the Market Mechanism," *Quarterly Journal of Economics* 84 (1970): 488–500. Two important papers that have applied the lemons problem analysis to financial markets are Stewart Myers and N. S. Majluf, "Corporate Financing and Investment Decisions When Firms Have Information That Investors Do Not Have," *Journal of Financial Economics* 13 (1984): 187–221; and Bruce Greenwald, Joseph E. Stiglitz, and Andrew Weiss, "Information Imperfections in the Capital Market and Macroeconomic Fluctuations," *American Economic Review* 74 (1984): 194–199.

American businesses. The presence of the lemons problem keeps securities markets such as the stock and bond markets from being effective in channeling funds from savers to borrowers.

Tools to Help Solve Adverse Selection Problems

In the absence of asymmetric information, the lemons problem goes away. If buyers know as much about the quality of used cars as sellers, so that all involved can tell a good car from a bad one, buyers will be willing to pay full value for good used cars. Because the owners of good used cars can now get a fair price, they will be willing to sell them in the market. The market will have many transactions and will do its intended job of channeling good cars to people who want them.

Similarly, if purchasers of securities can distinguish good firms from bad, they will pay the full value of securities issued by good firms, and good firms will sell their securities in the market. The securities market will then be able to move funds to the good firms that have the most productive investment opportunities.

Private Production and Sale of Information   The solution to the adverse selection problem in financial markets is to eliminate asymmetric information by furnishing the people supplying funds with full details about the individuals or firms seeking to finance their investment activities. One way to get this material to saver-lenders is to have private companies collect and produce information that distinguishes good from bad firms and then sell it. In the United States, companies such as Standard and Poor's, Moody's, and Value Line gather information on firms' balance sheet positions and investment activities, publish these data, and sell them to subscribers (individuals, libraries, and financial intermediaries involved in purchasing securities).

The system of private production and sale of information does not completely solve the adverse selection problem in securities markets, however, because of the **free-rider problem**. The free-rider problem occurs when people who do not pay for information take advantage of the information that other people have paid for. The free-rider problem suggests that the private sale of information will be only a partial solution to the lemons problem. To see why, suppose that you have just purchased information that tells you which firms are good and which are bad. You believe that this purchase is worthwhile because you can make up the cost of acquiring this information, and then some, by purchasing the securities of good firms that are undervalued. However, when our savvy (free-riding) investor Irving sees you buying certain securities, he buys right along with you, even though he has not paid for any information. If many other investors act as Irving does, the increased demand for the undervalued good securities will cause their low price to be bid up immediately to reflect the securities' true value. Because of all these free riders, you can no longer buy the securities for less than their true value. Now because you will not gain any profits from purchasing the information, you realize that you never should have paid for this information in the first place. If other investors come to the same realization, private firms and individuals may not be able to sell enough of this information to make it worth their while to gather and produce it. The weakened ability of private firms to profit from selling information will mean that less information is produced in the marketplace, so adverse selection (the lemons problem) will still interfere with the efficient functioning of securities markets.

Government Regulation to Increase Information   The free-rider problem prevents the private market from producing enough information to eliminate all the asymmetric information that leads to adverse selection. Could financial markets benefit from government intervention? The government could, for instance, produce information to help investors distinguish good from bad firms and provide it to the public free of charge. This solution, however, would involve the government in releasing negative information about firms, a practice that might be politically difficult. A second possibility (and one followed by the United States and most governments throughout the world) is for the government to regulate securities markets in a way that encourages firms to reveal honest information about themselves so that investors can determine how good or bad the firms are. In the United States, the Securities and Exchange Commission (SEC) is the government agency that requires firms selling their securities to have independent audits, in which accounting firms certify that the firm is adhering to standard accounting principles and disclosing accurate information about sales, assets, and earnings. Similar regulations are found in other countries. However, disclosure requirements do not always work well, as the recent collapse of Enron and accounting scandals at other corporations, such as WorldCom and Parmalat (an Italian company) suggest (see the FYI box, "The Enron Implosion").

The asymmetric information problem of adverse selection in financial markets helps explain why financial markets are among the most heavily regulated sectors in the economy (fact 5). Government regulation to increase information for investors is needed to reduce the adverse selection problem, which interferes with the efficient functioning of securities (stock and bond) markets.

Although government regulation lessens the adverse selection problem, it does not eliminate it. Even when firms provide information to the public about their sales, assets,

FYI   The Enron Implosion

Until 2001, Enron Corporation, a firm that specialized in trading in the energy market, appeared to be spectacularly successful. It had a quarter of the energy-trading market and was valued as high as $77 billion in August 2000 (just a little over a year before its collapse), making it the seventh-largest corporation in the United States at that time. However, toward the end of 2001, Enron came crashing down. In October 2001, Enron announced a third-quarter loss of $618 million and disclosed accounting "mistakes." The SEC then engaged in a formal investigation of Enron's financial dealings with partnerships led by its former finance chief. It became clear that Enron was engaged in a complex set of transactions by which it was keeping substantial amounts of debt and financial contracts off of its balance sheet. These transactions enabled Enron to hide its financial difficulties. Despite securing as much as $1.5 billion of new financing from J. P. Morgan Chase and Citigroup, the company was forced to declare bankruptcy in December 2001, up to then the largest bankruptcy in U.S. history.

The Enron collapse illustrates that government regulation can lessen asymmetric information problems, but cannot eliminate them. Managers have tremendous incentives to hide their companies' problems, making it hard for investors to know the true value of the firm.

The Enron bankruptcy not only increased concerns in financial markets about the quality of accounting information supplied by corporations, but also led to hardship for many of the firm's former employees, who found that their pensions had become worthless. Outrage against the duplicity of executives at Enron has been high, and several have been indicted, with some being already convicted and sent to jail.

or earnings, they still have more information than investors: There is a lot more to knowing the quality of a firm than statistics can provide. Furthermore, bad firms have an incentive to make themselves look like good firms, because this would enable them to fetch a higher price for their securities. Bad firms will slant the information they are required to transmit to the public, thus making it harder for investors to sort out the good firms from the bad.

Financial Intermediation   So far we have seen that private production of information and government regulation to encourage provision of information lessen, but do not eliminate, the adverse selection problem in financial markets. How, then, can the financial structure help promote the flow of funds to people with productive investment opportunities when there is asymmetric information? A clue is provided by the structure of the used-car market.

An important feature of the used-car market is that most used cars are not sold directly by one individual to another. An individual considering buying a used car might pay for privately produced information by subscribing to a magazine like *Consumer Reports* to find out if a particular make of car has a good repair record. Nevertheless, reading *Consumer Reports* does not solve the adverse selection problem, because even if a particular make of car has a good reputation, the specific car someone is trying to sell could be a lemon. The prospective buyer might also bring the used car to a mechanic for a once-over. But what if the prospective buyer doesn't know a mechanic who can be trusted or if the mechanic would charge a high fee to evaluate the car?

Because these roadblocks make it hard for individuals to acquire enough information about used cars, most used cars are not sold directly by one individual to another. Instead, they are sold by an intermediary, a used-car dealer who purchases used cars from individuals and resells them to other individuals. Used-car dealers produce information in the market by becoming experts in determining whether a car is a peach or a lemon. Once they know that a car is good, they can sell it with some form of a guarantee: either a guarantee that is explicit, such as a warranty, or an implicit guarantee, in which they stand by their reputation for honesty. People are more likely to purchase a used car because of a dealer's guarantee, and the dealer is able to make a profit on the production of information about automobile quality by being able to sell the used car at a higher price than the dealer paid for it. If dealers purchase and then resell cars on which they have produced information, they avoid the problem of other people free-riding on the information they produced.

Just as used-car dealers help solve adverse selection problems in the automobile market, financial intermediaries play a similar role in financial markets. A financial intermediary, such as a bank, becomes an expert in producing information about firms, so that it can sort out good credit risks from bad ones. Then it can acquire funds from depositors and lend them to the good firms. Because the bank is able to lend mostly to good firms, it is able to earn a higher return on its loans than the interest it has to pay to its depositors. The resulting profit that the bank earns gives it the incentive to engage in this information production activity.

An important element in the bank's ability to profit from the information it produces is that it avoids the free-rider problem by primarily making private loans rather than by purchasing securities that are traded in the open market. Because a private loan is not traded, other investors cannot watch what the bank is doing and bid up the loan's price to the point that the bank receives no compensation for the information it has produced. The bank's role as an intermediary that holds mostly nontraded loans is the key to its success in reducing asymmetric information in financial markets.

Our analysis of adverse selection indicates that financial intermediaries in general—and banks in particular, because they hold a large fraction of nontraded loans—should play a greater role in moving funds to corporations than securities markets do. Our analysis thus explains facts 3 and 4: why indirect finance is so much more important than direct finance and why banks are the most important source of external funds for financing businesses.

Another important fact that is explained by the analysis here is the greater importance of banks in the financial systems of developing countries. As we have seen, when the quality of information about firms is better, asymmetric information problems will be less severe, and it will be easier for firms to issue securities. Information about private firms is harder to collect in developing countries than in industrialized countries; therefore, the smaller role played by securities markets leaves a greater role for financial intermediaries such as banks. A corollary of this analysis is that as information about firms becomes easier to acquire, the role of banks should decline. A major development in the past twenty years in the United States has been huge improvements in information technology. Thus the analysis here suggests that the lending role of financial institutions such as banks in the United States should have declined, and this is exactly what has occurred (see Chapter 12).

Our analysis of adverse selection also explains fact 6, which questions why large firms are more likely to obtain funds from securities markets, a direct route, rather than from banks and financial intermediaries, an indirect route. The better known a corporation is, the more information about its activities is available in the marketplace. Thus it is easier for investors to evaluate the quality of the corporation and determine whether it is a good firm or a bad one. Because investors have fewer worries about adverse selection with well-known corporations, they will be willing to invest directly in their securities. Our adverse selection analysis thus suggests that there should be a pecking order for firms that can issue securities. Hence we have an explanation for fact 6: The larger and more established a corporation is, the more likely it will be to issue securities to raise funds.

Collateral and Net Worth   Adverse selection interferes with the functioning of financial markets only if a lender suffers a loss when a borrower is unable to make loan payments and thereby defaults. *Collateral*, property promised to the lender if the borrower defaults, reduces the consequences of adverse selection because it reduces the lender's losses in the event of a default. If a borrower defaults on a loan, the lender can sell the collateral and use the proceeds to make up for the losses on the loan. For example, if you fail to make your mortgage payments, the lender can take title to your house, auction it off, and use the receipts to pay off the loan. Lenders are thus more willing to make loans secured by collateral, and borrowers are willing to supply collateral because the reduced risk for the lender makes it more likely they will get the loan in the first place and perhaps at a better loan rate. The presence of adverse selection in credit markets thus provides an explanation for why collateral is an important feature of debt contracts (fact 7).

Net worth (also called **equity capital**), the difference between a firm's assets (what it owns or is owed) and its liabilities (what it owes), can perform a similar role to collateral. If a firm has a high net worth, then even if it engages in investments that cause it to have negative profits and so defaults on its debt payments, the lender can take title to the firm's net worth, sell it off, and use the proceeds to recoup some of the losses from the loan. In addition, the more net worth a firm has in the first place, the less likely it is to default, because the firm has a cushion of assets that it can use to pay off its loans. Hence, when firms seeking credit have high net worth, the consequences of adverse selection are less important and lenders are more willing to make loans. This analysis lies behind the often-heard lament, "Only the people who don't need money can borrow it!"

Summary   So far we have used the concept of adverse selection to explain seven of the eight facts about financial structure introduced earlier: The first four emphasize the importance of financial intermediaries and the relative unimportance of securities markets for the financing of corporations; the fifth, that financial markets are among the most heavily regulated sectors of the economy; the sixth, that only large, well-established corporations have access to securities markets; and the seventh, that collateral is an important feature of debt contracts. In the next section, we will see that the other asymmetric information concept of moral hazard provides additional reasons for the importance of financial intermediaries and the relative unimportance of securities markets for the financing of corporations, the prevalence of government regulation, and the importance of collateral in debt contracts. In addition, the concept of moral hazard can be used to explain our final fact (fact 8): why debt contracts are complicated legal documents that place substantial restrictions on the behavior of the borrower.

HOW MORAL HAZARD AFFECTS THE CHOICE BETWEEN DEBT AND EQUITY CONTRACTS

Moral hazard is the asymmetric information problem that occurs after the financial transaction takes place, when the seller of a security may have incentives to hide information and engage in activities that are undesirable for the purchaser of the security. Moral hazard has important consequences for whether a firm finds it easier to raise funds with debt than with equity contracts.

Moral Hazard in Equity Contracts: The Principal–Agent Problem

Equity contracts, such as common stock, are claims to a share in the profits and assets of a business. Equity contracts are subject to a particular type of moral hazard called the **principal–agent problem**. When managers own only a small fraction of the firm they work for, the stockholders who own most of the firm's equity (called the *principals*) are not the same people as the managers of the firm, who are the *agents* of the owners. This separation of ownership and control involves moral hazard, in that the managers in control (the agents) may act in their own interest rather than in the interest of the stockholder-owners (the principals) because the managers have less incentive to maximize profits than the stockholder-owners do.

To understand the principal–agent problem more fully, suppose that your friend Steve asks you to become a silent partner in his ice-cream store. The store requires an investment of $10,000 to set up and Steve has only $1,000. So you purchase an equity stake (stock shares) for $9,000, which entitles you to 90% of the ownership of the firm, while Steve owns only 10%. If Steve works hard to make tasty ice cream, keeps the store clean, smiles at all the customers, and hustles to wait on tables quickly, after all expenses (including Steve's salary), the store will have $50,000 in profits per year, of which Steve receives 10% ($5,000) and you receive 90% ($45,000).

But if Steve doesn't provide quick and friendly service to his customers, uses the $50,000 in income to buy artwork for his office, and even sneaks off to the beach while he should be at the store, the store will not earn any profit. Steve can earn the additional $5,000 (his 10% share of the profits) over his salary only if he works hard and forgoes unproductive investments (such as art for his office). Steve might decide that the extra $5,000 just isn't enough to make him expend the effort to be a good manager; he might decide that it would be worth his while only if he earned an extra $10,000. If Steve feels this way, he does not have enough incentive to be a good manager and will end up with a beautiful office, a good tan, and a store that doesn't show any profits. Because the store won't show any profits, Steve's decision not to act in your interest will cost you $45,000 (your 90% of the profits if he had chosen to be a good manager instead).

The moral hazard arising from the principal–agent problem might be even worse if Steve were not totally honest. Because his ice-cream store is a cash business, Steve has the incentive to pocket $50,000 in cash and tell you that the profits were zero. He now gets a return of $50,000, and you get nothing.

Further indications that the principal–agent problem created by equity contracts can be severe are provided by recent scandals in corporations such as Enron and Tyco International, in which managers have been accused of diverting funds for their own personal use. Besides pursuing personal benefits, managers might also pursue corporate strategies (such as the acquisition of other firms) that enhance their personal power but do not increase the corporation's profitability.

The principal–agent problem would not arise if the owners of a firm had complete information about what the managers were up to and could prevent wasteful expenditures or fraud. The principal–agent problem, which is an example of moral hazard, arises only because a manager, such as Steve, has more information about his activities than the stockholder does—that is, there is asymmetric information. The principal–agent problem would also not arise if Steve alone owned the store and there were no separation of ownership and control. If this were the case, Steve's hard work and avoidance of unproductive investments would yield him a profit (and extra income) of $50,000, an amount that would make it worth his while to be a good manager.

Tools to Help Solve the Principal–Agent Problem

Production of Information: Monitoring   You have seen that the principal–agent problem arises because managers have more information about their activities and actual profits than stockholders do. One way for stockholders to reduce this moral hazard problem is for them to engage in a particular type of information production, the monitoring of the firm's activities: auditing the firm frequently and checking on what the management is doing. The problem is that the monitoring process can be expensive in terms of time and money, as reflected in the name economists give it, **costly state verification**. Costly state verification makes the equity contract less desirable, and it explains, in part, why equity is not a more important element in our financial structure.

As with adverse selection, the free-rider problem decreases the amount of information production that would reduce the moral hazard (principal–agent) problem. In this example, the free-rider problem decreases monitoring. If you know that other stockholders are paying to monitor the activities of the company you hold shares in, you can take a free ride on their activities. Then you can use the money you save by not engaging in monitoring to vacation on a Caribbean island. If you can do this, though, so can other stockholders. Perhaps all the stockholders will go to the islands, and no one will spend any resources on monitoring the firm. The moral hazard problem for shares of common stock will then be severe, making it hard for firms to issue them to raise capital (providing an additional explanation for fact 1).

Government Regulation to Increase Information   As with adverse selection, the government has an incentive to try to reduce the moral hazard problem created by asymmetric information, which provides another reason why the financial system is so heavily regulated (fact 5). Governments everywhere have laws to force firms to adhere to standard accounting principles that make profit verification easier. They also pass laws to impose stiff criminal penalties on people who commit the fraud of hiding and stealing profits. However, these measures can be only partly effective. Catching this kind of fraud is not easy; fraudulent managers have the incentive to make it very hard for government agencies to find or prove fraud.

Financial Intermediation   Financial intermediaries have the ability to avoid the free-rider problem in the face of moral hazard, and this is another reason why indirect finance is so important (fact 3). One financial intermediary that helps reduce the moral hazard arising from the principal–agent problem is the **venture capital firm**. Venture capital firms pool the resources of their partners and use the funds to help budding entrepreneurs start new businesses. In exchange for the use of the venture capital, the firm receives an equity share in the new business. Because verification of earnings and profits is so important in eliminating moral hazard, venture capital firms usually insist on having several of their own people participate as members of the managing body of the firm, the board of directors, so that they can keep a close watch on the firm's activities. When a venture capital firm supplies start-up funds, the equity in the firm is not marketable to anyone *except* the venture capital firm. Thus other investors are unable to take a free ride on the venture capital firm's verification activities. As a result of this arrangement, the venture capital firm is able to garner the full benefits of its verification activities and is given the appropriate incentives to reduce the moral hazard problem. Venture capital firms have been important in the development of the high-tech sector in the United States, which has resulted in job creation, economic growth, and increased international competitiveness.

Debt Contracts   Moral hazard arises with an equity contract, which is a claim on profits in all situations, whether the firm is making or losing money. If a contract could be structured so that moral hazard would exist only in certain situations, there would be a reduced need to monitor managers, and the contract would be more attractive than the equity contract. The debt contract has exactly these attributes because it is a contractual agreement by the borrower to pay the lender *fixed* dollar amounts at periodic intervals. When the firm has high profits, the lender receives the contractual payments and does not need to know the exact profits of the firm. If the managers are hiding profits or are pursuing activities that are personally beneficial but don't increase profitability, the lender doesn't care as long as these activities do not interfere with the ability of the firm to make its debt payments on time. Only when the firm cannot meet its debt payments, thereby being in a state of default, is there a need for the lender to verify the state of the firm's profits. Only in this situation do lenders involved in debt contracts need to act more like equity holders; now they need to know how much income the firm has to get their fair share.

The less frequent need to monitor the firm, and thus the lower cost of state verification, helps explain why debt contracts are used more frequently than equity contracts to raise capital. The concept of moral hazard thus helps explain fact 1, why stocks are not the most important source of financing for businesses.[4]

HOW MORAL HAZARD INFLUENCES FINANCIAL STRUCTURE IN DEBT MARKETS

Even with the advantages just described, debt contracts are still subject to moral hazard. Because a debt contract requires the borrowers to pay out a fixed amount and lets them keep any profits above this amount, the borrowers have an incentive to take on investment projects that are riskier than the lenders would like.

For example, suppose that because you are concerned about the problem of verifying the profits of Steve's ice-cream store, you decide not to become an equity partner. Instead, you lend Steve the $9,000 he needs to set up his business and have a debt contract that pays you an interest rate of 10%. As far as you are concerned, this is a sure-fire investment because there is a strong and steady demand for ice cream in your neighborhood. However, once you give Steve the funds, he might use them for purposes other than you intended. Instead of opening up the ice-cream store, Steve might use your $9,000 loan to invest in chemical research equipment because he thinks he has a 1-in-10 chance of inventing a diet ice cream that tastes every bit as good as the premium brands but has no fat or calories.

Obviously, this is a very risky investment, but if Steve is successful, he will become a multimillionaire. He has a strong incentive to undertake the riskier investment with your money, because the gains to him would be so large if he succeeded. You would clearly be very unhappy if Steve used your loan for the riskier investment, because if he were unsuccessful, which is highly likely, you would lose most, if not all, of the money you gave him. And if he were successful, you wouldn't share in his success—you would still get only a 10% return on the loan because the principal and interest payments are fixed. Because of the potential moral hazard (that Steve might use your money to finance a very risky venture), you would probably not make the loan to Steve, even though an ice-cream store in the neighborhood is a good investment that would provide benefits for everyone.

Tools to Help Solve Moral Hazard in Debt Contracts

Net Worth and Collateral   When borrowers have more at stake because their net worth (the difference between their assets and their liabilities) is high or the collateral they have pledged to the lender is valuable, the risk of moral hazard—the temptation to act in a manner that lenders find objectionable—will be greatly reduced because the borrowers themselves have a lot to lose. Another way to say this is that if borrowers

---

[4]Another factor that encourages the use of debt contracts rather than equity contracts in the United States is our tax code. Debt interest payments are a deductible expense for American firms, whereas dividend payments to equity shareholders are not.

have more "skin in the game" because they have higher net worth or pledge collateral, they are likely to take less risk at the lender's expense. Let's return to Steve and his ice-cream business. Suppose that the cost of setting up either the ice-cream store or the research equipment is $100,000 instead of $10,000. So Steve needs to put $91,000 of his own money into the business (instead of $1,000) in addition to the $9,000 supplied by your loan. Now if Steve is unsuccessful in inventing the no-calorie nonfat ice cream, he has a lot to lose—the $91,000 of net worth ($100,000 in assets minus the $9,000 loan from you). He will think twice about undertaking the riskier investment and is more likely to invest in the ice-cream store, which is more of a sure thing. Thus, when Steve has more of his own money (net worth) in the business, and hence more skin in the game, you are more likely to make him the loan. Similarly, if you have pledged your house as collateral, you are less likely to go to Las Vegas and gamble away your earnings that month because you might not be able to make your mortgage payments and might lose your house.

One way of describing the solution that high net worth and collateral provides to the moral hazard problem is to say that it makes the debt contract **incentive-compatible**; that is, it aligns the incentives of the borrower with those of the lender. The greater the borrower's net worth and collateral pledged, then the greater the borrower's incentive to behave in the way that the lender expects and desires, the smaller the moral hazard problem in the debt contract, and the easier it is for the firm or household to borrow. Conversely, when the borrower's net worth and collateral are lower, the moral hazard problem is greater, and it is harder to borrow.

Monitoring and Enforcement of Restrictive Covenants   As the example of Steve and his ice-cream store shows, if you could make sure that Steve doesn't invest in anything riskier than the ice-cream store, it would be worth your while to make him the loan. You can ensure that Steve uses your money for the purpose *you* want it to be used for by writing provisions (restrictive covenants) into the debt contract that restrict his firm's activities. By monitoring Steve's activities to see whether he is complying with the restrictive covenants and enforcing the covenants if he is not, you can make sure that he will not take on risks at your expense. Restrictive covenants are directed at reducing moral hazard either by ruling out undesirable behavior or by encouraging desirable behavior. There are four types of restrictive covenants that achieve this objective:

1. Covenants to discourage undesirable behavior. Covenants can be designed to lower moral hazard by keeping the borrower from engaging in the undesirable behavior of undertaking risky investment projects. Some covenants mandate that a loan can be used only to finance specific activities, such as the purchase of particular equipment or inventories. Others restrict the borrowing firm from engaging in certain risky business activities, such as purchasing other businesses.

2. Covenants to encourage desirable behavior. Restrictive covenants can encourage the borrower to engage in desirable activities that make it more likely that the loan will be paid off. One restrictive covenant of this type requires the breadwinner in a household to carry life insurance that pays off the mortgage upon that person's death. Restrictive covenants of this type for businesses focus on encouraging the borrowing firm to keep its net worth high because higher borrower net worth reduces moral hazard and makes it less likely that the lender will suffer losses. These restrictive covenants typically specify that the firm must maintain minimum holdings of certain assets relative to the firm's size.

*3. **Covenants to keep collateral valuable**.* Because collateral is an important protection for the lender, restrictive covenants can encourage the borrower to keep the collateral in good condition and make sure that it stays in the possession of the borrower. This is the type of covenant ordinary people encounter most often. Automobile loan contracts, for example, require the car owner to maintain a minimum amount of collision and theft insurance and prevent the sale of the car unless the loan is paid off. Similarly, the recipient of a home mortgage must have adequate insurance on the home and must pay off the mortgage when the property is sold.

*4. **Covenants to provide information**.* Restrictive covenants also require a borrowing firm to provide information about its activities periodically in the form of quarterly accounting and income reports, thereby making it easier for the lender to monitor the firm and reduce moral hazard. This type of covenant may also stipulate that the lender has the right to audit and inspect the firm's books at any time.

We now see why debt contracts are often complicated legal documents with numerous restrictions on the borrower's behavior (fact 8): Debt contracts require complicated restrictive covenants to lower moral hazard.

Financial Intermediation   Although restrictive covenants help reduce the moral hazard problem, they do not eliminate it completely. It is almost impossible to write covenants that rule out *every* risky activity. Furthermore, borrowers may be clever enough to find loopholes in restrictive covenants that make them ineffective.

Another problem with restrictive covenants is that they must be monitored and enforced. A restrictive covenant is meaningless if the borrower can violate it knowing that the lender won't check up or is unwilling to pay for legal recourse. Because monitoring and enforcement of restrictive covenants are costly, the free-rider problem arises in the debt securities (bond) market just as it does in the stock market. If you know that other bondholders are monitoring and enforcing the restrictive covenants, you can free-ride on their monitoring and enforcement. But other bondholders can do the same thing, so the likely outcome is that not enough resources are devoted to monitoring and enforcing the restrictive covenants. Moral hazard therefore continues to be a severe problem for marketable debt.

As we have seen before, financial intermediaries—particularly banks—have the ability to avoid the free-rider problem as long as they make primarily private loans. Private loans are not traded, so no one else can free-ride on the intermediary's monitoring and enforcement of the restrictive covenants. The intermediary making private loans thus receives the benefits of monitoring and enforcement and will work to shrink the moral hazard problem inherent in debt contracts. The concept of moral hazard has provided us with additional reasons why financial intermediaries play a more important role in channeling funds from savers to borrowers than marketable securities do, as described in facts 3 and 4.

Summary

The presence of asymmetric information in financial markets leads to adverse selection and moral hazard problems that interfere with the efficient functioning of those markets. Tools to help solve these problems involve the private production and sale of information, government regulation to increase information in financial markets, the importance of collateral and net worth to debt contracts, and the use of monitoring and restrictive covenants. A key finding from our analysis is that the existence of the free-rider

SUMMARY TABLE 1

Asymmetric Information Problems and Tools to Solve Them

Asymmetric Information Problem	Tools to Solve It	Explains Fact Number
Adverse selection	Private production and sale of information	1, 2
	Government regulation to increase information	5
	Financial intermediation	3, 4, 6
	Collateral and net worth	7
Moral hazard in equity contracts (principal–agent problem)	Production of information: monitoring	1
	Government regulation to increase information	5
	Financial intermediation	3
	Debt contracts	1
Moral hazard in debt contracts	Collateral and net worth	6, 7
	Monitoring and enforcement of restrictive covenants	8
	Financial intermediation	3, 4

Note: List of facts:
1. Stocks are not the most important source of external financing.
2. Marketable securities are not the primary source of finance.
3. Indirect finance is more important than direct finance.
4. Banks are the most important source of external funds.
5. The financial system is heavily regulated.
6. Only large, well-established firms have access to securities markets.
7. Collateral is prevalent in debt contracts.
8. Debt contracts have numerous restrictive covenants.

problem for traded securities such as stocks and bonds indicates that financial intermediaries—particularly banks—should play a greater role than securities markets in financing the activities of businesses. Economic analysis of the consequences of adverse selection and moral hazard has helped explain the basic features of our financial system and has provided solutions to the eight facts about our financial structure outlined at the beginning of this chapter.

To help you keep track of all the tools that help solve asymmetric information problems, Table 1 summarizes the asymmetric information problems and tools that help solve them. In addition, it notes how these tools and asymmetric information problems explain the eight facts of financial structure described at the beginning of the chapter.

APPLICATION ✦ Financial Development and Economic Growth

Recent research has found that an important reason why many developing countries or ex-communist countries like Russia (which are referred to as *transition countries*) experience very low rates of growth is that their financial systems are underdeveloped (a situation referred to as *financial repression*.[5] The economic analysis of financial structure helps explain how an underdeveloped financial system leads to a low state of economic development and economic growth.

The financial systems in developing and transition countries face several difficulties that keep them from operating efficiently. As we have seen, two important tools used to help solve adverse selection and moral hazard problems in credit markets are collateral and restrictive covenants. In many developing countries, the system of property rights (the rule of law, constraints on government expropriation, absence of corruption) functions poorly, making it hard to use these two tools effectively. In these countries, bankruptcy procedures are often extremely slow and cumbersome. For example, in many countries, creditors (holders of debt) must first sue the defaulting debtor for payment, which can take several years; then, once a favorable judgment has been obtained, the creditor has to sue again to obtain title to the collateral. The process can take in excess of five years, and by the time the lender acquires the collateral, it may well have been neglected and thus have little value. In addition, governments often block lenders from foreclosing on borrowers in politically powerful sectors such as agriculture. Where the market is unable to use collateral effectively, the adverse selection problem will be worse, because the lender will need even more information about the quality of the borrower so that it can screen out a good loan from a bad one. The result is that it will be harder for lenders to channel funds to borrowers with the most productive investment opportunities. There will be less productive investment, and hence a slower-growing economy. Similarly, a poorly developed or corrupt legal system may make it extremely difficult for lenders to enforce restrictive covenants. Thus they may have a much more limited ability to reduce moral hazard on the part of borrowers and so will be less willing to lend. Again the outcome will be less productive investment and a lower growth rate for the economy. The importance of an effective legal system in promoting economic growth suggests that lawyers play a more positive role in the economy than we give them credit for (see the FYI box, "Should We Kill *All* the Lawyers?")

Governments in developing and transition countries often use their financial systems to direct credit to themselves or to favored sectors of the economy by setting interest rates at artificially low levels for certain types of loans, by creating development finance institutions to make specific types of loans, or by directing existing institutions to lend to certain entities. As we have seen, private institutions have an incentive to solve adverse selection and moral hazard problems and lend to borrowers with the most productive investment opportunities. Governments have less incentive to do so because they are not driven by the profit motive and thus their directed credit programs may not channel funds to sectors that will produce high growth for the economy. The outcome is again likely to result in less efficient investment and slower growth.

In addition, banks in many developing and transition countries are owned by their governments. Again, because of the absence of the profit motive, these **state-owned banks** have little incentive to allocate their capital to the most productive uses. Not surprisingly, the primary loan customer of these state-owned banks is often the government, which does not always use the funds wisely.

---

[5]See World Bank, *Finance for Growth: Policy Choices in a Volatile World* (World Bank and Oxford University Press, 2001) and Frederic S. Mishkin, *The Next Great Globalization: How Disadvantaged Nations can Harness, Their Financial Systems to Get Rich* (Princeton University Press, 2006) for a survey of the literature linking economic growth with financial development and a list of additional references.

FYI   Should We Kill *All* the Lawyers?

Lawyers are often an easy target for would-be comedians. Countless jokes center on ambulance-chasing and shifty filers of frivolous lawsuits. Hostility to lawyers is not just a recent phenomenon: in Shakespeare's *Henry VI*, written in the late sixteenth century, Dick the Butcher recommends, "The first thing we do, let's kill all the lawyers." Is Shakespeare's Dick the Butcher right?

Most legal work is actually not about ambulance chasing, criminal law, and frivolous lawsuits. Instead, it involves the writing and enforcement of contracts, which is how property rights are established. Property rights are essential to protect investments. A good system of laws, by itself, does not provide incentives to invest, because property rights without enforcement are meaningless. This is where lawyers come in. When someone encroaches on your land or makes use of your property without your permission, a lawyer can stop him or her. Without lawyers, you would be unwilling to invest. With zero or limited investment, there would be little economic growth.

The United States has more lawyers per capita than any other country in the world. It is also among the richest countries in the world with a financial system that is superb at getting capital to new productive uses such as the technology sector. Is this just a coincidence? Or could the U.S. legal system actually be beneficial to its economy? Recent research suggests the American legal system, which is based on the Anglo-Saxon legal system, is an advantage of the U.S. economy.*

*See Rafael La Porta, Florencio Lopez-de-Silanes, Andrei Shleifer, and Robert W. Vishny, "Legal Determinants of External Finance," *The Journal of Finance* 52, 3 (July 1997), 1131–1150; and Rafael La Porta, Florencio Lopez-de-Silanes, Andrei Shleifer, and Robert W. Vishny, "Law and Finance," *Journal of Political Economy* 106, 6 (December 1998), 1113–1155.

We have seen that government regulation can increase the amount of information in financial markets to make them work more efficiently. Many developing and transition countries have an underdeveloped regulatory apparatus that retards the provision of adequate information to the marketplace. For example, these countries often have weak accounting standards, making it very hard to ascertain the quality of a borrower's balance sheet. As a result, asymmetric information problems are more severe, and the financial system is severely hampered in channeling funds to the most productive uses.

The institutional environment of a poor legal system, weak accounting standards, inadequate government regulation, and government intervention through directed credit programs and state ownership of banks all help explain why many countries stay poor while others grow richer.

APPLICATION   ✦   Is China a Counter-Example to the Importance of Financial Development?

Although China appears to be on its way to becoming an economic powerhouse, its financial development remains in the early stages. The country's legal system is weak so that financial contracts are difficult to enforce, while accounting standards are lax so that high-quality information about creditors is hard to find. Regulation of the banking system is still in its formative stages, and the banking sector is dominated by large state-owned banks. Yet the Chinese economy has enjoyed one of the highest growth rates in the world over the last twenty years. How has China been able to grow so rapidly given its low level of financial development?

As noted above, China is in an early state of development, with a per capita income that is still less than $5,000, one-eighth of the per capita income in the United States. With an extremely high savings rate, averaging around 40% over the last two decades, the country has been able to rapidly build up its capital stock and shift a massive pool of underutilized labor from the subsistence-agriculture sector into higher-productivity activities that use capital. Even though available savings have not been allocated to their most productive uses, the huge increase in capital combined with the gains in productivity from moving labor out of low-productivity, subsistence agriculture have been enough to produce high growth.

As China gets richer, however, this strategy is unlikely to continue to work. The Soviet Union provides a graphic example. In the 1950s and 1960s, the Soviet Union shared many characteristics with modern-day China: high growth fueled by a high savings rate, a massive buildup of capital, and shifts of a large pool of underutilized labor from subsistence agriculture to manufacturing. During this high-growth phase, however, the Soviet Union was unable to develop the institutions needed to allocate capital efficiently. As a result, once the pool of subsistence laborers was used up, the Soviet Union's growth slowed dramatically and it was unable to keep up with the Western economies. Today no one considers the Soviet Union to have been an economic success story, and its inability to develop the institutions necessary to sustain financial development and growth was an important reason for the demise of this superpower.

To move into the next stage of development, China will need to allocate its capital more efficiently, which requires that it must improve its financial system. The Chinese leadership is well aware of this challenge: The government has announced that state-owned banks are being put on the path to privatization. In addition, the government is engaged in legal reform to make financial contracts more enforceable. New bankruptcy law is being developed so that lenders have the ability to take over the assets of firms that default on their loan contracts. Whether the Chinese government will succeed in developing a first-rate financial system, thereby enabling China to join the ranks of developed countries, is a big question mark.

CONFLICTS OF INTEREST

Earlier in this chapter, we saw how financial institutions play an important role in the financial system. Specifically, their expertise in interpreting signals and collecting information from their customers gives them a cost advantage in the production of information. Furthermore, because they are collecting, producing, and distributing this information, financial institutions can use the information over and over again in as many ways as they would like, thereby realizing economies of scale. By providing multiple financial services to their customers, such as offering them bank loans or selling their bonds for them, they can also achieve **economies of scope**; that is, they can lower the cost of information production for each service by applying one information resource to many different services. A bank, for example, can evaluate how good a credit risk a corporation is when making a loan to the firm, which then helps the bank decide whether it would be easy to sell the bonds of this corporation to the public. Additionally, by providing multiple financial services to their customers, financial institutions develop broader and longer-term relationships with firms. These relationships both reduce the cost of producing information and increase economies of scope.

What Are Conflicts of Interest and Why Do We Care?

Although the presence of economies of scope may substantially benefit financial institutions, it also creates potential costs in terms of **conflicts of interest**. Conflicts of interest are a type of moral hazard problem that arise when a person or institution has multiple objectives (interests) and, as a result, has conflicts between those objectives. Conflicts of interest are especially likely to occur when a financial institution provides multiple services. The potentially competing interests of those services may lead an individual or firm to conceal information or disseminate misleading information. Here we use the analysis of asymmetric information problems to understand why conflicts of interest are important, why they arise, and what can be done about them.

We care about conflicts of interest because a substantial reduction in the quality of information in financial markets increases asymmetric information problems and prevents financial markets from channeling funds into the most productive investment opportunities. Consequently, the financial markets and the economy become less efficient.

Why Do Conflicts of Interest Arise?

Three types of financial service activities have led to prominent conflicts-of-interest problems in financial markets in recent years:[6] underwriting and research in investment banks, auditing and consulting in accounting firms, and credit assessment and consulting in credit-rating agencies. Why do combinations of these activities so often produce conflicts of interest?

Underwriting and Research in Investment Banking   Investment banks perform two tasks: They *research* companies issuing securities, and they *underwrite* these securities by selling them to the public on behalf of the issuing corporations. Investment banks often combine these distinct financial services because information synergies are possible: That is, information produced for one task may also be useful in the other task. A conflict of interest arises between the brokerage and underwriting services because the banks are attempting to simultaneously serve two client groups—the security-issuing firms and the security-buying investors. These client groups have different information needs. Issuers benefit from optimistic research, whereas investors desire unbiased research. However, the same information will be produced for both groups to take advantages of economies of scope. When the potential revenues from underwriting greatly exceed the brokerage commissions from selling, the bank will have a strong incentive to alter the information provided to investors to favor the issuing firm's needs or else risk losing the firm's business to competing investment banks. For example, an internal

---

[6]Another important type of conflict of interest arises in universal banking, in which banks engage in multiple financial service activities, including commercial banking, investment banking, and insurance. For further analysis of these conflicts of interest, see Andrew Crockett, Trevor Harris, Frederic S. Mishkin, and Eugene N. White, *Conflicts of Interest in the Financial Services Industry: What Should We Do About Them?*, Geneva Reports on the World Economy 4 (International Center for Monetary and Banking Studies and Centre for Economic Policy Research: Geneva and London, 2003).

Morgan Stanley memo excerpted in the *Wall Street Journal* on July 14, 1992, stated, "Our objective . . . is to adopt a policy, fully understood by the entire firm, including the Research Department, that we do not make negative or controversial comments about our clients as a matter of sound business practice."

Because of directives like this one, analysts in investment banks might distort their research to please issuers, and indeed this seems to have happened during the stock market tech boom of the 1990s. Such actions undermine the reliability of the information that investors use to make their financial decisions and, as a result, diminish the efficiency of securities markets.

Another common practice that exploits conflicts of interest is **spinning**. Spinning occurs when an investment bank allocates hot, but underpriced, **initial public offerings (IPOs)**—that is, shares of newly issued stock—to executives of other companies in return for their companies' future business with the investment banks. Because hot IPOs typically immediately rise in price after they are first purchased, spinning is a form of kickback meant to persuade executives to use that investment bank. When the executive's company plans to issue its own shares, he or she will be more likely to go to the investment bank that distributed the hot IPO shares, which is not necessarily the investment bank that would get the highest price for the company's securities. This practice may raise the cost of capital for the firm, thereby diminishing the efficiency of the capital market.

Auditing and Consulting in Accounting Firms   Traditionally, an auditor checks the books of companies and monitors the quality of the information produced by firms to reduce the inevitable information asymmetry between the firm's managers and its shareholders. In auditing, threats to truthful reporting arise from several potential conflicts of interest. The conflict of interest that has received the most attention in the media occurs when an accounting firm provides its client with both auditing services and nonaudit consulting services such as advice on taxes, accounting, management information systems, and business strategy. Supplying clients with multiple services allows for economies of scale and scope, but creates two potential sources of conflicts of interest. First, auditors may be willing to skew their judgments and opinions to win consulting business from these same clients. Second, auditors may be auditing information systems or tax and financial plans put in place by their nonaudit counterparts within the firm, and therefore may be reluctant to criticize the systems or advice. Both types of conflicts may lead to biased audits, with the result that less reliable information is available in financial markets and investors find it difficult to allocate capital efficiently.

Another conflict of interest arises when an auditor provides an overly favorable audit to solicit or retain audit business. The unfortunate collapse of Arthur Andersen— once one of the five largest accounting firms in the United States—suggests that this may be the most dangerous conflict of interest (see the FYI box).

Credit Assessment and Consulting in Credit-Rating Agencies   Investors use credit ratings (e.g., Aaa or Baa) that reflect the probability of default to determine the creditworthiness of particular debt securities. As a consequence, debt ratings play a major role in the pricing of debt securities and in the regulatory process. Conflicts of interest can arise when multiple users with divergent interests (at least in the short term) depend on the credit ratings. Investors and regulators are seeking a well-researched, impartial assessment of credit quality; the issuer needs a favorable rating. In the credit-rating industry, the issuers of securities pay a rating firm such as Standard and

Poor's or Moody's to have their securities rated. Because the issuers are the parties paying the credit-rating agency, investors and regulators worry that the agency may bias its ratings upward to attract more business from the issuer.

Another kind of conflict of interest may arise when credit-rating agencies also provide ancillary consulting services. Debt issuers often ask rating agencies to advise them on how to structure their debt issues, usually with the goal of securing a favorable rating. In this situation, the credit-rating agencies would be auditing their own work and would experience a conflict of interest similar to the one found in accounting firms that provide both auditing and consulting services. Furthermore, credit-rating agencies may deliver favorable ratings to garner new clients for the ancillary consulting business. The possible decline in the quality of credit assessments issued by rating agencies could increase asymmetric information in financial markets, thereby diminishing their ability to allocate credit. Such conflicts of interest came to the forefront because of the damaged reputations of the credit-rating agencies during the subprime financial crisis starting in 2007 (see the FYI box, "Credit-Rating Agencies and the Subprime Financial Crisis.")

What Has Been Done to Remedy Conflicts of Interest?

Two major policy measures were implemented to deal with conflicts of interest: the Sarbanes-Oxley Act and the Global Legal Settlement.

FYI   The Demise of Arthur Andersen

In 1913, Arthur Andersen, a young accountant who had denounced the slipshod and deceptive practices that enabled companies to fool the investing public, founded his own firm. Up until the early 1980s, auditing was the most important source of profits within this firm. However, by the late 1980s, the consulting part of the business experienced high revenue growth with high profit margins, while audit profits slumped in a more competitive market. Consulting partners began to assert more power within the firm, and the resulting internal conflicts split the firm in two. Arthur Andersen (the auditing service) and Andersen Consulting were established as separate companies in 2000.

During the period of increasing conflict before the split, Andersen's audit partners had been under increasing pressure to focus on boosting revenue and profits from audit services. Many of Arthur Andersen's clients that later went bust—Enron, WorldCom, Qwest, and Global Crossing—were also the largest

clients in Arthur Andersen's regional offices. The combination of intense pressure to generate revenue and profits from auditing and the fact that some clients dominated regional offices translated into tremendous incentives for regional office managers to provide favorable audit stances for these large clients. The loss of a client like Enron or WorldCom would have been devastating for a regional office and its partners, even if that client contributed only a small fraction of the overall revenue and profits of Arthur Andersen.

The Houston office of Arthur Andersen, for example, ignored problems in Enron's reporting. Arthur Andersen was indicted in March 2002 and then convicted in June 2002 for obstruction of justice for impeding the SEC's investigation of the Enron collapse. Its conviction—the first ever against a major accounting firm—barred Arthur Andersen from conducting audits of publicly traded firms. This development contributed to the firm's demise.

Sarbanes-Oxley Act of 2002   The public outcry over the corporate and accounting scandals led in 2002 to the passage of the Public Accounting Return and Investor Protection Act, more commonly referred to as the Sarbanes-Oxley Act, after its two principal authors in Congress. This act increased supervisory oversight to monitor and prevent conflicts of interest:

- It established a Public Company Accounting Oversight Board (PCAOB), overseen by the SEC, to supervise accounting firms and ensure that audits are independent and controlled for quality.
- It increased the SEC's budget to supervise securities markets.

Sarbanes-Oxley also directly reduced conflicts of interest:

- It made it illegal for a registered public accounting firm to provide any nonaudit service to a client contemporaneously with an impermissible audit (as determined by the PCAOB).

FYI   Credit-Rating Agencies and the Subprime Financial Crisis

The credit-rating agencies have come under severe criticism for the role they played during the subprime financial crisis. Credit-rating agencies advised clients on how to structure complex financial instruments that paid out cash flows from subprime mortgages. At the same time, they were rating these identical products, leading to the potential for severe conflicts of interest. Specifically, the large fees they earned from advising clients on how to structure products that they were rating meant they did not have sufficient incentives to make sure their ratings were accurate.

When housing prices began to fall and subprime mortgages began to default, it became crystal clear that the ratings agencies had done a terrible job of assessing the risk in the subprime products they had helped to structure. Many AAA-rated products had to be downgraded over and over again until they reached junk status. The resulting massive losses on these assets were one reason why so many financial institutions who were holding them got into trouble, with absolutely disastrous consequences for the economy, as discussed in the next chapter.

Criticisms of the credit-rating agencies led the SEC to propose comprehensive reforms in 2008. The SEC concluded that the credit-rating agencies' models for rating subprime products were not fully developed and that conflicts of interest may have played a role in producing inaccurate ratings. To address conflicts of interest, the SEC prohibited credit-rating agencies from structuring the same products they rate, prohibited anyone who participates in determining a credit rating from negotiating the fee that the issuer pays for it, and prohibited gifts from bond-issuers to those who rate them in any amount over $25. In order to make credit-rating agencies more accountable, the SEC's new rules also required more disclosure of how the credit-rating agencies determine ratings. For example, credit-rating agencies were required to disclose historical ratings performance, including the dates of downgrades and upgrades, information on the underlying assets of a product that were used by the credit-rating agencies to rate a product, and the kind of research they used to determine the rating. In addition, the SEC required the rating agencies to differentiate the ratings on structured products from those issued on bonds. The expectation is that these reforms will bring increased transparency to the ratings process and reduce conflicts of interest that played such a large role in the subprime debacle.

Sarbanes-Oxley provided incentives for investment banks not to exploit conflicts of interest:

- It beefed up criminal charges for white-collar crime and obstruction of official investigations.

Sarbanes-Oxley also had measures to improve the quality of information in the financial markets:

- It required a corporation's chief executive officer (CEO) and chief financial officer (CFO), as well as its auditors, to certify that periodic financial statements and disclosures of the firm (especially regarding off-balance-sheet transactions) are accurate (Section 404).
- It required members of the audit committee (the subcommittee of the board of directors that oversees the company's audit) to be "independent"; that is, they cannot be managers in the company or receive any consulting or advisory fee from the company.

Global Legal Settlement of 2002   The second major policy measure arose out of a lawsuit brought by New York Attorney General Eliot Spitzer against the ten largest investment banks (Bear Stearns, Credit Suisse First Boston, Deutsche Bank, Goldman Sachs, J. P. Morgan, Lehman Brothers, Merrill Lynch, Morgan Stanley, Salomon Smith Barney, and UBS Warburg). A global settlement was reached on December 20, 2002, with these investment banks by the SEC, the New York Attorney General, NASD, NASAA, NYSE, and New York state regulators. Like Sarbanes-Oxley, this settlement directly reduced conflicts of interest:

- It required investment banks to sever the links between research and securities underwriting.
- It banned spinning.

The Global Legal Settlement also provided incentives for investment banks not to exploit conflicts of interest:

- It imposed $1.4 billion of fines on the accused investment banks.

The global settlement had measures to improve the quality of information in financial markets:

- It required investment banks to make their analysts' recommendations public.
- Over a five-year period, investment banks were required to contract with at least three independent research firms that would provide research to their brokerage customers.

It is too early to evaluate the impact of the Sarbanes-Oxley Act and the Global Legal Settlement, but the most controversial elements were the separation of functions (research from underwriting, and auditing from nonaudit consulting). Although such a separation of functions may reduce conflicts of interest, it might also diminish economies of scope and thus potentially lead to a reduction of information in financial markets. In addition, there is a serious concern that implementation of these measures, particularly Sarbanes-Oxley, is too costly and is leading to a decline in U.S. capital markets (see the FYI box "Has Sarbanes-Oxley Led to a Decline in U.S. Capital Markets?").

FYI   **Has Sarbanes–Oxley Led to a Decline in U.S. Capital Markets?**

There has been much debate in the United States in recent years regarding the impact of Sarbanes-Oxley, especially Section 404, on U.S. capital markets. Section 404 requires both management and company auditors to certify the accuracy of their financial statements. There is no question that Sarbanes-Oxley has led to increased costs for corporations, and this is especially true for smaller firms with revenues of less than $100 million, where the compliance costs have been estimated to exceed 1% of sales. These higher costs could result in smaller firms listing abroad and discourage IPOs in the United States, thereby shrinking U.S. capital markets relative to those abroad. However, improved accounting standards could work to encourage stock market listings and IPOs because better information could raise the valuation of common stocks.

Critics of Sarbanes-Oxley have cited it, as well as higher litigation and weaker shareholder rights, as the cause of declining U.S. stock listings and IPOs, but other factors are likely at work. The European financial system experienced a major liberalization in the 1990s, along with the introduction of the euro, that helped make its financial markets more integrated and efficient. As a result, it became easier for European firms to list in their home countries. The fraction of European firms that list in their home countries has risen to over 90% currently from around 60% in 1995. As the importance of the United States in the world economy has diminished because of the growing importance of other economies, the U.S. capital markets have become less dominant over time. This process is even more evident in the corporate bond market. In 1995, corporate bond issues were double that of Europe, while issues of corporate bonds in Europe now exceed those in the United States.

SUMMARY

1. There are eight basic facts about U.S. financial structure. The first four emphasize the importance of financial intermediaries and the relative unimportance of securities markets for the financing of corporations; the fifth recognizes that financial markets are among the most heavily regulated sectors of the economy; the sixth states that only large, well-established corporations have access to securities markets; the seventh indicates that collateral is an important feature of debt contracts; and the eighth presents debt contracts as complicated legal documents that place substantial restrictions on the behavior of the borrower.

2. Transaction costs freeze many small savers and borrowers out of direct involvement with financial markets. Financial intermediaries can take advantage of economies of scale and are better able to develop expertise to lower transaction costs, thus enabling their savers and borrowers to benefit from the existence of financial markets.

3. Asymmetric information results in two problems: adverse selection, which occurs before the transaction, and moral hazard, which occurs after the transaction. Adverse selection refers to the fact that bad credit risks are the ones most likely to seek loans, and moral hazard refers to the risk of the borrower's engaging in activities that are undesirable from the lender's point of view.

4. Adverse selection interferes with the efficient functioning of financial markets. Tools to help reduce the adverse selection problem include private production and sale of information, government regulation to increase information, financial intermediation, and collateral and net worth. The free-rider problem occurs when people who do not pay for information take advantage of information that other people have paid for. This problem explains why financial intermediaries, particularly banks, play a more important role in financing the activities of businesses than securities markets do.

5. Moral hazard in equity contracts is known as the principal–agent problem, because managers (the agents) have less incentive to maximize profits than stockholders (the principals). The principal–agent problem explains why debt contracts are so much more prevalent in financial markets than equity contracts. Tools to help reduce the principal–agent problem include monitoring, government regulation to increase information, and financial intermediation.

6. Tools to reduce the moral hazard problem in debt contracts include net worth, monitoring and enforcement of restrictive covenants, and financial intermediaries.

7. Conflicts of interest arise when financial service providers or their employees are serving multiple interests and have incentives to misuse or conceal information needed for the effective functioning of financial markets. We care about conflicts of interest because they can substantially reduce the amount of reliable information in financial markets, thereby preventing them from channeling funds to parties with the most productive investment opportunities. Three types of financial service activities have had the greatest potential for conflicts of interest: underwriting and research in investment banking, and auditing and consulting in accounting firms. Two major policy measures have been implemented to deal with conflicts of interest: the Sarbanes-Oxley Act of 2002 and the Global Legal Settlement of 2002, which arose from a lawsuit by the New York attorney general against the ten largest investment banks.

KEY TERMS

agency theory, p. 174

collateral, p. 171

conflicts of interest, p. 190

costly state verification, p. 181

economies of scope, p. 189

free-rider problem, p. 176

incentive-compatible, p. 184

initial public offering (IPO), p. 191

net worth (equity capital), p. 179

principal–agent problem, p. 180

restrictive covenants, p. 172

secured debt, p. 171

spinning, p. 191

state-owned banks, p. 187

unsecured debt, p. 171

venture capital firm, p. 182

QUESTIONS AND PROBLEMS

All questions and problems are available in myeconlab *at*
www.myeconlab.com/mishkin.

1. How can economies of scale help explain the existence of financial intermediaries?

2. Describe two ways in which financial intermediaries help lower transaction costs in the economy.

3. Would moral hazard and adverse selection still arise in financial markets if information were not asymmetric? Explain.

4. How do standard accounting principles help financial markets work more efficiently?

5. Do you think the lemons problem would be more severe for stocks traded on the New York Stock Exchange or those traded over-the-counter? Explain.

6. Which firms are most likely to use bank financing rather than to issue bonds or stocks to finance their activities? Why?

7. How can the existence of asymmetric information provide a rationale for government regulation of financial markets?

8. Would you be more willing to lend to a friend if she put all of her life savings into her business than you would if she had not done so? Why?

9. Wealthy people often worry that others will seek to marry them only for their money. Is this a problem of adverse selection?

10. The more collateral there is backing a loan, the less the lender has to worry about adverse selection. Is this statement true, false, or uncertain? Explain your answer.

11. How does the free-rider problem aggravate adverse selection and moral hazard problems in financial markets?

12. Explain how the separation of ownership and control in American corporations might lead to poor management.

13. Why can the provision of several types of financial services by one firm lead to a lower cost of information production?

14. How does the provision of several types of financial services by one firm lead to conflicts of interest?

15. How can conflicts of interest make financial service firms less efficient?

16. Describe two conflicts of interest that occur when underwriting and research are provided by a single investment firm.

17. How does spinning lead to a less efficient financial system?

18. Describe two conflicts of interest that occur in accounting firms.

19. Which provisions of Sarbanes-Oxley do you think are beneficial, and which are not?

20. Which provisions of the Global Legal Settlement do you think are beneficial, and which are not?

WEB EXERCISES

1. In this chapter we discuss the lemons problem and its effect on the efficient functioning of a market. This theory was initially developed by George Akerlof. Go to www.nobel.se/economics/laureates/2001/public.html. This site reports that Akerlof, Spence, and Stiglitz were awarded the Nobel prize in economics in 2001 for their work. Read this report down through the section on George Akerlof. Summarize his research ideas in one page.

WEB REFERENCES

http://nobelprize.org/nobel_prizes/economics/laureates/2001/public.html

A complete discussion of the lemons problem on a site dedicated to Nobel prize winners.

 MyEconLab CAN HELP YOU GET A BETTER GRADE

If your exam were tomorrow, would you be ready? For each chapter, MyEconLab Practice Test and Study Plans pinpoint which sections you have mastered and which ones you need to study. That way, you are more efficient with your study time, and you are better prepared for your exams.

To see how it works, turn to page 20 and then go to: www.myeconlab.com/mishkin

9 Financial Crises and the Subprime Meltdown

Preview

Financial crises are major disruptions in financial markets characterized by sharp declines in asset prices and firm failures. Beginning in August of 2007, defaults in the subprime mortgage market (for borrowers with weak credit records) sent a shudder through the financial markets, leading to the worst U.S. financial crisis since the Great Depression. In Congressional testimony, Alan Greenspan, former Chairman of the Fed, described the subprime financial crisis as a "once-in-a-century credit tsunami." Wall Street firms and commercial banks suffered hundreds of billions of dollars of losses. Households and businesses found they had to pay higher rates on their borrowings—and it was much harder to get credit. All over the world, stock markets crashed, with the U.S market falling by 40% from its peak. Many financial firms, including commercial banks, investment banks, and insurance companies, went belly up.

Why did this financial crisis occur? Why have financial crises been so prevalent throughout U.S. history, as well as in so many other countries, and what insights do they provide on the current crisis? Why are financial crises almost always followed by severe contractions in economic activity? We will examine these questions in this chapter by developing a framework to understand the dynamics of financial crises. Building on Chapter 8, we make use of agency theory, the economic analysis of the effects of asymmetric information (adverse selection and moral hazard) on financial markets and the economy, to see why financial crises occur and why they have such devastating effects on the economy. We will then apply the analysis to explain the course of events in a number of past financial crises throughout the world, including the most recent subprime crisis.

FACTORS CAUSING FINANCIAL CRISES

In the previous chapter we saw that a well-functioning financial system solves asymmetric information problems so that capital is allocated to its most productive uses. A **financial crisis** occurs when an increase in asymmetric information from a disruption in the financial system causes severe adverse selection and moral hazard problems that render financial markets incapable of channeling funds efficiently from savers to households and firms with productive investment opportunities. When financial markets fail to function efficiently, economic activity contracts sharply.

To understand why financial crises occur and, more specifically, how they lead to contractions in economic activity, we need to examine the factors that cause them. Six categories of factors play an important role in financial crises: asset market effects on balance sheets, deterioration in financial institutions' balance sheets, banking crisis, increases in uncertainty, increases in interest rates, and government fiscal imbalances. We will examine each of these factors and their impact on lending, investment, and economic activity.

Asset Market Effects on Balance Sheets

The state of borrowers' balance sheets has important implications for the severity of asymmetric information problems in the financial system.

Stock Market Decline   A sharp decline in the stock market is one factor that can cause a serious deterioration in borrowing firms' balance sheets. In turn, this deterioration can increase adverse selection and moral hazard problems in financial markets and provoke a financial crisis. A decline in the stock market means that the net worth of corporations has fallen, because share prices are the valuation of a corporation's net worth. The decline in net worth makes lenders less willing to lend because, as we have seen, the net worth of a firm plays a role similar to that of collateral. When the value of collateral declines, it provides less protection to lenders, meaning that losses on loans are likely to be more severe. Because lenders are now less protected against the consequences of adverse selection, they decrease their lending, which in turn causes investment and aggregate output to decline. In addition, the decline in corporate net worth as a result of a stock market decline increases moral hazard by providing incentives for borrowing firms to make risky investments, as they now have less to lose if their investments go sour. The resulting increase in moral hazard makes lending less attractive—another reason why a stock market decline and the resultant decline in net worth leads to decreased lending and economic activity.

Unanticipated Decline in the Price Level   In economies with moderate inflation, which characterizes most industrialized countries, many debt contracts with fixed interest rates are typically of fairly long maturity, ten years or more. In this institutional environment, unanticipated declines in the aggregate price level also decrease the net worth of firms. Because debt payments are contractually fixed in nominal terms, an unanticipated decline in the price level raises the value of borrowing firms' liabilities in real terms (increases the burden of the debt) but does not raise the real value of firms' assets. The result is that net worth in real terms (the difference between assets and liabilities in real terms) declines. A sharp drop in the price level therefore causes a substantial decline in real net worth for borrowing firms and an increase in adverse selection and moral hazard problems facing lenders. An unanticipated decline in the aggregate price level thus leads to a drop in lending and economic activity.

Unanticipated Decline in the Value of the Domestic Currency   Because of uncertainty about the future value of the domestic currency in developing countries (and in some industrialized countries), many nonfinancial firms, banks, and governments in developing countries find it easier to issue debt denominated in foreign currencies rather than in their own currency. This can lead to a financial crisis in a similar fashion to an unanticipated decline in the price level. With debt contracts denominated in foreign currency, when there is an unanticipated decline in the value of the domestic currency, the debt burden of domestic firms increases. Since assets are typically denominated in domestic currency, there is a resulting deterioration in firms' balance sheets and a decline in net worth, which then increases adverse selection and moral hazard problems along the lines just described. The increase in asymmetric information problems leads to a decline in investment and economic activity.

Asset Write-Downs   Asset price declines also lead to a write-down of the value of the assets side of the balance sheets of financial institutions. This deterioration in their balance sheets can also lead to a contraction of lending, as the next factor indicates.

Deterioration in Financial Institutions' Balance Sheets

Financial institutions, particularly banks, play a major role in financial markets because they are well positioned to engage in information-producing activities that facilitate productive investment for the economy. The state of banks' and other financial intermediaries' balance sheets has an important effect on lending. Suppose financial institutions suffer a deterioration in their balance sheets and so have a substantial contraction in their capital. They will have fewer resources to lend, and lending will decline. The contraction in lending then leads to a decline in investment spending, which slows economic activity.

Banking Crisis

If the deterioration in financial institutions' balance sheets is severe enough, they will start to fail. Fear can spread from one institution to another, causing even healthy ones to go under. Because banks have deposits that can be pulled out very quickly, they are particularly prone to contagion of this type. A **bank panic** occurs when multiple banks fail simultaneously. The source of the contagion is asymmetric information. In a panic, depositors, fearing for the safety of their deposits (in the absence of or with limited amounts of deposit insurance) and not knowing the quality of banks' loan portfolios, withdraw their deposits to the point that the banks fail. When a large number of banks fail in a short period of time, there is a loss of information production in financial markets and a direct loss of banks' financial intermediation.

The decrease in bank lending during a banking crisis decreases the supply of funds available to borrowers, which leads to higher interest rates. Bank panics result in an increase in adverse selection and moral hazard problems in credit markets: These problems produce an even sharper decline in lending to facilitate productive investments and lead to an even more severe contraction in economic activity.

Increases in Uncertainty

A dramatic increase in uncertainty in financial markets, due perhaps to the failure of a prominent financial or nonfinancial institution, a recession, or a stock market crash, makes it hard for lenders to screen good from bad credit risks. The resulting inability of lenders to solve the adverse selection problem makes them less willing to lend, which leads to a decline in lending, investment, and aggregate economic activity.

Increases in Interest Rates

As we saw in Chapter 8, individuals and firms with the riskiest investment projects are those who are willing to pay the highest interest rates. If increased demand for credit or a decline in the money supply market drives up interest rates sufficiently, good credit risks are less likely to want to borrow while bad credit risks are still willing to borrow. Because of the resulting increase in adverse selection, lenders will no longer want to make loans. The substantial decline in lending will lead to a substantial decline in investment and aggregate economic activity.

Increases in interest rates also play a role in promoting a financial crisis through their effect on cash flow, the difference between cash receipts and expenditures. A firm with sufficient cash flow can finance its projects internally, and there is no asymmetric information because it knows how good its own projects are. (Indeed, American businesses fund around two-thirds of their investments with internal funds.) An increase in interest rates and therefore in household and firm interest payments decreases their cash flow. With less cash flow, the firm has fewer internal funds and must raise funds from an external source, say, a bank, which does not know the firm as well as its owners or managers. How can the bank be sure if the firm will invest in safe projects or instead take on big risks and then be unlikely to pay back the loan? Because of this increased adverse selection and moral hazard, the bank may choose not to lend firms, even those with good risks, the money to undertake potentially profitable investments. Thus when cash flow drops as a result of an increase in interest rates, adverse selection and moral hazard problems become more severe, again curtailing lending, investment, and economic activity.

Government Fiscal Imbalances

In emerging market countries (Argentina, Brazil, Ecuador, Russia, and Turkey are recent examples), government fiscal imbalances may create fears of default on government debt. As a result, demand from individual investors for government bonds may fall, causing the government to force financial institutions to purchase them. If the debt then declines in price—which, as we have seen in Chapter 6, will occur if a government default is likely—financial institutions' balance sheets will weaken and their lending will contract for the reasons described earlier. Fears of default on the government debt can also spark a foreign exchange crisis in which the value of the domestic currency falls sharply because investors pull their money out of the country. The decline in the domestic currency's value will then lead to the destruction of the balance sheets of firms with large amounts of debt denominated in foreign currency. These balance sheet problems lead to an increase in adverse selection and moral hazard problems, a decline in lending, and a contraction of economic activity.

DYNAMICS OF PAST U.S. FINANCIAL CRISES

The subprime crisis has dominated recent news headlines, but it is only one of a number of financial crises in U.S. history. We will now examine trends in past crises—and uncover insights on present-day challenges along the way.

Financial crises in the United States have progressed in two and sometimes three stages. To help you understand how these crises have unfolded, refer to Figure 1, a diagram that identifies the stages and sequence of events in U.S. financial crises.

Stage One: Initiation of Financial Crisis

There are several possible ways that financial crises start—mismanagement of financial liberalization/innovation, asset price booms and busts, spikes in interest rates, or a general increase in uncertainty when there are failures of major financial institutions.

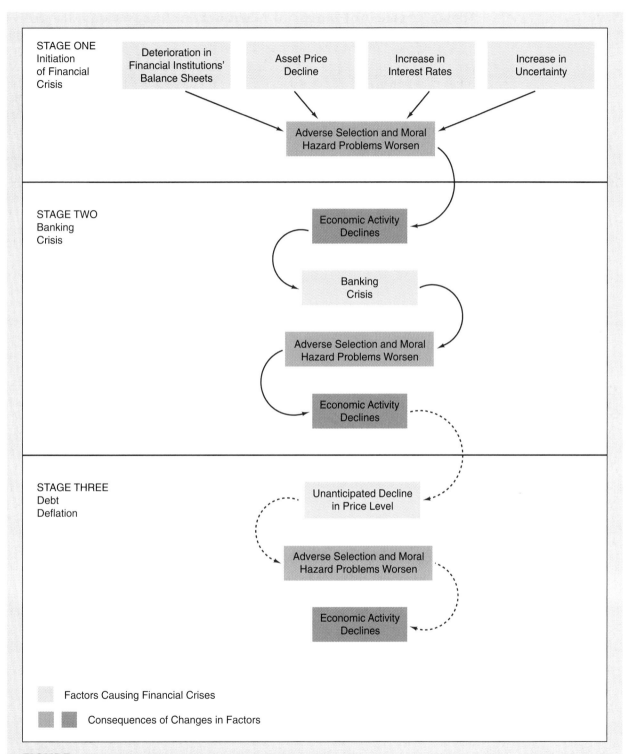

FIGURE 1   Sequence of Events in U.S. Financial Crises
The solid arrows in Stages One and Two trace the sequence of events in a typical financial crisis; the dotted arrows show the additional set of events that occur if the crisis develops into a debt deflation, Stage Three in our discussion.

Mismanagement of Financial Liberalization/Innovation   The seeds of a financial crisis are often sown when countries engage in **financial liberalization**, the elimination of restrictions on financial markets and institutions, or when major financial innovations are introduced to the marketplace, as occurred recently with subprime residential mortgages. Financial innovation or liberalization is highly beneficial in the long run because it facilitates the process of financial development discussed in the previous chapter, which leads to a more efficient financial system that can allocate capital better. However, financial liberalization or innovation has a dark side: if managed improperly, it can lead financial institutions to take on excessive risk. With restrictions lifted or new financial products introduced, financial institutions frequently go on a lending spree, often called a **credit boom**, and expand their lending at a rapid pace. Unfortunately, the managers of these financial institutions may not have the expertise to manage risk appropriately in these new lines of business. Even if the required managerial expertise is initially present, the rapid growth of credit will likely outstrip the information resources available to these institutions, leading to overly risky lending.

As we will discuss in Chapter 11, most governments try to prevent bank panics and encourage banks to keep on lending during bad times by providing a government safety net. If depositors and other providers of funds to banks are protected from losses, they will keep on supplying banks with funds so banks can continue to lend and will not fail. However, there is a catch: The government safety net weakens market discipline for the bank. With a safety net, depositors know that they will not lose anything if a bank fails. Thus the bank can still acquire funds even if it takes on excessive risk. The government safety net therefore increases the moral hazard incentive for banks to take on greater risk than they otherwise would, because if their risky, high-interest loans pay off, the banks make a lot of money; if they don't and the bank fails, taxpayers pay most of the bill for the safety net that protects the banks' depositors. In other words, banks can play the game of "heads, I win: tails, the taxpayer loses."

The presence of a government safety net requires regulation and government supervision of the financial system to prevent excessive risk taking. However, new lines of business and rapid credit growth stretch the resources of the government's supervisory agencies. Financial supervisors find themselves without the expertise or the additional resources needed to appropriately monitor the new lending activities. Without this monitoring, risk-taking can explode.

Eventually, this risk-taking comes home to roost. Losses on loans begin to mount and the drop in the value of the loans (on the asset side of the balance sheet) falls relative to liabilities, thereby driving down the net worth (capital) of banks and other financial institutions. With less capital, these financial institutions cut back on their lending, a process that is called **deleveraging**. Furthermore, with less capital, banks and other financial institutions become riskier, causing depositors and other potential lenders to these institutions to pull out their funds. Fewer funds mean fewer loans and a credit freeze. The lending boom turns into a lending crash.

As we have seen, banks and other financial intermediaries play a crucial role in financial markets because they are well suited to collect information about businesses and industries. This ability in turn enables these institutions to distinguish good loan prospects from bad ones. When financial intermediaries deleverage and cut back on their lending, no one else can step in to collect this information and make these loans. The ability of the financial system to cope with the asymmetric information problems of adverse selection and moral hazard is therefore severely hampered (as shown in the arrow pointing from the first factor in the top row of Figure 1). As loans become scarcer, firms are no longer able to fund their attractive investment opportunities; they decrease their spending and economic activity contracts.

Asset Price Boom and Bust   Asset prices, in the stock market and real estate, can be driven well above their fundamental economic values by investor psychology (dubbed "irrational exuberance" by Alan Greenspan when he was Chairman of the Federal Reserve). The result is an **asset-price bubble**, such as the tech stock market bubble of the late 1990s or the recent housing price bubble that we will discuss later in this chapter.

Asset-price bubbles are often also driven by credit booms, in which the large increase in credit is used to fund purchases of assets, thereby driving up their price. When the bubble bursts and asset prices realign with fundamental economic values, the resulting decline in net worth increases asymmetric information (as shown by the arrow pointing from the second factor in the top row of Figure 1), making borrowers less credit-worthy and causing a contraction in lending and spending along the lines we discussed in the previous section.

The asset price bust can also, as we have seen, lead to a deterioration in financial institutions' balance sheets (as shown by the arrow pointing from the second factor in the top row of Figure 1), which causes them to deleverage, further contributing to the decline in economic activity.

Spikes in Interest Rates   Many nineteenth-century U.S. financial crises were precipitated by increases in interest rates, either when interest rates shot up in London, which at the time was the world's financial center, or when bank panics led to a scramble for liquidity in the United States that produced sharp upward spikes in interest rates (sometimes rising by 100 percentage points in a couple of days).

The higher interest rates led to a decline in cash flow for households and firms and a reduction in the number of good credit risks who are willing to borrow, both of which increase adverse selection and moral hazard (as shown by the arrow pointing from the third factor in the top row of Figure 1), causing a decline in economic activity.

Increase in Uncertainty   Financial crises in the United States almost always have started when uncertainty is high, either after a recession has begun or the stock market has crashed. The failure of a major financial institution is a particularly important source of heightened uncertainty that features prominently in financial crises. Examples in U.S. history abound: the Ohio Life Insurance and Trust Company in 1857; Jay Cooke and Company in 1873; Grant and Ward in 1884; the Knickerbocker Trust Company in 1907; the Bank of the United States in 1930; and Bear Stearns, Lehman Brothers, and AIG in 2008. With information harder to come by in a period of high uncertainty, adverse selection and moral hazard problems increase, leading to a decline in lending and economic activity (as shown by the arrow pointing from the last factor in the top row of Figure 1).

Stage Two: Banking Crisis

Because of the worsening business conditions and uncertainty about their banks' health, depositors begin to withdraw their funds from banks and a banking crisis or bank panic often ensues. The resulting decline in the number of banks results in a loss of their information capital, worsening adverse selection and moral hazard problems in the credit markets, leading to a further spiraling down of the economy. Figure 1 represents this progression in the Stage Two portion. Bank panics were a feature of all U.S. financial crises during the nineteenth and twentieth centuries until World War II, occurring every twenty years or so—1819, 1837, 1857, 1873, 1884, 1893, 1907, and 1930–33.

For the typical U.S. financial crisis, there is then a sorting out of firms that are insolvent (had a negative net worth) from healthy firms by bankruptcy proceedings. The same process occurs for banks, often with the help of public and private authorities. Once this sorting out is complete, uncertainty in financial markets declines, the stock market recovers, and interest rates fall. The overall result is that adverse selection and moral hazard problems diminish and the financial crisis subsides. With the financial markets able to operate well again, the stage is set for the recovery of the economy, bringing us to the next possible stage.

Stage Three: Debt Deflation

If, however, the economic downturn leads to a sharp decline in prices, the recovery process can be short-circuited. In this situation, shown as Stage Three in Figure 1, a process called **debt deflation** occurs, in which a substantial unanticipated decline in the price level sets in, leading to a further deterioration in firms' net worth because of the increased burden of indebtedness. With debt deflation, the adverse selection and moral hazard problems become more severe so that lending, investment spending, and aggregate economic activity remain depressed for a long time. The most significant financial crisis that included debt deflation was the Great Depression, the worst economic contraction in U.S. history.

APPLICATION ✦ The Mother of All Financial Crises: The Great Depression

In 1928 and 1929, prices doubled in the U.S. stock market. Federal Reserve officials viewed the stock market boom as excessive speculation. To curb it, they pursued a tight monetary policy to raise interest rates; the Fed got more than it bargained for when the stock market crashed in October 1929, falling by 20%.

Although the 1929 crash had a great impact on the minds of a whole generation, most people forget that by the middle of 1930, more than half of the stock market decline had been reversed. Indeed, credit market conditions remained quite stable and there was little evidence that a major financial crisis was underway.

What might have been a normal recession turned into something far different, however, when adverse shocks to the agricultural sector led to bank failures in agricultural regions that then spread to the major banking centers. A sequence of bank panics followed from October 1930 until March 1933. More than one-third of U.S. banks went out of business (events described in more detail in Chapter 14).

The continuing decline in stock prices after mid-1930 (by mid-1932 stocks had declined to 10% of their value at the 1929 peak) and the increase in uncertainty from the unsettled business conditions created by the economic contraction worsened adverse selection and moral hazard problems in the credit markets. The loss of one-third of the banks reduced the amount of financial intermediation. Intensified adverse selection and moral hazard problems decreased the ability of financial markets to channel funds to firms with productive investment opportunities. As our analysis predicts, the amount of outstanding commercial loans fell by half from 1929 to 1933, and investment spending collapsed, declining by 90% from its 1929 level.

The short-circuiting of the process that kept the economy from recovering quickly, which it does in most recessions, occurred because of a fall in the price level by 25% in the 1930–1933 period. This huge decline in prices triggered a debt deflation in which net worth fell because of the increased burden of indebtedness borne by firms. The decline in net worth and the resulting increase in adverse selection and moral hazard problems in the credit markets led to a prolonged economic contraction in which unemployment rose to 25% of the labor force. The financial crisis in the Great Depression was the worst ever experienced in the United States, and it explains why this economic contraction was also the most severe ever experienced by the nation.[1]

THE SUBPRIME FINANCIAL CRISIS OF 2007–2008

Now that our framework for analyzing financial crises is in place, we are prepared to tackle the most recent U.S. financial crisis. Mismanagement of financial innovation in the subprime residential mortgage market and a bursting of a bubble in housing prices were the underlying forces behind the financial crisis of 2007–2008.

Financial Innovations Emerge in the Mortgage Markets

Before 2000, only the most credit-worthy (prime) borrowers were able to obtain residential mortgages. Advances in computer technology and new statistical techniques, known as data mining, however, led to enhanced, quantitative evaluation of the credit risk for a new class of riskier residential mortgages. **Subprime mortgages** are mortgages for borrowers with less-than-stellar credit records. **Alt-A mortgages** are mortgages for borrowers with higher expected default rates than prime (A-paper), but with better credit records than subprime borrowers. Households with credit records could now be assigned a numerical credit score, known as a FICO score (named after the Fair Isaac Corporation that developed it), that would predict how likely they would be to default on their loan payments. In addition, by lowering transaction costs, computer technology enabled the bundling together of smaller loans (like mortgages) into standard debt securities, a process known as **securitization**.

The ability to cheaply bundle and quantify the default risk of the underlying high-risk mortgages in a standardized debt security called **mortgage-backed securities** provided a new source of financing for these mortgages. The financial innovation of subprime and alt-A mortgages was born. Financial innovation didn't stop there. **Financial engineering**, the development of new, sophisticated financial instruments products, led to **structured credit products** that are derived from cash flows of underlying assets and can be tailored to have particular risk characteristics that appeal to

[1]For a discussion of the role of asymmetric information problems in the Great Depression period, see Ben Bernanke, "Nonmonetary Effects of the Financial Crisis in the Propagation of the Great Depression," *American Economic Review* 73 (1983): 257–276, and Charles Calomiris, "Financial Factors and the Great Depression," *Journal of Economic Perspectives* (Spring 1993): 61–85.

investors with differing preferences. Particularly notorious were **collateralized debt obligations (CDOs)**, which paid out the cash flows from subprime mortgage-backed securities in different tranches, with the highest-rated tranch paying out first, while lower ones paid out less if there were losses on the mortgage-backed securities. There were even CDO2s and CDO3s that sliced and diced risk even further, paying out the cash flows from CDOs and CDO2s.

Housing Price Bubble Forms

Aided by liquidity from cash flows surging into the United States from countries like China and India, the subprime mortgage market took off after the recession was over in 2001, becoming over a trillion dollar market by 2007. The development of the subprime mortgage market was lauded by economists and politicians alike because it led to a "democratization of credit" and helped raise U.S. homeownership rates to the highest levels in history. The asset price boom in housing, which took off after the 2000–2001 recession was over, also helped stimulate the growth of the subprime market. Higher housing prices meant that subprime borrowers could refinance their houses with even larger loans when their homes appreciated in value. Subprime borrowers were also unlikely to default because they could always sell their house to pay off the loan, making investors happy because the securities backed by cash flows from subprime mortgages had high returns. The growth of the subprime mortgage market, in turn, increased the demand for houses and so fueled the boom in housing prices.

Agency Problems Arise

But all was not well in the subprime mortgage market. All the agency problems described in the previous chapter were coming to the fore. The subprime mortgage market was based on a so-called **originate-to-distribute** business model, in which the mortgage was originated by a separate party, typically a mortgage broker, and then distributed to an investor as an underlying asset in a security. Unfortunately, the originate-to-distribute model is subject to the principal–agent problem because the agent for the investor, the mortgage originator, has little incentive to make sure that the mortgage is a good credit risk. Once the mortgage broker earns her fee, why should she care if the borrower makes good on his payment? The more volume the broker originates, the more she makes.

Not surprisingly, given these incentives, mortgage brokers often did not make a strong effort to evaluate whether the borrower could pay off the loan. Adverse selection then became especially severe: Risk-loving investors were able to obtain loans to acquire houses that would be very profitable if housing prices went up, but they could just "walk away" from houses if housing prices went down. The principal–agent problem also created incentives for mortgage brokers to encourage households to take on mortgages they could not afford, or to commit fraud by falsifying information on borrowers' mortgage applications in order to qualify them for their mortgages. Compounding this problem was lax regulation of originators, who were not required to disclose information to borrowers that would have helped them assess whether they could afford the loans.

The agency problems went even deeper. Commercial and investment banks, who were earning large fees by underwriting mortgage-backed securities and structured credit products like CDOs, also had weak incentives to make sure that the ultimate holders of the securities would be paid off. The credit-rating agencies that were evaluating these securities also were subject to conflicts of interest: they were earning fees from rating them and also from advising clients on how to structure these securities to get the highest ratings. The integrity of these ratings was thus more likely to be compromised.

Information Problems Surface

Although financial engineering has the potential benefit to create products and services that better match investors' risk appetites, it, too, has a dark side. The structured products like CDOs, CDO2s, and CDO3s can get so complicated that it can be hard to value the cash flows of the underlying assets for a security or to determine who actually owns these assets. Indeed, in a speech in October 2007, Ben Bernanke, the chairman of the Federal Reserve, joked that he "would like to know what those damn things are worth." In other words, the increased complexity of structured products can actually destroy information, thereby making asymmetric information worse in the financial system and increasing the severity of adverse selection and moral hazard problems.

Housing Price Bubble Bursts

As housing prices rose and profitability for mortgage originators and lenders was high, the underwriting standards for subprime mortgages fell to lower and lower standards. Riskier borrowers were able to obtain mortgages, and the amount of the mortgage relative to the value of the house, the loan-to-value ratio (LTV), rose. Borrowers were often able to get piggyback, second, and third mortgages on top of their original 80% LTV mortgage, so that they had to put almost no money down. When asset prices rise too far out of line with fundamentals, however, they must come down, and eventually the housing price bubble burst. With housing prices falling after their peak in 2006, the rot in the financial system began to be revealed. The decline in housing prices led to many subprime borrowers finding that their mortgages were "underwater," that is, the value of the house fell below the amount of the mortgage. When this happened, struggling homeowners had tremendous incentives to walk away from their homes and just send the keys back to the lender. Defaults on mortgages shot up sharply, eventually leading to over 1 million mortgages in foreclosure.

Crisis Spreads Globally

Although the problem originated in the United States, the wake-up call came from Europe, a sign of how extensive the globalization of financial markets had become. After Fitch and Standard & Poor's announced ratings downgrades on mortgage-backed securities and CDOs totaling more than $10 billion, the asset-based commercial paper market seized up and a French investment house, BNP Paribas, suspended redemption of shares held in some of its money market funds on August 7, 2008. Despite huge injections of liquidity into the financial system by the European Central Bank and the Federal Reserve, which will be discussed later in Chapter 15, banks began to horde cash and were unwilling to lend to each other. As can be seen in Figure 2, the Treasury Bill-to-Eurodollar rate (TED) spread, a good measure of liquidity in the interbank market, shot up from an average of 40 basis points (0.40 percentage points) during the first half of 2007 to a peak of 240 by August 20, 2007. The drying up of credit led to the first major bank failure in the United Kingdom in over 100 years when Northern Rock, which had relied on wholesale short-term borrowing rather than deposits for its funding, collapsed in September 2008.

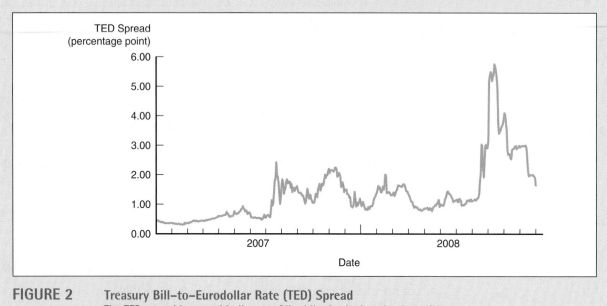

FIGURE 2   Treasury Bill–to–Eurodollar Rate (TED) Spread
The TED spread is a good indicator of liquidity in the interbank market.
Source: www.federalreserve.gov/releases/h15/data.htm

Banks' Balance Sheets Deteriorate

The decline in U.S. housing prices, which now accelerated, led to rising defaults on mortgages. As a result, the value of mortgage-backed securities and CDOs collapsed, leading to ever-larger write-downs at banks and other financial institutions. The balance sheets of these institutions deteriorated because of the losses from their holdings of these securities and because many of these institutions had to take back onto their balance sheets some of the *structured investment vehicles (SIVs)* they had sponsored. **Structured investment vehicles** are similar to CDOs in that they pay off cash flows from pools of assets such as mortgages; instead of issuing long-term debt as in CDOs, they issued asset-backed commercial paper. With weaker balance sheets, these banks and other financial institutions began to deleverage, selling off assets and restricting the availability of credit to both households and businesses. With no one else able to step in to collect information and make loans, adverse selection and moral hazard problems increased in the credit markets, leading to a slowing of the U.S. economy, and rising unemployment levels.

High-Profile Firms Fail

In March of 2008, Bear Stearns, the fifth-largest investment bank, which had invested heavily in subprime-related securities, had a run on its funding and was forced to sell itself to J.P. Morgan for less than 5% of what it was worth just a year earlier. In order to broker the deal, the Federal Reserve had to take over $30 billion of Bear Stearn's hard-to-value assets. In July, Fannie Mae and Freddie Mac, the two privately owned government-sponsored enterprises that together insured over $5 trillion of mortgages or mortgage-backed assets, had to be propped up by the U.S. Treasury and the Federal Reserve after suffering substantial losses from their holdings of subprime securities. In early September 2008, they were then put into conservatorship (in effect run by the government).

Worse was yet to come. On Monday, September 15, 2008, after suffering losses in the subprime market, Lehman Brothers, the fourth-largest investment bank by asset size with over $600 billion in assets and 25,000 employees, filed for bankruptcy, making it the largest bankruptcy filing in U.S. history. The day before, Merrill Lynch, the third-largest investment bank, which also suffered large losses on its holding of subprime securities, announced its sale to Bank of America for a price 60% below its price a year earlier. On Tuesday, September 16, AIG, an insurance giant with assets over $1 trillion, suffered an extreme liquidity crisis when its credit rating was downgraded. It had written over $400 billion of insurance contracts called credit default swaps (discussed in Web Chapter 1) which had to make payouts on possible losses from subprime mortgage securities. The Federal Reserve then stepped in with an $85 billion loan to keep AIG afloat (with total loans from the Fed and the government later increased to $173 billion).

Also on September 16, as a result of its losses from exposure to Lehman Brothers' debt, one large money market mutual fund, the Reserve Primary Fund, with over $60 billion of assets, "broke the buck"—that is, it could no longer redeem its shares at the par value of $1. A run on money market funds then ensued, with the Treasury putting in place a temporary guarantee for all money market mutual fund redemptions in order to stem withdrawals. On September 25, 2008, Washington Mutual (WAMU), the sixth-largest bank in the United States with over $300 billion in assets, was put into receivership by the FDIC and sold to J.P. Morgan, making it the largest bank failure in U.S. history.

Bailout Package Debated

The financial crisis then took an even more virulent turn after the House of Representatives, fearing the wrath of constituents who were angry about bailing out Wall Street, voted down a $700 billion dollar bailout package proposed by the Bush administration on Monday, September 29, 2008. The Emergency Economic Stabilization Act was finally passed on Friday, October 3. The stock market crash accelerated, with the week beginning on October 6 showing the worst weekly decline in U.S. history. Credit spreads went through the roof over the next three weeks, with the Treasury Bill-to-Eurodollar rate (TED) spread going to over 500 basis points (5.00 percentage points), the highest value in its history (see Figure 2). The crisis then spread to Europe with a string of failures of financial institutions.

Recovery in Sight?

The increase in uncertainty from the failures of so many financial institutions, the deterioration in financial institutions' balance sheets, and the decline in the stock market of over 40% from its peak all increased the severity of adverse selection and moral hazard problems in the credit markets. The resulting decline in lending led to the U.S. unemployment rate rising to above 7% by the end of 2008, with worse likely to come. The financial crisis led to a slowing of economic growth worldwide and massive government bailouts of financial institutions (see the Global box, "The Treasury Asset Relief Plan and Government Bailouts").

Global   The Treasury Asset Relief Plan and Government Bailouts

The Economic Recovery Act of 2008 had several provisions to promote recovery from the subprime financial crisis. The most important was the Treasury Asset Relief Plan (TARP), which authorized the Treasury to spend $700 billion purchasing subprime mortgage assets from troubled financial institutions or to inject capital into banking institutions. The hope was that by buying subprime assets, their price would rise above fire-sale levels, thus creating a market for them, while at the same time increasing capital in financial institutions. Along with injections of capital, this would enable these institutions to start lending again. In addition, the act raised the federal deposit insurance limit temporarily from $100,000 to $250,000 in order to limit withdrawals from banks and required the Treasury, as the owner of these assets, to encourage the servicers of the underlying mortgages to restructure them to minimize foreclosures. Shortly thereafter, the FDIC put in place a guarantee for certain debt newly issued by banks, and the Treasury guaranteed for a year money market mutual fund shares at par value.

The spreading bank failures in Europe in the fall of 2008 led to bailouts of financial institutions: the Netherlands, Belgium, and Luxembourg injected $16 billion to prop up Fortis, a major European bank; the Netherlands injected $13 billion into ING, a banking and insurance giant; Germany provided a $50 billion rescue package for Hypo Real Estate Holdings; and Iceland took over its three largest banks after its banking system collapsed. Ireland's government guaranteed all the deposits of its commercial banks as well as interbank lending, as did Greece. Spain implemented a bailout package similar to the United States' to buy up to 50 billion euros ($70 billion) of assets in its banks in order to encourage them to lend. The U.K. Treasury set up a bailout plan with a similar price tag to that of the U.S. Treasury's plan of 400 billion pounds ($699 billion). It guaranteed 250 billion pounds of bank liabilities, added 100 billion pounds to a facility that swaps these assets for government bonds, and allowed the U.K. government to buy up to 50 billion pounds of equity stakes in British banks. Bailout plans to the tune of over $100 billion in South Korea, $200 billion in Sweden, $400 billion in France, and $500 billion in Germany, all of which guaranteed the debt of their banks as well as injecting capital into them, then followed. Both the scale of these bailout packages and the degree of international coordination was unprecedented.

DYNAMICS OF FINANCIAL CRISES IN EMERGING MARKET ECONOMIES

Before the subprime crisis, economists looked abroad for recent examples of financial crises. **Emerging market economies**, economies in an earlier stage of market development that have recently opened up to the flow of goods, services, and capital from the rest of the world, are particularly vulnerable. With the opening up of their economies to markets, emerging market countries have been no stranger to devastating financial crises in recent years. The dynamics of financial crises in emerging market economies have many of the same elements as those found in the United States, but with some important differences. Figure 3 outlines the key stages and sequence of events in financial crises in these economies that we will address in this section.

Stage One: Initiation of Financial Crisis

In contrast to U.S. crises that have been triggered by a number of different factors, financial crises in emerging market countries develop along two basic paths: one involving the

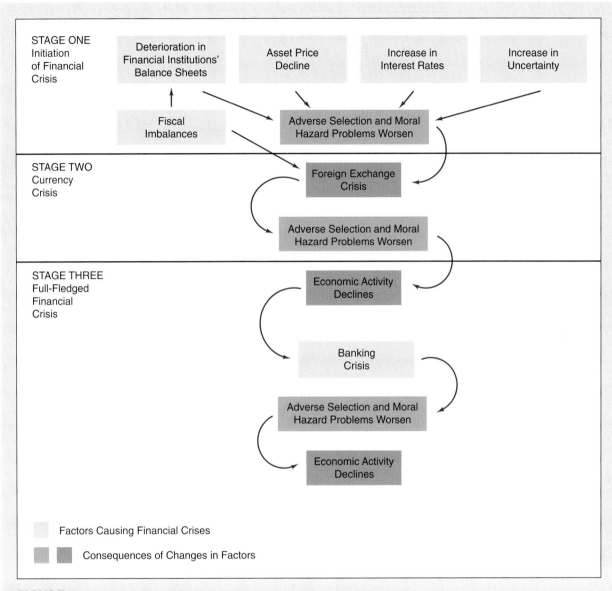

FIGURE 3   Sequence of Events in Emerging Market Financial Crises
The arrows trace the sequence of events during financial crises.

mismanagement of financial liberalization/globalization and the other involving severe fiscal imbalances.

Path One: Mismanagement of Financial Liberalization/Globalization

As has occurred in the United States, the seeds of a financial crisis in emerging market countries are often sown when countries liberalize their financial systems. Liberalization occurs by eliminating restrictions on financial institutions and markets domestically and opening up their economies to flows of capital and financial firms from other nations, a process called **financial globalization**.

Emerging market countries typically have very weak supervision by bank regulators and a lack of expertise in the screening and monitoring of borrowers by banking institutions. Consequently, the lending boom that results after a financial liberalization often leads to even riskier lending than is typical in advanced countries like the United States, and enormous loan losses result. The financial globalization process adds fuel to the fire because it allows domestic banks to borrow abroad. The banks pay high interest rates to attract foreign capital and so can rapidly increase their lending. The capital inflow is further stimulated by government policies that keep exchange rates fixed to the dollar, which give foreign investors a sense of lower risk.

At some point, all of the highly risky lending starts producing high loan losses, which then lead to a deterioration in bank balance sheets and banks cut back on their lending. Just as in advanced countries like the United States, the lending boom ends in a lending crash. In emerging market countries, banks play an even more important role in the financial system than in advanced countries because securities markets and other financial institutions are not as well developed. The decline in bank lending thus means that there are really no other players to solve adverse selection and moral hazard problems (as shown by the arrow pointing from the first factor in the top row of Figure 3). The deterioration in their balance sheets therefore has even more negative impacts on lending and economic activity than in advanced countries.

The story told so far suggests that a lending boom and crash are inevitable outcomes of financial liberalization and globalization in emerging market countries, but this is not the case. They only occur when there is an institutional weakness that prevents the nation from successfully handling the liberalization/globalization process. More specifically, if prudential regulation and supervision to limit excessive risk-taking were strong, the lending boom and bust would not happen. Why does regulation and supervision instead end up being weak? The answer is the principal-agent problem discussed in the previous chapter that encourages powerful domestic business interests to pervert the financial liberalization process. Politicians and prudential supervisors are ultimately agents for voters-taxpayers (principals); that is, the goal of politicians and prudential supervisors is, or should be, to protect the taxpayers' interest. Taxpayers almost always bear the cost of bailing out the banking sector if losses occur.

Once financial markets have been liberalized, powerful business interests that own banks will want to prevent the supervisors from doing their job properly. Powerful business interests who contribute heavily to politicians' campaigns are often able to persuade politicians to weaken regulations that restrict their banks from engaging in high-risk/high-payoff strategies. After all, if bank owners achieve growth and expand bank lending rapidly, they stand to make a fortune. But, if the bank gets in trouble, the government is likely to bail it out and the taxpayer foots the bill. In addition, these business interests can also make sure that the supervisory agencies, even in the presence of tough regulations, lack the resources to effectively monitor banking institutions or to close them down.

As we will see in Chapter 11, powerful business interests also have acted to prevent supervisors from doing their job properly in advanced countries like the United States. The weaker institutional environment in emerging market countries makes this perversion of the financial liberalization process even worse. In emerging market economies, business interests are far more powerful than they are in advanced economies where a better-educated public and a free press monitor (and punish) politicians and bureaucrats who are not acting in the public interest. Not surprisingly, then, the cost to the society of the principal–agent problem we have been describing here is particularly high in emerging market economies.

Path Two: Severe Fiscal Imbalances   The second path through which emerging market countries experience a financial crisis is government fiscal imbalances that entail substantial budget deficits that need to be financed. The recent financial crisis in Argentina in 2001–2002 is of this type; other recent crises, for example in Russia in 1998, Ecuador in 1999, and Turkey in 2001, also have some elements of deficit-driven fiscal imbalances.

When Willie Sutton, a famous bank robber, was asked why he robbed banks, he answered, "Because that's where the money is." Governments in emerging market countries have the same attitude. When they face large fiscal imbalances and cannot finance their debt, they often cajole or force banks to purchase government debt. Investors who lose confidence in the ability of the government to repay this debt unload the bonds, which causes their prices to plummet. Now the banks that are holding this debt have a big hole on the asset side of their balance sheets, with a huge decline in their net worth. The deterioration in bank balance sheets then causes a decline in bank lending and can even lead to a bank panic. Severe fiscal imbalances spill over into and weaken the banking system (as shown by the arrow from the factor in the second row of Figure 3), which leads to a worsening of adverse selection and moral hazard problems.

Additional Factors   Other factors also play a role in the first stage in some crises. For example, another precipitating factor in some crises is a rise in interest rates that comes from events abroad, such as a tightening of monetary policy. When interest rates rise, riskier firms are most willing to pay the higher interest rates, so the adverse selection problem is more severe. In addition, the higher interest rates reduce firms' cash flows, forcing them to seek funds in external capital markets in which asymmetric problems are greater. Increases in interest rates abroad that raise domestic interest rates can then increase adverse selection and moral hazard problems (as shown by the arrow from the second factor in the top row of Figure 3).

Because asset markets are not as large in emerging market countries as they are in advanced countries, they play a less prominent role in financial crises. Asset price declines in the stock market do, nevertheless, decrease the net worth of firms and so increase adverse selection problems. There is less collateral for lenders to grab on to which increases moral hazard problems because with lower net worth the owners of the firm have less to lose if they engage in riskier activities. Asset price declines can therefore have some role in worsening adverse selection and moral hazard problems directly (as shown by the arrow pointing from the third factor in the first row of Figure 3) as well as indirectly by causing a deterioration in banks' balance sheets from asset write-downs.

As in advanced countries, when an emerging market economy is in a recession or a prominent firm fails, people become more uncertain about the returns on investment projects. In emerging market countries, another source of uncertainty can come from their political systems, which are often notoriously unstable. When uncertainty increases, it becomes harder for lenders to screen out good credit risks from bad and to monitor the activities of firms to whom they have loaned money, so that adverse selection and moral hazard problems worsen (as shown by the arrow pointing from the last factor in the first row of Figure 3).

Stage Two: Currency Crisis

As the effects of any or all of the factors in stage one in Figure 3 build on each other, participants in the foreign exchange market sense an opportunity: they can make huge profits if they bet on a depreciation of the currency. As we will describe in more detail in Chapter 17, a currency that is fixed against the U.S. dollar now becomes subject to a **speculative attack**, in which speculators engage in massive sales of the currency. As the currency sales flood the market, supply far outstrips demand, the value of the currency collapses, and a currency crisis ensues (see the Stage Two section of Figure 3). High interest rates abroad, increases in uncertainty, and falling asset prices all play a role. The deterioration in bank balance sheets and severe fiscal imbalances, however, are the two key factors that trigger the speculative attacks and plunge the economies into a full-scale, vicious downward spiral of currency crisis, financial crisis, and meltdown.

How Deterioration of Bank Balance Sheets Triggers Currency Crises

When banks and other financial institutions are in trouble, governments have a limited number of options. Defending their currencies by raising interest rates should encourage capital inflows. If the government raises interest rates, banks must pay more to obtain funds. This increase in costs decreases bank profitability, which may lead them to insolvency. Thus when the banking system is in trouble, the government and central bank are now between a rock and a hard place: If they raise interest rates too much they will destroy their already weakened banks, and if they don't, they can't maintain the value of their currency.

Speculators in the market for foreign currency are able to recognize the troubles in a country's financial sector and realize when the government's ability to defend the currency is limited. They will seize an almost sure-thing bet because the currency has only one way to go, downward in value. Speculators engage in a feeding frenzy and sell the currency in anticipation of its decline, which will provide them with huge profits. These sales rapidly use up the country's holdings of reserves of foreign currency because the country has to sell its reserves to buy the domestic currency and keep it from falling in value. Once the country's central bank has exhausted its holdings of foreign currency reserves, the cycle ends. It no longer has the resources to intervene in the foreign exchange market and must let the value of the domestic currency fall; that is, the government must allow a devaluation.

How Severe Fiscal Imbalances Trigger Currency Crises

We have seen that severe fiscal imbalances can lead to a deterioration of bank balance sheets, and so can help produce a currency crisis along the lines just described. Fiscal imbalances can also directly trigger a currency crisis. When government budget deficits spin out of control, foreign and domestic investors begin to suspect that the country may not be able to pay back its government debt and so will start pulling money out of the country and selling the domestic currency. Recognition that the fiscal situation is out of control thus results in a speculative attack against the currency, which eventually results in its collapse.

Stage Three: Full-Fledged Financial Crisis

When debt contracts are denominated in foreign currency (dollars), as is typically the case in emerging market countries, and there is an unanticipated depreciation or devaluation of the domestic currency (for example, pesos), the debt burden of domestic firms increases in terms of domestic currency. That is, it takes more pesos to pay back the dollarized debt. Since the goods and services produced by most firms are priced in the domestic currency, the firms' assets do not rise in value in terms of pesos, while the debt does. The depreciation of the domestic currency increases the value of debt relative to assets, and the firm's net worth declines. The decline in net worth then increases adverse selection and moral hazard problems described earlier. A decline in investment and economic activity then follows (as shown by the Stage Three section of Figure 3).

We now see how the institutional structure of debt markets in emerging market countries interacts with the currency devaluations to propel the economies into full-fledged financial crises. Economists often call a concurrent currency and financial crisis the "twin crises." Many firms in these emerging market countries have debt denominated in foreign currency like the dollar and the yen. Depreciation of their currencies thus results in increases in their indebtedness in domestic currency terms, even though the value of their assets remains unchanged.

The collapse of a currency also can lead to higher inflation. The central banks in most emerging market countries have little credibility as inflation fighters. Thus a sharp depreciation of the currency after a currency crisis leads to immediate upward pressure on import prices. A dramatic rise in both actual and expected inflation will likely follow. The resulting increase in interest payments causes reductions in firms' cash flow, which lead to increased asymmetric information problems since firms are now more dependent on external funds to finance their investment. As the asymmetric information analysis suggests, the resulting increase in adverse selection and moral hazard problems leads to a reduction in investment and economic activity.

As shown in Figure 3, further deterioration in the economy occurs. The collapse in economic activity and the deterioration of cash flow and balance sheets of firms and households means that many of them are no longer able to pay off their debts, resulting in substantial losses for banks. Sharp rises in interest rates also have a negative effect on banks' profitability and balance sheets. Even more problematic for the banks is the sharp increase in the value of their foreign currency-denominated liabilities after the devaluation. Thus bank balance sheets are squeezed from both sides—the value of their assets falls as the value of their liabilities rises.

Under these circumstances, the banking system will often suffer a banking crisis in which many banks are likely to fail (as happened in the United States during the Great Depression). The banking crisis and the contributing factors in the credit markets explain a further worsening of adverse selection and moral hazard problems and a further collapse of lending and economic activity in the aftermath of the crisis.

 APPLICATION   ✦   **Financial Crises in Mexico, 1994–1995; East Asia, 1997–1998; and Argentina, 2001–2002**

When emerging market countries opened up their markets to the outside world in the 1990s, they had high hopes that globalization would stimulate economic growth and eventually make them rich. Instead of leading to high economic growth and reduced poverty, however, many of them experienced financial crises that were every bit as devastating as the Great Depression was in the United States.

The most dramatic of these crises were the Mexican crisis, which started in 1994; the East Asian crisis, which started in July 1997; and the Argentine crisis, which started in 2001. We now apply the asymmetric information analysis of the dynamics of financial crises to explain why a developing country can shift dramatically from a path of high growth before a financial crisis—as was true in Mexico and particularly the East

Asian countries of Thailand, Malaysia, Indonesia, the Philippines, and South Korea—to a sharp decline in economic activity.[2]

Before their crises, Mexico and the East Asian countries had achieved a sound fiscal policy. The East Asian countries ran budget surpluses, and Mexico ran a budget deficit of less than 1% of GDP, a number that most advanced countries, including the United States, would be thrilled to have today. The key precipitating factor driving these crises was the deterioration in banks' balance sheets because of increasing loan losses. When financial markets in these countries were liberalized and opened to foreign capital markets in the early 1990s, a lending boom ensued. Bank credit to the private non-financial business sector accelerated sharply, with lending expanding at 15% to 30% per year. Because of weak supervision by bank regulators, aided and abetted by powerful business interests (see the Global box on "Perversion of the Financial Liberalization/ Globalization Process: Chaebols and the South Korean Crisis") and a lack of expertise in screening and monitoring borrowers at banking institutions, losses on loans began to mount, causing an erosion of banks' net worth (capital). As a result of this erosion, banks had fewer resources to lend. This lack of lending led to a contraction of economic activity along the lines outlined in the previous section.

In contrast to Mexico and the East Asian countries, Argentina had a well-supervised banking system, and a lending boom did not occur before the crisis. The banks were in surprisingly good shape before the crisis, even though a severe recession had begun in 1998. This recession led to declining tax revenues and a widening gap between expenditures and taxes. The subsequent severe fiscal imbalances were so large that the government had trouble getting both citizens and foreigners to buy enough of its bonds, so it coerced banks into absorbing large amounts of government debt. Investors soon lost confidence in the ability of the Argentine government to repay this debt. The price of the debt plummeted, leaving big holes in banks' balance sheets. This weakening helped lead to a decline in lending and a contraction of economic activity, as in Mexico and East Asia.

Consistent with the U.S. experience in the nineteenth and early twentieth centuries, another precipitating factor in the Mexican and Argentine (but not East Asian) financial crises was a rise in interest rates abroad. Before the Mexican crisis, in February 1994, and before the Argentine crisis, in mid-1999, the Federal Reserve began a cycle of raising the federal funds rate to head off inflationary pressures. Although the Fed's monetary policy actions were successful in keeping U.S. inflation in check, they put upward pressure on interest rates in both Mexico and Argentina. The rise in interest rates in Mexico and Argentina directly added to increased adverse selection and moral hazard problems in their financial markets. As discussed earlier, it was more likely that the parties willing to take on the most risk would seek loans, and the higher interest payments led to a decline in firms' cash flow.

Also consistent with the U.S. experience, stock market declines and increases in uncertainty initiated and contributed to full-blown financial crises in Mexico, Thailand, South Korea, and Argentina. (The stock market declines in Malaysia, Indonesia, and the Philippines, on the other hand, occurred simultaneously with the onset of these crises.)

---

[2]This application does not examine four recent crises, those in Russia, Brazil, Ecuador, and Turkey. Russia's financial crisis in August 1998 can also be explained with the asymmetric information story here, but it is more appropriate to view it as a symptom of a wider breakdown in the economy. The Brazilian crisis in January 1999 has features of a more traditional balance-of-payments crisis (see Chapter 18) rather than a financial crisis. Ecuador's crisis of 1999 and the Turkish crisis of 2001 have features of both types of emerging market financial crises discussed in the application, with mismanagement of financial liberalization/globalization and severe fiscal imbalances playing a prominent role.

Global   **The Perversion of the Financial Liberalization/Globalization Process**

Chaebols and the South Korean Crisis

Although there are similarities with the perversion of the financial liberalization/globalization process that occurred in many emerging market economies, South Korea exhibited some particularly extraordinary elements because of the unique role of the chaebols, large, family-owned conglomerates. Because of their massive size—sales of the top five chaebols were nearly 50% of GDP right before the crisis—the chaebols were politically very powerful. The chaebols' influence extended the government safety net far beyond the financial system because the government had a long-standing policy of viewing the chaebols as being "too big to fail." With this policy in place, the chaebols would receive direct government assistance or directed credit if they got into trouble. Not surprisingly, given this guarantee, chaebols borrowed like crazy and were highly leveraged.

In the 1990s, the chaebols were in trouble: they weren't making any money. From 1993 to 1996, the return on assets for the top 30 chaebols was never much more than 3% (a comparable figure for U.S. corporations is 15–20%). In 1996 right before the crisis hit, the rate of return on assets had fallen to 0.2%. Furthermore, only the top five chaebols had any profits: the sixth to thirtieth chaebols never had a rate of return on assets much above 1% and in many years had negative rates of returns. With this poor profitability and the already high leverage, any banker would pull back on lending to these conglomerates if there were no government safety net. Because the banks knew the government would make good on the chaebol's loans if they were in default, the opposite occurred: Banks continued to lend to the chaebols and, in effect, threw good money after bad.

Even though the chaebols were getting substantial financing from commercial banks, it was not enough to feed their insatiable appetite for more credit. The chaebols decided that the way out of their troubles was to pursue growth, and they needed massive amounts of funds to do it. Even with the vaunted Korean national savings rate of over 30%, there just were not enough loanable funds to finance the chaebols' planned expansion. Where could they get it? The answer was in the international capital markets.

The chaebols encouraged the Korean government to accelerate the process of opening up Korean financial markets to foreign capital as part of the liberalization process. In 1993, the government expanded the ability of domestic banks to make loans denominated in foreign currency by expanding the types of loans for which this was possible. At the same time, the Korean government effectively allowed unlimited short-term foreign borrowing by financial institutions, but maintained quantity restrictions on long-term borrowing as a means of managing capital flows into the country. Opening up short-term but not long-term to foreign capital flows made no economic sense. It is short-term capital flows that make an emerging market economy financially fragile: *Short-term* capital can fly out of the country extremely rapidly if there is any whiff of a crisis.

Opening up primarily to short-term capital, however, made complete political sense: The chaebols needed the money and it is much easier to borrow short-term funds at lower interest rates in the international market because long-term lending is much riskier for foreign creditors. Keeping restrictions on long-term international borrowing, however, allowed the government to say that it was still restricting foreign capital inflows and to claim that it was opening up to foreign capital in a prudent manner. In the aftermath of these changes, Korean banks opened 28 branches in foreign countries that gave them access to foreign funds.

Although Korean financial institutions now had access to foreign capital, the chaebols still had a problem. They were not allowed to own commercial banks and so the chaebols might not get all of the bank loans that they needed. What was the answer? The chaebols needed to get their hands on financial institutions that they could own, that were allowed to borrow abroad, and that were subject to very little regulation. The financial institution could then engage in connected lending by borrowing foreign funds and then lending them to the chaebols who owned the institution.

(continued)

The Perversion of the Financial Liberalization/Globalization Process (*continued*)

An existing type of financial institution specific to South Korea perfectly met the chaebols' requirements: the merchant bank. Merchant banking corporations were wholesale financial institutions that engaged in underwriting securities, leasing, and short-term lending to the corporate sector. They obtained funds for these loans by issuing bonds and commercial paper and by borrowing from inter-bank and foreign markets.

At the time of the Korean crisis, merchant banks were allowed to borrow abroad and were virtually unregulated. The chaebols saw their opportunity. Government officials, often lured with bribery and kickbacks, allowed many finance companies (some already owned by the chaebols) that were not allowed to borrow abroad to be converted into merchant banks, which could. In 1990 there were only six merchant banks and all of them were foreign affiliated. By 1997, after the chaebols had exercised their political influence, there were 30 merchant banks, sixteen of which were owned by chaebols, two of which were foreign owned but in which chaebols were major stock holders, and twelve of which were independent of the chaebols, but Korean owned. The chaebols were now able to exploit connected lending with a vengeance: The merchant banks channeled massive amounts of funds to their chaebol owners, where they flowed into unproductive investments in steel, automobile production, and chemicals. When the loans went sour, the stage was set for a disastrous financial crisis.

The Mexican economy was hit by political shocks in 1994 (specifically, the assassination of the ruling party's presidential candidate, Luis Colosio, and an uprising in the southern state of Chiapas) that created uncertainty, while the ongoing recession increased uncertainty in Argentina. Right before their crises, Thailand and South Korea experienced major failures of financial and nonfinancial firms that increased general uncertainty in financial markets.

As we have seen, an increase in uncertainty and a decrease in net worth as a result of a stock market decline increases asymmetric information problems. It becomes harder to screen out good from bad borrowers. The decline in net worth decreases the value of firms' collateral and increases their incentives to make risky investments because there is less equity to lose if the investments are unsuccessful. The increase in uncertainty and stock market declines that occurred before the crises, along with the deterioration in banks' balance sheets, worsened adverse selection and moral hazard problems and made the economies ripe for a serious financial emergency.

At this point, full-blown speculative attacks developed in the foreign exchange market, plunging these countries into a full-scale crisis. With the Colosio assassination, the Chiapas uprising, and the growing weakness in the banking sector, the Mexican peso came under attack. Even though the Mexican central bank intervened in the foreign exchange market and raised interest rates sharply, it was unable to stem the attacks and was forced to devalue the peso on December 20, 1994. In the case of Thailand, concerns about the large current account deficit and weakness in the Thai financial system, culminating with the failure of a major finance company, Finance One, led to a successful speculative attack. The Thai central bank was forced to allow the baht to depreciate in July 1997. Soon thereafter, speculative attacks developed against the other countries in the region, leading to the collapse of the Philippine peso, the Indonesian rupiah, the Malaysian ringgit, and the South Korean won. In Argentina, a full-scale banking panic began in October–November 2001. This, along with realization that the government was going to default on its debt, also led to a speculative attack on the Argentine peso, resulting in its collapse on January 6, 2002.

The institutional structure of debt markets in Mexico and East Asia now interacted with the currency devaluations to propel the economies into full-fledged financial crises. Because so many firms in these countries had debt denominated in foreign currencies like the dollar and the yen, depreciation of their currencies resulted in increases in their indebtedness in domestic currency terms, even though the value of their assets remained unchanged. When the peso lost half its value by March 1995 and the Thai, Philippine, Malaysian, and South Korean currencies lost between one-third and one-half of their value by the beginning of 1998, firms' balance sheets took a big negative hit, causing a dramatic increase in adverse selection and moral hazard problems. This negative shock was especially severe for Indonesia and Argentina, which saw the value of their currencies fall by more than 70%, resulting in insolvency for firms with substantial amounts of debt denominated in foreign currencies.

The collapse of currencies also led to a rise in actual and expected inflation in these countries. Market interest rates rose sky-high (to around 100% in Mexico and Argentina). The resulting increase in interest payments caused reductions in household and firm cash flows. A feature of debt markets in emerging-market countries, like those in Mexico, East Asia, and Argentina, is that debt contracts have very short durations, typically less than one month. Thus the rise in short-term interest rates in these countries made the effect on cash flow and hence on balance sheets substantial. As our asymmetric information analysis suggests, this deterioration in households' and firms' balance sheets increased adverse selection and moral hazard problems in the credit markets, making domestic and foreign lenders even less willing to lend.

Consistent with the theory of financial crises outlined in this chapter, the sharp decline in lending helped lead to a collapse of economic activity, with real GDP growth falling sharply. Further deterioration in the economy occurred because the collapse in economic activity and the deterioration in the cash flow and balance sheets of both firms and households worsened banking crises. Many firms and households were no longer able to pay off their debts, resulting in substantial losses for the banks. Even more problematic for the banks were their many short-term liabilities denominated in foreign currencies. The sharp increase in the value of these liabilities after the devaluation led to a further deterioration in the banks' balance sheets. Under these circumstances, the banking system would have collapsed in the absence of a government safety net—as it did in the United States during the Great Depression. With the assistance of the International Monetary Fund, these countries were in some cases able to protect depositors and avoid a bank panic. However, given the loss of bank capital and the need for the government to intervene to prop up the banks, the banks' ability to lend was nevertheless sharply curtailed. As we have seen, a banking crisis of this type hinders the ability of the banks to lend and also makes adverse selection and moral hazard problems worse in financial markets, because banks are less capable of playing their traditional financial intermediation role. The banking crisis, along with other factors that increased adverse selection and moral hazard problems in the credit markets of Mexico, East Asia, and Argentina, explains the collapse of lending and hence economic activity in the aftermath of the crisis.

Following their crises, Mexico began to recover in 1996, while the crisis countries in East Asia tentatively began their recovery in 1999, with a stronger recovery later. Argentina was still in a severe depression in 2003, but subsequently the economy bounced back. In all these countries, the economic hardship caused by the financial crises was tremendous. Unemployment rose sharply, poverty increased substantially, and even the social fabric of the society was stretched thin. For example, after the financial crises, Mexico City and Buenos Aires became crime-ridden, while Indonesia experienced waves of ethnic violence.

SUMMARY

1. A financial crisis occurs when a disruption in the financial system causes an increase in asymmetric information that makes adverse selection and moral hazard problems far more severe, thereby rendering financial markets incapable of channeling funds to households and firms with productive investment opportunities, and causing a sharp contraction in economic activity. Six categories of factors play an important role in financial crises: asset market effects on balance sheets, deterioration in financial institutions' balance sheets, banking crisis, increases in uncertainty, increases in interest rates, and government fiscal imbalances.

2. There are several possible ways that financial crises can start in advanced countries like the United States: mismanagement of financial liberalization/innovation, asset price booms and busts, spikes in interest rates, or a general increase in uncertainty when there are failures of major financial institutions. The result is a substantial increase in adverse selection and moral hazard problems that lead to a contraction of lending and a decline in economic activity. The worsening business conditions and deterioration in bank balance sheets then triggers the second stage of the crisis, the simultaneous failure of many banking institutions, that is, a banking crisis. The resulting decline in the number of banks causes a loss of their information capital, leading to a further decline of lending and a spiraling down of the economy. In some instances, the resulting economic downturn leads to a sharp decline of prices, which increases the real liabilities of firms and therefore lowers their net worth, leading to a debt deflation. The decline in firms' net worth worsens adverse selection

and moral hazard problems, so that lending, investment spending, and aggregate economic activity remain depressed for a long time. The most significant financial crisis in U.S. history, that which led to the Great Depression, displayed the debt deflation phenomenon.

3. The financial crisis starting in 2007 was triggered by mismanagement of financial innovations involving subprime residential mortgages and the bursting of a housing price bubble.

4. Financial crises in emerging market countries develop along two basic paths: one involving the mismanagement of financial liberalization/globalization that weakens bank balance sheets and the other involving severe fiscal imbalances. Both lead to a speculative attack on the domestic currency, and eventually to a currency crisis in which there is a sharp decline in the currency's value. The decline in the value of the domestic currency causes a sharp rise in the debt burden of domestic firms, which leads to a decline in firms' net worth, as well as increases in inflation and interest rates. Adverse selection and moral hazard problems then worsen, leading to a collapse of lending and economic activity. The worsening economic conditions and increases in interest rates result in substantial losses for banks, leading to a banking crisis, which further depresses lending and aggregate economic activity.

5. The financial crises in Mexico in 1994–1995, East Asia in 1997–1998, and Argentina in 2001–2002 led to great economic hardship and weakened the social fabric of these countries.

KEY TERMS

alt-A mortgages, p. 207

asset-price bubble, p. 205

bank panic, p. 201

collateralized debt obligations (CDOs), p. 208

credit boom, p. 204

debt deflation, p. 206

deleveraging, p. 204

emerging market economies, p. 212

financial crisis, p. 199

financial engineering, p. 207

financial globalization, p. 213

financial liberalization, p. 204

mortgage-backed securities, p. 207

originate-to-distribute model, p. 208

securitization, p. 207

speculative attack, p. 216

structured credit products, p. 207

structured investment vehicles (SIVs), p. 210

subprime mortgages, p. 207

QUESTIONS AND PROBLEMS

All questions and problems are available in ⓧmyeconlab
at www.myeconlab.com/mishkin.

1. How can a bursting of an asset-price bubble in the stock market help trigger a financial crisis?

2. How does an unanticipated decline in the price level cause a drop in lending?

3. When can a decline in the value of a country's currency exacerbate adverse selection and moral hazard problems? Why?

4. How can a decline in real estate prices cause deleveraging and a decline in lending?

5. How does a deterioration in balance sheets of financial institutions and the simultaneous failures of these institutions cause a decline in economic activity?

6. How does a general increase in uncertainty as a result of a failure of a major financial institution lead to an increase in adverse selection and moral hazard problems?

7. What are the two ways that spikes in interest rates lead to an increase in adverse selection and moral hazard problems?

8. How can government fiscal imbalances lead to a financial crisis?

9. How can financial liberalizations lead to financial crises?

10. What role does weak financial regulation and supervision play in causing financial crises?

11. Why do debt deflations occur in advanced countries, but not in emerging market countries?

12. What technological innovations led to the development of the subprime mortgage market?

13. Why is the originate-to-distribute business model subject to the principal–agent problem?

14. True, false, or uncertain: Financial engineering always leads to a more efficient financial system.

15. How did a decline in housing prices help trigger the subprime financial crisis starting in 2007?

16. How can opening up to capital flows from abroad lead to a financial crisis?

17. Why are more resources not devoted to adequate prudential supervision of the financial system to limit excessive risk taking, when it is clear that this supervision is needed to prevent financial crises?

18. Why does the "twin crises" phenomenon of currency and banking crises occur in emerging market countries?

19. How can a currency crisis lead to higher interest rates?

20. How can a deterioration in bank balance sheets lead to a currency crisis?

WEB EXERCISE

1. This chapter discusses how an understanding of adverse selection and moral hazard can help us better understand financial crises. The greatest financial crisis faced by the United States was the Great Depression of 1929–1933. Go to www.amatecon.com/greatdepression.html. This site contains a brief discussion of the factors that led to the Great Depression. Write a one-page summary explaining how adverse selection and moral hazard contributed to the Great Depression.

2. Go to the International Monetary Fund's Financial Crisis page at www.imf.org/external/np/exr/key/finstab.htm.

Report on the most recent three countries that the IMF has given emergency loans to in response a financial crisis. According to the IMF, what caused the crisis in each country?

3. One of the countries hardest hit by the global financial crisis of 2008 was Iceland. Go to assets.opencrs.com/rpts/RS22988_20081120.pdf and summarize the causes and events that lead to the crisis in Iceland.

WEB REFERENCES

www.amatecon.com/gd/gdtimeline.html

A time line of the Great Depression

www.imf.org

The international Monetary Fund is an organization of 185 countries that works on global policy coordination (both monetary and trade), stable and sustainable economic prosperity, and the reduction of poverty.

www.publicpolicy.umd.edu/news/Reinhart%20paper.pdf

Paper by Carmen Reinhart and Kenneth Rogoff comparing the 2007 subprime crisis to other international crises.

www.earth.columbia.edu/sitefiles/File/about/director/pubs/paper27.pdf

Non-technical paper by Steven Radelet and Jeffrey Sachs on the causes of the East Asian financial crisis.

assets.opencrs.com/rpts/RS22988_20081120.pdf

The Congressional Research Service (CRS) report to congress about Iceland's financial crisis of 2008.

 MyEconLab CAN HELP YOU GET A BETTER GRADE

If your exam were tomorrow, would you be ready? For each chapter, MyEconLab Practice Test and Study Plans pinpoint which sections you have mastered and which ones you need to study. That way, you are more efficient with your study time, and you are better prepared for your exams.

To see how it works, turn to page 20 and then go to: www.myeconlab.com/mishkin

10 Banking and the Management of Financial Institutions

Preview

Because banking plays such a major role in channeling funds to borrowers with productive investment opportunities, this financial activity is important in ensuring that the financial system and the economy run smoothly and efficiently. In the United States, banks (depository institutions) supply more than $10 trillion in credit annually. They provide loans to businesses, help us finance our college educations or the purchase of a new car or home, and provide us with services such as checking and savings accounts.

In this chapter, we examine how banking is conducted to earn the highest profits possible: how and why banks make loans, how they acquire funds and manage their assets and liabilities (debts), and how they earn income. Although we focus on commercial banking, because this is the most important financial intermediary activity, many of the same principles are applicable to other types of financial intermediation.

THE BANK BALANCE SHEET

To understand how banking works, we start by looking at the bank **balance sheet**, a list of the bank's assets and liabilities. As the name implies, this list balances; that is, it has the characteristic that

$$\text{total assets} = \text{total liabilities} + \text{capital}$$

A bank's balance sheet is also a list of its *sources* of bank funds (liabilities) and *uses* to which the funds are put (assets). Banks obtain funds by borrowing and by issuing other liabilities such as deposits. They then use these funds to acquire assets such as securities and loans. Banks make profits by charging an interest rate on their asset holdings of securities and loans that is higher than the interest and other expenses on their liabilities. The balance sheet of all commercial banks as of December 2008 appears in Table 1.

Liabilities

A bank acquires funds by issuing (selling) liabilities, such as deposits, which are the *sources of funds* the bank uses. The funds obtained from issuing liabilities are used to purchase income-earning assets.

225

TABLE 1

Balance Sheet of All Commercial Banks (items as a percentage of the total, December 2008)

Assets (Uses of Funds)*		Liabilities (Sources of Funds)	
Reserves and cash items	8%	Checkable deposits	6%
Securities		Nontransaction deposits	
U.S. government and agency	10	Small-denomination time deposits	
U.S. state and local government		(< $100,000) + savings deposits	37
and other securities	12	Large-denomination time deposits	16
Loans		Borrowings	31
Commercial and industrial	13	Bank capital	10
Real estate	31		
Consumer	7		
Interbank	3		
Other	7		
Other assets (for example,			
physical capital)	9		
Total	100	Total	100

*In order of decreasing liquidity.

Source: www.federalreserve.gov/releases/h8/current/.

Checkable Deposits   Checkable deposits are bank accounts that allow the owner of the account to write checks to third parties. Checkable deposits include all accounts on which checks can be drawn: non-interest-bearing checking accounts (demand deposits), interest-bearing NOW (negotiable order of withdrawal) accounts, and money market deposit accounts (MMDAs). Introduced with the Depository Institutions Act in 1982, MMDAs have features similar to those of money market mutual funds and are included in the checkable deposits category. However, MMDAs are not subject to reserve requirements (discussed later in the chapter) as checkable deposits are and are not included in the M1 definition of money. Table 1 shows that the category of checkable deposits is an important source of bank funds, making up 6% of bank liabilities. Once checkable deposits were the most important source of bank funds (more than 60% of bank liabilities in 1960), but with the appearance of new, more attractive financial instruments, such as money market deposit accounts, the share of checkable deposits in total bank liabilities has shrunk over time.

Checkable deposits and money market deposit accounts are payable on demand; that is, if a depositor shows up at the bank and requests payment by making a withdrawal, the bank must pay the depositor immediately. Similarly, if a person who receives a check written on an account from a bank, presents that check at the bank, it must pay the funds out immediately (or credit them to that person's account).

A checkable deposit is an asset for the depositor because it is part of his or her wealth. Because the depositor can withdraw funds and the bank is obligated to pay, checkable deposits are a liability for the bank. They are usually the lowest-cost source of bank funds because depositors are willing to forgo some interest to have access to a liquid asset that they can use to make purchases. The bank's costs of maintaining checkable deposits include interest payments and the costs incurred in servicing these accounts—processing, preparing, and sending out monthly statements, providing efficient tellers (human or otherwise), maintaining an impressive building and conveniently located branches, and advertising and marketing to entice customers to deposit their funds with a given bank. In recent years, interest paid on deposits (checkable and nontransaction) has accounted for around 25% of total bank operating expenses, while the costs involved in servicing accounts (employee salaries, building rent, and so on) have been approximately 50% of operating expenses.

Nontransaction Deposits   Nontransaction deposits are the primary source of bank funds (53% of bank liabilities in Table 1). Owners cannot write checks on nontransaction deposits, but the interest rates paid on these deposits are usually higher than those on checkable deposits. There are two basic types of nontransaction deposits: savings accounts and time deposits (also called certificates of deposit, or CDs).

Savings accounts were once the most common type of nontransaction deposit. In these accounts, to which funds can be added or from which funds can be withdrawn at any time, transactions and interest payments are recorded in a monthly statement or in a passbook held by the owner of the account.

Time deposits have a fixed maturity length, ranging from several months to over five years, and assess substantial penalties for early withdrawal (the forfeiture of several months' interest). Small-denomination time deposits (deposits of less than $100,000) are less liquid for the depositor than passbook savings, earn higher interest rates, and are a more costly source of funds for the banks.

Large-denomination time deposits (CDs) are available in denominations of $100,000 or more and are typically bought by corporations or other banks. Large-denomination CDs are negotiable; like bonds, they can be resold in a secondary market before they mature. For this reason, negotiable CDs are held by corporations, money market mutual funds, and other financial institutions as alternative assets to Treasury bills and other short-term bonds. Since 1961, when they first appeared, negotiable CDs have become an important source of bank funds (16% in Table 1).

Borrowings   Banks also obtain funds by borrowing from the Federal Reserve System, the Federal Home Loan banks, other banks, and corporations. Borrowings from the Fed are called **discount loans** (also known as *advances*). Banks also borrow reserves overnight in the federal (fed) funds market from other U.S. banks and financial institutions. Banks borrow funds overnight to have enough deposits at the Federal Reserve to meet the amount required by the Fed. (The *federal funds* designation is somewhat confusing, because these loans are not made by the U.S. federal government or by the Federal Reserve, but rather by banks to other banks.) Other sources of borrowed funds are loans made to banks by their parent companies (bank holding companies), loan arrangements with corporations (such as repurchase agreements), and borrowings of Eurodollars (deposits denominated in U.S. dollars residing in foreign banks or foreign branches of U.S. banks). Borrowings have become a more important source of bank funds over time: In 1960, they made up only 2% of bank liabilities; currently, they are 31% of bank liabilities.

Bank Capital   The final category on the liabilities side of the balance sheet is bank capital, the bank's net worth, which equals the difference between total assets and liabilities (10% of total bank assets in Table 1). Bank capital is raised by selling new equity (stock) or from retained earnings. Bank capital is a cushion against a drop in the value of its assets, which could force the bank into insolvency (having liabilities in excess of assets, meaning that the bank can be forced into liquidation).

Assets

A bank uses the funds that it has acquired by issuing liabilities to purchase income-earning assets. Bank assets are thus naturally referred to as *uses of funds*, and the interest payments earned on them are what enable banks to make profits.

Reserves   All banks hold some of the funds they acquire as deposits in an account at the Fed. **Reserves** are these deposits plus currency that is physically held by banks (called **vault cash** because it is stored in bank vaults overnight). Although reserves earn a low interest rate, banks hold them for two reasons. First, some reserves, called **required reserves**, are held because of **reserve requirements**, the regulation that for every dollar of checkable deposits at a bank, a certain fraction (10 cents, for example) must be kept as reserves. This fraction (10% in the example) is called the **required reserve ratio**. Banks hold additional reserves, called **excess reserves**, because they are the most liquid of all bank assets and a bank can use them to meet its obligations when funds are withdrawn, either directly by a depositor or indirectly when a check is written on an account.

Cash Items in Process of Collection   Suppose that a check written on an account at another bank is deposited in your bank and the funds for this check have not yet been received (collected) from the other bank. The check is classified as a cash item in process of collection, and it is an asset for your bank because it is a claim on another bank for funds that will be paid within a few days.

Deposits at Other Banks   Many small banks hold deposits in larger banks in exchange for a variety of services, including check collection, foreign exchange transactions, and help with securities purchases. This is an aspect of a system called *correspondent banking*.

Collectively, reserves, cash items in process of collection, and deposits at other banks are referred to as *cash items*. In Table 1, they constitute only 8% of total assets, and their importance has been shrinking over time: In 1960, for example, they accounted for 20% of total assets.

Securities   A bank's holdings of securities are an important income-earning asset: Securities (made up entirely of debt instruments for commercial banks, because banks are not allowed to hold stock) account for 22% of bank assets in Table 1, and they provide commercial banks with about 10% of their revenue. These securities can be classified into three categories: U.S. government and agency securities, state and local government securities, and other securities. The U.S. government and agency securities are the most liquid because they can be easily traded and converted into cash with low transaction costs. Because of their high liquidity, short-term U.S. government securities are called **secondary reserves**.

Banks hold state and local government securities because state and local governments are more likely to do business with banks that hold their securities. State and local government and other securities are both less marketable (less liquid) and riskier than U.S. government securities, primarily because of default risk: There is some possibility that the issuer of the securities may not be able to make its interest payments or pay back the face value of the securities when they mature.

Loans   Banks make their profits primarily by issuing loans. In Table 1, some 61% of bank assets are in the form of loans, and in recent years they have generally produced more than half of bank revenues. A loan is a liability for the individual or corporation receiving it, but an asset for a bank, because it provides income to the bank. Loans are typically less liquid than other assets, because they cannot be turned into cash until the loan matures. If the bank makes a one-year loan, for example, it cannot get its funds back until the loan comes due in one year. Loans also have a higher probability of default than other assets. Because of the lack of liquidity and higher default risk, the bank earns its highest return on loans.

As you saw in Table 1, the largest categories of loans for commercial banks are commercial and industrial loans made to businesses and real estate loans. Commercial banks also make consumer loans and lend to each other. The bulk of these interbank loans are overnight loans lent in the federal funds market. The major difference in the balance sheets of the various depository institutions is primarily in the type of loan in which they specialize. Savings and loans and mutual savings banks, for example, specialize in residential mortgages, while credit unions tend to make consumer loans.

Other Assets   The physical capital (bank buildings, computers, and other equipment) owned by the banks is included in this category.

BASIC BANKING

Before proceeding to a more detailed study of how a bank manages its assets and liabilities to make the highest profit, you should understand the basic operation of a bank.

In general terms, banks make profits by selling liabilities with one set of characteristics (a particular combination of liquidity, risk, size, and return) and using the proceeds to buy assets with a different set of characteristics. This process is often referred to as *asset transformation*. For example, a savings deposit held by one person can provide the funds that enable the bank to make a mortgage loan to another person. The bank has, in effect, transformed the savings deposit (an asset held by the depositor) into a mortgage loan (an asset held by the bank). Another way this process of asset transformation is described is to say that the bank "borrows short and lends long" because it makes long-term loans and funds them by issuing short-dated deposits.

The process of transforming assets and providing a set of services (check clearing, record keeping, credit analysis, and so forth) is like any other production process in a firm. If the bank produces desirable services at low cost and earns substantial income on its assets, it earns profits; if not, the bank suffers losses.

To make our analysis of the operation of a bank more concrete, we use a tool called a **T-account**. A T-account is a simplified balance sheet, with lines in the form of a T, that lists only the changes that occur in balance sheet items starting from some initial balance sheet position. Let's say that Jane Brown has heard that the First National Bank provides excellent service, so she opens a checking account with a $100 bill. She now has a $100 checkable deposit at the bank, which shows up as a $100 liability on the bank's balance sheet. The bank now puts her $100 bill into its vault so that the bank's assets rise by the $100 increase in vault cash. The T-account for the bank looks like this:

First National Bank

Assets		Liabilities	
Vault cash	+$100	Checkable deposits	+$100

Because vault cash is also part of the bank's reserves, we can rewrite the T-account as follows:

Assets		Liabilities	
Reserves	+$100	Checkable deposits	+$100

Note that Jane Brown's opening of a checking account leads to *an increase in the bank's reserves equal to the increase in checkable deposits.*

If Jane had opened her account with a $100 check written on an account at another bank, say, the Second National Bank, we would get the same result. The initial effect on the T-account of the First National Bank is as follows:

Assets		Liabilities	
Cash items in process of collection	+$100	Checkable deposits	+$100

Checkable deposits increase by $100 as before, but now the First National Bank is owed $100 by the Second National Bank. This asset for the First National Bank is entered in the T-account as $100 of cash items in process of collection because the First National Bank will now try to collect the funds that it is owed. It could go directly to the Second National Bank and ask for payment of the funds, but if the two banks are in separate states, that would be a time-consuming and costly process. Instead, the First National Bank deposits the check in its account at the Fed, and the Fed collects the funds from the Second National Bank. The result is that the Fed transfers $100 of reserves from the Second National Bank to the First National Bank, and the final balance sheet positions of the two banks are as follows:

First National Bank				Second National Bank			
Assets		Liabilities		Assets		Liabilities	
Reserves	+$100	Checkable deposits	+$100	Reserves	−$100	Checkable deposits	−$100

The process initiated by Jane Brown can be summarized as follows: When a check written on an account at one bank is deposited in another, the bank receiving the deposit gains reserves equal to the amount of the check, while the bank on which the check is written sees its reserves fall by the same amount. Therefore, **when a bank receives additional deposits, it gains an equal amount of reserves; when it loses deposits, it loses an equal amount of reserves**.

Now that you understand how banks gain and lose reserves, we can examine how a bank rearranges its balance sheet to make a profit when it experiences a change in its deposits. Let's return to the situation when the First National Bank has just received the extra $100 of checkable deposits. As you know, the bank is obliged to keep a certain fraction of its checkable deposits as required reserves. If the fraction (the required reserve ratio) is 10%, the First National Bank's required reserves have increased by $10, and we can rewrite its T-account as follows:

First National Bank

Assets		Liabilities	
Required reserves	+$10	Checkable deposits	+$100
Excess reserves	+$90		

Let's see how well the bank is doing as a result of the additional checkable deposits. Servicing the extra $100 of checkable deposits is costly, because the bank must keep records, pay tellers, pay for check clearing, and so forth. Since reserves earn little interest the bank is taking a loss! The situation is even worse if the bank makes interest payments on the deposits, as with NOW accounts. If it is to make a profit, the bank must put to productive use all or part of the $90 of excess reserves it has available. One way to do this is to invest in securities. The other is to make loans; as we have seen, loans account for approximately 60% of the total value of bank assets (uses of funds). Because lenders are subject to the asymmetric information problems of adverse selection and moral hazard (discussed in Chapter 8), banks take steps to reduce the incidence and severity of these problems. Bank loan officers evaluate potential borrowers using what are called the "five C's": character, capacity (ability to repay), collateral, conditions (in the local and national economies), and capital (net worth) before they agree to lend. (Later in this chapter is a more detailed discussion of the methods banks use to reduce the risk involved in lending.)

Let us assume that the bank chooses not to hold any excess reserves but to make loans instead. The T-account then looks like this:

Assets		Liabilities	
Required reserves	+$10	Checkable deposits	+$100
Loans	+$90		

The bank is now making a profit because it holds short-term liabilities such as checkable deposits and uses the proceeds to fund longer-term assets such as loans with higher interest rates. As mentioned earlier, this process of asset transformation is frequently described by saying that banks are in the business of "borrowing short and lending long." For example, if the loans have an interest rate of 10% per year, the bank earns $9 in income from its loans over the year. If the $100 of checkable deposits is in a NOW account with a 5% interest rate and it costs another $3 per year to service the account, the cost per year of these deposits is $8. The bank's profit on the new deposits is then $1 per year, plus any interest that is paid on required reserves.

GENERAL PRINCIPLES OF BANK MANAGEMENT

Now that you have some idea of how a bank operates, let's look at how a bank manages its assets and liabilities to earn the highest possible profit. The bank manager has four primary concerns. The first is to make sure that the bank has enough ready cash to pay its depositors when there are **deposit outflows**—that is, when deposits are lost because depositors make withdrawals and demand payment. To keep enough cash on hand, the bank must engage in **liquidity management**, the acquisition of sufficiently liquid assets to meet the bank's obligations to depositors. Second, the bank manager must pursue an acceptably low level of risk by acquiring assets that have a low rate of default and by diversifying asset holdings (**asset management**). The third concern is to acquire funds at low cost (**liability management**). Finally, the manager must decide the amount of capital the bank should maintain and then acquire the needed capital (**capital adequacy management**).

To understand bank and other financial institution management fully, we must go beyond the general principles of bank asset and liability management described next and look in more detail at how a financial institution manages its assets. The two sections following this one provide an in-depth discussion of how a financial institution manages **credit risk**, the risk arising because borrowers may default, and how it manages **interest-rate risk**, the riskiness of earnings and returns on bank assets that results from interest-rate changes.

Liquidity Management and the Role of Reserves

Let us see how a typical bank, the First National Bank, can deal with deposit outflows that occur when its depositors withdraw cash from checking or savings accounts or write checks that are deposited in other banks. In the example that follows, we assume that the bank has ample excess reserves and that all deposits have the same required reserve ratio of 10% (the bank is required to keep 10% of deposits as reserves). Suppose that the First National Bank's initial balance sheet is as follows:

Assets		Liabilities	
Reserves	$20 million	Deposits	$100 million
Loans	$80 million	Bank capital	$ 10 million
Securities	$10 million		

The bank's required reserves are 10% of $100 million, or $10 million. Given that it holds $20 million of reserves, the First National Bank has excess reserves of $10 million.

If a deposit outflow of $10 million occurs, the bank's balance sheet becomes

Assets		Liabilities	
Reserves	$10 million	Deposits	$90 million
Loans	$80 million	Bank capital	$10 million
Securities	$10 million		

The bank loses $10 million of deposits *and* $10 million of reserves, but because its required reserves are now 10% of only $90 million ($9 million), its reserves still exceed this amount by $1 million. In short, ***if a bank has ample excess reserves, a deposit outflow does not necessitate changes in other parts of its balance sheet.***

The situation is quite different when a bank holds insufficient excess reserves. Let's assume that instead of initially holding $10 million in excess reserves, the First National Bank makes additional loans of $10 million, so that it holds no excess reserves. Its initial balance sheet would then be

Assets		Liabilities	
Reserves	$10 million	Deposits	$100 million
Loans	$90 million	Bank capital	$ 10 million
Securities	$10 million		

When it suffers the $10 million deposit outflow, its balance sheet becomes

Assets		Liabilities	
Reserves	$ 0	Deposits	$90 million
Loans	$90 million	Bank capital	$10 million
Securities	$10 million		

After $10 million has been withdrawn from deposits and hence reserves, the bank has a problem: It has a reserve requirement of 10% of $90 million, or $9 million, but it has no reserves! To eliminate this shortfall, the bank has four basic options. One is to acquire reserves to meet a deposit outflow by borrowing them from other banks in the federal funds market or by borrowing from corporations.[1] If the First National Bank

---

[1] One way that the First National Bank can borrow from other banks and corporations is by selling negotiable certificates of deposit. This method for obtaining funds is discussed in the section on liability management.

acquires the $9 million shortfall in reserves by borrowing it from other banks or corporations, its balance sheet becomes

Assets		Liabilities	
Reserves	$ 9 million	Deposits	$90 million
Loans	$90 million	Borrowings from other	$ 9 million
Securities	$10 million	banks or corporations	
		Bank capital	$10 million

The cost of this activity is the interest rate on these borrowings, such as the federal funds rate.

A second alternative is for the bank to sell some of its securities to help cover the deposit outflow. For example, it might sell $9 million of its securities and deposit the proceeds with the Fed, resulting in the following balance sheet:

Assets		Liabilities	
Reserves	$ 9 million	Deposits	$90 million
Loans	$90 million	Bank capital	$10 million
Securities	$ 1 million		

The bank incurs some brokerage and other transaction costs when it sells these securities. The U.S. government securities that are classified as secondary reserves are very liquid, so the transaction costs of selling them are quite modest. However, the other securities the bank holds are less liquid, and the transaction cost can be appreciably higher.

A third way that the bank can meet a deposit outflow is to acquire reserves by borrowing from the Fed. In our example, the First National Bank could leave its security and loan holdings the same and borrow $9 million in discount loans from the Fed. Its balance sheet would then be

Assets		Liabilities	
Reserves	$ 9 million	Deposits	$90 million
Loans	$90 million	Borrowings	$ 9 million
Securities	$10 million	from the Fed	
		Bank capital	$10 million

The cost associated with discount loans is the interest rate that must be paid to the Fed (called the **discount rate**).

Finally, a bank can acquire the $9 million of reserves to meet the deposit outflow by reducing its loans by this amount and depositing the $9 million it then receives with the Fed, thereby increasing its reserves by $9 million. This transaction changes the balance sheet as follows:

Assets		Liabilities	
Reserves	$ 9 million	Deposits	$90 million
Loans	$81 million	Bank capital	$10 million
Securities	$10 million		

The First National Bank is once again in good shape because its $9 million of reserves satisfies the reserve requirement.

However, this process of reducing its loans is the bank's costliest way of acquiring reserves when there is a deposit outflow. If the First National Bank has numerous short-term loans renewed at fairly short intervals, it can reduce its total amount of loans outstanding fairly quickly by *calling in* loans—that is, by not renewing some loans when they come due. Unfortunately for the bank, this is likely to antagonize the customers whose loans are not being renewed because they have not done anything to deserve such treatment. Indeed, they are likely to take their business elsewhere in the future, a very costly consequence for the bank.

A second method for reducing its loans is for the bank to sell them off to other banks. Again, this is very costly because other banks do not personally know the customers who have taken out the loans and so may not be willing to buy the loans at their full value (This is just the lemons adverse selection problem described in Chapter 8.)

The foregoing discussion explains why banks hold excess reserves even though loans or securities earn a higher return. When a deposit outflow occurs, holding excess reserves allows the bank to escape the costs of (1) borrowing from other banks or corporations, (2) selling securities, (3) borrowing from the Fed, or (4) calling in or selling off loans. ***Excess reserves are insurance against the costs associated with deposit outflows. The higher the costs associated with deposit outflows, the more excess reserves banks will want to hold.***

Just as you and I would be willing to pay an insurance company to insure us against a casualty loss such as the theft of a car, a bank is willing to pay the cost of holding excess reserves (the opportunity cost, the earnings forgone by not holding income-earning assets such as loans or securities) to insure against losses due to deposit outflows. Because excess reserves, like insurance, have a cost, banks also take other steps to protect themselves; for example, they might shift their holdings of assets to more liquid securities (secondary reserves).

Asset Management

Now that you understand why a bank has a need for liquidity, we can examine the basic strategy a bank pursues in managing its assets. To maximize its profits, a bank must simultaneously seek the highest returns possible on loans and securities, reduce risk, and make adequate provisions for liquidity by holding liquid assets. Banks try to accomplish these three goals in four basic ways.

First, banks try to find borrowers who will pay high interest rates and are unlikely to default on their loans. They seek out loan business by advertising their borrowing rates and by approaching corporations directly to solicit loans. It is up to the bank's loan officer to decide if potential borrowers are good credit risks who will make interest and principal payments on time (i.e., engage in screening to reduce the adverse selection problem). Typically, banks are conservative in their loan policies; the default rate is usually less than 1%. It is important, however, that banks not be so conservative that they miss out on attractive lending opportunities that earn high interest rates.

Second, banks try to purchase securities with high returns and low risk. Third, in managing their assets, banks must attempt to lower risk by diversifying. They accomplish this by purchasing many different types of assets (short- and long-term, U.S. Treasury, and municipal bonds) and approving many types of loans to a number of customers. Banks that have not sufficiently sought the benefits of diversification often come to regret it later. For example, banks that had overspecialized in making loans to energy companies, real estate developers, or farmers suffered huge losses in the 1980s with the slump in energy, property, and farm prices. Indeed, many of these banks went broke because they had "put too many eggs in one basket."

Finally, the bank must manage the liquidity of its assets so that it can satisfy its reserve requirements without bearing huge costs. This means that it will hold liquid securities even if they earn a somewhat lower return than other assets. The bank must decide, for example, how much in excess reserves must be held to avoid costs from a deposit outflow. In addition, it will want to hold U.S. government securities as secondary reserves so that even if a deposit outflow forces some costs on the bank, these will not be terribly high. Again, it is not wise for a bank to be too conservative. If it avoids all costs associated with deposit outflows by holding only excess reserves, the bank suffers losses because reserves earn low interest, while the bank's liabilities are costly to maintain. The bank must balance its desire for liquidity against the increased earnings that can be obtained from less liquid assets such as loans.

Liability Management

Before the 1960s, liability management was a staid affair: For the most part, banks took their liabilities as fixed and spent their time trying to achieve an optimal mix of assets. There were two main reasons for the emphasis on asset management. First, more than 60% of the sources of bank funds were obtained through checkable (demand) deposits that by law could not pay any interest. Thus banks could not actively compete with one another for these deposits by paying interest on them, and so their amount was effectively a given for an individual bank. Second, because the markets for making overnight loans between banks were not well developed, banks rarely borrowed from other banks to meet their reserve needs.

Starting in the 1960s, however, large banks (called **money center banks**) in key financial centers, such as New York, Chicago, and San Francisco, began to explore ways in which the liabilities on their balance sheets could provide them with reserves and liquidity. This led to an expansion of overnight loan markets, such as the federal funds market, and the development of new financial instruments such as negotiable CDs (first developed in 1961), which enabled money center banks to acquire funds quickly.[2]

---

[2]Because small banks are not as well known as money center banks and so might be a higher credit risk, they find it harder to raise funds in the negotiable CD market. Hence they do not engage nearly as actively in liability management.

This new flexibility in liability management meant that banks could take a different approach to bank management. They no longer needed to depend on checkable deposits as the primary source of bank funds and as a result no longer treated their sources of funds (liabilities) as given. Instead, they aggressively set target goals for their asset growth and tried to acquire funds (by issuing liabilities) as they were needed.

For example, today, when a money center bank finds an attractive loan opportunity, it can acquire funds by selling a negotiable CD. Or, if it has a reserve shortfall, it can borrow funds from another bank in the federal funds market without incurring high transaction costs. The federal funds market can also be used to finance loans. Because of the increased importance of liability management, most banks now manage both sides of the balance sheet together in an *asset–liability management (ALM) committee.*

The greater emphasis on liability management explains some of the important changes over the past three decades in the composition of banks' balance sheets. While negotiable CDs and bank borrowings have greatly increased in importance as a source of bank funds in recent years (rising from 2% of bank liabilities in 1960 to 47% by the beginning of 2009), checkable deposits have decreased in importance (from 61% of bank liabilities in 1960 to 6% at the end of 2008). Newfound flexibility in liability management and the search for higher profits have also stimulated banks to increase the proportion of their assets held in loans, which earn higher income (from 46% of bank assets in 1960 to 61% at the end of 2008).

Capital Adequacy Management

Banks have to make decisions about the amount of capital they need to hold for three reasons. First, bank capital helps prevent *bank failure*, a situation in which the bank cannot satisfy its obligations to pay its depositors and other creditors and so goes out of business. Second, the amount of capital affects returns for the owners (equity holders) of the bank. Third, a minimum amount of bank capital (bank capital requirements) is required by regulatory authorities.

How Bank Capital Helps Prevent Bank Failure   Let's consider two banks with identical balance sheets, except that the High Capital Bank has a ratio of capital to assets of 10% while the Low Capital Bank has a ratio of 4%.

High Capital Bank				Low Capital Bank			
Assets		Liabilities		Assets		Liabilities	
Reserves	$10 million	Deposits	$90 million	Reserves	$10 million	Deposits	$96 million
Loans	$90 million	Bank capital	$10 million	Loans	$90 million	Bank capital	$ 4 million

Suppose that both banks get caught up in the euphoria of the housing market, only to find that $5 million of their housing loans became worthless later. When these bad loans are written off (valued at zero), the total value of assets declines by $5 million. As a consequence, bank capital, which equals total assets minus liabilities, also declines by $5 million. The balance sheets of the two banks now look like this:

High Capital Bank				Low Capital Bank			
Assets		Liabilities		Assets		Liabilities	
Reserves	$10 million	Deposits	$90 million	Reserves	$10 million	Deposits	$96 million
Loans	$85 million	Bank	$ 5 million	Loans	$85 million	Bank	−$ 1 million
		capital				capital	

The High Capital Bank takes the $5 million loss in stride because its initial cushion of $10 million in capital means that it still has a positive net worth (bank capital) of $5 million after the loss. The Low Capital Bank, however, is in big trouble. Now the value of its assets has fallen below its liabilities, and its net worth is now −$1 million. Because the bank has a negative net worth, it is insolvent: It does not have sufficient assets to pay off all holders of its liabilities. When a bank becomes insolvent, government regulators close the bank, its assets are sold off, and its managers are fired. Because the owners of the Low Capital Bank will find their investment wiped out, they would clearly have preferred the bank to have had a large enough cushion of bank capital to absorb the losses, as was the case for the High Capital Bank. We therefore see an important rationale for a bank to maintain a sufficient level of capital: *A bank maintains bank capital to lessen the chance that it will become insolvent*.

How the Amount of Bank Capital Affects Returns to Equity Holders

Because owners of a bank must know whether their bank is being managed well, they need good measures of bank profitability. A basic measure of bank profitability is the **return on assets (ROA)**, the net profit after taxes per dollar of assets:

$$\text{ROA} = \frac{\text{net profit after taxes}}{\text{assets}}$$

The return on assets provides information on how efficiently a bank is being run, because it indicates how much profits are generated on average by each dollar of assets.

However, what the bank's owners (equity holders) care about most is how much the bank is earning on their equity investment. This information is provided by the other basic measure of bank profitability, the **return on equity (ROE)**, the net profit after taxes per dollar of equity (bank) capital:

$$\text{ROE} = \frac{\text{net profit after taxes}}{\text{equity capital}}$$

There is a direct relationship between the return on assets (which measures how efficiently the bank is run) and the return on equity (which measures how well the owners are doing on their investment). This relationship is determined by the **equity multiplier (EM)**, the amount of assets per dollar of equity capital:

$$\text{EM} = \frac{\text{assets}}{\text{equity capital}}$$

To see this, we note that

$$\frac{\text{net profit after taxes}}{\text{equity capital}} = \frac{\text{net profit after taxes}}{\text{assets}} \times \frac{\text{assets}}{\text{equity capital}}$$

which, using our definitions, yields

$$\text{ROE} = \text{ROA} \times \text{EM} \tag{1}$$

The formula in Equation 1 tells us what happens to the return on equity when a bank holds a smaller amount of capital (equity) for a given amount of assets. As we have seen, the High Capital Bank initially has $100 million of assets and $10 million of equity, which gives it an equity multiplier of 10 (=$100 million/$10 million). The Low Capital Bank, by contrast, has only $4 million of equity, so its equity multiplier is higher, equaling 25 (=$100 million/$4 million). Suppose that these banks have been equally well run so that they both have the same return on assets, 1%. The return on equity for the High Capital Bank equals 1% × 10 = 10%, while the return on equity for the Low Capital Bank equals 1% × 25 = 25%. The equity holders in the Low Capital Bank are clearly a lot happier than the equity holders in the High Capital Bank because they are earning more than twice as high a return. We now see why owners of a bank may not want it to hold too much capital. *Given the return on assets, the lower the bank capital, the higher the return for the owners of the bank.*

Trade-off Between Safety and Returns to Equity Holders   We now see that bank capital has both benefits and costs. Bank capital benefits the owners of a bank in that it makes their investment safer by reducing the likelihood of bankruptcy. But bank capital is costly because the higher it is, the lower will be the return on equity for a given return on assets. In determining the amount of bank capital, managers must decide how much of the increased safety that comes with higher capital (the benefit) they are willing to trade off against the lower return on equity that comes with higher capital (the cost).

In more uncertain times, when the possibility of large losses on loans increases, bank managers might want to hold more capital to protect the equity holders. Conversely, if they have confidence that loan losses won't occur, they might want to reduce the amount of bank capital, have a high equity multiplier, and thereby increase the return on equity.

Bank Capital Requirements   Banks also hold capital because they are required to do so by regulatory authorities. Because of the high costs of holding capital for the reasons just described, bank managers often want to hold less bank capital relative to assets than is required by the regulatory authorities. In this case, the amount of bank capital is determined by the bank capital requirements. We discuss the details of bank capital requirements and their important role in bank regulation in Chapter 11.

APPLICATION ✦ Strategies for Managing Bank Capital

Suppose that as the manager of the First National Bank, you have to make decisions about the appropriate amount of bank capital. Looking at the balance sheet of the bank, which like the High Capital Bank has a ratio of bank capital to assets of 10% ($10 million of capital and $100 million of assets), you are concerned that the large amount of bank capital is causing the return on equity to be too low. You conclude that the bank has a capital surplus and should increase the equity multiplier to increase the return on equity. What should you do?

To lower the amount of capital relative to assets and raise the equity multiplier, you can do any of three things: (1) You can reduce the amount of bank capital by buying back some of the bank's stock. (2) You can reduce the bank's capital by paying out higher dividends to its stockholders, thereby reducing the bank's retained earnings. (3) You can keep bank capital constant but increase the bank's assets by acquiring new funds—say, by issuing CDs—and then seeking out loan business or purchasing more securities with these new funds. Because you think that it would enhance your position with the stockholders, you decide to pursue the second alternative and raise the dividend on the First National Bank stock.

Now suppose that the First National Bank is in a similar situation to the Low Capital Bank and has a ratio of bank capital to assets of 4%. You now worry that the bank is short on capital relative to assets because it does not have a sufficient cushion to prevent bank failure. To raise the amount of capital relative to assets, you now have the following three choices: (1) You can raise capital for the bank by having it issue equity (common stock). (2) You can raise capital by reducing the bank's dividends to shareholders, thereby increasing retained earnings that it can put into its capital account. (3) You can keep capital at the same level but reduce the bank's assets by making fewer loans or by selling off securities and then using the proceeds to reduce its liabilities. Suppose that raising bank capital is not easy to do at the current time because capital markets are tight or because shareholders will protest if their dividends are cut. Then you might have to choose the third alternative and decide to shrink the size of the bank.

Our discussion of strategies for managing bank capital for the First National Bank leads to the following conclusion that deserves some emphasis: *A shortfall of bank capital is likely to lead to a bank reducing its assets and therefore a contraction in lending*. In past years, many banks experienced capital shortfalls and had to restrict asset and lending growth. The important consequences of this for the credit markets is illustrated by the application that follows.

APPLICATION ✦ How a Capital Crunch Caused a Credit Crunch in 2008

The dramatic slowdown in the growth of credit in the wake of the financial crisis starting in 2007 triggered a "credit crunch" in which credit was hard to get. As a result, the performance of the economy in 2008 was very poor. What caused the credit crunch?

Our analysis of how a bank manages its capital indicates that the 2008 credit crunch was caused, at least in part, by the capital crunch, in which shortfalls of bank capital led to slower credit growth.

As we discussed in the previous chapter, there was a major boom and bust in the housing market that led to huge losses for banks from their holdings of securities backed by residential mortgages. In addition, banks had to take back onto their balance sheets many of the structured investment vehicles (SIVs) they had sponsored. The losses that reduced bank capital, along with the need for more capital to support the assets coming back onto their balance sheets, led to capital shortfalls: Banks had to either raise new capital or restrict asset growth by cutting back on lending. Banks did raise some capital but with the growing weakness of the economy, raising new capital was extremely difficult, so banks also chose to tighten their lending standards and reduce lending. Both of these helped produce a weak economy in 2008.

✦

MANAGING CREDIT RISK

As seen in the earlier discussion of general principles of asset management, banks and other financial institutions must make successful loans that are paid back in full (and so subject the institution to little credit risk) if they are to earn high profits. The economic concepts of adverse selection and moral hazard (discussed in Chapters 2 and 8) provide a framework for understanding the principles that financial institutions have to follow to reduce credit risk and make successful loans.[3]

Adverse selection in loan markets occurs because bad credit risks (those most likely to default on their loans) are the ones who usually line up for loans; in other words, those who are most likely to produce an *adverse* outcome are the most likely to be *selected.* Borrowers with very risky investment projects have much to gain if their projects are successful, so they are the most eager to obtain loans. Clearly, however, they are the least desirable borrowers because of the greater possibility that they will be unable to pay back their loans.

Moral hazard exists in loan markets because borrowers may have incentives to engage in activities that are undesirable from the lender's point of view. In such situations, it is more likely that the lender will be subjected to the *hazard* of default. Once borrowers have obtained a loan, they are more likely to invest in high-risk investment projects—projects that pay high returns to the borrowers if successful. The high risk, however, makes it less likely that they will be able to pay the loan back.

To be profitable, financial institutions must overcome the adverse selection and moral hazard problems that make loan defaults more likely. The attempts of financial institutions to solve these problems help explain a number of principles for managing credit risk: screening and monitoring, establishment of long-term customer relationships, loan commitments, collateral and compensating balance requirements, and credit rationing.

Screening and Monitoring

Asymmetric information is present in loan markets because lenders have less information about the investment opportunities and activities of borrowers than borrowers do. This situation leads to two information-producing activities by banks and other financial institutions—screening and monitoring. Indeed, Walter Wriston, a former head of Citicorp, the largest bank corporation in the United States, was often quoted as stating that the business of banking is the production of information.

Screening   Adverse selection in loan markets requires that lenders screen out the bad credit risks from the good ones so that loans are profitable to them. To accomplish effective screening, lenders must collect reliable information from prospective borrowers. Effective screening and information collection together form an important principle of credit risk management.

When you apply for a consumer loan (such as a car loan or a mortgage to purchase a house), the first thing you are asked to do is fill out forms that elicit a great deal of

---

[3]Other financial intermediaries, such as insurance companies, pension funds, and finance companies, also make private loans, and the credit risk management principles we outline here apply to them as well.

information about your personal finances. You are asked about your salary, your bank accounts and other assets (such as cars, insurance policies, and furnishings), and your outstanding loans; your record of loan, credit card, and charge account repayments; the number of years you've worked and who your employers have been. You also are asked personal questions such as your age, marital status, and number of children. The lender uses this information to evaluate how good a credit risk you are by calculating your credit score, a statistical measure derived from your answers that predicts whether you are likely to have trouble making your loan payments. Deciding on how good a risk you are cannot be entirely scientific, so the lender must also use judgment. The loan officer, whose job is to decide whether you should be given the loan, might call your employer or talk to some of the personal references you supplied. The officer might even make a judgment based on your demeanor or your appearance. (This is why most people dress neatly and conservatively when they go to a bank to apply for a loan.)

The process of screening and collecting information is similar when a financial institution makes a business loan. It collects information about the company's profits and losses (income) and about its assets and liabilities. The lender also has to evaluate the likely future success of the business. So in addition to obtaining information on such items as sales figures, a loan officer might ask questions about the company's future plans, the purpose of the loan, and the competition in the industry. The officer may even visit the company to obtain a firsthand look at its operations. The bottom line is that, whether for personal or business loans, bankers and other financial institutions need to be nosy.

Specialization in Lending   One puzzling feature of bank lending is that a bank often specializes in lending to local firms or to firms in particular industries, such as energy. In one sense, this behavior seems surprising, because it means that the bank is not diversifying its portfolio of loans and thus is exposing itself to more risk. But from another perspective, such specialization makes perfect sense. The adverse selection problem requires that the bank screen out bad credit risks. It is easier for the bank to collect information about local firms and determine their creditworthiness than to collect comparable information on firms that are far away. Similarly, by concentrating its lending on firms in specific industries, the bank becomes more knowledgeable about these industries and is therefore better able to predict which firms will be able to make timely payments on their debt.

Monitoring and Enforcement of Restrictive Covenants   Once a loan has been made, the borrower has an incentive to engage in risky activities that make it less likely that the loan will be paid off. To reduce this moral hazard, financial institutions must adhere to the principle for managing credit risk that a lender should write provisions (restrictive covenants) into loan contracts that restrict borrowers from engaging in risky activities. By monitoring borrowers' activities to see whether they are complying with the restrictive covenants and by enforcing the covenants if they are not, lenders can make sure that borrowers are not taking on risks at their expense. The need for banks and other financial institutions to engage in screening and monitoring explains why they spend so much money on auditing and information-collecting activities.

Long-Term Customer Relationships

An additional way for banks and other financial institutions to obtain information about their borrowers is through long-term customer relationships, another important principle of credit risk management.

If a prospective borrower has had a checking or savings account or other loans with a bank over a long period of time, a loan officer can look at past activity on the accounts and learn quite a bit about the borrower. The balances in the checking and savings accounts tell the banker how liquid the potential borrower is and at what time of year the borrower has a strong need for cash. A review of the checks the borrower has written reveals the borrower's suppliers. If the borrower has borrowed previously from the bank, the bank has a record of the loan payments. Thus long-term customer relationships reduce the costs of information collection and make it easier to screen out bad credit risks.

The need for monitoring by lenders adds to the importance of long-term customer relationships. If the borrower has borrowed from the bank before, the bank has already established procedures for monitoring that customer. Therefore, the costs of monitoring long-term customers are lower than those for new customers.

Long-term relationships benefit the customers as well as the bank. A firm with a previous relationship will find it easier to obtain a loan at a low interest rate because the bank has an easier time determining if the prospective borrower is a good credit risk and incurs fewer costs in monitoring the borrower.

A long-term customer relationship has another advantage for the bank. No bank can think of every contingency when it writes a restrictive covenant into a loan contract; there will always be risky borrower activities that are not ruled out. However, what if a borrower wants to preserve a long-term relationship with a bank because it will be easier to get future loans at low interest rates? The borrower then has the incentive to avoid risky activities that would upset the bank, even if restrictions on these risky activities are not specified in the loan contract. Indeed, if a bank doesn't like what a borrower is doing even when the borrower isn't violating any restrictive covenants, it has some power to discourage the borrower from such activity: The bank can threaten not to let the borrower have new loans in the future. Long-term customer relationships therefore enable banks to deal with even unanticipated moral hazard contingencies.

Loan Commitments

Banks also create long-term relationships and gather information by issuing **loan commitments** to commercial customers. A loan commitment is a bank's commitment (for a specified future period of time) to provide a firm with loans up to a given amount at an interest rate that is tied to some market interest rate. The majority of commercial and industrial loans are made under the loan commitment arrangement. The advantage for the firm is that it has a source of credit when it needs it. The advantage for the bank is that the loan commitment promotes a long-term relationship, which in turn facilitates information collection. In addition, provisions in the loan commitment agreement require that the firm continually supply the bank with information about the firm's income, asset and liability position, business activities, and so on. A loan commitment arrangement is a powerful method for reducing the bank's costs for screening and information collection.

Collateral and Compensating Balances

Collateral requirements for loans are important credit risk management tools. Collateral, which is property promised to the lender as compensation if the borrower defaults, lessens the consequences of adverse selection because it reduces the lender's losses in the case of a loan default. It also reduces moral hazard because the borrower has more to lose from a default. If a borrower defaults on a loan, the lender can sell the collateral and use the proceeds to make up for its losses on the loan. One particular form of collateral required when a bank makes commercial loans is called **compensating balances**: A firm receiving a loan must keep a required minimum amount of funds in a checking account at the bank. For example, a business getting a $10 million loan may be required to keep compensating balances of at least $1 million in its checking account at the bank. This $1 million in compensating balances can then be taken by the bank to make up some of the losses on the loan if the borrower defaults.

Besides serving as collateral, compensating balances help increase the likelihood that a loan will be paid off. They do this by helping the bank monitor the borrower and consequently reduce moral hazard. Specifically, by requiring the borrower to use a checking account at the bank, the bank can observe the firm's check payment practices, which may yield a great deal of information about the borrower's financial condition. For example, a sustained drop in the borrower's checking account balance may signal that the borrower is having financial trouble, or account activity may suggest that the borrower is engaging in risky activities; perhaps a change in suppliers means that the borrower is pursuing new lines of business. Any significant change in the borrower's payment procedures is a signal to the bank that it should make inquiries. Compensating balances therefore make it easier for banks to monitor borrowers more effectively and are another important credit risk management tool.

Credit Rationing

Another way in which financial institutions deal with adverse selection and moral hazard is through **credit rationing**: refusing to make loans even though borrowers are willing to pay the stated interest rate or even a higher rate. Credit rationing takes two forms. The first occurs when a lender refuses to make a loan *of any amount* to a borrower, even if the borrower is willing to pay a higher interest rate. The second occurs when a lender is willing to make a loan but restricts the size of the loan to less than the borrower would like.

At first you might be puzzled by the first type of credit rationing. After all, even if the potential borrower is a credit risk, why doesn't the lender just extend the loan but at a higher interest rate? The answer is that adverse selection prevents this solution. Individuals and firms with the riskiest investment projects are exactly those that are willing to pay the highest interest rates. If a borrower took on a high-risk investment and succeeded, the borrower would become extremely rich. But a lender wouldn't want to make such a loan precisely because the credit risk is high; the likely outcome is that the borrower will *not* succeed and the lender will not be paid back. Charging a higher interest rate just makes adverse selection worse for the lender; that is, it increases the likelihood that the lender is lending to a bad credit risk. The lender would therefore rather not make any loans at a higher interest rate; instead, it would engage in the first type of credit rationing and would turn down loans.

Financial institutions engage in the second type of credit rationing to guard against moral hazard: They grant loans to borrowers, but not loans as large as the borrowers want. Such credit rationing is necessary because the larger the loan, the greater the benefits from moral hazard. If a bank gives you a $1,000 loan, for example, you are likely to take actions that enable you to pay it back because you don't want to hurt your credit rating for the future. However, if the bank lends you $10 million, you are more likely to fly down to Rio to celebrate. The larger your loan, the greater your incentives to engage in activities that make it less likely that you will repay the loan. Because more borrowers repay their loans if the loan amounts are small, financial institutions ration credit by providing borrowers with smaller loans than they seek.

MANAGING INTEREST-RATE RISK

With the increased volatility of interest rates that occurred in the 1980s, banks and other financial institutions became more concerned about their exposure to interest-rate risk, the riskiness of earnings and returns that is associated with changes in interest rates. To see what interest-rate risk is all about, let's again take a look at the First National Bank, which has the following balance sheet:

First National Bank

Assets		Liabilities	
Rate-sensitive assets	$20 million	Rate-sensitive liabilities	$50 million
Variable-rate and		Variable-rate CDs	
short-term loans		Money market deposit	
Short-term securities		accounts	
Fixed-rate assets	$80 million	Fixed-rate liabilities	$50 million
Reserves		Checkable deposits	
Long-term loans		Savings deposits	
Long-term securities		Long-term CDs	
		Equity capital	

A total of $20 million of its assets are rate-sensitive, with interest rates that change frequently (at least once a year), and $80 million of its assets are fixed-rate, with interest rates that remain unchanged for a long period (over a year). On the liabilities side, the First National Bank has $50 million of rate-sensitive liabilities and $50 million of fixed-rate liabilities. Suppose that interest rates rise by 5 percentage points on average, from 10% to 15%. The income on the assets increases by $1 million (=5% × $20 million of rate-sensitive assets), while the payments on the liabilities increase by $2.5 million (=5% × $50 million of rate-sensitive liabilities). The First National Bank's profits now decline by $1.5 million (=$1 million − $2.5 million). Conversely, if interest rates fall by 5 percentage points, similar reasoning tells us that the First National Bank's profits increase by $1.5 million. This example illustrates the following point: *If a bank has more rate-sensitive liabilities than assets, a rise in interest rates will reduce bank profits and a decline in interest rates will raise bank profits*.

Gap and Duration Analysis

The sensitivity of bank profits to changes in interest rates can be measured more directly using **gap analysis**, in which the amount of rate-sensitive liabilities is subtracted from the amount of rate-sensitive assets. In our example, this calculation (called the "gap") is

−$30 million (= $20 million − $50 million). By multiplying the gap times the change in the interest rate, we can immediately obtain the effect on bank profits. For example, when interest rates rise by 5 percentage points, the change in profits is 5% × −$30 million, which equals −$1.5 million, as we saw.

The analysis we just conducted is known as *basic gap analysis*, and it can be refined in two ways. Clearly, not all assets and liabilities in the fixed-rate category have the same maturity. One refinement, the *maturity bucket approach*, is to measure the gap for several maturity subintervals, called *maturity buckets*, so that effects of interest-rate changes over a multiyear period can be calculated. The second refinement, called *standardized gap analysis*, accounts for the differing degrees of rate sensitivity for different rate-sensitive assets and liabilities.

An alternative method for measuring interest-rate risk, called **duration analysis**, examines the sensitivity of the market value of the bank's total assets and liabilities to changes in interest rates. Duration analysis is based on what is known as Macaulay's concept of *duration*, which measures the average lifetime of a security's stream of payments.[4] Duration is a useful concept because it provides a good approximation of the sensitivity of a security's market value to a change in its interest rate:

$$\text{percent change in market value of security} \approx$$
$$-\text{percentage-point change in interest rate} \times \text{duration in years}$$

where ≈ denotes "approximately equals."

Duration analysis involves using the average (weighted) duration of a financial institution's assets and of its liabilities to see how its net worth responds to a change in interest rates. Going back to our example of the First National Bank, suppose that the average duration of its assets is three years (that is, the average lifetime of the stream of payments is three years), while the average duration of its liabilities is two years. In addition, the First National Bank has $100 million of assets and, say, $90 million of liabilities, so its bank capital is 10% of assets. With a 5-percentage-point increase in interest rates, the market value of the bank's assets falls by 15% (= −5% × 3 years), a decline of $15 million on the $100 million of assets. However, the market value of the liabilities falls by 10% (= −5% × 2 years), a decline of $9 million on the $90 million of liabilities. The net result is that the net worth (the market value of the assets minus the liabilities) has declined by $6 million, or 6% of the total original asset value. Similarly, a 5-percentage-point decline in interest rates increases the net worth of the First National Bank by 6% of the total asset value.

As our example makes clear, both duration analysis and gap analysis indicate that the First National Bank will suffer if interest rates rise but will gain if they fall. Duration analysis and gap analysis are thus useful tools for telling a manager of a financial institution its degree of exposure to interest-rate risk.

---

[4]Algebraically, Macaulay's duration, D, is defined as

$$D = \sum_{\tau=1}^{N} \tau \frac{CP_\tau}{(1+i)^\tau} \bigg/ \sum_{\tau=1}^{N} \frac{CP_\tau}{(1+i)^\tau}$$

where
τ = time until cash payment is made
CP_τ = cash payment (interest plus principal) at time τ
i = interest rate
N = time to maturity of the security

For a more detailed discussion of duration gap analysis using the concept of Macaulay's duration, you can look at an appendix to this chapter that is on this book's website at www.myeconlab.com/mishkin.

APPLICATION ✦ Strategies for Managing Interest-Rate Risk

Suppose that as the manager of the First National Bank, you have done a duration and gap analysis for the bank as discussed in the text. Now you need to decide which alternative strategies you should pursue to manage the interest-rate risk.

If you firmly believe that interest rates will fall in the future, you may be willing to take no action because you know that the bank has more rate-sensitive liabilities than rate-sensitive assets and so will benefit from the expected interest-rate decline. However, you also realize that the First National Bank is subject to substantial interest-rate risk because there is always a possibility that interest rates will rise rather than fall. What should you do to eliminate this interest-rate risk? One thing you could do is to shorten the duration of the bank's assets to increase their rate sensitivity. Alternatively, you could lengthen the duration of the liabilities. By this adjustment of the bank's assets and liabilities, the bank's income will be less affected by interest-rate swings.

One problem with eliminating the First National Bank's interest-rate risk by altering the balance sheet is that doing so might be very costly in the short run. The bank may be locked into assets and liabilities of particular durations because of where its expertise lies. Fortunately, recently developed financial instruments known as financial derivatives—financial forwards and futures, options, and swaps—can help the bank reduce its interest-rate risk exposure but do not require that the bank rearrange its balance sheet.

OFF-BALANCE-SHEET ACTIVITIES

Although asset and liability management has traditionally been the major concern of banks, in the more competitive environment of recent years banks have been aggressively seeking out profits by engaging in off-balance-sheet activities.[5] **Off-balance-sheet activities** involve trading financial instruments and generating income from fees and loan sales, activities that affect bank profits but do not appear on bank balance sheets. Indeed, off-balance-sheet activities have been growing in importance for banks: The income from these activities as a percentage of assets has nearly doubled since 1980.

Loan Sales

One type of off-balance-sheet activity that has grown in importance in recent years involves income generated by loan sales. A **loan sale**, also called a *secondary loan participation*, involves a contract that sells all or part of the cash stream from a specific loan and thereby removes the loan so that it no longer is an asset on the bank's balance sheet. Banks earn profits by selling loans for an amount slightly greater than the amount of the original loan. Because the high interest rate on these loans makes them attractive, institutions are willing to buy them, even though the higher price means that they earn a

---

[5]Managers of financial institutions also need to know how well their banks are doing at any point in time. A second appendix to this chapter discusses how bank performance is measured; it can be found on the book's website at www.myeconlab.com/mishkin.

slightly lower interest rate than the original interest rate on the loan, usually on the order of 0.15 percentage points.

Generation of Fee Income

Another type of off-balance-sheet activity involves the generation of income from fees that banks receive for providing specialized services to their customers, such as making foreign exchange trades on a customer's behalf, servicing a mortgage-backed security by collecting interest and principal payments and then paying them out, guaranteeing debt securities such as banker's acceptances (by which the bank promises to make interest and principal payments if the party issuing the security cannot), and providing backup lines of credit. There are several types of backup lines of credit. We have already mentioned the most important, the loan commitment, under which for a fee the bank agrees to provide a loan at the customer's request, up to a given dollar amount, over a specified period of time. Credit lines are also now available to bank depositors with "overdraft privileges"—these bank customers can write checks in excess of their deposit balances and, in effect, write themselves a loan. Other lines of credit for which banks get fees include standby letters of credit to back up issues of commercial paper and other securities and credit lines (called *note issuance facilities*, NIFs, and *revolving underwriting facilities*, RUFs) for underwriting Euronotes, which are medium-term Eurobonds.

Off-balance-sheet activities involving guarantees of securities and backup credit lines increase the risk a bank faces. Even though a guaranteed security does not appear on a bank's balance sheet, it still exposes the bank to default risk: If the issuer of the security defaults, the bank is left holding the bag and must pay off the security's owner. Backup credit lines also expose the bank to risk because the bank may be forced to provide loans when it does not have sufficient liquidity or when the borrower is a very poor credit risk.

Banks also earn fees by creating financial instruments like the structured investment vehicles (SIVs) mentioned in the previous chapter and selling them off to investors. However, as became clear during the subprime financial crisis starting in 2008, when they decline in value, many of these financial instruments have to be taken back onto the balance sheet of the bank (like Citigroup) sponsoring them, because to do otherwise would severely damage the reputation of the bank. Even though these financial instruments at first appear to be off-balance sheet, in reality they are back on the balance sheet if they are subjected to large losses. To their regret, banks such as Citigroup ended up taking large losses on these financial instruments during the subprime financial crisis, indicating that these off-balance-sheet vehicles exposed banks to just as much risk as if they had been part of their balance sheets from the outset.

Trading Activities and Risk Management Techniques

We have already mentioned that banks' attempts to manage interest-rate risk led them to trading in financial futures, options for debt instruments, and interest-rate swaps. Banks engaged in international banking also conduct transactions in the foreign exchange market. All transactions in these markets are off-balance-sheet activities because they do not have a direct effect on the bank's balance sheet. Although bank trading in these markets is often directed toward reducing risk or facilitating other bank business, banks also try to outguess the markets and engage in speculation. This speculation can be a very risky business and indeed has led to bank insolvencies, the most dramatic being the failure of Barings, a British bank, in 1995.

Global   Barings, Daiwa, Sumitomo, and Société Générale: Rogue Traders and the Principal–Agent Problem

The demise of Barings, a venerable British bank more than a century old, is a sad morality tale of how the principal–agent problem operating through a rogue trader can take a financial institution that has a healthy balance sheet one month and turn it into an insolvent tragedy the next.

In July 1992, Nick Leeson, Barings's new head clerk at its Singapore branch, began to speculate on the Nikkei, the Japanese version of the Dow Jones stock index. By late 1992, Leeson had suffered losses of $3 million, which he hid from his superiors by stashing the losses in a secret account. He even fooled his superiors into thinking he was generating large profits, thanks to a failure of internal controls at his firm, which allowed him to execute trades on the Singapore exchange *and* oversee the bookkeeping of those trades. (As anyone who runs a cash business, such as a bar, knows, there is always a lower likelihood of fraud if more than one person handles the cash. Similarly for trading operations, you never mix management of the back room with management of the front room; this principle was grossly violated by Barings management.)

Things didn't get better for Leeson, who by late 1994 had losses exceeding $250 million. In January and February 1995, he bet the bank. On January 17, 1995, the day of the earthquake in Kobe, Japan, he lost $75 million, and by the end of the week had lost more than $150 million. When the stock market declined on February 23, leaving him with a further loss of $250 million, he called it quits and fled Singapore. Three days later, he turned himself in at the Frankfurt airport. By the end of his wild ride, Leeson's losses, $1.3 billion in all, ate up Barings's capital and caused the bank to fail. Leeson was subsequently convicted and sent to jail in Singapore for his activities. He was released in 1999 and apologized for his actions.

Our asymmetric information analysis of the principal–agent problem explains Leeson's behavior and the danger of Barings's management lapse. By letting Leeson control both his own trades and the back room, it increased asymmetric information, because it reduced the principal's (Barings's) knowledge about Leeson's trading activities. This lapse increased the moral hazard incentive for him to take risks at the bank's expense, as he was now less likely to be caught. Furthermore, once he had experienced large losses, he had even greater incentives to take on even higher risk because if his bets worked out, he could reverse his losses and keep in good standing with the company, whereas if his bets soured, he had little to lose because he was out of a job anyway. Indeed, the bigger his losses, the more he had to gain by bigger bets, which explains the escalation of the amount of his trades as his losses mounted. If Barings's managers had understood the principal-agent problem, they would have been more vigilant at finding out what Leeson was up to, and the bank might still be here today.

Unfortunately, Nick Leeson is no longer a rarity in the rogue traders' billionaire club, those who have lost more than $1 billion. Over eleven years, Toshihide Iguchi, an officer in the New York branch of Daiwa Bank, also had control of both the bond trading operation and the back room, and he racked up $1.1 billion in losses over the period. In July 1995, Iguchi disclosed his losses to his superiors, but the management of the bank did not disclose them to its regulators. The result was that Daiwa was slapped with a $340 million fine and the bank was thrown out of the country by U.S. bank regulators.

Yasuo Hamanaka is another member of the billionaire club. In July 1996, he topped Leeson's and Iguchi's record, losing $2.6 billion for his employer, the Sumitomo Corporation, one of Japan's top trading companies. Jerome Kerviel's loss for his bank, Société Générale, in January 2008 set the all time record for a rogue trader: His unauthorized trades cost the French bank $7.2 billion.

The moral of these stories is that management of firms engaged in trading activities must reduce the principal–agent problem by closely monitoring their traders' activities, or the rogues' gallery will continue to grow.

Trading activities, although often highly profitable, are dangerous because they make it easy for financial institutions and their employees to make huge bets quickly. A particular problem for management of trading activities is that the principal–agent problem, discussed in Chapter 8, is especially severe. Given the ability to place large bets, a trader (the agent), whether she trades in bond markets, in foreign exchange markets or in financial derivatives, has an incentive to take on excessive risks: If her trading strategy leads to large profits, she is likely to receive a high salary and bonuses, but if she takes large losses, the financial institution (the principal) will have to cover them. As the Barings Bank failure in 1995 so forcefully demonstrated, a trader subject to the principal-agent problem can take an institution that is quite healthy and drive it into insolvency very rapidly (see the Global box).

To reduce the principal-agent problem, managers of financial institutions must set up internal controls to prevent debacles like the one at Barings. Such controls include the complete separation of the people in charge of trading activities from those in charge of the bookkeeping for trades. In addition, managers must set limits on the total amount of traders' transactions and on the institution's risk exposure. Managers must also scrutinize risk assessment procedures using the latest computer technology. One such method involves the value-at-risk approach. In this approach, the institution develops a statistical model with which it can calculate the maximum loss that its portfolio is likely to sustain over a given time interval, dubbed the value at risk, or VaR. For example, a bank might estimate that the maximum loss it would be likely to sustain over one day with a probability of 1 in 100 is $1 million; the $1 million figure is the bank's calculated value at risk. Another approach is called "stress testing." In this approach, a manager asks models what would happen if a doomsday scenario occurs; that is, she looks at the losses the institution would sustain if an unusual combination of bad events occurred. With the value-at-risk approach and stress testing, a financial institution can assess its risk exposure and take steps to reduce it.

United States bank regulators have become concerned about the increased risk that banks are facing from their off-balance-sheet activities, and, as we will see in Chapter 11, are encouraging banks to pay increased attention to risk management. In addition, the Bank for International Settlements is developing additional bank capital requirements based on value-at-risk calculations for a bank's trading activities.

SUMMARY

1. The balance sheet of commercial banks can be thought of as a list of the sources and uses of bank funds. The bank's liabilities are its sources of funds, which include checkable deposits, time deposits, discount loans from the Fed, borrowings from other banks and corporations, and bank capital. The bank's assets are its uses of funds, which include reserves, cash items in process of collection, deposits at other banks, securities, loans, and other assets (mostly physical capital).

2. Banks make profits through the process of asset transformation: They borrow short (accept deposits) and lend long (make loans). When a bank takes in additional deposits, it gains an equal amount of reserves;

when it pays out deposits, it loses an equal amount of reserves.

3. Although more-liquid assets tend to earn lower returns, banks still desire to hold them. Specifically, banks hold excess and secondary reserves because they provide insurance against the costs of a deposit outflow. Banks manage their assets to maximize profits by seeking the highest returns possible on loans and securities while at the same time trying to lower risk and making adequate provisions for liquidity. Although liability management was once a staid affair, large (money center) banks now actively seek out sources of funds by issuing liabilities such as negotiable CDs or by actively

borrowing from other banks and corporations. Banks manage the amount of capital they hold to prevent bank failure and to meet bank capital requirements set by the regulatory authorities. However, they do not want to hold too much capital because by so doing they will lower the returns to equity holders.

4. The concepts of adverse selection and moral hazard explain many credit risk management principles involving loan activities: screening and monitoring, establishment of long-term customer relationships and loan commitments, collateral and compensating balances, and credit rationing.

5. With the increased volatility of interest rates that occurred in the 1980s, financial institutions became more concerned about their exposure to interest-rate

risk. Gap and duration analyses tell a financial institution if it has more rate-sensitive liabilities than assets (in which case a rise in interest rates will reduce profits and a fall in interest rates will raise profits). Financial institutions manage their interest-rate risk by modifying their balance sheets but can also use strategies involving financial derivatives.

6. Off-balance-sheet activities consist of trading financial instruments and generating income from fees and loan sales, all of which affect bank profits but are not visible on bank balance sheets. Because these off-balance-sheet activities expose banks to increased risk, bank management must pay particular attention to risk assessment procedures and internal controls to restrict employees from taking on too much risk.

KEY TERMS

asset management, p. 232

balance sheet, p. 225

capital adequacy management, p. 232

compensating balance, p. 244

credit rationing, p. 244

credit risk, p. 232

deposit outflows, p. 232

discount loans, p. 227

discount rate, p. 234

duration analysis, p. 246

equity multiplier (EM), p. 238

excess reserves, p. 228

gap analysis, p. 245

interest-rate risk, p. 232

liability management, p. 232

liquidity management, p. 232

loan commitment, p. 243

loan sale, p. 247

money center banks, p. 236

off-balance-sheet activities, p. 247

required reserve ratio, p. 228

required reserves, p. 228

reserve requirements, p. 228

reserves, p. 228

return on assets (ROA), p. 238

return on equity (ROE), p. 238

secondary reserves, p. 228

T-account, p. 229

vault cash, p. 228

QUESTIONS AND PROBLEMS

All questions and problems are available in myeconlab *at* www.myeconlab.com/mishkin.

1. Why might a bank be willing to borrow funds from other banks at a higher rate than it can borrow from the Fed?

2. Rank the following bank assets from most to least liquid:
   a. Commercial loans
   b. Securities
   c. Reserves
   d. Physical capital

3. Using the T-accounts of the First National Bank and the Second National Bank, describe what happens when Jane Brown writes a $50 check on her account at the First National Bank to pay her friend Joe Green, who in turn deposits the check in his account at the Second National Bank.

4. What happens to reserves at the First National Bank if one person withdraws $1,000 of cash and another person deposits $500 of cash? Use T-accounts to explain your answer.

5. The bank you own has the following balance sheet:

Assets		Liabilities	
Reserves	$ 75 million	Deposits	$500 million
Loans	$525 million	Bank capital	$100 million

If the bank suffers a deposit outflow of $50 million with a required reserve ratio on deposits of 10%, what actions must you take to keep your bank from failing?

6. If a deposit outflow of $50 million occurs, which balance sheet would a bank rather have initially, the balance sheet in Problem 5 or the following balance sheet? Why?

Assets		Liabilities	
Reserves	$100 million	Deposits	$500 million
Loans	$500 million	Bank capital	$100 million

7. Why has the development of overnight loan markets made it more likely that banks will hold fewer excess reserves?

8. If the bank you own has no excess reserves and a sound customer comes in asking for a loan, should you automatically turn the customer down, explaining that you don't have any excess reserves to lend out? Why or why not? What options are available for you to provide the funds your customer needs?

9. If a bank finds that its ROE is too low because it has too much bank capital, what can it do to raise its ROE?

10. If a bank is falling short of meeting its capital requirements by $1 million, what three things can it do to rectify the situation?

11. Why is being nosy a desirable trait for a banker?

12. A bank almost always insists that the firms it lends to keep compensating balances at the bank. Why?

13. "Because diversification is a desirable strategy for avoiding risk, it never makes sense for a bank to specialize in making specific types of loans." Is this statement true, false, or uncertain? Explain your answer.

14. Suppose that you are the manager of a bank whose $100 billion of assets have an average duration of four years and whose $90 billion of liabilities have an average duration of six years. Conduct a duration analysis for the bank, and show what will happen to the net worth of the bank if interest rates rise by 2 percentage points. What actions could you take to reduce the bank's interest-rate risk?

15. Suppose that you are the manager of a bank that has $15 million of fixed-rate assets, $30 million of rate-sensitive assets, $25 million of fixed-rate liabilities, and $20 million of rate-sensitive liabilities. Conduct a gap analysis for the bank, and show what will happen to bank profits if interest rates rise by 5 percentage points. What actions could you take to reduce the bank's interest-rate risk?

WEB EXERCISES

1. Table 1 reports the balance sheet of all commercial banks based on aggregate data found in the Federal Reserve *Bulletin*. Compare this table to the most recent balance sheet reported by Bank of America. Go to www.bankofamerica.com/investor/index.cfm?section =700 and click on Annual Reports to view the balance sheet. Does Bank of America have more or less of its portfolio in loans than the average bank? Which type of loan is most common?

2. It is relatively easy to find up-to-date information on banks because of their extensive reporting requirements. Go to www2.fdic.gov/qbp/. This site is sponsored by the Federal Deposit Insurance Corporation. You will find summary data on financial institutions. Go to the most recent Quarterly Banking Profile. Scroll to the bottom and open Table 1-A.
   a. Have banks' return on assets been increasing or decreasing over the last few years?
   b. Has the core capital been increasing, and how does it compare to the capital ratio reported in Table 1 in the text?
   c. How many institutions are currently reporting to the FDIC?

WEB REFERENCES

www.bankofamerica.com/investor/index.cfm?section=700
Click on Annual Reports to view the balance sheet.

www.federalreserve.gov/boarddocs/SupManual/default.
htm#trading

The Federal Reserve Bank Trading and Capital Market
Activities Manual offers an in-depth discussion of a wide

range of risk management issues encountered in trading
operations.

 MyEconLab CAN HELP YOU GET A BETTER GRADE

If your exam were tomorrow, would you be ready? For each chapter, MyEconLab Practice Test and Study Plans pinpoint which sections you have mastered and which ones
you need to study. That way, you are more efficient with your study time, and you are
better prepared for your exams.

To see how it works, turn to page 20 and then go to: www.myeconlab.com/mishkin

11 Economic Analysis of Financial Regulation

Preview

As we have seen in the previous chapters, the financial system is among the most heavily regulated sectors of the economy, and banks are among the most heavily regulated of financial institutions. In this chapter, we develop an economic analysis of why regulation of the financial system takes the form it does.

Unfortunately, the regulatory process may not always work very well, as evidenced by the recent subprime meltdown and other financial crises, not only in the United States but in many countries throughout the world. Here we also use our economic analysis of financial regulation to explain the worldwide crises in banking and to consider how the regulatory system can be reformed to prevent future disasters.

ASYMMETRIC INFORMATION AND FINANCIAL REGULATION

In earlier chapters, we have seen how asymmetric information—the fact that different parties in a financial contract do not have the same information—leads to adverse selection and moral hazard problems that have an important impact on the financial system. The concepts of asymmetric information, adverse selection, and moral hazard are especially useful in understanding why government has chosen the form of financial regulation we see in the United States and in other countries. There are nine basic categories of financial regulation: the government safety net, restrictions on asset holdings, capital requirements, prompt corrective action, chartering and examination, assessment of risk management, disclosure requirements, consumer protection, and restrictions on competition.

Government Safety Net

As we saw in Chapter 8, financial intermediaries, like banks are particularly well suited to solving adverse selection and moral hazard problems because they make private loans that help avoid the free-rider problem. However, this solution to the free-rider problem creates another asymmetric information problem, because depositors lack information about the quality of these private loans. This asymmetric information problem leads to several reasons why the financial system might not function well.

Bank Panics and the Need for Deposit Insurance   Before the FDIC started operations in 1934, a **bank failure** (in which a bank is unable to meet its obligations to pay its depositors and other creditors and so must go out of business) meant that depositors would have to wait to get their deposit funds until the bank was liquidated (until its assets had been turned into cash); at that time, they would be paid only a fraction of the value of their deposits. Unable to learn if bank managers were taking on too much risk or were outright crooks, depositors would be reluctant to put money in the bank, thus making banking institutions less viable. Second, depositors' lack of information about the quality of bank assets can lead to bank panics, which, as we saw in Chapter 9, can have serious harmful consequences for the economy. To see this, consider the following situation. There is no deposit insurance, and an adverse shock hits the economy. As a result of the shock, 5% of the banks have such large losses on loans that they become insolvent (have a negative net worth and so are bankrupt). Because of asymmetric information, depositors are unable to tell whether their bank is a good bank or one of the 5% that are insolvent. Depositors at bad *and* good banks recognize that they may not get back 100 cents on the dollar for their deposits and will want to withdraw them. Indeed, because banks operate on a "sequential service constraint" (a first-come, first-served basis), depositors have a very strong incentive to show up at the bank first, because if they are last in line, the bank may run out of funds and they will get nothing. Uncertainty about the health of the banking system in general can lead to runs on banks both good and bad, and the failure of one bank can hasten the failure of others (referred to as the *contagion effect*). If nothing is done to restore the public's confidence, a bank panic can ensue.

Indeed, bank panics were a fact of American life in the nineteenth and early twentieth centuries, with major ones occurring every 20 years or so in 1819, 1837, 1857, 1873, 1884, 1893, 1907, and 1930–1933. Bank failures were a serious problem even during the boom years of the 1920s, when the number of bank failures averaged around 600 per year.

A government safety net for depositors can short-circuit runs on banks and bank panics, and by providing protection for the depositor, it can overcome reluctance to put funds in the banking system. One form of the safety net is deposit insurance, a guarantee such as that provided by the Federal Deposit Insurance Corporation (FDIC) in the United States in which depositors are paid off in full on the first $100,000 they have deposited in a bank if the bank fails. (FDIC coverage was temporarily raised to $250,000 during the subprime financial crisis in October 2008.) With fully insured deposits, depositors don't need to run to the bank to make withdrawals—even if they are worried about the bank's health—because their deposits will be worth 100 cents on the dollar no matter what. From 1930 to 1933, the years immediately preceding the creation of the FDIC, the number of bank failures averaged more than 2,000 per year. After the establishment of the FDIC in 1934, bank failures averaged fewer than 15 per year until 1981.

The FDIC uses two primary methods to handle a failed bank. In the first, called the *payoff method*, the FDIC allows the bank to fail and pays off deposits up to the $100,000 insurance limit (with funds acquired from the insurance premiums paid by the banks who have bought FDIC insurance). After the bank has been liquidated, the FDIC lines up with other creditors of the bank and is paid its share of the proceeds from the liquidated assets. Typically, when the payoff method is used, account holders with deposits in excess of the $100,000 limit get back more than 90 cents on the dollar, although the process can take several years to complete.

In the second method, called the *purchase and assumption method*, the FDIC reorganizes the bank, typically by finding a willing merger partner who assumes (takes over) all of the failed bank's liabilities so that no depositor or other creditor loses a penny. The FDIC often sweetens the pot for the merger partner by providing it with subsidized loans or by buying some of the failed bank's weaker loans. The net effect of the purchase and assumption method is that the FDIC has guaranteed *all* liabilities and deposits, not just deposits under the $100,000 limit. The purchase and assumption method is typically more costly for the FDIC than the payoff method, but nevertheless was the FDIC's most common procedure for dealing with a failed bank before new banking legislation in 1991.

In recent years, government deposit insurance has been growing in popularity and has spread to many countries throughout the world. Whether this trend is desirable is discussed in the Global box, "The Spread of Government Deposit Insurance Throughout the World: Is This a Good Thing?".

Other Forms of the Government Safety Net   Deposit insurance is not the only form of government safety net. In other countries, governments have often stood ready to provide support to domestic banks facing runs even in the absence of explicit deposit insurance. Furthermore, banks are not the only financial intermediaries that can pose a systemic threat to the financial system, as our discussion of financial crises in Chapter 9 has illustrated. When financial institutions are very large or highly interconnected with other financial institutions or markets, their failure has the potential to bring down the entire financial system. Indeed, as we saw in Chapter 9, this is exactly what happened with Bear Stearns and Lehman Brothers, two investment banks, and AIG, an insurance company, during the subprime financial crisis in 2008.

One way governments provide support is through lending from the central bank to troubled institutions, as the Federal Reserve did during the subprime financial crisis (more on this in Chapter 15). This form of support is often referred to as the "lender of

---

 Global   **The Spread of Government Deposit Insurance Throughout the World: Is This a Good Thing?**

For the first 30 years after federal deposit insurance was established in the United States, only six countries emulated the United States and adopted deposit insurance. However, this began to change in the late 1960s, with the trend accelerating in the 1990s, when the number of countries adopting deposit insurance topped 70. Government deposit insurance has taken off throughout the world because of growing concern about the health of banking systems, particularly after the increasing number of banking crises in recent years (documented at the end of this chapter). Has this spread of deposit insurance been a good thing? Has it helped improve the performance of the financial system and prevent banking crises?

The answer seems to be no under many circumstances. Research at the World Bank has found that, on average, the adoption of explicit government deposit insurance is associated with less banking sector stability and a higher incidence of banking crises.* Furthermore, on average, it seems to retard financial development. However, the negative effects of deposit insurance appear only in countries with weak institutional environments: an absence of rule of law, ineffective regulation and supervision of the financial sector, and high corruption. This is exactly what might be expected because, as we will see later in this chapter, a strong institutional environment is needed to limit the moral hazard incentives for banks to engage in the excessively risky behavior encouraged by deposit insurance. The problem is that developing a strong institutional environment may be very difficult to achieve in many emerging market countries. This leaves us with the following conclusion: Adoption of deposit insurance may be exactly the wrong medicine for promoting stability and efficiency of banking systems in emerging market countries.

*See World Bank, *Finance for Growth: Policy Choices in a Volatile World* (Oxford: World Bank and Oxford University Press, 2001).

last resort" role of the central bank. In other cases, funds are provided directly to troubled institutions, as was done by the U.S. Treasury and by other governments in 2008 during a particularly virulent phase of the subprime financial crisis. Governments can also take over (nationalize) troubled institutions and guarantee that all creditors will be repaid their loans in full.

Moral Hazard and the Government Safety Net   Although a government safety net can help protect depositors and other creditors and prevent, or ameliorate, financial crises, it is a mixed blessing. The most serious drawback of the government safety net stems from moral hazard, the incentives of one party to a transaction to engage in activities detrimental to the other party. Moral hazard is an important concern in insurance arrangements in general because the existence of insurance provides increased incentives for taking risks that might result in an insurance payoff. For example, some drivers with automobile collision insurance that has a low deductible might be more likely to drive recklessly, because if they get into an accident, the insurance company pays most of the costs for damage and repairs.

Moral hazard is a prominent concern in government arrangements to provide a safety net. With a safety net depositors and creditors know that they will not suffer losses if a financial institution fails, so they do not impose the discipline of the marketplace on these institutions by withdrawing funds when they suspect that the financial institution is taking on too much risk. Consequently, financial institutions with a government safety net have an incentive to take on greater risks than they otherwise would, with taxpayers paying the bill if the bank subsequently goes belly up. Financial institutions have been given the following bet: "Heads I win, tails the taxpayer loses."

Adverse Selection and the Government Safety Net   A further problem with a government safety net like deposit insurance arises because of adverse selection, the fact that the people who are most likely to produce the adverse outcome insured against (bank failure) are those who most want to take advantage of the insurance. For example, bad drivers are more likely than good drivers to take out automobile collision insurance with a low deductible. Because depositors and creditors protected by a government safety net have little reason to impose discipline on financial institutions, risk-loving entrepreneurs might find the financial industry a particularly attractive one to enter—they know that they will be able to engage in highly risky activities. Even worse, because protected depositors and creditors have so little reason to monitor the financial institution's activities, without government intervention outright crooks might also find finance an attractive industry for their activities because it is easy for them to get away with fraud and embezzlement.

"Too Big to Fail"   The moral hazard created by a government safety net and the desire to prevent financial institution failures have presented financial regulators with a particular quandary. Because the failure of a very large financial institution makes it more likely that a major financial disruption will occur, financial regulators are naturally reluctant to allow a big institution to fail and cause losses to its depositors and creditors. Indeed, consider Continental Illinois, one of the ten largest banks in the United States when it became insolvent in May 1984. Not only did the FDIC guarantee depositors up to the $100,000 insurance limit, but it also guaranteed accounts exceeding $100,000 and even prevented losses for Continental Illinois bondholders. Shortly thereafter, the Comptroller of the Currency (the regulator of national banks) testified to Congress that eleven of the largest banks would receive a similar treatment to that of

Continental Illinois. Although the comptroller did not use the term "too big to fail" (it was actually used by Congressman Stewart McKinney in those hearings), this term is now applied to a policy in which the government provides guarantees of repayment of large uninsured creditors of the largest banks, so that no depositor or creditor suffers a loss, even when they are not automatically entitled to this guarantee. The FDIC would do this by using the purchase and assumption method, giving the insolvent bank a large infusion of capital and then finding a willing merger partner to take over the bank and its deposits. The too-big-to-fail policy was extended to big banks that were not even among the eleven largest. (Note that "too big to fail" is somewhat misleading because when a financial institution is closed or merged into another financial institution, the managers are usually fired and the stockholders in the financial institution lose their investment.)

One problem with the too-big-to-fail policy is that it increases the moral hazard incentives for big banks. If the FDIC were willing to close a bank using the payoff method, paying depositors only up to the $100,000 limit, large depositors with more than $100,000 would suffer losses if the bank failed. Thus they would have an incentive to monitor the bank by examining the bank's activities closely and pulling their money out if the bank was taking on too much risk. To prevent such a loss of deposits, the bank would be more likely to engage in less risky activities. However, once large depositors know that a bank is too big to fail, they have no incentive to monitor the bank and pull out their deposits when it takes on too much risk: No matter what the bank does, large depositors will not suffer any losses. The result of the too-big-to-fail policy is that big banks might take on even greater risks, thereby making bank failures more likely.[1]

Similarly, the too-big-to-fail policy increases the moral hazard incentives for nonbank financial institutions that are extended a government safety net. Knowing that the financial institution will get bailed out, creditors have little incentive to monitor the institution and pull their money out when the institution is taking on excessive risk. As a result, large or interconnected financial institutions will be more likely to engage in highly risky activities, making it more likely that a financial crisis will occur.

Financial Consolidation and the Government Safety Net   With financial innovation and the passage of the Riegle-Neal Interstate Banking and Branching Efficiency Act of 1994 and the Gramm-Leach-Bliley Financial Services Modernization Act in 1999, financial consolidation has been proceeding at a rapid pace, leading to both larger and more complex financial organizations. Financial consolidation poses two challenges to financial regulation because of the existence of the government safety net. First, the increased size of financial institutions as a result of financial consolidation increases the too-big-to-fail problem, because there will now be more large institutions whose failure would expose the financial system to systemic (systemwide) risk. Thus more financial institutions are likely to be treated as too big to fail, and the increased moral hazard incentives for these large institutions to take on greater risk can then increase the fragility of the financial system. Second, financial consolidation of banks

---

[1] Evidence reveals, as our analysis predicts, that large banks took on riskier loans than smaller banks and that this led to higher loan losses for big banks; see John Boyd and Mark Gertler, "U.S. Commercial Banking: Trends, Cycles and Policy," *NBER Macroeconomics Annual*, 1993, pp. 319–368.

with other financial services firms means that the government safety net may be extended to new activities such as securities underwriting, insurance, or real estate activities, as has occurred during the subprime financial crisis in 2008. This increases incentives for greater risk taking in these activities that can also weaken the fabric of the financial system. Limiting the moral hazard incentives for the larger, more complex financial organizations that have arisen as a result of recent changes in legislation will be one of the key issues facing banking regulators in the aftermath of the subprime financial crisis.

Restrictions on Asset Holdings

As we have seen, the moral hazard associated with a government safety net encourages too much risk taking on the part of financial institutions. Bank regulations that restrict asset holdings are directed at minimizing this moral hazard, which can cost the taxpayers dearly.

Even in the absence of a government safety net, financial institutions still have the incentive to take on too much risk. Risky assets may provide the financial institution with higher earnings when they pay off; but if they do not pay off and the institution fails, depositors and creditors are left holding the bag. If depositors and creditors were able to monitor the bank easily by acquiring information on its risk-taking activities, they would immediately withdraw their funds if the institution was taking on too much risk. To prevent such a loss of funds, the institution would be more likely to reduce its risk-taking activities. Unfortunately, acquiring information on an institution's activities to learn how much risk it is taking can be a difficult task. Hence most depositors and many creditors are incapable of imposing discipline that might prevent financial institutions from engaging in risky activities. A strong rationale for government regulation to reduce risk taking on the part of financial institutions therefore existed even before the establishment of government safety nets like federal deposit insurance.

Because banks are most prone to panics, they are subjected to strict regulations to restrict their holding of risky assets such as common stocks. Bank regulations also promote diversification, which reduces risk by limiting the dollar amount of loans in particular categories or to individual borrowers. With the extension of the government safety net during the subprime financial crisis, it is likely that nonbank financial institutions may face greater restrictions on their holdings of risky assets. There is a danger, however, that these restrictions may become so onerous that the efficiency of the financial system will be impaired.

Capital Requirements

Government-imposed capital requirements are another way of minimizing moral hazard at financial institutions. When a financial institution is forced to hold a large amount of equity capital, the institution has more to lose if it fails and is thus more likely to pursue less risky activities. In addition, as was illustrated in Chapter 10, capital functions as a cushion when bad shocks occur, making it less likely that the financial institution will fail, thereby directly adding to the safety and soundness of financial institutions.

Capital requirements for banks take two forms. The first type is based on the **leverage ratio**, the amount of capital divided by the bank's total assets. To be classified as well capitalized, a bank's leverage ratio must exceed 5%; a lower leverage ratio, especially one below 3%, triggers increased regulatory restrictions on the bank. Through most of the 1980s, minimum bank capital in the United States was set solely by specifying a minimum leverage ratio.

In the wake of the Continental Illinois and savings and loans bailouts, regulators in the United States and the rest of the world have become increasingly worried about banks' holdings of risky assets and about the increase in banks' **off-balance-sheet activities**, activities that involve trading financial instruments and generating income from fees, which do not appear on bank balance sheets but nevertheless expose banks to risk. An agreement among banking officials from industrialized nations set up the **Basel Committee on Banking Supervision** (because it meets under the auspices of the Bank for International Settlements in Basel, Switzerland), which has implemented the **Basel Accord** that deals with a second type of capital requirements, risk-based capital requirements. The Basel Accord, which required that banks hold as capital at least 8% of their risk-weighted assets, has been adopted by more than 100 countries, including the United States. Assets and off-balance-sheet activities were allocated into four categories, each with a different weight to reflect the degree of credit risk. The first category carries a zero weight and includes items that have little default risk, such as reserves and government securities issued by the Organization for Economic Cooperation and Development (OECD—industrialized) countries. The second category has a 20% weight and includes claims on banks in OECD countries. The third category has a weight of 50% and includes municipal bonds and residential mortgages. The fourth category has the maximum weight of 100% and includes loans to consumers and corporations. Off-balance-sheet activities are treated in a similar manner by assigning a credit-equivalent percentage that converts them to on-balance-sheet items to which the appropriate risk weight applies. The 1996 Market Risk Amendment to the Basel Accord set minimum capital requirements for risks in banks' trading accounts.

Over time, limitations of the Basel Accord have become apparent, because the regulatory measure of bank risk as stipulated by the risk weights can differ substantially from the actual risk the bank faces. This has resulted in **regulatory arbitrage**, a practice in which banks keep on their books assets that have the same risk-based capital requirement but are relatively risky, such as a loan to a company with a very low credit rating, while taking off their books low-risk assets, such as a loan to a company with a very high credit rating. The Basel Accord could thus lead to increased risk taking, the opposite of its intent. To address these limitations, the Basel Committee on Bank Supervision has released proposals for a new capital accord, often referred to as Basel 2, but it is not clear if it is workable (see the Global box, "Basel 2: How Well Will It Work?").

The Basel Committee's work on bank capital requirements is never-ending. Indeed, with the extension of the government safety net to nonbank financial institutions during the subprime financial crisis, capital requirements for these other financial institutions will receive more scrutiny in the future. As the financial industry changes, regulation of capital must change with it to ensure the safety and soundness of financial institutions. It is increasingly likely that the Basel Committee will have an even greater role in exploring capital requirements for a wider range of financial institutions in the future.

Prompt Corrective Action

If the amount of a financial institution's capital falls to low levels, there are two serious problems. First, the bank is more likely to fail because it has a smaller capital cushion if it suffers loan losses or other asset write-downs. Second, with less capital, a financial

Global   Basel 2: How Well Will It Work?

Starting in June 1999, the Basel Committee on Banking Supervision released several proposals to reform the original 1988 Basel Accord. These efforts have culminated in what bank supervisors refer to as Basel 2, which is based on three pillars.

1. Pillar 1 links capital requirements for large, internationally active banks more closely to actual risk of three types: market risk, credit risk, and operational risk. It does so by specifying many more categories of assets with different risk weights in its standardized approach. Alternatively, it allows sophisticated banks to pursue an internal ratings-based approach that permits banks to use their own models of credit risk.

2. Pillar 2 focuses on strengthening the supervisory process, particularly in assessing the quality of risk management in banking institutions and evaluating whether these institutions have adequate procedures to determine how much capital they need.

3. Pillar 3 focuses on improving market discipline through increased disclosure of details about a bank's credit exposures, its amount of reserves and capital, the officials who control the bank, and the effectiveness of its internal rating system.

Although Basel 2 makes great strides toward limiting excessive risk taking by internationally active banking institutions, it has greatly increased the complexity of the accord. The document describing the original Basel Accord was 26 pages, while the final draft of Basel 2 exceeded 500 pages. The original timetable called for the completion of the final round of consultation by the end of 2001, with the new rules taking effect by 2004. However, criticism from banks, trade associations, and national regulators led to several postponements. The final draft was not published until June 2004 and Basel 2 started to be implemented at the beginning of 2008 by European banks. United States banks submitted plans for compliance with Basel 2 in 2008, but full implementation did not occur until 2009. Only the dozen or so largest U.S. banks are subject to Basel 2: all others will be allowed to use a simplified version of the standards it imposes.

There are several serious criticisms of Basel 2 that cast doubts on how well it will work. First, its complexity could make it unworkable. Second, risk weights in the standardized approach are heavily reliant on credit ratings. Since these credit ratings have proved to be very unreliable on subprime mortgage products during the recent financial crisis, there are serious doubts that the standardized approach using credit ratings will produce reliable risk weights. Third, Basel 2 is very procyclical. That is, it demands that banks hold less capital when times are good, but more when times are bad, thereby exacerbating credit cycles. Because the probability of default and expected losses for different classes of assets rises during bad times, Basel 2 may require more capital at exactly the time when capital is most short. This has been a particularly serious concern in the aftermath of the subprime financial crisis. As a result of this crisis, banks' capital balances eroded, leading to a cutback on lending that was a big drag on the economy. Basel 2 may make this cutback in lending even worse, doing even more harm to the economy.

institution has less "skin in the game" and is therefore more likely to take on excessive risks. In other words, the moral hazard problem becomes more severe, making it more likely that the institution will fail and the taxpayer will be left holding the bag. To prevent this, the Federal Deposit Insurance Corporation Improvement Act of 1991 adopted prompt corrective action provisions that require the FDIC to intervene earlier and more vigorously when a bank gets into trouble.

Banks are now classified into five groups based on bank capital. Group 1, classified as "well capitalized," are banks that significantly exceed minimum capital requirements and are allowed privileges such as the ability to do some securities underwriting. Banks in group 2, classified as "adequately capitalized," meet minimum capital requirements and are not subject to corrective actions but are not allowed the privileges of the well-capitalized banks. Banks in group 3, "undercapitalized," fail to meet capital requirements. Banks in groups 4 and 5 are "significantly undercapitalized" and "critically undercapitalized," respectively, and are not allowed to pay interest on their deposits at rates that are higher than average. In addition, for group 3 banks, the FDIC is required to take prompt corrective actions such as requiring them to submit a capital restoration plan, restrict their asset growth, and seek regulatory approval to open new branches or develop new lines of business. Banks that are so undercapitalized as to have equity capital that amounts to less than 2% of assets fall into group 5, and the FDIC must take steps to close them down.

Financial Supervision: Chartering and Examination

Overseeing who operates financial institutions and how they are operated, referred to as **financial supervision** or **prudential supervision**, is an important method for reducing adverse selection and moral hazard in the financial industry. Because financial institutions can be used by crooks or overambitious entrepreneurs to engage in highly speculative activities, such undesirable people would be eager to run a financial institution. Chartering financial institutions is one method for preventing this adverse selection problem; through chartering, proposals for new institutions are screened to prevent undesirable people from controlling them.

Regular on-site examinations, which allow regulators to monitor whether the institution is complying with capital requirements and restrictions on asset holdings, also function to limit moral hazard. Bank examiners give banks a *CAMELS rating*. The acronym is based on the six areas assessed: capital adequacy, asset quality, management, earnings, liquidity, and sensitivity to market risk. With this information about a bank's activities, regulators can enforce regulations by taking such formal actions as *cease and desist orders* to alter the bank's behavior or even close a bank if its CAMELS rating is sufficiently low. Actions taken to reduce moral hazard by restricting banks from taking on too much risk help reduce the adverse selection problem further, because with less opportunity for risk taking, risk-loving entrepreneurs will be less likely to be attracted to the banking industry. Note that the methods regulators use to cope with adverse selection and moral hazard have their counterparts in private financial markets (see Chapters 8 and 10). Chartering is similar to the screening of potential borrowers, regulations restricting risky asset holdings are similar to restrictive covenants that prevent borrowing firms from engaging in risky investment activities, capital requirements act like restrictive covenants that require minimum amounts of net worth for borrowing firms, and regular examinations are similar to the monitoring of borrowers by lending institutions.

A commercial bank obtains a charter either from the Comptroller of the Currency (in the case of a national bank) or from a U.S. state banking authority (in the case of a state bank). To obtain a charter, the people planning to organize the bank must submit an application that shows how they plan to operate the bank. In evaluating the application, the regulatory authority looks at whether the bank is likely to be sound by examining the quality of the bank's intended management, the likely earnings of the bank, and the amount of the bank's initial capital. Before 1980, the chartering agency typically explored the issue of whether the community needed a new bank. Often a new bank charter would not be granted if existing banks in a community would be hurt by its presence. Today this anticompetitive stance (justified by the desire to prevent failures of existing banks) is no longer as strong in the chartering agencies.

Once a bank has been chartered, it is required to file periodic (usually quarterly) *call reports* that reveal the bank's assets and liabilities, income and dividends, ownership, foreign exchange operations, and other details. The bank is also subject to examination by the bank regulatory agencies to ascertain its financial condition at least once a year. To avoid duplication of effort, the three U.S. government agencies work together and usually accept each other's examinations. This means that, typically, national banks are examined by the Office of the Comptroller of the Currency, the U.S. state banks that are members of the Federal Reserve System are examined by the Fed, and insured non-member state banks are examined by the FDIC.

Bank examinations are conducted by bank examiners, who sometimes make unannounced visits to the bank (so that nothing can be "swept under the rug" in anticipation of their examination). The examiners study a bank's books to see whether it is complying with the rules and regulations that apply to its holdings of assets. If a bank is holding securities or loans that are too risky, the bank examiner can force the bank to get rid of them. If a bank examiner decides that a loan is unlikely to be repaid, the examiner can force the bank to declare the loan worthless (to write off the loan, which reduces the bank's capital). If, after examining the bank, the examiner feels that it does not have sufficient capital or has engaged in dishonest practices, the bank can be declared a "problem bank" and will be subject to more frequent examinations.

Assessment of Risk Management

Traditionally, on-site examinations have focused primarily on assessment of the quality of a financial institution's balance sheet at a point in time and whether it complies with capital requirements and restrictions on asset holdings. Although the traditional focus is important for reducing excessive risk taking by financial institutions, it is no longer felt to be adequate in today's world, in which financial innovation has produced new markets and instruments that make it easy for financial institutions and their employees to make huge bets easily and quickly. In this new financial environment, a financial institution that is healthy at a particular point in time can be driven into insolvency extremely rapidly from trading losses, as forcefully demonstrated by the failure of Barings in 1995 (discussed in Chapter 10). Thus an examination that focuses only on a financial institution's position at a point in time may not be effective in indicating whether it will, in fact, be taking on excessive risk in the near future.

This change in the environment for financial institutions has resulted in a major shift in thinking about the prudential supervisory process throughout the world. Bank examiners, for example, are now placing far greater emphasis on evaluating the soundness of a bank's management processes with regard to controlling risk. This shift in thinking was reflected in a new focus on risk management in the Federal Reserve System's 1993 guidelines to examiners on trading and derivatives activities. The focus was expanded and formalized in the Trading Activities Manual issued early in 1994, which provided bank examiners with tools to evaluate risk management systems. In late 1995, the Federal Reserve and the Comptroller of the Currency announced that they would be assessing risk management processes at the banks they supervise. Now bank examiners give a separate risk management rating from 1 to 5 that feeds into the overall management rating as part of the CAMELS system. Four elements of sound risk management are assessed to come up with the risk management rating: (1) the quality of oversight provided by the board of directors and senior management, (2) the adequacy of policies and limits for all activities that present significant risks, (3) the quality of the risk measurement and monitoring systems, and (4) the adequacy of internal controls to prevent fraud or unauthorized activities on the part of employees.

This shift toward focusing on management processes is also reflected in recent guidelines adopted by the U.S. bank regulatory authorities to deal with interest-rate risk. These guidelines require the bank's board of directors to establish interest-rate risk limits, appoint officials of the bank to manage this risk, and monitor the bank's risk exposure. The guidelines also require that senior management of a bank develop formal risk management policies and procedures to ensure that the board of directors' risk limits are not violated and to implement internal controls to monitor interest-rate risk and compliance with the board's directives. Particularly important is the implementation of *stress testing*, which calculates losses under dire scenarios, or value-at-risk (VaR) calculations, which measure the size of the loss on a trading portfolio that might happen 1% of the time—say, over a two-week period. In addition to these guidelines, bank examiners will continue to consider interest-rate risk in deciding the bank's capital requirements.

Disclosure Requirements

The free-rider problem described in Chapter 8 indicates that individual depositors and creditors will not have enough incentive to produce private information about the quality of a financial institution's assets. To ensure that there is better information in the marketplace, regulators can require that financial institutions adhere to certain standard accounting principles and disclose a wide range of information that helps the market assess the quality of an institution's portfolio and the amount of its exposure to risk. More public information about the risks incurred by financial institutions and the quality of their portfolios can better enable stockholders, creditors, and depositors to evaluate and monitor financial institutions and so act as a deterrent to excessive risk taking.

Disclosure requirements are a key element of financial regulation. Basel 2 puts a particular emphasis on disclosure requirements with one of its three pillars focusing on increasing market discipline by mandating increased disclosure by banking institutions of their credit exposure, amount of reserves, and capital. The Securities Act of 1933 and the Securities and Exchange Commission (SEC), which was established in 1934, also impose disclosure requirements on any corporation, including financial institutions, that issues publicly traded securities. In addition, it has required financial institutions to provide additional disclosure regarding their off-balance-sheet positions and more information about how they value their portfolios.

Regulation to increase disclosure is needed to limit incentives to take on excessive risk and to improve the quality of information in the marketplace so that investors can make informed decisions, thereby improving the ability of financial markets to allocate capital to its most productive uses. The efficiency of markets is assisted by the SEC's disclosure requirements mentioned above, as well as its regulation of brokerage firms, mutual funds, exchanges, and credit-rating agencies to ensure that they produce reliable information and protect investors. The Sarbanes-Oxley Act of 2002, discussed in Chapter 8, took disclosure of information even further by increasing the incentives to produce accurate audits of corporate income statements and balance sheets, established the Public Company Accounting Oversight Board (PCAOB) to oversee the audit industry, and putting in place regulations to limit conflicts of interest in the financial services industry.

Particularly controversial in the wake of the subprime financial crisis is the move to so-called **mark-to-market accounting**, also called **fair-value accounting**, in which assets are valued in the balance sheet at what they could sell for in the market (see the FYI box, "Mark-to-Market Accounting and the Subprime Financial Crisis").

Consumer Protection

The existence of asymmetric information also suggests that consumers may not have enough information to protect themselves fully. Consumer protection regulation has taken several forms. The Consumer Protection Act of 1969 (more commonly referred to as the Truth in Lending Act) requires all lenders, not just banks, to provide informa-

FYI   Mark-to-Market Accounting and the Subprime Financial Crisis

The controversy over mark-to-market accounting has made accounting a hot topic. Mark-to-market accounting was made standard practice in the U.S. accounting industry in 1993. The rationale behind mark-to-market accounting is that market prices provide the best basis for estimating the true value of assets, and hence capital, in the firm. Before mark-to-market accounting, firms relied on traditional historical-cost (book value) basis in which the value of an asset was set at its initial purchase price. The problem with historical-cost accounting is that fluctuations in the value of assets and liabilities because of changes in interest rates or default are not reflected in the calculation of the firm's equity capital. Yet changes in the market value of assets and liabilities—and hence changes in the market value of equity capital—are what indicates if a firm is in good shape, or alternatively, if it is getting into trouble and may therefore be more susceptible to moral hazard.

Mark-to-market accounting, however, is subject to a major flaw. At times markets stop working, as occurred during the subprime financial crisis. The price of an asset sold at a time of financial distress does not reflect its fundamental value. That is, the fire-sale liquidation value of an asset can at times be well below the present value of its expected future cash flows. Many people, particularly bankers, have criticized mark-to-market accounting during the recent subprime financial crisis episode, claiming that it has been an important factor driving the crisis. They claim that the seizing up of financial markets has led to market prices being well below fundamental values. Mark-to-market accounting requires that the financial firms' assets be marked down in value. This markdown creates a shortfall in capital that leads to a cutback in lending, which causes a further deterioration in asset prices, which in turn causes a further cutback in lending. The resulting adverse feedback loop can then make the financial crisis even worse. Although the criticisms of mark-to-market accounting have some validity, some of the criticism by bankers is self-serving. The criticism was made only when asset values were falling, when mark-to-market accounting was painting a bleaker picture of banks' balance sheets, as opposed to when asset prices were booming, when it made banks' balance sheets look very good.

The criticisms of mark-to-market accounting led to a Congressional focus on mark-to-market accounting that resulted in a provision in the Emergency Economic Stabilization Act of 2008, discussed in Chapter 9, that required the SEC, in consultation with the Federal Reserve and the U.S. Treasury, to submit a study of mark-to-market accounting applicable to financial institutions. Who knew that accounting could even get politicians worked up!

tion to consumers about the cost of borrowing, including a standardized interest rate (called the *annual percentage rate*, or *APR*) and the total finance charges on the loan. The Fair Credit Billing Act of 1974 requires creditors, especially credit card issuers, to provide information on the method of assessing finance charges and requires that billing complaints be handled quickly. Both of these acts are administered by the Federal Reserve System under Regulation Z.

Congress has also passed legislation to reduce discrimination in credit markets. The Equal Credit Opportunity Act of 1974 and its extension in 1976 forbid discrimination by lenders based on race, gender, marital status, age, or national origin. It is administered by the Federal Reserve under Regulation B. The Community Reinvestment Act (CRA) of 1977 was enacted to prevent "redlining," a lender's refusal to lend in a particular area (marked off by a hypothetical red line on a map). The Community Reinvestment Act requires that banks show that they lend in all areas in which they take deposits, and if banks are found to be in noncompliance with the act, regulators can reject their applications for mergers, branching, or other new activities.

The subprime mortgage crisis has illustrated the need for greater consumer protection because so many borrowers took out loans with terms that they did not understand and which were well beyond their means to repay. The result was millions of foreclosures, with many households losing their homes. Because weak consumer protection regulation played a prominent role in this crisis, there have been increasing demands to strengthen this regulation, as is discussed in the FYI box, "The Subprime Mortgage Crisis and Consumer Protection Regulation."

Restrictions on Competition

Increased competition can also increase moral hazard incentives for financial institutions to take on more risk. Declining profitability as a result of increased competition could tip the incentives of financial institutions toward assuming greater risk in an effort to maintain former profit levels. Thus governments in many countries have instituted regulations to protect financial institutions from competition. These regulations have taken two forms in the United States in the past. First were restrictions on branching, described in Chapter 12, which reduced competition between banks, but were eliminated in 1994. The second form involved preventing nonbank institutions from competing with banks by engaging in banking business, as embodied in the Glass-Steagall Act, which was repealed in 1999.

Although restricting competition propped up the health of banks, restrictions on competition also had serious disadvantages: They led to higher charges to consumers and decreased the efficiency of banking institutions, which did not have to compete as vigorously. Thus, although the existence of asymmetric information provided a rationale for anticompetitive regulations, it did not mean that they would be beneficial. Indeed, in recent years, the impulse of governments in industrialized countries to restrict competition has been waning.

Summary

Asymmetric information analysis explains what types of financial regulations are needed to reduce moral hazard and adverse selection problems in the financial system. However, understanding the theory behind regulation does not mean that regulation and supervision of the financial system are easy in practice. Getting regulators and

FYI   The Subprime Mortgage Crisis and Consumer Protection Regulation

Because of the principal–agent problem inherent in the originate-to-distribute model for subprime mortgages discussed in Chapter 9, there were weak incentives for mortgage originators, typically mortgage brokers who were virtually unregulated, to ensure that subprime borrowers had an ability to pay back their loans. After all, mortgage brokers keep their large fees from mortgage originations even if sometime down the road the borrowers default on their loans and lose their houses. With these incentives, mortgage brokers weakened their underwriting standards, leading to subprime mortgage products such as "no-doc loans," more pejoratively referred to as "liar loans," in which borrowers did not have to produce documentation about their assets or income. A particular infamous variant of the no-doc loan was dubbed the NINJA loan because it was issued to borrowers with No Income, No Job, and No Assets. Mortgage brokers also had incentives to put households into very complicated mortgage products borrowers could not understand and which they couldn't afford to pay. In some cases, mortgage brokers even engaged in fraud by falsifying information on borrowers' mortgage applications in order to qualify them for mortgage loans.

Lax consumer protection regulation was an important factor in producing the subprime mortgage crisis. Mortgage originators were not required to disclose information to borrowers that would have helped them better understand complicated mortgage products and whether they could afford to repay them. Outrage over the surge of foreclosures has been an important stimulus for new regulation to provide better information to mortgage borrowers and to ban so-called "unfair and deceptive" practices. Under Regulation Z of the Truth in Lending Act, in July of 2008, the Federal Reserve issued a final rule for subprime mortgage loans with the following four elements: 1) a ban on lenders making loans without regard to borrowers' ability to repay the loan from income and assets other than the home's value, 2) a ban on no-doc loans, 3) a ban on prepayment penalties (i.e., a penalty for paying back the loan early) if the interest payment can change in the first four years of the loan, and 4) a requirement that lenders establish an escrow account for property taxes and homeowner's insurance to be paid into on a monthly basis. In addition, the rule stipulated the following new regulations for all mortgage loans, not just subprime mortgages: 1) a prohibition on mortgage brokers coercing a real estate appraiser to misstate a home's value, 2) a prohibition on putting one late fee on top of another and a requirement to credit consumers' loan payments as of the date of receipt, 3) a requirement for lenders to provide a good-faith estimate of the loan costs within three days after a household applies for a loan, and 4) a ban on a number of misleading advertising practices, including representing that a rate or payment is "fixed" when the payment can change.

Members of Congress have also stepped in, making legislation to further strengthen consumer protection regulation on subprime mortgages increasingly likely.

supervisors to do their job properly is difficult for several reasons. First, as we will see in the discussion of financial innovation in Chapter 12, in their search for profits, financial institutions have strong incentives to avoid existing regulations by loophole mining. Thus regulation applies to a moving target: Regulators are continually playing cat-and-mouse with financial institutions—financial institutions think up clever ways to avoid regulations, which then lead regulators to modify their regulation activities. Regulators continually face new challenges in a dynamically changing financial system—and unless they can respond rapidly to change, they may not be able to keep financial institutions from taking on excessive risk. This problem can be exacerbated if regulators and supervisors do not have the resources or expertise to keep up with clever people in financial institutions seeking to circumvent the existing regulations.

Financial regulation and supervision are difficult for two other reasons. In the regulation and supervision game, the devil is in the details. Subtle differences in the details may have unintended consequences; unless regulators get the regulation and supervision just right, they may be unable to prevent excessive risk taking. In addition, regulated firms may lobby politicians to lean on regulators and supervisors to go easy on them. For all these reasons, there is no guarantee that regulators and supervisors will be successful in promoting a healthy financial system. These same problems bedevil financial regulators in other countries besides the United States, as the Global box, "International Financial Regulation," indicates. Indeed, as we will see, financial regulation and supervision have not always worked well, leading to banking crises in the United States and throughout the world.

Global   International Financial Regulation

Because asymmetric information problems in the banking industry are a fact of life throughout the world, financial regulation in other countries is similar to that in the United States. Financial institutions are chartered and supervised by government regulators, just as they are in the United States. Disclosure requirements for financial institutions and corporations issuing securities are similar in other developed countries. Deposit insurance is also a feature of the regulatory systems in most other countries, although its coverage is often smaller than in the United States and is intentionally not advertised. We have also seen that capital requirements are in the process of being standardized across countries with agreements like the Basel Accord.

Particular problems in financial regulation occur when financial institutions operate in many countries and thus can readily shift their business from one country to another. Financial regulators closely examine the domestic operations of financial institutions in their country, but they often do not have the knowledge or ability to keep a close watch on operations in other countries, either by domestic institutions' foreign affiliates or by foreign institutions with domestic branches. In addition, when a financial institution operates in many countries, it is not always clear which national regulatory authority should have

primary responsibility for keeping the institution from engaging in overly risky activities.

The difficulties inherent in international financial regulation were highlighted by the collapse of the Bank of Credit and Commerce International (BCCI). BCCI, which was operating in more than 70 countries, including the United States and the United Kingdom, was supervised by Luxembourg, a tiny country unlikely to be up to the task. When massive fraud was discovered, the Bank of England closed BCCI down, but not before depositors and stockholders were exposed to huge losses. Cooperation among regulators in different countries and standardization of regulatory requirements provide potential solutions to the problems of international financial regulation. The world has been moving in this direction through agreements like the Basel Accord and oversight procedures announced by the Basel Committee in July 1992, which require a bank's worldwide operations to be under the scrutiny of a single home-country regulator with enhanced powers to acquire information on the bank's activities. Also, the Basel Committee ruled that regulators in other countries can restrict the operations of a foreign bank if they feel that it lacks effective oversight. Whether agreements of this type will solve the problem of international financial regulation in the future is an open question.

Because so many laws regulating the financial system have been passed in the United States, it is hard to keep track of them all. As a study aid, Table 1 lists the major financial legislation since the beginning of the twentieth century and its key provisions.

TABLE 1

Major Financial Legislation in the United States

Federal Reserve Act (1913)
Created the Federal Reserve System

McFadden Act of 1927
Effectively prohibited banks from branching across U.S. state lines
Put national and state banks on equal footing regarding branching

Banking Acts of 1933 (Glass-Steagall) and 1935
Created the FDIC
Separated commercial banking from the securities industry
Prohibited interest on checkable deposits and restricted such deposits to commercial banks
Put interest-rate ceilings on other deposits

Securities Act of 1933 and Securities Exchange Act of 1934
Required that investors receive financial information on securities offered for public sale
Prohibited misrepresentations and fraud in the sale of securities
Created the Securities and Exchange Commission (SEC)

Investment Company Act of 1940 and Investment Advisers Act of 1940
Regulated investment companies, including mutual funds
Regulated investment advisers

Bank Holding Company Act and Douglas Amendment (1956)
Clarified the status of bank holding companies (BHCs)
Gave the Federal Reserve regulatory responsibility for BHCs

Depository Institutions Deregulation and Monetary Control Act (DIDMCA) of 1980
Gave thrift institutions wider latitude in activities
Approved NOW and sweep accounts nationwide
Phased out interest-rate ceilings on deposits
Imposed uniform reserve requirements on depository institutions
Eliminated usury ceilings on loans
Increased deposit insurance to $100,000 per account

Depository Institutions Act of 1982 (Garn–St. Germain)
Gave the FDIC and the FSLIC emergency powers to merge banks and thrifts across state lines
Allowed depository institutions to offer money market deposit accounts (MMDAs)
Granted thrifts wider latitude in commercial and consumer lending

Competitive Equality in Banking Act (CEBA) of 1987
Provided $10.8 billion to the FSLIC
Made provisions for regulatory forbearance in depressed areas

TABLE 1 *(continued)*
Major Financial Legislation in the United States

Financial Institutions Reform, Recovery, and Enforcement Act (FIRREA) of 1989
Provided funds to resolve S&L failures
Eliminated the FSLIC and the Federal Home Loan Bank Board
Created the Office of Thrift Supervision to regulate thrifts
Created the Resolution Trust Corporation to resolve insolvent thrifts
Raised deposit insurance premiums
Reimposed restrictions on S&L activities

Federal Deposit Insurance Corporation Improvement Act (FDICIA) of 1991
Recapitalized the FDIC
Limited brokered deposits and the too-big-to-fail policy
Set provisions for prompt corrective action
Instructed the FDIC to establish risk-based premiums
Increased examinations, capital requirements, and reporting requirements
Included the Foreign Bank Supervision Enhancement Act (FBSEA), which strengthened the Fed's authority
   to supervise foreign banks

Riegle-Neal Interstate Banking and Branching Efficiency Act of 1994
Overturned prohibition of interstate banking
Allowed branching across U.S. state lines

Gramm-Leach-Bliley Financial Services Modernization Act of 1999
Repealed Glass-Steagall and removed the separation of banking and securities industries

Sarbanes-Oxley Act of 2002
Created Public Company Accounting Oversight Board (PCAOB)
Prohibited certain conflicts of interest
Required certification by CEO and CFO of financial statements and independence of audit committee

Federal Deposit Insurance Reform Act of 2005
Merged the Bank Insurance Fund and the Savings Association Insurance Fund
Increased deposit insurance on indivdual retirement accounts to $250,000 per account
Authorized FDIC to revise its system of risk-based premiums

THE 1980s SAVINGS AND LOAN AND BANKING CRISIS

Before the 1980s, financial regulation in the United States seemed largely effective in promoting a safe and sound banking system. In contrast to the pre-1934 period, when bank failures were common and depositors frequently suffered losses, the period from 1934 to 1980 was one in which bank failures were a rarity, averaging fifteen per year for commercial banks and fewer than five per year for savings and loan associations (S&Ls). After 1981, this rosy picture changed dramatically. Failures in both commercial banks and S&Ls climbed to levels more than ten times greater than in earlier years, as

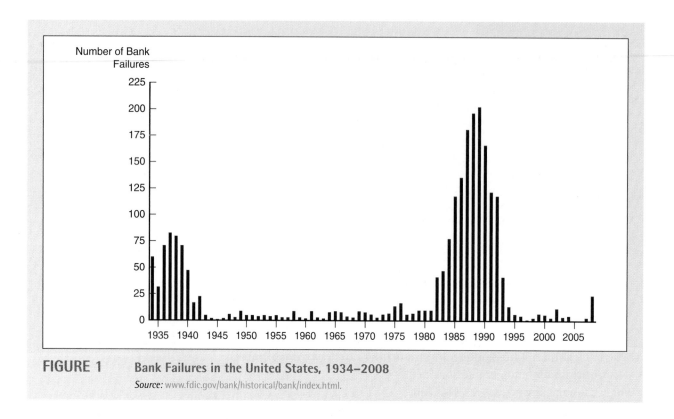

Number of Bank Failures

FIGURE 1 **Bank Failures in the United States, 1934–2008**

Source: www.fdic.gov/bank/historical/bank/index.html.

can be seen in Figure 1. Why did this happen? How did a regulatory system that seemed to be working well for half a century find itself in so much trouble.

The story starts with the burst of financial innovation in the 1960s, 1970s, and early 1980s. As we will see in Chapter 12, financial innovation decreased the profitability of certain traditional lines of business for commercial banks. Banks now faced increased competition for their sources of funds from new financial institutions, such as money market mutual funds, even as they were losing commercial lending business to the commercial paper market and securitization.

With the decreasing profitability of their traditional business, by the mid-1980s commercial banks were forced to seek out new and potentially risky business to keep their profits up. Specifically, they placed a greater percentage of their total loans in real estate and in credit extended to assist corporate takeovers and leveraged buyouts (called highly leveraged transaction loans). The existence of deposit insurance increased moral hazard for banks because insured depositors had little incentive to keep the banks from taking on too much risk. Regardless of how much risk banks were taking, deposit insurance guaranteed that depositors would not suffer any losses.

Adding fuel to the fire, financial innovation produced new financial instruments that widened the scope of risk taking. New markets in financial futures, junk bonds, swaps, and other instruments made it easier for banks to take on extra risk—making the moral hazard problem more severe. New legislation that deregulated the banking industry in the early 1980s, the Depository Institutions Deregulation and Monetary Control Act (DIDMCA) of 1980 and the Depository Institutions (Garn–St. Germain) Act of 1982, gave expanded powers to the S&Ls and mutual savings banks to engage in new risky activities. These thrift institutions, which had been restricted almost entirely to making loans for home mortgages, now were allowed to have up to 40% of their assets in commercial real estate loans, up to 30% in consumer lending, and up to 10% in commercial loans and leases. In the wake of this legislation, S&L regulators allowed up to 10% of assets to be in junk bonds or in direct investments (common stocks, real estate, service corporations, and operating subsidiaries).

In addition, DIDMCA increased the mandated amount of federal deposit insurance from $40,000 per account to $100,000 and phased out restrictions on the interest rate that could be paid on deposits. Banks and S&Ls that wanted to pursue rapid growth and take on risky projects could now attract the necessary funds by issuing larger-denomination insured certificates of deposit with interest rates much higher than those being offered by their competitors. Without deposit insurance, high interest rates would not have induced depositors to provide the high-rolling banks with funds because of the realistic expectation that they might not get the funds back. But with deposit insurance and the widespread use of the FDIC's purchase and assumption method to handle failed banks, the government was guaranteeing that all deposits were safe, so depositors were more than happy to make deposits in banks with the highest interest rates.

As a result of these forces, commercial banks and savings and loans did take on excessive risks and began to suffer substantial losses. The outcome was that bank failures rose to a level of 200 per year by the late 1980s. The resulting losses for the FDIC meant that it had to be recapitalized. Legislation in 1989 (The Financial Institutions Reform, Recovery, and Enforcement Act of 1989, FIRREA) and the Federal Deposit Insurance Corporation and Improvement Act of 1991, FDICIA, provided a bailout of the savings and loan and commercial banking industries and reregulated the banking industry. The cost of the bailout to U.S. taxpayers was on the order of $150 billion, 3% of GDP.[2]

BANKING CRISES THROUGHOUT THE WORLD

Because misery loves company, it may make you feel better to know that the United States has by no means been alone in suffering banking crises. Indeed, as Figure 2 and Table 2 illustrate, banking crises have struck a large number of countries throughout the world, and many of them have been substantially worse than the one we experienced in the 1980s.

"Déjà vu All Over Again"

In the banking crises in these different countries, history keeps repeating itself. The parallels between the banking crisis episodes in all these countries are remarkably similar, creating a feeling of déjà vu. They all started with financial liberalization or innovation, with weak bank regulatory systems and a government safety net. Although financial liberalization is generally a good thing because it promotes competition and can make a

---

[2]The full story of the S&L and banking crisis of the 1980s is a fascinating one, with juicy scandals, even involving Senator John McCain, who was a presidential candidate in 2008. An appendix to this chapter found on this book's website at www.myeconlab.com/mishkin discusses in more detail why this crisis happened, as well as the legislation in 1989 and 1991 that dealt with this crisis.

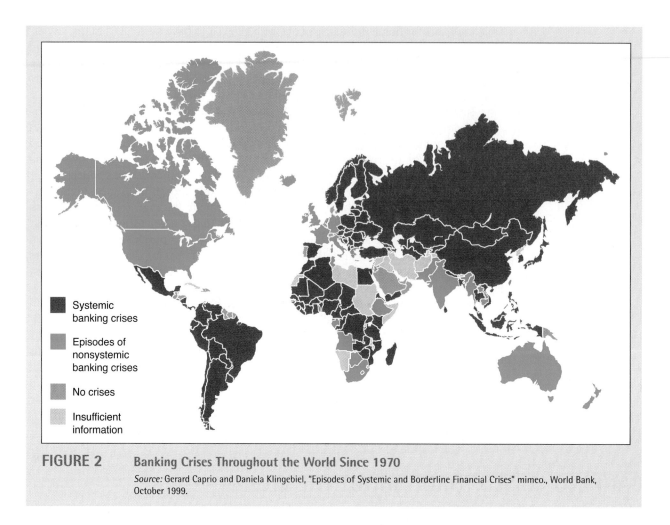

FIGURE 2   **Banking Crises Throughout the World Since 1970**

Source: Gerard Caprio and Daniela Klingebiel, "Episodes of Systemic and Borderline Financial Crises" mimeo., World Bank, October 1999.

financial system more efficient, it can lead to an increase in moral hazard, with more risk taking on the part of banks if there is lax regulation and supervision; the result can then be banking crises.[3]

However, the banking crisis episodes listed in Table 2 do differ in that deposit insurance has not played an important role in many of the countries experiencing banking crises. For example, the size of the Japanese equivalent of the FDIC, the Deposit Insurance Corporation, was so tiny relative to the FDIC that it did not play a prominent role in the banking system and exhausted its resources almost immediately with the first bank failures. This example indicates that deposit insurance is not to blame for some of these banking crises. However, what is common to all the countries discussed here is the existence of a government safety net, in which the government stands ready to bail out banks whether deposit insurance is an important feature of the regulatory environment or not. It is the existence of a government safety net, and not deposit insurance per se, that increases moral hazard incentives for excessive risk taking on the part of banks.

---

[3]An appendix to this chapter can be found on this book's website, www.myeconlab.com/mishkin, discusses in detail many of the episodes of banking crises listed in Table 2.

TABLE 2		
The Cost of Rescuing Banks in Several Countries		
Date	**Country**	**Cost as a Percentage of GDP**
1980–1982	Argentina	55
1997–2002	Indonesia	55
1990s–ongoing	China	47
1996–2000	Jamaica	44
1981–1983	Chile	42
1997–2002	Thailand	35
1993–1994	Macedonia	32
2000–ongoing	Turkey	31
1977–1983	Israel	30
1997–2002	South Korea	28
1988–1991	Cote d'Ivoire	25
1991–ongoing	Japan	24
1994–1995	Venezuela	22
1998–2001	Ecuador	20
1994–2000	Mexico	19
1997–2001	Malaysia	16
1992–1994	Slovenia	15
1998–ongoing	Philippines	13
1994–1999	Brazil	13
1995–2000	Paraguay	13
1989–1991	Czech Republic	12
1997–1998	Taiwan	12
1991–1994	Finland	11
1989–1990	Jordan	10
1991–1995	Hungary	10
1990–1993	Norway	8
1991–1994	Sweden	4
1988–1991	United States	3

Source: Gerard Caprio, Daniela Klingebiel, Luc Laeven, and Guillermo Noguera, *Banking Crises Database* (updated October 2003), http://www1.worldbank.org/finance/html/database_sfd.html.

WHITHER FINANCIAL REGULATION AFTER THE SUBPRIME FINANCIAL CRISIS?

The recent subprime financial crisis, discussed in detail in Chapter 9, has led to banking crises throughout the world, and it is too soon to tell how large the costs of rescuing the banks will be as a result of this episode (which is why they are not listed in Table 2). Given the size of the bailouts and the nationalization of so many financial institutions, the system of financial regulation will surely never be the same. Here we can speculate on where financial regulation might be heading as a result of this crisis.

The financial innovations of subprime and Alt-A mortgages and structured credit products like collateralized debt obligations helped trigger the crisis. Although these innovations have the positive potential for promoting the "democratization of credit," that is, increasing the access of poorer members of society to credit, they went horribly wrong because of the agency problems of the originate-to-distribute business model. Future regulation will surely focus on limiting these agency problems to make the originate-to-distribute model and the financial system overall work better. Eight types of regulation likely to be seen in the future are described below.

Increased Regulation of Mortgage Brokers

Mortgage brokers, who did not have proper incentives to make sure that borrowers could afford to pay back mortgages and were virtually unregulated, are now likely to be subjected to more regulatory scrutiny. Licensing requirements for mortgage originators are likely to be tightened up, and more regulations will require them to disclose mortgage terms more clearly and prevent them from encouraging borrowers to take on more debt than they can afford.

Fewer Subprime Mortgage Products

Some of the complex mortgage products that were offered to subprime borrowers may be banned by regulation. Even with full disclosure of these products' characteristics, they may still be so complicated that subprime borrowers, who are unlikely to be financially sophisticated, cannot understand them and make informed choices. Government ban or regulation of certain mortgage products might help prevent subprime borrowers from "getting in over their heads" again in the future.

Regulation Compensation

Compensation schemes for all the parties in the chain from origination of mortgages to the eventual distribution of mortgage-related securities may be constrained by government regulation. The high fees and executive compensation that have so outraged the public created incentives for the financial industry to push out securities that turned out to be much more risky than advertised and have proved to be disastrous.

Higher Capital Requirements

Regulation and supervision of financial institutions to ensure that they have enough capital to cope with the amount of risk they take are likely to be strengthened. Given the risks they were taking, investment banks did not have enough capital relative to their assets and their risky activities. Similarly the capital at AIG was not sufficient to cover the high risk it was taking by issuing credit insurance. Capital requirements will almost surely be beefed up for these institutions. Capital requirements at banks are also likely to be tightened up, particularly for some of their off-balance sheet activities. Banks' sponsoring of structured investment vehicles (SIVs), which were supposedly off balance sheet but came back on the balance sheet once the SIVs got into trouble, indicate that some off-balance-sheet activities should be treated as though they were on the balance sheet.

Additional Regulation of Privately Owned Government-Sponsored Enterprises

New regulations are needed to rein in privately owned government-sponsored enterprises such as Fannie Mae and Freddie Mac. There are four routes that the government might take here:

1. Fully privatize them by taking away their government sponsorship, thereby removing the implicit backing for their debt.
2. Completely nationalize them by taking away their private status and make them government agencies.
3. Leave them as privately owned government-sponsored enterprises, but strengthen regulations to restrict the amount of risk they take and to impose higher capital standards.
4. Leave them as privately owned government-sponsored enterprises, but force them to shrink dramatically in size so they no longer expose the taxpayer to huge losses or pose a systemic risk to the financial system when they fail.

Heightened Regulation to Limit Financial Institutions' Risk Taking

With the extension of the government safety net to a wider range of financial institutions, regulation will be needed to limit risk taking by financial firms. This will require stricter regulation of investment banks—some of this will automatically occur because the largest ones that have survived are now part of bank holding companies and thus will be regulated and supervised like banks—as well as insurance companies, which as the AIG example suggests, can threaten the health of the entire financial system when they take on excessive risk.

Increased Regulation of Credit-Rating Agencies

Regulations to restrict conflicts of interest at credit-rating agencies and to give them greater incentives to provide reliable ratings have already been strengthened, but even more is likely to be done. The inaccurate ratings provided by credit-rating agencies helped promote risk taking throughout the financial system and led to investors not having the information they needed to make informed choices about their investments. The reliance on credit ratings in the Basel 2 capital requirements may also have to be rethought, given the poor performance of credit-rating agencies in recent years.

Additional Regulation of Derivatives

More regulations both on disclosure and how derivatives are traded are likely to be put in place, particularly on derivatives such as credit-default swaps. As is discussed in Web Chapter 2 on financial derivatives, these derivatives ended up being "weapons of mass destruction" that helped lead to a financial meltdown when AIG had to be rescued after making overly extensive use of them. Preventing this from happening again will be a high priority.

The Danger of Overregulation

As a result of the subprime financial crisis, the world of financial regulation will never be the same. Although it is clear that more regulation is needed to prevent such a crisis from ever occurring again, there is a substantial danger that too much or poorly designed regulation could hamper the efficiency of the financial system. If new regulations choke off financial innovation that can benefit both households and businesses, economic growth in the future will suffer.

SUMMARY

1. The concepts of asymmetric information, adverse selection, and moral hazard help explain the eight types of financial regulation that we see in the United States and other countries: the government safety net, restrictions on financial institutions' asset holdings, capital requirements, financial institution supervision, assessment of risk management, disclosure requirements, consumer protection, and restrictions on competition.

2. Financial innovation and deregulation increased adverse selection and moral hazard problems in the 1980s and resulted in huge losses for U.S. S&Ls, banks, and taxpayers. Similar crises occurred in other countries.

3. The parallels between the banking crisis episodes that have occurred in countries throughout the world are striking, indicating that similar forces are at work.

KEY TERMS

bank failure, p. 255

Basel Accord, p. 261

Basel Committee on Banking Supervision, p. 261

fair-value accounting, p. 266

financial supervision (prudential supervision), p. 263

leverage ratio, p. 260

mark-to-market accounting, p. 266

off-balance-sheet activities, p. 261

regulatory arbitrage, p. 261

QUESTIONS AND PROBLEMS

All questions and problems are available in myeconlab *at* www.myeconlab.com/mishkin.

1. Give one example each of moral hazard and adverse selection in private insurance arrangements.

2. If casualty insurance companies provided fire insurance without any restrictions, what kind of adverse selection and moral hazard problems might result?

3. What U.S. bank regulation is designed to reduce adverse selection problems for deposit insurance? Will it always work?

4. What U.S. bank regulations are designed to reduce moral hazard problems created by deposit insurance? Will they completely eliminate the moral hazard problem?

5. What are the costs and benefits of a too-big-to-fail policy?

6. Why did the U.S. S&L crisis not occur until the 1980s?

7. Why is regulatory forbearance a dangerous strategy for a deposit insurance agency?

8. The FIRREA legislation of 1989 is the most comprehensive U.S. banking legislation since the 1930s. Describe its major features.

9. What steps were taken in the FDICIA of 1991 to improve the functioning of federal deposit insurance?

10. Some advocates of campaign reform believe that government funding of political campaigns and restrictions on campaign spending might reduce the principal–agent problem in the U.S. political system. Do you agree? Explain your answer.

11. How can the U.S. S&L crisis be blamed on the principal–agent problem?

12. Do you think that eliminating or limiting the amount of deposit insurance would be a good idea? Explain your answer.

13. Do you think that removing the impediments to a nationwide banking system will be beneficial to the economy? Explain your answer.

14. How could higher deposit insurance premiums for banks with riskier assets benefit the U.S. economy?

15. How has the too-big-to-fail policy been limited in the FDICIA legislation? How might limiting the too-big-to-fail policy help reduce the risk of a future banking crisis?

WEB EXERCISES

1. www.fdic.gov/regulations/laws/important/index.html. This site reports on the most significant pieces of legislation affecting banks since the 1800s. Summarize the most recently enacted bank regulation listed on this site.

2. The Office of the Comptroller of the Currency is responsible for many of the regulations affecting bank operations. Go to www.occ.treas.gov/. Click on "Legal and Regulatory" and then on "Law and Regulations." Now click on the 12 CFR Parts 1 to 199. What does Part 1 cover? How many parts are there in 12 CFR? Open Part 18. What topic does it cover? Summarize its purpose.

WEB REFERENCES

www.ny.frb.org/banking/supervisionregulate.html
View bank regulation information.

www.federalreserve.gov/Regulations/default.htm
Access regulatory publications of the Federal Reserve Board.

www.fdic.gov/regulations/laws/important/index.html
Describes the most important laws that have affected the banking industry in the United States.

www.fdic.gov/bank/historical/bank/index.html
Search for data on bank failures in any year.

 MyEconLab **CAN HELP YOU GET A BETTER GRADE**

If your exam were tomorrow, would you be ready? For each chapter, MyEconLab Practice Test and Study Plans pinpoint which sections you have mastered and which ones you need to study. That way, you are more efficient with your study time, and you are better prepared for your exams.

To see how it works, turn to page 20 and then go to: www.myeconlab.com/mishkin

12

Banking Industry: Structure and Competition

Preview

The operations of individual banks (how they acquire, use, and manage funds to make a profit) are roughly similar throughout the world. In all countries, banks are financial intermediaries in the business of earning profits. When you consider the structure and operation of the banking industry as a whole, however, the United States is in a class by itself. In most countries, four or five large banks typically dominate the banking industry, but in the United States there are on the order of 7,000 commercial banks, 1,200 savings and loan associations, 400 mutual savings banks, and 8,000 credit unions.

Is more better? Does this diversity mean that the American banking system is more competitive and therefore more economically efficient and sound than banking systems in other countries? What in the American economic and political system explains this large number of banking institutions? In this chapter, we try to answer these questions by examining the historical trends in the banking industry and its overall structure.

We start by examining the historical development of the banking system in the United States and how financial innovation has increased the competitive environment for the banking industry and is causing fundamental changes in it. We go on to look at the commercial banking industry in detail and then discuss the thrift industry, which includes savings and loan associations, mutual savings banks, and credit unions. We spend more time on commercial banks because they are by far the largest depository institutions, accounting for more than two-thirds of the deposits in the banking system. In addition to looking at the U.S. banking system, we examine the forces behind the growth in international banking to see how it has affected the United States.

HISTORICAL DEVELOPMENT OF THE BANKING SYSTEM

The modern commercial banking industry in the United States began when the Bank of North America was chartered in Philadelphia in 1782. With the success of this bank, other banks opened for business, and the American banking industry was off and running. (As a study aid, Figure 1 provides a time line of the most important dates in the history of American banking before World War II.)

A major controversy involving the industry in its early years was whether the national (federal) government or the states should charter banks. The Federalists, particularly Alexander Hamilton, advocated greater centralized control of banking and federal chartering of banks. Their efforts led to the creation in 1791 of the Bank of the United States, which had elements of both a private bank and a **central bank**, a government institution

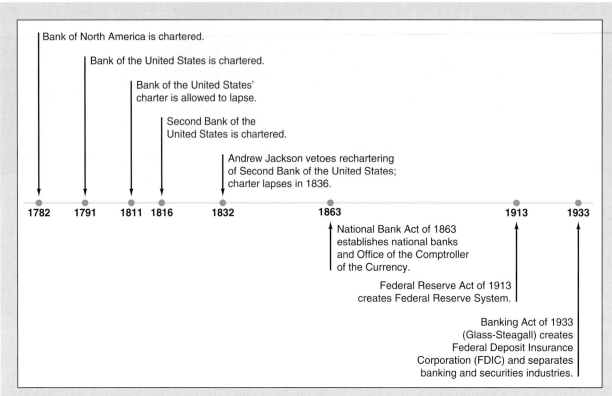

Bank of North America is chartered.

Bank of the United States is chartered.

Bank of the United States' charter is allowed to lapse.

Second Bank of the United States is chartered.

Andrew Jackson vetoes rechartering of Second Bank of the United States; charter lapses in 1836.

1782   1791   1811   1816   1832   1863   1913   1933

National Bank Act of 1863 establishes national banks and Office of the Comptroller of the Currency.

Federal Reserve Act of 1913 creates Federal Reserve System.

Banking Act of 1933 (Glass-Steagall) creates Federal Deposit Insurance Corporation (FDIC) and separates banking and securities industries.

FIGURE 1   Time Line of the Early History of Commercial Banking in the United States

that has responsibility for the amount of money and credit supplied in the economy as a whole. Agricultural and other interests, however, were quite suspicious of centralized power and hence advocated chartering by the states. Furthermore, their distrust of moneyed interests in the big cities led to political pressures to eliminate the Bank of the United States, and in 1811 their efforts met with success, when its charter was not renewed. Because of abuses by state banks and the clear need for a central bank to help the federal government raise funds during the War of 1812, Congress was stimulated to create the Second Bank of the United States in 1816. Tensions between advocates and opponents of centralized banking power were a recurrent theme during the operation of this second attempt at central banking in the United States, and with the election of Andrew Jackson, a strong advocate of states' rights, the fate of the Second Bank was sealed. After the election in 1832, Jackson vetoed the rechartering of the Second Bank of the United States as a national bank, and its charter lapsed in 1836.

Until 1863, all commercial banks in the United States were chartered by the banking commission of the state in which each operated. No national currency existed, and banks obtained funds primarily by issuing *banknotes* (currency circulated by the banks that could be redeemed for gold). Because banking regulations were extremely lax in many states, banks regularly failed due to fraud or lack of sufficient bank capital; their banknotes became worthless.

To eliminate the abuses of the state-chartered banks (called **state banks**), the National Bank Act of 1863 (and subsequent amendments to it) created a new banking system of federally chartered banks (called **national banks**), supervised by the Office of the Comptroller of the Currency, a department of the U.S. Treasury. This legislation was originally intended to dry up sources of funds to state banks by imposing a prohibitive tax on their banknotes while leaving the banknotes of the federally chartered banks untaxed. The state banks cleverly escaped extinction by acquiring funds through deposits. As a result, today the United States has a **dual banking system** in which banks supervised by the federal government and banks supervised by the states operate side by side.

Central banking did not reappear in the United States until the Federal Reserve System (the Fed) was created in 1913 to promote an even safer banking system. All national banks were required to become members of the Federal Reserve System and became subject to a new set of regulations issued by the Fed. State banks could choose (but were not required) to become members of the system, and most did not because of the high costs of membership stemming from the Fed's regulations.

During the Great Depression years 1930–1933, some 9,000 bank failures wiped out the savings of many depositors at commercial banks. To prevent future depositor losses from such failures, banking legislation in 1933 established the Federal Deposit Insurance Corporation (FDIC), which provided federal insurance on bank deposits. Member banks of the Federal Reserve System were required to purchase FDIC insurance for their depositors, and non–Federal Reserve commercial banks could choose to buy this insurance (almost all of them did). The purchase of FDIC insurance made banks subject to another set of regulations imposed by the FDIC.

Because investment banking activities of the commercial banks were blamed for many bank failures, provisions in the banking legislation in 1933 (also known as the Glass-Steagall Act) prohibited commercial banks from underwriting or dealing in corporate securities (though allowing them to sell new issues of government securities) and limited banks to the purchase of debt securities approved by the bank regulatory agencies. Likewise, it prohibited investment banks from engaging in commercial banking activities. In effect, the Glass-Steagall Act separated the activities of commercial banks from those of the securities industry.

Under the conditions of the Glass-Steagall Act, which was repealed in 1999, commercial banks had to sell off their investment banking operations. The First National Bank of Boston, for example, spun off its investment banking operations into the First Boston Corporation, now part of one of the most important investment banking firms in America, Credit Suisse First Boston. Investment banking firms typically discontinued their deposit business, although J. P. Morgan discontinued its investment banking business and reorganized as a commercial bank; however, some senior officers of J. P. Morgan went on to organize Morgan Stanley, another one of the largest investment banking firms today.

Multiple Regulatory Agencies

Commercial bank regulation in the United States has developed into a crazy quilt of multiple regulatory agencies with overlapping jurisdictions. The U.S. Office of the Comptroller of the Currency has the primary supervisory responsibility for the 1,850 national banks that own more than half of the assets in the commercial banking system. The Federal Reserve and the state banking authorities have joint primary responsibility for the 900 state banks that are members of the Federal Reserve System. The Fed also has regulatory responsibility over companies that own one or more banks (called **bank holding companies**) and secondary responsibility for the national banks. The FDIC and the state banking authorities jointly supervise the 4,800 state banks that have FDIC insurance but are not members of the Federal Reserve System. The state banking authorities have sole jurisdiction over the fewer than 500 state banks without FDIC insurance. (Such banks hold less than 0.2% of the deposits in the U.S. commercial banking system.)

If you find the U.S. bank regulatory system confusing, imagine how confusing it is for the banks, which have to deal with multiple regulatory agencies. Several proposals have been raised by the U.S. Treasury to rectify this situation by centralizing the regulation of all depository institutions under one independent agency. However, none of these proposals has been successful in Congress, and whether there will be regulatory consolidation in the future is highly uncertain.

FINANCIAL INNOVATION AND THE GROWTH OF THE "SHADOW BANKING SYSTEM"

Although banking institutions are still the most important financial institutions in the U.S. economy, in recent years the traditional banking business of making loans that are funded by deposits has been in decline. Some of this business has been replaced by the **shadow banking system**, in which bank lending has been replaced by lending via the securities market.

To understand how the U.S. banking industry has evolved over time, we must first understand the process of financial innovation, which has transformed the entire financial system. Like other industries, the financial industry is in business to earn profits by selling its products. If a soap company perceives that there is a need in the marketplace for a laundry detergent with fabric softener, it develops a product to fit the need. Similarly, to maximize their profits, financial institutions develop new products to satisfy their own needs as well as those of their customers; in other words, innovation—which can be extremely beneficial to the economy—is driven by the desire to get (or stay) rich. This view of the innovation process leads to the following simple analysis: *A change in the financial environment will stimulate a search by financial institutions for innovations that are likely to be profitable*.

Starting in the 1960s, individuals and financial institutions operating in financial markets were confronted with drastic changes in the economic environment: Inflation and interest rates climbed sharply and became harder to predict, a situation that changed demand conditions in financial markets. The rapid advance in computer technology changed supply conditions. In addition, financial regulations became more burdensome. Financial institutions found that many of the old ways of doing business were no longer profitable; the financial services and products they had been offering to the public were not selling. Many financial intermediaries found that they were no longer able to acquire funds with their traditional financial instruments, and without these funds they would soon be out of business. To survive in the new economic environment, financial institutions had to research and develop new products and services that would meet customer needs and prove profitable, a process referred to as **financial engineering**. In their case, necessity was the mother of innovation.

Our discussion of why financial innovation occurs suggests that there are three basic types of financial innovation: responses to changes in demand conditions, responses to changes in supply conditions, and avoidance of existing regulations. These three motivations often interact to produce particular financial innovations. Now that we have a framework for understanding why financial institutions produce innovations, let's look at examples of how financial institutions in their search for profits have produced financial innovations of the three basic types.

Responses to Changes in Demand Conditions: Interest-Rate Volatility

The most significant change in the economic environment that altered the demand for financial products in recent years has been the dramatic increase in the volatility of interest rates. In the 1950s, the interest rate on three-month U.S. Treasury bills fluctuated between 1.0% and 3.5%; in the 1970s, it fluctuated between 4.0% and 11.5%; in the 1980s, it ranged from 5% to more than 15%. Large fluctuations in interest rates lead to substantial capital gains or losses and greater uncertainty about returns on investments. Recall that the risk that is related to the uncertainty about interest-rate movements and returns is called *interest-rate risk*, and high volatility of interest rates, such as we saw in the 1970s and 1980s, leads to a higher level of interest-rate risk.

We would expect the increase in interest-rate risk to increase the demand for financial products and services that could reduce that risk. This change in the economic environment would thus stimulate a search for profitable innovations by financial institutions that meet this new demand and would spur the creation of new financial instruments that help lower interest-rate risk. Two examples of financial innovations that appeared in the 1970s confirm this prediction: the development of adjustable-rate mortgages and financial derivatives.

Adjustable-Rate Mortgages   Like other investors, financial institutions find that lending is more attractive if interest-rate risk is lower. They would not want to make a mortgage loan at a 10% interest rate and two months later find that they could obtain 12% in interest on the same mortgage. To reduce interest-rate risk, in 1975 savings and loans in California began to issue adjustable-rate mortgages; that is, mortgage loans on which the interest rate changes when a market interest rate (usually the Treasury bill rate) changes. Initially, an adjustable-rate mortgage might have a 5% interest rate. In six months, this interest rate might increase or decrease by the amount of the increase or decrease in, say, the six-month Treasury bill rate, and the mortgage payment would change. Because adjustable-rate mortgages allow mortgage-issuing institutions to earn higher interest rates on existing mortgages when market rates rise, profits remain high during these periods.

This attractive feature of adjustable-rate mortgages has encouraged mortgage-issuing institutions to issue adjustable-rate mortgages with lower initial interest rates than on conventional fixed-rate mortgages, making them popular with many households. However, because the mortgage payment on a variable-rate mortgage can increase, many households continue to prefer fixed-rate mortgages. Hence both types of mortgages are widespread.

Financial Derivatives   Given the greater demand for the reduction of interest-rate risk, commodity exchanges such as the Chicago Board of Trade recognized that if they could develop a product that would help investors and financial institutions to protect themselves from, or **hedge**, interest-rate risk, then they could make profits by selling this new instrument. **Futures contracts**, in which the seller agrees to provide a certain standardized commodity to the buyer on a specific future date at an agreed-on price, had been around for a long time. Officials at the Chicago Board of Trade realized that if they created futures contracts in financial instruments, which are called

financial derivatives because their payoffs are linked to (i.e., derived from) previously issued securities, they could be used to hedge risk. Thus, in 1975, financial derivatives were born.

Responses to Changes in Supply Conditions: Information Technology

The most important source of the changes in supply conditions that stimulate financial innovation has been the improvement in computer and telecommunications technology. This technology, called *information technology,* has had two effects. First, it has lowered the cost of processing financial transactions, making it profitable for financial institutions to create new financial products and services for the public. Second, it has made it easier for investors to acquire information, thereby making it easier for firms to issue securities. The rapid developments in information technology have resulted in many new financial products and services that we examine here.

Bank Credit and Debit Cards   Credit cards have been around since well before World War II. Many individual stores (Sears, Macy's, Goldwater's) institutionalized charge accounts by providing customers with credit cards that allowed them to make purchases at these stores without cash. Nationwide credit cards were not established until after World War II, when Diners Club developed one to be used in restaurants all over the world. Similar credit card programs were started by American Express and Carte Blanche, but because of the high cost of operating these programs, cards were issued only to selected persons and businesses that could afford expensive purchases.

A firm issuing credit cards earns income from loans it makes to credit card holders and from payments made by stores on credit card purchases (a percentage of the purchase price, say 5%). A credit card program's costs arise from loan defaults, stolen cards, and the expense involved in processing credit card transactions.

Seeing the success of Diners Club, American Express, and Carte Blanche, bankers wanted to share in the profitable credit card business. Several commercial banks attempted to expand the credit card business to a wider market in the 1950s, but the cost per transaction of running these programs was so high that their early attempts failed.

In the late 1960s, improved computer technology, which lowered the transaction costs for providing credit card services, made it more likely that bank credit card programs would be profitable. The banks tried to enter this business again, and this time their efforts led to the creation of two successful bank credit card programs: BankAmericard (originally started by Bank of America but now an independent organization called Visa) and MasterCharge (now MasterCard, run by the Interbank Card Association). These programs have become phenomenally successful; more than 200 million of their cards are in use. Indeed, bank credit cards have been so profitable that nonfinancial institutions such as Sears (which launched the Discover card), General Motors, and AT&T have also entered the credit card business. Consumers have benefited because credit cards are more widely accepted than checks to pay for purchases (particularly abroad), and they allow consumers to take out loans more easily.

The success of bank credit cards has led these institutions to come up with a new financial innovation, *debit cards*. Debit cards often look just like credit cards and can be used to make purchases in an identical fashion. However, in contrast to credit cards, which extend the purchaser a loan that does not have to be paid off immediately, a debit card purchase is immediately deducted from the card holder's bank account. Debit cards depend even more on low costs of processing transactions, because their profits are generated entirely from the fees paid by merchants on debit card purchases at their stores. Debit cards have grown extremely popular in recent years.

Electronic Banking   The wonders of modern computer technology have also enabled banks to lower the cost of bank transactions by having the customer interact with an electronic banking (e-banking) facility rather than with a human being. One important form of an e-banking facility is the **automated teller machine (ATM)**, an electronic machine that allows customers to get cash, make deposits, transfer funds from one account to another, and check balances. The ATM has the advantage that it does not have to be paid overtime and never sleeps, thus being available for use 24 hours a day. Not only does this result in cheaper transactions for the bank, but it also provides more convenience for the customer. Because of their low cost, ATMs can be put at locations other than a bank or its branches, further increasing customer convenience. The low cost of ATMs has meant that they have sprung up everywhere and now number more than 250,000 in the United States alone. Furthermore, it is now as easy to get local currency from an ATM when you are traveling abroad as it is to get cash from your local bank.

With the drop in the cost of telecommunications, banks have developed another financial innovation, *home banking*. It is now cost-effective for banks to set up an electronic banking facility in which the bank's customer is linked up with the bank's computer to carry out transactions by using either a telephone or a personal computer. Now a bank's customers can conduct many of their bank transactions without ever leaving the comfort of home. The advantage for the customer is the convenience of home banking, while banks find that the cost of transactions is substantially less than having the customer come to the bank. The success of ATMs and home banking has led to another innovation, the **automated banking machine (ABM)**, which combines in one location an ATM, an Internet connection to the bank's website, and a telephone link to customer service.

With the decline in the price of personal computers and their increasing presence in the home, we have seen a further innovation in the home banking area, the appearance of a new type of banking institution, the **virtual bank**, a bank that has no physical location but rather exists only in cyberspace. In 1995, Security First Network Bank, based in Atlanta but now owned by Royal Bank of Canada, became the first virtual bank, offering an array of banking services on the Internet—accepting checking account and savings deposits, selling certificates of deposits, issuing ATM cards, providing bill-paying facilities, and so on. The virtual bank thus takes home banking one step further, enabling the customer to have a full set of banking services at home 24 hours a day. In 1996, Bank of America and Wells Fargo entered the virtual banking market, to be followed by many others, with Bank of America now being the largest Internet bank in the United States. Will virtual banking be the predominant form of banking in the future (see the FYI box, "Will 'Clicks' Dominate 'Bricks' in the Banking Industry?")?

Junk Bonds   Before the advent of computers and advanced telecommunications, it was difficult to acquire information about the financial situation of firms that might want to sell securities. Because of the difficulty in screening out bad from good credit

FYI   **Will "Clicks" Dominate "Bricks" in the Banking Industry?**

With the advent of virtual banks ("clicks") and the convenience they provide, a key question is whether they will become the primary form in which banks do their business, eliminating the need for physical bank branches ("bricks") as the main delivery mechanism for banking services. Indeed, will stand-alone Internet banks be the wave of the future?

The answer seems to be no. Internet-only banks such as Wingspan (owned by Bank One), First-e (Dublin-based), and Egg (a British Internet-only bank owned by Prudential) have had disappointing revenue growth and profits. The result is that pure online banking has not been the success that proponents had hoped for. Why has Internet banking been a disappointment?

There are several strikes against Internet banking. First, bank depositors want to know that their savings are secure, and so are reluctant to put their money into new institutions without a long track record. Second, customers worry about the security of their

online transactions and whether their transactions will truly be kept private. Traditional banks are viewed as being more secure and trustworthy in terms of releasing private information. Third, customers may prefer services provided by physical branches. For example, banking customers seem to prefer to purchase long-term savings products face-to-face. Fourth, Internet banking has run into technical problems—server crashes, slow connections over phone lines, mistakes in conducting transactions—that will probably diminish over time as technology improves.

The wave of the future thus does not appear to be pure Internet banks. Instead it looks like "clicks and bricks" will be the predominant form of banking, in which online banking is used to complement the services provided by traditional banks. Nonetheless, the delivery of banking services is undergoing massive changes, with more and more banking services delivered over the Internet and the number of physical bank branches likely to decline in the future.

risks, the only firms that were able to sell bonds were very well-established corporations that had high credit ratings.[1] Before the 1980s, then, only corporations that could issue bonds with ratings of Baa or above could raise funds by selling newly issued bonds. Some firms that had fallen on bad times, known as *fallen angels*, had previously issued long-term corporate bonds that now had ratings that had fallen below Baa, bonds that were pejoratively dubbed "junk bonds."

With the improvement in information technology in the 1970s, it became easier for investors to acquire financial information about corporations, making it easier to screen out bad from good credit risks. With easier screening, investors were more willing to buy long-term debt securities from less well-known corporations with lower credit ratings. With this change in supply conditions, we would expect that some smart individual would pioneer the concept of selling new public issues of junk bonds, not for fallen angels but for companies that had not yet achieved investment-grade status. This is exactly what Michael Milken of Drexel Burnham Lambert, an investment banking firm, started to do in 1977. Junk bonds became an important factor in the corporate bond market, with the amount outstanding exceeding $200 billion by the late 1980s. Although there was a sharp slowdown in activity in the junk bond market

---

[1]The discussion of adverse selection problems in Chapter 8 provides a more detailed analysis of why only well-established firms with high credit ratings were able to sell securities.

after Milken was indicted for securities law violations in 1989, it heated up again in the 1990s and 2000s.

Commercial Paper Market   *Commercial paper* is a short-term debt security issued by large banks and corporations. The commercial paper market has undergone tremendous growth since 1970, when there was $33 billion outstanding, to over $1.7 trillion outstanding at the end of 2008. Indeed, commercial paper has been one of the fastest-growing money market instruments.

Improvements in information technology also help provide an explanation for the rapid rise of the commercial paper market. We have seen that the improvement in information technology made it easier for investors to screen out bad from good credit risks, thus making it easier for corporations to issue debt securities. Not only did this make it easier for corporations to issue long-term debt securities as in the junk bond market, but it also meant that they could raise funds by issuing short-term debt securities such as commercial paper more easily. Many corporations that used to do their short-term borrowing from banks now frequently raise short-term funds in the commercial paper market instead.

The development of money market mutual funds has been another factor in the rapid growth in the commercial paper market. Because money market mutual funds need to hold liquid, high-quality, short-term assets such as commercial paper, the growth of assets in these funds to around $2.6 trillion has created a ready market in commercial paper. The growth of pension and other large funds that invest in commercial paper has also stimulated the growth of this market.

Securitization   An important example of a financial innovation arising from improvements in both transaction and information technology is securitization, one of the most important financial innovations in the past two decades, which played an especially prominent role in the development of the subprime mortgage market in the mid-2000s. **Securitization** is the process of transforming otherwise illiquid financial assets (such as residential mortgages, auto loans, and credit card receivables), which have typically been the bread and butter of banking institutions, into marketable capital market securities. As we have seen, improvements in the ability to acquire information have made it easier to sell capital market securities. In addition, with low transaction costs because of improvements in computer technology, financial institutions find that they can cheaply bundle together a portfolio of loans (such as mortgages) with varying small denominations (often less than $100,000), collect the interest and principal payments on the mortgages in the bundle, and then "pass them through" (pay them out) to third parties. By dividing the portfolio of loans into standardized amounts, the financial institution can then sell the claims to these interest and principal payments to third parties as securities. The standardized amounts of these securitized loans make them liquid securities, and the fact that they are made up of a bundle of loans helps diversify risk, making them desirable. The financial institution selling the securitized loans makes a profit by servicing the loans (collecting the interest and principal payments and paying them out) and charging a fee to the third party for this service.

Avoidance of Existing Regulations

The process of financial innovation we have discussed so far is much like innovation in other areas of the economy: It occurs in response to changes in demand and supply conditions. However, because the financial industry is more heavily regulated than other industries, government regulation is a much greater spur to innovation in this industry. Government regulation leads to financial innovation by creating incentives for firms to skirt regulations that restrict their ability to earn profits. Edward Kane, an economist at Boston College, describes this process of avoiding regulations as "loophole mining." The economic analysis of innovation suggests that when the economic environment changes such that regulatory constraints are so burdensome that large profits can be made by avoiding them, loophole mining and innovation are more likely to occur.

Because banking is one of the most heavily regulated industries in America, loophole mining is especially likely to occur. The rise in inflation and interest rates from the late 1960s to 1980 made the regulatory constraints imposed on this industry even more burdensome, leading to financial innovation.

Two sets of regulations have seriously restricted the ability of banks to make profits: reserve requirements that force banks to keep a certain fraction of their deposits as reserves (vault cash and deposits in the Federal Reserve System) and restrictions on the interest rates that can be paid on deposits. For the following reasons, these regulations have been major forces behind financial innovation.

1. Reserve requirements. The key to understanding why reserve requirements led to financial innovation is to recognize that they act, in effect, as a tax on deposits. Because up until 2008 the Fed did not pay interest on reserves, the opportunity cost of holding them was the interest that a bank could otherwise earn by lending the reserves out. For each dollar of deposits, reserve requirements therefore imposed a cost on the bank equal to the interest rate, i, that could be earned if the reserves could be lent out times the fraction of deposits required as reserves, r. The cost of $i \times r$ imposed on the bank was just like a tax on bank deposits of $i \times r$ per dollar of deposits.

It is a great tradition to avoid taxes if possible, and banks also play this game. Just as taxpayers look for loopholes to lower their tax bills, banks seek to increase their profits by mining loopholes and by producing financial innovations that allow them to escape the tax on deposits imposed by reserve requirements.

2. Restrictions on interest paid on deposits. Until 1980, legislation prohibited banks in most U.S. states from paying interest on checking account deposits, and through Regulation Q, the Fed set maximum limits on the interest rate that could be paid on time deposits. To this day, banks are not allowed to pay interest on corporate checking accounts. The desire to avoid these **deposit rate ceilings** also led to financial innovations.

If market interest rates rose above the maximum rates that banks paid on time deposits under Regulation Q, depositors withdrew funds from banks to put them into higher-yielding securities. This loss of deposits from the banking system restricted the amount of funds that banks could lend (called **disintermediation**) and thus limited bank profits. Banks had an incentive to get around deposit rate ceilings, because by so doing, they could acquire more funds to make loans and earn higher profits.

We can now look at how the desire to avoid restrictions on interest payments and the tax effect of reserve requirements led to two important financial innovations.

Money Market Mutual Funds Money market mutual funds issue shares that are redeemable at a fixed price (usually $1) by writing checks. For example, if you buy 5,000 shares for $5,000, the money market fund uses these funds to invest in short-term money market securities (Treasury bills, certificates of deposit, commercial paper) that provide you with interest payments. In addition, you are able to write checks up to the $5,000 held as shares in the money market fund. Although money market fund shares effectively function as checking account deposits that earn interest, they are not legally deposits and so are not subject to reserve requirements or prohibitions on interest payments. For this reason, they can pay higher interest rates than deposits at banks.

The first money market mutual fund was created by two Wall Street mavericks, Bruce Bent and Henry Brown, in 1970. However, the low market interest rates from 1970 to 1977 (which were just slightly above Regulation Q ceilings of 5.25% to 5.5%) kept them from being particularly advantageous relative to bank deposits. In early 1978, the situation changed rapidly as inflation rose and market interest rates began to climb over 10%, well above the 5.5% maximum interest rates payable on savings accounts and time deposits under Regulation Q. In 1977, money market mutual funds had assets of less than $4 billion; in 1978, their assets climbed to close to $10 billion; in 1979, to more than $40 billion; and in 1982, to $230 billion. Currently, their assets are around $3 trillion. To say the least, money market mutual funds have been a successful financial innovation, which is exactly what we would have predicted to occur in the late 1970s and early 1980s when interest rates soared beyond Regulation Q ceilings.

In a supreme irony, risky investments by a money market mutual fund founded by Bruce Brent almost brought down the money market mutual fund industry during the subprime financial crisis in 2008 (see the FYI box, "Bruce Bent and the Money Market Mutual Fund Panic of 2008").

FYI   Bruce Bent and the Money Market Mutual Fund Panic of 2008

Bruce Bent, one of the originators of money market mutual funds, almost brought down the industry during the subprime financial crisis in the fall of 2008. Mr. Bent told his shareholders in a letter written in July 2008 that the fund was managed on a basis of "unwavering discipline focused on protecting your principal." He also wrote the Securities and Exchange Commission in September, 2007, "When I first created the money market fund back in 1970, it was designed with the tenets of safety and liquidity." He added that these principles had "fallen by the wayside as portfolio managers chased the highest yield and compromised the integrity of the money fund." Alas, Bent did not follow his own advice, and his fund, the Reserve Primary Fund, bought risky assets so that its yield was higher than the industry average.

When Lehman Brothers went into bankruptcy on September 15, 2008, the Reserve Primary Fund, with assets over $60 billion, was caught holding the bag on $785 million of Lehman's debt, which then had to be marked down to zero. The resulting losses meant that on September 16, Bent's fund could no longer afford to redeem its shares at the par value of $1, a situation known as "breaking the buck." Bent's shareholders began to pull their money out of the fund, causing it to lose 90% of its assets.

The fear that this could happen to other money market mutual funds led to a classic panic in which shareholders began to withdraw their funds at an alarming rate. The whole money market mutual fund industry looked like it could come crashing down. To prevent this, the Federal Reserve and the U.S. Treasury rode to the rescue on September 19. The Fed set up a facility, discussed in Chapter 15, to make loans to purchase commercial paper from money market mutual funds so they could meet the demands for redemptions from their investors. The Treasury then put in a temporary guarantee for all money market mutual fund redemptions and the panic subsided.

Not surprisingly, given the extension of a government safety net to the U.S. money market mutual fund industry, there are calls to regulate this industry more heavily. The U.S. money market mutual fund industry will never be the same.

Sweep Accounts   Another innovation that enables banks to avoid the "tax" from reserve requirements is the **sweep account**. In this arrangement, any balances above a certain amount in a corporation's checking account at the end of a business day are "swept out" of the account and invested in overnight securities that pay interest. Because the "swept out" funds are no longer classified as checkable deposits, they are not subject to reserve requirements and thus are not "taxed." They also have the advantage that they allow banks in effect to pay interest on these checking accounts, which otherwise is not allowed under existing regulations. Because sweep accounts have become so popular, they have lowered the amount of required reserves to the degree that most banking institutions do not find reserve requirements binding: In other words, they voluntarily hold more reserves than they are required to.

The financial innovations of sweep accounts and money market mutual funds are particularly interesting because they were stimulated not only by the desire to avoid a costly regulation, but also by a change in supply conditions—in this case, information technology. Without low-cost computers to process inexpensively the additional transactions required by these innovations, they would not have been profitable and therefore would not have been developed. Technological factors often combine with other incentives, such as the desire to get around a regulation, to produce innovation.

Financial Innovation and the Decline of Traditional Banking

The traditional financial intermediation role of banking has been to make long-term loans and to fund them by issuing short-term deposits, a process of asset transformation commonly referred to as "borrowing short and lending long." Here we examine how financial innovations have created a more competitive environment for the banking industry, causing the industry to change dramatically, with its traditional banking business going into decline.

In the United States, the importance of commercial banks as a source of funds to nonfinancial borrowers has shrunk dramatically. As we can see in Figure 2, in 1974, commercial banks provided close to 40% of these funds; by 2008, their market share was down to below 29%. The decline in market share for thrift institutions has been even more precipitous, from more than 20% in the late 1970s to 4% today. Another way of viewing the declining role of banking in traditional financial intermediation is to look at the size of banks' balance sheet assets relative to those of other financial intermediaries. Commercial banks' share of total financial intermediary assets has fallen from about 40% in the 1960–1980 period to 18% by the end of 2008. Similarly, the share of total financial intermediary assets held by thrift institutions has declined even more from the 20% level of the 1960–1980 period to about 2.5% by 2008.

To understand why traditional banking business has declined in size we need to look at how the financial innovations described earlier have caused banks to suffer declines in their cost advantages in acquiring funds—that is, on the liabilities side of their balance sheet—while at the same time they have lost income advantages on the assets side of their balance sheet. The simultaneous decline of cost and income advantages has resulted in reduced profitability of traditional banking and an effort by banks to leave this business and engage in new and more profitable activities.

Decline in Cost Advantages in Acquiring Funds (Liabilities)   Until 1980, U.S. banks were subject to deposit rate ceilings that restricted them from paying any interest on checkable deposits and (under Regulation Q) limited them to paying a maximum

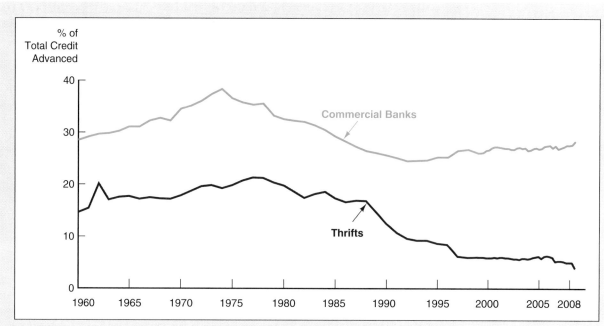

FIGURE 2   **U.S. Bank Share of Total Nonfinancial Borrowing, 1960–2008**
Source: Federal Reserve Flow of Funds Accounts; Federal Reserve Bulletin.

interest rate of a little more than 5% on time deposits. Until the 1960s, these restrictions worked to the banks' advantage because their major source of funds (in excess of 60%) was checkable deposits, and the zero interest cost on these deposits meant that the banks had a very low cost of funds. Unfortunately, this cost advantage for banks did not last. The rise in inflation beginning in the late 1960s led to higher interest rates, which made investors more sensitive to yield differentials on different assets. The result was the *disintermediation* process, in which people began to take their money out of banks, with their low interest rates on both checkable and time deposits, and began to seek out higher-yielding investments. At the same time, attempts to get around deposit rate ceilings and reserve requirements led to the financial innovation of money market mutual funds, which put the banks at an even further disadvantage because depositors could now obtain checking-account-like services while earning high interest on their money market mutual fund accounts. One manifestation of these changes in the financial system was that the low-cost source of funds, checkable deposits, declined dramatically in importance for banks, falling from more than 60% of bank liabilities to 6% today.

The growing difficulty for banks in raising funds led to their supporting legislation in the 1980s that eliminated Regulation Q ceilings on time deposit interest rates and allowed checkable deposit accounts that paid interest. Although these changes in regulation helped make banks more competitive in their quest for funds, it also meant that their cost of acquiring funds had risen substantially, thereby reducing their earlier cost advantage over other financial institutions.

Decline in Income Advantages on Uses of Funds (Assets)   The loss of cost advantages on the liabilities side of the balance sheet for American banks is one reason that they have become less competitive, but they have also been hit by a decline in income advantages on the assets side from the financial innovations we discussed earlier—junk bonds, securitization, and the rise of the commercial paper market. The resulting loss of income advantages for banks relative to these innovations has resulted in a loss of market share and has led to the growth of the shadow banking system, which has made use of these innovations to enable borrowers to bypass the traditional banking system.

We have seen that improvements in information technology have made it easier for firms to issue securities directly to the public. This has meant that instead of going to banks to finance short-term credit needs, many of the banks' best business customers now find it cheaper to go instead to the commercial paper market for funds. In addition, the commercial paper market has allowed finance companies, which depend primarily on commercial paper to acquire funds, to expand their operations at the expense of banks. Finance companies, which lend to many of the same businesses that borrow from banks, have increased their market share relative to banks: Before 1980, finance company loans to business equaled about 30% of commercial and industrial bank loans; currently, they account for more than 50%.

The emergence of the junk bond market has also eaten into banks' loan business. Improvements in information technology have made it easier for corporations to sell their bonds to the public directly, thereby bypassing banks. Although *Fortune* 500 companies started taking this route in the 1970s, now lower-quality corporate borrowers are using banks less often because they have access to the junk bond market.

We have also seen that improvements in computer technology have led to securitization, whereby illiquid financial assets such as bank loans and mortgages are transformed into marketable securities. Computers enable other financial institutions to originate loans because they can now accurately evaluate credit risk with statistical methods, while computers have lowered transaction costs, making it possible to bundle these loans and sell them as securities. When default risk can be easily evaluated with computers, banks no longer have an advantage in making loans. Without their former advantages, banks have lost loan business to other financial institutions even though the banks themselves are involved in the process of securitization. Securitization has been a particular problem for mortgage-issuing institutions such as S&Ls, because most residential mortgages are now securitized.

Banks' Responses   In any industry, a decline in profitability usually results in an exit from the industry (often due to widespread bankruptcies) and a shrinkage of market share. This occurred in the banking industry in the United States during the 1980s via consolidations and bank failures (discussed in Chapter 11).

In an attempt to survive and maintain adequate profit levels, many U.S. banks faced two alternatives. First, they could attempt to maintain their traditional lending activity by expanding into new and riskier areas of lending. For example, U.S. banks increased their risk taking by placing a greater percentage of their total funds in commercial real estate loans, traditionally a riskier type of loan. In addition, they increased lending for corporate takeovers and leveraged buyouts, which are highly leveraged transaction loans. The decline in the profitability of banks' traditional business may thus have helped lead to the crisis in banking in the 1980s and early 1990s that we discussed in the last chapter as well as the subprime financial crisis starting in 2007.

The second way banks have sought to maintain former profit levels is to pursue new off-balance-sheet activities that are more profitable and in effect embrace the shadow banking system. U.S. commercial banks did this during the early 1980s, more than doubling the share of their income coming from off-balance-sheet, non-interest-income activities. Nontraditional bank activities can be riskier and, therefore, result in excessive risk taking by banks. Indeed, they led to a substantial weakening of bank balance sheets during the subprime financial crisis as was discussed in Chapter 9.

The decline of banks' traditional business has thus meant that the banking industry has been driven to seek out new lines of business. This could be beneficial because by so doing, banks can keep vibrant and healthy. Indeed, bank profitability was high up until 2007, and nontraditional, off-balance-sheet activities played an important role in the high bank profits. However, the new directions in banking have lead to increased risk taking, and thus the decline in traditional banking has required regulators to be more vigilant. It also poses new challenges for bank regulators, who, as we saw in Chapter 11, must now be far more concerned about banks' off-balance-sheet activities.

Decline of Traditional Banking in Other Industrialized Countries

Forces similar to those in the United States have been leading to the decline of traditional banking in other industrialized countries. The loss of banks' monopoly power over depositors has occurred outside the United States as well. Financial innovation and deregulation are occurring worldwide and have created attractive alternatives for both depositors and borrowers. In Japan, for example, deregulation opened a wide array of new financial instruments to the public, causing a disintermediation process similar to that in the United States. In European countries, innovations have steadily eroded the barriers that have traditionally protected banks from competition.

In other countries, banks also faced increased competition from the expansion of securities markets and the growth of the shadow banking system. Both financial deregulation and fundamental economic forces in other countries have improved the availability of information in securities markets, making it easier and less costly for firms to finance their activities by issuing securities rather than going to banks. Further, even in countries where securities markets have not grown, banks have still lost loan business because their best corporate customers have had increasing access to foreign and offshore capital markets, such as the Eurobond market. In smaller economies, like Australia, which still do not have as well-developed corporate bond or commercial paper markets, banks have lost loan business to international securities markets. In addition, the same forces that drove the securitization process in the United States have been at work in other countries and have undercut the profitability of traditional banking in these countries as well. The United States has not been unique in seeing its banks face a more difficult competitive environment. Thus, although the decline of traditional banking occurred earlier in the United States than in other countries, the same forces have caused a decline in traditional banking abroad.

STRUCTURE OF THE U.S. COMMERCIAL BANKING INDUSTRY

There are approximately 7,000 commercial banks in the United States, far more than in any other country in the world. As Table 1 indicates, we have an extraordinary number of small banks. Forty percent of the banks have less than $100 million in assets. Far more typical is the size distribution in Canada or the United Kingdom, where five or fewer banks dominate the industry. In contrast, the ten largest commercial banks in the United States (listed in Table 2) together hold just 53% of the assets in their industry.

Most industries in the United States have far fewer firms than the commercial banking industry; typically, large firms tend to dominate these industries to a greater extent

TABLE 1

Size Distribution of Insured Commercial Banks, September 30, 2008

Assets	Number of Banks	Share of Banks (%)	Share of Assets Held (%)
Less than $100 million	2,882	40.3	1.9
$100 million–$1 billion	3,755	52.6	11.4
$1 billion–$10 billion	425	6.0	12.8
More than $10 billion	84	1.2	73.9
Total	7,146	100.00	100.00

Source: www2.fdic.gov/qbp/2008sep/cb4.html.

than in the commercial banking industry. (Consider the computer software industry, which is dominated by Microsoft, or the automobile industry, which is dominated by General Motors, Ford, Daimler-Chrysler, Toyota, and Honda.) Does the large number of banks in the commercial banking industry and the absence of a few dominant firms suggest that commercial banking is more competitive than other industries?

Restrictions on Branching

The presence of so many commercial banks in the United States actually reflects past regulations that restricted the ability of these financial institutions to open **branches** (additional offices for the conduct of banking operations). Each state had its own regulations on the type and number of branches that a bank could open. Regulations on

TABLE 2

Ten Largest U.S. Banks, December 30, 2008

Bank	Assets ($ millions)	Share of All Commercial Bank Assets (%)
1. J. P. Morgan Chase, Columbus, OH	1,746,242	14.06
2. Bank of America Corp., Charlotte, NC	1,471,631	11.85
3. Citibank, Las Vegas, NV	1,227,040	9.88
4. Wachovia Bank Held By Wells Fargo & Co., Charlotte, NC	635,476	5.12
5. Wells Fargo, Sioux Falls, SD	538,958	4.34
6. U.S. Bank, Cincinnati, OH	261,776	2.11
7. Bank of NY Mellon, New York, NY	195,164	1.57
8. Suntrust Bank, Atlanta, GA	185,099	1.49
9. HSBC Bank USA, McLean, VA	181,604	1.46
10. State Street B&T Corp., Boston, MA	171,228	1.38
Total	6,614,218	53.26

Source: www.federalreserve.gov/releases/h8/20081229.

both coasts, for example, tended to allow banks to open branches throughout a state; in the middle part of the country, regulations on branching were more restrictive. The McFadden Act of 1927, which was designed to put national banks and state banks on an equal footing (and the Douglas Amendment of 1956, which closed a loophole in the McFadden Act), effectively prohibited banks from branching across state lines and forced all national banks to conform to the branching regulations in the state where their headquarters were located.

The McFadden Act and state branching regulations constituted strong anticompetitive forces in the commercial banking industry, allowing many small banks to stay in existence, because larger banks were prevented from opening a branch nearby. If competition is beneficial to society, why have regulations restricting branching arisen in America? The simplest explanation is that the American public has historically been hostile to large banks. States with the most restrictive branching regulations were typically ones in which populist antibank sentiment was strongest in the nineteenth century. (These states usually had large farming populations whose relations with banks periodically became tempestuous when banks would foreclose on farmers who couldn't pay their debts.) The legacy of nineteenth-century politics was a banking system with restrictive branching regulations and hence an inordinate number of small banks. However, as we will see later in this chapter, branching restrictions have been eliminated, and we are heading toward nationwide banking.

Response to Branching Restrictions

An important feature of the U.S. banking industry is that competition can be repressed by regulation but not completely quashed. As we saw earlier in this chapter, the existence of restrictive regulation stimulates financial innovations that get around these regulations in the banks' search for profits. Regulations restricting branching have stimulated similar economic forces and have promoted the development of two financial innovations: bank holding companies and automated teller machines.

Bank Holding Companies   A holding company is a corporation that owns several different companies. This form of corporate ownership has important advantages for banks. It has allowed them to circumvent restrictive branching regulations, because the holding company can own a controlling interest in several banks even if branching is not permitted. Furthermore, a bank holding company can engage in other activities related to banking, such as the provision of investment advice, data processing and transmission services, leasing, credit card services, and servicing of loans in other states.

The growth of the bank holding companies has been dramatic over the past three decades. Today bank holding companies own almost all large banks, and more than 90% of all commercial bank deposits are held in banks owned by holding companies.

Automated Teller Machines   Another financial innovation that avoided the restrictions on branching is the automated teller machine (ATM). Banks realized that if they did not own or rent the ATM, but instead let it be owned by someone else and paid for each transaction with a fee, the ATM would probably not be considered a branch of the bank and thus would not be subject to branching regulations. This is exactly what the regulatory agencies and courts in most states concluded. Because they enable banks to widen their markets, a number of these shared facilities (such as Cirrus and NYCE) have been established nationwide. Furthermore, even when an ATM is owned by a bank, states typically have special provisions that allow wider establishment of ATMs than is permissible for traditional "brick and mortar" branches.

As we saw earlier in this chapter, avoiding regulation was not the only reason for the development of the ATM. The advent of cheaper computer and telecommunications technology enabled banks to provide ATMs at low cost, making them a profitable innovation. This example further illustrates that technological factors often combine with incentives such as the desire to avoid restrictive regulations like branching restrictions to produce financial innovation.

BANK CONSOLIDATION AND NATIONWIDE BANKING

As we can see in Figure 3, after a remarkable period of stability from 1934 to the mid-1980s, the number of commercial banks began to fall dramatically. Why has this sudden decline taken place?

The U.S. banking industry hit some hard times in the 1980s and early 1990s, with bank failures running at a rate of over 100 per year from 1985 to 1992 (more on this later in the chapter; also see Chapter 11). But bank failures are only part of the story. In the years 1985–1992, the number of U.S. banks declined by 3,000—more than double the number of failures. And in the period 1992–2007, when the banking industry returned to health, the number of commercial banks declined by a little over 3,800, less than 5% of which were bank failures, and most of these were of small banks. Thus we see that bank failures played an important, though not predominant, role in the decline in the number of U.S. banks in the 1985–1992 period and an almost negligible role in the decline in the number of banks up through 2007. The subprime

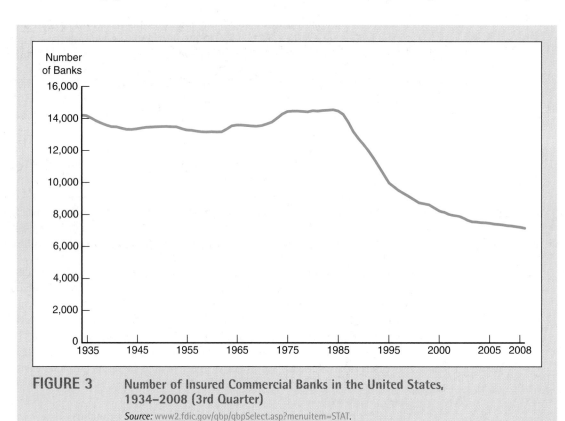

FIGURE 3   **Number of Insured Commercial Banks in the United States, 1934–2008 (3rd Quarter)**

Source: www2.fdic.gov/qbp/qbpSelect.asp?menuitem=STAT.

financial crisis has, however, led to additional declines in the number of banks because of bank failures.

So what explains the rest of the story? The answer is bank consolidation. Banks have been merging to create larger entities or have been buying up other banks. This gives rise to a new question: Why has bank consolidation been taking place in recent years?

As we have seen, loophole mining by banks has reduced the effectiveness of branching restrictions, with the result that many states have recognized that it would be in their best interest if they allowed ownership of banks across U.S. state lines. The result has been the formation of reciprocal regional compacts in which banks in one state are allowed to own banks in other states in the region. In 1975, Maine enacted the first interstate banking legislation that allowed out-of-state bank holding companies to purchase banks in that state. In 1982, Massachusetts enacted a regional compact with other New England states to allow interstate banking, and many other regional compacts were adopted thereafter until by the early 1990s, almost all states allowed some form of interstate banking.

With the barriers to interstate banking breaking down in the early 1980s, banks recognized that they could gain the benefits of diversification because they would now be able to make loans in many states rather than just one. This gave them the advantage that if one state's economy was weak, another state in which they operated might have a strong economy, thus decreasing the likelihood that loans in different states would default at the same time. In addition, allowing banks to own banks in other states meant that they could increase their size through out-of-state acquisition of banks or by merging with banks in other states. Mergers and acquisitions explain the first phase of banking consolidation, which has played such an important role in the decline in the number of banks since 1985. Another result of the loosening of restrictions on interstate branching is the development of a new class of banks, the **superregional banks**, bank holding companies that have begun to rival the money center banks in size but whose headquarters are not in one of the money center cities (New York, Chicago, and San Francisco). Examples of these superregional banks are Bank of America of Charlotte, North Carolina, and Banc One of Columbus, Ohio.

Not surprisingly, the advent of the Web and improved computer technology is another factor driving bank consolidation. Economies of scale have increased, because large upfront investments are required to set up many information technology platforms for financial institutions. To take advantage of these economies of scale, banks have needed to get bigger, and this development has led to additional consolidation. Information technology has also been increasing **economies of scope**, the ability to use one resource to provide many different products and services. For example, details about the quality and creditworthiness of firms not only inform decisions about whether to make loans to them, but also can be useful in determining at what price their shares should trade. Similarly, once you have marketed one financial product to an investor, you probably know how to market another. Business people describe economies of scope by saying that there are "synergies" between different lines of business, and information technology is making these synergies more likely. The result is that consolidation is taking place not only to make financial institutions bigger, but also to increase the combination of products and services they can provide. This consolidation has had two consequences. First, different types of financial intermediaries are encroaching on each other's territory, making them more alike. Second, consolidation has led to the development of what the Federal Reserve has named **large, complex banking organizations (LCBOs)**. This development has been facilitated by the repeal of the Glass-Steagall restrictions on combinations of banking and other financial service industries discussed in the next section.

The Riegle-Neal Interstate Banking and Branching Efficiency Act of 1994

Banking consolidation in the United States was given further stimulus by the passage in 1994 of the Riegle-Neal Interstate Banking and Branching Efficiency Act. This legislation expands the regional compacts to the entire nation and overturns the McFadden Act and Douglas Amendment's prohibition of interstate banking. Not only does this act allow bank holding companies to acquire banks in any other state, notwithstanding any state laws to the contrary, but bank holding companies can also merge the banks they own into one bank with branches in different states. States were, however, given the option of opting out of interstate branching, but only Texas did so, although it later reversed its position and now allows it.

The Riegle-Neal Act finally established the basis for a true nationwide banking system. Although interstate banking was accomplished previously by out-of-state purchase of banks by bank holding companies, until 1994 interstate branching was virtually nonexistent, because very few states had enacted interstate branching legislation. Allowing banks to conduct interstate banking through branching is especially important, because many bankers feel that economies of scale cannot be fully exploited through the bank holding company structure, but only through branching networks in which all of the bank's operations are fully coordinated.

Nationwide banks have now emerged in the United States. Starting with the merger in 1998 of Bank of America and NationsBank, which created the first bank with branches on both coasts, consolidation in the banking industry has created some banking organizations with operations in almost all of the fifty U.S. states.

What Will the Structure of the U.S. Banking Industry Look Like in the Future?

Now that true nationwide banking in the United States is a reality, the benefits of bank consolidation for the banking industry have increased substantially, driving the next phase of mergers and acquisitions and accelerating the decline in the number of commercial banks. With great changes occurring in the structure of this industry, the question naturally arises: What will the industry look like in ten years?

One view is that the industry will become more like that in many other countries (see the Global box, "Comparison of Banking Structure in the United States and Abroad") and the United States will end up with only a couple of hundred banks. A more extreme view is that the industry will look like that of Canada or the United Kingdom, with a few large banks dominating the industry. Research on this question, however, comes up with a different answer. The structure of the U.S. banking industry will still be unique, but not to the degree it once was. Most experts predict that the consolidation surge will settle down as the U.S. banking industry approaches several thousand, rather than several hundred, banks.[2]

---

[2]For example, see Allen N. Berger, Anil K. Kashyap, and Joseph Scalise, "The Transformation of the U.S. Banking Industry: What a Long, Strange Trip It's Been," *Brookings Papers on Economic Activity* 2 (1995): 55–201; and Timothy Hannan and Stephen Rhoades, "Future U.S. Banking Structure, 1990–2010," *Antitrust Bulletin* 37 (1992) 737–798. For a more detailed treatment of the bank consolidation process taking place in the United States, see Frederic S. Mishkin, "Bank Consolidation: A Central Banker's Perspective," in *Mergers of Financial Institutions*, ed. Yakov Amihud and Geoffrey Wood (Boston: Kluwer Academic Publishers, 1998), pp. 3–19.

Global   **Comparison of Banking Structure in the United States and Abroad**

The structure of the commercial banking industry in the United States is radically different from that in other industrialized nations. The United States is the only country that is just now developing a true national banking system in which banks have branches throughout the country. One result is that there are many more banks in the United States than in other industrialized countries. In contrast to the United States, which has on the order of 7,100 commercial banks, every other industrialized country has far less than 1,000. Japan, for example, has fewer than 100 commercial banks—a mere fraction of the number in the United States, even though its economy and population are half the size of those of the United States. Another result of the past restrictions on branching in the United States is that U.S. banks tend to be much smaller than those in other countries.

Banking consolidation will result not only in a smaller number of banks, but as the mergers between Chase Manhattan Bank and Chemical Bank and between Bank of America and NationsBank suggest, a shift in assets from smaller banks to larger banks as well. Within ten years, the share of bank assets in banks with less than $100 million in assets is expected to halve, while the amount at the megabanks, those with more than $100 billion in assets, is expected to more than double. Indeed, the United States now has several trillion-dollar banks (e.g., Citibank, J. P. Morgan Chase, and Bank of America).

Are Bank Consolidation and Nationwide Banking Good Things?

Advocates of nationwide banking believe that it will produce more efficient banks and a healthier banking system less prone to bank failures. However, critics of bank consolidation fear that it will eliminate small banks, referred to as **community banks**, and that this will result in less lending to small businesses. In addition, they worry that a few banks will come to dominate the industry, making the banking business less competitive.

Most economists are skeptical of these criticisms of bank consolidation. As we have seen, research indicates that even after bank consolidation is completed, the United States will still have plenty of banks. The banking industry will thus remain highly competitive, probably even more so than now considering that banks that have been protected from competition from out-of-state banks will now have to compete with them vigorously to stay in business.

It also does not look as though community banks will disappear. When New York state liberalized its branching laws in 1962, there were fears that community banks upstate would be driven from the market by the big New York City banks. Not only did this not happen, but some of the big boys found that the small banks were able to run rings around them in the local markets. Similarly, California, which has had unrestricted statewide branching for a long time, continues to have a thriving population of community banks.

Economists see some important benefits from bank consolidation and nationwide banking. The elimination of geographic restrictions on banking will increase competition and drive inefficient banks out of business, increasing the efficiency of the banking sector. The move to larger banking organizations also means that there will be some increase in efficiency because they can take advantage of economies of scale and scope. The increased diversification of banks' loan portfolios may lower the probability of a banking crisis in the future. In the 1980s and early 1990s, bank failures were often concentrated in states with weak economies. For example, after the decline in oil prices in 1986, all of the major commercial banks in Texas, which had been very profitable, found themselves in trouble. At that time, banks in New England were doing fine. However, when the 1990–1991 recession hit New England hard, some New England banks started failing. With nationwide banking, a bank could make loans in both New England and Texas and would thus be less likely to fail, because when loans go sour in one location, they would likely be doing well in the other. Thus nationwide banking is seen as a major step toward creating a banking system that is less vulnerable to banking crises.

Two concerns remain about the effects of bank consolidation—that it may lead to a reduction in lending to small businesses and that banks rushing to expand into new geographic markets may take increased risks leading to bank failures. The jury is still out on these concerns, but most economists see the benefits of bank consolidation and nationwide banking as outweighing the costs.

SEPARATION OF THE BANKING AND OTHER FINANCIAL SERVICE INDUSTRIES

Another important feature of the structure of the banking industry in the United States until recently was the separation of the banking and other financial services industries—such as securities, insurance, and real estate—mandated by the Glass-Steagall Act of 1933. As pointed out earlier in the chapter, Glass-Steagall allowed commercial banks to sell new offerings of government securities but prohibited them from underwriting corporate securities or from engaging in brokerage activities. It also prevented banks from engaging in insurance and real estate activities. In turn, it prevented investment banks and insurance companies from engaging in commercial banking activities and thus protected banks from competition.

Erosion of Glass-Steagall

Despite the Glass-Steagall prohibitions, the pursuit of profits and financial innovation stimulated both banks and other financial institutions to bypass the intent of the Glass-Steagall Act and encroach on each other's traditional territory. Brokerage firms engaged in the traditional banking business of issuing deposit instruments with the development of money market mutual funds and cash management accounts. After the Federal Reserve used a loophole in Section 20 of the Glass-Steagall Act in 1987 to allow bank holding companies to underwrite previously prohibited classes of securities, banks began to enter this business. The loophole allowed affiliates of approved commercial banks to engage in underwriting activities as long as the revenue didn't exceed a specified amount, which started at 10% but was raised to 25% of the affiliates' total revenue. After the U.S. Supreme Court validated the Fed's action in July 1988, the Federal Reserve allowed J. P. Morgan, a commercial bank holding company, to underwrite corporate debt securities (in January 1989) and to underwrite stocks (in September 1990), with the privilege later extended to other bank holding companies. The regulatory agencies also allowed banks to engage in some real estate and some insurance activities.

The Gramm-Leach-Bliley Financial Services Modernization Act of 1999: Repeal of Glass-Steagall

Because restrictions on commercial banks' securities and insurance activities put American banks at a competitive disadvantage relative to foreign banks, bills to overturn Glass-Steagall appeared in almost every session of Congress in the 1990s. With the merger in 1998 of Citicorp, the second-largest bank in the United States, and Travelers Group, an insurance company that also owned the third-largest securities firm in the country (Salomon Smith Barney), the pressure to abolish Glass-Steagall became overwhelming. Legislation to eliminate Glass-Steagall finally came to fruition in 1999. This legislation, the Gramm-Leach-Bliley Financial Services Modernization Act of 1999, allows securities firms and insurance companies to purchase banks, and allows banks to underwrite insurance and securities and engage in real estate activities. Under this legislation, states retain regulatory authority over insurance activities, while the Securities and Exchange Commission continues to have oversight of securities activities. The Office of the Comptroller of the Currency has the authority to regulate bank subsidiaries engaged in securities underwriting, but the Federal Reserve continues to have the authority to oversee the bank holding companies under which all real estate and insurance activities and large securities operations will be housed.

Implications for Financial Consolidation

As we have seen, the Riegle-Neal Interstate Banking and Branching Efficiency Act of 1994 has stimulated consolidation of the U.S. banking industry. The financial consolidation process has been further hastened by the Gramm-Leach-Bliley Act of 1999, because the way is now open to consolidation in terms not only of the number of banking institutions, but also across financial service activities. Given that information technology is increasing economies of scope, mergers of banks with other financial service firms like that of Citicorp and Travelers have become increasingly common, and more mega-mergers are likely to be on the way. Banking institutions are becoming not only larger, but also increasingly complex organizations, engaging in the full gamut of financial service activities. The trend toward larger and more complex banking organizations has been accelerated by the subprime financial crisis of 2007–2008 (see the FYI box, "The Subprime Financial Crisis and the Demise of Large, Free-Standing Investment Banks").

Separation of Banking and Other Financial Services Industries Throughout the World

Not many other countries in the aftermath of the Great Depression followed the lead of the United States in separating the banking and other financial services industries. In fact, in the past this separation was the most prominent difference between banking regulation in the United States and in other countries. Around the world, there are three basic frameworks for the banking and securities industries.

The first framework is *universal banking*, which exists in Germany, the Netherlands, and Switzerland. It provides no separation at all between the banking and securities industries. In a universal banking system, commercial banks provide a full range of banking, securities, real estate, and insurance services, all within a single legal entity. Banks are allowed to own sizable equity shares in commercial firms, and often they do.

The *British-style universal banking system*, the second framework, is found in the United Kingdom and countries with close ties to it, such as Canada and Australia, and

FYI **The Subprime Financial Crisis and the Demise of Large, Free-Standing Investment Banks**

Although the move toward bringing financial service activities into larger, complex banking organizations was inevitable after the demise of Glass-Steagall, no one expected it to occur as rapidly as it did in 2008. Over a six month period from March to Septermber of 2008, all five of the largest, free-standing investment banks ceased to exist in their old form. When Bear Stearns, the fifth-largest investment bank, revealed its large losses from investments in subprime mortgage securities, it had to be bailed out by the Fed in March 2008; the price it paid was a forced sale to J.P. Morgan for less than one-tenth what it had been worth only a year or so before. The Bear Stearns bailout made it clear that the government safety net had been extended to investment banks. The tradeoff is that investment banks will be subject to more regulation, along the lines of commercial banks, in the future.

Next to go was Lehman Brothers, the fourth-largest investment bank, which declared bankruptcy on September 15. Only one day before, Merrill Lynch, the third-largest investment bank, which also suffered large losses on its holdings of subprime securities, announced its sale to Bank of America for less than half of its year-earlier price. Within a week Goldman Sachs and Morgan Stanley, the first- and second-largest investment banks, both of whom had smaller exposure to subprime securities, nevertheless saw the writing on the wall. They realized that they would soon become regulated on a similar basis and decided to become bank holding companies so they could access insured deposits, a more stable funding base.

It was the end of an era. Large, free-standing investment banking firms are now a thing of the past.

now the United States. The British-style universal bank engages in securities underwriting, but it differs from the German-style universal bank in three ways: Separate legal subsidiaries are more common, bank equity holdings of commercial firms are less common, and combinations of banking and insurance firms are less common.

The third framework features some legal separation of the banking and other financial services industries, as in Japan. A major difference between the U.S. and Japanese banking systems is that Japanese banks are allowed to hold substantial equity stakes in commercial firms, whereas American banks cannot. In addition, most American banks use a bank-holding-company structure, but bank holding companies are illegal in Japan. Although the banking and securities industries are legally separated in Japan under Section 65 of the Japanese Securities Act, commercial banks are increasingly being allowed to engage in securities activities and, like U.S. banks, are becoming more like British-style universal banks.

THRIFT INDUSTRY: REGULATION AND STRUCTURE

Not surprisingly, the regulation and structure of the thrift industry (savings and loan associations, mutual savings banks, and credit unions) closely parallels the regulation and structure of the commercial banking industry.

Savings and Loan Associations

Just as there is a dual banking system for commercial banks, savings and loan associations (S&Ls) can be chartered either by the federal government or by the states. Most

S&Ls, whether state or federally chartered, are members of the Federal Home Loan Bank System (FHLBS). Established in 1932, the FHLBS was styled after the Federal Reserve System. It has twelve district Federal Home Loan banks, which are supervised by the Office of Thrift Supervision.

Federal deposit insurance up to $100,000 (temporarily $250,000) per account for S&Ls is provided by the FDIC. The Office of Thrift Supervision regulates federally insured S&Ls by setting minimum capital requirements, requiring periodic reports, and examining the S&Ls. It is also the chartering agency for federally chartered S&Ls, and for these S&Ls it approves mergers and sets the rules for branching.

The branching regulations for S&Ls were more liberal than for commercial banks: In the past, almost all states permitted branching of S&Ls, and since 1980, federally chartered S&Ls were allowed to branch statewide in all states. Since 1981, mergers of financially troubled S&Ls were allowed across state lines, and nationwide branching of S&Ls is now a reality.

The FHLBS, like the Fed, makes loans to the members of the system (obtaining funds for this purpose by issuing bonds). However, in contrast to the Fed's discount loans, which are expected to be repaid quickly, the loans from the FHLBS often need not be repaid for long periods of time. In addition, the rates charged to S&Ls for these loans are often below the rates that the S&Ls must pay when they borrow in the open market. In this way, the FHLBS loan program provides a subsidy to the savings and loan industry (and implicitly to the housing industry, since most of the S&L loans are for residential mortgages).

As we saw in Chapter 11, the savings and loans in the United States experienced serious difficulties in the 1980s. Because savings and loans now engage in many of the same activities as commercial banks, many experts view having a separate charter and regulatory apparatus for S&Ls an anachronism that no longer makes sense.

Mutual Savings Banks

Of the 400 or so U.S. mutual savings banks, which are similar to S&Ls but are jointly owned by the depositors, approximately half are chartered by states. Although the mutual savings banks are primarily regulated by the states in which they are located, the majority have their deposits insured by the FDIC up to the limit of $100,000 ($250,000 temporarily) per account; these banks are also subject to many of the FDIC's regulations for state-chartered banks. As a rule, the mutual savings banks whose deposits are not insured by the FDIC have their deposits insured by state insurance funds.

The branching regulations for mutual savings banks are determined by the states in which they operate. Because these regulations are not particularly restrictive, there are few mutual savings banks with assets of less than $25 million.

Credit Unions

Credit unions are small cooperative lending institutions organized around a particular group of individuals with a common bond (e.g., union members or employees of a particular firm). They are the only depository institutions that are tax-exempt and can be chartered either by the states or by the federal government; more than half are federally chartered. The National Credit Union Administration (NCUA) issues federal charters and regulates federally chartered credit unions by setting minimum capital requirements, requiring periodic reports, and examining the credit unions. Federal deposit insurance (up to the $100,000-per-account limit, temporarily $250,000) is provided to both federally chartered and state-chartered credit unions by a subsidiary of the NCUA, the National Credit Union Share Insurance Fund (NCUSIF). Because the majority of credit union lending is for consumer loans with fairly short terms to maturity, these institutions did not suffer the financial difficulties of the S&Ls and mutual savings banks.

Because their members share a common bond, credit unions are typically quite small; most hold less than $10 million of assets. In addition, their ties to a particular industry or company make them more likely to fail when large numbers of workers in that industry or company are laid off and have trouble making loan payments. Recent regulatory changes allow individual credit unions to cater to a more diverse group of people by interpreting the common bond requirement less strictly, and this has encouraged an expansion in the size of credit unions that may help reduce credit union failures in the future.

Often a credit union's shareholders are dispersed over many states, and sometimes even worldwide, so branching across state lines and into other countries is permitted for federally chartered credit unions. The Navy Federal Credit Union, for example, whose shareholders are members of the U.S. Navy and Marine Corps, has branches throughout the world.

INTERNATIONAL BANKING

In 1960, only eight U.S. banks operated branches in foreign countries, and their total assets were less than $4 billion. Currently, around 100 American banks have branches abroad, with assets totaling more than $2.1 trillion. The spectacular growth in international banking can be explained by three factors.

First is the rapid growth in international trade and multinational (worldwide) corporations that has occurred since 1960. When American firms operate abroad, they need banking services in foreign countries to help finance international trade. For example, they might need a loan in a foreign currency to operate a factory abroad. And when they sell goods abroad, they need to have a bank exchange the foreign currency they have received for their goods into dollars. Although these firms could use foreign banks to provide them with these international banking services, many of them prefer to do business with the U.S. banks with which they have established long-term relationships and which understand American business customs and practices. As international trade has grown, international banking has grown with it.

Second, American banks have been able to earn substantial profits by being very active in global investment banking, in which they underwrite foreign securities. They also sell insurance abroad, and they derive substantial profits from these investment banking and insurance activities.

Third, American banks have wanted to tap into the large pool of dollar-denominated deposits in foreign countries known as Eurodollars. To understand the structure of U.S. banking overseas, let us first look at the Eurodollar market, an important source of growth for international banking.

Eurodollar Market

Eurodollars are created when deposits in accounts in the United States are transferred to a bank outside the country and are kept in the form of dollars. (For a discussion of the birth of the Eurodollar, see the Global box, "Ironic Birth of the Eurodollar Market.") For example, if Rolls-Royce PLC deposits a $1 million check, written on an account at an

Global   Ironic Birth of the Eurodollar Market

One of capitalism's great ironies is that the Eurodollar market, one of the most important financial markets used by capitalists, was fathered by the Soviet Union. In the early 1950s, during the height of the Cold War, the Soviets had accumulated a substantial amount of dollar balances held by banks in the United States. Because the Russians feared that the U.S. government might freeze these assets in the United States, they wanted to move the deposits to Europe, where they would be safe from expropriation. (This fear was not unjustified—consider the U.S. freeze on Iranian assets in 1979 and Iraqi assets in 1990.) However, they also wanted to keep the deposits in dollars so that they could be used in their international transactions. The solution to the problem was to transfer the deposits to European banks but to keep the deposits denominated in dollars. When the Soviets did this, the Eurodollar was born.

American bank, in its bank in London—specifying that the deposit is payable in dollars—$1 million in Eurodollars is created.[3] More than 90% of Eurodollar deposits are time deposits, more than half of them certificates of deposit with maturities of 30 days or more. The total amount of Eurodollars outstanding is on the order of $5.2 trillion, making the Eurodollar market one of the most important financial markets in the world economy.

Why would companies such as Rolls-Royce want to hold dollar deposits outside the United States? First, the dollar is the most widely used currency in international trade, so Rolls-Royce might want to hold deposits in dollars to conduct its international transactions. Second, Eurodollars are "offshore" deposits—they are held in countries that will not subject them to regulations such as reserve requirements or restrictions (called *capital controls*) on taking the deposits outside the country.[4]

The main center of the Eurodollar market is London, a major international financial center for hundreds of years. Eurodollars are also held outside Europe in locations that provide offshore status to these deposits—for example, Singapore, the Bahamas, and the Cayman Islands.

The minimum transaction in the Eurodollar market is typically $1 million, and approximately 75% of Eurodollar deposits are held by banks. Plainly, you and I are unlikely to come into direct contact with Eurodollars. The Eurodollar market is, however, an important source of funds to U.S. banks. Rather than using an intermediary and borrowing all the deposits from foreign banks, American banks decided that they could earn higher profits by opening their own branches abroad to attract these deposits. Consequently, the Eurodollar market has been an important stimulus to U.S. banking overseas.

Structure of U.S. Banking Overseas

United States banks have most of their foreign branches in Latin America, the Far East, the Caribbean, and London. The largest volume of assets is held by branches in London, because it is a major international financial center and the central location for the

---

[3]Note that the London bank keeps the $1 million on deposit at the American bank, so the creation of Eurodollars has not caused a reduction in the amount of bank deposits in the United States.

[4]Although most offshore deposits are denominated in dollars, some are denominated in other currencies. Collectively, these offshore deposits are referred to as Eurocurrencies. A Japanese yen-denominated deposit held in London, for example, is called a Euroyen.

Eurodollar market. Latin America and the Far East have many branches because of the importance of U.S. trade with these regions. Parts of the Caribbean (especially the Bahamas and the Cayman Islands) have become important as tax havens, with minimal taxation and few restrictive regulations. In actuality, the bank branches in the Bahamas and the Cayman Islands are "shell operations" because they function primarily as book-keeping centers and do not provide normal banking services.

An alternative corporate structure for U.S. banks that operate overseas is the **Edge Act corporation**, a special subsidiary engaged primarily in international banking. United States banks (through their holding companies) can also own a controlling interest in foreign banks and in foreign companies that provide financial services, such as finance companies. The international activities of U.S. banking organizations are governed primarily by the Federal Reserve's Regulation K.

In late 1981, the Federal Reserve approved the creation of **international banking facilities (IBFs)** within the United States that can accept time deposits from people and business outside the United States but are not subject to either reserve requirements or restrictions on interest payments. IBFs are also allowed to make loans to people and business outside the United States, but they are not allowed to make loans to domestic residents. States have encouraged the establishment of IBFs by exempting them from state and local taxes. In essence, IBFs are treated like foreign branches of U.S. banks and are not subject to domestic regulations and taxes. The purpose of establishing IBFs is to encourage American and foreign banks to do more banking business in the United States rather than abroad. From this point of view, IBFs were a success: Their assets climbed to nearly $200 billion in the first two years, and were $1.1 trillion at the end of 2008.

Foreign Banks in the United States

The growth in international trade has not only encouraged U.S. banks to open offices overseas, but has also encouraged foreign banks to establish offices in the United States. Foreign banks have been extremely successful in the United States. Currently, they hold more than 6.5% of total U.S. bank assets and do a large portion of all U.S. bank lending, with nearly a 22% market share for lending to U.S. corporations.

Foreign banks engage in banking activities in the United States by operating an agency office of the foreign bank, a subsidiary U.S. bank, or a branch of the foreign bank. An agency office can lend and transfer funds in the United States, but it cannot accept deposits from domestic residents. Agency offices have the advantage of not being subject to regulations that apply to full-service banking offices (such as requirements for FDIC insurance). A subsidiary U.S. bank is just like any other U.S. bank (it may even have an American-sounding name) and is subject to the same regulations, but it is owned by the foreign bank. A branch of a foreign bank bears the foreign bank's name and is usually a full-service office. Foreign banks may also form Edge Act corporations and IBFs.

Before 1978, foreign banks were not subject to many regulations that applied to domestic banks: They could open branches across state lines and were not expected to meet reserve requirements, for example. The passage of the International Banking Act of 1978, however, put foreign and domestic banks on a more equal footing. The act stipulated that foreign banks may open new full-service branches only in the state they designate as their home state or in states that allow the entry of out-of-state banks. Limited-service branches and agency offices in any other state are permitted, however, and foreign banks are allowed to retain any full-service branches opened before the act was ratified.

The internationalization of banking, both by U.S. banks going abroad and by foreign banks entering the United States, has meant that financial markets throughout the

TABLE 3	
Ten Largest Banks in the World, 2008	
Bank	**Assets (U.S. $ millions)**
1. The Royal Bank of Scotland Group plc, UK	3,782,880.00
2. Deutsche Bank AG, Germany	2,953,727.00
3. BNP Paribas SA, France	2,477,272.00
4. Barclays PLC, UK	2,442,996.00
5. Credit Agricole SA, France	2,067,577.00
6. UBS AG, Switzerland	2,007,224.00
7. Societe Generale, France	1,566,904.00
8 ABN AMRO Holding NV, Netherlands	1,498,849.00
9. ING Bank NV, Netherlands	1,453,382.00
10. The Bank of Tokyo-Mitsubishi UFJ Ltd, Japan	1,362,598.00

Source: http://topforeignstocks.com/2008/07/25/the-top-10-banks-in-the-world-2008/.

world have become more integrated. As a result, there is a growing trend toward international coordination of bank regulation, one example of which is the 1988 Basel Accord to standardize minimum bank capital requirements in industrialized countries, discussed in Chapter 11. Financial market integration has also encouraged bank consolidation abroad, culminating in the creation of the first trillion-dollar bank with the merger of the Industrial Bank of Japan, Dai-Ichi Kangyo Bank, and Fuji Bank, in 2002. Another development has been the importance of foreign banks in international banking. As is shown in Table 3, in 2008, all of the ten largest banking groups in the world were foreign. The implications of this financial market integration for the operation of our economy are examined further in Chapter 18 when we discuss the international financial system in more detail.

SUMMARY

1. The history of banking in the United States has left us with a dual banking system, with commercial banks chartered by the states and the federal government. Multiple agencies regulate commercial banks: the Office of the Comptroller, the Federal Reserve, the FDIC, and the state banking authorities.

2. A change in the economic environment will stimulate financial institutions to search for financial innovations. Changes in demand conditions, especially an increase in interest-rate risk; changes in supply conditions, especially improvements in information technology; and the desire to avoid costly regulations have been major driving forces behind financial innovation. Financial innovation has caused banks to suffer declines in cost advantages in acquiring funds and in income advantages on their assets. The resulting squeeze has hurt profitability in banks' traditional lines of business and has led to a decline in traditional banking.

3. Restrictive state branching regulations and the McFadden Act, which prohibited branching across state lines, led to a large number of small commercial banks. The large number of commercial banks in the United States reflected the past *lack* of competition, not the presence of vigorous competition. Bank holding companies and ATMs were important responses to branching restrictions that weakened the restrictions' anticompetitive effect.

4. Since the mid-1980s, bank consolidation has been occurring at a rapid pace. The first phase of bank consolidation was the result of bank failures and the reduced effectiveness of branching restrictions. The second phase has been stimulated by information technology and the Riegle-Neal Interstate Banking and Branching Efficiency Act of 1994, which establishes the basis for a nationwide banking system. Once banking consolidation has settled down, we are likely to be left with a banking system with several thousand banks. Most economists believe that the benefits of bank consolidation and nationwide banking will outweigh the costs.

5. The Glass-Steagall Act separated commercial banking from the securities industry. Legislation in 1999, however, repealed the Glass-Steagall Act, removing the separation of these industries.

6. The regulation and structure of the thrift industry (savings and loan associations, mutual savings banks, and credit unions) parallel closely the regulation and structure of the commercial banking industry. Savings and loans are primarily regulated by the Office of Thrift Supervision, and deposit insurance is administered by the FDIC. Mutual savings banks are regulated by the states, and federal deposit insurance is provided by the FDIC. Credit unions are regulated by the National Credit Union Administration, and deposit insurance is provided by the National Credit Union Share Insurance Fund.

7. With the rapid growth of world trade since 1960, international banking has grown dramatically. United States banks engage in international banking activities by opening branches abroad, owning controlling interests in foreign banks, forming Edge Act corporations, and operating international banking facilities (IBFs) located in the United States. Foreign banks operate in the United States by owning a subsidiary American bank or by operating branches or agency offices in the United States.

KEY TERMS

automated banking machine (ABM), p. 287

automated teller machine (ATM), p. 287

bank holding companies, p. 283

branches, p. 296

central bank, p. 281

community banks, p. 301

deposit rate ceilings, p. 290

disintermediation, p. 290

dual banking system, p. 283

economies of scope, p. 299

Edge Act corporation, p. 308

financial derivatives, p. 286

financial engineering, p. 284

futures contracts, p. 285

hedge, p. 285

international banking facilities (IBFs), p. 308

large, complex banking organizations (LCBOs), p. 299

national banks, p. 283

securitization, p. 289

shadow banking system, p. 284

state banks, p. 282

superregional banks, p. 299

sweep account, p. 292

virtual bank, p. 287

QUESTIONS AND PROBLEMS

All questions and problems are available in myeconlab *at* www.myeconlab.com/mishkin.

1. Why was the United States one of the last of the major industrialized countries to have a central bank?

2. Which regulatory agency has the primary responsibility for supervising the following categories of commercial banks?
   a. National banks
   b. Bank holding companies
   c. Non–Federal Reserve member state banks
   d. Federal Reserve member state banks

3. "The commercial banking industry in Canada is less competitive than the commercial banking industry in the United States because in Canada only a few large banks dominate the industry, while in the United States there are around 7,500 commercial banks." Is this statement true, false, or uncertain? Explain your answer.

4. Why did new technology make it harder to enforce limitations on bank branching?

5. Why has there been such a dramatic increase in bank holding companies?

6. Why is there a higher percentage of banks with less than $25 million of assets among commercial banks than among savings and loans and mutual savings banks?

7. Unlike commercial banks, savings and loans, and mutual savings banks, credit unions did not have restrictions on locating branches in other states. Why, then, are credit unions typically smaller than the other depository institutions?

8. What incentives have regulatory agencies created to encourage international banking? Why have they done this?

9. How could the approval of international banking facilities (IBFs) by the Fed in 1981 have reduced employment in the banking industry in Europe?

10. If the bank at which you keep your checking account is owned by Saudi Arabians, should you worry that your deposits are less safe than if the bank were owned by Americans?

11. If reserve requirements were eliminated in the future, as some economists advocate, what effects would this have on the size of money market mutual funds?

12. Why have banks been losing cost advantages in acquiring funds in recent years?

13. "If inflation had not risen in the 1960s and 1970s, the banking industry might be healthier today." Is this statement true, false, or uncertain? Explain your answer.

14. Why have banks been losing income advantages on their assets in recent years?

15. "The invention of the computer is the major factor behind the decline of the banking industry." Is this statement true, false, or uncertain? Explain your answer.

WEB EXERCISES

1. Go to www2.fdic.gov/hsob/index.asp. Select "Commercial Bank Reports," then "Number of Institutions, Branches, and Total Offices." Looking at the trend in bank branches, does the public appear to have more or less access to banking facilities? How many banks were there in 1934 and how many are there now? Does the graph indicate that the trend toward consolidation is continuing?

2. Despite the regulations that protect banks from failure, some do fail. Go to www2.fdic.gov/hsob/index.asp. Select the tab labeled "Failures and Assistance Transactions." How many bank failures occurred in the United States during the most recent complete calendar year? What were the total assets held by the banks that failed? How many banks failed in 1937?

WEB REFERENCES

www.fdic.gov/bank/

The FDIC gathers data about individual financial institutions and the banking industry.

www2.fdic.gov/hsob/index.asp

Visit this website to gather statistics on the banking industry.

MyEconLab CAN HELP YOU GET A BETTER GRADE

If your exam were tomorrow, would you be ready? For each chapter, MyEconLab Practice Test and Study Plans pinpoint which sections you have mastered and which ones you need to study. That way, you are more efficient with your study time, and you are better prepared for your exams.

To see how it works, turn to page 20 and then go to: www.myeconlab.com/mishkin

PART 4

Central Banking

CHAPTER 13
Central Banks: A Global
Perspective

•

CHAPTER 14
The Money Supply Process

•

CHAPTER 15
The Tools of Monetary Policy

•

CHAPTER 16
The Conduct of Monetary Policy:
Strategy and Tactics

Crisis and Response: The Federal Reserve's Monetary Policy and Liquidity Provision During the Subprime Crisis

The onset of the subprime financial crisis in August 2007 was a curve ball for Ben Bernanke, the Chairman of the Federal Reserve, and his fellow members of the FOMC. The subprime financial crisis, described by former Chairman Alan Greenspan as a "once-in-a-century credit tsunami," had the potential to devastate the economy.

The Federal Reserve resolved to come to the rescue. Starting in September of 2007, the Federal Reserve lowered the federal funds rate target bringing it down to zero by the end of 2008. At the same time, the Fed implemented large liquidity injections into the credit markets to try to get them lending again. In mid-August 2007, the Fed lowered the discount rate at which it lent to banks to just 50 basis points above the federal funds rate target from the normal 100 basis points. Over the course of the crisis, the Fed broadened its provision of liquidity to the financial system well outside of its traditional lending to depository institutions. Indeed, after the Fed made loans to assist in the takeover of Bear Stearns by J.P. Morgan in March of 2008, Paul Volcker, a former Chairman of the Federal Reserve, described the Fed's actions as going to the "very edge of its lawful and implied powers." The number of new Fed lending programs over the course of the crisis spawned a whole new set of acronyms, the TAF, TSLF, PDCF, AMLF, CPFF, and MMIFF, making the Fed sound like the Pentagon with code-named initiatives and weapons. Like the Pentagon, the Fed was fighting a war, although its weapons were financial rather than guns, tanks, or aircraft.

The recent subprime crisis has demonstrated the importance of central banks like the Federal Reserve to the health of the financial system and the economy. Chapter 13 outlines what central banks are trying to achieve, what motivates them, and how they are set up. Chapter 14 describes how the money supply is determined. In Chapter 15, we look at the tools that central banks like the Fed have at their disposal and how they use them. Chapter 16 extends the discussion of how monetary policy is conducted to focus on the broader picture of central banks' strategies and tactics.

13 Central Banks: A Global Perspective

Preview

Among the most important players in financial markets throughout the world are central banks, the government authorities in charge of monetary policy. Central banks' actions affect interest rates, the amount of credit, and the money supply, all of which have direct impacts not only on financial markets, but also on aggregate output and inflation. To understand the role that central banks play in financial markets and the overall economy, we need to understand how these organizations work. Who controls central banks and determines their actions? What motivates their behavior? Who holds the reins of power?

In this chapter, we look at the goals and institutional structure of major central banks, and focus particularly on the Federal Reserve System and the European Central Bank, two of the most important central banks in the world. We start by examining what central banks are trying to do, and then focus on the elements of the institutional structure of these two central banks that determine where the true power lies. By understanding who makes the decisions, we will have a better idea of how they are made. We then shall take a quick tour around the world to look at the organization of several other major central banks, in a number of industrial nations, emerging economies, and developing countries. Finally, we examine what explains central bank behavior and whether it is a good idea to make central banks independent by insulating them from politicians. With this context in place, we will be prepared to comprehend the actual conduct of monetary policy described in the following chapters.

THE PRICE STABILITY GOAL AND THE NOMINAL ANCHOR

Over the past few decades, policymakers throughout the world have become increasingly aware of the social and economic costs of inflation and more concerned with maintaining a stable price level as a goal of economic policy. Indeed, **price stability**, which central bankers define as low and stable inflation, is increasingly viewed as the most important goal of monetary policy. Price stability is desirable because a rising price level (inflation) creates uncertainty in the economy, and that uncertainty might hamper economic growth. For example, when the overall level of prices is changing, the information conveyed by the prices of goods and services is harder to interpret, which complicates decision making for consumers, businesses, and government, thereby leading to a less efficient financial system.

Not only do public opinion surveys indicate that the public is hostile to inflation, but a growing body of evidence also suggests that inflation leads to lower economic growth.[1] The most extreme example of unstable prices is *hyperinflation*, such as Argentina, Brazil, and Russia have experienced in the recent past. Hyperinflation has proved to be very damaging to the workings of the economy.

Inflation also makes it difficult to plan for the future. For example, it is more difficult to decide how much to put aside to provide for a child's college education in an inflationary environment. Furthermore, inflation can strain a country's social fabric: Conflict could result, because each group in the society may compete with other groups to make sure that its income keeps up with the rising level of prices. In the first half of 2008, the higher cost of living spawned violent rioting in countries ranging from Cote d'Ivoire and Egypt to Haiti, Indonesia, and the Philippines.

The Role of a Nominal Anchor

Because price stability is so crucial to the long-run health of an economy, a central element in successful monetary policy is the use of a **nominal anchor**, a nominal variable such as the nominal exchange rate, wage and price controls, or the money supply, which ties down the price level to achieve price stability. Adherence to a nominal anchor that keeps the nominal variable within a narrow range promotes price stability by directly promoting low and stable inflation expectations. A more subtle reason for a nominal anchor's importance is that it can limit the **time-inconsistency problem**, in which monetary policy conducted on a discretionary, day-by-day basis leads to poor long-run outcomes.[2]

The Time-Inconsistency Problem

The time-inconsistency problem is something we deal with continually in everyday life. We often have a plan that we know will produce a good outcome in the long run, but when tomorrow comes, we just can't help ourselves and we renege on our plan because doing so has short-run gains. For example, we make a New Year's resolution to go on a diet, but soon thereafter we can't resist having one more bite of that rocky road ice cream—and then another bite, and then another bite—and the weight begins to pile back on. In other words, we find ourselves unable to *consistently* follow a good plan over *time*; the good plan is said to be *time-inconsistent* and will soon be abandoned.

Monetary policymakers also face the time-inconsistency problem. They are always tempted to pursue a discretionary monetary policy that is more expansionary than firms or people expect because such a policy would boost economic output (or lower unemployment) in the short run. The best policy, however, is *not* to pursue expansionary policy, because decisions about wages and prices reflect workers' and firms' expectations about policy; when they see a central bank pursuing expansionary policy, workers and firms will raise their expectations about inflation, driving wages and prices up. The rise in wages and prices will lead to higher inflation, but will not result in higher output on average. (We examine this issue more formally in Chapter 25.)

---

[1] For example, see Stanley Fischer, "The Role of Macroeconomic Factors in Growth," *Journal of Monetary Economics* 32 (1993): 485–512.

[2] The time-inconsistency problem was first outlined in papers by Nobel Prize winners Finn Kydland and Edward Prescott, "Rules Rather Than Discretion: The Inconsistency of Optimal Plans," *Journal of Political Economy* 85 (1977): 473–491; Guillermo Calvo, "On the Time Consistency of Optimal Policy in the Monetary Economy," *Econometrica* 46 (November 1978): 1411–1428; and Robert J. Barro and David Gordon, "A Positive Theory of Monetary Policy in a Natural Rate Model," *Journal of Political Economy* 91 (August 1983): 589–610.

A central bank will have better inflation performance in the long run if it does not try to surprise people with an unexpectedly expansionary policy, but instead keeps inflation under control. However, even if a central bank recognizes that discretionary policy will lead to a poor outcome (high inflation with no gains in output), it still may not be able to pursue the better policy of inflation control, because politicians are likely to apply pressure on the central bank to try to boost output with overly expansionary monetary policy.

A clue as to how we should deal with the time-inconsistency problem comes from how-to books on parenting. Parents know that giving in to a child to keep him from acting up will produce a very spoiled child. Nevertheless, when a child throws a tantrum, many parents give him what he wants just to shut him up. Because parents don't stick to their "do not give in" plan, the child expects that he will get what he wants if he behaves badly, so he will throw tantrums over and over again. Parenting books suggest a solution to the time-inconsistency problem (although they don't call it that): Parents should set behavior rules for their children and stick to them.

A nominal anchor is like a behavior rule. Just as rules help to prevent the time-inconsistency problem in parenting by helping the adults to resist pursuing the discretionary policy of giving in, a nominal anchor can help prevent the time-inconsistency problem in monetary policy by providing an expected constraint on discretionary policy.

OTHER GOALS OF MONETARY POLICY

While price stability is the primary goal of most central banks, five other goals are continually mentioned by central bank officials when they discuss the objectives of monetary policy: (1) high employment, (2) economic growth, (3) stability of financial markets, (4) interest-rate stability, and (5) stability in foreign exchange markets.

High Employment

High employment is a worthy goal for two main reasons: (1) the alternative situation—high unemployment—causes much human misery, and (2) when unemployment is high, the economy has both idle workers and idle resources (closed factories and unused equipment), resulting in a loss of output (lower GDP).

Although it is clear that high employment is desirable, how high should it be? At what point can we say that the economy is at full employment? At first, it might seem that full employment is the point at which no worker is out of a job—that is, when unemployment is zero. But this definition ignores the fact that some unemployment, called *frictional unemployment*, which involves searches by workers and firms to find suitable matchups, is beneficial to the economy. For example, a worker who decides to look for a better job might be unemployed for a while during the job search. Workers often decide to leave work temporarily to pursue other activities (raising a family, travel, returning to school), and when they decide to re-enter the job market, it may take some time for them to find the right job.

Another reason that unemployment is not zero when the economy is at full employment is *structural unemployment*, a mismatch between job requirements and the skills or availability of local workers. Clearly, this kind of unemployment is undesirable. Nonetheless, it is something that monetary policy can do little about.

This goal for high employment is not an unemployment level of zero but a level above zero, consistent with full employment, at which the demand for labor equals the supply of labor. This level is called the **natural rate of unemployment**.

Although this definition sounds neat and authoritative, it leaves a troublesome question unanswered. What unemployment rate is consistent with full employment? In some cases, it is obvious that the unemployment rate is too high: The unemployment rate in excess of 20% during the Great Depression, for example, was clearly far too high. In the early 1960s, on the other hand, policymakers thought that a reasonable goal was 4%, a level that was probably too low, because it led to accelerating inflation. Current estimates of the natural rate of unemployment place it between $4\frac{1}{2}$ and 6%, but even this estimate is subject to much uncertainty and disagreement. It is possible, for example, that appropriate government policy, such as the provision of better information about job vacancies or job training programs, could decrease the natural rate of unemployment.

Economic Growth

The goal of steady economic growth is closely related to the high-employment goal because businesses are more likely to invest in capital equipment to increase productivity and economic growth when unemployment is low. Conversely, if unemployment is high and factories are idle, it does not pay for a firm to invest in additional plants and equipment. Although the two goals are closely related, policies can be specifically aimed at promoting economic growth by directly encouraging firms to invest or by encouraging people to save, which provides more funds for firms to invest. In fact, this is the stated purpose of *supply-side economics* policies, which are intended to spur economic growth by providing tax incentives for businesses to invest in facilities and equipment and for taxpayers to save more. There is also an active debate about what role monetary policy can play in boosting growth.

Stability of Financial Markets

As our analysis in Chapter 9 showed, financial crises can interfere with the ability of financial markets to channel funds to people with productive investment opportunities and lead to a sharp contraction in economic activity. The promotion of a more stable financial system in which financial crises are avoided is thus an important goal for a central bank. Indeed, as we will discuss in this chapter, the Federal Reserve System was created in response to the bank panic of 1907 to promote financial stability.

Interest-Rate Stability

Interest-rate stability is desirable because fluctuations in interest rates can create uncertainty in the economy and make it harder to plan for the future. Fluctuations in interest rates that affect consumers' willingness to buy houses, for example, make it more difficult for consumers to decide when to purchase a house and for construction firms to plan how many houses to build. A central bank may also want to reduce upward movements in interest rates for the reasons we will discuss in this chapter: Upward movements in interest rates generate hostility toward central banks and lead to demands that their power be curtailed.

The stability of financial markets is also fostered by interest-rate stability, because fluctuations in interest rates create great uncertainty for financial institutions. An increase in interest rates produces large capital losses on long-term bonds and mortgages, losses that can cause the failure of the financial institutions holding them. In recent years, more pronounced interest-rate fluctuations have been a particularly severe problem for savings and loan associations and mutual savings banks, many of which got into serious financial trouble in the 1980s and early 1990s.

Stability in Foreign Exchange Markets

With the increasing importance of international trade, the value of the domestic currency of a country relative to other foreign currencies has become a major consideration for the central banks. For example, a rise in the value of the national currency makes domestic industries less competitive with those abroad, and declines in the value of the national currency stimulate inflation in the economy. In addition, preventing large changes in the value of the domestic currency makes it easier for firms and individuals purchasing or selling goods abroad to plan ahead. Stabilizing extreme movements in the value of the domestic currency in foreign exchange markets is thus an important goal of monetary policy. In those countries which are very dependent on foreign trade, stability in foreign exchange markets takes on even greater importance.

SHOULD PRICE STABILITY BE THE PRIMARY GOAL OF MONETARY POLICY?

In the long run, there is no inconsistency between the price stability goal and the other goals mentioned earlier. The natural rate of unemployment is not lowered by high inflation, so higher inflation cannot produce lower unemployment or more employment in the long run. In other words, there is no long-run trade-off between inflation and employment. In the long run, price stability promotes economic growth as well as financial and interest-rate stability. Although price stability is consistent with the other goals in the long run, in the short run price stability often conflicts with the goals of high employment and interest-rate stability. For example, when the economy is expanding and unemployment is falling, the economy may become overheated, leading to a rise in inflation. To pursue the price stability goal, a central bank would prevent this overheating by raising interest rates, an action that would initially lower employment and increase interest-rate instability. How should a central bank resolve this conflict among goals?

Hierarchical Versus Dual Mandates

Because price stability is crucial to the long-run health of the economy, many countries have decided that price stability should be the primary, long-run goal for central banks. For example, the Maastricht Treaty, which created the European Central Bank, states, "The primary objective of the European System of Central Banks [ESCB] shall be to maintain price stability. Without prejudice to the objective of price stability, the ESCB shall support the general economic policies in the Community," which include objectives such as "a high level of employment" and "sustainable and non-inflationary growth." Mandates of this type, which put the goal of price stability first, and then say that as long as it is achieved other goals can be pursued, are known as **hierarchical mandates**. They are the directives governing the behavior of central banks such as the Bank of England, the Bank of Canada, and the Reserve Bank of New Zealand, as well as for the European Central Bank.

In contrast, the legislation defining the mission of the Federal Reserve states, "The Board of Governors of the Federal Reserve System and the Federal Open Market Committee shall maintain long-run growth of the monetary and credit aggregates commensurate with the economy's long-run potential to increase production, so as to promote effectively the goals of maximum employment, stable prices, and moderate long-term interest rates." Because, as we learned in Chapter 5, long-term interest rates will be very high if there is high inflation, this statement in practice is a **dual mandate** to achieve two co-equal objectives: price stability and maximum employment.

Is it better for an economy to operate under a hierarchical mandate or a dual mandate?

Price Stability as the Primary, Long-Run Goal of Monetary Policy

Because there is no inconsistency between achieving price stability in the long run and the natural rate of unemployment, these two types of mandates are not very different *if* maximum employment is defined as the natural rate of employment. In practice, however, there could be a substantial difference between these two mandates, because the public and politicians may believe that a hierarchical mandate puts too much emphasis on inflation control and not enough on reducing business-cycle fluctuations.

Because low and stable inflation rates promote economic growth, central bankers have come to realize that price stability should be the primary, long-run goal of monetary policy. Nevertheless, because output fluctuations should also be a concern of monetary policy, the goal of price stability should be seen as the primary goal only in the long run. It is likely that attempts to keep inflation at the same level in the short run, no matter what, would lead to excessive output fluctuations.

As long as price stability is a long-run goal, but not a short-run goal, central banks can focus on reducing output fluctuations by allowing inflation to deviate from the long-run goal for short periods of time and, therefore, can operate under a dual mandate. However, if a dual mandate leads a central bank to pursue short-run expansionary policies that increase output and employment without worrying about the long-run consequences for inflation, the time-inconsistency problem may recur. Concerns that a dual mandate could lead to an overly expansionary policy is a key reason why central bankers often favor hierarchical mandates, in which the pursuit of price stability takes precedence. Hierarchical mandates can also be a problem if they lead to a central bank behaving as what the Governor of the Bank of England, Mervyn King, has referred to as an "inflation nutter"—that is, a central bank that focuses solely on inflation control, even in the short run, and so undertakes policies that lead to large output fluctuations. The choice of which type of mandate is better for a central bank ultimately depends on the subtleties of how it will work in practice. Either type of mandate is acceptable as long as it operates to make price stability the primary goal in the long run, but not the short run.

ORIGINS OF THE FEDERAL RESERVE SYSTEM

Of all the central banks in the world, the Federal Reserve System probably has the most unusual structure. To understand why this structure arose, we must go back to before 1913, when the Federal Reserve System was created.

Before the twentieth century, a major characteristic of American politics was the fear of centralized power, as seen in the checks and balances of the Constitution and the preservation of states' rights. The open hostility of the American public to the existence of a central bank resulted in the demise of the first two experiments in central banking, whose function was to police the banking system. The First Bank of the United States was disbanded in 1811, and the national charter of the Second Bank of the United States expired in 1836, after its renewal was vetoed in 1832 by President Andrew Jackson.

Hence, in the nineteenth and early twentieth centuries, nationwide bank panics became a regular event, occurring every twenty years or so, culminating in the panic of 1907. The 1907 panic resulted in such widespread bank failures and such substantial losses to depositors that the public was finally convinced that a central bank was needed to prevent future panics.

The hostility of the American public to banks and centralized authority created great opposition to the establishment of a single central bank like the Bank of England. Because of the heated debates on these issues, a compromise was struck. In the great American tradition, Congress wrote an elaborate system of checks and balances into the Federal Reserve Act of 1913, which created the Federal Reserve System with its twelve regional Federal Reserve banks.

STRUCTURE OF THE FEDERAL RESERVE SYSTEM

The writers of the Federal Reserve Act wanted to diffuse power along regional lines, between the private sector and the government, and among bankers, business people, and the public. This initial diffusion of power has resulted in the evolution of the Federal Reserve System to include the following entities: the 12 **Federal Reserve banks**, the **Board of Governors of the Federal Reserve System**, the **Federal Open Market Committee (FOMC)**, the Federal Advisory Council, and around 2,900 member commercial banks.

Federal Reserve Banks

Each of the twelve Federal Reserve districts has one main Federal Reserve bank, which may have branches in other cities in the district. The locations of these districts, the Federal Reserve banks, and their branches are shown in Figure 1. The three largest Federal Reserve banks in terms of assets are those of New York, Chicago, and San Francisco—combined they hold more than 50% of the assets (discount loans, securities, and other holdings) of the Federal Reserve System. The New York bank, with around one-quarter of the assets, is the most important of the Federal Reserve banks.

Each of the Federal Reserve banks is a quasi-public (part private, part government) institution owned by the private commercial banks in the district that are members of the Federal Reserve System. These member banks have purchased stock in their district Federal Reserve bank (a requirement of membership), and the dividends paid by that stock are limited by law to 6% annually. The member banks elect six directors for each district bank; three more are appointed by the Board of Governors. Together, these nine directors appoint the president of the bank (subject to the approval of the Board of Governors).

The twelve Federal Reserve banks perform the following functions:

- Clear checks
- Issue new currency
- Withdraw damaged currency from circulation
- Administer and make discount loans to banks in their districts
- Evaluate proposed mergers and applications for banks to expand their activities

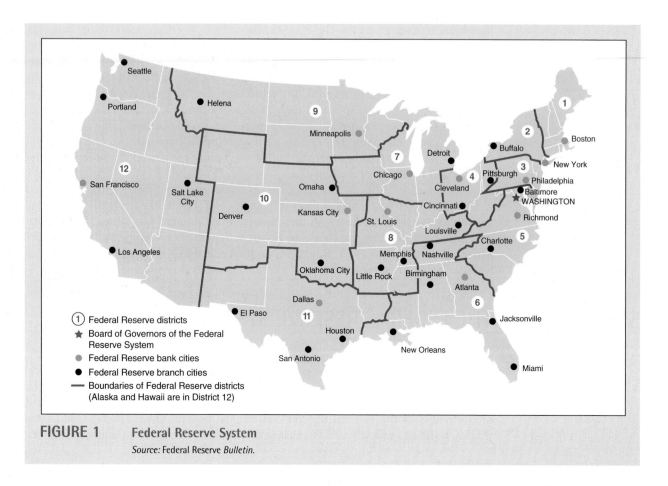

FIGURE 1 Federal Reserve System

Source: Federal Reserve *Bulletin.*

- Act as liaisons between the business community and the Federal Reserve System
- Examine bank holding companies and state-chartered member banks
- Collect data on local business conditions
- Use their staffs of professional economists to research topics related to the conduct of monetary policy

The twelve Federal Reserve banks are involved in monetary policy in several ways:

1. Their directors "establish" the discount rate (although the discount rate in each district is reviewed and determined by the Board of Governors).
2. They decide which banks, member and nonmember alike, can obtain discount loans from the Federal Reserve bank.
3. Their directors select one commercial banker from each bank's district to serve on the Federal Advisory Council, which consults with the Board of Governors and provides information that helps in the conduct of monetary policy.
4. Five of the twelve bank presidents each have a vote on the Federal Open Market Committee, which directs **open market operations** (the purchase and sale of government securities that affect both interest rates and the amount of reserves in the banking system). The president of the New York Fed is a permanent member of the FOMC, and therefore always has a vote on the FOMC, making it the most important of the banks; the other four votes allocated to the district banks rotate annually among the remaining eleven presidents.

Member Banks

All *national banks* (commercial banks chartered by the Office of the Comptroller of the Currency) are required to be members of the Federal Reserve System. Commercial banks chartered by the states are not required to be members, but they can choose to join. Currently, 38% of the commercial banks in the United States are members of the Federal Reserve System; this figure has declined from a peak figure of 49% in 1947.

Before 1980, only member banks were required to keep reserves as deposits at the Federal Reserve banks. Non-member banks were subject to reserve requirements determined by their states, which typically allowed them to hold much of their reserves in interest-bearing securities. Because at the time no interest was paid on reserves deposited at the Federal Reserve banks, it was costly to be a member of the system, and as interest rates rose, the relative cost of membership rose, and more and more banks left the system.

This decline in Fed membership was a major concern of the Board of Governors: one reason was that it lessened the Fed's control over the money supply, making it more difficult for the Fed to conduct monetary policy. The chairman of the Board of Governors repeatedly called for new legislation requiring all commercial banks to be members of the Federal Reserve System. One result of the Fed's pressure on Congress was a provision in the Depository Institutions Deregulation and Monetary Control Act of 1980: all depository institutions became subject (by 1987) to the same requirements to keep deposits at the Fed, so member and non-member banks would be on an equal footing in terms of reserve requirements. In addition, all depository institutions were given access to the Federal Reserve facilities, such as the discount window (discussed in Chapter 15) and Fed check clearing, on an equal basis. These provisions ended the decline in Fed membership and reduced the distinction between member and nonmember banks.

Board of Governors of the Federal Reserve System

At the head of the Federal Reserve System is the seven-member Board of Governors, headquartered in Washington, DC. Each governor is appointed by the president of the United States and confirmed by the Senate. To limit the president's control over the Fed and insulate the Fed from other political pressures, the governors can serve one full nonrenewable fourteen-year term plus part of another term, with one governor's term expiring every other January.[3] The governors (many are professional economists) are required to come from different Federal Reserve districts to prevent the interests of one region of the country from being overrepresented. The chairman of the Board of Governors is chosen from among the seven governors and serves a four-year, renewable term. It is expected that once a new chairman is chosen, the old chairman resigns from the Board of Governors, even if there are many years left to his or her term as a governor.

The Board of Governors is actively involved in decisions concerning the conduct of monetary policy. All seven governors are members of the FOMC and vote on the conduct of open market operations. Because there are only twelve voting members on this committee (seven governors and five presidents of the district banks), the Board has the majority of the votes. The Board also sets reserve requirements (within limits imposed by legislation) and effectively controls the discount rate by the "review and determination" process, whereby it approves or disapproves the discount rate "established" by the

---

[3]Although technically the governor's term is non-renewable, a governor can resign just before the term expires and then be reappointed by the president. This explains how one governor, William McChesney Martin, Jr., served for 28 years. Since Martin, the chairman from 1951 to 1970, retired from the board in 1970, the practice of allowing a governor to, in effect, serve a second full term has not been done and this is why Alan Greenspan had to retire from the Board after his fourteen-year term expired in 2006.

Federal Reserve banks. The chairman of the Board advises the president of the United States on economic policy, testifies in Congress, and speaks for the Federal Reserve System to the media. The chairman and other governors may also represent the United States in negotiations with foreign governments on economic matters. The Board has a staff of professional economists (larger than those of individual Federal Reserve banks), which provides economic analysis that the board uses in making its decisions.

The Board has substantial bank regulatory functions: it approves bank mergers and applications for new activities, specifies the permissible activities of bank holding companies, and supervises the activities of foreign banks in the United States.

Federal Open Market Committee (FOMC)

The FOMC usually meets eight times a year (about every six weeks) and makes decisions regarding the conduct of open market operations, which influence the money supply and interest rates. Indeed, the FOMC is often referred to as the "Fed" in the press: for example, when the media say that the Fed is meeting, they actually mean that the FOMC is meeting. The committee consists of the seven members of the Board of Governors, the president of the Federal Reserve Bank of New York, and the presidents of four other Federal Reserve banks. The chairman of the Board of Governors also presides as the chairman of the FOMC. Even though only the presidents of five of the Federal Reserve banks are voting members of the FOMC, the other seven presidents of the district banks attend FOMC meetings and participate in discussions. Hence they have some input into the committee's decisions.

Because open market operations are the most important policy tool that the Fed has for controlling the money supply, the FOMC is necessarily the focal point for policy-making in the Federal Reserve System. Although reserve requirements and the discount rate are not actually set by the FOMC, decisions in regard to these policy tools are effectively made there. The FOMC does not actually carry out securities purchases or sales. Instead, it issues directives to the trading desk at the Federal Reserve Bank of New York, where the manager for domestic open market operations supervises a roomful of people who execute the purchases and sales of the government or agency securities. The manager communicates daily with the FOMC members and their staffs concerning the activities of the trading desk.

HOW INDEPENDENT IS THE FED?

Stanley Fischer, who was a professor at MIT and is now governor of the Bank of Israel, has defined two different types of independence of central banks: **instrument independence**, the ability of the central bank to set monetary policy instruments, and **goal independence**, the ability of the central bank to set the goals of monetary policy. The Federal Reserve has both types of independence and is remarkably free of the political pressures that influence other government agencies. Not only are the members of the Board of Governors appointed for a fourteen-year term (and so cannot be ousted from office), but also the term is technically not renewable, eliminating some of the incentive for the governors to seek the approval of president and Congress.

Probably even more important to its independence from the whims of Congress is the Fed's independent and substantial source of revenue from its holdings of securities and, to a lesser extent, from its loans to banks. In recent years, for example, the Fed has

Inside the Fed   How Bernanke's Style Differs from Greenspan's

Every Federal Reserve chairman has a different style that affects how policy decisions are made at the Fed. There has been much discussion of how the current chairman of the Fed, Ben Bernanke, differs from Alan Greenspan, who was the chairman of the Federal Reserve Board for nineteen years from 1987 until 2006.

Alan Greenspan dominated the Fed like no other prior Federal Reserve chairman. His background was very different from that of Bernanke, who spent most of his professional life in academia at Princeton University. Greenspan, a disciple of Ayn Rand, is a strong advocate for laissez-faire capitalism and headed a very successful economic consulting firm, Townsend-Greenspan.* Greenspan has never been an economic theorist, but is rather famous for immersing himself in the data—literally so, because he is known to have done this in his bath tub at the beginning of the day—and often focused on rather obscure data series to come up with his forecasts. As a result, Greenspan did not rely exclusively on the Federal Reserve Board staff's forecast in making his policy decisions. A prominent example occurred during 1997, when the Board staff was forecasting a surge in inflation, which would have required a tightening of monetary policy. Yet Greenspan believed that inflation would not rise and convinced the FOMC

not to tighten monetary policy. Greenspan proved to be right and was dubbed the "maestro" by the media.

In contrast to Greenspan, Bernanke's background as a top academic economist has meant that he focuses on analytics in making his decisions. The result is a much greater use of model simulations in guiding policy discussions.

The FOMC decision-making process under Greenspan was one where the chairman for the most part made the decision about policy, while Bernanke's procedure is more democratic and enables participants to have greater influence over the chairman's vote.

Another big difference in style is in terms of transparency. Greenspan was famous for being obscure. Bernanke is known for being a particularly clear speaker. Finally, while Greenspan adopted more transparent communication with reluctance, Bernanke has been a much stronger supporter of transparency, having advocated that the Fed announce its inflation objective (see Chapter 16). Bernanke launched a major initiative in 2006 to study Federal Reserve communications that resulted in substantial increases in Fed transparency in November 2007.

*For biographical information on Alan Greenspan, see his autobiography, *The Age of Turbulence: Adventures in a New World* (New York: Penguin Press, 2007).

had net earnings after expenses of around $40 billion per year—not a bad living if you can find it! Because it returns the bulk of these earnings to the Treasury, it does not get rich from its activities, but this income gives the Fed an important advantage over other government agencies: it is not subject to the appropriations process usually controlled by Congress. Indeed, the Government Accountability Office, the auditing agency of the federal government, cannot audit the monetary policy or foreign exchange market functions of the Federal Reserve. Because the power to control the purse strings is usually synonymous with the power of overall control, this feature of the Federal Reserve System contributes to its independence more than any other factor.

Yet the Federal Reserve is still subject to the influence of Congress, because the legislation that structures it is written by Congress and is subject to change at any time. When legislators are upset with the Fed's conduct of monetary policy, they frequently threaten to take control of the Fed's finances and force it to submit a budget request like other government agencies. A recent example was the call by Senators Dorgan and Reid in 1996 for Congress to have budgetary authority over the nonmonetary activities of the

Federal Reserve. This is a powerful club to wield, and it certainly has some effect in keeping the Fed from straying too far from congressional wishes.

Congress also passed legislation in 1978, requiring the Federal Reserve to issue a *Monetary Policy Report to the Congress* semiannually, with accompanying testimony by the chairman of the Board of Governors, to explain how the conduct of monetary policy is consistent with the objectives given by the Federal Reserve Act.

The president can also influence the Federal Reserve. Because congressional legislation can affect the Fed directly or affect its ability to conduct monetary policy, the president can be a powerful ally through his influence on Congress. Second, although ostensibly a president might be able to appoint only one or two members to the Board of Governors during each presidential term, in actual practice the president appoints members far more often. One reason is that most governors do not serve out a full fourteen-year term. (Governors' salaries are substantially below what they can earn in the private sector or even at universities, thus providing an incentive for them to return to academia or take private sector jobs before their term expires.) In addition, the president is able to appoint a new chairman of the Board of Governors every four years, and a chairman who is not reappointed is expected to resign from the board so that a new member can be appointed.

STRUCTURE AND INDEPENDENCE OF THE EUROPEAN CENTRAL BANK

Until recently, the Federal Reserve had no rivals in terms of its importance in the central banking world. However, this situation changed in January 1999 with the start-up of the European Central Bank (ECB) and European System of Central Banks (ESCB), which now conduct monetary policy for countries that are members of the European Monetary Union. These countries, taken together, have a population that exceeds that of the United States and a GDP comparable with that of the United States. The Maastricht Treaty, which established the ECB and ESCB, patterned these institutions after the Deutsche Bundesbank, the German central bank, in that central banks for each country (referred to as *National Central Banks*, or *NCBs*) have a similar role to that of the *Lander Banks* (for a full review of how the *Lander Banks* operate, see the section about the Bundesbank). The decisions in the Eurosystem are taken in a centralized manner by the ECB, but implemented via the NCBs in a decentralized way.

Now let us acquaint ourselves with the institutions of the European Union. The ESCB encompasses the ECB and the National Central Banks of the 27 EU member states whether or not they use the euro as their domestic currency. The Eurosystem, on the other hand, comprises of the ECB and the NCBs of only the sixteen countries that have adopted the euro; Slovakia being the latest member to join the European Monetary Union in January 2009. As for the Euro area, it refers to only the EU countries using the euro as their currency. The ECB is owned by the sixteen NCBs and it was established as the center of the European System of Central Banks (ESCB) and the Eurosystem. While the ECB has a legal personality under public international law, the ESCB does not. It is intended that the Eurosystem and the ESCB coexist as long as there are EU Member States outside the euro area. Once all 27 members of the ESCB adopt the euro, both institutions will merge. Figure 2 shows the member nations of the ECB and the ESCB.

The decision-making process at the EMU takes place at three levels: the Governing Council, the Executive Board and the General Council. The Governing Council is the de facto decision maker; the Executive Board is responsible for the daily execution of

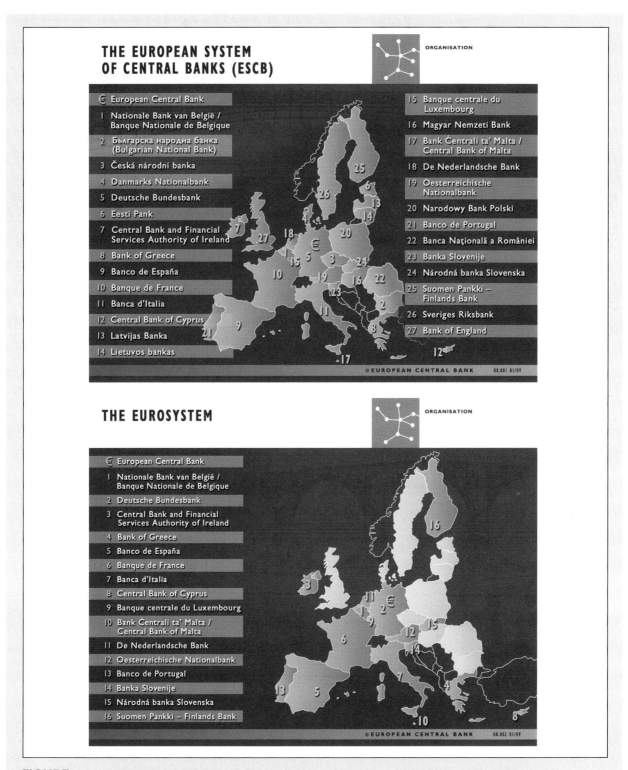

FIGURE 2   The European System of Central Banks vs. the Eurosystem

Source: Facts Presentation. ECB, January 2009, S 1&2. Copyright © European Central Bank, Frankfurt am Main, Germany. Figures are available free of charge via the ECB website.

decisions of the Governing Council; while the General Council undertakes minor roles as an advisory body.

Governing Council Executive Board and General Council

The Governing Council, the supreme decision-making body of the ECB, comprises the six members of the Executive Board, plus the governors of the National Central Banks of the 16 Euro area nations. The main responsibility of the Governing Council is to formulate the monetary policy for the Euro area. The monetary policy decisions of the Governing Council relate to meeting the general monetary objectives of the Euro zone, authorization of the NCBs to issue currency notes, changes in interest rates and supervising the proper management of foreign reserves. It is also responsible for giving guidelines to NCBs for the implementation of those decisions. The Governing Council convenes on a fortnightly basis at the Eurotower in Frankfurt, Germany. During its first meeting each month, members of the Governing Council assess the economic and monetary conditions and developments in the EMU in order to take decisions regarding its monthly monetary policies. During its second meeting, the council discusses issues pertaining to other responsibilities of the ECB and the detailed implementation process by each of the NCBs.

The Governing Council has decided that although its members have the legal right to vote, no formal vote will actually be taken; instead, the Council operates by consensus. One reason the Governing Council has decided not to take votes is because of worries that the casting of individual votes could lead the heads of National Central Banks to support a monetary policy that would be appropriate for their individual countries, but not necessarily for the countries in the European Monetary Union as a whole.

Just as the Federal Reserve releases the FOMC's decision on the setting of the policy interest rate (the federal funds rate) immediately after the meeting is over, the ECB does the same after the Governing Council meeting concludes (announcing the target for a similar short-term interest rate for interbank loans). However, whereas the Fed simply releases a statement about the setting of the monetary policy instruments, the ECB goes further by having a press conference in which the president and vice president of the ECB take questions from the news media. Holding such a press conference so soon after the meeting is tricky because it requires the president and vice president to be quick on their feet in dealing with the press. The first president of the ECB, Willem F. Duisenberg, caused uncomfortable situations at some of these press conferences, and the ECB came under some sharp criticism. His successor, Jean-Claude Trichet, a more successful communicator, has encountered fewer problems in this regard.

The Executive Board consists of the president, vice-president and four other members who are appointed by common agreement of the Heads of States of the Euro area countries. Its main tasks are to ensure the day-to-day implementation of the monetary policy through giving detailed instructions to all NCBs in accordance with the guidelines of the Governing Council. Moreover, the Executive Board is responsible for managing the daily business of the ECB.

Finally, The General Council includes the president and the vice-president of the ECB, representatives of the 16 Euro area countries and the 11 non-Euro zone EU Member States. The president of the EU Council and a member of the European Commission may attend the meetings of the General Council, but they have no voting rights. The General Council is a transitional body that will be dissolved once all EU Member States introduce the single currency. It performs advisory tasks to the ECB, collects statistical information and standardizes the accounting operations of the NCBs.

With more countries opting to join the European Monetary Union it becomes more difficult to reach a consensus. To deal with this potential problem, the Governing Council has decided on a complex system of rotation, somewhat like that for the FOMC, in which National Central Banks from the larger countries will vote more often than National Central Banks from the smaller countries. Moreover, once the member nations of the Euro zone reach 18, a two-third majority will be followed instead of the current consensus.

How Do National Central Banks Operate Within the Eurosystem?

The NCBs play an essential role in the ESCB and exercise powers delegated to them by the Governing Council. But the question that immediately comes to mind is how do individual National Central Banks act in accordance with ECB guidelines? In order to have a better understanding of the system, it is helpful to focus on one of the most significant members of the ECB, namely the Deutsche Bundesbank. The reason for selecting the Bundesbank is that it is the largest national central bank within the ECB and also more than half of the short-term inter-bank borrowing by Euro-area banks from the central banks is attributable to the Bundesbank. It also contributes almost 20% of the capital of the ECB. Moreover, the ECB was modeled after the Deutsche Bundesbank in a manner that fully ensures its independence.

Deutsche Bundesbank

In 1948, the Allied forces created the Bank deutscher Länder (BdL) to act as the central bank of the Federal Republic of Germany (West Germany). A two-tier central banking system was established comprising of the BdL and the Länder (or state) central banks whose presidents were appointed by the Länder governments. A higher council comprised of governors of the Länder central banks, a federal-appointed president and the president of the BdL. In this highly decentralized central banking system, the BdL assumed the main tasks of conducting monetary policy, coordinating the policies and tasks of the Länder central banks and managing the foreign exchange system of the country. In the meantime, the Länder central banks were greatly autonomous, with each state issuing currency notes, along with the BdL.

In 1957 the Bundesbank replaced the BdL as the new central bank of West Germany and a new structure was adopted. The Bundesbank, also nicknamed the "Buba" became the sole issuer of the Deutsche Mark currency notes and was required to cooperate with other policymaking institutions to ensure harmonious objectives and policies. The Central Bank Council comprised of ten central government representatives and eleven Länder central bank presidents, selected by the Länder governments. This structure served the dual objectives of coordinated policies, while ensuring that the Länder central banks still maintained some autonomy.

After the reunification of East and West Germany, the Bundesbank was reorganized in 1990 to allow for the incorporation of East Germany into the system. The composition of the council was altered, so that it comprised eight government appointees and nine Länder central bank presidents, while key states retained their central banks. This new structure of the Bundesbank strikes a balance between granting the federal or central government relative say in policy making, while preserving the majority status of the state central bank presidents. This guaranteed the continued independence of the Bundesbank.

Till 2008 the Bundesbank had nine regional offices and 47 branches throughout Germany. In 2008 it posted a profit of €6.3 billion, which accrued to Länder banks, since they are the legal owners of the Bundesbank. From 2009 the Executive Board of the

Bundesbank will consist of six instead of eight members. Three members will now be nominated by the Federal Government and three by the Bundesrat (or the German Federal Council) and all members are appointed by the President of Germany.

How does the ECB differ from the Bundesbank?

After its introduction in 2001, Germany adopted the euro as its currency to replace the Deutsche Mark. The Bundesbank no longer exists as an independent body, but is part of the European Central Bank. Its objectives are harmonious with those of the ECB, with the primary goal of price stability. The Governing Council of the ECB has the prime goal of targeting the annual rate of inflation in the Euro zone at approximately 2%.

The Bundesbank has five core tasks that it jointly performs with the ECB.

- The core function of the Bundesbank is to implement the Eurosystem monetary policy as laid down in the EC Treaty. It has to ensure stable prices and this is executed through voting in the monthly meeting of the Governing Council of the ECB where monetary policy decisions are made. The president of Bundesbank is a voting member in the Governing Council of the ECB and consults experts before voting each month. The Bundesbank does not have the right to issue currency notes and coins at its own discretion, but only after authorization from the ECB.
- It also performs the main function as the clearing house for its member banks and the banks' banker. All central banks within the Euro zone are now members of an advanced payment system, known as TARGET 2 that allows banks to make payments in real time and also permits them to use counter-payment as cover. The ECB does not have the task of supervising banks, but this task is delegated to each of the national banks such as the Bundesbank which is responsible for the supervision of the solvency, liquidity and risk management systems of 2,300 credit institutions in Germany. The Bundesbank also ensures that banks hold adequate capital requirements in accordance with the requirements of Basel Accord II.
- The Bundesbank is the state's banker and the Federal Government's fiscal agent. Moreover, the Bundesbank advises the government on issues of monetary policy.
- It also manages the currency reserves of Germany; the ECB has no say as to how much foreign reserves each of the national central banks should hold. But each NCB is required to contribute to the ECB foreign reserves equivalent to its contribution to the capital of the ECB.
- Finally, the Bundesbank may also cooperate with other international institutions to maintain a stable financial system. For example, during the current global financial crisis, it has cooperated with the Fed under a program called Term Auction Facility to improve dollar liquidity in the Euro area and to help stabilize the money market.

How Independent is the ECB?

Although the Federal Reserve is a highly independent central bank, the Maastricht Treaty, which established the Eurosystem, has made the ECB the most independent central bank in the world. Like the Board of Governors, the members of the Executive Board have long terms (eight years), while heads of National Central Banks are required to have terms at least five years long. Like the Fed, the Eurosystem determines its own budget, and the governments of the member countries are not allowed to issue instructions to the ECB. These elements of the Maastricht Treaty make the ECB highly independent.

Another element that grants the ECB more independence is that it is prohibited from granting loans to national public sector entities, in order to shield it from any influences by public authorities. Moreover, to ensure the independence of NCBs, the ECB strictly forbids them from taking instructions from European Community institutions, any government of an EU Member State or any other international body. This ensures total conformity of the NCBs, with monetary policy decisions undertaken by the Governing Council.

CENTRAL BANKS ROUND THE WORLD

Now let us tour the globe to examine the structure and degree of independence of central banks round the world. We shall first start with a selected number of industrial nations, followed by some central banks in transition economies and finally we shall take a look at how central banks operate in a number of developing countries.

Bank of Canada

Canada was late in establishing a central bank: the Bank of Canada was founded in 1934. Its directors are appointed by the government to three-year terms, and they appoint the governor, who has a seven-year term. A governing council, consisting of the four deputy governors and the governor, is the policymaking body comparable to the FOMC that makes decisions about monetary policy.

The Bank Act was amended in 1967 to give the ultimate responsibility for monetary policy to the government. So on paper, the Bank of Canada is not as essentially independent as the Federal Reserve. In practice, however, the Bank of Canada does essentially control monetary policy. In the event of a disagreement between the bank and the government, the minister of finance can issue a directive that the bank must follow. However, because the directive must be in writing and specific and applicable for a specified period, it is unlikely that such a directive would be issued, and none has been to date. The goal for monetary policy, a target for inflation, is set jointly by the Bank of Canada and the government, so the Bank of Canada has less goal independence than the Fed.

Bank of England

Founded in 1694, the Bank of England is one of the oldest central banks. The Bank Act of 1946 gave the government statutory authority over the Bank of England. The Court (equivalent to a board of directors) of the Bank of England is made up of the governor and two deputy governors, who are appointed for five-year terms, and sixteen non-executive directors, who are appointed for three-year terms.

Until 1997, the Bank of England was the least independent of the central banks examined in this chapter because the decision to raise or lower interest rates resided not within the Bank of England but with the Chancellor of the Exchequer (the equivalent of the U.S. Secretary of the Treasury or the Minister of Finance). All of this changed when the current Labour government came to power in May 1997. At this time, the Chancellor of the Exchequer, Gordon Brown, made a surprise announcement that the Bank of England would henceforth have the power to set interest rates. However, the

Bank was not granted total instrument independence: the government can overrule the Bank and set rates "in extreme economic circumstances" and "for a limited period." Nonetheless, as in Canada, because overruling the Bank would be so public and is supposed to occur only in highly unusual circumstances and for a limited time, it is likely to be a rare occurrence. Moreover, since 1997 the Bank of England has been stripped of two of its prime functions, namely the national debt management and the supervision of the banking sector. Both these roles were hived off to the Debt Management Office (DMO) and the Financial Services Authority (FSA) respectively.[4] Accordingly, the Bank of England is now totally focused on varying interest rates to achieve the inflation target set for it by the Chancellor of the Exchequer.

Because the United Kingdom is not a member of the European Monetary Union, the Bank of England makes its monetary policy decisions independently from the European Central Bank. The decision to set interest rates resides with the Monetary Policy Committee, made up of the governor, two deputy governors, two members appointed by the governor after consultation with the chancellor (normally central bank officials), plus four outside economic experts appointed by the chancellor. (Surprisingly, two of the four outside experts initially appointed to this committee were not British citizens— one was Dutch and the other American, although both were residents of the United Kingdom.) The inflation target for the Bank of England is set by the Chancellor of the Exchequer, so the Bank of England is also less goal-independent than the Fed.

Bank of Japan

The Bank of Japan (Nippon Ginko) was founded in 1882 during the Meiji Restoration. Monetary policy is determined by the Policy Board, which is composed of the governor, two vice-governors, and six outside members appointed by the cabinet and approved by the parliament, all of whom serve for five-year terms.

Until recently, the Bank of Japan was not formally independent of the government, with the ultimate power residing with the Ministry of Finance. However, the Bank of Japan Law, which took effect in April 1998 and was the first major change in the powers of the Bank of Japan in 55 years, changed this situation. In addition to stipulating that the objective of monetary policy is to attain price stability, the law granted greater instrument and goal independence to the Bank of Japan. Before this, the government had two voting members on the Policy Board, one from the Ministry of Finance and the other from the Economic Planning Agency. Now the government may send two representatives from these agencies to board meetings, but they no longer have voting rights, although they do have the ability to request delays in monetary policy decisions. In addition, the Ministry of Finance lost its authority to oversee many of the operations of the Bank of Japan, particularly the right to dismiss senior officials. However, the Ministry of Finance continues to have control over the part of the Bank's budget that is unrelated to monetary policy, which might limit its independence to some extent.

Central Banks in Transition Economies

In the early 1990s, of the elapsed century, socialism collapsed in a number of socialist countries in east and central Europe and the former USSR. As these countries were

---

[4]Even though the FSA was established with the role of consolidating the supervision of financial institutions under one institution, it was criticized for weak enforcement of regulations and for the inability to properly monitor and regulate the financial sector, hence contributing to the current global financial crisis.

moving from central planning and public ownership to more liberalization and private property rights, a number of institutions were changed, while totally new ones were created. This transition process was quite painful and cumbersome for many of these nations, as it entailed substantial structural changes and the formation of the previously non-existent markets.

Prior to 1990, most of the transition nations possessed one state-owned bank that assumed the dual roles of a commercial bank and a central bank, while a few others already possessed a separate central bank that supervised the operations of other state-owned banks. By the 1900s, the economies of these nations were in shambles, where the banking sector had a huge non-performing debt portfolio owed by the inefficient public sector firms. Moreover, with the abrupt introduction of markets to these economies they suffered from inflationary pressures due to the liberalization of prices, along with substantial deficits in their balance of payments and massive devaluations of their domestic currencies.

Hence, it was imperative to create new central banks, by breaking up the mono-bank into a central bank and a commercial bank, or to grant some degree of independence to the already existing ones. This required multiple central bank reforms in order to substantially upgrade both the instrument and the goal independence of these newly reformed institutions. Central bank independence in Eastern European nations and the Commonwealth of Independent Nations (the fifteen nations that gained their independence after the collapse of the USSR) was granted, albeit not being fully functional.

With the increase in the levels of law enforcement in transition economies, gradual central bank independence has been granted and implemented, leading to more successful solutions to the problems of inflation and bank supervision. Among the most independent central banks in transition nations are the Czech, Bulgarian and Hungarian central banks, which have proved successful in controlling inflation.

Central Banks in Developing Countries and Emerging Economies

Developing nations are those economies with a low-to-middle GDP. While such economies make up about 80% of the global population, they produce a little less than 20% of the world's GDP. An emerging economy, on the other hand, is a developing country or transition economy that is embarking on a new economic reform program in order to achieve higher economic performance, more efficiency in the capital markets and foreign exchange system reforms. Such nations are apt to attract considerable foreign investment both through financial markets as well as in their service sector and other productive industries. Even though the term is quite loosely used, emerging economies range from India and China to countries in Latin America, Africa, the Middle East and Asia.

Many of these nations are relative newcomers to the concept of central banking. The degree of independence of their central banks highly relates to the level of development of the financial sector and political institutions. Yet, one main barrier that renders the independence of central banks in some of these nations as futile is the low level of capitalization and their inability to generate sources of revenue. The case of the Central Bank of Costa Rica is a typical example of a relatively independent central bank, albeit lacking the necessary resources to provide it with de facto effectiveness to implement monetary policy. Another example of an emerging economy facing similar problems of insufficient capital is the Bank of Indonesia, which had insufficient capital at the turn of the century and hence was unable to extend credit assistance to the ailing banks during the 1997 Asian Crisis. For this reason, when central banks suffer from precarious financial conditions that may compromise the conduct of monetary policy, it becomes imperative to recapitalize central banks.

In order to ensure the independence and sovereignty of their central banks, many governments of developing nations and emerging economies have started to periodically increase the capital of their central banks. On the other hand, central banks of the Gulf Cooperation Council nations possess adequate capital but enjoy limited independence. This has urged them to try to form a multinational central bank to ensure independence from national government controls (see the Box "Will the Monetary Union of the Six-Nation Arab Gulf Cooperation Council be Achieved?")

Among the most independent central banks that freely implement monetary policy in Africa are the Reserve Bank of Africa and Central Bank of Egypt, which have considerable levels of independence from political pressures. However, this does not mean that these central banks are oblivious to the general macroeconomic goals of the country. On the contrary, in many cases central banks act in coordination with the fiscal agents of the government, especially at the time of crises.

Global   Will the Monetary Union of the Six-Nation Arab Gulf Cooperation Council be Achieved?

The Gulf Cooperation Council (GCC) is a trade bloc comprising six of the fastest growing Arab nations lying on the Persian Gulf, namely Bahrain, Kuwait, Oman, Qatar, Saudi Arabia and the United Arab Emirates. The GCC was established in May, 1981, but the GCC common market was founded only on January 1, 2008. The GCC common market removes all trade barriers between the member nations, and grants national treatment to GCC businesses and citizens. Its nominal GDP grew from $823 billion in 2007 to $1223 billion in 2008. Moreover, the GCC nations control nearly half the oil reserves in the world.

The heads of five of the central banks of these nations have decided at the dawn of 2009 to establish a new central bank that is expected to be named the Gulf Central Bank (GCB). Oman withdrew in 2006 in order to maintain independent monetary policy. The prime goal of the GCB would be to establish the long-awaited currency union in the 6 Arab Gulf nations by the end of 2010. The new common GCC currency is supposed to be named "khaliji" or "the gulf" and would be pegged to a basket of currencies including the US dollar, the euro, the Japanese yen and the British pound. The prime goal of the common currency, aside from facilitating trade, is to price oil in the new khaliji currency rather than in the volatile U.S. dollar. This is apt to enable these six nations to have a better grip of the prices of oil. Along the lines of the European Central Bank, the new Gulf Central Bank is expected to enjoy more independence than the national central banks that currently lack independence and freedom from their governments. Yet, on May 20th 2009 the United Arab Emirates, the second largest Arab economy after Saudi Arabia, has abruptly withdrawn from the currency union in protest at the decision to locate the GCB in Saudi Arabia's capital, Riyadh. This means that only four nations remain highly committed to the currency union. However, the United Arab Emirates has vowed to consider joining the currency union in case it proves to be successful.

People's Bank of China

The People's Bank of China (PBC), established in December, 1948, is an example of a relatively new central bank in an emerging economy. It acted as China's sole mono-bank, undertaking both commercial banking and central banking roles. This was the pattern of banking in most socialist regimes, since private banks were prohibited from operating in these economic systems. Only in 1980 did the State Council of China divide the commercial banking activities into four state-owned banks; in 1985 the People's Bank of China legally started its functions as a full-fledged central bank with its headquarters in Beijing and nine other regional offices. Since that date, gradual reforms have been introduced to grant the PBC control over the banking sector and the authority to implement monetary policy. However, the PBC is required to report its decisions, even before their implementation, to the State Council with regards to monetary policy, the volume of money supply, interest rates and foreign exchange rates. Thus, this high level of involvement of the State Council in its activities gives the PBC limited independence compared to most central banks in industrial nations.

Another serious problem inherent in the Chinese banking system is the large portfolio of bad debts, which amounted to $700 billion in 2007. This has compelled the PBC to bail out a number of state-owned banks.

Now let us turn our attention to how China has dealt with the banking sector in Hong Kong. In 1997, the UK ceded Hong Kong back to China. However, economically speaking, Hong Kong remains autonomous and independent of China, which is solely responsible for ensuring its military defense and conducting foreign relations on its behalf. Hence, Hong Kong remains as a free trade zone and maintains its own currency, the Hong Kong Dollar. In this context, the People's Bank of China is not responsible for the banking sector in Hong Kong, which is the responsibility of the Hong Kong Monetary Authority.

The HKMA is Hong Kong's central banking institution and was established in April 1993. It has four main functions: regulating and supervising banks and depository institutions; maintaining stability of the currency at the rate of HK$7.80 to one US dollar; managing Hong Kong's official reserves; and overseeing a robust and diverse financial infrastructure. However, the Hong Kong Monetary Authority issues only the 10 dollar bank notes and authorizes three commercial banks, The Hong Kong and Shanghai Banking Corporation Limited, the Standard Chartered Bank (Hong Kong) Limited, and the Bank of China (Hong Kong) Limited, to issue all other bank notes in Hong Kong. Compared to the People's Bank of China, HKMA is far more independent and is capable of maintaining a healthy banking sector.

Multinational Central Banks in Developing Countries

The ECB is not the only multinational central bank in the world, but some developing nations have established multinational central banks in order to enhance economic cooperation with other neighboring nations. Another reason is the lack of adequate funds and expertise necessary to establish such a complex regulatory and supervisory institution. The Eastern Caribbean Central Bank (ECCB) comprises of eight member nations, out of which six are independent nations, while two are territories of the United Kingdom. The ECCB was established on October 1, 1983 and currently consists of Antigua and Barbuda, Commonwealth of Dominica, Grenada, Montserrat, St Kitts and Nevis, Saint Lucia and Saint Vincent, The Grenadines and Anguilla. All of these countries are small, vulnerable economies that need to unite in order to achieve economic development. In a similar way to the European Central Bank, a chairman is elected annually on a rotating basis and the Monetary Council is responsible for conducting monetary policy and ensuring the stability of the common currency unit, the EC Dollar. However, unlike the ECB none of these nations possesses its own individual central bank.

Similar trends are followed in Africa, where most African nations have their own central banks, except for two regions that have multinational central banks. Banque Centrale des Etats de l'Afrique de l'Ouest, or the Central Bank of Western Africa, engulfs eight West African nations that use the West African CFA franc as their common currency. Similarly, six Central African nations are members of Banque des Etats de l'Afrique Centrale, or The Central Bank of Central Africa, and use the Central African CFA franc as their legal tender.

Central Bank Reforms in South America

In various Latin American countries central banks have found themselves in considerable financial distress, leading to recurrent banking crises. In the 1980s, Latin American countries were in an especially serious situation as three or four-digit rates of inflation were reported since the eighties of last century. For this reason, governments embarked on central bank reforms; Chile was the pioneer, where in 1989 its central bank was granted more independence in return for enhanced transparency and accountability. In order to reverse inflation, central banks in Brazil, Chile, Colombia, Mexico, and Peru adopted a nominal anchor by introducing inflation targeting. Moreover, since the 1990s most South American nations have started to separate central bank appointments from electoral calendars and granted central banks the right to conduct monetary policy without government interference. In exchange, central banks were made accountable for achieving specific inflation targets rather than focusing on economic growth.

Currency Unions in Developing Nations

Finally, some very poor and small developing countries unilaterally adopt the currency of larger "anchor" countries. For example, Panama, El Salvador, Ecuador, and a number of smaller Caribbean countries currently use the U.S. dollar, since they do not possess a domestic currency.[5] For example, Ecuador discarded its national currency, the sucre, in 2000 and adopted the U.S. dollar as its official currency. This was due to the fact that the exchange rate of the sucre declined from 25 sucres per U.S. dollar in 1980 to 25,000 in 2000. In such cases, the national central bank cannot carry out monetary policy and loses its ability to influence the value of the currency; this limits the role of the central bank to supervise banks in the country. Similarly, the African nations of Swaziland and Lesotho use the South African rand as their legal tender.

The Trend Toward Greater Independence

As our survey of the structure and independence of the major central banks indicates, in recent years we have seen a remarkable trend toward increasing independence. It used to be that the Federal Reserve was substantially more independent than almost all other central banks, with the exception of those in Germany and Switzerland. Now the newly established European Central Bank is far more independent than the Fed, and

---

[5]This is known as official dollarization, not to be confused with unofficial dollarization that occurs when the currency of a foreign country circulates widely side-by-side with the national currency.

greater independence has been granted to central banks such as the Bank of England and the Bank of Japan, putting them more on a par with the Fed, as well as to central banks in such diverse countries as New Zealand, Sweden, and the Euro nations. Both theory and experience suggest that more independent central banks produce better monetary policy, thus providing an impetus for this trend.

EXPLAINING CENTRAL BANK BEHAVIOR

One view of government bureaucratic behavior is that bureaucracies serve the public interest (this is the *public interest view*). Yet some economists have developed a theory of bureaucratic behavior that suggests other factors that influence how bureaucracies operate. The *theory of bureaucratic behavior* suggests that the objective of a bureaucracy is to maximize its own welfare, just as a consumer's behavior is motivated by the maximization of personal welfare and a firm's behavior is motivated by the maximization of profits. The welfare of a bureaucracy is related to its power and prestige. Thus this theory suggests that an important factor affecting a central bank's behavior is its attempt to increase its power and prestige.

What predictions does this view of a central bank suggest? One is that the central bank will fight vigorously to preserve its autonomy.

Another prediction is that central banks will try to avoid conflict with powerful groups that may threaten to curtail their power and reduce their autonomy. This behavior may take several forms.

The desire of central banks to hold as much power as possible also explains why they vigorously try to gain control over more banks. The campaign culminated in legislation that expanded jurisdiction of the Fed's reserve requirements to *all* banks.

Yet we must recognize that this view of a central bank as being solely concerned with its own self-interest is too extreme. Maximizing one's welfare does not rule out altruism. (You may give generously to a charity because it makes you feel good about yourself, but in the process you are helping a worthy cause.) Central banks are surely concerned that they conduct monetary policy in the public interest. However, much uncertainty and disagreement exist over what monetary policy should be.[6] When it is unclear what is in the public interest, other motives may influence the central bank's behavior. In these situations, the theory of bureaucratic behavior may be a useful guide to predicting what motivates the Fed and other central banks.

SHOULD THE CENTRAL BANKS BE INDEPENDENT?

As we have seen, an increasing number of nations have been giving more independence to their central banks. Politicians who strongly oppose a central bank policy often want to bring it under their supervision so as to impose a policy more to their liking. Should the central bank be independent, or would we be better off with a central bank under the control of the president or the parliament?

---

[6]One example of the uncertainty about how best to conduct monetary policy was discussed in Chapter 3. Economists are not sure how to measure money. So even if economists agreed that controlling the quantity of money is the appropriate way to conduct monetary policy (a controversial position, as we will see in later chapters), the Fed cannot be sure which monetary aggregate it should control.

The Case for Independence

The strongest argument for an independent central bank rests on the view that subjecting the central banks to more political pressures would impart an inflationary bias to monetary policy. In the view of many observers, politicians may be shortsighted because they are driven by the need to win their next election. With this as the primary goal, they are unlikely to focus on long-run objectives, such as promoting a stable price level. Instead, they will seek short-run solutions to problems, such as high unemployment and high interest rates, even if the short-run solutions have undesirable long-run consequences. For example, we saw in Chapter 5 that high money growth could lead initially to a drop in interest rates but may cause an increase later as inflation heats up. Would a central bank under the control of the parliament or the president be more likely to pursue a policy of excessive money growth when interest rates are high, even though it would eventually lead to inflation and even higher interest rates in the future? The advocates of an independent central bank say yes. They believe that a politically insulated central bank is more likely to be concerned with long-run objectives and thus be a defender of a sound dollar and a stable price level.

A variation on the preceding argument is that the political process in democratic societies could lead to a **political business cycle**, in which just before an election, expansionary policies are pursued to lower unemployment and interest rates. After the election, the bad effects of these policies—high inflation and high interest rates—cause problems, requiring contractionary policies that politicians hope the public will forget before the next election. There is some evidence that such a political business cycle exists in the United States, and a Federal Reserve under the control of Congress or the president may make the cycle even more pronounced.

Putting the central bank under the control of the treasury or fiscal agent of the government (making it more subject to influence by the president) is also considered dangerous because the central bank can be used to facilitate financing of large budget deficits by its purchases of government securities.[7] Government pressure on the central bank to "help out" could lead to more inflation in the economy. An independent central bank is better able to resist this pressure from the government.

Another argument for central bank independence is that control of monetary policy is too important to leave to politicians, a group that has repeatedly demonstrated a lack of expertise at making hard decisions on issues of great economic importance, such as reducing the budget deficit or reforming the banking system. Another way to state this argument is in terms of the principal-agent problem discussed in Chapters 8, 9, and 11. Both the central bank and politicians are agents of the public (the principals), and as we have seen, both politicians and the central bank have incentives to act in their own interest rather than in the interest of the public. The argument supporting central bank independence is that the principal-agent problem is worse for politicians than for the central bank because politicians have fewer incentives to act in the public interest.

Indeed, some politicians may prefer to have an independent central bank, which can be used as a public "whipping boy" to take some of the heat off their backs. It is possible that a politician who in private opposes an inflationary monetary policy will be forced to support such a policy in public for fear of not being re-elected. An independent central bank can pursue policies that are politically unpopular, yet in the public interest.

---

[7]Most central banks are prohibited from buying government securities directly from the fiscal agent of the government (except to roll over maturing securities); instead, central banks buy these securities on the open market. One possible reason for this prohibition is that the central bank would find it very costly to finance large fiscal budget deficits.

The Case Against Independence

Proponents of a central bank under the control of the president or the parliament argue that it is undemocratic to have monetary policy (which affects almost everyone in the economy) controlled by an elite group that is responsible to no one. The current lack of accountability of a central bank has serious consequences. If the central bank performs badly, there is no provision for replacing members (as there is with politicians). It is true that the central bank needs to pursue long-run objectives, but elected officials of the parliament vote on long-run issues also (foreign policy, for example).

The public holds the president, the cabinet, and the parliament responsible for the economic well-being of the country, yet they lack control over the government agency that may well be the most important factor in determining the health of the economy. In addition, to achieve a cohesive program that will promote economic stability, monetary policy must be coordinated with fiscal policy (management of government spending and taxation). Only by placing monetary policy under the control of the politicians who also control fiscal policy can these two policies be prevented from working at cross-purposes.

Another argument against central bank independence is that an independent central bank has not always used its freedom successfully. To cite an example, the Fed failed miserably in its stated role as lender of last resort during the Great Depression, and its independence certainly didn't prevent it from pursuing an overly expansionary monetary policy in the 1960s and 1970s that contributed to rapid inflation in this period.

Our earlier discussion also suggests that central banks are not immune from political pressures.[8] Independence may encourage them to pursue a course of narrow self-interest rather than the public interest.

There is yet no consensus on whether central bank independence is a good thing, although public support for independence of the central bank seems to have been growing in both the United States and abroad. As you may expect, people who like the central bank policies are more likely to support its independence, while those who dislike its policies advocate a less independent central bank.

Central Bank Independence and Macroeconomic Performance Throughout the World

We have seen that advocates of an independent central bank believe that macroeconomic performance will be improved by making the central bank more independent. Recent research seems to support this conjecture: when central banks are ranked from least independent to most independent, inflation performance is found to be the best for countries with the most independent central banks.[9] Although a more independent central bank appears to lead to a lower inflation rate, this is not achieved at the expense of poorer real economic performance. Countries with independent central banks are no

---

[8]For evidence on this issue, see Robert E. Weintraub, "Congressional Supervision of Monetary Policy," *Journal of Monetary Economics* 4 (1978): 341–362. Some economists suggest that lessening the independence of the Fed might even reduce the incentive for politically motivated monetary policy; see Milton Friedman, "Monetary Policy: Theory and Practice," *Journal of Money, Credit and Banking* 14 (1982): 98–118.

[9]Alberto Alesina and Lawrence H. Summers, "Central Bank Independence and Macroeconomic Performance: Some Comparative Evidence," *Journal of Money, Credit and Banking* 25 (1993): 151–162. However, Adam Posen, "Central Bank Independence and Disinflationary Credibility: A Missing Link," Federal Reserve Bank of New York Staff Report No. 1, May 1995, has cast some doubt on whether the causality runs from central bank independence to improved inflation performance.

more likely to have high unemployment or greater output fluctuations than countries with less independent central banks.

In the last few years maintaining low levels of inflation has become an important societal goal. In fact, since the 1990s the Bank of Israel has been granted more independence in order to target inflation, where the CPI is allowed to rise only within the range of 1% and 3% per annum. Inflation became a staggering problem from the mid-1980s for Israel which suffered from an extraordinary inflationary cycle during the 1980s, forcing it to adopt the new sheqel to replace the sheqel at the rate of 1:1000. The high level of independence of the Bank of Israel grants the Governor the sole responsibility of managing interest rates after consultations with directors and economists of the bank. Is this level of independence desirable? We must remember that is not the only macroeconomic goal. The current global financial crisis revealed to us that monetary policy may have devastating effects on other real economic variables. While increasing numbers of nations have granted their central banks more independence with the hope of maintaining low and stable inflation, there is always the danger that an independent central bank will not be accountable. Hence, delegating the power to implement far-reaching policies to an independent institution requires guaranteeing its accountability. For this reason, many policy makers have called for reforms that grant central banks instrument independence, while preserving the right of governments to establish policy goals. Only by making central banks accountable to the parliament would we be able to monitor their efficiency of central bank in achieving these policy goals.

SUMMARY

1. The six basic goals of monetary policy are price stability (the primary goal), high employment, economic growth, stability of financial markets, interest-rate stability, and stability in foreign exchange markets.

2. Having a strong nominal anchor is a key element in successful monetary policy. It helps promote price stability by tying down inflation expectations and limiting the time-inconsistency problem, in which monetary policymakers conduct monetary policy in a discretionary way that focuses on short-run objectives but produces poor long-run outcomes.

3. The Federal Reserve System was created in 1913 to lessen the frequency of bank panics. Because of public hostility to central banks and the centralization of power, the Federal Reserve System was created with many checks and balances to diffuse power.

4. The structure of the Federal Reserve System consists of twelve regional Federal Reserve banks, around 2,900 member commercial banks, the Board of Governors of the Federal Reserve System, the Federal Open Market Committee (FOMC), and the Federal Advisory Council. Although on paper the Federal Reserve System appears to be decentralized, in practice it has come to function as a unified central bank controlled by the Board of Governors, especially the board's chairman.

5. The Federal Reserve is more independent than most agencies of the U.S. government, but it is still subject to political pressures because the legislation that structures the Fed is written by Congress and can be changed at any time.

6. The European System of Central Banks has a fairly similar structure to the Federal Reserve System, with each member country having a National Central Bank, and an Executive Board of the European Central Bank being located in Frankfurt, Germany. The Governing Council, which is made up of the six members of the Executive Board (which includes the president of the European Central Bank) and the presidents of the National Central Banks, makes the decisions on monetary policy. The Eurosystem, which was established under the terms of the Maastricht Treaty, is even more independent than the Federal Reserve System because its charter cannot be changed by legislation. Indeed, it is the most independent central bank in the world.

7. Most developing nations and transition economies have reformed their central banks and granted them increasing levels of independence during the last decades of the twentieth century.

8. There has been a remarkable trend toward increasing independence of central banks throughout the world. Greater independence has been granted to central banks such as the Bank of England and the Bank of Japan in recent years, as well as to other central banks in such diverse countries as New Zealand and Sweden. Both theory and experience suggest that more independent central banks produce better monetary policy.

9. The theory of bureaucratic behavior suggests that one factor driving central banks' behavior might be an attempt to increase their power and prestige. This view explains many central bank actions, although central banks may also act in the public interest.

10. The case for an independent central bank rests on the view that curtailing its independence and subjecting it to more political pressures would impart an inflationary bias to monetary policy. An independent central bank can afford to take the long view and not respond to short-run problems that will result in expansionary monetary policy and a political business cycle. The case against an independent central bank holds that it is undemocratic to have monetary policy (so important to the public) controlled by an elite that is not accountable to the public. An independent central bank also makes the coordination of monetary and fiscal policy difficult.

KEY TERMS

Board of Governors of the Federal Reserve System, p. 321

dual mandate, p. 320

Federal Open Market Committee (FOMC), p. 321

Federal Reserve banks, p. 321

goal independence, p. 324

hierarchical mandates, p. 319

instrument independence, p. 324

natural rate of unemployment, p. 318

nominal anchor, p. 316

open market operations, p. 322

political business cycle, p. 338

price stability, p. 315

time-inconsistency problem, p. 316

QUESTIONS AND PROBLEMS

All questions and problems are available in (myeconlab) *at* www.myeconlab.com/mishkin.

1. Why was the Federal Reserve System set up with twelve regional Federal Reserve banks rather than one central bank, as in other countries?

2. What political realities might explain why the Federal Reserve Act of 1913 placed two Federal Reserve Banks in Missouri?

3. "The Federal Reserve System resembles the U.S. Constitution in that it was designed with many checks and balances." Discuss.

4. In what ways can the regional Federal Reserve Banks influence the conduct of monetary policy?

5. Which entities in the Federal Reserve System and the European Central Bank control the discount rate? Reserve requirements? Open market operations?

6. Do you think that the fourteen-year nonrenewable terms for governors effectively insulate the Board of Governors from political pressure?

7. Compare the structure and independence of the Federal Reserve System and the European System of Central Banks.

8. The Fed is the most independent of all U.S. government agencies. What is the main difference between it and other government agencies that explains the Fed's greater independence?

9. What is the primary tool that Congress uses to exercise some control over the Fed?

10. In the 1960s and 1970s, the Federal Reserve System lost member banks at a rapid rate. How can the theory of bureaucratic behavior explain the Fed's campaign for legislation to require all commercial banks to become members? Was the Fed successful in this campaign?

11. Explain why eleven states of the EU have opted not to adopt the euro as their domestic currency.

12. What are the main difficulties encountered by the newly established central banks in transition economies?

13. What are the reasons that compel some developing nations to adopt currency unions?

14. "The theory of bureaucratic behavior indicates that the Fed never operates in the public interest." Is this statement true, false, or uncertain? Explain your answer.

15. Why could eliminating the central bank's independence lead to a more pronounced political business cycle?

16. "The independence of the Fed leaves it completely unaccountable for its actions." Is this statement true, false, or uncertain? Explain your answer.

17. "The independence of the central bank has meant that it takes the long view and not the short view." Is this statement true, false, or uncertain? Explain your answer.

18. While the Fed promotes secrecy by not releasing the minutes of the FOMC meetings to Congress or the public immediately, the ECB holds a press conference after each of its meetings. Discuss the pros and cons of each of these policies.

WEB EXERCISES

1. Go to www.federalreserve.gov/ and click on "About the Fed." Then click on "The Federal Reserve System" and then on "Structure." According to the Federal Reserve, what is the most important responsibility of the Board of Governors?

2. Go to the previous site and click on "Monetary Policy." Then click on "Reports" and then go on "Beige Book." According to the summary of the most recently published book, is the economy weakening or strengthening?

WEB REFERENCES

www.federalreserve.gov/pubs/frseries/frseri.htm

Information on the structure of the Federal Reserve System.

www.federalreserve.gov/otherfrb.htm

Addresses and phone numbers of Federal Reserve Banks, branches, and RCPCs and links to the main pages of the 12 reserve banks and Board of Governors.

www.federalreserve.gov/bios/boardmembership.htm

Lists all the members of the Board of Governors of the Federal Reserve since its inception.

www.federalreserve.gov/fomc

Find general information on the FOMC; its schedule of meetings, statements, minutes, and transcripts; information on its members; and the "beige book."

www.ecb.int

The website for the European Central Bank.

www.bank-banque-canada.ca/

The website for the Bank of Canada.

www.bankofengland.co.uk/index.htm

The website for the Bank of England.

www.boj.or.jp/en/index.htm

The website for the Bank of Japan.

www.pbc.gov.cn/english

The website for the People's Bank of China.

MyEconLab CAN HELP YOU GET A BETTER GRADE

If your exam were tomorrow, would you be ready? For each chapter, MyEconLab Practice Test and Study Plans pinpoint which sections you have mastered and which ones you need to study. That way, you are more efficient with your study time, and you are better prepared for your exams.

To see how it works, turn to page 20 and then go to: www.myeconlab.com/mishkin

14

The Money Supply Process

Preview

As we saw in Chapter 5 and will see in later chapters on monetary theory, movements in the money supply affect interest rates and the overall health of the economy and thus affect us all. Because of its far-reaching effects on economic activity, it is important to understand how the money supply is determined. Who controls it? What causes it to change? How might control of it be improved? In this and subsequent chapters, we answer these questions by providing a detailed description of the *money supply process*, the mechanism that determines the level of the money supply.

Because deposits at banks are by far the largest component of the money supply, understanding how these deposits are created is the first step in understanding the money supply process. This chapter provides an overview of how the banking system creates deposits, and describes the basic principles of the money supply, needed to understand later chapters.

THREE PLAYERS IN THE MONEY SUPPLY PROCESS

The "cast of characters" in the money supply story is as follows:

1. The *central bank*—the government agency that oversees the banking system and is responsible for the conduct of monetary policy; in the United States, it is the Federal Reserve System
2. *Banks* (depository institutions)—the financial intermediaries that accept deposits from individuals and institutions and make loans: commercial banks, savings and loan associations, mutual savings banks, and credit unions
3. *Depositors*—individuals and institutions that hold deposits in banks

Of the three players, the central bank—the Federal Reserve System—is the most important. The Fed's conduct of monetary policy involves actions that affect its balance sheet (holdings of assets and liabilities), to which we turn now.

THE FED'S BALANCE SHEET

The operation of the Fed and its monetary policy involve actions that affect its balance sheet, its holdings of assets and liabilities. Here we discuss a simplified balance sheet that includes just four items that are essential to our understanding of the money supply process.[1]

Federal Reserve System

Assets	Liabilities
Government securities	Currency in circulation
Discount loans	Reserves

Liabilities

The two liabilities on the balance sheet, currency in circulation and reserves, are often referred to as the *monetary liabilities* of the Fed. They are an important part of the money supply story, because increases in either or both will lead to an increase in the money supply (everything else being constant). The sum of the Fed's monetary liabilities (currency in circulation and reserves) and the U.S. Treasury's monetary liabilities (Treasury currency in circulation, primarily coins) is called the **monetary base**. When discussing the monetary base, we will focus only on the monetary liabilities of the Fed because the monetary liabilities of the Treasury account for less than 10% of the base.[2]

1. Currency in circulation. The Fed issues currency (those green-and-gray pieces of paper in your wallet that say "Federal Reserve Note" at the top). Currency in circulation is the amount of currency in the hands of the public. Currency held by depository institutions is also a liability of the Fed, but is counted as part of the reserves.

Federal Reserve notes are IOUs from the Fed to the bearer and are also liabilities, but unlike most, they promise to pay back the bearer solely with Federal Reserve notes; that is, they pay off IOUs with other IOUs. Accordingly, if you bring a $100 bill to the Federal Reserve and demand payment, you will receive either two $50s, five $20s, ten $10s, or one hundred $1 bills.

People are more willing to accept IOUs from the Fed than from you or me because Federal Reserve notes are a recognized medium of exchange; that is, they are accepted as a means of payment and so function as money. Unfortunately, neither you nor I can convince people that our IOUs are worth anything more than the paper they are written on.[3]

---

[1] A detailed discussion of the Fed's balance sheet and the factors that affect the monetary base can be found in the appendix to this chapter, which you can find on this book's website at www.aw.com/mishkin.

[2] It is also safe to ignore the Treasury's monetary liabilities when discussing the monetary base because the Treasury cannot actively supply its monetary liabilities to the economy due to legal restrictions.

[3] The currency item on our balance sheet refers only to currency *in circulation*—that is, the amount in the hands of the public. Currency that has been printed by the U.S. Bureau of Engraving and Printing is not automatically a liability of the Fed. For example, consider the importance of having $1 million of your own IOUs printed up. You give out $100 worth to other people and keep the other $999,900 in your pocket. The $999,900 of IOUs does not make you richer or poorer and does not affect your indebtedness. You care only about the $100 of liabilities from the $100 of circulated IOUs. The same reasoning applies for the Fed in regard to its Federal Reserve notes.

For similar reasons, the currency component of the money supply, no matter how it is defined, includes only currency in circulation. It does not include any additional currency that is not yet in the hands of the public. The fact that currency has been printed but is not circulating means that it is not anyone's asset or liability and thus cannot affect anyone's behavior. Therefore, it makes sense not to include it in the money supply.

2. Reserves. All banks have an account at the Fed in which they hold deposits. **Reserves** consist of deposits at the Fed plus currency that is physically held by banks (called *vault cash* because it is stored in bank vaults). Reserves are assets for the banks but liabilities for the Fed, because the banks can demand payment on them at any time and the Fed is required to satisfy its obligation by paying Federal Reserve notes. As you will see, an increase in reserves leads to an increase in the level of deposits and hence in the money supply.

Total reserves can be divided into two categories: reserves that the Fed requires banks to hold (**required reserves**) and any additional reserves the banks choose to hold (**excess reserves**). For example, the Fed might require that for every dollar of deposits at a depository institution, a certain fraction (say, 10 cents) must be held as reserves. This fraction (10%) is called the **required reserve ratio**.

Assets

The two assets on the Fed's balance sheet are important for two reasons. First, changes in the asset items lead to changes in reserves, the monetary base, and consequently to changes in the money supply. Second, because these assets (government securities and discount loans) earn interest while the liabilities (currency in circulation and reserves) do not, the Fed makes billions of dollars every year—its assets earn income, and its liabilities cost nothing. Although it returns most of its earnings to the federal government, the Fed does spend some of it on "worthy causes," such as supporting economic research.

1. Government securities. This category of assets covers the Fed's holdings of securities issued by the U.S. Treasury. As you will see, one way the Fed can provide reserves to the banking system is by purchasing securities, thereby increasing its holdings of these assets. An increase in government securities held by the Fed leads to an increase in the money supply.

2. Discount loans. The second way the Fed can provide reserves to the banking system is by making discount loans to banks. For these banks, the discount loans they have taken out are referred to as *borrowings from the Fed* or, alternatively, as *borrowed reserves*. These loans appear as a liability on banks' balance sheets. An increase in discount loans can also be the source of an increase in the money supply. The interest rate charged banks for these loans is called the **discount rate**.

CONTROL OF THE MONETARY BASE

The *monetary base* (also called **high-powered money**) equals currency in circulation C plus the total reserves in banking system R.[4] The monetary base MB can be expressed as

$$MB = C + R$$

The Federal Reserve exercises control over the monetary base through its purchases or sale of government securities in the open market, called **open market operations**, and through its extension of discount loans to banks.

---

[4]Here currency in circulation includes both Federal Reserve currency (Federal Reserve notes) and Treasury currency (primarily coins).

Federal Reserve Open Market Operations

The primary way in which the Fed causes changes in the monetary base is through its open market operations. A purchase of bonds by the Fed is called an **open market purchase**, and a sale of bonds by the Fed is called an **open market sale**.

Open Market Purchase from a Bank   Suppose that the Fed purchases $100 of bonds from a bank and pays for them with a $100 check. To understand what occurs as a result of this transaction, we look at *T-accounts*, which list only the changes that occur in balance sheet items starting from the initial balance sheet position. The bank will either deposit the check in its account with the Fed or cash it in for currency, which will be counted as vault cash. Either action means that the bank will find itself with $100 more reserves and a reduction in its holdings of securities of $100. The T-account for the banking system, then, is

Banking System

Assets		Liabilities
Securities	−$100	
Reserves	+$100	

The Fed, meanwhile, finds that its liabilities have increased by the additional $100 of reserves, while its assets have increased by the $100 of additional securities that it now holds. Its T-account is

Federal Reserve System

Assets		Liabilities	
Securities	+$100	Reserves	+$100

The net result of this open market purchase is that reserves have increased by $100, the amount of the open market purchase. Because there has been no change of currency in circulation, the monetary base has also risen by $100.

Open Market Purchase from the Nonbank Public   To understand what happens when there is an open market purchase from the nonbank public, we must look at two cases. First, let's assume that the person or corporation that sells the $100 of bonds to the Fed deposits the Fed's check in the local bank. The nonbank public's T-account after this transaction is

Nonbank Public

Assets		Liabilities
Securities	−$100	
Checkable deposits	+$100	

When the bank receives the check, it credits the depositor's account with the $100 and then deposits the check in its account with the Fed, thereby adding to its reserves. The banking system's T-account becomes

Banking System

Assets		Liabilities	
Reserves	+$100	Checkable deposits	+$100

The effect on the Fed's balance sheet is that it has gained $100 of securities in its assets column, while it has an increase of $100 of reserves in its liabilities column:

Federal Reserve System

Assets		Liabilities	
Securities	+$100	Reserves	+$100

As you can see in the above T-account, when the Fed's check is deposited in a bank, the net result of the Fed's open market purchase from the nonbank public is identical to the effect of its open market purchase from a bank: Reserves increase by the amount of the open market purchase, and the monetary base increases by the same amount.

If, however, the person or corporation selling the bonds to the Fed cashes the Fed's check either at a local bank or at a Federal Reserve bank for currency, the effect on reserves is different.[5] This seller will receive currency of $100 while reducing holdings of securities by $100. The nonbank public's seller's T-account will be

Nonbank Public

Assets		Liabilities
Securities	−$100	
Currency	+$100	

---

[5]If the bond seller cashes the check at the local bank, the bank's balance sheet will be unaffected, because the $100 of vault cash that it pays out will be exactly matched by the deposit of the $100 check at the Fed. Thus its reserves will remain the same, and there will be no effect on its T-account. That is why a T-account for the banking system does not appear here.

The Fed now finds that it has exchanged $100 of currency for $100 of securities, so its T-account is

Federal Reserve System

Assets		Liabilities	
Securities	+$100	Currency in circulation	+$100

The net effect of the open market purchase in this case is that reserves are unchanged, while currency in circulation increases by the $100 of the open market purchase. Thus the monetary base increases by the $100 amount of the open market purchase, while reserves do not. This contrasts with the case in which the seller of the bonds deposits the Fed's check in a bank; in that case, reserves increase by $100, and so does the monetary base.

The analysis reveals that ***the effect of an open market purchase on reserves depends on whether the seller of the bonds keeps the proceeds from the sale in currency or in deposits***. If the proceeds are kept in currency, the open market purchase has no effect on reserves; if the proceeds are kept as deposits, reserves increase by the amount of the open market purchase.

The effect of an open market purchase on the monetary base, however, is always the same (the monetary base increases by the amount of the purchase) whether the seller of the bonds keeps the proceeds in deposits or in currency. The impact of an open market purchase on reserves is much more uncertain than its impact on the monetary base.

Open Market Sale   If the Fed sells $100 of bonds to a bank or the nonbank public, the monetary base will decrease by $100. For example, if the Fed sells the bonds to an individual who pays for them with currency, the buyer exchanges $100 of currency for $100 of bonds, and the resulting T-account is

Nonbank Public

Assets		Liabilities	
Securities	+$100		
Currency	−$100		

The Fed, for its part, has reduced its holdings of securities by $100 and has also lowered its monetary liability by accepting the currency as payment for its bonds, thereby reducing the amount of currency in circulation by $100:

Federal Reserve System

Assets		Liabilities	
Securities	−$100	Currency in circulation	−$100

The effect of the open market sale of $100 of bonds is to reduce the monetary base by an equal amount, although reserves remain unchanged. Manipulations of T-accounts in cases in which the buyer of the bonds is a bank or the buyer pays for the bonds with a check written on a checkable deposit account at a local bank lead to the same $100 reduction in the monetary base, although the reduction occurs because the level of reserves has fallen by $100.

The following conclusion can now be drawn from our analysis of open market purchases and sales: ***The effect of open market operations on the monetary base is much more certain than the effect on reserves.*** Therefore, the Fed can control the monetary base with open market operations more effectively than it can control reserves.

Open market operations can also be done in other assets besides government bonds and have the same effects on the monetary base we have described here.

Shifts from Deposits into Currency

Even if the Fed does not conduct open market operations, a shift from deposits to currency will affect the reserves in the banking system. However, such a shift will have no effect on the monetary base, another reason why the Fed has more control over the monetary base than over reserves.

Let's suppose that Jane Brown (who opened a $100 checking account at the First National Bank in Chapter 10) decides that tellers are so abusive in all banks that she closes her account by withdrawing the $100 balance in cash and vows never to deposit it in a bank again. The effect on the T-account of the nonbank public is

Nonbank Public

Assets		Liabilities
Checkable deposits	−$100	
Currency	+$100	

The banking system loses $100 of deposits and hence $100 of reserves:

Banking System

Assets		Liabilities	
Reserves	−$100	Checkable deposits	−$100

For the Fed, Jane Brown's action means that there is $100 of additional currency circulating in the hands of the public, while reserves in the banking system have fallen by $100. The Fed's T-account is

Federal Reserve System

Assets	Liabilities	
	Currency in circulation	+$100
	Reserves	−$100

The net effect on the monetary liabilities of the Fed is a wash; the monetary base is unaffected by Jane Brown's disgust at the banking system. But reserves are affected. Random fluctuations of reserves can occur as a result of random shifts into currency and out of deposits, and vice versa. The same is not true for the monetary base, making it a more stable variable.

Discount Loans

In this chapter so far we have seen how changes in the monetary base occur as a result of open market operations. However, the monetary base is also affected when the Fed makes a discount loan to a bank. When the Fed makes a $100 discount loan to the First National Bank, the bank is credited with $100 of reserves from the proceeds of the loan. The effects on the balance sheets of the banking system and the Fed are illustrated by the following T-accounts:

Banking System

Assets		Liabilities	
Reserves	+$100	Discount loans (borrowings from the Fed)	+$100

Federal Reserve System

Assets		Liabilities	
Discount loans (borrowings from the Fed)	+$100	Reserves	+$100

The monetary liabilities of the Fed have now increased by $100, and the monetary base, too, has increased by this amount. However, if a bank pays off a loan from the Fed, thereby reducing its borrowings from the Fed by $100, the T-accounts of the banking system and the Fed are as follows:

Banking System

Assets		Liabilities	
Reserves	−$100	Discount loans (borrowings from the Fed)	−$100

Federal Reserve System

Assets		Liabilities	
Discount loans (borrowings from the Fed)	−$100	Reserves	−$100

The net effect on the monetary liabilities of the Fed, and hence on the monetary base, is a reduction of $100. We see that the monetary base changes one-for-one with the change in the borrowings from the Fed.

Other Factors That Affect the Monetary Base

So far in this chapter, it seems as though the Fed has complete control of the monetary base through its open market operations and discount loans. However, the world is a little bit more complicated for the Fed. Two important items that affect the monetary base, but are not controlled by the Fed, are *float* and *Treasury deposits at the Fed*. When the Fed clears checks for banks, it often credits the amount of the check to a bank that has deposited it (increases the bank's reserves) before it debits (decreases the reserves of) the bank on which the check is drawn. The resulting temporary net increase in the total amount of reserves in the banking system (and hence in the monetary base) occurring from the Fed's check-clearing process is called **float**. When the U.S. Treasury moves deposits from commercial banks to its account at the Fed, leading to an increase in *Treasury deposits at the Fed*, it causes a deposit outflow at these banks like that shown in Chapter 10 and thus causes reserves in the banking system and the monetary base to decrease. Thus *float* (affected by random events such as the weather, which affects how quickly checks are presented for payment) and *Treasury deposits at the Fed* (determined by the U.S. Treasury's actions) both affect the monetary base but are not controlled by the Fed at all. Decisions by the U.S. Treasury to have the Fed intervene in the foreign exchange market also affect the monetary base.

Overview of the Fed's Ability to Control the Monetary Base

Our discussion above indicates that there are two primary features that determine the monetary base, open market operations and discount lending. Whereas, the amount of open market purchases or sales is completely controlled by the Fed's placing orders with dealers in bond markets, the central bank cannot unilaterally determine, and therefore cannot perfectly predict, the amount of borrowing by banks from the Fed. The Federal Reserve sets the discount rate (interest rate on discount loans), and then banks make decisions about whether to borrow. The amount of discount loans, though influenced by the Fed's setting of the discount rate, is not completely controlled by the Fed; banks' decisions play a role, too.

Therefore, we might want to split the monetary base into two components: one that the Fed can control completely and another that is less tightly controlled. The less tightly controlled component is the amount of the base that is created by discount loans from the Fed. The remainder of the base (called the **nonborrowed monetary base**) is under the Fed's control, because it results primarily from open market operations.[6] The nonborrowed monetary base is formally defined as the monetary base minus banks' borrowings from the Fed (discount loans), which are referred to as **borrowed reserves**:

$$MB_n = MB - BR$$

where
$\quad MB_n = $ nonborrowed monetary base
$\quad MB = $ monetary base
$\quad BR = $ borrowed reserves from the Fed

---

[6]Actually, there are other items on the Fed's balance sheet (discussed in the appendix on the website) that affect the magnitude of the nonborrowed monetary base. Because their effects on the nonborrowed base relative to open market operations are both small and predictable, these other items do not present the Fed with difficulties in controlling the nonborrowed base.

Factors not controlled at all by the Fed (for example, float and Treasury deposits with the Fed) undergo substantial short-run variations and can be important sources of fluctuations in the monetary base over time periods as short as a week. However, these fluctuations are usually predictable and so can be offset through open market operations. *Although float and Treasury deposits with the Fed undergo substantial short-run fluctuations, which complicate control of the monetary base, they do not prevent the Fed from accurately controlling it.*

MULTIPLE DEPOSIT CREATION: A SIMPLE MODEL

With our understanding of how the Federal Reserve controls the monetary base and how banks operate (Chapter 10), we now have the tools necessary to explain how deposits are created. When the Fed supplies the banking system with $1 of additional reserves, deposits increase by a multiple of this amount—a process called **multiple deposit creation**.

Deposit Creation: The Single Bank

Suppose that the $100 open market purchase described earlier was conducted with the First National Bank. After the Fed has bought the $100 bond from the First National Bank, the bank finds that it has an increase in reserves of $100. To analyze what the bank will do with these additional reserves, assume that the bank does not want to hold excess reserves because it earns little interest on them. We begin the analysis with the following T-account:

First National Bank			
Assets		Liabilities	
Securities	−$100		
Reserves	+$100		

Because the bank has no increase in its checkable deposits, required reserves remain the same, and the bank finds that its additional $100 of reserves means that its excess reserves have increased by $100. Let's say that the bank decides to make a loan equal in amount to the $100 increase in excess reserves. When the bank makes the loan, it sets up a checking account for the borrower and puts the proceeds of the loan into this account. In this way, the bank alters its balance sheet by increasing its liabilities with $100 of checkable deposits and at the same time increasing its assets with the $100 loan. The resulting T-account looks like this:

First National Bank			
Assets		Liabilities	
Securities	−$100	Checkable deposits	+$100
Reserves	+$100		
Loans	+$100		

The bank has created checkable deposits by its act of lending. Because checkable deposits are part of the money supply, the bank's act of lending has, in fact, created money.

In its current balance sheet position, the First National Bank still has excess reserves and so might want to make additional loans. However, these reserves will not stay at the bank for very long. The borrower took out a loan not to leave $100 idle at the First National Bank but to purchase goods and services from other individuals and corporations. When the borrower makes these purchases by writing checks, they will be deposited at other banks, and the $100 of reserves will leave the First National Bank. *A bank cannot safely make loans for an amount greater than the excess reserves it has before it makes the loan.*

The final T-account of the First National Bank is

First National Bank

Assets		Liabilities
Securities	−$100	
Loans	+$100	

The increase in reserves of $100 has been converted into additional loans of $100 at the First National Bank, plus an additional $100 of deposits that have made their way to other banks. (All the checks written on accounts at the First National Bank are deposited in banks rather than converted into cash, because we are assuming that the public does not want to hold any additional currency.) Now let's see what happens to these deposits at the other banks.

Deposit Creation: The Banking System

To simplify the analysis, let us assume that the $100 of deposits created by First National Bank's loan is deposited at Bank A and that this bank and all other banks hold no excess reserves. Bank A's T-account becomes

Bank A

Assets		Liabilities	
Reserves	+$100	Checkable deposits	+$100

If the required reserve ratio is 10%, this bank will now find itself with a $10 increase in required reserves, leaving it $90 of excess reserves. Because Bank A (like the First National Bank) does not want to hold on to excess reserves, it will make loans for the entire amount. Its loans and checkable deposits will then increase by $90, but when the borrower spends the $90 of checkable deposits, they and the reserves at Bank A will fall back down by this same amount. The net result is that Bank A's T-account will look like this:

Bank A

Assets		Liabilities	
Reserves	+$10	Checkable deposits	+$100
Loans	+$90		

If the money spent by the borrower to whom Bank A lent the $90 is deposited in another bank, such as Bank B, the T-account for Bank B will be

Bank B

Assets		Liabilities	
Reserves	+$90	Checkable deposits	+$90

The checkable deposits in the banking system have increased by another $90, for a total increase of $190 ($100 at Bank A plus $90 at Bank B). In fact, the distinction between Bank A and Bank B is not necessary to obtain the same result on the overall expansion of deposits. If the borrower from Bank A writes checks to someone who deposits them at Bank A, the same change in deposits would occur. The T-accounts for Bank B would just apply to Bank A, and its checkable deposits would increase by the total amount of $190.

Bank B will want to modify its balance sheet further. It must keep 10% of $90 ($9) as required reserves and has 90% of $90 ($81) in excess reserves and so can make loans of this amount. Bank B will make an $81 loan to a borrower, who spends the proceeds from the loan. Bank B's T-account will be

Bank B

Assets		Liabilities	
Reserves	+$ 9	Checkable deposits	+$90
Loans	+$81		

The $81 spent by the borrower from Bank B will be deposited in another bank (Bank C). Consequently, from the initial $100 increase of reserves in the banking system, the total increase of checkable deposits in the system so far is $271 (= $100 + $90 + $81).

Following the same reasoning, if all banks make loans for the full amount of their excess reserves, further increments in checkable deposits will continue (at Banks C, D, E, and so on), as depicted in Table 1. Therefore, the total increase in deposits from the initial $100 increase in reserves will be $1,000: The increase is tenfold, the reciprocal of the 10% (0.10) reserve requirement.

TABLE 1

Creation of Deposits (assuming 10% reserve requirement and a $100 increase in reserves)

Bank	Increase in Deposits ($)	Increase in Loans ($)	Increase in Reserves ($)
First National	0.00	100.00	0.00
A	100.00	90.00	10.00
B	90.00	81.00	9.00
C	81.00	72.90	8.10
D	72.90	65.61	7.29
E	65.61	59.05	6.56
F	59.05	53.14	5.91
.	.	.	.
.	.	.	.
.	.	.	.
Total for all banks	1,000.00	1,000.00	100.00

If the banks choose to invest their excess reserves in securities, the result is the same. If Bank A had taken its excess reserves and purchased securities instead of making loans, its T-account would have looked like this:

Bank A			
Assets		Liabilities	
Reserves	+$10	Checkable deposits	+$100
Securities	+$90		

When the bank buys $90 of securities, it writes a $90 check to the seller of the securities, who in turn deposits the $90 at a bank such as Bank B. Bank B's checkable deposits increase by $90, and the deposit expansion process is the same as before. ***Whether a bank chooses to use its excess reserves to make loans or to purchase securities, the effect on deposit expansion is the same.***

You can now see the difference in deposit creation for the single bank versus the banking system as a whole. Because a single bank can create deposits equal only to the amount of its excess reserves, it cannot by itself generate multiple deposit expansion. A single bank cannot make loans greater in amount than its excess reserves, because the bank will lose these reserves as the deposits created by the loan find their way to other banks. However, the banking system as a whole can generate a multiple expansion of deposits, because when a bank loses its excess reserves, these reserves do not leave the banking system even though they are lost to the individual bank. So as each bank makes a loan and creates deposits, the reserves find their way to another bank, which uses them to make additional loans and create additional deposits. As you have seen, this process continues until the initial increase in reserves results in a multiple increase in deposits.

The multiple increase in deposits generated from an increase in the banking system's reserves is called the **simple deposit multiplier**.[7] In our example with a 10% required reserve ratio, the simple deposit multiplier is 10. More generally, the simple deposit multiplier equals the reciprocal of the required reserve ratio, expressed as a fraction $(10 = 1/0.10)$, so the formula for the multiple expansion of deposits can be written as follows:

$$\Delta D = \frac{1}{r} \times \Delta R \tag{1}$$

where ΔD = change in total checkable deposits in the banking system
r = required reserve ratio (0.10 in the example)
ΔR = change in reserves for the banking system ($100 in the example)[8]

Deriving the Formula for Multiple Deposit Creation

The formula for the multiple creation of deposits can also be derived directly using algebra. We obtain the same answer for the relationship between a change in deposits and a change in reserves, but more quickly.

Our assumption that banks do not hold on to any excess reserves means that the total amount of required reserves for the banking system RR will equal the total reserves in the banking system R:

$$RR = R$$

The total amount of required reserves equals the required reserve ratio r times the total amount of checkable deposits D:

$$RR = r \times D$$

Substituting $r \times D$ for RR in the first equation

$$r \times D = R$$

and dividing both sides of the preceding equation by r gives

$$D = \frac{1}{r} \times R$$

Taking the change in both sides of this equation and using delta to indicate a change gives

$$\Delta D = \frac{1}{r} \times \Delta R$$

which is the same formula for deposit creation found in Equation 1.

---

[7]This multiplier should not be confused with the Keynesian multiplier, which is derived through a similar step-by-step analysis. That multiplier relates an increase in income to an increase in investment, whereas the simple deposit multiplier relates an increase in deposits to an increase in reserves.

[8]A formal derivation of this formula follows. Using the reasoning in the text, the change in checkable deposits is $100 (= $\Delta R \times 1$) plus $90 [= $\Delta R \times (1 - r)$] plus $81[= $\Delta R \times (1 - r)^2$], and so on, which can be rewritten as

$$\Delta D = \Delta R \times [1 + (1 - r) + (1 - r)^2 + (1 - r)^3 + \cdots]$$

Using the formula for the sum of an infinite series found in footnote 5 in Chapter 4, this can be rewritten as

$$\Delta D = \Delta R \times \frac{1}{1 - (1 - r)} = \frac{1}{r} \times \Delta R$$

This derivation provides us with another way of looking at the multiple creation of deposits, because it forces us to look directly at the banking system as a whole rather than at one bank at a time. For the banking system as a whole, deposit creation (or contraction) will stop only when all excess reserves in the banking system are gone; that is, the banking system will be in equilibrium when the total amount of required reserves equals the total amount of reserves, as seen in the equation $RR = R$. When $r \times D$ is substituted for RR, the resulting equation $R = r \times D$ tells us how high checkable deposits will have to be for required reserves to equal total reserves. Accordingly, a given level of reserves in the banking system determines the level of checkable deposits when the banking system is in equilibrium (when $ER = 0$); put another way, the given level of reserves supports a given level of checkable deposits.

In our example, the required reserve ratio is 10%. If reserves increase by $100, checkable deposits must rise by $1,000 for total required reserves also to increase by $100. If the increase in checkable deposits is less than this, say $900, then the increase in required reserves of $90 remains below the $100 increase in reserves, so there are still excess reserves somewhere in the banking system. The banks with the excess reserves will now make additional loans, creating new deposits, and this process will continue until all reserves in the system are used up. This occurs when checkable deposits rise by $1,000.

We can also see this by looking at the T-account of the banking system as a whole (including the First National Bank) that results from this process:

Banking System

Assets		Liabilities	
Securities	−$ 100	Checkable deposits	+$1,000
Reserves	+$ 100		
Loans	+$1,000		

The procedure of eliminating excess reserves by loaning them out means that the banking system (First National Bank and Banks A, B, C, D, and so on) continues to make loans up to the $1,000 amount until deposits have reached the $1,000 level. In this way, $100 of reserves supports $1,000 (ten times the quantity) of deposits.

Critique of the Simple Model

Our model of multiple deposit creation seems to indicate that the Federal Reserve is able to exercise complete control over the level of checkable deposits by setting the required reserve ratio and the level of reserves. The actual creation of deposits is much less mechanical than the simple model indicates. If proceeds from Bank A's $90 loan are not deposited but are kept in currency, nothing is deposited in Bank B and the deposit creation process ceases. The total increase in the money supply is now the $90 increase in currency plus the initial $100 of deposits deposited at Bank A, for a total of only $190—considerably less than the $1,000 we calculated with the simple model above. Another way of saying this is that currency has no multiple deposit expansion, while deposits do. Thus, if some proceeds from loans are used to raise the holdings of currency, there is less multiple expansion overall, and the money supply will not increase by as much as our simple model of multiple deposit creation tells us.

Another situation ignored in our model is one in which banks do not make loans or buy securities in the full amount of their excess reserves. If Bank A decides to hold on to all $90 of its excess reserves, no deposits would be made in Bank B, and this would also stop the deposit creation process. The total increase in deposits would be only $100 and not the $1,000 increase in our example. Hence, if banks choose to hold all or some of their excess reserves, the full expansion of deposits predicted by the simple model of multiple deposit creation again does not occur.

Our examples indicate that the Fed is not the only player whose behavior influences the level of deposits and therefore the money supply. Depositors' decisions regarding how much currency to hold and banks' decisions regarding the amount of excess reserves to hold can cause the money supply to change.

FACTORS THAT DETERMINE THE MONEY SUPPLY

Our critique of the simple model shows how we can expand on it to discuss all the factors that affect the money supply. Let's look at changes in each factor in turn, holding all other factors constant.

Changes in the Nonborrowed Monetary Base, MB_n

As shown earlier in the chapter, the Fed's open market purchases increase the nonborrowed monetary base, and its open market sales decrease it. Holding all other variables constant, an increase in MB_n arising from an open market purchase increases the amount of the monetary base and reserves, so that multiple deposit creation occurs and the money supply increases. Similarly, an open market sale that decreases MB_n shrinks the amount of the monetary base and reserves, thereby causing a multiple contraction of deposits and the money supply decrease. We have the following result: **The money supply is positively related to the nonborrowed monetary base MB_n.**

Changes in Borrowed Reserves, *BR*, from the Fed

An increase in discount loans from the Fed provides additional borrowed reserves, and thereby increases the amount of the monetary base and reserves, so that multiple deposit creation occurs and the money supply increases. If banks reduce the level of their discount loans, all other variables held constant, the monetary base and amount of reserves would fall, and the money supply would decrease. The result is this: **The money supply is positively related to the level of borrowed reserves, BR, from the Fed.**

Changes in the Required Reserve Ratio, *r*

If the required reserve ratio on checkable deposits increases while all other variables, such as the monetary base, stay the same, we have seen that there is less multiple deposit expansion, and hence the money supply falls. If, on the other hand, the required reserve ratio falls, multiple deposit expansion would be higher and the money supply would rise.

We now have the following result: **The money supply is negatively related to the required reserve ratio r.** In the past, the Fed sometimes used reserve requirements to affect the size of the money supply. In recent years, however, reserve requirements have become a less important factor in the determination of the money multiplier and the money supply, as we shall see in the next chapter.

Changes in Currency Holdings

As shown before, checkable deposits undergo multiple expansions while currency does not. Hence, when checkable deposits are converted into currency, holding the monetary base and other variables constant, there is a switch from a component of the money supply that undergoes multiple expansion to one that does not. The overall level of multiple expansion declines and the money supply falls. On the other hand, if currency holdings fall, there would be a switch into checkable deposits that undergo multiple deposit expansion, so the money supply would rise. This analysis suggests the following result: **The money supply is negatively related to currency holdings.**

Changes in Excess Reserves

When banks increase their holdings of excess reserves, those reserves are no longer being used to make loans, causing multiple deposit creation to stop dead in its tracks, thus causing a contraction of the money supply. If, on the other hand, banks chose to hold less excess reserves, loans and multiple deposit creation would go up and the money supply would rise. **The money supply is negatively related to the amount of excess reserves.**

Recall from Chapter 10 that the primary benefit to a bank of holding excess reserves is that they provide insurance against losses due to deposit outflows; that is, they enable the bank experiencing deposit outflows to escape the costs of calling in loans, selling securities, borrowing from the Fed or other corporations, or bank failure. If banks fear that deposit outflows are likely to increase (that is, if expected deposit outflows increase), they will want more insurance against this possibility and excess reserves will increase.

OVERVIEW OF THE MONEY SUPPLY PROCESS

We now have a model of the money supply process in which all three of the players—the Federal Reserve System, depositors, and banks—directly influence the money supply. As a study aid, Summary Table 1 charts the money supply response to the five factors discussed above and gives a brief synopsis of the reasoning behind them.

The variables are grouped by the player (or players) who is the primary influence behind the variable. The Federal Reserve, for example, influences the money supply by controlling the first three variables (called tools of the Fed). Depositors influence the money supply through their decisions about their holdings of currency, while banks influence the money supply with their decisions about excess reserves. However, because depositors' behavior influences bankers' expectations about deposit outflows, which as we have seen affects banks' decisions to hold excess reserves, depositors are also listed as a player determining excess reserves.

SUMMARY TABLE 1

Money Supply Response

Player	Variable	Change in Variable	Money Supply Response	Reason
Federal Reserve System	Nonborrowed monetary base, MB_n	↑	↑	More MB for deposit creation
	Borrowed reserves, BR	↑	↑	More MB for deposit creation
	Required reserve ratio, r	↑	↓	Less multiple deposit expansion
Depositors	Currency holdings	↑	↓	Less multiple deposit expansion
Depositors and banks	Excess reserves	↑	↓	Less loans and deposit creation

Note: Only increases (↑) in the variables are shown. The effects of decreases on the money supply would be the opposite of those indicated in the "Money Supply Response" column.

THE MONEY MULTIPLIER

The intuition in the section above is sufficient for you to understand how the money supply process works. For those of you who are more mathematically inclined, we can derive all of the above results using a concept called the **money multiplier**, denoted by **m**, which tells us how much the money supply changes for a given change in the monetary base. The relationship between the money supply, the money multiplier, and the monetary base is described by the following equation:

$$M = m \times MB \tag{2}$$

The money multiplier m tells us what multiple of the monetary base is transformed into the money supply. Because the money multiplier is larger than 1, the alternative name for the monetary base, *high-powered money*, is logical: a $1 change in the monetary base leads to more than a $1 change in the money supply.

Deriving the Money Multiplier

Let's assume that the desired holdings of currency C and excess reserves ER grows proportionally with checkable deposits D; in other words, we assume that the ratios of these items to checkable deposits are constants in equilibrium, as the braces in the following expressions indicate:

$$c = \{C/D\} = \text{currency ratio}$$

$$e = \{ER/D\} = \text{excess reserves ratio}$$

We will now derive a formula that describes how the currency ratio desired by depositors, the excess reserves ratio desired by banks, and the required reserve ratio set by the Fed affect the multiplier m. We begin the derivation of the model of the money supply with the following equation:

$$R = RR + ER$$

which states that the total amount of reserves in the banking system R equals the sum of required reserves RR and excess reserves ER. (Note that this equation corresponds to the equilibrium condition $RR = R$ earlier in the chapter, where excess reserves were assumed to be zero.)

The total amount of required reserves equals the required reserve ratio r times the amount of checkable deposits D:

$$RR = r \times D$$

Substituting $r \times D$ for RR in the first equation yields an equation that links reserves in the banking system to the amount of checkable deposits and excess reserves they can support:

$$R = (r \times D) + ER$$

A key point here is that the Fed sets the required reserve ratio r to less than 1. Thus \$1 of reserves can support more than \$1 of deposits, and the multiple expansion of deposits can occur.

Let's see how this works in practice. If excess reserves are held at zero ($ER = 0$), the required reserve ratio is set at $r = 0.10$, and the level of checkable deposits in the banking system is \$800 billion, then the amount of reserves needed to support these deposits is \$80 billion ($= 0.10 \times \$800$ billion). The \$80 billion of reserves can support ten times this amount in checkable deposits because multiple deposit creation will occur.

Because the monetary base MB equals currency C plus reserves R, we can generate an equation that links the amount of the monetary base to the levels of checkable deposits and currency by adding currency to both sides of the equation:

$$MB = R + C = (r \times D) + ER + C$$

Another way of thinking about this equation is to recognize that it reveals the amount of the monetary base needed to support the existing amounts of checkable deposits, currency, and excess reserves.

To derive the money multiplier formula in terms of the currency ratio $c = \{C/D\}$ and the excess reserves ratio $e = \{ER/D\}$, we rewrite the last equation, specifying C as $c \times D$ and ER as $e \times D$:

$$MB = (r \times D) + (e \times D) + (c \times D) = (r + e + c) \times D$$

We next divide both sides of the equation by the term inside the parentheses to get an expression linking checkable deposits D to the monetary base MB:

$$D = \frac{1}{r + e + c} \times MB \qquad (3)$$

Using the M1 definition of the money supply as currency plus checkable deposits ($M = D + C$) and again specifying C as $c \times D$,

$$M = D + (c \times D) = (1 + c) \times D$$

Substituting in this equation the expression for D from Equation 3, we have

$$M = \frac{1 + c}{r + e + c} \times MB \qquad (4)$$

We have derived an expression in the form of our earlier Equation 2. As you can see, the ratio that multiplies MB is the money multiplier, which tells how much the money supply changes in response to a given change in the monetary base (high-powered money). The money multiplier m is thus

$$m = \frac{1 + c}{r + e + c} \qquad (5)$$

It is a function of the currency ratio set by depositors c, the excess reserves ratio set by banks e, and the required reserve ratio set by the Fed r.

Intuition Behind the Money Multiplier

To get a feel for what the money multiplier means, let us construct a numerical example with realistic numbers for the following variables:

$$r = \text{required reserve ratio} = 0.10$$
$$C = \text{currency in circulation} = \$400 \text{ billion}$$
$$D = \text{checkable deposits} = \$800 \text{ billion}$$
$$ER = \text{excess reserves} = \$0.8 \text{ billion}$$
$$M = \text{money supply (M1)} = C + D = \$1,200 \text{ billion}$$

From these numbers we can calculate the values for the currency ratio c and the excess reserves ratio e:

$$c = \frac{\$400 \text{ billion}}{\$800 \text{ billion}} = 0.5$$

$$e = \frac{\$0.8 \text{ billion}}{\$800 \text{ billion}} = 0.001$$

The resulting value of the money multiplier is

$$m = \frac{1 + 0.5}{0.1 + 0.001 + 0.5} = \frac{1.5}{0.601} = 2.5$$

The money multiplier of 2.5 tells us that, given the required reserve ratio of 10% on checkable deposits and the behavior of depositors as represented by $c = 0.5$ and banks as represented by $e = 0.001$, a \$1 increase in the monetary base leads to a \$2.50 increase in the money supply (M1).

An important characteristic of the money multiplier is that it is less than the simple deposit multiplier of 10 found earlier in the chapter. The key to understanding this result is to realize that *although there is multiple expansion of deposits, there is no such expansion for currency*. Thus, if some portion of the increase in high-powered money finds its way into currency, this portion does not undergo multiple deposit expansion. In our simple model earlier in the chapter, we did not allow for this possibility, and so the increase in reserves led to the maximum amount of multiple deposit creation. However, in our current model of the money multiplier, the level of currency does increase when the monetary base MB and checkable deposits D increase because c is greater than zero. As previously stated, any increase in MB that goes into an increase in currency is not multiplied, so only part of the increase in MB is available to support checkable deposits that undergo multiple expansion. The overall level of multiple deposit expansion must be lower, meaning that the increase in M, given an increase in MB, is smaller than the simple model earlier in the chapter indicated.[9]

Money Supply Response to Changes in the Factors

By recognizing that the monetary base is $MB = MB_n + BR$, we can rewrite Equation 2 as:

$$M = m \times (MB_n + BR) \tag{6}$$

Now we can show algebraically all the results in Summary Table 1, which shows the money supply response to the changes in the factors.

As you can see from Equation 6, a rise in MB_n or BR raises the money supply M by a multiple amount because the money multiplier m is greater than one. We can see that a rise in the required reserve ratio lowers the money supply by calculating what happens to the value of the money multiplier using Equation 5 in our numerical example when r increases from 10% to 15% (leaving all other variables unchanged). The money multiplier then falls from 2.5 to

$$m = \frac{1 + 0.5}{0.15 + 0.001 + 0.5} = \frac{1.5}{0.651} = 2.3$$

which, as we would expect, is less than 2.5.

Similarly, we can see in our numerical example that a rise in currency lowers the money supply by calculating what happens to the money multiplier when c is raised from 0.50 to 0.75. The money multiplier then falls from 2.5 to

$$m = \frac{1 + 0.75}{0.1 + 0.001 + 0.75} = \frac{1.75}{0.851} = 2.06$$

---

[9]Another reason the money multiplier is smaller is that e is a constant fraction greater than zero, indicating that an increase in MB and D leads to higher excess reserves. The resulting higher amount of excess reserves means that the amount of reserves used to support checkable deposits will not increase as much as it otherwise would. Hence the increase in checkable deposits and the money supply will be lower, and the money multiplier will be smaller. However, because e is often tiny—around 0.001—the impact of this ratio on the money multiplier can be quite small. But there are periods when e is much larger and so has a more important role in lowering the money multiplier.

Finally, we can see that a rise in excess reserves lowers the money supply by calculating what happens to the money multiplier when e is raised from 0.001 to 0.005. The money multiplier declines from 2.5 to

$$m = \frac{1 + 0.5}{0.1 + 0.005 + 0.5} = \frac{1.5}{0.605} = 2.48$$

Note that although the excess reserves ratio has risen fivefold, there has been only a small decline in the money multiplier. This decline is small, because in recent years e has usually been extremely small, so changes in it have only a small impact on the money multiplier. However, there have been times, particularly during the recent subprime financial crisis and the Great Depression period that we examine in the next application, when this ratio was far higher, and its movements had a substantial effect on the money supply and the money multiplier.[10]

APPLICATION ✦ The Great Depression Bank Panics, 1930–1933

We can also use our money supply model to help us understand major movements in the money supply that have occurred in the past. In this application, we use the model to explain the monetary contraction that occurred during the Great Depression, the worst economic downturn in U.S. history. In Chapter 9, we discussed bank panics and saw that they could harm the economy by making asymmetric information problems more severe in credit markets, as they did during the Great Depression. Here we can see that another consequence of bank panics is that they can cause a substantial reduction in the money supply. As we will see in the chapters on monetary theory later in the book, such reductions can also cause severe damage to the economy.

Figure 1 traces the bank crisis during the Great Depression by showing the volume of deposits at failed commercial banks from 1929 to 1933. In their classic book *A Monetary History of the United States, 1867–1960*, Milton Friedman and Anna Schwartz describe the onset of the first banking crisis in late 1930 as follows:

> Before October 1930, deposits of suspended [failed] commercial banks had been somewhat higher than during most of 1929 but not out of line with experience during the preceding decade. In November 1930, they were more than double the highest value recorded since the start of monthly data in 1921. A crop of bank failures, particularly in Missouri, Indiana, Illinois, Iowa, Arkansas, and North Carolina, led to widespread attempts to convert checkable and time deposits into currency, and also, to a much lesser extent, into postal savings deposits. A contagion of fear spread among depositors, starting from the agricultural areas, which had experienced the heaviest impact of bank failures in the twenties. But failure of 256 banks with $180 million of deposits in November 1930 was followed by the failure of 532 with over $370 million of deposits in December (all figures seasonally unadjusted), the most dramatic being the failure on December 11 of the

---

[10]All the above results can be derived more generally from the Equation 5 formula as follows. When r or e increases, the denominator of the money multiplier increases, and therefore the money multiplier must decrease. As long as $r + e$ is less than 1 (as is the case using the realistic numbers as above), an increase in c raises the denominator of the money multiplier proportionally by more than it raises the numerator. The increase in c causes the multiplier to fall. For more background on the currency ratio c, consult the third Web appendix to this chapter at www.myeconlab.com/mishkin. Recall that the money multiplier in Equation 5 is for the M1 definition of money. A second appendix on the website discusses how the multiplier for M2 is determined.

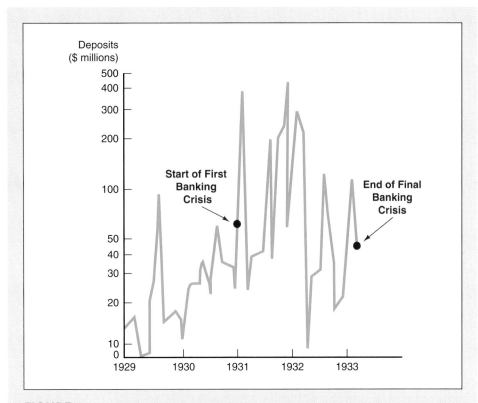

FIGURE 1   **Deposits of Failed Commercial Banks, 1929–1933**

Source: Milton Friedman and Anna Jacobson Schwartz, *A Monetary History of the United States, 1867–1960* (Princeton, NJ: Princeton University Press, 1963), p. 309.

Bank of United States with over $200 million of deposits. That failure was especially important. The Bank of United States was the largest commercial bank, as measured by volume of deposits, ever to have failed up to that time in U.S. history. Moreover, though it was just an ordinary commercial bank, the Bank of United States's name had led many at home and abroad to regard it somehow as an official bank, hence its failure constituted more of a blow to confidence than would have been administered by the fall of a bank with a less distinctive name.[11]

The first bank panic, from October 1930 to January 1931, is clearly visible in Figure 1 at the end of 1930, when there is a rise in the amount of deposits at failed banks. Because there was no deposit insurance at the time (the FDIC wasn't established until 1934), when a bank failed, depositors would receive only partial repayment of their deposits. Therefore, when banks were failing during a bank panic, depositors knew that they would be likely to suffer substantial losses on deposits and thus the expected return on deposits would be negative. The theory of asset demand predicts that with the onset of the first bank crisis, depositors would shift their holdings from checkable deposits to currency by withdrawing currency from their bank accounts, and

---

[11]Milton Friedman and Anna Jacobson Schwartz, *A Monetary History of the United States, 1867–1960* (Princeton, NJ: Princeton University Press, 1963), pp. 308–311.

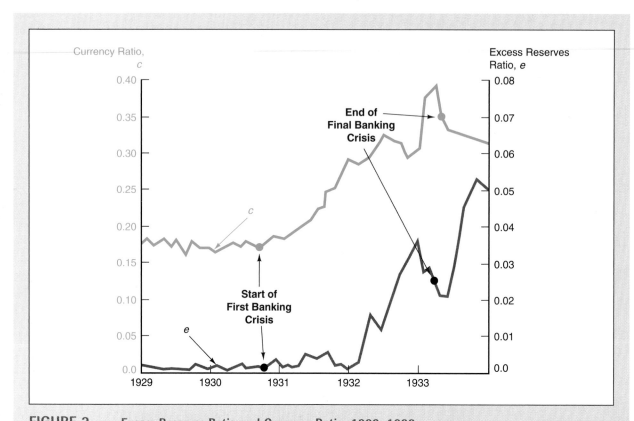

FIGURE 2 **Excess Reserves Ratio and Currency Ratio, 1929–1933**

Sources: Federal Reserve *Bulletin*; Milton Friedman and Anna Jacobson Schwartz, *A Monetary History of the United States, 1867–1960* (Princeton, NJ: Princeton University Press, 1963), p. 333.

c would rise. Our earlier analysis of the excess reserves ratio suggests that the resulting surge in deposit outflows would cause the banks to protect themselves by substantially increasing their excess reserves ratio e. Both of these predictions are borne out by the data in Figure 2. During the first bank panic (October 1930–January 1931) c began to climb. Even more striking is the behavior of e, which more than doubled from November 1930 to January 1931.

The money supply model predicts that when e and c increase, the money supply will contract. The rise in c results in a decline in the overall level of multiple deposit expansion, leading to a smaller money multiplier and a decline in the money supply, while the rise in e reduces the amount of reserves available to support deposits and also causes the money supply to decrease. Thus our model predicts that the rise in e and c after the onset of the first bank crisis would result in a decline in the money supply—a prediction borne out by the evidence in Figure 3.

Banking crises continued to occur from 1931 to 1933, and the pattern predicted by our model persisted: c continued to rise, and so did e. By the end of the crises in March 1933, the money supply (M1) had declined by over 25%—by far the largest decline in all of American history—and it coincided with the nation's worst economic contraction (see Chapter 9). Even more remarkable is that this decline occurred despite a 20% rise in the level of the monetary base—which illustrates how important the changes in c and e

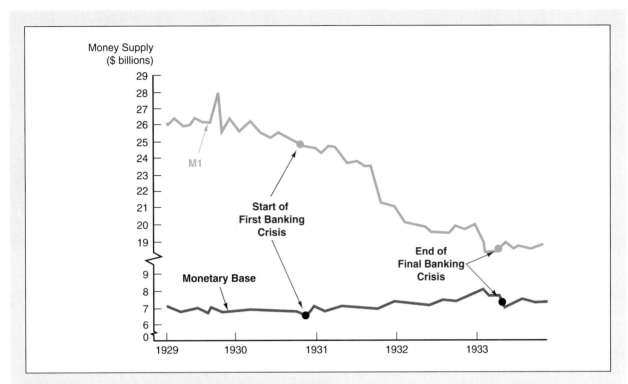

FIGURE 3   **M1 and the Monetary Base, 1929–1933**

Source: Milton Friedman and Anna Jacobson Schwartz, *A Monetary History of the United States, 1867–1960* (Princeton, NJ: Princeton University Press, 1963), p. 333.

during bank panics can be in the determination of the money supply. It also illustrates that the Fed's job of conducting monetary policy can be complicated by depositor and bank behavior.

✦

SUMMARY

1. There are three players in the money supply process: the central bank, banks (depository institutions), and depositors.

2. Four items in the Fed's balance sheet are essential to our understanding of the money supply process: the two liability items, currency in circulation and reserves, which together make up the monetary base, and the two asset items, government securities and discount loans.

3. The Federal Reserve controls the monetary base through open market operations and extension of discount loans to banks and has better control over the monetary base than over reserves. Although float and Treasury deposits with the Fed undergo substantial short-run fluctuations, which complicate control of the monetary base, they do not prevent the Fed from accurately controlling it.

4. A single bank can make loans up to the amount of its excess reserves, thereby creating an equal amount of deposits. The banking system can create a multiple expansion of deposits, because as each bank makes a loan and creates deposits, the reserves find their way to another bank, which uses them to make loans and create additional deposits. In the simple model of multiple deposit creation in which banks do not hold on to excess reserves and the public holds no currency, the multiple increase in checkable deposits (simple deposit multiplier) equals the reciprocal of the required reserve ratio.

5. The simple model of multiple deposit creation has serious deficiencies. Decisions by depositors to increase their holdings of currency or of banks to hold excess reserves will result in a smaller expansion of deposits than the simple model predicts. All four players—the Fed, banks, depositors, and borrowers from banks—are important in the determination of the money supply.

6. The money supply is positively related to the nonborrowed monetary base MB_n, which is determined by open market operations, and the level of borrowed reserves (discount loans) from the Fed, BR. The money supply is negatively related to the required reserve ratio, r, holdings of currency, and excess reserves. The model of the money supply process takes into account the behavior of all three players in the money supply process: the Fed through open market operations, discount lending, and setting of the required reserve ratio; depositors through their decisions about their holding of currency and banks through their decisions about excess reserves which are also influenced by depositors' decisions about deposit outflows.

7. The monetary base is linked to the money supply using the concept of the money multiplier, which tells us how much the money supply changes when there is a change in the monetary base.

KEY TERMS

borrowed reserves, p. 353

discount rate, p. 347

excess reserves, p. 347

float, p. 353

high-powered money, p. 347

monetary base, p. 346

money multiplier, p. 362

multiple deposit creation, p. 354

nonborrowed monetary base, p. 353

open market operations, p. 347

open market purchase, p. 348

open market sale, p. 348

required reserve ratio, p. 347

required reserves, p. 347

reserves, p. 347

simple deposit multiplier, p. 358

QUESTIONS AND PROBLEMS

All questions and problems are available in myeconlab *at* www.myeconlab.com/mishkin.

1. If the Fed sells $2 million of bonds to the First National Bank, what happens to reserves and the monetary base? Use T-accounts to explain your answer.

2. If the Fed sells $2 million of bonds to Irving the Investor, who pays for the bonds with a briefcase filled with currency, what happens to reserves and the monetary base? Use T-accounts to explain your answer.

3. If the Fed lends five banks an additional total of $100 million but depositors withdraw $50 million and hold it as currency, what happens to reserves and the monetary base? Use T-accounts to explain your answer.

4. The First National Bank receives an extra $100 of reserves but decides not to lend any of these reserves out. How much deposit creation takes place for the entire banking system?

Unless otherwise noted, the following assumptions are made in all the remaining problems: The required reserve ratio on checkable deposits is 10%, banks do not hold any excess reserves, and the public's holdings of currency do not change.

5. Using T-accounts, show what happens to checkable deposits in the banking system when the Fed lends an additional $1 million to the First National Bank.

6. Using T-accounts, show what happens to checkable deposits in the banking system when the Fed sells $2 million of bonds to the First National Bank.

7. Suppose that the Fed buys $1 million of bonds from the First National Bank. If the First National Bank and all other banks use the resulting increase in reserves to purchase securities only and not to make loans, what will happen to checkable deposits?

8. If the Fed buys $1 million of bonds from the First National Bank, but an additional 10% of any deposit is held as excess reserves, what is the total increase in checkable deposits? (*Hint:* Use T-accounts to show what happens at each step of the multiple expansion process.)

9. If a bank depositor withdraws $1,000 of currency from an account, what happens to reserves and checkable deposits?

10. If reserves in the banking system increase by $1 billion as a result of discount loans of $1 billion and checkable deposits increase by $9 billion, why isn't the banking system in equilibrium? What will continue to happen in the banking system until equilibrium is reached? Show the T-account for the banking system in equilibrium.

11. If the Fed reduces reserves by selling $5 million worth of bonds to the banks, what will the T-account of the banking system look like when the banking system is in equilibrium? What will have happened to the level of checkable deposits?

12. If a bank decides that it wants to hold $1 million of excess reserves, what effect will this have on checkable deposits in the banking system?

13. If a bank sells $10 million of bonds to the Fed to pay back $10 million on the discount loan it owes, what will be the effect on the level of checkable deposits?

14. If you decide to hold $100 less cash than usual and therefore deposit $100 in cash in the bank, what effect will this have on checkable deposits in the banking system if the rest of the public keeps its holdings of currency constant?

15. "The money multiplier is necessarily greater than 1." Is this statement true, false, or uncertain? Explain your answer.

16. During the Great Depression years, 1930–1933, the currency ratio c rose dramatically. What do you think happened to the money supply? Why?

17. During the Great Depression, the excess reserves ratio e rose dramatically. What do you think happened to the money supply? Why?

Using Economic Analysis to Predict the Future

18. The Fed buys $100 million of bonds from the public and also lowers r. What will happen to the money supply?

19. If the Fed sells $1 million of bonds and banks reduce their borrowings from the Fed by $1 million, predict what will happen to the money supply.

20. Predict what will happen to the money supply if there is a sharp rise in the currency ratio.

WEB EXERCISES

1. Go to www.federalreserve.gov/boarddocs/hh/ and find the most recent annual report of the Federal Reserve. Read the first section of the annual report that summarizes Monetary Policy and the Economic Outlook. Write a one-page summary of this section of the report.

2. Go to www.federalreserve.gov/releases/h6/hist/ and find the historical report of M1, M2. Compute the growth rate in each aggregate over each of the last three years (it will be easier to do if you move the data into Excel as demonstrated in Chapter 1). Does it appear that the Fed has been increasing or decreasing the rate of growth of the money supply? Is this consistent with what you understand the economy needs? Why?

3. An important aspect of the supply of money is reserve balances. Go to www.federalreserve.gov/Releases/h41/ and locate the most recent release. This site reports changes in factors that affect depository reserve balances.
   a. What is the current reserve balance?
   b. What is the change in reserve balances since a year ago?
   c. Based on parts a and b, does it appear that the money supply should be increasing or decreasing?

WEB REFERENCES

www.federalreserve.gov/boarddocs/rptcongress/annual04/default.htm

See the most recent Federal Reserve financial statement.

www.richmondfed.org/about_us/visit_us/tours/money_museum/index.cfm

A virtual tour of the Federal Reserve Bank of Richmond's money museum.

www.federalreserve.gov/Releases/h3/

The Federal Reserve website reports data about aggregate reserves and the monetary base. This site also reports on the volume of borrowings from the Fed.

www.federalreserve.gov/Releases/h6/

This site reports current and historical levels of M1 and M2, and other data on the money supply.

 MyEconLab CAN HELP YOU GET A BETTER GRADE

If your exam were tomorrow, would you be ready? For each chapter, MyEconLab Practice Test and Study Plans pinpoint which sections you have mastered and which ones you need to study. That way, you are more efficient with your study time, and you are better prepared for your exams.

To see how it works, turn to page 20 and then go to: www.myeconlab.com/mishkin

15

Tools of Monetary Policy

Preview

In the chapters describing the structure of the Federal Reserve System and the money supply process, we mentioned three policy tools that the Fed can use to manipulate the money supply and interest rates: open market operations, which affect the quantity of reserves and the monetary base; changes in borrowed reserves, which affect the monetary base; and changes in reserve requirements, which affect the money multiplier. Because the Fed's use of these policy tools has such an important impact on interest rates and economic activity, it is important to understand how the Fed wields them in practice and how relatively useful each tool is.

In recent years, the Federal Reserve has increasingly focused on the **federal funds rate** (the interest rate on overnight loans of reserves from one bank to another) as the primary instrument of monetary policy. Since February 1994, the Fed announces a federal funds rate target at each Federal Open Market Committee (FOMC) meeting, an announcement that is watched closely by market participants because it affects interest rates throughout the economy. Thus, to fully understand how the Fed's tools are used in the conduct of monetary policy, we must understand not only their effect on the money supply, but also their direct effects on the federal funds rate. The chapter therefore begins with a supply and demand analysis of the market for reserves to explain how the Fed's settings for the three tools of monetary policy determine the federal funds rate. We then go on to look in more detail at each of the three tools—open market operations, discount rate policy, and reserve requirements—to see how they are used in practice and to ask whether the use of these tools could be modified to improve the conduct of monetary policy. The chapter ends with a discussion of the tools of monetary policy used by other central banks besides the Federal Reserve.

THE MARKET FOR RESERVES AND THE FEDERAL FUNDS RATE

In Chapter 14, we saw how open market operations and discount lending (changes in borrowed reserves) affect the balance sheet of the Fed and the amount of reserves. The market for reserves is where the federal funds rate is determined, and this is why we turn to a supply and demand analysis of this market to analyze how all three tools of monetary policy affect the federal funds rate.

Demand and Supply in the Market for Reserves

The analysis of the market for reserves proceeds in a similar fashion to the analysis of the bond market we conducted in Chapter 5. We derive a demand and supply curve for reserves. Then the market equilibrium in which the quantity of reserves demanded equals the quantity of reserves supplied determines the federal funds rate, the interest rate charged on the loans of these reserves.

Demand Curve   To derive the demand curve for reserves, we need to ask what happens to the quantity of reserves demanded by banks, holding everything else constant, as the federal funds rate changes. Recall from Chapter 14 that the amount of reserves can be split up into two components: (1) required reserves, which equal the required reserve ratio times the amount of deposits on which reserves are required, and (2) excess reserves, the additional reserves banks choose to hold. Therefore, the quantity of reserves demanded by banks equals required reserves plus the quantity of excess reserves demanded. Excess reserves are insurance against deposit outflows, and the cost of holding these excess reserves is their opportunity cost, the interest rate that could have been earned on lending these reserves out, minus the interest rate that is earned on these reserves, i_{er}. Before 2008, the Federal Reserve did not pay interest on reserves, but since the fall of 2008, the Fed has paid interest on reserves at a level that is set at a fixed amount below the federal funds rate target and therefore changes when the target changes (see the Inside the Fed box, "Why Does the Fed Need to Pay Interest on Reserves?"). When the federal funds rate is above the rate paid on excess reserves, i_{er}, as the federal funds rate decreases, the opportunity cost of holding excess reserves falls. Holding everything else constant, including the quantity of required reserves, the quantity of reserves demanded rises. Consequently, the demand curve for reserves, R^d, slopes downward in Figure 1 when the federal funds rate is above i_{er}. If however, the federal funds rate begins to fall below the interest rate paid on excess reserves i_{er}, banks would not lend in the overnight market at a lower interest rate. Instead, they would just keep on adding to their holdings of excess reserves indefinitely. The result is that the demand curve for reserves, R^d, becomes flat (infinitely elastic) at i_{er} in Figure 1.

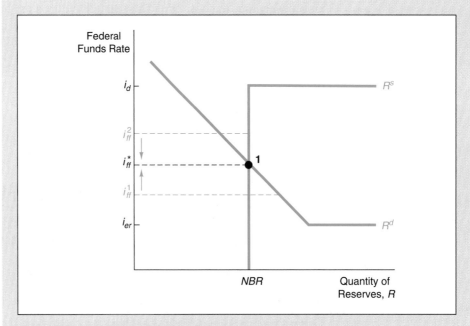

FIGURE 1   **Equilibrium in the Market for Reserves**
Equilibrium occurs at the intersection of the supply curve R^s and the demand curve R^d at point 1 and an interest rate of i^*_{ff}.

Inside the Fed   Why Does the Fed Need to Pay Interest on Reserves?

For years, the Federal Reserve asked Congress to pass legislation allowing the Fed to pay interest on reserves. In 2006 legislation was passed allowing the Fed to pay interest on reserves to go into effect in 2011, but the starting date was moved up to October 2008 during the subprime financial crisis. Why is paying interest on reserves so important to the Fed?

One argument for paying interest on reserves is that it reduces the effective tax on deposits, thereby increasing economic efficiency. As pointed out in Chapter 12, the opportunity cost for a bank of holding reserves is the interest the bank could earn by lending out the reserves minus the interest payment that it receives from the Fed. When there was no interest paid on reserves, this opportunity cost of holding them was quite high, and banks went to extraordinary measures to reduce them (for example, sweeping out deposits every night into repurchase agreements in order to reduce their required reserve balances). With the interest rate on reserves set close to the federal funds rate target, this opportunity cost is lowered dramatically, sharply reducing the need for banks to engage in unnecessary transactions to avoid this opportunity cost.

The second argument for paying interest on reserves is that it helps improve implementation of monetary policy. As we learned in Chapter 14, the amount of excess reserves fluctuates with changes in the opportunity cost of holding reserves. With the interest rate on reserves set at a fixed amount below the federal funds rate target, the opportunity cost of reserves no longer fluctuates as much. As a result, fluctuations in excess reserves are potentially reduced when interest rates change, which as we saw in Chapter 14, makes for less fluctuations and therefore tighter control of the money supply. In addition, as the supply and demand analysis of the market for reserves outlined in this chapter shows, paying interest on reserves puts a floor under the federal funds rate, and so limits fluctuations of the federal funds rate around its target level.

The third argument for paying interest on reserves became especially relevant during the subprime financial crisis of 2007–2008. As discussed below, during that period the Fed needed to provide liquidity to particular parts of the financial system using its lending facilities in order to limit the damage from the financial crisis. As the discussion of the Fed's balance sheet in Chapter 14 shows, when the Fed provides liquidity through its lending facilities, the monetary base and the amount of reserves will expand, which will raise the money supply and also cause the federal funds rate to decline, as the supply and demand analysis of the market for reserves in this chapter shows. In order to prevent this, the Fed can conduct offsetting, open market sales of its securities to "sterilize" the liquidity created by its lending and so keep the money supply and the federal funds rate at their prior levels. But doing so leads to a reduction of the holdings of these securities on the Fed's balance sheet. If the Fed were to run out of these securities, it would no longer be able to sterilize the liquidity created by its lending: In other words, it would have used up its balance sheet capacity to channel liquidity to specific sectors of the financial system that needed it, without altering monetary policy. This problem became particularly acute during the subprime financial crisis when the huge lending operations of the Fed caused a precipitous drop in the Fed's holdings of securities, raising fears that the Fed would not be able to engage in further lending operations.

Having the ability to pay interest on reserves helps solve this balance-sheet-capacity problem. With interest paid on reserves, the Fed can expand its lending facilities as much as it wants, and yet as our supply and demand analysis of the market for reserves demonstrates, the federal funds rate will not fall below the interest rate paid on reserves. If the interest rate paid on reserves is set close to the federal funds rate target, the expansion of the Fed's lending will then not drive down the federal funds rate much below its intended target. The Fed can then do all the lending

(continued)

Why Does the Fed Need to Pay Interest on Reserves? (*continued*)

it wants without having much of an effect on its monetary policy instrument, the federal funds rate.*

Given the huge expansion in the Fed's lending facilities during the subprime financial crisis, it is no surprise that Chairman Bernanke requested that Congress move up the date when the Fed could pay interest on reserves. This request was granted in the Emergency Economic Stabilization Act passed in October 2008.

*With interest paid on reserves, the expansion of Federal Reserve lending also would not lead to an expansion of the money supply. The supply and demand analysis of the market for reserves shows that once the federal funds rate hits the floor set by the interest rate paid on reserves, increasing the reserves supplied by increasing Fed lending leads to a continuing rise in excess reserves. However, as we saw in Chapter 14, the rise in reserves would not lead to a rise in the money supply: With the increase in reserves going into excess reserves, there would be no multiple deposit expansion and hence no increase in the money supply.

Supply Curve   The supply of reserves, R^s, can be broken up into two components: the amount of reserves that are supplied by the Fed's open market operations, called nonborrowed reserves (NBR), and the amount of reserves borrowed from the Fed, called *borrowed reserves* (BR). The primary cost of borrowing from the Fed is the interest rate the Fed charges on these loans, the discount rate (i_d), which is set at a fixed amount above the federal funds target rate and thus changes when the target changes. Because borrowing federal funds from other banks is a substitute for borrowing (taking out discount loans) from the Fed, if the federal funds rate i_{ff} is below the discount rate i_d, then banks will not borrow from the Fed and borrowed reserves will be zero because borrowing in the federal funds market is cheaper. Thus, as long as i_{ff} remains below i_d, the supply of reserves will just equal the amount of nonborrowed reserves supplied by the Fed, NBR, and so the supply curve will be vertical as shown in Figure 1. However, as the federal funds rate begins to rise above the discount rate, banks would want to keep borrowing more and more at i_d and then lending out the proceeds in the federal funds market at the higher rate, i_{ff}. The result is that the supply curve becomes flat (infinitely elastic) at i_d, as shown in Figure 1.

Market Equilibrium   Market equilibrium occurs where the quantity of reserves demanded equals the quantity supplied, $R^s = R^d$. Equilibrium therefore occurs at the intersection of the demand curve R^d and the supply curve R^s at point 1, with an equilibrium federal funds rate of i_{ff}^*. When the federal funds rate is above the equilibrium rate at i_{ff}^2, there are more reserves supplied than demanded (excess supply) and so the federal funds rate falls to i_{ff}^* as shown by the downward arrow. When the federal funds rate is below the equilibrium rate at i_{ff}^1, there are more reserves demanded than supplied (excess demand) and so the federal funds rate rises as shown by the upward arrow. (Note that Figure 1 is drawn so that i_d is above i_{ff}^* because the Federal Reserve now keeps the discount rate substantially above the target for the federal funds rate.)

How Changes in the Tools of Monetary Policy Affect the Federal Funds Rate

Now that we understand how the federal funds rate is determined, we can examine how changes in the three tools of monetary policy—open market operations, discount lending, and reserve requirements—affect the market for reserves and the equilibrium federal funds rate.

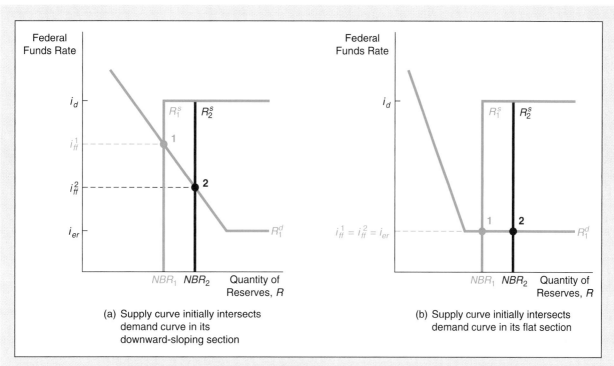

FIGURE 2   **Response to an Open Market Operation**
An open market purchase increases nonborrowed reserves and hence the reserves supplied, and shifts the supply curve from R_1^s to R_2^s. In panel (a), the equilibrium moves from point 1 to point 2, lowering the federal funds rate from i_{ff}^1 to i_{ff}^2. In panel (b), the equilibrium moves from point 1 to point 2, but the federal funds rate remains unchanged, $i_{ff}^1 = i_{ff}^2 = i_{er}$.

Open Market Operations   The effect of an open market operation depends on whether the supply curve initially intersects the demand curve in its downward-sloped section versus its flat section. Panel (a) of Figure 2 shows what happens if the intersection initially occurs on the downward-sloped section of the demand curve. We have already seen that an open market purchase leads to a greater quantity of reserves supplied; this is true at any given federal funds rate because of the higher amount of nonborrowed reserves, which rises from NBR_1 to NBR_2. An open market purchase therefore shifts the supply curve to the right from R_1^s to R_2^s and moves the equilibrium from point 1 to point 2, lowering the federal funds rate from i_{ff}^1 to i_{ff}^2.[1] The same reasoning implies that an open market sale decreases the quantity of nonborrowed reserves supplied, shifts the supply curve to the left, and causes the federal funds rate to rise. Because this is the typical situation—since the Fed usually keeps the federal funds rate target above the interest rate paid on reserves—the conclusion is that ***an open market purchase***

---

[1]We come to the same conclusion using the money supply framework in Chapter 14, along with the liquidity preference framework in Chapter 5. An open market purchase raises reserves and the money supply, and then the liquidity preference framework shows that interest rates fall as a result.

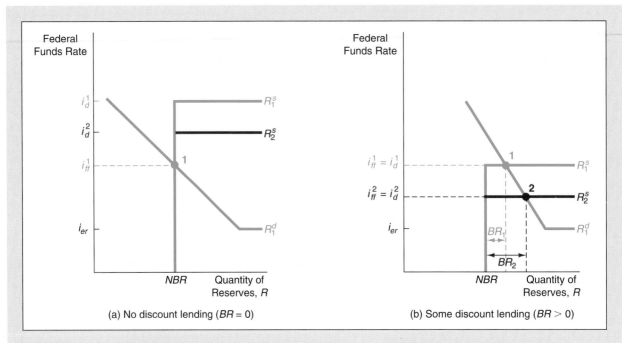

FIGURE 3   **Response to a Change in the Discount Rate**
In panel (a) when the discount rate is lowered by the Fed from i_d^1 to i_d^2, the horizontal section of the supply curve falls, as in R_2^s, and the equilibrium federal funds rate remains unchanged at i_{ff}^1. In panel (b) when the discount rate is lowered by the Fed from i_d^1 to i_d^2, the horizontal section of the supply curve R_2^s falls, and the equilibrium federal funds rate falls from i_{ff}^1 to i_{ff}^2 as borrowed reserves increase.

causes the federal funds rate to fall, whereas an open market sale causes the federal funds rate to rise.

However, if the supply curve initially intersects the demand curve on its flat section, as in panel (b) of Figure 2, open market operations have no effect on the federal funds rate. To see this, let's again look at an open market purchase that raises the quantity of reserves supplied, which shifts the demand curve from R_1^s to R_2^s, but now where initially $i_{ff}^1 = i_{er}$. The shift in the supply curve moves the equilibrium from point 1 to point 2, but the federal funds rate remains unchanged at i_{er} because **the interest rate paid on reserves, i_{er}, sets a floor for the federal funds rate**.

Discount Lending   The effect of a discount rate change depends on whether the demand curve intersects the supply curve in its vertical section versus its flat section. Panel (a) of Figure 3 shows what happens if the intersection occurs on the vertical section of the supply curve so there is no discount lending and borrowed reserves, *BR*, are zero. In this case, when the discount rate is lowered by the Fed from i_d^1 to i_d^2, the horizontal section of the supply curve falls, as in R_2^s, but the intersection of the supply and demand curves remains at point 1. Thus, in this case, there is no change in the equilibrium federal funds rate, which remains at i_{ff}^1. Because this is the typical situation—since the Fed now usually keeps the discount rate above its target for the federal funds rate—the conclusion is that *most changes in the discount rate have no effect on the federal funds rate*.

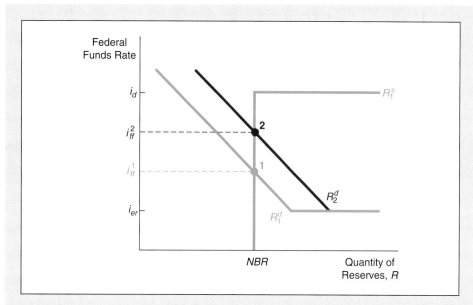

FIGURE 4   **Response to a Change in Required Reserves**
When the Fed raises reserve requirements, required reserves increase, which increases the demand for reserves. The demand curve shifts from R_1^d to R_2^d, the equilibrium moves from point 1 to point 2, and the federal fund rate rises from i_{ff}^1 to i_{ff}^2.

However, if the demand curve intersects the supply curve on its flat section, so there is some discount lending (i.e., $BR > 0$), as in panel (b) of Figure 3, changes in the discount rate do affect the federal funds rate. In this case, initially discount lending is positive and the equilibrium federal funds rate equals the discount rate, $i_{ff}^1 = i_d^1$. When the discount rate is lowered by the Fed from i_d^1 to i_d^2, the horizontal section of the supply curve R_2^s falls, moving the equilibrium from point 1 to point 2, and the equilibrium federal funds rate falls from i_{ff}^1 to i_{ff}^2 ($= i_d^2$) in panel (b).

Reserve Requirements   When the required reserve ratio increases, required reserves increase and hence the quantity of reserves demanded increases for any given interest rate. Thus a rise in the required reserve ratio shifts the demand curve to the right from R_1^d to R_2^d in Figure 4, moves the equilibrium from point 1 to point 2, and in turn raises the federal funds rate from i_{ff}^1 to i_{ff}^2.

The result is that *when the Fed raises reserve requirements, the federal funds rate rises*.[2]

Similarly, a decline in the required reserve ratio lowers the quantity of reserves demanded, shifts the demand curve to the left, and causes the federal funds rate to fall. *When the Fed decreases reserve requirements, the federal funds rate falls*.

---

[2]Because an increase in the required reserve ratio means that the same amount of reserves is able to support a smaller amount of deposits, a rise in the required reserve ratio leads to a decline in the money supply. Using the liquidity preference framework, the fall in the money supply results in a rise in interest rates, yielding the same conclusion in the text—that raising reserve requirements leads to higher interest rates.

APPLICATION ✦ How the Federal Reserve's Operating Procedures Limit Fluctuations in the Federal Funds Rate

An important advantage of the Fed's current procedures for operating the discount window and paying interest on reserves is that they limit fluctuations in the federal funds rate. We can use our supply and demand analysis of the market for reserves to see why.

Suppose that initially the equilibrium federal funds rate is at the federal funds rate target of i_{ff}^* in Figure 5. If the demand for reserves has a large unexpected increase, the demand curve would shift to the right to $R^{d''}$, where it now intersects the supply curve for reserves on the flat portion where the equilibrium federal funds rate i_{ff}'' equals the discount rate i_d. No matter how far the demand curve shifts to the right, the equilibrium federal funds rate i_{ff}'' will just stay at i_d because borrowed reserves will just continue to increase, matching the increase in demand. Similarly, if the demand for reserves has a large unexpected decrease, the demand curve would shift to the left to $R^{d'}$, and the supply curve intersects the demand curve on its flat portion where the equilibrium federal funds rate i_{ff}' equals the interest rate paid on reserves i_{er}. No matter how far the demand curve shifts to the left, the equilibrium federal funds rate i_{ff}' will stay at i_{er} because excess reserves will just keep on increasing so that the quantity demanded of reserves equals the quantity of nonborrowed reserves supplied.

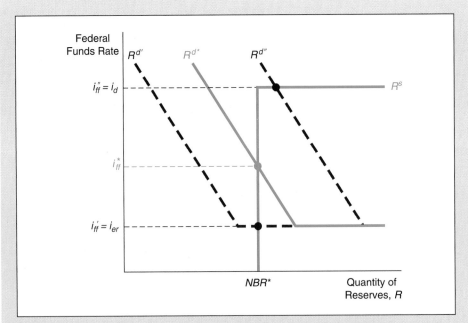

FIGURE 5   How the Federal Reserve's Operating Procedures Limit Fluctuations in the Federal Funds Rate
A rightward shift in the demand curve for reserves to $R^{d''}$ will raise the equilibrium federal funds rate to a maximum of $i_{ff}'' = i_d$ while a Leftward shift of the demand curve to $R^{d'}$ will lower the federal funds rate to a minimum of $i_{ff}' = i_{er}$.

Our analysis therefore shows that the ***Federal Reserve's operating procedures limit the fluctuations of the federal funds rate to between i_{er} and i_d***. If the range between i_{er} and i_d is kept narrow enough, then the fluctuations around the target rate will be small.

Now that we understand how the three tools of monetary policy—open market operations, discount lending, and reserve requirements—can be used by the Fed to manipulate the money supply and interest rates, we will look at each of them in turn to see how the Fed wields them in practice and how relatively useful each tool is.

OPEN MARKET OPERATIONS

Open market operations are the most important monetary policy tool, because they are the primary determinants of changes in interest rates and the monetary base, the main source of fluctuations in the money supply. Open market purchases expand reserves and the monetary base, thereby increasing the money supply and lowering short-term interest rates. Open market sales shrink reserves and the monetary base, decreasing the money supply and raising short-term interest rates. Now that we understand from Chapter 14 the factors that influence reserves and the monetary base, we can examine how the Federal Reserve conducts open market operations with the objective of controlling short-term interest rates and the money supply.

There are two types of open market operations: **Dynamic open market operations** are intended to change the level of reserves and the monetary base, and **defensive open market operations** are intended to offset movements in other factors that affect reserves and the monetary base, such as changes in Treasury deposits with the Fed or changes in float. The Fed conducts open market operations in U.S. Treasury and government agency securities, especially U.S. Treasury bills.[3] The Fed conducts most of its open market operations in Treasury securities because the market for these securities is the most liquid and has the largest trading volume. It has the capacity to absorb the Fed's substantial volume of transactions without experiencing excessive price fluctuations that would disrupt the market.

As we saw in Chapter 13, the decision-making authority for open market operations is the Federal Open Market Committee (FOMC), which sets a target for the federal funds rate. The actual execution of these operations, however, is conducted by the trading desk at the Federal Reserve Bank of New York. The best way to see how these transactions are executed is to look at a typical day at the trading desk, located in a newly built trading room on the ninth floor of the Federal Reserve Bank of New York.

A Day at the Trading Desk

The manager of domestic open market operations supervises the analysts and traders who execute the purchases and sales of securities in the drive to hit the federal funds

---

[3]To avoid conflicts of interest, the Fed does not conduct open market operations in privately issued securities. (For example, think of the conflict if the Federal Reserve purchased bonds issued by a company owned by the chairman's brother-in-law.)

rate target. To get a grip on what might happen in the federal funds market that day, her workday and that of her staff begins with a review of developments in the federal funds market the previous day and with an update on the actual amount of reserves in the banking system the day before. Later in the morning, her staff issues updated reports that contain detailed forecasts of what will be happening to some of the short-term factors affecting the supply and demand of reserves (discussed in Chapter 14). For example, if float is predicted to decrease because good weather throughout the country is speeding up check delivery, the manager of domestic open market operations knows that she will have to conduct a defensive open market operation (in this case, a *purchase* of securities) to offset the expected decline in reserves and the monetary base from the decreased float. However, if Treasury deposits with the Fed are predicted to fall, a defensive open market *sale* would be needed to offset the expected increase in reserves. The report also predicts the change in the public's holding of currency. If currency holdings are expected to rise, then, as we have seen in Chapter 14, reserves fall, and an open market purchase is needed to raise reserves back up again.

This information will help the manager of domestic open market operations and her staff decide how large a change in nonborrowed reserves is needed to reach the federal funds rate target. If the amount of reserves in the banking system is too large, many banks will have excess reserves to lend that other banks may have little desire to hold, and the federal funds rate will fall. If the level of reserves is too low, banks seeking to borrow reserves from the few banks that have excess reserves to lend may push the funds rate higher than the desired level. Also during the morning, the staff will monitor the behavior of the federal funds rate and contact some of the major participants in the funds market, which may provide independent information about whether a change in reserves is needed to achieve the desired level of the federal funds rate.

Early in the morning, members of the manager's staff contact several representatives of the **primary dealers**, government securities dealers (who operate out of private firms or commercial banks) that the open market desk trades with. Her staff finds out how the dealers view market conditions to get a feel for what may happen to the prices of the securities they trade in over the course of the day. They also call the Treasury to get updated information on the expected level of Treasury balances at the Fed to refine their estimates of the supply of reserves.

Shortly after 9 a.m., members of the Monetary Affairs Division at the Board of Governors are contacted, and the New York Fed's forecasts of reserve supply and demand are compared with the Board's. On the basis of these projections and the observed behavior of the federal funds market, the desk will formulate and propose a course of action to be taken that day, which may involve plans to add reserves to or drain reserves from the banking system through open market operations. If an operation is contemplated, the type, size, and maturity will be discussed.

At 9:20 a.m., a daily conference call is arranged linking the desk with the Office of the Director of Monetary Affairs at the Board of Governors and with one of the four voting Reserve Bank presidents outside of New York. During the call, a member of the open market operations unit will outline the desk's proposed reserve management strategy for the day. After the plan is approved, the desk is instructed to execute immediately any temporary open market operations that were planned for that day. (Outright operations, to be described shortly, may be conducted at other times of the day.)

The desk is linked electronically with its domestic open market trading counterparties by a computer system called TRAPS (Trading Room Automated Processing System), and all open market operations are now performed over this system. A message will be electronically transmitted simultaneously to all the primary dealers over TRAPS indicating the type and maturity of the operation being arranged. The dealers are given several minutes to respond via TRAPS with their propositions to buy or sell government securities. The propositions are then assembled and displayed on a computer screen for evaluation. The desk will select all propositions, beginning with the most attractively priced, up to the point where the desired amount is purchased or sold, and it will then notify each dealer via TRAPS which of its propositions have been chosen. The entire selection process is typically completed in a matter of minutes.

These temporary transactions are of two basic types. In a **repurchase agreement** (often called a **repo**), the Fed purchases securities with an agreement that the seller will repurchase them in a short period of time, anywhere from one to fifteen days from the original date of purchase. Because the effects on reserves of a repo are reversed on the day the agreement matures, a repo is actually a temporary open market purchase and is an especially desirable way of conducting a defensive open market purchase that will be reversed shortly. When the Fed wants to conduct a temporary open market sale, it engages in a **matched sale–purchase transaction** (sometimes called a **reverse repo**) in which the Fed sells securities and the buyer agrees to sell them back to the Fed in the near future.

At times, the desk may see the need to address a persistent reserve shortage or surplus and wish to arrange an operation that will have a more permanent impact on the supply of reserves. Outright transactions, which involve a purchase or sale of securities that is not self-reversing, are also conducted over TRAPS. These operations are traditionally executed at times of day when temporary operations are not being conducted.

Advantages of Open Market Operations

Open market operations have several advantages over the other tools of monetary policy.

1. Open market operations occur at the initiative of the Fed, which has complete control over their volume. This control is not found, for example, in discount operations, in which the Fed can encourage or discourage banks to borrow reserves by altering the discount rate but cannot directly control the volume of borrowed reserves.

2. Open market operations are flexible and precise; they can be used to any extent. No matter how small a change in reserves or the monetary base is desired, open market operations can achieve it with a small purchase or sale of securities. Conversely, if the desired change in reserves or the base is very large, the open market operations tool is strong enough to do the job through a very large purchase or sale of securities.

3. Open market operations are easily reversed. If a mistake is made in conducting an open market operation, the Fed can immediately reverse it. If the trading desk decides that the federal funds rate is too low because it has made too many open market purchases, it can immediately make a correction by conducting open market sales.

4. Open market operations can be implemented quickly; they involve no administrative delays. When the trading desk decides that it wants to change the monetary base or reserves, it just places orders with securities dealers, and the trades are executed immediately.

DISCOUNT POLICY

The facility at which banks can borrow reserves from the Federal Reserve is called the **discount window**. The easiest way to understand how the Fed affects the volume of borrowed reserves is by looking at how the discount window operates.

Operation of the Discount Window

The Fed's discount loans to banks are of three types: primary credit, secondary credit, and seasonal credit.[4] *Primary credit* is the discount lending that plays the most important role in monetary policy. Healthy banks are allowed to borrow all they want at very short maturities (usually overnight) from the primary credit facility, and it is therefore referred to as a **standing lending facility**.[5] The interest rate on these loans is the discount rate, and as we mentioned before, it is set higher than the federal funds rate target, usually by 100 basis points (one percentage point), and thus in most circumstances the amount of discount lending under the primary credit facility is very small. If the amount is so small, why does the Fed have this facility?

The answer is that the facility is intended to be a backup source of liquidity for sound banks so that the federal funds rate never rises too far above the federal funds target set by the FOMC. We have already seen how this works in Figure 5. When the demand for reserves has a large unexpected increase, no matter how far the demand curve shifts to the right, the equilibrium federal funds rate i''_{ff} will stay at i_d because borrowed reserves will just continue to increase, and the federal funds rate can rise no further. The primary credit facility has thus put a ceiling on the federal funds rate at i_d.

Secondary credit is given to banks that are in financial trouble and are experiencing severe liquidity problems. The interest rate on secondary credit is set at 50 basis points (0.5 percentage point) above the discount rate. The interest rate on these loans is set at a higher, penalty rate to reflect the less-sound condition of these borrowers. *Seasonal credit* is given to meet the needs of a limited number of small banks in vacation and agricultural areas that have a seasonal pattern of deposits. The interest rate charged on seasonal credit is tied to the average of the federal funds rate and certificate of deposit rates. The Federal Reserve has questioned the need for the seasonal credit facility because of improvements in credit markets and is thus contemplating eliminating it in the future.

Lender of Last Resort

In addition to its use as a tool to influence reserves, the monetary base, and the money supply, discounting is important in preventing and coping with financial panics. When the Federal Reserve System was created, its most important role was intended to be as the **lender of last resort**; to prevent bank failures from spinning out of control, it was

---

[4]The procedures for administering the discount window were changed in January 2003. The primary credit facility replaced an adjustment credit facility whose discount rate was typically set below market interest rates, so banks were restricted in their access to this credit. In contrast, now healthy banks can borrow all they want from the primary credit facility. The secondary credit facility replaced the extended credit facility, which focused somewhat more on longer-term credit extensions. The seasonal credit facility remains basically unchanged.

[5]This type of standard lending facility is commonly called a *Lombard facility* in other countries, and the interest rate changed on these loans is often called a *Lombard rate*. (This name comes from Lombardy, a region in northern Italy that was an important center of banking in the Middle Ages.)

to provide reserves to banks when no one else would, thereby preventing bank and financial panics. Discounting is a particularly effective way to provide reserves to the banking system during a banking crisis because reserves are immediately channeled to the banks that need them most.

Using the discount tool to avoid financial panics by performing the role of lender of last resort is an extremely important requirement of successful monetary policymaking. As we demonstrated with our money supply analysis in Chapter 14, the bank panics in the 1930–1933 period were the cause of the sharpest decline in the money supply in U.S. history, which many economists see as the driving force behind the collapse of the economy during the Great Depression. Financial panics can also severely damage the economy because they interfere with the ability of financial intermediaries and markets to move funds to people with productive investment opportunities (see Chapter 9).

Unfortunately, the discount tool has not always been used by the Fed to prevent financial panics, as the massive failures during the Great Depression attest. The Fed learned from its mistakes of that period and has performed admirably in its role of lender of last resort in the post–World War II period. The Fed has used its discount lending weapon several times to avoid bank panics by extending loans to troubled banking institutions, thereby preventing further bank failures.

At first glance, it might seem that the presence of the FDIC, which insures depositors up to a limit of $250,000 per account from losses due to a bank's failure, would make the lender-of-last-resort function of the Fed superfluous. There are two reasons why this is not the case. First, it is important to recognize that the FDIC's insurance fund amounts to around 1% of the total amount of deposits banks hold. If a large number of bank failures occurred, the FDIC would not be able to cover all the depositors' losses. Indeed, the large number of bank failures in the 1980s and early 1990s, described in Chapter 11, led to large losses and a shrinkage in the FDIC's insurance fund, which reduced the FDIC's ability to cover depositors' losses. This fact has not weakened the confidence of small depositors in the banking system because the Fed has been ready to stand behind the banks to provide whatever reserves are needed to prevent bank panics. Second, the $2 trillion of large-denomination deposits in the banking system are not guaranteed by the FDIC, because they exceed the $250,000 limit. A loss of confidence in the banking system could still lead to runs on banks from the large-denomination depositors, and bank panics could still occur despite the existence of the FDIC. The importance of the Federal Reserve's role as lender of last resort is, if anything, more important today because of the high number of bank failures experienced in the 1980s and early 1990s, and during the subprime financial crisis starting in 2007.

Not only can the Fed be a lender of last resort to banks, but it can also play the same role for the financial system as a whole. The existence of the Fed's discount window can help prevent and cope with financial panics that are not triggered by bank failures, as was the case during the Black Monday stock market crash of 1987, the terrorist destruction of the World Trade Center in September 2001 and the subprime financial crisis (see the two Inside the Fed boxes).

Although the Fed's role as the lender of last resort has the benefit of preventing bank and financial panics, it does have a cost. If a bank expects that the Fed will provide it with discount loans when it gets into trouble, it will be willing to take on more risk knowing that the Fed will come to the rescue. The Fed's lender-of-last-resort role has thus created a moral hazard problem similar to the one created by deposit insurance (discussed in Chapter 11): Banks take on more risk, thus exposing the deposit insurance agency, and hence taxpayers, to greater losses. The moral hazard problem is

Inside the Fed   Using Discount Policy to Prevent a Financial Panic

The Black Monday Stock Market Crash of 1987 and the Terrorist Destruction of the World Trade Center in September 2001. Although October 19, 1987, dubbed "Black Monday," will go down in the history books as the largest one-day percentage decline in stock prices to date (the Dow Jones Industrial Average declined by more than 20%), it was on Tuesday, October 20, 1987, that financial markets almost stopped functioning. Felix Rohatyn, one of the most prominent men on Wall Street, stated flatly: "Tuesday was the most dangerous day we had in 50 years."* Much of the credit for prevention of a market meltdown after Black Monday must be given to the Federal Reserve System and then-chairman of the Board of Governors, Alan Greenspan.

The stress of keeping markets functioning during the sharp decline in stock prices on Monday, October 19, meant that many brokerage houses and specialists (dealer-brokers who maintain orderly trading on the stock exchanges) were severely in need of additional funds to finance their activities. However, understandably enough, New York banks, as well as foreign and regional U.S. banks, growing very nervous about the financial health of securities firms, began to cut back credit to the securities industry at the very time when it was most needed. Panic was in the air. One chairman of a large specialist firm commented that on Monday, "from 2 p.m. on, there was total despair. The entire investment community fled the market. We were left alone on the field." It was time for the Fed, like the cavalry, to come to the rescue.

Upon learning of the plight of the securities industry, Alan Greenspan and E. Gerald Corrigan, then president of the Federal Reserve Bank of New York and the Fed official most closely in touch with Wall Street, became fearful of a spreading collapse of securities firms. To prevent this from occurring, Greenspan announced before the market opened on Tuesday, October 20, the Federal Reserve System's "readiness to serve as a source of liquidity to support the economic and financial system." In addition to this extraordinary announcement, the Fed made it clear that it would provide discount loans to any bank that would make loans to the securities industry, although this did not prove to be necessary. As one New York banker said, the Fed's message was, "We're here. Whatever you need, we'll give you."

The outcome of the Fed's timely action was that a financial panic was averted. The markets kept functioning on Tuesday, and a market rally ensued that day, with the Dow Jones Industrial Average climbing over 100 points.

A similar lender-of-last-resort operation was carried out in the aftermath of the destruction of the World Trade Center in New York City on Tuesday, September 11, 2001—the worst terrorist incident in U.S. history. Because of the disruption to the most important financial center in the world, the liquidity needs of the financial system skyrocketed. To satisfy these needs and to keep the financial system from seizing up, within a few hours of the incident, the Fed made an announcement similar to that made after the crash of 1987: "The Federal Reserve System is open and operating. The discount window is available to meet liquidity needs."** The Fed then proceeded to provide $45 billion to banks through the discount window, a 200-fold increase over the previous week. As a result of this action, along with the injection of as much as $80 billion of reserves into the banking system through open market operations, the financial system kept functioning. When the stock market reopened on Monday, September 17, trading was orderly, although the Dow Jones average did decline 7%.

The terrorists were able to bring down the twin towers of the World Trade Center, with nearly 3,000 dead. However, they were unable to bring down the U.S. financial system because of the timely actions of the Federal Reserve.

---

*"Terrible Tuesday: How the Stock Market Almost Disintegrated a Day After the Crash," *Wall Street Journal*, November 20, 1987, p. 1. This article provides a fascinating and more detailed view of the events described here and is the source of all the quotations cited.

**"Economic Front: How Policy Makers Regrouped to Defend the Financial System," *Wall Street Journal*, September 18, 2001, p. A1, provides more detail on this episode.

Inside the Fed   Federal Reserve Lender-of-Last-Resort Facilities During the Subprime Financial Crisis

The onset of the subprime financial crisis in August of 2007 led to a massive increase in Federal Reserve lender-of-last-resort facilities to contain the crisis.

In mid-August 2007, the Federal Reserve lowered the discount rate to just 50 basis points (0.5 percentage points) above the federal funds rate target from the normal 100 basis points. In March 2008, it narrowed the spread further by setting the discount rate at only 25 basis points above the federal funds rate target. In September 2007 and March 2008, it extended the term of discount loans: Before the crisis they were overnight or very short-term loans; in September the maturity of discount loans was extended to 30 days and to 90 days in March.

In December 2007, the Fed set up a temporary Term Auction Facility (TAF) in which it made discount loans at a rate determined through competitive auctions. This facility carried less of a stigma for banks than the normal discount window facility. It was more widely used than the discount window facility because it enabled banks to borrow at a rate less than the discount rate and because the rate was determined competitively, rather than being set at a penalty rate. While the TAF was a new facility for the Fed, the European Central Bank already had a similar facility. The TAF auctions started at amounts of $20 billion, but as the crisis worsened, the amounts were raised dramatically, with a total outstanding of over $400 billion.

On March 11, 2008, the Fed created the Term Securities Lending Facility (TSLF) in which it would lend Treasury securities to primary dealers for terms longer than overnight, as in existing lending programs, with the primary dealers pledging other securities. The TSLF's purpose was to supply more Treasury securities to primary dealers so they had sufficient Treasury securities to act as collateral, thereby helping the orderly functioning of financial markets. On the same day, the Fed authorized increases in reciprocal currency arrangements known as **swap lines**, in which it lent dollars to foreign central banks (in this case, the European Central Bank and the Swiss National Bank) in exchange for foreign currencies so that these central banks could in turn make dollar loans to their domestic banks. These swap lines were enlarged even further during the course of the crisis.

On March 14, 2008, as liquidity dried up for Bear Stearns, the Fed announced that it would in effect buy up $30 billion of Bear Stearns's mortgage-related assets in order to facilitate the purchase of Bear Stearns by J.P. Morgan.* The Fed took this extraordinary action because it believed that Bear Stearns was so interconnected with other financial institutions that its failure would have caused a massive fire-sale of assets and a complete seizing up of credit markets. The Fed took this action under an obscure provision of the Federal Reserve Act, section 13(3), that was put into the act during the Great Depression. It allowed the Fed under "unusual and exigent circumstances" to lend money to any individual, partnership, or corporation, as long as certain requirements were met. This broadening of the Fed's lender-of-last-resort actions outside of its traditional lending to depository institutions was described by Paul Volcker, a former chairman of the Federal Reserve, as the Fed going to the "very edge of its lawful and implied powers."

The broadening of the Fed's lender-of-last-resort activites using section 13(3) grew as the crisis deepened. On March 16, 2008, the Federal Reserve announced a new temporary credit facility, the Primary Dealer Credit Facility (PDCF), under which primary dealers, many of them investment banks, could borrow on similar terms to depository institutions using the traditional discount window facility. On September 19, 2008, after money market mutual funds were subject to large amounts of redemptions by investors, the Fed announced another temporary facility, the Asset-Backed Commercial Paper Money Market Mutual Fund Liquidity Facility (AMLF), in which the Fed would lend to primary dealers so that they could purchase asset-backed commercial paper from money market mutual funds. By so doing, money market mutual funds would be able to unload their asset-backed commercial paper when they needed to sell it to meet the demands for redemptions from their investors. A similar facility, the Money Market Investor Funding Facility (MMIFF), was set up on Octboer 21, 2008, to lend to special-purpose vehicles that could buy a wider range of money market mutual funds assets. On October 7, 2008, the Fed announced

(continued)

Federal Reserve Lender-of-Last-Resort Facilities During the Subprime Financial Crisis (*continued*)

another liquidity facility to promote the smooth functioning of the commercial paper market that had also begun to seize up, the Commercial Paper Funding Facility (CPFF). With this facility, the Fed could buy commercial paper directly from issuers at a rate 100 basis points above the expected federal funds rate over the term of the commercial paper. To restrict the facility to rolling over existing commercial paper, the Fed stipulated that each issuer could sell only an amount of commercial paper that was less than or equal to its average amount outstanding in August 2008. Then on November 25, 2008 the Fed announced two new liquidity facilities, the Term Asset-Backed Securities Loan Facility (TALF), in which it committed to the financing of $200 billion (later raised to $1 trillion) of asset-backed securities for a one-year period, and a Government Sponsored Entities Purchase Program, in which the Fed made a commitment to buy $100 billion of debt issued by Fannie Mae and Freddie Mac and other government-sponsored enterprises (GSEs), as well as $500 billion of mortgage-backed securities guaranteed by these GSEs.

In the aftermath of the Lehman Brothers failure, the Fed also extended large amounts of credit directly to financial institutions that needed to be bailed out. In late September, the Fed agreed to lend over $100 billion to prop up AIG and also authorized the Federal Reserve Bank of New York to purchase mortgage-backed and other risky securities from AIG to pump more liquidity into the company. In November, the Fed committed over $200 billion to absorb 90% of losses resulting from the federal government's guarantee of Citigroup's risky assets, while in January, it did the same thing for Bank of America, committing over $80 billion.

The expansion of the Fed's lender-of-last-resort programs during the subprime financial crisis was indeed remarkable, expanding the Fed's balance sheet by over one trillion dollars by the end of 2008, with expectations that the balance-sheet expansion would be far higher. The unprecedented expansion in the Fed's balance sheet demonstrated the Fed's commitment to get the financial markets working again.

*Technically, the purchase of these assets was in effect done with a non-recourse loan of $30 billion to J.P. Morgan, with the Fed bearing all the downside risk except for the first $1 billion, while getting all the gains if the assets were eventually sold for more than $30 billion. The effective purchase of commercial paper under the Asset-Backed Commercial Paper Money Market Mutual Fund Liquidity Facility, the Commercial Paper Funding Facility, and the Government Sponsored Entities Purchase Program was also done with non-recourse loans. Purchasing assets in this way conforms to section 13(3), which allows the Fed to make loans, but not purchase assets directly.

most severe for large banks, which may believe that the Fed and the FDIC view them as "too big to fail"; that is, they will always receive Fed loans when they are in trouble because their failure would be likely to precipitate a bank panic.

Similarly, Federal Reserve actions to prevent financial panic may encourage financial institutions other than banks to take on greater risk. They, too, expect the Fed to ensure that they could get loans if a financial panic seems imminent. When the Fed considers using the discount weapon to prevent panics, it therefore needs to consider the trade-off between the moral hazard cost of its role as lender of last resort and the benefit of preventing financial panics. This trade-off explains why the Fed must be careful not to perform its role as lender of last resort too frequently.

Advantages and Disadvantages of Discount Policy

The most important advantage of discount policy is that the Fed can use it to perform its role of lender of last resort. Experiences with the Black Monday crash, the terrorist attacks on September 11, 2001, and the subprime financial crisis starting in 2007 indicate that this role has become more important in the past couple of decades.

In the past, discount policy was used as a tool of monetary policy, with the discount rate changed to affect interest rates and the money supply. However, because the decisions to take out discount loans are made by banks and are therefore not completely controlled by the Fed, while open market operations are completely controlled by the Fed, the use of discount policy to conduct monetary policy has little to recommend it. This is why the Fed moved in January 2003 to the current system in which the discount facility is not used to set the federal funds rate, but is now a backup facility to prevent the federal funds rate from rising too far above its target or is used to provide liquidity during financial crises.

RESERVE REQUIREMENTS

As we saw in Chapter 14, changes in reserve requirements affect the money supply by causing the money supply multiplier to change. A rise in reserve requirements reduces the amount of deposits that can be supported by a given level of the monetary base and will lead to a contraction of the money supply. A rise in reserve requirements also increases the demand for reserves and raises the federal funds rate. Conversely, a decline in reserve requirements leads to an expansion of the money supply and a fall in the federal funds rate. The Fed has had the authority to vary reserve requirements since the 1930s; this once was a powerful way of affecting the money supply and interest rates, but is less important now.

The Depository Institutions Deregulation and Monetary Control Act of 1980 provided a simpler scheme for setting reserve requirements. All depository institutions, including commercial banks, savings and loan associations, mutual savings banks, and credit unions, are subject to the same reserve requirements: Required reserves on all checkable deposits—including non-interest-bearing checking accounts, NOW accounts, super-NOW accounts, and ATS (automatic transfer savings) accounts—are equal to 3% of the bank's first $48.3 million of checkable deposits[6] and 10% of the checkable deposits over $48.3 million, and the percentage set initially at 10% can be varied between 8% and 14%, at the Fed's discretion. In extraordinary circumstances, the percentage can be raised as high as 18%.

Disadvantages of Reserve Requirements as a Policy Tool

As we saw in Chapter 10, reserve requirements are no longer binding for most banks, so this tool is much less effective than it once was. Another disadvantage of using reserve requirements to control the money supply and interest rates is that raising the requirements can cause immediate liquidity problems for banks where reserve requirements are binding. When the Fed increased these requirements in the past, it usually softened the blow by conducting open market purchases or by making the discount loan window (borrowed reserves) more available, thereby providing reserves to banks that needed them. Continually fluctuating reserve requirements would also create more uncertainty for banks and make their liquidity management more difficult.

Since the policy tool of changing reserve requirements does not have much to recommend it, it is no longer used.

---

[6]The $48.3 million figure is as of the end of 2008. Each year, the figure is adjusted upward by 80% of the percentage increase in checkable deposits in the United States.

MONETARY POLICY TOOLS OF THE EUROPEAN CENTRAL BANK

Like the Federal Reserve, the European System of Central Banks (which is usually referred to as the European Central Bank) signals the stance of its monetary policy by setting a **target financing rate**, which in turn sets a target for the **overnight cash rate**. Like the federal funds rate, the overnight cash rate is the interest rate for very short-term interbank loans. The monetary policy tools used by the European Central Bank are similar to those used by the Federal Reserve and involve open market operations, lending to banks, and reserve requirements.

Open Market Operations

Like the Federal Reserve, the European Central Bank uses open market operations as its primary tool for conducting monetary policy and setting the overnight cash rate at the target financing rate. **Main refinancing operations** are the predominant form of open market operations and are similar to the Fed's repo transactions. They involve weekly **reverse transactions** (purchase or sale of eligible assets under repurchase or credit operations against eligible assets as collateral) that are reversed within two weeks. Credit institutions submit bids, and the European Central Bank decides which bids to accept. Like the Federal Reserve, the European Central Bank accepts the most attractively priced bids and makes purchases or sales to the point where the desired amount of reserves are supplied. In contrast to the Federal Reserve, which conducts open market operations in one location at the Federal Reserve Bank of New York, the European Central Bank decentralizes its open market operations by having them be conducted by the individual national central banks.

A second category of open market operations is the **longer-term refinancing operations**, which are a much smaller source of liquidity for the euro-area banking system and are similar to the Fed's outright purchases or sales of securities. These operations are carried out monthly and typically involve purchases or sales of securities with a maturity of three months. They are not used for signaling the monetary policy stance, but instead are aimed at providing euro-area banks access to longer-term funds.

Lending to Banks

As for the Fed, the next most important tool of monetary policy for the European Central Bank involves lending to banking institutions, which is carried out by the national central banks, just as discount lending is performed by the individual Federal Reserve Banks. This lending takes place through a standing lending facility called the **marginal lending facility**. There, banks can borrow (against eligible collateral) overnight loans from the national central banks at the **marginal lending rate**, which is set at 100 basis points above the target financing rate. The marginal lending rate provides a ceiling for the overnight market interest rate in the European Monetary Union, just as the discount rate does in the United States. Just as in the systems in the United States, Canada, Australia, and New Zealand, the Eurosystem has another standing facility, the **deposit facility**, in which banks are paid a fixed interest rate that is 100 basis points below the target financing rate. The prespecified interest rate on the deposit facility provides a floor for the overnight market interest rate, while the marginal lending rate sets a ceiling. This creates a channel/corridor, but with a much wider range of 100 basis points on either side.

Reserve Requirements

Like the Federal Reserve, the European Central Bank imposes reserve requirements such that all deposit-taking institutions are required to hold 2% of the total amount of checking deposits and other short-term deposits in reserve accounts with national central banks. All institutions that are subject to minimum reserve requirements have access to the European Central Bank's standing lending facilities and participate in open market operations. Like the Federal Reserve, the European Central Bank pays interest on reserves. Consequently, the banks' cost of complying with reserve requirements is low.

SUMMARY

1. A supply and demand analysis of the market for reserves yields the following results: When the Fed makes an open market purchase or lowers reserve requirements, the federal funds rate declines. When the Fed makes an open market sale or raises reserve requirements, the federal funds rate rises. Changes in the discount rate may also affect the federal funds rate.

2. The amount of an open market operation conducted on any given day by the trading desk of the Federal Reserve Bank of New York is determined by the amount of the dynamic open market operation intended to change reserves and the monetary base and by the amount of the defensive open market operation used to offset other factors that affect reserves and the monetary base. Open market operations are the primary tool used by the Fed to control the money supply because they occur at the initiative of the Fed, are flexible, are easily reversed, and can be implemented quickly.

3. The volume of discount loans (borrowed reserves) is affected by the discount rate. Besides its effect on the monetary base and the money supply, discount lending allows the Fed to perform its role as the lender of last resort. However, because the decisions by banks to take out discount loans (borrow reserves) are not controlled by the Fed, the use of discount policy to conduct monetary policy has little to recommend it.

4. Changing reserve requirements is too blunt a tool to use for controlling the money supply, and is no longer used as a policy tool.

5. The monetary policy tools used by the European Central Bank are similar to those used by the Federal Reserve System and involve open market operations, lending to banks, and reserve requirements. Main financing operations—open market operations in repos that are typically reversed within two weeks—are the primary tool to set the overnight cash rate at the target financing rate. The European Central Bank also operates standing lending facilities that operate to ensure that the overnight cash rate remains within 100 basis points of the target financing rate.

KEY TERMS

defensive open market operations, p. 381

deposit facility, p. 390

discount window, p. 384

dynamic open market operations, p. 381

federal funds rate, p. 373

lender of last resort, p. 384

longer-term refinancing operations, p. 390

main refinancing operations, p. 390

marginal lending facility, p. 390

marginal lending rate, p. 390

matched sale–purchase transaction (reverse repo), p. 383

overnight cash rate, p. 390

primary dealers, p. 382

repurchase agreement (repo), p. 383

reverse transactions, p. 390

standing lending facility, p. 384

swap lines, p. 387

target financing rate, p. 390

QUESTIONS AND PROBLEMS

All questions and problems are available in myeconlab *at* www.myeconlab.com/mishkin.

1. If the manager of the open market desk hears that a snowstorm is about to strike New York City, making it difficult to present checks for payment there and so raising the float, what defensive open market operations will the manager undertake?

2. During Christmastime, when the public's holdings of currency increase, what defensive open market operations typically occur? Why?

3. If the Treasury has just paid for a supercomputer and as a result its deposits with the Fed fall, what defensive open market operations will the manager of the open market desk undertake?

4. If float decreases below its normal level, why might the manager of domestic operations consider it more desirable to use repurchase agreements to affect the monetary base rather than an outright purchase of bonds?

5. Most open market operations are currently repurchase agreements. What does this tell us about the likely volume of defensive open market operations relative to dynamic open market operations?

6. "The only way that the Fed can affect the level of borrowed reserves is by adjusting the discount rate." Is this statement true, false, or uncertain? Explain your answer.

7. Using the supply and demand analysis of the market for reserves, show what happens to the federal funds rate, holding everything else constant, if the economy is surprisingly strong, leading to an increase in the amount of checkable deposits.

8. If there is a switch from deposits into currency, what happens to the federal funds rate? Use the supply and demand analysis of the market for reserves to explain your answer.

9. "Discounting is no longer needed because the presence of the FDIC eliminates the possibility of bank panics." Discuss.

10. The benefits of using Fed discount operations to prevent bank panics are straightforward. What are the costs?

11. You often read in the newspaper that the Fed has just lowered the discount rate. Does this signal that the Fed is moving to a more expansionary monetary policy? Why or why not?

12. How can the procyclical movement of interest rates (rising during business cycle expansions and falling during business cycle contractions) lead to a procyclical movement in the money supply as a result of Fed discounting? Why might this movement of the money supply be undesirable?

13. "If reserve requirements were eliminated, it would be harder to control interest rates." True, false, or uncertain?

14. "Considering that raising reserve requirements to 100% makes complete control of the money supply possible, Congress should authorize the Fed to raise reserve requirements to this level." Discuss.

15. Compare the use of open market operations, discounting, and changes in reserve requirements to control the money supply on the following criteria: flexibility, reversibility, effectiveness, and speed of implementation.

WEB EXERCISES

1. Go to www.federalreserve.gov/fomc/. This site reports activity by the FOMC. Scroll down to Calendar and click on the statement released after the last meeting. Summarize this statement in one paragraph. Be sure to note whether the committee has decided to increase or decrease the federal funds rate target. Now review the statements of the last two meetings. Has the stance of the committee changed?

2. Go to www.federalreserve.gov/releases/h15/update/. What is the current federal funds rate? What is the current Federal Reserve discount rate (define this rate as well)? Have short-term rates increased or declined since the end of 2008?

WEB REFERENCES

www.federalreserve.gov/fomc/fundsrate.htm

This site lists historical federal funds rates and discusses Federal Reserve targets.

www.frbdiscountwindow.org/

Information on the operation of the discount window and data on current and historical interest rates.

www.federalreserve.gov/monetarypolicy/reservereq.htm

Historical data and discussion about reserve requirements.

www.federalreserve.gov/fomc

A discussion about the Federal Open Market Committee, list of current members, meeting dates, and other current information.

 MyEconLab CAN HELP YOU GET A BETTER GRADE

If your exam were tomorrow, would you be ready? For each chapter, MyEconLab Practice Test and Study Plans pinpoint which sections you have mastered and which ones you need to study. That way, you are more efficient with your study time, and you are better prepared for your exams.

To see how it works, turn to page 20 and then go to: www.myeconlab.com/mishkin

16

The Conduct of Monetary Policy: Strategy and Tactics

Preview

Getting monetary policy right is crucial to the health of the economy. Overly expansionary monetary policy leads to high inflation, which decreases the efficiency of the economy and hampers economic growth. Monetary policy that is too tight can produce serious recessions in which output falls and unemployment rises. It can also lead to deflation, a fall in the price level, such as occurred in the United States during the Great Depression and in Japan more recently. As we saw in Chapter 9, deflation can be especially damaging to an economy, because it promotes financial instability and can worsen financial crises.

Now that we understand the tools that central banks such as the Federal Reserve use to conduct monetary policy, we can consider how central banks *should* conduct monetary policy. To explore this subject, in this chapter we first examine three monetary policy strategies, all of which focus on price stability as the primary, long-run goal of monetary policy. We then look at tactics, that is, the choice and setting of the monetary policy instrument. After examining the strategies and tactics, we can evaluate the Fed's conduct of monetary policy in the past, with the hope that it will indicate where monetary policy may head in the future.

MONETARY TARGETING

In pursuing a strategy of **monetary targeting**, the central bank announces that it will achieve a certain value (the target) of the annual growth rate of a monetary aggregate, such as a 5% growth rate of M1 or a 6% growth rate of M2. The central bank then is accountable for hitting the target.

Monetary Targeting in the United States, Japan, and Germany

In the 1970s, monetary targeting was adopted by several countries—most notably, Germany, Switzerland, Canada, the United Kingdom, Japan, and the United States. Monetary targeting in practice was quite different from Milton Friedman's suggestion that the chosen monetary aggregate be targeted to grow at a constant rate. Indeed, in all of these countries, the central banks never adhered to strict, ironclad rules for monetary growth. In some of these countries, monetary targeting was not pursued very seriously.

United States In 1970, Arthur Burns was appointed chairman of the Board of Governors of the Federal Reserve, and soon thereafter the Fed stated that it was committing itself to the use of monetary targets to guide monetary policy. In 1975, in response to a congressional resolution, the Fed began to announce publicly its targets for money supply growth, though it often missed them. In October 1979, two months after Paul Volcker became chairman of the Board of Governors, the Fed switched to an operating procedure that focused more on nonborrowed reserves and control of the monetary aggregates and less on the federal funds rate. Despite the change in focus, the performance in hitting monetary targets was even worse: In all three years of the 1979–1982 period, the Fed missed its M1 growth target ranges. What went wrong?

There are several possible answers to this question. The first is that the U.S. economy was exposed to several shocks during this period that made monetary control more difficult: the acceleration of financial innovation and deregulation, which added new categories of deposits such as NOW accounts to the measures of monetary aggregates; the imposition by the Fed of credit controls from March to July 1980, which restricted the growth of consumer and business loans; and the back-to-back recessions of 1980 and 1981–1982.[1]

A more persuasive explanation for poor monetary control, however, is that controlling the money supply was never really the intent of Volcker's policy shift. Despite Volcker's statements about the need to target monetary aggregates, he was not committed to these targets. Rather, he was far more concerned with using interest-rate movements to wring inflation out of the economy. Volcker's primary reason for changing the Fed's operating procedure was to free his hand to manipulate interest rates and thereby fight inflation. It was necessary to abandon interest-rate targets if Volcker were to be able to raise interest rates sharply when a slowdown in the economy was required to dampen inflation. This view of Volcker's strategy suggests that the Fed's announced attachment to monetary aggregate targets may have been a smokescreen to keep the Fed from being blamed for the high interest rates that would result from the new interest-rate policy.

In 1982, with inflation in check, the Fed decreased its emphasis on monetary targets. In July 1993, Board of Governors chairman Alan Greenspan testified in Congress that the Fed would no longer use any monetary aggregates as a guide for conducting monetary policy.

The Bank of Canada and the Bank of England also made commitments to monetary targets around the same time as the Federal Reserve and had similar experiences to that in the United States. By the 1980s, they found that monetary aggregates were not a reliable guide to monetary policy and, like the Federal Reserve, abandoned monetary targeting. Gerald Bouey, the governor of the Bank of Canada, described his bank's experience colorfully by saying, "We didn't abandon monetary aggregates; they abandoned us."

Japan The increase in oil prices in late 1973 was a major shock for Japan, which experienced a huge jump in the inflation rate, to greater than 20% in 1974—a surge facilitated by money growth in 1973 in excess of 20%. The Bank of Japan, like the other

---

[1]Another explanation focuses on the technical difficulties of monetary control when using a nonborrowed reserves operating target under a system of lagged reserve requirements, in which required reserves for a given week are calculated on the basis of the level of deposits two weeks earlier. See David Lindsey, "Nonborrowed Reserve Targeting and Monetary Control," in *Improving Money Stock Control*, ed. Laurence Meyer (Boston: Kluwer-Nijhoff, 1983), pp. 3–41.

central banks discussed here, began to pay more attention to money supply growth rates. In 1978, the Bank of Japan began to announce "forecasts" at the beginning of each quarter for M2 + CDs. Although the Bank of Japan was not officially committed to monetary targeting, monetary policy appeared to be more money-focused after 1978. For example, after the second oil price shock in 1979, the Bank of Japan quickly reduced M2 + CDs growth, rather than allowing it to shoot up as occurred after the first oil shock. The Bank of Japan now conducts monetary policy with operating procedures that are similar in many ways to those of the Federal Reserve. It uses the interest rate in the Japanese interbank market (similar to the federal funds market) as its daily operating target, just as the Fed does.

The Bank of Japan's monetary policy performance during the 1978–1987 period was much better than the Fed's. Money growth in Japan slowed gradually, beginning in the mid-1970s, and was much less variable than in the United States. The outcome was a more rapid braking of inflation and a lower average inflation rate. In addition, these excellent results on inflation were achieved with lower variability in real output than in the United States.

In parallel with the United States, financial innovation and deregulation in Japan began to reduce the usefulness of the M2 + CDs monetary aggregate as an indicator of monetary policy. Because of concerns about the appreciation of the yen, the Bank of Japan significantly increased the rate of money growth from 1987 to 1989. Many observers blame speculation in Japanese land and stock prices (the *bubble economy*) on the increase in money growth. To reduce this speculation, in 1989 the Bank of Japan switched to a tighter monetary policy aimed at slower money growth. The aftermath was a substantial decline in land and stock prices and the collapse of the bubble economy.

As a result, the Japanese economy was in a slump for ten years, often referred to as the "lost decade." The collapse of land and stock prices helped provoke a severe banking crisis, discussed in Chapter 11, that was a serious drag on the economy. The resulting weakness of the economy even led to deflation, promoting further financial instability. The outcome has been an economy that has stagnated for over a decade. Many critics believe that the Bank of Japan has pursued overly tight monetary policy and needs to substantially increase money growth in order to lift the economy out of its stagnation.

Germany   Starting in the mid-1970s and continuing through the next two decades, both Germany and Switzerland engaged in monetary targeting. The success of monetary targeting in controlling inflation in these two countries explains why monetary targeting still has strong advocates and is an element of the official policy regime for the European Central Bank (see the Global box). Because the success of the German monetary targeting regime in producing low inflation has received the most attention, we'll concentrate on Germany's experience.

Germany's central bank, the Bundesbank, chose to focus on a narrow monetary aggregate called *central bank money*, the sum of currency in circulation and bank deposits weighted by the 1974 required reserve ratios. In 1988, the Bundesbank switched targets from central bank money to M3.

The key fact about the monetary targeting regime in Germany is that it was not a Friedman-type monetary targeting rule in which a monetary aggregate is kept on a constant-growth-rate path and is the primary focus of monetary policy. The Bundesbank allowed growth outside of its target ranges for periods of two to three years, and overshoots of its targets were subsequently reversed. Monetary targeting in Germany was instead primarily a method of communicating the strategy of monetary policy focused on long-run considerations and the control of inflation.

Global The European Central Bank's Monetary Policy Strategy

The European Central Bank (ECB) pursues a hybrid monetary policy strategy that has elements in common with the monetary-targeting strategy previously used by the Bundesbank but also includes some elements of inflation targeting.* Like inflation targeting, the ECB has an announced goal for inflation over the medium term of "below, but close to, 2%." The ECB's strategy has two key "pillars." First, monetary and credit aggregates are assessed for "their implications for future inflation and economic growth." Second, many other economic variables are used to assess the future economic outlook. (Until 2003, the ECB employed something closer to a monetary target,

setting a "reference value" for the growth rate of the M3 monetary aggregate.)

The ECB's strategy is somewhat unclear and has been subject to criticism for this reason. Although the "below, but close to, 2%" goal for inflation sounds like an inflation target, the ECB has repeatedly stated that it does not have an inflation target. This central bank seems to have decided to try to "have its cake and eat it, too" by not committing too strongly to either a monetary-targeting strategy or an inflation-targeting strategy. The resulting difficulty of assessing the ECB's strategy has the potential to reduce the accountability of the institution.

*For a description of the ECB's monetary policy strategy, go to the ECB's website at www.ecb.int.

The calculation of monetary target ranges put great stress on making policy transparent (clear, simple, and understandable) and on regular communication with the public. First and foremost, a numerical inflation goal was prominently featured in the setting of target ranges. Second, monetary targeting, far from being a rigid policy rule, was flexible in practice. The target ranges for money growth were missed about 50% of the time in Germany, often because of the Bundesbank's concern about other objectives, including output and exchange rates. Furthermore, the Bundesbank demonstrated its flexibility by allowing its inflation goal to vary over time and to converge gradually to the long-run inflation goal.

The monetary targeting regime in Germany demonstrated a strong commitment to clear communication of the strategy to the general public. The money growth targets were continually used as a framework to explain the monetary policy strategy, and the Bundesbank expended tremendous effort in its publications and in frequent speeches by central bank officials to communicate to the public what the central bank was trying to achieve. Given that the Bundesbank frequently missed its money growth targets by significant amounts, its monetary targeting framework is best viewed as a mechanism for transparently communicating how monetary policy is being directed to achieve inflation goals and as a means for increasing the accountability of the central bank.

There are two key lessons to be learned from our discussion of German monetary targeting. First, a monetary targeting regime can restrain inflation in the longer run, even when the regime permits substantial target misses. Thus adherence to a rigid policy rule is not necessary to obtain good inflation outcomes. Second, the key reason why monetary targeting was reasonably successful, despite frequent target misses, is that the objectives of monetary policy were clearly stated and the central bank actively engaged in communicating the strategy of monetary policy to the public, thereby enhancing the transparency of monetary policy and the accountability of the central bank.

As we will see in the next section, these key elements of a successful monetary-targeting regime—flexibility, transparency, and accountability—are also important elements in inflation-targeting regimes. German monetary policy was actually closer in practice to inflation targeting than it was to Friedman-like monetary targeting, and thus might best be thought of as "hybrid" inflation targeting.

Advantages of Monetary Targeting

One advantage of monetary targeting is that information on whether the central bank is achieving its target is known almost immediately—figures for monetary aggregates are typically reported within a couple of weeks. Thus monetary targets can send almost immediate signals to the public and markets about the stance of monetary policy and the intentions of the policymakers to keep inflation in check. In turn, these signals help fix inflation expectations and produce less inflation. Monetary targets also allow almost immediate accountability for monetary policy to keep inflation low, thus helping to constrain the monetary policymaker from falling into the time-inconsistency trap.

Disadvantages of Monetary Targeting

All of the above advantages of monetary aggregate targeting depend on a big *if*: There must be a strong and reliable relationship between the goal variable (inflation or nominal income) and the targeted monetary aggregate. If the relationship between the monetary aggregate and the goal variable is weak, monetary aggregate targeting will not work; this seems to have been a serious problem in the United States and other countries that pursued monetary targets. The weak relationship implies that hitting the target will not produce the desired outcome on the goal variable and thus the monetary aggregate will no longer provide an adequate signal about the stance of monetary policy. As a result, monetary targeting will not help fix inflation expectations and will not be a good guide for assessing central bank accountability. In addition, an unreliable relationship between monetary aggregates and goal variables makes it difficult for monetary targeting to serve as a communications device that increases the transparency of monetary policy and makes the central bank accountable to the public.

INFLATION TARGETING

Given the breakdown of the relationship between monetary aggregates and goal variables such as inflation, many countries have recently adopted inflation targeting as their monetary policy strategy to achieve price stability. New Zealand was the first country to formally adopt inflation targeting in 1990, followed by Canada in 1991, the United Kingdom in 1992, Sweden and Finland in 1993, and Australia and Spain in 1994. Israel, Chile, and Brazil, among others, have also adopted a form of inflation targeting.

Inflation targeting involves several elements: (1) public announcement of medium-term numerical objectives (targets) for inflation; (2) an institutional commitment to price stability as the primary, long-run goal of monetary policy and a commitment to achieve the inflation goal; (3) an information-inclusive approach in which many variables (not just monetary aggregates) are used in making decisions about monetary policy; (4) increased transparency of the monetary policy strategy through communication with the public and the markets about the plans and objectives of monetary policymakers; and (5) increased accountability of the central bank for attaining its inflation objectives.

Inflation Targeting in New Zealand, Canada, and the United Kingdom

We begin our look at inflation targeting with New Zealand, because it was the first country to adopt it. We then go on to look at the experiences in Canada and the United Kingdom, which were next to adopt this strategy.[2]

New Zealand   As part of a general reform of the government's role in the economy, the New Zealand parliament passed a new Reserve Bank of New Zealand Act in 1989, which became effective on February 1, 1990. Besides increasing the independence of the central bank, moving it from being one of the least independent to one of the most independent among the developed countries, the act committed the Reserve Bank to a sole objective of price stability. The act stipulated that the minister of finance and the governor of the Reserve Bank should negotiate and make public a Policy Targets Agreement, a statement that sets out the targets by which monetary policy performance will be evaluated, specifying numerical target ranges for inflation and the dates by which they are to be reached. An unusual feature of the New Zealand legislation is that the governor of the Reserve Bank is held highly accountable for the success of monetary policy. If the goals set forth in the Policy Targets Agreement are not satisfied, the governor is subject to dismissal.

The first Policy Targets Agreement, signed by the minister of finance and the governor of the Reserve Bank on March 2, 1990, directed the Reserve Bank to achieve an annual inflation rate within a 3–5% range. Subsequent agreements lowered the range to 0–2% until the end of 1996, when the range was changed to 0–3% and later to 1–3% in 2002. As a result of tight monetary policy, the inflation rate was brought down from above 5% to below 2% by the end of 1992 (see Figure 1, panel a), but at the cost of a deep recession and a sharp rise in unemployment. Since then, inflation has typically remained within the targeted range, with the exception of brief periods in 1995, 2000, and 2008 when it exceeded the range by a small amount. (Under the Reserve Bank Act, the governor could have been dismissed, but after parliamentary debates he retained his job.) Since 1992, New Zealand's growth rate has generally been high, with some years exceeding 5%, and unemployment has come down significantly.

Canada   On February 26, 1991, a joint announcement by the minister of finance and the governor of the Bank of Canada established formal inflation targets. The target ranges were 2–4% by the end of 1992, 1.5–3.5% by June 1994, and 1–3% by December 1996. After the new government took office in late 1993, the target range was set at 1–3% from

---

[2]For further discussion of experiences with inflation targeting, particularly in other countries, see Leonardo Leiderman and Lars E. O. Svensson, *Inflation Targeting* (London: Centre for Economic Policy Research, 1995); Frederic S. Mishkin and Adam Posen, "Inflation Targeting: Lessons from Four Countries," Federal Reserve Bank of New York, *Economic Policy Review* 3 (August 1997), 9–110; Ben S. Bernanke, Thomas Laubach, Frederic S. Mishkin, and Adam S. Posen, *Inflation Targeting: Lessons from the International Experience* (Princeton: Princeton University Press, 1999); and Frederick S. Mishkin and Klaus Schmidt-Hebbel, "Does Inflation Targeting Matter?" in Frederick S. Mishkin and Klaus Schmidt-Hebbel, eds., *Monetary Policy Under Inflation Targeting* (Santiago: Central Bank of Chile, 2007), pp. 19–372.

FIGURE 1   **Inflation Rates and Inflation Targets for New Zealand, Canada, and the United Kingdom, 1980–2008**

(a) New Zealand; (b) Canada; (c) United Kingdom

Source: Ben S. Bernanke, Thomas Laubach, Frederic S. Mishkin, and Adam S. Poson, *Inflation Targeting: Lessons from the International Experience* (Princeton: Princeton University Press, 1999), updates from the same sources, and www.rbnz.govt.nz/statistics/econind/a3/ha3.xls.

December 1995 until December 1998 and has been kept at this level. Canadian inflation has also fallen dramatically since the adoption of inflation targets, from above 5% in 1991, to a 0% rate in 1995, and to around 2% subsequently (see Figure 1, panel b). As was the case in New Zealand, however, this decline was not without cost: Unemployment soared to above 10% from 1991 until 1994, but then declined substantially.

United Kingdom   In October 1992, the United Kingdom adopted an inflation target as its nominal anchor, and the Bank of England began to produce an *Inflation Report*, a quarterly report on the progress being made in achieving that target. The inflation target range was initially set at 1–4% until the next election (spring 1997 at the latest), with the intent that the inflation rate should settle down to the lower half of the range (below 2.5%). In May 1997, the inflation target was set at 2.5% and the Bank of England was given the power to set interest rates henceforth, granting it a more independent role in monetary policy.

Before the adoption of inflation targets, inflation had already been falling in the United Kingdom, with a peak of 9% at the beginning of 1991 and a rate of 4% at the time of adoption (see Figure 1, panel c). By the third quarter of 1994, it was at 2.2%, within the intended range. Subsequently inflation rose, climbing slightly above the 2.5% level by the end of 1995, but then fell and has remained close to the target since then except for 2008. In December 2003, the target was changed to 2.0% for a slightly different measure of inflation. Meanwhile, growth of the U.K. economy was strong until 2008 causing a substantial reduction in the unemployment rate.

Advantages of Inflation Targeting

Inflation targeting has several advantages over monetary targeting as a strategy for the conduct of monetary policy. With inflation targeting, stability in the relationship between money and inflation is not critical to its success, because it does not rely on this relationship. An inflation target allows the monetary authorities to use all available information, not just one variable, to determine the best settings for monetary policy.

Inflation targeting also has the key advantage that it is readily understood by the public and is thus highly transparent. Monetary targets, in contrast, are less likely to be easily understood by the public, and if the relationship between the growth rates of monetary aggregates and the inflation goal variable is subject to unpredictable shifts, as has occurred in many countries, monetary targets lose their transparency because they are no longer able to accurately signal the stance of monetary policy.

Because an explicit numerical inflation target increases the accountability of the central bank, inflation targeting has the potential to reduce the likelihood that the central bank will fall into the time-inconsistency trap of trying to expand output and employment in the short run by pursuing overly expansionary monetary policy. A key advantage of inflation targeting is that it can help focus the political debate on what a central bank can do in the long run—that is, control inflation, rather than what it cannot do, permanently increase economic growth and the number of jobs through expansionary monetary policy. Thus inflation targeting has the potential to reduce political pressures on the central bank to pursue inflationary monetary policy and thereby to reduce the likelihood of the time-inconsistency problem.

Inflation-targeting regimes also put great stress on making policy transparent and on regular communication with the public. Inflation-targeting central banks have frequent communications with the government, some mandated by law and some in response to informal inquiries, and their officials take every opportunity to make public speeches on their monetary policy strategy. While these techniques are also commonly used in countries that have not adopted inflation targeting, inflation-targeting central banks have taken public outreach a step further: Not only do they engage in extended public information campaigns, including the distribution of glossy brochures, but they also publish documents like the Bank of England's *Inflation Report*. The publication of these documents is particularly noteworthy, because they depart from the usual dull-looking, formal reports of central banks and use fancy graphics, boxes, and other eye-catching design elements to engage the public's interest.

The above channels of communication are used by central banks in inflation-targeting countries to explain the following concepts to the general public, financial market participants, and politicians: (1) the goals and limitations of monetary policy, including the rationale for inflation targets; (2) the numerical values of the inflation targets and how they were determined; (3) how the inflation targets are to be achieved, given current economic conditions; and (4) reasons for any deviations from targets. These communications have improved private sector planning by reducing uncertainty about monetary policy, interest rates, and inflation; they have promoted public debate of monetary policy, in part by educating the public about what a central bank can and cannot achieve; and they have helped clarify the responsibilities of the central bank and of politicians in the conduct of monetary policy.

Another key feature of inflation-targeting regimes is the tendency toward increased accountability of the central bank. Indeed, transparency and communication go hand in hand with increased accountability. The strongest case of accountability of a central bank in an inflation-targeting regime is in New Zealand, where the government has the right to dismiss the Reserve Bank's governor if the inflation targets are breached, even for one quarter. In other inflation-targeting countries, the central bank's accountability is less formalized. Nevertheless, the transparency of policy associated with inflation targeting has tended to make the central bank highly accountable to the public and the government. Sustained success in the conduct of monetary policy as measured against a pre-announced and well-defined inflation target can be instrumental in building public support for a central bank's independence and for its policies. This building of public support and accountability occurs even in the absence of a rigidly defined and legalistic standard of performance evaluation and punishment.

The performance of inflation-targeting regimes has been quite good. Inflation-targeting countries seem to have significantly reduced both the rate of inflation and inflation expectations beyond what would likely have occurred in the absence of inflation targets. Furthermore, once down, inflation in these countries has stayed down; following disinflations, the inflation rate in targeting countries has not bounced back up during subsequent cyclical expansions of the economy.

Disadvantages of Inflation Targeting

Critics of inflation targeting cite four disadvantages of this monetary policy strategy: delayed signaling, too much rigidity, the potential for increased output fluctuations, and low economic growth. We look at each in turn and examine the validity of these criticisms.

Delayed Signaling   In contrast to monetary aggregates, inflation is not easily controlled by the monetary authorities. Furthermore, because of the long lags in the effects of monetary policy, inflation outcomes are revealed only after a substantial lag. Thus an inflation target is unable to send immediate signals to both the public and markets about the stance of monetary policy. However, we have seen that the signals provided by monetary aggregates may not be very strong. Hence it is not at all clear that monetary targeting is superior to inflation targeting on these grounds.

Too Much Rigidity   Some economists have criticized inflation targeting because they believe it imposes a rigid rule on monetary policymakers and limits their ability to respond to unforeseen circumstances. However, useful policy strategies exist that are "rule-like" in that they involve forward-looking behavior that limits policymakers from systematically engaging in policies with undesirable long-run consequences. Such policies avoid the time-inconsistency problem and would best be described as "constrained discretion."

Indeed, inflation targeting can be described exactly in this way. Inflation targeting, as actually practiced, is far from rigid and is better described as "flexible inflation targeting." First, inflation targeting does not prescribe simple and mechanical instructions on how the central bank should conduct monetary policy. Rather, it requires the central bank to use all available information to determine which policy actions are appropriate to achieve the inflation target. Unlike simple policy rules, inflation targeting never requires the central bank to focus solely on one key variable. Second, inflation targeting as practiced contains a substantial degree of policy discretion. Inflation targets have been modified depending on economic circumstances, as we have seen. Moreover, central banks under inflation-targeting regimes have left themselves considerable scope to respond to output growth and fluctuations through several devices.

Potential for Increased Output Fluctuations   An important criticism of inflation targeting is that a sole focus on inflation may lead to monetary policy that is too tight when inflation is above target and thus may lead to larger output fluctuations. Inflation targeting does not, however, require a sole focus on inflation—in fact, experience has shown that inflation targeters display substantial concern about output fluctuations. All the inflation targeters have set their inflation targets above zero.[3] For example, currently New Zealand has the lowest midpoint for an inflation target, 1.5%, while Canada and Sweden set the midpoint of their inflation target at 2%; and the United Kingdom and Australia currently have their midpoints at 2.5%.

The decision by inflation targeters to choose inflation targets above zero reflects the concern of monetary policymakers that particularly low inflation can have substantial negative effects on real economic activity. Deflation (negative inflation in which the price level actually falls) is especially to be feared because of the possibility that it may promote financial instability and precipitate a severe economic contraction (Chapter 9). The deflation in Japan in recent years has been an important factor in the weakening of the Japanese financial system and economy. Targeting inflation rates of above zero makes periods of deflation less likely. This is one reason why some economists both within and outside of Japan have been calling on the Bank of Japan to adopt an inflation target at levels of 2% or higher.

Inflation targeting also does not ignore traditional stabilization goals. Central bankers in inflation-targeting countries continue to express their concern about fluctuations in output and employment, and the ability to accommodate short-run stabilization goals to some degree is built into all inflation-targeting regimes. All inflation-targeting countries have been willing to minimize output declines by gradually lowering medium-term inflation targets toward the long-run goal.

---

[3]Consumer price indexes have been found to have an upward bias in the measurement of true inflation, so it is not surprising that inflation targets would be chosen to exceed zero. However, the actual targets have been set to exceed the estimates of this measurement bias, indicating that inflation targeters have decided to have targets for inflation that exceed zero even after measurement bias is accounted for.

Low Economic Growth   Another common concern about inflation targeting is that it will lead to low growth in output and employment. Although inflation reduction has been associated with below-normal output during disinflationary phases in inflation-targeting regimes, once low inflation levels were achieved, output and employment returned to levels at least as high as they were before. A conservative conclusion is that once low inflation is achieved, inflation targeting is not harmful to the real economy. Given the strong economic growth after disinflation in many countries (such as New Zealand) that have adopted inflation targets, a case can be made that inflation targeting promotes real economic growth, in addition to controlling inflation.

MONETARY POLICY WITH AN IMPLICIT NOMINAL ANCHOR

In recent years, the United States has achieved excellent macroeconomic performance (including low and stable inflation) until the subprime financial crisis occurred, without using an explicit nominal anchor such as a monetary aggregate or an inflation target. Although the Federal Reserve has not articulated an explicit strategy, a coherent strategy for the conduct of monetary policy exists nonetheless. This strategy involves an implicit but not an explicit nominal anchor in the form of an overriding concern by the Federal Reserve to control inflation in the long run. In addition, it involves forward-looking behavior in which there is careful monitoring for signs of future inflation using a wide range of information, coupled with periodic "preemptive strikes" by monetary policy against the threat of inflation.

As emphasized by Milton Friedman, monetary policy effects have long lags. In industrialized countries with a history of low inflation, the inflation process seems to have tremendous inertia: Estimates from large macroeconometric models of the U.S. economy, for example, suggest that monetary policy takes over a year to affect output and over two years to have a significant impact on inflation. For countries that have experienced highly variable inflation, and therefore have more flexible prices, the lags may be shorter.

The presence of long lags means that monetary policy cannot wait to respond until inflation has begun. If the central bank waits until overt signs of inflation appear, it will already be too late to maintain stable prices, at least not without a severe tightening of policy: Inflation expectations will already be embedded in the wage- and price-setting process, creating an inflation momentum that will be hard to halt. Inflation becomes much harder to control once it has been allowed to gather momentum, because higher inflation expectations become ingrained in various types of long-term contracts and pricing agreements.

To prevent inflation from getting started, therefore, monetary policy needs to be forward-looking and preemptive. That is, depending on the lags from monetary policy to inflation, monetary policy needs to act long before inflationary pressures appear in the economy. For example, suppose it takes roughly two years for monetary policy to have a significant impact on inflation. In this case, even if inflation is currently low but policymakers believe inflation will rise over the next two years with an unchanged stance of monetary policy, they must tighten monetary policy *now* to prevent the inflationary surge.

Under Alan Greenspan, the Federal Reserve was successful in pursuing a preemptive monetary policy. For example, as discussed later in the chapter, the Fed raised interest rates from 1994 to 1995 before a rise in inflation got a toehold. As a result, inflation not only did not rise, but fell slightly. This preemptive, forward-looking monetary policy strategy is clearly also a feature of inflation-targeting regimes, because monetary policy instruments are adjusted to take account of the long lags in their effects in an effort to hit future inflation targets. However, the Fed's policy regime might best be described as a "just do it" policy, and differs from inflation targeting in that it does not officially have a nominal anchor and is much less transparent in its monetary policy strategy.

Advantages of the "Just Do It" Approach

The Fed's "just do it" approach, which has some of the key elements of inflation targeting, has many of the same advantages. It also does not rely on a stable money-inflation relationship. As with inflation targeting, the central bank uses many sources of information to determine the best settings for monetary policy. The Fed's forward-looking behavior and stress on price stability also help to discourage overly expansionary monetary policy, thereby ameliorating the time-inconsistency problem.

Another key argument for the "just do it" strategy is its demonstrated success. The Federal Reserve reduced inflation in the United States from double-digit levels in 1980 to an average rate close to 3% over the last fifteen years, which is arguably consistent with the price stability goal. At the same time, economic growth has been high, averaging around 3% over the same period, with relatively steady growth up until the sub-prime financial crisis hit the economy hard. Indeed, up until recently, the performance of the U.S. economy was the envy of the industrialized world.

Disadvantages of the "Just Do It" Approach

Given the success of the "just do it" strategy in the United States, why should the United States consider other monetary policy strategies? (If it ain't broke, why fix it?) The answer is that the "just do it" strategy has some disadvantages that may cause it to work less well in the future.

One disadvantage of the strategy is its lack of transparency. The Fed's close-mouthed approach about its intentions gives rise to a constant guessing game about what it is going to do. This high level of uncertainty leads to unnecessary volatility in financial markets and creates doubt among producers and the general public about the future course of inflation and output. Furthermore, the opacity of its policymaking makes it hard to hold the Federal Reserve accountable to Congress and the general public: The Fed can't be held accountable if there are no predetermined criteria for judging its performance. Low accountability may make the central bank more susceptible to the time-inconsistency problem, whereby it may pursue short-term objectives at the expense of long-term ones.

Probably the most serious problem with the "just do it" approach is its strong dependence on the preferences, skills, and trustworthiness of the individuals in charge of the central bank. In recent years in the United States, Federal Reserve chairmen Alan Greenspan and Ben Bernanke and other Federal Reserve officials have emphasized forward-looking policies and inflation control, with great success. The Fed's prestige and credibility with the American public have risen accordingly. But the Fed's leadership will periodically change, and there is no guarantee that it will be committed to the same approach. Nor is there any guarantee that the relatively good working relationship that has existed between the Fed and the executive branch will always continue. In a different economic or political environment, the Fed might face strong pressure to engage in over-expansionary policies, raising the possibility that time inconsistency may become a more serious problem. In the past, after a successful period of low inflation, the Federal Reserve has reverted to inflationary monetary policy—the 1970s are one example—and without an explicit nominal anchor, this could certainly happen again.

Another disadvantage of the "just do it" approach is that it has some inconsistencies with democratic principles. As described in Chapter 13, there are good reasons—notably, insulation from short-term political pressures—for the central bank to have some degree of independence, and the evidence does generally support central bank independence. Yet the practical economic arguments for central bank independence coexist uneasily with the presumption that government policies should be made democratically, rather than by an elite group.

In contrast, inflation targeting can make the institutional framework for the conduct of monetary policy more consistent with democratic principles and avoid some of

---

Inside the Fed   Chairman Bernanke and Inflation Targeting

Ben Bernanke, a former professor at Princeton University, became the Federal Reserve chairman in February 2006, after serving as a member of the Board of Governors from 2002–2005 and then as chairman of the Council of Economic Advisors. Bernanke is a world-renowned expert on monetary policy and while an academic wrote extensively on inflation targeting, including articles and a book written with the author of this text.*

Bernanke's writings suggest that he is a strong proponent of inflation targeting and increased transparency in central banks. In an important speech given at a conference at the Federal Reserve Bank of St. Louis in 2004 he described how the Federal Reserve might approach a movement toward inflation targeting: The Fed should announce a numerical value for its long-run inflation goal.** Bernanke emphasized that announcing a numerical objective for inflation would be completely consistent with the Fed's dual mandate of achieving price stability and maximum employment, and therefore might be called a *mandate-consistent inflation objective*, because it would be set above zero to avoid deflations, which have harmful effects on employment. In addition, it would not be intended to be a short-run target that might lead to excessively tight control of inflation at the expense of overly high employment fluctuations.

Since becoming Fed chairman, Bernanke has made it clear that any movement toward inflation targeting must result from a consensus within the FOMC. After Chairman Bernanke set up a subcommittee to discuss Federal Reserve communication, which included discussions about announcing a specific numerical inflation objective, the FOMC made a partial step in the direction of inflation targeting in November of 2007 when it announced a new communication strategy that lengthened the horizon for FOMC participants' inflation projections to three years. In many cases, the three-year horizon will be sufficiently long so that the projection for inflation under "appropriate policy" will reflect each participant's inflation objective because at that horizon inflation should converge to the long-run objective. A couple of relatively minor modifications could move the Fed even further toward inflation targeting. The first modification requires lengthening the horizon for the inflation projection. The goal would be to set a time sufficiently far off so that inflation would almost surely converge to its long-run value by then. Second, the FOMC participants would need to be willing to reach a consensus on a single value for the mandate-consistent inflation objective. With these two modifications, the longer-run inflation projections would in effect be an announcement of a specific numerical objective for the inflation rate and so serve as a flexible version of inflation targeting.*** Whether the Federal Reserve will move in this direction in the future is still highly uncertain.

*Ben S. Bernanke and Frederic S. Mishkin, "Inflation Targeting: A New Framework for Monetary Policy," *Journal of Economic Perspectives*, vol. 11, no. 2 (1997), Ben S. Bernanke, Frederic S. Mishkin and Adam S. Posen, "Inflation Targeting: Fed Policy After Greenspan," *Milken Institute Review*, (Fourth Quarter, 1999): 48–56, Ben S. Bernanke, Frederic S. Mishkin and Adam S. Posen, "What Happens When Greenspan is Gone," *Wall Street Journal*, January 5, 2000: p. A22, and Ben S. Bernanke, Thomas Laubach, Frederic S. Mishkin and Adam S. Posen, *Inflation Targeting: Lessosns from the International Experience* (Princeton, NJ: Princeton University Press 1999).

**Ben S. Bernanke, "Inflation Targeting," Federal Reserve Bank of St. Louis, *Review*, vol 86, no. 4 (July/August 2004), pp. 165–168.

***See Frederic S. Mishkin, "Whither Federal Reserve Communications," speech given at the Petersen Institute for International Economics, Washington, DC, July 28, 2008, http://www.federalreserve.gov/newsevents/speech/mishkin20080.

SUMMARY TABLE 1

Advantages and Disadvantages of Different Monetary Policy Strategies

	Monetary Targeting	Inflation Targeting	Implicit Nominal Anchor
Advantages	Immediate signal on achievement of target	Simplicity and clarity of target	Does not rely on stable money–inflation relationship
		Does not rely on stable money-inflation relationship	Demonstrated success in United States
		Increased accountability of central bank	
		Reduced effects of inflationary shocks	
Disadvantages	Relies on stable money-inflation relationship	Delayed signal about achievement of target	Lack of transparency
		Could impose rigid rule (though has not in practice)	Success depends on individuals in charge
		Larger output fluctuations if sole focus on inflation (though not in practice)	Low accountability

the above problems. The inflation-targeting framework promotes the accountability of the central bank to elected officials, who are given some responsibility for setting the goals for monetary policy and then monitoring the economic outcomes. However, under inflation targeting as it has generally been practiced, the central bank has complete control over operational decisions, so that it can be held accountable for achieving its assigned objectives.

The Fed's monetary policy strategy may move more toward inflation targeting in the future, particularly since chairman Ben Bernanke has been an advocate of inflation targeting (see the Inside the Fed box, "Chairman Bernanke and Inflation Targeting").

As a study aid, the advantages and disadvantages of monetary targeting as well as the other monetary policy strategies are listed in Summary Table 1.

TACTICS: CHOOSING THE POLICY INSTRUMENT

Now that we are familiar with the alternative strategies for monetary policy, let's look at how monetary policy is conducted on a day-to-day basis. Central banks directly control the tools of monetary policy—open market operations, reserve requirements, and the discount rate—but knowing the tools and the strategies for implementing a monetary

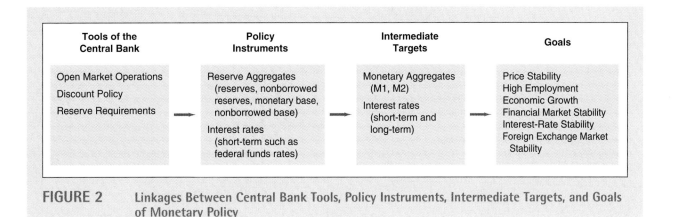

Tools of the Central Bank	Policy Instruments	Intermediate Targets	Goals
Open Market Operations Discount Policy Reserve Requirements	Reserve Aggregates (reserves, nonborrowed reserves, monetary base, nonborrowed base) Interest rates (short-term such as federal funds rates)	Monetary Aggregates (M1, M2) Interest rates (short-term and long-term)	Price Stability High Employment Economic Growth Financial Market Stability Interest-Rate Stability Foreign Exchange Market Stability

FIGURE 2   Linkages Between Central Bank Tools, Policy Instruments, Intermediate Targets, and Goals of Monetary Policy

policy does not tell us whether policy is easy or tight. The **policy instrument** (also called an **operating instrument**) is a variable that responds to the central bank's tools and indicates the stance (easy or tight) of monetary policy. A central bank like the Fed has at its disposal two basic types of policy instruments: reserve aggregates (total reserves, nonborrowed reserves, the monetary base, and the nonborrowed base) and interest rates (federal funds rate and other short-term interest rates). (Central banks in small countries can choose another policy instrument, the exchange rate, but we leave this topic to Chapter 18.) The policy instrument might be linked to an **intermediate target**, such as a monetary aggregate like M2 or a long-term interest rate. Intermediate targets stand between the policy instrument and the goals of monetary policy (e.g., price stability, output growth); they are not as directly affected by the tools of monetary policy, but might be more closely linked to the goals of monetary policy. As a study aid, Figure 2 shows a schematic of the linkages between the tools of monetary policy, policy instruments, intermediate targets, and the goals of monetary policy.

As an example, suppose the central bank's employment and inflation goals are consistent with a nominal GDP growth rate of 5%. The central bank might believe that the 5% nominal GDP growth rate will be achieved by a 4% growth rate for M2 (an intermediate target), which will in turn be achieved by a growth rate of 3% for nonborrowed reserves (the policy instrument). Alternatively, the central bank might believe that the best way to achieve its objectives would be to set the federal funds rate (a policy instrument) at, say, 4%. Can the central bank choose to target both the nonborrowed-reserves and the federal-funds-rate policy instruments at the same time? The answer is no. The application of supply and demand analysis to the market for reserves we developed in Chapter 15 explains why a central bank must choose one or the other.

Let's first see why choosing an aggregate target involves losing control of the interest rate. Figure 3 contains a supply and demand diagram for the market for reserves. Although the central bank expects the demand curve for reserves to be at R^{d*}, it fluctuates between $R^{d'}$ and $R^{d''}$ because of unexpected fluctuations in deposits (and hence required reserves) and changes in banks' desire to hold excess reserves. If the central bank has a nonborrowed reserves target of NBR^* (say, because it has a target growth rate of the money supply of 4%), it expects that the federal funds rate will be i_{ff}^*. However, as the figure indicates, the fluctuations in the reserves demand curve between $R^{d'}$ and $R^{d''}$ will result in a fluctuation in the federal funds rate between i_{ff}' and i_{ff}''. Pursuing an aggregate target implies that interest rates will fluctuate.

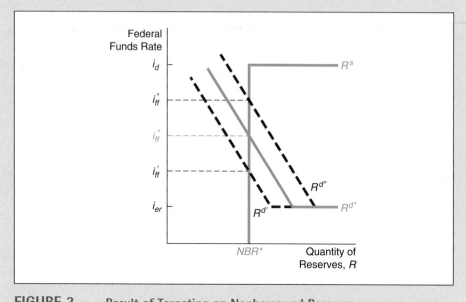

FIGURE 3   **Result of Targeting on Nonborrowed Reserves**
Targeting on nonborrowed reserves of NBR^* will lead to fluctuations in the federal funds rate between i'_{ff} and i''_{ff} because of fluctuations in the demand for reserves between $R^{d'}$ and $R^{d''}$.

The supply and demand diagram in Figure 4 shows the consequences of an interest-rate target set at i^*_{ff}. Again the central bank expects the reserves demand curve to be at R^{d*}, but it fluctuates between $R^{d'}$ and $R^{d''}$ due to unexpected changes in deposits or banks' desire to hold excess reserves. If the demand curve rises to $R^{d''}$, the federal funds rate will begin to rise above i^*_{ff} and the central bank will engage in open market purchases of bonds until it raises the supply of nonborrowed reserves to NBR'', at which point the equilibrium federal funds rate is again at i^*_{ff}. Conversely, if the demand curve falls to $R^{d'}$ and lowers the federal funds rate, the central bank would keep making open market sales until nonborrowed reserves fall to NBR' and the federal funds rate returns to i^*_{ff}. The central bank's adherence to the interest-rate target thus leads to a fluctuating quantity of nonborrowed reserves and the money supply.

The conclusion from the supply and demand analysis is that interest-rate and reserve (monetary) aggregate targets are incompatible. A central bank can hit one or the other, but not both. Because a choice between them has to be made, we need to examine what criteria should be used to select a policy instrument.

Criteria for Choosing the Policy Instrument

Three criteria apply when choosing a policy instrument: The instrument must be observable and measurable, it must be controllable by the central bank, and it must have a predictable effect on the goals.

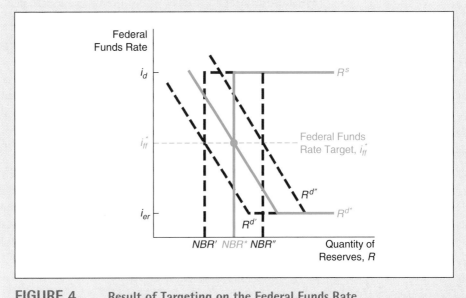

FIGURE 4   **Result of Targeting on the Federal Funds Rate**
Targeting on the interest rate i_{ff}^* will lead to fluctuation in nonborrowed reserves because of fluctuations in the demand for reserves between $R^{d'}$ and $R^{d''}$.

Observability and Measurability   Quick observability and accurate measurement of a policy instrument is necessary, because it will be useful only if it signals the policy stance rapidly. Reserve aggregates like nonborrowed reserves are straightforward to measure, but there is still some lag in reporting of reserve aggregates (a delay of two weeks). Short-term interest rates like the federal funds rate, by contrast, not only are easy to measure, but also are observable immediately. Thus, it seems that interest rates are more observable and measurable than are reserves and, therefore, are a better policy instrument.

However, as we learned in Chapter 4, the interest rate that is easiest to measure and observe is the nominal interest rate. It is typically a poor measure of the real cost of borrowing, which indicates with more certainty what will happen to the real GDP. This real cost of borrowing is more accurately measured by the real interest rate—that is, the nominal interest rate adjusted for expected inflation ($i_r = i - \pi^e$). Unfortunately, real interest rates are extremely difficult to measure, because we do not have a direct way to measure expected inflation. Given that both interest rates and aggregates have observability and measurability problems, it is not clear whether one should be preferred to the other as a policy instrument.

Controllability   A central bank must be able to exercise effective control over a variable if it is to function as a useful policy instrument. If the central bank cannot control the policy instrument, knowing that it is off track does little good, because the central bank has no way of getting it back on track.

Because of shifts in and out of currency, even reserve aggregates such as nonborrowed reserves are not completely controllable. Conversely, the Fed can control short-term interest rates such as the federal funds rate very tightly. It might appear, therefore, that short-term interest rates would dominate reserve aggregates on the controllability criterion. However, a central bank cannot set short-term real interest rates because it does not have control over expectations of inflation. Once again, a clear-cut case cannot be made that short-term interest rates are preferable to reserve aggregates as a policy instrument, or vice versa.

Predictable Effect on Goals   The most important characteristic of a policy instrument is that it must have a predictable effect on a goal. If a central bank can accurately and quickly measure the price of tea in China and can completely control its price, what good will that do? The central bank cannot use the price of tea in China to affect unemployment or the price level in its country. Because the ability to affect goals is so critical to the usefulness of any policy instrument, the tightness of the link from reserve or monetary aggregates to goals (output, employment, and inflation) or, alternatively, from interest rates to these goals, is a matter of much debate. In recent years, most central banks have concluded that the link between interest rates and goals such as inflation is tighter than the link between aggregates and inflation. For this reason, central banks throughout the world now generally use short-term interest rates as their policy instrument.

TACTICS: THE TAYLOR RULE

As we have seen, the Federal Reserve and most other central banks currently conduct monetary policy by setting a target for short-term interest rates like the federal funds rate. But how should this target be chosen?

John Taylor of Stanford University has come up with an answer, called the **Taylor rule**. The Taylor rule indicates that the federal (fed) funds rate should be set equal to the inflation rate plus an "equilibrium" real fed funds rate (the real fed funds rate that is consistent with full employment in the long run) plus a weighted average of two gaps: (1) an inflation gap, current inflation minus a target rate, and (2) an output gap, the percentage deviation of real GDP from an estimate of its potential full employment level.[4] This rule can be written as follows:

$$\text{Federal funds rate target} = \text{inflation rate} + \text{equilibrium real fed funds rate}$$
$$+ \tfrac{1}{2} (\text{inflation gap}) + \tfrac{1}{2} (\text{output gap})$$

Taylor has assumed that the equilibrium real fed funds rate is 2% and that an appropriate target for inflation would also be 2%, with equal weights of $\tfrac{1}{2}$ on the inflation and output gaps. For an example of the Taylor rule in practice, suppose that the inflation rate were at 3%, leading to a positive inflation gap of 1% (= 3% − 2%), and real GDP was 1% above its potential, resulting in a positive output gap of 1%. Then the Taylor rule suggests that the federal funds rate should be set at 6% [= 3% inflation + 2% equilibrium real fed funds rate + $\tfrac{1}{2}$ (1% inflation gap) + $\tfrac{1}{2}$ (1% output gap)].

An important feature of the Taylor rule is that the coefficient on the inflation gap is positive and equal to $\tfrac{1}{2}$. If the inflation rate rises by 1 percentage point, then the federal

---

[4]John B. Taylor, "Discretion Versus Policy Rules in Practice," *Carnegie-Rochester Conference Series on Public Policy* 39 (1993): 195–214. A more intuitive discussion with a historical perspective can be found in John B. Taylor, "A Historical Analysis of Monetary Policy Rules," in *Monetary Policy Rules*, ed. John B. Taylor (Chicago: University of Chicago Press, 1999), pp. 319–341.

funds target is raised by 1.5 percentage points, and so by more than one-to-one. In other words, a rise in inflation by 1 percentage point leads to a real federal funds rate increase of $\frac{1}{2}$ percentage point. The principle that the monetary authorities should raise nominal interest rates by more than the increase in the inflation rate has been named the **Taylor principle**, and it is critical to the success of monetary policy. Suppose the Taylor principle is not followed and nominal rates rise by *less* than the rise in the inflation rate so that real interest rates *fall* when inflation rises. There will then be serious instability because a rise in inflation leads to an effective easing of monetary policy, which then leads to even higher inflation in the future. Indeed, this was a feature of monetary policy in the 1970s that led to a loss of the nominal anchor and the era of the so-called "Great Inflation," when inflation rates climbed to double-digit levels. Fortunately, since 1979, the Taylor principle has become a feature of monetary policy, with much happier outcomes on both the inflation and aggregate output fronts.

The presence of an output gap in the Taylor rule might indicate that the Fed should care not only about keeping inflation under control, but also about minimizing business-cycle fluctuations of output around its potential. Caring about both inflation and output fluctuations is consistent with many statements by Federal Reserve officials that controlling inflation and stabilizing real output are important concerns of the Fed.

An alternative interpretation of the presence of the output gap in the Taylor rule is that the output gap is an indicator of future inflation as stipulated in **Phillips curve theory**. Phillips curve theory indicates that changes in inflation are influenced by the state of the economy relative to its productive capacity, as well as by other factors. This productive capacity can be measured by potential GDP, which is a function of the natural rate of unemployment, the rate of unemployment consistent with full employment. A related concept is the **NAIRU**, the **nonaccelerating inflation rate of unemployment**, the rate of unemployment at which there is no tendency for inflation to change.[5] Simply put, the theory states that when the unemployment rate is above NAIRU with output below potential, inflation will come down, but if it is below NAIRU with output above potential, inflation will rise. Prior to 1995, the NAIRU was thought to reside around 6%. However, with the decline in unemployment to around the 4% level in the late 1990s, with no increase (and even a slight decrease) in inflation, some critics have questioned the value of Phillips curve theory. Either they claim that it just doesn't work any more or, alternatively, they believe that there is great uncertainty about the value of NAIRU, which may have fallen to below 5% for reasons that are not absolutely clear. Phillips curve theory is now highly controversial, and many economists believe that it should not be used as a guide for the conduct of monetary policy.

As Figure 5 shows, the Taylor rule does a pretty good job of describing the Fed's setting of the federal funds rate under chairmen Greenspan and Bernanke. (It did not work very well in the 1970s, which reflects that the Taylor principle was not being followed, which explains why monetary policy outcomes were so poor.) Does this mean that the Fed should fire all its economists and put a computer in charge that just has to compute the Taylor rule setting for the federal funds rate? This would certainly save the taxpayers a lot of money.

There are several reasons why the answer is no. First, monetary policy has long lags, that is, it takes a long time for policy actions to affect the economy. Therefore, monetary

---

[5]There are, however, subtle differences between the two concepts, as is discussed in Arturo Estrella and Frederic S. Mishkin, "The Role of NAIRU in Monetary Policy: Implications of Uncertainty and Model Selection," in *Monetary Policy Rules*, ed. John Taylor (Chicago: University of Chicago Press, 1999): pp. 405–430.

policy necessarily needs to be forward looking. Good monetary policy requires that the Fed forecast where inflation and economic activity are going to be in the future, and then adjust the policy instrument accordingly. The Fed will therefore look at a much wider range of information than just the current inflation rate and output gap in setting policy, as is done in the Taylor rule. Second, no one really knows what the true model of the economy is. Monetary policymakers therefore need to apply a lot of judgment in deciding the appropriate stance of monetary policy. In other words, the conduct of monetary policy is as much an art as it is a science. The Taylor rule leaves out all the art, and so is unlikely to produce the best monetary policy outcomes. Third, the economy is changing all the time, so the Taylor rule coefficients would be unlikely to stay constant. Fourth, financial crises such as the recent subprime meltdown may require very different monetary policy because changes in credit spreads may alter the relationship between the federal funds rate and other interest rates more relevant to investment decisions, and therefore to economic activity. The bottom line is that putting monetary policy on autopilot using the Taylor rule with fixed coefficients would be a bad idea.

Given the above reasons, it is no surprise that the Taylor rule does not explain all the movements in the federal funds rate in Figure 5. For this reason, financial institutions hire Fed watchers, as described in the Inside the Fed box. The Taylor rule is, however, useful as a guide to monetary policy. If the setting of the policy instrument is very different from what the Taylor rule suggests, then policymakers should ask whether they have a good reason for deviating from this rule. If they don't, as during the Burns era in the 1970s, then they might be making a mistake. Indeed, the FOMC does make use of Taylor rule estimates in exactly this way. These estimates are made available to FOMC participants to help them in making their decisions at each FOMC meeting.

Inside the Fed   Fed Watchers

As we have seen, the most important player in the determination of the U.S. money supply and interest rates is the Federal Reserve. When the Fed wants to inject reserves into the system, it conducts open market purchases of bonds, which cause bond prices to increase and their interest rates to fall, at least in the short term. If the Fed withdraws reserves from the system, it sells bonds, thereby depressing their price and raising their interest rates. From a longer-run perspective, if the Fed pursues an expansionary monetary policy with high money growth, inflation will rise and, as we saw in Chapter 5, interest rates will rise as well. Contractionary monetary policy is likely to lower inflation in the long run and lead to lower interest rates.

Knowing what actions the Fed might be taking can thus help investors and financial institutions to predict the future course of interest rates with greater accuracy. Because, as we have seen, changes in interest rates have a major impact on investors and financial institutions' profits, they are particularly interested in scrutinizing the Fed's behavior. To assist in this task, financial institutions hire *Fed watchers*, experts on Federal Reserve behavior who may have worked in the Federal Reserve System and so have an insider's view of Federal Reserve operations. A Fed watcher who can accurately predict the course of monetary policy is a very valuable commodity, and successful Fed watchers therefore often earn very high salaries, well into the six-figure range and sometimes even higher.

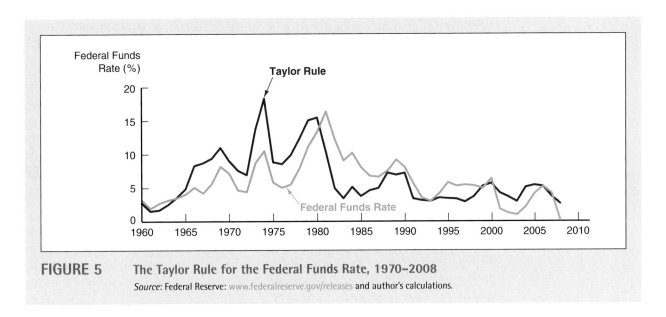

FIGURE 5   The Taylor Rule for the Federal Funds Rate, 1970–2008

Source: Federal Reserve: www.federalreserve.gov/releases and author's calculations.

CENTRAL BANKS' RESPONSE TO ASSET-PRICE BUBBLES: LESSONS FROM THE SUBPRIME CRISIS

Over the centuries, economies have been periodically subject to **asset-price bubbles**, pronounced increases in asset prices that depart from fundamental values, which eventually burst resoundingly. The story of the subprime financial crisis, discussed in Chapter 9, indicates how costly these bubbles can be. The bursting of the asset-price bubble in the housing market brought down the financial system, leading to an economic downturn, a rise in unemployment, disrupted communities, and direct hardship for families forced to leave their homes after foreclosures.

The high cost of asset-price bubbles raises the question: What should central banks do about them? Should they use monetary policy to try to pop bubbles? Are there regulatory measures they can take to rein in asset-price bubbles? To answer these questions, we need to ask whether there are different kinds of bubbles that require different types of response.

Two Types of Asset-Price Bubbles

There are two types of asset-price bubbles: one that is driven by credit and a second that is driven purely by overly optimistic expectations (which former chairman of the Fed, Alan Greenspan, referred to as "irrational exuberance").

Credit-Driven Bubbles   When a credit boom begins, it can spill over into an asset-price bubble: Easier credit can be used to purchase particular assets and thereby raise their prices. The rise in asset values, in turn, encourages further lending for these assets, either because it increases the value of collateral, making it easier to borrow, or because it raises the value of capital at financial institutions, which gives them more capacity to lend. The lending for these assets can then increase demand for them further and hence raise their prices even more. This feedback loop—in which a credit boom drives up asset prices, which in turn fuels the credit boom, which drives asset prices even higher, and so on—can generate a bubble in which asset prices rise well above their fundamental values.

Credit-driven bubbles are particularly dangerous, as the recent subprime financial crisis has demonstrated. When asset prices come back down to earth and the bubble bursts, the collapse in asset prices then leads to a reversal of the feedback loop in which loans go sour, lenders cut back on credit supply, the demand for assets declines further, and prices drop even more. These were exactly the dynamics in housing markets during the subprime financial crisis. Driven by a credit boom in subprime lending, housing prices rose way above fundamental values; but when housing prices crashed, credit shriveled up and housing prices plummeted.

The resulting losses on subprime loans and securities eroded the balance sheets of financial institutions, causing a decline in credit (deleveraging) and a sharp fall in business and household spending, and therefore in economic activity. As we saw during the subprime financial crisis, the interaction between housing prices and the health of financial institutions following the collapse of the housing price bubble endangered the operation of the financial system as a whole and had dire consequences for the economy.

Bubbles Driven Solely by Irrational Exuberance   Bubbles that are driven solely by overly optimistic expectations, but which are not associated with a credit boom, pose much less risk to the financial system. For example, the bubble in technology stocks in the late 1990s described in Chapter 7 was not fueled by credit, and the bursting of the tech-stock bubble was not followed by a marked deterioration in financial institutions' balance sheets. The bursting of the tech-stock bubble thus did not have a very severe impact on the economy and the recession that followed was quite mild. Bubbles driven solely by irrational exuberance are therefore far less dangerous than those driven by credit booms.

Should Central Banks Respond to Bubbles?

Under Alan Greenspan, the Federal Reserve took the position that it should not respond to bubbles. He argued that bubbles are nearly impossible to identify. If central banks or government officials knew that a bubble was in progress, why wouldn't market participants know as well? If so, then a bubble would be unlikely to develop, because market participants would know that prices were getting out of line with fundamentals. This argument applies very strongly to asset-price bubbles that are driven by irrational exuberance, as is often the case for bubbles in the stock market. Unless central bank or government officials are smarter than market participants, which is unlikely given the especially high wages that savvy market participants garner, they will be unlikely to identify when bubbles of this type are occurring. There is then a strong argument for not responding to these kinds of bubbles.

On the other hand, when asset-price bubbles are rising rapidly at the same time that credit is booming, there is a greater likelihood that asset prices are deviating from fundamentals, because laxer credit standards are driving asset prices upward. In this case, central bank or government officials have a greater likelihood of identifying that a bubble is in progress; this was indeed the case during the housing market bubble in the United States because these officials did have information that lenders had weakened lending standards and that credit extension in the mortgage markets was rising at abnormally high rates.

Should Monetary Policy Try to Prick Asset-Price Bubbles?

Not only are credit-driven bubbles possible to identify, but as we saw above, they are the ones that are capable of doing serious damage to the economy. There is thus a much stronger case that central banks should respond to possible credit-driven bubbles. But what is the appropriate response? Should monetary policy be used to try to prick a possible asset-price bubble that is associated with a credit boom by raising interest rates above what is desirable for keeping the economy on an even keel? Or are there other measures that are more suited to deal with credit-driven bubbles?

There are three strong arguments against using monetary policy to prick bubbles by raising interest rates more than is necessary for achieving price stability and minimizing economic fluctuations. First, even if an asset-price bubble is of the credit-driven variety and so can be identified, the effect of raising interest rates on asset prices is highly uncertain. Although some economic analysis suggests that raising interest rates can diminish rises in asset prices, raising interest rates may be very ineffective in restraining the bubble, because market participants expect such high rates of return from buying bubble-driven assets. Furthermore, raising interest rates has often been found to cause a bubble to burst more severely, thereby increasing the damage to the economy. Another way of saying this is that bubbles are departures from normal behavior, and it is unrealistic to expect that the usual tools of monetary policy will be effective in abnormal conditions.

Second, there are many different asset prices, and at any one time a bubble may be present in only a fraction of assets. Monetary policy actions are a very blunt instrument in such a case, as such actions would be likely to affect asset prices in general, rather than the specific assets that are experiencing a bubble.

Third, monetary policy actions to prick bubbles can have harmful affects on the aggregate economy. If interest rates are raised significantly to curtail a bubble, the economy will slow, people will lose jobs, and inflation can fall below its desirable level. Indeed, as the first two argument suggest, the rise in interest rates necessary to prick a bubble may be so high that it can only be done at great cost to workers and the economy. This is not to say that monetary policy should not respond to asset prices per se. As we will see in Chapter 23, the level of asset prices does affect aggregate demand and thus the evolution of the economy. Monetary policy should react to fluctuations in asset prices to the extent that they affect inflation and economic activity.

Although it is controversial, the basic conclusion from the above reasoning is that monetary policy should not be used to prick bubbles.

Are Other Types of Policy Responses Appropriate?

As argued above, there is a case for responding to credit-driven bubbles because they are more identifiable and can do great damage to the economy, but monetary policy does not seem to be the way to do it. Regulatory policy to affect what is happening in credit markets in the aggregate, referred to as **macroprudential regulation**, on the other hand, does seem to be the right tool for the job of reigning in credit-driven bubbles.

Financial regulation and supervision, either by central banks or other government entities, with the usual elements of a well-functioning prudential regulatory and supervisory system described in Chapter 11 can prevent excessive risk taking that can trigger a credit boom, which in turn leads to an asset-price bubble. These elements include adequate disclosure and capital requirements, prompt corrective action, close monitoring of financial institutions' risk-management procedures, and close supervision to enforce compliance with regulations. More generally, regulation should focus on preventing future feedback loops from credit booms to asset prices, asset prices to credit booms, credit booms to asset prices, and so on. As the subprime financial crisis demonstrated, the rise in asset prices that accompanied the credit boom resulted in higher capital buffers at financial institutions, supporting further lending in the context of unchanging capital requirements; in the bust, the value of the capital dropped precipitously, leading to a cut in lending. Capital requirements that are countercyclical, that is, adjusted upward during a boom and downward during a bust, might help eliminate the pernicious feedback loops that promote credit-driven bubbles.

A rapid rise in asset prices accompanied by a credit boom provides a signal that market failures or poor financial regulation and supervision might be causing a bubble to form. Central banks and other government regulators could then consider implementing policies to rein in credit growth directly or implement measures to make sure credit standards are sufficiently high.

An important lesson from the subprime financial crisis is that central banks and other regulators should not have a laissez-faire attitude and let credit-driven bubbles proceed without any reaction. Appropriate macroprudential regulation can help limit credit-driven bubbles and improve the perfomance of both the financial system and the economy.

FED POLICY PROCEDURES: HISTORICAL PERSPECTIVE

The well-known adage "The road to hell is paved with good intentions" applies as much to the Federal Reserve as it does to human beings. Understanding a central bank's goals and the strategies it can use to pursue them cannot tell us how monetary policy is actually conducted. To understand the practical results of the theoretical underpinnings, we have to look at how the Fed has actually conducted policy in the past. This historical perspective will not only show us how the U.S. central bank carries out its duties but will also help us interpret the Fed's activities and see where U.S. monetary policy may be heading in the future.

The Early Years: Discount Policy as the Primary Tool

When the Fed was created, changing the discount rate was the primary tool of monetary policy—the Fed had not yet discovered that open market operations were a more powerful tool for influencing the money supply, and the Federal Reserve Act made no provisions for changes in reserve requirements. The guiding principle for the conduct of monetary policy was that as long as loans were being made for "productive" purposes—that is, to support the production of goods and services—providing reserves to the banking system to make these loans would not be inflationary. This theory, now thoroughly discredited, became known as the **real bills doctrine**. In practice, it meant that the Fed would make loans to member commercial banks when they showed up at the discount window with *eligible paper*, loans to facilitate the production and sale of goods and services. (Since the 1920s, the Fed has not conducted discount operations in this way.) The Fed's act of making loans to member banks was initially called *rediscounting*, because the original bank loans to businesses were made by discounting (loaning less than) the face value of the loan, and the Fed would be discounting them again. (Over time, when the Fed's emphasis on eligible paper diminished, the Fed's loans to banks became known as *discounts*, and the interest rate on these loans the *discount rate*, which is the terminology we use today.)

By the end of World War I, the Fed's policy of rediscounting eligible paper and keeping interest rates low to help the Treasury finance the war had led to a raging inflation; in 1919 and 1920, the inflation rate averaged 14%. The Fed decided that it could no longer follow the passive policy prescribed by the real bills doctrine because it was inconsistent with the goal of price stability, and for the first time the Fed accepted the responsibility of playing an active role in influencing the economy. In January 1920, the Fed raised the discount rate from $4\frac{3}{4}\%$ to 6%, the largest jump in its history, and eventually raised it further, to 7% in June 1920, where it remained for nearly a year. The result of this policy was a sharp decline in the money supply and an especially sharp recession in 1920–1921. Although the blame for this severe recession can clearly be laid at the Fed's doorstep, in one sense the Fed's policy was very successful: After an initial decline in the price level, the inflation rate went to zero, paving the way for the prosperous Roaring Twenties.

Discovery of Open Market Operations

In the early 1920s, a particularly important event occurred: The Fed accidentally discovered open market operations. When the Fed was created, its revenue came exclusively from the interest it received on the discount loans it made to member banks. After the 1920–1921 recession, the volume of discount loans shrank dramatically, and the Fed was pressed for income. It solved this problem by purchasing income-earning securities. In doing so, the Fed noticed that reserves in the banking system grew and there was a multiple expansion of bank loans and deposits. This result is obvious to us now (we studied the multiple deposit creation process in Chapter 14), but to the Fed at that time it was a revelation. A new monetary policy tool was born, and by the end of the 1920s, it was the most important weapon in the Fed's arsenal.

The Great Depression

The stock market boom in 1928 and 1929 created a dilemma for the Fed. It wanted to temper the boom by raising the discount rate, but it was reluctant to do so, because that would mean raising interest rates to businesses and individuals who had legitimate needs for credit. Finally, in August 1929, the Fed raised the discount rate, but by then it was too late; the speculative excesses of the market boom had already occurred, and the Fed's action merely hastened the stock market crash and pushed the economy into recession.

The weakness of the economy, particularly in the agricultural sector, led to what Milton Friedman and Anna Schwartz labeled a "contagion of fear" that triggered substantial withdrawals from banks, building to a full-fledged panic in November and December 1930. For the next two years, the Fed sat idly by while one bank panic after another occurred, culminating in the final panic in March 1933, at which point the new president, Franklin Delano Roosevelt, declared a bank holiday. (Why the Fed failed to engage in its lender-of-last-resort role during this period is discussed in the Inside the Fed box on bank panics.) The spate of bank panics from 1930 to 1933 were the most severe in U.S. history, and Roosevelt aptly summed up the problem in his statement, "The only thing we have to fear is fear itself." By the time the panics were over in March 1933, more than one-third of the commercial banks in the United States had failed.

Inside the Fed   Bank Panics of 1930–1933: Why Did the Fed Let Them Happen?

The Federal Reserve System was totally passive during the bank panics of the Great Depression period and did not perform its intended role of lender of last resort to prevent them. In retrospect, the Fed's behavior seems quite extraordinary, but hindsight is always clearer than foresight.

The primary reason for the Fed's inaction was that Federal Reserve officials did not understand the negative impact that bank failures could have on the money supply and on economic activity. Friedman and Schwartz report that the Federal Reserve officials "tended to regard bank failures as regrettable consequences of bank management or bad banking practices, or as inevitable reactions to prior speculative excesses, or as a consequence but hardly a cause of the financial and economic collapse in process." In addition, bank failures in the early stages of the bank panics "were concentrated among smaller banks and,

since the most influential figures in the system were big-city bankers who deplored the existence of smaller banks, their disappearance may have been viewed with complacency."[*]

Friedman and Schwartz also point out that political infighting may have played an important role in the passivity of the Fed during this period. The Federal Reserve Bank of New York, which until 1928 was the dominant force in the Federal Reserve System, strongly advocated an active program of open market purchases to provide reserves to the banking system during the bank panics. However, other powerful figures in the Federal Reserve System opposed the New York bank's position, and the bank was outvoted. (Friedman and Schwartz's discussion of the politics of the Federal Reserve System during this period makes for fascinating reading, and you might enjoy their highly readable book.)

[*]Milton Friedman and Anna Jacobson Schwartz, *A Monetary History of the United States, 1867–1960* (Princeton, NJ: Princeton University Press, 1963), p. 358.

In Chapter 14, we examined how the bank panics of this period led to a decline in the money supply of more than 25%. The resulting unprecedented decline in the money supply during this period is thought by many economists, particularly monetarists, to have been the major contributing factor to the severity of the depression, never equaled before or since.

Reserve Requirements as a Policy Tool

The Thomas Amendment to the Agricultural Adjustment Act of 1933 provided the Federal Reserve's Board of Governors with emergency power to alter reserve requirements with the approval of the president of the United States. In the Banking Act of 1935, this emergency power was expanded to allow the Fed to alter reserve requirements without the president's approval.

The first use of reserve requirements as a tool of monetary control proved that the Federal Reserve was capable of adding to the blunders that it had made during the bank panics of the early 1930s. By the end of 1935, banks had increased their holdings of excess reserves to unprecedented levels, a sensible strategy considering their discovery during the 1930–1933 period that the Fed would not always perform its intended role as lender of last resort. Bankers now understood that they would have to protect themselves against a bank run by holding substantial amounts of excess reserves. The Fed viewed these excess reserves as a nuisance that made it harder to exercise monetary control. Specifically, the Fed worried that these excess reserves might be lent out and would produce "an uncontrollable expansion of credit in the future."[6]

To improve monetary control, the Fed raised reserve requirements in three steps: August 1936, January 1937, and May 1937. The result of this action was, as we would expect from our money supply model, a slowdown of money growth toward the end of 1936 and an actual decline in 1937. The recession of 1937–1938, which commenced in May 1937, was a severe one and was especially upsetting to the American public because even at its outset unemployment was intolerably high. So not only does it appear that the Fed was at fault for the severity of the Great Depression contraction in 1929–1933, but, to add insult to injury, it was responsible for aborting the subsequent recovery. The Fed's disastrous experience with varying its reserve requirements made it far more cautious in the use of this policy tool in the future.

War Finance and the Pegging of Interest Rates: 1942–1951

With the entrance of the United States into World War II in late 1941, U.S. government spending skyrocketed, and to finance it the Treasury issued huge amounts of bonds. The Fed agreed to help the Treasury finance the war cheaply by pegging interest rates at the low levels that had prevailed before the war: $\frac{3}{8}$% on Treasury bills and $2\frac{1}{2}$% on long-term Treasury bonds. Whenever interest rates rose above these levels and the price of bonds began to fall, the Fed would make open market purchases, thereby bidding up bond prices and driving interest rates down again. The result was a rapid growth in the monetary base and the money supply. The Fed had thus in effect relinquished its control of monetary policy to meet the financing needs of the government.

When the war ended, the Fed continued to peg interest rates, and because there was little pressure on them to rise, this policy did not result in an explosive growth in the money supply. When the Korean War broke out in 1950, however, interest rates began to climb, and the Fed found that it was again forced to expand the monetary base at a rapid rate. Because inflation began to heat up (the consumer price index rose 8% between 1950 and 1951), the Fed decided that it was time to reassert its control over monetary policy by abandoning the interest-rate peg. An often bitter debate ensued between the Fed and the Treasury, which wanted to keep its interest costs down and so favored a continued pegging of interest rates at low levels. In March 1951, the Fed and the Treasury came to an agreement known as the Accord, in which pegging was abandoned but the Fed promised that it would not allow interest rates to rise precipitously. After Eisenhower's election as president in 1952, the Fed was given complete freedom to pursue its monetary policy objectives.

Targeting Money Market Conditions: the 1950s and 1960s

With its freedom restored, the Federal Reserve, then under the chairmanship of William McChesney Martin, Jr., took the view that monetary policy should be grounded in intuitive judgment based on a feel for the money market. The policy procedure that resulted can be described as one in which the Fed targeted on money market conditions, and particularly on interest rates.

---

[6]Milton Friedman and Anna Jacobson Schwartz, *A Monetary History of the United States, 1867–1960* (Princeton, NJ: Princeton University Press, 1963), p. 524.

An important characteristic of this policy procedure was that it led to more rapid growth in the money supply when the economy was expanding and a slowing of money growth when the economy was in recession. The *procyclical monetary policy* (a positive association of money supply growth with the business cycle) is explained by the following step-by-step reasoning. As we learned in Chapter 5, a rise in national income ($Y\uparrow$) leads to a rise in market interest rates ($i\uparrow$). With the rise in interest rates, the Fed would purchase bonds to bid their price up and lower interest rates to their target level. The resulting increase in the monetary base caused the money supply to rise and the business-cycle expansion to be accompanied by a faster rate of money growth. In summary:

$$Y\uparrow \Rightarrow i\uparrow \Rightarrow MB\uparrow \Rightarrow M\uparrow$$

In a recession, the opposite sequence of events would occur, and the decline in income would be accompanied by a slower rate of growth in the money supply ($Y\downarrow \Rightarrow M\downarrow$).

A further problem with using interest rates as the primary operating instrument is that they may encourage an inflationary spiral to get out of control. As we saw in Chapter 5, when inflation and hence expected inflation rises, nominal interest rates rise via the Fisher effect. If the Fed attempted to prevent this increase by purchasing bonds, this would also lead to a rise in the monetary base and the money supply:

$$\pi\uparrow \Rightarrow \pi^e\uparrow \Rightarrow i\uparrow \Rightarrow MB\uparrow \Rightarrow M\uparrow$$

Higher inflation could thus lead to an increase in the money supply, which would increase inflationary pressures further.

By the late 1960s, the rising chorus of criticism of procyclical monetary policy by such prominent monetarist economists such as Milton Friedman, Karl Brunner, and Allan Meltzer and concerns about inflation finally led the Fed to abandon its focus on money market conditions.

Targeting Monetary Aggregates: the 1970s

In 1970, after Arthur Burns was appointed chairman of the Board of Governors, the Fed committed itself to the use of monetary aggregates as intermediate targets. Did monetary policy cease to be procyclical? A glance at Figure 4 in Chapter 1 indicates that monetary policy was as procyclical in the 1970s as in the 1950s and 1960s. What went wrong? Why did the conduct of monetary policy not improve? The answers to these questions lie in the Fed's operating procedures during the period, which suggest that its commitment to targeting monetary aggregates was not very strong.

Every six weeks, the Federal Open Market Committee would set target ranges for the growth rates of various monetary aggregates and would determine what federal funds rate (the interest rate on funds loaned overnight between banks) it thought consistent with these aims. The target ranges for the growth in monetary aggregates were fairly broad—a typical range for M1 growth might be 3% to 6%; for M2, 4% to 7%—while the range for the federal funds rate was a narrow band, say, from $7\frac{1}{2}$% to $8\frac{1}{4}$%. The trading desk at the Federal Reserve Bank of New York was then instructed to meet both sets of targets, but as we saw earlier, interest-rate targets and monetary aggregate targets might not be compatible. If the two targets were incompatible—say, the federal funds rate began to climb higher than the top of its target band when M1 was growing too rapidly—the trading desk was instructed to give precedence to the federal funds rate target. In the situation just described, this would mean that although M1 growth was too high, the trading desk would make open market purchases to keep the federal funds rate within its target range.

The Fed was actually using the federal funds rate as its operating instrument. During the six-week period between FOMC meetings, an unexpected rise in output (which would cause the federal funds rate to hit the top of its target band) would then induce open market purchases and a too-rapid growth of the money supply. When the FOMC met again, it would try to get money supply growth back on track by raising the target range on the federal funds rate. However, if income continued to rise unexpectedly, money growth would overshoot again. This is exactly what occurred from June 1972 to June 1973, when the economy boomed unexpectedly: M1 growth greatly exceeded its target, increasing at approximately an 8% rate, while the federal funds rate climbed from $4\frac{1}{2}$% to $8\frac{1}{2}$%. The economy soon became overheated, and inflationary pressures began to mount.

The opposite chain of events occurred at the end of 1974, when the economic contraction was far more severe than anyone had predicted. The federal funds rate fell dramatically, from over 12% to 5%, and persistently bumped against the bottom of its target range. The trading desk conducted open market sales to keep the federal funds rate from falling, and money growth dropped precipitously, actually turning negative by the beginning of 1975. Clearly, this sharp drop in money growth when the United States was experiencing one of the worst economic contractions of the postwar era was a serious mistake.

Using the federal funds rate as an operating instrument promoted a procyclical monetary policy despite the Fed's lip service to monetary aggregate targets. If the Federal Reserve really intended to pursue monetary aggregate targets, it seems peculiar that it would have chosen an interest rate for an operating instrument rather than a reserve aggregate. The explanation for the Fed's choice of an interest rate as an operating instrument is that it was still very concerned with achieving interest-rate stability and was reluctant to relinquish control over interest-rate movements. The incompatibility of the Fed's policy procedure with its stated intent of targeting on the monetary aggregates had become very clear by October 1979, when the Fed's policy procedures underwent drastic revision.

New Fed Operating Procedures: October 1979–October 1982

In October 1979, two months after Paul Volcker became chairman of the Board of Governors, the Fed finally de-emphasized the federal funds rate as an operating instrument by widening its target range more than fivefold: A typical range might be from 10% to 15%. The primary operating instrument became nonborrowed reserves, which the Fed would set after estimating the volume of discount loans the banks would borrow. Not surprisingly, the federal funds rate underwent much greater fluctuations after it was de-emphasized as an operating instrument. What is surprising, however, is that the deemphasis of the federal funds target did not result in improved monetary control: After October 1979, the fluctuations in the rate of money supply growth *increased* rather than decreased as would have been expected. In addition, the Fed missed its M1 growth target ranges in all three years of the 1979–1982 period.

In this chapter we saw that the likely reason for the target misses was that Volcker was not serious about controlling monetary aggregates, but rather wanted to avoid being blamed for the high interest rates that would be necessary to bring inflation down. Interest-rate movements during this period support this interpretation of

Fed strategy. After the October 1979 announcement, short-term interest rates were driven up by nearly 5%, until in March 1980 they exceeded 15%. With the imposition of credit controls in March 1980 and the rapid decline in real GDP in the second quarter of 1980, the Fed eased up on its policy and allowed interest rates to decline sharply. When recovery began in July 1980, inflation remained persistent, still exceeding 10%. Because the inflation fight was not yet won, the Fed tightened the screws again, sending short-term rates above the 15% level for a second time. The 1981–1982 recession and its large decline in output and high unemployment began to bring inflation down. With inflationary psychology apparently broken, interest rates were allowed to fall.

The Fed's anti-inflation strategy during the October 1979–October 1982 period was neither intended nor likely to produce smooth growth in the monetary aggregates. Indeed, the large fluctuations in interest rates and the business cycle, along with financial innovation, helped generate volatile money growth.

De-Emphasis of Monetary Aggregates: October 1982–Early 1990s

In October 1982, with inflation in check, the Fed returned, in effect, to a policy of smoothing interest rates. It did this by placing less emphasis on monetary aggregate targets and shifting to borrowed reserves (discount loan borrowings) as an operating instrument. To see how a borrowed reserves target produces interest-rate smoothing, let's consider what happens when the economy expands $(Y\uparrow)$ so that interest rates are driven up. The rise in interest rates $(i\uparrow)$ increases the incentives for banks to borrow more from the Fed, so borrowed reserves rise $(DL\uparrow)$. To prevent the resulting rise in borrowed reserves from exceeding the target level, the Fed must lower interest rates by bidding up the price of bonds through open market purchases. The outcome of targeting on borrowed reserves, then, is that the Fed prevents a rise in interest rates. In doing so, however, the Fed's open market purchases increase the monetary base $(MB\uparrow)$ and lead to a rise in the money supply $(M\uparrow)$, which produces a positive association of money and national income $(Y\uparrow \Rightarrow M\uparrow)$. Schematically,

$$Y\uparrow \Rightarrow i\uparrow \Rightarrow DL\uparrow \Rightarrow MB\uparrow \Rightarrow M\uparrow$$

A recession causes the opposite chain of events: The borrowed reserves target prevents interest rates from falling and results in a drop in the monetary base, leading to a fall in the money supply $(Y\downarrow \Rightarrow M\downarrow)$.

The de-emphasis on monetary aggregates and the change to a borrowed reserves target led to much smaller fluctuations in the federal funds rate after October 1982 but continued to have large fluctuations in money supply growth. Finally, in February 1987, the Fed announced that it would no longer even set M1 targets. The abandonment of M1 targets was defended on two grounds. The first was that the rapid pace of financial innovation and deregulation had made the definition and measurement of money very difficult. The second is that there had been a breakdown in the stable relationship between M1 and economic activity (discussed in Chapter 19). These two arguments suggested that a monetary aggregate such as M1 might no longer be a reliable guide for monetary policy. As a result, the Fed switched its focus to the broader monetary aggregate M2, which it felt had a more stable relationship with economic activity. However, in the early 1990s, this relationship also broke down, and in July 1993, Board of Governors chairman Alan Greenspan testified in

Congress that the Fed would no longer use any monetary targets, including M2, as a guide for conducting monetary policy. Finally, legislation in 2000 amending the Federal Reserve Act dropped the requirement that the Fed report target ranges for monetary aggregates to Congress.

Federal Funds Targeting Again: Early 1990s and Beyond

Having abandoned monetary aggregates as a guide for monetary policy, the Federal Reserve returned to using a federal funds target in the early 1990s. In February 1994, the Fed adopted a new policy procedure. Instead of keeping the federal funds target secret, as it had done previously, the Fed now announced any federal funds rate target change. As mentioned in Chapter 13, around 2:15 p.m., after every FOMC meeting, the Fed now announces whether the federal funds rate target has been raised, lowered, or kept the same. As a result of these announcements, the outcome of the FOMC meeting is now big news, and the media devote much more attention to FOMC meetings, because announced changes in the federal funds rate feed into changes in other interest rates that affect consumers and businesses.

Preemptive Strikes Against Inflation

The recognition that monetary policy needs to be more forward looking has prompted the Fed to be more preemptive. Starting in February 1994, after the economy returned to rapid growth, but the unemployment rate was still high—well above 6%—the Fed began a preemptive strike to head off future inflationary pressures that ultimately raised the federal funds rate from 3% to 6% by February 1995. This preemptive strike against inflation was highly successful because inflation actually fell from around the 3% to the 2% level.

With strong growth of the economy in 1999 and heightened concerns about inflation, the Fed began to raise the federal funds rate from $4\frac{3}{4}\%$ in June 1999 to $6\frac{1}{2}\%$ in May 2000. In this case, the Fed was a little too late in its preemptive strike and inflation rose from around 2% to over 3% by 2000.

After the economy's return to steady growth following the 2001 recession, the Fed again started raising interest rates at a "measured pace" of 25 basis points (0.25 percentage point) at every single FOMC meeting, starting from an extremely low level of 1% in June 2004 to $5\frac{1}{4}\%$ by June 2006. Although the Fed did begin to act when unemployment was high, well above 5%, the measured pace of the federal funds rate increases put the Fed a little behind the curve: Inflation crept up from around the 2% to the 3% level, and then jumped dramatically in 2008 to the 5% level with the surge in energy and other commodity prices.

By the standards of the 1970s and 1980s, the Fed's preemptive strikes worked quite well in keeping inflation within a fairly narrow range. Nonetheless, sometimes the preemptive strikes against inflation were not quite preemptive enough.

Preemptive Strikes Against Economic Downturns and Financial Disruptions: LTCM, Enron, and the Subprime Meltdown

The Fed has also acted preemptively against negative shocks to aggregate demand and especially to those associated with financial disruptions. It lowered the federal funds rate in early 1996 to deal with a possible slowing of the economy and then took the dramatic step in late September and mid-October of 1998 of reducing the federal funds rate target by $\frac{3}{4}$ of a percentage point when the collapse of Long Term Capital Management led to concerns about the health of the financial system. The financial markets soon calmed down and the economy kept on expanding.

With the weakening of the economy in January 2001 (just before the start of the recession in March 2001), the Fed began to ease monetary policy aggressively, taking the federal funds rate down by 1 percentage point even before the recession began, from 6% to 5%. The Federal Reserve then lowered the federal funds rate down to 1% by June of 2003. The result was a very mild recession in which the unemployment rate did not go much above 6%.

With the onset of the subprime financial crisis in August 2007, the Fed began to ease policy even in the face of a strong economy with growth above 3% in the third quarter of 2007, unemployment below 5%, and inflation rising because of the increase in energy prices. The potential for the financial disruption to weaken the economy and to produce an adverse feedback loop—in which credit markets worsened, which would weaken economic activity, which in turn would weaken credit markets further—encouraged the Fed to take preemptive action, cutting the federal funds rate by $\frac{1}{2}$ percentage point in September. At the same time, the Fed implemented large liquidity injections into the credit markets to try to get them working again (discussed in the previous chapter). By October 2008, unfortunately, the subprime financial crisis reached a particularly vicious stage, with an appreciable weakening of the economy. Subsequent easing of monetary policy lowered the federal funds rate to zero in December 2008.

These preemptive attacks against negative shocks to aggregate demand were particularly successful during the Greenspan era in keeping economic fluctuations very mild. The economic expansion from 1991 to 2001 was the longest in U.S. history, and the subsequent recession in 2001 was quite mild. The magnitude of the financial disruption during the subprime financial crisis, however, was so great that the preemptive actions by the Federal Reserve were not enough to contain the crisis, and the economy suffered accordingly.

 International Considerations

The increasing importance of international trade to the American economy has also brought international considerations to the forefront of Federal Reserve policymaking in recent years. By 1985, the strength of the dollar had contributed to a deterioration in American competitiveness with foreign businesses. In public pronouncements, Chairman Volcker and other Fed officials made it clear that the dollar was at too high a value and needed to come down. Because, as we will see in Chapter 17, expansionary monetary policy is one way to lower the value of the dollar, it is no surprise that the Fed engineered an acceleration in the growth rates of the monetary aggregates in 1985 and 1986 and that the value of the dollar declined. By 1987, policymakers at the Fed agreed that the dollar had fallen sufficiently, and sure enough, monetary growth in the United States slowed. These monetary policy actions by the Fed were encouraged by the process of **international policy coordination** in which countries agreed to enact policies cooperatively.

International considerations also played a role in the Fed's decision to lower the federal funds rate by $\frac{3}{4}$ of a percentage point in the fall of 1998. Concerns about the potential for a worldwide financial crisis in the wake of the collapse of the Russian financial system at that time and weakness in economies abroad, particularly in Asia, stimulated the Fed to take a dramatic step to calm down markets. International considerations, although not the primary focus of the Federal Reserve, are likely to be a major factor in the conduct of U.S. monetary policy in the future.

SUMMARY

1. Monetary targeting has the advantage that information on whether the central bank is achieving its target is known almost immediately. Monetary targeting suffers from the disadvantage that it works well only if there is a reliable relationship between the monetary aggregate and the goal variable, inflation—a relationship that has often not held in different countries.

2. Inflation targeting has several advantages: (1) It enables monetary policy to focus on domestic considerations; (2) stability in the relationship between money and inflation is not critical to its success; (3) it is readily understood by the public and is highly transparent; (4) it increases accountability of the central bank; and (5) it appears to ameliorate the effects of inflationary shocks. It does have some disadvantages, however: (1) Inflation is not easily controlled by the monetary authorities, so that an inflation target is unable to send immediate signals to both the public and markets; (2) it might impose a rigid rule on policymakers, although this has not been the case in practice; and (3) a sole focus on inflation may lead to larger output fluctuations, although this has also not been the case in practice.

3. In recent years, the Federal Reserve has had a strategy of having an implicit, not an explicit, nominal anchor. This strategy has the following advantages: (1) It enables monetary policy to focus on domestic considerations; (2) it does not rely on a stable money–inflation relationship; and (3) it has had a demonstrated success, producing low inflation with the longest business-cycle expansion in U.S. history. However, it does have some disadvantages: (1) It has a lack of transparency; (2) it is strongly dependent on the preferences, skills, and trustworthiness of individuals in the central bank and the government; and (3) it has some inconsistencies with democratic principles, because the central bank is not highly accountable.

4. Because interest-rate and aggregate policy instruments are incompatible, a central bank must choose between them on the basis of three criteria: measurability, controllability, and the ability to affect goal variables predictably. Central banks now typically use short-term interest rates as their policy instrument.

5. The Taylor rule indicates that the federal funds rate should be set equal to the inflation rate plus an "equilibrium" real funds rate plus a weighted average of two gaps: (1) an inflation gap, current inflation minus a target rate, and (2) an output gap, the percentage deviation of real GDP from an estimate of its potential full employment level. The output gap in the Taylor rule could represent an indicator of future inflation as stipulated in Phillips curve theory. However, this theory is controversial, because high output relative to potential as measured by low unemployment has not seemed to produce higher inflation in recent years.

6. There are two types of bubbles, credit-driven bubbles that are highly dangerous and so deserve a response from central banks, and bubbles driven solely by irrational exuberance, which do not. Although there are strong arguments against using monetary policy to prick bubbles, appropriate macroprudential regulation to rein in credit-driven bubbles can improve the performance of both the financial system and the economy.

7. The historical record of the Fed's conduct of monetary policy reveals that the Fed has switched its operating targets many times, returning to a federal funds target in recent years, with preemptive strikes against both inflation and economic downturns.

KEY TERMS

asset-price bubble, p. 415

inflation targeting, p. 399

intermediate target, p. 409

international policy coordination, p. 426

macroprudential regulation, p. 417

monetary targeting, p. 395

nonaccelerating inflation rate of
unemployment (NAIRU), p. 413

operating instrument, p. 409

Phillips curve theory, p. 413

policy instrument, p. 409

real bills doctrine, p. 418

Taylor principle, p. 413

Taylor rule, p. 412

QUESTIONS AND PROBLEMS

All questions and problems are available in (X)myeconlab *at* www.myeconlab.com/mishkin.

1. "Unemployment is a bad thing, and the government should make every effort to eliminate it." Do you agree or disagree? Explain your answer.

2. Classify each of the following as either a policy instrument or an intermediate target, and explain why.
   a. The ten-year Treasury bond rate
   b. The monetary base
   c. M2

3. "If the demand for reserves did not fluctuate, the Fed could pursue both an aggregate target and an interest-rate target at the same time." Is this statement true, false, or uncertain? Explain your answer.

4. If the Fed has an interest-rate target, why will an increase in the demand for reserves lead to a rise in the money supply?

5. What procedures can the Fed use to control the federal funds rate? Why does control of this interest rate imply that the Fed will lose control of nonborrowed reserves?

6. Compare the monetary base to M2 on the grounds of controllability and measurability. Which do you prefer as an intermediate target? Why?

7. "Interest rates can be measured more accurately and more quickly than reserve aggregates. Hence an interest rate is preferred over the reserve aggregates as a policy instrument." Do you agree or disagree? Explain your answer.

8. What are the benefits of using a nominal anchor for the conduct of monetary policy?

9. Give an example of the time-inconsistency problem that you experience in your everyday life.

10. What incentives arise for a central bank to fall into the time-inconsistency trap of pursuing overly expansionary monetary policy?

11. What are the advantages of monetary targeting as a strategy for the conduct of monetary policy?

12. What is the big *if* necessary for the success of monetary targeting? Does the experience with monetary targeting suggest that the big *if* is a problem?

13. What methods have inflation-targeting central banks used to increase communication with the public and increase the transparency of monetary policymaking?

14. Why might inflation targeting increase support for the independence of the central bank to conduct monetary policy?

15. "Because the public can see whether a central bank hits its monetary targets almost immediately, whereas it takes time before the public can see whether an inflation target is achieved, monetary targeting makes central banks more accountable than inflation targeting does." Is this statement true, false, or uncertain? Explain your answer.

16. "Because inflation targeting focuses on achieving the inflation target, it will lead to excessive output fluctuations." Is this statement true, false, or uncertain? Explain your answer.

17. "A central bank with a dual mandate will achieve lower unemployment in the long run than a central bank with a hierarchical mandate in which price stability takes precedence." Is this statement true, false, or uncertain?

18. What are the key advantages and disadvantages of the monetary strategy used in the United States under Alan Greenspan in which the nominal anchor is only implicit?

19. What is the advantage that monetary targeting, inflation targeting, and a monetary strategy with an implicit, but not an explicit, nominal anchor have in common?

20. How can bank behavior and the Fed's behavior cause money supply growth to be procyclical (rising in booms and falling in recessions)?

WEB EXERCISES

1. The Federal Open Market Committee (FOMC) meets about every six weeks to assess the state of the economy and to decide what actions the central bank should take. The minutes of this meeting are released three weeks after the meeting; however, a brief press release is made available immediately. Find the schedule of minutes and press releases at www.federalreserve.gov/fomc/.

   a. When was the last scheduled meeting of the FOMC? When is the next meeting?

   b. Review the press release from the last meeting. What did the committee decide to do about short-term interest rates?

   c. Review the most recently published meeting minutes. What areas of the economy seemed to be of most concern to the committee members?

2. It is possible to access other central bank websites to learn about their structure. One example is the European Central bank. Go to www.ecb.int/index.html. On the ECB home page, find information about the ECB's strategy for monetary policy.

3. Many countries have central banks that are responsible for their nation's monetary policy. Go to www.bis.org/cbanks.htm and select one of the central banks (for example, Norway). Review that bank's website to determine its policies regarding application of monetary policy. How does this bank's policies compare to those of the U.S. central bank?

WEB REFERENCES

www.federalreserve.gov/pf/pf.htm

Review what the Federal Reserve reports as its primary purposes and functions.

www.economagic.com/

A comprehensive listing of sites that offer a wide variety of economic summary data and graphs.

www.federalreserve.gov/releases/H3

Historic and current data on the aggregate reserves of depository institutions and the monetary base.

www.federalreserve.gov/aboutthefed/relatedWebSites.htm

The Federal Reserve provides links to other central bank Web pages.

 MyEconLab CAN HELP YOU GET A BETTER GRADE

If your exam were tomorrow, would you be ready? For each chapter, MyEconLab Practice Test and Study Plans pinpoint which sections you have mastered and which ones you need to study. That way, you are more efficient with your study time, and you are better prepared for your exams.

To see how it works, turn to page 20 and then go to: www.myeconlab.com/mishkin

PART 5

International Finance and Monetary Policy

CHAPTER 17
The Foreign Exchange Market:
Exchange Rates and Applications

•

CHAPTER 18
The International Financial
System

Crisis and Response: Foreign Exchange Market Turmoil and the IMF

From 2002 until 2008, the U.S. dollar steadily declined in value relative to other currencies. Indeed, a major concern of policymakers was that the dollar might crash, with adverse effects on both economic activity and inflation. With the credit markets seizing up in September and October of 2008, an amazing thing happened. Instead of continuing its decline, the dollar appreciated sharply. The same "flight to quality" that led investors to step up their purchases of U.S. Treasury securities also led them to want to hold more U.S. dollars, thereby bidding up the dollar's value.

The dollar's higher value made imported goods—ranging from flat-screen televisions to wines—cheaper to purchase and traveling abroad more affordable. But this good news for the U.S. dollar was often bad news for other currencies. Many countries in Latin America and Eastern Europe now found their currencies in free fall. The International Monetary Fund (IMF) stepped in and set up a new lending facility to make loans to distressed countries with fewer strings attached than was true for the IMF's previous lending programs. The IMF started making loans to the tune of billions of dollars. The IMF, which had looked like it was on the sidelines as the subprime financial crisis spread worldwide, now was moving to front and center.

The subprime crisis has demonstrated that events in the United States have worldwide ramifications and that international financial institutions like the IMF have an important role in responding to make sure that the international financial system continues to work well. Chapter 17 outlines how the foreign exchange market functions and how exchange rates between different countries' currencies are determined. In Chapter 18, we examine how the international financial system operates and how it affects monetary policy.

17

The Foreign Exchange Market: Exchange Rates and Applications

Preview

In the mid-1980s, American businesses became less competitive with their foreign counterparts; subsequently, in the 1990s and 2000s, their competitiveness increased. Did this swing in competitiveness occur primarily because American management fell down on the job in the 1980s and then got its act together afterwards? Not really. American business became less competitive in the 1980s because American dollars became worth more in terms of foreign currencies, making American goods more expensive relative to foreign goods. By the 1990s and 2000s, the value of the U.S. dollar had fallen appreciably from its highs in the mid-1980s, making American goods cheaper and American businesses more competitive.

The price of one currency in terms of another is called the **exchange rate**. As you can see in Figure 1, exchange rates are highly volatile. The exchange rate affects the economy and our daily lives, because when the domestic currency becomes more valuable relative to foreign currencies, foreign goods become cheaper in the domestic market and domestic goods become more expensive for foreigners. When the domestic currency falls in value, foreign goods become more expensive in the domestic market and domestic goods become cheaper for foreigners.

Fluctuations in the exchange rate also affect both inflation and output, and are an important concern to monetary policymakers. When the domestic currency falls in value, the higher prices of imported goods feed directly into a higher price level and inflation. At the same time, a declining domestic currency, which makes domestic (exported) goods cheaper for foreigners, increases the demand for domestic goods and leads to higher production and output.

We begin our study of international finance by examining the **foreign exchange market**, the financial market where exchange rates are determined.

FOREIGN EXCHANGE MARKET

Most countries of the world have their own currencies: The United States has its dollar; the European Monetary Union, its euro; Brazil, its real; and China, its yuan. Trade between countries involves the mutual exchange of different currencies (or, more usually, bank deposits denominated in different currencies). When an American firm buys foreign goods, services, or financial assets, for example, U.S. dollars (typically, bank deposits denominated in U.S. dollars) must be exchanged for foreign currency (bank deposits denominated in the foreign currency).

The trading of currencies and bank deposits denominated in particular currencies takes place in the foreign exchange market. Transactions conducted in the foreign

433

FIGURE 1   **Exchange Rates, 1990–2008**
Dollar prices of selected currencies. Note that a rise in these plots indicates a strengthening of the currency (weakening of the dollar).

Source: Federal Reserve: www.federalreserve.gov/releases/h10/hist.

exchange market determine the rates at which currencies are exchanged, which in turn determine the cost of purchasing foreign goods and financial assets.

What Are Foreign Exchange Rates?

The currency of a country has to be valued in terms of another currency. In most cases, global currencies are widely quoted against the two major currencies in the world: the U.S. dollar and the euro. However, most countries also quote their national currencies against currencies other than the dollar and the euro; these are known as currency cross rates. The Following the Financial News box, "Foreign Exchange Rates", on the opposite page shows how cross rates are quoted for the four major currencies in the world.

There are two kinds of exchange rate transactions. The predominant ones, called **spot transactions**, involve the immediate (two-day) exchange of bank deposits. The **spot exchange rate** is the exchange rate for the spot transaction, and the **forward exchange**

Following the Financial News   Foreign Exchange Rates

Log on to the website of the *Financial Times* and select the cross rates for as many currencies as you wish. The following quotations are for spot transactions for only eight currencies, where payment takes place two working days from the day the transaction was made. As you can see, each currency is quoted against the four major global currencies: the euro, the U.S. dollar, the pound sterling and the Japanese yen.

Currency Cross Rates

	GBP £	EUR €	USD $	JPY ¥
Australia 1.00AUD	0.49480	0.56580	0.80100	76.3300
Canada 1.00CAD	0.56630	0.64740	0.91701	87.3400
European Union 1.00EUR	0.87420	N/A	1.41570	134.840
Hong Kong 1.00HKD	0.07972	0.09120	0.12901	12.2914
Japan 1.00JPY	0.00648	0.00742	0.01050	N/A
Switzerland 1.00CHF	0.57880	0.66180	0.93782	89.2800
United Kingdom 1.00GBP	N/A	1.14300	1.61880	154.200
United States 1.00USD	0.61740	0.70640	N/A	95.330

Source: Based on "Markets Data: Currencies," *Financial Times,* May 29 2009. http://markets.ft.com/ft/markets/currencies.asp

rate is the exchange rate for the **forward transaction**. Forward transactions involve the exchange of bank deposits at some specified future date, usually one, three, six or twelve months. While the rate is decided upon today, the actual transfer of funds occurs in the future, thereby protecting against foreign exchange rate fluctuations. Most importers and exporters engage in forward transactions in order to hedge against foreign exchange risks.

When a currency increases in value, it experiences **appreciation**; when it falls in value and is worth fewer foreign currency units, it undergoes **depreciation**.

At the beginning of 1999, for example, the euro was valued at U.S. $1.18, as indicated in the box on the opposite page; on May 29, 2009, the euro was valued at U.S. $1.4157. The euro *appreciated* by 19.97%: $(1.4157 - 1.18/1.18) = 0.1997 = 19.97\%$.

Let us take another example. In May 2003, the pound was valued at 1.3780 euros; on May 29, 2009, the pound was traded for 1.1430 euros. The pound *depreciated* by 17.05%: (1.1430 − 1.3780/1.3780) = 0.1705 = 17.05%.

Why Are Exchange Rates Important?

Exchange rates are important because they affect the relative price of domestic and foreign goods. The dollar price of French goods to an American is determined by the interaction of two factors: the price of French goods in euros and the euro/dollar exchange rate.

Suppose that Wanda the Winetaster, an American, decides to buy a bottle of 1961 (a very good year) Château Lafite Rothschild to complete her wine cellar. If the price of the wine in France is 1,000 euros and the exchange rate is $1.28 to the euro, the wine will cost Wanda $1,280 (=1,000 euros × $1.28/euro). Now suppose that Wanda delays her purchase by two months, at which time the euro has appreciated to $1.40 per euro. If the domestic price of the bottle of Lafite Rothschild remains 1,000 euros, its dollar cost will have risen from $1,280 to $1,400.

The same currency appreciation, however, makes the price of foreign goods in that country less expensive. At an exchange rate of $1.28 per euro, a Dell computer priced at $2,000 costs Pierre the Programmer $1,563 euros; if the exchange rate increases to $1.40 per euro, the computer will cost only 1,429 euros.

A depreciation of the euro lowers the cost of French goods in America but raises the cost of American goods in France. If the euro drops in value to $1.00, Wanda's bottle of Lafite Rothschild will cost her only $1,000 instead of $1,280, and the Dell computer will cost Pierre 2,000 euros rather than $1,563.

Such reasoning leads to the following conclusion: **When a country's currency appreciates (rises in value relative to other currencies), the country's goods abroad become more expensive and foreign goods in that country become cheaper (holding domestic prices constant in the two countries). Conversely, when a country's currency depreciates, its goods abroad become cheaper and foreign goods in that country become more expensive.**

Depreciation of a currency makes it easier for domestic manufacturers to sell their goods abroad and makes foreign goods less competitive in domestic markets. From 2002 to 2008, the depreciated dollar helped U.S. industries sell more goods, but it hurt American consumers because foreign goods were more expensive. The prices of French wine and cheese and the cost of vacationing abroad all rose as a result of the weak dollar.

How Is Foreign Exchange Traded?

You cannot go to a centralized location to watch exchange rates being determined; currencies are not traded on exchanges such as the New York Stock Exchange. Instead, the foreign exchange market is organized as an over-the-counter market in which several hundred dealers (mostly banks) stand ready to buy and sell deposits denominated in foreign currencies. Because these dealers are in constant telephone and computer contact, the market is very competitive; in effect, it functions no differently from a centralized market.

An important point to note is that while banks, companies, and governments talk about buying and selling currencies in foreign exchange markets, they do not take a fistful of dollar bills and sell them for British pound notes. Rather, most trades involve the buying and selling of bank deposits denominated in different currencies. So when we say that a bank is buying dollars in the foreign exchange market, what we actually mean is that the bank is buying *deposits denominated in dollars*. The volume in this market is colossal, exceeding $3 trillion per day.

Trades in the foreign exchange market consist of transactions in excess of $1 million. The market that determines the exchange rates in the Following the Financial News box is not where one would buy foreign currency for a trip abroad. Instead, we buy foreign currency in the retail market from dealers such as American Express or from banks. Because retail prices are higher than wholesale, when we buy foreign exchange, we obtain fewer units of foreign currency per dollar, that is, we pay a higher price for foreign currency, than exchange rates in the box indicate.

EXCHANGE RATES IN THE LONG RUN

Like the price of any good or asset in a free market, exchange rates are determined by the interaction of supply and demand. To simplify our analysis of exchange rates in a free market, we divide it into two parts. First, we examine how exchange rates are determined in the long run; then we use our knowledge of the long-run determinants of the exchange rates to help us understand how they are determined in the short run.

Law of One Price

The starting point for understanding how exchange rates are determined is a simple idea called the **law of one price**: If two countries produce an identical good, and transportation costs and trade barriers are very low, the price of the good should be the same throughout the world no matter which country produces it. Suppose that American steel costs $100 per ton and identical Japanese steel costs 10,000 yen per ton. For the law of one price to hold, the exchange rate between the yen and the dollar must be 100 yen per dollar ($0.01 per yen) so that one ton of American steel sells for 10,000 yen in Japan (the price of Japanese steel) and one ton of Japanese steel sells for $100 in the United States (the price of U.S. steel). If the exchange rate were 200 yen to the dollar, Japanese steel would sell for $50 per ton in the United States or half the price of American steel, and American steel would sell for 20,000 yen per ton in Japan, twice the price of Japanese steel. Because American steel would be more expensive than Japanese steel in both countries and is identical to Japanese steel, the demand for American steel would go to zero. Given a fixed dollar price for American steel, the resulting excess supply of American steel will be eliminated only if the exchange rate falls to 100 yen per dollar, making the price of American steel and Japanese steel the same in both countries.

Theory of Purchasing Power Parity

One of the most prominent theories of how exchange rates are determined is the **theory of purchasing power parity (PPP)**. It states that exchange rates between any two currencies will adjust to reflect changes in the price levels of the two countries. The theory of PPP is simply an application of the law of one price to national price levels rather than to individual prices. Suppose that the yen price of Japanese steel rises 10% (to 11,000 yen) relative to the dollar price of American steel (unchanged at $100). For the law of one price to hold, the exchange rate must rise to 110 yen to the dollar, a 10% appreciation of the dollar. Applying the law of one price to the price levels in the two countries produces the theory of purchasing power parity, which maintains that if the Japanese price level rises 10% relative to the U.S. price level, the dollar will appreciate by 10%.

Another way of thinking about purchasing power parity is through a concept called the **real exchange rate**, the rate at which domestic goods can be exchanged for foreign goods. In effect, it is the price of domestic goods relative to the price of foreign goods denominated in the domestic currency. For example, if a basket of goods in New York costs $50, while the cost of the same basket of goods in Tokyo costs $75 because it costs 7500 yen while the exchange rate is at 100 yen per dollar, then the real exchange rate is 0.66 (=$50/$75). The real exchange rate is below 1.0, indicating that it is cheaper to buy the basket of goods in the United States than in Japan. The real exchange rate for the U.S. dollar is currently low against many other currencies, and this is why we are seeing New York overwhelmed by so many foreign tourists going on shopping sprees. It is the real exchange rate that indicates whether a currency is relatively cheap or not. Another way of describing the theory of PPP is to say that it predicts the real exchange rate is always equal to 1.0, so that the purchasing power of the dollar is the same as the purchasing power of other currencies such as the yen or the euro.

As our U.S./Japanese example demonstrates, the theory of PPP suggests that if one country's price level rises relative to another's, its currency should depreciate (the other country's currency should appreciate). As you can see in Figure 2, this prediction is borne out in the long run. From 1973 to the end of 2005, the British price level rose 89% relative to the U.S. price level, and as the theory of PPP predicts, the dollar appreciated against the pound—though by 58%, an amount smaller than the 89% increase predicted by PPP.

Yet, as the same figure indicates, PPP theory often has little predictive power in the short run. From early 1985 to the end of 1987, for example, the British price level rose relative to that of the United States. Instead of appreciating, as PPP theory predicts, the U.S. dollar actually depreciated by 40% against the pound. So even though PPP theory provides some guidance to the long-run movement of exchange rates, it is not perfect

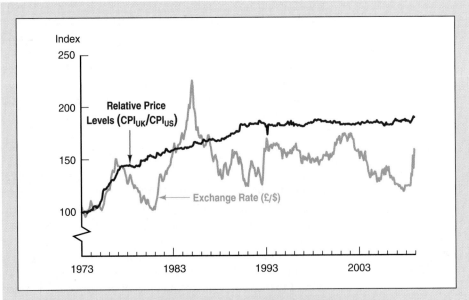

FIGURE 2   **Purchasing Power Parity, United States/United Kingdom, 1973–2008 (Index: March 1973 = 100.)**

Source: ftp.bls.gov/pub/special.requests/cpi/cpiai.txt.

and in the short run is a particularly poor predictor. What explains PPP theory's failure to predict well?

Why the Theory of Purchasing Power Parity Cannot Fully Explain Exchange Rates

The PPP conclusion that exchange rates are determined solely by changes in relative price levels rests on the assumption that all goods are identical in both countries and that transportation costs and trade barriers are very low. When this assumption is true, the law of one price states that the relative prices of all these goods (that is, the relative price level between the two countries) will determine the exchange rate. The assumption that goods are identical may not be too unreasonable for American and Japanese steel, but is it a reasonable assumption for American and Japanese cars? Is a Toyota the equivalent of a Chevrolet?

Because Toyotas and Chevys are obviously not identical, their prices do not have to be equal. Toyotas can be more expensive relative to Chevys and both Americans and Japanese will still purchase Toyotas. Because the law of one price does not hold for all goods, a rise in the price of Toyotas relative to Chevys will not necessarily mean that the yen must depreciate by the amount of the relative price increase of Toyotas over Chevys.

PPP theory furthermore does not take into account that many goods and services (whose prices are included in a measure of a country's price level) are not traded across borders. Housing, land, and services such as restaurant meals, haircuts, and golf lessons are not traded goods. So even though the prices of these items might rise and lead to a higher price level relative to another country's, there would be little direct effect on the exchange rate.

Factors That Affect Exchange Rates in the Long Run

In the long run, four major factors affect the exchange rate: relative price levels, trade barriers, preferences for domestic versus foreign goods, and productivity. We examine how each of these factors affects the exchange rate while holding the others constant.

The basic reasoning proceeds along the following lines: Anything that increases the demand for domestically produced goods that are traded relative to foreign traded goods tends to appreciate the domestic currency because domestic goods will continue to sell well even when the value of the domestic currency is higher. Similarly, anything that increases the demand for foreign goods relative to domestic goods tends to depreciate the domestic currency because domestic goods will continue to sell well only if the value of the domestic currency is lower. In other words, *if a factor increases the demand for domestic goods relative to foreign goods, the domestic currency will appreciate; if a factor decreases the relative demand for domestic goods, the domestic currency will depreciate*.

Relative Price Levels   In line with PPP theory, when prices of American goods rise (holding prices of foreign goods constant), the demand for American goods falls and the dollar tends to depreciate so that American goods can still sell well. By contrast, if prices of Japanese goods rise so that the relative prices of American goods fall, the demand for American goods increases, and the dollar tends to appreciate, because American goods will continue to sell well even with a higher value of the domestic currency. *In the long run, a rise in a country's price level (relative to the foreign price* *level) causes its currency to depreciate, and a fall in the country's relative price level causes its currency to appreciate.*

Trade Barriers Barriers to free trade such as **tariffs** (taxes on imported goods) and **quotas** (restrictions on the quantity of foreign goods that can be imported) can affect the exchange rate. Suppose that the United States increases its tariff or puts a lower quota on Japanese steel. These increases in trade barriers increase the demand for American steel, and the dollar tends to appreciate because American steel will still sell well even with a higher value of the dollar. *Increasing trade barriers causes a country's currency to appreciate in the long run.*

Preferences for Domestic Versus Foreign Goods If the Japanese develop an appetite for American goods—say, for Florida oranges and American movies—the increased demand for American goods (exports) tends to appreciate the dollar, because the American goods will continue to sell well even at a higher value for the dollar. Likewise, if Americans decide that they prefer Japanese cars to American cars, the increased demand for Japanese goods (imports) tends to depreciate the dollar. *Increased demand for a country's exports causes its currency to appreciate in the long run; conversely, increased demand for imports causes the domestic currency to depreciate.*

Productivity When productivity in a country rises, it tends to rise in domestic sectors that produce traded goods rather than nontraded goods. Higher productivity, therefore, is associated with a decline in the price of domestically produced traded goods relative to foreign traded goods. As a result, the demand for domestic traded goods rises, and the domestic currency tends to appreciate. If, however, a country's productivity lags behind that of other countries, its traded goods become relatively more expensive, and the currency tends to depreciate. *In the long run, as a country becomes more productive relative to other countries, its currency appreciates.*[1]

Our long-run theory of exchange rate behavior is summarized in Table 1. We use the convention that the exchange rate E is quoted so that an appreciation of the domestic currency corresponds to a rise in the exchange rate. In the case of the United States, this means that we are quoting the exchange rate as units of foreign currency per dollar (say, euros per dollar).[2]

EXCHANGE RATES IN THE SHORT RUN: A SUPPLY AND DEMAND ANALYSIS

We have developed a theory of the long-run behavior of exchange rates. However, because factors driving long-run changes in exchange rates move slowly over time, if we are to understand why exchange rates exhibit such large changes (sometimes several

---

[1] A country might be so small that a change in productivity or the preferences for domestic or foreign goods would have no effect on prices of these goods relative to foreign goods. In this case, changes in productivity or changes in preferences for domestic or foreign goods affect the country's income but will not necessarily affect the value of the currency. In our analysis, we are assuming that these factors can affect relative prices and consequently the exchange rate.

[2] Exchange rates can be quoted either as units of foreign currency per domestic currency or as units of domestic currency per foreign currency. In professional writing, many economists quote exchange rates as units of domestic currency per foreign currency so that an appreciation of the domestic currency is portrayed as a fall in the exchange rate. The opposite convention is used in the text here, because it is more intuitive to think of an appreciation of the domestic currency as a rise in the exchange rate.

Factors That Affect Exchange Rates in the Long Run

Factor	Change in Factor	Response of the Exchange Rate, E^*
Domestic price level†	↑	↓
Trade barriers†	↑	↑
Import demand	↑	↓
Export demand	↑	↑
Productivity†	↑	↑

*Units of foreign currency per dollar: ↑ indicates domestic currency appreciation; ↓, depreciation.

†Relative to other countries.

Note: Only increases (↑) in the factors are shown; the effects of decreases in the variables on the exchange rate are the opposite of those indicated in the "Response" column.

percent) from day to day, we must develop a supply and demand analysis of how current exchange rates (spot exchange rates) are determined in the short run.

The key to understanding the short-run behavior of exchange rates is to recognize that an exchange rate is the price of domestic assets (bank deposits, bonds, equities, etc., denominated in the domestic currency) in terms of foreign assets (similar assets denominated in the foreign currency). Because the exchange rate is the price of one asset in terms of another, the natural way to investigate the short-run determination of exchange rates is with a supply and demand analysis that uses an asset market approach, which relies heavily on the theory of asset demand developed in Chapter 5. As you will see, however, the long-run determinants of the exchange rate we have just outlined also play an important role in the short-run asset market approach.[3]

In the past, supply and demand approaches to exchange rate determination emphasized the role of import and export demand. The more modern asset market approach used here emphasizes stocks of assets rather than the flows of exports and imports over short periods, because export and import transactions are small relative to the amount of domestic and foreign assets at any given time. For example, foreign exchange transactions in the United States each year are well over 25 times greater than the amount of U.S. exports and imports. Thus, over short periods, decisions to hold domestic or foreign assets play a much greater role in exchange rate determination than the demand for exports and imports does.

---

[3]For a further description of the modern asset market approach to exchange rate determination that we use here, see Paul Krugman and Maurice Obstfeld, *International Economics*, 8th ed. (Boston: Pearson Addison Wesley, 2009).

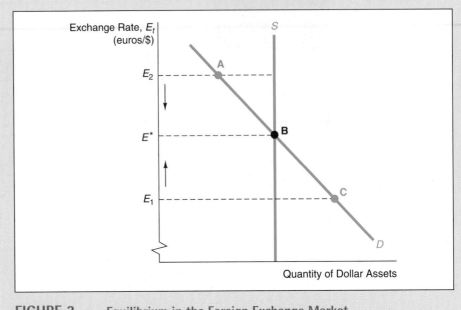

FIGURE 3   **Equilibrium in the Foreign Exchange Market**
Equilibrium in the foreign exchange market occurs at point B, the intersection of the demand curve *D* and the supply curve *S* at an exchange rate of *E**.

Supply Curve for Domestic Assets

We start by discussing the supply curve. In this analysis we treat the United States as the home country, so domestic assets are denominated in dollars. For simplicity, we use euros to stand for any foreign country's currency, so foreign assets are denominated in euros.

The quantity of dollar assets supplied is primarily the quantity of bank deposits, bonds, and equities in the United States, and for all practical purposes we can take this amount as fixed with respect to the exchange rate. The quantity supplied at any exchange rate does not change, so the supply curve, *S*, is vertical, as shown in Figure 3.

Demand Curve for Domestic Assets

The demand curve traces out the quantity demanded at each current exchange rate by holding everything else constant, particularly the expected future value of the exchange rate. We write the current exchange rate (the spot exchange rate) as E_t, and the expected exchange rate for the next period as E_{t+1}^e. As the theory of asset demand suggests, the most important determinant of the quantity of domestic (dollar) assets demanded is the relative expected return of domestic assets. Let's see what happens as the current exchange rate E_t falls.

Suppose we start at point A in Figure 3 where the current exchange rate is at E_2. With the future expected value of the exchange rate held constant at E_{t+1}^e, a lower value of the exchange rate, say at *E**, implies that the dollar is more likely to rise in value, that is appreciate. The greater expected rise (appreciation) of the dollar, the higher is the relative expected return on dollar (domestic) assets. The theory of asset demand then tells us that because dollar assets are now more desirable to hold, the quantity of dollar assets demanded will rise, as is shown by point B in Figure 3. If the current exchange rate falls even further to E_1, there is an even higher expected appreciation of the dollar, a higher expected return, and therefore an even greater quantity of dollar assets demanded. This is shown in point C in Figure 3. The resulting demand curve, D, which connects these points, is downward sloping, indicating that at lower current values of the dollar (everything else equal), the quantity demanded of dollar assets is higher.

Equilibrium in the Foreign Exchange Market

As in the usual supply and demand analysis, the market is in equilibrium when the quantity of dollar assets demanded equals the quantity supplied. In Figure 3, equilibrium occurs at point B, the intersection of the demand and supply curves. At point B, the exchange rate is E^*.

Suppose that the exchange rate is at E_2, which is higher than the equilibrium exchange rate of E^*. As we see in Figure 3, the quantity of dollar assets supplied is then greater than the quantity demanded, a condition of excess supply. Given that more people want to sell dollar assets than want to buy them, the value of the dollar will fall. As long as the exchange rate remains above the equilibrium exchange rate, there will continue to be an excess supply of dollar assets, and the dollar will fall in value until it reaches the equilibrium exchange rate of E^*.

Similarly, if the exchange rate is less than the equilibrium exchange rate at E_1, the quantity of dollar assets demanded will exceed the quantity supplied, a condition of excess demand. Given that more people want to buy dollar assets than want to sell them, the value of the dollar will rise until the excess demand disappears and the value of the dollar is again at the equilibrium exchange rate of E^*.

EXPLAINING CHANGES IN EXCHANGE RATES

The supply and demand analysis of the foreign exchange market illustrates how and why exchange rates change. We can simplify this analysis by assuming the amount of dollar assets is fixed: The supply curve is vertical at a given quantity and does not shift. Under this assumption, we need look at only those factors that shift the demand curve for dollar assets to explain how exchange rates change over time.

Shifts in the Demand for Domestic Assets

As we have seen, the quantity of domestic (dollar) assets demanded depends on the relative expected return of dollar assets. To see how the demand curve shifts, we need to determine how the quantity demanded changes, holding the current exchange rate, E_t, constant, when other factors change.

For insight into which direction the demand curve shifts, suppose you are an investor who is considering putting funds into domestic (dollar) assets. When a factor changes, decide whether at a given level of the current exchange rate, holding all other variables constant, you would earn a higher or lower expected return on dollar assets versus foreign assets. This decision tells you whether you want to hold more or fewer dollar assets and thus whether the quantity demanded increases or decreases at each

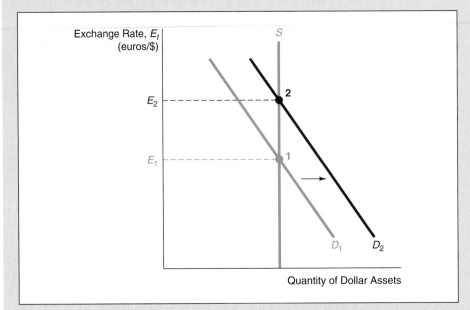

FIGURE 4   **Response to an Increase in the Domestic Interest Rate, i^D**
When the domestic interest rate i^D increases, the relative expected
return on domestic (dollar) assets increases and the demand curve
shifts to the right. The equilibrium exchange rate rises from E_1 to E_2.

level of the exchange rate. Knowing the direction of the change in the quantity
demanded at each exchange rate tells you which way the demand curve shifts. In other
words, if the relative expected return of dollar assets rises holding the current exchange
rate constant, the demand curve shifts to the right. If the relative expected return falls,
the demand curve shifts to the left.

Domestic Interest Rate, i^D   Suppose that dollar assets pay an interest rate of i^D.
When the domestic interest rate on dollar assets i^D rises, holding the current exchange
rate E_t and everything else constant, the return on dollar assets increases relative to foreign assets, so people will want to hold more dollar assets. The quantity of dollar assets
demanded increases at every value of the exchange rate, as shown by the rightward shift
of the demand curve in Figure 4 from D_1 to D_2. The new equilibrium is reached at point 2,
the intersection of D_2 and S, and the equilibrium exchange rate rises from E_1 to E_2. ***An
increase in the domestic interest rate i^D shifts the demand curve for domestic assets, D,
to the right and causes the domestic currency to appreciate (E ↑).***

  Conversely, if i^D falls, the relative expected return on dollar assets falls, the demand
curve shifts to the left, and the exchange rate falls. ***A decrease in the domestic interest
rate i^D shifts the demand curve for domestic assets, D, to the left and causes the
domestic currency to depreciate (E ↓).***

Foreign Interest Rate, i^F   Suppose that the foreign asset pays an interest rate of i^F.
When the foreign interest rate i^F rises, holding the current exchange rate and everything

FIGURE 5   **Response to an Increase in the Foreign Interest Rate, i^F**
When the foreign interest rate i^F increases, the relative expected return on domestic (dollar) assets falls and the demand curve shifts to the left. The equilibrium exchange rate falls from E_1 to E_2.

else constant, the return on foreign assets rises relative to dollar assets. Thus the relative expected return on dollar assets falls. Now people want to hold fewer dollar assets, and the quantity demanded decreases at every value of the exchange rate. This scenario is shown by the leftward shift of the demand curve in Figure 5 from D_1 to D_2. The new equilibrium is reached at point 2, when the value of the dollar has fallen. Conversely, a decrease in i^F raises the relative expected return on dollar assets, shifts the demand curve to the right, and raises the exchange rate. To summarize, ***an increase in the foreign interest rate i^F shifts the demand curve D to the left and causes the domestic currency to depreciate; a fall in the foreign interest rate i^F shifts the demand curve D to the right and causes the domestic currency to appreciate***.

Changes in the Expected Future Exchange Rate, E^e_{t+1}   Expectations about the future value of the exchange rate play an important role in shifting the current demand curve, because the demand for domestic assets, like the demand for any durable good, depends on the future resale price. Any factor that causes the expected future exchange rate, E^e_{t+1}, to rise increases the expected appreciation of the dollar. The result is a higher relative expected return on dollar assets, which increases the demand for dollar assets at every exchange rate, thereby shifting the demand curve to the right in Figure 6 from D_1 to D_2. The equilibrium exchange rate rises to point 2 at the intersection of the D_2 and S curves. ***A rise in the expected future exchange rate, E^e_{t+1}, shifts the demand curve to the right and causes an appreciation of the domestic currency.*** Using the same reasoning, ***a fall in the expected future exchange rate, E^e_{t+1}, shifts the demand curve to the left and causes a depreciation of the currency***.

FIGURE 6   **Response to an Increase in the Expected Future Exchange Rate, E_{t+1}^e**
When the expected future exchange rate increases, the relative expected return on domestic (dollar) assets rises and the demand curve shifts to the right. The equilibrium exchange rate rises from E_1 to E_2.

Earlier in the chapter we discussed the determinants of the exchange rate in the long run: the relative price level, relative trade barriers, import and export demand, and relative productivity (refer to Summary Table 1). These four factors influence the expected future exchange rate. The theory of purchasing power parity suggests that if a higher American price level relative to the foreign price level is expected to persist, the dollar will depreciate in the long run. A higher expected relative American price level should thus have a tendency to lower E_{t+1}^e, lower the relative expected return on dollar assets, shift the demand curve to the left, the lower the current exchange rate.

Similarly, the other long-run determinants of the exchange rate can influence the relative expected return on dollar assets and the current exchange rate. Briefly, the following changes, all of which increase the demand for domestic goods relative to foreign goods, will raise E_{t+1}^e: (1) expectations of a fall in the American price level relative to the foreign price level; (2) expectations of higher American trade barriers relative to foreign trade barriers; (3) expectations of lower American import demand; (4) expectations of higher foreign demand for American exports; and (5) expectations of higher American productivity relative to foreign productivity. By increasing E_{t+1}^e, all of these changes increase the relative expected return on dollar assets, shift the demand curve to the right, and cause an appreciation of the domestic currency, the dollar.

Recap: Factors That Change the Exchange Rate

Summary Table 2 outlines all the factors that shift the demand curve for domestic assets and thereby cause the exchange rate to change. Shifts in the demand curve occur when

SUMMARY TABLE 2

Factors That Shift the Demand Curve for Domestic Assets and Affect the Exchange Rate

Factor	Change in Factor	Change in Quantity Demanded of Domestic Assets at Each Exchange Rate	Response of Exchange Rate, E_t	
Domestic interest rate, i^D	↑	↑	↑	
Foreign interest rate, i^F	↑	↓	↓	
Expected domestic price level*	↑	↓	↓	
Expected trade barriers*	↑	↑	↑	
Expected import demand	↑	↓	↓	
Expected export demand	↑	↑	↑	
Expected productivity*	↑	↑	↑	

*Relative to other countries.

Note: Only increases (↑) in the factors are shown; the effects of decreases in the variables on the exchange rate are the opposite of those indicated in the "Response" column.

one factor changes, holding everything else constant, including the current exchange rate. Again, the theory of asset demand tells us that changes in the relative expected return on dollar assets are the source of shifts in the demand curve.

Let's review what happens when each of the seven factors in Table 2 changes. Remember that to understand which direction the demand curve shifts, consider what happens to the relative expected return on dollar assets when the factor changes. If the relative expected return rises, holding the current exchange rate constant, the demand curve shifts to the right. If the relative expected return falls, the demand curve shifts to the left.

1. When the interest rates on domestic assets i^D rise, the expected return on dollar assets rises at each exchange rate and so the quantity demanded increases. The demand curve therefore shifts to the right, and the equilibrium exchange rate rises, as is shown in the first row of Table 2.

2. When the foreign interest rate i^F rises, the return on foreign assets rises, so the relative expected return on dollar assets falls. The quantity demanded of dollar assets then falls, the demand curve shifts to the left, and the exchange rate declines, as in the second row of Table 2.

3. When the expected price level is higher, our analysis of the long-run determinants of the exchange rate indicates that the value of the dollar will fall in the future. The expected return on dollar assets thus falls, the quantity demanded declines, the demand curve shifts to the left, and the exchange rate falls, as in the third row of Table 2.

4. With higher expected trade barriers, the value of the dollar is higher in the long run and the expected return on dollar assets is higher. The quantity demanded of dollar assets thus rises, the demand curve shifts to the right, and the exchange rate rises, as in the fourth row of Table 2.

5. When expected import demand rises, we expect the exchange rate to depreciate in the long run, so the expected return on dollar assets falls. The quantity demanded of dollar assets at each value of the current exchange rate therefore falls, the demand curve shifts to the left, and the exchange rate declines, as in the fifth row of Table 2.

6. When expected export demand rises, the opposite occurs because the exchange rate is expected to appreciate in the long run. The expected return on dollar assets rises, the demand curve shifts to the right, and the exchange rate rises, as in the sixth row of Table 2.

7. With higher expected domestic productivity, the exchange rate is expected to appreciate in the long run, so the expected return on domestic assets rises. The quantity demanded at each exchange rate therefore rises, the demand curve shifts to the right, and the exchange rate rises, as in the seventh row of Table 2.

APPLICATION ✦ Changes in the Equilibrium Exchange Rate: Two Examples

Our analysis has revealed the factors that affect the value of the equilibrium exchange rate. Now we use this analysis to take a closer look at the response of the exchange rate to changes in interest rates and money growth.

Changes in Interest Rates

Changes in domestic interest rates i^D are often cited as a major factor affecting exchange rates. For example, we see headlines in the financial press like this one: "Dollar Recovers as Interest Rates Edge Upward." But is the view presented in this headline always correct?

Not necessarily, because to analyze the effects of interest rate changes, we must carefully distinguish the sources of the changes. The Fisher equation (Chapter 4) states that a nominal interest rate such as i^D equals the *real* interest rate plus expected inflation: $i = i_r + \pi^e$. The Fisher equation thus indicates that the interest rate i^D can change for two reasons: Either the real interest rate i_r changes or the expected inflation rate π^e changes. The effect on the exchange rate is quite different, depending on which of these two factors is the source of the change in the nominal interest rate.

Suppose that the domestic real interest rate increases so that the nominal interest rate i^D rises while expected inflation remains unchanged. In this case, it is reasonable to assume that the expected appreciation of the dollar will be unchanged because expected inflation is unchanged. In this case, the increase in i^D increases the relative expected return on dollar assets, increases the quantity of dollar assets demanded at each level of the exchange rate, and shifts the demand curve to the right. We end up with the situation depicted in Figure 4, which analyzes an increase in i^D, holding everything else constant. Our model of the foreign exchange market produces the following result: **When domestic real interest rates rise, the domestic currency appreciates**.

When the nominal interest rate rises because of an increase in expected inflation, we get a different result from the one shown in Figure 4. The rise in expected domestic inflation leads to a decline in the expected appreciation of the dollar, which is typically thought to be larger than the increase in the domestic interest rate i^D.[4] As a result, at any given exchange rate, the relative expected return on domestic (dollar) assets falls, the demand curve shifts to the left, and the exchange rate falls from E_1 to E_2 as shown in Figure 7. Our analysis leads to this conclusion: **When domestic interest rates rise due to an expected increase in inflation, the domestic currency depreciates**.

Because this conclusion is completely different from the one reached when the rise in the domestic interest rate is associated with a higher real interest rate, we must always distinguish between *real* and *nominal* measures when analyzing the effects of interest rates on exchange rates.

Changes in the Money Supply

Suppose that the Federal Reserve decides to increase the level of the money supply in an attempt to reduce unemployment, which it believes to be excessive. The higher money supply will lead to a higher American price level in the long run (as we will see in Chapter 22) and hence to a lower expected future exchange rate. The resulting decline in the expected appreciation of the dollar lowers the quantity of dollar assets demanded at each level of the exchange rate and shifts the demand curve to the left. In addition, the higher money supply will lead to a higher real money supply M/P, because the price level does not immediately increase in the short run. As suggested in Chapter 5,

---

[4]This conclusion is standard in asset market models of exchange rate determination; see Rudiger Dornbusch, "Expectations and Exchange Rate Dynamics," *Journal of Political Economy* 84 (1976): 1061–1076. It is also consistent with empirical evidence that suggests that nominal interest rates do not rise one-for-one with increases in expected inflation. See Frederic S. Mishkin, "The Real Interest Rate: An Empirical Investigation," *Carnegie-Rochester Conference Series on Public Policy* 15 (1981): 151–200; and Lawrence Summers, "The Nonadjustment of Nominal Interest Rates: A Study of the Fisher Effect," in *Macroeconomics, Prices and Quantities*, ed. James Tobin (Washington, DC: Brookings Institution, 1983), pp. 201–240.

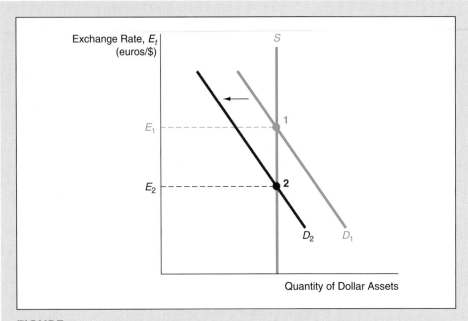

FIGURE 7   **Effect of a Rise in the Domestic Interest Rate as a Result of an Increase in Expected Inflation**
Because a rise in domestic expected inflation leads to a decline in expected dollar appreciation that is larger than the increase in the domestic interest rate, the relative expected return on domestic (dollar) assets falls. The demand curve shifts to the left, and the equilibrium exchange rate falls from E_1 to E_2.

the resulting rise in the real money supply causes the domestic interest rate to fall, which also lowers the relative expected return on dollar assets, providing a further reason why the demand curve shifts to the left. As we can see in Figure 8, the demand curve shifts to D_2, and the exchange rate declines from E_1 to E_2. The conclusion: **A higher domestic money supply causes the domestic currency to depreciate**.

Exchange Rate Overshooting

Our analysis of the effect of an increase in the money supply on the exchange rate is not yet over—we still need to look at what happens to the exchange rate in the long run. A basic proposition in monetary theory, called **monetary neutrality**, states that in the long run, a one-time percentage rise in the money supply is matched by the same one-time percentage rise in the price level, leaving unchanged the real money supply and all other economic variables such as interest rates. An intuitive way to understand this proposition is to think of what would happen if our government announced overnight that an old dollar would now be worth 100 new dollars. The money supply in new dollars would be 100 times its old value and the price level would also be 100 times higher, but nothing in the economy would really have changed: Real and nominal interest rates and the real money supply would remain the same. Monetary neutrality tells us that in

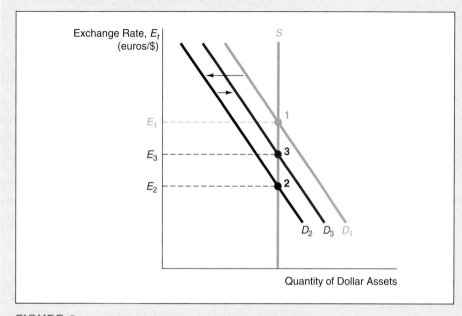

FIGURE 8   **Effect of a Rise in the Money Supply**
A rise in the money supply leads to a higher domestic price level,
which in turn leads to a lower expected future exchange rate. In
addition, the higher money supply leads to a decline in domestic
interest rates. The decline in both the expected appreciation of the
dollar and the domestic interest rate lowers the relative expected
return on dollar assets, shifting the demand curve leftward from D_1 to
D_2. In the short run, the equilibrium exchange rate falls from E_1 to E_2.
In the long run, however, the interest rate rises back up again to its
initial level and the demand curve shifts rightward to D_3. The exchange
rate rises from E_2 to E_3 in the long run.

the long run, the rise in the money supply would not lead to a change in the domestic
interest rate so it would rise back to its old level. The demand curve would shift to the
right to D_3, but not all the way back to D_1, because the price level will still be higher in
the long run. As we can see in Figure 8, this means that the exchange rate would rise
from E_2 to E_3 in the long run.

The phenomenon we have described here in which the exchange rate falls by more
in the short run than it does in the long run when the money supply increases is called
exchange rate overshooting. It is important because, as we will see in the following
application, it can help explain why exchange rates exhibit so much volatility.

Another way of thinking about why exchange rate overshooting occurs is to recognize that when the domestic interest rate falls in the short run, equilibrium in the foreign exchange market means that the expected return on foreign deposits must be
lower. With the foreign interest rate given, this lower expected return on foreign
deposits means that there must be an expected appreciation of the dollar (depreciation
of the euro) for the expected return on foreign deposits to decline when the domestic

interest rate falls. This can occur only if the current exchange rate falls below its long-run value.

APPLICATION ✦ Why Do Some Nations Peg Their Currencies?

So far, we have been discussing the exchange rates for currencies that are freely floating and tradable on foreign exchange markets. Till 1971, all currencies in the world were pegged against the U.S. dollar, which was valued at US $35 per ounce of gold. Since the dollar was unable to maintain this price towards gold, all major economies followed a floating rate regime.

Yet, a number of central banks in developing nations still peg their currencies against either the U.S. dollar, or a basket of major currencies including the euro, the Japanese yen, the pound sterling and the Swiss franc to create a stable environment for foreign investment. With a pegged or fixed currency, investors will not have to worry about daily fluctuations and foreign direct investment will pour into the economy, owing to greater confidence in the stability of the pegged currency.

However, since a peg is difficult to maintain in the long run, these fixed systems have resulted in financial panics in the past, since the central banks generally maintain an overvalued currency. Fearing that the central banks may no longer be able to meet the demands to convert the local currency into the foreign currency at the pegged rate, savers and investors may panic and rush to convert their local currency into foreign currency. A scenario such as this resulted in the financial crisis of Mexico in 1994, where the Bank of Mexico was forced to devalue the peso by 30%. Similarly, the 1997 Thai financial crisis resulted in the local currency, the bhat, losing 50% of its value as the Thai Central Bank floated its currency.

In order to avoid these negative effects, some central banks may choose to have a "floating," or "crawling" peg, whereby it re-evaluates and adjusts the value of the peg periodically. Among the countries that use this method are the Arab oil-rich nations, whose GDP is highly dependent on oil. This is to reduce shocks to the economy, especially given the immense volatility of oil prices.

APPLICATION ✦ The Euro Foreign Exchange Rate and Oil Prices

One of the reasons that urged the sixteen Euro zone nations to adopt the euro was to hedge against fluctuations in foreign exchange rates. Moreover, with the single currency stimulating further economic integration, prices will converge towards one sole price within the Euro zone. Since 1999 the euro has appreciated against all currencies including the pound sterling and the U.S. dollar. There are a number of factors responsible for speeding up the rise of the exchange rate of the euro following the global financial crisis, as shown in Figure 9. First, as a method of financing the hefty expenditures in bailout plans and expansionary fiscal programs, the U.S. debt is expected to exceed $12 trillion. Demand for the euro has increased relative to the dollar, since foreigners are skeptical that the U.S. may devalue the dollar to be able to repay its outstanding debt. Second, with these expectations of the decline in the exchange rate of the dollar, global traders will diversify into other non-dollar denominated assets, thus increasing demand for the euro, sterling and other currencies. Moreover, with an increasing number

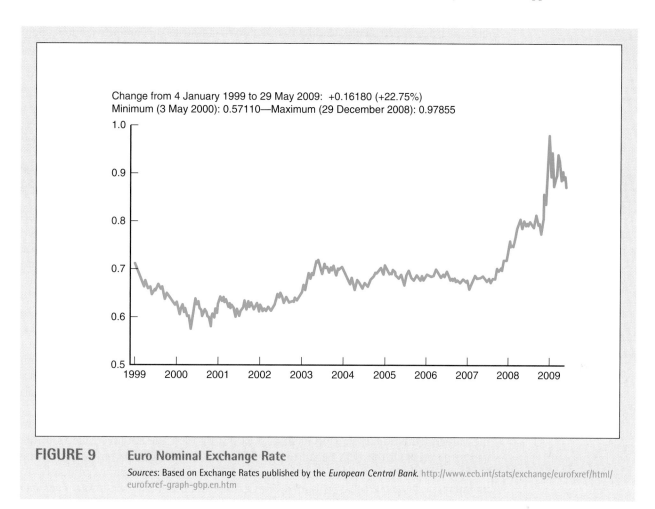

FIGURE 9   **Euro Nominal Exchange Rate**

Sources: Based on Exchange Rates published by the *European Central Bank*. http://www.ecb.int/stats/exchange/eurofxref/html/
eurofxref-graph-gbp.en.htm

of countries joining the European Union and the mounting volume of trade with the EU, demand for the euro is apt to increase. One more reason for the appreciation of the euro is the decline in trust in the U.S. dollar as a foreign reserve currency. In fact, since the outburst of the financial crisis, the euros held in global reserves increased by 180% to reach €1.1 trillion compared to $2.7 trillion held in U.S. dollars.

However, very much as the rate of inflation affects the exchange rate, the exchange rate in turn affects inflation. Let us see how this riddle works. Just before the summer of 2008, the price of a barrel of oil exceeded U.S. $100 or 375 Saudi riyals. Saudi Arabia is one of the few countries that peg its currency against the U.S. dollar; hence if the dollar declines by 20% against the euro, so does the value of the riyal, rendering all imports dearer to Saudi Arabian citizens. But since the energy prices have declined to hit a record low of U.S. $40 in February 2009, Saudi Arabia, along with other member nations of the Organization of Petroleum Exporting Countries (OPEC), retaliated by raising the price of oil by limiting its supply. Furthermore, since oil is priced in U.S. dollars, whenever the dollar declines oil-producing countries tend to raise oil prices to maintain profit margins in their domestic currencies. Hence, an appreciation of the euro, or, in other words, a depreciation of the dollar will drive oil-producing nations to raise the price of petroleum, leading to inflation in countries that are heavily dependent on imported oil.

APPLICATION ✦ The Global Financial Crisis and the Euro

As the subprime financial crisis erupted in the U.S. in August 2007, the U.S. dollar began an accelerated decline in value, falling by 9% against the euro to reach its lowest level on 15 July 2008. However, its gradual rebound started in August 2008. How can a subprime problem born in the U.S. have such substantial effects on the exchange rate of the euro? In order to answer this question, we have to examine the effect of interest rates on the foreign exchange market, first in 2007 and again in 2008.

During 2007, the negative effects of the subprime crisis on U.S. economic activity had started to become visible and were mostly confined to the United States. From September 2007 to December 2008, the Fed responded by substantially lowering the discount rate, as well as the target range for the federal funds rate, between 0% and 0.25%. Yet, the ECB did not lower interest rates. Following a policy of inflation targeting, the main concern of the ECB before the spread of the crisis was to neutralize the effect of the high oil prices that reached a peak of U.S. $147 per barrel in July of 2008. With this interest rate differential between the U.S. dollar and the euro, the relative expected return on dollar assets thus declined, shifting the demand curve for dollar assets to the left, as shown in Figure 5, leading to a decline in the equilibrium exchange rate. Our analysis of the foreign exchange market thus explains why the early phase of the subprime crisis led to a rise in the value of the euro against the dollar in 2007.

Let us now turn to the fall in the value of the euro and the corresponding rise in the value of the dollar, starting in August 2008. By then the spillover effects of the subprime crisis in the U.S. began to spread violently throughout the world, hitting European banks most harshly. In reaction, the ECB had no option but to gradually cut its interest rates by 325 basis points from October 2008 to reach the lowest ever rate of 1%. Most other central banks round the world have followed suit as a measure against economic contractionary pressures. With interest rates for the euro and the dollar converging, the former being 0.25% and the latter around 1%, what do you expect to happen to the relative expected returns for both the euro and the dollar? Your answer may be that for most people, interest rates at 0.25% are no different from zero interest rates. But there is another factor at force. When the global financial crisis reached a particularly virulent stage in September and October of 2008, both Americans and foreigners then wanted to put their money in the safest assets possible: U.S. Treasury securities. The resulting increase in the demand for dollar assets provided a strong reason for the demand curve for dollar assets to shift out to the right, thereby helping to produce a sharp appreciation of the dollar. The expected decline in foreign interest rates then increased the relative expected return of dollar assets, leading to a rightward shift in the demand curve, and a rise in the value of the dollar, as shown in Figure 4.

APPLICATION ✦ Reading the *Financial Times*: The "LEX" Column

Now after accumulating enough theoretical knowledge about how foreign exchange markets operate, let us turn to other factors that may have an influence on foreign exchange rates. It is best that we test our knowledge by following some releases in the

Following the Financial News   The "LEX" Column

The LEX column is a daily feature that appears on the back page of the first section of the *Financial Times* (FT). The LEX is the agenda-setting column of the FT and it comprises a wide set of analyses and opinions covering current business, economic and financial topics, usually from a global perspective. The following is an example of a contemporary topic relating to the effect of the global financial crisis on the credit rating of the U.K. and other indebted countries.

Sterling

FINANCIAL TIMES (LONDON, ENGLAND)

Well, it was nice while it lasted. The pound has had a good run this year. Since December's trough, sterling's trade-weighted exchange rate has risen 9 per cent—a big move and one due a correction, or at least a pause. A review of Britain's credit rating provided the excuse yesterday. Sterling tumbled and gilts fell after Standard & Poor's cut the UK's debt outlook to negative, warning the country's ratio of debt to gross domestic product could soon double to 100 per cent and the stay there.

There is, though, little new about such calculations. Sure, new data showed that government borrowing almost quintupled to £8.5bn in April compared with the same month the year before while tax receipts fell almost 10 per cent. But a high debt/GDP ratio need not be disastrous, as economic historians often point out. After all, British national debt was that high after the second world war, even if

it was a period of austerity for those who lived through it. Sugar rationing was lifted only in 1953 and, to save foreign exchange, bananas were a rarity.

What does matter is how long UK debt continues to rise. For now, gilt spreads over German Bunds remain tighter than for any other big European economy. But at some point markets will demand compensation for the growing credit risk. The government to be formed after elections that are due at the latest in the middle of next year, therefore, needs to slow growth in the national debt and then reverse it. This will be a painful and unpopular task, as squabbling over the public purse always is. It is probably no accident that the governments of other European countries that have debt to GDP ratios of about 100 per cent, such as Italy, Greece and Belgium, are characterised by fractious, fragile and fleeting coalitions.

financial press. Let us take the example of the LEX column, which appears on a daily basis in the *Financial Times* and discusses global developments relating to a vast range of foreign exchange, financial and business issues.

The column entitled "Sterling", in the Following the Financial News box above, discusses yet another factor that may affect the foreign exchange rates relating to the current financial crisis. In order to emerge out of the current crisis, many nations including the U.S. and the U.K. have increased their foreign borrowings, in order to finance their expansionary fiscal expenditure program needed for economic recovery. In response, the credit rating firm, Standard & Poor's, downgraded the debt outlook of the U.K. on May 22, 2009, due to its mounting debt/GDP ratio. The immediate effect was a slide in the value of the pound, soon to be followed by its rebound by the end of the same trading day. Normally, you would expect the demand for assets denominated in sterling to decline and the demand for other currencies (including the U.S. dollar) to rise. This would have resulted in a rightward shift in the demand curve for the dollar. But this has not happened, since the U.S., France, Germany, Italy and a number of other nations equally suffer from high debt/GDP ratios. If anything, this downgrading of the credit worthiness of the U.K. rings an alarm bell for the dire need for the U.K. to reduce its public deficit more rapidly once the economy embarks on its recovery path. Otherwise, the value of sterling will take a downward slide, especially if other nations prove more successful in settling their foreign debt.

SUMMARY

1. Foreign exchange rates (the price of one country's currency in terms of another's) are important because they affect the price of domestically produced goods sold abroad and the cost of foreign goods bought domestically.

2. The theory of purchasing power parity suggests that long-run changes in the exchange rate between two countries' currencies are determined by changes in the relative price levels in the two countries. Other factors that affect exchange rates in the long run are tariffs and quotas, import demand, export demand, and productivity.

3. In the short run, exchange rates are determined by changes in the relative expected return on domestic assets, which cause the demand curve to shift. Any

factor that changes the relative expected return on domestic assets will lead to changes in the exchange rate. Such factors include changes in the interest rates on domestic and foreign assets as well as changes in any of the factors that affect the long-run exchange rate and hence the expected future exchange rate. Changes in the money supply lead to exchange rate overshooting, causing the exchange rate to change by more in the short run than in the long run.

4. The asset market approach to exchange rate determination can explain both the volatility of exchange rates and the rise of the dollar in the 1980–1984 period and its subsequent fall.

KEY TERMS

appreciation, p. 435

capital mobility, p. 461

depreciation, p. 435

exchange rate, p. 433

exchange rate overshooting, p. 451

foreign exchange market, p. 433

forward exchange rate, p. 434

forward transaction, p. 435

interest parity condition, p. 461

law of one price, p. 437

monetary neutrality, p. 450

quotas, p. 440

real exchange rate, p. 437

spot exchange rate, p. 434

spot transaction, p. 434

tariffs, p. 440

theory of purchasing power parity (PPP), p. 437

QUESTIONS AND PROBLEMS

All questions and problems are available in myeconlab *at* www.myeconlab.com/mishkin.

1. When the euro appreciates, is an American more likely to drink California or French wine?

2. "A country is always worse off when its currency is weak (falls in value)." Is this statement true, false, or uncertain? Explain your answer.

3. In a newspaper, check the exchange rates for the foreign currencies listed in the Following the Financial News box on page 435. Which of these currencies have appreciated and which have depreciated since May 29, 2009?

4. If the Japanese price level rises by 5% relative to the price level in the United States, what does the theory of purchasing power parity predict will happen to the value of the Japanese yen in terms of dollars?

5. If the demand for a country's exports falls at the same time that tariffs on imports are raised, will the country's currency tend to appreciate or depreciate in the long run?

6. In the mid- to late 1970s, the yen appreciated relative to the dollar even though Japan's inflation rate was higher than America's. How can this be explained by an improvement in the productivity of Japanese industry relative to American industry?

Using Economic Analysis to Predict the Future
Answer the remaining questions by drawing the appropriate exchange market diagrams.

7. The president of the United States announces that he will reduce inflation with a new anti-inflation program. If the public believes him, predict what will happen to the exchange rate for the U.S. dollar.

8. If the British central bank prints money to reduce unemployment, what will happen to the value of the pound in the short run and the long run?

9. If the Indian government unexpectedly announces that it will be imposing higher tariffs on foreign goods one year from now, what will happen to the value of the Indian rupee today?

10. If nominal interest rates in America rise but real interest rates fall, predict what will happen to the U.S. exchange rate.

11. If American auto companies make a breakthrough in automobile technology and are able to produce a car that gets 60 miles to the gallon, what will happen to the U.S. exchange rate?

12. If Mexicans go on a spending spree and buy twice as much French perfume, Japanese TVs, English sweaters, Swiss watches, and Italian wine, what will happen to the value of the Mexican peso?

13. If expected inflation drops in Europe so that interest rates fall there, predict what will happen to the exchange rate for the U.S. dollar.

14. If the European central bank decides to contract the money supply to fight inflation, what will happen to the value of the U.S. dollar?

15. If there is a strike in France, making it harder to buy French goods, what will happen to the value of the euro?

WEB EXERCISES

1. The Federal Reserve maintains a website that lists the exchange rates between the U.S. dollar and many other currencies. Go to www.newyorkfed.org/markets/foreignex.html. Go to the historical data from 1999 and later and find the euro.
   a. What has the percentage change in the euro–dollar exchange rate been between introduction and now?
   b. What has been the annual percentage change in the euro–dollar exchange rate for each year since the euro's introduction?

2. International travelers and business people frequently need to accurately convert from one currency to another. It is often easy to find the rate needed to convert the U.S. dollar into another currency. It can be more difficult to find exchange rates between two non-U.S. currencies. Go to www.xe.com/ucc/full/. This site lets you convert from any currency into any other currency. How many Lithuanian litas can you currently buy with one Chilean peso?

WEB REFERENCES

www.newyorkfed.org/markets/foreignex.html

Get detailed information about the foreign exchange market in the United States.

http://quotes.ino.com/chart/

Go to this website and click on "Foreign Exchange" to get market rates and time charts for the exchange rate of the U.S. dollar to major world currencies.

www.oecd.org/department/0,3355,en_2649_34347_1_1_1_1_1,00.html

The purchasing power parities home page includes the PPP program overview, statistics, research, publications, and OECD meetings on PPP.

www.federalreserve.gov/releases/

The Federal Reserve reports current and historical exchange rates for many countries.

http://fx.sauder.ubc.ca

The Pacific Exchange Rate Service at the University of British Columbia's Sauder School of Business provides information on how market conditions are affecting exchange rates and allows easy plotting of exchange rate data.

 MyEconLab CAN HELP YOU GET A BETTER GRADE

If your exam were tomorrow, would you be ready? For each chapter, MyEconLab Practice Test and Study Plans pinpoint which sections you have mastered and which ones you need to study. That way, you are more efficient with your study time, and you are better prepared for your exams.

To see how it works, turn to page 20 and then go to: www.myeconlab.com/mishkin

17 The Interest Parity Condition

All the results in the text can be derived with a concept that is widely used in international finance. The *interest parity condition* shows the relationship between domestic interest rates, foreign interest rates, and the expected appreciation of the domestic currency. To derive this condition, we examine how expected returns on domestic and foreign assets are compared.

COMPARING EXPECTED RETURNS ON DOMESTIC AND FOREIGN ASSETS

As in the chapter we treat the United States as the home country, so domestic assets are denominated in dollars. For simplicity, we use euros to stand for any foreign country's currency, so foreign assets are denominated in euros. To illustrate further, suppose that dollar assets pay an interest rate of i^D and do not have any possible capital gains, so that they have an expected return payable in dollars of i^D. Similarly, foreign assets have an interest rate of i^F and an expected return payable in the foreign currency, euros, of i^F. To compare the expected returns on dollar assets and foreign assets, investors must convert the returns into the currency unit they use.

First let us examine how François the Foreigner compares the returns on dollar assets and foreign assets denominated in his currency, the euro. When he considers the expected return on dollar assets in terms of euros, he recognizes that it does not equal i^D; instead, the expected return must be adjusted for any expected appreciation or depreciation of the dollar. If François expects the dollar to appreciate by 3%, for example, the expected return on dollar assets in terms of euros would be 3% higher than i^D because the dollar is expected to become worth 3% more in terms of euros. Thus, if the interest rate on dollar assets is 4%, with an expected 3% appreciation of the dollar, the expected return on dollar assets in terms of euros is 7%: the 4% interest rate plus the 3% expected appreciation of the dollar. Conversely, if the dollar were expected to depreciate by 3% over the year, the expected return on dollar assets in terms of euros would be only 1%: the 4% interest rate minus the 3% expected depreciation of the dollar.

Writing the current exchange rate (the spot exchange rate) as E_t and the expected exchange rate for the next period as E_{t+1}^e, the expected rate of appreciation of the dollar is $(E_{t+1}^e - E_t)/E_t$. Our reasoning indicates that the expected return on dollar assets

459

R^D in terms of foreign currency can be written as the sum of the interest rate on dollar assets plus the expected appreciation of the dollar.[1]

$$R^D \text{ in terms of euros} = i^D + \frac{E^e_{t+1} - E_t}{E_t}$$

However, François's expected return on foreign assets R^F in terms of euros is just i^F. Thus, in terms of euros, the relative expected return on dollar assets (that is, the difference between the expected return on dollar assets and euro assets) is calculated by subtracting i^F from the expression above to yield

$$\text{Relative } R^D = i^D - i^F + \frac{E^e_{t+1} - E_t}{E_t} \tag{1}$$

As the relative expected return on dollar assets increases, foreigners will want to hold more dollar assets and fewer foreign assets.

Next let us look at the decision to hold dollar assets versus euro assets from Al the American's point of view. Following the same reasoning we used to evaluate the decision for François, we know that the expected return on foreign assets R^F in terms of dollars is the interest rate on foreign assets i^F plus the expected appreciation of the foreign currency, equal to minus the expected appreciation of the dollar, $(E^e_{t+1} - E_t)/E_t$:

$$R^F \text{ in terms of dollars} = i^F - \frac{E^e_{t+1} - E_t}{E_t}$$

If the interest rate on euro assets is 5%, for example, and the dollar is expected to appreciate by 3%, then the expected return on euro assets in terms of dollars is 2%. Al earns the 5% interest rate, but he expects to lose 3% because he expects the euro to be worth 3% less in terms of dollars as a result of the dollar's appreciation.

Al's expected return on the dollar assets R^D in terms of dollars is just i^D. Hence, in terms of dollars, the relative expected return on dollar assets is calculated by subtracting the expression just given from i^D to obtain

$$\text{Relative } R^D = i^D - \left(i^F - \frac{E^e_{t+1} - E_t}{E_t} \right) = i^D - i^F + \frac{E^e_{t+1} - E_t}{E_t}$$

---

[1]This expression is actually an approximation of the expected return in terms of euros, which can be more precisely calculated by thinking how a foreigner invests in dollar assets. Suppose that François decides to put one euro into dollar assets. First he buys $1/E_t$ of U.S. dollar assets (recall that E_t, the exchange rate between dollar and euro assets, is quoted in euros per dollar), and at the end of the period he is paid $(1 + i^D)(1/E_t)$ in dollars. To convert this amount into the number of euros he expects to receive at the end of the period, he multiplies this quantity by E^e_{t+1}. François's expected return on his initial investment of one euro can thus be written as $(1 + i^D)(E^e_{t+1}/E_t)$ minus his initial investment of one euro:

$$(1 + i^D)\left(\frac{E^e_{t+1}}{E_t}\right) - 1$$

This expression can be rewritten as

$$i^D\left(\frac{E^e_{t+1}}{E_t}\right) + \frac{E^e_{t+1} - E_t}{E_t}$$

which is approximately equal to the expression in the text because, E^e_{t+1}/E_t is typically close to 1. To see this, consider the example in the text in which $i^D = 0.04$; $(E^e_{t+1} - E_t)/E_t = 0.03$, so $E^e_{t+1}/E_t = 1.03$. Then François's expected return on dollar assets is $(0.04 \times 1.03) + 0.03 = 0.0712 = 7.12\%$, rather than the 7% reported in the text.

This equation is the same as Equation 1 describing François's relative expected return on dollar assets (calculated in terms of euros). The key point here is that the relative expected return on dollar assets is the same—whether it is calculated by François in terms of euros or by Al in terms of dollars. Thus, as the relative expected return on dollar assets increases, both foreigners and domestic residents respond in exactly the same way—both will want to hold more dollar assets and fewer foreign assets.

INTEREST PARITY CONDITION

We currently live in a world in which there is **capital mobility**: Foreigners can easily purchase American assets, and Americans can easily purchase foreign assets. If there are few impediments to capital mobility and we are looking at assets that have similar risk and liquidity—say, foreign and American bank deposits—then it is reasonable to assume that the assets are perfect substitutes (that is, equally desirable). When capital is mobile and when assets are perfect substitutes, if the expected return on dollar assets is above that on foreign assets, both foreigners and Americans will want to hold only dollar assets and will be unwilling to hold foreign assets. Conversely, if the expected return on foreign assets is higher than on dollar assets, both foreigners and Americans will not want to hold any dollar assets and will want to hold only foreign assets. For existing supplies of both dollar assets and foreign assets to be held, it must therefore be true that there is no difference in their expected returns; that is, the relative expected return in Equation 1 must equal zero. This condition can be rewritten as

$$i^D = i^F - \frac{E_{t+1}^e - E_t}{E_t} \tag{2}$$

This equation, which is called the **interest parity condition**, states that the domestic interest rate equals the foreign interest rate minus the expected appreciation of the domestic currency. Equivalently, this condition can be stated in a more intuitive way: The domestic interest rate equals the foreign interest rate plus the expected appreciation of the foreign currency. If the domestic interest rate is higher than the foreign interest rate, there is a positive expected appreciation of the foreign currency, which compensates for the lower foreign interest rate. A domestic interest rate of 5% versus a foreign interest rate of 3% means that the expected appreciation of the foreign currency must be 2% (or, equivalently, that the expected depreciation of the dollar must be 2%).

There are several ways to look at the interest parity condition. First, recognize that interest parity means simply that the expected returns are the same on both dollar assets and foreign assets. To see this, note that the left side of the interest parity condition (Equation 2) is the expected return on dollar assets, while the right side is the expected return on foreign assets, both calculated in terms of a single currency, the U.S. dollar. Given our assumption that domestic and foreign assets are perfect substitutes (equally desirable), the interest parity condition is an equilibrium condition for the foreign exchange market. Only when the exchange rate is such that expected returns on domestic and foreign assets are equal—that is, when interest parity holds—investors will be willing to hold both domestic and foreign assets.

With some algebraic manipulation, we can rewrite the interest parity condition in Equation 2 as

$$E_t = \frac{E_{t+1}^e}{i^F - i^D + 1}$$

This equation produces exactly the same results that we find in the supply and demand analysis in the text: If i^D rises, the denominator falls and so E_t rises. If i^F rises, the denominator rises and so E_t falls. If E_{t+1}^e rises, the numerator rises and so E_t rises.

18 The International Financial System

Preview

As the economies of the world grow more interdependent, a country's monetary policy can no longer be conducted without taking international considerations into account. In this chapter, we examine how international financial transactions and the structure of the international financial system affect monetary policy. We also examine the evolution of the international financial system during the past half century and consider where it may be heading in the future.

INTERVENTION IN THE FOREIGN EXCHANGE MARKET

In Chapter 17, we analyzed the foreign exchange market as if it were a completely free market that responds to all market pressures. Like many other markets, however, the foreign exchange market is not free of government intervention; central banks regularly engage in international financial transactions called **foreign exchange interventions** to influence exchange rates. In our current international environment, exchange rates fluctuate from day to day, but central banks attempt to influence their countries' exchange rates by buying and selling currencies. We can use the exchange rate analysis we developed in Chapter 17 to explain the impact of central bank intervention on the foreign exchange market.

Foreign Exchange Intervention and the Money Supply

The first step in understanding how central bank intervention in the foreign exchange market affects exchange rates is to see the impact on the monetary base from a central bank sale in the foreign exchange market of some of its holdings of assets denominated in a foreign currency (called **international reserves**). Suppose that the Fed decides to sell $1 billion of its foreign assets in exchange for $1 billion of U.S. currency. (This transaction is conducted at the foreign exchange desk at the Federal Reserve Bank of New York—see the Inside the Fed box.) The Fed's purchase of dollars has two effects. First, it reduces the Fed's holding of international reserves by $1 billion. Second, because the Fed's purchase of currency removes it from the hands of the public,

Inside the Fed   A Day at the Federal Reserve Bank of New York's Foreign Exchange Desk

Although the U.S. Treasury is primarily responsible for U.S. foreign exchange policy, decisions to intervene in the foreign exchange market are made jointly by the U.S. Treasury and the Federal Reserve's FOMC (Federal Open Market Committee). The actual conduct of foreign exchange intervention is the responsibility of the foreign exchange desk at the Federal Reserve Bank of New York, which is right next to the open market desk.

The manager of foreign exchange operations at the New York Fed supervises the traders and analysts who follow developments in the foreign exchange market. Every morning at 7:30, a trader on staff who has arrived at the New York Fed in the predawn hours speaks on the telephone with counterparts at the U.S. Treasury and provides an update on overnight activity in overseas financial and foreign exchange markets. Later in the morning, at 9:30, the manager and his or her staff hold a conference call with senior staff at the Board of Governors of the Federal Reserve in Washington. In the afternoon, at 2:30, they have a second conference call, which is a joint briefing of officials at the board and the Treasury.

Although by statute the Treasury has the lead role in setting foreign exchange policy, it strives to reach a consensus among all three parties—the Treasury, the Board of Governors, and the Federal Reserve Bank of New York. If they decide that a foreign exchange intervention is necessary that day—an unusual occurrence, as a year may go by without a U.S. foreign exchange intervention—the manager instructs his traders to carry out the agreed-on purchase or sale of foreign currencies. Because funds for exchange rate intervention are held separately by the Treasury (in its Exchange Stabilization Fund) and the Federal Reserve, the manager and his or her staff are not trading the funds of the Federal Reserve Bank of New York; rather, they act as an agent for the Treasury and the FOMC in conducting these transactions.

As part of their duties, before every FOMC meeting, the staff help prepare a lengthy document full of data for the FOMC members, other Reserve Bank presidents, and Treasury officials. It describes developments in the domestic and foreign markets over the previous five or six weeks, a task that keeps them especially busy right before the FOMC meeting.

currency in circulation falls by $1 billion. We can see this in the following T-account for the Federal Reserve:

Federal Reserve System			
Assets		Liabilities	
Foreign assets (international reserves)	−$1 billion	Currency in circulation	−$1 billion

Because the monetary base is made up of currency in circulation plus reserves, this decline in currency implies that the monetary base has fallen by $1 billion.

If instead of paying for the foreign assets sold by the Fed with currency, the persons buying the foreign assets pay for them by checks written on accounts at domestic banks, then the Fed deducts the $1 billion from the reserve deposits it holds for these banks. The result is that deposits with the Fed (reserves) decline by $1 billion, as shown in the following T-account:

Federal Reserve System

Assets		Liabilities	
Foreign assets (international reserves)	−$1 billion	Deposits with the Fed (reserves)	−$1 billion

In this case, the outcome of the Fed sale of foreign assets and the purchase of dollar deposits is a $1 billion decline in reserves and, as before, a $1 billion decline in the monetary base because reserves are also a component of the monetary base.

We now see that the outcome for the monetary base is exactly the same when a central bank sells foreign assets to purchase domestic bank deposits or domestic currency. This is why when we say that a central bank has purchased its domestic currency, we do not have to distinguish whether it actually purchased currency or bank deposits denominated in the domestic currency. We have thus reached an important conclusion: *A central bank's purchase of domestic currency and corresponding sale of foreign assets in the foreign exchange market leads to an equal decline in its international reserves and the monetary base.*

We could have reached the same conclusion by a more direct route. A central bank sale of a foreign asset is no different from an open market sale of a government bond. We learned in our exploration of the money supply process that an open market sale leads to an equal decline in the monetary base; therefore, a sale of foreign assets also leads to an equal decline in the monetary base. By similar reasoning, a central bank purchase of foreign assets paid for by selling domestic currency, like an open market purchase, leads to an equal rise in the monetary base. Thus we reach the following conclusion: *A central bank's sale of domestic currency to purchase foreign assets in the foreign exchange market results in an equal rise in its international reserves and the monetary base.*

The intervention we have just described, in which a central bank allows the purchase or sale of domestic currency to have an effect on the monetary base, is called an **unsterilized foreign exchange intervention**. But what if the central bank does not want the purchase or sale of domestic currency to affect the monetary base? All it has to do is to counter the effect of the foreign exchange intervention by conducting an offsetting open market operation in the government bond market. For example, in the case of a $1 billion purchase of dollars by the Fed and a corresponding $1 billion sale of foreign assets, which, as we have seen, would decrease the monetary base by $1 billion, the Fed can conduct an open market purchase of $1 billion of government bonds, which would increase the monetary base by $1 billion. The resulting T-account for the foreign exchange intervention and the offsetting open market operation leaves the monetary base unchanged:

Federal Reserve System

Assets		Liabilities	
Foreign assets (international reserves)	−$1 billion	Monetary base	0
Government bonds	+$1 billion		

A foreign exchange intervention with an offsetting open market operation that leaves the monetary base unchanged is called a **sterilized foreign exchange intervention**.

Now that we understand that there are two types of foreign exchange interventions—unsterilized and sterilized—let's look at how each affects the exchange rate.

Unsterilized Intervention

Your intuition might lead you to suspect that if a central bank wants to lower the value of the domestic currency, it should sell its currency in the foreign exchange market and purchase foreign assets. Indeed, this intuition is correct for the case of an unsterilized intervention.

Recall that in an unsterilized intervention, if the Federal Reserve decides to sell dollars so that it can buy foreign assets in the foreign exchange market, this works just like an open market purchase of bonds to increase the monetary base. Hence the sale of dollars leads to an increase in the money supply, and we find ourselves analyzing a similar situation to that described in Figure 8 of Chapter 17, which is reproduced here as Figure 1.[1] The higher money supply leads to a higher U.S. price level in the long run and so to a lower expected future exchange rate. The resulting decline in the expected appreciation of the dollar lowers the relative expected return on dollar assets and shifts the demand curve to the left. In addition, the increase in the money supply will lead to a higher real money supply in the short run, which causes the interest rate on dollar assets to fall, also lowering the relative expected return on dollar assets, and providing another reason for the demand curve to shift to the left. The demand curve shifts from D_1 to D_2, and the exchange rate falls to E_2. Because the domestic interest rate will rise back to its initial level in the long run, the relative expected return of dollar assets will increase somewhat, sending the demand curve to D_3, but not all the way back to D_1 because the price level will still be higher in the long run. The exchange rate thus rises from E_2 to E_3, which is still below the initial value of E_1. The result is the same one we found in the previous chapter, in which there is exchange rate overshooting—that is, the exchange rate falls by more in the short run than in the long run.

Our analysis leads us to the following conclusion about unsterilized interventions in the foreign exchange market: *An unsterilized intervention in which domestic currency is sold to purchase foreign assets leads to a gain in international reserves, an increase in the money supply, and a depreciation of the domestic currency.*

The reverse result is found for an unsterilized intervention in which domestic currency is purchased by selling foreign assets. The purchase of domestic currency by selling foreign assets (reducing international reserves) works like an open market sale to reduce the monetary base and the money supply. The decrease in the money supply raises the interest rate on dollar assets and lowers the long-run price level, thereby

---

[1] An unsterilized intervention in which the Fed sells dollars increases the amount of dollar assets slightly because it leads to an increase in the monetary base while leaving the amount of government bonds in the hands of the public unchanged. The curve depicting the supply of dollar assets would thus shift to the right slightly, which also works toward lowering the exchange rate, yielding the same conclusion derived from Figure 1. Because the resulting increase in the monetary base would be only a minuscule fraction of the total amount of dollar assets outstanding, the supply curve would shift by an imperceptible amount. This is why Figure 1 is drawn with the supply curve unchanged.

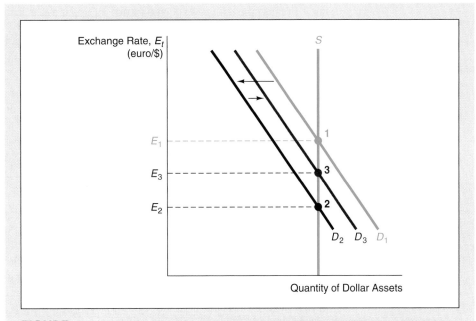

FIGURE 1   **Effect of a Sale of Dollars and a Purchase of Foreign Assets**
A sale of dollars and the consequent open market purchase of foreign assets increase the monetary base. The resulting rise in the money supply leads to a decline in domestic interest rates and a higher domestic price level in the long run, which produces a lower expected future exchange rate. The decline in both the expected appreciation of the dollar and the domestic interest rate lowers the relative expected return on dollar assets, shifting the demand curve leftward from D_1 to D_2. In the short run, the equilibrium exchange rate falls from E_1 to E_2. In the long run, the interest rate rises back to its initial level and the demand curve shifts rightward to D_3. The exchange rate rises from E_2 to E_3 in the long run.

increasing the future expected exchange rate. The resulting increase in the relative expected return on dollar assets means that people will buy more dollar assets, so the demand curve shifts to the right and the exchange rate rises. *An unsterilized intervention in which domestic currency is purchased by selling foreign assets leads to a drop in international reserves, a decrease in the money supply, and an appreciation of the domestic currency.*

Sterilized Intervention

The key point to remember about a sterilized intervention is that the central bank engages in offsetting open market operations, so that there is no impact on the monetary base and the money supply. In the context of the model of exchange rate determination we have developed here, it is straightforward to show that a sterilized intervention has almost *no effect* on the exchange rate. A sterilized intervention leaves the money supply unchanged and so has no direct way of affecting interest rates or the expected future exchange rate.[2] Because the relative expected return on dollar assets is unaffected, the demand curve would remain at D_1 in Figure 1, and the exchange rate would remain unchanged at E_1.

At first it might seem puzzling that a central bank purchase or sale of domestic currency that is sterilized does not lead to a change in the exchange rate. A central bank sterilized purchase of domestic currency cannot raise the exchange rate, because with no effect on the domestic money supply or interest rates, any resulting rise in the exchange rate would mean that there would be an excess supply of dollar assets. With more people willing to sell dollar assets than to buy them, the exchange rate would have to fall back to its initial equilibrium level, where the demand and supply curves intersect.

BALANCE OF PAYMENTS

Because international financial transactions such as foreign exchange interventions have considerable effects on monetary policy, it is worth knowing how these transactions are measured. The **balance of payments** is a bookkeeping system for recording all receipts and payments that have a direct bearing on the movement of funds between a nation (private sector and government) and foreign countries. Here we examine the key items in the balance of payments that you often hear about in the media.

The **current account** shows international transactions that involve currently produced goods and services. The difference between merchandise exports and imports, the net receipts from trade, is called the **trade balance**. When merchandise imports are greater than exports (by $820.8 billion in 2008), we have a trade deficit; if exports are greater than imports, we have a trade surplus.

Additional items included in the current account are the net receipts (cash flows received from abroad minus cash flows sent abroad) from three categories: investment income, service transactions, and unilateral transfers (gifts, pensions, and foreign aid). In 2008, for example, net investment income was $127.6 billion for the United States because Americans received more investment income from abroad than they paid out. Americans bought less in services from foreigners than foreigners bought from Americans, so net services generated $139.7 billion in receipts. Because Americans made more unilateral transfers to foreign countries (especially foreign aid) than foreigners made to the United States, net unilateral transfers were negative $119.7 billion. The sum of the previous three items plus the trade balance is the current account balance, which in 2008 showed a deficit of $673.2 billion (−$820.8 + $127.6 + $139.7 − $119.7 = −$673.2).

Another important item in the balance of payments is the **capital account**, the net receipts from capital transactions (e.g., purchases of stocks and bonds, bank loans, etc.). In 2008 the capital account was −$2.6 billion, indicating that $2.6 billion more capital flowed out of the United States than came in. Another way of saying this is that the

---

[2]A sterilized intervention changes the amount of foreign securities relative to domestic securities in the hands of the public, called a *portfolio balance effect*. Through this effect, the central bank might be able to affect the interest differential between domestic and foreign assets, which in turn affects the relative expected return of domestic assets. Empirical evidence has not revealed this portfolio balance effect to be significant. However, a sterilized intervention *could* indicate what central banks want to happen to the future exchange rate and so might provide a signal about the course of future monetary policy. In this way a sterilized intervention could lead to shifts in the demand curve for domestic assets and ultimately affect the exchange rate. However, the future change in monetary policy—not the sterilized intervention—is the source of the exchange rate effect. For a further discussion of the signaling and portfolio balance effects and the possible differential effects of sterilized versus unsterilized intervention, see Paul Krugman and Maurice Obstfeld, *International Economics*, 7th ed. (Boston: Addison-Wesley, 2006).

Global   Why the Large U.S. Current Account Deficit Worries Economists

The massive U.S. current account deficit in recent years, which now is around 5% of GDP, worries economists for several reasons. First, it indicates that at current exchange rate values, foreigners' demand for U.S. exports is far less than Americans' demand for imports. As we saw in the previous chapter, low demand for U.S. exports and high U.S. demand for imports may lead to a future decline in the value of the U.S. dollar. Some economists estimate that this decline could be very large, with the U.S. dollar depreciating by as much as 50%.

Second, the current account deficit means that foreigners' claims on U.S. assets are growing, and these claims will have to be paid back at some point.

Americans are mortgaging their future to foreigners; when the bill comes due, Americans will be poorer. Furthermore, if Americans have a greater preference for dollar assets than foreigners do, the movement of American wealth to foreigners could decrease the demand for dollar assets over time, also causing the dollar to depreciate.

The hope is that the eventual decline in the dollar resulting from the large U.S. current account deficit will be a gradual one, occurring over a period of several years. If the decline is precipitous, however, it could potentially disrupt financial markets and hurt the U.S. economy.

United States had a net capital outflow of $2.6 billion.[3] The sum of the current account and the capital account equals the **official reserve transactions balance** (net change in government international reserves), which was negative $675.8 billion in 2008 (−$673.2 − $2.6 = −$675.8 billion). When economists refer to a surplus or deficit in the balance of payments, they actually mean a surplus or deficit in the official reserve transactions balance.

Because the balance of payments must balance, the official reserve transactions balance, which equals the current account plus the capital account, tells us the net amount of international reserves that must move between governments (as represented by their central banks) to finance international transactions: i.e.,

$$\text{Current account} \ + \ \text{capital account} \ = \ \text{net change in government international reserves}$$

This equation shows us why the current account receives so much attention from economists and the media. The current account balance tells us whether the United States (private sector and government combined) is increasing or decreasing its claims on foreign wealth. A surplus indicates that America is increasing its claims on foreign wealth and thus is increasing its holdings of foreign assets (both good things for Americans); a deficit (as in 2008) indicates that the United States is reducing its holdings of foreign assets and foreign countries are increasing their claims on the United States.[4] The large U.S. current account deficit in recent years, which is over $600 billion, has raised serious concerns that these large deficits may have negative consequences for the U.S. economy (see the Global box, "Why the Large U.S. Current Account Deficit Worries Economists").

[3]The capital account balance number reported here includes a statistical discrepancy item that represents errors due to unrecorded transactions involving smuggling and other capital flows (−$39 billion in 2004). Many experts believe that the statistical discrepancy item, which keeps the balance of payments in balance, is primarily the result of large hidden capital flows, and this is why it is included in the capital account balance.

[4]The current account balance can also be viewed as showing the amount by which total saving exceeds private sector and government investment in the United States. Total U.S. saving equals the increase in total wealth held by the U.S. private sector and government. Total investment equals the increase in the U.S. capital stock (wealth physically in the United States). The difference between them is the increase in U.S. claims on foreign wealth.

EXCHANGE RATE REGIMES IN THE INTERNATIONAL FINANCIAL SYSTEM

Exchange rate regimes in the international financial system are classified into two basic types: fixed and floating. In a **fixed exchange rate regime**, the value of a currency is pegged relative to the value of one other currency (called the **anchor currency**) so that the exchange rate is fixed in terms of the anchor currency. In a **floating exchange rate regime**, the value of a currency is allowed to fluctuate against all other currencies. When countries intervene in foreign exchange markets in an attempt to influence their exchange rates by buying and selling foreign assets, the regime is referred to as a **managed float regime** (or a **dirty float**).

In examining past exchange rate regimes, we start with the gold standard of the late nineteenth and early twentieth centuries.

Gold Standard

Before World War I, the world economy operated under the **gold standard**, a fixed exchange rate regime in which the currency of most countries was convertible directly into gold at fixed rates, so exchange rates between currencies were also fixed. American dollar bills, for example, could be turned in to the U.S. Treasury and exchanged for approximately $\frac{1}{20}$ ounce of gold. Likewise, the British Treasury would exchange $\frac{1}{4}$ ounce of gold for £1 sterling. Because an American could convert $20 into 1 ounce of gold, which could be used to buy £4, the exchange rate between the pound and the dollar was effectively fixed at $5 to the pound. The fixed exchange rates under the gold standard had the important advantage of encouraging world trade by eliminating the uncertainty that occurs when exchange rates fluctuate.

As long as countries abided by the rules under the gold standard and kept their currencies backed by and convertible into gold, exchange rates remained fixed. However, adherence to the gold standard meant that a country had no control over its monetary policy, because its money supply was determined by gold flows between countries. Furthermore, monetary policy throughout the world was greatly influenced by the production of gold and gold discoveries. When gold production was low in the 1870s and 1880s, the money supply throughout the world grew slowly and did not keep pace with the growth of the world economy. The result was deflation (falling price levels). Gold discoveries in Alaska and South Africa in the 1890s greatly expanded gold production, causing money supplies to increase rapidly and price levels to rise (inflation) until World War I.

The Bretton Woods System

After World War II, the victors set up a fixed exchange rate system that became known as the **Bretton Woods system**, after the New Hampshire town in which the agreement was negotiated in 1944. The Bretton Woods system remained in effect until 1971.

The Bretton Woods agreement created the **International Monetary Fund (IMF)**, headquartered in Washington, DC, which had 30 original member countries in 1945 and currently has over 180. The IMF was given the task of promoting the growth of world trade by setting rules for the maintenance of fixed exchange rates and by making loans to countries that were experiencing balance-of-payments difficulties. As part of its role of monitoring the compliance of member countries with its rules, the IMF also took on the job of collecting and standardizing international economic data.

The Bretton Woods agreement also set up the International Bank for Reconstruction and Development, commonly referred to as the **World Bank**. Headquartered in Washington, DC, it provides long-term loans to help developing countries build dams, roads, and other physical capital that would contribute to their economic development. The funds for these loans are obtained primarily by issuing World Bank bonds, which are sold in the capital markets of the developed countries. In addition, the General Agreement on Tariffs and Trade (GATT), headquartered in Geneva, Switzerland, was set up to monitor rules for the conduct of trade between countries (tariffs and quotas). The GATT has since evolved into the **World Trade Organization (WTO)**.

Because the United States emerged from World War II as the world's largest economic power, with over half of the world's manufacturing capacity and the greater part of the world's gold, the Bretton Woods system of fixed exchange rates was based on the convertibility of U.S. dollars into gold (for foreign governments and central banks only) at $35 per ounce. The fixed exchange rates were to be maintained by intervention in the foreign exchange market by central banks in countries besides the United States that bought and sold dollar assets, which they held as international reserves. The U.S. dollar, which was used by other countries to denominate the assets that they held as international reserves, was called the **reserve currency**. Thus an important feature of the Bretton Woods system was the establishment of the United States as the reserve currency country.

The Bretton Woods system was abandoned in 1971. From 1979 to 1990, however, the European Union instituted among its members its own fixed exchange rate system, the European Monetary System (EMS). In the *exchange rate mechanism (ERM)* in this system, the exchange rate between any pair of currencies of the participating countries was not supposed to fluctuate outside narrow limits, called the "snake." In practice, all of the countries in the EMS pegged their currencies to the German mark.

Even after the breakup of the Bretton Woods system, the U.S. dollar has kept its position as the reserve currency in which most international financial transactions are conducted. However, with the creation of the euro in 1999, the supremacy of the U.S. dollar may be subject to a serious challenge (see the Global box below).

Global   The Euro's Challenge to the Dollar

With the creation of the European Monetary System and the euro in 1999, the U.S. dollar is facing a challenge to its position as the key reserve currency in international financial transactions. Adoption of the euro increases integration of Europe's financial markets, which could rival those in the United States. The resulting increase in the use of euros in financial markets will make it more likely that international transactions are carried out in the euro. The economic clout of the European Union rivals that of the United States: Both have a similar share of world GDP (around 20%) and world exports (around 15%). If the European Central Bank can make sure that inflation remains low so that the euro becomes a sound currency, this should bode well for the euro.

However, for the euro to eat into the dollar's position as a reserve currency, the European Union must function as a cohesive political entity that can exert its influence on the world stage. There are serious doubts on this score, however, particularly with the "no" votes on the European constitution by France and the Netherlands in 2005. Most analysts think it will be a long time before the euro beats out the dollar in international financial transactions.

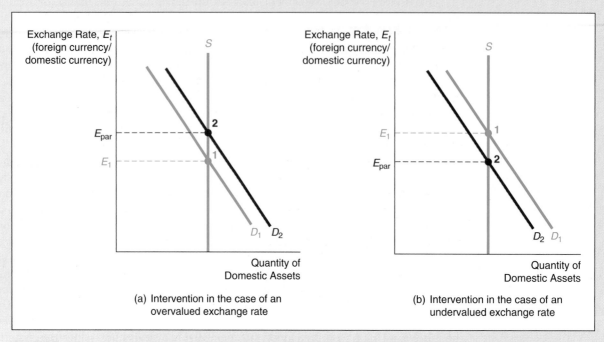

FIGURE 2 **Intervention in the Foreign Exchange Market Under a Fixed Exchange Rate Regime**
In panel (a), the exchange rate at E_{par} is overvalued. To keep the exchange rate at E_{par} (point 2), the central bank must purchase domestic currency to shift the demand curve to D_2. In panel (b), the exchange rate at E_{par} is undervalued, so the central bank must sell domestic currency to shift the demand curve to D_2 and keep the exchange rate at E_{par} (point 2).

How a Fixed Exchange Rate Regime Works

Figure 2 shows how a fixed exchange rate regime works in practice by using the supply and demand analysis of the foreign exchange market we learned in the previous chapter. Panel (a) describes a situation in which the domestic currency is fixed relative to an anchor currency at E_{par}, while the demand curve has shifted left to D_1, perhaps because foreign interest rates have risen, thereby lowering the relative expected return of domestic assets. At E_{par}, the exchange rate is now *overvalued*: The demand curve D_1 intersects the supply curve at an exchange rate E_1, which is lower than the fixed (par) value of the exchange rate E_{par}. To keep the exchange rate at E_{par}, the central bank must intervene in the foreign exchange market to purchase domestic currency by selling foreign assets. This action, like an open market sale, means that both the monetary base and the money supply decline, driving up the interest rate on domestic assets, i^{D}.[5] This increase in the domestic interest rate raises the relative expected return on domestic assets, shifting the demand curve to the right. The central bank will continue purchasing

---

[5]Because the exchange rate will continue to be fixed at E_{par}, the expected future exchange rate remains unchanged and so does not need to be addressed in the analysis.

domestic currency until the demand curve reaches D_2 and the equilibrium exchange rate is at E_{par} at point 2 in panel (a).

We have thus come to the conclusion that **when the domestic currency is overvalued, the central bank must purchase domestic currency to keep the exchange rate fixed, but as a result it loses international reserves.**

Panel (b) in Figure 2 describes the situation in which the demand curve has shifted to the right to D_1 because the relative expected return on domestic assets has risen and hence the exchange rate is undervalued: The initial demand curve D_1 intersects the supply curve at exchange rate E_1, which is above E_{par}. In this situation, the central bank must sell domestic currency and purchase foreign assets. This action works like an open market purchase to increase the money supply and lower the interest rate on domestic assets i^D. The central bank keeps selling domestic currency and lowering i^D until the demand curve shifts all the way to D_2, where the equilibrium exchange rate is at E_{par}—point 2 in panel (b). Our analysis thus leads us to the following result: **When the domestic currency is undervalued, the central bank must sell domestic currency to keep the exchange rate fixed, but as a result, it gains international reserves.**

As we have seen, if a country's currency is overvalued, its central bank's attempts to keep the currency from depreciating will result in a loss of international reserves. If the country's central bank eventually runs out of international reserves, it cannot keep its currency from depreciating, and a **devaluation** must occur, in which the par exchange rate is reset at a lower level.

If, by contrast, a country's currency is undervalued, its central bank's intervention to keep the currency from appreciating leads to a gain of international reserves. As we will see shortly, the central bank might not want to acquire these international reserves, and so it might want to reset the par value of its exchange rate at a higher level (a **revaluation**).

If there is perfect capital mobility—that is, if there are no barriers to domestic residents purchasing foreign assets or foreigners purchasing domestic assets—then a sterilized exchange rate intervention cannot keep the exchange rate at E_{par} because, as we saw earlier in the chapter, the relative expected return of domestic assets is unaffected. For example, if the exchange rate is overvalued, a sterilized purchase of domestic currency will leave the relative expected return and the demand curve unchanged—so pressure for a depreciation of the domestic currency is not removed. If the central bank keeps purchasing its domestic currency but continues to sterilize, it will just keep losing international reserves until it finally runs out of them and is forced to let the value of the currency seek a lower level.

One important implication of the foregoing analysis is that a country that ties its exchange rate to an anchor currency of a larger country loses control of its monetary policy. If the larger country pursues a more contractionary monetary policy and decreases its money supply, this would lead to lower expected inflation in the larger country, thus causing an appreciation of the larger country's currency and a depreciation of the smaller country's currency. The smaller country, having locked in its exchange rate to the anchor currency, will now find its currency overvalued and will therefore have to sell the anchor currency and buy its own to keep its currency from depreciating. The result of this foreign exchange intervention will then be a decline in the smaller country's international reserves, a contraction of its monetary base, and thus a decline in its money supply. Sterilization of this foreign exchange intervention is not an option because this would just lead to a continuing loss of international reserves until the smaller country was forced to devalue its currency.

The smaller country no longer controls its monetary policy, because movements in its money supply are completely determined by movements in the larger country's money supply.

Another way to see that when a country fixes its exchange rate to a larger country's currency it loses control of its monetary policy is through the interest parity condition discussed in the appendix to the previous chapter. There we saw that when there is capital mobility, the domestic interest rate equals the foreign interest rate minus the expected appreciation of the domestic currency. With a fixed exchange rate, expected appreciation of the domestic currency is zero, so that the domestic interest rate equals the foreign interest rate. Therefore changes in the monetary policy in the large anchor country that affect its interest rate are directly transmitted to interest rates in the small country. Furthermore, because the monetary authorities in the small country cannot make their interest rate deviate from that of the larger country, they have no way to use monetary policy to affect their economy.

APPLICATION ✦ How Did China Accumulate Over $2 Trillion of International Reserves?

By 2009, China had accumulated over $2 trillion of international reserves. How did the Chinese get their hands on this vast amount of foreign assets? After all, China is not yet a rich country.

The answer is that China pegged its exchange rate to the U.S. dollar at a fixed rate of 12 cents to the yuan (also called renminbi) in 1994. Because of China's rapidly growing productivity and an inflation rate that is lower than in the United States, the long-run value of the yuan has increased, leading to a higher relative expected return for yuan assets and a rightward shift of the demand for yuan assets. As a result, the Chinese have found themselves in the situation depicted in panel (b) of Figure 2, in which the yuan is undervalued. To keep the yuan from appreciating above E_{par} to E_1 in the figure, the Chinese central bank has been engaging in massive purchases of U.S. dollar assets. Today the Chinese government is one of the largest holders of U.S. government bonds in the world.

The pegging of the yuan to the U.S. dollar has created several problems for Chinese authorities. First, the Chinese now own a lot of U.S. assets, particularly U.S. Treasury securities, which have very low returns. Second, the undervaluation of the yuan has meant that Chinese goods are so cheap abroad that many countries have threatened to erect trade barriers against these goods if the Chinese government does not allow an upward revaluation of the yuan. Third, as we learned earlier in the chapter, the Chinese purchase of dollar assets has resulted in a substantial increase in the Chinese monetary base and money supply, which has the potential to produce high inflation in the future. Because the Chinese authorities have created substantial roadblocks to capital mobility, they have been able to sterilize most of their exchange rate interventions while maintaining the exchange rate peg. Nevertheless, they still worry about inflationary pressures. In July 2005, China finally made its peg somewhat more flexible by letting the value of the yuan rise 2.1% and subsequently allowed it to appreciate at a gradual pace. The central bank also indicated that it would no longer fix the yuan to the U.S. dollar, but would instead maintain its value relative to a basket of currencies.

Why did the Chinese authorities maintain this exchange rate peg for so long despite the problems? One answer is that they wanted to keep their export sector humming by keeping the prices of their export goods low. A second answer might be that they wanted to accumulate a large amount of international reserves as a "war chest" that could be sold to buy yuan in the event of a speculative attack against the yuan at some future date. Given the pressure on the Chinese government to further revalue its currency from government officials in the United States and Europe, there are likely to be further adjustments in China's exchange rate policy in the future.

How the Bretton Woods System Worked   Under the Bretton Woods system, exchange rates were supposed to change only when a country was experiencing a "fundamental disequilibrium"—that is, large persistent deficits or surpluses in its balance of payments. To maintain fixed exchange rates when countries had balance-of-payments deficits and were losing international reserves, the IMF would loan deficit countries international reserves contributed by other members. As a result of its power to dictate loan terms to borrowing countries, the IMF could encourage deficit countries to pursue contractionary monetary policies that would strengthen their currency or eliminate their balance-of-payments deficits. If the IMF loans were not sufficient to prevent depreciation of a currency, the country was allowed to devalue its currency by setting a new, lower exchange rate.

A notable weakness of the Bretton Woods system was that although deficit countries losing international reserves could be pressured into devaluing their currencies or pursuing contractionary policies, the IMF had no way to force surplus countries to revise their exchange rates upward or pursue more expansionary policies. Particularly troublesome in this regard was the fact that the reserve currency country, the United States, could not devalue its currency under the Bretton Woods system even if the dollar was overvalued. When the United States attempted to reduce domestic unemployment in the 1960s by pursuing an inflationary monetary policy, a fundamental disequilibrium of an overvalued dollar developed. Because surplus countries were not willing to revise their exchange rates upward, adjustment in the Bretton Woods system did not take place, and the system collapsed in 1971. Attempts to patch up the Bretton Woods system with the Smithsonian Agreement in December 1971 proved unsuccessful, and by 1973, America and its trading partners had agreed to allow exchange rates to float.

Managed Float

Although most exchange rates are currently allowed to change daily in response to market forces, central banks have not been willing to give up their option of intervening in the foreign exchange market. Preventing large changes in exchange rates makes it easier for firms and individuals purchasing or selling goods abroad to plan into the future. Furthermore, countries with surpluses in their balance of payments frequently do not want to see their currencies appreciate, because it makes their goods more expensive abroad and foreign goods cheaper in their country. Because an appreciation might hurt sales for domestic businesses and increase unemployment, surplus countries have often sold their currency in the foreign exchange market and acquired international reserves.

Countries with balance-of-payments deficits do not want to see their currency lose value, because it makes foreign goods more expensive for domestic consumers and can stimulate inflation. To keep the value of the domestic currency high, deficit countries have often bought their own currency in the foreign exchange market and given up international reserves.

The current international financial system is a hybrid of a fixed and a flexible exchange rate system. Rates fluctuate in response to market forces but are not determined solely by them. Furthermore, many countries continue to keep the value of their currency fixed against other currencies, as was the case in the European Monetary System before the introduction of the euro (to be described shortly).

Another important feature of the current system is the continuing de-emphasis of gold in international financial transactions. Not only has the United States suspended convertibility of dollars into gold for foreign central banks, but since 1970 the IMF has been issuing a paper substitute for gold, called **special drawing rights (SDRs)**. Like gold in the Bretton Woods system, SDRs function as international reserves. Unlike gold, whose quantity is determined by gold discoveries and the rate of production, SDRs can be created by the IMF whenever it decides that there is a need for additional international reserves to promote world trade and economic growth.

The use of gold in international transactions was further de-emphasized by the IMF's elimination of the official gold price in 1975 and by the sale of gold by the U.S. Treasury and the IMF to private investors in an effort to demonetize it. Currently, the price of gold is determined in a free market. Investors who want to speculate in it are able to purchase and sell gold at will, as are jewelers and dentists who use gold in their businesses.

European Monetary System (EMS)

In March 1979, eight members of the European Economic Community (Germany, France, Italy, the Netherlands, Belgium, Luxembourg, Denmark, and Ireland) set up the European Monetary System (EMS), in which they agreed to fix their exchange rates vis-à-vis one another and to float jointly against the U.S. dollar. Spain joined the EMS in June 1989, the United Kingdom in October 1990, and Portugal in April 1992. The EMS created a new monetary unit, the *European currency unit* (ECU), whose value was tied to a basket of specified amounts of European currencies.

The exchange rate mechanism (ERM) of the European Monetary System worked as follows. The exchange rate between every pair of currencies of the participating countries was not allowed to fluctuate outside narrow limits around a fixed exchange rate. (The limits were typically ±2.25% but were raised to ±15% in August 1993.) When the exchange rate between two countries' currencies moved outside these limits, the central banks of both countries were supposed to intervene in the foreign exchange market. If, for example, the French franc depreciated below its lower limit against the German mark, the Bank of France was required to buy francs and sell marks, thereby giving up international reserves. Similarly, the German central bank was required to intervene to sell marks and buy francs and consequently increase its international reserves. The EMS thus required that intervention be symmetric when a currency fell outside the limits, with the central bank with the weak currency giving up international reserves and the one with the strong currency gaining them. Central bank intervention was also very common even when the exchange rate was within the limits, but in this case, if one central bank intervened, no others were required to intervene as well.

A serious shortcoming of fixed exchange rate systems such as the Bretton Woods system or the European Monetary System is that they can lead to foreign exchange crises involving a "speculative attack" on a currency—massive sales of a weak currency or purchases of a strong currency that cause a sharp change in the exchange rate. In the following application, we use our model of exchange rate determination to understand how the September 1992 exchange rate crisis that rocked the European Monetary System came about.

APPLICATION ✦ The Foreign Exchange Crisis of September 1992

In the aftermath of German reunification in October 1990, the German central bank, the Bundesbank, faced rising inflationary pressures, with inflation having accelerated from below 3% in 1990 to near 5% by 1992. To get monetary growth under control and to dampen inflation, the Bundesbank raised German interest rates to near double-digit levels. Figure 3 shows the consequences of these actions by the Bundesbank in the foreign exchange market for British pounds. Note that in the diagram, the pound is the domestic currency and the German mark (deutsche mark, DM, Germany's currency before the advent of the euro in 1999) is the foreign currency.

The increase in German interest rates i^F lowered the relative expected return of British pound assets and shifted the demand curve to D_2 in Figure 3. The intersection of the supply and demand curves at point 2 was now below the lower exchange rate limit at that time (2.778 marks per pound, denoted E_{par}). To increase the value of the pound relative to the mark and to restore the mark/pound exchange rate to within the exchange rate mechanism limits, one of two things had to happen. The Bank of England would have to pursue a contractionary monetary policy, thereby raising British interest rates sufficiently to shift the demand curve back to D_1 so that the equilibrium would

FIGURE 3   **Foreign Exchange Market for British Pounds in 1992**
The realization by speculators that the United Kingdom would soon devalue the pound decreased the relative expected return on British pound assets, resulting in a leftward shift of the demand curve from D_2 to D_3. The result was the need for a much greater purchase of pounds by the British central bank to raise the interest rate so that the demand curve would shift back to D_1 and keep the exchange rate E_{par} at 2.778 German marks per pound.

remain at point 1, where the exchange rate would remain at E_{par}. Alternatively, the Bundesbank would have to pursue an expansionary monetary policy, thereby lowering German interest rates. Lower German interest rates would raise the relative expected return on British assets and shift the demand curve back to D_1 so the exchange rate would be at E_{par}.

The catch was that the Bundesbank, whose primary goal was fighting inflation, was unwilling to pursue an expansionary monetary policy, and the British, who were facing their worst recession in the postwar period, were unwilling to pursue a contractionary monetary policy to prop up the pound. This impasse became clear when in response to great pressure from other members of the EMS, the Bundesbank was willing to lower its lending rates by only a token amount on September 14 after a speculative attack was mounted on the currencies of the Scandinavian countries. So at some point in the near future, the value of the pound would have to decline to point 2. Speculators now knew that the depreciation of the pound was imminent. As a result, the relative expected return of the pound fell sharply, shifting the demand curve left to D_3 in Figure 3.

As a result of the large leftward shift of the demand curve, there was now a huge excess supply of pound assets at the par exchange rate E_{par}, which caused a massive sell-off of pounds (and purchases of marks) by speculators. The need for the British central bank to intervene to raise the value of the pound now became much greater and required a huge rise in British interest rates. After a major intervention effort on the part of the Bank of England, which included a rise in its lending rate from 10% to 15%, which still wasn't enough, the British were finally forced to give up on September 16: They pulled out of the ERM indefinitely and allowed the pound to depreciate by 10% against the mark.

Speculative attacks on other currencies forced devaluation of the Spanish peseta by 5% and the Italian lira by 15%. To defend its currency, the Swedish central bank was forced to raise its daily lending rate to the astronomical level of 500%! By the time the crisis was over, the British, French, Italian, Spanish, and Swedish central banks had intervened to the tune of $100 billion; the Bundesbank alone had laid out $50 billion for foreign exchange intervention. Because foreign exchange crises lead to large changes in central banks' holdings of international reserves and thus significantly affect the official reserve asset items in the balance of payments, these crises are also referred to as **balance-of-payments crises**.

The attempt to prop up the European Monetary System was not cheap for these central banks. It is estimated that they lost $4 to $6 billion as a result of exchange rate intervention during the crisis. What the central banks lost, the speculators gained. A speculative fund run by George Soros ran up $1 billion of profits during the crisis, and Citibank traders reportedly made $200 million. When an exchange rate crisis comes, life can certainly be sweet for exchange rate speculators.

APPLICATION ✦ Recent Foreign Exchange Crises in Emerging Market Countries: Mexico 1994, East Asia 1997, Brazil 1999, and Argentina 2002

Major currency crises in emerging market countries have been a common occurrence in recent years. We can use Figure 3 to understand the sequence of events during the currency crises in Mexico in 1994, East Asia in 1997, Brazil in 1999, and Argentina in 2002. To do so, we just need to recognize that dollars are the foreign currency, while the domestic currency was either pesos, baht, or reals. (Note that the exchange rate label on the vertical axis would be in terms of dollars/domestic currency and that the label on the horizontal axis would be the quantity of domestic currency (say, pesos) assets.

In Mexico in March 1994, political instability (the assassination of the ruling party's presidential candidate) sparked investors' concerns that the peso might be devalued. The result was that the relative expected return on domestic assets fell, thus moving the demand curve from D_1 to D_2 in Figure 3. In the case of Thailand in May 1997, the large current account deficit and the weakness of the Thai financial system raised similar concerns about the devaluation of the domestic currency, with the same effect on the demand curve. In Brazil in late 1998 and Argentina in 2001, concerns about fiscal situations that could lead to the printing of money to finance the deficit, and thereby raise inflation, also meant that a devaluation was more likely to occur. The concerns thus lowered the relative expected return on domestic assets and shifted the demand curve from D_1 to D_2. In all of these cases, the result was that the intersection of the supply and demand curves was below the pegged value of the domestic currency at E_{par}.

To keep their domestic currencies from falling below E_{par}, these countries' central banks needed to buy the domestic currency and sell dollars to raise interest rates and shift the demand curve to the right, in the process losing international reserves. At first, the central banks were successful in containing the speculative attacks. However, when more bad news broke, speculators became even more confident that these countries could not defend their currencies. (The bad news was everywhere: In Mexico, there was an uprising in Chiappas and revelations about problems in the banking system; in Thailand, there was a failure of a major financial institution; Brazil had a worsening fiscal situation, along with a threat by a governor to default on his state's debt; and in Argentina, a full-scale bank panic and an actual default on the government debt occurred.) As a result, the relative expected returns on domestic assets fell further, and the demand curve moved much farther to the left to D_3, and the central banks lost even more international reserves. Given the stress on the economy from rising interest rates and the loss of reserves, eventually the monetary authorities could no longer continue to defend the currency and were forced to give up and let their currencies depreciate. This scenario happened in Mexico in December 1994, in Thailand in July 1997, in Brazil in January 1999, and in Argentina in January 2002.

Concerns about similar problems in other countries then triggered speculative attacks against them as well. This contagion occurred in the aftermath of the Mexican crisis (jauntily referred to as the "Tequila effect") with speculative attacks on other Latin American currencies, but there were no further currency collapses. In the East Asian crisis, however, fears of devaluation spread throughout the region, leading to a scenario akin to that depicted in Figure 3. Consequently, one by one, Indonesia, Malaysia, South Korea, and the Philippines were forced to devalue sharply. Even Hong Kong, Singapore, and Taiwan were subjected to speculative attacks, but because these countries had healthy financial systems, the attacks were successfully averted.

As we saw in Chapter 9, the sharp depreciations in Mexico, East Asia, and Argentina led to full-scale financial crises that severely damaged these countries' economies. The foreign exchange crisis that shocked the European Monetary System in September 1992 cost central banks a lot of money, but the public in European countries were not seriously affected. By contrast, the public in Mexico, Argentina, and the crisis countries of East Asia were not so lucky: The collapse of these currencies triggered by speculative attacks led to the financial crises described in Chapter 9, producing severe depressions that caused hardship and political unrest.

CAPITAL CONTROLS

Because capital flows were an important element in the currency crises in Mexico and East Asia, politicians and some economists have advocated that emerging market countries avoid financial instability by restricting capital mobility. Are capital controls a good idea?

Controls on Capital Outflows

Capital outflows can promote financial instability in emerging market countries, because when domestic residents and foreigners pull their capital out of a country, the resulting capital outflow forces a country to devalue its currency. This is why some politicians in emerging market countries have recently found capital controls particularly attractive. For example, Prime Minister Mahathir of Malaysia instituted capital controls in 1998 to restrict outflows in the aftermath of the East Asian crisis.

Although these controls sound like a good idea, they suffer from several disadvantages. First, empirical evidence indicates that controls on capital outflows are seldom effective during a crisis because the private sector finds ingenious ways to evade them and has little difficulty moving funds out of the country.[6] Second, the evidence suggests that capital flight may even increase after controls are put into place, because confidence in the government is weakened. Third, controls on capital outflows often lead to corruption, as government officials get paid off to look the other way when domestic residents are trying to move funds abroad. Fourth, controls on capital outflows may lull governments into thinking they do not have to take the steps to reform their financial systems to deal with the crisis, with the result that opportunities are lost to improve the functioning of the economy.

Controls on Capital Inflows

Although most economists find the arguments against controls on capital outflows persuasive, controls on capital inflows receive more support. Supporters reason that if speculative capital cannot come in, then it cannot go out suddenly and create a crisis. Our analysis of the financial crises in East Asia in Chapter 9 provides support for this view by suggesting that capital inflows can lead to a lending boom and excessive risk taking on the part of banks, which then helps trigger a financial crisis.

However, controls on capital inflows have the undesirable feature that they may block from entering a country funds that would be used for productive investment opportunities. Although such controls may limit the fuel supplied to lending booms through capital flows, over time they produce substantial distortions and misallocation of resources as households and businesses try to get around them. Indeed, just as with controls on capital outflows, controls on capital inflows can lead to corruption. There are serious doubts whether capital controls can be effective in today's environment, in which trade is open and where there are many financial instruments that make it easier to get around these controls.

On the other hand, there is a strong case for improving bank regulation and supervision so that capital inflows are less likely to produce a lending boom and encourage excessive risk taking by banking institutions. For example, restricting banks in how fast

---

[6]See Sebastian Edwards, "How Effective are Capital Controls?," *Journal of Economic Perspectives* 13, (Winter 2000): 65–84.

their borrowing can grow might substantially limit capital inflows. Supervisory controls that focus on the sources of financial fragility, rather than the symptoms, can enhance the efficiency of the financial system, rather than hampering it.

THE ROLE OF THE IMF

The International Monetary Fund was originally set up under the Bretton Woods system to help countries deal with balance-of-payments problems and stay with the fixed exchange rates by lending to deficit countries. When the Bretton Woods system of fixed exchange rates collapsed in 1971, the IMF took on new roles.

The IMF continues to function as a data collector and provide technical assistance to its member countries. Although the IMF no longer attempts to encourage fixed exchange rates, its role as an international lender has become more important recently. This role first came to the fore in the 1980s during the Third World debt crisis, in which the IMF assisted developing countries in repaying their loans. The financial crises in Mexico in 1994–1995 and in East Asia in 1997–1998 led to huge loans by the IMF to these and other affected countries to help them recover from their financial crises and to prevent the spread of these crises to other countries. This role, in which the IMF acts like an international lender of last resort to cope with financial instability, is indeed highly controversial.

Should the IMF Be an International Lender of Last Resort?

As we saw in Chapter 15, in industrialized countries when a financial crisis occurs and the financial system threatens to seize up, domestic central banks can address matters with a lender-of-last-resort operation to limit the degree of instability in the banking system. In emerging market countries, however, where the credibility of the central bank as an inflation-fighter may be in doubt and debt contracts are typically short-term and denominated in foreign currencies, a lender-of-last-resort operation becomes a double-edged sword—as likely to exacerbate the financial crisis as to alleviate it. For example, when the U.S. Federal Reserve engaged in a lender-of-last-resort operation during the 1987 stock market crash and after the 2001 terrorist destruction of the World Trade Center (Chapter 15), there was almost no sentiment in the markets that there would be substantially higher inflation. However, for a central bank with less inflation-fighting credibility than the Fed, central bank lending to the financial system in the wake of a financial crisis—even under the lender-of-last-resort rhetoric—may well arouse fears of inflation spiraling out of control, causing an even greater currency depreciation and still greater deterioration of balance sheets. The resulting increase in moral hazard and adverse selection problems in financial markets, along the lines discussed in Chapter 9, would only worsen the financial crisis.

Central banks in emerging market countries therefore have only a very limited ability to successfully engage in a lender-of-last-resort operation. However, liquidity provided by an international lender of last resort does not have these undesirable consequences, and in helping to stabilize the value of the domestic currency, it strengthens domestic balance sheets. Moreover, an international lender of last resort may be able to prevent contagion, the situation in which a successful speculative attack on one emerging market currency leads to attacks on other emerging market currencies, spreading financial and economic disruption as it goes. Because a lender of last resort for emerging market countries is needed at times, and because it cannot be provided domestically, there is a strong rationale for an international institution to fill this role. Indeed, since Mexico's financial crisis in 1994, the International Monetary Fund and other international agencies have stepped into the lender-of-last-resort role and provided emergency lending to countries threatened by financial instability.

However, support from an international lender of last resort brings risks of its own, especially the risk that the perception it is standing ready to bail out irresponsible financial institutions may lead to excessive risk taking of the sort that makes financial crises more likely. In the Mexican and East Asian crises, governments in the crisis countries used IMF support to protect depositors and other creditors of banking institutions from losses. This safety net creates a well-known moral hazard problem because the depositors and other creditors have less incentive to monitor these banking institutions and withdraw their deposits if the institutions are taking on too much risk. The result is that these institutions are encouraged to take on excessive risks. Indeed, critics of the IMF— most prominently, the Congressional Commission headed by Professor Alan Meltzer of Carnegie-Mellon University—contend that IMF lending in the Mexican crisis, which was used to bail out foreign lenders, set the stage for the East Asian crisis, because these lenders expected to be bailed out if things went wrong, and thus provided funds that were used to fuel excessive risk taking.[7]

An international lender of last resort must find ways to limit this moral hazard problem, or it can actually make the situation worse. The international lender of last resort can make it clear that it will extend liquidity only to governments that put the proper measures in place to prevent excessive risk taking. In addition, it can reduce the incentives for risk taking by restricting the ability of governments to bail out stockholders and large uninsured creditors of domestic financial institutions. Some critics of the IMF believe that the IMF has not put enough pressure on the governments to which it lends to contain the moral hazard problem.

One problem that arises for international organizations like the IMF engaged in lender-of-last-resort operations is that they know that if they don't come to the rescue, the emerging market country will suffer extreme hardship and possible political instability. Politicians in the crisis country may exploit these concerns and engage in a game of chicken with the international lender of last resort: They resist necessary reforms, hoping that the IMF will cave in. Elements of this game were present in the Mexican crisis of 1994 and were also a particularly important feature of the negotiations between the IMF and Indonesia during the East Asian crisis.

How Should the IMF Operate?

The IMF would produce better outcomes if it made clear that it will not play this game. Just as giving in to ill-behaved children may be the easy way out in the short run, but supports a pattern of poor behavior in the long run, some critics worry that the IMF may not be tough enough when confronted by short-run humanitarian concerns. For example, these critics have been particularly critical of the IMF's lending to the Russian government, which resisted adopting appropriate reforms to stabilize its financial system.

The IMF has also been criticized for imposing on the East Asian countries so-called austerity programs that focus on tight macroeconomic policies rather than on microeconomic policies to fix the crisis-causing problems in the financial sector. Such programs

---

[7]See International Financial Institution Advisory Commission, *Report* (IFIAC: Washington, DC, 2000).

are likely to increase resistance to IMF recommendations, particularly in emerging market countries. Austerity programs allow politicians in these countries to label institutions such as the IMF as being anti-growth, rhetoric that helps the politicians mobilize the public against the IMF and avoid doing what they really need to do to reform the financial system in their country. IMF programs focused instead on reforms of the financial sector would increase the likelihood that the IMF will be seen as a helping hand in the creation of a more efficient financial system.

An important historical feature of successful lender-of-last-resort operations is that the faster the lending is done, the lower the amount that actually has to be lent. An excellent example involving the Federal Reserve occurred in the aftermath of the stock market crash on October 19, 1987 (Chapter 15). At the end of that day, to service their customers' accounts, securities firms needed to borrow several billion dollars to maintain orderly trading. However, given the unprecedented developments, banks were nervous about extending further loans to these firms. Upon learning this, the Federal Reserve engaged in an immediate lender-of-last-resort operation, making it clear that it would provide liquidity to banks making loans to the securities industry. What is striking about this episode is that the extremely quick intervention of the Fed not only resulted in a negligible impact of the stock market crash on the economy, but also meant that the amount of liquidity that the Fed needed to supply to the economy was not very large.

The ability of the Fed to engage in a lender-of-last-resort operation within a day of a substantial shock to the financial system stands in sharp contrast to the amount of time it has taken the IMF to supply liquidity during the recent crises in emerging market countries. Because IMF lending facilities were originally designed to provide funds after a country was experiencing a balance-of-payments crisis and because the conditions for the loan had to be negotiated, it took several months before the IMF made funds available. By this time, the crisis had gotten much worse—and much larger sums of funds were needed to cope with the crisis, often stretching the resources of the IMF. One reason central banks can lend so much more quickly than the IMF is that they have set up procedures in advance to provide loans, with the terms and conditions for this lending agreed upon beforehand. The need for quick provision of liquidity, to keep the loan amount manageable, argues for similar credit facilities at the international lender of last resort, so that funds can be provided quickly, as long as the borrower meets conditions such as properly supervising its banks or keeping budget deficits low.

The flaws in IMF lending programs discussed above led to countries avoiding borrowing from the IMF in recent years. Countries did not want to be subjected to harsh austerity programs and also were unhappy with IMF delays in disbursing funds during a crisis. As an alternative to the IMF, countries built up substantial cushions of international reserves to deal with balance-of-payments problems on their own. IMF lending therefore shrunk to very low levels, even creating a shortfall of revenue for its operations because it was no longer earning income by making loans. The IMF was at risk of becoming irrelevant—until the subprime financial crisis. With the subprime financial crisis, the IMF's role as an international lender of last resort returned, as can be seen in the Global box, "The Subprime Financial Crisis and the IMF."

The debate on whether the world will be better off with the IMF operating as an international lender of last resort is currently a hot one. Much attention is being focused on making the IMF more effective in performing this role, and redesign of the IMF is at the center of proposals for a new international financial architecture to help reduce international financial instability.

Global   The Subprime Financial Crisis and the IMF

Because financial institutions in emerging market countries had limited exposure to subprime mortgages, the early stages of the subprime financial crisis had little impact on their economies. However, when the subprime crisis became more virulent in October of 2008, a number of emerging market countries, as well as Iceland and former communist countries, found that foreigners were pulling funds out of their financial systems, putting not only domestic banks under stress, but also causing a sharp depreciation of their currencies.

The role of the IMF as an international lender of last resort now came to the fore. Toward the end of October, the IMF extended $25 billion in loans to Hungary, $16.5 billion to the Ukraine, and $2 billion to Iceland. These loans stipulated that the countries would have to undergo belt-tightening in order to get their fiscal houses in order.

The IMF recognized, however, that, as the Managing Director of the IMF, Dominique Strauss-Kahn put it, "exceptional times call for an exceptional response," and that a new type of lending program was needed to overcome the reluctance of countries

to borrow from it during the crisis at hand. The IMF created a new lending program at the end of October 2008 called the Short-Term Liquidity Facility, with $100 billion of funds. It provides three-month loans to countries whose economies are judged by the IMF to be basically sound, but under stress. These condition-free loans could be disbursed very quickly. In addition, these loans would not have austerity programs attached to them, making them far more attractive to potential borrowing countries.

In 1999, the IMF tried to implement a similar facility called the Contingent Credit Line, but it was unsuccessful because it required preapproval from the IMF, and countries were reluctant to apply for it because doing so might suggest that they were likely to get into trouble. The new Short-Term Liquidity Facility does not require countries to apply for it. The IMF can just determine that a country has access and give them a loan if they need it. It is too soon to determine whether this new lending facility will overcome some of the criticisms leveled against previous IMF lending programs, but it does appear to be a step in the right direction.

INTERNATIONAL CONSIDERATIONS AND MONETARY POLICY

Our analysis in this chapter so far has suggested several ways in which monetary policy can be affected by international matters. Awareness of these effects can have significant implications for the way monetary policy is conducted.

Direct Effects of the Foreign Exchange Market on the Money Supply

When central banks intervene in the foreign exchange market, they acquire or sell off international reserves, and their monetary base is affected. When a central bank intervenes in the foreign exchange market, it gives up some control of its money supply. For example, in the early 1970s, the German central bank faced a dilemma. In attempting to keep the German mark from appreciating too much against the U.S. dollar, the Germans acquired huge quantities of international reserves, leading to a rate of money growth that the German central bank considered inflationary.

The Bundesbank could have tried to halt the growth of the money supply by stopping its intervention in the foreign exchange market and reasserting control over its own money supply. Such a strategy has a major drawback when the central bank is under pressure not to allow its currency to appreciate: The lower price of imports and higher price of exports as a result of an appreciation in its currency will hurt domestic producers and increase unemployment.

Because the U.S. dollar has been a reserve currency, the U.S. monetary base and money supply have been less affected by developments in the foreign exchange market. As long as foreign central banks, rather than the Fed, intervene to keep the value of the dollar from changing, American holdings of international reserves are unaffected. The ability to conduct monetary policy is typically easier when a country's currency is a reserve currency.[8]

Balance-of-Payments Considerations

Under the Bretton Woods system, balance-of-payments considerations were more important than they are under the current managed float regime. When a nonreserve currency country is running balance-of-payments deficits, it necessarily gives up international reserves. To keep from running out of these reserves, under the Bretton Woods system it had to implement contractionary monetary policy to strengthen its currency—exactly what occurred in the United Kingdom before its devaluation of the pound in 1967. When policy became expansionary, the balance of payments deteriorated, and the British were forced to "slam on the brakes" by implementing a contractionary policy. Once the balance of payments improved, policy became more expansionary until the deteriorating balance of payments again forced the British to pursue a contractionary policy. Such on-again, off-again actions became known as a "stop-go" policy, and the domestic instability it created was criticized severely.

Because the United States is a major reserve currency country, it can run large balance-of-payments deficits without losing huge amounts of international reserves. This does not mean, however, that the Federal Reserve is never influenced by developments in the U.S. balance of payments. Current account deficits in the United States suggest that American businesses may be losing some of their ability to compete because the value of the dollar is too high. In addition, large U.S. balance-of-payments deficits lead to balance-of-payments surpluses in other countries, which can in turn lead to large increases in their holdings of international reserves (this was especially true under the Bretton Woods system). Because such increases put a strain on the international financial system and may stimulate world inflation, the Fed worries about U.S. balance-of-payments and current account deficits. To help shrink these deficits, the Fed might pursue a more contractionary monetary policy.

Exchange Rate Considerations

Unlike balance-of-payments considerations, which have become less important under the current managed float system, exchange rate considerations now play a greater role in the conduct of monetary policy. If a central bank does not want to see its currency fall in value, it may pursue a more contractionary monetary policy of reducing the money supply to raise the domestic interest rate, thereby strengthening its currency. Similarly, if a country experiences an appreciation in its currency, its domestic industry may suffer from increased foreign competition and may pressure the central bank to pursue a higher rate of money growth so as to lower the exchange rate.

---

[8]However, the central bank of a reserve currency country must worry about a shift away from the use of its currency for international reserves.

The pressure to manipulate exchange rates seems to be greater for central banks in countries other than the United States, but even the Federal Reserve is not completely immune. The growing tide of protectionism stemming from the inability of American firms to compete with foreign firms because of the strengthening dollar from 1980 to early 1985 stimulated congressional critics of the Fed to call for a more expansionary monetary policy to lower the value of the dollar. As we saw in Chapter 16, the Fed let money growth surge. A policy to bring the dollar down was confirmed in the Plaza Agreement of September 1985, in which the finance ministers from the five most important industrial nations in the free world (the United States, Japan, West Germany, the United Kingdom, and France) agreed to intervene in foreign exchange markets to achieve a decline in the dollar. The dollar continued to fall rapidly after the Plaza Agreement, and the Fed played an important role in this decline by continuing to expand the money supply at a rapid rate.

TO PEG OR NOT TO PEG: EXCHANGE-RATE TARGETING AS AN ALTERNATIVE MONETARY POLICY STRATEGY

In Chapter 16, we discussed several monetary policy strategies that could be followed to promote price stability: monetary targeting, inflation targeting, and monetary policy with an implicit (not explicit) nominal anchor. One other strategy also uses a strong nominal anchor to promote price stability: **exchange-rate targeting** (sometimes referred to as an **exchange rate peg**).

Targeting the exchange rate is a monetary policy strategy with a long history. It can take the form of fixing the value of the domestic currency to a commodity such as gold, the key feature of the gold standard described earlier in the chapter. More recently, fixed exchange rate regimes have involved fixing the value of the domestic currency to that of a large, low-inflation country like the United States (the *anchor country*). Another alternative is to adopt a *crawling target* or *peg*, in which a currency is allowed to depreciate at a steady rate so that the inflation rate in the pegging country can be higher than that of the anchor country.

Advantages of Exchange-Rate Targeting

Exchange-rate targeting has several advantages. First, the nominal anchor of an exchange-rate target directly contributes to keeping inflation under control by tying the inflation rate for internationally traded goods to that found in the anchor country. It does this because the foreign price of internationally traded goods is set by the world market, while the domestic price of these goods is fixed by the exchange-rate target. For example, until 2002 in Argentina the exchange rate for the Argentine peso was exactly one to the dollar, so that a bushel of wheat traded internationally at five dollars had its price set at five pesos. If the exchange-rate target is credible (i.e., expected to be adhered to), the exchange-rate target has the added benefit of anchoring inflation expectations to the inflation rate in the anchor country.

Second, an exchange-rate target provides an automatic rule for the conduct of monetary policy that helps mitigate the time-inconsistency problem described in Chapter 13. As we saw earlier in the chapter, an exchange-rate target forces a tightening of monetary policy when there is a tendency for the domestic currency to depreciate or a loosening of policy when there is a tendency for the domestic currency to appreciate, so that discretionary monetary policy is less of an option. The central bank will therefore be constrained from falling into the time-inconsistency trap of trying to expand output and employment in the short-run by pursuing overly expansionary monetary policy.

Third, an exchange-rate target has the advantage of simplicity and clarity, which makes it easily understood by the public. A "sound currency" is an easy-to-understand rallying cry for monetary policy. In the past, for example, this aspect was important in France, where an appeal to the "franc fort" (strong franc) was often used to justify tight monetary policy.

Given its advantages, it is not surprising that exchange-rate targeting has been used successfully to control inflation in industrialized countries. Both France and the United Kingdom, for example, successfully used exchange-rate targeting to lower inflation by tying the values of their currencies to the German mark. In 1987, when France first pegged its exchange rate to the mark, its inflation rate was 3%, two percentage points above the German inflation rate. By 1992, its inflation rate had fallen to 2%, a level that can be argued is consistent with price stability, and was even below that in Germany. By 1996, the French and German inflation rates had converged, to a number slightly below 2%. Similarly, after pegging to the German mark in 1990, the United Kingdom was able to lower its inflation rate from 10% to 3% by 1992, when it was forced to abandon the exchange rate mechanism (ERM).

Exchange-rate targeting has also been an effective means of reducing inflation quickly in emerging market countries. For example, before the devaluation in Mexico in 1994, its exchange-rate target enabled it to bring inflation down from levels above 100% in 1988 to below 10% in 1994.

Disadvantages of Exchange-Rate Targeting

Despite the inherent advantages of exchange-rate targeting, there are several serious criticisms of this strategy. The problem (as we saw earlier in the chapter) is that with capital mobility the targeting country can no longer pursue its own independent monetary policy and use it to respond to domestic shocks that are independent of those hitting the anchor country. Furthermore, an exchange-rate target means that shocks to the anchor country are directly transmitted to the targeting country, because changes in interest rates in the anchor country lead to a corresponding change in interest rates in the targeting country.

A striking example of these problems occurred when Germany was reunified in 1990. In response to concerns about inflationary pressures arising from reunification and the massive fiscal expansion required to rebuild East Germany, long-term German interest rates rose until February 1991 and short-term rates rose until December 1991. This shock to the anchor country in the exchange rate mechanism (ERM) was transmitted directly to the other countries in the ERM whose currencies were pegged to the mark, and their interest rates rose in tandem with those in Germany. Continuing adherence to the exchange-rate target slowed economic growth and increased unemployment in countries such as France that remained in the ERM and adhered to the exchange-rate peg.

A second problem with exchange-rate targets is that they leave countries open to speculative attacks on their currencies. Indeed, one aftermath of German reunification was the foreign exchange crisis of September 1992. As we saw earlier, the tight monetary policy in Germany following reunification meant that the countries in the ERM were subjected to a negative demand shock that led to a decline in economic growth and a rise in unemployment. It was certainly feasible for the governments of these countries to keep their exchange rates fixed relative to the mark in these circumstances, but speculators began to question whether these countries' commitment to the exchange-rate peg would weaken. Speculators reasoned that these countries would not tolerate the rise in unemployment resulting from keeping interest rates high enough to fend off attacks on their currencies.

At this stage, speculators were, in effect, presented with a one-way bet, because the currencies of countries like France, Spain, Sweden, Italy, and the United Kingdom could go in only one direction and depreciate against the mark. Selling these currencies before the likely depreciation occurred gave speculators an attractive profit opportunity with potentially high expected returns. The result was the speculative attack in September 1992. Only in France was the commitment to the fixed exchange rate strong enough so that France did not devalue. The governments in the other countries were unwilling to defend their currencies at all costs and eventually allowed their currencies to fall in value.

The different responses of France and the United Kingdom after the September 1992 exchange-rate crisis illustrates the potential cost of an exchange-rate target. France, which continued to peg its currency to the mark and was thus unable to use monetary policy to respond to domestic conditions, found that economic growth remained slow after 1992 and unemployment increased. The United Kingdom, on the other hand, which dropped out of the ERM exchange-rate peg and adopted inflation targeting, had much better economic performance: Economic growth was higher, the unemployment rate fell, and yet its inflation was not much worse than France's.

In contrast to industrialized countries, emerging market countries (including the transition countries of Eastern Europe) may not lose much by giving up an independent monetary policy when they target exchange rates. Because many emerging market countries have not developed the political or monetary institutions that allow the successful use of discretionary monetary policy, they may have little to gain from an independent monetary policy, but a lot to lose. Thus they would be better off by, in effect, adopting the monetary policy of a country like the United States through targeting exchange rates than by pursuing their own independent policy. This is one of the reasons that so many emerging market countries have adopted exchange-rate targeting.

Nonetheless, exchange-rate targeting is highly dangerous for these countries, because it leaves them open to speculative attacks that can have far more serious consequences for their economies than for the economies of industrialized countries. Indeed, the successful speculative attacks in Mexico in 1994, East Asia in 1997, and Argentina in 2002 plunged their economies into full-scale financial crises that devastated their economies.

An additional disadvantage of an exchange-rate target is that it can weaken the accountability of policymakers, particularly in emerging market countries. Because exchange-rate targeting fixes the exchange rate, it eliminates an important signal that can help constrain monetary policy from becoming too expansionary and thereby limit the time-inconsistency problem. In industrialized countries, particularly in the United States, the bond market provides an important signal about the stance of monetary policy. Overly expansionary monetary policy or strong political pressure to engage in overly expansionary monetary policy produces an inflation scare in which inflation expectations surge, interest rates rise because of the Fisher effect (described in Chapter 5), and there is a sharp decline in long-term bond prices. Because both central banks and the politicians want to avoid this kind of scenario, overly expansionary monetary policy will be less likely.

In many countries, particularly emerging market countries, the long-term bond market is essentially nonexistent. Under a floating exchange rate regime, however, if monetary policy is too expansionary, the exchange rate will depreciate. In these countries the daily fluctuations of the exchange rate can, like the bond market in the

United States, provide an early warning signal that monetary policy is too expansionary. Just as the fear of a visible inflation scare in the bond market constrains central bankers from pursuing overly expansionary monetary policy and constrains politicians from putting pressure on the central bank to engage in overly expansionary monetary policy, fear of exchange-rate depreciations can make overly expansionary monetary policy, and the time-inconsistency problem, less likely.

The need for signals from the foreign exchange market may be even more acute for emerging market countries, because the balance sheets and actions of their central banks are not as transparent as they are in industrialized countries. Targeting the exchange rate can make it even harder to ascertain the central bank's policy actions. The public is less able to keep a watch on the central bank and the politicians pressuring it, which makes it easier for monetary policy to become too expansionary.

When Is Exchange-Rate Targeting Desirable for Industrialized Countries?

Given the above disadvantages with exchange-rate targeting, when might it make sense? In industrialized countries, the biggest cost to exchange-rate targeting is the loss of an independent monetary policy to deal with domestic considerations. If an independent, domestic monetary policy can be conducted responsibly, this can be a serious cost indeed, as the comparison between the post-1992 experiences of France and the United Kingdom indicates. However, not all industrialized countries have found that they are capable of conducting their own monetary policy successfully, either because the central bank is not independent or because political pressures on the central bank lead to an inflationary bias in monetary policy. In these cases, giving up independent control of domestic monetary policy may not be a great loss, while the gain of having monetary policy determined by a better-performing central bank in the anchor country can be substantial.

Italy provides an example: It was not a coincidence that the Italian public had the most favorable attitude of all those in Europe toward the European Monetary Union. The past record of Italian monetary policy was not good, and the Italian public recognized that having monetary policy controlled by more responsible outsiders had benefits that far outweighed the costs of losing the ability to focus monetary policy on domestic considerations.

A second reason why industrialized countries might find targeting exchange rates useful is that it encourages integration of the domestic economy with its neighbors. Clearly this was the rationale for long-standing pegging of the exchange rate to the deutsche mark by countries such as Austria and the Netherlands, and the more recent exchange-rate pegs that preceded the European Monetary Union.

To sum up, exchange-rate targeting for industrialized countries is probably not the best monetary policy strategy to control the overall economy unless (1) domestic monetary and political institutions are not conducive to good monetary policymaking or (2) there are other important benefits of an exchange-rate target that have nothing to do with monetary policy.

When Is Exchange-Rate Targeting Desirable for Emerging Market Countries?

In countries whose political and monetary institutions are particularly weak and who therefore have been experiencing continued bouts of hyperinflation, a characterization that applies to many emerging market (including transition) countries, exchange-rate targeting may be the only way to break inflationary psychology and stabilize the economy. In this situation, exchange-rate targeting is the stabilization policy of last resort. However, if the exchange-rate targeting regimes in emerging market countries are not always transparent, they are more likely to break down, often resulting in disastrous financial crises.

Are there exchange-rate strategies that make it less likely that the exchange-rate regime will break down in emerging market countries? Two such strategies that have received increasing attention in recent years are currency boards and dollarization.

Currency Boards

One solution to the problem of lack of transparency and commitment to the exchange-rate target is the adoption of a **currency board**, in which the domestic currency is backed 100% by a foreign currency (say, dollars) and in which the note-issuing authority, whether the central bank or the government, establishes a fixed exchange rate to this foreign currency and stands ready to exchange domestic currency for the foreign currency at this rate whenever the public requests it. A currency board is just a variant of a fixed exchange-rate target in which the commitment to the fixed exchange rate is especially strong because the conduct of monetary policy is in effect put on autopilot, and taken completely out of the hands of the central bank and the government. In contrast, the typical fixed or pegged exchange-rate regime does allow the monetary authorities some discretion in their conduct of monetary policy because they can still adjust interest rates or print money.

A currency board arrangement thus has important advantages over a monetary policy strategy that just uses an exchange-rate target. First, the money supply can expand only when foreign currency is exchanged for domestic currency at the central bank. Thus the increased amount of domestic currency is matched by an equal increase in foreign exchange reserves. The central bank no longer has the ability to print money and thereby cause inflation. Second, the currency board involves a stronger commitment by the central bank to the fixed exchange rate and may therefore be effective in bringing down inflation quickly and in decreasing the likelihood of a successful speculative attack against the currency.

Although they solve the transparency and commitment problems inherent in an exchange-rate target regime, currency boards suffer from some of the same shortcomings: the loss of an independent monetary policy and increased exposure of the economy to shocks from the anchor country, and the loss of the central bank's ability to create money and act as a lender of last resort. Other means must therefore be used to cope with potential banking crises. Also, if there is a speculative attack on a currency board, the exchange of the domestic currency for foreign currency leads to a sharp contraction of the money supply, which can be highly damaging to the economy.

Currency boards have been established in the territory of Hong Kong (1983), and countries such as Argentina (1991), Estonia (1992), Lithuania (1994), Bulgaria (1997), and Bosnia (1998). Argentina's currency board, which operated from 1991 to 2002 and required the central bank to exchange U.S. dollars for new pesos at a fixed exchange rate of 1 to 1, is one of the most interesting. For more on this subject, see the Global box, "Argentina's Currency Board."

Dollarization

Another solution to the problems created by a lack of transparency and commitment to the exchange-rate target is **dollarization**, the adoption of a sound currency, like the U.S. dollar, as a country's money. Indeed, dollarization is just another variant of a fixed

Global   Argentina's Currency Board

Argentina has had a long history of monetary instability, with inflation rates fluctuating dramatically and sometimes surging to beyond 1,000% per year. To end this cycle of inflationary surges, Argentina decided to adopt a currency board in April 1991. The Argentine currency board worked as follows. Under Argentina's convertibility law, the peso/dollar exchange rate was fixed at one to one, and a member of the public could go to the Argentine central bank and exchange a peso for a dollar, or vice versa, at any time.

The early years of Argentina's currency board looked stunningly successful. Inflation, which had been running at an 800% annual rate in 1990, fell to less than 5% by the end of 1994, and economic growth was rapid, averaging almost 8% per year from 1991 to 1994. In the aftermath of the Mexican peso crisis, however, concern about the health of the Argentine economy resulted in the public pulling money out of the banks (deposits fell by 18%) and exchanging pesos for dollars, thus causing a contraction of the Argentine money supply. The result was a sharp drop in Argentine economic activity, with real GDP shrinking by more than 5% in 1995 and the unemployment rate jumping above 15%. Only in 1996 did the economy begin to recover.

Because the central bank of Argentina had no control over monetary policy under the currency board system, it was relatively helpless to counteract the contractionary monetary policy stemming from the public's behavior. Furthermore, because the currency board did not allow the central bank to create pesos and lend them to the banks, it had very little capability to act as a lender of last resort. With help from international agencies, such as the IMF, the World Bank, and the Interamerican Development Bank, which lent Argentina more than $5 billion in 1995 to help shore up its banking system, the currency board survived.

However, in 1998 Argentina entered another recession, which was both severe and very long lasting. By the end of 2001, unemployment reached nearly 20%, a level comparable to that experienced in the United States during the Great Depression of the 1930s. The result has been civil unrest and the fall of the elected government, as well as a major banking crisis and a default on nearly $150 billion of government debt. Because the Central Bank of Argentina had no control over monetary policy under the currency board system, it was unable to use monetary policy to expand the economy and get out of its recession. Furthermore, because the currency board did not allow the central bank to create pesos and lend them to banks, it had very little capability to act as a lender of last resort. In January 2002, the currency board finally collapsed and the peso depreciated by more than 70%. The result was the full-scale financial crisis described in Chapter 9, with inflation shooting up and an extremely severe depression. Clearly, the Argentine public is not as enamored of its currency board as it once was.

exchange-rate target with an even stronger commitment mechanism than a currency board provides. A currency board can be abandoned, allowing a change in the value of the currency, but a change of value is impossible with dollarization: A dollar bill is always worth one dollar, whether it is held in the United States or outside of it.

Dollarization has been advocated as a monetary policy strategy for emerging market countries: It was discussed actively by Argentine officials in the aftermath of the devaluation of the Brazilian real in January 1999 and was adopted by Ecuador in March 2000. Dollarization's key advantage is that it completely avoids the possibility of a speculative attack on the domestic currency (because there is none). (Such an attack is still a danger even under a currency board arrangement.)

Dollarization is subject to the usual disadvantages of an exchange-rate target (the loss of an independent monetary policy, increased exposure of the economy to shocks from the anchor country, and the inability of the central bank to create money and act as a lender of last resort). Dollarization has one additional disadvantage not characteristic of currency boards or other exchange-rate target regimes. Because a country adopting dollarization no longer has its own currency, it loses the revenue that a government receives by issuing money, which is called **seignorage**. Because governments (or their central banks) do not have to pay interest on their currency, they earn revenue (seignorage) by using this currency to purchase income-earning assets such as bonds. In the case of the Federal Reserve in the United States, this revenue is on the order of $30 billion per year. If an emerging market country dollarizes and gives up its currency, it needs to make up this loss of revenue somewhere, which is not always easy for a poor country.

SUMMARY

1. An unsterilized central bank intervention in which the domestic currency is sold to purchase foreign assets leads to a gain in international reserves, an increase in the money supply, and a depreciation of the domestic currency. Available evidence suggests, however, that sterilized central bank interventions have little long-term effect on the exchange rate.

2. The balance of payments is a bookkeeping system for recording all payments between a country and foreign countries that have a direct bearing on the movement of funds between them. The official reserve transactions balance is the sum of the current account balance plus the items in the capital account. It indicates the amount of international reserves that must be moved between countries to finance international transactions.

3. Before World War I, the gold standard was predominant. Currencies were convertible into gold, thus fixing exchange rates between countries. After World War II, the Bretton Woods system and the IMF were established to promote a fixed exchange rate system in which the U.S. dollar, the reserve currency, was convertible into gold. The Bretton Woods system collapsed in 1971. We now have an international financial system that has elements of a managed float and a fixed exchange rate system. Some exchange rates fluctuate from day to day, although central banks intervene in the foreign exchange market, while other exchange rates are fixed.

4. Controls on capital outflows receive support because they may prevent domestic residents and foreigners from pulling capital out of a country during a crisis and make devaluation less likely. Controls on capital inflows make sense under the theory that if speculative capital cannot flow in, then it cannot go out suddenly and create a crisis. However, capital controls suffer from several disadvantages: They are seldom effective, they lead to corruption, and they may allow governments to avoid taking the steps needed to reform their financial systems to deal with the crisis.

5. The IMF has recently taken on the role of an international lender of last resort. Because central banks in emerging market countries are unlikely to be able to perform a lender-of-last-resort operation successfully, an international lender of last resort like the IMF is needed to prevent financial instability. However, the IMF's role as an international lender of last resort creates a serious moral hazard problem that can encourage excessive risk taking and make a financial crisis more likely, but refusing to lend may be politically hard to do. In addition, it needs to be able to provide liquidity quickly during a crisis to keep manageable the amount of funds lent.

6. Three international considerations affect the conduct of monetary policy: direct effects of the foreign exchange market on the money supply, balance-of-payments considerations, and exchange rate considerations. Inasmuch as the United States has been a reserve currency country in the post–World War II period, U.S. monetary policy has been less affected by developments in the foreign exchange market and its balance of payments than is true for other countries. However, in recent years, exchange rate considerations have been playing a more prominent role in influencing U.S. monetary policy.

7. Exchange-rate targeting has the following advantages as a monetary policy strategy: (1) It directly keeps inflation under control by tying the inflation rate for internationally traded goods to that found in the anchor country to whom its currency is pegged; (2) it provides an automatic rule for the conduct of monetary policy that helps mitigate the time-inconsistency problem; and (3) it is simple and clear. Exchange-rate targeting also has serious disadvantages: (1) It results in a loss of independent monetary policy; (2) it leaves the country open to speculative attacks; and (3) it can weaken the accountability of policymakers because the exchange-rate signal is lost. Two strategies that make it less likely that the exchange-rate regime will break down are currency boards, in which the central bank stands ready to automatically exchange domestic for foreign currency at a fixed rate, and dollarization, in which a sound currency like the U.S. dollar is adopted as the country's money.

KEY TERMS

anchor currency, p. 470

balance of payments, p. 468

balance-of-payments crisis, p. 478

Bretton Woods system, p. 470

capital account, p. 468

currency board, p. 490

current account, p. 468

devaluation, p. 473

dollarization, p. 490

exchange-rate peg, p. 486

exchange-rate targeting, p. 486

fixed exchange rate regime, p. 470

floating exchange rate regime, p. 470

foreign exchange interventions, p. 463

gold standard, p. 470

International Monetary Fund (IMF), p. 470

international reserves, p. 463

managed float regime (dirty float), p. 470

official reserve transactions balance, p. 469

reserve currency, p. 471

revaluation, p. 473

seignorage, p. 492

special drawing rights (SDRs), p. 476

sterilized foreign exchange intervention, p. 466

trade balance, p. 468

unsterilized foreign exchange intervention, p. 465

World Bank, p. 471

World Trade Organization (WTO), p. 471

QUESTIONS AND PROBLEMS

All questions and problems are available in myeconlab *at* www.myeconlab.com/mishkin.

1. If the Federal Reserve buys dollars in the foreign exchange market but conducts an offsetting open market operation to sterilize the intervention, what will be the impact on international reserves, the money supply, and the exchange rate?

2. If the Federal Reserve buys dollars in the foreign exchange market but does not sterilize the intervention, what will be the impact on international reserves, the money supply, and the exchange rate?

3. For each of the following, identify in which part of the balance-of-payments account it appears (current account, capital account, or net change in international reserves) and whether it is a receipt or a payment.

    a. A British subject's purchase of a share of Johnson & Johnson stock

    b. An American's purchase of an airline ticket from Air France

    c. The Swiss government's purchase of U.S. Treasury bills

    d. A Japanese's purchase of California oranges

    e. $50 million of foreign aid to Honduras

    f. A loan by an American bank to Mexico

    g. An American bank's borrowing of Eurodollars

4. Why does a balance-of-payments deficit for the United States have a different effect on its international

reserves than a balance-of-payments deficit for the Netherlands?

5. Under the gold standard, if Britain became more productive relative to the United States, what would happen to the money supply in the two countries? Why would the changes in the money supply help preserve a fixed exchange rate between the United States and Britain?

6. What is the exchange rate between dollars and Swiss francs if one dollar is convertible into $\frac{1}{20}$ ounce of gold and one Swiss franc is convertible into $\frac{1}{40}$ ounce of gold?

7. If a country's par exchange rate was undervalued during the Bretton Woods fixed exchange rate regime, what kind of intervention would that country's central bank be forced to undertake, and what effect would it have on its international reserves and the money supply?

8. How can a large balance-of-payments surplus contribute to the country's inflation rate?

9. "If a country wants to keep its exchange rate from changing, it must give up some control over its money supply." Is this statement true, false, or uncertain? Explain your answer.

10. Why can balance-of-payments deficits force some countries to implement a contractionary monetary policy?

11. "Balance-of-payments deficits always cause a country to lose international reserves." Is this statement true, false, or uncertain? Explain your answer.

12. How can persistent U.S. balance-of-payments deficits stimulate world inflation?

13. "Inflation is not possible under the gold standard." Is this statement true, false, or uncertain? Explain your answer.

14. Why is it that in a pure flexible exchange rate system, the foreign exchange market has no direct effects on the money supply? Does this mean that the foreign exchange market has no effect on monetary policy?

15. "The abandonment of fixed exchange rates after 1973 has meant that countries have pursued more independent monetary policies." Is this statement true, false, or uncertain? Explain your answer.

16. What are the key advantages of exchange-rate targeting as a monetary policy strategy?

17. Why did the exchange-rate peg lead to difficulties for the countries in the ERM when German reunification occurred?

18. How can exchange-rate targets lead to a speculative attack on a currency?

19. Why may the disadvantage of exchange-rate targeting of not having an independent monetary policy be less of an issue for emerging market countries than for industrialized countries?

20. How can the long-term bond market help reduce the time-inconsistency problem for monetary policy? Can the foreign exchange market also perform this role?

21. When is exchange-rate targeting likely to be a sensible strategy for industrialized countries? When is exchange-rate targeting likely to be a sensible strategy for emerging market countries?

22. What are the advantages and disadvantages of a currency board over a monetary policy that just uses an exchange-rate target?

23. What are the key advantages and disadvantages of dollarization over other forms of exchange-rate targeting?

WEB EXERCISES

1. The Federal Reserve publishes information online that explains the workings of the foreign exchange market. One such publication can be found at www.ny.frb.org/education/addpub/usfxm. Review the table of contents and open Chapter 10, the evolution of the international monetary system. Read this chapter and write a one-page summary that discusses why each monetary standard was dropped in favor of the succeeding one.

2. The International Monetary Fund stands ready to help nations facing monetary crises. Go to www.imf.org. Click on the tab labeled "About IMF." What is the stated purpose of the IMF? How many nations participate and when was it established?

WEB REFERENCES

http://research.stlouisfed.org/fred2

This website contains exchange rates, balance of payments, and trade data.

www.imf.org/external/np/exr/facts/sdr.htm

Find information about special drawing rights, allocation, valuation, and SDR users' guide.

http://users.erols.com/kurrency/intro.htm

A detailed discussion of the history, purpose, and function of currency boards.

 MyEconLab CAN HELP YOU GET A BETTER GRADE

If your exam were tomorrow, would you be ready? For each chapter, MyEconLab Practice Test and Study Plans pinpoint which sections you have mastered and which ones you need to study. That way, you are more efficient with your study time, and you are better prepared for your exams.

To see how it works, turn to page 20 and then go to: www.myeconlab.com/mishkin

PART 6

Monetary Theory

CHAPTER 19
The Demand for Money

•

CHAPTER 20
The *ISLM* Model

•

CHAPTER 21
Monetary and Fiscal Policy in
the *ISLM* Model

•

CHAPTER 22
Aggregate Demand and Supply
Analysis

•

CHAPTER 23
Transmission Mechanisms of
Monetary Policy: The Evidence

•

CHAPTER 24
Money and Inflation

•

CHAPTER 25
Rational Expectations:
Implications for Policy

Crisis and Response:
The Perfect Storm of 2007–2008

In 2007 and 2008, the U.S. economy was hit by a perfect storm of formidable shocks. Higher demand for oil from rapidly growing developing countries like China and India and slowing of production in places like Mexico, Russia, and Nigeria drove up oil prices sharply from around the $60 per barrel level at the beginning of 2007. By the end of the year, oil prices had risen to $100 per barrel and reached a peak of over $140 in July of 2008. The oil price shock was both contractionary and inflationary, and as a result led to both higher inflation and unemployment—and many unhappy drivers at gas pumps.

If this supply shock were not bad enough, the subprime financial crisis hit the economy starting in August of 2007 and caused a contraction in both household and business spending. This shock led to a further rise in unemployment, with some weakening of inflationary pressure further down the road.

The result of this perfect storm of adverse shocks was a rise in U.S. unemployment from the 4.6% level in 2006 and 2007 to over 8% by early 2009. Inflation also accelerated from 2.5% in 2006 to over 5% by the middle of 2008, but with the increase in the unemployment rate and the decline of oil and other commodity prices by the fall of 2008, inflation rapidly came back down again.

Although the Fed's aggressive monetary policy aimed to address the contractionary forces in the economy, lawmakers wanted additional action. In February of 2008 and then again in February 2009, the U.S. Congress passed stimulus packages, first of $150 billion and then of $787 billion. However, although both stimulus packages helped boost GDP, they were overwhelmed by the continuing worsening of the financial crisis, and the economy went into a tailspin.

The impact of the perfect storm of adverse shocks highlights that we need to understand how monetary and other government policies affect the price level and economic activity. Chapter 19 discusses how theories of the demand for money have evolved. Chapters 20 and 21 outline the *ISLM* model, which explains how interest rates and total output in the economy are determined. In Chapter 22, we develop a basic tool, aggregate supply and demand analysis, that will enable us to study the effect of monetary policy on output and prices. Chapter 23 outlines how monetary policy affects the aggregate economy. In Chapter 24, we expand on aggregate supply and demand analysis in order to understand the inflation process. Chapter 25 examines the rational expectations revolution in monetary theory and what it implies for analyzing the impact of monetary policy on inflation and economic activity.

19 The Demand for Money

Preview

In earlier chapters, we spent a lot of time and effort learning what the money supply is, how it is determined, and what role central banks, such as the Federal Reserve System, play in it. Now we are ready to explore the role of the money supply in determining the price level and total production of goods and services (aggregate output) in the economy. The study of the effect of money on the economy is called **monetary theory**, and we examine this branch of economics in the chapters of Part 6.

When economists mention *supply,* the word *demand* is sure to follow, and the discussion of money is no exception. The supply of money is an essential building block in understanding how monetary policy affects the economy, because it suggests the factors that influence the quantity of money in the economy. Not surprisingly, another essential part of monetary theory is the demand for money.

This chapter describes how the theories of the demand for money have evolved. We begin with the classical theories refined at the start of the twentieth century by economists such as Irving Fisher, Alfred Marshall, and A. C. Pigou; then we move on to the Keynesian theories of the demand for money. We end with Milton Friedman's modern quantity theory.

A central question in monetary theory is whether or to what extent the quantity of money demanded is affected by changes in interest rates. Because this issue is crucial to how we view money's effects on aggregate economic activity, we focus on the role of interest rates in the demand for money.[1]

QUANTITY THEORY OF MONEY

Developed by the classical economists in the nineteenth and early twentieth centuries, the quantity theory of money is a theory of how the nominal value of aggregate income is determined. Because it also tells us how much money is held for a given amount of aggregate income, it is a theory of the demand for money. The most important feature of this theory is that it suggests that interest rates have no effect on the demand for money.

---

[1]In Chapter 21, we will see that the responsiveness of the quantity of money demanded to changes in interest rates has important implications for the relative effectiveness of monetary policy and fiscal policy in influencing aggregate economic activity.

Velocity of Money and Equation of Exchange

The clearest exposition of the classical quantity theory approach is found in the work of the American economist Irving Fisher, in his influential book *The Purchasing Power of Money,* published in 1911. Fisher wanted to examine the link between the total quantity of money M (the money supply) and the total amount of spending on final goods and services produced in the economy $P \times Y$, where P is the price level and Y is aggregate output (income). (Total spending $P \times Y$ is also thought of as aggregate nominal income for the economy or as nominal GDP.) The concept that provides the link between M and $P \times Y$ is called the **velocity of money** (often reduced to *velocity*), the average number of times per year (turnover) that a dollar is spent in buying the total amount of goods and services produced in the economy. Velocity V is defined more precisely as total spending $P \times Y$ divided by the quantity of money M:

$$V = \frac{P \times Y}{M} \tag{1}$$

If, for example, nominal GDP ($P \times Y$) in a year is $5 trillion and the quantity of money is $1 trillion, velocity is 5, meaning that the average dollar bill is spent five times in purchasing final goods and services in the economy.

By multiplying both sides of this definition by M, we obtain the **equation of exchange**, which relates nominal income to the quantity of money and velocity:

$$M \times V = P \times Y \tag{2}$$

The equation of exchange thus states that the quantity of money multiplied by the number of times that this money is spent in a given year must equal nominal income (the total nominal amount spent on goods and services in that year).[2]

As it stands, Equation 2 is nothing more than an identity—a relationship that is true by definition. It does not tell us, for instance, that when the money supply M changes, nominal income ($P \times Y$) changes in the same direction; a rise in M, for example, could be offset by a fall in V that leaves $M \times V$ (and therefore $P \times Y$) unchanged. To convert the equation of exchange (an *identity*) into a *theory* of how nominal income is determined requires an understanding of the factors that determine velocity.

Irving Fisher reasoned that velocity is determined by the institutions in an economy that affect the way individuals conduct transactions. If people use charge accounts and credit cards to conduct their transactions, as they can today, and consequently use money less often when making purchases, less money is required to conduct the transactions generated by nominal income (M falls relative to $P \times Y$), and velocity ($P \times Y$)/M

---

[2]Fisher actually first formulated the equation of exchange in terms of the nominal value of transactions in the economy PT:

$$MV_T = PT$$

where $\quad P$ = average price per transaction

$\quad\quad\quad T$ = number of transactions conducted in a year

$\quad\quad\quad V_T = PT/M$ = transactions velocity of money

Because the nominal value of transactions T is difficult to measure, the quantity theory has been formulated in terms of aggregate output Y as follows: T is assumed to be proportional to Y so that $T = vY$, where v is a constant of proportionality. Substituting vY for T in Fisher's equation of exchange yields $MV_T = vPY$, which can be written as Equation 2 in the text, in which $V = V_T/v$.

will increase. Conversely, if it is more convenient for purchases to be paid for with cash or checks (both of which are money), more money is used to conduct the transactions generated by the same level of nominal income, and velocity will fall. Fisher took the view that the institutional and technological features of the economy would affect velocity only slowly over time, so velocity would normally be reasonably constant in the short run.

Quantity Theory

Fisher's view that velocity is fairly constant in the short run transforms the equation of exchange into the **quantity theory of money**, which states that nominal income is determined solely by movements in the quantity of money: When the quantity of money M doubles, $M \times V$ doubles and so must $P \times Y$, the value of nominal income. To see how this works, let's assume that velocity is 5, nominal income (GDP) is initially $5 trillion, and the money supply is $1 trillion. If the money supply doubles to $2 trillion, the quantity theory of money tells us that nominal income will double to $10 trillion ($= 5 \times \$2$ trillion).

Because the classical economists (including Fisher) thought that wages and prices were completely flexible, they believed that the level of aggregate output Y produced in the economy during normal times would remain at the full-employment level, so Y in the equation of exchange could also be treated as reasonably constant in the short run. The quantity theory of money then implies that if M doubles, P must also double in the short run, because V and Y are constant. In our example, if aggregate output is $5 trillion, the velocity of 5 and a money supply of $1 trillion indicate that the price level equals 1 because 1 times $5 trillion equals the nominal income of $5 trillion. When the money supply doubles to $2 trillion, the price level must also double to 2 because 2 times $5 trillion equals the nominal income of $10 trillion.

For the classical economists, the quantity theory of money provided an explanation of movements in the price level: *Movements in the price level result solely from changes in the quantity of money*.

Quantity Theory of Money Demand

Because the quantity theory of money tells us how much money is held for a given amount of aggregate income, it is, in fact, a theory of the demand for money. We can see this by dividing both sides of the equation of exchange by V, thus rewriting it as

$$M = \frac{1}{V} \times PY$$

where nominal income $P \times Y$ is written as PY. When the money market is in equilibrium, the quantity of money M that people hold equals the quantity of money demanded M^d, so we can replace M in the equation by M^d. Using k to represent the quantity $1/V$ (a constant, because V is a constant), we can rewrite the equation as

$$M^d = k \times PY \tag{3}$$

Equation 3 tells us that because k is a constant, the level of transactions generated by a fixed level of nominal income PY determines the quantity of money M^d that people demand. Therefore, Fisher's quantity theory of money suggests that the demand for

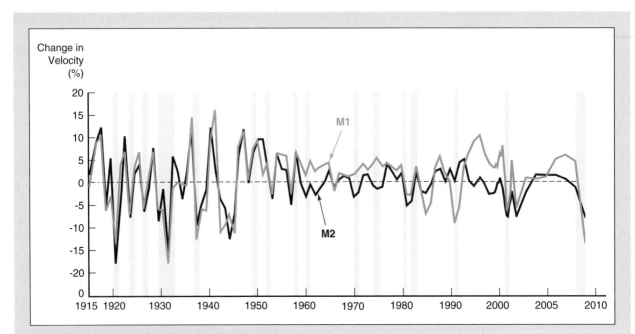

FIGURE 1   **Change in the Velocity of M1 and M2 from Year to Year, 1915–2008**
Shaded areas indicate recessions. Velocities are calculated using nominal GNP before 1959 and
nominal GDP thereafter.

Sources: Economic Report of the President; Banking and Monetary Statistics; www.federalreserve.gov/releases/h6/hist/h6hist1.txt.

money is purely a function of income, and interest rates have no effect on the demand
for money.[3]

Fisher came to this conclusion because he believed that people hold money only to
conduct transactions and have no freedom of action in terms of the amount they want
to hold. The demand for money is determined (1) by the level of transactions generated
by the level of nominal income PY and (2) by the institutions in the economy that affect
the way people conduct transactions and thus determine velocity and hence k.

IS VELOCITY A CONSTANT?

The classical economists' conclusion that nominal income is determined by movements in the money supply rested on their belief that velocity PY/M could be treated
as reasonably constant.[4] Is it reasonable to assume that velocity is constant? To answer
this, let's look at Figure 1, which shows the year-to-year changes in velocity from

---

[3]While Fisher was developing his quantity theory approach to the demand for money, a group of classical economists in Cambridge, England led by Alfred Marshall and A. C. Pigou, came to similar conclusions, although with
slightly different reasoning. They derived Equation 3 by recognizing that two properties of money motivate people
to hold it: its utility as a medium of exchange and as a store of wealth.

[4]Actually, the classical conclusion still holds if velocity grows at some uniform rate over time that reflects changes
in transaction technology. Hence the concept of a constant velocity should more accurately be thought of here as
a lack of upward and downward fluctuations in velocity.

1915 to 2008 (nominal income is represented by nominal GDP and the money supply by M1 and M2).

What we see in Figure 1 is that even in the short run, velocity fluctuates too much to be viewed as a constant. Prior to 1950, velocity exhibited large swings up and down. This may reflect the substantial instability of the economy in this period, which included two world wars and the Great Depression. (Velocity actually falls, or at least its rate of growth declines, in years when recessions are taking place.) After 1950, velocity appears to have more moderate fluctuations, yet there are large differences in the growth rate of velocity from year to year. The percentage change in M1 velocity (GDP/M1) from 1981 to 1982, for example, was −2.5%, whereas from 1980 to 1981 velocity grew at a rate of 4.2%. This difference of 6.7% means that nominal GDP was 6.7% lower than it would have been if velocity had kept growing at the same rate as in 1980–1981.[5] The drop is enough to account for the severe recession that took place in 1981–1982. After 1982, M1 velocity appears to have become even more volatile, a fact that has puzzled researchers when they examine the empirical evidence on the demand for money (discussed later in this chapter). M2 velocity remained more stable than M1 velocity after 1982, with the result that the Federal Reserve dropped its M1 targets in 1987 and began to focus more on M2 targets. However, instability of M2 velocity in the early 1990s resulted in the Fed's announcement in July 1993 that it no longer felt that any of the monetary aggregates, including M2, was a reliable guide for monetary policy.

Until the Great Depression, economists did not recognize that velocity declines sharply during severe economic contractions. Why did the classical economists not recognize this fact when it is easy to see in the pre-Depression period in Figure 1? Unfortunately, accurate data on GDP and the money supply did not exist before World War II. (Only after the war did the government start to collect these data.) Economists had no way of knowing that their view of velocity as a constant was demonstrably false. The decline in velocity during the Great Depression years was so great, however, that even the crude data available to economists at that time suggested that velocity was not constant. This explains why, after the Great Depression, economists began to search for other factors influencing the demand for money that might help explain the large fluctuations in velocity.

Let us now examine the theories of money demand that arose from this search for a better explanation of the behavior of velocity.

KEYNES'S LIQUIDITY PREFERENCE THEORY

In his famous 1936 book *The General Theory of Employment, Interest, and Money*, John Maynard Keynes abandoned the classical view that velocity was a constant and developed a theory of money demand that emphasized the importance of interest rates. His theory of the demand for money, which he called the **liquidity preference theory**, asked the question: Why do individuals hold money? He postulated that there are three motives behind the demand for money: the transactions motive, the precautionary motive, and the speculative motive.

---

[5]We reach a similar conclusion if we use M2 velocity. The percentage change in M2 velocity (GDP/M2) from 1981 to 1982 was −5.0%, whereas from 1980 to 1981 it was +2.3%. This difference of 7.3% means that nominal GDP was 7.3% lower than it would have been if M2 velocity had kept growing at the same rate as in 1980–1981.

Transactions Motive

In the classical approach, individuals are assumed to hold money because it is a medium of exchange that can be used to carry out everyday transactions. Following the classical tradition, Keynes emphasized that this component of the demand for money is determined primarily by the level of people's transactions. Because he believed that these transactions were proportional to income, like the classical economists, he took the transactions component of the demand for money to be proportional to income.

Precautionary Motive

Keynes went beyond the classical analysis by recognizing that in addition to holding money to carry out current transactions, people hold money as a cushion against an unexpected need. Suppose that you've been thinking about buying a fancy sound system; you walk by a store that is having a 50%-off sale on the one you want. If you are holding money as a precaution for just such an occurrence, you can purchase the stereo right away; if you are not holding precautionary money balances, you cannot take advantage of the sale. Precautionary money balances also come in handy if you are hit with an unexpected bill—say, for car repair or hospitalization.

Keynes believed that the precautionary money balances people want to hold are determined primarily by the level of transactions that they expect to make in the future and that these transactions are proportional to income. Therefore, he postulated, the demand for precautionary money balances is proportional to income.

Speculative Motive

If Keynes had ended his theory with the transactions and precautionary motives, income would be the only important determinant of the demand for money, and he would not have added much to the classical approach. However, Keynes took the view that people also hold money as a store of wealth. He called this reason for holding money the *speculative motive*. Because he believed that wealth is tied closely to income, the speculative component of money demand would be related to income. However, Keynes looked more carefully at other factors that influence the decisions regarding how much money to hold as a store of wealth, especially interest rates.

Keynes divided the assets that can be used to store wealth into two categories: money and bonds. He then asked the following question: Why would individuals decide to hold their wealth in the form of money rather than bonds?

Thinking back to the discussion of the theory of asset demand (Chapter 5), you would want to hold money if its expected return was greater than the expected return from holding bonds. Keynes assumed that the expected return on money was zero because in his time, unlike today, most checkable deposits did not earn interest. For bonds, there are two components of the expected return: the interest payment and the *expected* rate of capital gains.

You learned in Chapter 4 that when interest rates rise, the price of a bond falls. If you expect interest rates to rise, you expect the price of the bond to fall and therefore expect to suffer a negative capital gain—that is, a capital loss. If you expect the rise in interest rates to be substantial enough, the capital loss might outweigh the interest payment, and your *expected* return on the bond would be negative. In this case, you would want to store your wealth as money because its expected return is higher; its zero return exceeds the negative return on the bond.

Keynes assumed that individuals believe that interest rates gravitate to some normal value (an assumption less plausible in today's world). If interest rates are below this normal value, individuals expect the interest rate on bonds to rise in the future and so expect to suffer capital losses on them. As a result, individuals will be more likely to hold their wealth as money rather than bonds, and the demand for money will be high.

What would you expect to happen to the demand for money when interest rates are above the normal value? In general, people will expect interest rates to fall, bond prices to rise, and capital gains to be realized. At higher interest rates, they are more likely to expect the return from holding a bond to be positive, thus exceeding the expected return from holding money. They will be more likely to hold bonds than money, and the demand for money will be quite low. From Keynes's reasoning, we can conclude that as interest rates rise, the demand for money falls, and therefore **money demand is negatively related to the level of interest rates**.

Putting the Three Motives Together

In putting the three motives for holding money balances together into a demand for money equation, Keynes was careful to distinguish between nominal quantities and real quantities. Money is valued in terms of what it can buy. If, for example, all prices in the economy double (the price level doubles), the same nominal quantity of money will be able to buy only half as many goods. Keynes thus reasoned that people want to hold a certain amount of **real money balances** (the quantity of money in real terms)—an amount that his three motives indicated would be related to real income Y and to interest rates i. Keynes wrote down the following demand for money equation, known as the *liquidity preference function*, which says that the demand for real money balances M^d/P is a function of (related to) i and Y:[6]

$$\frac{M^d}{P} = f(\underset{-}{i}, \underset{+}{Y}) \tag{4}$$

The minus sign below i in the liquidity preference function means that the demand for real money balances is negatively related to the interest rate i, and the plus sign below Y means that the demand for real money balances and real income Y are positively related. Keynes's conclusion that the demand for money is related not only to income but also to interest rates is a major departure from Fisher's view of money demand, in which interest rates have no effect on the demand for money.

The money demand function in Equation 4 is the same one used in our analysis of money demand in Chapter 5 and in Chapter 20 that describes the *ISLM* model. Because money demand is negatively related to the interest rate, a fall in i leads to a rise in the quantity of money demanded M^d, and so the money demand curve is downward sloping as in Figure 8 in Chapter 5. By deriving the liquidity preference function for velocity PY/M, we can see that Keynes's theory of the demand for money implies that velocity

---

[6]The classical economists' money demand equation can also be written in terms of real money balances by dividing both sides of Equation 3 by the price level P to obtain:

$$\frac{M^d}{P} = k \times Y$$

is not constant, but instead fluctuates with movements in interest rates. The liquidity preference equation can be rewritten as

$$\frac{P}{M^d} = \frac{1}{f(i, Y)}$$

Multiplying both sides of this equation by Y and recognizing that M^d can be replaced by M because they must be equal in money market equilibrium, we solve for velocity:

$$V = \frac{PY}{M} = \frac{Y}{f(i, Y)} \tag{5}$$

We know that the demand for money is negatively related to interest rates; when i goes up, $f(i, Y)$ declines, and therefore velocity rises. In other words, a rise in interest rates encourages people to hold lower real money balances for a given level of income; therefore, the rate at which money turns over (velocity) must be higher. This reasoning implies that because interest rates have substantial fluctuations, the liquidity preference theory of the demand for money indicates that velocity has substantial fluctuations as well.

An interesting feature of Equation 5 is that it explains some of the velocity movements in Figure 1, in which we noted that when recessions occur, velocity falls or its rate of growth declines. What fact regarding the cyclical behavior of interest rates (discussed in Chapter 5) might help us explain this phenomenon? You might recall that interest rates are procyclical, rising in expansions and falling in recessions. The liquidity preference theory indicates that a rise in interest rates will cause velocity to rise also. The procyclical movements of interest rates should induce procyclical movements in velocity, and that is exactly what we see in Figure 1.

Keynes's model of the speculative demand for money provides another reason why velocity might show substantial fluctuations. What would happen to the demand for money if the view of the normal level to which interest rates gravitate changes? For example, what if people expect the future normal interest rate to be higher than the current normal interest rate? Because interest rates are then expected to be higher in the future, more people will expect the prices of bonds to fall and will anticipate capital losses. The expected returns from holding bonds will decline, and money will become more attractive relative to bonds. As a result, the demand for money will increase. This means that $f(i, Y)$ will increase and so velocity will fall. Velocity will change as expectations about future normal levels of interest rates change, and unstable expectations about future movements in normal interest rates can lead to instability of velocity. This is one more reason why Keynes rejected the view that velocity could be treated as a constant.

In summary, Keynes's liquidity preference theory postulated three motives for holding money: the transactions motive, the precautionary motive, and the speculative motive. Although Keynes took the transactions and precautionary components of the demand for money to be proportional to income, he reasoned that the speculative motive would be negatively related to the level of interest rates.

Keynes's model of the demand for money has the important implication that velocity is not constant, but instead is positively related to interest rates, which fluctuate substantially. His theory also rejected the constancy of velocity, because changes in people's expectations about the normal level of interest rates would cause shifts in the demand for money that would cause velocity to shift as well. Thus Keynes's liquidity preference theory casts doubt on the classical quantity theory that nominal income is determined primarily by movements in the quantity of money.

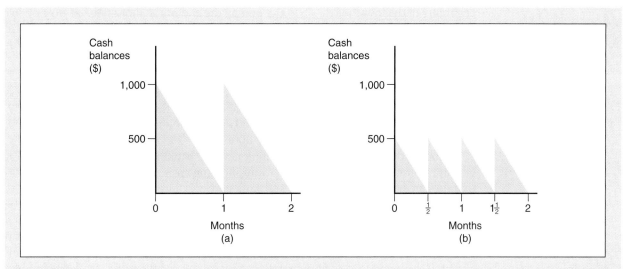

FIGURE 2   **Cash Balances in the Baumol–Tobin Model**
In panel (a), the $1,000 payment at the beginning of the month is held entirely in cash and is spent at a constant rate until it is exhausted by the end of the month. In panel (b), half of the monthly payment is put into cash and the other half into bonds. At the middle of the month, cash balances reach zero and bonds must be sold to bring balances up to $500. By the end of the month, cash balances again dwindle to zero.

FURTHER DEVELOPMENTS IN THE KEYNESIAN APPROACH

After World War II, economists began to take the Keynesian approach to the demand for money even further by developing more precise theories to explain the three Keynesian motives for holding money. Because interest rates were viewed as a crucial element in monetary theory, a key focus of this research was to understand better the role of interest rates in the demand for money.

Transactions Demand

William Baumol and James Tobin independently developed similar demand for money models, which demonstrated that even money balances held for transactions purposes are sensitive to the level of interest rates.[7] In developing their models, they considered a hypothetical individual who receives a payment once a period and spends it over the course of this period. In their model, money, which earns zero interest, is held only because it can be used to carry out transactions.

To refine this analysis, let's say that Grant Smith receives $1,000 at the beginning of the month and spends it on transactions that occur at a constant rate during the course of the month. If Grant keeps the $1,000 in cash to carry out his transactions, his money balances follow the sawtooth pattern displayed in panel (a) of Figure 2. At the

---

[7]William J. Baumol, "The Transactions Demand for Cash: An Inventory Theoretic Approach," *Quarterly Journal of Economics* 66 (1952): 545–556; and James Tobin, "The Interest Elasticity of the Transactions Demand for Cash," *Review of Economics and Statistics* 38 (1956): 241–247.

beginning of the month he has $1,000, and by the end of the month he has no cash left because he has spent it all. Over the course of the month, his holdings of money will on average be $500 (his holdings at the beginning of the month, $1,000, plus his holdings at the end of the month, $0, divided by 2).

At the beginning of the next month, Grant receives another $1,000 payment, which he holds as cash, and the same decline in money balances begins again. This process repeats monthly, and his average money balance during the course of the year is $500. Since his yearly nominal income is $12,000 and his holdings of money average $500, the velocity of money ($V = PY/M$) is $12,000/$500 = 24.

Suppose that as a result of taking a money and banking course, Grant realizes that he can improve his situation by not always holding cash. In January, then, he decides to hold part of his $1,000 in cash and puts part of it into an income-earning security such as bonds. At the beginning of each month, Grant keeps $500 in cash and uses the other $500 to buy a Treasury bond. As you can see in panel (b), he starts out each month with $500 of cash, and by the middle of the month, his cash balance has run down to zero. Because bonds cannot be used directly to carry out transactions, Grant must sell them and turn them into cash so that he can carry out the rest of the month's transactions. At the middle of the month, then, Grant's cash balance rises back up to $500. By the end of the month, the cash is gone. When he again receives his next $1,000 monthly payment, he again divides it into $500 of cash and $500 of bonds, and the process continues. The net result of this process is that the average cash balance held during the month is $500/2 = $250—just half of what it was before. Velocity has doubled to $12,000/$250 = 48.

What has Grant Smith gained from his new strategy? He has earned interest on $500 of bonds that he held for half the month. If the interest rate is 1% per month, he has earned an additional $2.50 ($= \frac{1}{2} \times \$500 \times 1\%$) per month.

Sounds like a pretty good deal, doesn't it? In fact, if he had kept $333.33 in cash at the beginning of the month, he would have been able to hold $666.67 in bonds for the first third of the month. Then he could have sold $333.33 of bonds and held on to $333.34 of bonds for the next third of the month. Finally, two-thirds of the way through the month, he would have had to sell the remaining bonds to raise cash. The net result of this is that Grant would have earned $3.33 per month [$= (\frac{1}{3} \times \$666.67 \times 1\%) \times (\frac{1}{3} \times \$333.34 \times 1\%)$]. This is an even better deal. His average cash holdings in this case would be $333.33/2 = $166.67. Clearly, the lower his average cash balance, the more interest he will earn.

As you might expect, there is a catch to all this. In buying bonds, Grant incurs transaction costs of two types. First, he must pay a straight brokerage fee for the buying and selling of the bonds. These fees increase when average cash balances are lower because Grant will be buying and selling bonds more often. Second, by holding less cash, he will have to take time to sell the bonds to get the cash. Because time is money, this must also be counted as part of the transaction costs.

Grant faces a trade-off. If he holds very little cash, he can earn a lot of interest on bonds, but he will incur greater transaction costs. If the interest rate is high, the benefits of holding bonds will be high relative to the transaction costs, and he will hold more bonds and less cash. Conversely, if interest rates are low, the transaction costs involved in holding a lot of bonds may outweigh the interest payments, and Grant would then be better off holding more cash and fewer bonds.

The conclusion of the Baumol-Tobin analysis may be stated as follows: As interest rates increase, the amount of cash held for transactions purposes will decline, which in turn means that velocity will increase as interest rates increase.[8] Put another way, the ***transactions component of the demand for money is negatively related to the level of interest rates***.

The basic idea in the Baumol-Tobin analysis is that there is an opportunity cost of holding money—the interest that can be earned on other assets. There is also a benefit to holding money—the avoidance of transaction costs. When interest rates increase, people will try to economize on their holdings of money for transactions purposes, because the opportunity cost of holding money has increased. By using simple models, Baumol and Tobin revealed something that we might not otherwise have seen: that the transactions demand for money, and not just the speculative demand, will be sensitive to interest rates. The Baumol-Tobin analysis presents a nice demonstration of the value of economic modeling.[9]

The idea that as interest rates increase, the opportunity cost of holding money increases so that the demand for money falls, can be stated equivalently with the terminology of expected returns used in Chapter 5. As interest rates increase, the expected return on the other asset, bonds, increases, causing the relative expected return on money to fall, thereby lowering the demand for money. These two explanations are in fact identical, because as we saw in Chapter 5, changes in the opportunity cost of an asset are just a description of what is happening to the relative expected return. Baumol and Tobin used opportunity cost terminology in their work on the transactions demand for money, and that is why we use this terminology here.

Precautionary Demand

Models that explore the precautionary motive of the demand for money have been developed along lines similar to the Baumol-Tobin framework, so we will not go into great detail about them here. We have already discussed the benefits of holding precautionary money balances, but weighed against these benefits must be the opportunity cost of the interest forgone by holding money. We therefore have a trade-off similar to the one for transactions balances. As interest rates rise, the opportunity cost of holding precautionary balances rises, so the holdings of these money balances fall. We then have a result similar to the one found for the Baumol-Tobin analysis.[10] ***The precautionary demand for money is negatively related to interest rates***.

Speculative Demand

Keynes's analysis of the speculative demand for money was open to several serious criticisms. It indicated that an individual holds only money as a store of wealth when the

---

[8]Similar reasoning leads to the conclusion that as brokerage fees increase, the demand for transactions money balances increases as well. When these fees rise, the benefits from holding transactions money balances increase because by holding these balances, an individual will not have to sell bonds as often, thereby avoiding these higher brokerage costs. The greater benefits to holding money balances relative to the opportunity cost of interest forgone, then, lead to a higher demand for transactions balances.

[9]The mathematics behind the Baumol-Tobin model can be found in an appendix to this chapter on this book's website at www.myeconlab.com/mishkin.

[10]These models of the precautionary demand for money also reveal that as uncertainty about the level of future transactions grows, the precautionary demand for money increases. This is so because greater uncertainty means that individuals are more likely to incur transaction costs if they are not holding precautionary balances. The benefit of holding such balances then increases relative to the opportunity cost of forgone interest, and so the demand for them rises.

expected return on bonds is less than the expected return on money and holds only bonds when the expected return on bonds is greater than the expected return on money. Only when people have expected returns on bonds and money that are exactly equal (a rare instance) would they hold both. Keynes's analysis therefore implies that practically no one holds a diversified portfolio of bonds and money simultaneously as a store of wealth. Because diversification is apparently a sensible strategy for choosing which assets to hold, the fact that it rarely occurs in Keynes's analysis is a serious shortcoming of his theory of the speculative demand for money.

Tobin developed a model of the speculative demand for money that attempted to avoid this criticism of Keynes's analysis.[11] His basic idea was that not only do people care about the expected return on one asset versus another when they decide what to hold in their portfolio, but they also care about the riskiness of the returns from each asset. Specifically, Tobin assumed that most people are risk-averse—that they would be willing to hold an asset with a lower expected return if it is less risky. An important characteristic of money is that its return is certain; Tobin assumed it to be zero. Bonds, by contrast, can have substantial fluctuations in price, and their returns can be quite risky and sometimes negative. So even if the expected returns on bonds exceed the expected return on money, people might still want to hold money as a store of wealth because it has less risk associated with its return than bonds do.

The Tobin analysis also shows that people can reduce the total amount of risk in a portfolio by diversifying—that is, by holding both bonds and money. The model suggests that individuals will hold bonds and money simultaneously as stores of wealth. Because this is probably a more realistic description of people's behavior than Keynes's, Tobin's rationale for the speculative demand for money seems to rest on more solid ground.

Tobin's attempt to improve on Keynes's rationale for the speculative demand for money was only partly successful, however. It is still not clear that the speculative demand even exists. What if there are assets that have no risk—like money—but earn a higher return? Will there be any speculative demand for money? No, because an individual will always be better off holding such an asset rather than money. The resulting portfolio will enjoy a higher expected return yet has no higher risk. Do such assets exist in the American economy? The answer is yes. United States Treasury bills and other assets that have no default risk provide certain returns that are greater than those available on money. Therefore, why would anyone want to hold money balances as a store of wealth (ignoring for the moment transactions and precautionary reasons)?

Although Tobin's analysis did not explain why money is held as a store of wealth, it was an important development in our understanding of how people should choose among assets. Indeed, his analysis was an important step in the development of the academic field of finance, which examines asset pricing and portfolio choice (the decision to buy one asset over another).

To sum up, further developments of the Keynesian approach have attempted to give a more precise explanation for the transactions, precautionary, and speculative demand for money. The attempt to improve Keynes's rationale for the speculative demand for money has been only partly successful; it is still not clear that this demand even exists. However, the models of the transactions and precautionary demand for money indicate that these components of money demand are negatively related to interest rates. Hence

---

[11]James Tobin, "Liquidity Preference as Behavior Towards Risk," *Review of Economic Studies* 25 (1958): 65–86.

Keynes's proposition that the demand for money is sensitive to interest rates—suggesting that velocity is not constant and that nominal income might be affected by factors other than the quantity of money—is still supported.

FRIEDMAN'S MODERN QUANTITY THEORY OF MONEY

In 1956, Milton Friedman developed a theory of the demand for money in a famous article, "The Quantity Theory of Money: A Restatement."[12] Although Friedman frequently referred to Irving Fisher and the quantity theory, his analysis of the demand for money was actually closer to that of Keynes.

Like his predecessors, Friedman pursued the question of why people choose to hold money. Instead of analyzing the specific motives for holding money, as Keynes did, Friedman simply stated that the demand for money must be influenced by the same factors that influence the demand for any asset. Friedman then applied the theory of asset demand to money.

The theory of asset demand (Chapter 5) indicates that the demand for money should be a function of the resources available to individuals (their wealth) and the expected returns on other assets relative to the expected return on money. Like Keynes, Friedman recognized that people want to hold a certain amount of real money balances (the quantity of money in real terms). From this reasoning, Friedman expressed his formulation of the demand for money as follows:

$$\frac{M^d}{P} = f(\underset{+}{Y_p}, \underset{-}{r_b - r_m}, \underset{-}{r_e - r_m}, \underset{-}{\pi^e - r_m}) \tag{6}$$

where M^d/P = demand for real money balances

Y_p = Friedman's measure of wealth, known as *permanent income* (technically, the present discounted value of all expected future income, but more easily described as expected average long-run income)

r_m = expected return on money

r_b = expected return on bonds

r_e = expected return on equity (common stocks)

π^e = expected inflation rate

The signs underneath the equation indicate whether the demand for money is positively (+) related or negatively (−) related to the terms that are immediately above them.[13]

---

[12]Milton Friedman, "The Quantity Theory of Money: A Restatement," in *Studies in the Quantity Theory of Money*, ed. Milton Friedman (Chicago: University of Chicago Press, 1956), pp. 3–21.

[13]Friedman also added to his formulation a term *h* that represented the ratio of human to nonhuman wealth. He reasoned that if people had more permanent income coming from labor income and thus from their human capital, they would be less liquid than if they were receiving income from financial assets. In this case, they might want to hold more money because it is a more liquid asset than the alternatives. The term *h* plays no essential role in Friedman's theory and has no important implications for monetary theory. That is why we ignore it in the money demand function.

Let us look in more detail at the variables in Friedman's money demand function and what they imply for the demand for money.

Because the demand for an asset is positively related to wealth, money demand is positively related to Friedman's wealth concept, permanent income (indicated by the plus sign beneath it). Unlike our usual concept of income, permanent income (which can be thought of as expected average long-run income) has much smaller short-run fluctuations, because many movements of income are transitory (short-lived). For example, in a business cycle expansion, income increases rapidly, but because some of this increase is temporary, average long-run income does not change very much. Hence in a boom, permanent income rises much less than income. During a recession, much of the income decline is transitory, and average long-run income (hence permanent income) falls less than income. One implication of Friedman's use of the concept of permanent income as a determinant of the demand for money is that the demand for money will not fluctuate much with business cycle movements.

An individual can hold wealth in several forms besides money. Friedman categorized them into three types of assets: bonds, equity (common stocks), and goods. The incentives for holding these assets rather than money are represented by the expected return on each of these assets relative to the expected return on money, the last three terms in the money demand function. The minus sign beneath each indicates that as each term rises, the demand for money will fall.

The expected return on money r_m, which appears in all three terms, is influenced by two factors:

1. The services provided by banks on deposits included in the money supply, such as provision of receipts in the form of canceled checks or the automatic paying of bills. When these services are increased, the expected return from holding money rises.

2. The interest payments on money balances. NOW accounts and other deposits that are included in the money supply currently pay interest. As these interest payments rise, the expected return on money rises.

The terms $r_b - r_m$ and $r_e - r_m$ represent the expected return on bonds and equity relative to money; as they rise, the relative expected return on money falls, and the demand for money falls. The final term, $\pi^e - r_m$, represents the expected return on goods relative to money. The expected return from holding goods is the expected rate of capital gains that occurs when their prices rise and hence is equal to the expected inflation rate π^e. If the expected inflation rate is 10%, for example, then goods' prices are expected to rise at a 10% rate, and their expected return is 10%. When $\pi^e - r_m$ rises, the expected return on goods relative to money rises, and the demand for money falls.

DISTINGUISHING BETWEEN THE FRIEDMAN AND KEYNESIAN THEORIES

There are several differences between Friedman's theory of the demand for money and the Keynesian theories. One is that by including many assets as alternatives to money, Friedman recognized that more than one interest rate is important to the operation of the aggregate economy. Keynes, for his part, lumped financial assets other than money into one big category—bonds—because he felt that their returns generally move together. If this is so, the expected return on bonds will be a good indicator of the expected return on other financial assets, and there will be no need to include them separately in the money demand function.

Also in contrast to Keynes, Friedman viewed money and goods as substitutes; that is, people choose between them when deciding how much money to hold. That is why Friedman included the expected return on goods relative to money as a term in his money demand function. The assumption that money and goods are substitutes indicates that changes in the quantity of money may have a direct effect on aggregate spending.

In addition, Friedman stressed two issues in discussing his demand for money function that distinguish it from Keynes's liquidity preference theory. First, Friedman did not take the expected return on money to be a constant, as Keynes did. When interest rates rise in the economy, banks make more profits on their loans, and they want to attract more deposits to increase the volume of their now more profitable loans. If there are no restrictions on interest payments on deposits, banks attract deposits by paying higher interest rates on them. Because the industry is competitive, the expected return on money held as bank deposits then rises with the higher interest rates on bonds and loans. The banks compete to get deposits until there are no excess profits, and in doing so they close the gap between interest earned on loans and interest paid on deposits. The net result of this competition in the banking industry is that $r_b - r_m$ stays relatively constant when the interest rate i rises.[14]

What if there are restrictions on the amount of interest that banks can pay on their deposits? Will the expected return on money be a constant? As interest rates rise, will $r_b - r_m$ rise as well? Friedman thought not. He argued that although banks might be restricted from making pecuniary payments on their deposits, they can still compete on the quality dimension. For example, they can provide more services to depositors by hiring more tellers, paying bills automatically, or making more cash machines available at more accessible locations. The result of these improvements in money services is that the expected return from holding deposits will rise. So despite the restrictions on pecuniary interest payments, we might still find that a rise in market interest rates will raise the expected return on money sufficiently so that $r_b - r_m$ will remain relatively constant. *Unlike Keynes's theory, which indicates that interest rates are an important determinant of the demand for money, Friedman's theory suggests that changes in interest rates should have little effect on the demand for money.*

Therefore, Friedman's money demand function was essentially one in which permanent income is the primary determinant of money demand, and his money demand equation can be approximated by

$$\frac{M^d}{P} = f(Y_p) \tag{7}$$

In Friedman's view, the demand for money was insensitive to interest rates—not because he viewed the demand for money as insensitive to changes in the incentives for holding other assets relative to money, but rather because changes in interest rates should have little effect on these incentive terms in the money demand function. The incentive

---

[14]Friedman suggested that there is some increase in $r_b - r_m$ when i rises because part of the money supply (especially currency) is held in forms that cannot pay interest in a pecuniary or nonpecuniary form. See, for example, Milton Friedman, "Why a Surge of Inflation Is Likely Next Year," *Wall Street Journal*, September 1, 1983, p. 24.

terms remain relatively constant, because any rise in the expected returns on other assets as a result of the rise in interest rates would be matched by a rise in the expected return on money.

The second issue Friedman stressed was the stability of the demand for money function. In contrast to Keynes, Friedman suggested that random fluctuations in the demand for money are small and that the demand for money can be predicted accurately by the money demand function. When combined with his view that the demand for money is insensitive to changes in interest rates, this means that velocity is highly predictable. We can see this by writing down the velocity that is implied by the money demand equation (Equation 7):

$$V = \frac{Y}{f(Y_p)} \qquad (8)$$

Because the relationship between Y and Y_p is usually quite predictable, a stable money demand function (one that does not undergo pronounced shifts, so that it predicts the demand for money accurately) implies that velocity is predictable as well. If we can predict what velocity will be in the next period, a change in the quantity of money will produce a predictable change in aggregate spending. Even though velocity is no longer assumed to be constant, the money supply continues to be the primary determinant of nominal income as in the quantity theory of money. Therefore, Friedman's theory of money demand is indeed a restatement of the quantity theory, because it leads to the same conclusion about the importance of money to aggregate spending.

You may recall that we said that the Keynesian liquidity preference function (in which interest rates are an important determinant of the demand for money) is able to explain the procyclical movements of velocity that we find in the data. Can Friedman's money demand formulation explain this procyclical velocity phenomenon as well?

The key clue to answering this question is the presence of permanent income rather than measured income in the money demand function. What happens to permanent income in a business cycle expansion? Because much of the increase in income will be transitory, permanent income rises much less than measured income. Friedman's money demand function then indicates that the demand for money rises only a small amount relative to the rise in measured income, and as Equation 8 indicates, velocity rises. Similarly, in a recession, the demand for money falls less than measured income, because the decline in permanent income is small relative to measured income, and velocity falls. In this way, we have the procyclical movement in velocity.

To summarize, Friedman's theory of the demand for money used a similar approach to that of Keynes but did not go into detail about the motives for holding money. Instead, Friedman made use of the theory of asset demand to indicate that the demand for money will be a function of permanent income and the expected returns on alternative assets relative to the expected return on money. There are two major differences between Friedman's theory and Keynes's. Friedman believed that changes in interest rates have little effect on the expected returns on other assets relative to money. Thus, in contrast to Keynes, he viewed the demand for money as insensitive to interest rates. In addition, he differed from Keynes in stressing that the money demand function does not undergo substantial shifts and is therefore stable. These two differences also indicate that velocity is predictable, yielding a quantity theory conclusion that money is the primary determinant of aggregate spending. The conclusion that money is the primary determinant of aggregate spending was the basis of **monetarism**, the view that the money supply is the primary source of movements in the price level and aggregate output.

EMPIRICAL EVIDENCE ON THE DEMAND FOR MONEY

As we have seen, the alternative theories of the demand for money can have very different implications for our view of the role of money in the economy. Which of these theories is an accurate description of the real world is an important question, and it is the reason why evidence on the demand for money has been at the center of many debates on the effects of monetary policy on aggregate economic activity. Here we examine the empirical evidence on the two primary issues that distinguish the different theories of money demand and affect their conclusions about whether the quantity of money is the primary determinant of aggregate spending: Is the demand for money sensitive to changes in interest rates, and is the demand for money function stable over time?[15]

Interest Rates and Money Demand

Earlier in the chapter, we saw that if interest rates do not affect the demand for money, velocity is more likely to be a constant—or at least predictable—so that the quantity theory view that aggregate spending is determined by the quantity of money is more likely to be true. However, the more sensitive the demand for money is to interest rates, the more unpredictable velocity will be, and the less clear the link between the money supply and aggregate spending will be. Indeed, there is an extreme case of ultrasensitivity of the demand for money to interest rates, called the *liquidity trap*, in which monetary policy has no direct effect on aggregate spending, because a change in the money supply has no effect on interest rates. (If the demand for money is ultrasensitive to interest rates, a tiny change in interest rates produces a very large change in the quantity of money demanded. Hence, in this case, the demand for money is completely flat in the supply and demand diagrams of Chapter 5. Therefore, a change in the money supply that shifts the money supply curve to the right or left results in it intersecting the flat money demand curve at the same unchanged interest rate.)

The evidence on the interest sensitivity of the demand for money found by different researchers is remarkably consistent. Neither extreme case is supported by the data: In situations in which nominal interest rates have not hit a floor of zero, the demand for money is sensitive to interest rates, and there is little evidence that a liquidity trap has ever existed. However, as we saw in Chapter 4, when interest rates fall to zero, they can go no lower. In this situation, a liquidity trap has occurred because the demand for money is now completely flat. Indeed, Japan has been experiencing a liquidity trap of this type in recent years, which is one reason why it has been difficult for Japanese monetary authorities to stimulate the economy.

---

[15]If you are interested in a more detailed discussion of the empirical research on the demand for money, you can find it in an appendix to this chapter on this book's website at www.myeconlab.com/mishkin.

Stability of Money Demand

If the money demand function, like Equation 4 or 6, is unstable and undergoes substantial unpredictable shifts, as Keynes thought, then velocity is unpredictable, and the quantity of money may not be tightly linked to aggregate spending, as it is in the modern quantity theory. The stability of the money demand function is also crucial to whether the Federal Reserve should target interest rates or the money supply (see Chapter 16). Thus it is important to look at the question of whether the money demand function is stable, because it has important implications for how monetary policy should be conducted.

By the early 1970s, evidence strongly supported the stability of the money demand function. However, after 1973, the rapid pace of financial innovation, which changed which items could be used as money, led to substantial instability in estimated money demand functions. The recent instability of the money demand function calls into question whether our theories and empirical analyses are adequate. It also has important implications for the way monetary policy should be conducted, because it casts doubt on the usefulness of the money demand function as a tool to provide guidance to policymakers. In particular, because the money demand function has become unstable, velocity is now harder to predict, and as discussed in Chapter 16, setting rigid money supply targets to control aggregate spending in the economy may not be an effective way to conduct monetary policy.

SUMMARY

1. Irving Fisher developed a transactions-based theory of the demand for money in which the demand for real balances is proportional to real income and is insensitive to interest-rate movements. An implication of his theory is that velocity, the rate at which money turns over, is constant. This generates the quantity theory of money, which implies that aggregate spending is determined solely by movements in the quantity of money.

2. The classical view that velocity can be effectively treated as a constant is not supported by the data. The nonconstancy of velocity became especially clear to the economics profession after the sharp drop in velocity during the years of the Great Depression.

3. John Maynard Keynes suggested three motives for holding money: the transactions motive, the precautionary motive, and the speculative motive. His resulting liquidity preference theory views the transactions and precautionary components of money demand as proportional to income. However, the speculative component of money demand is viewed as sensitive to interest rates as well as to expectations about the future movements of interest rates. This theory, then, implies that velocity is unstable and cannot be treated as a constant.

4. Further developments in the Keynesian approach provided a better rationale for the three Keynesian motives for holding money. Interest rates were found to be important to the transactions and precautionary components of money demand as well as to the speculative component.

5. Milton Friedman's theory of money demand used a similar approach to that of Keynes. Treating money like any other asset, Friedman used the theory of asset demand to derive a demand for money that is a function of the expected returns on other assets relative to the expected return on money and permanent income. In contrast to Keynes, Friedman believed that the demand for money is stable and insensitive to interest-rate movements. His belief that velocity is predictable (though not constant) in turn leads to the quantity theory conclusion that money is the primary determinant of aggregate spending.

6. There are two main conclusions from the research on the demand for money: The demand for money is sensitive to interest rates, but there is little evidence that it is or has been ultrasensitive (liquidity trap). Since 1973, money demand has been found to be unstable, with the most likely source of the instability being the rapid pace of financial innovation.

KEY TERMS

equation of exchange, p. 500

liquidity preference theory, p. 503

monetarism, p. 515

monetary theory, p. 499

quantity theory of money, p. 501

real money balances, p. 505

velocity of money, p. 500

QUESTIONS AND PROBLEMS

All questions and problems are available in Wmyeconlab *at* www.myeconlab.com/mishkin.

1. Suppose the money supply *M* has been growing at 10% per year, and nominal GDP *PY* has been growing at 20% per year. The data are as follows (in billions of dollars):

	2010	2011	2012
M	100	110	121
PY	1,000	1,200	1,440

   Calculate the velocity in each year. At what rate is velocity growing?

2. Calculate what happens to nominal GDP if velocity remains constant at 5 and the money supply increases from $200 billion to $300 billion.

3. What happens to nominal GDP if the money supply grows by 20% but velocity declines by 30%?

4. If credit cards were made illegal by congressional legislation, what would happen to velocity? Explain your answer.

5. If velocity and aggregate output are reasonably constant (as the classical economists believed), what happens to the price level when the money supply increases from $1 trillion to $4 trillion?

6. If velocity and aggregate output remain constant at 5 and 1,000, respectively, what happens to the price level if the money supply declines from $400 billion to $300 billion?

7. Looking at Figure 1 in the chapter, when were the two largest falls in velocity? What do declines like this suggest about how velocity moves with the business cycle? Given the data in Figure 1, is it reasonable to assume, as the classical economists did, that declines in

aggregate spending are caused by declines in the quantity of money?

8. Using data from the *Economic Report of the President*, calculate velocity for the M2 definition of the money supply for each of the past five years. Does velocity appear to be constant?

9. In Keynes's analysis of the speculative demand for money, what will happen to money demand if people suddenly decide that the normal level of the interest rate has declined? Why?

10. Why is Keynes's analysis of the speculative demand for money important to his view that velocity will undergo substantial fluctuations and thus cannot be treated as constant?

11. If interest rates on bonds go to zero, what does the Baumol-Tobin analysis suggest Grant Smith's average holdings of money balances should be?

12. If brokerage fees go to zero, what does the Baumol-Tobin analysis suggest Grant Smith's average holdings of money should be?

13. "In Tobin's analysis of the speculative demand for money, people will hold both money and bonds, even if bonds are expected to earn a positive return." Is this statement true, false, or uncertain? Explain your answer.

14. Both Keynes's and Friedman's theories of the demand for money suggest that as the relative expected return on money falls, demand for it will fall. Why does Friedman think that money demand is unaffected by changes in interest rates? Why did Keynes think that money demand is affected by changes in interest rates?

15. Why does Friedman's view of the demand for money suggest that velocity is predictable, whereas Keynes's view suggests the opposite?

WEB EXERCISES

1. Refer to Figure 1. The formula for computing the velocity of money is GDP/M1. Go to www.research.stlouisfed.org/fred2 and look up the GDP. Next go to www.federalreserve.gov/Releases/h6/Current/ and find M1. Compute the most recent year's velocity of money and compare it to its level in 2002. Has it risen or fallen? Suggest reasons for its change since that time.

2. John Maynard Keynes is among the most well-known economic theorists. Go to cepa.newschool.edu/het/profiles/keynes.htm and write a one-page summary of his life and contributions.

WEB REFERENCES

www.usagold.com/gildedopinion/puplava/20020614.html

A summary of how various factors affect the velocity of money.

cepa.newschool.edu/het/profiles/keynes.htm

A brief history of John Maynard Keynes.

 MyEconLab CAN HELP YOU GET A BETTER GRADE

If your exam were tomorrow, would you be ready? For each chapter, MyEconLab Practice Test and Study Plans pinpoint which sections you have mastered and which ones you need to study. That way, you are more efficient with your study time, and you are better prepared for your exams.

To see how it works, turn to page 20 and then go to: www.myeconlab.com/mishkin

20 The *ISLM* Model

Preview

In the media, you often see forecasts of GDP and interest rates by economists and government agencies. At times, these forecasts seem to come from a crystal ball, but economists actually make their predictions using a variety of economic models. One model widely used by economic forecasters is the *ISLM* model, which was developed by Sir John Hicks in 1937 and is based on the analysis in John Maynard Keynes's influential book *The General Theory of Employment, Interest, and Money*, published in 1936.[1] The *ISLM* model explains how interest rates and total output produced in the economy (aggregate output or, equivalently, aggregate income) are determined, given a fixed price level (a reasonable assumption in the short run).

The *ISLM* model is valuable not only because it can be used in economic forecasting, but also because it provides a deeper understanding of how government policy can affect aggregate economic activity. In Chapter 21 we use it to evaluate the effects of monetary and fiscal policy on the economy and to learn some lessons about how monetary policy might best be conducted.

In this chapter, we begin by developing the simplest framework for determining aggregate output, in which all economic actors (consumers, firms, and others) except the government play a role. Government fiscal policy (spending and taxes) is then added to the framework to see how it can affect the determination of aggregate output. Finally, we achieve a complete picture of the *ISLM* model by adding monetary policy variables: the money supply and the interest rate.

DETERMINATION OF AGGREGATE OUTPUT

Keynes was especially interested in understanding movements of aggregate output because he wanted to explain why the Great Depression had occurred and how government policy could be used to increase employment in a similar economic situation. Keynes's analysis started with the recognition that the total quantity demanded of an economy's output was the sum of four types of spending: (1) **consumer expenditure** (*C*), the total demand for consumer goods and services (hamburgers, electronics, rock concerts, visits to the doctor, and so on); (2) **planned investment spending** (*I*), the total planned spending by businesses on new physical capital (machines, computers, factories, raw materials, and the like) plus planned spending on new homes;

---

[1] John Hicks, "Mr. Keynes and the Classics: A Suggested Interpretation," *Econometrica* (1937): 147–159.

(3) **government spending** (G), the spending by all levels of government on goods and services (aircraft carriers, government workers, red tape, and so forth); and (4) **net exports** (NX), the net foreign spending on domestic goods and services, equal to exports minus imports.[2] The total quantity demanded of an economy's output, called **aggregate demand** (Y^{ad}), can be written as

$$Y^{ad} = C + I + G + NX \tag{1}$$

Using the common-sense concept from supply and demand analysis, Keynes recognized that equilibrium would occur in the economy when total quantity of output supplied (aggregate output produced) Y equals quantity of output demanded Y^{ad}:

$$Y = Y^{ad} \tag{2}$$

When this equilibrium condition is satisfied, producers are able to sell all of their output and have no reason to change their production. Keynes's analysis explains two things: (1) why aggregate output is at a certain level (which involves understanding which factors affect each component of aggregate demand) and (2) how the sum of these components can add up to an output smaller than the economy is capable of producing, resulting in less than full employment of resources.

Keynes was especially concerned with explaining the low level of output and employment during the Great Depression. Because inflation was not a serious problem during this period, he assumed that output could change without causing a change in prices. ***Keynes's analysis assumes that the price level is fixed***; that is, dollar amounts for variables such as consumer expenditure, investment, and aggregate output do not have to be adjusted for changes in the price level to tell us how much the real quantities of these variables change. Because the price level is assumed to be fixed, when we talk in this chapter about changes in nominal quantities, we are talking about changes in real quantities as well.

Our discussion of Keynes's analysis begins with a simple framework of aggregate output determination in which the role of government, net exports, and the possible effects of money and interest rates are ignored. Because we are assuming that government spending and net exports are zero ($G = 0$ and $NX = 0$), we need examine only consumer expenditure and investment spending to explain how aggregate output is determined. This simple framework is unrealistic, because both government and monetary policy are left out of the picture, and because it makes other simplifying assumptions, such as a fixed price level. Still, the model is worth studying, because its simplified view helps us understand the key factors that explain how the economy works. It also clearly illustrates the Keynesian idea that the economy can come to rest at a level of aggregate output below the full-employment level. Once you understand this simple framework, we can proceed to more complex and more realistic models.

Consumer Expenditure and the Consumption Function

Ask yourself what determines how much you spend on consumer goods and services. Your likely response is that your income is the most important factor, because if your income rises, you will be willing to spend more. Keynes reasoned similarly that consumer

---

[2]Imports are subtracted from exports in arriving at the net exports component of the total quantity demanded of an economy's output because imports are already counted in *C, I,* and *G* but do not add to the demand for the economy's output.

TABLE 1

Consumption Function: Schedule of Consumer Expenditure *C* When *mpc* = 0.5 and *a* = 200 ($ billions)

Point in Figure 1	Disposable income Y_D (1)	Change in Disposable Income ΔY_D (2)	Change in Consumer Expenditure ΔC (0.5 × ΔY_D) (3)	Consumer Expenditure C (4)
E	0	—	—	200 (= a)
F	400	400	200	400
G	800	400	200	600
H	1,200	400	200	800

expenditure is related to **disposable income**, the total income available for spending, equal to aggregate income (which is equivalent to aggregate output) minus taxes ($Y - T$). He called this relationship between disposable income Y_D and consumer expenditure C the **consumption function** and expressed it as follows:

$$C = a + (mpc \times Y_D) \tag{3}$$

The term *a* stands for **autonomous consumer expenditure**, the amount of consumer expenditure that is independent of disposable income and is the intercept of the consumption function line. It tells us how much consumers will spend when disposable income is 0 (they still must have food, clothing, and shelter). If *a* is $200 billion when disposable income is 0, consumer expenditure will equal $200 billion.[3]

The term *mpc*, the **marginal propensity to consume**, is the slope of the consumption function line ($\Delta C/\Delta Y_D$) and reflects the change in consumer expenditure that results from an additional dollar of disposable income. Keynes assumed that *mpc* was a constant between the values of 0 and 1. If, for example, a $1.00 increase in disposable income leads to an increase in consumer expenditure of $0.50, then *mpc* = 0.5.

A numerical example of a consumption function using the values of *a* = 200 and *mpc* = 0.5 will clarify the preceding concepts. The $200 billion of consumer expenditure at a disposable income of 0 is listed in the first row of Table 1 and is plotted as point E in Figure 1. (Remember that throughout this chapter, dollar amounts for all variables in the figures correspond to real quantities, because Keynes assumed that the price level is fixed.) Because *mpc* = 0.5, when disposable income increases by $400 billion, the change in consumer expenditure—ΔC in column 3 of Table 1—is $200 billion (0.5 × $400 billion). Thus, when disposable income is $400 billion, consumer expenditure is $400 billion (initial value of $200 billion when income is 0 plus the $200 billion change in consumer expenditure). This combination of consumer expenditure and disposable income is listed in the second row of Table 1 and is plotted as point F in

---

[3]Consumer expenditure can exceed income if people have accumulated savings to tide them over during bad times. An alternative is to have parents who will give you money for food (or to pay for school) when you have no income. The situation in which consumer expenditure is greater than disposable income is called *dissaving*.

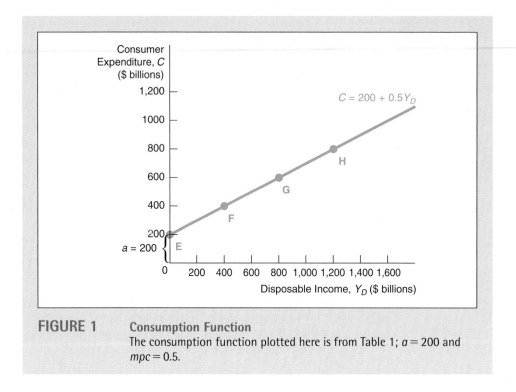

FIGURE 1   **Consumption Function**
The consumption function plotted here is from Table 1; $a = 200$ and $mpc = 0.5$.

Figure 1. Similarly, at point G, where disposable income has increased by another $400 billion to $800 billion, consumer expenditure will rise by another $200 billion to $600 billion. By the same reasoning, at point H, at which disposable income is $1,200 billion, consumer expenditure will be $800 billion. The line connecting these points in Figure 1 graphs the consumption function.

Investment Spending

It is important to understand that there are two types of investment. The first type, **fixed investment**, is the spending by firms on equipment (machines, computers, airplanes) and structures (factories, office buildings, shopping centers) and planned spending on residential housing. The second type, **inventory investment**, is spending by firms on additional holdings of raw materials, parts, and finished goods, calculated as the change in holdings of these items in a given time period—say a year. (The FYI box explains how economists' use of the word *investment* differs from everyday use of the term.)

Suppose that Dell, a company that produces personal computers, has 100,000 computers sitting in its warehouses on December 31, 2009, ready to be shipped to dealers. If each computer has a wholesale price of $1,000, Dell has an inventory worth $100 million. If by December 31, 2010, its inventory of personal computers has risen to $150 million, its inventory investment in 2010 is $50 million, the *change* in the level of its inventory over the course of the year ($150 million minus $100 million). Now suppose that there is a drop in the level of inventories; inventory investment will then be negative.

Dell may also have additional inventory investment if the level of raw materials and parts that it is holding to produce these computers increases over the course of the year.

FYI   Meaning of the Word *Investment*

Economists use the word *investment* somewhat differently than other people do. When noneconomists say that they are making an investment, they are normally referring to the purchase of common stocks or bonds, purchases that do not necessarily involve newly produced goods and services. But when economists speak of investment spending, they are referring to the purchase of *new* physical assets such as new machines or new houses—purchases that add to aggregate demand.

If on December 31, 2009, it holds $20 million of computer chips used to produce its computers and on December 31, 2010, it holds $30 million, it has an additional $10 million of inventory investment in 2010.

An important feature of inventory investment is that—in contrast to fixed investment, which is always planned—some inventory investment can be unplanned. Suppose that the reason Dell finds itself with an additional $50 million of computers on December 31, 2010, is that $50 million less of its computers were sold in 2010 than expected. This $50 million of inventory investment in 2010 was unplanned. In this situation, Dell is producing more computers than it can sell and will cut production.

Planned investment spending, a component of aggregate demand Y^{ad}, is equal to planned fixed investment plus the amount of inventory investment *planned* by firms. Keynes mentioned two factors that influence planned investment spending: interest rates and businesses' expectations about the future. How these factors affect investment spending is discussed later in this chapter. For now, planned investment spending will be treated as a known value. At this stage, we want to explain how aggregate output is determined for a given level of planned investment spending; we can then examine how interest rates and business expectations influence aggregate output by affecting planned investment spending.

Equilibrium and the Keynesian Cross Diagram

We have now assembled the building blocks (consumer expenditure and planned investment spending) that will enable us to see how aggregate output is determined when we ignore the government and net exports. Although unrealistic, this stripped-down analysis clarifies the basic principles of output determination. In the following sections, government and net exports enter the picture and makes our model more realistic.

The diagram in Figure 2, known as the *Keynesian cross diagram*, shows how aggregate output is determined. The vertical axis measures aggregate demand, and the horizontal axis measures the level of aggregate output. The 45° line shows all the points at which aggregate output Y equals aggregate demand Y^{ad}; that is, it shows all the points at which the equilibrium condition $Y = Y^{ad}$ is satisfied. Because government spending and net exports are zero ($G = 0$ and $NX = 0$), aggregate demand is

$$Y^{ad} = C + I$$

Because there is no government sector to collect taxes, there are none in our simplified economy; disposable income Y_D then equals aggregate output Y (remember that aggregate income and aggregate output are equivalent; see the appendix to Chapter 1). Thus

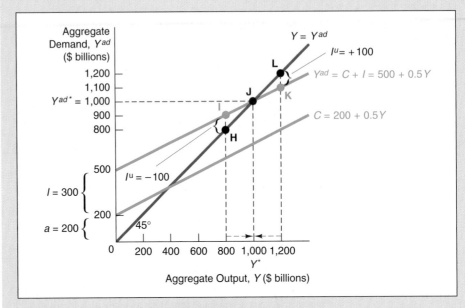

FIGURE 2   **Keynesian Cross Diagram**
When $I = 300$ and $C = 200 + 0.5Y$, equilibrium output occurs at $Y^* = 1,000$, where the aggregate demand function $Y^{ad} = C + I$ intersects with the 45° line $Y = Y^{ad}$.

the consumption function with $a = 200$ and $mpc = 0.5$ plotted in Figure 1 can be written as $C = 200 + 0.5Y$ and is plotted in Figure 2. Given that planned investment spending is $300 billion, aggregate demand can then be expressed as follows:

$$Y^{ad} = C + I = 200 + 0.5Y + 300 = 500 + 0.5Y$$

This equation, plotted in Figure 2, represents the quantity of aggregate demand at any given level of aggregate output and is called the **aggregate demand function**.

The aggregate demand function $Y^{ad} = C + I$ is the vertical sum of the consumption function line ($C = 200 + 0.5Y$) and planned investment spending ($I = 300$). The point at which the aggregate demand function crosses the 45° line $Y = Y^{ad}$ indicates the equilibrium level of aggregate demand and aggregate output. In Figure 2, equilibrium occurs at point J, with both aggregate output Y^* and aggregate demand Y^{ad*} at $1,000 billion.

As you learned in Chapter 5, the concept of equilibrium is useful only if there is a tendency for the economy to settle there. To see whether the economy heads toward the equilibrium output level of $1,000 billion, let's first look at what happens if the amount of output produced in the economy is above the equilibrium level at $1,200 billion. At this level of output, aggregate demand is $1,100 billion (point K), $100 billion less than the $1,200 billion of output (point L on the 45° line). Because output exceeds aggregate demand by $100 billion, firms are saddled with $100 billion of unsold inventory. To keep from accumulating unsold goods, firms will cut production. As long as it is above the equilibrium level, output will exceed aggregate demand and firms will cut production, sending aggregate output toward the equilibrium level.

Another way to observe a tendency of the economy to head toward equilibrium at point J is from the viewpoint of inventory investment. When firms do not sell all output produced, they add unsold output to their holdings of inventory, and inventory investment increases. At an output level of $1,200 billion, for instance, the $100 billion of unsold goods leads to $100 billion of unplanned inventory investment, which firms do not want. Companies will decrease production to reduce inventory to the desired level, and aggregate output will fall (indicated by the arrow near the horizontal axis). This viewpoint means that unplanned inventory investment for the entire economy I^u equals the excess of output over aggregate demand. In our example, at an output level of $1,200 billion, $I^u = $100 billion. If I^u is positive, firms will cut production and output will fall. Output will stop falling only when it has returned to its equilibrium level at point J, where $I^u = 0$.

What happens if aggregate output is below the equilibrium level of output? Let's say output is $800 billion. At this level of output, aggregate demand at point I is $900 billion, $100 billion higher than output (point H on the 45° line). At this level, firms are selling $100 billion more goods than they are producing, so inventory falls below the desired level. The negative unplanned inventory investment ($I^u = -$100 billion) will induce firms to increase their production so that they can raise inventory to the desired levels. As a result, output rises toward the equilibrium level, shown by the arrow in Figure 2. As long as output is below the equilibrium level, unplanned inventory investment will remain negative, firms will continue to raise production, and output will continue to rise. We again see the tendency for the economy to settle at point J, where aggregate demand Y equals output Y^{ad} and unplanned inventory investment is zero ($I^u = 0$).

Expenditure Multiplier

Now that we understand that equilibrium aggregate output is determined by the position of the aggregate demand function, we can examine how different factors shift the function and consequently change aggregate output. We will find that either a rise in planned investment spending or a rise in autonomous consumer expenditure shifts the aggregate demand function upward and leads to an increase in aggregate output.

Output Response to a Change in Planned Investment Spending   Suppose that a new electric motor is invented that makes all factory machines three times more efficient. Because firms are suddenly more optimistic about the profitability of investing in new machines that use this new motor, planned investment spending increases by $100 billion from an initial level of $I_1 = $300 billion to $I_2 = $400 billion. What effect does this have on output?

The effects of this increase in planned investment spending are analyzed in Figure 3 using a Keynesian cross diagram. Initially, when planned investment spending I_1 is $300 billion, the aggregate demand function is Y_1^{ad}, and equilibrium occurs at point 1, where output is $1,000 billion. The $100 billion increase in planned investment spending adds directly to aggregate demand and shifts the aggregate demand function upward to Y_2^{ad}. Aggregate demand now equals output at the intersection of Y_2^{ad} with the 45° line $Y = Y^{ad}$ (point 2). As a result of the $100 billion increase in planned investment spending, equilibrium output rises by $200 billion to $1,200 billion ($Y_2$). For every dollar increase in planned investment spending, aggregate output has increased twofold.

The ratio of the change in aggregate output to a change in planned investment spending, $\Delta Y/\Delta I$, is called the **expenditure multiplier**. (This multiplier should not be confused with the money supply multiplier developed in Chapter 14, which measures the ratio of the change in the money supply to the change in the monetary base.) In Figure 3, the expenditure multiplier is 2.

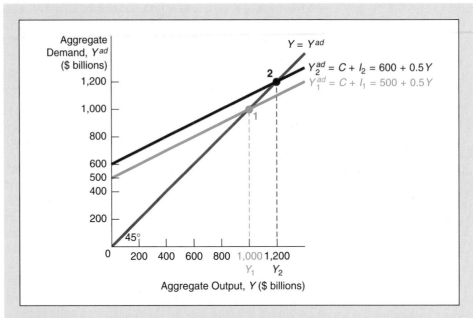

FIGURE 3   **Response of Aggregate Output to a Change in Planned Investment**
A $100 billion increase in planned investment spending from $I_1 = 300$ to $I_2 = 400$ shifts the aggregate demand function upward from Y_1^{ad} to Y_2^{ad}. The equilibrium moves from point 1 to point 2, and equilibrium output rises from $Y_1 = 1,000$ to $Y_2 = 1,200$.

Why does a change in planned investment spending lead to an even larger change in aggregate output so that the expenditure multiplier is greater than 1? The expenditure multiplier is greater than 1 because an increase in planned investment spending, which raises output, leads to an additional increase in consumer expenditure ($mpc \times \Delta Y$). The increase in consumer expenditure, in turn, raises aggregate demand and output further, resulting in a multiple change of output from a given change in planned investment spending. This conclusion can be derived algebraically by solving for the unknown value of Y in terms of a, mpc, and I, resulting in the following equation:[4]

$$Y = (a + I) \times \frac{1}{1 - mpc} \qquad (4)$$

---

[4]Substituting the consumption function $C = a + (mpc \times Y)$ into the aggregate demand function $Y^{ad} = C + I$ yields

$$Y^{ad} = a + (mpc \times Y) + I$$

In equilibrium, where aggregate output equals aggregate demand,

$$Y = Y^{ad} = a + (mpc \times Y) + I$$

Subtracting the term $mpc \times Y$ from both sides of this equation to collect the terms involving Y on the left side, we have

$$Y - (mpc \times Y) = Y(1 - mpc) = a + I$$

Dividing both sides by $1 - mpc$ to solve for Y leads to Equation 4 in the text.

Because *I* is multiplied by the term $1/(1 - mpc)$, this equation tells us that a $1 change in *I* leads to a $$1/(1 - mpc)$ change in aggregate output; thus $1/(1 - mpc)$ is the expenditure multiplier. When $mpc = 0.5$, the change in output for a $1 change in *I* is $2 $[= 1/(1 - 0.5)]$; if $mpc = 0.8$, the change in output for a $1 change in *I* is $5. The larger the marginal propensity to consume, the higher the expenditure multiplier.

Response to Changes in Autonomous Spending   Because *a* is also multiplied by the term $1/(1 - mpc)$ in Equation 4, a $1 change in autonomous consumer expenditure *a* also changes aggregate output by $1/(1 - mpc)$, the amount of the expenditure multiplier. Therefore, we see that the expenditure multiplier applies equally well to changes in autonomous consumer expenditure. In fact, Equation 4 can be rewritten as

$$Y = A \times \frac{1}{1 - mpc} \tag{5}$$

in which *A* = autonomous spending = *a* + *I*.

This rewritten equation tells us that any change in autonomous spending, whether from a change in *a*, in *I*, or in both, will lead to a multiplied change in *Y*. If both *a* and *I* decrease by $100 billion each, so that *A* decreases by $200 billion, and $mpc = 0.5$, the expenditure multiplier is 2 $[= 1/(1 - 0.5)]$, and aggregate output *Y* will fall by $2 \times 200 billion = $400 billion. Conversely, a rise in *I* by $100 billion that is offset by a $100 billion decline in *a* will leave autonomous spending *A*, and hence *Y*, unchanged. The expenditure multiplier $1/(1 - mpc)$ can therefore be defined more generally as the ratio of the change in aggregate output to the change in autonomous spending $(\Delta Y/\Delta A)$.

Another way to reach this conclusion—that any change in autonomous spending will lead to a multiplied change in aggregate output—is to recognize that the shift in the aggregate demand function in Figure 3 did not have to come from an increase in *I*; it could also have come from an increase in *a*, which directly raises consumer expenditure and therefore aggregate demand. Alternatively, it could have come from an increase in both *a* and *I*. Changes in the attitudes of consumers and firms about the future, which cause changes in their spending, will result in multiple changes in aggregate output.

Keynes believed that changes in autonomous spending are dominated by unstable fluctuations in planned investment spending, which is influenced by emotional waves of optimism and pessimism—factors he labeled "**animal spirits**." His view was colored by the collapse in investment spending during the Great Depression, which he saw as the primary reason for the economic contraction. We will examine the consequences of this fall in investment spending in the following application.

APPLICATION   ✦   The Collapse of Investment Spending and the Great Depression

From 1929 to 1933, the U.S. economy experienced the largest percentage decline in investment spending ever recorded. One explanation for the investment collapse was the ongoing set of financial crises during this period, described in Chapter 9. In 2000 dollars, investment spending fell from $232 billion to $38 billion—a decline of over 80%. What does the Keynesian analysis developed so far suggest should have happened to aggregate output in this period?

Figure 4 demonstrates how the $194 billion drop in planned investment spending would shift the aggregate demand function downward from Y_1^{ad} to Y_2^{ad}, moving the economy from point 1 to point 2. Aggregate output would then fall sharply; real GDP

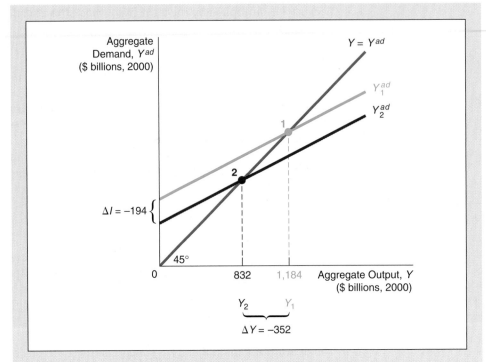

FIGURE 4   **Response of Aggregate Output to the Collapse of Investment Spending, 1929–1933**
The decline of $194 billion (in 2000 dollars) in planned investment spending from 1929 to 1933 shifted the aggregate demand function down from Y_1^{ad} to Y_2^{ad} and caused the economy to move from point 1 to point 2, where output fell by $352 billion.

Source: Economic Report of the President.

actually fell by $352 billion (a multiple of the $194 billion drop in investment spending), from $1,184 billion to $832 billion (in 2000 dollars). Because the economy was at full employment in 1929, the fall in output resulted in massive unemployment, with over 25% of the labor force unemployed in 1933.

Government's Role

After witnessing the events in the Great Depression, Keynes took the view that an economy would continually suffer major output fluctuations because of the volatility of autonomous spending, particularly planned investment spending. He was especially worried about sharp declines in autonomous spending, which would inevitably lead to large declines in output and an equilibrium with high unemployment. If autonomous spending fell sharply, as it did during the Great Depression, how could an economy be restored to higher levels of output and more reasonable levels of unemployment? Not by an increase in autonomous investment and consumer spending, because the business outlook was so grim. Keynes's answer to this question involved looking at the role of government in determining aggregate output.

Keynes realized that government spending and taxation could also affect the position of the aggregate demand function and hence be manipulated to restore the economy to full employment. As shown in the aggregate demand equation $Y^{ad} = C + I + G + NX$, government spending G adds directly to aggregate demand. Taxes, however, do not affect aggregate demand directly, as government spending does. Instead, taxes lower the amount of income that consumers have available for spending and affect aggregate demand by influencing consumer expenditure. When there are taxes, disposable income Y_D does not equal aggregate output; it equals aggregate output Y minus taxes T: $Y_D = Y - T$. The consumption function $C = a + (mpc \times Y_D)$ can be rewritten as follows:

$$C = a + [mpc \times (Y - T)] = a + (mpc \times Y) - (mpc \times T) \qquad (6)$$

This consumption function looks similar to the one used in the absence of taxes, but it has the additional term $-(mpc \times T)$ on the right side. This term indicates that if taxes increase by $100, consumer expenditure declines by mpc multiplied by this amount; if $mpc = 0.5$, consumer expenditure declines by $50. This occurs because consumers view $100 of taxes as equivalent to a $100 reduction in income and reduce their expenditure by the marginal propensity to consume times this amount.

To see how the inclusion of government spending and taxes modifies our analysis, first we will observe the effect of a positive level of government spending on aggregate output in the Keynesian cross diagram of Figure 5. Let's say that in the absence of government spending or taxes, the economy is at point 1, where the aggregate demand function $Y_1^{ad} = C + I = 500 + 0.5Y$ crosses the 45° line $Y = Y^{ad}$. Here equilibrium output is at $1,000 billion. Suppose, however, that the economy reaches full employment at an aggregate output level of $1,800 billion. How can government spending be used to restore the economy to full employment at $1,800 billion of aggregate output?

If government spending is set at $400 billion, the aggregate demand function shifts upward to $Y_2^{ad} = C + I + G = 900 + 0.5Y$. The economy moves to point 2, and aggregate output rises by $800 billion to $1,800 billion. Figure 5 indicates that aggregate output is positively related to government spending and that a change in government spending leads to a multiplied change in aggregate output, equal to the expenditure multiplier, $1/(1 - mpc) = 1/(1 - 0.5) = 2$. Therefore, declines in planned investment spending that produce high unemployment (as occurred during the Great Depression) can be offset by raising government spending.

What happens if the government decides that it must collect taxes of $400 billion to balance the budget? Before taxes are raised, the economy is in equilibrium at the same point 2 found in Figure 5. Our discussion of the consumption function (which allows for taxes) indicates that taxes T reduce consumer expenditure by $mpc \times T$ because there is T less income now available for spending. In our example, $mpc = 0.5$, so consumer expenditure and the aggregate demand function shift downward by $200 billion ($= 0.5 \times 400$); at the new equilibrium, point 3, the level of output has declined by twice this amount (the expenditure multiplier) to $1,400 billion.

Although you can see that aggregate output is negatively related to the level of taxes, it is important to recognize that the change in aggregate output from the $400 billion increase in taxes ($\Delta Y = -\$400$ billion) is smaller than the change in aggregate output from the $400 billion increase in government spending ($\Delta Y = \$800$ billion). If both taxes and government spending are raised equally—by $400 billion, as occurs in going from point 1 to point 3 in Figure 5—aggregate output will rise.

The Keynesian framework indicates that the government can play an important role in determining aggregate output by changing the level of government spending or taxes. If the economy enters a deep recession, in which output drops severely and unemployment climbs, the analysis we have just developed provides a prescription for restoring the economy

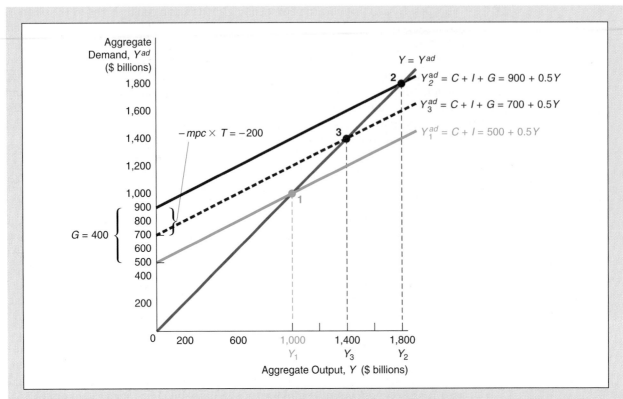

FIGURE 5 **Response of Aggregate Output to Government Spending and Taxes**
With no government spending or taxes, the aggregate demand function is Y_1^{ad}, and equilibrium output is $Y_1 = 1,000$. With government spending of $400 billion, the aggregate demand function shifts upward to Y_2^{ad}, and aggregate output rises by $800 billion to $Y_2 = \$1,800$ billion. Taxes of $400 billion lower consumer expenditure and the aggregate demand function by $200 billion from Y_2^{ad} to Y_3^{ad}, and aggregate output falls by $400 billion to $Y_3 = \$1,400$ billion.

to health. The government might raise aggregate output by increasing government spending, or it could lower taxes and reverse the process described in Figure 5 (that is, a tax cut makes more income available for spending at any level of output, shifting the aggregate demand function upward and causing the equilibrium level of output to rise).

Role of International Trade

International trade also plays a role in determining aggregate output because net exports (exports minus imports) are a component of aggregate demand. To analyze the effect of net exports in the Keynesian cross diagram of Figure 6, suppose that initially net exports are equal to zero ($NX_1 = 0$) so that the economy is at point 1, where the aggregate demand function $Y_1^{ad} = C + I + G + NX_1 = 500 + 0.5Y$ crosses the 45° line $Y = Y_1^{ad}$. Equilibrium output is again at $1,000 billion. Now foreigners suddenly get an urge to buy more American products so that net exports rise to $100 billion ($NX_2 = 100$). The $100 billion increase in net exports adds directly to aggregate demand and shifts the aggregate demand function upward to $Y_2^{ad} = C + I + G + NX_2 = 600 + 0.5Y$. The economy moves to point 2, and aggregate output rises by $200 billion to $1,200 billion ($Y_2$).

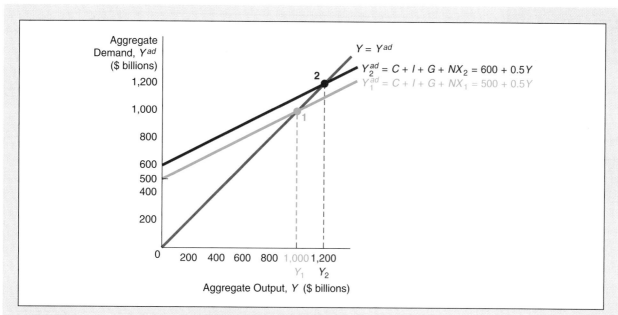

FIGURE 6   **Response of Aggregate Output to a Change in Net Exports**
A $100 billion increase in net exports from $NX_1 = 0$ to $NX_2 = 100$ shifts the aggregate demand function upward from Y_1^{ad} to Y_2^{ad}. The equilibrium moves from point 1 to point 2, and equilibrium output rises from $Y_1 = \$1,000$ billion to $Y_2 = \$1,200$ billion.

Figure 6 indicates that, just as we found for planned investment spending and government spending, a rise in net exports leads to a multiplied rise in aggregate output, equal to the expenditure multiplier, $1/(1 - mpc) = 1/(1 - 0.5) = 2$. Therefore, changes in net exports can be another important factor affecting fluctuations in aggregate output.

Summary of the Determinants of Aggregate Output

Our analysis of the Keynesian framework so far has identified five autonomous factors (factors independent of income) that shift the aggregate demand function and hence the level of aggregate output:

1. Changes in autonomous consumer expenditure (a)
2. Changes in planned investment spending (I)
3. Changes in government spending (G)
4. Changes in taxes (T)
5. Changes in net exports (NX)

The effects of changes in each of these variables on aggregate output are summarized in Table 2 and discussed next in the text.

Changes in Autonomous Consumer Spending (a)   A rise in autonomous consumer expenditure a (say, because consumers become more optimistic about the economy when the stock market booms) directly raises consumer expenditure and shifts the aggregate demand function upward, resulting in an increase in aggregate output. A decrease in a causes consumer expenditure to fall, leading ultimately to a decline in

SUMMARY TABLE 2

Response of Aggregate Output *Y* to Autonomous Changes in *a, I, G, T,* and *NX*

Variable	Change in Variable	Response of Aggregate Output, *Y*	
Autonomous consumer expenditure, *a*	↑	↑	
Investment *I*	↑	↑	
Government spending *G*	↑	↑	
Taxes, *T*	↑	↓	
Net exports, *NX*	↑	↑	

Note: Only increases (↑) in the variables are shown; the effects of the decreases in the variables on aggregate output would be the opposite of the those increased in the "Response" column.

aggregate output. Therefore, **aggregate output is positively related to autonomous consumer expenditure *a*.**

Changes in Planned Investment Spending (*I*)   A rise in planned investment spending adds directly to aggregate demand, raising the aggregate demand function and aggregate output. A fall in planned investment spending lowers aggregate demand and causes aggregate output to fall. Therefore, **aggregate output is positively related to planned investment spending *I*.**

Changes in Government Spending (G)   A rise in government spending also adds directly to aggregate demand and raises the aggregate demand function, increasing aggregate output. A fall directly reduces aggregate demand, lowers the aggregate demand function, and causes aggregate output to fall. Therefore, ***aggregate output is positively related to government spending G.***

Changes in Taxes (T)   A rise in taxes does not affect aggregate demand directly, but does lower the amount of income available for spending, reducing consumer expenditure. The decline in consumer expenditure then leads to a fall in the aggregate demand function, resulting in a decline in aggregate output. A lowering of taxes makes more income available for spending, raises consumer expenditure, and leads to higher aggregate output. Therefore, ***aggregate output is negatively related to the level of taxes T.***

Changes in Net Exports (NX)   A rise in net exports adds directly to aggregate demand and raises the aggregate demand function, increasing aggregate output. A fall directly reduces aggregate demand, lowers the aggregate demand function, and causes aggregate output to fall. Therefore, ***aggregate output is positively related to net exports NX.***

Size of the Effects from the Five Factors   The aggregate demand function in the Keynesian cross diagrams shifts vertically by the full amount of the change in a, I, G, or NX, resulting in a multiple effect on aggregate output through the effects of the expenditure multiplier, $1/(1 - mpc)$. A change in taxes has a smaller effect on aggregate output, because consumer expenditure changes only by mpc times the change in taxes $(-mpc \times \Delta T)$, which in the case of $mpc = 0.5$ means that aggregate demand shifts vertically by only half of the change in taxes.

If there is a change in one of these autonomous factors that is offset by a change in another (say, I rises by \$100 billion, but a, G, or NX falls by \$100 billion or T rises by \$200 billion when $mpc = 0.5$), the aggregate demand function will remain in the same position, and aggregate output will remain unchanged.[5]

---

[5]These results can be derived algebraically as follows. Substituting the consumption function allowing for taxes (Equation 6) into the aggregate demand function (Equation 1), we have

$$Y^{ad} = a - (mpc \times T) + (mpc \times Y) + I + G + NX$$

If we assume that taxes T are unrelated to income, we can define autonomous spending in the aggregate demand function to be

$$A = a - (mpc \times T) + I + G + NX$$

The expenditure equation can be rewritten as

$$Y^{ad} = A + (mpc \times Y)$$

In equilibrium, aggregate demand equals aggregate output:

$$Y = A + (mpc \times Y)$$

which can be solved for Y. The resulting equation

$$Y = A \times \frac{1}{1 - mpc}$$

is the same equation that links autonomous spending and aggregate output in the text (Equation 5), but it now allows for additional components of autonomous spending in A. We see that any increase in autonomous expenditure leads to a multiple increase in output. Thus any component of autonomous spending that enters A with a positive sign (a, I, G, and NX) will have a positive relationship with output, and any component with a negative sign ($-mpc \times T$) will have a negative relationship with output. This algebraic analysis also shows us that any rise in a component of A that is offset by a movement in another component of A, leaving A unchanged, will leave output unchanged.

THE *ISLM* MODEL

So far, our analysis has excluded monetary policy. We now include money and interest rates in the Keynesian framework to develop the more intricate *ISLM* model of how aggregate output is determined, in which monetary policy plays an important role. Why another complex model? The *ISLM* model is versatile and allows us to understand economic phenomena that cannot be analyzed with the simpler Keynesian cross framework used earlier. The *ISLM* model will help us understand how monetary policy affects economic activity and interacts with fiscal policy (changes in government spending and taxes) to produce a certain level of aggregate output; how the level of interest rates is affected by changes in investment spending as well as by changes in monetary and fiscal policy; how monetary policy is best conducted; and how the *ISLM* model generates the aggregate demand curve, an essential building block for the aggregate supply and demand analysis used in Chapter 22 and thereafter.

Like our simplified Keynesian model, the full *ISLM* model examines an equilibrium in which aggregate output produced equals aggregate demand, and, because it assumes a fixed price level, in which real and nominal quantities are the same. The first step in constructing the *ISLM* model is to examine the effect of interest rates on planned investment spending and hence on aggregate demand. Next we use a Keynesian cross diagram to see how the interest rate affects the equilibrium level of aggregate output. The resulting relationship between equilibrium aggregate output and the interest rate is known as the **IS curve**.

Just as a demand curve alone cannot tell us the quantity of goods sold in a market, the *IS* curve by itself cannot tell us what the level of aggregate output will be because the interest rate is still unknown. We need another relationship, called the **LM curve**, to describe the combinations of interest rates and aggregate output for which the quantity of money demanded equals the quantity of money supplied. When the *IS* and *LM* curves are combined in the same diagram, the intersection of the two determines the equilibrium level of aggregate output as well as the interest rate. Finally, we will have obtained a more complete analysis of the determination of aggregate output in which monetary policy plays an important role.

Equilibrium in the Goods Market: The *IS* Curve

In Keynesian analysis, the primary way that interest rates affect the level of aggregate output is through their effects on planned investment spending and net exports. After explaining why interest rates affect planned investment spending and net exports, we will use Keynesian cross diagrams to learn how interest rates affect equilibrium aggregate output.[6]

Interest Rates and Planned Investment Spending   Businesses make investments in physical capital (machines, factories, and raw materials) as long as they expect to earn more from the physical capital than the interest cost of a loan to finance

---

[6]More modern Keynesian approaches suggest that consumer expenditure, particularly for consumer durables (cars, furniture, appliances), is influenced by the interest rate. This interest sensitivity of consumer expenditure can be allowed for in the model here by defining planned investment spending more generally to include the interest-sensitive component of consumer expenditure.

the investment. When the interest rate is high, few investments in physical capital will earn more than the cost of borrowed funds, so planned investment spending is low. When the interest rate is low, many investments in physical capital will earn more than the interest cost of borrowed funds. Therefore, when interest rates are lower, business firms are more likely to undertake an investment in physical capital, and planned investment spending will be higher.

Even if a company has surplus funds and does not need to borrow to undertake an investment in physical capital, its planned investment spending will be affected by the interest rate. Instead of investing in physical capital, it could purchase a security, such as a bond. If the interest rate on this security is high, the opportunity cost (forgone interest earnings) of an investment is high, and planned investment spending will be low, because the firm would probably prefer to purchase the security than to invest in physical capital. As the interest rate and the opportunity cost of investing fall, planned investment spending will increase because investments in physical capital are more likely than the security to earn greater income for the firm.

The relationship between the amount of planned investment spending and any given level of the interest rate is illustrated by the investment schedule in panel (a) of Figure 7. The downward slope of the schedule reflects the negative relationship between planned investment spending and the interest rate. At a low interest rate i_1, the level of planned investment spending I_1 is high; for a high interest rate i_3, planned investment spending I_3 is low.

Interest Rates and Net Exports As discussed in more detail in Chapter 17, when interest rates rise in the United States (with the price level fixed), U.S. dollar assets become more attractive relative to assets denominated in foreign currencies, thereby causing an increased demand for dollar assets and thus a rise in the exchange rate. The higher value of the dollar resulting from the rise in interest rates makes domestic goods more expensive than foreign goods, thereby causing a fall in net exports. The resulting negative relationship between interest rates and net exports is shown in panel (b) of Figure 7. At a low interest rate i_1, the exchange rate is low and net exports NX_1 are high; at a high interest rate i_3, the exchange rate is high and net exports NX_3 are low.

Deriving the *IS* Curve We can now use what we have learned about the relationship of interest rates to planned investment spending and net exports in panels (a) and (b) to examine the relationship between interest rates and the equilibrium level of aggregate output (holding government spending and autonomous consumer expenditure constant). The three levels of planned investment spending and net exports in panels (a) and (b) are represented in the three aggregate demand functions in the Keynesian cross diagram of panel (c). The lowest interest rate i_1 has the highest level of both planned investment spending I_1 and net exports NX_1, and hence the highest aggregate demand function Y_1^{ad}. Point 1 in panel (d) shows the resulting equilibrium level of output Y_1, which corresponds to interest rate i_1. As the interest rate rises to i_2, both planned investment spending and net exports fall, to I_2 and NX_2, respectively, so equilibrium output falls to Y_2. Point 2 in panel (d) shows the lower level of output Y_2, which corresponds to interest rate i_2. Finally, the highest interest rate i_3 leads to the lowest level of planned investment spending and net exports, and hence the lowest level of equilibrium output, which is plotted as point 3.

The line connecting the three points in panel (d), the *IS* curve, shows the combinations of interest rates and equilibrium aggregate output for which aggregate output produced equals aggregate demand. The negative slope indicates that higher interest

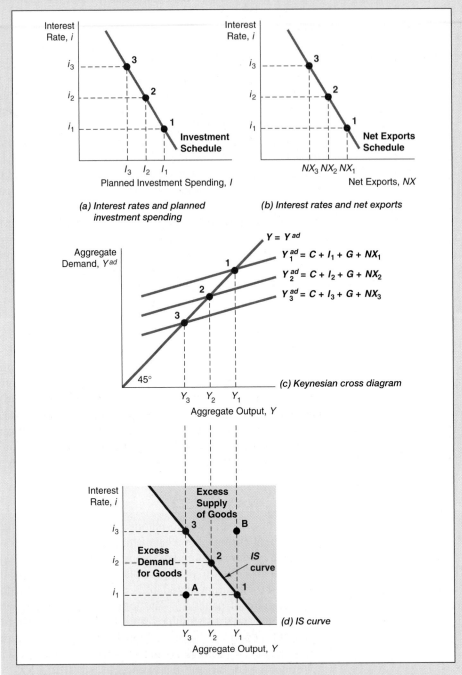

FIGURE 7   **Deriving the *IS* Curve**

The investment schedule in panel (a) shows that as the interest rate rises from i_1 to i_2 to i_3, planned investment spending falls from I_1 to I_2 to I_3. Panel (b) shows that net exports also fall from NX_1 to NX_2 to NX_3 as the interest rate rises. Panel (c) then indicates the levels of equilibrium output Y_1, Y_2, and Y_3 that correspond to those three levels of planned investment and net exports. Finally, panel (d) plots the level of equilibrium output corresponding to each of the three interest rates; the line that connects these points is the *IS* curve.

rates result in lower planned investment spending and net exports, and hence lower equilibrium output.

What the *IS* Curve Tells Us   The *IS* curve traces out the points at which the total quantity of goods produced equals the total quantity of goods demanded. It describes points at which the goods market is in equilibrium. For each given level of the interest rate, the *IS* curve tells us what aggregate output must be for the goods market to be in equilibrium. As the interest rate rises, planned investment spending and net exports fall, which in turn lowers aggregate demand; aggregate output must be lower for it to equal aggregate demand and satisfy goods market equilibrium.

The *IS* curve is a useful concept because output tends to move toward points on the curve that satisfy goods market equilibrium. If the economy is located in the area to the right of the *IS* curve, it has an excess supply of goods. At point B, for example, aggregate output Y_1 is greater than the equilibrium level of output Y_3 on the *IS* curve. This excess supply of goods results in unplanned inventory accumulation, which causes output to fall toward the *IS* curve. The decline stops only when output is again at its equilibrium level on the *IS* curve.

If the economy is located in the area to the left of the *IS* curve, it has an excess demand for goods. At point A, aggregate output Y_3 is below the equilibrium level of output Y_1 on the *IS* curve. The excess demand for goods results in an unplanned decrease in inventory, which causes output to rise toward the *IS* curve, stopping only when aggregate output is again at its equilibrium level on the *IS* curve.

Significantly, equilibrium in the goods market does not produce a unique equilibrium level of aggregate output. Although we now know where aggregate output will head for a given level of the interest rate, we cannot determine aggregate output because we do not know what the interest rate is. To complete our analysis of aggregate output determination, we need to introduce another market that produces an additional relationship that links aggregate output and interest rates. The market for money fulfills this function with the *LM* curve. When the *LM* curve is combined with the *IS* curve, a unique equilibrium that determines both aggregate output and the interest rate is obtained.

Equilibrium in the Market for Money: The *LM* Curve

Just as the *IS* curve is derived from the equilibrium condition in the goods market (aggregate output equals aggregate demand), the *LM* curve is derived from the equilibrium condition in the market for money, which requires that the quantity of money demanded equal the quantity of money supplied. The main building block in Keynes's analysis of the market for money is the demand for money he called *liquidity preference*. Let us briefly review his theory of the demand for money (discussed at length in Chapters 5 and 19).

Keynes's liquidity preference theory states that the demand for money in real terms M^d/P depends on income Y (aggregate output) and interest rates i. The demand for money is positively related to income for two reasons. First, a rise in income raises the level of transactions in the economy, which in turn raises the demand for money because it is used to carry out these transactions. Second, a rise in income increases the demand for money because it increases the wealth of individuals who want to hold more assets, one of which is money. The opportunity cost of holding money is the interest sacrificed by not holding other assets (such as bonds) instead. As interest rates rise, the opportunity cost of holding money rises, and the demand for money falls. According to

FIGURE 8 **Deriving the *LM* Curve**
Panel (a) shows the equilibrium levels of the interest rate in the market for money that arise when aggregate output is at Y_1, Y_2, and Y_3. Panel (b) plots the three levels of the equilibrium interest rate i_1, i_2, and i_3 corresponding to these three levels of output; the line that connects these points is the *LM* curve.

the liquidity preference theory, the demand for money is positively related to aggregate output and negatively related to interest rates.

Deriving the *LM* Curve In Keynes's analysis, the level of interest rates is determined by equilibrium in the market for money (when the quantity of money demanded equals the quantity of money supplied). Figure 8 depicts what happens to equilibrium in the market for money as the level of output changes. Because the *LM* curve is derived holding the real money supply at a fixed level, it is fixed at the level of $\overline{M}/P$ in panel (a).[7] Each level of aggregate output has its own money demand curve because as aggregate output changes, the level of transactions in the economy changes, which in turn changes the demand for money.

When aggregate output is Y_1, the money demand curve is $M^d(Y_1)$: It slopes downward because a lower interest rate means that the opportunity cost of holding money is lower, so the quantity of money demanded is higher. Equilibrium in the market for money occurs at point 1, at which the interest rate is i_1. When aggregate output is at the higher level Y_2, the money demand curve shifts rightward to $M^d(Y_2)$ because the higher level of output means that at any given interest rate, the quantity of money demanded is higher. Equilibrium in the market for money now occurs at point 2, at which the interest rate is at the higher level of i_2. Similarly, a still higher level of aggregate output Y_3 results in an even higher level of the equilibrium interest rate i_3.

---

[7]As pointed out in earlier chapters on the money supply process, the money supply is positively related to interest rates, so the M^s curve in panel (a) should actually have a positive slope. The M^s curve is assumed to be vertical in panel (a) to simplify the graph, but allowing for a positive slope leads to identical results.

Panel (b) plots the equilibrium interest rates that correspond to the different output levels, with points 1, 2, and 3 corresponding to the equilibrium points 1, 2, and 3 in panel (a). The line connecting these points is the *LM* curve, which shows the combinations of interest rates and output for which the market for money is in equilibrium. The positive slope arises because higher output raises the demand for money and thus raises the equilibrium interest rate.

What the *LM* Curve Tells Us   The *LM* curve traces out the points that satisfy the equilibrium condition that the quantity of money demanded equals the quantity of money supplied. For each given level of aggregate output, the *LM* curve tells us what the interest rate must be for there to be equilibrium in the market for money. As aggregate output rises, the demand for money increases and the interest rate rises, so that money demanded equals money supplied and the market for money is in equilibrium.

Just as the economy tends to move toward the equilibrium points represented by the *IS* curve, it also moves toward the equilibrium points on the *LM* curve. If the economy is located in the area to the left of the *LM* curve, there is an excess supply of money. At point A, for example, the interest rate is i_3 and aggregate output is Y_1. The interest rate is above the equilibrium level, and people are holding more money than they want to. To eliminate their excess money balances, they will purchase bonds, which causes the price of the bonds to rise and their interest rate to fall. (The inverse relationship between the price of a bond and its interest rate is discussed in Chapter 4.) As long as an excess supply of money exists, the interest rate will fall until it comes to rest on the *LM* curve.

If the economy is located in the area to the right of the *LM* curve, there is an excess demand for money. At point B, for example, the interest rate i_1 is below the equilibrium level, and people want to hold more money than they currently do. To acquire this money, they will sell bonds and drive down bond prices, and the interest rate will rise. This process will stop only when the interest rate rises to an equilibrium point on the *LM* curve.

ISLM APPROACH TO AGGREGATE OUTPUT AND INTEREST RATES

Now that we have derived the *IS* and *LM* curves, we can put them into the same diagram (Figure 9) to produce a model that enables us to determine both aggregate output and the interest rate. The only point at which the goods market and the market for money are in simultaneous equilibrium is at the intersection of the *IS* and *LM* curves, point E. At this point, aggregate output equals aggregate demand (*IS*) and the quantity of money demanded equals the quantity of money supplied (*LM*). At any other point in the diagram, at least one of these equilibrium conditions is not satisfied, and market forces move the economy toward the general equilibrium, point E.

To learn how this works, let's consider what happens if the economy is at point A, which is on the *IS* curve but not the *LM* curve. Even though at point A the goods market is in equilibrium, so that aggregate output equals aggregate demand, the interest rate is above its equilibrium level, so the demand for money is less than the supply. Because people have more money than they want to hold, they will try to get rid of it by buying bonds. The resulting rise in bond prices causes a fall in interest rates, which in turn causes both planned investment spending and net exports to rise, and thus aggregate output rises. The economy then moves down along the *IS* curve, and the process

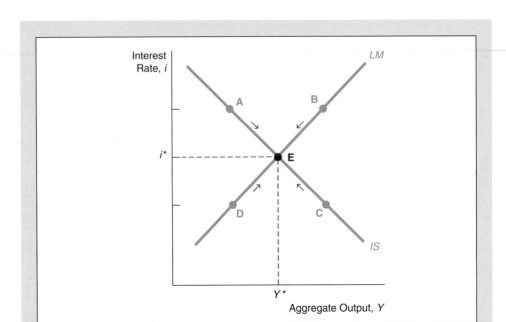

FIGURE 9   *ISLM* **Diagram: Simultaneous Determination of Output and the Interest Rate**
Only at point E, when the interest rate is i^* and output is Y^*, is there equilibrium simultaneously in both the goods market (as measured by the *IS* curve) and the market for money (as measured by the *LM* curve). At other points, such as A, B, C, or D, one of the two markets is not in equilibrium, and there will be a tendency to head toward the equilibrium, point E.

continues until the interest rate falls to i^* and aggregate output rises to Y^*—that is, until the economy is at equilibrium point E.

If the economy is on the *LM* curve but off the *IS* curve at point B, it will also head toward the equilibrium at point E. At point B, even though money demand equals money supply, output is higher than the equilibrium level and exceeds aggregate demand. Firms are unable to sell all their output, and unplanned inventory accumulates, prompting firms to cut production and lower output. The decline in output means that the demand for money will fall, lowering interest rates. The economy then moves down along the *LM* curve until it reaches equilibrium point E.

We have finally developed a model, the *ISLM* model, that tells us how both interest rates and aggregate output are determined when the price level is fixed. Although we have demonstrated that the economy will head toward an aggregate output level of Y^*, there is no reason to assume that at this level of aggregate output the economy is at full employment. If the unemployment rate is too high, government policymakers might want to increase aggregate output to reduce it. The *ISLM* apparatus indicates that they can do this by manipulating monetary and fiscal policy. We will conduct an *ISLM* analysis of how monetary and fiscal policy can affect economic activity in the next chapter.

SUMMARY

1. In the simple Keynesian framework in which the price level is fixed, output is determined by the equilibrium condition in the goods market that aggregate output equals aggregate demand. Aggregate demand equals the sum of consumer expenditure, planned investment spending, government spending, and net exports. Consumer expenditure is described by the consumption function, which indicates that consumer expenditure will rise as disposable income increases. Keynes's analysis shows that aggregate output is positively related to autonomous consumer expenditure, planned investment spending, government spending, and net exports and negatively related to the level of taxes. A change in any of these factors leads, through the expenditure multiplier, to a multiple change in aggregate output.

2. The *ISLM* model determines aggregate output and the interest rate for a fixed price level using the *IS* and *LM* curves. The *IS* curve traces out the combinations of the interest rate and aggregate output for which the goods market is in equilibrium, and the *LM* curve traces out the combinations for which the market for money is in equilibrium. The *IS* curve slopes downward, because higher interest rates lower planned investment spending and net exports and so lower equilibrium output. The *LM* curve slopes upward, because higher aggregate output raises the demand for money and so raises the equilibrium interest rate.

3. The simultaneous determination of output and interest rates occurs at the intersection of the *IS* and *LM* curves, where both the goods market and the market for money are in equilibrium. At any other level of interest rates and output, at least one of the markets will be out of equilibrium, and forces will move the economy toward the general equilibrium point at the intersection of the *IS* and *LM* curves.

KEY TERMS

aggregate demand, p. 520

aggregate demand function, p. 524

"animal spirits," p. 527

autonomous consumer expenditure, p. 521

consumer expenditure, p. 519

consumption function, p. 521

disposable income, p. 521

expenditure multiplier, p. 525

fixed investment, p. 522

government spending, p. 520

inventory investment, p. 522

IS curve, p. 534

LM curve, p. 534

marginal propensity to consume, p. 521

net exports, p. 520

planned investment spending, p. 519

QUESTIONS AND PROBLEMS

All questions and problems are available in myeconlab *at* www.myeconlab.com/mishkin.

1. Calculate the value of the consumption function at each level of disposable income in Table 1 if $a = 100$ and $mpc = 0.9$.

2. Why do companies cut production when they find that their unplanned inventory investment is greater than zero? If they didn't cut production, what effect would this have on their profits? Why?

3. Plot the consumption function $C = 100 + 0.75Y$ on graph paper.

a. Assuming no government sector or net exports, if planned investment spending is 200, what is the equilibrium level of aggregate output? Show this equilibrium level on the graph you have drawn.

b. If businesses become more pessimistic about the profitability of investment and planned investment spending falls by 100, what happens to the equilibrium level of output?

4. If the consumption function is $C = 100 + 0.8Y$ and planned investment spending is 200, what is the equilibrium level of output? If planned investment falls by 100, how much does the equilibrium level of output fall?

5. Why are the multipliers in Problems 3 and 4 different? Explain intuitively why one is higher than the other.

6. If firms suddenly become more optimistic about the profitability of investment and planned investment spending rises by $100 billion, while consumers become more pessimistic and autonomous consumer spending falls by $100 billion, what happens to aggregate output?

7. "A rise in planned investment spending by $100 billion at the same time that autonomous consumer expenditure falls by $50 billion has the same effect on aggregate output as a rise in autonomous consumer expenditure alone by $50 billion." Is this statement true, false, or uncertain? Explain your answer.

8. If the consumption function is $C = 100 + 0.75Y$, $I = 200$, and government spending is 200, what will be the equilibrium level of output? Demonstrate your answer with a Keynesian cross diagram. What happens to aggregate output if government spending rises by 100?

9. If the marginal propensity to consume is 0.5, how much would government spending have to rise to increase output by $1,000 billion?

10. Suppose that government policymakers decide that they will change taxes to raise aggregate output by $400 billion, and $mpc = 0.5$. By how much will taxes have to be changed?

11. What happens to aggregate output if both taxes and government spending are lowered by $300 billion and $mpc = 0.5$? Explain your answer.

12. Will aggregate output rise or fall if an increase in autonomous consumer expenditure is matched by an equal increase in taxes?

13. If a change in the interest rate has no effect on planned investment spending or net exports, trace out what happens to the equilibrium level of aggregate output as interest rates fall. What does this imply about the slope of the *IS* curve?

14. Using a supply and demand diagram for the market for money, show what happens to the equilibrium level of the interest rate as aggregate output falls. What does this imply about the slope of the *LM* curve?

15. "If the point describing the combination of the interest rate and aggregate output is not on either the *IS* curve or the *LM* curve, the economy will have no tendency to head toward the intersection of the two curves." Is this statement true, false, or uncertain? Explain your answer.

WEB EXERCISES

1. Go to www.fgn.unisg.ch/eurmacro/Tutor/keynesiancross.html. Make sure the following settings are used: $t = 0$, $G = 200$, $c = 0.8$, and $m = 0.0$. Click on the "memorize" button. Note the value of equilibrium output. Now, decrease G by 50. What is the value of equilibrium output? What is the implied multiplier?

2. Go to www.fgn.unisg.ch/eurmacro/Tutor/keynesiancross.html. Make sure the following settings are used: $t = 0.25$, $G = 400$; $c = 0.8$, and $m = 0.0$. Click the "memorize" button. Note the value of equilibrium output. Now, decrease G by 50. What is the value of equilibrium output? What is the implied multiplier? Compare your answer with the answer to Web Exercise Question 1.

WEB REFERENCES

http://research.stlouisfed.org/fred2

Information about the macroeconomic variables discussed in this chapter.

 MyEconLab CAN HELP YOU GET A BETTER GRADE

If your exam were tomorrow, would you be ready? For each chapter, MyEconLab Practice Test and Study Plans pinpoint which sections you have mastered and which ones you need to study. That way, you are more efficient with your study time, and you are better prepared for your exams.

To see how it works, turn to page 20 and then go to: www.myeconlab.com/mishkin

21

Monetary and Fiscal Policy in the *ISLM* Model

Preview

Since World War II, U.S. government policymakers have tried to promote high employment without causing inflation. If the U.S. economy experiences a recession such as the one that began in December 2007, policymakers have two principal sets of tools that they can use to affect aggregate economic activity: *monetary policy*, the control of interest rates or the money supply, and *fiscal policy*, the control of government spending and taxes.

The *ISLM* model can help policymakers predict what will happen to aggregate output and interest rates if they decide to increase the money supply or increase government spending. In this way, *ISLM* analysis enables us to answer some important questions about the usefulness and effectiveness of monetary and fiscal policy in influencing economic activity.

But which is better? When is monetary policy more effective than fiscal policy at controlling the level of aggregate output, and when is it less effective? Will fiscal policy be more effective if it is conducted by changing government spending rather than changing taxes? Should the monetary authorities conduct monetary policy by manipulating the money supply or interest rates?

In this chapter, we use the *ISLM* model to help answer these questions and to learn how the model generates the aggregate demand curve featured prominently in the aggregate demand and supply framework (examined in Chapter 22), which is used to understand changes not only in aggregate output but also in the price level. Our analysis will show why economists focus so much attention on topics such as the stability of the demand for money function and whether the demand for money is strongly influenced by interest rates.

First, however, let's examine the *ISLM* model in more detail to see how the *IS* and *LM* curves developed in Chapter 20 shift and the implications of these shifts. (We continue to assume that the price level is fixed so that real and nominal quantities are the same.)

FACTORS THAT CAUSE THE *IS* CURVE TO SHIFT

You have already learned that the *IS* curve describes equilibrium points in the goods market—the combinations of aggregate output and interest rate for which aggregate output produced equals aggregate demand. The *IS* curve shifts whenever a change in autonomous factors (factors independent of aggregate output) occurs that is unrelated to the interest rate. (A change in the interest rate that affects equilibrium aggregate output causes only a movement along the *IS* curve.) We have already identified five candidates as autonomous factors that can shift aggregate demand and hence affect the level of equilibrium output. We can now ask how changes in each of these factors affect the *IS* curve.

1. Changes in Autonomous Consumer Expenditure. A rise in autonomous consumer expenditure shifts the aggregate demand function upward and shifts the *IS* curve to the right (see Figure 1). To see how this shift occurs, suppose that the *IS* curve is initially at IS_1 in panel (a) and a huge oil field is discovered in Wyoming, perhaps containing more oil than fields in Saudi Arabia. Consumers now become more optimistic about the future health of the economy, and autonomous consumer expenditure rises. What happens to the equilibrium level of aggregate output as a result of this rise in autonomous consumer expenditure when the interest rate is held constant at i_A?

The IS_1 curve tells us that equilibrium aggregate output is at Y_A when the interest rate is at i_A (point A). Panel (b) shows that this point is an equilibrium in the goods market because the aggregate demand function Y_1^{ad} at an interest rate i_A crosses the 45° line $Y = Y^{ad}$ at an aggregate output level of Y_A. When autonomous consumer expenditure rises because of the oil discovery, the aggregate demand function shifts upward to Y_2^{ad} and equilibrium output rises to $Y_{A'}$. This rise in equilibrium output from Y_A to $Y_{A'}$ when the interest rate is i_A is plotted in panel (a) as a movement from point A to point A'. The same analysis can be applied to every point on the initial IS_1 curve; therefore, the rise in autonomous consumer expenditure shifts the *IS* curve to the right from IS_1 to IS_2 in panel (a).

A decline in autonomous consumer expenditure reverses the direction of the analysis. For any given interest rate, the aggregate demand function shifts downward, the equilibrium level of aggregate output falls, and the *IS* curve shifts to the left.

2. Changes in Investment Spending Unrelated to the Interest Rate. In Chapter 20, we learned that changes in the interest rate affect planned investment spending and hence the equilibrium level of output. This change in investment spending merely causes a movement along the *IS* curve and not a shift. A rise in planned investment spending unrelated to the interest rate (say, because companies become more confident about investment profitability after the Wyoming oil discovery) shifts the aggregate demand function upward, as in panel (b) of Figure 1. For any given interest rate, the equilibrium level of aggregate output rises, and the *IS* curve will shift to the right, as in panel (a).

A decrease in investment spending because companies become more pessimistic about investment profitability shifts the aggregate demand function downward for any given interest rate; the equilibrium level of aggregate output falls, shifting the *IS* curve to the left.

3. Changes in Government Spending. An increase in government spending will also cause the aggregate demand function at any given interest rate to shift upward, as in panel (b). The equilibrium level of aggregate output rises at any given interest rate, and the *IS* curve shifts to the right. Conversely, a decline in government spending shifts the aggregate demand function downward, and the equilibrium level of output falls, shifting the *IS* curve to the left.

4. Changes in Taxes. Unlike changes in other factors that directly affect the aggregate demand function, a decline in taxes shifts the aggregate demand function by raising consumer expenditure and shifting the aggregate demand function upward at any given interest rate. A decline in taxes raises the equilibrium level of aggregate output at any given interest rate and shifts the *IS* curve to the right (as in Figure 1). Recall, however, that a change in taxes has a smaller effect on aggregate demand than an equivalent change in government spending. So for a given change in taxes, the *IS* curve will shift less than for an equal change in government spending.

A rise in taxes lowers the aggregate demand function and reduces the equilibrium level of aggregate output at each interest rate. Therefore, a rise in taxes shifts the *IS* curve to the left.

5. Changes in Net Exports Unrelated to the Interest Rate. As with planned investment spending, changes in net exports arising from a change in interest rates merely cause a

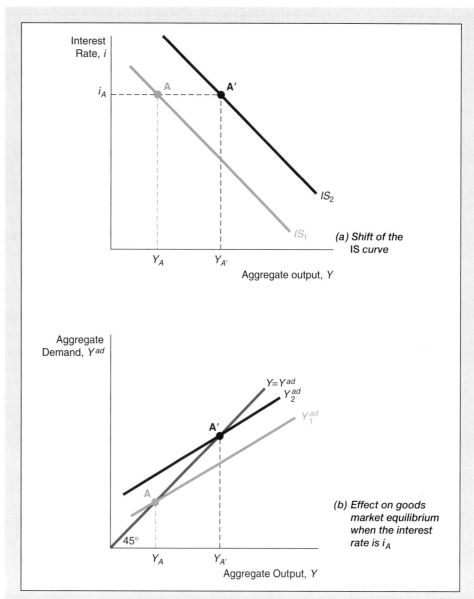

FIGURE 1   Shift in the *IS* Curve

The *IS* curve will shift from IS_1 to IS_2 as a result of (1) an increase in autonomous consumer spending, (2) an increase in planned investment spending due to business optimism, (3) an increase in government spending, (4) a decrease in taxes, or (5) an increase in net exports that is unrelated to interest rates. Panel (b) shows how changes in these factors lead to the rightward shift in the *IS* curve using a Keynesian cross diagram. For any given interest rate (here i_A), these changes shift the aggregate demand function upward and raise equilibrium output from Y_A to Y_A'.

movement along the *IS* curve and not a shift. An autonomous rise in net exports unrelated to the interest rate—say, because American-made jeans become more chic than French-made jeans—shifts the aggregate demand function upward and causes the *IS* curve to shift to the right, as in Figure 1. Conversely, an autonomous fall in net exports shifts the aggregate demand function downward, and the equilibrium level of output falls, shifting the *IS* curve to the left.

FACTORS THAT CAUSE THE *LM* CURVE TO SHIFT

The *LM* curve describes the equilibrium points in the market for money—the combinations of aggregate output and interest rate for which the quantity of money demanded equals the quantity of money supplied. Whereas five factors can cause the *IS* curve to shift (changes in autonomous consumer expenditure, planned investment spending unrelated to the interest rate, government spending, taxes, and net exports unrelated to the interest rate), only two factors can cause the *LM* curve to shift: autonomous changes in money demand and changes in the money supply. How do changes in these two factors affect the *LM* curve?

1. Changes in the Money Supply. A rise in the money supply shifts the *LM* curve to the right, as shown in Figure 2. To see how this shift occurs, suppose that the *LM* curve is initially at LM_1 in panel (a) and the Federal Reserve conducts open market purchases that increase the money supply. If we consider point A, which is on the initial LM_1 curve, we can examine what happens to the equilibrium level of the interest rate, holding output constant at Y_A.

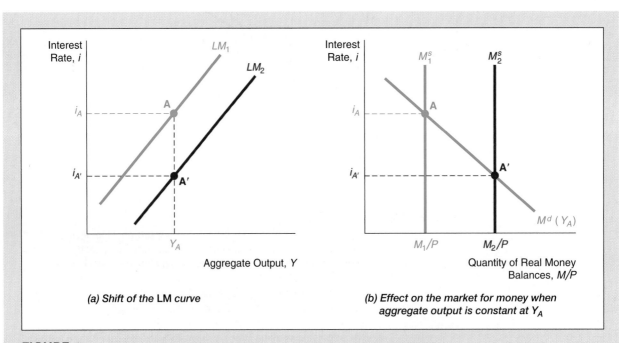

(a) Shift of the LM *curve*

(b) Effect on the market for money when aggregate output is constant at Y_A

FIGURE 2   Shift in the *LM* Curve from an Increase in the Money Supply
The *LM* curve shifts to the right from LM_1 to LM_2 when the money supply increases because, as indicated in panel (b), at any given level of aggregate output (say, Y_A), the equilibrium interest rate falls (point A to A').

Panel (b), which contains a supply and demand diagram for the market for money, depicts the equilibrium interest rate initially as i_A at the intersection of the supply curve for money M_1^s and the demand curve for money M^d. The rise in the quantity of money supplied shifts the supply curve to M_2^s, and, holding output constant at Y_A, the equilibrium interest rate falls to $i_{A'}$. In panel (a), this decline in the equilibrium interest rate from i_A to $i_{A'}$ is shown as a movement from point A to point A'. The same analysis can be applied to every point on the initial LM_1 curve, leading to the conclusion that at any given level of aggregate output, the equilibrium interest rate falls when the money supply increases. Thus LM_2 is below and to the right of LM_1.

Reversing this reasoning, a decline in the money supply shifts the *LM* curve to the left. A decline in the money supply results in a shortage of money at points on the initial *LM* curve. This condition of excess demand for money can be eliminated by a rise in the interest rate, which reduces the quantity of money demanded until it again equals the quantity of money supplied.

2. Autonomous Changes in Money Demand. The theory of asset demand outlined in Chapter 5 indicates that there can be an autonomous rise in money demand (that is, a change not caused by a change in the price level, aggregate output, or the interest rate). For example, an increase in the volatility of bond returns would make bonds riskier relative to money and would increase the quantity of money demanded at any given interest rate, price level, or amount of aggregate output. The resulting autonomous increase in the demand for money shifts the *LM* curve to the left, as shown in Figure 3. Consider point A on the initial LM_1 curve. Suppose that a massive financial panic occurs, sending many companies into bankruptcy. Because bonds have become a riskier asset, people want to shift from holding bonds to holding money; they will hold more money at

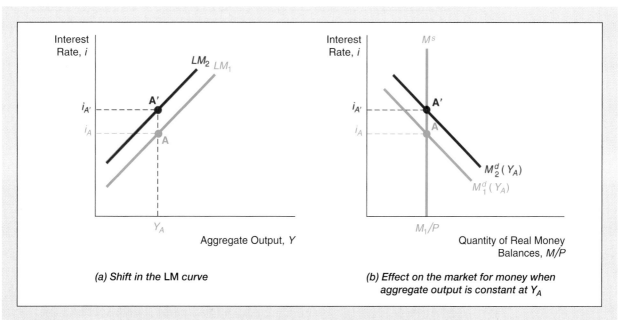

(a) Shift in the LM *curve*

(b) Effect on the market for money when aggregate output is constant at Y_A

FIGURE 3   **Shift in the *LM* Curve When Money Demand Increases**
The *LM* curve shifts to the left from LM_1 to LM_2 when money demand increases because, as indicated in panel (b), at any given level of aggregate output (say, Y_A), the equilibrium interest rate rises (point A to A').

all interest rates and output levels. The resulting increase in money demand at an output level of Y_A is shown by the shift of the money demand curve from M_1^d to M_2^d in panel (b). The new equilibrium in the market for money now indicates that if aggregate output is constant at Y_A, the equilibrium interest rate will rise to $i_{A'}$, and the point of equilibrium moves from A to A'.

Conversely, an autonomous decline in money demand would lead to a rightward shift in the *LM* curve. The fall in money demand would create an excess supply of money, which is eliminated by a rise in the quantity of money demanded that results from a decline in the interest rate.

CHANGES IN EQUILIBRIUM LEVEL OF THE INTEREST RATE AND AGGREGATE OUTPUT

You can now use your knowledge of factors that cause the *IS* and *LM* curves to shift for the purpose of analyzing how the equilibrium levels of the interest rate and aggregate output change in response to changes in monetary and fiscal policies.

Response to a Change in Monetary Policy

Figure 4 illustrates the response of output and interest rate to an increase in the money supply. Initially, the economy is in equilibrium for both the goods market and the

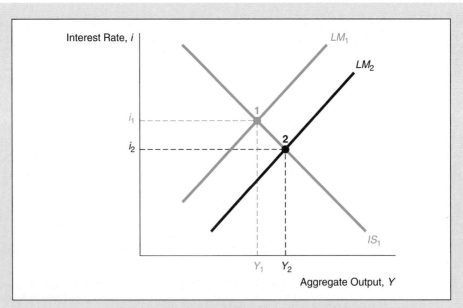

FIGURE 4   **Response of Aggregate Output and the Interest Rate to an Increase in the Money Supply**
The increase in the money supply shifts the *LM* curve to the right from LM_1 to LM_2; the economy moves to point 2, where output has increased to Y_2 and the interest rate has declined to i_2.

market for money at point 1, the intersection of IS_1 and LM_1. Suppose that at the resulting level of aggregate output Y_1, the economy is suffering from an unemployment rate of 10%, and the Federal Reserve decides it should try to raise output and reduce unemployment by raising the money supply. Will the Fed's change in monetary policy have the intended effect?

The rise in the money supply causes the LM curve to shift rightward to LM_2, and the equilibrium point for both the goods market and the market for money moves to point 2 (intersection of IS_1 and LM_2). As a result of an increase in the money supply, the interest rate declines to i_2, as we found in Figure 2, and aggregate output rises to Y_2; the Fed's policy has been successful in improving the health of the economy.

For a clear understanding of why aggregate output rises and the interest rate declines, think about exactly what has happened in moving from point 1 to point 2. When the economy is at point 1, the increase in the money supply (rightward shift of the LM curve) creates an excess supply of money, resulting in a decline in the interest rate. The decline causes investment spending and net exports to rise, which in turn raises aggregate demand and causes aggregate output to rise. The excess supply of money is eliminated when the economy reaches point 2 because both the rise in output and the fall in the interest rate have raised the quantity of money demanded until it equals the new higher level of the money supply.

A decline in the money supply reverses the process; it shifts the LM curve to the left, causing the interest rate to rise and output to fall. Accordingly, ***aggregate output is positively related to the money supply***; aggregate output expands when the money supply increases and falls when it decreases.

Response to a Change in Fiscal Policy

Suppose that the Federal Reserve is not willing to increase the money supply when the economy is suffering from a 10% unemployment rate at point 1. Can the U.S. government come to the rescue and manipulate government spending and taxes to raise aggregate output and reduce the massive unemployment?

The *ISLM* model demonstrates that it can. Figure 5 depicts the response of output and the interest rate to an expansionary fiscal policy (increase in government spending or decrease in taxes). An increase in government spending or a decrease in taxes causes the *IS* curve to shift to IS_2, and the equilibrium point for both the goods market and the market for money moves to point 2 (intersection of IS_2 with LM_1). The result of the change in fiscal policy is a rise in aggregate output to Y_2 and a rise in the interest rate to i_2. Note the difference in the effect on the interest rate between an expansionary fiscal policy and an expansionary monetary policy. In the case of an expansionary fiscal policy, the interest rate rises, whereas in the case of an expansionary monetary policy, the interest rate falls.

Why does an increase in government spending or a decrease in taxes move the economy from point 1 to point 2, causing a rise in both aggregate output and the interest rate? An increase in government spending raises aggregate demand directly; a decrease in taxes makes more income available for spending and raises aggregate demand by raising consumer expenditure. The resulting increase in aggregate demand causes aggregate output to rise. The higher level of aggregate output raises the quantity of money demanded, creating an excess demand for money, which in turn causes the interest rate to rise. At point 2, the excess demand for money created by a rise in aggregate output has been eliminated by a rise in the interest rate, which lowers the quantity of money demanded.

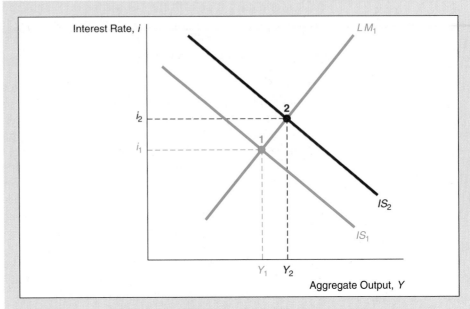

FIGURE 5   Response of Aggregate Output and the Interest Rate to an Expansionary Fiscal Policy
Expansionary fiscal policy (a rise in government spending or a decrease in taxes) shifts the *IS* curve to the right from IS_1 to IS_2; the economy moves to point 2, aggregate output increases to Y_2, and the interest rate rises to i_2.

A contractionary fiscal policy (decrease in government spending or increase in taxes) reverses the process described in Figure 5; it causes aggregate demand to fall, which shifts the *IS* curve to the left and causes both aggregate output and the interest rate to fall. *Aggregate output and the interest rate are positively related to government spending and negatively related to taxes.*

As a study aid, Summary Table 1 indicates the effect on aggregate output and interest rates of a change in the seven factors that shift the *IS* and *LM* curves.

APPLICATION ✦ The Economic Stimulus Act of 2008

In February 2008, the U.S. Congress passed the Economic Stimulus Act of 2008 in order to counter the contractionary effects on the economy from the subprime financial crisis. The most important feature of the legislation was the issuance of over $100 billion of rebate checks to low and middle-income taxpayers, although the bill also included tax incentives for businesses to invest and help for homeowners who were facing foreclosure.

Our *ISLM* analysis can indicate the likely impact of this legislation. The tax rebates serve exactly like a tax cut, similar to the situation depicted in Figure 5, which shows the response to expansionary fiscal policy. The *IS* curve shifts to the right, which would raise both interest rates and aggregate output. In addition, the tax incentives to businesses in the stimulus package would lead to a rise in investment, which provides another reason for the *IS* curve to shift to the right and interest rates and output to rise.

SUMMARY TABLE 1

Effects from Factors That Shift the *IS* and *LM* Curves

Factor	Autonomous Change in Factor	Response	Reason	
Consumer expenditure, C	↑	$Y\uparrow, i\uparrow$	$C\uparrow \Rightarrow Y^{ad}\uparrow \Rightarrow$ *IS* shifts right	
Investment, I	↑	$Y\uparrow, i\uparrow$	$I\uparrow \Rightarrow Y^{ad}\uparrow \Rightarrow$ *IS* shifts right	
Government spending, G	↑	$Y\uparrow, i\uparrow$	$G\uparrow \Rightarrow Y^{ad}\uparrow \Rightarrow$ *IS* shifts right	
Taxes, T	↑	$Y\downarrow, i\downarrow$	$T\uparrow \Rightarrow C\downarrow \Rightarrow Y^{ad}\downarrow \Rightarrow$ *IS* shifts left	
Net exports, NX	↑	$Y\uparrow, i\uparrow$	$NX\uparrow \Rightarrow Y^{ad}\uparrow \Rightarrow$ *IS* shifts right	
Money supply, M^s	↑	$Y\uparrow, i\downarrow$	$M^s\uparrow \Rightarrow i\downarrow \Rightarrow$ *LM* shifts right	
Money demand, M^d	↑	$Y\downarrow, i\uparrow$	$M^d\uparrow \Rightarrow i\uparrow \Rightarrow$ *LM* shifts left	

Note: Only increases (↑) in the factors are shown. The effect of decreases in the factors would be the opposite of those indicated in the "Response" column.

Although economists have estimated that the stimulus package did increase spending a little bit and so had some of the effects described in Figure 5, the continuing deterioration in credit market conditions overwhelmed the expansionary effect of the stimulus package. As a result, aggregate spending actually fell rather than rising. Consequently, instead of the *IS* curve shifting to the right, as depicted in Figure 5, the *IS* curve shifted to the left and aggregate output and interest rates ended up declining rather than rising during this period.

With the ongoing deterioration in the economy, the incoming Obama administration quickly passed an additional $787 billion stimulus package. How effective it will be in turning around the economy is an open question.

EFFECTIVENESS OF MONETARY VERSUS FISCAL POLICY

Our discussion of the effects of fiscal and monetary policy suggests that a government can easily lift an economy out of a recession by implementing any of a number of policies (changing the money supply, government spending, or taxes). But how can policymakers decide which of these policies to use if faced with too much unemployment? Should they decrease taxes, increase government spending, raise the money supply, or do all three? And if they decide to increase the money supply, by how much? Economists do not pretend to have all the answers, and although the *ISLM* model will not clear the path to aggregate economic bliss, it can help policymakers decide which policies may be most effective under certain circumstances.

Monetary Policy Versus Fiscal Policy: The Case of Complete Crowding Out

The *ISLM* model developed so far in this chapter shows that both monetary and fiscal policy affect the level of aggregate output. To understand when monetary policy is more effective than fiscal policy, we will examine a special case of the *ISLM* model in which money demand is unaffected by the interest rate (money demand is said to be interest-inelastic) so that monetary policy affects output but fiscal policy does not.

Consider the slope of the *LM* curve if the demand for money is unaffected by changes in the interest rate. If point 1 in panel (a) of Figure 6 is such that the quantity of money demanded equals the quantity of money supplied, then it is on the *LM* curve. If the interest rate rises to, say, i_2, the quantity of money demanded is unaffected, and it will continue to equal the *unchanged* quantity of money supplied only if aggregate output remains *unchanged* at Y_1 (point 2). Equilibrium in the market for money will occur at the same level of aggregate output regardless of the interest rate, and the *LM* curve will be vertical, as shown in both panels of Figure 6.

Suppose that the economy is suffering from a high rate of unemployment, which policymakers try to eliminate with either expansionary fiscal or monetary policy. Panel (a) depicts what happens when an expansionary fiscal policy (increase in government spending or cut in taxes) is implemented, shifting the *IS* curve to the right from IS_1 to IS_2. As you can see in panel (a), the fiscal expansion has no effect on output; aggregate output remains at Y_1 when the economy moves from point 1 to point 2.

In our earlier analysis, expansionary fiscal policy always increased aggregate demand and raised the level of output. Why doesn't that happen in panel (a)? The answer is that

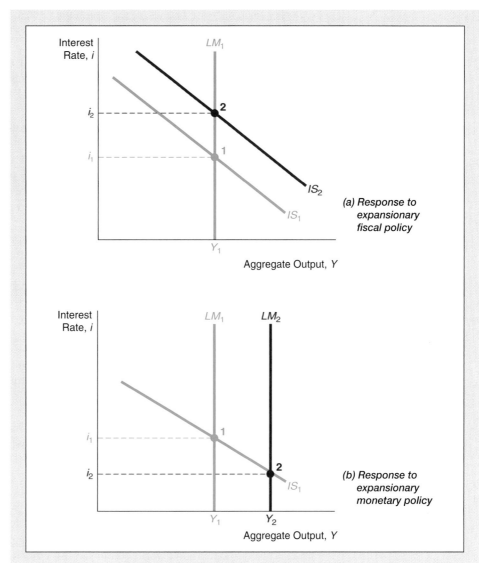

FIGURE 6   **Effectiveness of Monetary and Fiscal Policy When Money Demand Is Unaffected by the Interest Rate**
When the demand for money is unaffected by the interest rate, the *LM* curve is vertical. In panel (a), an expansionary fiscal policy (increase in government spending or a cut in taxes) shifts the *IS* curve from IS_1 to IS_2 and leaves aggregate output unchanged at Y_1. In panel (b), an increase in the money supply shifts the *LM* curve from LM_1 to LM_2 and raises aggregate output from Y_1 to Y_2. Therefore, monetary policy is effective, but fiscal policy is not.

because the *LM* curve is vertical, the rightward shift of the *IS* curve raises the interest rate to i_2, which causes investment spending and net exports to fall enough to offset completely the increased spending of the expansionary fiscal policy. Put another way, increased spending that results from expansionary fiscal policy has *crowded out* investment spending and net exports, which decrease because of the rise in the interest rate. This situation in which expansionary fiscal policy does not lead to a rise in output is frequently referred to as a case of **complete crowding out**.[1]

Panel (b) shows what happens when the Federal Reserve tries to eliminate high unemployment through an expansionary monetary policy (increase in the real money supply, M/P). Here the LM curve shifts to the right from LM_1 to LM_2, because at each interest rate, output must rise so that the quantity of money demanded rises to match the increase in the money supply. Aggregate output rises from Y_1 to Y_2 (the economy moves from point 1 to point 2), and expansionary monetary policy does affect aggregate output in this case.

We conclude from the analysis in Figure 6 that if the demand for money is unaffected by changes in the interest rate (money demand is interest-inelastic), monetary policy is effective but fiscal policy is not. An even more general conclusion can be reached: ***The less interest-sensitive money demand is, the more effective monetary policy is relative to fiscal policy.***[2]

Because the interest sensitivity of money demand is important to policymakers' decisions regarding the use of monetary or fiscal policy to influence economic activity, the subject has been studied extensively by economists and has been the focus of many debates. Findings on the interest sensitivity of money demand are discussed in Chapter 19.

APPLICATION ✦ Targeting Money Supply Versus Interest Rates

In the 1970s and early 1980s, central banks in many countries pursued a strategy of *monetary targeting*—that is, they used their policy tools to make the money supply equal a target value. However, as we saw in Chapter 16, many of these central banks abandoned monetary targeting in the 1980s to pursue interest-rate targeting instead because of the breakdown of the stable relationship between the money supply and economic activity. The *ISLM* model has important implications for which variable a central bank should target and we can apply it to explain why central banks have abandoned monetary targeting for interest-rate targeting.[3]

As we saw in Chapter 16, when the Federal Reserve attempts to hit a reserve aggregate or a money supply target, it cannot at the same time pursue an interest-rate target; it can hit one target or the other but not both. Consequently, it needs to know which of these two targets will produce more accurate control of aggregate output.

In contrast to the textbook world you have been inhabiting, in which the *IS* and *LM* curves are assumed to be fixed, the real world is one of great uncertainty in which *IS* and *LM* curves shift because of unanticipated changes in autonomous spending and

---

[1]When the demand for money is affected by the interest rate, the usual case in which the LM curve slopes upward but is not vertical, some crowding out occurs. The rightward shift of the IS curve also raises the interest rate, which causes investment spending and net exports to fall somewhat. However, as Figure 5 indicates, the rise in the interest rate is not sufficient to reduce investment spending and net exports to the point where aggregate output does not increase. Thus expansionary fiscal policy increases aggregate output, and only partial crowding out occurs.

[2]This result and many others in this and the previous chapter can be obtained more directly by using algebra. An algebraic treatment of the *ISLM* model can be found in an appendix to this chapter, which is on this book's website at www.myeconlab.com/mishkin.

[3]The classic paper on this topic is William Poole, "The Optimal Choice of Monetary Policy Instruments in a Simple Macro Model," *Quarterly Journal of Economics* 84 (1970): 192–216. A less mathematical version of his analysis, far more accessible to students, is contained in William Poole, "Rules of Thumb for Guiding Monetary Policy," in *Open Market Policies and Operating Procedures: Staff Studies* (Washington, DC: Board of Governors of the Federal Reserve System, 1971).

FIGURE 7   **Money Supply and Interest-Rate Targets When the** *IS* **Curve Is Unstable and the** *LM* **Curve Is Stable**
The unstable *IS* curve fluctuates between *IS′* and *IS″*. The money supply target produces smaller fluctuations in output (Y'_M to Y''_M) than the interest-rate target (Y'_I to Y''_I). Therefore, the money supply target is preferred.

money demand. To understand whether the Fed should use a money supply target or an interest-rate target, we need to look at two cases: one in which uncertainty about the *IS* curve is far greater than uncertainty about the *LM* curve, and another in which uncertainty about the *LM* curve is far greater than uncertainty about the *IS* curve.

The *ISLM* diagram in Figure 7 illustrates the outcome of the two targeting strategies for the case in which the *IS* curve is unstable and uncertain, so it fluctuates around its expected value of *IS** from *IS′* to *IS″*, while the *LM* curve is stable and certain, so it stays at *LM**. Because the central bank knows that the expected position of the *IS* curve is at *IS** and desires aggregate output of *Y**, it will set its interest-rate target at *i** so that the expected level of output is *Y**. This policy of targeting the interest rate at *i** is labeled "Interest-Rate Target."

How would the central bank keep the interest rate at its target level of *i**? Recall from Chapter 16 that the Fed can hit its interest-rate target by buying and selling bonds when the interest rate differs from *i**. When the *IS* curve shifts out to *IS″*, the interest rate would rise above *i** with the money supply unchanged. To counter this rise in interest rates, however, the central bank would need to buy bonds just until their price is driven back up so that the interest rate comes back down to *i**. (The result of these open market purchases, as we have seen in Chapters 13 and 14, is that the monetary base and the money supply rise until the *LM* curve shifts to the right to intersect the *IS″* curve at *i**—not shown in the diagram for simplicity.) When the interest rate is below *i**, the central bank needs to sell bonds to lower their price and raise the interest rate back up to i^*. (These open market sales reduce the monetary base and the money supply until the *LM* curve shifts to the left to intersect the *IS* curve at i^*—again not shown in the diagram.) The result of pursuing the interest-rate target is that aggregate output fluctuates between Y_I' and Y_I'' in Figure 7.

If, instead, the Fed pursues a money supply target, it will set the money supply so that the resulting *LM* curve *LM** intersects the *IS** curve at the desired output level of Y^*. This policy of targeting the money supply is labeled "Money Supply Target." Because it is not changing the money supply and so keeps the *LM* curve at *LM**, aggregate output will fluctuate between Y_M' and Y_M'' under the money supply target policy.

As you can see in the figure, the money supply target leads to smaller output fluctuations around the desired level than the interest-rate target. A rightward shift of the *IS* curve to *IS''*, for example, causes the interest rate to rise, given a money supply target, and this rise in the interest rate leads to a lower level of investment spending and net exports and hence to a smaller increase in aggregate output than occurs under an interest-rate target. Because smaller output fluctuations are desirable, the conclusion is that ***if the* IS *curve is more unstable than the* LM *curve, a money supply target is preferred*.

The outcome of the two targeting strategies for the case of a stable *IS* curve and an unstable *LM* curve caused by unanticipated changes in money demand is illustrated in Figure 8. Again, the interest-rate and money supply targets are set so that the expected level of aggregate output equals the desired level Y^*. Because the *LM* curve is now

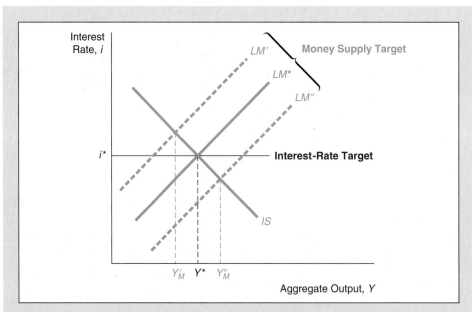

FIGURE 8   **Money Supply and Interest-Rate Targets When the *LM* Curve Is Unstable and the *IS* Curve Is Stable**
The unstable *LM* curve fluctuates between *LM'* and *LM''*. The money supply target then produces bigger fluctuations in output (Y_M' to Y_M'') than the interest-rate target (which leaves output fixed at Y^*). Therefore, the interest-rate target is preferred.

unstable, it fluctuates between LM' and LM'' even when the money supply is fixed, causing aggregate output to fluctuate between Y'_M and Y''_M.

The interest-rate target, by contrast, is not affected by uncertainty about the LM curve, because it is set by the Fed's adjustment of the money supply whenever the interest rate tries to depart from i^*. When the interest rate begins to rise above i^* because of an increase in money demand, the central bank again just buys bonds, driving up their price and bringing the interest rate back down to i^*. The result of these open market purchases is a rise in the monetary base and the money supply. Similarly, if the interest rate falls below i^*, the central bank sells bonds to lower their price and raise the interest rate back to i^*, thereby causing a decline in the monetary base and the money supply. The only effect of the fluctuating LM curve, then, is that the money supply fluctuates more as a result of the interest-rate target policy. The outcome of the interest-rate target is that output will be exactly at the desired level with no fluctuations.

Because smaller output fluctuations are desirable, the conclusion from Figure 8 is that *if the* **LM** *curve is more unstable than the* **IS** *curve, an interest-rate target is preferred*.

We can now see why many central banks decided to abandon monetary targeting for interest-rate targeting in the 1980s. With the rapid proliferation of new financial instruments whose presence can affect the demand for money (see Chapter 19), money demand (which is embodied in the LM curve) became highly unstable in many countries. Thus central banks in these countries recognized that they were more likely to be in the situation depicted in Figure 8 and decided that they would be better off with an interest-rate target than a money supply target.[4]

ISLM MODEL IN THE LONG RUN

So far in our *ISLM* analysis, we have been assuming that the price level is fixed so that nominal values and real values are the same. This is a reasonable assumption for the short run, but in the long run the price level does change. To see what happens in the *ISLM* model in the long run, we make use of the concept of the **natural rate level of output** (denoted by Y_n), which is the rate of output at which the price level has no tendency to rise or fall. When output is above the natural rate level, the booming economy will cause prices to rise; when output is below the natural rate level, the slack in the economy will cause prices to fall.

---

[4]It is important to recognize, however, that the crucial factor in deciding which target is preferred is the *relative* instability of the IS and LM curves. Although the LM curve has been unstable recently, the evidence supporting a stable IS curve is also weak. Instability in the money demand function does not automatically mean that money supply targets should be abandoned for an interest-rate target. Furthermore, the analysis so far has been conducted assuming that the price level is fixed. More realistically, when the price level can change, so that there is uncertainty about expected inflation, the case for an interest-rate target is less strong. As we learned in Chapters 4 and 5, the interest rate that is more relevant to investment decisions is not the nominal interest rate but the real interest rate (the nominal interest rate minus expected inflation). Hence when expected inflation rises, at each given nominal interest rate, the real interest rate falls and investment and net exports rise, shifting the IS curve to the right. Similarly, a fall in expected inflation raises the real interest rate at each given nominal interest rate, lowers investment and net exports, and shifts the IS curve to the left. In the real world, expected inflation undergoes large fluctuations, so the IS curve in Figure 8 will also have substantial fluctuations, making it less likely that the interest-rate target is preferable to the money supply target.

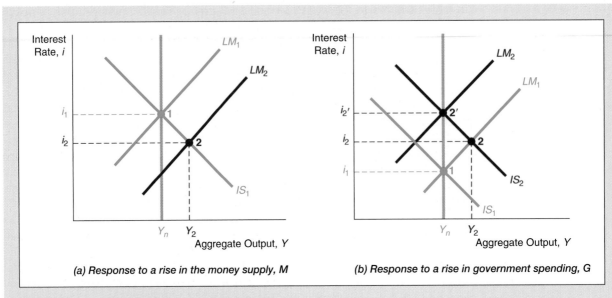

(a) Response to a rise in the money supply, M   **(b) Response to a rise in government spending, G**

FIGURE 9   *ISLM* Model in the Long Run

In panel (a), a rise in the money supply causes the *LM* curve to shift rightward to LM_2, and the equilibrium moves to point 2, where the interest rate falls to i_2 and output rises to Y_2. Because output at Y_2 is above the natural rate level Y_n, the price level rises, the real money supply falls, and the *LM* curve shifts back to LM_1; the economy has returned to the original equilibrium at point 1. In panel (b), an increase in government spending shifts the *IS* curve to the right to IS_2, and the economy moves to point 2, at which the interest rate has risen to i_2 and output has risen to Y_2. Because output at Y_2 is above the natural rate level Y_n, the price level begins to rise, real money balances M/P begin to fall, and the *LM* curve shifts to the left to LM_2. The long-run equilibrium at point 2' has an even higher interest rate at $i_{2'}$, and output has returned to Y_n.

Because we now want to examine what happens when the price level changes, we can no longer assume that real and nominal values are the same. The spending variables that affect the *IS* curve (consumer expenditure, investment spending, government spending, and net exports) describe the demand for goods and services and are *in real terms*; they describe the physical quantities of goods that people want to buy. Because these quantities do not change when the price level changes, a change in the price level has no effect on the *IS* curve, which describes the combinations of the interest rate and aggregate output *in real terms* that satisfy goods market equilibrium.

Figure 9 shows what happens in the *ISLM* model when output rises above the natural rate level, which is marked by a vertical line at Y_n. Suppose that initially the *IS* and *LM* curves intersect at point 1, where output $Y = Y_n$. Panel (a) examines what happens to output and interest rates when there is a rise in the money supply. As we saw in Figure 2, the rise in the money supply causes the *LM* curve to shift to LM_2, and the equilibrium moves to point 2 (the intersection of IS_1 and LM_2), where the interest rate falls to i_2 and output rises to Y_2. However, as we can see in panel (a), the level of output at Y_2 is greater than the natural rate level Y_n, and so the price level begins to rise.

In contrast to the *IS* curve, which is unaffected by a rise in the price level, the *LM* curve is affected by the price level rise because the liquidity preference theory states that the demand for money *in real terms* depends on real income and interest rates. This makes sense because money is valued in terms of what it can buy. However, the money supply the media reports in dollars is not the money supply in real terms; it is a nominal quantity. As the price level rises, the quantity of money *in real terms* falls, and the effect on the *LM* curve is identical to a fall in the nominal money supply with the price level fixed. The lower value of the real money supply creates an excess demand for money, causing the interest rate to rise at any given level of aggregate output, and the *LM* curve shifts back to the left. As long as the level of output exceeds the natural rate level, the price level will continue to rise, shifting the *LM* curve to the left, until finally output is back at the natural rate level Y_n. This occurs when the *LM* curve has returned to LM_1, where real money balances M/P have returned to the original level and the economy has returned to the original equilibrium at point 1. The result of the expansion in the money supply in the long run is that the economy has the same level of output and interest rates.

The fact that the increase in the money supply has left output and interest rates unchanged in the long run is referred to as **long-run monetary neutrality**. The only result of the increase in the money supply is a higher price level, which has increased proportionally to the increase in the money supply so that real money balances M/P are unchanged.

Panel (b) looks at what happens to output and interest rates when there is expansionary fiscal policy such as an increase in government spending. As we saw earlier, the increase in government spending shifts the *IS* curve to the right to IS_2, and in the short run the economy moves to point 2 (the intersection of IS_2 and LM_1), where the interest rate has risen to i_2 and output has risen to Y_2. Because output at Y_2 is above the natural rate level Y_n, the price level begins to rise, real money balances M/P begin to fall, and the *LM* curve shifts to the left. Only when the *LM* curve has shifted to LM_2 and the equilibrium is at point $2'$, where output is again at the natural rate level Y_n, does the price level stop rising and the *LM* curve come to rest. The resulting long-run equilibrium at point $2'$ has an even higher interest rate at $i_{2'}$ and output has not risen from Y_n. Indeed, what has occurred in the long run is complete crowding out: The rise in the price level, which has shifted the *LM* curve to LM_2, has caused the interest rate to rise to $i_{2'}$, causing investment and net exports to fall enough to offset the increased government spending completely. What we have discovered is that even though complete crowding out does not occur in the short run in the *ISLM* model (unless the *LM* curve is vertical), it does occur in the long run.

Our conclusion from examining what happens in the *ISLM* model from an expansionary monetary or fiscal policy is that *although monetary and fiscal policy can affect output in the short run, neither affects output in the long run*. Clearly, an important issue in deciding on the effectiveness of monetary and fiscal policy to raise output is how soon the long run occurs. This is a topic that we explore in the next chapter.

ISLM MODEL AND THE AGGREGATE DEMAND CURVE

We now examine further what happens in the *ISLM* model when the price level changes. When we conduct the *ISLM* analysis with a changing price level, we find that as the price level falls, the level of aggregate output rises. Thus we obtain a relationship between the price level and quantity of aggregate output for which the goods market and the market for money are in equilibrium, called the **aggregate demand curve**. This aggregate demand curve is a central element in the aggregate supply and demand analysis

FIGURE 10   Deriving the Aggregate Demand Curve
The *ISLM* diagram in panel (a) shows that with a given nominal money supply as the price level rises from P_1 to P_2 to P_3, the *LM* curve shifts to the left, and equilibrium output falls. The combinations of the price level and equilibrium output from panel (a) are then plotted in panel (b), and the line connecting them is the aggregate demand curve *AD*.

of Chapter 22, which allows us to explain changes not only in aggregate output but also in the price level.

Deriving the Aggregate Demand Curve

Now that you understand how a change in the price level affects the *LM* curve, we can analyze what happens in the *ISLM* diagram when the price level changes. This exercise is carried out in Figure 10. Panel (a) contains an *ISLM* diagram for a given value of the nominal money supply. Let us first consider a price level of P_1. The *LM* curve at this price level is *LM* (P_1), and its intersection with the *IS* curve is at point 1, where output is Y_1. The equilibrium output level Y_1 that occurs when the price level is P_1 is also plotted in panel (b) as point 1. If the price level rises to P_2, then *in real terms* the money supply has fallen. The effect on the *LM* curve is identical to a decline in the nominal money supply when the price level is fixed: The *LM* curve will shift leftward to *LM* (P_2). The new equilibrium level of output has fallen to Y_2, because planned investment and net exports fall when the interest rate rises. Point 2 in panel (b) plots this level of output for price level P_2. A further increase in the price level to P_3 causes a further decline in the real money supply, leading to a further increase in the interest rate and a further decline in planned investment and net exports, and output declines to Y_3. Point 3 in panel (b) plots this level of output for price level P_3.

The line that connects the three points in panel (b) is the aggregate demand curve *AD*, and it indicates the level of aggregate output consistent with equilibrium in the goods market and the market for money at any given price level. This aggregate demand curve has the usual downward slope, because a higher price level reduces the money supply in real terms, raises interest rates, and lowers the equilibrium level of aggregate output.

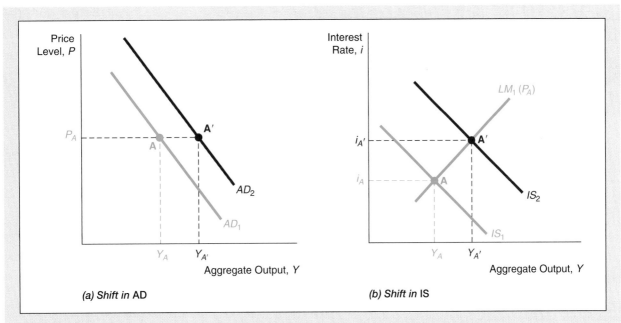

(a) *Shift in* AD	(b) *Shift in* IS

FIGURE 11   **Shift in the Aggregate Demand Curve Caused by a Shift in the *IS* Curve**
Expansionary fiscal policy, a rise in net exports, or more optimistic consumers and firms shift the *IS* curve to the right in panel (b), and at a price level of P_A, equilibrium output rises from Y_A to $Y_{A'}$. This change in equilibrium output is shown as a movement from point A to point A' in panel (a); hence the aggregate demand curve shifts to the right, from AD_1 to AD_2.

Factors That Cause the Aggregate Demand Curve to Shift

ISLM analysis demonstrates how the equilibrium level of aggregate output changes for a given price level. A change in any factor (except a change in the price level) that causes the *IS* or *LM* curve to shift causes the aggregate demand curve to shift. To see how this works, let's first look at what happens to the aggregate demand curve when the *IS* curve shifts.

Shifts in the *IS* Curve   Five factors cause the *IS* curve to shift: changes in autonomous consumer spending, changes in investment spending related to business confidence, changes in government spending, changes in taxes, and autonomous changes in net exports. How changes in these factors lead to a shift in the aggregate demand curve is examined in Figure 11.

Suppose that initially the aggregate demand curve is at AD_1 and there is a rise in, for example, government spending. The *ISLM* diagram in panel (b) shows what then happens to equilibrium output, holding the price level constant at P_A. Initially, equilibrium output is at Y_A at the intersection of IS_1 and LM_1. The rise in government spending (holding the price level constant at P_A) shifts the *IS* curve to the right and raises equilibrium output to $Y_{A'}$. In panel (a), this rise in equilibrium output is shown as a movement from point A to point A', and the aggregate demand curve shifts to the right (to AD_2).

The conclusion from Figure 11 is that ***any factor that shifts the* IS *curve shifts the aggregate demand curve in the same direction***. Therefore, "animal spirits" that encourage a rise in autonomous consumer spending or planned investment spending, a rise in government spending, a fall in taxes, or an autonomous rise in net exports—all of which shift the *IS* curve to the right—will also shift the aggregate demand curve to the

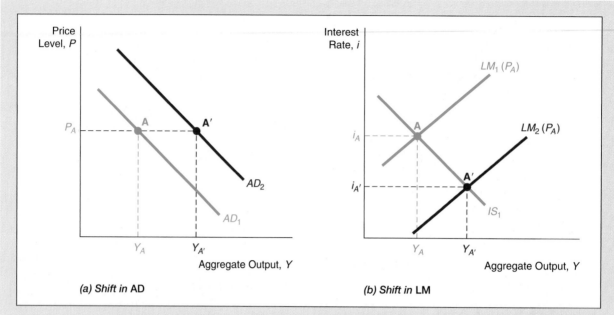

FIGURE 12   **Shift in the Aggregate Demand Curve Caused by a Shift in the *LM* Curve**
A rise in the money supply or a fall in money demand shifts the *LM* curve to the right in panel (b), and at a price level of P_A, equilibrium output rises from Y_A to $Y_{A'}$. This change in equilibrium output is shown as a movement from point A to point A' in panel (a); hence the aggregate demand curve shifts to the right, from AD_1 to AD_2.

right. Conversely, a fall in autonomous consumer spending, a fall in planned investment spending, a fall in government spending, a rise in taxes, or a fall in net exports will cause the aggregate demand curve to shift to the left.

Shifts in the *LM* Curve   Shifts in the *LM* curve are caused by either an autonomous change in money demand (not caused by a change in *P*, *Y*, or *i*) or a change in the money supply. Figure 12 shows how either of these changes leads to a shift in the aggregate demand curve. Again, we are initially at the AD_1 aggregate demand curve, and we look at what happens to the level of equilibrium output when the price level is held constant at P_A. A rise in the money supply shifts the *LM* curve to the right and raises equilibrium output to $Y_{A'}$. This rise in equilibrium output is shown as a movement from point A to point A' in panel (a), and the aggregate demand curve shifts to the right.

Our conclusion from Figure 12 is similar to that of Figure 11: ***Holding the price level constant, any factor that shifts the LM curve shifts the aggregate demand curve in the same direction***. Therefore, a decline in money demand as well as an increase in the money supply, both of which shift the *LM* curve to the right, also shift the aggregate demand curve to the right. The aggregate demand curve will shift to the left, however, if the money supply declines or money demand rises.

You have now derived and analyzed the aggregate demand curve—an essential element in the aggregate demand and supply framework that we examine in Chapter 22. The aggregate demand and supply framework is particularly useful, because it demonstrates how the price level is determined and enables us to examine factors that affect aggregate output when the price level varies.

SUMMARY

1. The IS curve is shifted to the right by a rise in autonomous consumer spending, a rise in planned investment spending related to business confidence, a rise in government spending, a fall in taxes, or an autonomous rise in net exports. A movement in the opposite direction of these five factors will shift the IS curve to the left.

2. The *LM* curve is shifted to the right by a rise in the money supply or an autonomous fall in money demand; it is shifted to the left by a fall in the money supply or an autonomous rise in money demand.

3. A rise in the money supply raises equilibrium output, but lowers the equilibrium interest rate. Expansionary fiscal policy (a rise in government spending or a fall in taxes) raises equilibrium output, but, in contrast to expansionary monetary policy, also raises the interest rate.

4. The less interest-sensitive money demand is, the more effective monetary policy is relative to fiscal policy.

5. The *ISLM* model provides the following conclusion about the conduct of monetary policy: When the *IS* curve is more unstable than the *LM* curve, pursuing a money supply target provides smaller output fluctuations than pursuing an interest-rate target and is preferred; when the *LM* curve is more unstable than the *IS* curve, pursuing an interest-rate target leads to smaller output fluctuations and is preferred.

6. The conclusion from examining what happens in the *ISLM* model from an expansionary monetary or fiscal policy is that although monetary and fiscal policy can affect output in the short run, neither affects output in the long run.

7. The aggregate demand curve tells us the level of aggregate output consistent with equilibrium in the goods market and the market for money for any given price level. It slopes downward because a lower price level creates a higher level of the real money supply, lowers the interest rate, and raises equilibrium output. The aggregate demand curve shifts in the same direction as a shift in the *IS* or *LM* curve; hence it shifts to the right when government spending increases, taxes decrease, "animal spirits" encourage consumer and business spending, autonomous net exports increase, the money supply increases, or money demand decreases.

KEY TERMS

aggregate demand curve, p. 559

complete crowding out, p. 554

long-run monetary neutrality, p. 559

natural rate level of output, p. 557

QUESTIONS AND PROBLEMS

All questions and problems are available in *at* www.myeconlab.com/mishkin.

1. If taxes and government spending rise by equal amounts, what will happen to the position of the *IS* curve? Explain this outcome with a Keynesian cross diagram.

2. What happened to the *IS* curve during the Great Depression when investment spending collapsed? Why?

3. What happens to the position of the *LM* curve if the Fed decides that it will decrease the money supply to fight inflation and if, at the same time, the demand for money falls?

4. "An excess demand for money resulting from a rise in the demand for money can be eliminated only by a rise in the interest rate." Is this statement true, false, or uncertain? Explain your answer.

In Problems 5–15, demonstrate your answers with an **ISLM** *diagram.*

5. In late 1969, the Federal Reserve reduced the money supply while the government raised taxes. What do you think should have happened to interest rates and aggregate output?

6. "The high level of interest rates and the rapidly growing economy during Ronald Reagan's third and fourth years as president can be explained by a tight monetary policy combined with an expansionary fiscal policy." Do you agree with this statement? Why or why not?

7. Suppose that the Federal Reserve wants to keep interest rates from rising when the government sharply increases military spending. How can the Fed do this?

8. Evidence indicates that lately the demand for money has become quite unstable. Why is this finding important to Federal Reserve policymakers?

9. "As the price level rises, the equilibrium level of output determined in the *ISLM* model also rises." Is this statement true, false, or uncertain? Explain your answer.

10. What will happen to the position of the aggregate demand curve if the money supply is reduced when government spending increases?

11. How will an equal rise in government spending and taxes affect the position of the aggregate demand curve?

12. If money demand is unaffected by changes in the interest rate, what effect will a rise in government spending have on the position of the aggregate demand curve?

Using Economic Analysis to Predict the Future

13. Predict what will happen to interest rates and aggregate output if a stock market crash causes autonomous consumer expenditure to fall.

14. Predict what will happen to interest rates and aggregate output when there is an autonomous export boom.

15. If a series of defaults in the bond market make bonds riskier and as a result the demand for money rises, predict what will happen to interest rates and aggregate output.

WEB EXERCISES

1. An excellent way to learn about how changes in various factors affect the *IS* and *LM* curves is to visit www .fgn.unisg.ch/eurmacro/tutor/islm.html. This site, sponsored by the World Bank, allows you to make changes and to observe immediately their impact on the *ISLM* model.
   a. Increase G from 200 to 500. What happens to the interest rate?
   b. Reduce *t* to 0.1. What happens to aggregate out-put *Y*?
   c. Increase M to 450. What happens to the interest rate and aggregate output?

2. Looking at the same site as you used in question 1, www.fgn.unisg.ch/eurmacro/Tutor/islm.html, the exogenous parameters in this simulation are the MPC (c), the sensitivity of money demand to income (k), the sensitivity of money demand to the interest rate (h), and the sensitivity of investment to the interest rate (b). For each of these parameters, explain what happens in the *IS/LM* graph when they are *increased*. What happens to equilibrium output and the equilibrium level of the interest rate?

WEB REFERENCES

ingrimayne.com/econ/optional/ISLM/Limitations.html
A paper discussing limitations of *ISLM* analysis.

faculty.washington.edu/danby/islm/islmindx.htm
An animated explanation of *ISLM*.

 MyEconLab CAN HELP YOU GET A BETTER GRADE

If your exam were tomorrow, would you be ready? For each chapter, MyEconLab Practice Test and Study Plans pinpoint which sections you have mastered and which ones you need to study. That way, you are more efficient with your study time, and you are better prepared for your exams.

To see how it works, turn to page 20 and then go to: www.myeconlab.com/mishkin

22 Aggregate Demand and Supply Analysis

Preview

In earlier chapters, we focused considerable attention on monetary policy, because it touches our everyday lives by affecting the prices of the goods we buy and the quantity of available jobs. In this chapter, we develop a basic tool, aggregate demand and supply analysis, that will enable us to study the effects of monetary policy on output and prices. **Aggregate demand** is the total quantity of an economy's final goods and services demanded at different price levels. **Aggregate supply** is the total quantity of final goods and services that firms in the economy want to sell at different price levels. As with other supply and demand analyses, the actual quantity of output and the price level are determined by equating aggregate demand and aggregate supply.

Aggregate demand and supply analysis will enable us to explore how aggregate output and the price level are determined. (The Following the Financial News box indicates where and how often data on aggregate output and the price level are published.) Not only will the analysis help us interpret recent episodes in the business cycle, but it will also enable us to understand the debates on how economic policy should be conducted.

AGGREGATE DEMAND

The first building block of aggregate supply and demand analysis is the **aggregate demand curve**, which describes the relationship between the quantity of aggregate output demanded and the price level when all other variables are held constant.

Aggregate demand is made up of four component parts: **consumer expenditure**, the total demand for consumer goods and services; **planned investment spending**,[1] the total planned spending by business firms on new machines, factories, and other capital goods, plus planned spending on new homes; **government spending**, spending by all levels of government (federal, state, and local) on goods and services (paper clips, computers, computer programming, missiles, government workers, and so on); and **net exports**, the net foreign spending on domestic goods and services, equal to exports minus imports. Using the symbols C for consumer expenditure, I for planned investment spending, G for government spending, and NX for net exports, we can write the following expression for aggregate demand Y^{ad}:

$$Y^{ad} = C + I + G + NX \qquad (1)$$

---

[1]Recall that economists restrict use of the word *investment* to the purchase of new physical capital, such as a new machine or a new house, that adds to expenditure.

Following the Financial News
Aggregate Output, Unemployment, and the Price Level

Newspapers and Internet sites periodically report data that provide information on the level of aggregate output, unemployment, and the price level in the United States. Here is a list of the relevant data series, their frequency, and when they are published.

Aggregate Output and Unemployment

Real GDP: Quarterly (January–March, April–June, July–September, October–December); published three to four weeks after the end of a quarter.

Industrial production: Monthly. Industrial production is not as comprehensive a measure of aggregate output as real GDP, because it measures only manufacturing output; the estimate for the previous month is reported in the middle of the following month.

Unemployment rate: Monthly; previous month's figure is usually published on the Friday of the first week of the following month.

Price Level

GDP deflator: Quarterly. This comprehensive measure of the price level (described in the appendix to Chapter 1) is published at the same time as the real GDP data.

Consumer price index (CPI): Monthly. The CPI is a measure of the price level for consumers (also described in the appendix to Chapter 1); the value for the previous month is published in the third or fourth week of the following month.

Producer price index (PPI): Monthly. The PPI is a measure of the average level of wholesale prices charged by producers and is published at the same time as industrial production data.

Deriving the Aggregate Demand Curve

Examining the effects of changes in the price level on individual components of aggregate demand is one way to derive the aggregate demand curve. The aggregate demand curve is downward-sloping because a lower price level ($P\downarrow$), holding the nominal quantity of money (M) constant, leads to a larger quantity of money in real terms (in terms of the goods and services that it can buy, $M/P\uparrow$). The larger quantity of money in real terms ($M/P\uparrow$) that results from the lower price level causes interest rates to fall ($i\downarrow$), as suggested in Chapter 5. The resulting lower cost of financing purchases of new physical capital makes investment more profitable and stimulates planned investment spending ($I\uparrow$). Because, as shown in Equation 1, the increase in planned investment spending adds directly to aggregate demand ($Y^{ad}\uparrow$), the lower price level leads to a higher level of the quantity of aggregate output demanded ($P\downarrow \Rightarrow Y^{ad}\uparrow$) and so the aggregate demand curve slopes down as in Figure 1. Schematically, we can write the mechanism just described as follows:

$$P\downarrow \Rightarrow M/P\uparrow \Rightarrow i\downarrow \Rightarrow I\uparrow \Rightarrow Y^{ad}\uparrow$$

Another mechanism that generates a downward-sloping aggregate demand curve operates through international trade. Because a lower price level ($P\downarrow$) leads to a larger quantity of money in real terms ($M/P\uparrow$) and lower interest rates ($i\downarrow$), U.S. dollar assets become less attractive relative to assets denominated in foreign currencies, thereby causing a decline in the demand for dollar assets and a decline in the exchange rate for the dollar, denoted by $E\downarrow$ (as in Chapter 17). The lower value of the dollar, which makes domestic goods cheaper relative to foreign goods, then causes net exports to rise, which in turn increases aggregate demand:

$$P\downarrow \Rightarrow M/P\uparrow \Rightarrow i\downarrow \Rightarrow E\downarrow \Rightarrow NX\uparrow \Rightarrow Y^{ad}\uparrow$$

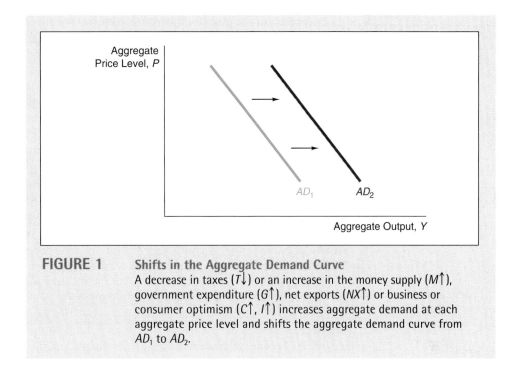

FIGURE 1   **Shifts in the Aggregate Demand Curve**
A decrease in taxes ($T\downarrow$) or an increase in the money supply ($M\uparrow$), government expenditure ($G\uparrow$), net exports ($NX\uparrow$) or business or consumer optimism ($C\uparrow$, $I\uparrow$) increases aggregate demand at each aggregate price level and shifts the aggregate demand curve from AD_1 to AD_2.

The fact that the aggregate demand curve is downward sloping can also be derived from the quantity theory of money analysis in Chapter 19. The equation of exchange, $MV = PY$, indicates that if velocity stays constant, a constant money supply (M) implies that nominal aggregate spending (PY) is also constant. When the price level falls ($P\downarrow$), aggregate demand must necessarily rise ($Y^{ad}\uparrow$) to keep aggregate spending at the same level.

Factors That Shift the Aggregate Demand Curve

The quantity theory analysis directly shows that an increase in the money supply ($M\uparrow$) shifts the aggregate demand curve to the right, because with velocity constant the higher money supply raises nominal aggregate spending ($PY\uparrow$) and hence at a given price level, the quantity of aggregate demand increases ($Y^{ad}\uparrow$). Hence an increase in the quantity of money increases the quantity of aggregate demand at each price level and shifts the aggregate demand curve to the right from AD_1 to AD_2 in Figure 1. The components approach to aggregate demand also indicates that changes in the money supply causes the aggregate demand curve to shift via the two mechanisms shown in the schematics above. For a given price level, a rise in the money supply causes the real money supply to increase ($M/P\uparrow$), which leads to a decline in interest rates ($i\downarrow$), an increase in investment and net exports (I, $NX\uparrow$), and an increase in the quantity of aggregate demand ($Y^{ad}\uparrow$), shifting the aggregate demand curve to the right from AD_1 to AD_2.[2]

---

[2]A complete demonstration of the components approach to the aggregate demand curve is given in Chapters 20 and 21.

In contrast to the quantity theory, the components approach suggests that other factors (manipulation of government spending and taxes, changes in net exports, and changes in consumer and business spending) are also important causes of shifts in the aggregate demand curve. For instance, if the government spends more $(G\uparrow)$ or net exports increase $(NX\uparrow)$, the quantity of aggregate output demanded at each price level rises, and the aggregate demand curve shifts to the right. A decrease in government taxes $(T\downarrow)$ leaves consumers with more income to spend, so consumer expenditure rises $(C\uparrow)$. The quantity of aggregate output demanded at each price level also rises, and the aggregate demand curve shifts to the right. Finally, if consumer and business optimism increases, consumer expenditure and planned investment spending rise $(C\uparrow, I\uparrow)$, again shifting the aggregate demand curve to the right. John Maynard Keynes described waves of optimism and pessimism as "**animal spirits**" and considered them a major factor affecting the aggregate demand curve and an important source of business cycle fluctuations.

Summary   Both the quantity theory and the components approach to aggregate demand agree that the aggregate demand curve slopes downward and shifts in response to changes in the money supply. However, in the quantity theory approach, there is only one important source of movements in the aggregate demand curve—changes in the money supply. The components approach suggests that other factors—fiscal policy, net exports, and "animal spirits"—are equally important sources of shifts in the aggregate demand curve. Our discussion of the quantity theory and the components approach indicates that six factors can shift the aggregate demand curve: the money supply, government spending, taxes, net exports, consumer optimism, and business optimism. The last two ("animal spirits") affect willingness to spend. The possible effect on the aggregate demand curve of these six factors (often referred to as **demand shocks**) is summarized in Table 1.

AGGREGATE SUPPLY

To complete our analysis we need to derive an **aggregate supply curve**, the relationship between the quantity of output supplied and the price level. In the typical supply and demand analysis, we have only one supply curve, but because prices and wages take time to adjust to their long-run level, the aggregate supply curve differs in the short and the long runs. First, we examine the long-run aggregate supply curve. We then derive the short-run aggregate supply curve and see how it shifts over time as the economy moves from the short run to the long run.

Long-Run Aggregate Supply Curve

The amount of output that can be produced in the economy in the long run is determined by the amount of capital in the economy, the amount of labor supplied at full employment, and the available technology. As discussed in Chapter 16, some unemployment cannot be helped because it is either frictional or structural. Thus at full employment, unemployment is not at zero, but is rather at a level above zero at which the demand for labor equals the supply of labor. This **natural rate of unemployment** is where the economy gravitates to in the long run.[3] Many economists believe that the natural rate of unemployment is currently around 5%.

---

[3]A related concept is the *nonaccelerating inflation rate of unemployment* (NAIRU), the rate of unemployment at which there is no tendency for the inflation rate to change.

SUMMARY TABLE 1

Factors That Shift the Aggregate Demand Curve

Factor	Change	Shift in the Aggregate Demand Curve
Money supply, M	↑	
Government spending, G	↑	
Taxes, T	↑	
Net exports, NX	↑	
Consumer optimism, C	↑	
Business optimism, I	↑	

Note: Only increases (↑) in the factors are shown. The effect of decreases in the factors would be the opposite of those indicated in the "Shift" column. Note that the quantity theory approach views the money supply as the only important cause of shifts in the aggregate demand curve.

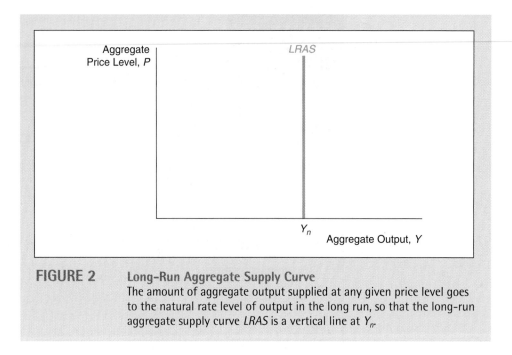

FIGURE 2   Long-Run Aggregate Supply Curve
The amount of aggregate output supplied at any given price level goes to the natural rate level of output in the long run, so that the long-run aggregate supply curve *LRAS* is a vertical line at Y_n.

The level of aggregate output produced at the natural rate of unemployment is called the **natural rate of output**; it is where the economy settles in the long run for any price level. Hence the long-run aggregate supply curve (*LRAS*) is vertical at the natural rate of output, denoted by Y_n, as drawn in Figure 2.

Short-Run Aggregate Supply Curve

Because wages and prices take time to adjust to economic conditions, a process described by saying that wages and prices are *sticky*, the aggregate supply curve (AS_1) in the short run is upward-sloping, as depicted in Figure 3. To understand why the short-run aggregate supply curve is upward-sloping, we have to look at the factors that cause the quantity of output supplied to change. Because the goal of business firms is to maximize profits, the quantity of output supplied is determined by the profit made on each unit of output. If profit rises, more aggregate output will be produced, and the quantity of output supplied will increase; if it falls, less output will be produced, and the quantity of aggregate output supplied will fall.

Profit on a unit of output equals the price for the unit minus the costs of producing it. In the short run, costs of many factors that go into producing goods and services are fixed; wages, for example, are often fixed for periods of time by labor contracts, and raw materials are often bought by firms under long-term contracts that fix the price. Because these costs of production are fixed in the short run, when the overall price level rises, the price for a unit of output will rise relative to the costs of producing it, and the profit per unit will rise. Because the higher price level results in higher profits in the short run, firms increase production, and the quantity of aggregate output supplied rises, resulting in an upward-sloping short-run aggregate supply curve.

Frequent mention of the *short run* in the preceding paragraph hints that the relationship between the price level and aggregate output embodied in the upward-sloping,

FIGURE 3   **Aggregate Supply Curve in the Short Run**
A rise in the costs of production shifts the short-run supply curve leftward from AS_1 to AS_2.

short-run aggregate supply curve (AS_1 in Figure 3) may not remain fixed as time passes. To see what happens over time, we need to understand what makes the aggregate supply curve shift.[4]

Shifts in the Short-Run Aggregate Supply Curve

We have seen that the profit on a unit of output determines the quantity of output supplied. If the cost of producing a unit of output rises, profit on a unit of output falls, and the quantity of output supplied at each price level falls. To learn what this implies for the position of the aggregate supply curve, let's consider what happens at a price level of P_1 when the costs of production increase. Now that firms are earning a lower profit per unit of output, they reduce production at that price level, and the quantity of aggregate output supplied falls from point A to point A'. Applying the same reasoning at price level P_2 indicates that the quantity of aggregate output supplied falls from point B to point B'. What we see is that *the short-run aggregate supply curve shifts to the left when costs of production increase and to the right when costs decrease.*

Factors That Shift the Short-Run Aggregate Supply Curve

The factors that cause the short-run aggregate supply curve to shift are ones that affect the costs of production: (1) tightness of the labor market, (2) expectations of inflation, (3) workers' attempts to push up their real wages, and (4) changes in the production costs that are unrelated to wages (such as energy costs). The first three factors shift the

---

[4]The aggregate supply curve is closely linked to the Phillips curve discussed in Chapter 16. More information on the Phillips and aggregate supply curves can be found in an appendix to this chapter, which is on this book's website at www.myeconlab.com/mishkin.

short-run aggregate supply curve by affecting wage costs; the fourth affects other costs of production.

Tightness of the Labor Market   If the economy is booming and the labor market is tight ($Y > Y_n$), employers may have difficulty hiring qualified workers and may even have a hard time keeping their present employees. Because the demand for labor now exceeds supply in this tight labor market, employers will raise wages to attract needed workers, and the costs of production will rise. The higher costs of production lower the profit per unit of output at each price level, and the short-run aggregate supply curve shifts to the left (see Figure 3).

By contrast, if the economy enters a recession and the labor market is slack ($Y < Y_n$), because the demand for labor is less than the supply, workers who cannot find jobs will be willing to work for lower wages. In addition, employed workers may be willing to make wage concessions to keep their jobs. Therefore, in a slack labor market in which the quantity of labor demanded is less than the quantity supplied, wages and hence costs of production will fall, the profit per unit of output will rise, and the short-run aggregate supply curve will shift to the right.

The effects of tightness of the labor market on the short-run aggregate supply curve can be summarized as follows: **When aggregate output is above the natural rate, the short-run aggregate supply curve shifts to the left; when aggregate output is below the natural rate, the short-run aggregate supply curve shifts to the right**.

Expected Price Level   Workers and firms care about wages in real terms—that is, in terms of the goods and services that wages can buy. When the price level increases, a worker earning the same nominal wage will be able to buy fewer goods and services. A worker who expects the price level to rise will thus demand a higher nominal wage to keep the real wage from falling. For example, if Chuck the Construction Worker expects prices to increase by 5%, he will want a wage increase of at least 5% (more, if he thinks he deserves an increase in real wages). Similarly, if Chuck's employer knows that the houses he is building will rise in value at the same rate as inflation (5%), he will be willing to pay Chuck 5% more. An increase in the expected price level leads to higher wages, which in turn raise the costs of production, lower the profit per unit of output at each price level, and shift the aggregate supply curve to the left (see Figure 3). Therefore, *a rise in the expected price level causes the aggregate supply curve to shift to the left; the greater the expected increase in price level (that is, the higher the expected inflation), the larger the shift*.

Wage Push   Suppose that Chuck and his fellow construction workers decide to strike and succeed in obtaining higher real wages. This wage push will then raise the costs of production, and the aggregate supply curve will shift leftward. *A successful wage push by workers will cause the aggregate supply curve to shift to the left*.

Changes in Production Costs Unrelated to Wages   Changes in technology and in the supply of raw materials (called **supply shocks**) can also shift the aggregate supply curve. A negative supply shock, such as a reduction in the availability of raw materials (like oil), which raises their price, increases production costs and shifts the aggregate supply curve leftward. A positive supply shock, such as unusually good weather that leads to a bountiful harvest and lowers the cost of food, will reduce

SUMMARY TABLE 2

Factors That Shift the Short-Run Aggregate Supply Curve

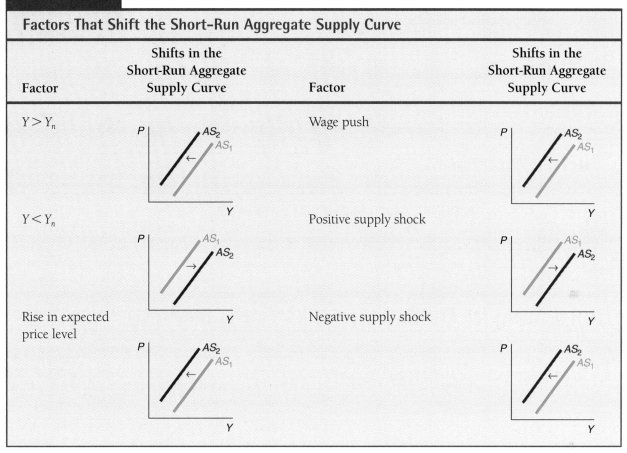

Factor	Shifts in the Short-Run Aggregate Supply Curve	Factor	Shifts in the Short-Run Aggregate Supply Curve
$Y > Y_n$		Wage push	
$Y < Y_n$		Positive supply shock	
Rise in expected price level		Negative supply shock	

production costs and shift the aggregate supply curve rightward. Similarly, the development of a new technology that lowers production costs, perhaps by raising worker productivity, can be considered a positive supply shock that shifts the aggregate supply curve to the right.

The effect on the aggregate supply curve of changes in production costs unrelated to wages (supply shocks) can be summarized as follows: ***A negative supply shock that raises production costs shifts the aggregate supply curve to the left; a positive supply shock that lowers production costs shifts the aggregate supply curve to the right.***[5] As a study aid, factors that shift the short-run aggregate supply curve are listed in Summary Table 2.

---

[5]Developments in the foreign exchange market can also shift the aggregate supply curve by changing domestic production costs. As discussed in more detail in Chapter 17, an increase in the value of the dollar makes foreign goods cheaper in the United States. The decline in prices of foreign goods and hence foreign factors of production lowers U.S. production costs and thus raises the profit per unit of output at each price level in the United States. An increase in the value of the dollar therefore shifts the aggregate supply curve to the right. Conversely, a decline in the value of the dollar, which makes foreign factors of production more expensive, shifts the aggregate supply curve to the left.

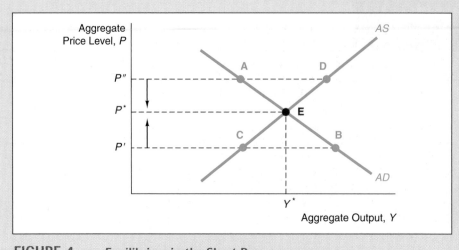

FIGURE 4   **Equilibrium in the Short Run**
Equilibrium occurs at point E at the intersection of the aggregate
demand curve *AD* and the short-run aggregate supply curve *AS*.

EQUILIBRIUM IN AGGREGATE SUPPLY AND DEMAND ANALYSIS

The equilibrium level of aggregate output and the price level will occur at the point where the quantity of aggregate output demanded equals the quantity of aggregate output supplied. However, in the context of aggregate supply and demand analysis, there are two types of equilibrium: short-run and long-run.

Equilibrium in the Short Run

Figure 4 illustrates a short-run equilibrium in which the quantity of aggregate output demanded equals the quantity of output supplied—that is, where the short-run aggregate demand curve *AD* and the aggregate supply curve *AS* intersect at point E. The equilibrium level of aggregate output equals Y^*, and the equilibrium price level equals P^*.

As in our earlier supply and demand analyses, equilibrium is a useful concept only if there is a tendency for the economy to head toward it. We can see that the economy heads toward the equilibrium at point E by first looking at what happens when we are at a price level above the equilibrium price level P^*. If the price level is at P'', the quantity of aggregate output supplied at point D is greater than the quantity of aggregate output demanded at point A. Because people want to sell more goods and services than others want to buy (a condition of *excess supply*), the prices of goods and services will fall, and the aggregate price level will drop, as shown by the downward arrow. This decline in the price level will continue until it has reached its equilibrium level of P^* at point E.

When the price level is below the equilibrium price level, say at P', the quantity of output demanded is greater than the quantity of output supplied. Now the price level will rise, as shown by the upward arrow, because people want to buy more goods than others want to sell (a condition of *excess demand*). This rise in the price level will continue until it has again reached its equilibrium level of P^* at point E.

Equilibrium in the Long Run

Usually in supply and demand analysis, once we find the equilibrium at which the quantity demanded equals the quantity supplied, there is no need for additional discussion. In *aggregate* supply and demand analysis, however, that is not the case. Even when the quantity of aggregate output demanded equals the quantity supplied, forces operate that can cause the equilibrium to move over time if $Y^* \neq Y_n$. To understand why, we must remember that if costs of production change, the aggregate supply curve will shift.

As we saw earlier, the short-run aggregate supply curve will not remain stationary when aggregate output and unemployment differ from their natural rate: When $Y > Y_n$, labor markets are tight, production costs rise at any given price level, and the short-run aggregate supply curve shifts to the left; when $Y < Y_n$, labor markets are slack, production costs fall at any given price level, and the aggregate supply curve shifts to the right. Only when aggregate output and unemployment are at their natural rates is there no pressure from the labor market for wages to rise or fall. Under these conditions, there is no reason for the short-run aggregate supply to shift.

We look at how the short-run equilibrium changes over time in response to two situations: when short-run equilibrium is initially above the natural rate level and when it is initially below the natural rate level.

In panel (a) of Figure 5, the initial equilibrium occurs at point 1, the intersection of the aggregate demand curve *AD* and the initial short-run aggregate supply curve AS_1. Because the level of equilibrium output Y_1 is greater than the natural rate level Y_n, unemployment is less than its natural rate, and excessive tightness exists in the labor market. This tightness drives wages up, raises production costs, and shifts the aggregate supply curve to AS_2. The equilibrium is now at point 2, and output falls to Y_2. Because aggregate output Y_2 is still above the natural rate level, Y_n, wages continue to be driven up, eventually shifting the aggregate supply curve to AS_3. The equilibrium reached at point 3 is on the vertical long-run aggregate supply curve (*LRAS*) at Y_n and is a long-run equilibrium. Because output is at the natural rate level, there is no further pressure on wages to rise and thus no further tendency for the aggregate supply curve to shift.

The movements in panel (a) indicate that the economy will not remain at a level of output higher than the natural rate level because the short-run aggregate supply curve will shift to the left, raise the price level, and cause the economy (equilibrium) to slide upward along the aggregate demand curve until it comes to rest at a point on the long-run aggregate supply curve at the natural rate level of output Y_n.

In panel (b), the initial equilibrium at point 1 is one at which output Y_1 is below the natural rate level. Because unemployment is higher than its natural rate, wages begin to fall, shifting the short-run aggregate supply curve rightward until it comes to rest at AS_3. The economy (equilibrium) slides downward along the aggregate demand curve until it reaches the long-run equilibrium point 3, the intersection of the aggregate demand curve (*AD*) and the long-run aggregate supply curve (*LRAS*) at Y_n. Here, as in panel (a), the economy comes to rest when output has again returned to the natural rate level.

A striking feature of both panels of Figure 5 is that regardless of where output is initially, it returns eventually to the natural rate level. This feature is described by saying that the economy has a **self-correcting mechanism**.

An important issue for policymakers is how rapidly this self-correcting mechanism works. Many economists believe that the self-correcting mechanism takes a long time, so the approach to long-run equilibrium is slow. This view is reflected in Keynes's often quoted remark, "In the long run, we are all dead." These economists view the self-correcting mechanism as slow, because wages are inflexible, particularly

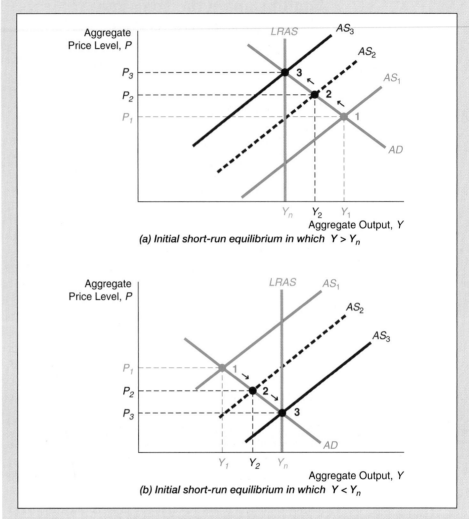

FIGURE 5   Adjustment to Long-Run Equilibrium in Aggregate Supply and Demand Analysis

In both panels, the initial short-run equilibrium is at point 1 at the intersection of AD and AS_1. In panel (a), $Y_1 > Y_n$ so the short-run aggregate supply curve keeps shifting to the left until it reaches AS_3, where output has returned to Y_n. In panel (b), $Y_1 < Y_n$ so the short-run aggregate supply curve keeps shifting to the right until output is again returned to Y_n. Hence in both cases, the economy displays a self-correcting mechanism that returns it to the natural rate level of output.

in the downward direction when unemployment is high. The resulting slow wage and price adjustments mean that the aggregate supply curve does not move quickly to restore the economy to the natural rate of unemployment. Hence when unemployment is high, these economists, many of whom are followers of Keynes and are thus also known as **Keynesians**, are more likely to see the need for active government policy to restore the economy to full employment.

Other economists believe that wages are sufficiently flexible that the wage and price adjustment process is reasonably rapid. As a result of this flexibility, adjustment of the aggregate supply curve to its long-run position and the economy's return to the natural rate levels of output and unemployment will occur quickly. Thus these economists see much less need for active government policy to restore the economy to the natural rate levels of output and unemployment when unemployment is high. Indeed, Milton Friedman and his followers, known as **monetarists**, advocate the use of a rule whereby the money supply or the monetary base grows at a constant rate so as to minimize fluctuations in aggregate demand that might lead to output fluctuations. We will return in Chapter 24 to the debate about whether government policy should react in a discretionary fashion to keep the economy near full employment.

Changes in Equilibrium Caused by Aggregate Demand Shocks

With an understanding of the distinction between the short-run and long-run equilibria, you are now ready to analyze what happens when an economy's aggregate demand curve shifts. Figure 6 depicts the effect of a rightward shift in the aggregate demand curve due to positive demand shocks: an increase in the money supply ($M\uparrow$), an increase in government spending ($G\uparrow$), an increase in net exports ($NX\uparrow$), a decrease in taxes ($T\downarrow$), or an increase in the willingness of consumers and businesses to spend because they become more optimistic ($C\uparrow, I\uparrow$). The figure has been drawn so that the economy initially is in long-run equilibrium at point 1, where the initial aggregate demand curve AD_1 intersects the short-run aggregate supply AS_1 curve at Y_n. When the

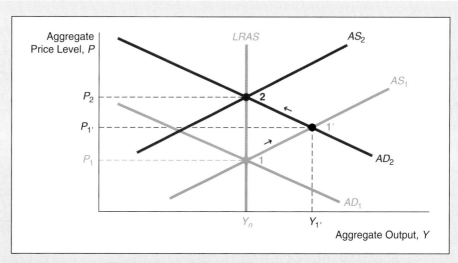

FIGURE 6   **Response of Output and the Price Level to a Shift in the Aggregate Demand Curve**
A shift in the aggregate demand curve from AD_1 to AD_2 moves the economy from point 1 to point 1'. Because $Y_{1'} > Y_n$, the short-run aggregate supply curve begins to shift leftward, eventually reaching AS_2, where output returns to Y_n and the price level has risen to P_2.

aggregate demand curve shifts rightward to AD_2, the economy moves to point 1′, and both output and the price level rise. However, the economy will not remain at point 1′ in the long run, because output at $Y_{1'}$ is above the natural rate level. Wages will rise, increasing the cost of production at all price levels, and the short-run aggregate supply curve will eventually shift leftward to AS_2, where it finally comes to rest. The economy (equilibrium) thus slides up the aggregate demand curve from point 1′ to point 2, which is the point of long-run equilibrium at the intersection of AD_2 and the long-run aggregate supply curve (*LRAS*) at Y_n. *Although the initial short-run effect of the rightward shift in the aggregate demand curve is a rise in both the price level and output, the ultimate long-run effect is only a rise in the price level*.

Changes in Equilibrium Caused by Aggregate Supply Shocks

Our understanding of the distinction between short-run and long-run equilibria allows us to analyze what happens when aggregate supply shocks shift the short-run aggregate supply curve. Suppose that the economy is initially at the natural rate level of output at point 1 when the short-run aggregate supply curve shifts from AS_1 to AS_2 in Figure 7 because of a negative supply shock (a sharp rise in energy prices, for example). The economy will move from point 1 to point 2, where the price level rises but aggregate output *falls*. A situation of a rising price level but a falling level of aggregate output, as pictured in Figure 7, has been labeled *stagflation* (a combination of words *stagnation* and *inflation*). At point 2, output is below the natural rate level, so wages fall and shift the short-run aggregate supply curve back to where it was initially at AS_1. The result is that the economy (equilibrium) slides down the aggregate demand curve AD_1 (assuming that the aggregate demand curve remains in the same position) and returns to the long-run equilibrium at point 1. *Although a leftward shift in the short-run aggregate*

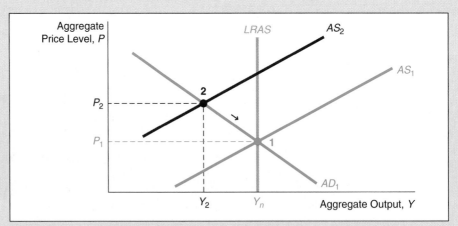

FIGURE 7   **Response of Output and the Price Level to a Shift in Short–Run Aggregate Supply**
A shift in the short-run aggregate supply curve from AS_1 to AS_2 moves the economy from point 1 to point 2. Because $Y_2 < Y_n$, the short-run aggregate supply curve begins to shift back to the right, eventually returning to AS_1, where the economy is again at point 1.

supply curve initially raises the price level and lowers output, the ultimate effect is that output and price level are unchanged (holding the aggregate demand curve constant).

Shifts in the Long-Run Aggregate Supply Curve: Real Business Cycle Theory and Hysteresis

To this point, we have assumed that the natural rate level of output Y_n and hence the long-run aggregate supply curve are given. However, over time, the natural rate level of output increases as a result of economic growth. If the productive capacity of the economy is growing at a steady rate of 3% per year, for example, every year Y_n will grow by 3% and the long-run aggregate supply curve at Y_n will shift to the right by 3%. To simplify the analysis when Y_n grows at a steady rate, Y_n and the long-run aggregate supply curve are drawn as fixed in the aggregate demand and supply diagrams. Keep in mind, however, that the level of aggregate output pictured in these diagrams is actually best thought of as the level of aggregate output relative to its normal rate of growth (trend).

The usual assumption when conducting aggregate demand and supply analysis is that shifts in either the aggregate demand curve or the aggregate supply curve have no effect on the natural rate level of output (which grows at a steady rate). Movements of aggregate output around the Y_n level in the diagram then describe short-run (business cycle) fluctuations in aggregate output. However, some economists take issue with the assumption that Y_n is unaffected by aggregate demand and supply shocks.

One group, led by Edward Prescott of the University of Minnesota, has developed a theory of aggregate economic fluctuations called **real business cycle theory**, in which aggregate supply (real) shocks do affect the natural rate level of output Y_n. This theory views shocks to tastes (workers' willingness to work, for example) and technology (productivity) as the major driving forces behind short-run fluctuations in the business cycle, because these shocks lead to substantial short-run fluctuations in Y_n. Shifts in the aggregate demand curve, perhaps as a result of changes in monetary policy, by contrast are not viewed as being particularly important to aggregate output fluctuations. Because real business cycle theory views most business cycle fluctuations as resulting from fluctuations in the natural rate level of output, it does not see much need for activist policy to eliminate high unemployment. Real business cycle theory is highly controversial and is the subject of intensive research.[6]

Another group of economists disagrees with the assumption that the natural rate level of output Y_n is always at the full employment level and is unaffected by aggregate demand shocks. These economists contend that the natural rate level of unemployment and output are subject to **hysteresis**, a departure from full employment levels as a result of past high unemployment.[7] When unemployment rises because of a reduction of aggregate demand that shifts the *AD* curve inward, the natural rate of unemployment is viewed as rising above the full employment level. This could occur because the unemployed become discouraged and fail to look hard for work or because employers

[6]See Charles Plosser, "Understanding Real Business Cycles," *Journal of Economic Perspectives* (1989): 51–77, for a nontechnical discussion of real business cycle theory.

[7]For a further discussion of hysteresis, see Olivier Blanchard and Lawrence Summers, "Hysteresis in the European Unemployment Problem," *NBER Macroeconomics Annual*, 1986, 1, ed. Stanley Fischer (Cambridge, MA.: MIT Press, 1986), pp. 15–78.

may be reluctant to hire workers who have been unemployed for a long time, seeing it as a signal that the worker is undesirable. The outcome is that the natural rate of unemployment shifts upward after unemployment has become high, and Y_n falls below the full employment level. In this situation, the self-correcting mechanism will be able to return the economy only to the natural rate levels of output and unemployment, not to the full employment level. Only with expansionary policy to shift the aggregate demand curve to the right and raise aggregate output can the natural rate of unemployment be lowered (Y_n raised) to the full employment level. Proponents of hysteresis are thus more likely to promote activist, expansionary policies to restore the economy to full employment.

Conclusions

Aggregate demand and supply analysis yields the following conclusions (under the usual assumption that the natural rate level of output is unaffected by aggregate demand and supply shocks):

1. A shift in the aggregate demand curve—which can be caused by changes in monetary policy (the money supply), fiscal policy (government spending or taxes), international trade (net exports), or "animal spirits" (business and consumer optimism)—affects output only in the short run and has no effect in the long run. Furthermore, the initial change in the price level is less than is achieved in the long run, when the aggregate supply curve has fully adjusted.

2. A shift in the aggregate supply curve—which can be caused by changes in expected inflation, workers' attempts to push up real wages, or a supply shock—affects output and prices only in the short run and has no effect in the long run (holding the aggregate demand curve constant).

3. The economy has a self-correcting mechanism, which will return it to the natural rate levels of unemployment and aggregate output over time.

APPLICATION ✦ Explaining Past Business Cycle Episodes

Aggregate supply and demand analysis is an extremely useful tool for analyzing aggregate economic activity; we will apply it to several business cycle episodes. To simplify our analysis, we always assume in all five examples that aggregate output is initially at the natural rate level.

Vietnam War Buildup, 1964–1970

America's involvement in Vietnam began to escalate in the early 1960s, and after 1964, the United States was fighting a full-scale war. Beginning in 1965, the resulting increases in military expenditure raised government spending, while at the same time the Federal Reserve increased the rate of money growth in an attempt to keep interest rates from rising. What does aggregate supply and demand analysis suggest should have happened to aggregate output and the price level as a result of the Vietnam War buildup?

The rise in government spending and the higher rate of money growth would shift the aggregate demand curve to the right (shown in Figure 6). As a result, aggregate output would rise, unemployment would fall, and the price level would rise. Table 3 demonstrates that this is exactly what happened: The unemployment rate fell steadily

TABLE 3

Unemployment and Inflation During the Vietnam War Buildup, 1964–1970

Year	Unemployment Rate (%)	Inflation (Year to Year) (%)
1964	5.0	1.3
1965	4.4	1.6
1966	3.7	2.9
1967	3.7	3.1
1968	3.5	4.2
1969	3.4	5.5
1970	4.8	5.7

Source: Economic Report of the President.

from 1964 to 1969, remaining well below what economists now think was the natural rate of unemployment during that period (around 5%), and inflation began to rise. As Figure 6 predicts, unemployment would eventually begin to return to the natural rate level because of the economy's self-correcting mechanism. This is exactly what we saw occurring in 1970, when the inflation rate rose even higher and unemployment increased.

Negative Supply Shocks, 1973–1975 and 1978–1980

In 1973, the U.S. economy was hit by a series of negative supply shocks. As a result of the oil embargo stemming from the Arab–Israeli war of 1973, the Organization of Petroleum Exporting Countries (OPEC) was able to engineer a quadrupling of oil prices by restricting oil production. In addition, a series of crop failures throughout the world led to a sharp increase in food prices. Another factor was the termination of U.S. wage and price controls in 1973 and 1974, which led to a push by workers to obtain wage increases that had been prevented by the controls. The triple thrust of these events caused the aggregate supply curve to shift sharply leftward, and as the aggregate demand and supply diagram in Figure 7 predicts, both the price level and unemployment began to rise dramatically (see Table 4).

TABLE 4

Unemployment and Inflation During the Negative Supply Shocks Periods, 1973–1975 and 1978–1980

Year	Unemployment Rate (%)	Inflation (Year to Year) (%)	Year	Unemployment Rate (%)	Inflation (Year to Year) (%)
1973	4.8	6.2	1978	6.0	7.6
1974	5.5	11.0	1979	5.8	11.3
1975	8.3	9.1	1980	7.0	13.5

Source: Economic Report of the President.

TABLE 5		
Unemployment and Inflation During the Favorable Supply Shocks Period, 1995–1999		
Year	Unemployment Rate (%)	Inflation (Year to Year) (%)
1995	5.6	2.8
1996	5.4	3.0
1997	4.9	2.3
1998	4.5	1.6
1999	4.2	2.2

Source: Economic Report of the President.

The 1978–1980 period was almost an exact replay of the 1973–1975 period. By 1978, the economy had just about fully recovered from the 1973–1975 supply shocks, when poor harvests and a doubling of oil prices (as a result of the overthrow of the Shah of Iran) again led to another sharp leftward shift of the aggregate supply curve. The pattern predicted by Figure 7 played itself out again—inflation and unemployment both shot upward (see Table 4).

Favorable Supply Shocks, 1995–1999

In February 1994, the Federal Reserve began to raise interest rates, because it believed the economy would be reaching the natural rate of output and unemployment in 1995 and might become overheated thereafter. As we can see in Table 5, however, the economy continued to grow rapidly, with unemployment falling to below 5%, well below what many economists believed to be the natural rate level, and yet inflation continued to fall, declining to around 2%. Can aggregate demand and supply analysis explain what happened?

The answer is yes. Two favorable supply shocks hit the economy in the late 1990s. First, changes in the health care industry, such as the emergence of health maintenance organizations (HMOs), reduced medical care costs substantially relative to other goods and services. Second, the computer revolution finally began to have a favorable impact on productivity, raising the potential growth rate of the economy (which journalists dubbed the "new economy"). The outcome was a rightward shift in the aggregate supply curve, producing the opposite result depicted in Figure 7: Aggregate output rose, and unemployment fell, while inflation also declined.

Negative Demand Shocks, 2001–2004

In 2000, the U.S. economy was experiencing a business cycle boom when it was hit by a series of negative shocks to aggregate demand. First, the "tech bubble" burst in March 2000 and the stock market fell sharply. Second, the September 11, 2001, terrorist attacks weakened both consumer and business confidence. Third, the Enron bankruptcy in late 2001 and other corporate accounting scandals in 2002 revealed that corporate financial data were not to be trusted. The result was that interest rates on

TABLE 6

Unemployment and Inflation During the Negative Demand Shocks Period, 2000–2004

Year	Unemployment Rate (%)	Inflation (Year to Year) (%)
2000	4.0	3.4
2001	4.7	2.8
2002	5.8	1.6
2003	6.0	2.3
2004	5.5	2.7

Source: *Economic Report of the President.*

corporate bonds rose because their riskiness increased (see Chapter 6), making it more expensive for corporations to finance their investments.

All of these shocks decreased household and business spending, causing a drop in aggregate demand and a shift of the aggregate demand curve to the left. The situation was exactly the opposite to that shown in Figure 6, and our aggregate demand and supply analysis predicts that unemployment would rise and inflation would fall. As we can see in Table 6, this prediction is what came to pass. Unemployment, which had been at 4% in 2000, rose to 6% in 2003, while the annual rate of inflation fell from 3.4% to 1.6%. By 2004, the self-correcting mechanism feature of aggregate demand and supply analysis began to come into play, with the unemployment rate dropping back to 5.5%.

The Perfect Storm of 2007–2008: Negative Supply Shocks and the Subprime Financial Crisis

Higher demand for oil from rapidly growing developing countries like China and India and slowing of production in places like Mexico, Russia, and Nigeria drove up oil prices sharply from around the $60 per barrel level at the beginning of 2007. By the end of the year, oil prices had risen to $100 per barrel and reached a peak of over $140 in July of 2008. the run up of oil prices along with other commodity prices caused the aggregate supply curve to shift sharply leftward. As the aggregate demand and supply diagram in Figure 7 indicates, the result was rises in both unemployment and inflation.

If this supply shock were not bad enough, the subprime financial crisis hit the economy starting in August of 2007, reaching a more virulent phase in the fall of 2008. As discussed in Chapter 9, the subprime financial crisis caused a contraction in both household and business spending leading to a drop in aggregate demand and a shift of the aggregate demand curve to the left, the exact opposite of the situation depicted in Figure 6. Aggregate demand and supply analysis indicates that this would lead to a rise in unemployment, with some weakening of inflationary pressure. As our aggregate demand and supply analysis predicts, and as Table 7 shows, the result of this perfect storm of negative shocks was a recession starting in December of 2007, with unemployment rising from the 4.6% level in 2006 and 2007 to 5.5% in June 2008 and

TABLE 7		
Unemployment and Inflation During the Perfect Storm of 2007–2008		
Year	**Unemployment Rate (%)**	**Inflation (Year to Year) (%)**
2006	4.6	2.5
2007	4.6	4.1
2008, June	5.5	5.0
2008, Dec.	7.2	0.1

Source: Economic Report of the President.

to 7.2% in December. Also, as the aggregate demand and supply analysis predicts, inflation accelerated from 2.5% in 2006 to 5.0% in June 2008. With the increase in the unemployment rate and the sharp decline of oil and other commodity prices after the mid year, inflation fell rapidly to 0.1% in December 2008.

SUMMARY

1. The aggregate demand curve indicates the quantity of aggregate output demanded at each price level, and it is downward-sloping. The primary sources of shifts in the aggregate demand curve are changes in the money supply, fiscal policy (government spending and taxes), net exports, and the willingness of consumers and businesses to spend ("animal spirits").

2. The long-run aggregate supply curve is vertical at the natural rate level of output. The short-run aggregate supply curve slopes upward, because a rise in the price level raises the profit earned on each unit of production, and the quantity of output supplied rises. Four factors can cause the aggregate supply curve to shift: tightness of the labor market as represented by

unemployment relative to the natural rate, expectations of inflation, workers' attempts to push up their real wages, and supply shocks unrelated to wages that affect production costs.

3. Equilibrium in the short run occurs at the point where the aggregate demand curve intersects the short-run aggregate supply curve. Although this is where the economy heads temporarily, it has a self-correcting mechanism, which leads it to settle permanently at the long-run equilibrium where aggregate output is at its natural rate level. Shifts in either the aggregate demand or the short-run aggregate supply curve can produce changes in aggregate output and the price level in the short run.

KEY TERMS

aggregate demand, p. 565

aggregate demand curve, p. 565

aggregate supply, p. 565

aggregate supply curve, p. 568

"animal spirits," p. 568

consumer expenditure, p. 565

demand shocks, p. 568

government spending, p. 565

hysteresis, p. 579

Keynesians, p. 576

monetarists, p. 577

natural rate of output, p. 570

natural rate of unemployment, p. 568

net exports, p. 565

planned investment spending, p. 565

real business cycle theory, p. 579

self-correcting mechanism, p. 575

supply shocks, p. 572

QUESTIONS AND PROBLEMS

All questions and problems are available in ⓧmyeconlab *at* www.myeconlab.com/mishkin.

1. If exports fall while imports rise, what happens to the aggregate demand curve?

2. If government expenditure goes down while taxes are raised to balance the budget, what happens to the aggregate demand curve?

3. Suppose that government spending is raised at the same time that the money supply is lowered. What will happen to the position of the aggregate demand curve?

4. Why does the aggregate demand curve shift when "animal spirits" change?

5. If the dollar increases in value relative to foreign currencies so that foreign goods become cheaper in the United States, what will happen to the position of the short-run aggregate supply curve? The aggregate demand curve?

6. "Profit-maximizing behavior on the part of firms explains why the short-run aggregate supply curve is upward-sloping." Is this statement true, false, or uncertain? Explain your answer.

7. If huge budget deficits cause the public to think that there will be higher inflation in the future, what is likely to happen to the short-run aggregate supply curve when budget deficits rise?

8. If a pill were invented that made workers twice as productive but their wages did not change, what would happen to the position of the short-run aggregate supply curve?

9. When aggregate output is below the natural rate level, what will happen to the price level over time if the aggregate demand curve remains unchanged? Why?

10. Show how aggregate demand and supply analysis can explain why both aggregate output and the price level fell sharply when investment spending collapsed during the Great Depression.

11. "An important difference between Keynesians and monetarists rests on how long they think the long run actually is." Is this statement true, false, or uncertain? Explain your answer.

Using Economic Analysis to Predict the Future

12. Predict what will happen to aggregate output and the price level if the Federal Reserve increases the money supply at the same time that Congress implements an income tax cut.

13. Suppose that the public believes that a newly announced anti-inflation program will work and so lowers its expectations of future inflation. What will happen to aggregate output and the price level in the short run?

14. Proposals have come before the U.S. Congress that advocate the implementation of a national sales tax. Predict the effect of such a tax on both the aggregate supply and demand curves and on aggregate output and the price level.

15. When there is a decline in the value of the dollar, some experts expect it to lead to a dramatic improvement in the ability of American firms to compete abroad. Predict what would happen to output and the price level in the United States as a result.

WEB EXERCISES

1. As this book went to press, the United States was in a recession with an increasing unemployment rate. Go to research.stlouisfed.org/fred2/categories/12 and click on the Series ID link "UNRATE" (Civilian Unemployment Rate). What has happened to the unemployment rate since the last reported figure in Table 7?

2. In the beginning of 2009, the Federal Open Market Committee warned in their statement dated January 28, 2009 that ". . . the Committee sees some risk that

inflation could persist for a time below rates that best foster economic growth and price stability in the longer term." Go to research.stlouisfed.org/fred2/categories/9 and click on the Series ID link "CPIAUCSL" (Consumer Price Index for All Urban Consumers: All Items-SA). Then click on the link "% Chg. From Yr. Ago." What has happened to the inflation rate since the last reported figure in Table 7?

WEB REFERENCES

www.bls.gov

The home page of the Bureau of Labor Statistics lists information on unemployment and price levels.

www.census.gov/compendia/statab

Statistics on the U.S. economy in an easy-to-understand format.

www.research.stlouisfed.org/fred2/

A database of U.S. economic data hosted by the Federal Reserve Bank of St. Louis.

 MyEconLab CAN HELP YOU GET A BETTER GRADE

If your exam were tomorrow, would you be ready? For each chapter, MyEconLab Practice Test and Study Plans pinpoint which sections you have mastered and which ones you need to study. That way, you are more efficient with your study time, and you are better prepared for your exams.

To see how it works, turn to page 20 and then go to: www.myeconlab.com/mishkin

23 Transmission Mechanisms of Monetary Policy: The Evidence

Preview

Since 1980, the U.S. economy has been on a roller coaster, with output, unemployment, and inflation undergoing drastic fluctuations. At the start of the 1980s, inflation was running at double-digit levels, and the recession of 1980 was followed by one of the shortest economic expansions on record. After a year, the economy plunged into the 1981–1982 recession, the most severe economic contraction in the postwar era—the unemployment rate climbed to over 10%, and only then did the inflation rate begin to come down to below the 5% level. The 1981–1982 recession was then followed by a long economic expansion that reduced the unemployment rate to below 6% in the 1987–1990 period. With Iraq's invasion of Kuwait and a rise in oil prices in the second half of 1990, the economy again plunged into recession. Subsequent growth in the economy was sluggish at first but eventually sped up, lowering the unemployment rate to below 5% in the late 1990s. In March 2001, the economy slipped into recession, with the unemployment rate climbing to around 6%. By 2007, a recovery brought the unemployment rate below 5%, but with the onset of the subprime financial crisis, the economy entered a recession in December of 2007 and the unemployment rate began to rise again. In light of large fluctuations in aggregate output (reflected in the unemployment rate) and inflation, and the economic instability that accompanies them, policymakers face the following dilemma: What policy or policies, if any, should be implemented to reduce fluctuations in output and inflation in the future?

To answer this question, monetary policymakers must have an accurate assessment of the timing and effect of their policies on the economy. To make this assessment, they need to understand the mechanisms through which monetary policy affects the economy. In this chapter, we examine empirical evidence on the effect of monetary policy on economic activity. We first look at a framework for evaluating empirical evidence and then use this framework to understand why there are still deep disagreements on the importance of monetary policy to the economy. We then go on to examine the transmission mechanisms of monetary policy and evaluate the empirical evidence on them to better understand the role that monetary policy plays in the economy. We will see that these monetary transmission mechanisms emphasize the link between the financial system (which we studied in the first three parts of this book) and monetary theory, the subject of this part.

FRAMEWORK FOR EVALUATING EMPIRICAL EVIDENCE

To develop a framework for understanding how to evaluate empirical evidence, we need to recognize that there are two basic types of empirical evidence in economics and other scientific disciplines: **Structural model evidence** examines whether one variable affects

587

another by using data to build a model that explains the channels through which this variable affects the other; **reduced-form evidence** examines whether one variable has an effect on another simply by looking directly at the relationship between the two variables.

Suppose that you were interested in whether drinking coffee leads to heart disease. Structural model evidence would involve developing a model that analyzed data on how coffee is metabolized by the human body, how it affects the operation of the heart, and how its effects on the heart lead to heart attacks. Reduced-form evidence would involve looking directly at whether coffee drinkers tend to experience heart attacks more frequently than non–coffee drinkers.

How you look at evidence—whether you focus on structural model evidence or reduced-form evidence—can lead to different conclusions. This is particularly true for the debate on the importance of monetary policy to economic fluctuations.

Structural Model Evidence

The components analysis of aggregate demand discussed in Chapter 22 is specific about the channels through which the money supply affects economic activity (called the **transmission mechanisms of monetary policy**). This approach examines the effect of changes in the money supply on economic activity by building a **structural model**, a description of how the economy operates using a collection of equations that describe the behavior of firms and consumers in many sectors of the economy. These equations then show the channels through which monetary and fiscal policy affect aggregate output and spending. A structural model might have behavioral equations that describe the workings of monetary policy with the following schematic diagram:

$$M \longrightarrow \boxed{i \longrightarrow I \longrightarrow} \longrightarrow Y$$

The model describes the transmission mechanism of monetary policy as follows: The change in the money supply M affects interest rates i, which in turn affect investment spending I, which in turn affects aggregate output or aggregate spending Y. Structural model evidence on the relationship between M and Y looks at empirical evidence on the specific channels of monetary influence, such as the link between interest rates and investment spending.

Reduced-Form Evidence

The quantity theory approach to aggregate demand does not describe specific ways in which the money supply affects aggregate spending. Instead, it suggests that the effect of money on economic activity should be examined by looking at whether movements in Y are tightly linked to (have a high correlation with) movements in M. Reduced-form evidence analyzes the effect of changes in M on Y as if the economy were a black box whose workings cannot be seen. The reduced-form way of looking at the evidence can be represented by the following schematic diagram, in which the economy is drawn as a black box with a question mark:

Advantages and Disadvantages of Structural Model Evidence

The structural model approach has the advantage of giving us an understanding of how the economy works. If the structure is correct—if it contains all the transmission mechanisms and channels through which monetary policy can affect economic activity—the structural model approach has three major advantages over the reduced-form approach.

1. Because we can evaluate each transmission mechanism separately to see whether it is plausible, we can gather more evidence on whether monetary policy has an important effect on economic activity. If we find that monetary policy significantly affects economic activity, for example, we will have more confidence that changes in monetary policy actually cause the changes in economic activity; that is, we will have more confidence on the direction of causation between M and Y.

2. Knowing how changes in monetary policy affect economic activity may help us predict the effect of changes in M on Y more accurately. For example, expansions in the money supply might be found to be less effective when interest rates are low. Then, when interest rates are higher, we would be able to predict that an expansion in the money supply would have a larger impact on Y than would otherwise be the case.

3. By knowing how the economy operates, we may be able to predict how institutional changes in the economy might affect the link between changes in M and Y. For instance, before 1980, when Regulation Q was still in effect, restrictions on interest payments on savings deposits meant that the average consumer would not earn more on savings when interest rates rose. Since the termination of Regulation Q, the average consumer now earns more on savings when interest rates rise. If we understand how changes in the interest rates paid on savings affect consumer spending, we might be able to say that a change in monetary policy, which affects interest rates, will have a different effect today than it would have had before 1980. Because of the rapid pace of financial innovation, the advantage of being able to predict how institutional changes affect the link between changes in M and Y may be more important now than in the past.

These three advantages of the structural model approach suggest that it is better than the reduced-form approach *if we know the correct structure of the model.* Put another way, structural model evidence is only as good as the structural model it is based on; it is best only if all the transmission mechanisms are fully understood. This is a big *if*, as failing to include one or two relevant transmission mechanisms for monetary policy in the structural model might result in a serious misjudgment about the impact of changes in M on Y.

However, structural models may ignore the transmission mechanisms for monetary policy that are most important. For example, if the most important monetary transmission mechanisms involve consumer spending rather than investment spending, the structural model (such as the $M\uparrow \Rightarrow i\downarrow \Rightarrow I\uparrow \Rightarrow Y\uparrow$ model we used earlier), which focuses on investment spending for its monetary transmission mechanism, may underestimate the importance of an increase in the money supply to economic activity.

Advantages and Disadvantages of Reduced-Form Evidence

The main advantage of reduced-form evidence over structural model evidence is that no restrictions are imposed on the way monetary policy affects the economy. If we are not sure that we know what all the monetary transmission mechanisms are, we may be more likely to spot the full effect of changes in M on Y by looking at whether movements in Y correlate highly with movements in M.

FYI   **Perils of Reverse Causation: A Russian Folk Tale**

A Russian folk tale illustrates the problems that can arise from reverse causation. As the story goes, there once was a severe epidemic in the Russian countryside and many doctors were sent to the towns where the epidemic was at its worst. The peasants in the towns noticed that wherever doctors went, many people were dying. So to reduce the death rate, they killed all the doctors.

Were the peasants better off? Clearly not.

The most notable objection to reduced-form evidence is that it may misleadingly suggest that changes in M cause changes in Y when that is not the case. A basic principle applicable to all scientific disciplines, including economics, states that **correlation does not necessarily imply causation**. That movement of one variable is linked to another doesn't necessarily mean that one variable *causes* the other.

Suppose, for example, you notice that wherever criminal activity abounds, more police patrol the street. Should you conclude from this evidence that police patrols cause criminal activity and recommend pulling police off the street to lower the crime rate? The answer is clearly no, because police patrols do not cause criminal activity; criminal activity causes police patrols. This situation is called **reverse causation** and can produce misleading conclusions when interpreting correlations (see the FYI box, "Perils of Reverse Causation: A Russian Folk Tale").

The reverse causation problem may be present when examining the link between changes in money and aggregate output or spending. Our discussion of the conduct of monetary policy in Chapter 16 suggested that when the Federal Reserve has an interest-rate target, higher output may lead to a higher money supply. If most of the correlation between M and Y occurs because of the Fed's interest-rate target, controlling the money supply will not help control aggregate output, because it is actually changes in Y that are causing changes in M, rather than the other way around.

Another facet of the correlation–causation question is that an outside factor, yet unknown, could be the driving force behind two variables that move together. Coffee drinking might be associated with heart disease not because coffee drinking causes heart attacks but because coffee drinkers tend to be people who are under a lot of stress and the stress causes heart attacks. Getting people to stop drinking coffee, then, would not lower the incidence of heart disease. Similarly, if there is an unknown outside factor that causes M and Y to move together, controlling M will not improve control of Y (see the FYI box, "Perils of Ignoring an Outside Driving Factor: How to Lose a Presidential Election").

Conclusions

No clear-cut case can be made that reduced-form evidence is preferable to structural model evidence, or vice versa. The structural model approach offers an understanding of how the economy works. If the structure is correct, it predicts the effect of monetary policy more accurately, allows predictions of the effect of monetary policy when institutions change, and provides more confidence in the direction of causation between M and Y. If the structure of the model is not correctly specified because it leaves out important transmission mechanisms of monetary policy, it could be very misleading.

FYI   Perils of Ignoring an Outside Driving Factor: How to Lose a Presidential Election

Ever since Muncie, Indiana, was dubbed "Middletown" by two sociology studies over half a century ago, it has produced a vote for president that closely mirrors the national vote; that is, in every election, there has been a very high correlation between Muncie's vote and the national vote. Noticing this, a political adviser to a presidential candidate recommends that the candidate's election will be assured if *all* the candidate's campaign funds are spent in Muncie. Should the presidential candidate promote or fire this adviser? Why?

It is very unlikely that the vote in a small town like Muncie drives the vote in a national election. Rather,

it is more likely that national preferences are a third driving factor that determines the vote in Muncie and also determines the vote in the national election. Changing the vote in Muncie will thus only break the relationship between that town's vote and national preferences and will have almost no impact on the election. Spending all the campaign money on this town will therefore be a waste of money.

The presidential candidate should definitely fire the adviser.

The reduced-form approach does not restrict the way monetary policy affects the economy and may be more likely to spot the full effect of changes in M on Y. However, reduced-form evidence cannot rule out reverse causation, whereby changes in output cause changes in money, or the possibility that an outside factor drives changes in both output and money. A high correlation of money and output might then be misleading, because controlling the money supply would not help control the level of output.

Armed with the framework to evaluate empirical evidence we have outlined here, we can now use it to evaluate the empirical debate on the importance of monetary policy to economic fluctuations.

APPLICATION   ✦   The Debate on the Importance of Monetary Policy to Economic Fluctuations

We can apply our understanding of the advantages and disadvantages of structural model versus reduced-form evidence to a debate that has been going on for more than 70 years: How important is monetary policy to economic fluctuations? The followers of Milton Friedman, known as *monetarists*, tended to focus on reduced-form evidence and found that changes in the money supply are very important to economic fluctuations. Early followers of John Maynard Keynes, known as *Keynesians*, focused on structural model evidence based on the components approach to determination of aggregate demand, which was less likely to find that monetary policy is important. We evaluate the evidence that monetarists and Keynesians brought to bear on the importance of monetary policy using the analysis we developed in the previous section.

Early Keynesian Evidence on the Importance of Money

Although Keynes proposed his theory for analyzing aggregate economic activity in 1936, his views reached their peak of popularity among economists in the 1950s and early 1960s, when the majority of economists had accepted his framework. Although most Keynesians currently believe that monetary policy has important effects on economic activity, the early Keynesians of the 1950s and early 1960s characteristically held the view that *monetary policy does not matter at all* to movements in aggregate output and hence to the business cycle.

Their belief in the ineffectiveness of monetary policy stemmed from three pieces of structural model evidence:

1. During the Great Depression, interest rates on U.S. Treasury securities fell to extremely low levels; the three-month Treasury bill rate, for example, declined to below 1%. Early Keynesians believed monetary policy affected aggregate demand solely through its effect on nominal interest rates, which in turn affected investment spending; they believed that low interest rates during the Great Depression indicated that monetary policy was easy (expansionary) because it encouraged investment spending and so could not have played a contractionary role during this period. Because monetary policy was not capable of explaining why the worst economic contraction in U.S. history had taken place, early Keynesians concluded that changes in the money supply have no effect on aggregate output—in other words, money doesn't matter.

2. Early empirical studies found no linkage between movements in nominal interest rates and investment spending. Because early Keynesians saw this link as the channel through which changes in the money supply affect aggregate demand, finding that the link was weak also led them to the conclusion that changes in the money supply have no effect on aggregate output.

3. Surveys of business people revealed that their decisions on how much to invest in new physical capital were not influenced by market interest rates. This evidence further confirmed that the link between interest rates and investment spending was weak, strengthening the conclusion that money doesn't matter. The result of this interpretation of the evidence was that most economists paid only scant attention to monetary policy before the mid-1960s.

Objections to Early Keynesian Evidence

While Keynesian economics was reaching its ascendancy in the 1950s and 1960s, a small group of economists at the University of Chicago, led by Milton Friedman, adopted what was then the unfashionable view that money *does* matter to aggregate demand. Friedman and his disciples, who later became known as monetarists, objected to the early Keynesian interpretation of the evidence on the grounds that the structural model used by the early Keynesians was severely flawed. Because structural model evidence is only as good as the model it is based on, the monetarist critique of this evidence needs to be taken seriously.

In 1963, Friedman and Anna Schwartz, a researcher at the National Bureau of Economic Research, published their classic monetary history of the United States, which showed that contrary to the early Keynesian beliefs, monetary policy during the Great Depression was not easy; indeed, it had never been more contractionary.[1] Friedman and Schwartz documented the massive bank failures of this period and the resulting decline in the money supply—the largest ever experienced in the United States (see Chapter 14). Hence monetary policy could explain the worst economic contraction in U.S. history,

---

[1]Milton Friedman and Anna Jacobson Schwartz, *A Monetary History of the United States, 1867–1960* (Princeton, NJ: Princeton University Press, 1963).

and the Great Depression could not be singled out as a period that demonstrates the ineffectiveness of monetary policy.

A Keynesian could still counter Friedman and Schwartz's argument that monetary policy was contractionary during the Great Depression by citing the low level of interest rates. But were these interest rates really so low? Referring to Figure 1 in Chapter 6, you will note that although interest rates on U.S. Treasury securities and high-grade corporate bonds were low during the Great Depression, interest rates on lower-grade bonds, such as Baa corporate bonds, rose to unprecedented high levels during the sharpest part of the contraction phase (1930–1933). By the standard of these lower-grade bonds, then, interest rates were high and monetary policy was tight.

There is a moral to this story. Although much aggregate economic analysis proceeds as though there is only *one* interest rate, we must always be aware that there are *many* interest rates, which may tell different stories. During normal times, most interest rates move in tandem, so lumping them all together and looking at one representative interest rate may not be too misleading. But that is not always so. Unusual periods (like the Great Depression), when interest rates on different securities begin to diverge, do occur. This is exactly the kind of situation in which a structural model (like the early Keynesians') that looks at only the interest rates on a low-risk security such as a U.S. Treasury bill or bond can be very misleading.

There is a second, potentially more important reason why the early Keynesian structural model's focus on nominal interest rates provides a misleading picture of the tightness of monetary policy during the Great Depression. In a period of deflation, when there is a declining price level, low *nominal* interest rates do not necessarily indicate that the cost of borrowing is low and that monetary policy is easy—in fact, the cost of borrowing could be quite high. If, for example, the public expects the price level to decline at a 10% rate, then even though nominal interest rates are at zero, the real cost of borrowing would be as high as 10%. (Recall from Chapter 4 that the real interest rate equals the nominal interest rate, 0, in this case, minus the expected rate of inflation, −10%, so the real interest rate equals $0 - (-10\%) = 10\%$.)

You can see in Figure 1 that this is exactly what happened during the Great Depression: Real interest rates on U.S. Treasury bills were far higher during the 1931–1933 contraction phase of the depression than was the case throughout the next 40 years.[2] As a result, movements of *real* interest rates indicate that, contrary to the early Keynesians' beliefs, monetary policy was extremely tight during the Great Depression. Because an important role for monetary policy during this depressed period could no longer be ruled out, most economists were forced to rethink their position regarding whether money matters.

Monetarists also objected to the early Keynesian structural model's view that a weak link between nominal interest rates and investment spending indicates that investment spending is unaffected by monetary policy. A weak link between *nominal* interest rates and investment spending does not rule out a strong link between *real* interest rates and investment spending. As depicted in Figure 1, nominal interest rates are often a very

---

[2]In the 1980s, real interest rates rose to exceedingly high levels, approaching those of the Great Depression period. Research has tried to explain this phenomenon, some of which points to monetary policy as the source of high real rates in the 1980s. For example, see Oliver J. Blanchard and Lawrence H. Summers, "Perspectives on High World Interest Rates," *Brookings Papers on Economic Activity* 2 (1984): 273–324; and John Huizinga and Frederic S. Mishkin, "Monetary Policy Regime Shifts and the Unusual Behavior of Real Interest Rates," *Carnegie-Rochester Conference Series on Public Policy* 24 (1986): 231–274.

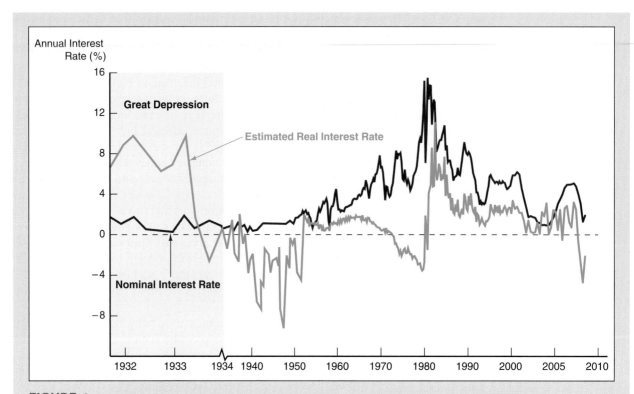

FIGURE 1   **Real and Nominal Interest Rates on Three-Month Treasury Bills, 1931–2008**

Sources: Nominal rates from www.federalreserve.gov/releases/h15/update/. The real rate is constructed using the procedure outlined in Frederic S. Mishkin, "The Real Interest Rate: An Empirical Investigation," *Carnegie-Rochester Conference Series on Public Policy* 15 (1981): 151–200. This involves estimating expected inflation as a function of past interest rates, inflation, and time trends and then subtracting the expected inflation measure from the nominal interest rate.

misleading indicator of real interest rates—not only during the Great Depression, but in later periods as well. Because real interest rates more accurately reflect the true cost of borrowing, they should be more relevant to investment decisions than nominal interest rates. Accordingly, the two pieces of early Keynesian evidence indicating that nominal interest rates have little effect on investment spending do not rule out a strong effect of changes in the money supply on investment spending and hence on aggregate demand.

Monetarists also asserted that interest-rate effects on investment spending might be only one of many channels through which monetary policy affects aggregate demand. Monetary policy could then have a major impact on aggregate demand even if interest-rate effects on investment spending are small, as was suggested by the early Keynesians.

Early Monetarist Evidence on the Importance of Money

In the early 1960s, Milton Friedman and his followers published a series of studies based on reduced-form evidence that promoted the case for a strong effect of money on economic activity. In general, reduced-form evidence can be broken down into three categories: *timing evidence*, which looks at whether the movements in one variable typically occur before another; *statistical evidence*, which performs formal statistical tests on the correlation of the movements of one variable with another; and *historical evidence*, which examines specific past episodes to see whether movements in one variable appear to cause another. Let's look at the monetarist evidence on the importance of money that falls into each of these three categories.

Timing Evidence   Monetarist timing evidence reveals how the rate of money supply growth moves relative to the business cycle. The evidence on this relationship was first presented by Friedman and Schwartz in a famous paper published in 1963.[3] Friedman and Schwartz found that in every business cycle over nearly a century that they studied, the money growth rate always declined before output did. On average, the peak in the rate of money growth occurred 16 months before the peak in the level of output. However, this lead time could vary, ranging from a few months to more than two years. The conclusion that these authors reached on the basis of this evidence is that money growth causes business cycle fluctuations, but its effect on the business cycle operates with "long and variable lags."

Timing evidence is based on the philosophical principle first stated in Latin as *post hoc, ergo propter hoc*, which means that if one event occurs after another, the second event must have been caused by the first. This principle is valid only if we know that the first event is an *exogenous* event, an event occurring as a result of an independent action that could not possibly be caused by the event following it or by some outside factor that might affect both events. If the first event is exogenous, when the second event follows the first we can be more confident that the first event is causing the second.

An example of an exogenous event is a controlled experiment. A chemist mixes two chemicals; suddenly his lab blows up and he with it. We can be absolutely sure that the cause of his demise was the act of mixing the two chemicals together. The principle of *post hoc, ergo propter hoc* is extremely useful in scientific experimentation.

Unfortunately, economics does not enjoy the precision of hard sciences like physics or chemistry. Often we cannot be sure that an economic event, such as a decline in the rate of money growth, is an exogenous event—it could have been caused by an outside factor or by the event it is supposedly causing. When another event (such as a decline in output) typically follows the first event (a decline in money growth), we cannot conclude with certainty that one caused the other. Timing evidence is clearly of a reduced-form nature because it looks directly at the relationship of the movements of two variables. Money growth could lead output, or both could be driven by an outside factor.

Because timing evidence is of a reduced-form nature, there is also the possibility of reverse causation, in which output growth causes money growth. How can this reverse causation occur while money growth still leads output? There are several ways in which this can happen, but we will deal with just one example.[4]

---

[3]Milton Friedman and Anna Jacobson Schwartz, "Money and Business Cycles," *Review of Economics and Statistics* 45, Suppl. (1963): 32–64.

[4]A famous article by James Tobin, "Money and Income: *Post Hoc, Ergo Propter Hoc*," *Quarterly Journal of Economics* 84 (1970): 301–317, describes an economic system in which changes in aggregate output cause changes in the growth rate of money but changes in the growth rate of money have no effect on output. Tobin shows that such a system with reverse causation could yield timing evidence similar to that found by Friedman and Schwartz.

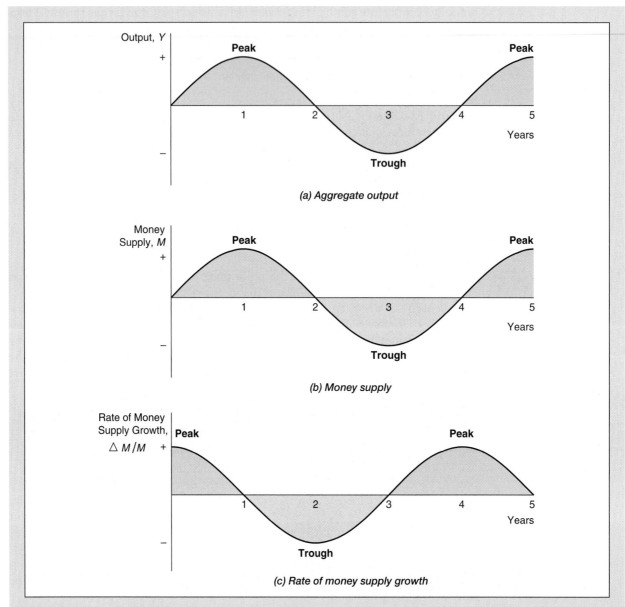

FIGURE 2 **Hypothetical Example in Which Money Growth Leads Output**
Although neither *M* nor *Y* in panels (a) and (b) leads the other (that is, their peaks and troughs coincide), $\Delta M/M$ has its peaks and troughs one year ahead of *M* and *Y*, thus leading both series. (Note that *M* and *Y* in panels (a) and (b) are drawn as movements around a positive average value; a plus sign indicates a value above the average, and a minus sign indicates a value below the average, not a negative value.)

Suppose that you are in a hypothetical economy with a very regular business cycle movement, plotted in panel (a) of Figure 2, that is four years long (four years from peak to peak). Let's assume that in our hypothetical economy, there is reverse causation from output to the money supply and movements in the money supply and output are perfectly correlated; that is, the money supply *M* and output *Y* move upward and downward at the same time. The result is that the peaks and troughs of the *M* and *Y* series in panels (a) and (b) occur at exactly the same time. Therefore, no lead or lag relationship exists between them.

Now let's construct the rate of money supply growth from the money supply series in panel (b). This is done in panel (c). What is the rate of growth of the money supply at its peaks in years 1 and 5? At these points, it is not growing at all; the rate of growth is zero. Similarly, at the trough in year 3, the growth rate is zero. When the money supply is declining from its peak in year 1 to its trough in year 3, it has a negative growth rate, and its decline is fastest sometime between years 1 and 3 (year 2). Translating to panel (c), the rate of money growth is below zero from years 1 to 3, with its most negative value reached at year 2. By similar reasoning, you can see that the growth rate of money is positive in years 0 to 1 and 3 to 5, with the highest values reached in years 0 and 4. When we connect all these points together, we get the money growth series in panel (c), in which the peaks are at years 0 and 4, with a trough in year 2.

Now let's look at the relationship of the money growth series of panel (c) with the level of output in panel (a). As you can see, the money growth series consistently has its peaks and troughs exactly one year before the peaks and troughs of the output series. We conclude that in our hypothetical economy, the rate of money growth always decreases one year before output does. This evidence does not, however, imply that money growth *drives* output. In fact, by assumption, we know that this economy is one in which causation actually runs from output to the level of money supply, and there is no lead or lag relationship between the two. Only by our judicious choice of using the *growth rate* of the money supply rather than its *level* have we found a leading relationship.

This example shows how easy it is to misinterpret timing relationships. Furthermore, by searching for what we hope to find, we might focus on a variable, such as a growth rate, rather than a level, which suggests a misleading relationship. Timing evidence can be a dangerous tool for deciding on causation.

Stated even more forcefully, "one person's lead is another person's lag." For example, you could just as easily interpret the relationship of money growth and output in Figure 2 to say that the money growth rate lags output by three years—after all, the peaks in the money growth series occur three years after the peaks in the output series. In short, you could say that output leads money growth.

We have seen that timing evidence is extremely hard to interpret. Unless we can be sure that changes in the leading variable are exogenous events, we cannot be sure that the leading variable is actually causing the following variable. And it is all too easy to find what we seek when looking for timing evidence. Perhaps the best way of describing this danger is to say that "timing evidence may be in the eyes of the beholder."

Statistical Evidence   Monetarist statistical evidence examined the correlations between money and aggregate output or aggregate spending by performing formal statistical tests. Again in 1963 (obviously a vintage year for the monetarists), Milton Friedman and David Meiselman published a paper that proposed the following test of a monetarist model against a model used by early Keynesians.[5] In the Keynesian components framework, investment and government spending were sources of fluctuations in

---

[5]Milton Friedman and David Meiselman, "The Relative Stability of Monetary Velocity and the Investment Multiplier," in *Stabilization Policies,* ed. Commission on Money and Credit (Upper Saddle River, NJ: Prentice-Hall, 1963), pp. 165–268

aggregate demand, so Friedman and Meiselman constructed a "Keynesian" autonomous expenditure variable A equal to investment spending plus government spending. They characterized the Keynesian components model as saying that A should be highly correlated with aggregate spending Y, while the money supply M should not. In the monetarist model, the money supply is the source of fluctuations in aggregate spending, and M should be highly correlated with Y, while A should not.

A logical way to find out which model is better would be to see which is more highly correlated with Y: M or A. When Friedman and Meiselman conducted this test for many different periods of U.S. data, they discovered that *the monetarist model wins!*[6] They concluded that monetarist analysis gives a better description than Keynesian analysis of how aggregate spending is determined.

Several objections were raised against the Friedman–Meiselman evidence:

1. The standard criticisms of this reduced-form evidence are the ones we have already discussed: Reverse causation could occur, or an outside factor might drive both series.

2. The test may not be fair because the Keynesian components model is characterized too simplistically. Keynesian structural models commonly include hundreds of equations. The one-equation "Keynesian" model that Friedman and Meiselman tested may not adequately capture the effects of autonomous expenditure. Furthermore, Keynesian models usually include the effects of other variables. By ignoring them, the effect of monetary policy might be overestimated and the effect of autonomous expenditure underestimated.

3. The Friedman–Meiselman measure of autonomous expenditure A might be constructed poorly, preventing the "Keynesian" model from performing well. For example, orders for military hardware affect aggregate demand before they appear as spending in the autonomous expenditure variable that Friedman and Meiselman used. A more careful construction of the autonomous expenditure variable should take account of the placing of orders for military hardware. When the autonomous expenditure variable was constructed more carefully by critics of the Friedman–Meiselman study, they found that the results were reversed: The "Keynesian" model won.[7] A later study on the appropriateness of various ways of determining autonomous expenditure does not give a clear-cut victory to either the "Keynesian" or the monetarist model.[8]

Historical Evidence The monetarist historical evidence found in Friedman and Schwartz's *A Monetary History* has been very influential in gaining support for the monetarist position. We have already seen that the book was extremely important as a criticism of early Keynesian thinking, showing as it did that the Great Depression was not a period of easy monetary policy and that the depression could be attributed to the sharp decline in the money supply from 1930 to 1933 resulting from bank panics. In addition, the book documented in great detail that the growth rate of money leads

---

[6]Friedman and Meiselman did not actually run their tests using the Y variable because they felt that this gave an unfair advantage to the Keynesian model in that A is included in Y. Instead, they subtracted A from Y and tested for the correlation of $Y - A$ with M or A.

[7]See, for example, Albert Ando and Franco Modigliani, "The Relative Stability of Monetary Velocity and the Investment Multiplier," *American Economic Review* 55 (1965): 693–728.

[8]See William Poole and Edith Kornblith, "The Friedman-Meiselman CMC Paper: New Evidence on an Old Controversy," *American Economic Review* 63 (1973): 908–917.

business cycles, because it declines before every recession. This timing evidence is, of course, subject to all the criticisms raised earlier.

The historical evidence contains one feature, however, that makes it different from other monetarist evidence we have discussed so far. Several episodes occur in which changes in the money supply appear to be exogenous events. These episodes are almost like controlled experiments, so the *post hoc, ergo propter hoc* principle is far more likely to be valid: If the decline in the growth rate of the money supply is soon followed by a decline in output in these episodes, much stronger evidence is presented that money growth is the driving force behind the business cycle.

One of the best examples of such an episode is the increase in reserve requirements in 1936–1937 (discussed in Chapter 16), which led to a sharp decline in the money supply and in its rate of growth. The increase in reserve requirements was implemented because the Federal Reserve wanted to improve its control of monetary policy; it was not implemented in response to economic conditions. We can thus rule out reverse causation from output to the money supply. Also, it is hard to think of an outside factor that could have driven the Fed to increase reserve requirements and that could also have directly affected output. Therefore, the decline in the money supply in this episode can probably be classified as an exogenous event with the characteristics of a controlled experiment. Soon after this experiment, the very severe recession of 1937–1938 occurred. We can conclude with confidence that in this episode, the change in the money supply due to the Fed's increase in reserve requirements was indeed the source of the business cycle contraction that followed.

A Monetary History also documented other historical episodes, such as the bank panics of 1907 and other years in which the decline in money growth again appears to have been an exogenous event. The fact that recessions have frequently followed apparently exogenous declines in money growth is very strong evidence that changes in the growth rate of the money supply do have an impact on aggregate output. Recent work by Christina and David Romer, both of the University of California, Berkeley, applies the historical approach to more recent data using more sophisticated statistical techniques and also finds that monetary policy shifts have had an important impact on the aggregate economy.[9]

Overview of the Monetarist Evidence

Where does this discussion of the monetarist evidence leave us? We have seen that because of reverse causation and outside-factor possibilities, there are some serious doubts about the conclusions that can be drawn from timing and statistical evidence alone. However, some of the historical evidence in which exogenous declines in money growth are followed by business cycle contractions does provide stronger support for the monetarist position. When historical evidence is combined with timing and statistical evidence, the conclusion that monetary policy does matter seems warranted.

As you can imagine, the economics profession was shaken by the appearance of the monetarist evidence, because up to that time most economists believed that money does

---

[9]Christina Romer and David Romer, "Does Monetary Policy Matter? A New Test in the Spirit of Friedman and Schwartz," *NBER Macroeconomics Annual, 1989,* 4, ed. Stanley Fischer (Cambridge, MA.: MIT Press, 1989), pp. 121–170.

FYI   Real Business Cycle Theory and the Debate on Money and Economic Activity

New entrants to the debate on money and economic activity are advocates of *real business cycle theory*, which states that real shocks to tastes and technology (rather than monetary shocks) are the driving forces behind business cycles. Proponents of this theory are critical of the monetarist view that money matters to business cycles because they believe that the correlation of output with money reflects reverse causation; that is, the business cycle drives money, rather than the other way

around. An important piece of evidence they offer to support the reverse causation argument is that almost none of the correlation between money and output comes from the monetary base, which is controlled by the monetary authorities.* Instead, the money–output correlation stems from other sources of money supply movements that, as we saw in Chapter 14, are affected by the actions of banks and depositors, and are more likely to be influenced by the business cycle.

*Robert King and Charles Plosser, "Money, Credit and Prices in a Real Business Cycle," *American Economic Review* 74 (1984): 363–380; and Charles Plosser, "Understanding Real Business Cycles," *Journal of Economic Perspectives* 3 (Summer 1989): 51–78.

---

not matter at all. Monetarists had demonstrated that this early Keynesian position was probably wrong, and it won them a lot of converts. Recognizing the fallacy of the position that money does not matter does not necessarily mean that we must accept the position that money is *all* that matters. Many Keynesian economists shifted their views toward the monetarist position, but not all the way. Instead, they adopted an intermediate position: They allowed that money, fiscal policy, net exports, and "animal spirits" all contributed to fluctuations in aggregate demand. The result has been a convergence of the views on the importance of monetary policy to economic activity. However, proponents of a new theory of aggregate fluctuations called *real business cycle theory* are more critical of the monetarist reduced-form evidence that money is important to business cycle fluctuations because they believe there is reverse causation from the business cycle to money (see the FYI box, "Real Business Cycle Theory and the Debate on Money and Economic Activity").

TRANSMISSION MECHANISMS OF MONETARY POLICY

After the successful monetarist attack on the early Keynesian position, economic research went in two directions. One direction was to use more sophisticated monetarist reduced-form models to test for the importance of money to economic activity.[10] The second direction was to pursue a structural model approach and to develop a better

---

[10]The most prominent example of more sophisticated reduced-form research is the St. Louis model, which was developed at the Federal Reserve Bank of St. Louis in the late 1960s and early 1970s. It provided support for the monetarist position, but is subject to the same criticisms of reduced-form evidence outlined in the text. The St. Louis model was first outlined in Leonall Andersen and Jerry Jordan, "Monetary and Fiscal Actions: A Test of Their Relative Importance in Economic Stabilization," Federal Reserve Bank of St. Louis *Review* 50 (November 1968): 11–23.

understanding of channels (other than interest-rate effects on investment) through which monetary policy affects aggregate demand. In this section we examine some of these channels, or *transmission mechanisms*, beginning with interest-rate channels, because they are the key monetary transmission mechanism in the *ISLM* and *AD/AS* models you have seen in Chapters 20, 21, and 22.

Traditional Interest-Rate Channels

The traditional components view of the monetary transmission mechanism can be characterized by the following schematic, which shows the effect of an expansionary monetary policy:

$$\text{Expansionary monetary policy} \Rightarrow i_r \downarrow \Rightarrow I \uparrow \Rightarrow Y \uparrow \tag{1}$$

where an expansionary monetary policy leads to a fall in real interest rates ($i_r \downarrow$), which in turn lowers the cost of capital, causing a rise in investment spending ($I \uparrow$), thereby leading to an increase in aggregate demand and a rise in output ($Y \uparrow$).

Although Keynes originally emphasized this channel as operating through businesses' decisions about investment spending, the search for new monetary transmission mechanisms recognized that consumers' decisions about housing and **consumer durable expenditure** (spending by consumers on durable items such as automobiles and refrigerators) also are investment decisions. Thus the interest-rate channel of monetary transmission outlined in Equation 1 applies equally to consumer spending, in which *I* also represents residential housing and consumer durable expenditure.

An important feature of the interest-rate transmission mechanism is its emphasis on the *real* (rather than the nominal) interest rate as the rate that affects consumer and business decisions. In addition, it is often the real *long*-term interest rate (not the real short-term interest rate) that is viewed as having the major impact on spending. How is it that changes in the short-term nominal interest rate induced by a central bank result in a corresponding change in the real interest rate on both short- and long-term bonds? The key is the phenomenon known as *sticky prices*, the fact that the aggregate price level adjusts slowly over time, meaning that expansionary monetary policy, which lowers the short-term nominal interest rate, also lowers the short-term *real* interest rate. The expectations hypothesis of the term structure described in Chapter 6, which states that the long-term interest rate is an average of expected future short-term interest rates, suggests that a lower real short-term interest rate, as long as it persists, leads to a fall in the real long-term interest rate. These lower real interest rates then lead to rises in business fixed investment, residential housing investment, inventory investment, and consumer durable expenditure, all of which produce the rise in aggregate output.

That the real interest rate rather than the nominal rate affects spending provides an important mechanism for how monetary policy can stimulate the economy, even if nominal interest rates hit a floor of zero during a deflationary episode. With nominal interest rates at a floor of zero, a commitment to future expansionary monetary policy can raise the expected price level ($P^e \uparrow$) and hence expected inflation ($\pi^e \uparrow$), thereby lowering the real interest rate ($i_r = [i - \pi^e] \downarrow$) even when the nominal interest rate is fixed at zero and stimulating spending through the interest-rate channel:

$$\text{Expansionary monetary policy} \Rightarrow P^e \uparrow \Rightarrow \pi^e \uparrow \Rightarrow i_r \downarrow \Rightarrow I \uparrow \Rightarrow Y \uparrow \tag{2}$$

This mechanism thus indicates that monetary policy can still be effective even when nominal interest rates have already been driven down to zero by the monetary authorities.

Indeed, this mechanism is a key element in monetarist discussions of why the U.S. economy was not stuck in a liquidity trap (in which increases in the money supply might be unable to lower interest rates, discussed in Chapter 19) during the Great Depression and why expansionary monetary policy could have prevented the sharp decline in output during that period.

Some economists, such as John Taylor of Stanford University, take the position that there is strong empirical evidence for substantial interest-rate effects on consumer and investment spending through the cost of capital, making the interest-rate monetary transmission mechanism a strong one. His position is highly controversial, and many researchers, including Ben Bernanke, now the chairman of the Fed, and Mark Gertler of New York University, believe that the empirical evidence does not support strong interest-rate effects operating through the cost of capital.[11] Indeed, these researchers see the empirical failure of traditional interest-rate monetary transmission mechanisms as having provided the stimulus for the search for other transmission mechanisms of monetary policy.

These other transmission mechanisms fall into two basic categories: those operating through asset prices other than interest rates and those operating through asymmetric information effects on credit markets (the **credit view**). (These mechanisms are summarized in the schematic diagram in Figure 3.)

Other Asset Price Channels

As we saw earlier in the chapter, a key monetarist objection to the Keynesian analysis of monetary policy effects on the economy is that it focuses on only one asset price, the interest rate, rather than on many asset prices. Monetarists envision a transmission mechanism in which other relative asset prices and real wealth transmit monetary effects onto the economy. In addition to bond prices, two other asset prices receive substantial attention as channels for monetary policy effects: foreign exchange rates and the prices of equities (stocks).

Exchange Rate Effects on Net Exports   With the growing internationalization of economies throughout the world and the advent of flexible exchange rates, more attention has been paid to how monetary policy affects exchange rates, which in turn affect net exports and aggregate output.

This channel also involves interest-rate effects, because, as we saw in Chapter 17, when domestic real interest rates fall, domestic dollar assets become less attractive relative to assets denominated in foreign currencies. As a result, the value of dollar assets relative to other currency assets falls, and the dollar depreciates (denoted by $E\downarrow$). The lower value of the domestic currency makes domestic goods cheaper than foreign goods, thereby causing a rise in net exports ($NX\uparrow$) and hence in aggregate output ($Y\uparrow$). The schematic for the monetary transmission mechanism that operates through the exchange rate is

$$\text{Expansionary monetary policy} \Rightarrow i_r\downarrow \Rightarrow E\downarrow \Rightarrow NX\uparrow \Rightarrow Y\uparrow \qquad (3)$$

---

[11]See John Taylor, "The Monetary Transmission Mechanism: An Empirical Framework," *Journal of Economic Perspectives* 9 (Fall 1995): 11–26, and Ben Bernanke and Mark Gertler, "Inside the Black Box: The Credit Channel of Monetary Policy Transmission," *Journal of Economic Perspectives* 9 (Fall 1995): 27–48.

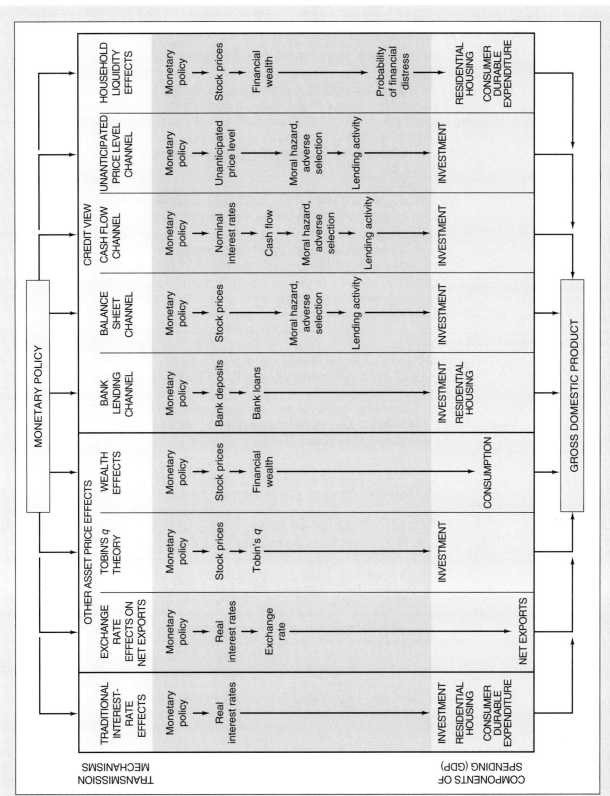

FIGURE 3 The Link Between Monetary Policy and GDP: Monetary Transmission Mechanisms

Recent research has found that this exchange rate channel plays an important role in how monetary policy affects the domestic economy.[12]

Tobin's *q* Theory James Tobin developed a theory, referred to as *Tobin's q theory*, that explains how monetary policy can affect the economy through its effects on the valuation of equities (stock). Tobin defines *q* as the market value of firms divided by the replacement cost of capital. If *q* is high, the market price of firms is high relative to the replacement cost of capital, and new plant and equipment capital is cheap relative to the market value of firms. Companies can then issue stock and get a high price for it relative to the cost of the facilities and equipment they are buying. Investment spending will rise, because firms can buy a lot of new investment goods with only a small issue of stock.

Conversely, when *q* is low, firms will not purchase *new* investment goods because the market value of firms is low relative to the cost of capital. If companies want to acquire capital when *q* is low, they can buy another firm cheaply and acquire old capital instead. Investment spending, the purchase of new investment goods, will then be very low. Tobin's *q* theory gives a good explanation for the extremely low rate of investment spending during the Great Depression. In that period, stock prices collapsed, and by 1933, stocks were worth only one-tenth of their value in late 1929; *q* fell to unprecedented low levels.

The crux of this discussion is that a link exists between Tobin's q and investment spending. But how might monetary policy affect stock prices? Quite simply, when monetary policy is expansionary, the public finds that it has more money than it wants and so gets rid of it through spending. One place the public spends is in the stock market, increasing the demand for stocks and consequently raising their prices.[13] Combining this with the fact that higher stock prices (P_s) will lead to a higher *q* and thus higher investment spending *I* leads to the following transmission mechanism of monetary policy:[14]

$$\text{Expansionary monetary policy} \Rightarrow P_s \uparrow \Rightarrow q \uparrow \Rightarrow I \uparrow \Rightarrow Y \uparrow \qquad (4)$$

Wealth Effects In their search for new monetary transmission mechanisms, researchers also looked at how consumers' balance sheets might affect their spending decisions. Franco Modigliani was the first to take this tack, using his famous life cycle hypothesis of consumption. **Consumption** is spending by consumers on nondurable goods and services.[15] It differs from *consumer expenditure* in that it does not include spending on consumer durables. The basic premise of Modigliani's theory is that

---

[12]For example, see Ralph Bryant, Peter Hooper, and Catherine Mann, *Evaluating Policy Regimes: New Empirical Research in Empirical Macroeconomics* (Washington, DC: Brookings Institution, 1993); and John B. Taylor, *Macroeconomic Policy in a World Economy: From Econometric Design to Practical Operation* (New York: Norton, 1993).

[13]See James Tobin, "A General Equilibrium Approach to Monetary Theory," *Journal of Money, Credit, and Banking* 1 (1969): 15–29. A somewhat more Keynesian story with the same outcome is that the increase in the money supply lowers interest rates on bonds so that the yields on alternatives to stocks fall. This makes stocks more attractive relative to bonds, so demand for them increases, raises their price, and thereby lowers their yield.

[14]An alternative way of looking at the link between stock prices and investment spending is that higher stock prices lower the yield on stocks and reduce the cost of financing investment spending through issuing equity. This way of looking at the link between stock prices and investment spending is formally equivalent to Tobin's q theory; see Barry Bosworth, "The Stock Market and the Economy," *Brookings Papers on Economic Activity* 2 (1975): 257–290.

[15]Consumption also includes another small component, the services that a consumer receives from the ownership of housing and consumer durables.

consumers smooth out their consumption over time. Therefore, what determines consumption spending is the lifetime resources of consumers, not just today's income.

An important component of consumers' lifetime resources is their financial wealth, a major component of which is common stocks. When stock prices rise, the value of financial wealth increases, thereby increasing the lifetime resources of consumers, and consumption should rise. Considering that, as we have seen, expansionary monetary policy can lead to a rise in stock prices, we now have another monetary transmission mechanism:

$$\text{Expansionary monetary policy} \Rightarrow P_s\uparrow \Rightarrow \text{wealth}\uparrow \Rightarrow \text{consumption}\uparrow \Rightarrow Y\uparrow \quad (5)$$

Modigliani's research found this relationship to be an extremely powerful mechanism that adds substantially to the potency of monetary policy.[16]

The wealth and Tobin's q channels allow for a general definition of equity, so they can also be applied to the housing market, where housing is equity. An increase in house prices, which raises their prices relative to replacement cost, leads to a rise in Tobin's q for housing, thereby stimulating its production. Similarly, housing and land prices are extremely important components of wealth, so rises in these prices increase wealth, thereby raising consumption. Monetary expansion, which raises land and housing prices through the Tobin's q and wealth mechanisms described here, thus leads to a rise in aggregate demand.

Credit View

Dissatisfaction with the conventional stories that interest-rate effects explain the impact of monetary policy on expenditures on durable assets has led to a new explanation based on the problem of asymmetric information in financial markets (see Chapter 8). This explanation, referred to as the *credit view*, proposes that two types of monetary transmission channels arise as a result of information problems in credit markets: those that operate through effects on bank lending and those that operate through effects on firms' and households' balance sheets.[17]

Bank Lending Channel   The bank lending channel is based on the analysis in Chapter 8, which demonstrated that banks play a special role in the financial system because they are especially well suited to solve asymmetric information problems in credit markets. Because of banks' special role, certain borrowers will not have access to the credit markets unless they borrow from banks. As long as there is no perfect substitutability of retail bank deposits with other sources of funds, the bank lending channel of monetary transmission operates as follows: Expansionary monetary policy, which increases bank reserves and bank deposits, increases the quantity of bank loans available.

---

[16]See Franco Modigliani, "Monetary Policy and Consumption," in *Consumer Spending and Money Policy: The Linkages* (Boston: Federal Reserve Bank, 1971), pp. 9–84.

[17]Surveys of the credit view can be found in Ben Bernanke, "Credit in the Macroeconomy," Federal Reserve Bank of New York *Quarterly Review* (Spring 1993): 50–70; Ben Bernanke and Mark Gertler, "Inside the Black Box: The Credit Channel of Monetary Policy Transmission," *Journal of Economic Perspectives* 9 (Fall 1995): 27–48; Stephen G. Cecchetti, "Distinguishing Theories of the Monetary Transmission Mechanism," Federal Reserve Bank of St. Louis *Review* 77 (May–June 1995): 83–97; and R. Glenn Hubbard, "Is There a 'Credit Channel' for Monetary Policy?" Federal Reserve Bank of St. Louis *Review* 77 (May–June 1995): 63–74.

Because many borrowers are dependent on bank loans to finance their activities, this increase in loans will cause investment (and possibly consumer) spending to rise. Schematically, the monetary policy effect is

$$\text{Expansionary monetary policy} \Rightarrow \text{bank deposits}\uparrow$$
$$\Rightarrow \text{bank loans}\uparrow \Rightarrow I\uparrow \Rightarrow Y\uparrow \tag{6}$$

An important implication of the credit view is that monetary policy will have a greater effect on expenditure by smaller firms, which are more dependent on bank loans, than it will on large firms, which can get funds directly through stock and bond markets (and not only through banks).

Though this result has been confirmed by researchers, doubts about the bank lending channel have been raised in the literature, and there are reasons to suspect that the bank lending channel in the United States may not be as powerful as it once was.[18] The first reason this channel is not as powerful is that current U.S. regulations no longer impose restrictions on banks that hinder their ability to raise funds (see Chapter 12). Prior to the mid-1980s, certificates of deposit (CDs) were subjected to reserve requirements and Regulation Q deposit rate ceilings, which made it hard for banks to replace deposits that flowed out of the banking system during a monetary contraction. With these regulatory restrictions abolished, banks can more easily respond to a decline in bank reserves and a loss of retail deposits by issuing CDs at market interest rates that do not have to be backed up by required reserves. Second, the worldwide decline of the traditional bank lending business (also discussed in Chapter 12) has rendered the bank lending channel less potent. Nonetheless, many economists believe that the bank lending channel played an important role in the slow recovery in the United States from the 1990–1991 recession.

Balance Sheet Channel   Even though the bank lending channel may be declining in importance, it is by no means clear that this is the case for the other credit channel, the balance sheet channel. Like the bank lending channel, the balance sheet channel arises from the presence of asymmetric information problems in credit markets. In Chapter 8, we saw that the lower the net worth of business firms, the more severe the adverse selection and moral hazard problems in lending to these firms. Lower net worth means that lenders in effect have less collateral for their loans, so their potential losses from adverse selection are higher. A decline in net worth, which raises the adverse selection problem, thus leads to decreased lending to finance investment spending. The lower net worth of businesses also increases the moral hazard problem because it means that owners have a lower equity stake in their firms, giving them more incentive to engage in risky investment projects. Because taking on riskier investment projects makes it more likely that lenders will not be paid back, a decrease in businesses' net worth leads to a decrease in lending and hence in investment spending.

Monetary policy can affect firms' balance sheets in several ways. Expansionary monetary policy, which causes a rise in stock prices ($P_s\uparrow$) along the lines described earlier, raises the net worth of firms and so leads to higher investment spending ($I\uparrow$) and

---

[18]For example, see Valerie Ramey, "How Important Is the Credit Channel in the Transmission of Monetary Policy?" *Carnegie-Rochester Conference Series on Public Policy* 39 (1993): 1–45; and Allan H. Meltzer, "Monetary, Credit (and Other) Transmission Processes: A Monetarist Perspective," *Journal of Economic Perspectives* 9 (Fall 1995): 49–72.

aggregate demand ($Y\uparrow$) because of the decrease in adverse selection and moral hazard problems. This leads to the following schematic for one balance sheet channel of monetary transmission:

$$\text{Expansionary monetary policy} \Rightarrow P_s\uparrow \Rightarrow \text{firms' net worth}\uparrow \Rightarrow \text{adverse selection}\downarrow,$$
$$\text{moral hazard}\downarrow \Rightarrow \text{lending}\uparrow \Rightarrow I\uparrow \Rightarrow Y\uparrow \qquad (7)$$

Cash Flow Channel   Another balance sheet channel operates by affecting *cash flow*, the difference between cash receipts and cash expenditures. Expansionary monetary policy, which lowers nominal interest rates, also causes an improvement in firms' balance sheets because it raises cash flow. The rise in cash flow increases the liquidity of the firm (or household) and thus makes it easier for lenders to know whether the firm (or household) will be able to pay its bills. The result is that adverse selection and moral hazard problems become less severe, leading to an increase in lending and economic activity. The following schematic describes this additional balance sheet channel:

$$\text{Expansionary monetary policy} \Rightarrow i\downarrow \Rightarrow \text{firms' cash flow}\uparrow \Rightarrow \text{adverse selection}\downarrow,$$
$$\text{moral hazard}\downarrow \Rightarrow \text{lending}\uparrow \Rightarrow I\uparrow \Rightarrow Y\uparrow \qquad (8)$$

An important feature of this transmission mechanism is that *nominal* interest rates affect firms' cash flow. Thus this interest-rate mechanism differs from the traditional interest-rate mechanism discussed earlier, in which the real interest rate affects investment. Furthermore, the short-term interest rate plays a special role in this transmission mechanism, because interest payments on short-term (rather than long-term) debt typically have the greatest impact on households' and firms' cash flow.

A related mechanism involving adverse selection through which expansionary monetary policy that lowers interest rates can stimulate aggregate output involves the credit-rationing phenomenon. As discussed in Chapter 10, credit rationing occurs in cases where borrowers are denied loans even when they are willing to pay a higher interest rate. This is because individuals and firms with the riskiest investment projects are exactly the ones who are willing to pay the highest interest rates, for if the high-risk investment succeeds, they will be the primary beneficiaries. Thus higher interest rates increase the adverse selection problem, and lower interest rates reduce it. When expansionary monetary policy lowers interest rates, less risk-prone borrowers make up a higher fraction of those demanding loans, so lenders are more willing to lend, raising both investment and output, along the lines of parts of the schematic in Equation 8.

Unanticipated Price Level Channel   A third balance sheet channel operates through monetary policy effects on the general price level. Because in industrialized countries debt payments are contractually fixed in nominal terms, an unanticipated rise in the price level lowers the value of firms' liabilities in real terms (decreases the burden of the debt) but should not lower the real value of the firms' assets. Monetary expansion that leads to an unanticipated rise in the price level ($P\uparrow$) therefore raises real net worth, which lowers adverse selection and moral hazard problems, thereby leading to a rise in investment spending and aggregate output as in the following schematic:

$$\text{Expansionary monetary policy} \Rightarrow \text{unanticipated } P\uparrow \Rightarrow \text{firms' real net worth}\uparrow$$
$$\Rightarrow \text{adverse selection }\downarrow, \text{moral hazard}\downarrow \Rightarrow \text{lending}\uparrow \Rightarrow I\uparrow \Rightarrow Y\uparrow \qquad (9)$$

FYI   Consumers' Balance Sheets and the Great Depression

The years between 1929 and 1933 witnessed the worst deterioration in consumers' balance sheets ever seen in the United States. The stock market crash in 1929, which caused a slump that lasted until 1933, reduced the value of consumers' wealth by $737 billion (in 2000 dollars), and as expected, consumption dropped sharply (by over $100 billion). Because of the decline in the price level in that period, the level of real debt consumers owed also increased sharply (by over 20%). Consequently, the value of financial assets relative to the amount of debt declined sharply, increasing the likelihood of financial distress. Not surprisingly, spending on consumer durables and housing fell precipitously: From 1929 to 1933, consumer durable expenditure declined by over 50%, while expenditure on housing declined by 80%.*

*For further discussion of the effect of consumers' balance sheets on spending during the Great Depression, see Frederic S. Mishkin, "The Household Balance Sheet and the Great Depression," *Journal of Economic History* 38 (1978): 918–937.

The view that unanticipated movements in the price level affect aggregate output has a long tradition in economics: It is the key feature in the debt-deflation view of the Great Depression outlined in Chapter 9.

Household Liquidity Effects   Although most of the literature on the credit channel focuses on spending by businesses, the credit view should apply equally well to consumer spending, particularly on consumer durables and housing. Declines in bank lending induced by a monetary contraction should cause a decline in durables and housing purchases by consumers who do not have access to other sources of credit. Similarly, increases in interest rates cause a deterioration in household balance sheets, because consumers' cash flow is adversely affected.

Another way of looking at how the balance sheet channel may operate through consumers is to consider liquidity effects on consumer durable and housing expenditures, which were found to be important factors during the Great Depression (see the FYI box, "Consumers' Balance Sheets and the Great Depression"). In the liquidity effects view, balance sheet effects work through their impact on consumers' desire to spend rather than on lenders' desire to lend. Because of asymmetric information about their quality, consumer durables and housing are very illiquid assets. If, as a result of a bad income shock, consumers needed to sell their consumer durables or housing to raise money, they would expect a big loss because they could not get the full value of these assets in a distress sale. (This is just a manifestation of the lemons problem described in Chapter 8.) In contrast, if consumers held financial assets (such as money in the bank, stocks, or bonds), they could easily sell them quickly for their full market value and raise the cash. Hence, if consumers expect a higher likelihood of finding themselves in financial distress, they would rather hold fewer illiquid consumer durable or housing assets and more liquid financial assets.

A consumer's balance sheet should be an important influence on his or her estimate of the likelihood of suffering financial distress. Specifically, when consumers have a large amount of financial assets relative to their debts, their estimate of the probability of financial distress is low, and they will be more willing to purchase consumer durables or housing. When stock prices rise, the value of financial assets rises as well; consumer durable expenditure will also rise because consumers have a more secure financial position and a lower estimate of the likelihood of suffering financial distress.

This leads to another transmission mechanism for monetary policy, operating through the link between money and stock prices:[19]

$$\text{Expansionary monetary policy} \Rightarrow P_s \uparrow \Rightarrow \text{value of households' financial assets} \uparrow$$
$$\Rightarrow \text{likelihood of financial distress} \downarrow$$
$$\Rightarrow \text{consumer durable and housing expenditure} \uparrow \Rightarrow Y \uparrow \qquad (10)$$

The illiquidity of consumer durable and housing assets provides another reason why a monetary expansion, which lowers interest rates and thereby raises cash flow to consumers, leads to a rise in spending on consumer durables and housing. A rise in consumer cash flow decreases the likelihood of financial distress, which increases the desire of consumers to hold durable goods or housing, thus increasing spending on them and hence aggregate output. The only difference between this view of cash flow effects and that outlined in Equation 8 is that it is not the willingness of lenders to lend to consumers that causes expenditure to rise but the willingness of consumers to spend.

Why Are Credit Channels Likely to Be Important?

There are three reasons to believe that credit channels are important monetary transmission mechanisms. First, a large body of evidence on the behavior of individual firms supports the view that credit market imperfections of the type crucial to the operation of credit channels do affect firms' employment and spending decisions.[20] Second, there is evidence that small firms (which are more likely to be credit-constrained) are hurt more by tight monetary policy than large firms, which are unlikely to be credit-constrained.[21] Third, and maybe most compelling, the asymmetric information view of credit market imperfections at the core of the credit channel analysis is a theoretical construct that has proved useful in explaining many other important phenomena, such as why many of our financial institutions exist, why our financial system has the structure that it has, and why financial crises are so damaging to the economy (topics discussed in Chapters 8 and 9). The best support for a theory is its demonstrated usefulness in a wide range of applications. By this standard, the asymmetric information theory supporting the existence of credit channels as an important monetary transmission mechanism has much to recommend it.

APPLICATION   ✦   The Subprime Recession

With the advent of the subprime financial crisis in the summer of 2007, the Fed began a very aggressive easing of monetary policy. The Fed dropped the target federal funds rate from $5\frac{1}{4}\%$ to 0% over a fifteen-month period from September 2007 to December 2008. At first, it appeared that the Fed's actions would keep the growth slowdown mild and prevent a recession. However, the economy proved to be weaker than the Fed or private forecasters expected, with a recession beginning in December of 2007. Why did

---

[19]See Frederic S. Mishkin, "What Depressed the Consumer? The Household Balance Sheet and the 1973–1975 Recession," *Brookings Papers on Economic Activity* 1 (1977): 123–164.

[20]For a survey of this evidence, see Hubbard, "Is There a 'Credit Channel' for Monetary Policy?" (note 17).

[21]See Mark Gertler and Simon Gilchrist, "Monetary Policy, Business Cycles, and the Behavior of Small Manufacturing Firms," *Quarterly Journal of Economics* 109 (May 1994): 309–340.

the economy become so weak despite this unusually rapid reduction in the Fed's policy instrument?

The subprime meltdown led to negative effects on the economy from many of the channels we have outlined above. The rising level of subprime mortgage defaults, which led to a decline in the value of mortgage-backed securities and CDOs, led to large losses on the balance sheets of financial institutions. With weaker balance sheets, these financial institutions began to deleverage and cut back on their lending. With no one else to collect information and make loans, adverse selection and moral hazard problems increased in credit markets, leading to a slowdown of the economy. Credit spreads also went through the roof with the increase in uncertainty from failures of so many financial markets. The decline in the stock market and housing prices also weakened the economy, because it lowered household wealth. The decrease in household wealth led to restrained consumer spending and weaker investment, because of the resulting drop in Tobin's q.

With all these channels operating, it is no surprise that despite the Fed's aggressive lowering of the federal funds rate, the economy still took a bit hit.

LESSONS FOR MONETARY POLICY

What useful implications for central banks' conduct of monetary policy can we draw from the analysis in this chapter? There are four basic lessons to be learned.

1. It is dangerous always to associate the easing or the tightening of monetary policy with a fall or a rise in short-term nominal interest rates. Because most central banks use short-term nominal interest rates—typically, the interbank rate—as the key operating instrument for monetary policy, there is a danger that central banks and the public will focus too much on short-term nominal interest rates as an indicator of the stance of monetary policy. Indeed, it is quite common to see statements that always associate monetary tightenings with a rise in the interbank rate and monetary easings with a decline in the rate. This view is highly problematic, because—as we have seen in our discussion of the Great Depression period—movements in nominal interest rates do not always correspond to movements in real interest rates, yet it is typically the real and not the nominal interest rate that is an element in the channel of monetary policy transmission. For example, we have seen that during the contraction phase of the Great Depression in the United States, short-term interest rates fell to near zero, yet real interest rates were extremely high. Short-term interest rates that are near zero therefore do not indicate that monetary policy is easy if the economy is undergoing deflation, as was true during the contraction phase of the Great Depression. As Milton Friedman and Anna Schwartz have emphasized, the period of near-zero short-term interest rates during the contraction phase of the Great Depression was one of highly contractionary monetary policy, rather than the reverse.

2. Other asset prices besides those on short-term debt instruments contain important information about the stance of monetary policy because they are important elements in various monetary policy transmission mechanisms. As we have seen in this chapter, economists have come a long way in understanding that other asset prices besides interest rates have major effects on aggregate demand. As we saw in Figure 3, other asset prices, such as stock prices, foreign exchange rates, and housing and land prices, play an important role in monetary transmission mechanisms. Furthermore, the discussion of such additional channels as those operating through the exchange rate, Tobin's *q*, and wealth effects provides additional reasons why other asset prices play such an important role in the monetary transmission mechanisms. Although there are strong disagreements among economists about which channels of monetary transmission are the most important—not surprising, given that economists, particularly those in academia, always like to disagree—they do agree that other asset prices play an important role in the way monetary policy affects the economy.

The view that other asset prices besides short-term interest rates matter has important implications for monetary policy. When we try to assess the stance of policy, it is critical that we look at other asset prices in addition to short-term interest rates. For example, if short-term interest rates are low or even zero and yet stock prices are low, land prices are low, and the value of the domestic currency is high, monetary policy is clearly tight, *not* easy.

3. ***Monetary policy can be highly effective in reviving a weak economy even if short-term interest rates are already near zero***. We have recently entered a world where inflation is not always the norm. Japan, for example, recently experienced a period of deflation when the price level was actually falling. One common view is that when a central bank has driven down short-term nominal interest rates to near zero, there is nothing more that monetary policy can do to stimulate the economy. The transmission mechanisms of monetary policy described here indicate that this view is false. As our discussion of the factors that affect the monetary base in Chapter 14 indicated, expansionary monetary policy to increase liquidity in the economy can be conducted with open market purchases, which do not have to be solely in short-term government securities. For example, purchases of foreign currencies, like purchases of government bonds, lead to an increase in the monetary base and in the money supply. This increased liquidity and a commitment to future expansionary monetary policy helps revive the economy by raising general price-level expectations and by reflating other asset prices, which then stimulate aggregate demand through the channels outlined here. Therefore, monetary policy can be a potent force for reviving economies that are undergoing deflation and have short-term interest rates near zero. Indeed, because of the lags inherent in fiscal policy and the political constraints on its use, expansionary monetary policy is the key policy action required to revive an economy experiencing deflation.

4. ***Avoiding unanticipated fluctuations in the price level is an important objective of monetary policy, thus providing a rationale for price stability as the primary long-run goal for monetary policy***. As we saw in Chapter 16, central banks in recent years have been putting greater emphasis on price stability as the primary long-run goal for monetary policy. Several rationales have been proposed for this goal, including the undesirable effects of uncertainty about the future price level on business decisions and hence on productivity, distortions associated with the interaction of nominal contracts and the tax system with inflation, and increased social conflict stemming from inflation. The discussion here of monetary transmission mechanisms provides an additional reason why price stability is so important. As we have seen, unanticipated movements in the price level can cause unanticipated fluctuations in output, an undesirable outcome. Particularly important in this regard is the knowledge that, as we saw in Chapter 9, price deflation can be an important factor leading to a prolonged financial crisis, as occurred during the Great Depression. An understanding of the monetary transmission mechanisms thus makes it clear that the goal of price stability is desirable, because it reduces uncertainty about the future price level. Thus the price stability goal implies that a negative inflation rate is at least as undesirable as too high an inflation rate.

Indeed, because of the threat of financial crises, central banks must work very hard to prevent price deflation.

APPLICATION ✦ Applying the Monetary Policy Lessons to Japan

Until 1990, it looked as if Japan might overtake the United States in per capita income. Since then, the Japanese economy has been stagnating, with deflation and low growth. As a result, Japanese living standards have been falling further and further behind those in the United States. Many economists take the view that Japanese monetary policy is in part to blame for the poor performance of the Japanese economy. Could applying the four lessons outlined in the previous section have helped Japanese monetary policy perform better?

The first lesson suggests that it is dangerous to think that declines in interest rates always mean that monetary policy has been easing. In the mid-1990s, when short-term interest rates began to decline, falling to near zero in the late 1990s and early 2000s, the monetary authorities in Japan took the view that monetary policy was sufficiently expansionary. Now it is widely recognized that this view was incorrect, because the falling and eventually negative inflation rates in Japan meant that real interest rates were actually quite high and that monetary policy was tight, not easy. If the monetary authorities in Japan had followed the advice of the first lesson, they might have pursued a more expansionary monetary policy, which would have helped boost the economy.

The second lesson suggests that monetary policymakers should pay attention to other asset prices in assessing the stance of monetary policy. At the same time interest rates were falling in Japan, stock and real estate prices were collapsing, thus providing another indication that Japanese monetary policy was not easy. Recognizing the second lesson might have led Japanese monetary policymakers to recognize sooner that they needed a more expansionary monetary policy.

The third lesson indicates that monetary policy can still be effective even if short-term interest rates are near zero. Officials at the Bank of Japan have frequently claimed that they have been helpless in stimulating the economy, because short-term interest rates had fallen to near zero. Recognizing that monetary policy can still be effective even when interest rates are near zero, as the third lesson suggests, would have helped them to take monetary policy actions that would have stimulated aggregate demand by raising other asset prices and inflationary expectations.

The fourth lesson indicates that unanticipated fluctuations in the price level should be avoided. If the Japanese monetary authorities had adhered to this lesson, they might have recognized that allowing deflation to occur could be very damaging to the economy and would be inconsistent with the goal of price stability. Indeed, critics of the Bank of Japan have suggested that the bank should announce an inflation target to promote the price stability objective, but the bank has resisted this suggestion.

Heeding the advice from the four lessons in the previous section might have led to a far more successful conduct of monetary policy in Japan in recent years.[22]

---

[22]For a more detailed critique of recent monetary policy in Japan, see Takatoshi Ito and Frederic S. Mishkin, "Two Decades of Japanese Monetary Policy and the Deflation Problem," *National Bureau of Economic Research Working Paper No. 10878* (November 2004).

SUMMARY

1. There are two basic types of empirical evidence: structural model evidence and reduced-form evidence. Both have advantages and disadvantages. The main advantage of structural model evidence is that it provides us with an understanding of how the economy works and gives us more confidence in the direction of causation between money and output. However, if the structure is not correctly specified, because it ignores important monetary transmission mechanisms, it could seriously underestimate the effectiveness of monetary policy. Reduced-form evidence has the advantage of not restricting the way monetary policy affects economic activity and so may be more likely to capture the full effects of monetary policy. However, reduced-form evidence cannot rule out the possibility of reverse causation or an outside driving factor, which could lead to misleading conclusions about the importance of money.

2. The early Keynesians believed that money does not matter, because they found weak links between interest rates and investment and because low interest rates on Treasury securities convinced them that monetary policy was easy during the worst economic contraction in U.S. history, the Great Depression. Monetarists objected to this interpretation of the evidence on the grounds that (a) the focus on nominal rather than real interest rates may have obscured any link between interest rates and investment; (b) interest-rate effects on investment might be only one of many channels through which monetary policy affects aggregate demand; and (c) by the standards of real interest rates and interest rates on lower-grade bonds, monetary policy was extremely contractionary during the Great Depression.

3. Early monetarist evidence falls into three categories: timing, statistical, and historical. Because of reverse causation and outside-factor possibilities, some serious doubts exist regarding conclusions that can be drawn from timing and statistical evidence alone. However, some of the historical evidence in which exogenous declines in money growth are followed by recessions provides stronger support for the monetarist position that money matters. As a result of empirical research, Keynesian and monetarist opinion has converged to the view that money does matter to aggregate economic activity and the price level. However, Keynesians do not agree with the monetarist position that money is *all* that matters.

4. The transmission mechanisms of monetary policy include traditional interest-rate channels that operate through the cost of capital and affect investment; other asset price channels such as exchange rate effects, Tobin's *q* theory, and wealth effects; and the credit view channels—the bank lending channel, the balance sheet channel, the cash flow channel, the unanticipated price level channel, and household liquidity effects.

5. Four lessons for monetary policy can be drawn from this chapter: (a) It is dangerous always to associate monetary policy easing or tightening with a fall or a rise in short-term nominal interest rates; (b) other asset prices besides those on short-term debt instruments contain important information about the stance of monetary policy because they are important elements in the monetary policy transmission mechanisms; (c) monetary policy can be highly effective in reviving a weak economy even if short-term interest rates are already near zero; and (d) avoiding unanticipated fluctuations in the price level is an important objective of monetary policy, thus providing a rationale for price stability as the primary long-run goal for monetary policy.

KEY TERMS

consumer durable expenditure, p. 601

consumption, p. 604

credit view, p. 602

reduced-form evidence, p. 588

reverse causation, p. 590

structural model, p. 588

structural model evidence, p. 587

transmission mechanisms of monetary policy, p. 588

⌐IONS AND PROBLEMS

All questions and problems are available in 〔myeconlab〕 *at* www.myeconlab.com/mishkin.

1. Suppose that a researcher is trying to determine whether jogging is good for a person's health. She examines this question in two ways. In method A, she examines whether joggers live longer than nonjoggers. In method B, she examines whether jogging reduces cholesterol in the bloodstream and lowers blood pressure; then she asks whether lower cholesterol and blood pressure prolong life. Which of these two methods will produce reduced-form evidence and which will produce structural model evidence?

2. If research indicates that joggers do not have lower cholesterol and blood pressure than nonjoggers, is it still possible that jogging is good for your health? Give a concrete example.

3. If research indicates that joggers live longer than non-joggers, is it possible that jogging is not good for your health? Give a concrete example.

4. Suppose that you plan to buy a car and want to know whether a General Motors car is more reliable than a Ford. One way to find out is to ask owners of both cars how often their cars go into the shop for repairs. Another way is to visit the factories producing the cars and see which one is built better. Which procedure will provide reduced-form evidence and which structural model evidence?

5. If the GM car you plan to buy has a better repair record than a Ford, does this mean that the GM car is necessarily more reliable? (GM car owners might, for example, change their oil more frequently than Ford owners.)

6. Suppose that when you visit the Ford and GM car factories to examine how the cars are built, you have time only to see how well the engine is put together. If Ford engines are better built than GM engines, does that mean that the Ford will be more reliable than the GM car?

7. How might bank behavior (described in Chapter 14) lead to causation running from output to the money supply? What does this say about evidence that finds a strong correlation between money and output?

8. What operating procedures of the Fed (described in Chapter 16) might explain how movements in output could cause movements in the money supply?

9. "In every business cycle in the past 100 years, the rate at which the money supply is growing always decreases before output does. Therefore, the money supply causes business cycle movements." Do you agree? What objections can you raise against this argument?

10. How did the research strategies of Keynesian and monetarist economists differ after they were exposed to the earliest monetarist evidence?

11. In the 1973–1975 recession, the value of common stocks in real terms fell by nearly 50%. How might this decline in the stock market have affected aggregate demand and thus contributed to the severity of this recession? Be specific about the mechanisms through which the stock market decline affected the economy.

12. "The cost of financing investment is related only to interest rates; therefore, the only way that monetary policy can affect investment spending is through its effects on interest rates." Is this statement true, false, or uncertain? Explain your answer.

13. Predict what will happen to stock prices if the money supply rises. Explain why you are making this prediction.

14. Franco Modigliani found that the most important transmission mechanisms of monetary policy involve consumer expenditure. Describe how at least two of these mechanisms work.

15. "The monetarists have demonstrated that the early Keynesians were wrong in saying that money doesn't matter at all to economic activity. Therefore, we should accept the monetarist position that money is all that matters." Do you agree? Why or why not?

WEB EXERCISES

1. Figure 1 shows the relationship between estimated real interest rates and nominal interest rates. Go to www.martincapital.com/ and click on "charts and data," then on "nominal versus real market rates" to find data showing the spread between real interest rates and nominal interest rates. Discuss how the current spread differs from that shown most recently in Figure 1. What are the implications of this change?

2. Figure 2 discusses business cycles. Go to www.econlib.org/library/Enc1/Recessions.html and review the material reported on recessions.
   a. What is the formal definition of a recession?
   b. What are the problems with the definition?
   c. What are the three D's used by the National Bureau of Economic Research (NBER) to define a recession?
   d. Review Chart 1. What trend is apparent about the length of recessions?

WEB REFERENCES

www.martincapital.com/

Click on "charts and data," then on "nominal versus real market rates" to find up-to-the-minute data showing the spread between real rates and nominal rates.

www.conference-board.org/economics/bci

A site with extensive data on the factors that define business cycles.

 MyEconLab CAN HELP YOU GET A BETTER GRADE

If your exam were tomorrow, would you be ready? For each chapter, MyEconLab Practice Test and Study Plans pinpoint which sections you have mastered and which ones you need to study. That way, you are more efficient with your study time, and you are better prepared for your exams.

To see how it works, turn to page 20 and then go to: www.myeconlab.com/mishkin

24

Money and Inflation

Preview

Since the early 1960s, when the inflation rate hovered between 1% and 2%, the economy has suffered from higher and more variable rates of inflation. By the late 1960s, the inflation rate had climbed beyond 5%, and by 1974, it reached the double-digit level. After moderating somewhat during the 1975–1978 period, it shot above 10% in 1979 and 1980, slowed to around 5% from 1982 to 1990, declined further to around 2% in the late 1990s, and then climbed above the 5% level in 2008. Inflation, the condition of a continually rising price level, has become a major concern of politicians and the public, and how to control it frequently dominates the discussion of economic policy.

How do we prevent the inflationary fire from igniting and end the roller-coaster ride in the inflation rate of the past 40 years? Milton Friedman provided an answer in his famous proposition that "inflation is always and everywhere a monetary phenomenon." He postulated that the source of all inflation episodes is a high growth rate of the money supply: Simply by reducing the growth rate of the money supply to low levels, inflation can be prevented.

In this chapter, we use aggregate demand and supply analysis from Chapter 22 to reveal the role of monetary policy in creating inflation. You will find that as long as inflation is defined as the condition of a continually and rapidly rising price level, almost all economists agree with Friedman's proposition that inflation is a monetary phenomenon.

But what *causes* inflation? How does inflationary monetary policy come about? You will see that inflationary monetary policy is an offshoot of other government policies: the attempt to hit high employment targets or the running of large budget deficits. Examining how these policies lead to inflation will point us toward ways of preventing it at minimum cost in terms of unemployment and output loss.

MONEY AND INFLATION: EVIDENCE

The evidence for Friedman's statement is straightforward. **Whenever a country's inflation rate is extremely high for a sustained period of time, its rate of money supply growth is also extremely high**. Indeed, this is exactly what we saw in Figure 6 in Chapter 1, which shows that the countries with the highest inflation rates have also had the highest rates of money growth.

Evidence of this type seems to support the proposition that extremely high inflation is the result of a high rate of money growth. Keep in mind, however, that you are looking at reduced-form evidence, which focuses solely on the correlation of two variables:

617

money growth and the inflation rate. As with all reduced-form evidence, reverse causation (inflation causing money supply growth) or an outside factor that drives both money growth and inflation could be involved.

How might you rule out these possibilities? First, you might look for historical episodes in which an increase in money growth appears to be an exogenous event; a high inflation rate for a sustained period following the increase in money growth would provide strong evidence that high money growth is the driving force behind the inflation. Luckily for our analysis, such clear-cut episodes—hyperinflations (extremely rapid inflations with inflation rates exceeding 50% per month)—have occurred, the most notorious being the German hyperinflation of 1921–1923.

German Hyperinflation, 1921–1923

In 1921, the need to make reparations and reconstruct the economy after World War I caused the German government's expenditures to greatly exceed revenues. The government could have obtained revenues to cover these increased expenditures by raising taxes, but that solution was, as always, politically unpopular and would have taken much time to implement. The government could also have financed the expenditure by borrowing from the public, but the amount needed was far in excess of its capacity to borrow. There was only one route left: the printing press. The government could pay for its expenditures simply by printing more currency (increasing the money supply) and using it to make payments to the individuals and companies that were providing it with goods and services. As shown in Figure 1, this is exactly what the German government did; in late 1921, the money supply began to increase rapidly, and so did the price level.

In 1923, the budgetary situation of the German government deteriorated even further. Early that year, the French invaded the Ruhr, because Germany had failed to make its scheduled reparations payments. A general strike in the region then ensued to protest the French action, and the German government actively supported this "passive resistance" by making payments to striking workers. As a result, government expenditures climbed dramatically, and the government printed currency at an even faster rate to finance this spending. As displayed in Figure 1, the result of the explosion in the money supply was that the price level blasted off, leading to an inflation rate for 1923 that exceeded 1 million percent!

The invasion of the Ruhr and the printing of currency to pay striking workers fit the characteristics of an exogenous event. Reverse causation (that the rise in the price level caused the French to invade the Ruhr) is highly implausible, and it is hard to imagine a third factor that could have been a driving force behind both inflation and the explosion in the money supply. Therefore, the German hyperinflation qualifies as a "controlled experiment" that supports Friedman's proposition that inflation is a monetary phenomenon.

Recent Episodes of Rapid Inflation

Only one country has recently topped Germany in the high inflation league. In 2008, Zimbabwe's inflation rate went to over 2 million percent officially (but unofficially over 10 million percent). In July, the Zimbabwean central bank issued a new $100 billion bank note. That's a lot of zeros.

The explanation for Zimbabwe's hyperinflation is the same as Germany's during its hyperinflation: extremely high money growth because the weak government of Robert

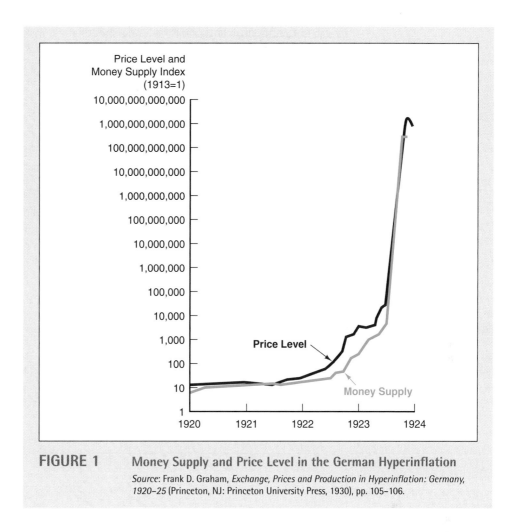

FIGURE 1   **Money Supply and Price Level in the German Hyperinflation**

Source: Frank D. Graham, *Exchange, Prices and Production in Hyperinflation: Germany, 1920–25* (Princeton, NJ: Princeton University Press, 1930), pp. 105–106.

Mugabe was unwilling to finance government expenditures by raising taxes, which led to a very high budget deficit financed by money creation.

Note that the inflation rate is high in all cases in which the high rate of money growth can be classified as an exogenous event. This is strong evidence that high money growth causes high inflation.

MEANING OF INFLATION

You may have noticed that all the empirical evidence on the relationship of money growth and inflation discussed so far looks only at cases in which the price level is continually rising at a rapid rate and so inflation is persistent. It is this definition of inflation that Friedman and other economists use when they make statements such as "inflation is always and everywhere a monetary phenomenon." This is not what your friendly newscaster means when reporting the monthly inflation rate on the nightly news. The newscaster is only telling you how much, in percentage terms, the price level has changed from the previous month. For example, when you hear that the monthly inflation rate is 1% (12% annual rate), this indicates only that the price level has risen by 1% in that month. This could be a one-shot change, in which the high inflation rate is merely temporary, not sustained. Only if the inflation rate remains high persistently for, say, several years will economists say that inflation has been high.

Accordingly, Milton Friedman's proposition actually says that upward movements in the price level are a monetary phenomenon *only* if this is a sustained process. When *inflation* is defined as a persistent and rapid rise in the price level, almost all economists agree with Friedman's proposition that money alone is to blame.

VIEWS OF INFLATION

Now that we understand what Friedman's proposition means, we can use the aggregate demand and supply analysis learned in Chapter 22 to show that large and persistent upward movements in the price level (high inflation) can occur only if there is a continually growing money supply.

How Money Growth Produces Inflation

First, let's look at the outcome of a continually growing money supply (see Figure 2). Initially, the economy is at point 1, with output at the natural rate level and the price level at P_1 (the intersection of the aggregate demand curve AD_1 and the short-run aggregate supply curve AS_1). If the money supply increases steadily over the course of the year, the aggregate demand curve shifts rightward to AD_2. At first, for a very brief time, the economy may move to point $1'$ and output may increase above the natural rate level

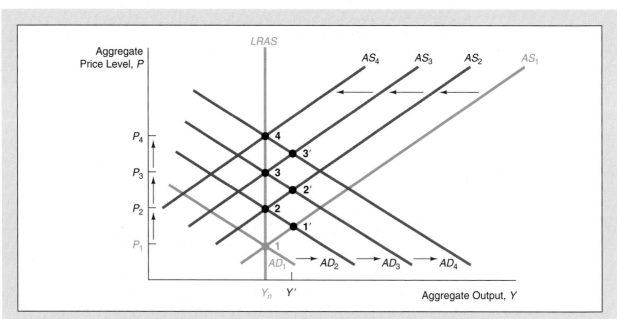

FIGURE 2   **Response to a Continually Growing Money Supply**
A continually growing money supply shifts the aggregate demand curve to the right from AD_1 to AD_2 to AD_3 to AD_4, while the short-run aggregate supply curve shifts to the left from AS_1 to AS_2 to AS_3 to AS_4. The result is that the price level rises continually from P_1 to P_2 to P_3 to P_4.

to Y′, but the resulting decline in unemployment below the natural rate level will cause wages to rise, and the short-run aggregate supply curve will quickly begin to shift leftward. It will stop shifting only when it reaches AS_2, at which time the economy has returned to the natural rate level of output on the long-run aggregate supply curve.[1] At the new equilibrium, point 2, the price level has increased from P_1 to P_2.

If the money supply increases the next year, the aggregate demand curve will shift to the right again to AD_3, and the short-run aggregate supply curve will shift from AS_2 to AS_3; the economy will move to point 2′ and then to point 3, where the price level has risen to P_3. If the money supply continues to grow in subsequent years, the economy will continue to move to higher and higher price levels. As long as the money supply grows, this process will continue, and inflation will occur. **High money growth produces high inflation**.

Can Other Factors Besides Money Growth Produce a Sustained Inflation?

In the aggregate demand and supply analysis in Chapter 22, you learned that other factors besides changes in the money supply (such as fiscal policy and supply shocks) can affect the aggregate demand and supply curves. Doesn't this suggest that these other factors can generate persistent high inflation? The answer, surprisingly, is no. To see why high inflation is always a monetary phenomenon, let's dig a little deeper into aggregate demand and supply analysis to see whether other factors can generate high inflation in the absence of a high rate of money growth.

Can Fiscal Policy by Itself Produce Inflation?   To examine this question, let's look at Figure 3, which demonstrates the effect of a one-shot permanent increase in government expenditure (say, from $500 billion to $600 billion) on aggregate output and the price level. Initially, we are at point 1, where output is at the natural rate level and the price level is P_1. The increase in government expenditure shifts the aggregate demand curve to AD_2, and we move to point 1′, where output is above the natural rate level at $Y_{1'}$. Because of this, the short-run aggregate supply curve will begin to shift leftward, eventually reaching AS_2, where it intersects the aggregate demand curve AD_2 at point 2, at which output is again at the natural rate level and the price level has risen to P_2.

The net result of a one-shot permanent increase in government expenditure is a one-shot permanent increase in the price level. What happens to the inflation rate? When we move from point 1 to 1′ to 2, the price level rises, and we have a positive inflation rate. But when we finally get to point 2, the inflation rate returns to zero. We see that the one-shot increase in government expenditure leads to only a *temporary* increase in the inflation rate, not to persistent inflation in which the price level is continually rising.

If government spending increases continually, however, we *could* get a continuing rise in the price level. It appears, then, that aggregate demand and supply analysis could reject Friedman's proposition that inflation is always the result of money growth. The problem with this argument is that a continually increasing level of government expenditure is not a feasible policy. There is a limit on the total amount of possible government expenditure; the government cannot spend more than 100% of GDP. In fact, well before

---

[1]There is a possibility that the short-run aggregate supply curve may immediately shift in toward AS_2, because workers and firms may expect the increase in the money supply, so expected inflation will be higher. In this case, the movement to point 2 will be very rapid, and output need not rise above the natural rate level. (Some support for this scenario from the theory of rational expectations is discussed in Chapter 25.)

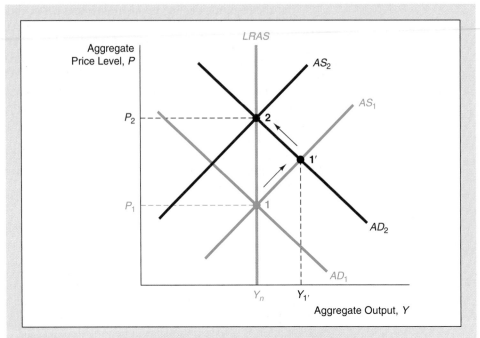

FIGURE 3   **Response to a One-Shot Permanent Increase in Government Expenditure**

A one-shot permanent increase in government expenditure shifts the aggregate demand curve rightward from AD_1 to AD_2, moving the economy from point 1 to point 1′. Because output now exceeds the natural rate level Y_n, the short-run aggregate supply curve eventually shifts leftward to AS_2, and the price level rises from P_1 to P_2, a one-shot permanent increase but not a continuing increase.

this limit is reached, the political process would stop the increases in government spending. As revealed in the continual debates in Congress over balanced budgets and government spending, both the public and politicians have a particular target level of government spending they deem appropriate; although small deviations from this level might be tolerated, large deviations would not. Indeed, public and political perceptions impose tight limits on the degree to which government expenditures can increase.

What about the other side of fiscal policy—taxes? Could continual tax cuts generate an inflation? Again the answer is no. The analysis in Figure 3 also describes the price and output response to a one-shot decrease in taxes. There will be a one-shot increase in the price level, but the increase in the inflation rate will be only temporary. We can increase the price level by cutting taxes even more, but this process would have to stop—once taxes reach zero, they can't be reduced further. We must conclude, then, that ***persistent high inflation cannot be driven by fiscal policy alone***.[2]

---

[2]The argument here demonstrates that "animal spirits" also cannot be the source of inflation. Although consumer and business optimism, which stimulates these groups' spending, can produce a one-shot shift in the aggregate demand curve and a temporary inflation, it cannot produce continuing shifts in the aggregate demand curve and persistent inflation. The reasoning is the same as before: Consumers and businesses cannot continue to raise their spending without limit because their spending cannot exceed 100% of GDP.

FIGURE 4   **Response to a Supply Shock**
A negative supply shock (or a wage push) shifts the short-run aggregate supply curve leftward to AS_2 and results in high unemployment at point 1′. As a result, the short-run aggregate supply curve shifts back to the right to AS_1, and the economy returns to point 1, where the price level has returned to P_1.

Can Supply-Side Phenomena by Themselves Produce Inflation?

Because supply shocks and workers' attempts to increase their wages can shift the short-run aggregate supply curve leftward, you might suspect that these supply-side phenomena by themselves could stimulate inflation. Again, we can show that this suspicion is incorrect.

Suppose that a negative supply shock—for example, an oil embargo—raises oil prices (or workers could have successfully pushed up their wages). As displayed in Figure 4, the negative supply shock shifts the short-run aggregate supply curve from AS_1 to AS_2. If the money supply remains unchanged, leaving the aggregate demand curve at AD_1, we move to point 1′, where output $Y_{1'}$ is below the natural rate level and the price level $P_{1'}$ is higher. The short-run aggregate supply curve will now shift back to AS_1, because unemployment is above the natural rate, and the economy slides down AD_1 from point 1′ to point 1. The net result of the supply shock is that we return to full employment at the initial price level, and there is no continuing inflation. Additional negative supply shocks that again shift the short-run aggregate supply curve leftward will lead to the same outcome: The price level will rise temporarily, but persistent inflation will not result. The conclusion that we have reached is the following: **Supply-side phenomena cannot be the source of persistent high inflation.**[3]

---

[3]Supply-side phenomena that alter the natural rate level of output (and shift the long-run aggregate supply curve at Y_n) can produce a permanent one-shot change in the price level. However, this resulting one-shot change results in only a temporary inflation, not a continuing rise in the price level.

Summary

Our aggregate demand and supply analysis shows that persistent high inflation can occur only with a high rate of money growth. As long as we recognize that inflation refers to a continuing increase in the price level at a rapid rate, we now see why Milton Friedman was correct when he said that "Inflation is always and everywhere a monetary phenomenon."

ORIGINS OF INFLATIONARY MONETARY POLICY

Although we now know *what* must occur to generate a persistent rapid inflation—a high rate of money growth—we still can't understand *why* persistent high inflation occurs until we have learned how and why inflationary monetary policies come about. If everyone agrees that inflation is not a good thing for an economy, why do we see so much of it? Why do governments pursue inflationary monetary policies? Because there is nothing intrinsically desirable about inflation and because we know that a high rate of money growth doesn't happen of its own accord, it must follow that in trying to achieve other goals, governments end up with a high money growth rate and high inflation. In this section, we will examine the government policies that are the most common sources of inflation.

High Employment Targets and Inflation

The first goal most governments pursue that often results in inflation is high employment. The U.S. government is committed by law (the Employment Act of 1946 and the Humphrey-Hawkins Act of 1978) to promoting high employment. Though it is true that both laws require a commitment to a high level of employment consistent with a stable price level, in practice the U.S. government has often pursued a high employment target with little concern about the inflationary consequences of its policies. This was true especially in the mid-1960s and 1970s, when the U.S. government began to take a more active role in attempting to stabilize unemployment.

Two types of inflation can result from an activist stabilization policy to promote high employment: **cost-push inflation**, which occurs because of negative supply shocks or a push by workers to get higher wages, and **demand-pull inflation**, which results when policymakers pursue policies that shift the aggregate demand curve to the right. We will now use aggregate demand and supply analysis to examine how a high employment target can lead to both types of inflation.

Cost-Push Inflation   In Figure 5, the economy is initially at point 1, the intersection of the aggregate demand curve AD_1 and the short-run aggregate supply curve AS_1. Suppose that workers decide to seek higher wages, either because they want to increase their real wages (wages in terms of the goods and services they can buy) or because they expect inflation to be high and wish to keep up with inflation. The effect of such an increase (similar to a negative supply shock) is to shift the short-run aggregate supply curve leftward to AS_2.[4] If government fiscal and monetary policy remains unchanged, the economy would move to point 1′ at the intersection of the new short-run

---

[4]The cost-push inflation we describe here might also occur as a result either of firms' attempts to obtain higher prices or of negative supply shocks.

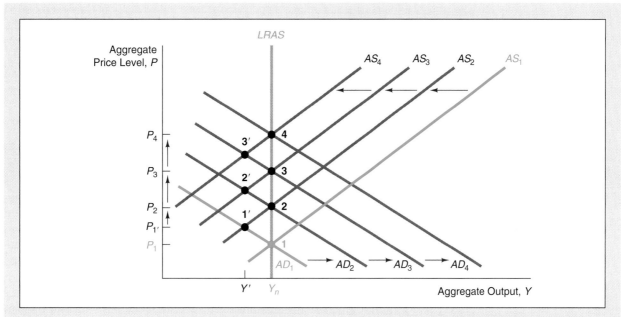

FIGURE 5   Cost-Push Inflation with an Activist Policy to Promote High Employment
In a cost-push inflation, the leftward shifts of the short-run aggregate supply curve from AS_1 to AS_2 to AS_3 and so on cause a government with a high employment target to shift the aggregate demand curve to the right continually to keep unemployment and output at their natural rate levels. The result is a continuing rise in the price level from P_1 to P_2 to P_3 and so on.

aggregate supply curve AS_2 and the aggregate demand curve AD_1. Output would decline to Y', below its natural rate level Y_n, and the price level would rise to $P_{1'}$.

What would activist policymakers with a high employment target do if this situation developed? Because of the drop in output and resulting increase in unemployment, they would implement policies to raise the aggregate demand curve to AD_2, so that we would return to the natural rate level of output at point 2 and price level P_2. The workers who have increased their wages have not fared too badly. The government has stepped in to make sure that there is no excessive unemployment, and they have achieved their goal of higher wages. Because the government has, in effect, given in to the demands of workers for higher wages, an activist policy with a high employment target is often referred to as an **accommodating policy**.

The workers, having had their cake and eaten it, too, might be encouraged to seek even higher wages. In addition, other workers might now realize that their wages have fallen relative to their fellow workers', and because they don't want to be left behind, these workers will seek to increase their wages. The result is that the short-run aggregate supply curve shifts leftward again, to AS_3. Unemployment develops again when we move to point $2'$, and the activist policies will once more be used to shift the aggregate demand curve rightward to AD_3 and return the economy to full employment at a price level of P_3. If this process continues, the result will be a continuing increase in the price level—a persistent cost-push inflation.

What role does monetary policy play in a cost-push inflation? A cost-push inflation can occur only if the aggregate demand curve is shifted continually to the right. The first shift of the aggregate demand curve to AD_2 could be achieved by a one-shot increase in government expenditure or a one-shot decrease in taxes. But what about the next required rightward shift of the aggregate demand curve to AD_3, and the next, and the next? The limits on the maximum level of government expenditure and the minimum level of taxes would prevent the use of this expansionary fiscal policy for very long. Hence it cannot be used continually to shift the aggregate demand curve to the right. But the aggregate demand curve *can* be shifted continually rightward by continually increasing the money supply—that is, by going to a higher rate of money growth. Therefore, *a persistent cost-push inflation is a monetary phenomenon because it cannot occur without the monetary authorities pursuing an accommodating policy of a higher rate of money growth*.

Demand-Pull Inflation   The goal of high employment can lead to inflationary monetary policy in another way. Even at full employment, some unemployment is always present because of frictions in the labor market, which make it difficult to immediately match unemployed workers with employers. An unemployed autoworker in Detroit may not know about a job opening in the electronics industry in California or, even if he or she did, may not want to move or be retrained. So the unemployment rate when there is full employment (the natural rate of unemployment) will be greater than zero. If policymakers set a target for unemployment that is too low because it is less than the natural rate of unemployment, this can set the stage for a higher rate of money growth and a resulting persistent inflation. Again we can show how this can happen using an aggregate supply and demand diagram (see Figure 6).

If policymakers have an unemployment target (say, 4%) that is below the natural rate (estimated to be between $4\frac{1}{2}\%$ and $5\frac{1}{2}\%$ currently), they will try to achieve an output

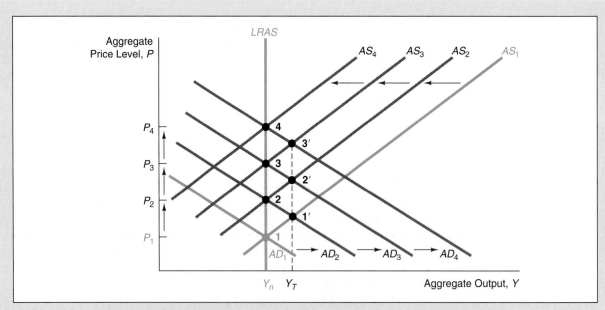

FIGURE 6   **Demand–Pull Inflation: The Consequence of Setting Too Low an Unemployment Target**
Too low an unemployment target (too high an output target of Y_T) causes the government to shift the aggregate demand curve rightward from AD_1 to AD_2 to AD_3 and so on, while the short-run aggregate supply curve shifts leftward from AS_1 to AS_2 to AS_3 and so on. The result is a continuing rise in the price level known as a demand-pull inflation.

target greater than the natural rate level of output. This target level of output is marked Y_T in Figure 6. Suppose that we are initially at point 1; the economy is at the natural rate level of output but below the target level of output Y_T. To hit the unemployment target of 4%, policymakers enact policies to increase aggregate demand, and the effects of these policies shift the aggregate demand curve until it reaches AD_2 and the economy moves to point 1′. Output is at Y_T, and the 4% unemployment rate goal has been reached.

If the targeted unemployment rate was at the natural rate level between $4\frac{1}{2}\%$ and $5\frac{1}{2}\%$, there would be no problem. However, because at Y_T the 4% unemployment rate is below the natural rate level, wages will rise and the short-run aggregate supply curve will shift in to AS_2, moving the economy from point 1′ to point 2. The economy is back at the natural rate of unemployment, but at a higher price level of P_2. We could stop there, but because unemployment is again higher than the target level, policymakers would again shift the aggregate demand curve rightward to AD_3 to hit the output target at point 2′, and the whole process would continue to drive the economy to point 3 and beyond. The overall result is a steadily rising price level—a persistent inflation.

How can policymakers continually shift the aggregate demand curve rightward? We have already seen that they cannot do it through fiscal policy, because of the limits on raising government expenditures and reducing taxes. Instead they will have to resort to expansionary monetary policy: a continuing increase in the money supply and hence a high money growth rate.

Pursuing too low an unemployment rate target or, equivalently, too high an output target is the source of inflationary monetary policy in this situation, but it seems senseless for policymakers to do this. They have not gained the benefit of a permanently higher level of output but have generated the burden of an inflation. If, however, they do not realize that the target rate of unemployment is below the natural rate, the process that we see in Figure 6 will be well under way before they realize their mistake.

Because the inflation described results from policymakers' pursuing policies that shift the aggregate demand curve to the right, it is called a *demand-pull inflation*. In contrast, a *cost-push inflation* occurs when workers push their wages up. Is it easy to distinguish between them in practice? The answer is no. We have seen that both types of inflation will be associated with higher money growth, so we cannot distinguish between them on this basis. Yet as Figures 5 and 6 demonstrate, demand-pull inflation will be associated with periods when unemployment is below the natural rate level, whereas cost-push inflation is associated with periods when unemployment is above the natural rate level. To decide which type of inflation has occurred, we can look at whether unemployment has been above or below its natural rate level. This would be easy if economists and policymakers actually knew how to measure the natural rate of unemployment; unfortunately, this difficult research question is still not fully resolved by the economics profession. In addition, the distinction between cost-push and demand-pull inflation is blurred, because a cost-push inflation can be initiated by a demand-pull inflation: When a demand-pull inflation produces higher inflation rates, expected inflation will eventually rise and cause workers to demand higher wages so that their real wages do not fall. In this way, demand-pull inflation can eventually trigger cost-push inflation.

Budget Deficits and Inflation

Our discussion of the evidence on money and inflation suggested that budget deficits are another possible source of inflationary monetary policy. To see if this could be the case, we need to look at how a government finances its budget deficits.

Government Budget Constraint   Because the government has to pay its bills just as we do, it has a budget constraint. There are two ways we can pay for our spending: raise revenue (by working) or borrow. The government also enjoys these two options: raise revenue by levying taxes or go into debt by issuing government bonds. Unlike us, however, it has a third option: The government can create money and use it to pay for the goods and services it buys.

Methods of financing government spending are described by an expression called the **government budget constraint**, which states the following: The government budget deficit *DEF*, which equals the excess of government spending *G* over tax revenue *T*, must equal the sum of the change in the monetary base ΔMB and the change in government bonds held by the public ΔB. Algebraically, this expression can be written as follows:

$$DEF = G - T = \Delta MB + \Delta B \tag{1}$$

To see what the government budget constraint means in practice, let's look at the case in which the only government purchase is a $100 million supercomputer. If the government convinces the electorate that such a computer is worth paying for, it will probably be able to raise the $100 million in taxes to pay for it, and the budget deficit will equal zero. The government budget constraint then tells us that no issue of money or bonds is needed to pay for the computer, because the budget is balanced. If taxpayers think that the supercomputer is too expensive and refuse to pay taxes for it, the budget constraint indicates that the government must pay for it by selling $100 million of new bonds to the public or by, in effect, printing $100 million of currency to pay for the computer. In either case, the budget constraint is satisfied; the $100 million deficit is balanced by the change in the stock of government bonds held by the public ($\Delta B =$ $100 million) or by the change in the monetary base ($\Delta MB =$ $100 million).

The government budget constraint thus reveals two important facts: *If the government deficit is financed by an increase in bond holdings by the public, there is no effect on the monetary base and hence on the money supply. But, if the deficit is not financed by increased bond holdings by the public, the monetary base and the money supply increase.*

There are several ways to understand why a deficit leads to an increase in the monetary base when the public's bond holdings do not increase. The simplest case is when the government's treasury has the legal right to issue currency to finance its deficit. Financing the deficit is then very straightforward: The government just pays for the spending that is in excess of its tax revenues with new currency. Because this increase in currency adds directly to the monetary base, the monetary base rises and the money supply with it through the process of multiple deposit creation described in Chapter 14.

In the United States, however, and in many other countries, the government does not have the right to issue currency to pay for its bills. In this case, the government must finance its deficit by first issuing bonds to the public to acquire the extra funds to pay its bills. Yet if these bonds do not end up in the hands of the public, the only alternative is that they are purchased by the central bank. For the government bonds not to end up in the hands of the public, the central bank must conduct an open market purchase, which, as we saw in Chapter 14, leads to an increase in the monetary base and in the money supply. This method of financing government spending is called **monetizing the debt** because, as the two-step process described indicates, government debt issued to finance government spending has been removed from the hands of the public and has been replaced by high-powered money. This method of financing, or the more direct method when a government just issues the currency directly, is also, somewhat inaccurately, referred to as **printing money** because high-powered money (the monetary base) is created in the process. The use of the word *printing* is misleading because what is essential to this method of financing government spending is that the monetary base increases when the central bank conducts open market purchases, just as it would if more currency were put in circulation.

We thus see that a budget deficit can lead to an increase in the money supply if it is financed by the creation of high-powered money. However, earlier in this chapter you have seen that persistent inflation can develop only when the stock of money grows continually. Can a budget deficit financed by printing money do this? The answer is yes, if the budget deficit persists for a substantial period of time. In the first period, if the deficit is financed by money creation, the money supply will rise, shifting the aggregate demand curve to the right and leading to a rise in the price level (see Figure 2). If the budget deficit is still present in the next period, it has to be financed all over again. The money supply will rise again, and the aggregate demand curve will again shift to the right, causing the price level to rise further. As long as the deficit persists and the government resorts to printing money to pay for it, this process will continue. *Financing a persistent deficit by money creation will lead to a sustained inflation*.

A critical element in this process is that the deficit is persistent. If temporary, it would not produce an inflation because the situation would then be similar to that shown in Figure 3, in which there is a one-shot increase in government expenditure. In the period when the deficit occurs, there will be an increase in money to finance it, and the resulting rightward shift of the aggregate demand curve will raise the price level. If the deficit disappears in the next period, there is no longer a need to print money. The aggregate demand curve will not shift further, and the price level will not continue to rise. Hence the one-shot increase in the money supply from the temporary deficit generates only a one-shot increase in the price level, and a persistent inflation does not develop.

To summarize, *a deficit can be the source of a sustained inflation only if it is persistent rather than temporary and if the government finances it by creating money rather than by issuing bonds to the public*.

If inflation is the result, why do governments frequently finance persistent deficits by creating money? The answer is the key to understanding how budget deficits may lead to inflation.

Budget Deficits and Money Creation in Other Countries   Although the United States has well-developed money and capital markets in which huge quantities of its government bonds, both short- and long-term, can be sold, this is not the situation in many developing countries. If developing countries run budget deficits, they cannot finance them by issuing bonds and must resort to their only other alternative, printing money. As a result, when they run large deficits relative to GDP, the money supply grows at substantial rates, and a persistent inflation results.

Earlier we cited Germany in the 1920s and Zimbabwe more recently who had high inflation rates and high money growth as evidence that inflation is a monetary phenomenon. The Latin American countries that had high money growth are precisely the ones that had persistent and extremely large budget deficits relative to GDP. The only way to finance the deficits was to print more money, so the ultimate source of their high inflation rates was their large budget deficits.

In all episodes of hyperinflation, huge government budget deficits are also the ultimate source of inflationary monetary policies. The budget deficits during hyperinflations are so large that even if a capital market exists to issue government bonds, it does not have sufficient capacity to handle the quantity of bonds that the government wishes to sell. In this situation, the government must also resort to the printing press to finance the deficits.

Budget Deficits and Money Creation in the United States So far we have seen why budget deficits in some countries must lead to money creation and inflation. Either the deficit is huge, or the country does not have sufficient access to capital markets in which it can sell government bonds. But neither of these scenarios seems to describe the situation in the United States. True, the United States' deficits were large in the 1980s, early 1990s and mid-2000s, but even so, the magnitude of these deficits relative to GDP was small compared to the deficits of countries that have experienced hyperinflations: The U.S. deficit as a percentage of GDP reached a peak of 6% in 1983, whereas Argentina's budget deficit sometimes exceeded 15% of GDP. Furthermore, because the United States has the best-developed government bond market of any country in the world, it can issue large quantities of bonds when it needs to finance its deficit.

Whether the budget deficit can influence the monetary base and the money supply depends critically on how the Federal Reserve chooses to conduct monetary policy. If the Fed pursues a policy goal of preventing high interest rates (a possibility, as we have seen in Chapter 16), many economists contend that a budget deficit will lead to the printing of money. Their reasoning, using the supply and demand analysis of the bond market in Chapter 5, is as follows: When the Treasury issues bonds to the public, the supply of bonds rises (from B_1^s to B_2^s in Figure 7), causing bond prices to fall from P_1 to P_2 and hence interest rates to rise. If the Fed considers the rise in interest rates undesirable, it will buy bonds to prop up bond prices and reduce interest rates. The net result is that the government budget deficit can lead to Federal Reserve open market purchases, which raise the monetary base (create high-powered money) and raise the money supply. If the budget deficit persists so that the quantity of bonds supplied keeps on growing, the upward pressure on interest rates will continue, the Fed will purchase bonds again and again, and the money supply will continually rise, resulting in a persistent inflation.

Economists such as Robert Barro of Harvard University, however, do not agree that budget deficits influence the monetary base in the manner just described. Their analysis (which Barro named **Ricardian equivalence** after the nineteenth-century British economist David Ricardo) contends that when the government runs deficits and issues bonds, the public recognizes that it will be subject to higher taxes in the future to pay off these bonds. The public then saves more in anticipation of these future taxes, with the net result that the public demand for bonds increases to match the increased supply. The demand curve for bonds shifts rightward to B_R^d in Figure 7, leaving the bond price and interest rate unchanged. There is now no need for the Fed to purchase bonds to keep the interest rate from rising.

To sum up, although persistent high inflation is "always and everywhere a monetary phenomenon" in the sense that it cannot occur without a high rate of money growth, there are reasons why this inflationary monetary policy might come about. The two underlying reasons are the adherence of policymakers to a high employment target and the presence of persistent government budget deficits.

APPLICATION ✦ Explaining the Rise in U.S. Inflation, 1960–1980

Now that we have examined the underlying sources of inflation, let's apply this knowledge to understanding the causes of the rise in U.S. inflation from 1960 to 1980.

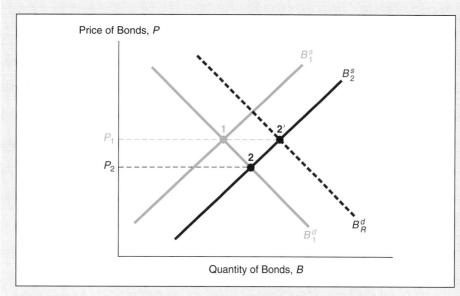

FIGURE 7   **Interest Rates and the Government Budget Deficit**
When the Treasury issues bonds to finance the budget deficit, the supply curve for bonds shifts rightward from B_1^s to B_2^s. Many economists take the position that the equilibrium moves to point 2 because the bond demand curve remains unchanged, with the result that the bond price falls from P_1 to P_2 and the interest rate rises. Adherents of Ricardian equivalence, however, suggest that the demand curve for bonds also increases to B_R^d, moving the equilibrium to point 2′, where the bond price is unchanged at P_1, so that the interest rate does not rise and there is no need for the Fed to buy bonds and increase the money supply.

Figure 8 documents the rise in inflation in those years. At the beginning of the period, the inflation rate was close to 1% at an annual rate; by the late 1970s, it was averaging around 8%. How does the analysis of this chapter explain this rise in inflation?

The conclusion that inflation is a monetary phenomenon is given a fair amount of support by the period from 1960 through 1980. As Figure 8 shows, in this period, there is a close correspondence between movements in the inflation rate and the monetary growth rate from two years earlier. (The money growth rates are from two years earlier, because research indicates that a change in money growth takes that long to affect the inflation rate.) The rise in inflation from 1960 to 1980 can be attributed to the rise in the money growth rate over this period. But you have probably noticed that in 1974–1975 and 1979–1980, the inflation rate is well above the money growth rate from two years earlier. You may recall from Chapter 22 that temporary upward bursts of the inflation rate in those years can be attributed to supply shocks from oil and food price increases that occurred in 1973–1975 and 1978–1981.

However, the linkage between money growth and inflation after 1980 is not at all evident in Figure 8, which explains why in 1982 the Fed announced that it would no longer use M1 as a basis to set monetary policy (see Chapter 16). The breakdown of the relationship between money growth and inflation is the result of substantial gyrations

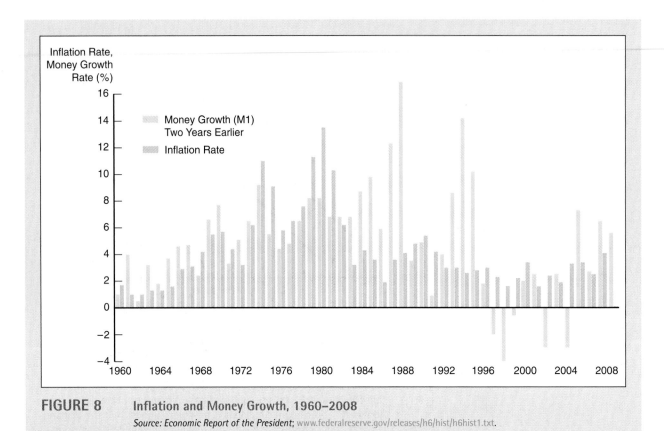

FIGURE 8   **Inflation and Money Growth, 1960–2008**

Source: Economic Report of the President; www.federalreserve.gov/releases/h6/hist/h6hist1.txt.

in velocity in the 1980s and 1990s (documented in Chapter 19). For example, the early 1980s was a period of rapid disinflation (a substantial fall in the inflation rate), yet the money growth rates in Figure 8 do not display a visible downward trend until after the disinflation was over. (The disinflationary process in the 1980s will be discussed in another application later in this chapter.) Although some economists see the 1980s and 1990s as evidence against the money–inflation link, others view this as an unusual period characterized by large fluctuations in interest rates and by rapid financial innovation that made the correct measurement of money far more difficult (see Chapter 3). In their view, this period was an aberration, and the close correspondence of money and inflation is sure to reassert itself. However, this has not yet occurred.

What is the underlying cause of the increased rate of money growth that we see occurring from 1960 to 1980? We have identified two possible sources of inflationary monetary policy: government adherence to a high employment target and budget deficits. Let's see if budget deficits can explain the move to an inflationary monetary policy by plotting the ratio of government debt to GDP in Figure 9. This ratio provides a reasonable measure of whether government budget deficits put upward pressure on interest rates. Only if this ratio is rising might there be a tendency for budget deficits to raise interest rates, because the public is then being asked to hold more government bonds relative to their capacity to buy them. Surprisingly, over the course of the 20-year period from 1960 to 1980, this ratio was falling, not rising. Thus U.S. budget deficits in this period did not raise interest rates and so could not have encouraged the Fed to

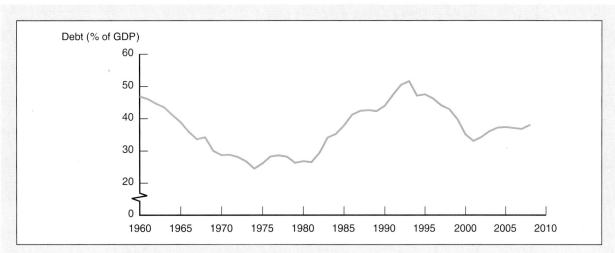

FIGURE 9   Government Debt-to-GDP Ratio, 1960–2008
Source: Economic Report of the President.

expand the money supply by buying bonds. Therefore, Figure 9 tells us that we can rule out budget deficits as a source of the rise in inflation in this period.

Because politicians were frequently bemoaning the budget deficits in this period, why did deficits not lead to an increase in the debt–GDP ratio? The reason is that in this period, U.S. budget deficits were sufficiently small that the increase in the stock of government debt was still slower than the growth in nominal GDP, and the ratio of debt to GDP declined. You can see that interpreting budget deficit numbers is a tricky business.[5]

We have ruled out budget deficits as the instigator; what else could be the underlying cause of the higher rate of money growth and more rapid inflation in the 1960s and 1970s? Figure 10, which compares the actual unemployment rate to the natural rate of unemployment, shows that the economy was experiencing unemployment below the natural rate in all but one year between 1965 and 1973. This suggests that in 1965–1973, the American economy was experiencing the demand-pull inflation described in Figure 6.

Policymakers apparently pursued policies that continually shifted the aggregate demand curve to the right in trying to achieve an output target that was too high, thus causing the continual rise in the price level outlined in Figure 6. This occurred because policymakers, economists, and politicians had become committed in the mid-1960s to a target unemployment rate of 4%, the level of unemployment they thought was consistent with price stability. In hindsight, most economists today agree that the natural rate of unemployment was substantially higher in this period, on the order of 5% to 6%,

---

[5]Another way of understanding the decline in the debt–GDP ratio is to recognize that a rise in the price level reduces the value of the outstanding government debt in real terms—that is, in terms of the goods and services it can buy. So even though budget deficits did lead to a somewhat higher nominal amount of debt in this period, the continually rising price level (inflation) produced a lower real value of the government debt. The decline in the real amount of debt at the same time that real GDP was rising in this period then resulted in the decline in the debt–GDP ratio. For a fascinating discussion of how tricky it is to interpret deficit numbers, see Robert Eisner and Paul J. Pieper, "A New View of the Federal Debt and Budget Deficits," *American Economic Review* 74 (1984): 11–29.

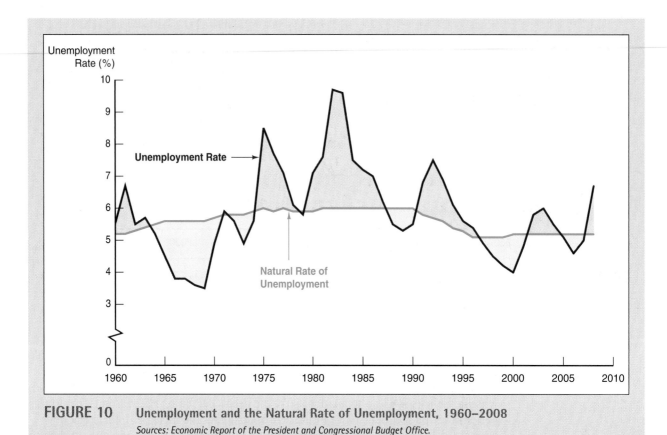

FIGURE 10   **Unemployment and the Natural Rate of Unemployment, 1960–2008**
Sources: Economic Report of the President and Congressional Budget Office.

as shown in Figure 10. The result of the inappropriate 4% unemployment target was the beginning of the most sustained inflationary episode in American history.

After 1975, the unemployment rate was regularly above the natural rate of unemployment, yet inflation continued. It appears that we have the phenomenon of a cost-push inflation described in Figure 5 (the impetus for which was the earlier demand-pull inflation). The persistence of inflation can be explained by the public's knowledge that government policy continued to be concerned with achieving high employment. With a higher rate of expected inflation arising initially from the demand-pull inflation, the aggregate supply curve in Figure 5 continued to shift leftward, causing a rise in unemployment that policymakers would try to eliminate by shifting the aggregate demand curve to the right. The result was a continuation of the inflation that had started in the 1960s.

THE DISCRETIONARY/NONDISCRETIONARY POLICY DEBATE

All economists have similar policy goals—they want to promote high employment and price stability—and yet they often have different views on how policy should be conducted. Advocates of **discretionary policy**, that is, policy to eliminate high

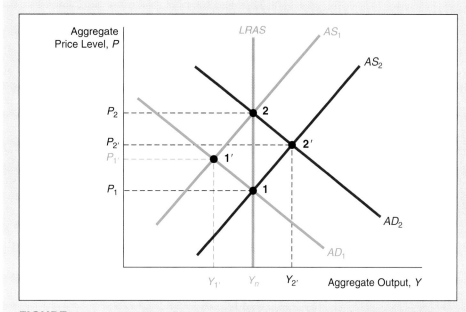

FIGURE 11 — **The Choice Between Discretionary and Nondiscretionary Policy**
When the economy has moved to point 1', the policymaker has two
choices of policy: the nondiscretionary policy of doing nothing and
letting the economy return to point 1 or the discretionary policy of
shifting the aggregate demand curve to AD_2 to move the economy to
point 2.

unemployment whenever it appears, regard the self-correcting mechanism through
wage and price adjustment (see Chapter 22) as very slow. Opponents of discretionary
policy, by contrast, believe that the performance of the economy would be improved
if the government avoided discretionary policy reactions to eliminate unemployment.
We will explore this policy debate by first looking at what the policy responses might
be when the economy experiences high unemployment.

Responses to High Unemployment

Suppose that policymakers confront an economy that has moved to point 1' in Figure 11.
At this point, aggregate output $Y_{1'}$ is lower than the natural rate level, and the economy
is suffering from high unemployment. Policymakers have two viable choices: If they are
proponents of nondiscretionary policy and do nothing, the short-run aggregate supply
curve will eventually shift rightward over time, driving the economy from point 1' to
point 1, where full employment is restored. The discretionary policy alternative is to try
to eliminate the high unemployment by attempting to shift the aggregate demand curve
rightward to AD_2 by pursuing expansionary policy (an increase in the money supply,
increase in government spending, or lowering of taxes). If policymakers could shift the
aggregate demand curve to AD_2 instantaneously, the economy would immediately move
to point 2, where there is full employment. However, several types of lags prevent this
immediate movement from occurring.

1. The *data lag* is the time it takes for policymakers to obtain the data that tell them what is happening in the economy. Accurate data on GDP, for example, are not available until several months after a given quarter is over.

2. The *recognition lag* is the time it takes for policymakers to be sure of what the data are signaling about the future course of the economy. For example, to minimize errors, the National Bureau of Economic Research (the organization that officially dates business cycles) will not declare the economy to be in recession until at least six months after it has determined that one has begun.

3. The *legislative lag* represents the time it takes to pass legislation to implement a particular policy. The legislative lag does not exist for most monetary policy actions such as open market operations. It is, however, important for the implementation of fiscal policy, when it can sometimes take six months to a year to get legislation passed to change taxes or government spending.

4. The *implementation lag* is the time it takes for policymakers to change policy instruments once they have decided on the new policy. Again, this lag is unimportant for the conduct of open market operations because the Fed's trading desk can purchase or sell bonds almost immediately upon being told to do so by the Federal Open Market Committee. Actually implementing fiscal policy may take time, however; for example, getting government agencies to change their spending habits takes time, as does changing tax tables.

5. The *effectiveness lag* is the time it takes for the policy actually to have an impact on the economy. An important argument against discretionary policy is that the effectiveness lag is long (often a year or longer) and variable (i.e., there is substantial uncertainty about how long this lag is).

Discretionary and Nondiscretionary Positions

Now that we understand the considerations that affect decisions by policymakers on whether to pursue discretionary versus nondiscretionary policy, we can examine when each of these policies would be preferable.

Case for Discretionary Policy   Advocates of discretionary policies view the wage and price adjustment process as extremely slow. They believe that nondiscretionary policy is costly, because the slow movement of the economy back to full employment results in a large loss of output. This means that, even though the five lags described may result in delay of a year or two before the aggregate demand curve shifts to AD_2, the short-run aggregate supply curve likewise moves very little during this time. The appropriate path for policymakers to pursue is thus a discretionary policy of moving the economy to point 2 in Figure 11.

Case for a Nondiscretionary Policy   Opponents of discretionary policy view the wage and price adjustment process as more rapid than advocates of discretionary policies do and consider nondiscretionary policy less costly because output is soon back at the natural rate level. They suggest that a discretionary policy of shifting the aggregate demand curve to AD_2 is costly, because it produces more volatility in both the price level and output. The reason for this volatility is that the time it takes to shift the aggregate demand curve to AD_2 is substantial, whereas the wage and price adjustment process is more rapid. Hence, before the aggregate demand curve shifts to the right, the short-run aggregate supply curve will have shifted rightward to AS_2, and the economy will have moved from point 1′ to point 1, where it has returned to the natural rate level of output Y_n. After adjustment to the AS_2 curve is complete, the shift of the aggregate demand curve to AD_2 finally takes effect, leading the economy to point 2′ at the intersection of AD_2 and AS_2. Aggregate output at $Y_{2'}$ is now greater than the natural rate level ($Y_{2'} > Y_n$), so the short-run aggregate supply curve will now shift leftward back to AS_1, moving the economy to point 2, where output is again at the natural rate level.

Although the discretionary policy eventually moves the economy to point 2 as policymakers intended, it leads to a sequence of equilibrium points—1′, 1, 2′, and 2—at which both output and the price level have been highly variable: Output overshoots its target level of Y_n, and the price level falls from $P_{1'}$ to P_1 and then rises to $P_{2'}$ and eventually to P_2. Because this variability is undesirable, policymakers would be better off pursuing nondiscretionary policy which just lets the economy move to point 1.

Expectations and the Discretionary/Nondiscretionary Debate

Our analysis of inflation in the 1970s demonstrated that expectations about policy can be an important element in the inflation process. Allowing for expectations about policy to affect how wages are set (the wage-setting process) provides an additional reason for pursuing a nondiscretionary policy.

Do Expectations Favor Nondiscretionary Policy?   Does the possibility that expectations about policy matter to the wage-setting process strengthen the case for nondiscretionary policy? The case for discretionary policy states that with slow wage and price adjustment, the discretionary policy returns the economy to full employment at point 2 far more quickly than it takes to get to full employment at point 1 if nothing is done. However, the argument for discretionary policy does not allow for the possibility (1) that expectations about policy matter to the wage-setting process and (2) that the economy might initially have moved from point 1 to point 1′ because an attempt by workers to raise their wages or a negative supply shock shifted the short-run aggregate supply curve from AS_2 to AS_1. We must therefore ask the following question about discretionary policy: Will the short-run aggregate supply curve continue to shift to the left after the economy has reached point 2, leading to cost-push inflation?

The answer to this question is yes *if* expectations about policy matter. Our discussion of cost-push inflation in Figure 5 suggested that if workers know that policy will be accommodating in the future, they will continue to push their wages up, and the short-run aggregate supply curve will keep shifting leftward. As a result, policymakers are forced to accommodate the cost push by continuing to shift the aggregate demand curve to the right to eliminate the unemployment that develops. The accommodating, discretionary policy with its high employment target has the hidden cost or disadvantage that it may well lead to inflation.[6]

The main advantage of a nonaccommodating, nondiscretionary policy, in which policymakers do not try to shift the aggregate demand curve in response to the cost push, is that it will prevent inflation. As depicted in Figure 4, the result of an upward push on wages in the face of a nonaccommodating, nondiscretionary policy will be a

---

[6]The issue that is being described here is the time-inconsistency problem described in Chapter 16.

period of unemployment above the natural rate level, which will eventually shift the short-run aggregate supply curve and the price level back to their initial positions. The main criticism of this policy is that the economy will suffer protracted periods of unemployment when the short-run aggregate supply curve shifts leftward. Workers, however, would probably not push for higher wages to begin with if they knew that policy would be nonaccommodating, because their wage gains will lead to a protracted period of unemployment. A nonaccommodating, nondiscretionary policy may have not only the advantage of preventing inflation but also the hidden benefit of discouraging leftward shifts in the short-run aggregate supply curve that lead to excessive unemployment.

In conclusion, *if workers' opinions about whether policy is accommodating or nonaccommodating matter to the wage-setting process, the case for discretionary policy is much weaker*.

Do Expectations About Policy Matter to the Wage-Setting Process?

The answer to this question is crucial to deciding whether discretionary or nondiscretionary policy is preferred and so has become a major topic of current research for economists, but the evidence is not yet conclusive. We can ask, however, whether expectations about policy do affect people's behavior in other contexts. This information will help us know if expectations regarding whether policy is accommodating are important to the wage-setting process.

As any good negotiator knows, convincing your opponent that you will be nonaccommodating is crucial to getting a good deal. If you are bargaining with a car dealer over price, for example, you must convince him that you can just as easily walk away from the deal and buy a car from a dealer on the other side of town. This principle also applies to conducting foreign policy—it is to your advantage to convince your opponent that you will go to war (be nonaccommodating) if your demands are not met. Similarly, if your opponent thinks that you will be accommodating, he will almost certainly take advantage of you. Finally, anyone who has dealt with a two-year-old child knows that the more you give in (pursue an accommodating policy), the more demanding the child becomes. People's expectations about policy *do* affect their behavior. Consequently, it is quite plausible that expectations about policy also affect the wage-setting process.[7]

Discretionary Versus Nondiscretionary: Conclusions

The following conclusions can be generated from our analysis: Advocates of discretionary policy believe in the use of policy to eliminate excessive unemployment whenever it develops, because they view the wage and price adjustment process as sluggish and unresponsive to expectations about policy. Proponents of nondiscretionary policy, by contrast, believe that a discretionary policy that reacts to excessive unemployment is counterproductive, because wage and price adjustment is rapid and because expectations about policy can matter to the wage-setting process. Pro-

---

[7]A recent development in monetary theory, new classical macroeconomics, strongly suggests that expectations about policy are crucial to the wage-setting process and the movements of the aggregate supply curve. We will explore why new classical macroeconomics comes to this conclusion in Chapter 25, when we discuss the implications of the rational expectations hypothesis, which states that expectations are formed using all available information, including expectations about policy.

ponents of nondiscretionary policy thus advocate the use of a policy rule to keep the aggregate demand curve from fluctuating away from the trend rate of growth of the natural rate level of output. Monetarists, who oppose discretionary policy and who also see money as the sole source of fluctuations in the aggregate demand curve, in the past advocated a policy rule whereby the Federal Reserve keeps the money supply growing at a constant rate. This monetarist rule is referred to as a **constant-money-growth-rate rule**. Because of the unstable velocity of M1 and M2, monetarists such as Bennett McCallum and Alan Meltzer of Carnegie-Mellon University have advocated a rule for the growth of the monetary base that is adjusted for past velocity changes.

As our analysis indicates, an important element for the success of a nonaccommodating, nondiscretionary policy rule is that it be *credible*: The public must believe that policymakers will be tough and not accede to a cost push by shifting the aggregate demand curve to the right to eliminate unemployment. In other words, government policymakers need credibility as inflation-fighters in the eyes of the public. Otherwise, workers will be more likely to push for higher wages, which will shift the aggregate supply curve leftward after the economy reaches full employment at a point such as point 2 in Figure 11 and will lead to unemployment or inflation (or both). Alternatively, a credible, nonaccommodating, nondiscretionary policy rule has the benefit that it makes a cost push less likely and thus helps prevent inflation and potential increases in unemployment. The following application suggests that recent historical experience is consistent with the importance of credibility to successful policymaking.

APPLICATION ✦ Importance of Credibility to Volcker's Victory over Inflation

In the period from 1965 through the 1970s, policymakers had little credibility as inflation-fighters—a well-deserved reputation, as they pursued a discretionary, accommodating policy to achieve high employment. As we have seen, the outcome was not a happy one. Inflation soared to double-digit levels, while the unemployment rate remained high. To wring inflation out of the system, the Federal Reserve under Chairman Paul Volcker put the economy through two back-to-back recessions in 1980 and 1981–1982 (see Chapter 16). (The data on inflation, money growth, and unemployment in this period are shown in Figures 8 and 10.) Only after the 1981–1982 recession—the most severe in the postwar period, with unemployment above the 10% level—did Volcker establish credibility for the Fed's anti-inflation policy. By the end of 1982, inflation was running at a rate of less than 5%.

One indication of Volcker's credibility came in 1983, when the money growth rate accelerated dramatically and yet inflation did not rise. Workers and firms were convinced that if inflation reared its head, Volcker would pursue a nonaccommodating policy of quashing it. They did not raise wages and prices, which would have shifted the aggregate supply curve leftward and would have led to both inflation and unemployment. The success of Volcker's anti-inflation policy continued throughout the rest of his term as chairman, which ended in 1987; unemployment fell steadily, while the inflation rate remained below 5%. Volcker's triumph over inflation was achieved because he obtained credibility the hard way—he earned it.

SUMMARY

1. Milton Friedman's famous proposition that "inflation is always and everywhere a monetary phenomenon" is supported by the following evidence: Every country that has experienced a sustained, high inflation has also experienced a high rate of money growth.

2. Aggregate demand and supply analysis shows that high inflation can occur only if there is a high rate of money growth. As long as we recognize that by inflation we mean a rapid and continuing increase in the price level, almost all economists agree with Friedman's proposition.

3. Although high inflation is "always and everywhere a monetary phenomenon" in the sense that it cannot occur without a high rate of money growth, there are reasons why inflationary monetary policy comes about. The two underlying reasons are the adherence of policymakers to a high employment target and the presence of persistent government budget deficits.

4. Advocates of discretionary policy believe in the use of policy to eliminate excessive unemployment whenever it occurs because they view wage and price adjustment as sluggish and unresponsive to expectations about policy. Opponents of discretionary policy take the opposite view and believe that discretionary policy is counterproductive. In addition, they regard the credibility of a nonaccommodating anti-inflation policy as crucial to its success.

KEY TERMS

accommodating policy, p. 625

constant-money-growth-rate rule, p. 639

cost-push inflation, p. 624

demand-pull inflation, p. 624

discretionary policy, p. 634

government budget constraint, p. 628

monetizing the debt, p. 628

printing money, p. 629

Ricardian equivalence, p. 630

QUESTIONS AND PROBLEMS

All questions and problems are available in (X myeconlab) *at* www.myeconlab.com/mishkin.

1. "There are frequently years when the inflation rate is high and yet money growth is quite low. Therefore, the statement that inflation is a monetary phenomenon cannot be correct." Comment.

2. Why do economists focus on historical episodes of hyperinflation to decide whether inflation is a monetary phenomenon?

3. "Because increases in government spending raise the aggregate demand curve, fiscal policy by itself can be the source of inflation." Is this statement true, false, or uncertain? Explain your answer.

4. "A cost-push inflation occurs as a result of workers' attempts to push up their wages. Therefore, inflation does not have to be a monetary phenomenon." Is this statement true, false, or uncertain? Explain your answer.

5. "Because government policymakers do not consider inflation desirable, their policies cannot be the source of inflation." Is this statement true, false, or uncertain? Explain your answer.

6. "A budget deficit that is only temporary cannot be the source of inflation." Is this statement true, false, or uncertain? Explain your answer.

7. How can the Fed's desire to prevent high interest rates lead to inflation?

8. "If the data and recognition lags could be reduced, discretionary policy would more likely be beneficial to the economy." Is this statement true, false, or uncertain? Explain your answer.

9. "The more sluggish wage and price adjustment is, the more variable output and the price level are when a discretionary policy is pursued." Is this statement true, false, or uncertain? Explain your answer.

10. "If the public believes that the monetary authorities will pursue a discretionary policy, a cost-push inflation is more likely to develop." Is this statement true, false, or uncertain? Explain your answer.

11. Why are discretionary policies to eliminate unemployment more likely to lead to inflation than nondiscretionary policies?

12. "The less important expectations about policy are to movements of the aggregate supply curve, the stronger the case is for discretionary policy to eliminate unemployment." Is this statement true, false, or uncertain? Explain your answer.

13. If the economy's self-correcting mechanism works slowly, should the government necessarily pursue discretionary policy to eliminate unemployment?

14. "To prevent inflation, the Fed should follow Teddy Roosevelt's advice: 'Speak softly and carry a big stick.'" What would the Fed's "big stick" be? What is the statement trying to say?

15. In a speech early in the Iraq-Kuwait crisis in 1990, President George H. W. Bush stated that although his heart went out to the hostages held by Saddam Hussein, he would not let this hostage-taking deter the United States from insisting on the withdrawal of Iraq from Kuwait. Do you think that Bush's position made sense? Explain why or why not.

WEB EXERCISES

1. Figure 8 reports the inflation rate from 1960 to 2008. As this chapter states, inflation continues to be a major factor in economic policy. Go to ftp://ftp.bls.gov/pub/special.requests/cpi/cpiai.txt. Move data into Excel using the method described at the end of Chapter 1. Delete all but the first and last column (date and annual CPI). Graph this data and compare it to Figure 8.
   a. Has inflation increased or decreased since the end of 2008?
   b. When was inflation at its highest?
   c. When was inflation at its lowest?
   d. Have we ever had a period of deflation? If so, when?
   e. Have we ever had a period of hyperinflation? If so, when?

2. It can be an interesting exercise to compare the purchasing power of the dollar over different periods in history. Go to www.bls.gov/cpi/ and scroll down to the link to the "inflation calculator." Use this calculator to compute the following:
   a. If a new home cost $125,000 in 2008, what would it have cost in 1950?
   b. The average household income in 2008 was about $40,000. How much would this have been in 1945?
   c. An average new car cost about $20,000 in 2008. What would this have cost in 1945?
   d. Using the results you found in Exercises b and c, does a car consume more or less of average household income in 2008 than in 1945?

WEB REFERENCES

www.bls.gov/cpi/

The home page of the Bureau of Labor Statistics, which reports inflation numbers.

ftp://ftp.bls.gov/pub/special.requests/cpi/cpiai.txt

Download historical inflation statistics going back to 1913. This data can easily be moved into Microsoft Excel using the procedure discussed at the end of Chapter 1.

http://www.gpoaccess.gov/eop

The *Economic Report of the President* reports debt levels and gross domestic product, along with many other economic statistics.

MyEconLab CAN HELP YOU GET A BETTER GRADE

If your exam were tomorrow, would you be ready? For each chapter, MyEconLab Practice Test and Study Plans pinpoint which sections you have mastered and which ones you need to study. That way, you are more efficient with your study time, and you are better prepared for your exams.

To see how it works, turn to page 20 and then go to: www.myeconlab.com/mishkin

25 Rational Expectations: Implications for Policy

Preview

After World War II, economists, armed with models (such as the *ISLM* model) that described how government policies could be used to manipulate employment and output, felt that discretionary policies could reduce the severity of business cycle fluctuations without creating inflation. In the 1960s and 1970s, these economists got their chance to put their policies into practice (see Chapter 24), but the results were not what they had anticipated. The economic record for that period is not a happy one: Inflation accelerated, the rate often climbing above 10%, while unemployment figures deteriorated from those of the 1950s.[1]

In the 1970s and 1980s, economists, including Robert Lucas of the University of Chicago and Thomas Sargent, now at New York University, used the rational expectations theory discussed in Chapter 7 to examine why discretionary policies appear to have performed so poorly. Their analysis cast doubt on whether macroeconomic models can be used to evaluate the potential effects of policy and on whether policy can be effective when the public *expects* that it will be implemented. Because the analysis of Lucas and Sargent has such strong implications for the way policy should be conducted, it has been labeled the *rational expectations revolution.*[2]

This chapter examines the analysis behind the rational expectations revolution. We start first with the Lucas critique, which indicates that because expectations are important in economic behavior, it may be quite difficult to predict what the outcome of a discretionary policy will be. We then discuss the effect of rational expectations on the aggregate demand and supply analysis developed in Chapter 22 by exploring three models that incorporate expectations in different ways.

A comparison of all three models indicates that the existence of rational expectations makes discretionary policies less likely to be successful and raises the issue of credibility as an important element affecting policy outcomes. With rational expectations, an essential ingredient to a successful anti-inflation policy is the credibility of the policy in the eyes of the public. The rational expectations revolution is now at the center of many of the current debates in monetary theory that have major implications for how monetary and fiscal policy should be conducted.

---

[1]Some of the deterioration can be attributed to supply shocks in 1973–1975 and 1978–1980.

[2]Other economists who have been active in promoting the rational expectations revolution are Robert Barro of Harvard University, Bennett McCallum of Carnegie-Mellon University, Edward Prescott of Arizona State, and Neil Wallace of Pennsylvania State University.

THE LUCAS CRITIQUE OF POLICY EVALUATION

In his famous paper "Econometric Policy Evaluation: A Critique," Robert Lucas presented an argument that had devastating implications for the usefulness of conventional **econometric models** (models whose equations are estimated with statistical procedures) for evaluating policy.[3] Economists developed these models for two purposes: to forecast economic activity and to evaluate the effects of different policies. Although Lucas's critique had nothing to say about the usefulness of these models as forecasting tools, he argued that they could not be relied on to evaluate the potential impact of particular policies on the economy.

Econometric Policy Evaluation

To understand Lucas's argument, we must first understand econometric policy evaluation: how econometric models are used to evaluate policy. For example, we can examine how the Federal Reserve uses its econometric model in making decisions about the future course of monetary policy. The model contains equations that describe the relationships among hundreds of variables. These relationships are assumed to remain constant and are estimated using past data. Let's say that the Fed wants to know the effect on unemployment and inflation of a decrease in the fed funds rate from 5% to 4%. It feeds the new, lower fed funds rate into a computer that contains the model, and the model then provides an answer about how much unemployment will fall as a result of the lower fed funds rate and how much the inflation rate will rise. Other possible policies, such as a rise in the fed funds rate by one percentage point, might also be fed into the model. After a series of these policies have been tried out, the policymakers at the Fed can see which policies produce the most desirable outcome for unemployment and inflation.

Lucas's challenge to this procedure for evaluating policies is based on a simple principle of rational expectations theory from Chapter 7: *The way in which expectations are formed (the relationship of expectations to past information) changes when the behavior of forecasted variables changes.* So when policy changes, the relationship between expectations and past information will change, and because expectations affect economic behavior, the relationships in the econometric model will change. The econometric model, which has been estimated with past data, is then no longer the correct model for evaluating the response to this policy change and may consequently prove highly misleading.

Example: The Term Structure of Interest Rates

The best way to understand Lucas's argument is to look at a concrete example involving only one equation typically found in econometric models: the term structure equation. The equation relates the long-term interest rate to current and past values of the short-term interest rate. It is one of the most important equations in macro econometric models because the long-term interest rate, not the short-term rate, is the one believed to have an impact on aggregate demand.

In Chapter 6, we learned that the long-term interest rate is related to an average of expected future short-term interest rates. Suppose that in the past, when the short-term rate rose, it quickly fell back down again; that is, any increase was temporary. Because

---

[3]*Carnegie-Rochester Conference Series on Public Policy* 1 (1976): 19–46.

rational expectations theory suggests that any rise in the short-term interest rate is expected to be only temporary, a rise should have only a minimal effect on the average of expected future short-term rates. It will cause the long-term interest rate to rise by a negligible amount. The term structure relationship estimated using past data will then show only a weak effect on the long-term interest rate of changes in the short-term rate.

Suppose the Fed wants to evaluate what will happen to the economy if it pursues a policy that is likely to raise the short-term interest rate from a current level of 5% to a permanently higher level of 8%. The term structure equation that has been estimated using past data will indicate that there will be just a small change in the long-term interest rate. However, if the public recognizes that the short-term rate is rising to a permanently higher level, rational expectations theory indicates that people will no longer expect a rise in the short-term rate to be temporary. Instead, when they see the interest rate rise to 8%, they will expect the average of future short-term interest rates to rise substantially, and so the long-term interest rate will rise greatly, not minimally as the estimated term structure equation suggests. You can see that evaluating the likely outcome of the change in Fed policy with an econometric model can be highly misleading.

The term structure example also demonstrates another aspect of the Lucas critique. The effects of a particular policy depend critically on the public's expectations about the policy. If the public expects the rise in the short-term interest rate to be merely temporary, the response of long-term interest rates, as we have seen, will be negligible. If, however, the public expects the rise to be more permanent, the response of long-term rates will be far greater. ***The Lucas critique points out not only that conventional econometric models cannot be used for policy evaluation, but also that the public's expectations about a policy will influence the response to that policy***.

The term structure equation discussed here is only one of many equations in econometric models to which the Lucas critique applies. In fact, Lucas uses the examples of consumption and investment equations in his paper. One attractive feature of the term structure example is that it deals with expectations in a financial market, a sector of the economy for which the theory and empirical evidence supporting rational expectations are very strong. The Lucas critique should also apply, however, to sectors of the economy for which rational expectations theory is more controversial, because the basic principle of the Lucas critique is not that expectations are always rational but rather that the formation of expectations changes when the behavior of a forecasted variable changes. This less stringent principle is supported by the evidence in sectors of the economy other than financial markets.

NEW CLASSICAL MACROECONOMIC MODEL

We now turn to the implications of rational expectations for the aggregate demand and supply analysis we studied in Chapter 22. The first model we examine that views expectations as rational is the *new classical macroeconomic model* developed by Robert Lucas and Thomas Sargent, among others. In the new classical model, all wages and prices are completely flexible with respect to expected changes in the price level; that is, a rise in the expected price level results in an immediate and equal rise in wages and prices because workers try to keep their *real* wages from falling when they expect the price level to rise.

This view of how wages and prices are set indicates that a rise in the expected price level causes an immediate leftward shift in the short-run aggregate supply curve, which leaves real wages unchanged and aggregate output at the natural rate (full-employment) level if expectations are realized. This model then suggests that anticipated policy has no effect on aggregate output and unemployment; only unanticipated policy has an effect.

Effects of Unanticipated and Anticipated Policy

First, let us look at the short-run response to an unanticipated (unexpected) policy such as an unexpected increase in the money supply.

In Figure 1, the short-run aggregate supply curve AS_1 is drawn for an expected price level P_1. The initial aggregate demand curve AD_1 intersects AS_1 at point 1, where the realized price level is at the expected price level P_1 and aggregate output is at the natural rate level Y_n. Because point 1 is also on the long-run aggregate supply curve at Y_n, there is no tendency for the aggregate supply to shift. The economy remains in long-run equilibrium.

Suppose the Fed suddenly decides the unemployment rate is too high and so makes a large open market purchase that is unexpected by the public. The money supply increases, and the aggregate demand curve shifts rightward to AD_2. Because this shift is unexpected, the expected price level remains at P_1 and the short-run aggregate supply

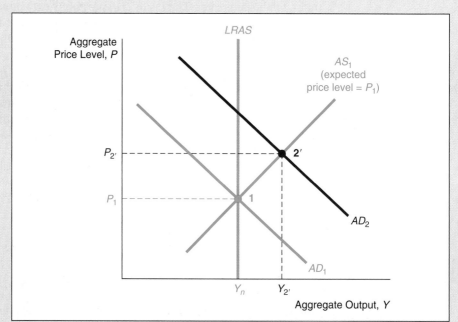

FIGURE 1 **Short-Run Response to Unanticipated Expansionary Policy in the New Classical Model**
Initially, the economy is at point 1 at the intersection of AD_1 and AS_1 (expected price level = P_1). An expansionary policy shifts the aggregate demand curve to AD_2, but because this is unexpected, the short-run aggregate supply curve remains fixed at AS_1. Equilibrium now occurs at point 2'—aggregate output has increased above the natural rate level to $Y_{2'}$, and the price level has increased to $P_{2'}$.

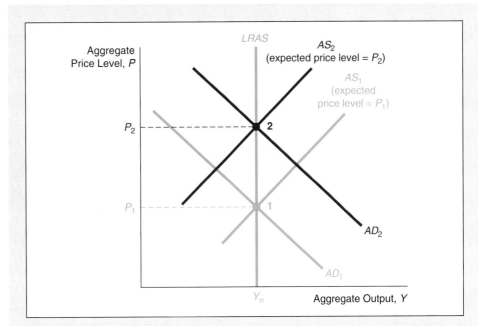

FIGURE 2   **Short–Run Response to Anticipated Expansionary Policy in the New Classical Model**
The expansionary policy shifts the aggregate demand curve rightward to AD_2, but because this policy is expected, the short-run aggregate supply curve shifts leftward to AS_2. The economy moves to point 2, where aggregate output is still at the natural rate level but the price level has increased to P_2.

curve remains at AS_1. Equilibrium is now at point $2'$, the intersection of AD_2 and AS_1. Aggregate output increases above the natural rate level to $Y_{2'}$ and the realized price level increases to $P_{2'}$.

If, by contrast, the public expects that the Fed will make these open market purchases to lower unemployment because they have seen the Fed do this in the past, the expansionary policy will be anticipated. The outcome of such anticipated expansionary policy is illustrated in Figure 2. Because expectations are rational, workers and firms recognize that an expansionary policy will shift the aggregate demand curve to the right and will expect the aggregate price level to rise to P_2. Workers will demand higher wages so that their real earnings will remain the same when the price level rises. The short-run aggregate supply curve then shifts leftward to AS_2 and intersects AD_2 at point 2, an equilibrium point where aggregate output is at the natural rate level Y_n and the price level has risen to P_2.

The new classical macroeconomic model demonstrates that aggregate output does not increase as a result of anticipated expansionary policy and that the economy immediately moves to a point of long-run equilibrium (point 2) where aggregate output is at the natural rate level. Although Figure 2 suggests why this occurs, we have not yet proved why an anticipated expansionary policy shifts the short-run aggregate supply curve to exactly AS_2 (corresponding to an expected price level of P_2) and hence why aggregate output *necessarily* remains at the natural rate level. The proof is somewhat difficult and is dealt with in the FYI box, "Proof of the Policy Ineffectiveness Proposition."

FYI **Proof of the Policy Ineffectiveness Proposition**

The proof that in the new classical macroeconomic model aggregate output *necessarily* remains at the natural rate level when there is anticipated expansionary policy is as follows. In the new classical model, the expected price level for the short-run aggregate supply curve occurs at its intersection with the long-run aggregate supply curve (see Figure 2). The optimal forecast of the price level is given by the intersection of the aggregate supply curve with the anticipated aggregate demand curve AD_2. If the short-run aggregate supply curve is to the right of AS_2 in Figure 2, it will intersect AD_2 at a price level lower than the expected level (which is the intersection of this aggregate supply curve and the long-run aggregate supply curve). The optimal forecast of the price level will then not equal the expected price level, thereby violating the rationality of expectations. A similar argument can be made to show that when the short-run aggregate supply curve is to the left of AS_2, the assumption of rational expectations also is violated. Only when the short-run aggregate supply curve is at AS_2 (corresponding to an expected price level of P_2) are expectations rational because the optimal forecast equals the expected price level. As we see in Figure 2, the AS_2 curve implies that aggregate output remains at the natural rate level as a result of the anticipated expansionary policy.

The new classical model has the word *classical* associated with it because when policy is anticipated, the new classical model has a property that is associated with the classical economists of the nineteenth and early twentieth centuries: Aggregate output remains at the natural rate level. Yet the new classical model allows aggregate output to fluctuate away from the natural rate level as a result of *unanticipated* movements in the aggregate demand curve. The conclusion from the new classical model is a striking one: ***Anticipated policy has no effect on the business cycle; only unanticipated policy matters.***[4]

This conclusion has been called the **policy ineffectiveness proposition**, because it implies that one anticipated policy is just like any other; it has no effect on output fluctuations. You should recognize that this proposition does not rule out output effects from policy changes. If the policy is a surprise (unanticipated), it will have an effect on output.[5]

Can an Expansionary Policy Lead to a Decline in Aggregate Output?

Another important feature of the new classical model is that an expansionary policy, such as an increase in the rate of money growth, can lead to a *decline* in aggregate output if the public expects an even more expansionary policy than the one actually implemented. There will be a surprise in the policy, but it will be negative and drive output down. Policymakers cannot be sure if their policies will work in the intended direction.

---

[4]The new classical view, in which anticipated policy has no effect on the business cycle, does not imply that anticipated policy has no effect on the overall health of the economy. For example, the new classical analysis does not rule out possible effects of anticipated policy on the natural rate of output Y_n, which can benefit the public.

[5]Thomas Sargent and Neil Wallace, "'Rational' Expectations, the Optimal Monetary Instrument, and the Optimal Money Supply Rule," *Journal of Political Economy* 83 (1975): 241–254, first demonstrated the full implications of the policy ineffectiveness proposition.

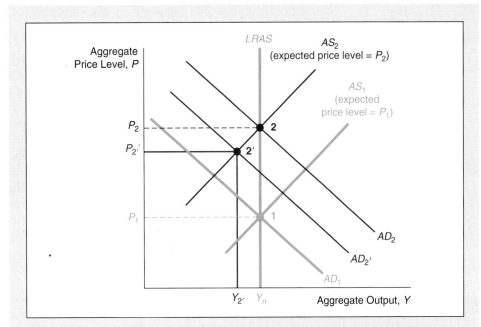

FIGURE 3   **Short-Run Response to an Expansionary Policy That Is Less Expansionary Than Expected in the New Classical Model**
Because the public expects the aggregate demand curve to shift to AD_2, the short-run aggregate supply curve shifts to AS_2 (expected price level = P_2). When the actual expansionary policy falls short of the public's expectation (the aggregate demand curve merely shifts to $AD_{2'}$), the economy ends up at point $2'$, at the intersection of $AD_{2'}$ and AS_2. Despite the expansionary policy, aggregate output falls to $Y_{2'}$.

To see how an expansionary policy can lead to a decline in aggregate output, let us turn to the aggregate supply and demand diagram in Figure 3. Initially we are at point 1, the intersection of AD_1 and AS_1; output is Y_n, and the price level is P_1. Now suppose that the public expects the Fed to increase the money supply to shift the aggregate demand curve to AD_2. As we saw in Figure 2, the short-run aggregate supply curve shifts leftward to AS_2, because the price level is expected to rise to P_2. Suppose that the expansionary policy engineered by the Fed actually falls short of what was expected so that the aggregate demand curve shifts only to $AD_{2'}$. The economy will move to point $2'$, the intersection of the short-run aggregate supply curve AS_2 and the aggregate demand curve $AD_{2'}$. The result of the mistaken expectation is that output falls to $Y_{2'}$, while the price level rises to $P_{2'}$ rather than P_2. An expansionary policy that is less expansionary than anticipated leads to an output movement directly opposite to that intended.

Implications for Policymakers

The new classical model, with its policy ineffectiveness proposition, has two important lessons for policymakers: It illuminates the distinction between the effects of anticipated versus unanticipated policy actions, and it demonstrates that policymakers cannot know the outcome of their decisions without knowing the public's expectations regarding them.

At first you might think that policymakers can still use discretionary policy to stabilize the economy. Once they figure out the public's expectations, they can know what effect their policies will have. There are two catches to such a conclusion. First, it may be nearly impossible to find out what the public's expectations are, given that the public consists of over 300 million U.S. citizens. Second, even if it were possible, policymakers would run into further difficulties, because the public has rational expectations and will try to guess what policymakers plan to do. Public expectations do not remain fixed while policymakers are plotting a surprise—the public will revise its expectations, and policies will have no predictable effect on output.[6]

Where does this lead us? Should the Fed and other policymaking agencies pack up, lock the doors, and go home? In a sense, the answer is yes. The new classical model implies that discretionary stabilization policy cannot be effective and might have undesirable effects on the economy. Policymakers' attempts to use discretionary policy may create a fluctuating policy stance that leads to unpredictable policy surprises, which in turn cause undesirable fluctuations around the natural rate level of aggregate output. To eliminate these undesirable fluctuations, the Fed and other policymaking agencies should abandon discretionary policy and generate as few policy surprises as possible.

As we have seen in Figure 2, even though anticipated policy has no effect on aggregate output in the new classical model, it *does* have an effect on the price level. The new classical macroeconomists care about anticipated policy and suggest that policy rules be designed so that the price level will remain stable.

NEW KEYNESIAN MODEL

In the new classical model, all wages and prices are completely flexible with respect to expected changes in the price level; that is, a rise in the expected price level results in an immediate and equal rise in wages and prices. Many economists who accept rational expectations as a working hypothesis do not accept the characterization of wage and price flexibility in the new classical model. These critics of the new classical model, called *new Keynesians*, object to complete wage and price flexibility and identify factors in the economy that prevent some wages and prices from rising fully with a rise in the expected price level.

Long-term labor contracts are one source of rigidity that prevents wages and prices from responding fully to changes in the expected price level (called **wage-price stickiness**). For example, workers might find themselves at the end of the first year of a three-year wage contract that specifies the wage rate for the coming two years. Even if new information appeared that would make them raise their expectations of the inflation rate and the future price level, they could not do anything about it because they are locked into a wage agreement. Even with a high expectation about the price level, the wage rate will not adjust. In two years, when the contract is renegotiated, both workers

---

[6]This result follows from one of the implications of rational expectations: The forecast error of expectations about policy (the deviation of actual policy from expectations of policy) must be unpredictable. Because output is affected only by unpredictable (unanticipated) policy changes in the new classical model, policy effects on output must be unpredictable as well.

and firms may build the expected inflation rate into their agreement, but they cannot do so immediately.

Another source of rigidity is that firms may be reluctant to change wages frequently even when there are no explicit wage contracts, because such changes may affect the work effort of the labor force. For example, a firm may not want to lower workers' wages when unemployment is high, because this might result in poorer worker performance. Price stickiness may also occur because firms engage in fixed-price contracts with their suppliers or because it is costly for firms to change prices frequently. All of these rigidities (which diminish wage and price flexibility), even if they are not present in all wage and price arrangements, suggest that an increase in the expected price level might not translate into an immediate and complete adjustment of wages and prices.

Although the new Keynesians do not agree with the complete wage and price flexibility of the new classical macroeconomics, they nevertheless recognize the importance of expectations to the determination of short-run aggregate supply and are willing to accept rational expectations theory as a reasonable characterization of how expectations are formed. The model they have developed, the *new Keynesian model*, assumes that expectations are rational but does not assume complete wage and price flexibility; instead, it assumes that wages and prices are sticky. Its basic conclusion is that unanticipated policy has a larger effect on aggregate output than anticipated policy (as in the new classical model). However, in contrast to the new classical model, the policy ineffectiveness proposition does not hold in the new Keynesian model: Anticipated policy *does* affect aggregate output and the business cycle.

Effects of Unanticipated and Anticipated Policy

In panel (a) of Figure 4, we look at the short-run response to an unanticipated expansionary policy for the new Keynesian model. The analysis is identical to that of the new classical model. We again start at point 1, where the aggregate demand curve AD_1 intersects the short-run aggregate supply curve AS_1 at the natural rate level of output and price level P_1. When the Fed pursues its expansionary policy of purchasing bonds and raising the money supply, the aggregate demand curve shifts rightward to AD_2. Because the expansionary policy is unanticipated, the expected price level remains unchanged, leaving the short-run aggregate supply curve unchanged. Thus the economy moves to point U, where aggregate output has increased to Y_U and the price level has risen to P_U.

In panel (b), we see what happens when the Fed's expansionary policy that shifts the aggregate demand curve from AD_1 to AD_2 is anticipated. Because the expansionary policy is anticipated and expectations are rational, the expected price level increases, causing wages to increase and the short-run aggregate supply curve to shift to the left. Because of rigidities that do not allow *complete* wage and price adjustment, the short-run aggregate supply curve does not shift all the way to AS_2 as it does in the new classical model. Instead, it moves to AS_A, and the economy settles at point A, the intersection of AD_2 and AS_A. Aggregate output has risen above the natural rate level to Y_A, while the price level has increased to P_A. ***Unlike the new classical model, in the new Keynesian model anticipated policy does have an effect on aggregate output.***

We can see in Figure 4 that Y_U is greater than Y_A, meaning that the output response to unanticipated policy is greater than to anticipated policy. It is greater because the short-run aggregate supply curve does not shift when policy is unanticipated, causing a lower price level and hence a higher level of output. We see that ***like the new classical model, the new Keynesian model distinguishes between the effects of anticipated versus unanticipated policy, with unanticipated policy having a greater effect.***

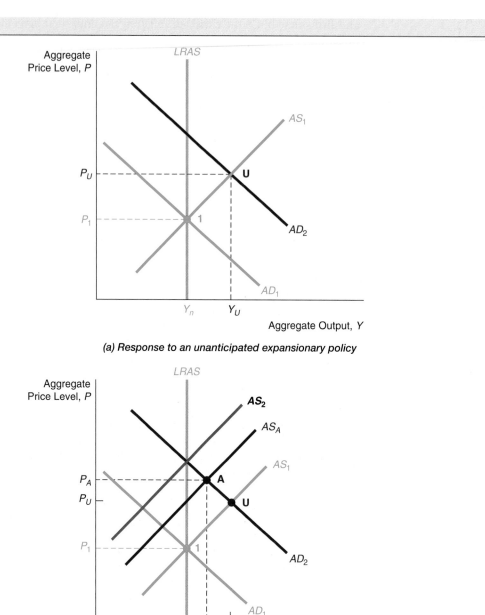

(a) Response to an unanticipated expansionary policy

(b) Response to an anticipated expansionary policy

FIGURE 4   **Short-Run Response to Expansionary Policy in the New Keynesian Model**
The expansionary policy that shifts aggregate demand to AD_2 has a bigger effect on output when it is unanticipated than when it is anticipated. When the expansionary policy is unanticipated in panel (a), the short-run aggregate supply curve does not shift, and the economy moves to point U, so that aggregate output increases to Y_U and the price level rises to P_U. When the policy is anticipated in panel (b), the short-run aggregate supply curve shifts to AS_A (but not all the way to AS_2 because rigidities prevent complete wage and price adjustment), and the economy moves to point A so that aggregate output rises to Y_A (which is less than Y_U) and the price level rises to P_A (which is higher than P_U).

Implications for Policymakers

Because the new Keynesian model indicates that anticipated policy has an effect on aggregate output, it does not rule out beneficial effects from discretionary stabilization policy, in contrast to the new classical model. It does warn policymakers that designing such a policy will not be an easy task, because the effects of anticipated and unanticipated policy can be quite different. As in the new classical model, to predict the outcome of their actions, policymakers must be aware of the public's expectations about those actions. Policymakers face similar difficulties in devising successful policies in both the new classical and new Keynesian models.

COMPARISON OF THE TWO NEW MODELS WITH THE TRADITIONAL MODEL

To obtain a clearer picture of the impact of the rational expectations revolution on our analysis of the aggregate economy, we can compare the two rational expectations models (the new classical macroeconomic model and the new Keynesian model) to a model that we call, for lack of a better name, the *traditional model*. In the traditional model, expectations are *not* rational. That model uses adaptive expectations (mentioned in Chapter 7), expectations based solely on past experience. The traditional model views expected inflation as an average of past inflation rates. This average is not affected by the public's predictions of future policy; hence predictions of future policy do not affect the aggregate supply curve.

First we will examine the short-run output and price responses in the three models. Then we will examine the implications of these models for both stabilization and anti-inflation policies. As a study aid, the comparison of the three models is summarized in Table 1. You may want to refer to the table as we proceed with the comparison.

Short-Run Output and Price Responses

Figure 5 compares the response of aggregate output and the price level to an expansionary policy in the three models. Initially, the economy is at point 1, the intersection of the aggregate demand curve AD_1 and the short-run aggregate supply curve AS_1. When the expansionary policy occurs, the aggregate demand curve shifts to AD_2. If the expansionary policy is *unanticipated*, all three models show the same short-run output response. The traditional model views the short-run aggregate supply curve as given in the short run, while the other two view it as remaining at AS_1 because there is no change in the expected price level when the policy is a surprise. Hence, when policy is *unanticipated*, all three models indicate a movement to point $1'$, where the AD_2 and AS_1 curves intersect and where aggregate output and the price level have risen to $Y_{1'}$ and $P_{1'}$ respectively.

The response to the *anticipated* expansionary policy is, however, quite different in the three models. In the traditional model in panel (a), the short-run aggregate supply curve remains at AS_1 even when the expansionary policy is anticipated, because adaptive expectations imply that anticipated policy has no effect on expectations and hence on aggregate supply. It indicates that the economy moves to point $1'$, which is where it moved when the policy was unanticipated. The traditional model does not distinguish between the effects of anticipated and unanticipated policy: Both have the same effect on output and prices.

SUMMARY TABLE 1

The Three Models

Model	Response to Unanticipated Expansionary Policy	Response to Anticipated Expansionary Policy	Can Discretionary Policy Be Beneficial?	Response to Unanticipated Anti-inflation Policy	Response to Anticipated Anti-inflation Policy	Is Credibility Important to Successful Anti-inflation Policy?
Traditional model	$Y\uparrow, P\uparrow$	$Y\uparrow, P\uparrow$ by same amount as when policy is unanticipated	Yes	$Y\downarrow, \pi\downarrow$	$Y\downarrow, \pi\downarrow$ by same amount as when policy is unanticipated	No
New classical macro-economic model	$Y\uparrow, P\uparrow$	Y unchanged, $P\uparrow$ by more than when policy is unanticipated	No	$Y\downarrow, \pi\downarrow$	Y unchanged, $\pi\downarrow$ by more than when policy is unanticipated	Yes
New Keynesian model	$Y\uparrow, P\uparrow$	$Y\uparrow$ by less than when policy is unanticipated, $P\uparrow$ by more than when policy is unanticipated	Yes, but designing a beneficial policy is difficult	$Y\downarrow, \pi\downarrow$	$Y\downarrow$ by less than when policy is unanticipated, $\pi\downarrow$ by more than when policy is unanticipated	Yes

Note: π represents the inflation rate.

In the new classical model in panel (b), the short-run aggregate supply curve shifts leftward to AS_2 when policy is anticipated, because when expectations of the higher price level are realized, aggregate output will be at the natural rate level. Thus it indicates that the economy moves to point 2; aggregate output does not rise, but prices do, to P_2. This outcome is quite different from the move to point 1' when policy is unanticipated. The new classical model distinguishes between the short-run effects of anticipated and unanticipated policies: Anticipated policy has no effect on output, but unanticipated policy does. However, anticipated policy has a bigger impact than unanticipated policy on price level movements.

The new Keynesian model in panel (c) is an intermediate position between the traditional and new classical models. It recognizes that anticipated policy affects the aggregate supply curve, but due to rigidities such as long-term contracts, wage and price adjustment is not as complete as in the new classical model. Hence the short-run aggregate supply curve shifts only to $AS_{2'}$ in response to anticipated policy, and the economy

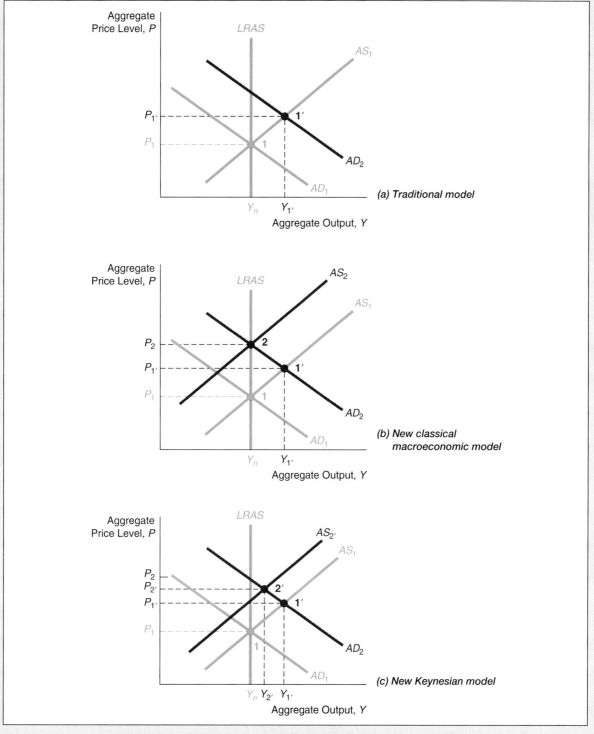

FIGURE 5   **Comparison of the Short-Run Response to Expansionary Policy in the Three Models**
Initially, the economy is at point 1. The expansionary policy shifts the aggregate demand curve from AD_1 to AD_2. In the traditional model, the expansionary policy moves the economy to point 1′ whether the policy is anticipated or not. In the new classical model, the expansionary policy moves the economy to point 1′ if it is unanticipated and to point 2 if it is anticipated. In the new Keynesian model, the expansionary policy moves the economy to point 1′ if it is unanticipated and to point 2′ if it is anticipated.

moves to point $2'$, where output at $Y_{2'}$ is lower than the $Y_{1'}$ level reached when the expansionary policy is unanticipated. But the price level at $P_{2'}$ is higher than the level $P_{1'}$ that resulted from the unanticipated policy. Like the new classical model, the new Keynesian model distinguishes between the effects of anticipated and unanticipated policies: Anticipated policy has a smaller effect on output than unanticipated policy does but a larger effect on the price level. However, in contrast to the new classical model, anticipated policy does affect output fluctuations.

Stabilization Policy

The three models have different views of the effectiveness of *stabilization policy*, policy intended to reduce output fluctuations. Because the effects of anticipated and unanticipated policy are identical in the traditional model, policymakers do not have to concern themselves with the public's expectations. This makes it easier for them to predict the outcome of their policy, an essential matter if their actions are to have the intended effect. In the traditional model, it is possible for discretionary policy to stabilize output fluctuations.

The new classical model takes the extreme position that discretionary stabilization policy serves to aggravate output fluctuations. In this model, only unanticipated policy affects output; anticipated policy does not matter. Policymakers can affect output only by surprising the public. Because the public is assumed to have rational expectations, it will always try to guess what policymakers plan to do.

In the new classical model, the conduct of policy can be viewed as a game in which the public and the policymakers are always trying to outfox each other by guessing the other's intentions and expectations. The sole possible outcome of this process is that discretionary stabilization policy will have no predictable effect on output and cannot be relied on to stabilize economic activity. Instead, it may create a lot of uncertainty about policy that will increase random output fluctuations around the natural rate level of output. Such an undesirable effect is exactly the opposite of what the discretionary stabilization policy is trying to achieve. The outcome in the new classical view is that policy-makers should be nondiscretionary and promote as much certainty about their policy actions as possible.

The new Keynesian model again takes an intermediate position between the traditional and the new classical models. Contrary to the new classical model, it indicates that anticipated policy *does* matter to output fluctuations. Policymakers can count on some output response from their anticipated policies and can use them to stabilize the economy.

In contrast to the traditional model, however, the new Keynesian model recognizes that the effects of anticipated and unanticipated policy will not be the same. Policymakers will encounter more uncertainty about the outcome of their actions, because they cannot be sure to what extent the policy is anticipated. Hence a discretionary policy is less likely to operate always in the intended direction and is less likely to achieve its goals. The new Keynesian model raises the possibility that a discretionary policy could be beneficial, but uncertainty about the outcome of policies in this model may make the design of such a beneficial policy extremely difficult.

Anti-inflation Policies

So far we have focused on the implications of these three models for policies whose intent is to eliminate fluctuations in output. By the end of the 1970s, the high inflation rate (then over 10%) helped shift the primary concern of policymakers to the reduction of inflation. What do these models have to say about anti-inflation policies designed to eliminate upward movements in the price level? The aggregate demand and supply diagrams in Figure 6 will help us answer the question.

Suppose that the economy has settled into a sustained 10% inflation rate caused by a high rate of money growth that shifts the aggregate demand curve so that it moves up by 10% every year. If this inflation rate has been built into wage and price contracts, the short-run aggregate supply curve shifts and rises at the same rate. We see this in Figure 6 as a shift in the aggregate demand curve from AD_1 in year 1 to AD_2 in year 2, while the short-run aggregate supply curve moves from AS_1 to AS_2. In year 1, the economy is at point 1 (intersection of AD_1 and AS_1); in the second year, the economy moves to point 2 (intersection of AD_2 and AS_2), and the price level has risen 10%, from P_1 to P_2. (Note that the figure is not drawn to scale.)

Now suppose that a new Federal Reserve chairman is appointed who decides that inflation must be stopped. He convinces the FOMC to stop the high rate of money growth so that the aggregate demand curve will not rise from AD_1. The policy of halting money growth immediately could be costly if it leads to a fall in output. Let's use our three models to explore the degree to which aggregate output will fall as a result of an anti-inflation policy.

First, look at the outcome of this policy in the traditional model's view of the world in panel (a). The movement of the short-run aggregate supply curve to AS_2 is already set in place and is unaffected by the new policy of keeping the aggregate demand curve at AD_1 (whether the effort is anticipated or not). The economy moves to point 2′ (the intersection of the AD_1 and AS_2 curves), and the inflation rate slows down because the price level increases only to $P_{2'}$ rather than P_2. The reduction in inflation has not been without cost: Output has declined to $Y_{2'}$, which is well below the natural rate level.

In the traditional model, estimates of the cost in terms of lost output for each 1% reduction in the inflation rate are around 4% of a year's real GDP. The high cost of reducing inflation in the traditional model is one reason why some economists are reluctant to advocate an anti-inflation policy of the sort tried here. They question whether the cost of high unemployment is worth the benefits of a reduced inflation rate.

If you adhere to the new classical philosophy, you would not be as pessimistic about the high cost of reducing the inflation rate. If the public *expects* the monetary authorities to stop the inflationary process by ending the high rate of money growth, it will occur without any output loss. In panel (b), the aggregate demand curve will remain at AD_1, but because this is expected, wages and prices can be adjusted so that they will not rise, and the short-run aggregate supply curve will remain at AS_1 instead of moving to AS_2. The economy will stay put at point 1 (the intersection of AD_1 and AS_1), and aggregate output will remain at the natural rate level while inflation is stopped because the price level is unchanged.

An important element in the story is that the anti-inflation policy be anticipated by the public. If the policy is *not* expected, the aggregate demand curve remains at AD_1, but the short-run aggregate supply curve continues its shift to AS_2. The outcome of the unanticipated anti-inflation policy is a movement of the economy to point 2′. Although the inflation rate slows in this case, it is not entirely eliminated as it was when the anti-inflation policy was anticipated. Even worse, aggregate output falls below the natural rate level to $Y_{2'}$. An anti-inflation policy that is unanticipated, then, is far less desirable than one that is anticipated.

The new Keynesian model in panel (c) also leads to the conclusion that an unanticipated anti-inflation policy is less desirable than an anticipated one. If the policy of

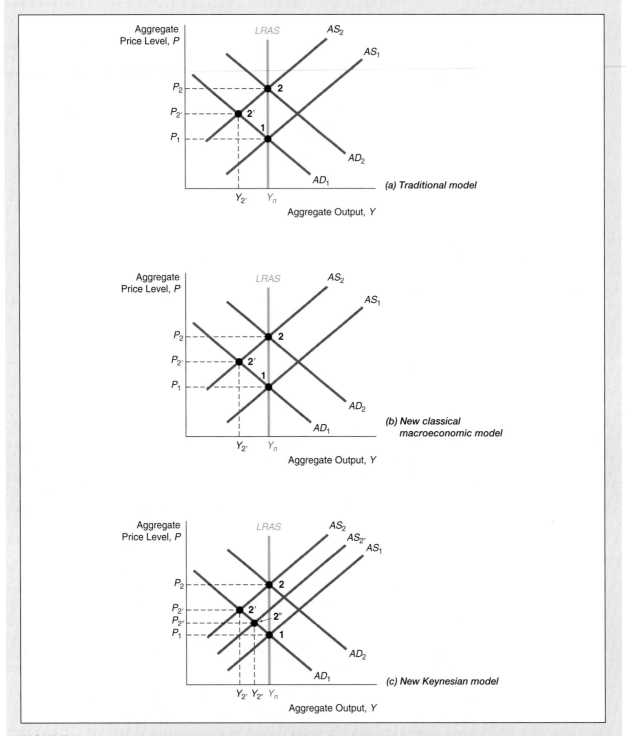

FIGURE 6   Anti-inflation Policy in the Three Models

With an ongoing inflation in which the economy is moving from point 1 to point 2, the aggregate demand curve is shifting from AD_1 to AD_2 and the short-run aggregate supply curve from AS_1 to AS_2. The anti-inflation policy, when implemented, prevents the aggregate demand curve from rising, holding it at AD_1. (a) In the traditional model, the economy moves to point 2′ whether the anti-inflation policy is anticipated or not. (b) In the new classical model, the economy moves to point 2′ if the policy is unanticipated and stays at point 1 if it is anticipated. (c) In the new Keynesian model, the economy moves to point 2′ if the policy is unanticipated and to point 2″ if it is anticipated.

keeping the aggregate demand curve at AD_1 is *not* expected, the short-run aggregate supply curve will continue its shift to AS_2, and the economy moves to point $2'$ at the intersection of AD_1 and AS_2. The inflation rate slows, but output declines to $Y_{2'}$, well below the natural rate level.

If, by contrast, the anti-inflation policy is *expected*, the short-run aggregate supply curve will not move all the way to AS_2. Instead it will shift only to $AS_{2''}$ because some wages and prices (but not all) can be adjusted, so wages and the price level will not rise at their previous rates. Instead of moving to point $2'$ (as occurred when the anti-inflation policy was not expected), the economy moves to point $2''$, the intersection of the AD_1 and $AS_{2''}$ curves. The outcome is more desirable than when the policy is unanticipated— the inflation rate is lower (the price level rises only to $P_{2''}$ and not $P_{2'}$), and the output loss is smaller as well ($Y_{2''}$ is higher than $Y_{2'}$).

Credibility in Fighting Inflation

Both the new classical and new Keynesian models indicate that for an anti-inflation policy to be successful in reducing inflation at the lowest output cost, the public must believe (expect) that it will be implemented. In the new classical view of the world, the best anti-inflation policy (when it is credible) is to go "cold turkey." The rise in the aggregate demand curve from AD_1 should be stopped immediately. Inflation would be eliminated at once with no loss of output *if the policy is credible*. In a new Keynesian world, the cold-turkey policy, *even if credible*, is not as desirable, because it will produce some output loss.

John Taylor, a proponent of the new Keynesian model, has demonstrated that a more gradual approach to reducing inflation may be able to eliminate inflation without producing a substantial output loss.[7] An important catch here is that this gradual policy must somehow be made credible, which may be harder to achieve than a cold-turkey anti-inflation policy, which demonstrates immediately that the policymakers are serious about fighting inflation. Taylor's contention that inflation can be reduced with little output loss may be overly optimistic.

Incorporating rational expectations into aggregate supply and demand analysis indicates that a successful anti-inflation policy must be credible. Evidence that credibility plays an important role in successful anti-inflation policies is provided by the dramatic end of the Bolivian hyperinflation in 1985 (see the Global box). But establishing credibility is easier said than done. You might think that an announcement by policymakers at the Federal Reserve that they plan to pursue an anti-inflation policy might do the trick. The public would expect this policy and would act accordingly. However, that conclusion implies that the public will believe the policymakers' announcement. Unfortunately, that is not how the real world works.

Our historical review of Federal Reserve policymaking in Chapter 16 suggests that the Fed has not always done what it set out to do. In fact, during the 1970s, the chairman of the Federal Reserve Board, Arthur Burns, repeatedly announced that the Fed would pursue a vigorous anti-inflation policy. The actual policy pursued, however, had quite a different outcome: The rate of growth of the money supply increased rapidly during the period, and inflation soared. Such episodes reduced the credibility of the Federal Reserve in the eyes of the public and, as predicted by the new classical and new

---

[7]John Taylor, "The Role of Expectations in the Choice of Monetary Policy," in *Monetary Policy Issues in the 1980s* (Kansas City: Federal Reserve Bank, 1982), pp. 47–76.

Global   Ending the Bolivian Hyperinflation: A Successful Anti-inflation Program

The most remarkable anti-inflation program in recent times was implemented in Bolivia. In the first half of 1985, Bolivia's inflation rate was running at 20,000% and rising. Indeed, the inflation rate was so high that the price of a movie ticket often rose while people waited in line to buy it. In August 1985, Bolivia's new president announced his anti-inflation program, the New Economic Policy. To rein in money growth and establish credibility, the new government took drastic actions to slash the budget deficit by shutting down many state-owned enterprises, eliminating subsidies, freezing public sector salaries, and collecting a new wealth tax. The finance ministry was put on a new footing; the budget was balanced on a day-by-day basis. Without exceptions, the finance minister would not authorize spending in excess of the amount of tax revenue that had been collected the day before. ·

The rule of thumb that a reduction of 1% in the inflation rate requires a 4% loss of a year's aggregate output indicates that ending the Bolivian hyperinflation would have required halving Bolivian aggregate output for 1,600 years! Instead, the Bolivian inflation was stopped in its tracks within one month, and the output loss was minor (less than 5% of GDP).

Certain hyperinflations before World War II were also ended with small losses of output using policies similar to Bolivia's,* and a more recent anti-inflation program in Israel that also involved substantial reductions in budget deficits sharply reduced inflation without any clear loss of output. There is no doubt that credible anti-inflation policies can be highly successful in eliminating inflation.

*For an excellent discussion of the end of four hyperinflations in the 1920s, see Thomas Sargent, "The Ends of Four Big Inflations," in *Inflation: Causes and Consequences,* ed. Robert E. Hall (Chicago: University of Chicago Press, 1982), pp. 41–98.

Keynesian models, had serious consequences. The reduction of inflation that occurred from 1981 to 1984 was bought at a very high cost; the 1981–1982 recession that helped bring the inflation rate down was the most severe recession in the post–World War II period.

The U.S. government can play an important role in establishing the credibility of anti-inflation policy. We have seen that large budget deficits may help stimulate inflationary monetary policy, and when the government and the Fed announce that they will pursue a restrictive anti-inflation policy, it is less likely that they will be believed *unless* the federal government demonstrates fiscal responsibility. Another way to say this is to use the old adage, "Actions speak louder than words." When the U.S. government takes actions that will help the Fed adhere to anti-inflation policy, the policy will be more credible. Unfortunately, this lesson has sometimes been ignored by politicians in the United States and in other countries.

APPLICATION   ✦   Credibility and the Reagan Budget Deficits

The Reagan administration was strongly criticized for creating huge budget deficits by cutting taxes in the early 1980s. In the aggregate supply and demand framework, we usually think of tax cuts as stimulating aggregate demand and increasing aggregate output. Could the expectation of large budget deficits have helped create a more severe recession in 1981–1982 after the Federal Reserve implemented an anti-inflation monetary policy?

Some economists answer yes, using diagrams like panels (b) and (c) of Figure 6. They claim that the prospect of large budget deficits made it harder for the public to believe that an anti-inflationary policy would actually be pursued when the Fed announced its intention to do so. Consequently, the short-run aggregate supply curve would continue to rise from AS_1 to AS_2 as in panels (b) and (c). When the Fed actually kept the aggregate demand curve from rising to AD_2 by slowing the rate of money growth in 1980–1981 and allowing interest rates to rise, the economy moved to a point like 2′ in panels (b) and (c), and significant unemployment resulted. As our analysis in panels (b) and (c) of Figure 6 predicts, the inflation rate did slow substantially, falling below 5% by the end of 1982, but this was very costly: Unemployment reached a peak of 10.7%.

If the Reagan administration had actively tried to reduce deficits instead of raising them by cutting taxes, what might have been the outcome of the anti-inflation policy? Instead of moving to point 2′, the economy might have moved to point 2″ in panel (c)—or even to point 1 in panel (b), if the new classical macroeconomists are right. Reduction of budget deficits thus could have led to an even more rapid reduction in inflation and a smaller loss of output.

Reagan is not the only head of state who ran large budget deficits while espousing an anti-inflation policy. Britain's Prime Minister Margaret Thatcher preceded Reagan in this activity, and economists such as Thomas Sargent assert that the reward for her policy was a climb of unemployment in Britain to unprecedented levels.[8]

Although many economists agree that the Fed's anti-inflation program lacked credibility, especially in its initial phases, not all of them agree that the Reagan budget deficits were the cause of that lack of credibility. The conclusion that the Reagan budget deficits helped create a more severe recession in 1981–1982 is controversial.

IMPACT OF THE RATIONAL EXPECTATIONS REVOLUTION

The theory of rational expectations has caused a revolution in the way most economists now think about the conduct of monetary and fiscal policies and their effects on economic activity. One result of this revolution is that economists are now far more aware of the importance of expectations to economic decision making and to the outcome of particular policy actions. Although the rationality of expectations in all markets is still controversial, most economists now accept the following principle suggested by rational expectations: Expectations formation will change when the behavior of forecasted variables changes. As a result, the Lucas critique of policy evaluation using conventional econometric models is now taken seriously by most economists. The Lucas critique also demonstrates that the effect of a particular policy depends critically on the public's expectations about that policy. This observation has made economists much less certain that policies will have their intended effect. An important result of the rational expectations revolution is that economists are no longer as confident in the success of discretionary stabilization policies as they once were.

---

[8]Thomas Sargent, "Stopping Moderate Inflations: The Methods of Poincaré and Thatcher," in *Inflation, Debt, and Indexation,* ed. Rudiger Dornbusch and M. H. Simonsen (Cambridge, MA: MIT Press, 1983), pp. 54–96, discusses the problems that Thatcher's policies caused and contrasts them with more successful anti-inflation policies pursued by the Poincaré government in France during the 1920s.

Has the rational expectations revolution convinced economists that there is no role for discretionary stabilization policy? Those who adhere to the new classical macroeconomics think so. Because anticipated policy does not affect aggregate output, discretionary policy can lead only to unpredictable output fluctuations. Pursuing a nondiscretionary policy in which there is no uncertainty about policy actions is then the best we can do. Such a position is not accepted by many economists, because the empirical evidence on the policy ineffectiveness proposition is mixed. Some studies find that only unanticipated policy matters to output fluctuations, while other studies find a significant impact of anticipated policy on output movements.[9] In addition, some economists question whether the degree of wage and price flexibility required in the new classical model actually exists.

The result is that many economists take an intermediate position that recognizes the distinction between the effects of anticipated versus unanticipated policy but believe that anticipated policy can affect output. They are still open to the possibility that discretionary stabilization policy can be beneficial, but they recognize the difficulties of designing it.

The rational expectations revolution has also highlighted the importance of credibility to the success of anti-inflation policies. Economists now recognize that if an anti-inflation policy is not believed by the public, it may be less effective in reducing the inflation rate when it is actually implemented and may lead to a larger loss of output than is necessary. Achieving credibility (not an easy task in that policymakers often say one thing but do another) should then be an important goal for policymakers. To achieve credibility, policymakers must be consistent in their course of action.

The rational expectations revolution has caused major rethinking about the way economic policy should be conducted and has forced economists to recognize that we may have to accept a more limited role for what policy can do for us. Rather than attempting to fine-tune the economy so that all output fluctuations are eliminated, we may have to settle for policies that create less uncertainty and thereby promote a more stable economic environment.

---

[9]Studies with findings that only unanticipated policy matters include Thomas Sargent, "A Classical Macroeconometric Model for the United States," *Journal of Political Economy* 84 (1976): 207–237; Robert J. Barro, "Unanticipated Money Growth and Unemployment in the United States," *American Economic Review* 67 (1977): 101–115; and Robert J. Barro and Mark Rush, "Unanticipated Money and Economic Activity," in *Rational Expectations and Economic Policy,* ed. Stanley Fischer (Chicago: University of Chicago Press, 1980), pp. 23–48. Studies that find a significant impact of anticipated policy are Frederic S. Mishkin, "Does Anticipated Monetary Policy Matter? An Econometric Investigation," *Journal of Political Economy* 90 (1982): 22–51; and Robert J. Gordon, "Price Inertia and Policy Effectiveness in the United States, 1890–1980," *Journal of Political Economy* 90 (1982): 1087–1117.

SUMMARY

1. The simple principle (derived from rational expectations theory) that expectation formation changes when the behavior of forecasted variables changes led to the famous Lucas critique of econometric policy evaluation. Lucas argued that when policy changes, expectations formation changes; hence the relationships in an econometric model will change. An econometric model that has been estimated on the basis of past data will no longer be the correct model for evaluating the effects of this policy change and may prove to be highly misleading. The Lucas critique also points out that the effects of a particular policy depend critically on the public's expectations about the policy.

2. The new classical macroeconomic model assumes that expectations are rational and that wages and prices are completely flexible with respect to the expected price level. It leads to the policy ineffectiveness proposition that anticipated policy has no effect on output; only unanticipated policy matters.

3. The new Keynesian model also assumes that expectations are rational but views wages and prices as sticky. Like the new classical model, the new Keynesian model distinguishes between the effects from anticipated and unanticipated policy: Anticipated policy has a smaller effect on aggregate output than unanticipated policy. However, anticipated policy does matter to output fluctuations.

4. The new classical model indicates that discretionary policy can be only counterproductive, while the new Keynesian model suggests that activist policy might be beneficial. However, because both models indicate that there is uncertainty about the outcome of a particular policy, the design of a beneficial discretionary policy may be very difficult. A traditional model in which expectations about policy have no effect on the short-run aggregate supply curve does not distinguish between the effects of anticipated or unanticipated policy. This model favors discretionary policy, because the outcome of a particular policy is less uncertain.

5. If expectations about policy affect the short-run aggregate supply curve, as they do in the new classical and new Keynesian models, an anti-inflation policy will be more successful (will produce a faster reduction in inflation with smaller output loss) if it is credible.

6. The rational expectations revolution has forced economists to be less optimistic about the effective use of discretionary stabilization policy and has made them more aware of the importance of credibility to successful policymaking.

KEY TERMS

econometric models, p. 644   policy ineffectiveness proposition, p. 648   wage-price stickiness, p. 650

QUESTIONS AND PROBLEMS

All questions and problems are available in myeconlab *at* www.myeconlab.com/mishkin.

1. If the public expects the Fed to pursue a policy that is likely to raise short-term interest rates permanently to 12% but the Fed does not go through with this policy change, what will happen to long-term interest rates? Explain your answer.

2. If consumer expenditure is related to consumers' expectations of their average income in the future, will an income tax cut have a larger effect on consumer expenditure if the public expects the tax cut to last for one year or for ten years?

Use an aggregate demand and supply diagram to illustrate your answer in all the following questions.

3. Having studied the new classical model, the new chairman of the Federal Reserve Board has thought up a surefire plan for reducing inflation and lowering unemployment. He announces that the Fed will lower the rate of money growth from 10% to 5% and then persuades the FOMC to keep the rate of money growth at 10%. If the new classical view of the world is correct, can his plan achieve the goals of lowering inflation and unemployment? How? Do you think his plan will work? If the traditional model's view of the world is correct, will the Fed chairman's surefire plan work?

4. "The costs of fighting inflation in the new classical and new Keynesian models are lower than in the traditional model." Is this statement true, false, or uncertain? Explain your answer.

5. The new classical model is an offshoot of the monetarist framework because it has a similar view of aggregate supply. What are the differences and similarities between the monetarist and new classical views of aggregate supply?

6. "The new classical model does not eliminate policymakers' ability to reduce unemployment because they can always pursue policies that are more expansionary than the public expects." Is this statement true, false, or uncertain? Explain your answer.

7. Which principle of rational expectations theory is used to prove the proposition that stabilization policy can have no predictable effect on aggregate output in the new classical model?

8. "The Lucas critique by itself casts doubt on the ability of discretionary stabilization policy to be beneficial." Is this statement true, false, or uncertain? Explain your answer.

9. "The more credible the policymakers who pursue an anti-inflation policy, the more successful that policy will be." Is this statement true, false, or uncertain? Explain your answer.

10. Many economists are worried that a high level of budget deficits may lead to inflationary monetary policies in the future. Could these budget deficits have an effect on the current rate of inflation?

Using Economic Analysis to Predict the Future

11. Suppose that a treaty is signed limiting armies throughout the world. The result of the treaty is that the public expects military and hence government spending to be reduced. If the new classical view of the economy is correct and government spending does affect the aggregate demand curve, predict what will happen to aggregate output and the price level when government spending is reduced in line with the public's expectations.

12. How would your prediction differ in Problem 11 if the new Keynesian model provides a more realistic description of the economy? What if the traditional model provides the most realistic description of the economy?

13. The chairman of the Federal Reserve Board announces that over the next year, the rate of money growth will be reduced from its current rate of 10% to a rate of 2%. If the chairman is believed by the public but the Fed actually reduces the rate of money growth to 5%, predict what will happen to the inflation rate and aggregate output if the new classical view of the economy is correct.

14. How would your prediction differ in Problem 13 if the new Keynesian model provides a more accurate description of the economy? What if the traditional model provides the most realistic description of the economy?

15. If, in a surprise victory, a new administration is elected to office that the public believes will pursue inflationary policy, predict what might happen to the level of output and inflation even before the new administration comes into power. Would your prediction differ depending on which of the three models—traditional, new classical, and new Keynesian—you believed in?

WEB EXERCISES

1. Robert Lucas won the Nobel Prize in economics. Go to nobelprize.org/nobel_prizes/economics/ and locate the press release on Robert Lucas. What was his Nobel Prize awarded for? When was it awarded?

WEB REFERENCES

http://homepage.newschool.edu/het/profiles/lucas.htm

A brief biography of Robert Lucas, including a list of his publications.

www.federalreserve.gov/pubs/feds/2001/200113/200113pap.pdf

The Federal Reserve recently published a paper discussing the new Keynesian model and price stickiness.

 MyEconLab CAN HELP YOU GET A BETTER GRADE

accommodating policy An activist policy in pursuit of a high employment target. **625**

adaptive expectations Expectations of a variable based on an average of past values of the variable. **152**

adverse selection The problem created by asymmetric information *before* a transaction occurs: The people who are the most undesirable from the other party's point of view are the ones who are most likely to want to engage in the financial transaction. **41**

agency theory The analysis of how asymmetric information problems affect economic behavior. **174**

aggregate demand The total quantity of output demanded in the economy at different price levels. **520, 565**

aggregate demand curve A relationship between the price level and the quantity of aggregate output demanded when the goods and money markets are in equilibrium. **559, 565**

aggregate demand function The relationship between aggregate output and aggregate demand that shows the quantity of aggregate output demanded for each level of aggregate output. **524**

aggregate income The total income of factors of production (land, labor, capital) in the economy. **21**

aggregate output The total production of final goods and services in the economy. **8**

aggregate price level The average price of goods and services in an economy. **8**

aggregate supply The quantity of aggregate output supplied by the economy at different price levels. **565**

aggregate supply curve The relationship between the quantity of output supplied and the price level. **568**

alt-A mortages Mortgages for borrowers with higher expected default rates than prime borrowers, but with better credit records than subprime borrowers. **207**

anchor currency A currency to which other countries' currencies are pegged. **470**

"animal spirits" Waves of optimism and pessimism that affect consumers' and businesses' willingness to spend. **527, 568**

appreciation Increase in a currency's value. **435**

arbitrage Elimination of a riskless profit opportunity in a market. **157**

asset A financial claim or piece of property that is a store of value. **3**

asset management The acquisition of assets that have a low rate of default and diversification of asset holdings to increase profits. **232**

asset market approach An approach to determine asset prices using stocks of assets rather than flows. **97**

asset price bubbles Increases in asset prices in the stock and real estate markets that are driven well above their fundamental economic values by investor psychology. **205**

asset transformation The process of turning risky assets into safer assets for investors by creating and selling assets with risk characteristics that people are comfortable with and then using the funds acquired by selling these assets to purchase other assets that may have far more risk. **40**

asymmetric information The unequal knowledge that each party to a transaction has about the other party. **41**

automated banking machine (ABM) One location that provides an automated teller machine (ATM), an Internet connection to the bank's Web site, and a telephone link to customer service. **287**

automated teller machine (ATM) An electronic machine that provides banking services 24-hours a day. **287**

autonomous consumer expenditure The amount of consumer expenditure that is independent of disposable income. **521**

balance of payments A bookkeeping system for recording all payments that have a direct bearing on the movement of funds between a country and foreign countries. **468**

balance-of-payments crisis A foreign exchange crisis stemming from problems in a country's balance of payments. **478**

balance sheet A list of the assets and liabilities of a bank (or firm) that balances: Total assets equal total liabilities plus capital. **225**

bank failure A situation in which a bank cannot satisfy its obligations to pay its depositors and other creditors and so goes out of business. **255**

bank holding companies Companies that own one or more banks. **283**

bank panic The simultaneous failure of many banks, as during a financial crisis. **201**

banks Financial institutions that accept money deposits and make loans (such as commercial banks, savings and loan associations, and credit unions). **7**

Basel Accord An agreement that required that banks hold as capital at least 8% of their risk-weighted assets. **261**

Basel Committee on Banking Supervision An international committee of bank supervisors that meets under the auspices of the Bank for International Settlements in Basel, Switzerland. **261**

behavioral finance A subfield of finance that applies concepts from other social sciences such as anthropology, sociology, and, particularly, psychology to understand the behavior of securities prices. **162**

Board of Governors of the Federal Reserve System A board with seven governors (including the chairman) that plays an essential role in decision making within the Federal Reserve System. **321**

bond A debt security that promises to make payments periodically for a specified period of time. **3**

borrowed reserves A bank's borrowings from the Fed. **353**

branches Additional offices of banks that conduct banking operations. **296**

Bretton Woods system The international monetary system in use from 1945 to 1971 in which exchange rates were fixed and the U.S. dollar was freely convertible into gold (by foreign governments and central banks only). **470**

brokers Agents for investors; they match buyers with sellers. **28**

bubble A situation in which the price of an asset differs from its fundamental market value. **161**

budget deficit The excess of government expenditure over tax revenues. **12**

budget surplus The excess of tax revenues over government expenditures. **12**

business cycles The upward and downward movement of aggregate output produced in the economy. **8**

capital Wealth, either financial or physical, that is employed to produce more wealth. **27**

capital account An account that describes the flow of capital between a country and other countries. **468**

capital adequacy management A bank's decision about the amount of capital it should maintain and then acquisition of the needed capital. **232**

capital market A financial market in which longer-term debt (generally with original maturity of greater than one year) and equity instruments are traded. **24**

capital mobility A situation in which foreigners can easily purchase a country's assets and the country's residents can easily purchase foreign assets. **461**

cash flow The difference between cash receipts and cash expenditures.

cash flows Cash payments to the holder of a security. **69, 147**

central bank The government agency that oversees the banking system and is responsible for the amount of money and credit supplied in the economy; in the United States, the Federal Reserve System. **10, 281**

collateral Property that is pledged to the lender to guarantee payment in the event that the borrower is unable to make debt payments. **171**

collateralized debt obligations (CDOs) Securities that paid out cash flows from subprime mortgaged-backed securities in different tranches, with the highest tranch paying out first, while lower ones paid out less if there were losses. **208**

commodity money Money made up of precious metals or another valuable commodity. **57**

common stock A security that is a claim on the earnings and assets of a company. **5**

community banks Small banks with local roots. **295**

compensating balance A required minimum amount of funds that a firm receiving a loan must keep in a checking account at the lending bank. **244**

complete crowding out The situation in which expansionary fiscal policy, such as an increase in government spending, does not lead to a rise in output because there is an exactly offsetting movement in private spending. **554**

conflicts of interest A manifestation of the moral hazard problem, particularly when a financial institution provides multiple services and the potentially competing interests of those services may lead to a concealment of information or dissemination of misleading information. **190**

consol A perpetual bond with no maturity date and no repayment of principal that periodically makes fixed coupon payments. **77**

constant-money-growth-rate rule A policy rule advocated by monetarists, whereby the Federal Reserve keeps the money supply growing at a constant rate. **639**

consumer durable expenditure Spending by consumers on durable items such as automobiles and household appliances. **601**

consumer expenditure The total demand for (spending on) consumer goods and services. **519, 565**

consumption Spending by consumers on nondurable goods and services (including services related to the ownership of homes and consumer durables). **604**

consumption function The relationship between disposable income and consumer expenditure. **521**

costly state verification Monitoring a firm's activities, an expensive process in both time and money. **181**

cost-push inflation Inflation that occurs because of the push by workers to obtain higher wages. **624**

coupon bond A credit market instrument that pays the owner a fixed interest payment every year until the maturity date, when a specified final amount is repaid. **72**

coupon rate The dollar amount of the yearly coupon payment expressed as a percentage of the face value of a coupon bond. **72**

credit boom A lending spree when financial institutions expand their lending at a rapid pace. **204**

credit rationing A lender's refusal to make loans even though borrowers are willing to pay the stated interest rate or even a higher rate or restriction of the size of loans made to less than the full amount sought. **244**

credit-rating agencies Investment advisory firms that rate the quality of corporate and municipal bonds in terms of the probability of default. **126**

credit risk The risk arising from the possibility that the borrower will default. **232**

credit view Monetary transmission mechanisms operating through asymmetric information effects on credit markets. **602**

currency   Paper money (such as dollar bills) and coins. **30, 53**

currency board   A monetary regime in which the domestic currency is backed 100% by a foreign currency (say, dollars) and in which the note-issuing authority, whether the central bank or the government, establishes a fixed exchange rate to this foreign currency and stands ready to exchange domestic currency at this rate whenever the public requests it. **490**

current account   An account that shows international transactions involving currently produced goods and services. **468**

current yield   An approximation of the yield to maturity that equals the yearly coupon payment divided by the price of a coupon bond. **78**

dealers   People who link buyers with sellers by buying and selling securities at stated prices. **30**

debt deflation   A situation in which a substantial decline in the price level sets in, leading to a further deterioration in firms' net worth because of the increased burden of indebtedness. **206**

default   A situation in which the party issuing a debt instrument is unable to make interest payments or pay off the amount owed when the instrument matures. **30, 123**

default-free bonds   Bonds with no default risk, such as U.S. government bonds. **124**

defensive open market operations   Open market operations intended to offset movements in other factors that affect the monetary base (such as changes in Treasury deposits with the Fed or changes in float). **381**

deleveraging   When financial institutions cut back on their lending because they have less capital. **204**

demand curve   A curve depicting the relationship between quantity demanded and price when all other economic variables are held constant. **94**

demand-pull inflation   Inflation that results when policymakers pursue policies that shift the aggregate demand curve. **624**

demand shocks   Shocks that can shift the aggregate demand curve, including changes in the money supply, changes in government expenditure and taxes, changes in net exports, and changes in consumer and business spending. **568**

deposit facility   The European Central Bank's standing facility in which banks are paid a fixed interest rate 100 basis points below the target financing rate. **390**

deposit outflows   Losses of deposits when depositors make withdrawals or demand payment. **232**

deposit rate ceiling   Restriction on the maximum interest rate payable on deposits. **290**

depreciation   Decrease in a currency's value. **435**

devaluation   Resetting of the fixed value of a currency at a lower level. **473**

dirty float   An exchange rate regime in which countries attempt to influence their exchange rates by buying and selling currencies (also called a *managed float regime*). **470**

discount bond   A credit market instrument that is bought at a price below its face value and whose face value is repaid at the maturity date; it does not make any interest payments. Also called a zero-coupon bond. **72**

discount loans   A bank's borrowings from the Federal Reserve System; also known as advances. **227**

discount rate   The interest rate that the Federal Reserve charges banks on discount loans. **234, 347**

discount window   The Federal Reserve facility at which discount loans are made to banks. **384**

discretionary policy   Policy to eliminate high unemployment whenever it appears on a discretionary basis. **634**

disintermediation   A reduction in the flow of funds into the banking system that causes the amount of financial intermediation to decline. **290**

disposable income   Total income available for spending, equal to aggregate income minus taxes. **521**

diversification   Investing in a collection (**portfolio**) of assets whose returns do not always move together, with the result that overall risk is lower than for individual assets. **40**

dividends   Periodic payments made by equities to shareholders. **28, 147**

dollarization   The adoption of a sound currency, like the U.S. dollar, as a country's money. **490**

dual banking system   The system in the United States in which banks supervised by the federal government and banks supervised by the states operate side by side. **283**

dual mandate   A central bank mandate that features two co-equal objectives: price stability and maximum employment. **320**

duration analysis   A measurement of the sensitivity of the market value of a bank's assets and liabilities to changes in interest rates. **246**

dynamic open market operations   Open market operations that are intended to change the level of reserves and the monetary base. **381**

e-cash   Electronic money that is used on the Internet to purchase goods or services. **59**

econometric model   A model whose equations are estimated using statistical procedures. **644**

economies of scale   The reduction in transaction costs per dollar of transaction as the size (scale) of transactions increases. **34**

economies of scope   The ability to use one resource to provide many different products and services. **189, 299**

Edge Act corporation   A special subsidiary of a U.S. bank that is engaged primarily in international banking. **308**

effective exchange rate index   An index reflecting the value of a basket of representative foreign currencies. **452**

efficient market hypothesis   The application of the theory of rational expectations to financial markets. **155**

e-finance   A new means of delivering financial services electronically. **7**

electronic money (e-money)   Money that exists only in electronic form and substitutes for cash as well. **58**

emerging market economics   Economies in an earlier stage of market development that have recently opened up to the flow of goods, services, and capital from the rest of the world. **212**

equation of exchange   The equation $MV = PY$, which relates nominal income to the quantity of money. **500**

equities   Claims to share in the net income and assets of a corporation (such as common stock). **28**

equity capital   See *net worth*. **179**

equity multiplier (*EM*)   The amount of assets per dollar of equity capital. **238**

Eurobonds   Bonds denominated in a currency other than that of the country in which they are sold. **37**

Eurocurrencies   A variant of the Eurobond; foreign currencies deposited in banks outside the home country. **37**

Eurodollars   U.S. dollars that are deposited in foreign banks outside the United States or in foreign branches of U.S. banks. **37**

excess demand   A situation in which quantity demanded is greater than quantity supplied. **96**

excess reserves   Reserves in excess of required reserves. **228, 347**

excess supply   A situation in which quantity supplied is greater than quantity demanded. **96**

exchange rate   The price of one currency stated in terms of another currency. **433**

exchange rate overshooting   A phenomenon whereby the exchange rate changes by more in the short run than it does in the long run when the money supply changes. **451**

exchange-rate peg   Fixing the value of the domestic currency to the value of another currency, so the exchange rate is fixed. **486**

exchange-rate targeting   See *exchange-rate peg* **486**

exchanges   Secondary markets in which buyers and sellers of securities (or their agents or brokers) meet in one central location to conduct trades. **29**

expectations theory   The proposition that the interest rate on a long-term bond will equal the average of the short-term interest rates that people expect to occur over the life of the long-term bond. **132**

expected return   The return on an asset expected over the next period. **91**

expenditure multiplier   The ratio of a change in aggregate output to a change in investment spending (or autonomous spending). **525**

face value   A specified final amount paid to the owner of a coupon bond at the maturity date. Also called par value. **72**

fair-value accounting   In which assets are valued in the balance sheet of what they could sell for in the market. **266**

federal funds rate   The interest rate on overnight loans of deposits at the Federal Reserve. **33, 313**

Federal Open Market Committee (FOMC)   The committee that makes decisions regarding the conduct of open market operations; composed of the seven members of the Board of Governors of the Federal Reserve System, the president of the Federal Reserve Bank of New York, and the presidents of four other Federal Reserve banks on a rotating basis. **321**

Federal Reserve banks   The 12 district banks in the Federal Reserve System. **321**

Federal Reserve System (the Fed)   The central banking authority responsible for monetary policy in the United States. **12**

fiat money   Paper currency decreed by a government as legal tender but not convertible into coins or precious metal. **57**

financial crisis   A major disruption in financial markets that is characterized by sharp declines in asset prices and the failures of many financial and nonfinancial firms. **7, 199**

financial derivatives   Instruments that have payoffs that are linked to previously issued securities, used as risk reduction tools. **286**

financial engineering   The process of researching and developing new financial products and services that would meet customer needs and prove profitable. **207, 284**

financial globalization   The process of economies opening up to flows of capital and financial firms from other nations. **213**

financial intermediaries   Institutions (such as banks, insurance companies, mutual funds, pension funds, and finance companies) that borrow funds from people who have saved and then make loans to others. **6**

financial intermediation   The process of indirect finance whereby financial intermediaries link lender-savers and borrower-spenders. **39**

financial liberalization   The elimination or restrictions on financial markets. **204**

financial markets   Markets in which funds are transferred from people who have a surplus of available funds to people who have a shortage of available funds. **3**

financial panic   The widespread collapse of financial markets and intermediaries in an economy. **47**

financial supervision (prudential supervision)   Overseeing who operates financial institutions and how they are operated. **263**

fiscal policy   Policy that involves decisions about government spending and taxation. **12**

Fisher effect   The outcome that when expected inflation occurs, interest rates will rise; named after economist Irving Fisher. **104**

fixed exchange rate regime   A regime in which central banks buy and sell their own currencies to keep their exchange rates fixed at a certain level. **470**

fixed investment   Spending by firms on equipment (computers, airplanes) and structures (factories, office buildings) and planned spending on residential housing. **522**

fixed-payment loan   A credit market instrument that provides a borrower with an amount of money that is repaid by making a fixed payment periodically (usually monthly) for a set number of years. **72**

float   Cash items in process of collection at the Fed minus deferred-availability cash items. **353**

floating exchange rate regime   An exchange rate regime in which the value of currencies are allowed to fluctuate against one another. **470**

foreign bonds   Bonds sold in a foreign country and denominated in that country's currency. **37**

foreign exchange intervention   An international financial transaction in which a central bank buys or sells currency to influence foreign exchange rates. **463**

foreign exchange market   The market in which exchange rates are determined. **13, 433**

foreign exchange rate   See *exchange rate*. **13**

forward exchange rate   The exchange rate for a forward transaction. **434**

forward transaction   A transaction that involves the exchange of bank deposits denominated in different currencies at some specified future date. **435**

free-rider problem   The problem that occurs when people who do not pay for information take advantage of the information that other people have paid for. **176**

fully amortized loan   See *fixed-payment loan* **72**

futures contract   A contract in which the seller agrees to provide a certain standardized commodity to the buyer on a specific future date at an agreed-on price. **285**

gap analysis   A measurement of the sensitivity of bank profits to changes in interest rates, calculated by subtracting the amount of rate-sensitive liabilities from the amount of rate-sensitive assets. **245**

generalized dividend model   Calculates that the price of stock is determined only by the present value of the dividends. **149**

goal independence   The ability of the central bank to set the goals of monetary policy. **324**

gold standard   A fixed exchange rate regime under which a currency is directly convertible into gold. **470**

Gordon growth model   A simplified model to compute the value of a stock by assuming constant dividend growth. **149**

government budget constraint   The requirement that the government budget deficit equal the sum of the change in the monetary base and the change in government bonds held by the public. **628**

government spending   Spending by all levels of government on goods and services. **520, 565**

gross domestic product (GDP)   The value of all final goods and services produced in the economy during the course of a year. **12, 21**

hedge   To protect oneself against risk. **285**

hierarchical mandate   A mandate for the central bank that puts the goal of price stability first, but as long as it is achieved other goals can be pursued. **319**

high-powered money   The monetary base. **347**

hyperinflation   An extreme inflation in which the inflation rate exceeds 50% per month. **56**

hysteresis   A departure from full-employment levels as a result of past high unemployment. **579**

incentive-compatible   Having the incentives of both parties to a contract in alignment. **184**

income   The flow of earnings. **54**

indexed bond   A bond whose interest and principal payments are adjusted for changes in the price level, and whose interest rate thus provides a direct measure of a real interest rate. **86**

inflation   The condition of a continually rising price level. **8**

inflation rate   The rate of change of the price level, usually measured as a percentage change per year. **9**

inflation targeting   A monetary policy strategy that involves public announcement of a medium-term numerical target for inflation. **399**

initial public offering (IPO)   Shares of newly issued stock. **191**

instrument independence   The ability of the central bank to set monetary policy instruments. **324**

interest parity condition   The observation that the domestic interest rate equals the foreign interest rate plus the expected appreciation in the foreign currency. **461**

interest rate   The cost of borrowing or the price paid for the rental of funds (usually expressed as a percentage per year). **4**

interest-rate risk   The possible reduction in returns associated with changes in interest rates. **82, 232**

intermediate target   Any of a number of variables, such as monetary aggregates or interest rates, that have a direct effect on employment and the price level and that the Fed seeks to influence. **409**

intermediate-term   With reference to a debt instrument, having a maturity of between one and ten years. **28**

international banking facilities (IBFs)   Banking establishments in the United States that can accept time deposits from foreigners but are not subject to either reserve requirements or restrictions on interest payments. **308**

International Monetary Fund (IMF)   The international organization created by the Bretton Woods agreement whose objective is to promote the growth of world trade by making loans to countries experiencing balance-of-payments difficulties. **470**

international policy coordination   Agreements among countries to enact policies cooperatively. **426**

international reserves   Central bank holdings of assets denominated in foreign currencies. **463**

inventory investment   Spending by firms on additional holdings of raw materials, parts, and finished goods. **522**

inverted yield curve   A yield curve that is downward-sloping. **130**

investment banks   Firms that assist in the initial sale of securities in the primary market. **28**

IS curve   The relationship that describes the combinations of aggregate output and interest rates for which the total quantity of goods produced equals the total quantity demanded (goods market equilibrium). **534**

junk bonds   Bonds with ratings below Baa (or BBB) that have a high default risk. **126**

Keynesian   A follower of John Maynard Keynes who believes that movements in the price level and aggregate output are driven by changes not only in the money supply but also in government spending and fiscal policy and who does not regard the economy as inherently stable. **576**

large, complex banking organizations (LCBOs)   Large companies that provide banking as well as many other financial services. **299**

law of one price   The principle that if two countries produce an identical good, the price of this good should be the same throughout the world no matter which country produces it. **437**

lender of last resort   Provider of reserves to financial institutions when no one else would provide them to prevent a financial crisis. **384**

leverage ratio   A bank's capital divided by its assets. **260**

liabilities   IOUs or debts. **26**

liability management   The acquisition of funds at low cost to increase profits. **232**

liquid   Easily converted into cash. **29**

liquidity   The relative ease and speed with which an asset can be converted into cash. **56, 92**

liquidity management   The decisions made by a bank to maintain sufficient liquid assets to meet the bank's obligations to depositors. **232**

liquidity preference framework   A model developed by John Maynard Keynes that predicts the equilibrium interest rate on the basis of the supply of and demand for money. **109**

liquidity preference theory   John Maynard Keynes's theory of the demand for money. **503**

liquidity premium theory   The theory that the interest rate on a long-term bond will equal an average of short-term interest rates expected to occur over the life of the long-term bond plus a positive term (liquidity) premium. **136**

liquidity services   Services financial inermediaries provide to their customers to make it easier for them to conduct their transactions. **40**

LM curve   The relationship that describes the combinations of interest rates and aggregate output for which the quantity of money demanded equals the quantity of money supplied (money market equilibrium). **534**

loan commitment   A bank's commitment (for a specified future period of time) to provide a firm with loans up to a given amount at an interest rate that is tied to some market interest rate. **243**

loan sale   The sale under a contract (also called a secondary loan participation) of all or part of the cash stream from a specific loan, thereby removing the loan from the bank's balance sheet. **247**

longer-term refinancing operations   A category of open market operations by the European Central Bank that are similar to the Fed's outright purchases or sales of securities. **390**

long-run monetary neutrality   See *monetary neutrality*. **559**

long-term   With reference to a debt instrument, having a maturity of ten years or more. **28**

M1   A measure of money that includes currency, traveler's checks, and checkable deposits. **62**

M2   A measure of money that adds to M1: money market deposit accounts, money market mutual fund shares, small-denomination time deposits, savings deposits, overnight repurchase agreements, and overnight Eurodollars. **62**

macroprudential regulation   Regulatory policy to affect what is happening in the credit markets in the aggregate. **417**

main refinancing operations   Weekly reverse transactions (purchase or sale of eligible assets under repurchase agreements or credit operations against eligible assets as collateral) that are reversed within two weeks and are the primary monetary policy tool of the European Central Bank. **390**

managed float regime   An exchange rate regime in which countries attempt to influence their exchange rates by buying and selling currencies (also called a dirty float). **470**

marginal lending facility   The European Central Bank's standing lending facility in which banks can borrow (against eligible collateral) overnight loans from the national central bank at a rate 100 basis points above the target financing rate. **390**

marginal lending rate   The interest rate charged by the European Central Bank for borrowing at its marginal lending facility. **390**

marginal propensity to consume   The slope of the consumption function line that measures the change in consumer expenditure resulting from an additional dollar of disposable income. **521**

mark-to-market accounting   An accounting method in which assets are valued in the balance sheets at what they would sell for in the market. **260**

market equilibrium   A situation occurring when the quantity that people are willing to buy (demand) equals the quantity that people are willing to sell (supply). **96**

market fundamentals   Items that have a direct impact on future income streams of a security. **158**

matched sale–purchase transaction   An arrangement whereby the Fed sells securities and the buyer agrees to sell them back to the Fed in the near future; sometimes called a reverse repo. **383**

maturity   Time to the expiration date (maturity date) of a debt instrument. **28**

medium of exchange   Anything that is used to pay for goods and services. **54**

monetarism   The view that the money supply is the primary source of movements in the price level and aggregate output. **515**

monetarist   A follower of Milton Friedman who sees changes in the money supply as the primary source of movements in the price level and aggregate output and who views the economy as inherently stable. **577**

monetary aggregates   The measures of the money supply used by the Federal Reserve System (M1 and M2). **60**

monetary base   The sum of the Fed's monetary liabilities (currency in circulation and reserves) and the U.S. Treasury's monetary liabilities (Treasury currency in circulation, primarily coins). **346**

monetary neutrality   A proposition that in the long run, a percentage rise in the money supply is matched by the same percentage rise in the price level, leaving unchanged the real money supply and all other economic variables such as interest rates. **450, 559**

monetary policy   The management of the money supply and interest rates. **10**

monetary targeting   A monetary policy strategy in which the central bank announces that it will achieve a certain value (the target) of the annual growth rate of a monetary aggregate. **395**

monetary theory   The theory that relates changes in the quantity of money to changes in economic activity. **8, 499**

monetizing the debt   A method of financing government spending whereby the government debt issued to finance government spending is removed from the hands of the public and is replaced by high-powered money instead. Also called *printing money*. **628**

money (money supply)   Anything that is generally accepted in payment for goods or services or in the repayment of debts. **8**

money center banks   Large banks in key financial centers (New York, Chicago, San Francisco). **236**

money market   A financial market in which only short-term debt instruments (generally those with original maturity of less than one year) are traded. **29**

money multiplier   A ratio that relates the change in the money supply to a given change in the monetary base. **362**

money supply   The quantity of money. **8**

moral hazard   The risk that one party to a transaction will engage in behavior that is undesirable from the other party's point of view. **41**

mortgage-backed securities   Securities that cheaply bundle and quantify the default risk of the underlying high-risk mortgages. **207**

multiple deposit creation   The process whereby, when the Fed supplies the banking system with $1 of additional reserves, deposits increase by a multiple of this amount. **354**

NAIRU (nonaccelerating inflation rate of unemployment)   The rate of unemployment when demand for labor equals supply, consequently eliminating the tendency for the inflation rate to change. **413**

national banks   Federally chartered banks. **283**

natural rate level of output   The level of aggregate output produced at the natural rate of unemployment at which there is no tendency for wages or prices to change. **557, 570**

natural rate of unemployment   The rate of unemployment consistent with full employment at which the demand for labor equals the supply of labor. **318, 568**

net exports   Net foreign spending on domestic goods and services, equal to exports minus imports. **520, 565**

net worth   The difference between a firm's assets (what it owns or is owed) and its liabilities (what it owes). Also called *equity capital*. **179**

nominal anchor   A nominal variable such as the inflation rate, an exchange rate, or the money supply that monetary policymakers use to tie down the price level. **316**

nominal interest rate   An interest rate that does not take inflation into account. **84**

nonaccelerating inflation rate of unemployment   See *NAIRU*. **413**

nonborrowed monetary base   The monetary base minus discount loans (borrowed reserves). **353**

off-balance-sheet activities   Bank activities that involve trading financial instruments and the generation of income from fees and loan sales, all of which affect bank profits but are not visible on bank balance sheets. **247, 261**

official reserve transactions balance   The current account balance plus items in the capital account. **469**

open market operations   The Fed's buying or selling of bonds in the open market. **322, 347**

open market purchase   A purchase of bonds by the Fed. **348**

open market sale   A sale of bonds by the Fed. **348**

operating instrument   A variable that is very responsive to the central bank's tools and indicates the stance of monetary policy (also called a policy instrument). **409**

opportunity cost   The amount of interest (expected return) sacrificed by not holding an alternative asset. **110**

optimal forecast   The best guess of the future using all available information. **153**

originate-to-distribute model   A business model in which the mortgage is originated by a separate party, typically a mortgage broker, and then distributed to an investor as an underlying asset in a security. **208**

over-the-counter (OTC) market A secondary market in which dealers at different locations who have an inventory of securities stand ready to buy and sell securities "over the counter" to anyone who comes to them and is willing to accept their prices. **29**

overnight cash rate The interest rate for very-short-term interbank loans in the euro area. **390**

par value See *face value.* **72**

payments system The method of conducting transactions in the economy. **57**

perpetuity See *consol.* **77**

Phillips curve theory A theory suggesting that changes in inflation are influenced by the state of the economy relative to its production capacity, as well as to other factors. **413**

planned investment spending Total planned spending by businesses on new physical capital (e.g., machines, computers, apartment buildings) plus planned spending on new homes. **519, 565**

policy ineffectiveness proposition The conclusion from the new classical model that anticipated policy has no effect on output fluctuations. **648**

policy instrument A variable that is very responsive to the central bank's tools and indicates the stance of monetary policy (also called an operating instrument). **409**

political business cycle A business cycle caused by expansionary policies before an election. **338**

portfolio A collection or group of assets. **41**

preferred habitat theory A theory that is closely related to liquidity premium theory, in which the interest rate on a long-term bond equals an average of short-term interest rates expected to occur over the life of the long-term bond plus a positive term premium. **137**

present discounted value See *present value.* **69**

present value Today's value of a payment to be received in the future when the interest rate is *i.* Also called *present discounted value.* **69**

price stability Low and stable inflation. **315**

primary dealers Government securities dealers, operating out of private firms or commercial banks, with whom the Fed's open market desk trades. **382**

primary market A financial market in which new issues of a security are sold to initial buyers. **28**

principal–agent problem A moral hazard problem that occurs when the managers in control (the agents) act in their own interest rather than in the interest of the owners (the principals) due to different sets of incentives. **180**

printing money See *monetizing the debt.* **629**

prudential supervision See *financial supervision.* **263**

quantity theory of money The theory that nominal income is determined solely by movements in the quantity of money. **501**

quotas Restrictions on the quantity of foreign goods that can be imported. **440**

rate of capital gain The change in a security's price relative to the initial purchase price. **81**

rate of return See *return.* **80**

rational expectations Expectations that reflect optimal forecasts (the best guess of the future) using all available information. **153**

real bills doctrine A guiding principle (now discredited) for the conduct of monetary policy that states that as long as loans are made to support the production of goods and services, providing reserves to the banking system to make these loans will not be inflationary. **418**

real business cycle theory A theory that views real shocks to tastes and technology as the major driving force behind short-run business cycle fluctuations. **579**

real exchange rate The rate at which domestic goods can be exchanged for foreign goods; i.e., the price of domestic relative to foreign goods denominated in domestic currency. **437**

real interest rate The interest rate adjusted for expected changes in the price level (inflation) so that it more accurately reflects the true cost of borrowing. **84**

real money balances The quantity of money in real terms. **505**

real terms Terms reflecting actual goods and services one can buy. **85**

recession A period when aggregate output is declining. **8**

reduced-form evidence Evidence that examines whether one variable has an effect on another by simply looking directly at the relationship between the two variables. **588**

regulatory arbitrage A process in which banks keep on their books assets that have the same risk-based capital requirement but are relatively risky, such as a loan to a company with a very low credit rating, while taking off their books low-risk assets, such as a loan to a company with a very high credit rating. **261**

repurchase agreement (repo) An arrangement whereby the Fed, or another party, purchases securities with the understanding that the seller will repurchase them in a short period of time, usually less than a week. **383**

required reserve ratio The fraction of deposits that the Fed requires be kept as reserves. **228, 347**

required reserves Reserves that are held to meet the Fed's requirement that for every dollar of deposits at a bank, a certain fraction must be kept as reserves. **228, 347**

reserve currency A currency, such as the U.S. dollar, that is used by other countries to denominate the assets they hold as international reserves. **471**

reserve requirements Regulation making it obligatory for depository institutions to keep a certain fraction of their deposits in accounts with the Fed. **228**

reserves   Banks' holding of deposits in accounts with the Fed plus currency that is physically held by banks (vault cash). **228, 347**

residual claimant   The right as a stockholder to receive whatever remains after all other claims against the firm's assets have been satisfied. **147**

restrictive covenants   Provisions that restrict and specify certain activities that a borrower can engage in. **172**

return   The payments to the owner of a security plus the change in the security's value, expressed as a fraction of its purchase price. More precisely called the *rate of return*. **80**

return on assets (ROA)   Net profit after taxes per dollar of assets. **238**

return on equity (ROE)   Net profit after taxes per dollar of equity capital. **238**

revaluation   Resetting of the fixed value of a currency at a higher level. **473**

reverse causation   A situation in which one variable is said to cause another variable, when in reality the reverse is true. **590**

reverse repo   See *matched sale–purchase transaction*. **383**

reverse transactions   Purchase or sale of eligible assets by the European Central Bank under repurchase agreements or credit operations against eligible assets as collateral that are reversed within two weeks. **390**

Ricardian equivalence   Named after the nineteenth-century British economist David Ricardo, it contends that when the government runs deficits and issues bonds, the public recognizes that it will be subject to higher taxes in the future to pay off these bonds. **630**

risk   The degree of uncertainty associated with the return on an asset. **40, 92**

risk premium   The spread between the interest rate on bonds with default risk and the interest rate on default-free bonds. **124**

risk sharing   The process of creating and selling assets with risk characteristics that people are comfortable with and then using the funds acquired by selling these assets to purchase other assets that may have far more risk. **40**

risk structure of interest rates   The relationship among the interest rates on various bonds with the same term to maturity. **123**

secondary market   A financial market in which securities that have previously been issued (and are thus second-hand) can be resold. **28**

secondary reserves   Short-term U.S. government and agency securities held by banks. **228**

secured debt   Debt guaranteed by collateral. **171**

securitization   The process of transforming illiquid financial assets into marketable capital market instruments. **207, 289**

security   A claim on the borrower's future income that is sold by the borrower to the lender. Also called a financial instrument. **3**

segmented markets theory   A theory of term structure that sees markets for different-maturity bonds as completely separated and segmented such that the interest rate for bonds of a given maturity is determined solely by supply of and demand for bonds of that maturity. **135**

seignorage   The revenue a government receives by issuing money. **492**

self-correcting mechanism   A characteristic of the economy that causes output to return eventually to the natural rate level regardless of where it is initially. **575**

shadow banking system   A system in which bank lending is replaced by lending via the securities market. **284**

short sales   Borrowing stock from brokers and then selling the stock in the market, with the hope that a profit will be earned by buying the stock back again ("covering the short") after it has fallen in price. **162**

short-term   With reference to a debt instrument, having a maturity of one year or less. **28**

simple deposit multiplier   The multiple increase in deposits generated from an increase in the banking system's reserves in a simple model in which the behavior of depositors and banks plays no role. **358**

simple loan   A credit market instrument providing the borrower with an amount of funds that must be repaid to the lender at the maturity date along with an additional payment (interest). **70**

smart card   A stored-value card that contains a computer chip that lets it be loaded with digital cash from the owner's bank account whenever needed. **59**

special drawing rights (SDRs)   An IMF-issued paper substitute for gold that functions as international reserves. **476**

speculative attack   A situation in which speculators engage in massive sales of the currency. **216**

spinning   When an investment bank allocates shares of hot, but underpriced initial public offerings to executives of other companies in return for their companies' future business with the investment bank. **191**

spot exchange rate   The exchange rate for a spot transaction. **434**

spot transaction   The predominant type of exchange rate transaction, involving the immediate exchange of bank deposits denominated in different currencies. **434**

standing lending facility   A lending facility in which healthy banks are allowed to borrow all they want from a central bank. **384**

state banks   State-chartered banks. **282**

state-owned banks   Banks that are owned by governments. **187**

sterilized foreign exchange intervention   A foreign exchange intervention with an offsetting open market operation that leaves the monetary base unchanged. **466**

stock   A security that is a claim on the earnings and assets of a company. **5**

stockholders   Those who hold stock in a coproration. **147**

store of value   A repository of purchasing power over time. **56**

structural model   A description of how the economy operates, using a collection of equations that describe the behavior of firms and consumers in many sectors of the economy. **588**

structural model evidence   Evidence that examines whether one variable affects another by using data to build a model illustrating the channels through which this variable affects the other. **587**

structured credit products   Securities that are derived from cash flows of underlying assets and are tailored to have particular risk characteristics that appeal to investors with different preferences. **207**

structured investment vehicles (SIVs)   Securities similar to CDOs in that they pay off cash flows from pools of assets such as mortgages; however, instead of being issued as long-term debt as in CDOs, they are issued as asset-backed commercial paper. **210**

subprime mortgages   Mortgages for borrowers with less than stellar credit records. **207**

superregional banks   Bank holding companies similar in size to money center banks, but whose headquarters are not based in one of the money center cities (New York, Chicago, San Francisco). **299**

supply curve   A curve depicting the relationship between quantity supplied and price when all other economic variables are held constant. **95**

supply shock   Any change in technology or the supply of raw materials that can shift the aggregate supply curve. **572**

swap lines   Arrangements in which the Fed lent dollars to foreign central banks in exchange for foreign currencies. **387**

sweep account   An arrangement in which any balances above a certain amount in a corporation's checking account at the end of a business day are "swept out" of the account and invested in overnight repos that pay the corporation interest. **292**

T-account   A simplified balance sheet with lines in the form of a T that lists only the changes that occur in balance sheet items starting from some initial balance sheet position. **229**

target financing rate   The European Central Bank's target for the overnight cash rate, the interest rate for very-short-term interbank loans in the euro area. **390**

tariffs   Taxes on imported goods. **440**

Taylor principle   The principle that the monetary authorities should raise nominal interest rates by more than the increase in the inflation rate. **413**

Taylor rule   Economist John Taylor's monetary policy rule that explains how the federal funds rate target is set. **412**

term structure of interest rates   The relationship among interest rates on bonds with different terms to maturity. **123**

theory of asset demand   The theory that the quantity demanded of an asset is (1) usually positively related to wealth, (2) positively related to its expected return relative to alternative assets, (3) negatively related to the risk of its return relative to alternative assets, and (4) positively related to its liquidity relative to alternative assets. **93**

theory of efficient capital markets   See *efficient market hypothesis.* **155**

theory of purchasing power parity (PPP)   The theory that exchange rates between any two currencies will adjust to reflect changes in the price levels of the two countries. **437**

thrift institutions (thrifts)   Savings and loan associations, mutual savings banks, and credit unions. **43**

time-inconsistency problem   The problem that occurs when monetary policymakers conduct monetary policy in a discretionary way and pursue expansionary policies that are attractive in the short run but lead to bad long-run outcomes. **316**

trade balance   The difference between merchandise exports and imports. **468**

transaction costs   The time and money spent trying to exchange financial assets, goods, or services. **39**

transmission mechanisms of monetary policy   The channels through which the money supply affects economic activity. **588**

underwrite   Purchase securities from a corporation at a predetermined price and then resell them in the market. **28, 46**

unemployment rate   The percentage of the labor force not working. **8**

unexploited profit opportunity   A situation in which an investor can earn a higher than normal return. **157**

unit of account   Anything used to measure value in an economy. **55**

unsecured debt   Debt not guaranteed by collateral. **171**

unsterilized foreign exchange intervention   A foreign exchange intervention in which a central bank allows the purchase or sale of domestic currency to affect the monetary base. **465**

vault cash   Currency that is physically held by banks and stored in vaults overnight. **228**

velocity of money   The rate of turnover of money; the average number of times per year that a dollar is spent in buying the total amount of final goods and services produced in the economy. **500**

venture capital firm   A financial intermediary that pools the resources of its partners and uses the funds to help entrepreneurs start up new businesses. **182**

virtual bank   A bank that has no building but rather exists only in cyberspace. **287**

wage-price stickiness   When a source of rigidity prevents wages from responding fully to changes in the expected price level. **650**

wealth   All resources owned by an individual, including all assets. **54, 91**

World Bank   The International Bank for Reconstruction and Redevelopment, an international organization that provides long-term loans to assist developing countries in building dams, roads, and other physical capital that would contribute to their economic development. **471**

World Trade Organization (WTO)   An organization headquartered in Geneva, Switzerland, that monitors rules for the conduct of trade between countries (tariffs and quotas). **471**

yield curve   A plot of the interest rates for particular types of bonds with different terms to maturity. **130**

yield to maturity   The interest rate that equates the present value of payments received from a credit market instrument with its value today. **72**

zero-coupon bond   See *discount bond.* **72**

Italicized *t* refers to tables, *f* refers to figures, and *b* refers to boxed material.

ABM (automated banking machine), 287
Accommodating policy, 625
Accounting firms, conflicts of interest in auditing and consulting by, 191, 193, 193*b*
Adaptive expectations, 152–53
Adjustable-rate mortgages, 285
Adjustment credit facility, 384 n.4
Advances. *See* Discount loans (advances)
Adverse selection, 41–42, 174–80, 186*t*
  Akerlof's "lemons problem" as example of, 174–75
  as asymmetric information problem before transactions occur, 174
  bank management of credit risks and problem of, 241
  defined, 41
  government safety net and, 258
  in stock and bonds markets, 175–76
  tools to help solve problems of, 176–80
Adverse shocks, "perfect storm" of (2007–2008), 498, 583–84
Agency problems in subprime mortgage market, 208–9
Agency theory, 174
Aggregate demand, 520, 524, 565–68. *See also* Aggregate demand curve
  component parts of, 565
  defined, 565
  M. Friedman on importance of money to, 592–94
Aggregate demand and supply analysis, 565–86
  aggregate demand and, 565–68
  aggregate supply and, 568–73

explaining business cycle episodes, 580–84
  equilibrium in, 573–80
  implication of rational expectations for, 645–53
  inflation and, 620–24
  web references, 586
Aggregate demand curve, 559, 565
  deriving, 566–67
  factors causing shifts in, 567–68, 569*t*
  summary, 568
Aggregate demand curve, *ISLM* model and, 559–62
  deriving, 560, 560*f*
  factors causing shifts in, 561–62
Aggregate demand function, 524, 533, 533 n.5
Aggregate economic activity
  business cycles and, 580–84
  effectiveness of monetary versus fiscal policy in controlling, 552–57
  ISLM model and, 539–48
  ISLM model in long run and effects on, 557–59
Aggregate income, 21
  quantity theory of money on determining nominal value of, 499–503
Aggregate output, 8, 21, 499, 519–33
  aggregate demand and, 520, 565–68
  comparing three models on price responses to short-run, 653–56
  consumer expenditure, consumption function, and, 519, 520–22, 531, 532*t*
  effect of expansionary policy on, 648–49
  equilibrium, 523–25, 534
  expenditure multiplier and, 525–27

fiscal policy changes and response of, 549–50
  government spending and role of government in, 520, 528–30, 532*t*, 533
  inflation targeting and increased fluctuations in, 404
  international trade, net exports, and, 520, 530–31, 532*t*, 533
  ISLM model and, 534–40
  monetary policy change and response of, 548–49
  planned investment spending, 519, 522–23, 525–27, 532, 532*t*
  summary of determinants of, 531–33
  taxes and, 529–30, 532*t*, 533
  unemployment, price level, and, 566*b*
  of U.S. economy, 8
Aggregate price level
  defined, 8
  income and, 22
  money supply and, 10*f*
  three measures of, 22
Aggregate supply, 565, 568–73. *See also* Aggregate demand and supply analysis
  aggregate supply curve, 568
  defined, 565
Aggregate supply curve, 568–73
  factors affecting short-run, 571–73, 573*t*
  inflation and short-run, 621 n.1
  long-run, 568, 570, 570*f*
  shifts in long-run, 579–80
  shifts in short-term, 571
  short-run, 570–71, 571*f*
Agricultural Adjustment Act of 1933, 420
AIG insurance, 211, 388*b*
Akerlof, George, "lemons problem," 174–75, 175 n.3
Alt-A mortgages, 222
Anchor country, 486

Anchor currency, 470
"Animal spirits," J. M. Keynes on, 527, 568
  inflation and, 622 n.2
Annual percentage rate (APR), 267
Anticipated and unanticipated policy, effects of
  in new classical macroeconomic model, 646–48
  in new Keynesian model, 651, 652f
Applications, 15
  aggregate supply and demand analysis, and business cycle, 580–84
  applying lessons of monetary policy to Japan, 612
  bank capital, managing, 239–40
  China's international reserves, 474–75
  collapse of investment spending in Great Depression, 527–28
  crashes and rational expectations, efficient markets, 161–62
  credibility in Reagan era of budget deficits, 660–61
  credibility of Volcker's anti-inflation policy, 639
  credit crunch of 2008, 240
  currency pegging, 452
  debating importance of monetary policy to economic fluctuations, 591–600
  Economic Stimulus Act of 2008, 550, 552
  effects of Bush administration tax cuts on bond interest rates, 130
  equilibrium exchange rate, changes in, 448–52
  euro foreign exchange rate and oil prices, 452–54
  federal funds rate fluctuations, limiting of, 380–81
  financial crises in Mexico, East Asia, and Argentina, 217–21
  financial development and economic growth in transition countries, 186–87

financial development in China, 188–89
  foreign exchange crisis (1992), 477–78
  foreign exchange crises in emerging market countries (1994–2002), 478–79
  global financial crisis and the euro, 454
  Great Depression, 206–7, 366–69
  guide to investing in stock market, 158
  interest rates, 85
  interest-rate behavior, 103–7, 112, 114–18
  interpreting yield curves, 141
  monetary policy and stock prices, 151–52
  reading "Credit Markets" column of Wall Street Journal, 107–8
  reading the Financial Times:, The "LEX" Column, 454–55
  rise in U.S. inflation (1960–1980), explaining, 630–34
  simple present value, 71
  subprime collapse and Baa-Treasury spread, 127
  subprime crisis and stock market, 152
  subprime recession, 609–10
  targeting money supply versus interest rates, 554–57
  yield to maturity, 73, 74–75, 76, 78
Appreciation of currency, 435, 436, 439–40, 444–45, 449
Arbitrage, 157
Argentina
  currency board, 491b
  financial crises in (2002), 478–79
Arthur Anderson accounting firm, conflict of interest in Enron case and, 191, 193b
Asset(s)
  bank (see Bank capital)
  on bank balance sheets, 225, 226t, 228–29

defined, 3
  demand for (see Asset demand)
  diversification of, 40–41
  domestic (see Domestic assets)
  on Federal Reserve balance sheets, 347
  for financial intermediaries, 43t
  flows, 97
  foreign (see Foreign assets)
  management of, in banks, 232, 235–36
  portfolio of, 40
  return on (ROA), 238
  stocks (supply) of, 97
  value of, bubble in, 161
  value of, for select financial intermediaries, 44t
Asset-Backed Commercial Paper Money Market Mutual Fund Liquidity Facility (AMLF), 387b
Asset demand. See also Demand for money
  determinants of, 91–93
  for domestic assets, 442–48
  quantity of assets and demand determinants, 93t
  theory of, 91, 93 (see also Theory of asset demand)
Asset holdings, regulation of bank, 260
Asset-liability management committee, 237
Asset management, 251
Asset markets, effects of, on balance sheets, 200–1
  asset write-downs, 201
  currency-value decline, 200–1
  price-level decline, 200
  stock market decline, 200
Asset markets approach, 97
  applied to commodity markets (gold), 97 n.3
Asset price boom and bust, 205
Asset-price bubble, 205, 415
  credit-driven, 415–16
  driven by irrational exuberance, 416
  response of central banks to, 415–18

Asset price channels of monetary transmission mechanism, 602–5, 610–11
  exchange rate effects on net exports, 602
  Tobin's q theory, 604
  wealth effects, 604–5
Asset transformation, 40, 229, 232
Asset write-downs, 201
Asymmetric information, 41–42, 174
  adverse selection and, 174–80
  bank management of credit risks and problem of, 241
  bank panics and, 256
  conflicts of interest and, 190–94
  financial regulation and, 255–71
  moral hazards and, 180–83
  problems of, and tools to solve, 186t
  regulatory agencies and alleviation of, 46
  transaction cost and, 174
ATM. See Automated teller machines (ATM)
Australia, 295
Automated banking machines (ABM), 287
Automated teller machines (ATM), 7, 287
  as response to restrictions on bank branching, 297–98
Autonomous consumer expenditure, 521
  change in curve and, 544, 551t
  change in aggregate output due to, 527, 531–32, 532t

Bailouts, 211, 212b, 273
Balance(s), compensating, 243–44
Balance of payments, 468–69
  effects of, on monetary policy, 485
Balance-of-payments crises, 478
Balance sheet, bank, 225–29
  activities off, 247–50
  assets (uses of funds), 225, 228–29, 293–94
  capital adequacy management and, 237–40
  of commercial banks (2008), 226t

deterioration of, as factor of financial crises, 201, 210, 216
  interest-rate risk and, 245
  liabilities (sources of funds), 225–28, 292–93
  liquidity management and role of reverse in, 232–35
  as monetary transmission mechanism, 606–7
  T-account as simplified, 229–32
Balance sheet, consumers', and Great Depression, 608, 608b
Balance sheet, Federal Reserve, 345–47
Bank(s), 43–44. See also Banking; Banking industry
  balance sheets (see Balance sheet, bank)
  basic operation of, 229–32
  chartering of, 263–64
  classification of, according to capitalization, 262–63
  commercial (see Commercial banks)
  consolidation of, 298–302
  cost of rescuing, in select countries, 275t
  defined, 7
  Federal Reserve (see Federal Reserve Banks (FRBs))
  foreign, in U.S., 308–9
  global crises in, 273–75
  investment, 28, 44
  largest U.S., 296t
  merger partners for insolvent, 258–59
  monetary supply and, 345
  money center banks, 236
  multiple deposit creation by single, 354–55
  national, 283, 323
  open market purchase from, 348
  panic (see Bank panics)
  physical branches, versus internet-only, 288b
  regulation of (see Banking regulation)
  savings and loan (see Savings and loan associations (S&Ls))

as source of funding for businesses, 171
  state, 282, 323
  state-owned, 187
  superregional, 299
  supervision of, 263–64
  world's largest, 309t
Bank capital, 227–28, 262–63
  credit crunch of 2008 and, 240
  prevention of bank failure and role of, 237–38
  regulations on requirements for, 260–61
  return to equity holders and amount of, 238–39
  strategies for managing, 239–40
Bank credit and debit cards, 286–87
Bank examiners, 263
  Federal Reserve guidelines for, 263–64
Bank failures, 255–56, 271–73
  avoiding through capital adequacy management, 237–38
  European, 212b
  FDIC's two methods of handling, 256–57
  in Great Depression, 283
  in Japan, 274
  risks to depositors' funds in, 255–57
  in U.S. (1934–2008), 272f
Bank for International Settlements (BIS), 244
Bank holding companies, 283, 297
Bank Holding Company Act and Douglas Amendment (1956), 270t
Banking, 7, 225–53. See also Bank(s); Banking industry
  bank balance sheets, 225–29
  basic concepts of, 229–32
  crises, 205–4
  financial crises due to problems in, 201
  financial innovations and decline in traditional, 292–95
  international, 306–9
  management of, general principles, 232–40

Banking (*continued*)
  managing credit risk, 240–45
  managing credit risk, assessment of, 264–65
  managing interest-rate risk, 245–47
  multiple deposit creation and system of, 355–58
  nationwide, 298–302
  off-balance sheet activities in, 247–50
  regulation of (*see* Banking regulation)
  this book's approach to study of, 14–15
  universal, 303
  web references, 253
Banking Acts of 1933 and 1935, 270*t*, 420. *See also* Glass-Steagall Act
Banking industry, 281–312
  bank consolidation in, and nationwide banking, 298–302
  diversity of, 281
  financial innovation, and growth of "shadow banking system," 284–95
  foreign, in U.S., 308–9
  historical development of, 281–84
  international, 306–9
  regulation (*see* Banking regulation)
  separation of, from other financial service industries, 302–4
  structure of U.S. commercial, 295–98, 300–1
  thrift industry regulation and structure, 304–6
  time line of American, 282*f*
  web references, 311
Banking regulation. *See* Financial regulation
Bank lending, 35, 229, 234–35
  management of credit risks associated with, 241–245
  as monetary transmission mechanism, 605–6
  to other banks, 227
Banknotes, 53, 282

Bank of America, 211, 287, 300, 301, 388*b*
Bank of Canada, 331, 396, 400–1
  structure and independence of, 332
Bank of Credit and Commerce International (BCCI), 271*b*
Bank of England, 271*b*, 320, 321, 396, 402
  structure and independence of, 331–32
Bank of Japan, 332, 404
Bank of North America, 281, 282*f*
Bank of the United States, 281–82, 282*f*
Bank panics, 201
  founding of Federal Reserve system linked to, 321
  lack of information leading to, 256
  in U.S. during Great Depression, 366–69, 385, 419–20, 420*b*
Bank supervision, 263–64
Barings Bank, principal-agent problem and demise of, 249*b*, 264
Barro, Robert, 630, 643 n.2
Barter economy, 54
  transaction costs in, 54–55
  units of account lacking in, 55–56
Basel Accord, 261, 271*b*, 309
  reforms of, 262*b*
Basel 2, 261, 262*b*
Basel Committee on Banking Supervision, 261, 262*b*
Basic gap analysis, 245–46
Baumol, William, 507
Baumol-Tobin on transactions component on demand for money, 507–511
Bear Stearns, 210, 314, 387*b*
Behavioral finance, 162–63
Bent, Bruce, 291, 291*b*
Bernanke, Ben, 209, 314, 325, 406, 602
  inflation targeting policy, 407*b*, 408
BNP Paribus, 209
Board of Governors of the Federal Reserve System, 321, 323–24

governor terms of service, 323 n.3
Bolivia, hyperinflation in, 659, 660*b*
Bond(s), 26
  consol (perpetuity), 77
  convertible, 35
  corporate, 35 (*see also* Corporate bond(s))
  coupon, 72 (*see also* Coupon bond(s))
  defined, 3–4, 4 n.1
  discount (zero-coupon), 72
  effects of Bush administration tax cuts on interest rates of, 130
  indexed, 86, 87*b*
  interest rate and prices of, 80, 82–84
  interest rate and returns on, 81*t*
  interest rate on select, 4*f*
  interest-rate risk and returns on, 82–84
  interest rates on, with different maturities, 131*f*
  international, 37
  junk, 126
  market for (*see* Bond market)
  municipal (*see* Municipal bonds)
  negative relationship of interest rates and price of, 80
  rate of capital gain on, 80–82
  ratings on, 126*t*
  returns on, versus yield to maturity on, 80–82
  returns on, volatility, and maturity, 82–84
  state and local government, 35
  U.S. government, 35, 131*f*
  yields to maturity for long-term (1919–2008), 123, 124*f*
Bond market
  adverse selection (lemons problem) in, 175–76
  changes in equilibrium interest rates caused by supply-demand shifts in, 97–108
  supply and demand in, 94–97
  supply and demand in, and money supply, 114 n.6

Bond ratings, Moody's, Standard and Poor's, and Fitch, 126*t*

Borrowed reserves (*BR*), 347, 353
 defined, 353
 Federal Reserve controls on, 361
 money supply and, 360, 362*t*
 supply curve of reserves and, 376

Borrowers-lenders in financial markets, 25–26, 26*f*

Borrowings
 by banks, 227
 from Federal Reserve (borrowed reserves), 347

Bouey, Gerald, 396

BR. See Borrowed reserves (*BR*)

Branches (bank), 296
 bank responses to restrictions on, 297–98
 physical, versus internet banks, 288*b*
 regulatory restrictions on, 267, 296–97

Brazil, financial crisis in (1999), 478–79

Bretton Woods system (fixed exchange rate regime), 470–72, 481
 operation of, 475

British-style universal banking system, 303–4

Brokers, 28

Brown, Henry, 291

Brunner, Karl, 422

Bubble, 163
 asset-price, 415–18
 asset valuation and, 161–62
 housing price, 208, 209

Budget deficit/surplus
 defined, 12
 of federal government budget, and shifts in bond supply, 101*t*, 102–3
 government credibility in times of high deficits, 659–61
 inflation and deficits, 627–30
 money creation and deficits, 629–30
 as percentage of gross domestic product (1950–2008), 12*f*

Bundesbank
 foreign exchange crisis of 1992 and actions of, 477–78
 monetary targeting policy of, 397–98

Bureaucracies, behavior of, 337

Burns, Arthur, 659
 monetary policy of, 422–23

Bush, George W., administration bailout of 2008, 211
 effects of tax cuts in, on bond interest rates, 130

Business(es). *See also* Corporations
 failures of, in subprime crisis, 210–11
 sources of external funds for, in select countries, 169, 170*f*
 U.S. dollars held by, 629*b*

Business cycle(s)
 defined, 8
 money and, 8
 money growth and, in U.S. (1950–2008), 9*f*
 real business cycle theory, 579–80

yield curve as forecasting tool for, 141*b*

Business cycle episodes, aggregate supply and demand analysis and explanations of, 579–84
 favorable supply shocks (1995–1999), 582, 582*t*
 negative demand shocks (2001–2004), 582–83, 583*t*
 negative supply shocks (1973–1975, 1978–1980), 581–82, 581*t*
 subprime crisis (2007–2008), 583–84, 584*t*
 Vietnam War buildup (1964–1970), 580–81, 581*t*

Business cycle expansion changes in interest rate due to, 104–6, 105*f*, 106*f*

shift in demand for bonds and, 98

"Buy and hold" strategy, 161

c. See Currency ratio (*c*)

C. See Currency in circulation (monetary base) (*C*)

Call reports, bank, 264

CAMELS system for rating of banks, 263, 264

Canada
 central bank of, 331
 exchange rate on Canadian dollar, 434*f*
 inflation targeting in 400–2, 401*f*
 sources of external funds for nonfinancial businesses in, 170*f*

Capital account (balance of payments), 468

Capital adequacy management, 232, 237–40

Capital controls, 307
 on inflows, 480–81
 on outflows, 480

Capital market(s), 27
 Sarbanes-Oxley Act and, 195*b*

Capital market instruments, 33–35
 consumer and bank commercial loans as, 35
 corporate bonds as, 35
 mortgages as, 33–35
 principal, 33*t*
 state and local government bonds as, 35
 stocks as, 33
 U.S. government agency securities as, 35
 U.S. government securities as, 35

Capital mobility, 461

Capital requirements, 260–61
 higher, 276

Cash flows, 69, 147
 as monetary transmission mechanism, 607

Cash items, 226*t*, 228

Cash items in process of collection, 228

Cash management account, 302

Casualty insurance companies, 45

Causation, relationship to correlation, 590, 590*b*

CDs. *See* Certificates of deposit (CDs)
Cease and desist orders, 263
Central bank(s), 281–82, 315–43
of Canada, 331
channel/corridor for conducting monetary policy, 390
of England, 331–32
European, 326–31
explaining behaviors of, 337
Federal Reserve System, 320–26, (*see also* Federal Reserve System)
independence of, and global macroeconomic performance, 341
independence of, 324–26, 337–38
inflation targeting by, 399–405
of Japan, 332
as lender of last resort, 257, 481–80
monetary policy and, 10, 12, 390–91 (*see also* Monetary policy)
monetary supply and, 345
monetary targeting by, 395–99
structure and independence of select foreign, 331–37
web references on, 342
Central bank money, 497
Certificates of deposit (CDs), 31, 227, 606
negotiable bank, 31, 233 n.1, 236
Ceteris paribus (other things being equal), 94
Chaebols, 220
Channel/corridor for conducting monetary policy, 390
Chartering of banks, 263–64
Check(s), 57–58, 226
Checkable deposits (D), 226–27
decline of, 293
money multiplier and, 362, 363, 364
Chicago Board of Trade, 29
China, 498

economic development and financial development in, 188–89
international reserves held by, 474–75
People's Bank of, 60
Citibank, 478
Citigroup, 388b
Collateral, 31, 171–72
bank management of credit risk and loan requirements for, 243–44
restrictive covenants to preserve value of, 172, 187
solving adverse selection problem with, 179–80
solving moral hazard problem using, 183–84
Collateralized debt obligations (CDOs), 208
Commercial banks, 43–44. *See also* *Banking industry*
consolidation of American, 298–302
development of U.S., 281–84, 282f
financial innovation in American, 284–95
regulation of (*see* Financial regulation)
restrictions on branching of, 267, 296–97
size distribution of insured U.S., 296t
structure of industry in U.S., 295–98, 300–1
Commercial loans, 35
Commercial paper, 31, 289
Commercial Paper Funding Facility (CPFF), 388b
Commercial paper market as financial innovation, 289, 294
Commodities Futures Trading Commission (CFTC), 47t
Commodity markets, asset market approach applied to, 97 n.3
Commodity money, 57
Common stock, 5. *See also* Stock(s)
computing price of, 147–50
stock market and prices of, 150–52

Communication between central bank and public, 402–3
Community banks, 301
Community Reinvestment Act (CRA) of 1977, 267
Compensating balances, bank management of credit risk through use of, 243–44
Competition
limits on, among financial intermediaries, 48
restrictions on, banking regulation and, 267
Competitive Equality in Banking Act (CEBA) of 1987, 270t
Complete crowding out, 554
Comptroller of the Currency, 258, 263, 264
Conflicts of interest, 189–95
case study of Arthur Anderson accounting firm, 193b
credit-rating agencies and, 191–92, 192b
defined, 190
open market operations and potential, 381 n.3
policy measures for remedying, 193–95
reasons for caring about, 190
reasons for rise of, 190–92
subprime crisis and, 192b
Congress, U.S.
influence of, on Federal Reserve System, 324–26
Consol (perpetuity) bond, 77
bond price formula for, 77 n.3
Constant-money-growth-rate rule, 639
Consumer durable expenditure, 601
Consumer expenditures, 519
aggregate demand and, 565
aggregate output and, 519, 520–22, 531–32, 532t
consumption versus, 604–5
interest rate and, 534 n.6
IS curve shift and changes in autonomous, 544, 545f, 551t
Consumer loans, 35
Consumer Price Index (CPI), 22, 566b

upward bias in measuring true inflation, 404 n.3
Consumer Protection Act of 1969, 266–67
Consumer protection, financial regulation and, 266–67
subprime crisis and, 267, 268b
Consumption, 604
consumer expenditures versus, 604–5
services and, 604 n.15
Consumption function, 520–22
Contagion effect, bank panics and, 256
Continental Illinois bank, insolvency of, 258–59
Contingent Credit Line, 484b
Contract(s)
debt, 172
futures, 285
Contractual savings institutions, 44–45
fire and casualty insurance companies as, 45
life insurance companies as, 45
pension funds and government retirement funds as, 45
value of assets, 44t
Convertible bonds, 35
Corporate bond(s), 35
as capital market instrument, 35
response to increase in default risk on, 125f, 126, 127
Corporations. See also Business(es)
access of, to funding by securities market, 171
scandals involving, 177b, 193
Correlation, relationship to causation, 590, 590b
Correspondent banking, 228
Corrigan, E. Gerald, 386b
Costly state verification, 181
Cost-push inflation, 624–26, 627
Coupon bond(s), 72
relationship of interest rates to returns on, 76t, 81t
term to maturity and yield on, 136 n.4
yield to maturity, 76–78
Coupon rate, 72

CPI. See Consumer Price Index (CPI)
Crawling target (crawling peg), 486
Credibility of government anti-inflation policy, 659–60, 662
Regan-era budget deficits and, 660–61
P. Volcker's policies and, 639
Credit cards, 286–87
Credit crisis of 2008, 68, 240
Credit default swaps, 211
Credit-driven bubbles, 415–16
Credit market instruments, 72
"Credit markets" column of Wall Street Journal, 107–8
Credit-rating agencies, 126
increased regulation of, 277
potential conflict of interest in credit assessment and consulting in, 191–92
subprime crisis and, 192b
Credit rationing, 244, 607
Credit risk, managing bank, 232, 241–45
adverse selection and moral hazard issues applied to, 241
collateral and compensating balances and, 243–44
credit rationing and, 244–45
loan commitments and, 243
long-term customer relationships and, 242–43
screening and monitoring as, 184–85, 241–42
Credit Suisse First Boston, 283
Credit unions, 44, 305–6
Credit view as monetary transmission mechanism, 602, 603f, 605–9
balance sheet channel, 606–7
bank lending channel, 605–6
cash flow channel, 607
household liquidity effects, 608–9
importance of, 609
unanticipated price level channel, 607–8
Criminals, U.S. dollars held by, 63b

Currency, 30, 53–54
anchor, 470
appreciation and depreciation of, 435, 439–40, 444–45, 449
checks as replacement of, 57–58
crisis, 215–16
declines, in financial crises, 200
devaluation, and revaluation of, 473
dollar (see Dollar, U.S.)
Eurocurrencies, 37 (see also Euro (currency))
European currency unit (ECU), 476
exchange rate for different, 433, 434f (see also Foreign exchange rate(s))
Federal Reserve's shift from deposits into, 351–52
future society without, 59b
monetary aggregates and measurement of, 60
paper, 57
reserve, 471
speculative attacks on (see Speculative attacks on currency)
Currency boards, 490
in Argentina, 491b
Currency in circulation (monetary base) (C), 346, 347 n.4, 362, 363, 364. See also Monetary base (MB)
Currency ratio (c), 363, 364
changes in, and money multiplier, 368
excessive reserves ratio and (1929–1933), 368f
Current account (balance of payments), 468, 469 n.4
U.S. deficit in, 469b
Current yield (interest rates on long-term bonds), 78
Customer relations, bank management of credit risk by developing, 242–43

D. See Checkable deposits (D)
Daiwa Bank, 249b
Data, collecting and graphing, 15–17, 16f, 17f

Data lag time and economic results, 636
Dealers, 28
Debit cards, 58, 286–87
Debt
  monetizing government, 628–29
  secured and unsecured, 171
Debt contracts, 172
  incentive-compatible, 184
  reducing principal-agent and moral hazard problem in, 182–83
  tax considerations in, 183 n.4
Debt deflation, 206
Debt instruments
  maturity of, 28
  present value (present discounted value) applied to, 69–71
  raising funds through, 27–28, 170f, 170–71
Debt markets, moral hazard problem in, 183
  tools for solving, 183–6
Default, 30, 123
Default-free bonds, 124
Default risk, 123–27
  on corporate bonds, 125, 125f
Defensive open market operations, 381
Deflation, 404
Delayed signaling, inflation targeting and, 403–4
Deleveraging, 204
Demand
  for assets (see Asset demand)
  excess, 96
  for money (see Demand for money)
  shifts in, and effects on foreign exchange rate, 443–48
  shifts in, and effects on interest rates, 97
  shifts in, for money, and income and price levels, 111, 112f
Demand conditions, financial innovation as response to, 285–86
Demand curve for reserves, 374
Demand curve in bond market, 94–95, 95f

effects of shifts in, on equilibrium interest rates, 97–100
  factors affecting shifts in, 99t
  graphing of, 95 n.2
Demand deposits, money aggregates and measurement of, 60–62
Demand for money, 499–518
  distinguishing between Friedman and Keynesian theories of, 512–15
  empirical evidence on, 515–16
  M. Friedman's modern quantity theory of, 511–12
  further developments in Keynesian approach to, 506–11
  income, and shifts in, 111, 112t, 113, 113f
  J. M. Keynes's liquidity preference theory and, 109–15, 503–6, 537
  LM curve shifts, and autonomous changes in, 547f, 547, 551t
  quantity theory of money and, 499–502
  price level, and shifts in, 111, 112, 113f
  stability of, 516
  velocity of money and, 500, 502–3, 514
  web references, 518
Demand-pull inflation, 624, 626–27
Demand shocks, 568, 569t
  changes in equilibrium caused by aggregate, 577–78
  negative (2001–2004), 582–83
Deposit(s)
  bank, at other banks, 228
  checkable, 226–27, 362–64
  creation of multiple (see Multiple deposit creation)
  demand, 60–62
  of failed commercial banks, 367f
  Federal Reserve's shift from, into currency, 351–52
  money market, 62
  nontransaction, 227
  off-shore, 307

outflow of expected, affects on excess reserves ratio, 361
  regulation of interest rates paid on, 49, 290
  savings, 62
Deposit facility, 390
Deposit insurance, 48, 255–57. See also Federal Deposit Insurance Corporation (FDIC)
  global spread of, 258b
Depositors
  monetary supply and, 345
  threat of bank failure to, 255–57
Depository institutions, 42–44
  assets and liabilities of, 43t
  commercial banks as, 43–44
  credit unions as, 44
  primary liabilities and assets of, 43t
  savings and loans associations and mutual savings banks as, 44
  value of assets, 44t
Depository Institutions Act of 1982 (Garn-St.Germain Act), 226, 270t, 272
Depository Institutions Deregulation and Monetary Control Act (DIDMCA) of 1980, 270t, 272, 323, 389
Deposit outflows, management of bank, 232, 233, 234, 235
Deposit rate ceilings, 290
Depreciation of currency, 435, 436, 439–40, 444–45, 449
Derivatives, increased regulation of, 277
Devaluation of currency, 473
Developing countries, financial system in, 179, 186–88
Direct finance, 26
Dirty float (managed float regime), 470, 475–76
Disclosure requirements, banking regulations and, 265–66
Discount bond (zero-coupon bond), 72
  term to maturity and yield on, 136 n.4
  yield to maturity, 78–79
Discounting the future, 70

Discount loans (advances), 227, 234, 384–89, 418–19
  advantages and disadvantages of Federal Reserve's policy on, 388–89
  discount window and process of making, 384, 386b
  effects of, on federal funds rate, 378–79, 378f, 380–81
  European Central Bank and, 390
  Federal Reserve as lender of last resort and, 257, 384–85, 388, 419
  Federal Reserve balance-sheet assets and, 347
  Federal Reserve policy on, and averting financial crises, 386b
  interest on (discount rate), 347
  monetary base and, 352–53
  three types of, 384
Discount rate, 234
  defined, 347
  federal funds rate and, 378f, 378–79
  as primary Federal Reserve policy tool, 418–19
  set by Federal Reserve Board of Governors, 323
Discount window, 384
  operation of, 384
  primary credit and, 384
  secondary and seasonal credit, 384
Discount yield. See Yield on a discount basis
Discretionary policy, 634
Discretionary versus nondiscretionary policy debate, 634–39
  conclusions, 638–39
  expectations, 637–38
  positions, 636–37
  responses to high unemployment, 635–36
Disintermediation, 290, 293, 295
Disposable income, 521
Dissaving, 515 n.3
Diversification, 40, 510
  of bank assets, 236
Dividend(s), 28, 147

generalized valuation model of, 149
Gordon growth model of, 149–50, 150 n.1, 151
Dollar, U.S.
  adoption of, as second currency, 490–92
  challenge of euro to, 471b
  Eurodollars, 37, 227, 306–7, 307b
  foreign exchange rate for, 13–14, 13f
  individuals and groups holding, 52b
  sale of, and purchase of foreign assets, 467f
Dollarization, 490–92
Domestic assets
  comparing expected returns on foreign and, 459–61
  demand curve for, 442–43
  shifts in demand for, 443–46, 447t
  supply curve for, 442
Domestic goods, preferences for foreign goods over, and effects on exchange rate, 440
Douglas Amendment of 1956, 297, 300
Dow Jones Industrial Average (DJIA), 5, 147
  stock prices on (1950–2008), 6f
Dual banking system, 283
Dual mandates in monetary policy, 319–20
Duisenberg, Willem F., 328
Duration analysis, interest-rate risk measured using, 82 n.4, 246
Dynamics of financial crises in emerging market economies, 212–21, 213f
  currency crisis (stage two), 215–16
  fiscal imbalances, 215
  full-fledged crisis (stage three), 216–17
  initiation (stage one), 212–15
  in Mexico, East Asia, and Argentina, 217–21

mismanagement of financial liberalization/globalization, 213–14
Dynamics of past U.S financial crises, 202–6, 203f
  banking crisis (stage two), 205–6
  debt deflation (stage three), 206
  initiation (stage one), 202–5
Dynamic open market operations, 381

e. See Excess reserves ratio (e)
East Asian countries, financial crises in (1997), 478–79
E-Cash, 58–59
Econometric models, 644–45
Economic efficiency
  banking and, 225
  financial markets and, 27
  financial structure and promotion of, 169
  in markets (see Efficient market hypothesis)
  money and, 55
Economic fluctuations, importance of monetary policy to, 591–600
  early Keynesian evidence on, 591–92
  early monetarists evidence on, 594–99
  objections to Keynesian evidence, 592–94
  overview of monetarists evidence, 599–600
Economic forecasts
  determination of aggregate output, 519–33
  ISLM model, 534–40 (see also ISLM model)
  web references, 542
Economic growth
  financial development and, in China, 188–89
  financial development and, in transition countries, 186–88
  as goal of monetary policy, 318
  inflation targeting and low, 405
Economic Stimulus Act of 2008, 498, 550, 552

Economics, two types of empirical evidence in, 587–91
Economies of scale, 39
    bank consolidation and, 298–99
    reducing transaction costs with, 173
Economies of scope, 189–90
    bank consolidation and, 299
Edge Act corporation, 308
Effectiveness lag and economic policy, 636
Efficiency. *See* Economic efficiency
Efficient market hypothesis, 155–62
    applications to the real world and, 158–62
    market crashes and, 161–62
    rationale behind, 157–58
    stronger version of, 158
E-finance, 7
    future cashless society, 59*b*
    internet banking versus physical bank branches, 288*b*
Electronic banking (e-banking), 287
    physical bank branches versus, 288*b*
Electronic money (e-money), 58–59
Electronic payments, 58
Eligible paper, 418
Emergency Economic Stabilization Act of 2008, 168, 211, 266*b*
Emerging market countries
    exchange-rate targeting and, 489–90
    financial crises in, 212–21, 213*f*, 478–79
Emerging market economies, 212
E-money (electronic money), 58–59
Employment
    goal of high, 317–18
    inflation caused by policies targeting high, 624–27, 632
    Keynesians on government policy to restore, 576–77
    monetarists on, 577
Employment Act of 1946, 624
Enron Corporation scandal, 177*b*

conflict of interest in Arthur Anderson accounting firm and, 191, 193*b*
    principal-agent problem and, 181
Entrepreneurs, 26
Equal Credit Opportunity Act of 1974, 267
Equation of exchange, 500
Equations and formulas
    after-tax real interest rate, 86 n.8
    adaptive expectation of inflation, 153 n.2
    aggregate demand function, 533 n.5
    constant growth in dividends, 149–50
    current price of stocks, 148
    demand for money, 511
    equation of exchange, 500
    exchange rate monetary transmission mechanism, 602
    expected interest rates on bonds, 134
    expected return on domestic and foreign assets, 460
    expected return on securities, 156, 157
    expenditure multiplier, 526, 527
    Fisher equation, 84, 449
    generalized dividend model, 149
    government budget constraint, 628
    infinite series, 358 n.8
    interest parity condition, 461
    liquidity preference function, 505–6
    liquidity premium theory, 137
    Macaulay's duration, 246
    monetary base, 347
    money multiplier, 362–64
    multiple deposit creation, 358
    nonborrowed monetary base, 353
    permanent income and demand for money, 513
    present value, 70
    rate of capital gain, 81
    rational expectation, 154
    return on bond, 80

return on equity and equity multiplier, 238–39
    simple deposit multiplier, 358
    Tobin's q theory and monetary transmission mechanism, 604
    velocity of money, 500, 514
    wealth effects and monetary transmission mechanism, 605
    yield to maturity for discount bond, 79
    yield to maturity on consol (perpetuity), 77–78
    yield to maturity on coupon bond, 75–76
    yield to maturity on fixed-payment loan, 74
Equilibrium
    in aggregate output, 523–25, 548–50
    in foreign exchange market, 443
    in interest rate (*see* Equilibrium interest rate(s))
    in market for money, 110*f*, 537–39
    in market for reserves, 374*f*, 376
Equilibrium in aggregate supply and demand analysis, 574–80
    long run, 575–77
    short run, 574, 574*f*
Equilibrium exchange rate, 443
    changes in interest rates and effects on, 448–49, 450*f*
    changes in money supply and effects on, 449–50, 451*f*
    exchange rate overshooting and, 450–52
Equilibrium interest rate(s), 97–103
    bond market, 95*f*
    business cycle expansion and changes in, 104–6
    changes in, from liquidity preference framework viewpoint, 111–118
    effects of inflation on, 103–4, 103*f*, 104*f*
    financial news on, 107–8
    fiscal policy changes and response of, 549–50

monetary policy changes and response of, 548–49
shift in demand for bonds and changes in, 97–100
shift in supply of bonds and changes in, 101–3
Equilibrium price, 96–97
in bond market, 95f
Equity (equities). 28. See also Stock(s)
dividends of, 28
raising funds through, 170f, 170–71
return on (ROE), 238–39
Equity capital, 179. See also Net worth (equity capital)
Equity contracts, moral hazard (principal-agent) problem in, 180–81
tools to solve, 181–83
Equity holders
amount of bank capital and returns to, 238–39
tradeoff between safety and returns to, 239
Equity market. See also Stock market(s)
adverse selection (lemons problem) in, 175–76
Equity multiplier (EM), 238
ER. See Excess reserves (ER)
Euro (currency), 37
challenge of, to U.S. dollar, 471b
foreign exchange rate on, 434f
Eurobond(s), 37
Eurodollars, 37, 227
market for, 306–7
origins of, 307b
Eurodollar market, birth of, 307b
European Central Bank (ECB), 319, 326–31
governing council of, 328–29
independence of, 330–31
monetary policy and monetary targeting by, 398b
monetary policy tools of, 390–91
European currency unit (ECU), 476

European Monetary System (EMS), 476
European Monetary Union, 326, 328, 329
European System of Central Banks (ESCB), 326, 327t
Eurosystem, 326, 327f, 329, 330
Ex ante real interest rate, 84
Excel, graphing data on, 15, 17f, 18f
Excess demand, 96
Excess reserves (ER), 228, 347
demand curve for reserves and, 374
money supply and, 361, 362t
Excess reserves ratio (e)
currency ratio and (1929–1933), 368f
money multiplier and, 362–64, 365 n.9, 368–69
Excess supply, 96
Exchange(s), defined, 29
Exchange rate, 433, 434f. See also Foreign exchange rate(s)
Exchange rate mechanism (ERM), 472, 476, 487, 488
Exchange rate overshooting, 450–51
Exchange rate peg. See Exchange-rate targeting
Exchange rate regimes, 470–80
Bretton Woods system of fixed, 470–72, 475
European Monetary System and, 476
fixed, 470, 472–74
floating regime, 470
gold standard as fixed, 470
managed float and, 475–76
Exchange-rate targeting, 486–92
advantages, 486–87
currency boards and, 490, 491b
disadvantages, 487–89
dollarization and, 490–92
in emerging market countries, 489–90
in industrial countries, 489
Exogenous event, 595
Expectations
discretionary versus nondiscretionary debate on, 637–39

adaptive, 152–53
forecast error of, 154, 155
rational, 152 (see also Rational expectations; Rational expectations revolution)
theory of (see Theory of rational expectations)
Expectations theory on term structure of interest rates, 131, 132–35
critique of, 644–45
relationship to liquidity premium (preferred habitat) theory, 139f
Expected inflation
money supply and, 115, 117f
shifts in bond supply and, 101, 102, 102f, 103f
Expected profitability of investment opportunities, shifts in bond supply and, 101, 101t, 102, 102f
Expected return, 91
asset quantity and, 93t
calculating, 92 n.1
as determinant of asset demand, 91, 92
shift in demand for bonds and, 99t, 100
Expenditure multiplier, 525–27
Expertise, reducing transaction costs by making use of financial intermediaries', 173
Ex post real interest rate, 84
Face value (par value), 72
Factors causing financial crises, 199–202
asset market effects on balance sheets, 200–1 (see also Asset markets, effects of, on balance sheets)
banking crisis, 201
deterioration in financial institutions' balance sheets, 201
government fiscal imbalances, 202
interest rate increases, 201–2
uncertainty, 201
Factors of production, income from. See Aggregate income

Fads, stock market bubbles and, 163

Fair Credit Billing Act of 1974, 267

Fair Isaac Corporation, 207

Fair-value accounting, 266

FDIC. *See* Federal Deposit Insurance Corporation (FDIC)

Federal Advisory Council, 321

Federal Deposit Insurance Corporation (FDIC), 47*t*, 48, 255–60, 273, 283
  deposit insurance provided by, 256–57
  Federal Reserve as lender of last resort versus services of, 385, 386
  methods of handling bank failures by, 256–57

Federal Deposit Insurance Corporation Improvement Act (FDICIA) of 1991, 262, 270*t*, 273

Federal Deposit Insurance Reform Act of 2005, 270*t*

Federal (fed) funds, 31, 33

Federal funds rate, 31*b*, 33, 314, 373–781
  de-emphasis of, and emphasis on nonborrowed reserves (1979–1982), 423–26
  effect of monetary-policy tools on, 376–81
  as operating instrument, 422
  subprime crisis and, 609–10
  supply/demand in market for reserves and, 373–76
  targeting, 411*f*
  targeting (early 1990s and beyond), 425
  Taylor rule on, 412–14, 415*f*

Federal Home Loan Bank System (FHLBS), 305
  bank borrowings from, 227

Federal Home Loan Mortgage Corporation (FHLMC) "Freddie Mac," 35, 210, 277, 388*b*

Federalists, banking system and, 281

Federal National Mortgage Association (FNMA) "Fannie Mae," 35, 210, 277, 388*b*

Federal Open Market Committee (FOMC), 321, 322, 324, 636
  federal funds rate target announced at meetings of, 373
  open market operations responsibility of, 324, 381

Federal Reserve Act of 1913, 270*t*, 321, 326

Federal Reserve Banks (FRBs), 321, 321–22
  directors, 321
  functions, 321–22
  map, 322*f*
  monetary policy and, 322
  of New York, 322, 463, 464*b*

Federal Reserve System (the Fed), 12, 47*t*, 283, 320–26
  balance sheet of, 345–47
  bank borrowings from, 227
  banking regulations and, 302, 303, 308
  guidelines for bank examiners from, 264
  historical perspective on procedures and policies of, 418–26
  inflation-fighting policy, credibility of, 659–60
  independence of, 324–26, 338, 339
  influence of U.S. Congress and president on, 324–26
  as lender of last resort, 257, 339, 384–88, 419, 481
  measurement of monetary aggregates, 60–63
  mission, 320
  monetary policy and role of, 322, 345 (*see also* Monetary policy; Monetary policy tools; Money supply)
  monetary policy of, with implicit nominal anchor, 405–8
  monetary policy procedures, historical review, 418–26
  monetary targeting policy, 396
  origins of, 320–21
  predicting actions of, 414*b*
  subprime crisis and, 314
  structure of, 321–24
  T-accounts of, 346–47, 464–65

theory of bureaucratic behavior and, 337
  transparency/lack of transparency, 406
  web references, 343
  web site, 16*f*

Fed watchers, 414*b*

Fee income, bank generation of, as off-balance-sheet activity, 248

Fiat money, 57

FICO score, 207

Finance, 510

Finance, electronic. *See* E-finance

Finance companies, 45

Financial consolidation, government safety net and, 259–60

Financial crises, 7, 199–224. *See also* Stock market declines and crashes; Subprime financial crisis of 2007–2008
  of 2008, 68, 199
  asymmetric information and, 199
  defined, 199
  dynamics of, in emerging market countries, 212–221. *See also* Dynamics of financial crises in emerging market countries
  dynamics of past U.S., 202–7. *See also* Dynamics of past U.S. financial crises
  factors causing, 199–202. *See also* Factors causing financial crises
  Federal Reserve discount policy and avoidance of, 386*b*
  Great Depression as, 366–69, 385, 421–22
  financial crises in Mexico, East Asia, and Argentina, 217–21
  in United States, 7, 199, 366–69
  web references, 224

Financial derivatives, 285–86

Financial engineering, 207, 284

Financial globalization, 213
  mismanagement of, 213–14

Financial innovation, 7, 264, 284–95
  avoidance of existing regulations and, 289–92

decline of traditional banking linked to, 292–95
mismanagement of, 204–5
in mortgage markets, 207–8
as response to changes in supply conditions, and information technology, 286–89
as response to demand conditions, and interest rate volatility, 285–86
in savings and loan industry, 271–72
Financial institutions, 7. See also Bank(s)
Financial Institutions Reform, Recovery, and Enforcement Act (FIRREA) of 1989, 270t, 273
Financial instruments, 3, 25 See also Security (securities)
Financial intermediaries, 6
decline in commercial banks' role as, 292–95
function of, 39–42
global importance of, and securities markets, 40b
as indirect source of funding for businesses, 170f, 171
primary assets and liabilities of, 43t
regulation and restrictions on, to ensure soundness of, 47–49
role of, in reducing transaction costs, 39–40, 173
types of, 42–46
value of assets, 44t
Financial intermediation
defined, 39
solving adverse selection problem using, 178–79
solving moral hazard in debt contracts using, 185
solving principal-agent problem using, 182
Financial liberalization, 204
mismanagement of, 204–5, 213–14
perversion of, 219b
Financial markets
asymmetric information in, 41–42

bond market, 3–5 (see also Bond market)
debt and equity markets as, 27–28
defined, 3
exchanges, and over-the-counter markets as, 29
foreign exchange market, 13–14 (see also Foreign exchange market(s))
function of, 25–27
interest rates, 4–5 (see also Interest rate(s))
international, 36–38
money and capital markets as, 29
primary and secondary markets as, 28–29
reasons for studying, 3–7
stability of, as goal of monetary policy, 318
stock market, 5, 6f (see also Stock market(s))
structure of, 27–29
this book's approach to study of, 14–16
Financial panic, 47–48
Financial regulation, 255–79
assessment of risk management, 264–65
asymmetric information and, 255–71
avoidance of existing, as financial innovation, 289–92
bank capital requirements, 260–63
on bank reserves, 228
Basel Accord and Basel 2, 262b, 309
consumer protection, 266–67
disclosure requirements, 265–66
evolution of, 283
Glass-Steagall Act (see Glass-Steagall Act of 1933 and 1935)
government safety net and deposit insurance as category of, 255–60
Gramm-Leach-Bliley Financial Services Modernization Act (1999), 259, 270t, 303
international, 271b

International Banking Act (1978), 308
international banking crises and, 273–75
McFadden Act (see McFadden Act of 1927)
major U.S. banking legislation in 20th century, 270–71t
multiple agencies responsible for, 283–84
restrictions on asset holdings, 260
restrictions on bank branching, 267, 296–98
restrictions on competition as category, 267
Riegle-Neal Interstate Banking and Branching Efficiency Act (1994), 259, 270t, 300
savings and loan and banking crisis in 1980s and, 271–73
Financial regulation (continued)
subprime crisis and, 275–78
supervision through chartering and examinations, 263–64
web references, 279
Financial repression, 187
Financial services, separation of banking from, 302–4
Financial supervision (prudential supervision), 263
Financial system, 25–52, 169–197. See also International financial system
adverse selection in, 41, 174 (see also Adverse selection)
basic facts about structure of, 169–72
conflicts of interest in, 189–195
economic growth and development of, 188–89
effects of moral hazards in, 41–42, 174, 180–89 (see also Moral hazard)
financial intermediaries in, function of, 39–42
financial intermediaries in, types of, 42–46
financial market instruments in, 30–35

Financial system (*continued*)
  financial markets in, function of, 25–27
  flow of funds through, 25, 26f
  influence of adverse selection on structure of, 174–80
  internationalization of financial markets in, 36–38
  introduction to asymmetric information in, 174 (*see also* Asymmetric information)
  regulation of, 46–49, 171 (*see also* Banking regulation; Regulation of financial system)
  structure of, 6, 27–29
  transaction costs in, 172–74
  web references on, 52, 197
Financial Times Stock Exchange (FTSE) 100-Share Index (London), 37
Financing. *See* Funds
Fire insurance companies, 45
First Bank of the United States, 321
First Boston Corporation, 283
First National Bank of Boston, 283
Fiscal imbalances, government, 202
Fiscal policy
  defined, 12, 543
  changes in interest rate and aggregate output equilibriums as response to changes in, 548–50
  effectiveness of, versus monetary policy, 552–54
  expansionary, 554 n.1
  inflation and, 621–22
  ISLM model and effects of, 543–50
Fischer, Stanley, 324
Fisher, Irving, 84, 104, 499. *See also* Fisher effect; Fisher equation
  on velocity and quantity theory of money, 500–1
Fisher effect, 103–4, 104f, 488
Fisher equation
  effects of change in interest rate on equilibrium exchange rate, 449
  real interest rate defined by, 84
Fitch, bond ratings by, 126t

Fixed exchange rate regime, 470, 472–74
Fixed investment, 522
Fixed-payment (fully amortized) loan, 72
  yield to maturity, 74–75
Fixed-rate mortgages, 285
Float, effect of, on monetary base, 353
Floating exchange rate regime, 470
  managed, 475–76
Following the Financial News, 15
  aggregate output, unemployment, and price level, 566b
  credit markets column, 108
  "Currency Trading" column, 435b, 455b
  foreign exchange rates, 435b
  LEX column, 455b
  monetary aggregates, 61b
  money market rates, 31
  yield curves, 132
FOMC. *See* Federal Open Market Committee (FOMC)
Forecast. *See* Economic forecasts
Forecast error of expectations, 154, 155
Forecasting tools, yield curves, 141b
Foreign assets
  comparing expected returns on domestic and, 459–61
  sale of dollars, and purchase of, 467f
Foreign bonds, 37
Foreigners, U.S. dollars held by, 63b
Foreign exchange crises, 477–79
  in emerging market countries in 1990s, 478–79
  German Bundesbank actions on British pound (1992), 477–78
Foreign exchange interventions, 463–68
  defined, 463
  money supply and, 463–66
  sterilized, 466, 467–68
  unsterilized, 465, 466–67
Foreign exchange market, 13–14, 433–62. *See also* Foreign exchange rate(s)

crises in (*see* Foreign exchange crises)
  defined, 433
  effects of, on money supply, 484–85
  equilibrium in, 443
  financial crises and speculation in, 218
  interventions in, 463–68
  organization of, 436–37
  stability in, as goal of monetary policy, 319
  web references, 458
Foreign exchange rate(s), 13–14, 433–62
  changes in expected future, 445–46
  effects of, on monetary policy, 485–86
  effects of, on net exports, 602
  equilibrium exchange rate, 448–52
  exchange rate regimes in international financial system, 470–74
  explaining changes in, 443–48
  Following the Financial News about, 435b, 454–56
  importance of, 436
  long run, 437–40, 441t
  methods of quoting, 440 n.2
  over-the-counter market for trading, 436–37
  shifts in aggregates supply curve and, 573 n.5
  short run, 440–43
  subprime crisis and, 454
  targeting, as alternative monetary policy strategy, 486–92
  two categories of, 434
  for U.S. dollar (1973–2008), 13–14, 13f
Foreign goods, preferences for, over domestic goods, and effects on exchange rate, 440
Foreign stocks, 37
Formulas. *See* Equations and formulas
Fortis, 212b
Forward exchange rate, 434
Forward transactions, 435

France, exchange-rate targeting and, 488

Fraud, e-finance transactions and threat of, 59b

Free-rider problem, 176, 255, 265
adverse selection problems and, 176–77, 178
moral hazard problems and, 181, 185

Frictional unemployment, 317

Friedman, Milton, 9, 422
on Great Depression bank panics, 366–67, 419, 420b
on growth rate of money supply linked to inflation, 617, 619
on importance of money to aggregate demand, 592–94
J. M. Keynes's theories compared to, 512–15
on lags in monetary policy effects, 405
monetarists and, 577 (see also Monetarists)
monetarists' evidence on importance of money, and theories of, 594–99
on money supply and interest rates, 114–15
quantity theory of money of, 511–12

Fully amortized loan, 72

Funds
assets as uses of, on bank balance sheets, 225, 226t, 228–29
commercial banks' share of total nonfinancial borrowing, 293f
external sources of, in select countries, 169, 170f
flow of, through financial system, 25, 26f
liabilities as sources of, on bank balance sheets, 225–28, 226t, 292–93
raising, in debt and equity markets, 27–28

Futures contracts, 285

FYI
Bruce Bent and 2008 market mutual fund panic, 291b

consumer protection regulation and subprime crisis, 268b
consumers' balance sheets and Great Depression, 608b
credit-rating agencies and subprime crisis, 192b
demise of Arthur Andersen, 193b
Enron Corporation implosion, 177b
helping investors to select desired interest-rate risk, 83b
indexed bonds, 87b
individuals and groups holding U.S. dollars, 63b
investment, meaning of, 523b
investment advisers, 160b
lawyers in U.S., 188b
mark-to-market accounting and subprime crisis, 266b
perils of ignoring outside driving factors, 591b
perils of reverse causation, 590b
policy ineffectiveness proposition, 648b
real business cycle and debate on money and economic activity, 600b
Sarbanes-Oxley Act and capital markets, 195b
subprime crisis and investment banks, 304b
virtual banks, 288b
yield curve as forecasting tool, 141b

Gap analysis, 245–46

GDP. See Gross domestic product (GDP)

GDP deflator, 22, 566b

General Agreement on Tariffs and Trade (GATT), 471

Generalized dividend valuation model, 149

The General Theory of Employment, Interest, and Money (Keynes), 503, 519

Germany
central bank (see Bundesbank)
exchange-rate targeting and, 487

hyperinflation in, 56, 618, 619f
monetary targeting policy in, 397–99
sources of external funds for nonfinancial businesses in, 170f

Gertler, Mark, 602

Glass-Steagall Act of 1933 and 1935, 267, 270t, 283
erosion and repeal of, 302

Global Legal Settlement of 2002, 194

Global topics
Argentina's currency board, 491b
Basel 2 Accord on banking, 262b
banking structure in U.S. and abroad, 301b
birth of Eurodollar market, 307b
Bolivian hyperinflation, 660b
capital markets, 36b
central bank independence and macroeconomic performance, 341
challenge of euro to U.S. dollar, 461b
decline in traditional banking, 295
European Central Bank, monetary policy of, 398b
financial liberalization/globalization process, 219b
foreign exchange market stability, 319
government bailouts and Treasury Asset Relief Plan, 212b
hierarchical versus dual mandates in monetary policy, 319–20
importance of financial intermediaries to international securities markets, 40b
international financial regulation, 271b
internationalization of financial markets, 36–38
monetary targeting as monetary policy, 395–99
monetary union of the six-nation Arab Gulf Cooperation Council, 334
negative T-bill rates in Japan, 79b

Global topics (*continued*)
  rogue traders and principal-agent problem, 249*b*
  separation of banking and financial services industries, 303–4
  spread of government deposit insurance, 258*b*
  structure of global financial systems, 169–72
  subprime crisis and International Monetary Fund, 481*b*
  U.S. current account deficit (balance of payments), 469*b*
Goal independence, 324
Gold market, asset market approach to understanding, 97 n.3
Gold standard, 470
Good news, effect on stock prices, 160
Goods and services, total production of. *See* Aggregate output
Goods market, equilibrium in (*IS* curve), 534–37
Gordon growth model, 149–50, 152
  monetary policy, stock prices and, 152
Governing Council, European Central Bank, 328
Government bailouts, 211. *See also* Subprime mortgage crisis of 2007–2008
  Treasury Asset Relief Plan and, 212*b*
Government bonds. *See* Municipal bonds; State and local government bonds; U.S. government bonds
Government budget
  credibility issues in era of high deficits, 660–61
  inflation and constraints on, 628–29
  shifts in bond supply and, 101, 101*t*, 102, 102*f*
Government budget constraint, 628
Government debt-to-GDP ratio, 632–33, 633*f*
Government fiscal imbalances as cause of financial crises, 202

Government National Mortgage Association (GNMA) "Ginnie Mae," 35
Government policy. *See* Monetary policy
Government retirement funds, 45
Government safety net, financial regulation and, 255–60. *See also* Federal Deposit Insurance Corporation (FDIC)
  adverse selection and, 257–58
  development and use of deposit insurance, 255–57
  financial consolidation and, 259–60
  moral hazard and, 257, 273
  "too big to fail" problem and, 258–59
Government securities
  Federal Reserve balance-sheet assets, 347
  Federal Reserve purchase/sale of, 348–51 (*see also* Open market operations)
Government spending
  aggregate demand and, 565
  aggregate output and, 520, 528–30, 532*t*, 533
  change in *IS* and *LM* curves and, 544, 545*f*, 551*t*, 558*f*
  fiscal policy on control of taxes and, 543 (*see also* Fiscal policy)
  inflation and one-shot permanent increase in, 622*f*
Government-sponsored enterprises (GSEs), 388*b*
Government Sponsored Entities Purchase Program, 388*b*
Gramm-Leach-Bliley Financial Services Modernization Act of 1999, 259, 270*t*, 303
Great Britain. *See* United Kingdom
Great Depression, 283
  application on, 206–7
  asymmetric information problems in, 207 n.1
  bank failures during, 283
  collapse of investment spending in, 527–28

consumers' balance sheets and, 608, 608*b*
debt deflation and, 206
Federal Reserve operating tools in, 419–21
importance of money policy in, 592, 593, 593*f*, 594
money supply model applied to bank panics in (1930–1933), 366–69, 385
unemployment during, 318
velocity of money in, 503
Greenspan, Alan, 199, 314, 323 n.3, 325, 386*b*, 396, 413, 416
  monetary policy of, 396, 405, 406, 426
Gross domestic product (GDP)
  defined, 12, 21
  inflation and growth rate of, 23
  link between monetary policy and, 603*f*
  as measure of aggregate output, 21
  ratio of government debt to, 632–33, 633*f*
  real, versus nominal, 21–22
Growth rates, GDP, inflation rate and, 23

Hamanaka, Yasuo, 249*t*
Hamilton, Alexander, 281
Hedge, 285
Hicks, John, 519
Hierarchical mandates in monetary policy, 319–20
High-powered money, 347, 362. *See also* Monetary base (*MB*)
Historical evidence on importance of money to economic activity, 598–99
Home banking, 287
Hong Kong, 479
Hot tips on stock market investments, 159
Household liquidity effects as monetary transmission mechanism, 608–9
Housing price bubble, 208, 209
Humphrey-Hawkins Act of 1978, 624
Hungary, 484*b*

Hyperinflation, 56, 316, 629
  in Bolivia, 659, 660b
  in Germany (1921–1923), 56,
    618, 619f
  in Zimbabwe, 618–19
Hypo Real Estate Holdings, 212b
Hysteresis, 579

Iceland, 484b
Iguchi, Toshihide, 249b
IMF. See International Monetary
    Fund (IMF)
Implementation lag and economic
    policy, 636
Incentive-compatible debt con-
    tract, 184
Income
  aggregate output, 21
  bank generation of fee, 248
  defined, 54
  disposable, 521
  permanent, 511, 512
  shifts in demand for money and
    effects of, 111, 112, 113f
Income tax
  municipal bonds, risk structure
    of interest rates and, 128–29
  real interest rate after paying fed-
    eral, 86 n.8
Indexed bonds, 86, 87b
India, 498
Industrialized countries, exchange-
    rate targeting and, 489
Industrial production, 566b
Inflation, 617–42
  adaptive expectations and, 153
    n.2
  average rate of, versus average
    rate of money growth for
    select countries, 11f
  budget deficits and, 627–30,
    632–33
  causes of monetary policy lead-
    ing to, 624–34
  changes in interest rate due to,
    102, 103–4
  comparing three models on poli-
    cies to reduce, 656–59
  cost-push, 624–26, 627
  defined, 8

demand-pull, 626–27
discretionary versus nondiscre-
    tionary policy debate, 634–39
exchange-rate targeting to solve
    problem of, 486–87
expected, and money supply,
    115–16, 117f
expected, and rise in domestic
    interest rate, 450f
expected, and shifts in bond
    supply, 101, 101f, 102, 103–4
during favorable supply shocks
    (1995–1999), 582, 582t
fiscal policy and production of,
    621–22
GDP growth rate and, 23
high employment targets and,
    624–27
hyperinflation, 56, 316
meaning of, 619–20
money and, 8–9, 617–19
money growth and production
    of, 620–21, 632f
during negative demand shocks
    (2001–2004), 582–83, 583t
during negative supply shocks
    (1973–1975, 1978–1980),
    581–82, 581t
price stability as low and stable,
    315–16, 319–20
real versus nominal interest rates
    and effects of, 84–87
subprime crisis and, 583–84, 584t
supply-side phenomena and pro-
    duction of, 623
targeting (see Inflation targeting)
during Vietnam War Buildup
    (1964–1970), 580–81, 581t
web references, 641
yield curves as forecasting tool
    for, 141b
Inflation gap, 412–13
Inflation rate
  defined, 9
  in New Zealand, Canada, and
    United Kingdom (1980–2008),
    401f
  mandate-consistent objective of,
    407b
  in U.S., 406

Inflation targeting, 399–405
  advantages of, 402–3, 408t
  in Canada, 400–2, 401f
  disadvantages of, 403–5, 408t
  elements of, 399–400
  in New Zealand, 400, 401f
  in United Kingdom, 401f, 402
  in U.S. Federal Reserve, 407b
Information
  asymmetric, and lack of (see
    Asymmetric information)
  bank management of credit risk
    through production of,
    241–42
  increasing through government
    regulation, to reduce adverse
    selection problem, 46–47,
    176–78, 182
Information (continued)
  monitoring and increasing, to
    solve principal-agent problem,
    181–82
  private production and sale of,
    to reduce adverse selection
    problem, 176
  problems in subprime mortgage
    market, 209
  restrictive covenants to provide,
    185
  role of, in asset (stock) valuation,
    151
Information technology
  financial innovations in response
    to supply conditions based on,
    286–89
ING, 212b
Initial public offerings (IPOs),
    191
Innovation. See Financial innovation
Insider trading, 46
Inside the Fed
  bank panics and the Fed, 420b
  Bernanke vs. Greenspan, 325
  discount policy to prevent finan-
    cial crisis, 386b
  Fed watchers, 414b
  inflation targeting and Ben
    Bernanke, 407b
  lender of last resort during sub-
    prime crisis, 387–88

Inside the Fed (continued)
operation of Foreign Exchange
Desk of Federal Reserve Bank
of New York, 464b
paying interest on reserves,
375–76b
transparency, 407b
Instrument(s), financial market
capital market, 29
credit market, 72
debt, 27–28
money market, 29
Instrument independence, 324
Interest paid on deposits, 49
Interest parity condition, 459–62
Interest rate(s), 69–89. See also
Interest rates, behavior of
bond prices and, 80
bond returns and, 81t
Bush administration tax cuts,
effects on bond, 130
credit market instruments and, 72
defined, 4
demand for money, and
effects/lack of effects of, 499,
503–6, 509, 513, 515
distinction between returns and,
80–84
domestic, and shift in demand
for domestic assets, 444
effects of business cycle expansion on, 104–6, 105f, 106f
effects of higher expected, 98
effects of shifts in supply/demand
in bond market on, 94–103
equilibrium (see Equilibrium
interest rate(s))
equilibrium aggregate output
and (IS curve), 534–35, 536f
equilibrium exchange rates
affected by changes in,
448–49, 450f
Federal Reserve tools to manipulate (see Monetary-policy tools)
financial crises and increases in,
201–2
financial innovation in response
to volatility in, 285–86
foreign, and shifts in demand for
domestic assets, 444–45

government budget deficits and,
631f
graphing data of, 16f, 17f
inflation and changes in, 102,
103f, 104f
ISLM model approach to aggregate output and, 539–40
mean-reverting, 135 n.3
monetary policy and control of,
543 (see also Monetary policy)
money supply and, 113–14
negative, 79b
on overnight loans of reserves
between banks (see Federal
funds rate)
pegging of (1942–1951), 421
as policy instrument, 409
present value concept and,
69–71
real, versus nominal, 84–87
regulation of, paid on deposits,
49
relationship of higher growth
rate of money supply to,
113–18
return (rate of return) distinguished from, 80–84
risk, 82 (see also Interest-rate risk)
risk structure of, 123–30
on select bonds, 4f
simple, 70
spikes in, 205
stability of, as goal of monetary
policy, 318–19
standardized (annual percentage
rate), 267
targeting, 409–10, 412–13
term structure of, 123, 130–42,
644–45
on U.S. Treasury bonds, and rate
of money growth
(1950–2008), 10, 11f
web references on, 89
yield on a discount, and measurement of, 78–80
yield to maturity, and measurement of, 72–80
Interest-rate channels as monetary
transmission mechanism,
601–2

Interest-rate risk, 82, 232
bank management of, 245–47
bond returns and, 82–84
financial innovation in response
to, 285–86
helping investors to select
desired, 83b
management of bank, 232
nonexistent, 82 n.5
reinvestment risk and, 83 n.6
Interest rates, behavior of, 91–121
asset demand, determinants of,
91–93, 93t
equilibrium interest rates,
changes in, 97–108
liquidity reference framework,
and changes in equilibrium
interest rates, 111–18
liquidity reference framework,
and supply and demand in
market for money, 109–11
nominal interests rates and, 91
supply and demand in bond
markets, 94–97
web references, 121
Intermediate target, 409
Intermediate-term maturity of debt
instruments, 28
Internal rate of return, 73 n.1.
See also Yield to maturity
International Banking Act of 1978,
308
International banking facilities
(IBFs), 308
International bond market, 37
International financial data, average
inflation rate versus average
rate of money growth in select
countries (1995–2007), 11f
International financial regulation,
49, 271b
International financial system,
463–95
balance of payments and,
468–69
capital controls in, 480–81
exchange rate regimes in,
469–79
exchange rate targeting in,
486–92

foreign exchange interventions in, 463–68
monetary policy and, 484–86
role of International Monetary Fund in, 481–84
web references, 495
International Monetary Fund (IMF), 221, 432, 481–84
Bretton Woods system and, 470–72, 475
establishment of, 470, 481
as lender of last resort, 481–82
recommendations for, 482–83
subprime crisis and, 484b
International policy coordination, 426
International reserves, 463
China's nearly one trillion dollars in, 474–75
International stock markets, 37
International topics. See Global topics
International trade, net exports, and aggregate output, 520, 530–31, 532t, 533
Internet, banking services on, 287, 288b
Inventory investment, 522–23
Inverted yield curve, 130
Investing, practical guide to stock-market, 158–61
Investment(s)
aggregate output and planned, 519, 522–23
defined, 523b, 565 n.1
efficient markets and, 160–61
expected return on, and shifts in bond supply, 100, 101t, 102, 102f
fixed, 522
hot tips on, 159
inventory, 522–23
planned spending on (see Investment spending, planned)
present value of all cash flows and value of, 148
Investment advisors
performance of, 160b
value of published reports by, 158–59

Investment Advisers Act of 1940, 270t
Investment bank(s), 28, 46
conflicts of interest in research and underwriting by, 190–91
Global Legal Settlement of 2002, 194
subprime crisis, 304b
Investment Company Act of 1940, 270t
Investment-grade securities, 126
Investment intermediaries, 45–46
finance companies as, 45
investment banks as, 46
liabilities and assets of, 43t
money market mutual funds as, 46
mutual funds as, 46
value of assets, 44t
Investment spending
aggregate demand and planned, 565
aggregate output and planned, 519, 522–23, 524–25, 525–27, 527–28, 532, 532t
collapse of, in Great Depression, 527–28
IS curve and, 534–35, 536f, 544, 545f, 551t
link between stock prices and, 604 n.14
Investors. See also Investment(s)
efficient market prescription for, 160–61
practical guide for stock-market, 158–61
selection of desired interest-rate risk by, 83b
IS curve, 534–37
deriving, 535–37
factors causing shifts in, 543–46, 551t
information gained from, 537
interest rates, net exports, and, 535
interest rates, planning investment spending, and, 534–35
money supply targeting preferred for unstable, 556, 556f

shifts in aggregate demand curve caused by shifts in, 561-62, 561f
ISLM model, 519–42, 543–64
aggregate demand curve and, 559–62
aggregate output, interest rates, and, 539–40
algebraic treatment of, 554 n.2
ISLM model (continued)
changes in equilibrium levels on interest rates and aggregate output in, 548–50
defined, 534
equilibrium in goods market and IS curve of, 534–37
equilibrium in market for money and LM curve of, 534, 537–39
factors causing IS curve to shift in, 543–46, 551t
factors causing LM curve to shift in, 546–48, 551t
fiscal policy and changes in, 549–50
in long run, and concept of natural rate level of output, 557–59
monetary policy and changes in, 548–49, 552–54
web references, 542, 564
Italy, exchange-rate targeting and, 489

Jackson, Andrew, 321
Japan
applying monetary policy lessons to, 612
banking and financial crisis in, 274
bubble economy in 1980s, 396–97
central bank of, 332
deflation in, 404
disintermediation process in, 295
exchange rate on Japanese yet, 434f
explaining low interest rates in, 106–7

Japan (continued)
   monetary targeting policy in,
      396–97
   negative T-bill rates in, 79b
   stock market in, 37
   sources of external funds for non-
      financial businesses in, 170f
J. P. Morgan, 210, 211, 283, 302,
      314, 387b
Junk bonds, 126
   information technology and,
      287–89, 294
"Just do it" approach in monetary
      policy, 406–8

Kane, Edward, 290
Kerviel, Jerome, 249b
Keynes, John Maynard
   determination of aggregate out-
      put and theories of, 519–33
   followers of (see Keynesians)
   M. Friedman's theory compared
      to theories of, 512–15
   further developments in
      approach of, 507–11
   ISLM model and work of, 519
      (see also ISLM model)
   liquidity preference framework
      concept by, 109
   liquidity preference theory of,
      503–6, 537–38
   new Keynesian model and theo-
      ries of, 650–53
Keynesian multiplier, 358 n.7
Keynesian cross diagram, 523–25
Keynesians, 576, 591
   evidence of, on importance of
      money to economic fluctua-
      tions, 591–92
   failures of, in 1960s and 1970s,
      643
   on government economic policy,
      575–76
   new Keynesian model from, and
      critique of new classical
      model, 650–53
   objections to evidence of, 592–94
   rational expectations analysis of
      (see Rational expectations
      revolution)

King, Mervyn, 320
Kydland, Finn, 316 n.2

Labor market, aggregate supply
      curve affected by tightness of,
      572
Large, complex banking organiza-
      tions (LCBOs), 299
Latin American. See also names of
      specific countries, e.g.,
      Argentina; Mexico
   rapid inflation episodes in, 629
Law of one price, 437
Leeson, Nick, 249b
Legislation, major U.S. financial,
      270–71t
Legislative lag and economic pol-
      icy, 636
Lehman Brothers, 211, 291b, 388b
"Lemons problem," adverse selec-
      tion problem and, 174–80
   in stock and bond markets,
      175–76
   tools to help solve, 176–80
Lender of last resort
   Federal Reserve as, 257, 384–88,
      419, 481
   International Monetary Fund as,
      481–82
Lender-savers in financial markets,
      25, 26f
Lending, specialization in, 242
Leverage ratio, bank capital
      requirements of, 260
Liabilities, 26
   on bank balance sheets, 225,
      226t
   decline in cost advantage in
      acquiring, 292–93
   on Federal Reserve balance
      sheets, 346–47
Liability management in banks,
      232, 236–37
Life insurance companies, 45
Liquid
   defined, 29
   financial instruments as, 29
   money as, 56
Liquidity
   defined, 56

as determinant of asset demand,
      92, 93, 93t, 115
   risk structure of interest rates
      and factor of, 127–28
   shifts in demand for bonds and,
      99t, 100
Liquidity effect, 115, 116, 117f
Liquidity management, role of
      reserves in bank, 232–35
Liquidity preference, 537
Liquidity preference framework,
      109–18
   changes in income and, 111,
      113, 113f
   changes in money supply and,
      113–14, 114f
   changes in price levels and, 113,
      113f
   shifts in demand for money and,
      111
   shifts in supply of money and,
      111, 112t
   supply and demand in market
      for money, 109–11
Liquidity preference function,
      505–6
Liquidity preference theory, 503–6,
      537–38
   on demand for money in real
      terms, 558
   precautionary motive, 504
   speculative motive, 504–5
   transactions motive, 504
Liquidity premium theory of term
      structure of interest rates, 132,
      136–40
   relationship to expectations the-
      ory, 138f
   yield curves and market's expec-
      tations of future short-term
      interest rates according to, 139f
Liquidity services, 40
   reducing transaction costs with,
      173
Liquidity trap, 515
LM curve, 534, 537–39
   deriving, 538–39
   factors affecting shift in, 546–48,
      551t
   information gained from, 539

interest rate target preferred for unstable, 556f, 557
shifts in aggregate demand curve caused by shifts in, 562f, 562
Loan(s)
bank management of credit risks associated with issuing, 241–45
borrowings made by banks from other banks, 227
commercial real estate, 294
discount, 227
issued by banks, 35, 229, 234–35
fixed-payment (fully amortized), 72, 74–75
as monetary transmission mechanism, 605–6
simple, 70–71, 72, 73–74
specialization in lending, 242
Loan commitments, 243
Loan sales as off-balance-sheet activity, 247–48
Loan-to-value ratio (LTV), 209
Longer-term refinancing operations, 390
Long-run aggregate supply curve, 568, 570, 570t
equilibrium in, 575–77
shifts in, 579–80
Long-run exchange rates, 437–40
factors affecting, 439–40, 441t
law of one price and, 437
theory of purchasing power parity (PPP) and, 437–39
Long-run monetary neutrality, 559
Long-term bonds
interest rates on, 135
yield to maturity for (1919–2008), 123, 124f
Long Term Capital Management, 426
Long-term maturity of debt instruments, 28
Loophole mining, 290, 299
Loss aversion, 162
Lucas, Robert, 643
critique of models used to evaluate economic policies, 644–45

new classical macroeconomic model developed by T. Sargent and, 645–50

m. See Money multiplier (m)
M1 monetary aggregate, 60–63
See also Money supply
components of, 61t,62t
data reliability of, 63–64
growth rates (1999–2008), 64f
monetary base and, in Great Depression, 369f
money supply process, money multiplier, and, 362–66
money supply response to select variables, 362t
velocity of, 502f
M2 monetary aggregate, 60–64
components of, 61t,62t
data reliability of, 63–64
growth rates (1999–2008), 64f
interest rates and (1950–2008), 118f
velocity of, 502f
Maastricht Treaty, 319, 326, 330
Macaulay's concept of duration, 246
MB. See Monetary base (MB)
MBn. See Nonborrowed monetary base (MBn)
McCain, John, 273 n.2
McCallum, Bennett, 639, 643 n.2
McFadden Act of 1927, 270t, 297, 300
McKinney, Stewart, 259
Macroprudential regulation, 417
Magnitudes, real versus nominal, 21–22
Main refinancing operations, 390
Malaysia, 479
Managed float regime (dirty float), 70 475–76
Mandate-consistent inflation objective, 407b
Marginal lending facility, 390
Marginal lending rate, 390
Marginal propensity to consume (mpc), 521
Market clearing price. See Equilibrium price

Market equilibrium, 91, 96–97
in bond market, 95f
Market for money
equilibrium, and LM curve, 534, 537–38
money market compared to, 109 n.4
supply and demand in, 109–11
Market fundamentals, 158
Market Risk Amendment to Basel Accord (1996), 261
Mark-to-market accounting and subprime crisis, 266, 266b
Marshall, Alfred, 499, 502 n.3
Martin, William McChesney, Jr., 323 n.3
monetary policy of, 421–22
Matched sale-purchase transaction (reverse repo), 383
Maturity buckets, 246
Maturity of debt instruments, 28
term to, and interest rates, 130–42
Mean-reverting interest rates, 135 n.3
Medium of exchange, 54
money as, 54–55
Meiselman, David, 597
Meltzer, Allan, 422, 482, 639
Merger partners for insolvent banks, 258–59
Merrill Lynch, 211
Mexico, 498
financial crisis in (1994), 478–79
Microsoft Excel, graphing data on, 15, 17f, 18f
Modigliani, Franco, on life cycle hypothesis of consumption and wealth effects as monetary transmission mechanism, 604–605
Mondex, 59b
Monetarists, 577, 591
evidence of, on importance of money to economic fluctuations, 594–99
on government economic policy, 577
overview of monetarist evidence, 599–600

Monetary Affairs Division, Federal Reserve Board of Governors, 382

Monetary aggregates. *See also* M1 monetary aggregate; M2 monetary aggregate
de-emphasis of (1982–early 1990s), 424–25
targeting (1970s), 422–23
targeting annual growth rate of, 395–99

Monetary aggregates, measurement of, 60–64, 337 n.6. *See also* M1 monetary aggregate; M2 monetary aggregate
data reliability of, 63–64
financial news data on, 61*b*
growth rates of, 64

Monetary base (*MB*), 346–54, 362
defined, 346
discount loans and, 352–53
effect of unsterilized foreign exchange intervention on, 466 n.1
equation expressing, 347
money multiplier, money supply, and, 362–66
money supply (M1) and, during Great Depression bank crises, 369*f*
nonborrowed, 360
open market operations and control of, 348–51
other factors affecting, 353
overview of Federal Reserve's ability to control, 353–54
shifts from deposits into currency and control of, 351–52

Monetary History of the United States (1867–1960) (Friedman, Schwartz), 366–67, 592, 598–99

Monetary liabilities, Federal Reserve, 346–47

Monetary neutrality, 450–51

Monetary policy, 10–12, 315–20, 395–429
advantages/disadvantages of select strategies, 408*t*

changes in interest rate and aggregate output equilibriums as response to changes in, 548–50
channel/corridor for conducting, 390
choosing policy instruction (operating instrument), 408–12
effectiveness of, versus fiscal policy, 552–54
exchange-rate targeting as alternative strategy of, 486–92
Federal Reserve and, 322, 345, 373 (*see also* Monetary policy tools)
five additional goals of, 317–19
hierarchical versus dual mandates in, 319–20
historical perspective on procedures and tools of, 418–27
inflationary, origins of, 624–34
inflation targeting as, 399–405
international considerations for, 484–86
ISLM model and effects of, 543–52
link between GDP and, 603*f*
R. Lucas critique of models used to evaluate, 644–45
monetary targeting as, 395–99
money supply and (*see* Money supply)
nominal anchor in, 316, 317, 405–8
price stability as goal of, 315–17, 319–20
rational expectations and (*see* Rational expectations revolution; Theory of rational expectations)
role of central banks in setting, 315
Taylor rule in, 412–15
time-consistency problem and, 316–17
transmission mechanisms (*see* Monetary policy, transmission mechanisms of)
subprime crisis, asset-price bubbles, and, 415–18
web references, 429

Monetary policy, transmission mechanisms of, 600–9
credit view, 605–9
framework for evaluating empirical evidence and, 587–600
lessons for monetary policy, 610–12
other asset price channels, 602–5
traditional interest-rate channels, 601–2
web references, 615

Monetary policy tools, 373–93
de-emphasizing federal funds rate, and emphasis on nonborrowed reserves (1979–1982), 423–24
de-emphasizing monetary aggregates (1982–early 1990s), 424–25
discount loans policy, 384–89, 418–19 (*see also* Discount loans (advances); Discount rate)
effects of, on federal funds rate, 376–80
of European Central Bank, 390–91
federal funds rate and market for reserves, 373–81
in Great Depression, 419–20
international considerations affecting, 426–27
open markets operations as, 377–78, 381–83, 419 (*see also* Open market operations)
pegging interest rates and war financing (1942–1951), 421
preemptive strikes against economic downturns, 425–26
preemptive strikes against inflation, 425
reserve requirements, 389, 420–21 (*see also* Reserve requirements)
targeting federal funds (early 1990s and beyond), 425
targeting monetary aggregates (1970s), 422–23
targeting money market conditions (1950s, 1960s), 421–22
web references, 393

Monetary Policy Report to Congress, 326

Monetary targeting, 395–99
  advantages and disadvantages of, 399, 408*t*
  in U.S., Japan, and Germany, 395–99

Monetary theory, 8, 499
  determination of aggregate output, 519–25
  developments of Keynesian approach to, 506–11
  distinguishing between Friedman and Keynesian, 512–15
  M. Friedman's modern quantity theory of, 511–12
  ISLM model, 534–40
  J. M. Keynes's liquidity preference theory, 503–6
  quantity theory of, 499–502
  velocity of money. *See* Velocity of money

Monetizing the debt, 628

Money, 8–12, 53–66. *See also* Money supply
  budget deficits and creation of, 629–30
  business cycles and, 8
  checks as, 57–58
  commodity, 57
  demand for (*see* Demand for money)
  electronic payment and e-money as, 58–59
  fiat, 57
  functions of, 54–56
  inflation and, 8–9
  interests rates and, 10
  market (*see* Market for money; Money market)
  meaning of, 53–54
  measurement of, 60–63, 337 n.6
  monetary policy and, 8–12
  payments system and forms of, 57–59
  printing, 628–29, 630
  in prisoner-of-war camp, WWII, 55 n.1
  reliability of data on, 63–64

shifts in demand for 111, 112*t*
shifts in supply of, 111–12, 112*t*
this book's approach to study of, 14–15
web references on, 66

Money, importance of, to economic fluctuations, 591–600
  early Keynesian evidence on, 591–92
  early monetarist evidence on, 594–99
  objections to early Keynesian evidence on, 592–94
  overview of monetarist evidence, 599–600

Money center banks, 236

Money demand. *See* Demand for money

Money growth (M2 annual rate)
  average rate of, versus average inflation rate for select countries (1997–2007), 11*f*
  business cycles in U.S. and, (1950–2008), 9*f*
  hypothetical example of output and, 596*f*
  inflation and, 617–19, 620–21, 632*f*
  interest on U.S. Treasury bills and, 10, 11*f*, 118*f*
  rule of constant rate of, 639

Money market, 29–33
  market for money compared to, 109 n.4
  rates on, 33
  targeting conditions of, as operating tool, 421–22

Money market deposit accounts (MMDAs), 226
  money aggregates and measurement of, 62
  reducing transaction costs using, 173

Money market instrument(s), 30–33
  commercial paper as, 31
  federal (fed) funds, 31–33

negotiable bank certificates of deposit as, 31
repurchase agreements as, 31
U.S. Treasury Bills as, 30

Money Market Investor Funding Facility (MMIFF), 387*b*

Money market mutual funds, 46, 302
  as financial innovation, 289, 290–91
  money aggregates and measurement of, 62
  panic of 2008, 291*b*

Money multiplier (*m*), 362–66
  deriving, 362–64
  intuition behind, 364–65
  relationship to excess reserves ratio e, 365 n.9

Money supply, 8, 53, 345–72, 499. *See also* Money
  aggregate price levels and, 10*f*
  changes in, and effects on equilibrium exchange rate, 449–50, 451*f*
  changes in, and effects on interest rates, 113–15, 114*f*
  changes in, and effects on *LM* and *IS* curves curve, 546*f*, 546–47, 551*t*, 558*f*
  control of monetary base and, 347–54
  determining factors of, 360–61
  effects of foreign exchange market on, 484–85
  expected-inflation effect and, 115, 117*f*
  Federal Reserve manipulation of (*see* Monetary policy tools)
  Federal Reserve's balance sheet and, 345–47
  foreign exchange interventions and, 463–66
  higher rate of growth in, and relationship to interest rates, 115–18
  income effect and, 115
  inflation linked to growth rate of, 617–19, 620–21, 630–34

Money supply (*continued*)
  monetary base and, during Great
    Depression bank crises,
    366–69, 369*f*
  money multiplier ratio and
    model for determinants of,
    362–69
  multiple deposit creation, simple
    model of, 354–60
  overview of process of, 361–62
  price level effect and, 115
  relationship of growth rate in, to
    interest rates, 115–18
  three players in process of, 345
  web references on, 372
Monitoring and enforcement of
  restrictive covenants, bank
  management of credit risk
  through, 184–85, 236
Moody's Investors Service
  bond ratings by, 126*t*
Moral hazard, 41–42, 174,
  180–86, 186*t*
  bank management of credit risks
    and problem of, 241
  conflicts of interest as, 189–195
  in debt contracts, 183
  in equity contracts (principal-
    agent problem), 180–81
  government safety net (deposit
    insurance) and, 255–57, 258,
    259
  for lenders of last resort, 482
  summary on, 185–86
  tools to solve, in debt contracts,
    183–86
  tools to solve, in equity con-
    tracts, 181–83
Morgan Stanley, 283
Mortgages
  adjustable-rate, 285
  as capital market instrument,
    33–35
  innovations in market for, 207–8
  subprime, 207 (*see also* Subprime
    mortgage crisis of 2007–2008)
Mortgage-backed securities, 207
mpc (marginal propensity to
  consume), 521
Mugabe, Robert, 618–19

Multiple deposit creation, 354–60
  banking system and, 355–58
  critique of model for, 359–60
  formula for, 358–59
  by single banks, 354–55
Municipal bonds, 35
  interest rates on, 125*f*
  risk structure of interest rates,
    income tax considerations,
    and, 128–29
Muth, John, 153
Mutual funds, 45
  investing in, 161
  reducing transaction costs with,
    173
Mutual savings banks, 44, 305
MyEconlab, 20, 52, 66, 89, 121,
  145, 165, 197, 224, 253, 279,
  312, 343, 372, 393, 429, 458,
  495, 518, 542, 564, 586, 615,
  642, 664
NAIRU (nonaccelerating inflation
  rate of unemployment), 413
NASDAQ (National Association of
  Securities Dealers Automated
  Quotation System), 28, 147
National bank(s), 283
National Bank Act of 1863, 282
National Bureau of Economic
  Research, 636
National Central Banks (NCBs),
  326, 328, 329, 331
National Credit Union Administra-
  tion (NCUA), 47*t*, 305
National Credit Union Share Insur-
  ance Fund (NCUSIF), 48, 306
NationsBank, 300
Natural rate level of output, 557,
  570
Natural rate of unemployment,
  318, 568
  unemployment and
    (1960–2008), 634*f*
Negotiable bank certificates of
  deposit, 31, 233 n.1, 236
Net exports, 520
  aggregate demand and, 565
  aggregate output and, 520,
    530–31, 532*t*, 533
  calculating, 520 n.2

effects of exchange rates on, 602
  IS curve and, 535, 536*f*, 544,
    545*f*, 546, 551*t*
Net worth (equity capital), 179
  adverse selection problem and,
    179–80
  reducing moral hazard in debt
    contracts using, 183–84
New classical macroeconomic
  model, 645–50
  comparison of, with traditional
    (nonrational expectations)
    model, 653–60
  on effects of unanticipated and
    anticipated policy, 646–48
  on expansionary policy leading
    to decline in aggregate output,
    648–49
  implications of, for policymakers,
    649–50
  new Keynesian model as critique
    of, 650–53
New Keynesian model, 650–53
  comparison of, with traditional
    (nonrational expectations)
    model, 653–60
  effects of unanticipated and
    anticipated policy, 651, 652*f*
  implications of, for policymakers,
    653
New York Stock Exchange, 28,
  29
New Zealand, inflation targeting
  in, 400, 401*f*
Nigeria, 498
Nikkei 300 Average (Tokyo), 37
NINJA loan, 268*b*
No-doc loan, 268*b*
Nominal anchor, 316
  monetary policy with implicit, in
    U.S., 405–08
  price stability and, 315–17
  role of, 316
Nominal GDP, 21–22
Nominal income, movements in
  money supply and, 502–3
Nominal interest rates, 69
  behavior of (*see* Interest rates,
    behavior of)
  defined, 84

monetary policy and, 593 n.2, 594, 610
monetary transmission mechanisms and, 610
policy instrument and, 411–12
real interest rate versus, 84–86
for three-month Treasury bill (1953–2008), 86f
Nonaccelerating inflation rate of unemployment (NAIRU), 413, 568 n.3
Nonbank public, open market purchase from, 348–50
Nonborrowed monetary base (MBn), 353, 360
Nonborrowed reserves, targeting on, 409, 410b, 423–24
Nondiscretionary policy. See Discretionary versus nondiscretionary policy debate
Nontransaction deposits, 227
certificates of deposit (CDs), 31, 227, 606
Northern Rock, 209
NOW accounts (interest-bearing negotiable order of withdrawal), 226

Off-balance-sheet activities, 247–50, 261
bank search for profits and increased, 295
defined, 247
generation of fee income as, 248
loan sales as, 247–48
regulations on bank assets and, 261
trading activities and risk management techniques as, 248–50
Office of the Comptroller of the Currency, 47t, 48, 264, 283, 323
Office of Thrift Supervision (OTS), 47t, 305
Official reserve transactions balance, 469
Off-shore deposits, 307
One-period valuation model, 148
Open market operations, 322, 324, 348–51, 381–83

advantages of, 383
defensive, 381
defined, 322, 347
dynamic, 381
effects of, on federal funds rate, 377–78
of European Central Bank, 390
Federal Reserve use of, in 1920s, 419
management of trading desk, 381–83
open market sales, 350
purchase from bank, 348
purchase from nonbank public, 348–50
Open market purchase, 348
Open market sale, 348, 350
Operating instrument, 409. See also Policy instrument
Opportunity cost, 110
of holding money, 509
Optimal forecast, 153, 154
Orange County, California, municipal bond default, 128
Organization for Economic Cooperation and Development (OECD), 261
Originate-to-distribute model, 208
Output gap, 412
Overconfidence, stock market bubbles and, 163
Overnight cash rate, 390
Overregulation, danger of, 278
Over-the-counter (OTC) market defined, 29
foreign exchange market organized as, 436–37

Paper currency, 57
Parmalat Corporation, 177
Par value (face value) of bond, 72
Payments system, 57
evolution of, 57–59
Payoff method, bank failure and FDIC's, 256
PCE deflator, defined, 22
Pension funds, 45
"Perfect storm" of adverse shocks, (2007–2008), 498

Perfect substitutes, bonds with different maturities as, 132–33
Permanent income, 511, 512
Perpetuity(ies) (consol), 77–78
Personal consumption expenditures (PCE), 22
Phillips curve theory, 413
Pigou, A. C., 499, 502 n.3
Planned investment spending aggregate demand and, 565
aggregate output and, 519, 522–27, 527–28, 532t, 532
Plaza Agreement (1987), 486
Policy, monetary. See Monetary policy
Policy ineffectiveness proposition, 648, 648b
Policy instrument, 409–10
criteria for choosing, 410–12
Policy Targets Agreement, 400
Political business cycle, 338
Portfolio of assets, 40
Post hoc, ergo propter hoc principle, 595
Pound, British, 434f, 477, 477f
PPP. See Theory of purchasing power parity (PPP)
Precautionary motive for demand for money
further developments of, 509
J. Keynes on, 504
Preferred habitat theory, 137–40
yield curves and market's expectations of future short-term interest rates according to, 139f
Prescott, Edward, 316 n.2, 643 n.2
real business cycle theory of, 579
Present discounted value, 69
Present value, 69–71
application on calculating simple, 71
application on calculating value of lottery jackpot, 71
President, U.S., influence on Federal Reserve System, 326
Price(s), new classical macroeconomic model on, 645–50
Price and wage stickiness, 650–51

Price level, 9, 21, 22. *See also* Aggregate price level
  aggregate output, unemployment, and, 566*b*
  declines in financial crises, 200
  foreign exchange rates and relative, 439–40
  J. Keynes's assumption of fixed, 519
  natural rate level of output and, 557–59
  quantity of money and, 501
  shifts in aggregate demand curve caused by, 559–62
  shifts in demand for money affected by, 111, 113, 113*f*
  short-term aggregate supply curve affected by expected, 572
  unanticipated, as monetary transmission mechanism, 607–8, 611
Price-level effect, interest rates, money supply and, 115, 117*f*
Price response to short-run aggregate output, three models of, 653–56
Price stability, 315–20
  defined, 315
  as primary goal of monetary policy, 319–20
  role of nominal anchor, 316
  time-inconsistency problem, 316–17, 486
Primary credit, 384
Primary Dealer Credit Facility (PDCF), 387*b*
Primary dealers, open market operations, 382
Primary market, 28–29
Principal-agent problem, 180–81
  demise of Barings Bank caused by, 249*b*
  tools to help solve, 181–83
Printing money, 628–29, 630
Prisoner-of-war camp, development of money in World War II, 55 n.1
Procyclical monetary policy, 422

Producer price index (PPI), 566*b*
Production costs, changes in, unrelated to wages, and short-run aggregate supply curve, 572–73
Productivity, effects on foreign exchange rate, 440
Profit(s)
  financial innovation as search for increased, 284–85
  managing banks to earn maximum, 232–40
Property rights in developing countries, 187
Protectionism, 486
Prudential supervision, 263–64
Public Accounting Return and Investor Protection Act (Sarbanes-Oxley Act), 193–94
Public Company Accounting Oversight Board (PCAOB), 193, 265
Public interest view of bureaucratic behavior, 337
Purchase and assumption method, bank failures and FDIC's, 256–57
The Purchasing Power of Money (Fisher), 500

q theory, James Tobin's, 604
Quantity theory of money, 499–502
  M. Friedman's modern, 511–12
  velocity of money and, 500–1, 513, 514
"The Quantity Theory of Money: A Restatement" (Friedman), 511–12
Quotas, 440

r. See Required reserve ratio (*r*)
Rate of capital gain, 81–82
Rate of return. *See* Return(s) (rate of return)
Rational bubbles, 161
Rational expectations, 152–158, 638 n.7, 643–664. *See also* Rational expectations revolution; Theory of rational expectations
Rational expectations revolution, 643

comparison of new and traditional models from perspective of, 653–61
  impact of, 661–62
  R. Lucas critique of policy evaluation and, 644–45
  new classical macroeconomic model and, 645–50
  new Keynesian model and, 650–53
  web references, 664
government credibility in era of high budget deficits, 660–61
Real bills doctrine, 418
Real business cycle theory
  debate on money and economic activity, and, 600*b*
  shifts in long-run aggregate supply curve and, 579
Real estate loans, 294
Real exchange rate, 437
Real GDP, 21–22, 566*b*
Real interest rate, 69
  after-tax, 86 n.8
  application on calculating, 85
  defined, 84
  monetary policy and, 589 n.2, 590
  nominal interest rate versus, 84–85
  for three-month Treasury bill (1953–2008), 86*f*
  TIPS (Treasury Inflation Protection Securities) and, 87*b*
Real money balances, 505
Real terms, defined, 85
Recession(s), economic, 8
  shift in demand for bonds in, 98
Recognition lag time and economic policy, 636
Rediscounting, 418
Redlining, 267
Reduced-form evidence, 588
  advantages and disadvantages of, 589–90
  timing evidence as, 595
Reduced-form model, St. Louis model as, 600 n.10
Regulation B, 267

Regulation K, 308

Regulation of financial system, 46–49, 171

on banking (*see* Banking regulation)

on bank reserves, 228

ensuring soundness of financial intermediaries and role of, 47–49

increasing information to investors, and role of, 46–47, 176–77, 182

international, 49

principal U.S. regulatory agencies, 47*t*

reducing principal-agent problem using government, 182

to remedy conflicts of interest problems, 193–95

Regulation Q, 49, 290, 293, 589, 606

Regulation Z, 267, 268*b*

Regulatory arbitrage, 261

Reinvestment risk, 83 n.6

Repurchase agreements (repo), 31, 383

Required reserve ratio (*r*), 228, 347, 360, 360*t*

Required reserves, 228, 347

demand curve for reserves and, 374

Reserve Bank of New Zealand, 319

Reserve Bank of New Zealand Act of 1989, 400

Reserve(s), 228

federal funds rate on, and effects of monetary-policy tools, 379–81

international, 463, 474–75

liquidity management and role of bank, 232–35, 236

open market operations and, 348–51

secondary bank, 228

supply and demand in market for, 379–81

Reserve aggregates (total reserves, nonborrowed reserves, monetary base, nonborrowed base) as policy instrument, 409–10

Reserve currency, 471

Reserve Primary Fund, 211, 291*b*

Reserve requirements, 228, 233, 389. *See also* Required reserve ratio (*r*)

disadvantages of, 389

European Central Bank and, 391

federal funds rate and effects of, 379, 379*f*

as Federal Reserve policy tool, in 1930s, 420–21

financial innovations regarding, 290

Residual claimant(s), equity holders as, 28, 147

Restrictive covenants, 172, 187

monitoring and enforcement of, 184–85, 242

Return(s) (rate of return), 80

expected, as determinant of asset demand, 91, 92, 93*t*

interest rates distinguished from, 80–84

maturity and volatility of bond, 82–84

Return on assets (ROA), 238

Return on equity (ROE), 238

Revaluation of currency, 473

Reverse causation, 590

Reverse repo (matched sale-purchase transaction), 383

Reverse transactions, 390

Ricardian evidence, 630

Ricardo, David, 630

Riegle-Neal Interstate Banking and Branching Efficiency Act of 1994, 259, 270*t*, 300

Rigidity, inflation targeting and, 404

Risk

defined, 40, 92

as determinant of asset demand, 92–93, 93*t*

effects of, on shifts in demand for bonds, 99*t*, 100

interest-rate, 82–83

reinvestment, 83 n.6

Risk aversion, 92

Risk management

assessment of, 264–65

of credit risk, 241–45

of interest-rate risk, 245–47

Risk preference, 92

Risk premium, 124, 128

Risk sharing, role of financial intermediaries in, 40–41

Risk structure of interest rates, 123–30

default risk and, 123–27

income tax considerations and, 128–29

liquidity and, 127–28

summary, 129

web references, 144

Roosevelt, Franklin Delano, 419

R^s (supply curve of reserves), 376

Russia, 498

financial crisis in, 218 n.2

financial development and economic growth in, 186

Sarbanes-Oxley Act of 2002, 36*b*, 193–94, 265, 270*t*

capital markets and, 195*b*

Sargent, Thomas, 643, 661

new classical macroeconomic model developed by R. Lucas and, 645–50

Savings accounts, 227

Savings and loan associations (S&Ls), 44, 271–73, 304–5

bailout of (1989), 273

Savings deposits, money aggregates and measurement of, 61–62

Schwartz, Anna, 592–93, 599

on Great Depression bank panics, 366–67, 419, 420*b*

Screening, bank management of credit risk through, 241–42

Seasonal credit, 384

Secondary credit, 384

Secondary loan participation, 247

Secondary markets, 28–29

Secondary reserves, 228

Second Bank of the United States, 282, 321

Secured debt, 171

Securities Act of 1933, 46, 265, 270*t*

Securities and Exchange Commission (SEC), 46, 47*t*, 265
Securities Exchange Act of 1934, 270*t*
Securitization, 207, 289, 294
Security (securities), 26
  bank assets, 228–23
  defined, 3
  types of, traded in financial markets, 30–35
  underwriting, 28, 46
Security First Network Bank, 287
Security markets, importance of financial intermediaries to global, 40*b*
Segmented markets theory on term structure of interest rates, 135–36
Seignorage, 492
Self-correcting mechanism, 575
Services, consumption and, 604 n.15
Shadow banking system, 284. *See also* Financial innovation
Shell operations, 308
Shifts in supply and demand in bond market, 94, 97–103
Shocks, 498. *See also* Supply-side shocks
Short-run aggregate supply curve, 570–73
  equilibrium in, 574, 574*f*
  inflation and, 621 n.1
  shifts in, 571–73, 573*t*
Short-run exchange rates, 440–43
  comparing expected returns on domestic and foreign assets, and, 459–61
  demand curve for domestic assets and, 442–43
  equilibrium in foreign exchange market, 443
  interest parity condition and, 461–62
  supply curve for domestic assets and, 442
Short sales, 162
Short-Term Liquidity Facility, 484*b*
Short-term maturity of debt instruments, 28
  bonds, 135

Simple deposits multiplier, 358
Simple loan, 70–71, 72
  yield to maturity on, 73–74
Small-denomination time deposits, money aggregates and measurement of, 62
Smart card, 59
"Smart money" market, behavioral finance and, 162–63
Société Générale, 249*b*
Soros, George, 478
South Korea, 212*b*, 219*b*
Soviet Union, origins of Eurodollar market and role of, 307*b*
Special drawing rights (SDRs), 476
Specialization in lending, bank management of credit risk through, 242
Speculative attack(s), 216
  on currency, 476, 478
  exchange-rate targeting and, 487–88
Speculative motive for demand for money
  J. Keynes on, 504–5
  J. Tobin on, 509–11
Spending, four types of, and aggregate output, 519–31
Spinning, 191
Spitzer, Eliot, 194
Spot exchange rate, 434
Spot transactions, 434
Stabilization policies, comparing three models on, 656
Stagflation, 578
Standard and Poor's Corporation, bond ratings by, 126*t*
Standard and Poor's (S&P) 500 index, 147
Standing lending facility, 384
State and local government bonds, 32, 228–29
State bank(s), 187, 282, 323
State banking and insurance commissions, 47*t*
State-owned banks, 187
Statistical evidence on importance of money to economic activity, 597–98

Sterilized foreign exchange intervention, 466, 467–68
Sticky prices, 601
Stock(s). *See also* Security (securities)
  as capital market instrument, 33
  computing price of common, 147–50
  defined, 5
  investing in, 158–61 (*see also* Investment(s))
  money as, 54
  not most important source of external funds for businesses, 169–70
  prices of (*see* Stock prices)
Stock exchange, 28–29. *See also* Stock market(s)
Stockholders, 147
Stock market(s), 5, 27–29, 147–65
  adverse selection (lemons problem) in, 175–76
  behavior finance applied to study of stock prices and, 162–63
  bubbles in, 161–62, 162–63
  computing price of common stock, 147–50
  crashes in, 147, 161–62 (*see also* Stock market declines and crashes)
  efficient market hypothesis and rational expectations in, 155–58 (*see also* Efficient market hypothesis)
  international, 37
  practical guide to investing in, 158–62
  stock prices on (1950–2008), 6*f*
  stock prices set by, 150–52 (*see also* Stock prices)
  theory of rational expectations and stock prices in, 152–55
  web references on, 165
Stock market declines and crashes, 200. *See also* Financial crises
  "Black Monday," October 19, 1987, 5, 161–62, 386*b*
  crash of 1929, 46
  Great Depression and (*see* Great Depression)

high-tech bubble collapse of 2000, 5, 161–62

of October 2008, 68

rational expectations, efficient market hypothesis and, 161–62

terrorist attacks of September 11, 2001, and, 386*b*

Stock prices

good news on, 160

link between investment spending and, 604 n.14

monetary policy and, 151–52

prices of, measured on Dow Jones, 5, 6*f*

prices of, set by stock market, 150–52

Stored-value card, 58–59, 59*b*

Store of value, money as, 56

Stress testing of banks, 265

Stronger version of efficient market hypothesis, 158

Strauss-Kahn, Dominique, 484*b*

Structural model, 588, 600

Structural model evidence, 587, 588, 592

advantages and disadvantages of, 589

Structural unemployment, 317

Structured credit products, 207

Structured investment vehicles (SIVs), 210, 276

Subprime mortgage(s), 207

Subprime mortgage crisis of 2007–2008, 68, 147, 168, 207–12, 498

agency problems and, 208–9

Baa-Treasury spread and, 127

bailout packages and, 211, 212*b*

bank balance sheet deterioration and, 210

consumer protection regulation and, 267, 268*b*

credit-rating agencies and, 192*b*

dollar, value of, and, 454

Economic Stimulus Act of 2008 and, 550, 552

failure of firms in, 210–11

Federal Reserve lender-of-last-resort facilities during, 387–88*b*

Federal Reserve preemptive strikes against, 426

financial innovations and, 207–8

financial regulation and, 275–78

global spread of, 209

housing price bubble and, 208, 209

information problems and, 209

International Monetary Fund and, 481*b*

investment banks and, 304*b*

lessons from, in monetary policy, 415–18

mark-to-market accounting, 266*b*

negative supply shocks and, 583–84, 584*f*

recession and, 609–10

recovery from, 211

stock market and, 152

worldwide spread of, 432

Sumitomo Corporation, 249*b*

Superregional banks, 299

Supply

excess, 96

factors affecting bond, 101, 101*t*

inflation and phenomenon associated with, 623

of money, 112*t*, 113–114, 114*f*, 499 (*see also* Money supply)

shifts in bond, and effects on interest rates, 101–3

shocks in (*see* Supply shocks)

Supply and demand analysis, 97. *See also* Aggregate demand and supply analysis

in bond market, 94–97, 97–104, 99*f*

of fixed exchange rate regime, 472–74

foreign exchange rate, 437–40

market equilibrium, 96

in market for money, 109–11

in market for reserves, 373–76

for money, 111–14, 112*t*

Supply conditions, financial innovation in response to, 286–89

Supply curve, 95

for domestic assets, 442

in bond market, 95*f*, 95

of reserves (R^s), 376

Supply shocks, 572–73

changes in equilibrium caused by, 576-79

favorable (1995–1999), 582

inflation and, 623, 623*f*

negative (1973–1975, 1978–1980), 581–82, 643 n.1

subprime crisis and negative (2007–2008), 583–84

Supply side economic policy, 318

Sutton, Willie, 215

Swap lines, 387*b*

Sweep accounts, 292

T-account (simplified balance sheet), 229–32

Federal Reserve, 345–46, 464–65

multiple deposit creation and, 354–57, 359

open market operations and Federal Reserve, 348–52

Taiwan, 479

Target financing rate, 390

Tariffs, 440

Tax(es)

change in *IS* curve and changes in, 544, 545*f*, 551*t*

fiscal policy and control of government spending and, 543 (*see also* Fiscal policy)

government spending, aggregate output, and, 529–30, 532*t*, 533

Tax considerations

debt contracts and, 183 n.4

municipal bonds, risk structure of interest rates and, 128–29

Tax cuts, effects of Bush administration, on bond interest rates, 130

Tax havens, international banks as, 308

Taylor, John, 412, 602, 659

Taylor principal, 413

Taylor rule, 412–14

for federal funds rate, 415*f*

Tech-stock bubble, 416
Term Asset-Backed Securities Loan Facility (TALF), 388*b*
Term Auction Facility (TAF), 387*b*
Term Securities Lending Facility (TSLF), 387*b*
Term structure of interest rates, 123, 130–42
    evidence on, 140
    expectations theory on, 132–35, 640–41
    liquidity premium and preferred habitat theories, 136–40
    segmented markets theory on, 135–36
    summary, 140
    web references, 144
Terrorist attacks of September 11, 2001
    stock market and, 386*b*
Thailand, 479
Thatcher, Margaret, 661
Theory of asset demand, 91, 93, 125, 504
    autonomous rise in demand for money and, 547–48
    bank crises of Great Depression and, 366–69
Theory of bureaucratic behavior, 337
Theory of efficient capital markets, 155
Theory of purchasing power parity (PPP), 437–39
    failure of, to fully explain exchange rates, 439
Theory of rational expectations, 147, 152–55. *See also* Rational expectations; Rational expectations revolution
    efficient market hypothesis and, 155–62
    formal statement of, 154
    implications of, 155
    rationale behind, 154–55
    shortcomings of discretionary policies and analysis from perspective of, 643
Thomas Amendment, 420

Thrift institutions (thrifts), 43–44, 304–6
    credit unions, 44, 305–6
    mutual savings banks, 44, 305
    savings and loan associations, 44, 304–5
Time deposits, 227. *See also* Certificates of deposit (CDs)
Time-inconsistency problem, 316–17, 486
Timing evidence on importance of money for economic activity, 595–97
TIPS (Treasury Inflation Protection Securities), 87*b*
Tobin, James, 507
    Baumol-Tobin on transactions component on demand for money, 507–11
    q theory, 604
    on speculative demand for money, 509–11
"Too big to fail" problem and government safety net, 258–59
Trade, role of international, in determining aggregate output, 520, 530–31, 532*t*, 533
Trade balance, 468
Trade barriers, foreign exchange rates and effects of, 440, 448
Trading activities, as bank off-balance-sheet activity, 248–50
    principal-agent problem in, 249*b*, 250
Trading Activities Manual, 264
Traditional model (nonrational expectations model), comparison with new classical, and new Keynesian models, 653, 654*t*
    anti-inflation policies and, 656–59
    credibility in fighting inflation and, 659–61
    short-run output and prices responses and, 653–56, 655*f*
    stabilization policy and, 656
Transaction costs
    in barter economy, 54

    defined, 39
    influence of, on financial structure, 172–73
    role of financial intermediaries in reducing, 39–41, 173
    role of money in reducing, 54–55
Transactions motive for demand for money
    Baumol-Tobin analysis of, 507–93
    J. Keynes on, 504
Transition countries
    economic growth and financial development in, 186–88
    financial crises in, 212
Transmission mechanisms of monetary policy, 587–615
    credit view, 605–9
    defined, 588
    evaluating empirical evidence, 587–600
    monetary policy lessons, 610–12
    other asset price channels, 602–5
    traditional interest-rate channels, 601–2
    web references, 615
TRAPS (Trading Room Automated Processing System), 382–83
Treasury Asset Relief Plan (TARP) and government bailouts, 212*b*
Treasury bills. *See also* U.S. Treasury bills
    interest rates on, 129*f*
    negative interest, in Japan, 79*b*
Treasury bill-to-Eurodollar rate (TED), 209, 210*f*, 211
Treasury Inflation Protection Securities (TIPS), 87*b*
Trichet, Jean-Claude, 328
Truth in Lending Act, 266, 268*b*
Tyco International, principal-agent problem in, 181

Ukraine, 484*b*
Unanticipated and anticipated policy, effects of
    in new classical macroeconomic model, 646–48

in new Keynesian model, 651, 652*f*

Uncertainty
Federal Reserve's lack of transparency and, 406
financial crises and increases in, 201, 205
monetary policy and avoidance of, 337 n.6

Underwriting services, 28, 46
conflicts of interest in, 190–91

Unemployment
in 2006–2007, 498
in 2008, 211
aggregate output, price level, and, 566*b*
demand-pull inflation resulting from too low target for, 626*f*
during favorable supply shocks (1995–1999), 582, 582*t*
frictional, 317
Keynesians on government policy to reduce, 576–77
monetarists on, 577
natural rate of, 318, 568
natural rate of, in years 1960–2008, 634*f*
during negative demand shocks (2001–2004), 582–83, 583*t*
during negative supply shocks (1973–1975, 1978–1980), 581–82, 581*t*
nonaccelerating rate of, 413
responses to high, 635–36
structural, 317
subprime crisis and, 583–84, 584*t*
during Vietnam War buildup (1964–1970), 580–81, 581*t*

Unemployment rates, 8, 566*b*

Unexploited profit opportunity, 157–58

United Kingdom
budget deficits and inflation fighting in Thatcher-era, 661
central bank of, 331–32
exchange rate on British pound, 434*f*
exchange-rate targeting and, 488

foreign exchange market for British pound (1992), 477–78, 477*f*
inflation targeting in, 401*f*, 402
monetary policy in, 485
purchasing power parity between U.S. and (1973–2008), 438*f*

United States
banking industry in, 282–309
central bank (*see* Federal Reserve System)
dollar (*see* Dollar, U.S.)
financial crises in, 7 (*see also* Stock market declines and crashes)
government budget constraints and inflation in, 628–29
government budget deficits and money creation in, 630
purchasing power parity between United Kingdom and (1973–2008), 438*f*
sources of external funds for nonfinancial businesses in, 170*f*

U.S. economy
aggregate output, and unemployment rate in, 8
aggregate price level and money supply in (1950–2008), 10*f*
budget surplus/deficit, as percentage of gross domestic product (1950–2008), 12*f*
central bank in (*see* Federal Reserve System)
current account deficit (balance of payments), 468–69
effects of international financial markets on, 36–38
fluctuations in, since 1980s, 587
monetary policy and health of, 395 (*see also* Monetary policy)
monetary targeting in, 395, 396
money growth and business cycles in (1950–2008), 9*f*
payments system in, 57–59
rise in inflation (1960–1980), 630–34

U.S. government
budget of, and shifts in bond supply, 101*t*, 102
debt of, ratio to GDP, 632, 633*f*
inflation and budget deficits in, 627–30, 632–33
mortgage agencies, 35
regulation by (*see* Banking regulation; Regulation of financial system)

U.S. government agency securities, 35, 222

U.S. government bonds
interest rates on, 131*f*
yield curves for, 142*f*

U.S. government securities, 35, 228–27

U.S. Treasury
deposits of, at Federal Reserve, 353
monetary liability (monetary base) of, 346

U.S. Treasury bills, 30
business cycle and interest rates on three-month (1951–2008), 106*f*
as collateral for repurchase agreements, 31
as discount bonds, 78–79
expected inflation and interest rates on three-month (1982–2008), 104*f*
money growth (M2), and interest rates on three-month (1950–2008), 118*f*
real and nominal interest rates on three-month (1931–2008), 594*f*
real and nominal interest rates on three-month, (1953–2008), 86*f*
TIPS (Treasury Inflation Protection Securities), 87*b*
yield curve, 130, 132*b*

U.S. Treasury bonds
as default-free, 124, 125
indexed, 87*b*
interest rates on, and money growth, 10, 11*f*

Unit of account
  defined, 55
  money as providing, 55–56
Universal banking, 303–4
  potential conflict of interest in,
    190 n.6
Unsecured debt, 171
Unsterilized foreign exchange
    intervention, 465, 466–67
Used-car market, 175, 178
Uses of funds (bank assets), 225,
    226t, 228–29
  decline in income advantages of,
    293–94

Value-at-risk (VaR) calculations,
    265
Vanguard Group, 83b
Vault cash, 228
Velocity of money, 500–1, 505–6,
    513–14
  as constant, refuted, 502–3
  defined, 500
  of M1 and M2 (1915–2008), 502f
Venture capital firm, 182
Virtual bank, 287, 288b
Volcker, Paul, 314, 387b, 396, 426
  importance of credibility to
    inflation-fighting policies of, 639
  monetary policy of, 423–24

Wage(s), new classical macroeco-
    nomic model on, 645–50
Wage-price stickiness, 650
Wage push, short-term aggregate
    supply curve affected by, 572
Wage-setting, expectations about
    policy and process of, 638
Wallace, Neil, 643 n.2
Wall Street Journal
  "Following the Financial News"
    (see Following the Financial
    News)
  "Heard on the Street" column,
    158
Washington Mutual (WAMU), 211
Wealth
  defined, 54
  as determinant of asset demand,
    91, 92, 93t
  effect of, on demand for bonds,
    97, 98, 99t
  M. Friedman on, 511–12
  as monetary transmission mech-
    anism, 604–5
  money and bonds as two forms
    of storing, 109, 504
World Bank, 471
WorldCom Corporation, 177
World Trade Organization (WTO),
    471

World War II, pegging of interest
    rates in years 1942–1951, 421
Wriston, Walter, 241
Write-downs, asset, 201

Yield curve, 130
  application on interpreting, 141,
    142f
  as forecasting tool for inflation
    and business cycles, 141b
  inverted, 130
  liquidity premium (preferred
    habitat) theory on future short-
    term interest rates and, 139f
Yield to maturity, 69, 72–80.
    See also Interest rate(s)
  on coupon bond, 75–77
  curve on (see Yield curve)
  defined, 72–73
  on discount bond, 78–79
  on fixed-payment loan, 74–75
  for long-term bonds
    (1919–2008), 123, 124f
  perpetuity and, 77–78
  on simple loan, 73–74
  summary, 80

Zero-coupon bond. See Discount
    (zero-coupon) bond
Zimbabwe, inflation in, 618–19

Guide to Commonly Used Symbols

Symbol	Term
Δ	change in a variable
π^e	expected inflation
a	autonomous consumer expenditure
AD	aggregate demand curve
AS	aggregate supply curve
B^d	demand for bonds
B^s	supply of bonds
BR	borrowed reserves
c	currency ratio
C	yearly coupon payment
C	currency
C	consumer expenditure
D	demand curve
D	checkable deposits
DL	discount loans
e	excess reserves ratio
E_t	exchange (spot) rate
$(E^e_{t+1} - E_t)/E_t$	expected appreciation of domestic currency
EM	equity multiplier
ER	excess reserves
G	government spending
i	interest rate (yield to maturity)
i_d	discount rate
i^D	interest rate on domestic assets
i^F	interest rate on foreign assets
i_r	real interest rate
I	planned investment spending
IS	IS curve
LM	LM curve
m	money multiplier

Symbol	Term
M	money supply
M^d	demand for money
M^s	supply of money
M1	M1 monetary aggregate
M2	M2 monetary aggregate
MB	monetary base (high-powered money)
MB_n	nonborrowed monetary base
mpc	marginal propensity to consume
NBR	nonborrowed reserves
NX	net exports
P	price level
P^e	expected price level
P_s	stock prices
P_t	price of a security at time t
r	required reserve ratio for checkable deposits
R	reserves
R	return
R^e	expected return
R^D	expected return on domestic deposits
R^F	expected return on foreign deposits
ROA	return on assets
ROE	return on equity
RR	required reserves
S	supply curve
T	taxes
V	velocity of money
Y	aggregate output (national income)
Y^{ad}	aggregate demand
Y_n	natural rate level of output